The Universities
of the
Italian Renaissance

THE

NIVERSITIES

OF THE

ITALIAN RENAISSANCE

PAUL F. GRENDLER

THE JOHNS HOPKINS UNIVERSITY PRESS
Baltimore & London

*This book was brought to publication with the generous assistance
of the Gladys Krieble Delmas Foundation*

The Johns Hopkins University Press
2715 North Charles Street
Baltimore, Maryland 21218-4363
www.press.jhu.edu

Library of Congress Cataloging-in-Publication Data

Grendler, Paul F.
The universities of the Italian Renaissance / Paul F. Grendler.
p. cm.
Includes bibliographical references and index.
ISBN 0-8018-6631-6 (hardcover : alk. paper)
1. Universities and colleges—Italy—History. 2. Education, Humanistic—Italy—History.
3. Renaissance—Italy. I. Title.
LA797.G74 2001
378.45—dc21
00-011287

A catalog record for this book is available from the British Library.

To the memory of

CHARLES B. SCHMITT

(1933–1986)

and

PAUL OSKAR KRISTELLER

(1905–1999)

Contents

Illustrations

Tables

Preface

t Padua in the first week of June 1996, I sat in an upper-story room of the sixteenth-century Palazzo del Bo reading documents from the Archivio Antico dell'Università di Padova. The window overlooked the small square in front of the Palazzo. Early June is the time for the laureate (doctoral) examinations in Italy, some in progress in rooms below. As a successful candidate emerged, friends hailed the new doctor with a scatological serenade in dialect: "Dotore, Dotore, Dotore, pal buso del cul. Vaffan cul, vaffan cul." While the chant seems crude and insulting in English translation, the words floated on joy and laughter. Sometimes friends draped a large wreath around the neck of the new doctor.

As the examinations continued in the ensuing days, large handwritten and illustrated posters appeared on the front wall of the Palazzo del Bo to celebrate in verse and picture the accomplishments of new doctors. Signed by many friends, they were both elaborate and funny. The climax came with a placard chronicling the life of a certain "Dottoressa Barbara Pasqueta." The placard was a university version of the pasquinades (*pasquinata* = *Pasqueta*) attached to the famous statue in Rome. According to the placard, Dottoressa Pasqueta had enjoyed a life full of extraordinary academic and sexual exploits, all detailed in satirical verses and graphic illustrations. She obtained her degree with a minimum score of thirty-seven out of sixty points.

Sometimes the celebrations honoring the new doctor continued into the evening. One night I watched the festivities for a new laureate in front of the Palazzo. The graduate wore a swimsuit, apron, brown paint on her face, and flowers in her hair, making her into a wood nymph. She first delivered a short peroration on a platform. Friends abruptly ended her speech by putting tape over her mouth and tying her to a post. Upon release she went about the piazza selling vegetables from a basket, as comrades took pictures. Before long the group moved on, possibly to further celebration in home or tavern. *Gaudeamus igitur.*

These celebrations with their traditional goliardic elements embellished a pleasant passage of a dozen years devoted to researching and writing this book. I came to the project in unexpected fashion. Paul Oskar Kristeller, who published pioneering work on the subject in several articles of the 1950s and later, intended to write a book on Italian Renaissance universities. However, other projects intervened. He then persuaded Charles Schmitt, who had already written numerous articles on philosophy and science in Renaissance universities, and the University of Pisa in particular, to write such a book. In early April 1986, Charles wrote me that he had cleared his desk of other matters and was about to start the universities book. But first he had to go to the University of Padua to deliver some lectures. There he collapsed and died on April 15, 1986. His death was a great loss to scholarship and the end of a friendship that had begun in 1962.

Then one evening in midsummer of 1986, I received a telephone call from Professor Kristeller strongly urging me to write the book that Charles could not do. Surprised, I only promised to consider the possibility. As I finished a book on preuniversity education in Renaissance Italy, the idea attracted me more and more, because of the intrinsic importance of the topic and as a continuation of my previous investigation. As "Giovanni" finished Latin secondary school, why not follow him into the university, where he studied arts, medicine, law, or theology? After forwarding the book on schooling to the publisher in 1987, I began to study Italian Renaissance universities.

This book attempts to understand universities in the Italian Renaissance from 1400 to 1600. Part I provides overviews of the development of Italy's sixteen universities, including such mundane information as how many professors, students, and graduates each had and how the institution functioned. Part II follows in broad lines the old and new scholarly issues that exercised scholars and teachers in various disciplines. It notes institutional changes, such as the creation of professorships for new approaches, and the addition or subtraction of positions in traditional disciplines. Part III offers reasons for the decline of Italian universities in the seventeenth century.

The long-held view that Italian Renaissance universities resisted intellectual change is clearly wrong. But how much did they change? Did they welcome into their midst humanists with their criticism of established views? Did they make room for innovative scholarship in medicine, law, and other subjects? A gifted scholar's impact on his discipline depended greatly on whether universities made structural changes to accommodate a line of inquiry. Did only a few leading institutions, such as Bologna and Padua, make changes, or did the smaller universities follow suit? What did universities accomplish or fail to do during the Renaissance?

Only an examination of all sixteen Italian universities over a long period of time can answer such questions. This is the first attempt to see them as a whole. Fortunately, a renaissance of scholarship in the past ten to twenty years has yielded much new material on individual universities. The journey of discovery has always been interesting.

IT IS A PLEASURE TO THANK THOSE WHO HAVE HELPED ALONG THE WAY. My greatest debt is to John Monfasani, who read the entire manuscript, always offering good advice. He also provided photocopies of some hard-to-find articles. William A. Wallace, O.P., read Chapters 7, 8, 10, and 12, giving me the benefit of his extraordinary expertise in these areas. Ronald Witt read Chapter 6 carefully and rescued me from various errors. Giuliana Adorni, Joseph Black, Giuliano Catoni, J. Patrick Donnelly, Konrad Eisenbichler, Frederick J. McGinness, Nelson Minnich, Paul V. Murphy, Simona Negruzzo, John W. O'Malley, Guido Ruggiero, Erika Rummel, and Philip Stadter provided me with copies of hard-to-locate publications and documents or helped in other ways. Donald L. LaRocca, associate curator of Arms and Armor in the Metropolitan Museum of Art, explained Renaissance guns. Cynthia R. Arkin, associate director for Special Collections of the Biddle Law Library of the University of Pennsylvania Law School, was very helpful in the search for illustrations from law books. Archivists and librarians in Bologna, Florence, Macerata, Padua, Parma, Pavia, Rome, Vatican City, and Venice have aided my research. I particularly wish to thank Drs. Emilia Veronese and Luciana Rea of the Archivio Antico dell'Università di Padova; they steered me to materials I might otherwise have missed and pressed useful publications on me. On this side of the Atlantic, the libraries at the Catholic University of America, Centre for Reformation and Renaissance Studies at Victoria University in the University of Toronto, Columbia University, Columbia Law School, Duke University, the Newberry Library, the Pontifical Institute for Mediaeval Studies of St. Michael's College in the University of Toronto, University of North Carolina at Chapel Hill, University of Pennsylvania, and University of Toronto have been helpful. Alan Tuttle and Jean Houston of the National Humanities Center procured many books and photocopies for me. Grace Buonocore very carefully copyedited a long and complex manuscript.

Several agencies provided financial support, making possible extended periods of research. An Interpretive Research Grant from the National Endowment for the Humanities made it possible to spend the academic year 1989–90, and January to June 1992, on this book. The Social Sciences and Humanities Research Council of Canada provided a Research Time Stipend for 1988–89. With this financial support, I spent the academic years 1988–1990 in residence at the National Humanities Center, Research Triangle Park, North Carolina. The Gladys Krieble Delmas Foundation made possible a return trip to Padua and Venice in May and June 1996. The Social Sciences and Research Council of Canada provided a research grant for short research trips to Italy in 1996, 1997, and 1999. Finally, a Connaught Fellowship from the University of Toronto made possible a leave of absence from teaching, January to June 1997. I am grateful to all.

After a long and productive scholarly career, Paul Oskar Kristeller died just as this project was coming to an end. This book is fittingly dedicated to his memory and to that of Charles B. Schmitt. *Monumentum aere perennius;* they truly created durable monuments of learning.

Abbreviations

CHRP	*The Cambridge History of Renaissance Philosophy.* Edited by Charles B. Schmitt, Quentin Skinner, Eckhard Kessler, and Jill Kraye. Cambridge, 1988.
Cultura veneta	*Storia della cultura veneta.* Edited by Girolamo Arnaldi and Manlio Pastore Stocchi. Vol. 1: *Dalle Origini al Trecento.* Vol. 2: *Il Trecento.* Vol. 3 in 3 parts: *Dal Primo Quattrocento al Concilio di Trento.* Vol. 4 in 2 parts: *Il Seicento.*. Vol. 5 in 2 parts: *Il Settecento.* Vicenza, 1976–86.
DBI	*Dizionario biografico degli italiani.* Rome, 1960–.
DSB	*Dictionary of Scientific Biography.* Edited by Charles C. Gillispie et al. 18 vols. New York, 1970–80; second printing, New York, 1981.
GW	*Gesamtkatalog der Wiegendrucke.* Leipzig, 1925–
Medical Renaissance	*The Medical Renaissance of the Sixteenth Century.* Edited by A. Wear, R. K. French, and I. M. Lonie. Cambridge, 1985.
Quaderni	*Quaderni per la storia dell'Università di Padova*
Renaissance Humanism	*Renaissance Humanism: Foundations, Forms, and Legacy.* Edited by Albert Rabil Jr. 3 vols. Philadelphia, 1988.
La rinascita del sapere	*La rinascita del sapere: Libri e maestri dello studio ferrarese.* Edited by Patrizia Castelli. Venice, 1991.
Roma e lo Studium Urbis	*Roma e lo Studium Urbis: Spazio urbano e cultura dal Quattro al Seicento.* Atti del convegno, Roma, 7–10 giugno 1989. Rome, 1992.
RQ	*Renaissance Quarterly*
Sapere e/è potere	*Sapere e/è potere: Discipline, dispute, e professioni nell'Università medievale e moderna: Il caso bolognese a confronto.* Atti del 4° Convegno Bologna, 13–15 aprile 1989. Edited by Luisa Avellini, Andrea Cristiani, and Angela De Benedictis. 3 vols. Bologna, 1990.
Scienza e filosofia	*Scienza e filosofia all'Università di Padova nel Quattrocento.* Edited by Antonino Poppi. Padua and Trieste, 1983.
SMUB	*Studi e memorie per la storia dell'Università di Bologna*
L'Università di Pisa	*Storia dell'Università di Pisa.* Vol. 1 in 2 parts: *1343–1737.* Pisa, 1993.
L'Università di Siena.	*L'Università di Siena. 750 anni di storia.* Siena, 1991.
Universities in the Middle Ages	*A History of the University in Europe.* Vol. 1: *Universities in the Middle Ages.* Edited by Hilde de Ridder-Symoens. Cambridge, 1992.
Bu.	Busta
F.	Filza
FF.	Filze
f.	folio
R.	Registro

PART I

THE UNIVERSITIES OF ITALY

talian communes (city governments) and princes founded universities in waves. Both Bologna and Paris claimed the honor of first university in Europe; each began in the second half of the twelfth century. The universities of Padua, Naples, Siena, Rome, and Perugia followed between 1222 and 1308. After a pause, a second wave occurred between 1343 and 1445, with the establishment of Pisa, Florence, Pavia, Ferrara, Turin, and Catania. After another century-long pause, a third wave of late Renaissance foundations created the universities of Macerata, Salerno, Messina, and Parma between 1540 and 1601. Since the University of Florence moved to Pisa in 1473 to replace the Pisan *studium* (university), which had died, Renaissance Italy boasted fifteen at the beginning of the seventeenth century.

The Renaissance university had three missions. Its professors carried on research at a high level. They taught their disciplines to students. And the university awarded degrees recognizing the recipient as an expert in a discipline and authorizing him to teach it anywhere in Christendom. To carry out these missions, all Italian universities created similar structures of teaching, methods of awarding degrees, and relationships with the civil authority. Students came, lived, learned, and graduated.

The Universities of Renaissance Italy and Their Foundation Dates

CHAPTER I

Bologna and Padua

he Middle Ages created the university, the period's most magnificent and enduring achievement after the Christian Church. But the definition of *university* is not always clear. And Italian universities differed in important ways from their northern European counterparts, especially those of Paris and Oxford.

THE ITALIAN UNIVERSITY

A functioning, whole Italian university had two complementary parts. It possessed a papal or imperial charter authorizing it to confer license and doctoral degrees recognized throughout Christendom. A local college of doctors and the chancellor of the university, often the bishop or his representative, usually exercised the power bestowed by the charter. Possession of a papal or imperial charter permitted a commune to claim that a *studium generale* (university empowered to grant degrees) existed in the town.[1] But this did not necessarily mean

---

1. Verger's explanation of *studium generale* is worth quoting: "A *studium generale* was an institution of higher education founded on, or, at any rate, confirmed in its status by, an authority of a universal nature, such as the pope or (less frequently) the emperor, whose members enjoyed a certain number of rights, likewise universal in their application, which transcended all local divisions (such as towns, dioceses, principalities, and states). . . . Titles awarded in the universities were guaranteed by the founding authority and therefore regarded as being universally valid. This meant that the licenses (*licentiae docendi*) granted by the universities were licenses *ubique docendi,* entitling the holder to teach throughout Christendom. . . . As for the titles of doctor or master, the holding of them was regarded as a sign of the very highest intellectual competence and of equivalent value in all circumstances, no matter which university had granted them; and, as a consequence, they were supposed to allow access everywhere to the offices and honours reserved for the holders of this high rank." Verger, 1992, 35–36.

Verger's explanation assumes that *studium generale* meant that both the right to confer degrees and advanced teaching existed. But this was not always the case. Contemporary documents often used the terms *studium generale* and *studium* (*studio* in Italian) when a charter, but not a complete teaching university, existed. Modern historians faithfully following the documents use these terms, sometimes

that it was a whole university. A university also had to offer advanced instruction in law, arts, medicine, and sometimes theology. A complete, if small, functioning Italian university had a minimum of six to eight professors teaching civil law, canon law, medicine, logic, natural philosophy, and usually rhetoric, but not necessarily theology, in regular classes at an advanced level. Only the combination of charter and teaching made a university.

Providing advanced teaching in a variety of disciplines was considerably more difficult to accomplish than acquiring the right to award degrees. Popes and emperors handed out university charters practically for the asking, especially if a sum of money accompanied the request. A visiting emperor might present a university charter to his communal hosts as an expression of good will. A pope might award one in exchange for support against an antipope. A charter encouraged the commune to create a university, but that was all. It resembled a hunting license authorizing prince or commune to seek professors and the money to hire them. Raising money, hiring professors, and attracting students were difficult tasks. Lack of funds and internal or external political opposition often prevented a town from turning a charter into a functioning university. Communes with charters to award degrees but without advanced instruction were "paper universities," not teaching universities.[2]

Sometimes a commune with a charter achieved part of its goal. A number of Italian communes and courts appointed an advanced teacher of law or medicine, or both. A commune with one, two, or three men teaching some university subjects at an advanced level did not have a university, whether or not it possessed a charter. It might have an incomplete university.[3] The largest and best-known incomplete university in Italy was the Collegio Romano, founded by the Society of Jesus in 1551. It had many scholars who taught grammar, rhetoric, humanities, Greek, logic, natural philosophy, mathematics and astronomy, and theology at every level from elementary to advanced. Pope Paul IV in 1556 conferred on the Jesuits the power to award doctorates in arts and theology (but not law and medicine) to students of the Collegio Romano.[4] But it was not an Italian university, because it neither taught nor awarded degrees in law and medicine. It lacked the complete curriculum of an Italian university.

Italian universities differed from those in northern Europe and in Spain in several ways. They concentrated on law and medicine; arts and theology had less importance than in ultramontane universities. Italian universities granted doctoral degrees but almost never awarded bachelor's degrees. Most students at Italian universities were eighteen to twenty-five years of age, somewhat older

---

leaving the impression that teaching universities existed when they did not. Local pride in the institution encourages this tendency. The following pragmatic definition of an Italian university attempts to clarify a blurred picture.

2. Rashdall (1936, 2:325) defines *paper universities* as "universities for which Bulls were granted, but which never came into actual existence." I define a *paper university* as one that had a charter and awarded degrees but did not teach.

3. *Incomplete university* is my term.

4. Villoslada, 1954, 33–36.

than students at northern universities.[5] The majority of Italian professors were married laymen, rather than members of the clergy. Instruction at Italian universities occurred at "public" lectures, that is, lectures open to all, delivered by professors appointed and paid by the civil government. By contrast, much teaching at the universities of Paris and Oxford took place in colleges, which combined residence and teaching, especially for younger students. Clergymen were often college teachers in northern Europe. And instruction inside the college was not necessarily open to nonmembers of the college. By contrast, teaching colleges did not exist in Italian universities.

In this study the term *Italian university,* or just *university,* means a teaching institution that awarded doctorates and had a minimum of six to eight professors. Paid by the commune, the professors offered advanced instruction in the core subjects of law, medicine, and arts, which defined Italian universities. The host commune possessed a papal or imperial charter authorizing the conferral of license and doctoral degrees bearing the university's name.

Italy had sixteen universities between 1400 and 1601.[6] Bologna was the first.

BOLOGNA: SECOND HALF OF THE TWELFTH CENTURY

Bologna vied with Paris for the honor of being the first European university, and it provided the model for all others in southern Europe. The traditional account states that sometime in the late eleventh century students began to gather at the feet of lawyers who looked to Roman law as the guide to creating legal principles that enabled society to sort out the confusion between imperial claims, communal authority, and citizens' rights.[7] The most famous of these jurists was the Bolognese Irnerius (c. 1055–c. 1130), a practicing lawyer and judge involved in cases concerning imperial authority in northern Italy. He glossed (made detailed comments on) Justinian's *Corpus juris civilis* of the sixth century, and especially the *Digest,* in an effort to derive legal principles useful to medieval society. Others gathered to hear him, although it is not clear if he taught in a formal academic setting.

Other legists soon followed his example. About 1140 Gratian, a monk with legal experience living in a Bolognese monastery, made a compilation of church council decrees, papal letters, and extracts from patristic writings. He organized them so as to illustrate legal principles appropriate to the church and to eccle-

---

5. Marc-Antoine Muret's description of the ideal progress of studies (written 1572–85) clearly states that the student should begin university studies at the age of eighteen. Muret, 1737, 1:302–7; Renzi, 1986, 267–70. Abundant evidence from the lives of students and the ages when doctoral degrees were conferred supports Muret.

6. From this point onward, *university* means "a complete teaching university," unless otherwise indicated. See Chapter 4 for some paper and incomplete universities. Occasionally *studium* and *studio* are used for the sake of variety.

7. The following is based on Rashdall, 1936, vol. 1, ch. 4; Sorbelli, 1940, chs. 1–4; Stelling-Michaud, 1955, chs. 2 and 3; Hyde, 1972; Bellomo, 1995, 58–63, 65–68; and Southern, 1995, chs. 8 and 9, esp. 274–82. Although there is much more bibliography, these works are essential.

siastical issues. Gratian's work became the basis for the study of church legislation, although he probably did not teach.

Nevertheless, a number of men did begin to teach civil and canon law at Bologna, attracting a growing number of foreign (non-Bolognese) students to the city. Since these students had little or no legal existence away from their homes, they created a student association in order to assert certain legal rights. They were law students, after all. An imperial document of 1158 recognized such an association (*universitas*), although nothing else is known about the student organization at this time.

The combination of structured teaching and student associations marked the origin of the University of Bologna. In the nineteenth century the leaders of the University of Bologna decided that this had happened in 1088, so that there might be a grand celebration in 1888. Bologna then celebrated its nine-hundredth anniversary in 1988. But it is not likely that enough instruction and organization existed to merit the term *university* before the 1150s, and it might not have happened before the 1180s.[8]

The presence of teaching legists probably encouraged teachers in other fields to come to Bologna. *Ars dictaminis,* grammar, logic, philosophy based on Aristotle, mathematical arts, and especially medicine were taught there by the middle of the thirteenth century. Taddeo Alderotti (c. 1210–95) of Florence, who adapted Aristotelian natural philosophy to the needs of medicine, began to teach in Bologna about 1260.[9] He soon raised medicine to a prestigious position in the university. Recognizing the contribution of Alderotti and his pupils, the commune extended scholarly privileges and tax exemptions to them between 1274 and 1288. About this time a college of physicians composed of teachers began to examine candidates for medical degrees. A student organization for arts comparable to that of the law students developed at the end of the thirteenth century and in the first years of the fourteenth at Bologna. Like the law student *universitas,* it hired professors and imposed pedagogical conditions on them.

For the better part of the thirteenth century the Bolognese student associations exercised powers of which students everywhere dream: they appointed, paid, and dismissed the professors. The students' greatest strength lay in the threat to migrate to another town, taking with them the considerable income that wealthy foreign students brought to a host city.

However, the commune began to pay law professors' salaries in the 1220s, stopped in the 1230s, a high point for the student *universitates,* but resumed payments in 1280.[10] The commune also began to pay salaries to medical professors, possibly to Alderotti, certainly to his successors in the first decade of the fourteenth century. It is likely that the commune did so because paying academic

8. Hyde (1972, 34–37) and Southern (1995, 312–17) suggest the 1150s; Verger (1992, 47–49) prefers the 1180s; and Rüegg (1992, 4–6), the last years of the twelfth century. But all scholars recognize that the creation of the University of Bologna was an evolutionary process.

9. The following is based on Rashdall, 1936, 1:233–42; Siraisi, 1981, 13–24; and Sorbelli, 1940, ch. 4.

10. Rashdall, 1936, 1:210–11; Hyde, 1972, 44.

salaries almost guaranteed the stability of the university. As professors stayed in one place in order to receive regular salaries, students did as well, unless they could find another group of professors to teach them. And if students left, a stationary corps of teachers would attract new students. The decision to pay professorial salaries showed that the city viewed the university as an asset to the community, rather than as a group of wealthy young men who drove up housing costs, disturbed the peace, and violated women. The commune recognized that the university earned prestige for the city and poured income into the pockets of merchants, landlords, servants, and others. Bologna became a communally financed and ruled university by 1350.

The decision of the commune of Bologna to wrest control of the university from the students by paying professors was probably the most important decision in the early history of Italian universities. The civil government appointed professors and opened or closed the university. Student power did not completely disappear; the student organizations and many of their privileges remained, as did the regulations they imposed on professors, which the commune now enforced. But paying professorial salaries decided the issue of control. Every other Italian university followed the Bolognese example. Commune or prince ruled all Italian universities.

Pope and emperor, the twin towers of medieval authority, played no substantive role in the birth of the University of Bologna. The papacy entered only in 1219, when Honorius III decreed that the archdeacon of Bologna, an official of the Bolognese church, had to approve the granting of the *licentia docendi,* the license to teach.[11] This seems to have been only a claim, because teachers already conducted examinations and awarded degrees. A division of responsibilities developed, even though few records survive to document the process. A college of doctors examined a candidate who, if successful, received a degree sanctioned by the church, represented by the local bishop as chancellor of the university. The papally sanctioned degree gave the recipient the right to teach anywhere in Christendom. This permission became accepted as the right of the pope (later the emperor as well) to issue a charter authorizing the establishment of a *studium generale* with the authority to award degrees recognized throughout Christendom. In future centuries a city or prince wishing to create a university obtained a charter from pope, emperor, or both.

The first surviving faculty rolls of the University of Bologna come from the mid-fourteenth century. The commune of Bologna paid salaries to 17, 23, and 17 professors, respectively, the majority teaching law, in the three academic years 1351–52 through 1353–54.[12] However, these may not be complete rolls. The next surviving faculty roll comes from the academic year 1370–71, followed by almost all faculty rolls through the eighteenth century, the most complete set of

11. Rashdall, 1936, 1:221–24, 231–32; Sorbelli, 1940, 92; and Trombetti Budriesi, 1988, 140–53. The last includes much additional bibliography.

12. Sorbelli, 1912. The information comes from communal payment records, is somewhat confusing, and may be incomplete. The total annual amount may have reached 2,000 Bolognese lire.

surviving rolls for any Italian university. Bologna had the largest faculty in Italy throughout the Renaissance.

After growing steadily until reaching an average size of 97 in the decade of the 1440s, the number of teachers stabilized at 85 to 110 until the 1530s, when it fell to about 80. Bologna had more legists than artists until the decade 1510–19, when the artists temporarily dominated. Then from the 1540s through the end of the century, Bologna had more artists than legists. The reasons are twofold: Bologna added more professors of medicine and arts, as some subjects (e.g., anatomy, medical botany, and the humanities) grew in importance. Moreover, professors of theology and Scripture were added. By contrast, law declined because the university sharply reduced the number of canonists (see Ch. 13) and because student lectureships in law were seldom filled in the second half of the sixteenth century. Student lectureships in arts continued to be filled.

Examination of the distribution of professors by subject offers a more detailed picture of the faculty. In 1370–71 the university had 11 professors of civil law (called civilians), 7 professors of canon law, 3 professors of medical theory ("the philosophy of medicine and principles of physiology and pathology"), 2 of medical practice ("the specifics of diagnosis and treatment"),[13] 1 professor of surgery, 1 professor who taught both medicine and natural philosophy, a logician, an astrologer, a rhetorician, and a professor of notarial art, for a total of 29.[14] The university continued to grow. The roll of 1388–89 numbered 15 professors of canon law, 18 for civil law, 16 for theoretical and practical medicine and surgery, 5 natural philosophers, 2 moral philosophers, 3 logicians, 4 astronomers, 1 rhetorician, and 3 who taught notarial art, for a total of 67.

The faculty grew mostly through the addition of more professors in the traditional subjects in the fifteenth century. For example, the roll of 1426–27 listed 25 canonists, 28 civilians, 11 professors of medical theory, 10 for medical practice, 3 professors of surgery, 1 for orthopedics (*Ad lecturam dislocationum et fracturarum ossium*), 4 professors of natural and moral philosophy, 3 astrologers, 3 logicians, 4 professors of rhetoric and poetry, a professor of Greek, and a professor of notarial art, making a total of 94.[15] Although this was an early peak, Bologna still averaged 79 professors through the 1420s.

The distribution of faculty changed little in the course of the century. The rolls of the 1470s usually listed about 17 canonists, 23 civilians, 1 notary professor, 8 professors of medical theory, 3 or 4 professors of medical practice, 2 or 3 surgeons, 5 natural philosophers, 2 moral philosophers, 2 or 3 astronomers, 5 logicians, 4 professors of rhetoric and poetry, a professor of Greek, and 1 for Hebrew, an innovation. In addition, 2 student rectors and 5 to 11 unpaid student lecturers taught.

Having decided to pay professorial salaries, the commune created a civil magistracy to rule the university directly and to serve as a buffer between *studium*

---

13. Quoted from Siraisi, 1990, 73.
14. Dallari, 1888–1924, vol. 4: *Aggiunte,* 3–4.
15. Ibid., 51–53.

TABLE I.I

Average Annual Number of Professors at Bologna, 1370–1599

Years	Law	Arts & Medicine	Total
1370–79	18	13	31
1380–89	27	24	51
1390–99	43	30	73
1400–1409	33	24	57
1410–19	31	26	57
1420–29	46	33	79
1430–39	45	28	73
1440–49	59	38	97
1450–59	68	42	110
1460–69	54	36	90
1470–79	49	37	86
1480–89	50	35	85
1490–99	57	35	92
1500–1509	49	39	88
1510–19	44	47	91
1520–29	47	53	100
1530–39	43	37	80
1540–49	37	39	76
1550–59	38	41	79
1560–69	35	45	80
1570–79	28	49[a]	77
1580–89	30	56[b]	86
1590–99	34	52[c]	86

Source: Dallari, 1888–1924, 1, 2, and 4: *Aggiunte;* plus Zaoli, 1912 and 1920.

Note: The professorship (occasionally with two men) of notarial arts was listed in the arts faculty until 1458–59, when it moved to the law faculty. It is always classified as law in the table above, because it was closer to law than arts. The table includes one to three teaching student rectors of law and arts, when these positions were filled, which was less often after 1550. It includes the competitive student lectureships, which totaled eleven (six law, five arts and medicine) when all were filled. This was frequently not the case, which helps explain the fluctuation in numbers. A small number of incomplete rolls have not been included in the averages. The majority of rolls, especially after 1450, also list preuniversity teachers who taught beginning reading and writing, Latin grammar and reading, rhetoric, and arithmetic and geometry (i.e., abbaco) in different quarters of the city (see Grendler, 1989, 26–29, for further explanation). These teachers have been excluded. The small number of cases in which it is not clear whether a grammarian taught at the university or preuniversity level do not affect the overall averages.

[a] This includes an average of 1.5 professors of theology and Scripture, listed in the arts rolls.

[b] This includes an average of 2.5 professors of theology and Scripture, listed in the arts rolls.

[c] This includes an average of 4 professors of theology and Scripture, listed in the arts rolls.

and the higher ranks of government. In or about 1376 the commune appointed four citizens—a senator, a noble, a knight, and a merchant—to oversee the university.[16] Called Riformatori dello Studio (Reformers of the University), this magistracy negotiated with professors, determined stipends, compiled the annual roll, fixed the teaching schedule, and regulated the university in every way except the legal privileges of the students. The Riformatori reported to the highest council of the commune. Other cities and princes followed the Bolognese example by establishing a civil magistracy, often also called Riformatori dello Studio, to oversee the local university. In 1463 the Riformatori appointed a *punctator,* an official charged with visiting classes daily to make certain that professors delivered lectures, taught the required one or two hours, and had a minimum of five students in attendance. A professor deficient in any of these categories suffered financial penalties.[17] Other universities followed the Bolognese lead with similar legislation.

The University of Bologna flourished amid political instability. The city had a population of 32,000 in 1371, making it one of the five or six largest in Italy and clearly one of the wealthiest.[18] But Bologna did not enjoy political peace. A free commune throughout the university's formative period, Bologna maintained its independence under the overlordship of the papacy in the early fourteenth century. Communal strife intensified in the second half of the fourteenth century because no individual, faction, or outsider was strong enough to hold the city for long. Hence, Bologna alternated between free communal government, more or less direct papal rule through a legate, and princely rule by an outsider in the last half of the fourteenth century.

Constant strife and frequent change of office prompted the leading citizens in 1393 to concentrate authority in a council of patricians called the Sedici Riformatori, who would serve for life.[19] But instead of creating unity, the council served as a launching pad for men with princely ambitions, especially members of the Bentivoglio family. In addition, factions of patricians occasionally invited the papacy to exercise direct rule through a legate, invitations that the papacy eagerly accepted.

The pattern continued into the following century. Then Bologna underwent a major political change in 1445. After several abortive attempts, the Bentivoglio succeeded in becoming de facto "first citizens." Sante Bentivoglio (b. 1424) became prince of Bologna in everything but name in 1445 and remained so until his death in 1463. Giovanni II Bentivoglio (1443–1508), a second cousin, immediately succeeded him as "first citizen" and lasted until 1506.

The Bentivoglio still had to contend with the papacy. In 1447 Pope Nicholas V and Sante Bentivoglio created a mixed constitutional state.[20] The key provision was that the highest civil magistracy and the papal legate had to concur; the

16. Simeoni, 1940, 11–12. There is no study of this body.

17. ASB, Riformatori dello Studio, Appuntazioni dei lettori, 1465–1526, 1531–37, provides evidence that the *punctator* discharged his duty.

18. Salvioni, 1890, 45.

19. Ady, 1969, ch. 1, for this and the following paragraph.

20. Ibid., 37–41.

actions of one were invalid without the consent of the other. In other words, oligarchic commune dominated by the Bentivoglio and pope shared power; commune and legate would act in unison. This seemingly impossible arrangement worked because the papacy and the Bentivoglio, who dominated the Sedici Riformatori, wanted it to work. "First-citizen" members of the Bentivoglio family and papal legates supported each other for the next sixty years. The Bentivoglio dominated civic affairs, while the papacy determined foreign policy.

During the latter part of the century Giovanni II Bentivoglio increasingly became patron and prince of the university. In particular he drew the university humanists, who were Bolognese natives, into his orbit. Francesco da Pozzo (called Puteolano), Filippo Beroaldo the Elder, Antonio Urceo (called Il Codro), and Giovanni Garzoni, humanist and professor of medicine, tutored Bentivoglio children, praised the "first citizen" in their works, and enjoyed Bentivoglio patronage. As always, princely patronage had a price: losing the prince's favor meant dismissal for some professors.[21] The Bentivoglio also insisted that the university award a few degrees for political reasons.

The concord between Bentivoglio and papacy helped the university when Pope Nicholas V sent Cardinal Bessarion to be his legate (1450–55). The learned Bessarion immediately proposed improvements for the university which Nicholas V, who had taken an arts doctorate at Bologna in 1420 and had been bishop of the city, implemented through a bull. However, his attempt to add a professorship of music did not succeed.[22]

In 1384–85 the forty-four teaching professors received a total of about 4,900 lire bolognesi, a modest average salary of 111 Bolognese lire, paid quarterly.[23] Salary expenses then rose to 10,000 to 13,000 Bolognese lire annually in the second and third decades of the fifteenth century. Two or three law professors earned very high salaries, but the average was a modest 165 to 195 Bolognese lire, the equivalent of about 83 to 117 Florentine florins or Venetian ducats.[24] In addition, university statutes of 1405 permitted professors to collect small fees (sometimes called "bench money") from students attending their lectures. Doctoral examination fees and fiscal immunities increased professorial incomes.

21. Ibid., 144–45, 161–63.

22. For Nicholas V's degree, see Piana, 1966, 118–19. The roll of 1451–52 listed a professorship *Ad lecturam Musice* without a holder. Dallari notes that a name had been erased from the original document. Nothing more is heard of the music professorship. Dallari, 1888–1924, 1:32. There were no professors of music in Italian universities. The University of Pavia listed as a professor the musical theorist Francesco Gaffurio in the late fifteenth century, but he taught music at the Milanese court. See Ch. 3, "Pavia, 1361."

23. Dallari, 1888–1924, 1:3–5. Unlike most rolls, this one included salaries that totaled 3,415 Bolognese lire and 900 florins pegged at 33 soldi. Since the Bolognese lira was worth 20 soldi, the florin pegged at 33 soldi was worth 1.65 Bolognese lire. Hence, 900 florins can be converted to 1,485 Bolognese lire and added to 3,415 lire to get the total salary expenses of 4,900 Bolognese lire.

24. Zaoli, 1912, 136–50; Zaoli, 1920, 196–97, 202–5, 226–44. The Bolognese lira was worth 50 to 60 percent of the florin and ducat at this time. As always, such figures should be treated as approximate. Salvioni, 1890, 57–60; Spufford, 1986, 72–79. The Bolognese lira decreased in value against the florin and ducat in the sixteenth century.

Bologna financed the university through tax revenues.[25] In 1416 the commune assigned the revenues from several taxes, including that on pepper, to the university. This apparently proved inadequate. Hence, in 1433 the papal governor (Bologna having temporarily returned to direct rule by the papacy) assigned the revenues of a tax on all saleable goods coming into the city. Pope Eugenius IV confirmed this in 1437 and promised additional funds if needed. This tax financed the university through the rest of the century.

The College of Civil Law conferred 1,427 known combined licentiates and doctorates, or licentiates only, in civil law, or civil and canon law together (*utroque iure*), between 1378 and 1500. This was an average of 11.6 degrees per year.[26] Since there are some lacunae in the records, and because such records seldom included all recipients, the actual number is probably higher. Moreover, it is likely that Bologna awarded at least 5 canon law degrees and at least 7 arts and medicine doctorates annually. Hence, Bologna awarded a minimum of 24 degrees annually in the fifteenth century; the real number was undoubtedly higher.[27]

The geographical distribution of the civil law degree recipients demonstrates the international character of the student body. About 73 percent of the civil law and *utroque iure* degrees went to Italians and 26 percent to non-Italians.[28] Of the foreigners, the largest number came from France (29%), Germany (28%), Spain (21%), and England (11%). Students from what are now Austria, Belgium, Greece, the Netherlands, Poland, and Portugal also received civil law licentiates and doctorates between 1378 and 1500. Because the number of non-Italians acquiring civil law degrees was much greater after 1450 than earlier, it appears that the student body became more international in the course of the century.

But localism ruled in the faculty. Prominent Bolognese family names dominated every faculty roll of the fifteenth century. Indeed, son sometimes followed father into university teaching. A few political leaders held teaching posts. Antongaleazzo Bentivoglio took a degree in civil law in 1414 and held an ordinary professorship of civil law from 1418 to 1420 at a salary of 300 Bolognese lire, the third highest salary in law.[29] He then ruled the city for six months of 1420 before being driven into exile. Members of leading Bolognese families opposed to the Bentivoglio also held faculty positions. Bologna did not often hire foreign-that is, non-Bolognese—professors at this time, and they did not stay long.

Other communes countered faculty provincialism to a limited extent by hir-

25. This aspect of the university has been little studied. The following paragraph is based on ASB, Assunteria di Studio, Bu. 95, fascicle 1, which summarizes the decrees dealing with finances; plus Zaoli, 1920, esp. 201–5, and Zaccagnini, 1930, 46, 48, 50.

26. Trombetti Budriesi, 1988, 165–79.

27. Unfortunately, only limited records for arts and medicine degrees for the fifteenth century survive. Piana (1966, 113–74) located 92 arts degrees (7 per year) awarded between 1419 and 1431. And Bronzino, 1962, 1–7, based on a seventeenth-century source, lists 139 degrees in arts and medicine, an average of 7 per year, awarded from 1480 to 1499. Alidosi Pasquali (1980; first published in 1623) lists arts, medicine, and theology degrees, 1000–1623, in alphabetical order along with bits of biographical information for the recipients. But his information is incomplete.

28. Trombetti Budriesi, 1988, 172–75.

29. Zaoli, 1912, 146.

ing a few prominent foreign scholars at higher salaries. Pope Nicholas V in 1450 attempted to limit the salaries of Bolognese citizen professors to 600 Bolognese lire in an effort to accumulate money that could be used to attract distinguished foreigners.[30] But his decree had little effect on appointments or salaries. The vast majority of both Bolognese and foreign professors earned considerably less than 600 Bolognese lire before 1450 and remained far below this figure later. In the academic year 1470–71, seventy-two professors received a total of 14,535 Bolognese lire. One professor received 1,200 Bolognese lire, and two received 1,000. The next highest salary was 400, and the average stipend was 202 Bolognese lire.[31]

Certainly 14,500 Bolognese lire for university salaries was a large commitment of resources. But Bologna chose to hire numerous professors, mostly local men, at modest salaries, rather than fewer but more eminent professors, including expensive outsiders. Certainly the Bolognese policy had advantages. A large faculty meant that students could always find instruction on a particular subject or text. And because most locally born professors taught at Bologna their entire careers, the faculty had great stability.

Many professors bearing local names were able scholars, but few were commanding figures in their fields. An exception was Alessandro Achillini (1461/63–1512), a native of Bologna. Achillini took his degree at Bologna in 1484 and immediately began teaching there: logic until 1487, natural philosophy from 1487 to 1494, morning ordinary professor of medical theory from 1494 to 1497, and afternoon ordinary professor of natural philosophy from 1497 to 1500. Achillini then held both ordinary positions simultaneously: morning professor of medical theory and afternoon professor of natural philosophy, from 1500 until the fall of 1506. This meant that he delivered two lectures daily, which was very unusual. As a warm supporter of the Bentivoglio, Achillini left for Padua in early November 1506, when Giovanni II Bentivoglio lost power. After having taught for two years at Padua, he returned to Bologna in September 1508 to reclaim the same two positions in medicine and philosophy, which he held until his death in 1512. In 1509–10 Achillini received a salary of 900 Bolognese lire, the third highest after two legists.[32] He published many works in medicine, anatomy, and philosophy. He may have discovered, and he certainly was the first to describe, the small bones of the ear and the ileocaecal valve connecting the small and large intestines. As a philosopher Achillini maintained an Averroist interpretation of Aristotle.

The University of Bologna prospered in the fifteenth century despite the sharp and sometimes bloody competition for political power in the city. Commune and papal legate worked together to ensure that the university sailed se-

30. Zaccagnini, 1930, 50; Sorbelli, 1940, 235.

31. ASB, Riformatori dello Studio, Appuntazioni dei lettori, 1465–1526, 1531–37, a salary list of Nov. 2, 1470, no pag. The roll for 1470–71 in Dallari, 1888–1924, 1:82–85, lists 83 professors including 11 student lecturers who did not receive stipends.

32. See B. Nardi, 1958, 179–279; B. Nardi, 1960; Dallari, 1888–1924, vol. 1; and ASB, Assunteria di Studio, Bu. 92, roll of 1509–10, for his salary. Even though Dallari (1:198) lists him as teaching medicine at Bologna in 1507–8, B. Nardi (1958, 259) demonstrates that he did not return until September 1508.

renely through choppy political seas. The commune did not reduce the university appropriation in time of difficulty, and it maintained the size of the faculty when one regime replaced another. The papacy in its capacity as overlord and supranational authority issued bulls to support student and faculty privileges, encouraged foreign students to attend, and worked to strengthen the university.

BOLOGNA IN THE SIXTEENTH CENTURY

The Bolognese kept the papacy at a distance through the fifteenth century despite recognizing papal authority and making annual payments. But the papacy always viewed concessions granted to the commune as temporary. When Giovanni II Bentivoglio lost support within Bologna in the first years of the sixteenth century, Pope Julius II marched on the city. Giovanni II fled rather than face certain defeat, and papal troops entered the city in November 1506. Although he and other members of his family attempted to regain power in the next few years, their rule had ended.

But papal triumph did not signal Bolognese subjugation. After the death of Julius II in 1513, papacy and commune reinstated the terms of the agreement of 1447 under which they shared power. A Senate of forty (later fifty) life members drawn from the leading noble families of Bologna replaced the Sedici Riformatori. When a vacancy occurred, the pope chose a replacement from a group of four nominees presented by the Senate. The Senate later became hereditary. Communal legislative and fiscal structures remained in place. As before, Senate and legate had to act in accord under the principle that "the legate can do nothing without the Senate, and the Senate can do nothing without the legate."[33] The Bolognese mostly governed themselves in internal matters. And like a sovereign state, Bologna had a small armed force under the joint authority of Senate and legate and maintained a resident ambassador at the papal court. Bologna and its *contado* (the surrounding countryside under direct rule of the commune) remained a largely self-governing aristocratic republic within the papal state until the unification of Italy in the nineteenth century.[34]

Governance and fiscal support for the University of Bologna continued as before under the direct authority of the commune. Julius II confirmed in 1509 that the tax on goods coming into the city to be sold (called *grossa gabella*) would finance the university. It yielded income of slightly more than 25,000 Bolognese lire for the university in 1509–10 and similar or larger annual amounts in the next twenty years. Subsequent popes confirmed this financial arrangement in 1567 and 1586.[35] The Riformatori dello Studio chose the professors and determined

---

33. Nulla può il Legato senza il Senato, nulla il Senato senza il Legato. Quoted in Fanti, 1978, 216. This work and Colliva, 1977, provide good accounts of Bolognese politics and government after 1500.

34. Gleason, 1993, 277; Hughes, 1994, 9–11.

35. ASB, Assunteria di Studio, Bu. 95, fascicle 1, and ibid., Bu. 92, Diversorum. Lettori e collegi, secc. XVI–XVIII, fascicle 8, with fiscal rolls of 1509–10, 1523–24, and 1526–27.

stipends. A representative of the Senate and the legate ratified the actions of the Riformatori.

With increased funding the university had a large faculty. Bologna continued a policy of appointing three to six or more concurrent professors for the major professorships, such as the ordinary morning professor of civil law and ordinary morning professor of medical theory. But only the stipends, which were not published, indicated which person was considered to hold the first position. In the 1520s the faculty numbered 100, including the 6 student lecturers in law and 5 in arts, divided between 47 legists and 53 professors of arts and medicine. The law faculty now typically included about 24 professors of civil law, 21 professors of canon law, and 2 professors of notarial art. The arts and medicine faculty had approximately 18 professors of medical theory, 5 of medical practice, 5 professors of surgery, 5 natural philosophers, 2 metaphysicians, 5 logicians, 4 astronomers, 7 professors of rhetoric and poetry or humanities, a professor of Greek, and one to teach Hebrew or Hebrew and "Chaldean" (i.e., Aramaic). This large faculty received about 25,000 Bolognese lire in 1523–24 and 30,000 Bolognese lire in 1526–27. The average salary in 1526–27 was about 306 Bolognese lire.[36] University expenses remained at this high level. The commune spent a little more than 31,000 Bolognese lire on the university, all except about 1,000 of the amount for faculty salaries, in 1552–53. The star civilian Mariano Sozzini the Younger received 5,200 Bolognese lire, more than one-sixth of the total. The commune spent about 17,400 Bolognese lire for arts and medicine salaries alone in 1563–64.[37]

The Riformatori dello Studio took advantage of the ill fortune of the University of Padua in order to pursue the most famous philosopher of the day, Pietro Pomponazzi of Mantua (1462–1525). Pomponazzi had taught at Padua since 1488, with the exception of three years of private study. When war closed the University of Padua in 1509, Pomponazzi fled to Ferrara. When the Venetians did not immediately restore the Studio Padovano, the Bolognese persuaded him to come to Bologna to hold the position of ordinary professor of natural philosophy at a salary of 200 gold ducats (worth about 700 Bolognese lire at this time), less than he had earned at Padua.[38] Pomponazzi began teaching at Bologna either during the academic year 1511–12 or in the autumn of 1512.

The Bolognese had to pay considerably more to keep Pomponazzi. In 1514–15 he held two posts, ordinary professor of natural philosophy and extraordinary professor of moral philosophy with the obligation of lecturing on holidays. The Bolognese offered him a four-year contract at 400 ducats (1,250 Bolognese lire) to continue these two posts. But the Florentine government then offered him

36. ASB, Assunteria di Studio, Bu. 92, with fiscal rolls of 1523–24 and 1526–27.

37. Cavina, 1988, 437–40 (for 1552–53); Simili, 1956, 391–93 (1563–64).

38. Professorial contracts and correspondence between commune and professors indicated that the value of a gold ducat, a Florentine florin, and the scudo ranged between 3 and 4 Bolognese lire in the sixteenth century and may have been about 3.5 Bolognese lire at this time. By 1580 the scudo had risen to more than 4 Bolognese lire. McCuaig, 1989, 61–62.

500 florins to teach natural philosophy at Pisa. When the University of Pisa did not open for the academic year in the autumn of 1515, the Florentine authorities invited him to lecture at Florence. The Bolognese responded by using every means at their disposal to hold Pomponazzi. They took the high ground of begging Pope Leo X and Cardinal Giulio de' Medici to dissuade the younger Medici princes in Florence from pursuing him. They took the low road of denying Pomponazzi permission to move his effects out of Bologna. In October 1515 Pomponazzi signed a four-year contract with Bologna. However, the Florentines continued to pursue him. The Bolognese countered with an offer of an eight-year contract for 600 ducats (2,100 Bolognese lire), which Pomponazzi signed in late December 1518. Throughout this academic tug-of-war, Pomponazzi taught large classes and wrote his most famous book, *De immortalitate animae*, which was printed in 1516. He taught at Bologna until illness forced him to stop in 1524; he died in 1525.[39]

The Bolognese took further advantage of Paduan difficulties by hiring the eminent Carlo Ruini of Reggio (c. 1456–1530), who had also been teaching at Padua. Bologna appointed him its major afternoon ordinary professor of civil law in 1511 at a stipend of 3,000 Bolognese lire (about 857 gold ducats), a figure later raised to 4,320 Bolognese lire (about 1,234 gold ducats).[40] After Ruini's death the Bolognese pursued other famous non-Bolognese legists.

Although Bolognese legists taught *mos italicus*, the traditional legal method, a famous name was more important than methodological consistency. Hence, Bologna turned to the leading representative of the new humanistic jurisprudence, Andrea Alciato of Milan (1492–1550). Alciato agreed to come from Pavia to Bologna for 1,200 gold scudi per annum plus 200 scudi for moving expenses. He taught civil law at Bologna for four years, 1537 through 1541. However, pressure from Emperor Charles V, overlord of Lombardy, forced Alciato to agree to return to the University of Pavia at the end of 1541.[41] Bologna continued to pursue famous law professors throughout the century.

As the example of Alciato demonstrated, the commune had begun to hire a few eminent non-Bolognese professors. In 1513 the Senate decreed that the university might have four non-Bolognese professors on its rolls, one each in law, philosophy, medicine, and the humanities.[42] The commune did its best to ensure that these four would be the most famous scholars that money could buy. The

---

39. Costa, 1902–3b, with numerous letters; also see ASB, Assunteria di Studio, Bu. 52, fascicle 36, with several letters to and by Pomponazzi.

40. For a short biographical and bibliographical sketch, see Belloni, 1986, 180–82. For his salary, see ASB, Riformatori di Studio, Minute dei rotoli 1515–44, ff. 2ʳ, 6ʳ, 30ʳ; ASB, Assunteria di Studio, Bu. 53, Requisiti dei Lettori. Lettere R, vol. 24, fascicle 42; and ASB, Assunteria di Studio, Bu. 92. fiscal rolls for 1523–24 and 1525–26.

41. Costa (1902–3a) describes the pursuit of these legal scholars. Alciato's Bolognese salary is found in ASB, Assunteria di Studio, Requisiti dei Lettori, Bu. 30, fascicle 42, letter of Aug. 29, 1537. Incidentally, because war broke out in Lombardy in early 1542, Alciato did not immediately return to Pavia but went to Ferrara for 1,350 ducats.

42. Costa, 1902–3a, 330 n. 24, Senate decree of 1513, repeated in 1540 and 1578; Zaccagnini, 1930, 146–47.

Fig. 1. Carlo Ruini, *Lectura ultima super prima Infortiati.* 1538. Colophon: Venice: Battista Torti. *Special Collections Library, Biddle Law Library, University of Pennsylvania Law School.*

commune was not just interested in scholarship; it wanted eminent foreigners in order to attract students, especially ultramontanes. Nor did the university limit itself to four; it appointed some professors, especially in arts and medicine, from other parts of Italy.

Still, the non-Bolognese faculty constituted only a small fraction of the total. Law was almost exclusively staffed by local men through the rest of the century. Fortunately, Bologna and its territory had a strong intellectual tradition that produced many good scholars, especially in medicine. For example, Giulio Cesare Aranzio of Bologna (c. 1530–89) took a degree at Bologna in 1556 and taught surgery from 1556 to 1570 and anatomy from 1570 to 1588 there, making important discoveries about the human fetus.[43] Gaspare Tagliacozzi of Bologna (1545–99) took his degree in medicine at Bologna in 1570, was appointed to the newly established anatomy professorship, taught at Bologna until his death, and was a pioneer in plastic surgery. The Bolognese Ulisse Aldrovandi (1522–1605) developed natural history during his long teaching career (1553–1600).

Thanks to talented native sons and a few outsiders, Bologna achieved a level of scholarly eminence above all other Italian universities with the exception of Padua. The two institutions competed throughout the century; indeed, a significant number of well-known scholars taught at both.

As table 1.1 indicated, Bologna had 80 to 85 professors and student lecturers in the last third of the sixteenth century. The civilians numbered 20 to 23, and the canonists had dropped to 7 to 10. The faculty of arts and medicine of 45 to 50 persons had 9 professors of medical theory, 7 for practical medicine, 4 for surgery, and 1 for medical botany. There were about 8 natural philosophers including Aldrovandi, who taught "fossils, plants, and animals." Two astronomers, 1 mathematician, 3 humanists, 1 professor of Greek, 2 metaphysicians, and 1 or 2 logicians made up the rest. A professorship of Hebrew (sometimes Hebrew and Aramaic) came and went. The student rector of arts sometimes taught, as did up to 5 student lecturers, 1 each in medicine, natural philosophy, astronomy, rhetoric, and logic. Finally, the arts roll listed 1 to 4 professors of theology and Sacred Scripture, a new departure for Bologna (see Ch. 10, "Universities Reluctant to Teach Theology").

The university acquired its own quarters through the efforts of the papal legate. Classes had met in rented rooms throughout the city, but especially in the center. Stimulated by the example of the University of Padua, where all classes met in the university building by 1530, the papal legate agitated for a home for the Bolognese *studio*. Pope Pius IV, aware of the need from his student days at Bologna (he took a law degree *in utroque iure* in 1525), issued a bull in 1561 ordering the erection of a building. The Bolognese Senate strongly opposed the measure, as did the professors, who feared that part of their salaries would be diverted to construction costs. The legate prevailed, and the professors' fears were realized. Construction of the Archiginnasio building very near the cathedral of San Petronio in the center of the city began in March 1562. The city and the

43. Mondella, 1961.

faculty bore the construction costs of 64,000 Bolognese lire. The building was completed in time for the opening of the academic year in October 1563. The Archiginnasio had seven lecture halls for law, six for arts and medicine, space for a permanent anatomical theater (added after 1595), and two additional rooms for other purposes. Classes met in the Archiginnasio until 1803; it now houses the Biblioteca Archiginnasio, the city's major library. Numerous crests of student rectors, professors, and students decorate the walls.[44]

Bologna conferred a large number of degrees in the sixteenth century. It awarded an average of 25 doctorates in arts and medicine annually between 1550 and 1559, the decade with the highest number of known degrees in arts and medicine. In law, Bologna awarded an average of 55 degrees annually between 1583 and 1599.[45] It is likely that the total number of doctorates was greater than this sampling indicates, because documentation for university degrees is seldom complete.

Since Bologna boasted the largest faculty in Italy, it is likely that its enrollments were the highest. Bologna may have had average annual enrollments of 1,000 students from 1400 to 1450, about 1,500 for 1450–99, and 1,500 to 2,000 between 1500 and 1550. Enrollment probably held at about 2,000 at midcentury and then declined to 1,500 in the last years of the century. These are only estimates, because no precise information is available.[46] Enrollments could fluctuate considerably from year to year.

The city's population and physical size could accommodate a large student body. The inhabitants probably numbered slightly fewer than 40,000 at the end of the fourteenth century and possibly about 50,000 at the end of the fifteenth century. The sixteenth century saw steady growth to 62,000 in 1569 and 72,000 in 1587. Recession and famine then lowered the population to about 65,000 in the 1590s, and it remained at this level through the first two decades of the following century.[47]

Students frequently disturbed the peace. They commonly wore swords, and some carried firearms in the late sixteenth century. Clashes between students of different nations, or between students and the communal police force, could be bloody. When fighting produced a fatality, the Bolognese commune often executed the alleged killer, despite student claims of immunity from local prosecution. And the commune acted swiftly and brutally against any perceived threat of insurrection. In 1520 it decapitated a student accused of writing treason against the commune. On the other hand, the city sometimes bent over backward to avoid

44. Simeoni, 1940, ch. 2.

45. Bronzino (1962) provides a list of arts and medicine degrees, 1480 through 1800, based on university archival records. Simeoni (1940, 65) provides a count of law degrees, 1583–99, and arts degrees (the number a few less than Bronzino located), 1506–1600, based on the same records. Neither used notarial records, which might include additional doctorates.

46. See the Appendix for estimates of student enrollments for all universities. Simeoni (1940, 63) suggests a maximum student enrollment of "several thousands" at Bologna. Brizzi (1977, 444) estimates 2,000, and Fanti (1978, 228) suggests more than 1,000.

47. Salvioni, 1890, 72–77; Ginatempo and Sandri, 1990, 85, 100, 254–55.

antagonizing the students as a whole, fearing that they would leave for another university or overwhelm the city's small police force. When in 1560 a fight between students and police led to the death of a student, the authorities appeased the students by hanging a policeman who had allegedly thrown a rock at them.[48]

The University of Bologna sailed relatively serenely through the sixteenth century. Its large faculty of numerous local sons and some eminent outsiders seemed to satisfy students. The Riformatori dello Studio became a little more aristocratic in composition, as its four members typically included two nobles. Then in the 1520s the Bolognese Senate established its own subcommittee to deal with extraordinary university matters. Called the Assunteria di Studio, this committee of four senators gradually assumed control over the most important matters, such as professorial hiring and salaries. The Riformatori were reduced to scheduling and keeping track of missed lectures.[49]

The Bolognese consulted with their papal overlords about major university matters more often than previously, especially when attempting to appoint a distinguished foreign scholar. Then the Assunteria di Studio contacted the Bolognese ambassador to the Holy See, who would enlist the help of influential cardinals. Popes often helped in the recruitment of leading scholars.[50] Both commune and pontiff strove to maintain the university at the highest level. Indeed, the papacy put the interests of the University of Bologna ahead of those of other universities (Perugia, Macerata, Ferrara after 1598, and Rome itself) in the papal state.

Many future university scholars studied or took degrees at Bologna. So did five popes, Nicholas V (1447–55), Alexander VI (law degree in 1456; pope 1492–1503), Pius IV (1559–65), Gregory XIII (1572–85), and Gregory XV (1621–23). Nicholas V (Tommaso Parentucelli) took an arts degree in 1420.[51] The Bolognese-born Gregory XIII (Ugo Buoncampagni) took a law degree *in utroque iure* in 1530 and taught civil law at Bologna from 1530 to 1540 before moving to a curial post in Rome. Many future papal diplomats, curialists, bishops, and cardinals also studied at Bologna. Most of them took degrees in law, because law, rather than theology, positioned a clergyman for advancement in the Renaissance church. The Protestant Ulrich von Hutten also studied law at Bologna, in 1516–17.[52] Nicolaus Copernicus (1473–1543), who studied law and astronomy at Bologna from 1496 to 1501 (see Ch. 12, "Professors of Astrology, Astronomy, and Mathematics"), may have been Bologna's most famous student.

48. Zaccagnini, 1930, 187–91.

49. Simeoni, 1940, 11–12, who does not give a precise date for its establishment. I have found Assunteria records beginning in the mid-1520s. Comparing the surviving documents of Assunteria and Riformatori shows clearly that the former was the more important agency by the third quarter of the sixteenth century.

50. See the numerous letters concerning the recruitment of professors in ASB, Assunteria di Studio, Bu. 75, Lettere dell'ambasciadori agli Assunti, 1571–1694, and ibid., Bu. 79, Lettere di diversi all'Assunteria, 1575–1691.

51. His degree is recorded in Piana, 1966, 118–19.

52. Knod, 1970, 225.

Bologna awarded the second known doctorate to a woman, who then became the first female professor. The Bolognese Laura Maria Caterina Bassi (1711–78), the daughter of a professor of medicine, studied privately. She then participated in a public disputation with five professors on theses in logic, metaphysics, and physics before an assemblage of senators, professors, and the cardinal archbishop on April 17, 1732. So impressed were they that a doctoral examination was arranged. Bassi passed the examination on May 11, 1732, and received her degree on May 12. The commune then offered her a teaching position at 500 Bolognese lire. Her name appeared on the roll for the rest of her life, from 1732–33 through the academic year 1777–78 as a professor *Ad universam philosophiam* with the freedom to lecture on texts of her choosing ("ad beneplacitum"). However, she apparently did not lecture in the university building but at home. Although some male professors also taught at home, this seems to have been a concession to those who objected to the appointment of a woman. In later years Bassi also conducted physical experiments for advanced students, lectured frequently at the local academy of science, corresponded with Voltaire and Alessandro Volta among others, and received Emperor Joseph II, who admired her physical experiments.[53]

The Studio Bolognese was the first Italian university and set the pattern. When the commune began to pay faculty salaries and make appointments, it fixed the character of the Italian university as a civic enterprise teaching the secular subjects of law and medicine. The commune appointed citizens and residents of the city and its territory to the majority of teaching posts, a policy followed by most Italian universities. By 1400 the Studio Bolognese was a large institution attracting students from the entire European world. Political turbulence had few negative effects on the university. Although commune and papacy contested each other for political control of the city, they collaborated for the benefit of the university. So far as is known, it never closed between 1400 and 1600, a remarkable record for the times. Although Bologna began by teaching law, arts and medicine were equally important, perhaps more significant, in the sixteenth century. Bologna had the largest number of professors and probably the highest student enrollment among Italian universities. Overall, Bologna competed with Padua for the title of Italy's leading university.

PADUA, 1222

The traditional account states that the University of Padua began with a migration of teachers and students from Bologna in 1222.[54] Although little is known about the migration, various pieces of evidence confirm the presence of professors and students in law and other fields in the 1220s and 1230s. But the university may have closed under the harsh rule of Ezzelino da Romano, who

53. The bibliography on Bassi is too extensive to list here. See Comelli, 1912; Findlen, 1993; and Dallari, 1888–1924, vol. 3, pt. 1, pp. 336, 341, 346, 350, 355; vol. 3, pt. 2, pp. 5, 11, 16, 21, 26, 31, 37, 42, 47, and passim, 205, 211, for the rolls listing Bassi.

54. This short summary of the early history of the University of Padua is based on Rashdall, 1936, 2:9–21; especially on Siraisi, 1973, 15–31, 175–76; Arnaldi, 1977; and Kohl, 1998, 31–34, 199–200.

took control of the city in 1237. It revived at the end of his family's rule in 1260. In 1262 the commune guaranteed scholarly privileges and agreed to pay the salaries of professors of canon and civil law. Additional influxes of scholars and students from Bologna in 1262 and 1274 strengthened the university. Pope Urban IV granted papal recognition in 1264 by affirming that the doctors in the schools might examine students for degrees and that the bishop would confer the license to teach and the doctorate on successful candidates.

The communal government of Padua, and the Carrara ruling family after 1318, supported and guided the university through the fourteenth century. The commune appointed and paid the important professors of law, arts, and medicine by the time of the appearance of the first statutes in 1331. Nevertheless, the students continued to name the occupants of some lesser professorships in the fifteenth century and the first half of the sixteenth. As at Bologna, colleges of doctors of law and medicine, enrolling professors and some local lawyers and physicians who did not teach, conducted degree examinations. In the late thirteenth century the civil government barred Paduan citizens from academic positions funded by the commune. Although the Paduan prohibition against local professors did not endure, it signaled the city's determination to appoint able non-Paduans in order to build a faculty capable of attracting students from abroad. In 1346 Pope Clement VI enhanced the status of Padua with a bull describing it as an ancient *studium generale* in which all subjects except theology might be taught. In 1363 Pope Urban V authorized the establishment of a faculty of theology. By the late fourteenth century, the university boasted some well-known scholars and students from different parts of Europe.

In 1405 the Republic of Venice conquered Padua and incorporated the city into the Venetian state. The Venetian overlords made it clear from the beginning that they would strongly support the university. At first Venice and the commune of Padua were each to contribute half of 3,000 ducats for the expenses of the *studio*. But in September 1407 the Venetian Senate agreed to pay all the expenses up to a maximum of 4,000 ducats.[55] The Venetian government also ordered the embryonic and potentially competing *studii* of Treviso and Vicenza to close. On March 31, 1407, it decreed that all the republic's subjects desiring university degrees must study at Padua under pain of a fine of 500 ducats. This decree was repeated several times in the next two hundred years, but violators were never punished, so far as is known. Still, it signaled Venetian support.

---

55. Dupuigrenet Desroussilles, 1980, 611–12. This is the most recent and best narrative of the university and its relations with the Venetian government during the Renaissance. Briefer narratives include Favaro, 1922, 3–54; Rossetti, 1983; and Ohl, 1980, for the fifteenth century. The Venetian Senate records expressed university financial figures, including salaries, in ducats of account (worth 6 lire 4 soldi) throughout the fifteenth, sixteenth, and early seventeenth centuries. Nevertheless, professors were normally paid in Paduan florins worth 5 lire. Hence, when the Senate decreed that a professor should be paid 100 ducats (= 620 lire), he actually received 100 Paduan florins (= 500 lire). Although this account uses ducats when summarizing Venetian Senate acts and Paduan florins when quoting professorial salaries in salary rolls, the difference should be kept in mind. A few leading professors won contracts specifying payment in ducats or scudi in the sixteenth century.

Most important, the Venetian Senate took a keen and constructive interest in attracting students by making good faculty appointments and increasing salaries. A Senate directive of July 20, 1413, typified Venetian actions. A delegation of students had come to ask the Senate to provide "famous teachers" for the University of Padua. The Senate agreed: "Students follow famous teachers, and if provisions for this are not made, our *studium* will be ruined." The Senate decree went on to note that Raffaele Fulgosio, professor of civil law, had received an offer of 1,000 ducats from Parma but had agreed to remain in Padua for 850. The Senate concluded that since a famous professor of canon law was needed as well, one would be appointed at 600 ducats. With two famous law professors, students would come. If additional funds were needed for these appointments, the Senate directed that the proceeds from a tax on Paduan prostitutes should be applied to university salaries and that another professor might be released. Finally, the Senate expressed a desire to abolish the limit of 4,000 ducats for university expenses.[56]

The Venetian Senate returned to the university in 1414 by authorizing spending more than 4,000 ducats if needed, with the additional funds to come from new taxes to be imposed on Padua and its territory.[57] The Senate then delegated daily authority over the university to the two Venetian governors of Padua, subject to senatorial guidance. In addition, the Senate instructed the governors to choose four Paduan citizens called *reformatores studii* to oversee university affairs and to keep the governors informed on matters of teaching and discipline. But the Paduan *reformatores* had little, if any, influence and left few traces in the documents. The Venetian Senate made policy and decided all financial and appointment issues, usually after receipt of information from the Venetian governors of Padua or in response to complaints from students who came directly to the Senate.

Young Venetian nobles began to study and take degrees at the University of Padua. Some attended the classes of Padua's first humanist professor, Gasparino Barzizza, who taught rhetoric and "moral authors" from 1407 to 1421. These young nobles began to appreciate that humanistic studies and the university contributed to their personal development. They also concluded that the university could train the men needed to rule and administer the Venetian state as it expanded across northern Italy. These former students would eventually rule Venice and be in position to make the Paduan *studium,* now "their university," Italy's leader.[58]

The first surviving role comes from 1422–23. The University of Padua at that time had 16 professors of arts and medicine, 11 for law, and 2 teaching student rectors. It was fourth in size, after Bologna, Pavia, and Perugia. Professors and

56. "Quia scolares seguntur [= sequuntur] famosos doctores, et nisi ad hoc provideatur dictum nostrum studium destruitur." AAUP, F. 648, ff. 8ʳ, 9ʳ⁻ᵛ, 10ʳ⁻ᵛ, 11ʳ, 20ʳ, 23ʳ, 26ʳ⁻ᵛ, for various measures by the Senate on behalf of the *studio* from 1406 through 1413. Quotation from ibid., f. 26ᵛ.

57. For the Senate measure of Feb. 15, 1414, see AAUP, F. 505, no pag.

58. For more on Barzizza, see Ch. 6. See King, 1986, 315–449 passim, for biographies of Venetian nobles and others who attended the University of Padua. It is likely that former students played key roles in fifteenth-century legislation strengthening the university.

TABLE I.2
University of Padua Roll, 1422–1423

Arts and Medicine

Medical theory, ordinary A.M.	Antonio Cermisone,[a] 550 florins
	Galeazzo Santasofia,[b] 300florins
Medical theory, extraordinary nones P.M.	Stefano Dottori,[c] 50 florins
	Bartolomeo Montagnana,[d] 100 florins
Medical practice, hour 21	Bono Dal Fiume,[e] 40 florins
	Francesco Niasio,[f] 40 florins
Medical practice	Niccolò Cavazzoli,[g] 30 florins
Natural philosophy, ordinary	Antonio Acelo,[h] 100 florins
	Sigismondo Polcastro,[i] 60 florins
Natural philosophy, extraordinary	Giovanni Caldiera,[j] 20 florins
Surgery	Niccolò da Andria,[k] 20 florins
	Giovanni Matteo Regini,[l] 8 florins
Astrology	Prosdocimo Beldomandi,[m] 40 florins
Rhetoric	Vittorino Rambaldoni da Feltre,[n] 80 florins, resigned April 18, 1423; replaced by Giacomo Languschi,[o] 80 florins
Logic	Giovanni Fornaci,[p] 30 florins
	Gaetano da Thiene,[q] 40 florins
Medicine, extraordinary *in diebus festis*	Henricus da Alemania,[r], student rector of arts and medicine, 20 florins

Law

Canon law *Decretum*	Rainaldo da Camerino,[s] 100 florins
Decretals A.M.	Prosdocimo Conti,[t] 30 florins
Decretals P.M.	Giovanni Francesco Capodilista,[u] 200 florins
Sextus and *Clementinae*	Paolo Dotti,[v] 60 florins
	Bartolomeo Zabarella,[w] 40 florins
Civil law, ordinary, *Codex*	Raffaele Fulgosio,[x] 1000 florins
Infortiatum	Raffaele Raimondi (da Como),[y] 700 florins
Codex, extraordinary	Francesco Gennari,[z] 20 florins
Institutes	Giacomo Mussato,[aa] 15 florins
Civil law, extraordinary *in diebus festis*	Cristoforo da Pesaro,[bb], student rector of law, 34 florins
Civil law, extraordinary	Antonio Aristotele,[cc] 10 florins
Notarial art	Padovano Pizzacomini,[dd] 35 florins

Source: This is the first surviving Paduan roll, never before printed in its entirety. There are two copies, both later manuscripts. The first is AAUP, F. 648, ff. 35ʳ–36ᵛ, dated November 10, 1422, with additions throughout the academic year. Belloni (1986, 44–45), reprints the legists' part of the roll from this source. Another copy is BUP, Ms. 1673, f. 179ʳ. The AAUP source gives salaries in florins, the BUP ms. in ducats.

[a]Cermisone (d. 1441), from Padua, obtained a doctorate in arts (1387) and in medicine (1390) from

Padua, taught briefly at Florence and Pavia, and then was appointed to the above position in 1413, which he held until death. A well-known medical scholar in his time, Cermisone wrote hundreds of medical *consilia* and several treatises. Di Trocchio, 1979, and Pesenti, 1984, 72–91.

[b]Probably not a Paduan, Santasofia (d. 1427) was one of several members of his family who taught at Padua. He obtained a doctorate in medicine from Padua in 1390, taught briefly at Bologna and for several years at the University of Vienna, and then held the above position from 1407 to 1427. He wrote several short works. Pesenti, 1984, 182–86.

[c]Dottori (d. 1463), from Padua, obtained a doctorate in arts and medicine (1409) and in medicine (1419) from Padua. A follower of Cermisone, he held secondary medical professorships at Padua from 1422 until 1439, when he was confined in Venice for involvement in an anti-Venetian conspiracy. After release in 1441, he apparently no longer taught but still served as a promoter for degrees. Pesenti, 1984, 115–16, and Pesenti, 1992c.

[d]Named after a town about 50 kilometers southwest of Padua, Montagnana (d. after February 1452) was one of the most famous professors of medicine of his age. He obtained his doctorate in medicine from Padua in 1403 and then taught there probably from 1408 onward. He wrote numerous *consilia* and several treatises. Pesenti, 1984, 141–57.

[e]Dal Fiume (d. after 1449) obtained his medical doctorate from Padua in 1410, probably began teaching there by 1418, and continued until about 1450. Pesenti, 1984, 93–94.

[f]Niasio (d. 1427) came from the Euganean Hills near Padua. He obtained his doctorate in medicine from Padua in 1411 and taught there from 1414 until death. Pesenti, 1984, 159–60.

[g]Cavazzoli (d. after February 1430), a Venetian, obtained a doctorate in medicine from Padua in 1417 and taught there from 1422 to 1424. Pesenti, 1984, 72.

[h]Acelo taught at Padua (1422–30). Facciolati, 1978, pt. 2:102–3.

[i]Polcastro (1384–1473), from Vicenza, received a doctorate in arts from Padua in 1412, taught philosophy from 1419, obtained a doctorate in medicine in 1424, and taught medicine from 1426 to 1465. He wrote several short medical works. Pesenti, 1984, 167–70.

[j]Caldiera (1395/1400–74), a Venetian, is much better known as a humanist. He obtained doctorates in arts (1420) and medicine (1426) from Padua. He did not teach long at the university but was practicing medicine in Venice by 1431. He also made astrological predictions and wrote several humanistic treatises in praise of Venice. Cotton, 1973; and especially King, 1986, 344–45 and passim.

[k]Niccolò da Andria taught surgery at Padua from 1421 to 1434, perhaps longer, and then surgery at Ferrara (1457–58). Pesenti, 1984, 160–61; *I maestri di Ferrara*, 1991, 9.

[l]From Feltre, Regini obtained his doctorate in medicine from Padua in 1422, taught surgery in the years 1422–26, and then left teaching. Pesenti, 1984, 173.

[m]Beldomandi, or Beldemandis (1370/80–1428), a Paduan, obtained a doctorate in medicine from Padua in 1411 and taught there from 1422 to 1428. He composed influential works in musical theory, astronomy, astrology, and mathematics. Favaro, 1966, 1:89–90, and Monterosso Vacchelli and Vasoli, 1965.

[n]This is the famous Vittorino da Feltre (1373 or 1378–1446/47). In his biography, probably written between 1462 and 1465, Bartolomeo Sacchi (il Platina) wrote that Vittorino resigned his university post because of the insolence and licentiousness of the students. Platina, 1948, 9. The few months from November to April were Vittorino's only university teaching experience. He established his school at Mantua in the summer of 1423.

[o]Languschi (d. after 1452), a Venetian, was a notary for the Venetian republic in the years 1409–20. He taught from 1423 to 1428 and then became a papal secretary, but he did not sever his ties with Padua. He received a doctorate in arts from Padua in 1431 and was a minor humanist poet. Tomasini, 1986, 496; King, 1986, 286–87; and Davies, 1988, 12–22.

[p]The Venetian Fornaci (d. after 1458) received a doctorate in arts from Padua in 1421. He left Padua to teach logic at Bologna (1423–25). After obtaining a doctorate in medicine from Padua in 1431, he

TABLE 1.2, *continued*

taught natural philosophy and medicine at Bologna and Padua for the rest of his life. He wrote two medical works. Pesenti, 1984, 117–18.

qFrom Gaeta, Gaetano da Thiene (1387–1465) was appointed on October 18, 1422, in place of Giovanni da Sicilia, who was to be paid 10 florins. This was the beginning of a long and distinguished career. Gaetano became professor of natural philosophy in 1430 and wrote many works. *CHRP,* 818–19.

rAlready possessing a doctorate in arts, Henricus added the doctorate in medicine in 1425. Pesenti, 1984, 123–24. "Magister Thaddeus" replaced him at the same salary on April 9, 1423.

sFrom the Marches, Rainaldo received his doctorate in canon law in 1419 from Padua, apparently taught at Padua for two years, and later taught at Bologna. Belloni, 1986, 326.

tBorn into an important Paduan family, Conti (c. 1370–1438) obtained his doctorate *in utroque iure* at Padua in 1398 and began teaching canon law there about 1402. With the exception of about three years teaching at Siena, he spent the rest of his life teaching law at Padua and serving the Venetian state. He wrote important works in canon law. Kohl, 1983a, and Belloni, 1986, 303–6.

uCapodilista (c. 1375–1452), a Paduan, obtained doctorates in civil law (1401) and canon law (1403) at Padua. He taught either canon or civil law at Padua (1401–44), with a few absences, and published modestly. Several of his descendents also taught law at Padua; see chapter 5, "Doctorates from Counts Palatine." Tocci, 1965, and Belloni, 1986, 254–58.

vFrom a wealthy Paduan family, Dotti (1392–after 1455) obtained a doctorate in civil law from Padua in 1415 and began teaching there in 1422 or earlier. Dotti taught both canon and civil law at Padua, while also serving in numerous communal political offices. But in 1439 he was permanently exiled to Crete for his alleged involvement in a conspiracy to transfer Paduan allegiance to the Visconti of Milan. Dotti wrote several legal works. Belloni, 1986, 292–94, 323, and Di Renzo Villata, 1992.

wIt is not clear how long Zabarella (1400–1455), another Paduan, taught. He was bishop of Spalato (1428–39) and of Florence (1439–45) and then became a papal nuncio. Belloni, 1986, 323.

xFrom Piacenza, Fulgosio (1367–1427) obtained his doctorate *in utroque iure* at Pavia in 1390, began teaching there in 1389, and moved to Padua about 1409. Note that his salary had risen to 1,000 florins, matching the Parma offer (see above). Several of his works were printed in the sixteenth century. Belloni, 1986, 306–11.

yFrom Como, Raimondi (c. 1375–1427) obtained his doctorate *in utroque iure* from Pavia in 1398 and began teaching there about that time. He moved to Padua in 1410. Several of his works were later printed. Belloni, 1986, 311–13.

zGennari taught at Padua in the years 1422–25, but that is all that is known. Belloni, 1986, 339

aaMussato, a Paduan, taught in the years 1422–25, but that is all that is known. Belloni, 1986, 319.

bbNo further information.

ccAntonio came from Sulmona in the Abruzzi, but that is all that is known.

ddHe was obviously a Paduan, but nothing else is known.

rectors earned 3,772 florins; other expenses brought the total to a 3,810 florins.[59] Nine professors were Paduans, another 2 came from Paduan territory, and 3 from Venice. This was not extraordinary localism for the times but greater than Padua would demonstrate in the next century. The scholarly quality of the faculty was high, although not as distinguished as it would be later.

The size and subject distribution of the faculty remained about the same through the next dozen years. The 1424–25 roll listed 13 legists and 16 professors of arts and medicine including a teaching student rector.[60] The 1430–31 roll, possibly incomplete, listed 11 legists and 8 arts and medicine professors.[61] Arts and medicine alone had 17 professors and a teaching student rector in 1434–35 and 18 professors and a teaching student rector in 1435–36. If the legists continued to number about a dozen, then the university continued with about 30 professors. Then the arts and medicine component suddenly rose to 30 professors, plus the teaching student rector, in 1436–37. If law maintained its previous size, the university had about 43 professors at this time; if law also grew, the number was higher.[62]

In 1434 the Venetian Senate established an enduring fiscal scheme for financing the university. Like other Italian governments, it believed that the town hosting the university should bear the costs. The Senate decreed that a tax to be paid by the owners of vehicles (*carri*) plus a head or "mouth" (*boccadego*) tax in the town and territory of Padua would support the university. These two levies produced most of the income needed to pay university expenses through the rest of the fifteenth century as well as the sixteenth and seventeenth.[63]

The university suffered a crisis in enrollment at midcentury. In November 1457, the Venetian governors of Padua reported that student enrollment had dropped from a normal figure of 800 to only 300.[64] This is the earliest available information on the size of the student body. A normal enrollment of 800 suggests that Padua was second in size after Bologna at this time and 100 to 200 ahead of Pavia. It also suggests that the teaching complement numbered about 50.

The enrollment drop to 300 students generated a good deal of soul-searching by the Venetian authorities, who attributed the decline to internal weakness and

59. The arts and medicine beadle received 2 florins, the law beadle 8, rent for the rooms in which to hold law classes cost 12 florins, and the expenses of the office of rector of law were 16 florins. BUP, Ms. 1673, f. 179[r].

60. The law roll is found in AAUP, F. 648, f. 37[r], and printed in Belloni, 1986, 47. The artists' roll is found in Tomasini, 1986, 496.

61. The separate rolls for law, and arts and medicine, are found in AAUP, F. 648, ff. 53[r], 54[r], as well as in Venetian Senate records. Cessi (1909, 143 n. 1) prints the artists' roll, and Belloni (1986, 47–48) prints the jurists' roll with one addition.

62. AAUP, F. 648, ff. 79[r]–81[v], for the three rolls, 1434–37; Tomasini, 1986, 155–58, prints them. Law rolls for these years have not been located. No other rolls for the rest of the century have been found.

63. Dupruigrenet Desroussilles, 1980, 617–18.

64. AAUP, F. 648, f. 115[r]–[v], Nov. 8, 1457, for this and the following paragraph. See also Dupuigrenet Desroussilles, 1980, 615 (the same figures from an ASVe source), 618–19, and Lazzarini, 1950–51, who offers a good summary of the crisis.

external causes. Some professors missed so many classes that students refused to come to Padua. Famous but aging professors no longer attracted students. Two law professors had died. The fall of Constantinople (1453) and Italian political unrest kept some students away.

The Venetian government responded with a series of measures over the next twenty years designed to strengthen the university. In 1463 the Senate promulgated new university statutes and issued regulations fining professors absent from Padua without permission. The government then added teeth to the law requiring Venetian subjects to study at Padua: in addition to a fine, those who obtained degrees elsewhere were barred from employment by the Venetian state. This was a weighty threat, because the republic usually hired educated local men to serve as judges, assessors, and civil servants in its subject cities and territories. The Senate barred the two small schools of higher learning in Venice, the Scuola di Rialto for Aristotelian philosophy and the Scuola di San Marco for humanistic studies, from granting degrees, thus eliminating potential competition.[65] Finally, the Senate ordered the rolls to be prepared in May for the academic year beginning in November. Students would know in advance who would be teaching.[66]

The Senate expanded the faculty. In 1467 it added six "third places," two each in canon law, civil law, and medicine. This meant that in addition to the first ordinary professor in a subject and his concurrent, a third professor would also lecture. These third positions carried stipends of 20 florins and were reserved for recent graduates of the university.[67] Found in other universities as well, the junior positions added more teaching at little expense.

The Venetian Senate then severely limited localism in university appointments. In 1479 it ruled that Paduans could not be concurrents–that is, Paduan citizens could not hold simultaneously the first and second positions (teaching at the same hour) in any ordinary professorship in such fields as law, medicine, and natural philosophy.[68] And it forbade Venetian patricians and original citizens from holding professorships at Padua.[69] Finally, the Senate exempted all except the lowest-paid professors from the traditional student vote of approval. And if the students voted against someone the government preferred, it would overrule the students.[70]

Restricting localism in faculty hiring was a departure from customary practice. Prominent families in university towns across Italy looked to professorships as op-

---

65. It did permit the College of Physicians of Venice to grant degrees and to hold an annual anatomical dissection. See Ch. 4, "Paper Universities."

66. AAUP, F. 648, f. 210^{r-v}, Jan. 16, 1478 (probably 1479 because the Venetian calendar changed the year on Mar. 1).

67. Dupuigrenet Desroussilles, 1980, 624.

68. AAUP, F. 648, f. 212^v, Senate decree of Mar. 29, 1479.

69. Dupuigrenet Desroussilles, 1980, 623. Original citizens were a legal caste, just below the patriciate, conferring certain privileges barred to commoners. For example, only original citizens could hold high-ranking state secretaryships.

70. For example, on Dec. 4, 1503, the Senate decreed that, because student elections of professors led to "a thousand disturbances," all professors earning at least 60 florins and having taught for five years were no longer subject to student election. AAUP, F. 505, no pag. This was one of several such measures.

portunities, almost entitlements, for sons able to earn doctorates. The *padovani,* who had held a number of professorships, must not have been happy. But they were subjects obliged to obey. No doubt the alleged participation of some Paduan-born professors in conspiracies to overthrow Venetian rule was another reason to reduce their presence in the *studio.*[71] The Venetian Senate did recognize local academic excellence by appointing and paying well many able scholars from Padua over the next century and beyond. But they would be only a minority in the faculty.

Excluding the republic's own nobles and original citizens from academic posts was more surprising but not a great departure in practice. Many nobles studied at Padua, and some were conspicuously learned. But few, if any, had taught at Padua before the decree. Venetian ideology prized service to the state in public office, rather than university teaching. Indeed, the Venetian system of restricting political office to nobles, and high civil service positions to original citizens, emphasized the tradition. Exclusion from Paduan professorships was small loss compared with the opportunity to hold political offices and to enjoy the accompanying power and acclaim.

Efforts to improve the university continued. The Senate raised professorial salaries and recruited scholars from other universities for the important ordinary professorships in canon law, civil law, medical theory, and natural philosophy. In the last fifteen years of the century, the Venetian authorities made offers to scholars at the universities of Ferrara, Pavia, Pisa, Rome, and Siena, with some success.[72] The government found the money for higher salaries by diverting tax revenues collected in the subject towns of Bergamo, Treviso, and Verona. The Senate also expected Padua and its territory to pay more for the university.[73]

These measures bore fruit, as Padua boasted some famous scholars, such as Pietro Pomponazzi of Mantua, at the end of the fifteenth century. He obtained a doctorate in arts at Padua in 1487 and then was appointed extraordinary professor of natural philosophy, with Alessandro Achillini his concurrent, the following year. He ascended to first ordinary professor of natural philosophy, with Nicoletto Vernia his concurrent in the second position, in 1495. Pomponazzi left for three years of private study in Ferrara in 1496 but returned to Padua in 1499 at the same position, with Agostino Nifo as concurrent. He continued to teach at Padua until war broke out in 1509.[74] As his concurrents demonstrate, he was not the only eminent philosopher at Padua.

Padua probably had a faculty of close to 60 professors in the late fifteenth century.[75] The roll of 1500–1501 listed 31 law professors and 28 professors and

---

71. See the examples of Stefano Dottori and Paolo Dotti in the notes to table 1.2 and Dupuigrenet Desroussilles, 1980, 614–15.

72. AAUP, F. 648, ff. 262ʳ, 277ʳ, 294ʳ–295ᵛ, 302ʳ–ᵛ, 334ʳ, 339ʳ, 362ʳ, 394ʳ. There are also many examples of the Senate approving salary increments in the 1480s and 1490s. See F. 648.

73. AAUP, F. 648, ff. 137ʳ–ᵛ, 139ʳ–ᵛ (Apr. 18 and 20, 1461), 233ʳ–ᵛ (Oct. 24, 1480).

74. See Facciolati, 1978, 2:108–9; Pine, 1986, 43–45.

75. Facciolati, 1978, for all fields; Pesenti, 1984, for medicine; and Belloni, 1986, for law. They document that the university kept all the ordinary professorships filled. But because of rapid turnover, it is more difficult to track the less important ordinary and the extraordinary lectureships.

GYMNASIVM PATAVINVM

Fig. 2. Engraving of the Palazzo del Bo, seat of the University of Padua. Notice that most of the men in front of the building are wearing swords. Are they students? *From Iacopo Philippo Tomasini, Gymnasium Patavinum. Udine, 1654.*

one vacancy in the faculty of arts and medicine.[76] The legists divided into 14 canonists and 17 civilians. The faculty of arts included 12 professors of medicine (4 in medical theory, 4 for medical practice, 2 professors of surgery, and 2 to teach the third book of Avicenna). The roll of the faculty of arts also listed 2 theologians and 2 metaphysicians, the latter duo friars. Four professors of natural philosophy, 2 moral philosophers, 3 logicians plus one vacancy, 2 humanists, and a professor of mathematics and astrology completed the faculty. Bologna and Rome were larger, while Pavia had about the same number of professors at this time.

Enrollment recovered. Fragmentary information suggests that the University of Padua regained its former enrollment of 800 students and may have surpassed it. In June 1479, at the end of the academic year, the Venetian governors of Padua reported 300 ultramontane students in attendance.[77] Since it is very unlikely that ultramontane students constituted more than a third of the student body, and the fraction may have been smaller, enrollment may have reached 900 to 1,000.

The university acquired a permanent home. Until the end of the fifteenth century professors, with some financial help from the government, rented lecture rooms in various parts of the city.[78] Then in 1493 the government acquired for the legists a large building called Hospitium Bovis (Hotel of the Ox) in the center of the city. The Venetian government authorized extensive renovations, which continued through the following century and beyond, to make the building more suitable for teaching. In 1530 the arts professors also began to teach there. Called the Palazzo del Bo (possibly a contraction of "bovis"), it still houses the offices of the rector and the central administration of the university.[79] By all accounts, the Paduan *studium* flourished as the new century opened.

PADUA AFTER 1509

Disaster struck in 1509. The Venetian army suffered a crushing defeat at the battle of Agnadello (May 14, 1509) during the War of the League of Cambrai. The leading citizens of Padua immediately threw off Venetian rule and welcomed imperial forces into the city. But Paduan independence lasted only until Venetian troops recaptured the city in mid-July. Nevertheless, students stayed away, and some prominent professors fled, never to return. As noted above, Bologna took advantage of Paduan distress by hiring Pomponazzi and Carlo Ruini. The Venetians believed that several Paduan-born university professors had participated in the revolt, especially Bertuccio Bagarotti (c. 1445–1509), a professor of canon law who held high civic office during the brief imperial occupation. Even though his exact role is unclear, the republic hanged him as a rebel. It meted out lesser penalties to two other professors.[80]

---

76. The artists' roll comes from Marin Sanudo's *Diarii,* vol. 3, columns 654–56, and is reprinted in A. Favaro, 1918, 75–77; the law roll is found in Belloni, 1986, 48–50.

77. AAUP, F. 646, f. 436ʳ, June 12, 1479.

78. See Veronese Ceseracciu, 1995.

79. Rossetti, 1983, 23–25; Dupuigrenet Desroussilles, 1980, 647.

80. A. Favaro, 1918, 90–94, for the entries from Sanudo. Also Bagarotti, 1963, and Dupuigrenet

The university did not resume full operations for the duration of the war. The Senate directed the preparation of a roll for 1510–11 of eighteen professors but without first-place ordinary professors in several fields. This contrasted with 22 legists alone from the roll of 1509–10, prepared before the military defeat.[81] Some lectures were delivered, and a limited number of degrees were conferred in the next few years. On March 1, 1515, the university celebrated a solemn reopening with appropriate orations.[82] But this seems to have been only a gesture. It appears that the Paduan *studio* offered very little teaching to a handful of students during the war years.

The Venetians finished reconquering their mainland state in January 1517 and began to consider reopening the University of Padua as a functioning institution. The Venetian Senate met in September to confirm a roll of professors. In a surprising development, some senators objected to the move as premature. Proponents responded that students, including their own sons, wanted the university to reopen. Twenty-four young Venetian nobles had been studying at Padua at the time of the outbreak of war; they need to return to their studies, pleaded one senator.[83] Although university expenses would cost the treasury 7,000 ducats, foreign students coming to Padua would spend more than that, another senator argued. The Senate voted to reopen the university and confirmed an initial list of 4 professors of law and 15 for medicine and arts, mostly second-position ordinary professors, to be paid a total of 2,470 ducats. To fill the second places at Padua, the Venetians hired some current holders of first positions at Ferrara and Pavia. The roll of 1517 stated that several first-position ordinary professorships, including civil law in the morning and afternoon and medical practice, were to be left unfilled for the time being.[84] The unspent 5,500 ducats would be used to hire more-distinguished scholars for first positions in the future. This policy enabled the government to remake the faculty. Whether coincidence or not, humanism strongly influenced several of the new professors of arts and medicine appointed over the next two decades.

As the Venetian government rebuilt the university from 1517 onward, the Senate relied on three of its members to prepare faculty rolls. Senate documents began to refer to the trio as "Riformatori" of the university. In the following decades the trio became an elected commission, called the Riformatori dello Studio di Padova, charged with overseeing all aspects of the university. The Riformatori made recommendations for faculty appointments, salaries, and

Desroussilles, 1980, 625–26. The roll of 1509–10 listed him as afternoon ordinary professor of canon law. AAUP, F. 652, f. 1ʳ.

81. The list, which also included a teaching student rector of law, is found in A. Favaro, 1918, 91–92. See also Dupuigrenet Desroussilles, 1980, 626–27. For the legists' roll of 1509–10, which embodied Venetian plans before the disruptions, see AAUP, F. 652, fol. 1ʳ–ᵛ.

82. Tomasini, 1986, 402, and Piovan, 1997, 96–97.

83. It is not known if 24 was a typical number of Venetian nobles studying at Padua. Given that the patriciate numbered 1,500 to 2,500 males over the age of 18 during the sixteenth century, the figure seems low.

84. A. Favaro, 1918, 95–97.

many other matters, which the Senate almost always ratified. In time the Riformatori also oversaw book licensing and preuniversity schooling in Venice.[85]

A Senate law of 1557 established that the Riformatori would serve two-year terms, much longer than the normal six- to twelve-month terms for other offices in the Venetian government. They could not resign for another position before their term was completed, because, as the legislation stated, "the matters of the University of Padua are of such importance and honor to our state."[86] However, in 1563 the Senate decreed that patricians could hold the office of Riformatore dello Studio di Padova concurrently with other offices, an unusual concession. Hence, some of the most powerful nobles simultaneously ran the Venetian state and oversaw the university. The political weight of the Riformatori ensured that the Senate paid attention to the university's needs. Some Riformatori held degrees from Padua and were considered learned.

The University of Padua rebuilt its faculty and regained its intellectual leadership, or co-leadership with Bologna, among Italian and other European universities. Numerous scholars whose research is still remembered today taught at Padua in the sixteenth century. From about 1525 to 1560, the average faculty complement included 25 legists and 30 or 31 artists, plus teaching student rectors of law and arts. A typical arts and medicine roll began with 2 theologians, followed by 2 metaphysicians. Next came 13 professors of medicine: 2 ordinary and 3 extraordinary professors of medical theory, 2 ordinary and 3 extraordinary professors of medical practice, 2 professors who taught Avicenna (also considered medical theory), and a professorship of surgery, which later became anatomy. A professorship of medical botany (*Ad lecturam semplicium*) was added in 1533. Two ordinary professors and 3 extraordinary professors taught natural philosophy, and a moral philosopher taught Aristotle's *Ethics*. Five logicians, a professor of astronomy and mathematics, and 2 (sometimes 1) humanists, who taught rhetoric and Greek, respectively, completed the faculty. Salary expenses for a faculty of 55 to 60 came to 8,000 to 10,000 florins annually in these years.[87]

85. Dupruigrenet Desroussilles, 1980, 629–30; A. Favaro, 1918, 98, 99, 100, 104, for the entries from Sanudo's diaries referring to the Riformatori in 1517 and shortly thereafter. For the role of the Riformatori in censorship, see Grendler, 1977, 151–52, 154, 163, 274; for their role in overseeing Venetian preuniversity schools, see Grendler, 1989, 63–65, 67–68.

86. Le cose del Studio di Padoa, che sono di quella importantia, et honor al stato nostro. From the Senate law of July 29, 1557, in AAUP, F. 737, f. 15^r. See ibid., ff. 11^r–16^r, for copies of various laws regarding the Riformatori including that of 1563. See AAUP, F. 508, no foliation, and F. 737, ff. 18^r–21^r, for lists of the Riformatori. A. Favaro (1966, 2: 307–8) prints the names for the period 1587–1614. See Grendler, 1990a, 55, 63, 70, 72, 74, 75, 77, 78, 80, 81, 82, 83, 84, 85, and Grendler, 1990b, 12, for political biographies of some of the very powerful patricians who were Riformatori.

87. This and the following paragraph are based on examination of 24 rolls for law and 31 rolls for arts and medicine for the period 1520 through 1600 found in AAUP, FF. 242 and 651 (arts and medicine) and F. 652 (law). Law rolls and arts and medicine rolls are always listed separately in the documents, contrary to the practice of other universities. See also AAUP, Inventario 1320, with photocopies of some rolls drawn from other filze. Dott.a Elisabetta Barile is preparing the arts and medicine rolls for publication; a typescript of her work to date is available in AAUP. I am grateful for the opportunity to consult it. A. Favaro (1922, 15–17, 22–24) lists the locations of many rolls. The

The size of the teaching faculty diminished slightly in the last forty years of the century. The faculty of law had about 20 professors, the arts faculty approximately 24 professors with about 7 vacancies, for a total of about 44 active teachers through much of the 1560s and 1570s. In the 1590s the faculty of law remained at about 2l, while the arts faculty rose to an average of 28 professors, with perhaps 1 vacancy annually, for a total of 49 professors. The distribution of the professors across different subjects remained the same as earlier. Annual university expenses rose to 10,000 to 12,000 florins.

By the 1580s, all the revenue for the university again came from Padua and its territory, 85 percent from the vehicle and head taxes. Additional revenue came from a tax on notarial documents and testaments, a "one-time-only offering" of 1,000 ducats from the territory of Padua, a tax on documents required of foreign visitors, and funds that were originally intended to purchase firewood to warm the police who patrolled the streets of Padua but which were diverted to the university.[88] However, by the early seventeenth century, the taxes on Padua and its territory failed to meet university expenses. An official charged with finding a solution believed that the people of Padua could not pay more and recommended a reduction in professorial salaries.[89] The government did not reduce salaries. Rather, it paid them late, or not in full, or left positions vacant, as the seventeenth century went on.

Annual student attendance probably rose from 1,100 in the 1530s to a peak of 1,600 in the 1560s and then declined slightly later in the century. Four hundred ninety-one students matriculated in the law student associations (nations) in 1531. If Padua had an equal number of arts and medicine students, the total reached about 1,100, including the students from Venice and Padua, who were not eligible for membership in nations. The Venetian governors of Padua estimated the enrollment to be 1,300 in 1542.[90] In June 1547 another governor of Padua estimated that the university had more than 700 arts and medicine students, attributing the unusually high number to the excellence of the arts faculty.

---

roll of 1551–52 with salaries is printed in Gallo, 1963, 67–73. The arts roll of 1592–93 is printed in A. Favaro, 1966, 2: 111–13.

A small number of the rolls include salaries. See also AAUP, F. 505, unpaginated fascicle entitled "Ragguaglio della spesa dello Studio nelli tre secoli XVI, XVII, XVIII," with the salaries and other expenses for the academic year 1552–53. Twenty-three legists and 3 teaching students earned 4,334 florins, and 28 artists and a teaching rector of arts earned 5,836 florins, for a total of 10,170 florins.

88. BUP, Ms. 1676, f. 73ʳ, a large fold-out page entitled "Conto della spesa del Studio di Padoa per mesi vinti princianti [sic] primo novembre 1581 et finiti sesto Zugno 1583." It is a balance sheet for the twenty-month period compiled by "Anzolo Agostini essattor del studio" and dated July 1, 1583. The various taxes yielded 125,409 lire, 1 soldo, and 8 pence. Professorial salaries and additional expenses (a few other university officials and the botanical garden) amounted to 123,561 lire, 8 soldi, and 10 pence, which was a little less than 12,000 ducats of account worth 6 lire 4 soldi. Thus, the taxes gathered 1,847 lire, 12 soldi, and 10 pence, more than university expenses.

89. ASVe, Riformatori dello Studio di Padova, F. 429, "Discorso di Ingolfo Conti circa i danari per lo Studio di Padova, 1614 14 aprile, fatto alli Sig.ri Reformatori," unpaginated memorandum. The Riformatori had appointed Conti, a Paduan third-position professor of logic, to examine all aspects of the university. See Ch. 14, "Private Anatomy Teaching," for more on Conti.

90. The figures of 491 and 1,300 come from Dupuigrenet Desrouissilles, 1980, 631, 637.

IN NOMINE DOMINI
NOSTRI IESV CHRISTI AMEN.

Enerale,&nouum Principium interpretationum Nobiliſſ.&Florentiſſ.
Academiæ Dominorum Philoſophorum,&MedicorumCeleberrimi
PatauiniGymnaſiiAnni præſētis 1594. Feliciter incipiet die 3. Noueb.
ſub Felicib⁹ Auſpicijs,Illuſtriſſimorum D.D.ThomæMauroceni proSereniſſ. ,&
Illuſt.Duc.Dom.Veneto Prætoris, & Zacariæ Contareni Præfecti Patauii,Magni
fici Domini Sindici,& Dominorum Conſiliariorum Academiæ praedictae, cum
Lectionibus per horas diſtributis;Quas infraſcripti admodumR.Magiſtri,&Excel
lentiſſ.Domini Doctores,de mandato ipſius Mag.Domini Sindici,& DD.Conſi
liariorum aggredientur,& proſequentur ordine,vt infra diſpoſito,videlicet.

Ad Theologiam in via Sancti Thomæ.	
Reuerendus Pater D. Magiſter Angelus Andronicus Venetus.	Legent Lib.ſecundum ſententiarum,hora tertia mane.
Ad Theologiam in via Scoti.	
Reuerendus P.D.Mag.Hieronymus Pallanterius à Caſtro Bononienſi.	
Ad Lecturam Sacræ Scripturæ.	Leget quintum caput,& ſequentia Epiſt. Di.Pauli ad
Reuerendus Pater D.Magiſter Alphonſus Sotus Florentinus.	Hebreos diebus feſtinis hora ſecunda mane.
Ad Metaphyſicam in via Sancti Thomæ.	
Reuerendus Pater D. Magiſter Camillus Leonius Patauinus.	Legent lib.ſeptimum metaph.hora ſecunda mane.
Ad Metaphyſicam in via Scoti.	
Reuerendus Pater D.Magiſter Saluator Barthelatius de Aſſiſio.	
Ad Theoricam ordinariam Medicinæ.	
Excellentiſſimus D.Horatius Auguſtinus Marchinus in primo loco.	Legent Aphoriſmos Hippocratis hora prima mane.
Excellentiſſimus D.Albertinus Bottonus Patauinus in ſecundo loco .	
Ad Practicam ordinariam Medicinæ.	
Excellentiſſimus D.Alexander Maſſaria Vicentinus in primo loco.	Legent de Febribus hora prima poſt meridiem.
Excellentiſſimus D.Hercules Saxonia Patauinus, in ſecundo loco.	
Ad Philoſophiam ordinariam .	
Excellentiſſimus D.Franciſcus Piccolomineus Senenſis,in primo loco.	Legent primum Phyſicorum hora ſecunda poſt meridiem.
Excellentiſſimus D.Cæſar Cremoninus Centenſis in ſecundo loco.	
Ad Theoricam extraordinariam Medicinæ	
Excellentiſſimus D. Annibal Bimbiolus , in primo loco.	Legent primam primi Auicennæ hora meridiei.
Excellentiſſimus D. Nicolaus Truiſanus Patauinus, in altero loco.	
Ad Practicam extraordinariam Medicinæ.	Legent de Morbis particularibus à corde infra hora ſecun
Excellentiſſimus D.Æmilus Campilongius Patauinus, in primo loco.	da mane.
Excellentiſſimus D.Alexander Vigontia Patauinus, in altero loco.	
Ad Philoſophiam extraordinariam.	
Excellentiſſimus D.Camillus Bellonus Venetus , in primo loco.	Legent octauum Phyſicorum hora prima poſt mediem.
Exc.llentiſſimus D.Schinella de Coguibus Patauinus, in altero loco.	
Ad Philoſophiam Moralem Ariſtotelis.	Leget librum primum ethicorum hora prima poſt meridiem
Excell ntiſſimus ac adm R.D.Ioānes Bellonus Canonicus Patauinus.	diebus feſtis.
Ad Chirurgiam, & Anatomen.	Leget de partibus ſimilaribus,& diſſimilaribus, & earun
Excellentiſſimus D.Hieronymus Fabricius d'Aquapendente Etruſcus.	dem actionibus,& oſtione,& anatome. Item de luxa
	tionibus,& fracturis hora 3.mane.
Ad Lecturam tertij libri Auicennæ.	Leget de effectibus capitis hora ſecunda mane in diebus
Excellentiſſimus D. Antonius Niger Patauinus, in præcedentis loci.	feſtinis.
Excellen.iſſimus D.Hieronymus Fracanzanus Patauinus,in concurretia.	
Ad Lecturam Simplicium .	Leget libros de ſimplicium medicamentorum facultatibus
Excellentiſſimus D. Proſper Alpinus Maroſticenſis.	hora 3.poſt.merid.
Mag. D. Ioannes Antonius Coruultus Patauinus .	Incipiet docere, in horto die ſecunda Maij. 1595. Hora.22
Ad Logicam .	
Excell ntiſſimus D.Bernardinus Petrella Thuſcus, in primo loco.	Leget lib.ſecundum poſteriorum hora prima mane.
Excellentiſſimus D.Fauſtinus Summus Patauinus, in ſecundo loco.	
Excellent.ſſimus D.Priamus Buſinellus Patauinus, in tertio loco.	Leget lib.primum poſt in diebus feſtinis.hora 2. mane.
Ad Mathematicam .	
Excellentiſſimus D. Galileus d: G.ldei Florentinus.	Leget quintum lib.Euclidis,& Theoricas planetarum hora
	tertia poſt merid.
Ad Humanitatem Græcam,et Latinam.	Explicabit Topica Ciceronis , & adipodem Tyrannum So
Excellentiſſimus D.Antonius Riccobonus cinc.Rhod gn⁰,& Patauin⁰.	phoclis.

LAVS DEO OPTIMO MAXIMO.

Patauij,ex Officio Almæ Vniuerſitatis Artiſtarum præſcripti Gymn.Die 3.Nouemb. 1594.

Marcus Antonius Coradinus Canc. Mand.

PATAVII, Apud Laurentium Paſquatum. 1594.

But he lamented that the law students, normally twice the number of artists, had fallen to 300, making a total of 1,000.[91] In 1549 the Venetian governor stated that there were more than 1,200 students at Padua. Again he noted that there were more students in arts than in law, and for the same reason as earlier. In 1554 the estimate was 1,000 students.[92] Enrollment probably peaked at 1,500 to 1,600 students in the 1560s and may have been higher.[93] The Venetian governors estimated an enrollment of 1,500 students in 1609 and 1,200 students in 1611.[94]

The list of the law student nations demonstrates that they came from many lands. The non-Italian nations were Germany, Poland, Provence, Burgundy, England, Scotland, Spain (including Portuguese students), and "Ultramarine," which included Cyprus and Greece. The Italian nations were Rome, Sicily,

---

91. "Che non sonno più che 300 scholarj leggisti et di artisti ne sonno più de 700, che suole sempre essere al contrario che li legisti sogliono essere sempre doe fiate più delle artisti. Et questo aviene per la qualità delli lettori, che nelle arti sono moltj, et eccellenti." *Relazione* of Matteo Dandolo, June 8, 1547, in *Relazioni,* 1975, 17. Two Venetian patricians jointly ruled Padua as *capitano* (military governor) and *podestà* (chief judicial official) for terms of about two years. At the end of their tenure, one or both wrote summary reports (*relazioni*) for the Senate. The *relazioni* merit respect, because it was the duty of the governors to be well informed about Paduan affairs. When citing the *relazioni,* the name of the *capitano or podestà* is omitted except for direct quotations.

92. *Relazioni,* 1975, 24, 40.

93. This estimate comes indirectly. In early August, the law students balloted by nations for the student rectors of law and some minor professorships. Four hundred ninety-four legists voted in August 1562, 606 in August 1563, 763 in August 1564, and 732 in August 1565, 469 in August 1566, and 423 in August 1567, for the student rector of law. AAUP, F. 10, ff. 187^v–188^r, 220r–221v; F. 11, ff. 3^r–4^v, 64^r–65^v, 120^r–121^r, 169^r–170^v. The corresponding totals for the minor law professorships, 1562–65, were 470, 541, 727, and 720. AAUP, F. 646, f. 436^v. Woolfson (1998, 24, 26–27) presents these and additional election figures from the above and other AAUP archival sources.

The number who voted does not include all law students attending the University of Padua. At least twenty-five to fifty Venetians and Paduans, who did not have nations, must have studied law each year. In every election one or more small nations did not vote, because they lacked the minimum three or four students needed for a quorum. Moreover, there is no guarantee that all the eligible students were present to vote when the elections were held, because early August was in the middle of the five-month-long vacation. Some students must have left for home. Finally, student interest and participation in the elections of their representatives seem to have waxed and waned from year to year, as they do today in North American universities. For all these reasons the number of students who voted in rector elections can only be indicative of the total law enrollment.

No comparable records for the arts students for the sixteenth century have been located. But it seems reasonable to estimate that Padua had at least as many arts and medicine students as law students. Hence, if one doubles the number of law students who voted for student rectors to account for the arts and medicine students, then adds 50 to 100 to account for the Venetians, Paduans, and those students who did not vote, a conservative estimate makes the student enrollment at least 1,500 to 1,600 in the 1560s, and possibly higher.

In 1573 and 1574 the number of law students voting for the rector dropped to 183 and 255, respectively, mostly because only a small number of Italian law students voted. The number of Germans voting was comparable to the 1560s. AAUP, F. 12, ff. 42^{r-v}, 48^{r-v}, 95^v–96^v. Student participation in the election of rectors declined in the late sixteenth century. This suggests less interest in the elections, as happened at Bologna, and some decline in enrollment, rather than a drastic decline in enrollment.

94. *Relazioni,* 1975, 114, 142.

Ancona (the Marches), Milan, Lombardy, Tuscany, and Piedmont. The nations of Treviso, Friuli, and Dalmatia were part of the Venetian Terraferma state.[95] Approximately 19 percent of the law students came from the German nation, 11 percent were other non-Italians, 21 percent came from the Veneto, Padua, and Venice, and 49 percent came from the rest of Italy, in the years 1562–66.[96] The largest single group of non-Italian students was the Germans. A total of 10,536 Germans studied at Padua during the period 1546 through 1630, an average of 124 per year.[97] Two hundred German legists were in attendance in August 1564, possibly a high point for the century.[98]

An extraordinary number of famous Renaissance figures studied at Padua from 1400 to 1600.[99] Among Italians they included the historians and political theorists Donato Giannotti, Paolo Giovio, Francesco Guicciardini, and Paolo Paruta. Humanists who studied at Padua included Pietro Bembo, Aldo Manuzio the Younger, Niccolò Perotti, Giovanni Pico della Mirandola, Giovanni Pontano, and Pier Paolo Vergerio the Elder. Well-known Italian scholars in other fields who studied at Padua included Ulisse Aldrovandi, Girolamo Cardano, Francesco Patrizi da Cherso, and Bernardino Telesio. Torquato Tasso studied there in the years 1560–62 and 1564–65, as did Popes Eugenius IV (1431–47) and Sixtus IV (1471–84). So did saints Gaetano Thiene (founder of the Theatines) and Antonio Maria Zaccaria (one of the founders of the Barnabites). Elena Lucrezia Cornaro Piscopia (1646–84), a Venetian noblewoman, the first woman to receive a university degree, obtained a doctorate of philosophy at Padua on June 25, 1678, although she never attended university lectures.[100]

The University of Padua had an equally distinguished group of non-Italian students. The Poles included Nicolaus Copernicus plus many future prelates, nobles, and magistrates. As many as a thousand Hungarian students came to

95. This list comes from the balloting for law student rectors in AAUP, FF. 10, 11, and 12. For French students at Padua, see Rodinis, 1970; for Greek students, see Fabris, 1942, and Plumidis, 1971; for Spanish and Portuguese students, see Veronese Ceseracciu, 1978; for English students see Woolfson, 1998; for a survey of all foreign students, 1550–1700, see Fedalto, 1984.

96. This is based on analysis of the count of 3,056 students who balloted for the rectors of law in the years 1562–66. See note 93 for the references. Since Padua and Venice lacked nations, I have estimated that an additional 50 law students from these two towns were annually in attendance, making a total of 3,306 students. It is likely that the provenance of arts and medicine students was about the same as that of the legists. Of course, this distribution by nation might vary considerably from year to year and decade to decade. For additional comments on the provenance of students, see Dupruigrenet Desroussilles, 1980, 631–32.

97. Brugi, 1905, 41. See ibid., 17, 47, and 73, for additional information on the number of German students and the total number of students.

98. AAUP, F. 11, f. 3ᵛ.

99. This and the following paragraph are based on the summary lists with bibliography found in Fabris, 1939–40. The list is not definitive. It should also be emphasized that some of these famous individuals took no degree, or took degrees elsewhere, or have left no information about their degrees. Brief biographies of many of the individuals mentioned in this and the following paragraph can be found in *Encyclopedia of the Renaissance,* 1999.

100. See Grendler, 1999a, for a brief biography.

Padua between 1526 and 1660, including the humanists John de Csezmicze (Janos Pannonius) and Andre Dudith de Sbardellat (1533–89). The German group included Nicholas of Cusa (doctorate in canon law in 1423), plus the future humanists and scholars Joachim Camerarius, Konrad Peutinger, Willibald Pirkheimer, Hartman Schedel, Joachim von Watt (Vadianus), and Theodore Zwinger. The English group included John Colet, William Harvey (medical doctorate in 1602), William Latimer, Thomas Linacre, Richard Pace, the Jesuit Robert Parsons, Cardinal Reginald Pole, and Cuthbert Tunstall. Michael Servetus, Spanish physician and anti-Trinitarian, studied at Padua, as did the jurist and chancellor of France Michel de l'Hôpital. From Greece came John Argyropoulos, who was rector of arts in 1443–44 and took his degree in July 1444, and Massimo Margunious (1530–1602), future bishop and scholar from Crete. Padua even had an American student in the seventeenth century. Edmund Davie (d. before 1688), the son of an Englishman who immigrated to Boston, obtained a bachelor's degree at Harvard in 1674 and a medical doctorate at Padua in 1681. So far as can be determined, Davie was the first English-speaking North American to attend an Italian university.[101]

Padua was large enough to host a thousand and more students. The city had about 32,000 inhabitants in 1397, but plague reduced it to 18,000 in 1411. The city's population remained at 18,000 in 1435 and was probably only 19,000 at the end of the century. Then the population rose to 34,000 in 1545 and 35,000 to 40,000 later. The Great Plague of 1575–77 took about 10,000 lives, reducing the population to 30,000, where it remained for at least a decade. By the early seventeenth century, the city had recovered to 40,000. The Paduan territory held 100,000 to 144,000 souls through most of the sixteenth and early seventeenth centuries.[102]

However, the Venetian overlords had little good to say about the town. Poorer than any other in the Venetian state, Padua was a town that begged, a Venetian governor reported in 1549. Only a few families enjoyed incomes over a thousand ducats; the majority lived in little houses renting for 14 ducats annually. Padua lacked comfort, beautiful buildings, and healthy air; its citizens were mostly cowards. (He did not mention the artistic monuments of the city.) Only the university conferred distinction on this town, he concluded.[103]

But that distinction was enormous. The University of Padua had such a great reputation in Germany, Flanders, and France that northerners were awarded honors and granted management of important affairs simply because they studied at Padua, wrote a veteran Venetian diplomat in 1549. More than one governor proclaimed the university to be the heart and soul of Padua. "Without the

---

101. Rossetti, 1974.

102. Ginatempo and Sandri, 1990, 81–83; and *Relazioni,* 1975, xxii–xxiii, 37, 38, 68, 74, 77, 126. The Paduan territory had 122,414 persons and 5,647 vehicles in 1615. ASVe, Riformatori dello Studio di Padova, F. 429, "Descrittione del territorio di Padova," no pag., Feb. 28, 1615.

103. *Relazioni,* 1975, 22–24, statement of Bernardo Navagero.

university, Padua would not be Padua."[104] And, of course, the Venetians believed that it was "their" university. It did not belong to the Paduans.

The university contributed a great deal to the town's economy. Every student spent 80 to 100 ducats annually for eating, dressing, and living; some spent 500 to 1,000, the governors reported in 1549 and 1554. Although the majority of students could not have spent so freely as the very rich, a student body of 1,000 to 1,500, of whom 95 percent came from outside the city, contributed far more to the local economy than university costs of 10,000 florins.[105] The Paduans knew this. In 1547 guild leaders offered to make a financial contribution so that the university might hire a famous professor of law who would attract more students.[106]

Although Paduan leaders recognized the economic utility of the university, town-gown conflicts were common. One Venetian governor happily reported that clashes between students and townspeople had not produced any deaths or serious injuries during his two-year tenure.[107] Despite the shocking implications of his statement, deaths and serious injuries were infrequent. But students and townspeople often fought each other, and students among themselves. The Venetian authorities did their best to keep a lid on their "Latin Quarter."

Padua was fortunate enough to become a good university at an early date and to benefit from governmental policies that made it better. The Renaissance university at Padua inherited a strong intellectual tradition from its first two centuries. When the Republic of Venice replaced the Carrara family in 1405, it supported the university with enlightened policies. It made Padua the sole university for its large state at the expense of institutions of higher learning in Venice itself. The Senate passed measures to ensure adequate and regular funding. When the university faltered in the mid-fifteenth century, the Venetian government took decisive action to strengthen it.

The measures of the last forty years of the fifteenth century laid the foundations for the brilliance of the next century. The University of Padua filled the key positions in law, and especially in medicine and arts, with distinguished scholars and kept them filled. The university recovered strongly from a short closure in 1509 and a period of reduced activity from 1510 to 1517. Padua innovated more quickly than its rivals; it was the first to introduce a professorship of medical botany, to make clinical medicine part of the curriculum, and much else. The Venetians often appointed distinguished outsiders to the faculty. Indeed, localism played a smaller role in faculty appointments than in any other Italian university, with the exception of Rome, a lesser institution.

The leaders of the Venetian state were immensely proud of their university

104. Che senza il Studio, Padova non saria Padova. *Relazioni,* 1975, 24–25 (quote), by Bernardo Navagero. Since he had represented Venice at several foreign courts, Navagero could claim firsthand knowledge of northern views.

105. Ibid., 24, 40, 41, 49 (1549, 1554, and 1557).

106. Ibid., 11.

107. Ibid., 26 (1549).

and its faculty, especially in arts and medicine. A Venetian governor of Padua boasted in 1549 that one could not hope to hear a physician, philosopher, logician, or humanist better than those that were in Padua. There was no one to equal Giovanni Battista Da Monte in medicine, Marc'Antonio de' Passeri (called il Genova) in natural philosophy,[108] Bernardino Tomitano in logic, or Lazzaro Bonamico in Greek and Latin, he wrote.[109] In the century and a quarter between Pomponazzi's appointment in 1488 and Galilei's departure in 1610, the University of Padua may have enjoyed the most illustrious period of any university in the Renaissance or in modern Europe.

108. Passeri (1490/91–1563) was an anti-Alexandrist Aristotelian who differed with Pomponazzi. From Genoa, he took a degree in arts at Padua in 1511 or 1512 and taught at Padua from 1517 until his death. Even though he is little remembered today, he was immensely popular with students and Venetian nobles. In 1545, when he held the first-position ordinary professorship of natural philosophy, the Venetian Senate raised his salary to 600 florins. And in gratitude for the number of students he brought to the university plus his other merits, the Senate gave him another 600 florins with which to dower his daughter. AAUP, F. 571, f. 180ʳ, Dec. 5, 1545. Da Monte, Tomitano, and Bonamico are mentioned in the appropriate chapters below.

109. "Il Monti che legge medicina, il Genova che legge la philosophia, il Tomitano la logica et M. Lazaro la lingua greca et latina, ha cadaun di questi quatro, le scole tutte piene, et ognuno è riputato singular nella sua professione; et per cadaun di loro si intrattien gran numero de scolari. . . . Che non è così nel Studio delle arti, perchè non sperano di udir medico, philosopho, logico, nè humanista più eccelente di quelli che sono in Padua." *Relazioni,* 1975, 25, Bernardo Navagero's *relazione* of 1549. Navagero was a little less enthusiastic about the professors of law. He felt that they were as good as could be found in Italy, with the significant exceptions of Andrea Alciato and Mariano Sozzini the Younger, who taught at Pavia and Bologna, respectively.

CHAPTER 2

Naples, Siena, Rome, and Perugia

he grand medieval impulse to create universities continued with the founding of Naples, Siena, Rome, and Perugia by 1308.

NAPLES, 1224

Emperor Frederick II created the University of Naples by fiat in 1224, a great contrast to the spontaneous origins of Bologna and Padua. On the eve of an unsuccessful attempt to crush the Lombard League of northern Italian cities, the emperor issued a decree founding a university in his territory and forbidding his subjects of the realms of Naples and Sicily to study elsewhere.[1] His decree combined enthusiasm for learning with aversion to Bologna, where Italians learned too much about communal liberties, in his view. Naples was the first Italian university, and possibly the first in Europe, to be established by the will of the prince. But little is known about its first forty years, probably because Frederick and his immediate successors did little to help the Neapolitan *studio* grow.

Charles I of Anjou, the first of his dynasty to rule Naples and Sicily, revived the dormant university in 1266. In the following years Charles promulgated norms for professors and students and for the conferral of degrees. He also forbade other *studii* in the Kingdom of Naples except for the medical school at Salerno, which soon withered. And he ordered those obtaining degrees not to leave the kingdom to teach.

The University of Naples enjoyed a modest existence during the rest of the Angevin rule, which lasted until 1442. Probably 8 to 11 salaried professors constituted the teaching staff in the late thirteenth century and first half of the fourteenth.[2] The professors normally included 2 to 4 in civil law, 2 in canon law, 2

---

1. This account of the origins is based on Torraca, 1924. Origlia, 1973, is still useful. Rashdall, 1936, 2:21–26, is less valuable.

2. Monti, 1924, is the basic source for the Angevin period; see 76–87 for lists of known professors. Any count is tentative because of the paucity of sources.

or 3 in medicine, and perhaps 2 for natural philosophy or other subjects. A handful of extraordinary lecturers and recent graduates probably collected fees from their students but did not receive salaries.[3] The university taught no theology at this time. Instead, members of the Augustinian, Dominican, and Franciscan orders taught theology at their respective monasteries.[4] The university may have conferred an average of half a dozen medical degrees annually.[5] Since it was better known for law, it may have conferred more degrees in law than in arts.

The king of Naples initially conferred the doctorate. He examined the candidate or appointed examiners, who did not necessarily teach at the university or hold doctorates. In time Neapolitan practice conformed to that of other universities: colleges of law and medicine selected the examining committees and conducted doctoral examinations.[6] Degrees were conferred on the basis of papal authority received in a bull of 1465.[7]

Despite the acceptance of normal university practice, the Angevin and Aragonese rulers probably exercised tighter control over the university than did rulers elsewhere. The monarchs appointed professors without making use of an intermediate body, such as a group of *riformatori*. A crown-appointed grand chancellor presided over the colleges of law and medicine. Beginning in 1465, the monarch appointed a professor to be the rector, that is, the formal head of the university. Student rectors elected by the students filled this role in other universities, even though their power was limited. Numerous professors held governmental and court positions simultaneously, or nearly so. Legists were judges, councilors to the king, and ambassadors; professors of medicine were court physicians; and humanists tutored royal children.[8] Although none of this was unique to Naples, the links between *studio* and court were stronger.

A series of dynastic conflicts and civil wars disrupted the kingdom between 1345 and 1442. Little is known about the university in this period. The fact that few names of professors have been located suggests that the university barely functioned and was often closed. It did close at the death of Queen Giovanna II in 1435. After a long struggle, Alfonso I (the Magnanimous) of Aragon (b. 1396; ruled 1442–58) succeeded to the throne in 1442. He reopened the university in 1451.

Alfonso the Magnanimous and his successor, Ferrante I (b. 1431; ruled 1458–94), presided over a Neapolitan Renaissance, which included the university. The kings invited humanists and artists to Naples and supported their activities. The

3. Ibid., 31–32.

4. Ibid., 26–30. Theology continued to be taught in the monasteries during the Aragonese period. See Filangieri di Candida, 1924, 186.

5. Monti, 1924, 69.

6. Ibid., 51–52, 58–60.

7. Filangieri di Candida, 1924, 161, 197–99 for the bull.

8. Origlia, 1973, 1:242–68; Monti, 1924, 63, 100–102, 123–24; Filangieri di Candida, 1924, 168–69, 179–80, 183. These historians lament princely control over the University of Naples, compared with what they see as the autonomy enjoyed by other universities. However, the differences were more a matter of degree than substance.

Aragonese monarchs provided the university with twice as many professors as their Angevin predecessors. Twenty-two professors taught at Naples in 1465, earning 1,760 ducats in salaries.[9] The roll of 1465 included 4 humanists, a large number for the times, and remained at this figure through 1471; it then dropped to 2. The university continued at the level of 18 to 26 professors between 1468 and 1488. A complement of 20 professors included about 10 legists, 4 or 5 professors of medicine, 2 natural philosophers, a logician, and 2 to 4 humanists. They collectively earned about 1,900 ducats annually.

The monarchs filled professorships with subjects of the kingdom, some of them able scholars. The learned and productive Giuniano Maio (c. 1430–93) taught rhetoric and poetry at the university between 1465 and 1488. A few professors in law and medicine enjoyed considerable local fame but little renown in the larger academic world. The best known and highest paid of these was Giovanni Antonio Carafa of Naples, professor of canon law; he taught in the years 1467–74 and 1478–80, at a salary of 300 ducats. Outsiders were few: the Byzantine émigré Constantine Lascaris (1434–1501) taught Greek and eloquence at Naples for one year, 1465–66, for 100 ducats. The refusal or inability of the rulers to lure famous scholars by paying them the 500 to 1,000 ducats they earned at Bologna and Padua prevented the university from realizing its potential.[10] The Aragonese monarchs did attract to the court some major humanists, including Lorenzo Valla and Giovanni Gioviano Pontano. But they did not teach at the university.[11]

Until 1473 the professors taught in private houses for which the state paid rent. From 1474 through 1487 they taught in three rented rooms, which grew to five rooms after 1487, in three different monasteries. From about 1515 onward teaching was consolidated in three rented rooms, costing the state 50 ducats annually, at the monastery of San Domenico.[12]

Unfortunately, the university was closed as often as it was open during Aragonese rule. The dates of reopenings are well known, because the monarchy made them festive occasions. But the *studio* closed its doors quietly, leaving the exact dates and extent of teaching uncertain. After the closing of 1435, the university reopened its doors with great fanfare in 1451 and then furtively shut down in 1456. Another festive reopening occurred in 1465, and classes continued until the closing of 1474. The *studio* reopened again in the fall of 1478 for two academic years, followed by a long silence from 1480 to 1487. The university resumed teaching in 1487, only to shut down again, probably in 1496, in the aftermath of Charles VIII's invasion of the Kingdom of Naples. The frequent closures caused by war and lack of funds prevented the university from achieving the results that the relatively large number of professors promised.[13]

9. Filangieri di Candida, 1924, is the basic source for the Aragonese period. See esp. pp. 162, 198–99. See also Cannavale, 1980, 44–52, and De Frede, 1960, 191–93.

10. Monti, 1924, 78–100; Filangieri di Candida, 1924, 177–92.

11. Bentley (1987) offers an excellent overview of Neapolitan humanism and the court.

12. Cannavale, 1980, 23–25 and 54–78 passim.

13. Filangieri di Candida, 1924, 154–55, 158, 160, 166–67.

In 1503 the Kingdom of Naples lost its independence to Spain, which ruled the kingdom through resident viceroys. After being closed for more than a decade, the *studio* reopened in October 1507. It did not change under Spanish rule. As before, an official appointed by the state, now called the major chaplain, presided over the university.[14] Earlier practices, such as paying a mendicant order theologian to teach theology in his convent, prohibiting subjects from studying elsewhere, and refusing to recognize foreign degrees, continued. Like the Angevin and Aragonese monarchs before them, viceroys occasionally ignored the last prohibition in order to appoint professors who were not subjects of the kingdom. Not until 1615 did a viceroy attempt to make the university resemble the Spanish University of Salamanca.[15]

The university had 15 professors in 1507 and remained at 13 to 19 throughout the century. A theologian, a canonist, 7 civilians, 2 medical professors, 2 natural philosophers, a metaphysician, and a humanist constituted the faculty. Salaries gradually rose. Fifteen professors received a total of 560 ducats in 1507. Salary expenses rose to 1,000 ducats by the 1530s, to 2,000 ducats in the 1570s, and about 2,800 ducats in the 1590s.[16] Even though inflation absorbed some of the increase, faculty stipends clearly improved. The funds came from the central treasury of the monarchy rather than a designated tax, as was the custom elsewhere.

The university benefited from the political stability that Spanish rule provided. In contrast to the previous century, it suffered few interruptions. War, civil unrest, and especially plague closed its doors from 1527 to 1529, in 1531, probably in 1547, again in 1562, and in 1585. Professors continued to draw their salaries during some of the closures.[17]

A few famous scholars taught at Naples in the sixteenth century. The much traveled Agostino Nifo (1469/70–1538) taught medicine and philosophy during the academic year 1531–32 and perhaps earlier. Simone Porzio (1496–1554) taught natural philosophy from 1529 to 1545. Alessandro Turamini of Siena (1556–1605) taught civil law at Naples from 1592 to 1603. He received 200 ducats for moving expenses and a salary rising from 680 to 800 ducats, making him the highest-paid professor of the sixteenth century.[18]

Naples may have had 300 students in the late fifteenth century, 400 in the first half of the sixteenth, and 500 in the peaceable second half of the sixteenth.[19] The vast majority probably came from the huge city of Naples and its mainland

14. Cortese, 1924, is the basic source for the university during Spanish rule. A shorter version is found in Cortese, 1965, 31–119.

15. Cortese, 1924, 255–64.

16. Cannavale, 1980, 53–81; Cortese, 1924, 224–26.

17. Cortese, 1924, 205.

18. Cortese, 1924, 316–36, esp. 318, 326, 333; Cannavale, 1980, 33, 62–65, 72–81. Unfortunately, some rolls are missing, and others may be incomplete.

19. These are my estimates, based on the number of professors and comparisons with other universities. A contemporary observer stated that Naples had two thousand non-Neapolitan students in 1591. Another said that the university had five thousand students in 1607. Cortese, 1924, 255 and n. 3. These figures are not possible.

kingdom. Giovanni Boccaccio (1313–75) from Tuscany, a lackadaisical student of canon law at Naples from 1333 to 1339, was an exception.[20] The large number of Sicilians who attended northern Italian universities suggests that Naples failed to attract many students from the nearby island, even though it was part of the kingdom. The fact that Neapolitan subjects also attended the University of Rome in the sixteenth century (see later in this chapter) argues that the law banning subjects from studying elsewhere had little effect. The University of Naples was a second-tier university throughout the Renaissance.

SIENA, 1246

Siena was the first university in Tuscany. In 1240 the commune of Siena paid salaries to several teachers of law, grammar, and dialectic; it rented lecture rooms and may have invited non-Sienese students to come. The timing was not accidental, as students at Bologna were threatening to migrate because of a local dispute.[21] In 1246 or slightly earlier, the Sienese school received some form of limited imperial recognition, the exact nature of which is unclear.[22] Also in 1246, the commune began to send messengers to invite Tuscan students to come to Siena to study law. This was a traditional means of announcing the opening of the academic year of a university. Communal records also began to employ terminology appropriate to a *studium* in 1246. These actions marked the establishment of a university guided and sustained by the commune.

Siena drafted legislation for teacher contracts, the financing of the *studium,* and the immunities of teachers and students in 1275. Between 1240 and 1321, the University of Siena probably had an average teaching complement of about a dozen professors, distributed among 4 legists, 3 professors of medicine, 2 logicians, 2 grammarians, and 1 rhetorician.[23] The majority came from Siena or elsewhere in Tuscany, although seldom from the hated rival, Florence. The professors had modest accomplishments with one exception. "Pietro Ispano," who taught medicine at Siena probably from 1248 to 1250, perhaps 1247–52, was the famous Peter of Spain (b. 1210/15; elected Pope John XXI in 1276; d. 1277). One of the first western European scholars to comment on Aristotle, he wrote

20. Monti, 1924, 109

21. This paragraph is based on Prunai, 1949, and P. Nardi, 1991 and 1996, which are the latest reviews of the foundation and early history of the University of Siena. Davidsohn (1977, 255–62) provides a brief summary of the first decades. *Chartularium Studii Senensis* (1942) prints documents for the period 1240 through 1357.

22. Scholars have spent considerable effort investigating what happened in 1246 without reaching a consensus. For a survey of the differing views, see Minnucci, 1981b, 432–34, 440, and P. Nardi, 1982.

23. Since no rolls but only some communal appointment and payment records survive, any count must be tentative. The above is based on the (perhaps incomplete) list of professors uncovered by Prunai, 1949, 67–74. See also Fioravanti, 1991a, 255–56; Minnucci, 1991, 111–12; and Piccinni, 1991, 145. Garosi (1958) follows the teaching of medicine at Siena from 1240 to 1555. Here and elsewhere, teachers of Latin and abbaco described as "maestri" of the "Terzi" (administrative districts of Siena) are omitted, because they probably taught at a preuniversity level.

numerous works in medicine, philosophy, and theology. He also wrote *Summulae logicales,* the most published logic textbook of the Middle Ages and Renaissance; over 300 manuscripts and more than 150 pre-1600 printed editions survive.[24]

The University of Siena seized upon a new crisis at the University of Bologna in order to expand further. In the spring of 1321 the Bolognese authorities condemned to death a Spanish student for raping the daughter of a Bolognese notary.[25] Outraged by this perceived violation of their juridical privileges, the Bolognese students prepared to migrate. The Sienese commune welcomed Bolognese students and professors with 6,500 florins plus the loan of another 6,000 florins, for preparation of lodgings, moving expenses, and the purchase of books to be brought to Siena. They offered tax immunities and juridical privileges that put foreign students on an equal footing with Sienese citizens. The Sienese commune also paid the moving expenses of students who came from other universities. Since Siena was a thriving commercial center of about fifty thousand inhabitants in the late thirteenth century and early fourteenth, it could afford such a large outlay of money.[26] A number of Bolognese professors and students came to Siena.

The Bolognese government reached a reconciliation with its students in February 1323. They returned to Bologna, although a few Bolognese professors remained. The bold attempt to supplant Bologna as the leading university of Italy failed.

The University of Siena returned to the status of a successful provincial university. The faculty probably averaged twelve to fifteen professors in the early fourteenth century.[27] The majority came from Tuscany and Umbria and lacked national or international reputations. An exception was the famous jurist Cino da Pistoia (c. 1270–1336/37) who taught law from 1321 to 1326 and wrote vernacular poetry. It is likely that a large majority of the students also came from Tuscany and central Italy.

The commune realized that the university needed formal recognition from pope or emperor as a *studium generale* in order to attract ultramontane students. The vague privilege of 1246 from Frederick II carried insufficient weight. Moreover, the Sienese wanted papal recognition so that clergymen might enjoy the income of their benefices while studying away from home. Beginning in 1339 the Sienese annually begged for a papal privilege. Finally, Emperor Charles IV visited Siena and on August 16, 1357, conferred a new constitution that made the *studio* of Siena an imperial university.[28] The commune, in turn, granted the

---

24. See Minnucci, 1981b, 432; P. Nardi, 1991, 9; Piccinni, 1991, 145.

25. This and the following paragraphs are based on Prunai, 1950, and P. Nardi, 1991, 14–19.

26. Bowsky, 1970, 19, and Ginatempo and Sandri, 1990, 148, 260.

27. Only sparse payment records survive. From such evidence Zdekauer (1977, 14–15, 136–38) lists 20 professors in 1338–39; Prunai (1950, 29–30) counts 12. But the inclusion of several grammarians and abbaco teachers who probably taught at the preuniversity level, and the absence of professors of civil law in the payment records, make it hard to be certain. A realistic estimate seems to be 12 to 15 professors. See also Minnucci, 1991, 111–12, and Piccinni, 1991, 145–46.

28. Prunai, 1950, 18–23; P. Nardi, 1991, 19–22.

bishop the right to confer degrees and designated 2,000 florins for faculty salaries. Pope Gregory XII (1406–9) eventually conferred papal privileges on the Sienese university.[29] Thanks to imperial and papal approval, Siena seems to have had greater standing in contemporary eyes and probably began to attract more students.

The last thirty to forty years of the fourteenth century were difficult for most Italian universities, and Siena was no exception. War and the threat of war consumed communal treasure. The government tried to find more revenues for the university through new taxes and by obliging the clergy to help pay the salaries of professors, with little success. The university closed in 1402 and then reopened in 1404 with twenty professors. Again beset by financial problems, the commune in 1409 released all the Sienese professors while retaining the foreigners. Few students came. The university had reached a low ebb.

At this moment the commune took action to set the *studio* on the road to becoming an important Renaissance university. In 1404 the commune decided to establish a student residence in order to attract the ultramontane students whose presence was felt to be essential to the university's reputation.[30] It assigned the building and revenues of a lay confraternity, while an accommodating pope diverted some ecclesiastical revenues to the new establishment. Private donations of buildings and lands added to the patrimony of the proposed residential college. The Casa della Sapienza, or La Sapienza, opened its doors to ten university students in February 1416 and an additional ten in October. Thirty to forty mostly non-Italian students lived and boarded there by 1437.

Residents of La Sapienza had to be at least twenty years of age and to have already studied for one year. A student paid a once-only fee of 50 gold florins, which entitled him to board, room, and laundry at the residence for up to seven years. The price was raised to 60 gold ducats (a ducat was worth about the same as a florin) for seven years, and 40 gold ducats for three and one-half years, in the sixteenth century. These prices were probably lower than the normal cost of room and board. The student, in turn, was obliged to take his degree at Siena. The quasi-monastic rules of the Casa della Sapienza demanded that the students study, participate in religious exercises, and live sober lives, which did not always happen. Weapons were forbidden except for a personal sword. At one point twenty-five of the thirty places were reserved for legists. The Casa della Sapienza resembled private residence colleges, except that the state had created it in order to attract foreign students.

La Sapienza fulfilled the commune's hopes, as students competed for places. The 47 students in residence in 1474–75 included 10 Portuguese, 8 Germans, 3 Frenchmen, 2 Hungarians, and 2 Spaniards. The Germans then dominated for a while, filling two-thirds of the places in 1492. By the 1530s, the Casa della

29. Zdekauer, 1977, 32–33.

30. The following is based on Catoni, 1973, which includes the 1416 statutes of the Casa della Sapienza; Cascio Pratilli, 1975, 12–14, 63–68; Zdekauer, 1977, 33–37, 99–100; Minnucci and Košuta, 1989, 25–30, 319–20, 342–65, 384–89, 461–72; and Denley, 1991a, 43–48, 90–91. See Marrara, 1970, 320–27, for the statutes of 1602.

Sapienza again had a broader mix of Italian and foreign residents. Whether attracted by La Sapienza or coming for other reasons, German students were a very significant presence at Siena from the late fifteenth through the seventeenth centuries. After Padua and Bologna, Siena may have enrolled the largest number of Germans.[31]

The erection of La Sapienza was part of a general revitalization of the university. The commune appropriated greater sums, thus enabling it to appoint more professors at higher salaries. In 1432 the faculty numbered about 22 professors.[32] It had expanded to 44 professors (10 canonists, 13 civilians, 12 medical professors, 3 natural philosophers, and 6 logicians) in 1474.[33] The roll for the academic year 1492–93 listed 45 professors: 8 canonists, 14 civilians, 10 professors of medicine, 4 natural philosophers, 1 metaphysician, 3 logicans, 1 for astronomy, astrology, and mathematics, 2 professors of poetry, and 2 grammarians, who may have taught at the preuniversity level. Individual salaries ranged from a high of 690 florins to a low of 25, for a total of 5,515 florins.[34] (The Sienese gold florin was worth 4 lire.) Siena had 52 professors in the academic year 1500–1501: 3 theologians, 18 canonists, 13 civilians, 9 professors of medicine (or possibly medicine and philosophy), 4 logicians, 1 astrologer, and 4 humanists.[35] They earned 25 to 300 florins each, for a total of 4,625 florins. Siena, with 44 to 52 professors, ranked well behind Bologna and Pavia, slightly behind Padua, but ahead of all other Italian universities in faculty size at this time.

It is likely that the student body grew as well. In early November 1423, 115 students gathered in the communal palace for an official occasion. Thus, at least this many, and possibly more, students were in attendance when the university was at a low point.[36] It is likely that annual enrollment grew until it reached 400 to 500 in the last quarter of the century.

Several famous scholars taught at Siena during the fifteenth century. The best known were legists, beginning with the Sienese Mariano Sozzini the Elder (1397/1401–67), the first of a famous legal dynasty (see Ch. 13). He began teaching at Siena as a student lecturer in 1425 and was a professor from 1427 until death. Other well-known legists followed. Siena had a few eminent medical professors, including native son Ugo Benzi (1376–1439), who taught in the years 1405–9 and 1416–21.[37] Siena's most famous student was Aeneas Silvius Piccolomini (b. 1405; elected Pius II 1458; d. 1464) from a small town later renamed

31. For the residents of La Sapienza in 1474–75 and 1492, see Minnucci and Košuta, 1989, 98–101; for the German presence at Siena, see *I tedeschi dell'Università di Siena,* 1988.

32. Zdekauer, 1977, 56, 164. In addition to sources already cited for Siena in the fifteenth century, see Denley (1988), who compares Siena and Florence.

33. Minnucci and Košuta, 1989, 119–21. Garosi (1958, 226–80 and 525–54 passim) is particularly useful for medicine in the fifteenth century. Since fifteenth-century rolls have not been found, the faculty must be reconstructed from payment and other records.

34. Zdekauer, 1977, 191–93.

35. Mondolfo, 1897.

36. Catoni, 1973, 174 n. 85.

37. Benzi, 1966. For more on the professoriat in various fields, see Fioravanti, 1991a; Minnucci, 1991; and Piccinni, 1991.

Pienza in the Sienese state. He studied law under Mariano Sozzini but concentrated on classical Latin literature, from 1423 until the winter of 1431–32, when he left without a degree. Piccolomini probably also spent the years 1429–31 studying at Florence with the humanist Francesco Filelfo. Filelfo later taught Greek and Latin literature at Siena (1435–39), the only major humanist to teach there in the fifteenth and sixteenth centuries.

The commune directed the university through an administrative structure typical of universities ruled by communes.[38] A six-member (which became eight in the sixteenth century) magistracy called the Savi dello Studio (two of whose members were named Riformatori dello Studio) began sometime in the fourteenth century. Its responsibilities were clearly defined by 1400: it oversaw the university and the Casa della Sapienza. The Savi made appointment and salary recommendations to the highest assembly of the commune. In June or July the government confirmed contracts (usually for two years and almost always automatically renewed). The student organizations had little power.

Siena preferred foreign, that is, non-Sienese, professors in the century after 1321. It began to look more favorably on native sons in the period 1416–19, because they cost less. But Sienese professors remained few in number until 1437, when the commune decided that every professorship should have at least one Sienese occupant. The change was dramatic: by midcentury the number of foreigners and Sienese was about equal. By the end of the century, the faculty was 90 percent Sienese, and foreigners were rarely appointed in the sixteenth century.[39] Unlike Bologna, Siena did not attempt to leaven the local faculty with yeasty outsiders who might have raised the scholarly dough. The Sienese scholarly tradition produced several eminent legists but did less well in other subjects. Still, local professors produced stability and cost less than outsiders.

In 1484 a group of citizens petitioned the government to bring back one of its famous legal sons, Bartolomeo Sozzini (1436–1506), then teaching at Pisa. The petitioners argued that this was a good time to strengthen the University of Siena, because the universities of Padua, Pavia, Bologna, and Ferrara were almost deserted as a result of wars and famines and Perugia had greatly declined. Pisa stayed alive only through the reputation of Sozzini, whom the students would follow anywhere. If Siena could appoint Sozzini, more than three hundred foreign students would come, and the city would realize 15,000 florins in additional annual income.[40] Although it greatly exaggerated the perceived decline of other universities and overestimated the expected influx of students and income, the

---

38. Denley, 1991b, provides an excellent summary of how the commune ruled the university. See also Zdekauer, 1977, and Minnucci and Košuta, 1989, 366–83, for more on the Savi dello Studio.

39. In addition to the evidence from sixteenth-century rolls, see Denley, 1991b, 32–33.

40. "Che habiamo notitia tutti li Studii di Lombardia come Padua, Pavia, Bologna et Ferrara, per le guerre et carestie essere quasi derelicti, et anco Perogia grandemente declinata, et Pisa si tiene vivo solo con la reputatione del Sozino, a cui tuti li scolari di quella facultà verranno dietro; et havendo el Sozino potete tenere certo più che trecento scolari forestieri harà lo Studio vostro, li quali venendo non possano fare non mettino in la città fiorini 15.000 l'anno, tutti in beneficio de vostri buttigari et cittadini." Quoted in Bargagli, 1992, 308.

petition expressed soaring Sienese ambitions. The government wooed Sozzini assiduously, but he declined to come, partly because of a legal dispute with the Sienese commune.

Despite the failure to bring back Bartolomeo Sozzini, the University of Siena was doing well. The rolls of the late fifteenth century show it to have been a traditional institution emphasizing law and medicine. Siena lacked innovative philosophers and paid little attention to the humanities. But it did attract and graduate numerous law students. It conferred licentiates and doctorates on 1,675 recipients in the years 1484 through 1486 and 1496 through 1579. The distribution of degrees by subject matter was

Law (civil law, canon law, and *utroque iure*)	76.7%
Arts, Medicine, and Philosophy	16.9%
Theology	5.6%
Uncertain	0.8%

While law students were more likely than arts and medicine students to pursue their studies to completion with the doctorate, it is likely that the distribution of subject matter in the student body mirrored the degrees.[41]

Siena succeeded in attracting numerous non-Italians, especially Germans. Twenty-seven percent (454) of the degree recipients (1,675) were non-Italians, and 45 percent (205) of the non-Italians were Germans. Spanish degree recipients were a distant second, followed by degree recipients from areas that are modern France, Portugal, Belgium, the Netherlands, Austria, Poland, Czech Republic, Great Britain, Switzerland, Sweden, Cyprus, Lithuania, Montenegro, and Romania, in that order.

Tuscans constituted the largest number of Italian degree recipients, 46 percent. Very few of them were Florentines or Pisans, because Pisa was the seat of a rival Tuscan university and because the grand dukes of Tuscany wanted Florentines to attend the University of Pisa. But Siena attracted many students from the rest of Tuscany. Sicilians were the next largest group (17%) of Italian degree recipients, followed by Umbrians (12%) and men from the Marches (9%). Very few northern Italians came to Siena for degrees.

The sixteenth century brought wars, civil strife, and numerous changes of government to the Sienese republic. Nevertheless, the university continued to function. In 1531–43, the next years for which rolls are available, Siena had an average of 39 professors: 4 for canon law, 14 or 15 for civil law, 7 or 8 for

41. The figures in this and the following two paragraphs are based on the degrees discovered in notarial records in the Archivio Archivescovile di Siena and published by Minnucci (1981a, 1984, and 1985) and Minnucci and Morelli (1992 and 1998). See especially the introduction and summary tables by Minnucci in Minnucci and Morelli, 1998, ix–xxviii. Minnucci, 1995, is an earlier version of the introduction. Other degrees awarded through private channels, such as those conferred by counts palatine (see Ch. 5) were not included. Hence, the total number of degrees conferred was probably a little higher. Additional impressionistic data presented by Zdekauer (1977, 68–71, 96–98, 190–191) supports this surmise.

medicine, 6 for natural philosophy, 2 metaphysicians, 1 for astronomy, astrology, and mathematics, 3 humanists, and 1 logician.[42] Compared with the rolls of 1492–93 and 1500–1501, arts and medicine instruction had expanded slightly, while the number of canonists had decreased, shifts that occurred in most Italian universities. Theology had disappeared, to be partly replaced by metaphysics taught by members of the regular clergy from local monasteries. The 39 professors earned a total of 3,400 to 4,000 Sienese florins annually between 1531 and 1543, a lower amount than in 1500. The average salary was 80 to 100 florins, not a high figure. None of the professors was a major scholar, perhaps a consequence of the reduced communal appropriation for the university.

Unhappy with several aspects of communal governance of the university, the law professors went on strike in November 1532.[43] They demanded that the Savi dello Studio cease recommending appointments and determining salaries; they asked for an end to salary cuts; they objected to individuals simultaneously holding communal positions and professorships, with the result that they taught little; and they called for an end to holiday lectures. When the government promised to meet their demands, the legists agreed to return to teaching. But the students proclaimed vacation days and prevented the professors from lecturing until sometime in January 1533. By the beginning of the following academic year the government had still not acted, so more professors refused to teach. Finally in December 1533 the government acted. It removed the power to deal with professorial contracts from the Savi dello Studio and gave it to a newly created body of eight senators. The government agreed to increase salaries (although the amounts seem to have been slight), to take action against nonteaching professors, and to reduce vacations, so that more lectures would be available. The government acceded to the demands because it did not want "its" professors to leave for other universities, especially Pisa, which it believed would reopen shortly after being closed since 1526. (However, Pisa did not reopen until 1543).

The political situation went from bad to disastrous at midcentury. Siena's weakness created a political vacuum in central Italy which stronger powers were only too eager to fill. The French and especially the Spanish exerted increasing influence, while Florence stood ready to pounce. The Spanish stationed troops in the city from 1530; the brave Sienese drove them from the city in 1552. Charles V responded with a siege that starved the Sienese into surrender in 1555. He then sold the Sienese state to his ally, Cosimo I de' Medici, ruler of Florence, in 1557. Siena never regained its independence.

Although it is not clear whether the university remained open during the war and siege, it obviously suffered. The fluctuation in the annual number of degrees awarded showed the vicissitudes of the university in the sixteenth century. The 1520s were a period of intense warfare culminating in the Battle of Pavia in 1525 and the Sack of Rome in 1527. The Sienese *studio* recovered nicely in the 1540s and early 1550s. But then the number of degrees conferred dropped precipitously

42. The rolls are found in Minnucci and Košuta, 1989, 395–416.
43. See Minnucci and Košuta, 1989, 333–41, 373, 392–93, 572, for what follows.

in 1553 and remained very low through 1559, clearly the result of the siege and surrender of the republic. (See table 2.1.)

The University of Siena embarked on a new era in which the will of the Medici rulers determined its fate.[44] The Sienese asked Cosimo I to support the university; he evasively replied that he would do what was reasonable. Year after year the Sienese bombarded the grand duke with requests for new appointments and higher salaries. Cosimo saw matters differently. Pisa would be the favored international university in Tuscany, while Siena would become a small local university. He politely put off Sienese demands. For the academic year 1563–64, Siena had fourteen professors who earned about 1,100 florins, plus a handful of lecturers in *Institutes* (the introductory civil law text) and logic, who taught without salary. Pisa, by contrast, had forty-five professors.[45]

But then the fortunes of the Sienese *studio* improved. In 1567 Cosimo I turned over active management of the state to his son, the future grand duke Francesco I. The latter and his chief advisor heard Sienese requests on behalf of the university more sympathetically and responded pragmatically. While formally adhering to his father's policy favoring Pisa, Francesco I authorized the appointment of additional professors for Siena, always to be financed through Sienese funds. The professoriat grew to 20 for the academic year 1567–68 at a cost of 1,255 florins, to 25 in 1570–71 at a cost of 2,215 florins. When Francesco I became sole ruler after Cosimo I's death in 1574, the *studio* of Siena further expanded. It reached 39 professors costing about 2,280 florins in 1586–87 and 52 professors at 2,825 florins in 1588–89.[46] These numbers did not include Sienese citizens who, upon graduation, were obliged to teach gratis for a year.[47] Meanwhile, the faculty at Pisa held steady at about 45.

Sienese expansion came through adding numerous additional professors of law at extremely modest salaries. For example, the role of 1588–89 listed thirty-five legists, two-thirds of the total teaching staff. These multiple concurrents (professors teaching the same text at the same hour) received salaries of 25 or 35 florins. Nor did the rest of the faculty earn much more: the highest-paid professor received only 260 florins. A large supply of local degree holders made this approach possible. Siena had so many *dottori* that they were happy to teach for little, commented the grand duke's chief advisor in 1574.[48] One or two distinguished legists from elsewhere led the faculty, with the rest coming from Siena. Nevertheless, Siena once again had a vibrant university with a significant number of non-Italian students

These improvements did not satisfy the Sienese, who wanted to compete with more famous universities with broader curricula. The death of Francesco I in

44. Unless otherwise indicated, the following account to 1600 is based on Prunai, 1959; Marrara, 1970; Cascio Pratilli, 1975; and Catoni, 1991.

45. Cascio Pratilli, 1975, 175–76 and table on 201.

46. See the rolls in Cascio Pratilli, 1975, 175–87.

47. Prunai, 1959, 84. However, the extent of implementation of this policy is not clear. Cascio Pratilli (1975, 73–74) states that it added five to eight more teachers annually.

48. Cascio Pratilli, 1975, 40, 180–81.

TABLE 2.1

Average Annual Number of Doctorates Conferred at the University of Siena, 1484–1486, 1496–1513, 1516–1579

1484–86	10 per year
1496–99	16
1500–1509	21
1510–13	21
1516–19	10
1520–29	6
1530–39	11
1540–49	26
1550–52	33
1553–59	4
1560–69	24
1570–79	42

Source: Minnucci, 1981a, 1984, and 1985; Minnucci and Morelli, 1992 and 1998.
Note: The average for the entire period was 19.7 degrees conferred per year. The numbers of doctorates conferred in 1484, 1485, and 1486 were 2, 23, and 6, respectively. This may indicate that the documentation for 1484 and 1486 is incomplete and that the annual average should be higher. The years 1514 and 1515 have been eliminated from the table, because only 2 doctorates were noted in 1514 and none in 1515. Again, this probably indicated incomplete information, such as a shift from one notary to another.

October 1587 seemed to signal an opportunity for a bolder approach in 1588 and 1589. Not only did the Sienese continue to request permission to award higher salaries and make outside appointees, but they also sought the creation of three new posts. A professorship of simples (medical botany) would enable Siena to match Padua, Bologna, Ferrara, Pisa, and Pavia, all of which had created professorships of simples between 1533 and 1546. Second, the Sienese endorsed a request from their ultramontane students that the university add a professorship of humanistic jurisprudence called the *Pandects* professorship. Rome in 1567, Padua in 1578, and Bologna in 1588 had previously introduced this lectureship. Third, the Sienese wanted to create a professorship of Tuscan.

Most important, the Sienese proposed that all professors be chosen through open competitions (*concorsi*): applicants would dispute publicly before juries of academics and Sienese public officials. This was a revolutionary proposal, for all Italian universities filled posts through the mysterious process of reputation, recognition, and recommendation. A governmental committee inquired about and negotiated with professors reputed to be distinguished. It looked at recent local graduates from prominent families. Or a person of influence recommended a scholar with whom he was personally acquainted. The Sienese argued that new professorships and open competitions for posts would add learned non-Sienese to the faculty and strengthen the university. This, in turn, would attract more students, especially Germans.

After considerable discussion, the new sovereign Ferdinando I de' Medici (ruled 1587–1609) granted the Sienese much of what they wanted. But the reforms did not accomplish the desired ends. The teaching of medical botany began in the autumn of 1588, with the professorship going to a local physician and civic officeholder who was paid only 35 florins. The professorship of *Pandects* began in the fall of 1589 with the appointment of Francesco Accarigi (c. 1557–1622) at 130 florins. Although not a native, Accarigi earned his degree at Siena and was already there as a lowly extraordinary lecturer in civil law. Both Accarigi and his successors were chosen by the grand duke rather than through *concorsi*. Nor did the appointment meet the scholarly expectations of the German students, who hoped that it would mean the introduction of humanistic jurisprudence based on a direct reading of the ancient texts. But Accarigi and his successors followed *mos italicus*, the Italian traditional method of concentrating on medieval and Renaissance commentators.[49]

The chair of Tuscan began in the autumn of 1588 with the appointment of Diomede Borghesi (c. 1540–98), a Sienese who had studied at Siena, had links to the Medici court, and had written many works on vernacular grammar, poetry, and letters.[50] But attendance was restricted to German students. It appears that the government viewed the teaching of Tuscan as a service to ultramontane students rather than the promotion of scholarship on Tuscan language and literature.[51] Despite the limitations, the position was the first vernacular language professorship in Europe. Borghesi and his successors studied, lectured, and published on the Italian language. The university also promoted the vernacular by permitting the professors of anatomy, medical botany, and mathematics to lecture in Italian beginning in 1589.

The grand-ducal government only partially accepted public competitions. It inaugurated the *concorsi* but exempted many of the more important professorships. It also made ad interim provisional appointments that became permanent. The grand-ducal government simply would not allow that much power over the university to slip from its hands. Even the authorized *concorsi* did not work well. Distinguished non-Sienese academics refused to submit to this potentially embarrassing test of their competence. Local candidates also frustrated the competitions: only one man would enter a competition, or the candidates would arrange the outcome in advance. Sienese natives continued to claim the vast majority of the professorships, even when the commune sought prestigious outsiders. The competitions dwindled in importance and were suppressed in 1609. No other Italian university tried the Sienese innovation.

Even worse, a drastic reduction of the faculty accompanied the reforms. For the academic year 1589–90 the grand-ducal government slashed the number of professors from 52 to 35. They consisted of 16 professors of civil law, 2 for canon law, 1 theologian, 5 professors of medicine, 1 for simples, 5 philosophers, 2 logicians, a mathematician, a humanist, and the professor of Tuscan. The faculty remained at this level for the rest of the century and beyond. Elimination of many

49. Ibid., 41 n. 79, 73 n. 199, 93, 183, 185, 187.
50. Rossi, 1910; Beccaria, 1970; and Maraschio and Poggi Salani, 1991.
51. Prunai, 1959, 98–100; Cascio Pratilli, 1975, 83–84 n. 22, 88, 186, 188.

of the poorly paid *concorrenti* (concurrents) in law accomplished the reduction. At the same time, the Medici ruler partially responded to the Sienese demand for higher salaries by allowing the salary disbursement to rise slightly from about 2,800 florins to 3,100 florins. Hence, the average professorial salary rose from 54 florins to 91.

The government refused to support the University of Siena fully because Ferdinando I and his chief advisor decided to restore the earlier policy of promoting Pisa while restraining Siena. In contrast to the Sienese cuts, the University of Pisa grew from forty professors in 1588–89 to forty-seven in 1590–91. The grand-ducal government would no longer permit Siena to rival Pisa.

Its plans thwarted, the University of Siena remained a medium-sized, second-tier university still important as a destination for ultramontane students. A few professors, especially in medicine, had more than local scholarly reputations in the last third of the sixteenth century. However, the majority came from prominent local families, acquired degrees in Siena, and remained as ill-paid and relatively undistinguished academics. The *studio* seldom competed with more prominent institutions for eminent professors.

Most Italian students came from Siena and Tuscany; a minority came from the rest of Italy. Siena also continued to enroll Germans and other ultramontanes. The presence of a colony of German artisans in Siena probably helped to attract them, as did the grand duke's status as an imperial feudatory.[52] And the Medici indirectly aided recruitment of Germans by blocking the Sienese Inquisition from investigating ultramontane students suspected of heresy (see Ch. 5, "The Counter Reformation").

Despite its difficulties, the University of Siena probably maintained an enrollment of 400 to 500 through the first half of the century. Certainly Siena, as the only available Tuscan university, profited from Pisa's closure between 1526 and 1543. Siena still managed to enroll 242 students at the end of June 1553, a time of mounting political tensions with the emperor.[53] Enrollment probably returned to the level of 500 students in the last third of the century.

Numerous Sienese studied at the local university, and some became well-known scholars. So did some foreigners. The French Protestant humanistic juris-consult Jean de Coras (1513–72) obtained a civil law degree at Siena in April 1535. The important Croatian humanist Marin Držić (Darsa; 1508–67) studied humanities at Siena 1538–45 and was elected student rector. He departed without a degree-and without paying numerous creditors. Johann Albrecht Wid-manstetter (1506–57), scholar of Oriental matters, took a degree *in utroque iure* in 1539.[54]

Throughout its history the commune of Siena strongly supported its *studio*

52. Prunai, 1959, 122–24.

53. The only known surviving matriculation figures come from June 28–30, 1553, at which time 242 students, only a handful of them non-Italians, were matriculated. Minnucci and Košuta, 1989, 425–32. It is not clear if clergymen, who usually were not required to matriculate, were listed. Minnucci and Košuta (1989, 319) speculate that Siena had close to 500 students in 1542.

54. Ibid., 535, 537–38, 567.

despite political upheaval, war, and loss of independence. Indeed, supporting the university may have been the only policy upon which the fractious Sienese agreed. The commune maintained its commitment even though the population of the city dropped to between 14,000 and 17,000 in the fifteenth century and remained under 20,000 in the following century.[55] Siena was an important, conservative legal center in the fifteenth century and struggled to maintain that status in the next. The *studio* tried to be innovative and experimental in other ways but failed to achieve academic leadership outside of law. Nevertheless, the university attracted numerous ultramontane students throughout the Renaissance.

ROME, 1240S

It is not clear when the University of Rome began. Probably a limited amount of instruction in canon law and civil law, with theology taught in the local mendicant order monasteries, occurred in the 1240s, and a small amount of medical instruction came later in the century. In 1244 or 1245 Pope Innocent IV issued a document that proclaimed the establishment of a *studium generale,* using the name Studium Romanae Curiae (University of the Roman Curia) and Studium Curiae (University of the Curia). This terminology has led some scholars to postulate the existence of a university attached to the papal court, separate from the University of Rome (Studium Urbis), thought to have been founded later. It is more likely that Studium Romanae Curiae and Studium Urbis were two names used to describe a single entity, a Roman university that reflected the dual nature, papal and civic, of governance in Rome.[56]

An important clarifying document appeared on April 20, 1303, when Pope Boniface VIII issued a bull. It called the Studium Urbis (University of Rome) a *studium generale* and granted to its professors and students the customary legal immunities, plus the right to elect a rector. Another papal bull of August 1, 1318, affirmed and clarified the right of the University of Rome to award degrees in

55. Ginatempo and Sandri, 1990, 109, 148.

56. The first historian of the University of Rome, Giuseppe Carafa (Carafa, 1971, first published in 1751), did not believe that the Studium Romanae Curiae and Studium Urbis were separate and autonomous institutions. Then Filippo Maria Renazzi argued against Carafa that two distinct institutions existed until the city university absorbed the curial university by the late fifteenth century. Renazzi, 1971 (first published 1803–6), 1:21–56. Rashdall, 1936, 2:28–31; Creytens, 1942 (the most detailed account); Valentini 1936 and 1944; and others followed Renazzi. Doubts then began to surface about the existence of a curial university because so little evidence of pedagogical or other activity could be located. Paravicini Bagliani (1989) and Frova and Miglio (1992) accepted the existence of a curial university as a degree-granting entity but saw teaching occurring outside it. They also noted what appeared to be collaboration between the two bodies. Thus, they chipped away at the existence of a distinct curial university. Finally, Adorni (1992, 1995, and 1997) demonstrated that the term *Studium Curiae* appeared in university documents and contexts that were clearly municipal. On the basis of extensive investigation of the manuscript evidence, she argues that Rome had but one university, commonly called the Studium Urbis, which began in the 1240s or slightly earlier. She demonstrates that the names *Studium Curiae* and *Studium Urbis* referred to the same entity. The two names reflected the always complex dual juridical nature of a university ruled by both city government and pope.

civil and canon law, listing degree requirements very similar to those for other universities.[57] By the 1320s civic officials, the Roman clergy, and the papal vicar joined together to select professors. Taxes paid by subject towns such as Tivoli supported the university.

The University of Rome taught law, medicine, grammar, and logic, while the mendicant order monasteries taught theology, from the early fourteenth century onward. Although no rolls survive, the names of a few professors, usually modest scholars, in law, medicine, philosophy, grammar, and logic are known. For example, Angelo and Pietro degli Ubaldi, brothers of the famous Baldo degli Ubaldi, taught civil and canon law in Rome in the late 1370s and the 1380s.[58] But the professoriat may have been very small. Professors lectured in houses contiguous with or near the church of Sant'Eustachio, between the Pantheon and Piazza Navona, in the heart of the city. The university may have avoided closures in the fourteenth century despite Rome's turbulent political history. The absence of the papacy in Avignon (1309–77) did not seem to harm the university.

By contrast, the end of the Avignonese exile inaugurated a period of difficulty. Civil strife, the papal schism of 1378 to 1417, and natural disaster between about 1370 and 1431 had a "calamitous" impact on the university according to later documents. Classes were moved across the Tiber to the district of Trastevere in the 1370s. Pope Innocent VII announced his intention to restore the University of Rome on September 1, 1406. The humanist Leonardo Bruni, then in papal service, wrote the papal bull, which called for a full program of studies including the teaching of Greek. Unfortunately, Innocent VII died on November 6, 1406, without taking action.[59] The university remained open but did little.[60]

A new era for the University of Rome began in 1431. On October 10 of that year Pope Eugenius IV issued a bull that renewed the constitution of Boniface VIII and, most important, put the University of Rome on a firm financial basis. Henceforward, the proceeds of a tax of 17.5 percent levied on imported wine (called *gabella studii*) sold by the taverns of the city went to the university.[61] As Rome's importance as a destination for pilgrims and a center for Europe's ecclesiastical and political business swelled, the tax yielded large sums for the Studium Urbis. The pope also moved the university back to the neighborhood of Sant'Eustachio, where it remained until the twentieth century. The Renaissance university dates from this bull issued by a pontiff strongly committed to education.[62]

---

57. The bulls of 1303 and 1318 are found in Renazzi, 1971, 1:258–59, 266–68.

58. Renazzi, 1971, 1:80–81, 107–8. For the history of the university in the fourteenth century, see Renazzi, 1971, vol. 1, and Valentini, 1936 and 1944.

59. Griffiths, 1973.

60. See Valentini, 1936, 196–217, and Valentini, 1944, 388–89, which correct Renazzi, 1971, 1:103–4, who stated that the university closed.

61. Lee (1978, 153) calculated the percentage of the levy. This and the following paragraph are based on Renazzi, 1:116–26, 201–9, 274–77 (including documents), and Chambers, 1976, 70–71.

62. Eugenius IV also caused to be founded or renewed numerous cathedral schools across Italy. See Grendler, 1989, 9.

Additional measures clarified the mixed administrative structure of the university. A papal chamberlain, who was sometimes a cardinal relative of the reigning pontiff, exercised ultimate authority. Instead of students electing a student rector, the pope named a rector, who was frequently a bishop and sometimes a professor. The rector oversaw the preparation of an annual *rotulus* (list of professors and courses) when this finally became a legal requirement in 1514. In addition, the city government nominated a dozen citizens, from whom the chamberlain chose four, at least one of whom had to hold a doctorate of law, to serve as Riformatori dello Studio. The latter supervised the administration of the monies collected from the wine tax and the disbursement of funds for salaries and other expenses. Chamberlain, rector, and Riformatori served as buffers between university and pontiff, the ruler of the state. The degree of papal involvement in the university varied according to the wishes of individual pontiffs. Like other universities, Rome had colleges of law and arts outside the university which examined degree candidates.[63]

As the Renaissance flowered in Rome, intellectuals came to the city, some of them to teach at the Studium Urbis.[64] Antonio Roselli, a major legal scholar, came to Rome during the pontificate of Martin V (1417–31), taught canon law as ordinary professor, and wrote various works until his death in 1446.[65] George of Trebizond and Lorenzo Valla taught at the University of Rome in the 1440s and 1450s. The Studium Urbis became a significant institution boasting major intellectual figures.

Only in the 1470s did the size of the University of Rome become evident. It had 45 to 50 professors in 1473–74, 50 to 75 in 1481–84, and 42 to 49 in 1494–96.[66] In an average year during this quarter century, the faculty consisted of 20 to 25 professors of law (slightly more professors of civil than canon law), 10 to 15 professors of medicine, 4 to 10 humanists (i.e., teachers of rhetoric or Greek), 2 to 4 theologians, 4 professors of natural philosophy or metaphysics or both, 1 or 2 logicians, and occasionally an astronomer/mathematician. It was a typical faculty complement, except that the humanists were more numerous and the philosophers fewer. Professors collectively earned 4,000 to 8,000 Roman florins annually. As in other universities, salaries varied considerably, from a low of 25 Roman florins to a high of 600 Roman florins paid to the humanist Francesco Filelfo in 1475 and 1476.[67] As elsewhere, legists normally earned the highest

63. Adorni (1995, 323–55) prints the statutes of the legal college, which consisted of twelve local men, from a manuscript written between 1486 and 1492.

64. The basic study of the Renaissance in Rome is D'Amico, 1983. See also Stinger, 1985.

65. Renazzi, 1971, 1:128–29.

66. Payment records exist for 1473–74, 1481–84, and 1494–96. Chambers (1976), Lee (1978, 155–192), and especially Dorati da Empoli (1980) provide detailed summaries of these records. Lee (1984) discusses the university on the basis of these records and some others. Because the records are incomplete, often fail to indicate the subject taught, and are widely scattered among other materials, the above scholars arrive at slightly different numbers of professors. I have rounded the figures.

67. Lee, 1984, 133–41. Filelfo taught at Rome for only five months in the first half of 1475 and another few months in early 1476. A Roman florin was worth only 47 soldi (Lee, 1978, 165 n. 54), considerably less than the Florentine florin, worth 120 to 130 soldi at this time. Goldthwaite, 1980,

salaries, upwards of 500 Roman florins. Professors may not have received full salaries every year, but some humanists and legists also drew salaries from curial positions.

Pope Leo X (1513–21) aided the university with fiscal and administrative reforms. In November 1513 he restored to the university most revenues, some of which had been diverted to other purposes, from the tax on imported wine. And he may have added additional sums for professorial salaries in 1517 and 1518. At the same time, he tried to ensure that professors received their full salaries and on time. The pope ordered the rector and Riformatori to visit the university at least once a month and one Riformatore to visit classrooms twice a week. The city's representatives issued regulations intended to ensure that professors met their academic responsibilities. Law professors were forbidden to argue cases in the courts, which suggests that some may have neglected teaching for litigation.[68]

The University of Rome reached its peak faculty size during Leo X's pontificate. The *rotulus* of 1514, the earliest to be found, listed 87 professors (and one vacancy) for the academic year 1514–15.[69] They included 4 theologians, 11 canonists, 19 civilians, 15 professors of medicine, 5 natural philosophers, 2 metaphysicians, 2 moral philosophers, 4 logicians, 3 professors of mathematics and astrology, 18 rhetoricians, 3 professors of Greek, and a professor of medical botany (*Ad declarationem Simplicium Medicinae*), the first in any university.[70] The cohort of rhetoricians was by far the largest to be found anywhere: 6 ordinary professors of rhetoric lectured in the morning, another 5 lectured in the afternoon, 3 extraordinary professors of rhetoric lectured on holiday mornings, and another 4 on holiday afternoons. Twenty-one, or close to one-fourth of the entire professoriat, taught humanistic subjects—rhetoric, Greek, and moral philosophy. This large collection of talent cost a great deal of money—close to 16,000 Roman florins, two to four times as much as in the 1470s and 1480s.[71]

The faculty included some distinguished figures. The Aristotelian Agostino Nifo had previously taught at the universities of Padua and Naples. Leo X brought him to Rome as ordinary professor of philosophy at a salary of 300 gold ducats. He moved to the University of Pisa in 1519.[72] The peripatetic Luca Pacioli of Sansepolcro (c. 1445–1517), probably the best-known mathematician of his day, had previously taught at the Studium Urbis for a few months between 1487

---

430. The wine tax raised much more money than the amount spent on the university, but much of it was diverted to buildings, roads, and other purposes.

68. Renazzi, 1971, 2:25–27, 35–36.

69. Marini (1797) first discovered and printed it. Roscoe (1805, vol. 2, app., pp. 81–86) reprinted it. So did Renazzi (1971, 2:235–39), who identified most of the professors. It is also printed in *I maestri di Roma* (1991, 1–5). The thirteen (later fourteen) *maestri dei rioni*, elementary and secondary school teachers also listed on university rolls, are always omitted in the following discussion.

70. Giuliano da Foligno, about whom nothing is known, held the position.

71. The salaries listed on the *rotulus* amounted to about 12,960 florins (presumably Roman florins worth 47 soldi) plus 1,100 ducats, assumed to have the value of a Venetian ducat of account, which was 124 soldi. Thus, the total was close to 18,000 Roman florins. Because of the difficulty of comparing monies, the total should be viewed as approximate.

72. Renazzi, 1971, 2:45–46.

and 1489; he returned in 1514.[73] The rhetoricians included the well-known Roman humanists Tommaso Fedra Inghirami, Giovanni Battista Pio, and Raffaele Brandolini, as well as Filippo Beroaldo the Younger, who came from the University of Bologna.

The lack of surviving documents, except for the roll of 1514, makes it very difficult to evaluate the University of Rome between 1500 and 1527. Leo X and Clement VII (1523–34) certainly appointed eminent scholars to teach at the Studium Urbis.[74] But it is not likely that Rome had a student body of a size comparable to the large number of professors.[75] Despite the large size and high quality of the faculty, an air of improvisation hung over the Studium Urbis. Missed lectures seem to have been common occurrences and not viewed gravely. Professors complained that the papacy was late in paying their salaries or did not deliver the full amount. The same Medici pontiffs who warmly supported scholarship also mismanaged papal finances.[76] Despite Leo X's restoration of its income, Clement VII again diverted tax revenues intended for the university to other purposes in the 1520s.[77]

Numerous scholars came to Rome, because the Eternal City was so important and the patronage so rich. But they did not necessarily view university teaching as their most important activity in Rome, nor did they stay long.

The fundamental problem was that the university was not the intellectual center of Rome. Popes and cardinals often brought scholars to the Eternal City to undertake a scholarly project or to serve as personal physician, humanist secretary, or legal advisor. Appointment to the University of Rome might follow as a device to provide financial support to the scholar without draining the papal or cardinalatial purse. Hence, the primary purpose behind the appointment was not the establishment of a strong faculty to attract and teach students. In these circumstances some university professors put loyalty to pontiff, prelate, or their own ambitions ahead of university obligations. For example, the young Paolo Giovio (1486–1552), historian and future bishop, then making his way as a Roman courtier, lectured in moral philosophy in 1514–15 and in natural philosophy in 1515–16. But he also served a cardinal and spent much time interviewing political and military leaders about the Italian wars for his future histories. When Giovio traveled with his cardinal, he arranged for a substitute to lecture for him.[78] The University of Rome needed a core of essential professors in law and medicine to stay and teach for many years if it wished to acquire a great reputation and attract numerous students.

The Sack of Rome of May 1527 brought the Studium Urbis of the High

73. Jayawardene, 1981c, 269–70.

74. For Clement VII's efforts, see Renazzi, 1971, 2:81–87.

75. No data have been located on the number of students or the degrees granted before the second half of the sixteenth century. It is likely that most university documents were destroyed in the sack of 1527.

76. See the comments in Pastor, 1891–1953, 8:272–75.

77. Renazzi, 1971, 2:27, 87.

78. Zimmermann, 1995, 14–15.

Renaissance to a horrible end. After the pillaging troops finally left, Clement VII put all the revenues of the wine tax into repairing the city's walls.[79] The university remained closed for eight years.

Paul III (1534–49) reconstituted the university by restoring the *gabella studii* to its original purpose and making appointments. The University of Rome re-opened in the autumn of 1535 with 18 professors, which grew to 24 in 1539 and 21 in 1542.[80] Paul III and his successors guaranteed adequate funding, improved university quarters, and instituted administrative reforms. A congregation of cardinal-protectors oversaw the university, while city authority over the univer-sity diminished. A beadle visited each lecture to ensure that professors met their classes.[81] A document of 1568 referred to La Sapienza, which is the name of the university today.[82]

La Sapienza became a stable, medium-sized university. The faculty averaged 37 professors from 1548 through 1582.[83] It consisted of 4 or 5 theologians, a professor of Scripture, 3 canonists, 9 civilians, 5 or 6 professors of theoretical and practical medicine, a professor of surgery, another for medical botany, 2 logicians, 3 natural and/or moral philosophers, 1 or 2 metaphysicians, 3 professors of rhetoric, 2 for Greek, 1 for Hebrew, and a mathematician. The average faculty component decreased to 29 professors in the last twenty years of the century and to 27 in the first decade of the seventeenth century. University expenses grew from about 4,500 scudi to more than 7,000 scudi during the last forty years of the century.[84] Salaries gradually rose, possibly because of inflation. But Rome seldom hired star legists at astronomical salaries.

The distribution of faculty by subjects was typical of a medium-sized univer-sity, with two exceptions. La Sapienza had more theologians (see Ch. 10, "Uni-versities Teaching Theology Continuously"), and it emphasized the teaching of

79. Renazzi, 1971, 2:87–91.

80. For the three rolls, see *I maestri di Roma*, 1991, 7–15. For the university during Paul III's pontificate, see also Renazzi, 1971, 2:95–100, and Pastor, 1891–1953, 12:526–28. All the known rolls from 1514 onward, with many gaps for the sixteenth century, have been published in *I maestri di Roma* (1991), based on various *fondi* in ASR and ASVa. A small number of rolls had been published earlier: see Marini, 1797, esp. 126–27, 143–49; Renazzi, 2:245–48, 276–77; 3:221–22, 224–25; and Pometti, 1901.

81. See Renazzi, 1971, 2:93–167; Pometti, 1901, 71–72; Conte, 1985a, 13–18; and especially Conte 1985b. See also the scattered comments in Pastor, 1891–1953, 13:327–28, 16:409–10, 17:134; 20:589–90; 22:197–98; 24:450–51.

82. Renazzi, 1971, 2:166.

83. The following is based on *I maestri di Roma* (1991). Many of the rolls, especially those from ASVa, Miscellanea Armadio XI, vol. 93A, of the second half of the century provide additional information. Prepared by the beadle, Alessio Lorenzani, who served from 1552 to 1580, these are large sheets of paper listing professors, sometimes their salaries, lecture hours, and the texts read. Lorenzani often added comments about the teachers, the quality of their instruction, the number of their students, and the number of degrees awarded. Emanuele Conte and his collaborators have done an immense service in transcribing the rolls, most of which I examined before his volumes were published.

84. A scudo was worth a little less than a Venetian ducat or a Florentine florin. It is not known why salaries were now denominated in scudi rather than Roman florins.

ancient languages more than other universities. Rome boasted one and often two professors of Greek from the reopening of the university in 1535 through 1582. It had a professor of Hebrew throughout the second half of the century and into the following century, although he taught few students.[85]

In a remarkable development, a professor of Arabic grammar appeared in 1575–76. The beadle commented that the professor of Arabic had many students in the beginning of the year, but then the number dwindled to a handful of advanced students. Since there were only a few advanced students, it would be a good idea to accept beginners, the beadle suggested. He also felt that the religious orders should send some of their members to learn Arabic. This would be a good thing, because if they ever had to preach to the infidel, they would not be considered ignorant of Arabic.[86] The comment suggests that the introduction of Arabic may have been an experiment. If so, it was not continued; the next surviving roll (1579–80) had no teacher of Arabic. Perhaps professors of Greek, Hebrew, and Arabic were expected to help train the scholars who prepared new editions of the Vulgate Bible and the works of patristic and medieval Scholastic authors, the program of Catholic scholarly renewal under way.

Most instruction did not support religious scholarship but prepared men for secular careers. For example, La Sapienza did not emphasize canon law, even though law was the surest path to high position in the Italian church. It had only 2 or 3 canonists, compared with 7 to 9 civilians, after 1535. The university awarded many more civil law degrees, or degrees *in utroque iure,* than degrees in arts or theology (see Ch. 13, "Pavia and Rome").

La Sapienza had a more cosmopolitan faculty than most Italian universities, as Frenchmen, Spaniards, and Italians from different parts of the peninsula taught there. Romans and inhabitants of the papal state did not receive preference for university posts. Turnover was low, as the majority of professors spent many years at Rome.[87]

A few of the professors were well-known scholars. Romolo Amaseo of Udine (1489–1552), a humanist who had previously taught at Padua and Bologna, taught at Rome from 1544 to 1550.[88] The Frenchman Marc'Antoine Muret

85. Lorenzani, the beadle, wrote in 1575–76 that the professor of Hebrew "non multos habet scholares," but he also knew Chaldean (ancient Aramaic). *I maestri di Roma,* 1991, 102 (quote), 1027, 1034–35.

86. "Arabicus gramaticam. D. Andreas de Monte. Hic, cum primum agressus est, multos habuit auditores, modo subsequun[tur], sed pluries res ad triarios rediit, hic sic dicit et esse consentaneum videtur quomodo in hac lingua non sunt studiosi, quod bonum esset ut . . . religionibus mitteretur auditores ut inde haec lingua adisci posset, quodquidem bonum comprobandum est ut si quandoque ad predicandum inter infideles necesse foret non ignari haberentur." ASVa, Miscellanea Armadio XI, vol. 93A, roll of 1575–76, no foliation, comment of the beadle, Alessio Lorenzani; reprinted in *I maestri di Roma,* 1991, 103. I wish to thank Philip Stadter for helping me puzzle out the passage. I have been unable to learn more about Andrea da Monte, who earned only 50 scudi.

87. The beadle often indicated the number of years that a professor had taught at La Sapienza. See the rolls for 1574–76, 1579–80, 1587, 1592–95, in *I maestri di Roma,* 1991, 85–92, 98–104, 114–18, 125–27, and 129–42, as well as the lists of professors organized by subject at the end of the book.

88. Avesani, 1960, 663–64.

(1526–85) taught moral philosophy in the years 1562–67, the *Pandects,* that is, humanistic jurisprudence, the first such position in Italy, from 1567 to 1572, then rhetoric from 1572 until his death. Francesco Patrizi da Cherso (1529–97) taught Platonic philosophy at La Sapienza from 1592 to 1595 and perhaps later. Andrea Cesalpino (1524/25–1603), a well-published scholar on botany and the circulation of the blood, came from Pisa in 1592 to teach at Rome until his death.[89]

Another professor was hired for his ancestry and books. Aldo Manuzio the Younger (1547–97) taught rhetoric at Rome from 1588 to 1596. Numerous universities courted this scholarly mediocrity because they coveted the Aldine family library, which he owned. He began teaching at Rome to great acclaim, but attendance soon dropped to one or two students.[90]

Although located in the universal city, La Sapienza drew the vast majority of its students from the papal state and southern Italy. For example, law graduates came from Ancona, Aquila, Rimini, Viterbo, and Rome in the papal state. A larger number came from tiny towns and castles in Basilicata and Calabria, a few from such larger towns as Naples and Salerno, plus Sicily. A handful came from northern Italian towns. But only two non-Italians, a Pole and a Spaniard, obtained law degrees in the decade 1549 to 1558. This pattern continued for the rest of the century.[91] It appears that almost all the students studied exclusively in Rome, rather than moving from university to university, as wealthier students often did.[92]

La Sapienza may have had a student body of about 300 in the 1530s. This probably rose to 500 by 1550, to 750 by the 1580s, and then declined to 600 by the end of the century. Indirect evidence supporting these estimates comes from a document of 1628, in which a university official stated that La Sapienza had about 490 students (250 in law, 140 in medicine, and 100 in other fields) at that date. He lamented that this marked a decline from the late sixteenth century.[93] Another observer noted in 1623 that, because of the "ruin of the money of the Kingdom (of Naples)," fewer students came from the Neapolitan state than in the last third of the sixteenth century, because they could not afford to live away from home. Students from the papal state had the same difficulty.[94] Moreover, an enrollment

89. De Ferrari, 1980.

90. Renazzi, 1971, 3:46–47.

91. ASR, Archivio dell'Università di Roma, R. 227, "Registri dei Dottori e decreti togati, 3 marzo 1549–23 dicembre 1558." See ff. 190ʳ and 202ᵛ for the Spaniard and the Pole. Of course, the records do not always list the town or country of origin. See also ibid., R. 105, documents beginning in 1587, and Cagno, 1932, 170–72, 178–79.

92. See ASR, Archivio dell'Università di Roma, R. 105, for the period 1587 onward. This is a register of statements by law students that they had studied in a university for at least five years, one of the prerequisites for taking degree examinations. Two professors were required to confirm the students' assertions. All but one student studied exclusively at Rome; the exception had studied at Naples.

93. ASR, Archivio dell'Università di Roma, R. 83, f. 39bisʳ. The figures come at the end of a three-page *relazione* of 1628 discussing the university in some detail. Although the *relazione* is anonymous, it clearly comes from an official of the university, perhaps the beadle.

94. "La ruina delle monete di Regno dove venivano molti scolari à Roma, li quali al presente

rising from 300 to 750 seems consistent with the number of professors and law degrees awarded.[95] The city of Rome, which had 55,000 to 60,000 inhabitants in 1526, and probably more later, easily supported this number of students.[96]

The University of Rome had three phases. It began in the 1240s but remained a minor institution until the second half of the fifteenth century. The Studium Urbis had a large and talented faculty, especially in the humanities, from the 1470s until the sack of 1527. But other problems kept it from joining the company of Italy's leading universities. After 1535 Rome settled into a secure role as a middle-rank university. La Sapienza performed the traditional function of a regional university: it educated men from a nearby recruitment area who wished to become lawyers, civil servants, physicians, humanists, and teachers. It also offered instruction in theology and ancient languages to clergymen serving the papacy and universal church. But the Collegio Romano (founded 1551) of the Jesuits, and the *studia* of the mendicant orders, also attracted clergymen coming to Rome to study theology, philosophy, and the humanities.[97] With four universities within its state (Rome, Bologna, Perugia, and Macerata from 1540–41), the papacy encouraged Bologna to maintain its high international reputation. The University of Rome had to accept a lesser role.

PERUGIA, 1308

The free commune of Perugia set out to create a university modeled on that of Bologna. Although the commune initially may not have had a complete plan in mind, the University of Perugia came into existence through a series of logical steps.

In 1266 the governing council of Perugia, a major city of 23,000 to 28,000 inhabitants, approved expenses for a *studium*.[98] Nine years later the commune promised legal immunity to any scholar wishing to come to the *studium*. In 1276

---

mancano, non potevano mantenere, come ancora molti dello stato ecclesiastico, li quali prima potevano più facilmente mantenersi in Roma." ASR, Archivio dell'Università di Roma, R. 83, f. 28ᵛ, an anonymous report on the university dated 1623. Other reasons advanced for decline were the proliferation of private teaching, the lack of a famous legist on the faculty, and the diversion of funds from the *gabella studii* to other purposes. See also ibid., R. 86, for many complaints concerning the diversion of the proceeds of the *gabella studii* to other purposes in the first half of the seventeenth century.

95. La Sapienza awarded an average of seventy degrees annually *in utroque iure* in the second half of the sixteenth century, plus an unknown number of, but obviously fewer, degrees in medicine, arts, and theology. See ASR, Archivio dell'Università di Roma, R. 227, "Registri dei Dottori e decreti togati, 3 marzo 1549–23 dicembre 1558;" Cagno, 1932, esp. 168; and *I maestri di Roma,* 1991, 51, 59, 64, 74, 85, 96, 113. If most degree recipients studied at Rome, as seems to have been the case, one can cautiously extrapolate from the number of degrees to the enrollment.

96. Ginatempo and Sandri, 1990, 134, 148.

97. For an interesting discussion about rhetoric at the university and the Collegio Romano in the late sixteenth century, see McGinness, 1995a.

98. The following is based on Ermini, 1971, 1:15–29, 113, which supersedes all previous accounts, including Rashdall, 1936, 2:40–43. The population figures for the late thirteenth and early fourteenth centuries come from Ginatempo and Sandri, 1990, 129.

the commune invited students from the surrounding territory to come to Perugia to study with a professor of law or a professor of arts. In 1285 it appropriated a substantial amount of money to hire a professor of law and made other hires in the following years. In 1304 it authorized the formation of a student *universitas* with a rector. With the pieces of a university modeled on Bologna in place, the commune requested a papal bull for a *studium generale*, which Clement V granted on September 8, 1308. This date is taken as the founding date of the University of Perugia. Papal bulls of 1318 and 1321 established the forms for conferring degrees in civil and canon law and in medicine and arts. The bishop of Perugia conferred the license to teach and doctorate after an examination in which various doctors assisted.

The commune in 1306 established a minimum of 9 professors for the *studium:* 4 professors of civil law, 2 for canon law, and 1 each for medicine, logic, and grammar.[99] The teaching component remained at about this number, with some internal fluctuation, for the next few years. Then the university gradually expanded. It reached 12 in 1339 (3 professors of civil law, 4 of canon law, 3 professors of medicine, and 1 each of philosophy and logic). In this year 119 law students and 23 students of medicine, figures that may be incomplete, matriculated. The majority of students came from central Italy; others came from Germany, Bohemia, southern France, the Hispanic peninsula, and England.[100] Further expansion occurred late in the century. In 1396 the University of Perugia had 16 or more teachers evenly divided between law and arts: 3 professors of civil law, 4 of canon law, 5 of medicine, 1 for logic and philosophy, and another for astrology. A teacher of *ars notaria* (notarial art) and a teacher *Ad reactandum ossa* ("setting bones") were also included, as well as the occasional extraordinary professor. Perugia began the fifteenth century with 16 or more professors, about one-fourth the size of Bologna.[101]

In 1322 the commune created the Savi dello Studio, a magistracy consisting of ten members, two each from the five districts of the city, to oversee the university. Additional legislation of 1366 reduced their number to five and further defined their duties. Elected by the highest councils of the Perugian government to one-year terms, followed by five years of ineligibility, the Savi chose the professors and exercised all other authority over the university. The Savi lasted until 1625.[102]

The university's law faculty achieved great eminence in the fourteenth century, because the two most famous Italian legal scholars of all time studied and taught there. Bartolo da Sassoferrato (1313–57) studied at Perugia from 1326 or 1327 until 1333, took his degree at Bologna, and then taught at Perugia from 1342 or 1343 until his death. He founded the legal method called *mos italicus.* His

99. Ermini, 1971, 1:45.

100. Ibid., 85–86. Ermini opines that students from Perugia and clergymen from the local monasteries were not counted in the matriculation figures.

101. Ibid., 49–50. I exclude the *maestri di grammatica e autori,* who taught at the preuniversity level in various sections of the city, and two teachers of geometry, arithmetic, and/or abbaco, who also probably taught at the preuniversity level.

102. Ibid., 39–42.

most famous pupil was Baldo degli Ubaldi (1327?–1400) of Perugia. Baldo studied at Perugia and then taught there from about 1351 to 1357 and 1365 to
1376.[103] The method and works of these two scholars dominated Italian legal
education for the next two centuries and beyond.

Perugia began to lose its political independence in the late fourteenth century.
Although the papacy claimed ultimate sovereignty over Perugia, it initially authorized various individuals to rule the city. This had little effect on the university, because these rulers regularly confirmed communal autonomy over the
studium.[104] The papacy finally took direct control of the city in 1424, although
Perugia remained internally tumultuous. The papacy gradually asserted authority over the university after this date. In 1431 Pope Eugenius IV, always interested
in educational matters, decreed that the papal governor or legate had to endorse
professorial appointments made by the Savi dello Studio. Then in 1457 Calixtus
III recommended to the Savi a professor of medicine. And in 1467 the papal
governor met with the Savi to select professors and to determine salaries. After
this the commune steadily lost its power to oversee the university; by the end of
the sixteenth century, the Savi met infrequently.[105] Nevertheless, a little communal authority remained. Papal legates never exercised the personal control over
the Perugian *studio* which the dukes of Ferrara and kings of Naples wielded over
the universities in their states.

The commune supported the university with monies gathered through various imposts and gabelles. In 1366 the commune appropriated 2,000 gold florins
to pay the salaries of the professors and other expenses. This figure remained
constant until 1430, when, with papal approval, another 500 gold florins were
added. The papacy also helped in a small way to fund the university. But repeated
attempts in the later fifteenth century to increase funding beyond about 2,500
gold florins had little success.[106]

The law faculty was considerably larger than the faculty of arts and medicine
during the fifteenth century. Thirteen civilians and 6 canonists taught there in
1429–30; Perugia had more legists than Padua at this time. The number rose to
21 legists, with probably the some division between civil and canon law, in 1431–
32, while the arts and medicine complement numbered only 15: a theologian, 9
professors of medicine (including one *Ad reactandum ossa*), a philosopher, 3 grammarians (who may have taught at the preuniversity level), and an astrologer. Law
continued to dominate. In 1443–44, the faculty included 13 professors of civil
law and 11 for canon law. The medicine and arts faculty had 6 professors of
medicine (4 for medical theory, 1 for surgery and practical medicine, and 1 *Ad
reactandum ossa*), 3 philosophers, a man who taught both logic and philosophy,
and a humanist who taught rhetoric, Terence, and authors, making a total faculty
of 35 professors.[107] Perugia maintained a high reputation for the teaching of law,

103. Ibid., 137–52. See Ch. 13, "*Mos Italicus,*" for more on Bartolo and Baldo.
104. Ermini, 1971, 1:190–205.
105. Ibid., 241–48.
106. Ibid., 261–64.
107. Nicolini, 1961, with documents, and Ermini, 1971, 1:226–27, 234.

especially civil law, in the fifteenth century, as other legists continued the tradition of Bartolo and Baldo.

But Perugia fared less well in medicine and arts. Some relatively established medical scholars taught there, but only briefly. Ugo Caccini (called Maestro Ugolino da Montecatini), known for his treatise *De balneis,* on the therapeutic use of mineral and thermal waters, taught at Perugia toward the end of his career, from 1419 until about 1421. Benedetto Riguardati da Norca taught in the years 1422–27 and again in 1431, and Ugo Benzi da Siena taught from 1428 to 1430. In similar fashion, native son Mattiolo Mattioli (before 1410–before 1473) taught in Perugia from 1427 to 1430 and again in 1454. But he did the greater part of his teaching at Padua, where he became a famous medical scholar.[108] And Perugia had limited success in attracting humanists.

On the other hand, two accomplished mathematicians taught at Perugia. Luca Pacioli from Sansepolcro taught arithmetic, possibly at the preuniversity level, in Perugia from 1477 to 1480. He then taught at the university in the years 1487–88, 1500, and 1510–14. Pietro Antonio Cataldi (1552–1626) of Bologna began his career at Perugia (1569–83) before moving to Bologna.[109]

The university's budget did not grow until papal efforts eventually produced more revenue in the late sixteenth century. In 1535 Pope Paul III added 100 gold ducats from the Perugian papal treasury with which to pay supplementary sums to the oldest professors.[110] Nevertheless, the regular university appropriation remained at 2,550 florins in the mid-sixteenth century. This meant that the average salary was only 71 florins, below the scale at many other universities. Then Pope Sixtus V in 1587 made a determined effort to increase funding for the University of Perugia in the course of his reorganization of the finances of the papal state. He decreed that the university would get 3,526 scudi annually, plus another 1,500 scudi in annual contributions from various Perugian monasteries, confraternities, and merchant associations, and some designated taxes levied in the Perugian territory. (A scudo was worth a little less than a florin or ducat.) As might be expected, the institutions obliged to help support the university vigorously opposed the papal measure. Consequently, Clement VIII in 1593 lifted most of the institutional obligations in favor of trying to raise money for the *studio* in other ways. Despite the retreat from Sixtus's generosity, the university received about 4,000 scudi for its expenses in 1600, substantially more than it had earlier.[111]

Most universities had more arts and medicine professors than legists in the sixteenth century. But law maintained its superiority at Perugia. For example, in 1567–68 Perugia had 15 professors of civil law and 11 of canon law. The arts faculty numbered only 10 professors in the 1520s and then grew slightly to 15 or 16. A typical arts roll later in the century included 2 professors of theoretical medicine, 2 of practical medicine, 2 for surgery plus a vacation lecturer for surgery, and a

108. Ermini, 1971, 1:555–65; Pesenti, 1984, 133–40.
109. Ibid., 584–87; De Ferrari, 1979a.
110. Ermini, 1971, 1:278–79.
111. Ibid., 265–68.

professor of medicinal simples beginning in 1537. The arts faculty also included 1 logician, a professor of metaphysics, a vacation lecturer in moral philosophy, a mathematician, a vacation lecturer for mathematics, 2 humanists, and occasionally a vacation lecturer in the humanities. Vacation lecturers taught only between Easter and June 24, the Feast of the Nativity of Saint John the Baptist. The position was a Perugian variation on the extraordinary lecturerships found elsewhere.[112]

In 1600–1601, the law faculty had 13 professors and 2 vacation lecturers in civil law and 5 professors and 1 vacation lecturer in canon law, for a total of 21. The arts and medicine faculty numbered 13 professors and 5 vacation lecturers. They included 2 professors of theoretical medicine, 2 for practical medicine, 2 for surgery and anatomy, a professor of pharmacological theory, and another for pharmacological practice. Arts also included 4 philosophers (including a vacation lecturer for metaphysics and another for moral philosophy), 1 logician, 2 vacation lecturers for mathematics, and 2 professors plus 1 vacation lecturer in the humanities. The faculty numbered 31 ordinary professors and 8 vacation lecturers, for a total of 39.[113]

Perugia appointed a few reasonably well known legists in the sixteenth century but did not attract eminent professors in other fields. As in the previous century, a few important arts and medicine scholars taught briefly at Perugia early in their careers. Perugia's reputation and salaries could not hold them.

Professors lectured wherever they could, sometimes in private homes, sometimes in wretched rented quarters, through the fourteenth and fifteenth centuries. Aware of the problem from his teaching career at Perugia in the 1450s, Pope Sixtus IV in 1483 ordered the renovation of some shops next to the handsome Palazzo del Capitano in the Piazza del Sopramuro. This piazza, now renamed Piazza Matteotti, is built on the city walls in the heart of the city near the cathedral and Palazzo dei Priori, the seat of government. Sixtus IV provided 100 florins for the work, the money to be deducted from professors' stipends. But little happened until 1512, when the commune dedicated 1,000 florins to completing construction. Professors began to teach in the renovated building, now named the Palazzo della Vecchia Università, in 1514. Sixtus V further improved the building in 1590. The legists lectured on the second floor, the professors of arts and medicine on the third floor, which included an anatomical theater. The mathematician, the professor of medical botany, and a theologian lectured elsewhere. This building served the university until the early nineteenth century.[114]

Only fragmentary enrollment information has come to light. In May 1443, students balloting to elect a student lecturer numbered 114; how many did not vote is impossible to determine. In 1511 the university recorded 172 matriculants; whether this figure counted only new matriculants for that year or total enrollment is unknown. Moreover, matriculation records were never complete.[115]

112. Ibid., 228–29, 233–34, 570. Also see Ch. 5, "Organization of Instruction."
113. Ermini, 1971, 1:230, 235–36.
114. Ibid., 426–31.
115. Nicolini, 1961, 143–44, 153–56. Matriculation records list 5,188 names between 1511 and

In the absence of better information, one can only estimate enrollment on the basis of the number of professors, because governments seldom appointed and paid more professors than were needed to teach the students. Because the Perugian *studio* had about 35 professors and a certain eminence in law, it is likely that enrollment averaged 300 to 400 in the fifteenth century. Perugia's population of 20,000 to 25,000 inhabitants in the first half of the fifteenth century, perhaps rising to 30,000 in the 1490s, could easily provide lodging for this number of students.[116] Perugia had only about 28 professors teaching throughout the year and 8 vacation lecturers in the sixteenth century. Moreover, the universities of Rome and Macerata competed with Perugia for students within the papal state at this time. Hence, annual enrollments may have dropped to 200 to 300. Perugia's population also declined to 19,000 to 20,000 by the 1580s, still more than enough to support 200 to 300 students. Despite its small size, Perugia attracted a significant number of non-Italian students, especially Germans, most of whom came to study law. The German nation was the most important student group in Perugia throughout the history of the university. It had its own library numbering 268 titles in 1600.[117]

The commune of Perugia created the university through foresight and determination. Then the *studio* had great good fortune in that the founding fathers of late medieval and Renaissance civil jurisprudence taught there. The commune deserves full credit for appointing and retaining as long as possible the immensely influential Bartolo and Baldo. Perugia continued to be an important center for legal studies in the fifteenth century. Nevertheless, it always recruited most of its professors, including Bartolo and Baldo, locally, the sign of a provincial university. Nor did Perugia ever build an arts and medicine professoriat comparable to law. Perugia's illustrious legal tradition may have persuaded the leaders of the commune that it did not need to do much in arts and medicine in order to attract students. Steady but limited funding was another problem. And over time, Perugia's status as a subject commune probably also held back the university. Even though the papacy's intervention in university affairs was generally beneficial, three other universities within the papal state competed for its attention.[118] After 1500 the only eminent professors at Perugia were those passing through on their way to fame elsewhere. Perugia was a modest provincial university emphasizing law through most of the Renaissance.

1656, an annual average of 35.5. However, some years are missing, and matriculation records do not seem to have been scrupulously compiled. Ermini, 1971, 1:320.

116. Ginatempo and Sandri, 1990, 134.

117. Weigle, 1942 and 1954.

118. Throughout his excellent study, Ermini (1971) expresses a very negative view of the papacy. He especially blames it for what he sees as the university's decline in the fifteenth century. The evidence does not support this view. Indeed, comparison with the governing authorities of other universities demonstrates that the papacy supported the university moderately well. If the University of Perugia did not realize its potential after 1400, the commune of Perugia bore part of the responsibility.

CHAPTER 3

The Second Wave

Pisa, Florence, Pavia, Turin, Ferrara, and Catania

fter the heroic age of university foundations, communes and princes rested. Then the demand for educated professionals and the yearning for the prestige of a *studio* began anew. Italy doubled the number of its universities between 1343 and 1445. These new institutions were the Italian part of a new wave of university foundations washing across Europe.

PISA, 1343

The Commune of Pisa took advantage of Bolognese difficulties to establish a university.[1] In March 1338 Pope Benedict XII excommunicated the city of Bologna, thus provoking a migration of professors and students. The Commune of Pisa encouraged them to come to Pisa. It paid the rent for a house in which a medical man would teach in 1339, and it hired a medical professor in 1340. It appointed and paid several other professors, including Bartolo da Sassaferrato to teach civil law in 1339. Already known for his legal expertise, Bartolo did his first teaching at Pisa and remained until 1343. Having created the nucleus of a university, the commune petitioned for a charter, which Pope Clement VI granted on September 4, 1343. The charter established a *studium generale* that might teach and award degrees in canon and civil law, medicine, and theology. Pisa was the first Italian university authorized to award degrees in theology. The archbishop of Pisa or his vicar conferred all degrees after examination. The pontiff also permitted out-of-town clergymen to live off the income of their benefices for five years while studying at Pisa. Thus, Pisa had a university.

1. This account of the origins and history of the University of Pisa until 1473 is based on Fabroni, 1971, 1:14–74; Caturegli, 1942–44; Picotti, 1968; Del Gratta, 1993b, 33–34; Fioravanti, 1993, 259–66; Spagnesi, 1993, 191–202; and Tangheroni, 1993. Rashdall, 1936, 2:45–46, contains several errors. For Bartolo's appointment at Pisa, see Calasso, 1964, 642.

In the following sixty to seventy years, professors of law, medicine, grammar, and theology, including a few important scholars, taught at the *studio*. Baldo degli Ubaldi (c. 1327–1400) taught for one year, 1357–58. The grammarian Francesco da Buti (1324–1405) taught from 1355 to about 1360. He was called back at a much higher stipend in 1365 to lecture on Dante's *Commedia* and possibly on Horace and Persius. Classes met in the homes of professors or in rooms rented from local monasteries.

But the *studio* did not flourish. Plague, economic stagnation, and political turmoil drained Pisan energy and wealth in the second half of the fourteenth century. The university practically closed in 1359, as only five professors received salaries. In December 1382, the commune provided stipends enabling Pisans to study medicine and surgery outside the city, a sign that Pisa lacked medical instruction at that time. Although little can be stated with certainty because of the paucity of records, the *studio* may have functioned at the lowest level of viability—eight or nine professors—through much of this period.

The situation worsened. Giangaleazzo Visconti, duke of Milan, purchased Pisa from its local ruler in 1399. After Visconti's death in 1402, Pisa had to defend itself against Florentine aggression. The commune reduced support for the university in order to pay military expenses. But Florence conquered Pisa in 1406 and, because it had its own university, closed the Pisan *studio*. The latter became a paper university (see Ch. 4), as local colleges of doctors awarded sixty-one doctorates (forty-two in law) between 1406 and 1472.[2] But no teaching existed. Pisa lost its independence and university at the same time.

Then Lorenzo "the Magnificent" de' Medici, the political leader of Florence, did a volte-face. Following the example of the rulers of Venice and Milan, he decided to locate the state's university outside the capital city. He moved the Florentine *studio*, excepting a handful of introductory and humanistic positions, to Pisa in 1473.

The idea was not new. The Florentines had considered but then abandoned the idea of moving the university to Pisa in 1460. Lorenzo probably decided to move the *studio* for economic, dynastic, and prestige reasons. A university would bring much-needed money into a depressed town. Second, a university in the subject city of Pisa might be viewed as the creation of the prince in a way that the Florentine *studio*, founded long before the Medici ascendancy, could not. Indeed, the humanist professor Lorenzo Lippi portrayed the university as Lorenzo's gift to the people of Pisa in his oration opening the academic year 1473–74. And Lorenzo may have decided that the move would make it easier to create a good university that would add luster to the Medici name.[3] Ignoring the pleas of Arezzo, which eagerly sought the university, Lorenzo moved the Florentine *studio* to Pisa.

The University of Pisa reopened its doors in November 1473. Because the

---

2. Davies, 2000.

3. Documents of Dec. 18–22, 1472, authorizing the move to Pisa are found in Fabroni, 1971, 1:409–14, and Gherardi, 1973, 273–76. See also Fioravanti, 1991b and 1993, 267.

Florentine government added new faculty positions, the resurrected university was larger and stronger than the previous Florentine *studio*. The University of Pisa employed an average of 30 to 32 professors annually from 1473 to 1503: 1 theologian, 7 canonists, 10 or 11 professors of civil law, 6 professors of medicine, 2 or 3 philosophers, 1 mathematician (including Luca Pacioli, 1500–1503 and 1504–6), 2 logicians, and 1 or 2 humanists. Salary expenses ranged from 6,000 to 8,500 florins annually.[4] In a key development, Pope Sixtus IV in January 1475 authorized the Florentine republic to levy a tax of 5,000 ducats annually on the clergy of the state for five years for the university. In short, the clergy paid about two-thirds of the costs of the university. The papacy renewed this concession in 1487, 1493, and 1498.[5]

The university attracted 200 to 320 students annually between 1474 and 1495. The beadle reported an enrollment of 305 to 310 (215 to 220 law students and about 90 in arts and medicine) in November 1474, which he said was about the same as the previous year. Enrollment fell to 200 in early November 1484, because some professors were not present and fighting had broken out on the Tuscan-Genoese frontier. The number rose to about 260 in 1487 and 260 again in 1489. The university had 300 students (170 in law and 130 in arts) in November 1493, with the number expected to rise to 320 by Christmas. After the university was closed for the academic year 1494–95, it moved to Prato and opened with 100 students in November 1495, with more arriving daily.[6] The university awarded an average of 11 degrees annually between 1474 and 1505, 59 percent in law, 31 percent in arts and medicine, and 10 percent in theology.[7]

The resurrected university became peripatetic. Plague forced moves to Pistoia for the academic years 1478–80; to Prato, March to November 1482; and again to Prato, March to November 1486. When the Medici fled Florence in November 1494 as the French army marched on the city, Pisa threw off Florentine rule. This left the university in limbo, because Florence would not allow the professors, which it appointed and paid, to teach in a rebel town. Since the Pisans were not prepared to support the university either, classes did not meet at all in 1494–95. As Pisa remained rebellious, the Florentine government moved the university to Prato for the two academic years 1495–97. When plague struck Prato, the university moved to Florence in the fall of 1497, where it remained until 1503. It closed at that time, because the papal privilege allowing a tax on clerical benefices

4. See Verde, 1973–94, 1:287–383; Fabroni, 1971, 1:379–400 passim; and Del Gratta, 1993a. Detailed payment records are found in Verde, 1973–94, vol. 5.

5. Verde, 1973–94, 5:16–30, and Davies, 1998, 76–77, 136. The Florentine government had sought this concession in the past without success. Davies, 1998, 128.

6. The figures come from letters of the beadle in November of various years. He sometimes also listed the number of students attending the lectures of individual professors. The beadle usually did not give the number of clerical students (*preti* and *frati*). Hence, these have been estimated from the one occasion on which he did give their number (about thirty-eight in 1493). Verde, 1973–94, 4:144, 560, 718, 865, 866, 1102, 1188.

7. The precise numbers are civil law 87, canon law 56, *in utroque iure* 59, arts and medicine 107, theology 34, and surgery 1. Verde, 1973–94, 2:648–729. These are the known degrees; there probably were others.

to be diverted to university expenses expired and was not renewed.[8] The university reopened in 1505 in Florence for one or two years, before closing again in 1506 or 1507. In Florence, professors lectured in a building on Via dello Studio near the Duomo, while examinations were held in the Medici Riccardi palace on Via Larga (now Via Cavour). Thus, between 1473 and 1506, classes of the University of Pisa met in Pisa for 19 academic years, in Florence 7 years, in Prato about 2 years, in Pistoia 2 years, and not at all for 3 years. But it remained the University of Pisa, because degrees were awarded on the authority granted by the original charter to the archbishop of Pisa as vice-chancellor of the university.

Although Florence reconquered Pisa in 1509, the university remained closed. Then the restored Medici rulers of Florence reopened the university in Pisa in the fall of 1515 and rebuilt its faculty. Pope Leo X, head of the Medici clan and a generous, if profligate, patron of learning, provided 3,000 ducats from Tuscan ecclesiastical revenues. The faculty numbered 32 professors in 1515–16, averaged 40 in the following years, and reached a high of 42 in 1525–26. The professoriat normally included 1 theologian, 8 or 9 canonists, 10 to 12 professors of civil law, 6 or 7 professors of medicine, 4 or 5 philosophers, 1 metaphysician, 1 mathematician, 5 logicians, and 2 humanists.[9] The university awarded an average of 28 doctorates annually (and a total of 340) between December 1516 and November 1528, 77 percent in law, 21 percent in arts and medicine, and 2 percent in theology. The graduates came from Tuscany, the rest of Italy, France, Sicily, Germany, Sardinia, and England, in that order.[10]

After the university moved to Pisa in 1473, the Florentine government followed a tacit policy of excluding Pisans from the faculty. Only a handful of Pisans taught, for short periods of time and in minor positions. By contrast, the university hired numerous Florentines and other subjects of the Florentine state, although few were established scholars. It also hired a significant number of outsiders, some of them distinguished scholars commanding high salaries. Agostino Nifo from southern Italy taught natural philosophy from 1519 to 1522 at a salary of 1,225 florins. Filippo Decio (1454–1536) of Milan taught law at Florence in the years 1476–84, 1487–1502, and 1515–26. As his fame grew, he received a progressively higher salary that reached 2,625 florins in 1525–26. The Mantuan Pietro Pomponazzi, then teaching in Bologna, declined an offer in 1515.

The Medici governments (1473–94, 1512–27, and 1530 onward) supported the University of Pisa more strongly than the republican governments of 1494–1512 and 1527–30, which were preoccupied with war. Nor did the Medici allow their political allegiances to get in the way of attracting students. When war broke out between Habsburg emperor and French king, the pro-imperialist Medici

8. Verde, 1998, 109.

9. For this and the following paragraph, see the rolls with salaries in Fabroni, 1971, 1:379–400, and especially Del Gratta, 1993a. Fiscal rolls (i.e., lists of professors with payment records) for 1516–21 are found in ASF, Studio fiorentino e pisano, F. 8, ff. 131^r–139^r, 143^r–145^v. Although the rolls of 1522–25 are missing, Del Gratta's lists show that professors taught. Also see Picotti, 1968, 37–40, for the period 1504–43, and Verde, 1998, for the period 1504–28.

10. Verde, 1998, 113.

guaranteed safe passage to French students wishing to attend the Pisan *studio*. Plague emptied the university in June 1526, and the government officially closed it in December 1526.[11] It remained shut for seventeen years, as Florence underwent two more changes of government, a losing siege, and assassination of a Medici duke from 1527 through 1537.

Cosimo I de' Medici became the ruler of the Florentine state in 1537 and began to build a strong, centralized state. He and his successors restored and supported the University of Pisa for the sake of their subjects, in order to train loyal civil servants, and to win international acclaim as patrons of learning. The third, and most successful, period of the University of Pisa began when it reopened in early November 1543.[12]

Pisa began with 20 professors in 1543: 2 theologians, 2 canonists, 5 civilians, 3 professors of medicine, 2 philosophers, 2 logicians, 2 metaphysicians, 1 professor of Greek, and another for the humanities. They earned more than 4,700 florins, about 237 florins each, a respectable average salary. A large part of the financial support came from the diversion of the revenues of ecclesiastical benefices and sites in Tuscany to the university, renewed for five years by Pope Paul III in 1543 and made permanent in 1564.[13] The number of professors climbed to 45 in 1567–68. They included 2 theologians, 7 professors of canon law, 15 for civil law (plus 4 student lecturers), 8 professors of medicine, 1 for medical botany, 6 philosophers, 2 metaphysician, 2 logicians, 1 mathematician, and 1 humanist. They earned about 7,200 florins, an average of about 160 florins. The number of professors remained at about 45 for the rest of the century.[14] Another 4 or 5 professors continued to teach in Florence (see below).

Cosimo I and his successors pursued the same policies on faculty appointments as Lorenzo the Magnificent. They appointed numerous Florentines and other Tuscans, very few Pisans, and a small number of scholars from beyond Tuscany. Andrea Alciato (1492–1550) of Milan, probably the most famous legist of the century, declined an extravagantly generous offer.[15] But some excellent medical scholars did come. Realdo Colombo of Cremona (c. 1510–59) taught anatomy and surgery at Pisa from 1546 to 1548 and then moved to Rome. Gabriele Falloppia of Modena (1523–62) replaced him (1548–51) and then went to Padua. Others stayed longer. Luca Ghini of Corvara d'Imola (c. 1490–1556) came from Bologna in 1544 to assume the newly established professorship of medical botany and to help establish Pisa's botanical garden, which opened in late 1544 or in 1545. Pisa shared with Padua the honor of founding the first university botanical garden. Ghini remained until 1555. Andrea Cesalpino of Arezzo (1524/

11. Ibid., 116.

12. For the period 1543–1600, see Fabroni, 1971, vol. 2; Barsanti, 1993; Marrara, 1993; and Volpi Rosselli, 1993, in addition to previously mentioned sources.

13. Marrara, 1993, 79.

14. Cascio Pratilli, 1975, 194–97. Rolls for 1543–69 are found in FN, Ms. Corte d'appello, 3, ff. 2ᵛ–55ʳ. Rolls of 1585–86 and 1589–91 are printed in Galilei, 1966, 32–41.

15. See Abbondanza, 1958.

25–1603) took his degree at Pisa in 1551 and then taught medical botany at Pisa (1555–72) and practical medicine (1572–92) before going to Rome. Girolamo Mercuriale of Forlì (d. 1606) taught practical medicine from 1592 until his death. Galileo Galilei of Florence (1564–1642) studied at Pisa (1581–85) without taking a degree and then studied privately; he taught mathematics at Pisa (1589–92) before moving to Padua. Like mathematicians generally, Galilei received the low salary of 60 florins.[16] In contrast to the number of learned arts and medicine professors, Pisa had few distinguished professors of law after 1543.[17]

The grand-ducal regime exercised closer control over the renewed university than earlier governments. Instead of ruling the university through an intermediate body of elected officials serving short terms, such as the Ufficiali dello Studio in fifteenth-century Florence or Riformatori dello Studio found in other states, the Medici grand dukes ruled the university through appointed civil servants. A Provveditore dello Studio (overseer of the university) oversaw daily affairs. He initially visited the university twice a year and then resided in Pisa from 1575 onward. The Provveditore sent detailed reports on vacant positions, appointments, promotions, salaries, curriculum, and everything else. He increasingly ruled over disciplinary matters that elected student representatives had decided in the past. His reports went to the Auditore dello Studio, in effect, the minister for higher education, at the court. The Auditore dello Studio examined the reports, advised the grand duke, and executed the latter's commands. He also protected the university against the competing interests of other ministers. Individual Provveditori and Auditori held office for many years, which further increased their power. For example, the eminent legal scholar Lelio Torelli (1489–1576) was Auditore dello Studio from 1546 until his death.[18]

New university statutes of 1543 required graduates and professors to swear an oath of fealty to the grand duke of Tuscany. The government further insisted in 1575 that non-Tuscans could not include the saving clause *sine preiudicio mei Principis* ("without prejudice to my prince") when swearing the civil oath.[19] Since many non-Tuscan students continued to obtain degrees, the oath may have had little effect. But certainly non-Tuscans resented it. And, as elsewhere in Catholic lands, swearing an oath of loyalty to Catholicism, ordered by the papal bull *In sacrosancta beati Petri* of 1564, became a degree prerequisite in 1566. As a consequence, the number of German graduates dropped from twenty-five in the decade of 1560s to six in the 1570s, although Protestants still attended the university.[20] Some German students migrated to the University of Siena.[21]

16. Galilei, 1966, 32, 35, 39, 41, 43.

17. See Fabroni, 1971, 2:463–71; Schmitt, 1972 and 1983f; Cascio Pratilli, 1975, 147–55; De Ferrari, 1980; Barsanti, 1993; Iofrida, 1993; and Spagnesi, 1993.

18. Marrara, 1993, 89–99; Cascio Pratilli, 1975, 45–46 n. 91 and passim. For Torelli as legal scholar, see Ch. 13, "Humanistic Jurisprudence."

19. Quoted in Marrara, 1993, 174.

20. Del Gratta, 1980, table 4a, and Volpi Rosselli, 1993, 463.

21. Cascio Pratilli, 1975, 142–44; Mango Tomei, 1976, 37–40.

Pisa probably had only about 7,500 inhabitants in the late fifteenth century and no more than 10,000 in the next century.[22] The Florentine government dealt with the chronic shortage of good student housing by establishing residence colleges in 1545 and 1595, which provided free board and lodging for forty and thirty-five Tuscan students, respectively. These state-supported residence colleges had the added benefit of tying grateful subjects more closely to the regime. Private benefactors added additional residences for a few more students in 1568 and 1605.[23]

The University of Pisa awarded many more degrees than earlier, an average of seventy-one degrees annually in the period 1543–99; the number rose to eighty-eight annually in the years 1570–99.[24] Seventy percent of the graduates took degrees in law, 19 percent took degrees in arts, and 11 percent took degrees in theology between 1543 and 1600. However, the number of theology doctorates grew from a handful between 1543 and 1570 to parity with the number of arts degrees in the 1590s. About 55 percent of the graduates came from the grand duchy of Tuscany, 19 percent from the rest of peninsular Italy, 14 percent from Sicily, and 12 percent from foreign lands, notably Spain (7%) and Germany (1.5%). The government's close diplomatic and commercial relations with the Spanish crown helped attract Spanish students.

Pisa probably had a medium-sized student body.[25] Since the faculty grew from twenty to forty-five professors from 1543 onward and the number of degrees rose, it is likely that enrollment expanded. Pisa may have had 300 students annually in the 1540s, 400–500 students in residence in the 1550s and 1560s, and an average of 600 students annually from 1560 to the end of the century.[26]

22. Ginatempo and Sandri, 1990, 109, 112.

23. See Cascio Pratilli, 1975, 163–65; Mango Tomei, 1976, 68–72; and Ch. 5, "Residence Colleges," for further bibliography.

24. The precise figures are as follows: 1543–49: 23 doctorates annually; 1550–59: 52; 1560–69: 65; 1570–79: 85; 1580–89: 87; 1590–99: 92. See Del Gratta, 1980, and the summary tables in Volpi Rosselli, 1993, 462–68, for this and what follows.

25. It appears that a student was supposed to matriculate once in his career; indeed, an average of one hundred students matriculated annually in the years 1543–99. But the surviving matriculation records are of little help in determining enrollment, because a majority of students may not have matriculated at any time. For example, about 50 percent of the known graduates never matriculated, possibly because they did not want to pay the low fee of 12 soldi. Pisans, clergymen, students at the residence colleges, students holding offices in student organizations, and many others seldom matriculated. The Florentine government lamented their refusal to matriculate but never forced them to do so. See Del Gratta, 1980, esp. ix–xxii; see also Mango Tomei, 1976, 117–24, and Volpi Roselli, 1993, 377–81.

26. The estimate of a high figure of 600 students, with which I concur, comes from Schmitt, 1972, 249, 251, and Schmitt, 1983f, 24. It seems reasonable that a university of 45 professors and up to 90 graduates annually would have about 600 students in residence in a typical year. On the other hand, it is likely that attendance was lower before 1570, when the number of professors and graduates was lower. Most students took five or more years to obtain a degree. The students who did not graduate may be balanced by the number of Tuscan subjects who initially studied elsewhere and then returned to the university in their home state for final study and degree. Thus, they partially observed the grand-ducal decree that subjects must study at and graduate from Pisa.

After a promising start, the University of Pisa faltered in the late fourteenth century and died shortly after 1400. Lorenzo the Magnificent brought it back to life in 1473. Overcoming political upheaval, war, and plague, Pisa became a second-tier university between 1473 and 1526. Cosimo I revived the university again in 1543, the beginning of its greatest period. It had the fourth largest faculty (after Bologna, Padua, and Ferrara) and about as many students as Pavia, Rome, or Ferrara in the late sixteenth century. It created a botanical garden and employed some innovative professors in arts and medicine. Intellectually, Pisa trailed Padua and Bologna but may have ranked equal to, or just ahead of, Pavia, Rome, and Ferrara, especially in medicine, in the second half of the sixteenth century.

FLORENCE, 1348

Florence first tried to establish a university in the spring of 1321, when Bolognese students and professors threatened to migrate. Yearning for the prestige of hosting a university and greedy for the economic benefits from an influx of wealthy students, the Commune of Florence proclaimed the establishment of a *studium generale*. The commune appointed at least four professors and promised immunities to all. However, Florence did not offer as much as Siena, which already had a functioning university. Hence, Siena reaped the limited benefits of the Bolognese migration. After an additional two or three appointments in the early 1330s, the initial attempt to establish the Florentine *studio* came to a halt in 1334.[27]

Florence tried again in 1348. The commune appropriated 2,500 gold florins, more than enough for a small university, and appointed an undetermined number of professors. The Florentine *studio* began to teach in the autumn of 1348. On May 31, 1349, Pope Clement VI authorized it to grant degrees in the usual fields of canon and civil law, arts and medicine, and theology. A few months later, Florence awarded its first degree, in theology. But support flagged. The commune reduced the appropriation to 1,500 florins in 1350 but still tried to appoint eminent scholars. In 1351 it sent a long, eloquent letter full of classical references, drafted by Giovanni Boccaccio, inviting Francesco Petrarch to come back to his native land to teach. In an even more eloquent reply, with more classical references, Petrarch proclaimed his love for his *patria* but declined to come.[28] It is difficult to imagine Petrarch lecturing in a university, an environment that he scorned. Even though classes halted by 1354, Florence had managed to found a university.

The *studio* came back to life in the autumn of 1357 and taught without interruption through the academic year 1369–70. The annual appropriation rose to 2,500 florins before receding to 2,000 in the late 1360s. The small Florentine

27. For the early history of the Florentine *studio*, see Davidsohn, 1977, 269–79; Rashdall, 1936, 2:47–51; Brucker, 1969 and 1988; and Garfagnini, 1988. Documents for the period 1320 through 1354 are found in Gherardi, 1973, 107–27, 277–87.

28. Gherardi, 1973, 283–86, for the letters.

studio had 11 professors in 1357 but expanded to a high of 21 in 1367–68.[29] The average complement of 16 or 17 professors between 1357 and 1370 included 4 for civil law, 3 for canon law, 3 in medicine, 2 for philosophy and logic, 1 for *ars notaria* (notarial art), occasionally a rhetorician, and 3 or 4 theologians. This was a high point for theology; thereafter, Florence had one or no theologians on its roll. The mendicant order *studia* took charge of theology instruction.

The professors were a mixed lot. Boccaccio persuaded the commune to appoint Leonzio Pilato, a Greek from Calabria, to teach Greek, the first such professorship in western Europe. Pilato taught for two academic years, 1360–62, for 100 florins per annum, while he prepared Latin translations of Homer's *Iliad* and *Odyssey* for Boccaccio and Petrarch. Unfortunately, his word-for-word translation style failed to satisfy readers. Pilato then left, and his Florentine instruction produced no lasting results.[30] The famous Baldo degli Ubaldi of Perugia taught civil law from 1358 to 1364. But more typical of the professors were Florentines better known for their contributions in other areas of intellectual life than their university careers. The chronicler Filippo di Matteo Villani (1325?–1405) taught civil law in 1361–62 and later held the Dante lectureship (see below), in the years 1392–93 and 1394–96. Lapo di Lapo da Castiglionchio, a civic office holder of conservative views, taught canon law in 1357–58 and from 1362 to 1369.

A series of wars with the papacy and Milan as well as the Ciompi revolution of 1378 to 1381 disrupted Florentine life. The commune slashed the university's budget, and it closed in 1370. The commune then appointed a few lecturers *in civitate* (in the city) instead of *in studio*. When a number of leading citizens wanted all Florentines to know the works of the city's most famous author, the commune in 1373–74 appointed Giovanni Boccaccio *in civitate* to lecture on Dante for "all who wished to listen." One wonders if he lectured in Latin or the vernacular.[31] The commune also appointed two men *in civitate* to teach surgery and medicine, obviously to help the city's physicians and surgeons during the *studio's* closure.[32] Thus, the *in civitate* appointments served two purposes: they provided instruction for the general populace and helped fill the gap when the university was closed.

The university revived in the autumn of 1385. Although many faculty lists are missing, it seems to have had twenty to thirty professors annually from 1385 to 1407, at a cost of 2,000 to 3,000 florins. A handful were major scholars.[33] The commune promulgated university statutes in 1387.[34] And at some point in the late fourteenth century the government began to delegate authority to appoint

29. For lists of professors 1357 through 1446, see Park, 1980. See also Gherardi, 1973, such as the list of April 1366 on 314–15.

30. Park, 1980, 255–56, for the appointment. See also Weiss, 1977, 5–6, 186–89, 229–31, and Wilson, 1992, 2–7.

31. Gherardi, 1973, 162–63, 344–45; Park, 1980, 265; and Garfagnini, 1988, 194.

32. Park, 1985, 95, and Davies, 1998, 14–16, for explanation of *in civitate* appointments.

33. Davies, 1998, is the key source for the period 1385–1473. See also Abbondanza, 1959 (faculty roll for 1388); Brucker, 1969, 223, 229, 232; and Spagnesi, 1979 (faculty rolls 1391–97).

34. Gherardi, 1973, 1–104.

and pay professors to a group of elected officals called Ufficiali dello Studio. In 1392 they ordered the construction of a building for university teaching in the street now called Via dello Studio near the Duomo.[35]

After these relatively fruitful years, however, the university shut its doors again in 1407 upon the expensive conquest of Pisa and equally costly mobilization to meet the threat posed by Naples which followed. The *studio* reopened in 1413 and stayed open through 1446. But the number of professors rose and fell drastically according to the level of communal support. Between 1413 and 1423, the *studio* averaged 17 professors: 6 civil lawyers, 3 canon lawyers, 3 or 4 professors of medicine, 2 or 3 philosophers, with the remaining 2 rotating among logic, rhetoric, astrology, and the Dante lectureship.[36] The number dropped to an average of 8 for the period 1423–28, as Florence withheld funds from the university in order to prosecute a war against Milan. With peace and a levy on Florentine ecclesiastical incomes authorized by Pope Martin V in 1429 (it produced 1,500 florins annually, half or more of university expenses), the number of faculty rose to 27 between 1429 and 1433.[37] The *studio* dipped again during the political struggle between Cosimo de' Medici and his opponents. After Cosimo's victory in 1434, the university settled at an average of 22 faculty members through the academic year 1445–46.

But the lack of faculty stability must have prevented the university from acquiring a greater reputation and attracting more students. Not only did the number of professors rise and fall dramatically year by year, but the amount of instruction available for each discipline fluctuated more than in other universities of comparable size. For example, the number of professors of medicine typically varied between two and six. Relative stability of faculty size, continuous tenure by individual professors, and consistent offerings in each discipline were needed to attract students. But the *studio* did not provide them, and the commune seemed unconcerned. Indeed, it devoted only 0.5 percent of its peacetime budget to the university, a much smaller percentage than the communes of Pavia and Perugia gave to their universities.[38] The small number of prominent scholars, especially in the humanities, could not overcome these difficulties.

Because of the frequent closures and the lack of continuity, the University of Florence probably had low enrollments. It awarded only 107 known doctorates between 1385 and 1473, about 1.2 per year.[39] The low doctoral production and the moderately sized faculty suggest that the university may have had an average annual enrollment of 100 to 200 in the years 1413–73. Even though one or more

35. Davies, 1998, for information on the Ufficiali and p. 16 for the building.

36. For the list of professors, 1413–46, see Park, 1980, 268–308. These invaluable documents, which are fiscal records rather than rolls, also list communally funded grammarians, who probably taught at the preuniversity level, as their very low salaries suggest. Hence, they have been excluded from the counts of professors.

37. Gherardi, 1973, 218–20.

38. Brucker, 1969, 225.

39. Davies, 1998, 157–62. Even if another 107 doctorates remain to be discovered, the figure would be extremely low.

Germans, Frenchmen, Spaniards, and Portuguese obtained doctorates in Florence, it appears that the vast majority of students were Florentines and other Tuscans. Many Florentines studied elsewhere, especially law at Bologna, despite the protectionist legislation ordering them to study at the home university.[40]

The Florentine government occasionally tried to improve the university. In March 1429 the commune increased the appropriation with the argument that a better university would attract Florentines who studied elsewhere. The commune noted that 250 Florentines spent 5,000 florins annually studying abroad. If they attended the home university, the money would stay in Florence.[41] Borrowing the idea and the name from the Casa della Sapienza of Siena, the commune resolved to erect a state-supported student residence for forty or fifty students. But the project suffered many delays and was never realized. A building finally appeared by 1465 but was put to other purposes.[42]

The Florentine university began a deep decline in the late 1440s. It closed in 1449, when its funding was diverted to war expenses. It reopened in 1451, apparently with very few professors. It continued at a low level through the 1450s and 1460s. The philosopher John Argyropoulos, possibly the most famous scholar on the faculty, left in 1471, claiming that the commune owed him 1,200 florins in unpaid salary.[43]

In 1460 a leading Florentine proposed moving the university to Pisa.[44] The idea of moving the university to another town would have been unthinkable in Bologna, Padua, Siena, Perugia, Pavia, and elsewhere; indeed, some towns (such as Arezzo) eagerly wanted a university. Nevertheless, some Florentines hoped in 1460 to boost the sagging economy of the subject city of Pisa by giving it the Florentine *studio*. The ensuing debate brought to light sharp differences of opinion concerning its value.

Some of the speakers expressed common views about the benefits and risks of universities. If the university remained in Florence, the sons of the city could study and learn at lower cost than if they went elsewhere. But the financial benefits to the economy of Florence of keeping the university had to be weighed against the moral and political dangers of hosting unruly young males.

The Florentine leaders, however, voiced unusual negative views as well. One speaker strongly argued in favor of moving the university to Pisa because Florentine anti-intellectualism bred civic indifference to its *studio*. Florentines were so

40. Martines, 1968, 81 and 482–508 passim, for the legal studies of many Florentines.

41. "Troviamo fuori della città et provincia vostra circa ducento cinquanta scolari continuamente vivere, i quali traggono del nostro districto circa cinquemilia florini per anno." Gherardi, 1973, 211, Mar. 15–18, 1429. Molho, 1971, 134–35, first noted this. The figure of 250 studying abroad may have been unusually high at this time, because the Florentine *studio* was at a very low ebb between 1423 and 1428.

42. Gherardi, 1973; Brucker, 1982, 519–20; Denley, 1988, 201–2; and Davies, 1998, 17–18.

43. Davies, 1998, 127–30.

44. Brucker, 1982, for what follows; see also Davies, 1998, 72–74, 116–17; and Davies, 2000, 199–203.

devoted to making money that they had neither time nor energy for learning, he charged. Professors were unappreciated, and students became distracted in the large city. Since the *studio* had failed to become an eminent center for learning, why not move it to Pisa? Lacking a consensus, the government did not bring the measure to a vote. The university stayed in Florence for the time being. But the debate revealed lukewarm support for the university.

Prodded by Lorenzo de' Medici, the commune in December 1472 decided to transfer the university to Pisa as a five-year experiment.[45] Classes would begin in Pisa in November 1473.

The decision was the best alternative for a weak university. The lack of strong support had already condemned the University of Florence to second-rate status. And the contest between the Medici party and its opponents to win control of the Ufficiali dello Studio further weakened the university.[46] In the end Florence adopted the policy of other major Italian political capitals: they did not host important universities. Milan and Venice located their universities outside the seat of government. Rome had a university, but the most important *studio* in the papal state was in Bologna. The Neapolitan university never achieved greatness. Powerful capital cities focused on governance, conquest, and commerce; they were too busy shaping the world to study it. By contrast, subject cities and small states—Bologna, Ferrara, Macerata, Padua, Perugia, and Siena—saw the university as an important, often *the* most important, focus of civic pride and source of income and responded accordingly. Lorenzo de' Medici's decision brought Florentine policy into line with that of most other major Italian states.

However, the 1472 decision kept university humanities instruction ("degli oratori et poeti et degli ornamenti della lingua latina") in Florence.[47] Lorenzo and his supporters probably made this concession (1) to pacify those who wanted to hold on to the university, (2) to continue to provide humanistic instruction for those who did not wish to go to Pisa, and (3) to provide a supply of needy university students who would support themselves by teaching Latin to the children of leading citizens. Dividing the university between two locations was not uniquely Florentine. One to six professors of rhetoric listed on University of Pavia rolls actually lectured in Milan in the late fifteenth century (see below, and Ch. 6, "Court and Classroom").

For the next century and more, two to five professors, some of them eminent scholars, taught rhetoric, poetry, or Greek in Florence. By contrast, the University of Pisa had only one or two humanists, always minor figures. The first two

45. The measure is printed in Gherardi, 1973, 273–76, Dec. 18–22, 1472. It needed several days to pass through various councils. The votes were far from unanimous: 161 to 80, 103 to 48, and 92 to 33. A stated justification for the move was the lack of sufficient housing in Florence for the expected large number of students who would come to study at an improved university. However, Pisa also lacked sufficient student housing until state-supported student residences were built late in the sixteenth century. See Ch. 5, "Residence Colleges."

46. This is a major theme of Davies, 1998.

47. Quote in Gherardi, 1973, 274. Davies, 1998, 116–17, 134, suggested the third reason.

appointees to the Florentine positions in 1473 were Cristoforo Landino (1425–98), who had taught at Florence since at least 1456, and Andronico Callisto of Salonika, who taught Greek. In the later fifteenth and early sixteenth centuries Angelo Poliziano (1454–94, taught 1480–94), John Lascaris, John Argyropoulos (who returned in 1477), and other well-known scholars occupied these positions. From 1487 onward the Florentine cohort usually included two humanists and a theologian. In 1563–64, a professor of *Institutes* substituted for the theologian. In 1566–67, the group became two humanists, a theologian, and an *Institutes* professor. This group of four remained at least through 1590–91.[48] The Florentine professors were listed as part of the University of Pisa and were paid through the same magistracy, but that was all. They did not move between Florence and Pisa. They did not teach the subjects that led to degrees in law or medicine, but they offered higher education in a few subjects to Florentines. The Florentine rump of a university became one of several state-supported intellectual establishments, such as the Accademia Fiorentina, a fellowship of scholars sponsored and supported by the grand-ducal government from the 1540s onward.[49]

For a century and a quarter Florence had a small *studio* whose size and stature placed it in the lower half or lowest third of Italy's universities. Local men and other Tuscans, with the occasional outsider, made up the faculty; the university's most important appointees were in the humanities. The vast majority of students came from Florence and Tuscany. Lack of strong communal support led to numerous closures, much instability, and blocked improvement. Lorenzo de' Medici moved the university to Pisa in 1473, while maintaining a small group of professors in Florence.

PAVIA, 1361

Galeazzo II Visconti (ruled 1354–78) founded the University of Pavia. Members of the Visconti family had been conquering the cities and towns of Lombardy for about a century in order to create a strong territorial state with Milan as the capital. Galeazzo II now wanted a university to crown the achievement, and he needed lawyers and jurists to administer his state. But instead of choosing Milan, Galeazzo located the university 35 kilometers south in Pavia, a town of about 15,000 inhabitants on the Ticino River. Pavia with its rebellious past had

---

48. For the professors who taught in Florence in the years 1473–1503, see Verde, 1973–94, 1:296–383 passim. For the period 1516–21, see ASF, Studio fiorentino e pisano, F. 8, ff. 131ᵛ, 134ʳ, 135ʳ, 136ᵛ, 139ʳ, 143ʳ, 145ʳ, 154ʳ, 161ᵛ, 163ᵛ, 168ʳ, 171ʳ, with some repetition. The number of professors teaching in Florence temporarily rose to seven or eight in 1520–21. For the period 1557–69, see FN, Ms. Corte d'appello, 3, ff. 32ʳ, 34ʳ, 38ʳ, 39ᵛ, 42ʳ, 44ᵛ, 47ʳ, 49ʳ, 50ᵛ–51ʳ, 52ᵛ, 54ᵛ–55ʳ. The Florentine professors listed in the University of Pisa roll of 1590–91 are found in Galilei, 1966, 42. This roll places these four positions under the separate heading "Studio di Firenze." For more discussion of the humanists at the Florentine part of the university, see Ch. 6.

49. The links between leaders of the state and the Florentine humanist professors are key themes in Godman, 1998.

only reluctantly passed permanently under Visconti rule in 1359. Galeazzo may have chosen it to host the university as a gesture of benevolence or to acknowledge its distinguished tradition of legal studies going back to the ninth century.

On April 13, 1361, Galeazzo II obtained from Emperor Charles IV a charter for a *studium generale* with the power to award degrees. He then forbade his subjects to study anywhere but Pavia. The university opened its doors in the autumn of 1361 with at least four professors of law and possibly teachers in other subjects. It granted its first degree in 1367. Pope Boniface IX further recognized the University of Pavia on November 16, 1389, with a bull that authorized the granting of degrees in theology as well as the usual law, medicine, and arts.[50] The town, with its university, enormous castle (1360–65), and lovely nearby charter-house (begun 1396), became a showcase of Visconti grandeur.

The university had a large corps of professors by the 1380s. They numbered 35 in 1387, the first year for which a roll is available, and grew to an average of 51 professors between 1389 and 1394–95.[51] The faculty consisted of 1 professor of theology (sometimes teaching both theology and moral philosophy), 11 professors of canon law, 17 professors of civil law, 1 who taught notarial skills, 14 professors of medicine including 1 surgeon, one professor of astrology, a second who combined astrology and natural philosophy, 2 professors of natural philosophy, 2 logicians, and 1 professor of grammar and rhetoric. The concentration on law (28 professors of 51) and lack of emphasis on arts was distinctive. Baldo degli Ubaldi, who taught at Pavia from 1390 until his death in 1400, was the most famous scholar to teach there during its first forty years.

In late October 1398, just before the opening of the academic year, Duke Giangaleazzo Visconti (b. 1351; ruled 1385–1402) ordered the university to move to Piacenza, about 50 kilometers southeast of Pavia. The reasons are unclear: political displeasure with Pavia, ducal unhappiness over communal failure to pay promised salary increments to the professors, inadequate housing in Pavia, and the threat of plague are possibilities. In any case, classes began in Piacenza on December 4, 1398. The faculty grew to sixty-nine professors in Piacenza in 1399–1400 through the addition of several poorly paid minor lecturers, especially in law. At the same time, degrees were still awarded and limited teaching continued in Pavia. Negotiations began for a return to Pavia. Students and professors demanded that the Commune of Pavia make available three hundred houses with annual rents no higher than 4–5 percent of the value of the house. They claimed

50. Unless otherwise indicated, the history of the origins to 1450 is based on Vaccari, 1957, 1–73, and especially Maiocchi, 1971. Rashdall (1936, 2:51–53) offers a very brief account. See *Memorie di Pavia,* 1970, pt. 2:2–5, for the imperial and papal charters. For the medieval tradition of legal studies at Pavia, see Radding, 1988, 10–13, 74, 75, 78, 97, 171–74. Since there are no population figures for the late fourteenth century, the above estimate is based on what is known about the thirteenth and fifteenth centuries. Ginatempo and Sandri, 1990, 76, 78.

51. This paragraph is based on "fiscal rolls" published in Maiocchi, 1971, vol. 1, docs. 252, 305, 366, 430, and 432.

that this was the practice at Bologna and Padua, a statement that cannot be verified. The Commune of Pavia did not accept the housing demands but pledged improvements. It also promised to pay the moving expenses of professors and students if they returned. With ducal approval, the university moved back to Pavia in May 1402.[52]

Giangaleazzo Visconti died of the plague while besieging Florence in September 1402. His fourteen-year-old son Giovanni Maria (1388–1412), who combined personal cruelty and political ineptitude, succeeded him. Various nobles sought to manipulate him, while some towns escaped Visconti rule. In the turmoil the university suffered, as the faculty complement dropped to 43 in 1403–4 and to an average of 26 in the next five years.[53] It further sank to only 9 (paid only 950 florins) in 1409–10 and 12 in 1412–13. A major reason for Pavia's decline was competition from the new University of Parma, 110 kilometers southeast of Pavia. Formerly part of the Visconti state, Parma had escaped Visconti rule in 1409. It created a university that opened its doors in 1412 (see Ch. 4, "Parma, 1601"). Some professors and students fled declining Pavia for Parma.

Upon Giovanni Maria's assassination in 1412, his younger brother Filippo Maria Visconti (b. 1392; ruled 1412–47) became duke of Milan. As personally repugnant as his brother but politically far more able, Filippo Maria revived the fortunes of the state and the university, despite his numerous wars. The ducal government and the Commune of Pavia rebuilt the faculty to 22 professors paid close to 2,000 florins in 1415–16 and to 36 professors paid about 5,000 florins in 1419–20. Equally important, the new government eliminated competition. It first forbade subjects to teach or study at Parma and then regained control of the city in September 1420. The University of Parma closed its doors.

With the rival dispatched, the University of Pavia flourished. It employed an average of 44 professors paid close to 6,000 florins through the 1420s and early 1430s. The number of professors then rose to 54 in 1433–34 and reached the figure of about 65 professors earning close to 10,000 florins in the academic years 1441 through 1446. The professoriat rose again to more than 80 in 1446–47, at a salary expense of more than 11,000 florins.

The roll for the academic year 1446–47 listed 84 professors, of whom 43 taught law (23 civilians, 16 canonists, and 4 unclear). The faculty of arts and medicine included 21 professors of medicine and surgery, 4 for philosophy, 4 for logic, 2 for astrology, 2 *Ad lecturam Prognosticorum* (medical prognosis, possibly based on the Hippocratic text *Prognostics*), 2 for moral philosophy, 1 metaphysician, 2 rhetoricians, and 3 theologians.[54] However, many low-paid teaching posts, especially in

---

52. Nasalli Rocca, 1927; Vaccari, 1957, 47–51; and Maiocchi, 1971, vol. 1, docs. 682, 725, 728, 733, 751; vol. 2, pt. 1, docs. 3–6, 9, 11, 13–16, 19–21, 24.

53. The following paragraphs on the university in the years 1402–47 are based on Maiocchi, 1971, vols. 1 and 2, especially the rolls.

54. The roll is found in Maiocchi, 1971, vol. 2, pt. 2, doc. 640. The two student rectors have been excluded. The professors earned approximately 11,000 florins. However, the Pavese florin (fiorino) was worth only 32 soldi, rather than, for example, the Florentine florin worth 80 to 100 soldi at this time. See Maiocchi, 1971, vol. 2, pt. 1, doc. 479 of Nov. 30, 1434, for the value of the Pavese florin.

law, swelled the number of professors. For example, 6 men taught *Institutes* at salaries ranging from 20 to 80 florins, and 4 lectured on canon law on holidays for salaries of 20 to 50 florins. Pavia followed the usual pattern of paying the highest salaries to the ordinary professors of civil law and theoretical medicine but did not hire so-called stars at astronomically high stipends. The highest salary was 600 florins and the average less than 150 florins in 1446–47. As in other universities, salary payments were sometimes delayed or did not include the full amount promised, and occasionally they were not made at all. Although Pavia emphasized law, its most famous and controversial professor in the first half of the century was Lorenzo Valla, who taught from 1431 to 1433 but was driven out in the middle of the academic year (see Ch. 6, "Humanists Join the University").

Pavia had a unique system for choosing its professors during the Visconti-Sforza era. The officers of the student organizations met to decide which professors they wanted for the coming academic year. They communicated their list, or roll, to the two highest councils of the government, the Consiglio Segreto, which reported only to the duke, and the smaller Consiglio di Giustizia, a council of about five jurists. These councils decided appointments, salaries, and duration of contracts and produced the final roll. The student leaders and the Consiglio Segreto normally agreed on the major professors, whose appointments continued year after year. But the Consiglio Segreto, with input from the duke, sometimes differed considerably from the students on other positions. When that happened, the Consiglio Segreto and duke ignored the students. Recognizing the situation, men seeking university appointments normally wrote directly to the Consiglio Segreto and the duke. Tax revenues collected from Pavia and its region paid university salaries.[55]

When Duke Filippo Maria Visconti died in August 1447, the leading citizens of Milan proclaimed the Ambrosian Republic. In the spring of 1448 the republic announced a Milanese university with a roll of 23 professors, approximately a third of them drawn from the Studio Pavese. In the autumn the republic proclaimed the restoration of the ancient University of Milan that had flourished during the time of Saint Ambrose (c. 340–97).[56] (Although ancient Rome did not have universities in the medieval meaning of the word, some cities had publicly funded municipal schools, some of whose teachers taught at an advanced level. Milan, an important city in the second half of the fourth century, was one of them.) The republicans called on all Milanese students to attend and all Milanese *dottori* lecturing at other universities to return.

Pavia countered by placing itself under the protection of the major claimant of the ducal throne, Francesco Sforza, who confirmed the University of Pavia with the same faculty roll as before. The Studio Pavese began the academic year 1448–49 with forty-five professors, compared with seventy-six in the previous year.

55. Sottili, 1990, 418, 433–34, 447–48.
56. "Revocare el General Studio, il quale già multi anni in questa citade fu florentissimo, maxime al tempo de sancto Ambroxio nostro protectore." Proclamation of the Ambrosian Republic of Sept. 5, 1448, in Maiocchi, 1971, vol. 2, pt. 2, doc. 680, p. 531. For municipal schools in ancient Rome, see Marrou, 1964, 407–8.

The Pavians who prepared the roll proclaimed that, instead of four or six professors teaching a subject, they were keeping "the best" two, which were enough.[57]
If higher salaries defined "the best," the statement was partly true but also put a
good face on the defection of some leading professors to Milan. The Pavians
offered an inducement intended to add faculty: any citizen with a doctoral degree who wanted to teach civil or canon law would be hired at 30 florins per
annum so long as he taught every day and had at least four pupils. If they found
eight *dottori* to teach, this would silence many people at the small cost of 240
florins, they opined.[58]

When Francesco Sforza defeated the republicans and became the ruler of
Milan in February 1450, he put an immediate end to the University of Milan.
The University of Pavia then rapidly regained its previous faculty size. Between
1455 and the end of the century, the faculty ranged from 53 to 73 professors, plus
2 teaching student rectors, and averaged 60 professors.[59] The relative distribution
among fields remained approximately the same as in the first half of the century:
half taught law, the other half taught everything else. The most esteemed professors earned higher salaries than earlier. Possibly the best-known professor of
this era was Giason del Maino (1435–1519), who taught civil law at Pavia from
1467 to 1485, in 1490, and then from 1497 until his death. His salary in 1482 was
1,250 florins, the highest in the university.[60] His students included the future
legists Gianfrancesco Sannazari del Ripa and Andrea Alciato.

Even though the university resided in Pavia, a few professors, especially humanists teaching rhetoric or oratory, taught in Milan. The practice began in the
1430s. Guiniforte Barzizza (1406–63), son of the more famous and abler humanist Gasparino Barzizza (1360–1431), obtained his doctorate in arts from Pavia in
1422 and immediately became an extraordinary lecturer in moral philosophy
there. He probably continued to teach at Pavia until he was appointed to teach
oratory and moral philosophy in Milan in 1434. Exactly where and under what
circumstances he taught is not clear, but it clearly was an appointment to the
court. By 1439–40 he was back at Pavia. He continued to be listed on the
teaching roll at Pavia in the succeeding few years, even though he became ducal

57. "Basta de questi dui et sono li migliori [*sic*]." This statement dealing with extraordinary
lecturers of civil law is in a document of late 1448 which compares the rolls of 1446–48 with that of
1448–49. Maiocchi, 1971, vol. 2, pt. 2, doc. 688, p. 537, col. 2. This paragraph and the preceding one
are based on docs. 676, 680, 683, and 688, in ibid.

58. "Et non se trovarà may octo doctori che lezono et che habiano li schollari, lo cui sallario serà
floreni ccxl l'anno et serà uno fare tacere molte zente et la spexa serà pocha." Maiocchi, 1971, vol. 2,
pt. 2, doc. 688, p. 540.

59. The figures exclude the two student rectors. Approximately thirty rolls for the period 1450–
99 have been found. See the archival and printed references in n. 62 below. Zanetti (1962, table after
p. 428) and Sottili (1982, 544, 548) provide numerical summaries. In addition, several rolls have been
printed: a fiscal roll of 1452–53 and the roll of 1455–56 in *Documenti di Pavia*, 1994, docs. 61, 195; the
1467–68 roll in Ferrari, 1977, 47–48; rolls of 1480 and 1482 in Verde, 1973–94, 1:384–92; and the
1498–99 fiscal roll in Porro, 1878.

60. See the bio-bibliographical sketch in Belloni, 1986, 221–27, and the 1482 roll in Verde, 1973–
94, 1:389.

secretary, then ducal counsellor. Guiniforte probably went back and forth between Pavia and Milan according to the duke's wishes until 1447.[61]

After a hiatus of many years, a humanist again taught in Milan in the late
1460s. Two, three, and four humanists taught in Milan in the 1470s and 1480s.
Then six or seven professors of various subjects taught there in the 1490s: three or
four humanists taught rhetoric and oratory; Fazio Cardano (1445–1524), father
of Girolamo Cardano, taught the unlikely combination of mathematics and *Institutes*; the famous mathematician Luca Pacioli taught arithmetic and geometry;
and the well-known musical theorist Franchino Gaffurio (1451–1522) lectured
on music. A beadle was paid to take care of the room (*auditorium*) in which they
lectured. All these scholars were listed on the rolls of the University of Pavia but
described as "legentes Mediolani."[62]

When Demetrius Chalcondylas (1423–1511), one of the humanists appointed
to lecture in Milan, began his lectures on November 6, 1491, a contemporary
reported that he had an audience of "counsellors and other courtiers and a great
number of persons who work at their studies." In his prolusion Chalcondylas
praised letters and lauded Duke Ludovico Sforza for providing the opportunity
whereby the "youth of Milan" might become learned.[63]

Thus, the teaching at the court was intended for members of the court and
local students. Counsellors, secretaries, members of the chancery, and all manner
of courtiers, especially the younger ones, were an obvious audience. Although
appointment to the Sforza court came through family connections and patronage
rather than learning, many courtiers probably wanted to refine their skills and
add to their knowledge.

The subject matter of the lectures supports this view. The majority of the
professors were humanists, who would improve their listeners' Latin, Greek, and

61. Maiocchi, 1971, vol. 2, pts. 1 and 2, docs. 300, 304, 338, 353, 479, 480, 497, 522, 578, 579,
611, 619, 623, 627, 668, but several rolls are missing; Martellotti, 1965b.

62. Rolls of the 1470s, 1480s, and 1490s, which include the professors teaching at Milan, are
found in ASPv, Università, Bu. 22, ff. 155^r–157^r (1472–73), 158^r–159^r (1475–76), 165^r–167^r (1480–
81), 168^r–170^r (1481–82), 172^r–v (1482–83), 183^r–185^v (1486–87), 186^v–188^v (1487–88), 197^r–199^v
(1491–92), 200^r–203^r (1493–94), 204^r–206^v (1495–96), 207^r–210^r (1496–97), 212^v–213^r (1497–98),
222^v–223^v (1498–99); Bu. 23, roll of 1472–73, no pag.; Bu. 32, fasc. 72 (roll of 1476). A few rolls have
been printed; see n. 59. Sottili, 1982, 539–43, is an excellent guide to this material. There are some
interesting details about individual appointments in Rosso, 1996. Gaffurio, also *maestro di capella* at
Milan's cathedral from 1484, received a salary of 50 florins for lecturing on music. For more on him,
see Moyer, 1992, 67–92. However, the biographical information on p. 68 needs modification in light
of the above. The beadle was charged "ad curam et custodiam Auditorium Mediolani." ASPv,
Università, Bu. 22, ff. 212^v, 223^v. On Fazio Cardano, trained as a lawyer but also a published
mathematician consulted by Leonardo da Vinci, see M. Gliozzi, 1976, 758–59.

63. "Maestro Demetrio greco, hogi, alle XXI hore, ha facto principio al legere suo, dovi se li è
retrovato alcuni consilieri et altri cortesani cum gran numero de persone quale danno opera alli studii.
El principio suo è stato una oratione in laude de lettere, cum laudare etiam la Signoria Vostra, et
maxime per il gran studio quale epsa mette in fare che li gioveni milanesi siano eruditi." Letter of
Bartolomeo Calco to Ludovico il Moro Sforza, Nov. 6, 1491, Milan, in Banfi, 1983, 388–90 (quote
on 388). The letter is also quoted by Cammelli (1954, 111), who provides additional information on
Chalcondylas's Milanese career on 105–31.

knowledge of the classics. Secretaries and courtiers would be able to draft more eloquent letters with manifold classical allusions. The *Institutes* lecturer provided an introduction to civil law and its terminology. The mathematics and music lecturers provided skills to help men get ahead gracefully. Because courtiers could not simultaneously serve the duke and attend the Studio Pavese 35 kilometers distant, part of the university came to them. And the duke gained credit for offering educational opportunity to the youth of Milan.

The relationship between Milan and the University of Pavia was like that of Florence and the Univerity of Pisa after 1473. Pavia and Pisa were the universities of their respective states, teaching law, natural philosophy, medicine, and other university disciplines. But both the Milanese and Florentine governments also wished to keep a few university-level humanists and others nearby in order to teach local youths and to serve the state. Some professors were close to the regime in both Milan and Florence. For example, Chalcondylas simultaneously taught and was a member of the Milanese chancery, and Marcello Adriani taught and served as first chancellor of the Florentine republic after 1498.[64]

The University of Pavia attracted an enrollment of 600 to 700 through most of the fifteenth century. The students demanded 300 houses as a condition of their return from Piacenza in 1402. If at least two students lived in each house, with a few houses set aside for professors, then the enrollment would have been about 600. In 1460 the vice-chancellor of the university estimated student enrollment at 600, evenly split between law and medicine. Based on the number of students who voted for the rectors in early July 1470, the *podestà* of Pavia estimated that there were at least 600 students, 400 legists and 200 artists, in residence at that time. Since students from Pavia and its surrounding territory were not eligible to vote, and because not all students voted (no doubt some were absent because classes did not meet in July), the total was probably at least 700. When plague threatened the city in November 1476, enrollment fell to 260 and then rebounded. The Florentine ambassador put Pavia's enrollment at 600 to 700 students in 1480. Probably one-fourth were non-Italians, especially Germans. Some of the latter became professors in German universities or assumed other important posts in their native land.[65] Pavia had a population of 16,000 souls in 1480 and probably 10,000 to 16,000 at other times in the second half of the fifteenth century.[66]

The Italian wars between 1494 and 1559 devastated Pavia and its university. Because Lombardy was the major prize sought by France and Spain, armies marched back and forth through the area. As Pavia was considered the gateway to Milan and the bridge to Genoa, armies seldom bypassed the city. Pavia was sacked

---

64. Cammelli, 1954, 112, and Godman, 1998, 162, 167 and passim.

65. The various enrollment estimates and rector elections results are found in Sottili, 1982, 534–35 n. 23; Sottili, 1990, 400–18; Ferrari, 1977, 16; and Vaccari, 1957, 77. For subsequent careers of German graduates of Pavia, see Sottili, 1984.

66. Negruzzo, 1995, 29; Ginatempo and Sandri, 1990, 76, 78.

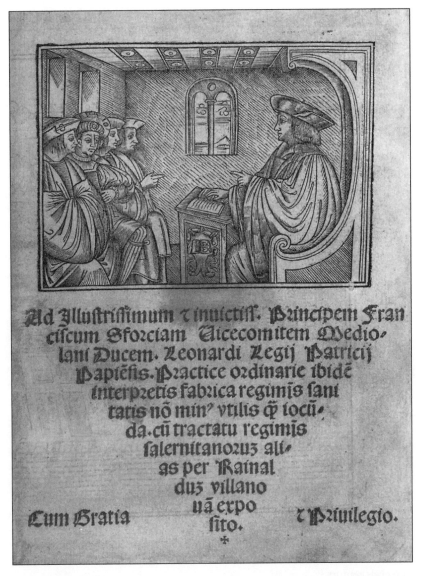

Ad Illuſtriſſimum ⁊ inuictiſſ. Principem Fran
ciſcum Sforciam Uicecomitem Mediolani Ducem. Leonardi Legij Patricij
Papieſis. Practice ordinarie ibidē
interpretis fabrica regiminis ſani
tatis nō min⁹ vtilis ꝗ̃ iocū-
da.cū tractatu regimis
ſalernitanoruz ali-
as per Rainal
duz villano
uā expo
ſito.
*

Cum Gratia ⁊ Priuilegio.

FIG. 4. Woodcut of professor lecturing to students. Title page of Leonardo Legio (or Leggi), *Fabrica regiminis sanitatis*. Pavia: Bernardino Garaldi, July 31, 1522. The title page indicates that Legio was an ordinary professor of medical practice at the University of Pavia. *Houghton Library, Harvard University.*

several times, suffered from plague, and saw its population dwindle to a low of 5,000 in 1536.[67]

Because no rolls and very few documents of any kind survive for the years between 1499–1500 and 1536–37, reconstructing the university's history during the wars is difficult. The university probably remained open for the first dozen years of the century. Students are known to have studied there between 1507 and 1512 (see Ripa and Alciato below). Then the university closed its doors in June 1512 and remained closed at least through early 1516. It may have reopened in the autumn of 1516 but closed again at an unknown date.[68] The duke promised in June and October 1522 that the university would now reopen, which probably happened.[69] Then in late 1524 Francis I of France laid siege to Pavia during his march on Milan. In the Battle of Pavia of February 24, 1525, one of the most important of the Italian wars, an imperial army routed the French and captured the French king. The French returned with a vengeance: they brutally sacked Pavia and partially destroyed the Visconti castle on October 4, 1527. Obviously, the university closed in late 1524 for an indefinite period. In October 1531, the Commune of Pavia asked Duke Francesco II Sforza to reopen the university, chiding him for his delay.[70] It may have reopened at this time or perhaps in November 1532.

A letter of 1533 complaining about misbehaving students and a roll of 1536–37 (listing 11 legists, 8 artists, and a student lecturer) confirm that the university taught between 1533 and 1537.[71] The number of professors was far below the seventy who taught in 1499–1500. Then a new peril loomed. When Francesco II Sforza died without heirs on November 1, 1535, Milan passed into the Spanish empire under Charles V. The change of rule produced immediate fiscal difficulties. On November 21, 1535, the commune wrote that students had arrived but that the professors were not disposed to teach because they had not been paid.[72] On November 2, 1537, Charles V ordered the university closed because of war, a decision that the Commune of Pavia criticized as based on only the "rumor of war."[73]

Surviving rolls indicate that the university taught in the years 1538–40, with twenty-six and twenty-three arts professors in the two academic years and an

---

67. Negruzzo, 1995, 28–29.

68. Ascheri, 1970, 22 n. 66. Also see the letter of Duke Francesco II Sforza of Sept. 18, 1516, announcing that after the recent closure caused by war, the university would reopen. ASPv, Università, Cartone 33, fasc. 98. Zorzoli (1986, 159–60 n. 51) lists some of the military and other disasters affecting Pavia in the half century.

69. ASPv, Università, Cartone 33, fasc. 104, ducal proclamations of June 5 and Oct. 7, 1522.

70. Ibid., fasc. 107, Oct. 1, 1531.

71. Ibid., fasc. 109, Apr. 29, 1533. The 1536–37 roll is found in ibid., Cartone 23, no pag., and in Cartone 21, pp. 235–38. There are some discrepancies between the two rolls. The roll of 1499–1500 is found in Cartone 21, pp. 217–20.

72. Ibid., Cartone 33, fasc. 111; also ibid., Cartone 30, ff. 27^v–28^v.

73. Ibid., Cartone 36, p. 10, printed edict; Cartone 33, fasc. 113, the commune's protest of Dec. 18, 1537.

unknown number of legists.[74] The university was ready to begin a new academic year in 1542, but the imperial government in Milan did not want to provide the funds for salaries because of the threat of war. Hence, the university was closed from 1542 to 1544. By late 1545 the university was again functioning, as the professors complained in May 1546 that they had not been paid.[75] About 350 students were in attendance in late 1546.[76]

Despite the great difficulties during this half century, the university trained and appointed some distinguished jurists. Gianfrancesco Sannazari della Ripa (c. 1480–1535) of Pavia took his law doctorate there between 1506 and 1508 and then taught at Pavia from 1507 or 1508 until 1512, when he moved to the University of Avignon. Through a combination of carrot and stick, Francesco II Sforza brought him back to teach at Pavia in 1533 at the high salary of 1,000 florins and with an appointment as Milanese senator. His younger rival Andrea Alciato of Milan (1492–1550) also studied at Pavia, probably in the years 1507–11, before taking his degree at Ferrara in 1516. He then embarked on a distinguished teaching and legal career that took him to several universities, including Avignon, where he and Sannazari della Ripa jousted. Alciato taught at Pavia from 1533 to 1537 and again from 1546 until his death.[77]

The university resumed a more normal existence by the end of the 1540s. Despite the incorporation of Lombardy into the Spanish empire, local Italians still directed the university. The Milanese Senate replaced the duke and his Consiglio Segreto as supreme authority over the university.[78] Even though official proclamations, such as warnings to the students to behave, were issued in the name of the king of Spain ("Yo el Rey"), the Senate decided appointments and resolved controversies. When the wars subsided, it rebuilt the university.

Twenty-eight professors (13 in law and 15 in arts) taught in the academic year 1548–49.[79] The numbers gradually rose: Pavia had 30 to 35 professors in the 1550s, 40 to 45 in the 1560s and 1570s, and 47 to 50 in the 1580s and 1590s; it reached the height of 60 in 1601–2. The typical roll of 1581–82 had 49 professors: 20 in law (16 civilians, 4 canonists), and 29 in theology, arts, and medicine (Scholastic theology 2, Sacred Scripture 1, metaphysics 2, natural philosophy 5, logic 3, medical theory 7, practical medicine 4, medical botany taught by one of the medical theory professors, surgery 2, anatomy 1, mathematics 1, and Greek and Latin oratory 1). Except for having only one humanist, the distribution of

74. Ibid., Cartone 21, pp. 240, 242.

75. Ibid., Cartone 33, fasc. 118–21.

76. This is the figure given by an agent of Duke Cosimo I de' Medici of Florence who was attempting to recruit Andrea Alciato for the University of Pisa. See the letter of Francesco Vinta of Dec. 31, 1546, Milan, quoted in Abbondanza, 1958, 402.

77. See Ascheri, 1970, and Abbondanza, 1960, for the biographies.

78. Rizzo, 1987, 70. The Senate now handled university matters, such as correspondence with Pavian authorities, requests for appointment, and so on.

79. ASPv, Università, Cartone 21, pp. 244–45; Zorzoli, 1982, 567 n. 48. For what follows, see the numerous rolls, almost year by year, in ibid., Cartone 20, no pag. Rizzo (1987, 73–74) offers a summary of the rolls and prints the roll of 1584–85 on 75–76 n. 35.

professors through the subjects was typical of a medium-sized university. Like other Italian universities, Pavia reduced the number of canonists, added new civil law positions, a professorship of medical botany (1546), and a botanical garden (1558), and increased the importance of anatomy. And the cohort teaching in Milan disappeared.

Pavia continued to award degrees during the wars, because this could be done even when teaching was suspended.[80] Then in the last forty years of the century it awarded many more degrees, especially in law. The number rose to an average of almost 40 annually and reached a peak of 114 in 1587.[81] As in the fifteenth century, the vast majority of the degrees went to Italians, especially men from Lombardy. But Germans, Dutchmen, Spaniards, and other foreigners continued to obtain degrees from Pavia.

However, the faculty became more provincial in the second half of the sixteenth century. An overwhelming majority of the professors in the faculty of law came from Pavia; Milanese citizens and men from other parts of the state made up the rest. The university adopted a career ladder for legists which encouraged stability at the price of provincialism. When a senior law vacancy occurred, the university did not seek an established scholar. Instead, everyone moved up a chair, leaving the lowest position, an *Institutes* lectureship, vacant. A new appointee who taught at a very low salary or for free filled it. The combination of a faculty drawn from Pavia and Lombardy and a career ladder meant that almost all professors spent their entire lives at Pavia. Despite these limitations, Pavia had some eminent legists in the late sixteenth century. The faculty of arts and medicine was slightly less dominated by local men, while the majority of friars who taught theology, Scripture, and metaphysics came from beyond Lombardy.[82]

Lectures were held in a Dominican convent and other rented rooms across the city until the sixteenth century. Despite the wars, the Milanese Senate in 1533 authorized the erection of a university building in the center of the city. Construction began in 1534 with the renovation of an older structure, to which a new

---

80. Pavia awarded one to six doctorates annually in 1525, 1527, 1529, 1530, and 1531. The number increased after 1541, for example, 23 in 1547 and 19 in 1556. ASPv, Università, Doctoratus, Bu. 1, for the period 1525–65. However, it is likely that many records of doctorates have disappeared in these war-torn decades.

81. Ibid., Bu. 1 (1525–65), 2 (1566–72), 3 (1573–77), 6 (1587–90), and 8 (1596–99). The university continued to award numerous doctorates in the following half century; see ibid., Bu. 27 (1651–52), which records 45 in 1651 and 40 in 1652.

The number of known doctorates awarded in the second half of the sixteenth century was higher than the number awarded between 1450 and 1499, when records for about 600 degrees (12 per year) have been found. However, Sottili believes that the total number for the period 1450–99 may have been 2,400 (48 annually) for several reasons, including the probability that many earlier records were destroyed in the first forty years of the sixteenth century. Sottili, 1990, 421–29, 450–51; the introductory comments of Sottili in *Documenti di Pavia,* 1994, 14; and *Lauree pavesi,* 1995. Certainly there were many more doctorates awarded in the fifteenth century than those for which documents have been located, but a number is difficult to estimate.

82. Zorzoli, 1982, 568–69; Zorzoli, 1986, 187; and Rizzo, 1987, 71–81, 121–22. For theology, see Negruzzo, 1995, 39 and passim. Other discussions of Pavia in the late sixteenth century are Barbieri, 1912, and Rizzo, 1989.

building was added. Much expansion over the centuries produced a large structure on the Strada Nuova which today contains offices, lecture rooms, and the university library.[83] Several endowed residences for university students were also built in the later sixteenth century. Pavia had more than five hundred students in November 1586; this was probably typical annual enrollment in the last forty years of the century.[84]

Pavia's most famous students came from Lombard noble ranks. Carlo Borromeo (1538–84), the future archbishop of Milan and saint, studied canon and civil law at Pavia between 1552 and 1559, taking his law doctorate in the last year. His younger cousin Federico Borromeo (1564–1631) came to Pavia in 1580 and took his theology degree in 1585. He also became archbishop of Milan and an important figure in the life of the state.

The University of Pavia concentrated on law. Its most famous professors taught law, and the majority of students, including many non-Italians, came to study that subject. But Pavia also had some major scholars in medicine, arts, and the humanities. Pavia ranked just behind Bologna and Padua in quality and number of faculty and students in the fifteenth century. It was equal to, and possibly the superior of, Bologna and Padua in law throughout much of the Renaissance. But it suffered more grievously than any other university during the Italian wars. It fell to a middle-rank position in the second half of the sixteenth century, trailing Padua, Bologna, Pisa, Rome, and Ferrara, especially in arts and medicine. The fortunes of the University of Pavia mirrored those of the Lombard state. It flourished when the Visconti-Sforza dukedom prospered, but it declined when Lombardy was devastated by war and lost its independence.

TURIN, 1411–1413

The University of Turin was the university of the county (later duchy) of Piedmont-Savoy, a sprawling agglomeration of French, Swiss, and Italian estates and towns circling the Alps.[85] Prince Ludovico d'Acaia, ruler of Turin and the rest of Piedmont for his brother, Amadeus VIII, count of Piedmont-Savoy, requested a bull to establish a university. Professors fleeing to Turin from the University of Pavia in the years of turmoil following the death in 1402 of Giangaleazzo Visconti, ruler of Lombardy, may have offered the opportunity. The Avignonese antipope Benedict XIII issued bulls of October 28, 1404, and November 27, 1405, authorizing a university at Turin.

But nothing happened until the autumn of 1411, when four professors of law appeared in Turinese communal records. Law instruction began, and the initial

---

83. Vaccari, 1957, 99–103; Rizzo, 1987, 87–90.

84. The number comes from a letter of Nov. 15, 1586, of the *podestà* of Pavia. Negruzzo, 1995, 48. Vaccari (1957, 140) also estimates annual enrollment at five hundred.

85. This account is based on Vallauri, 1970, the oldest history; Chiaudano, 1972a, 1972b, and 1972c; and Bellone, 1986. The latter works supplement and sometimes correct Vallauri. Naso, 1997, and Naso, 1998, are recent reviews of the fifteenth century, and Catarinella and Salsotto, 1998, the period 1536–1630. Rashdall (1936, 2:55–57) gives a very brief account.

doctorates were awarded in early 1412. The first professor of medicine was appointed for the academic year 1413–14. Theological teaching may also have begun at this time. Hence, most of the university subjects were being taught by 1413–14, although the number of professors is not known. Turin obtained an imperial charter in 1412 and a third papal bull in 1413 from John XXIII, another antipope. The new university probably wanted approval from all sides in this era of rival authorities. Ludovico d'Acaia appointed a magistracy called Riformatori dello Studio to oversee the university, and he asked the Commune of Turin for funds for faculty salaries. The commune responded with the very modest amount of 350 fiorini a piccoli. It also paid the rent for teaching quarters and made efforts to find housing for students. The University of Turin had begun.

It remained a tiny university until midcentury. Although no rolls survive for the century, 4 professors of law, 2 medical professors, and 2 theologians regularly appeared in communal records in the first twenty years of the university. These men were the nucleus of the faculty. Perhaps 2 or 3 junior extraordinary lecturers and a teaching rector of students joined them.

The university did not grow because it lacked support. The Riformatori regularly asked the commune for a larger appropriation for university salaries, and the commune regularly complained about the tax privileges enjoyed by professors and students. During one such standoff in February 1427, Count Amadeus VIII authorized the university to move to the smaller town of Chieri, 15 kilometers southwest of Turin.[86] When the same disputes between commune and university arose in Chieri, Ludovico of Savoy, lieutenant for Piedmont for his father, Amadeus VIII, in August 1434 ordered the university moved to Savigliano, about 50 kilometers directly south of Turin. But students and faculty complained about the high price of meat and the muddy streets of Savigliano, so Ludovico returned the university to Turin in October 1436. There it remained.

The stabilized university grew. In 1441 Duke Ludovico, now sole ruler of Piedmont-Savoy, assumed the expenses of professorial salaries up to an annual amount of 2,000 fiorini a piccoli. The commune agreed to pay the cost of renting rooms for teaching and to make a small contribution toward salaries, and it bore an increasing share of the costs over time.[87] The university had its own quarters from 1443, probably at Via San Francesco d'Assisi near the church of San Rocco. All this had a positive effect; Turin had at least 25 professors in 1452–53, 24 in 1456–57, and 22 in 1458–59.[88] Law dominated, as 9 law professors appeared in communal records in 1450 and 19 in 1452.[89] As many as 5 professors of medicine and 2 theologians also surfaced in communal records at midcentury, and 2 or 3

---

86. Vallauri (1970, 1:58–60) states that the *studio* moved to Chieri in 1421. Bellone (1986, 40–41) demonstrates that it remained in Turin until 1427.

87. Bellone, 1986, 63.

88. Naso, 1998, 106.

89. Bellone, 1986, 96–97. The information comes from miscellaneous records, rather than rolls or regular payment records. Hence, the number of names of professors discovered varies greatly from year to year.

philosophers and logicians may have taught. Hence, Turin had a small university with the normal range of lectureships.

The University of Pavia continued to provide faculty for Turin. Several natives of Lombardy took degrees at Pavia and then taught at Turin their entire professional lives. But they were not distinguished scholars, nor did the dukes bring in notable outsiders. Salaries remained at a low level; indeed, in 1470 several medical professors refused to teach until their salaries were raised.[90] The university also suffered from internal tensions. Piedmontese and Savoyard students fought each other. But both complained about high rents, probably the consequence of an inadequate supply of housing in a small town. Turin had at most 10,000 to 15,000 inhabitants at midcentury, and the figure may have been considerably smaller.[91] And the townspeople complained that the students molested women and girls, the same complaint heard in every other university town.

The largest number of students and graduates came from Turin, Biella, Chivasso, Ivrea, and Vercelli in the eastern half of Piedmont. The number of known degrees awarded in the fifteenth century was extremely modest, only about 25 in law, 12 in medicine, and 34 in theology. Obviously more degrees were awarded, but the records have disappeared.[92] Law graduates often found employment as judges and administrators in the state; medical graduates became communally paid physicians and surgeons.

The resident student body must have been small, perhaps one hundred or fewer in the early years, possibly about two hundred in the second half of the fifteenth century.[93] Although the dukes of Piedmont-Savoy ordered their subjects to attend the University of Turin, linguistic and geographical diversity led them elsewhere. Many French-speaking subjects went to Avignon, Montpellier, and Orléans; Italian-speaking subjects attended Padua and Pavia. The University of Turin remained a small, poorly funded university through the fifteenth century.

Nevertheless, the Studio Torinese seemed to prosper at the end of the fifteenth century and the beginning of the sixteenth. A number of sons of prominent Piedmontese families took degrees at Turin. So did at least 18 Frenchmen, 18 Englishmen, and 2 Scots, plus Germans and Spaniards, between 1497 and 1512.[94] Although degrees awarded to foreigners did not necessarily mean that they spent much time in Turin, they confirm that Turin had a modest place on the academic map.

90. Salaries ranged from average amounts of 5 to 20 florins to a maximum of 180 to 200 fiorini a piccoli. Bellone, 1986, 129 n. 54 and p. 82 for the threatened strike.

91. This is the estimate of Bellone, 1986, 128. By contrast, Ginatempo and Sandri (1990, 65, 67) put the figure at only 2,500 to 3,000 in 1415. If true, it is unlikely that the population climbed to 10,000 to 15,000 by midcentury.

92. Bellone, 1986, 111, 127, 136. There are many lacunae in the notarial files of the archepiscopal archive where degrees were recorded.

93. This figure is my estimate based on projections from the number of professors and graduates.

94. Vallauri, 1970, 1:126–27; Bellone, 1994.

At this time Turin awarded its most famous doctorate, to Desiderius Erasmus of Rotterdam (1466–1536). Erasmus arrived about the middle of August 1506 (when classes were not in session), was examined for the doctorate of theology, received the degree on September 4, 1506, and then left.[95] He did not study at Turin.

The Italian wars beginning in 1494 interrupted the university. Piedmont's location, between France and Lombardy, invited occupation by competing major powers. The lack of records makes it impossible to determine exactly when the university was open and when it was closed. Nevertheless, the university may have survived the first forty years of the Italian wars relatively well. Rolls for 1532–33 and 1534–35 indicate that Turin had 24 professors: 2 theologians, 5 professors of canon law plus a teaching student rector, 7 civilians, 5 professors of medicine, 1 for surgery, 1 philosopher, 1 logician, and 2 rhetoricians. They earned a total of about 4,500 florins.[96]

Turin was not so fortunate in the latter part of the Italian wars. War between France and Piedmont-Savoy broke out in 1535. The French captured Turin and several other Piedmontese towns in 1536; the Spanish occupied some of the rest. The university seems to have been closed through most of the lengthy French occupation; it did not teach in the years 1536–38, 1546–56, and 1558–60 and may have been closed in other years.[97]

The Peace of Cateau-Cambrésis (1559) brought the Italian wars to an end and obliged the French to withdraw, but gradually, from Piedmont-Savoy. Duke Emanuele Filiberto (b. 1528; ruled 1553–80) began to rebuild his battered state. One of the ablest Italian rulers of the century, the duke soon reestablished a university, but not in Turin. In December 1560 he gave permission for a university in Mondovì, a town of 22,000 some 90 kilometers south of Turin in the southernmost part of the state. Two reasons seem to have motivated him: the French still occupied Turin, and the Commune of Mondovì offered generous financial concessions. Duke and commune immediately set about assembling a faculty and obtaining the necessary privileges. Pope Pius IV authorized the granting of degrees on September 22, 1561, and Pius V confirmed the new university on January 17, 1566. In a break with past policy, the duke paid substantial sums in order to lure professors with established reputations from other institutions. By May 1565 the university at Mondovì had 21 professors: 8 legists, 4 medical professors, 1 anatomist, 1 professor of medical botany, 2 natural philosophers, 1 metaphysician, 2 logicians, 1 mathematician, and a humanist. They collectively earned about 5,200 scudi at the rate of 8 fiorini a piccoli to 1 scudo.[98]

95. For the circumstances, text, and English translation of Erasmus's doctorate, see Grendler, 1998.

96. The rolls are in Vallauri, 1970, 1:135–39.

97. Chiaudano, 1972c, 55, and Catarinella and Salsotto, 1998, 523.

98. The list of May 25, 1565, is found in Vallauri, 1970, 1:205–7. It is not a conventional roll, because some of the professors were already teaching, and a few were hired to begin in the autumn. Since professorial salaries were paid in scudi worth 8 florins in the late sixteenth century, it would

The communal council of Turin, citing long residence and historical privileges of the Studio Torinese, strenuously objected that the university belonged in Turin. Mondovì responded that its new papal privileges superseded the old ones. Turin's case probably became stronger when the French finally left the city in December 1562. Still, the duke would not return the university until Turin offered the duke 4,000 scudi (at the rate of 8 florins to 1 scudo), plus an annual contribution of 1,000 scudi for the university, double the offer from Mondovì. Now the duke's mind cleared. He ordered the faculty at Mondovì to move to Turin, and the renewed University of Turin began classes in early November 1566. The restoration of the university was part of a larger political strategy, the shift of the capital and the center of gravity of the state from French-speaking Chambéry on the French side of the Alps to Turin on the Italian side. The university at Mondovì had lasted from sometime during the academic year 1560–61 to the summer of 1566. However, the college of doctors of Mondovì retained the privilege of conferring degrees, becoming another paper university on the Italian landscape.

Most of the professors of the renewed Studio Torinese had been at Mondovì, but Emanuele Filiberto added a few distinguished outsiders. He invited Aimone Cravetta (1504–69), a subject born in Savigliano (Piedmont), then teaching at Pavia, to fill the major chair of civil law at the handsome salary of 1,000 gold scudi. Cravetta had taken his degree at Turin and taught briefly there; he then became a famous legist at other universities. When Cravetta declined to come, the duke ordered all his property at Savigliano confiscated. Cravetta then accepted the invitation.[99] When Cravetta died in October 1569, the duke hired another distinguished jurist to replace him. Guido Panciroli (1523–99) from Reggio nell'Emilia, then teaching at Padua, came to Turin in 1570 at 700 scudi. He remained through the academic year 1581–82, with his salary rising to 1,228 scudi, and then returned to Padua. Although the university tried to appoint scholars who had taught elsewhere to a few major chairs, men from Turin and Piedmont enjoyed preference for the rest.

Despite the examples of Cravetta and Panciroli, the restored university had more arts and medicine professors than legists. The average faculty size between 1566–67 and 1585–86 was 30 professors.[100] The 12 professors of law included at least 8 for civil law, including the relatively new fields of criminal law and feudal law, and 4 canonists. They received 35 to 40 percent of the salary appropriation, which averaged 5,400 scudi annually. In contrast to the pattern at other universities, law professors did not receive higher salaries than the rest.

The other 18 faculty included a theologian and a metaphysician, both posts

---

appear that salaries were far higher than in the fifteenth century. Nevertheless, the sixteenth-century scudo seems to have had about the same value as the fifteenth-century florin.

99. Chiaudano, 1972c, 62; Olmo, 1984.

100. All but one of the rolls (with salaries) for these twenty academic years are printed in Chiaudano, 1972a and 1972b.

filled by clergymen. Then came 3 professors of medical theory, 4 for practical medicine, and 1 for surgery or anatomy. The arts faculty also included a professor of medical botany, 3 natural philosophers, 2 logicians, a mathematician, and a Greek humanist *(humanista greco)*. A professorship in Scripture was added in 1580–81. The 18 collectively received 60 to 65 percent of the total appropriation. The greater emphasis on medicine and natural philosophy compared with the fifteenth century may have come from the duke, who took a great interest in science.

But the humanities hardly existed, because Duke Emanuele Filiberto made other arrangements. He decreed that the newly founded (1567) Jesuit college in Turin would teach the humanities to university students.[101] He dismissed the only Latin humanist on the faculty, Giovanni Battista Giraldi Cinzio of Ferrara (1504–73), who had been hired for the University of Mondovì and had taught at Turin for two academic years, 1566–68. The university roll listed annual payments to the Jesuit college, from 1567–68 through 1573–74, of 200 scudi, which was half Giraldi Cinzio's salary.

Happy with the humanities instruction of the Jesuits, the duke also wanted them to teach natural philosophy, logic, and theology. The Jesuits were willing, but commune and Riformatori strongly protested, and the matter was dropped.[102] Moreover, the university continued to employ a professor of Greek and had a professor of Latin humanities *(humanista latino)* for two years, 1575–77. Since payments to the Jesuit college ceased in 1574, it is not clear if it continued to teach the humanities to university students. In any case, between 1566 and 1586 the University of Turin had only the professor of Greek and a professor of Latin humanities for two years.[103]

In 1571 Duke Emanuele Filiberto appointed—seven outright, the other two from a short list proposed by the commune of Turin—nine Riformatori dello Studio to supervise the university. All came from the highest ranks of government and society.[104] They prepared the roll for the duke's approval and drafted instructions for the university. In 1579 Emanuele Filiberto created and appointed a new official, the Conservatore Generale, who oversaw daily activities, defended student privileges, and dealt with infractions of regulations. The authority of the student rector, never strong, hardly existed. The governance of the University of Turin paralleled the growth of princely absolutism in Piedmont-Savoy.

The commune directly and indirectly paid most university costs. A Turinese tax on wine and meat raised money for salaries; the proceeds went to the ducal treasury and then to the professors. But salaries were in arrears several times in the late sixteenth century, when the expenses of war drained the treasury. The commune also bore the cost of improving lecture halls. It purchased some houses at the corner of Via San Francesco d'Assisi and Via Garibaldi, across from the

101. For the following, see Chiaudano, 1972c, 63, and 1972b, 77–78; Scaglione, 1986, 136–42; and Scaduto, 1992, 329–32.

102. For more, see Grendler, in press.

103. It is not possible to follow the story further, because the rolls for 1586 to 1600 are missing. But no humanists appeared in the rolls of the first decade of the seventeenth century.

104. Catarinella and Salsotto, 1998, 527–28.

Palazzo di Città in the heart of the city, and created large teaching rooms on the second floors of these houses.

The University of Turin prospered in the last third of the sixteenth century. It had 500 students in 1571 and "at least 400" in 1597.[105] The vast majority were ducal subjects, who often went on to magistracies, diplomatic posts, and court positions in the state.

The fifteenth-century University of Turin was the smallest and least important of the northern Italian universities. It grew in size and stature after 1566 but remained a modest provincial university, even though it had some established professors from beyond Piedmont. The Studio Torinese primarily served the needs of the ruler and inhabitants of Piedmont-Savoy, especially those who spoke Italian. Piedmont-Savoy was a minor state in the Italian Renaissance but assumed great political importance in subsequent centuries. The university followed the same trajectory.

FERRARA, 1442

The traditional date for the beginning of the University of Ferrara is 1391. But Ferrara did not have a teaching university with enough professors to teach the basic subjects of canon and civil law, logic, natural philosophy, and medicine until 1442. The latter is the real foundation date.

Pope Boniface IX granted Ferrara a charter authorizing a *studio* with the power to award degrees in civil law, canon law, arts, medicine, and theology on March 4, 1391.[106] The university officially opened its doors on October 18 of that year, with two law professors, who also held other positions in the government. An additional four legists may have taught at that time, but no evidence of university-level arts and medicine instruction has been found. This partial *studio* closed in 1394 and then may have reopened again in 1402 with three legists teaching. After two more years, the university appropriation was diverted to the expenses of war, and teaching ceased in 1404. Marquis Niccolò III d'Este (ruled 1393–1441) tried to reopen the university in 1418, proposing that the communal government of Ferrara bear half of the expenses through a new tax to be levied by

105. Chiaudano, 1972c, 67, and 1972a, 156. The first estimate comes from a report of the papal ambassador; the second, from a communal report.

106. Very little is known about the period before 1442 because very little happened. Borsetti (1735; with corrections by G. Guarini, 1970; and response by Borsetti, 1970) is the basic source. However, Borsetti has many errors plus statements that cannot be confirmed because of the loss of university records through fire and theft. Modern studies of the origins of the partial *studio* and the fifteenth century began with Bottoni, 1892, which has errors. Better studies are Secco Suardo, 1983, 62–65 and passim; Pardi, 1972, 26–36; Solerti, 1892, 5–17; and Visconti, 1950, 6–14. Good recent reviews for the period 1391 through 1441, which do not change the basic story, are Samaritani, 1995, and Del Nero, 1996, 3–38, 44–45, 55–56, 66–68, 84, 99. Rashdall (1936, 2:53–55) offers a very brief survey. *I maestri di Ferrara* (1991, 3–6) lists one to five arts and medicine professors annually in the years 1391–1441. But these names come from Borsetti, who recorded many degree promoters as professors and made other errors. The editor of the volume discusses the problems with the sources on pp. xiii, xxvii–xviii.

the commune. The commune informed the prince that it would be happy to reopen the university but not to levy a new tax. Since neither ruler nor commune was willing to assume the financial obligation, no action was taken.

Thus, although possessing a charter and colleges of doctors empowered to award degrees in law, arts, medicine, and theology, Ferrara initially had only a tiny, incomplete teaching university, which soon closed. Nevertheless, the colleges awarded 108 known degrees from 1402 through 1441.[107] The vast majority of degree recipients stated that they had studied at other universities, typically Bologna or Padua. A handful affirmed that they studied at the Studio Ferrarese; all had local promoters. But it does not appear that the promoters were teaching professors. For example, Ugo Benzi of Siena (1376–1439), a famous medical scholar, served as promoter for several doctorates of medicine. He was personal physician to the ruler (1430–39) and taught privately but did not hold a professorship in Ferrara. Other promoters were probably not professors either but local lawyers and physicians with degrees, that is, the men who filled colleges of doctors in university towns and nonuniversity towns alike. The awarding of degrees and reference to the Studio Ferrarese do not prove that university teaching existed in Ferrara after 1402.

Marquis Leonello d'Este (b. 1407; ruled late December 1441–50) made the University of Ferrara a full teaching university in 1442. The great humanist pedagogue Guarino Guarini of Verona (1374–1460) probably strongly encouraged him. In 1429 Marquis Niccolò III d'Este had brought Guarini to Ferrara to be the personal tutor of his designated successor, Leonello, and to grace court marriages with Latin epithalamia. After his contract to tutor Leonello expired in 1435, Guarini remained at Ferrara as a well-paid communal teacher. He also operated his own boarding school for students of various ages. Guarini taught the classics, carried on an extensive correspondence, received visiting scholars, and made Ferrara a center of humanist activity.[108]

In a meeting of January 1442, Marquis Leonello d'Este and the commune agreed to create a university. The commune cited the usual reasons: a distinguished center of learning would bring renown to the city, local men would more easily obtain degrees, and an influx of students would bolster the city's economy. The commune levied a sales tax on meat and paid the greater part of faculty salaries; Leonello also contributed financially.[109] The university formally opened on October 18, 1442. Guarini delivered the inaugural oration, which praised both humanistic studies and university subjects. He became a humanities professor.

The first surviving list of professors had 12 in the faculty of law and 13 in the faculty of arts in 1449–50.[110] Ferrara quickly expanded to 40 to 45 professors and

---

107. Venturini, 1892, and especially Pardi, 1970, 10–17, who reworks and supplements Venturini. See also the comments of Pardi, 1972, 34–36. The degrees come from notarial records; others may await discovery.

108. For Guarini at Ferrara, see Sabbadini, 1964a, esp. paragraphs 200, 273–74, 305, 310–15.

109. See Gundersheimer, 1973, 101, for evidence that the prince helped.

110. The list, based on payment records and without indicating the individual lectureships, comes

to 49 in 1473–74. At that time the 22 legists included 6 ordinary professors and 2 extraordinary of canon law, 6 ordinary and 7 extraordinary professors of civil law, and 1 professor of notarial art. The 27 arts professors included 1 theologian, 4 professors of theoretical medicine, 5 professors of practical medicine, 2 professors of surgery, 2 professors of natural philosophy, 1 who taught both natural and moral philosophy, 7 logicians, 3 humanists, and 1 professor of astrology. They earned a little less than 11,000 lire marchesini.[111] The number then probably dropped to 25 to 30 professors in the last quarter of the fifteenth century.[112]

The ruler oversaw the university indirectly and sometimes directly. Two to six Riformatori dello Studio, some chosen by the city council, others by the ruler, appointed professors, determined salaries, and managed the university. They reported to the governing council (Consiglio dei XII Savi) of the commune of Ferrara. However, since the prince named the head and members of the Consiglio dei XII Savi, he exercised considerable indirect authority over the university. And the Este also intervened directly. For example, if the commune hesitated to hire a costly law professor, the duke appointed him anyway. On the whole, ducal interventions aided the university.

Ruler and commune shared university expenses until 1473, when it was decided that the commune would pay the entire cost of the university and the ruler would pay the higher costs of maintaining the city's fortifications.[113] But the university was a heavy burden for the city: in 1492 about 44 percent of the communal budget (11,000 of about 25,000 lire marchesini) went to the university.[114] To be sure, Ferrara professors did not often receive their entire stipends. The commune usually withheld 2 percent, and the ruler exacted additional sums to pay for the city's fortifications. In addition, professors were obliged to help meet wedding expenses of members of the large ruling family.[115]

The university suffered only brief interruptions in the second half of the

---

from Borsetti (1735, 57). Secco Suardo (1983, 204–5) reprints and interprets it in the light of additional information; Visconti (1950, 16) reprints it without comment or date. As the latter two versions differ slightly, Secco Suardo is preferred for its greater detail. *I maestri di Ferrara* (1991) lists 11 arts and medicine professors in 1449–50. As indicated in n. 106, the lists of arts, medicine, and theology professors given in *I maestri di Ferrara* are not always accurate for the fifteenth century. To cite one example, *I maestri di Ferrara* (1991) lists Theodore Gaza as teaching in the years 1441–43. But Monfasani (1994b) demonstrates that he taught at Ferrara in the years 1446–49. *I maestri di Ferrara* seems to be more reliable for the sixteenth century. Secco Suardo (1983, 210–65) presents lists of legists for the years 1451–74.

111. Secco Suardo, 1983, 265–68, based on Borsetti. Secco Suardo gives the date as "1474," which must be 1473–74. *I maestri di Ferrara* (1991, 14–15) lists thirty-six arts professors for that year, which seems too many. University expenses were much higher in some years, for example, 16,000 lire marchesini in 1485–86. Zambotti, 1937, 170. Sitta (1892, 100) states that 34 lire marchesini equaled one gold ducat at the end of the fourteenth century. It then lost value, to the point that it took 95 lire marchesini to equal one gold ducat in the late sixteenth century.

112. This is based on an average of thirteen arts professors listed in *I maestri di Ferrara* (1991, 15–20) and my estimate that Ferrara had an equal number of law professors.

113. Del Nero, 1996, 188.

114. Sitta, 1892, 110, 212–13.

115. Visconti (1950, 22) gives a brief summary of such exactions.

fifteenth century. It moved to Rovigo from 1463 to 1464 because of famine and practically closed in the years 1483–84 because of plague and famine. However, the period 1505–29 was very difficult. Famine caused the university to close its doors in 1505–6. War absorbed all available funds and forced the university to shut down between 1511 and 1513. The *studio* functioned with only six to eight professors between 1514 and 1518. And pestilence seems to have sharply reduced and perhaps closed the university again between 1523 and 1529. Duke Alfonso I (ruled 1505–34) formally reopened it in November 1529, and it gradually regained its former strength.[116]

From the 1540s until 1596, Ferrara had 45 to 50 professors, costing 10,000 to 14,000 lire marchesini.[117] One-third taught law; two-thirds taught medicine, arts, and theology. As in other universities at this time, Ferrara had many more civilians (about 11) than canonists (about 4), plus a professor of notarial art in the law faculty. The most distinguished legist by far was Andrea Alciato, who taught from 1542 to 1546, initially earning 1,200 gold scudi (equal to 4,260 lire marchesini), a figure that rose to 4,860. His salary in 1542–43 consumed half of the university appropriation and 10 percent of the communal budget.[118]

An average of 30 professors of arts and medicine included 4 professors of theoretical medicine, 2 to 4 professors of practical medicine, 2 professors of surgery, a professor of medical botany (*Ad lecturam simplicium medicamentorum*) beginning in 1543, a professor of anatomy from 1570 onward, and a professor *Ad lecturam Graecam operum Hippocratis,* who presumably lectured from the Greek text of Hippocrates. Probably the most distinguished physician was Antonio Musa Brasavola (1500–1555), professor of practical medicine from 1541 to 1555. The rest of the arts contingent included 4 or 5 natural philosophers, a moral philosopher, 2 metaphysics professors, and 2 theologians from 1569 onward. Six professors taught logic, and 3 to 4 men, some well known, taught the humanities. A professor of astronomy and mathematics completed the roll.

The most important innovation was the professorship of Platonic philosophy called *Ad lecturam Reipublicae Platonis* initially and then *Ad lecturam philosophiae Platonicae* from 1578 through 1592, held by Francesco Patrizi (1529–97). For two academic years, 1541–43, one "Abraam veneto" taught Hebrew (*Ad lectiones Hebraicas*), one of the few such posts in Italian universities.[119]

Classes met in several locations, including a Franciscan monastery for the legists, until 1560, when a fire destroyed the guild hall where the humanists taught. The commune then purchased a building from the Este. After remodel-

---

116. Pardi, 1972, 36–39; Visconti, 1950, 57–58; and *I maestri di Ferrara*, 1991, 21–24.

117. The following is based on Solerti, 1892; Pardi, 1972, 225–49; Franceschini, 1970, who presents composite lists of the faculty 1532–96; Franceschini, 1975; and *I maestri di Ferrara,* 1991, 26–49.

118. Abbondanza, 1960, 73; Franceschini, 1970, xii, 223; and Solerti, 1892, 24–25, who gives Alciato's highest salary as the equivalent of 4,985 lire marchesini.

119. Franceschini, 1970, 266. *I maestri di Ferrara* (1991, 27, 179) lists the professor of Hebrew as 1541–42 only.

ing, the Palazzo Paradiso (now called Palazzo dell'Università) housed all classes except theology from 1586 onward. It continues to serve the university today.[120]

Ferrara aggressively recruited students. In 1455 Duke Borso d'Este (ruled 1450–71, the Este having become dukes in 1450) gave the rector of the law students' organization 200 ducats to distribute to foreign students willing to come to Ferrara.[121] And like other rulers, Duke Ercole I (ruled 1471–1505) in 1485 forbade his subjects to study or take degrees outside Ferrara, an injunction repeated several times over the next hundred years.

Ferrara probably had 400 to 500 students from the late fifteenth century through the sixteenth, except for the periods of near closure. A professor of natural philosophy who had just moved from Pisa to Ferrara reported that Ferrara had more than 300 law students and more than 130 arts students in February 1488. He further opined that the University of Ferrara was better than the University of Pisa.[122] A student confirmed the figure for the law students. On January 28, 1481, a masked contingent from the Ferrarese court threw snowballs at a group of law students. The latter took up the challenge: about 300 law students donned masks for a two-hour snowball fight, and a good time was had by all.[123] Finally, a modern historian suggests an average resident student body of 500 in the century and a half after 1442.[124] Since the town of Ferrara had a population of 20,000 to 25,000 in the fifteenth century and grew to 42,000 in the late sixteenth century, it could easily house a student body of 400 to 500 students.[125]

A few of the students achieved considerable fame later. Aldo Manuzio (c. 1450–1515) studied at Ferrara in the late 1470s and did not leave permanently until 1482. The major German humanist Rudolf Agricola (1444–85) studied in

120. Quinterio, 1991.

121. Del Nero, 1996, 76.

122. "Per avixarvi del Studio di Ferrara, sapiati che qua è bono Studio in legie et in le arte nostre: in legie v'è più di 300 scholari, mentre in nostre facultade ve n'è più di 130. . . . Credo che stia meglio el Studio di Ferrara che el vostro da Pisa." Letter of Antonio Cittadini to Bernardo Pulci, the Florentine procurator, the official who oversaw the University of Pisa, of Feb. 3, 1488, Ferrara, printed in Verde, 1973–94, vol. 4, pt. 2, p. 723. From Faenza, Cittadini (d. c. 1518) was a professor of natural philosophy at Bologna (1465–66), of natural philosophy and medical theory at Ferrara (1468–82), of natural philosophy at Pisa (1482–1487/88), professor of practical medicine at Ferrara (1488–1505), then professor of medical theory at Padua (1505 to at least 1509). Cittadini also complained in the above letter that part of his Pisan salary had not been paid, and he wanted a higher salary from Pisa. For a brief biography, see Pesenti, 1984, 91–93. For his Pisan appointment, see Verde, 1973–94, 2:32–35; see also Verde, 1995, 86–87.

123. Zambotti, 1937, 84–85. The chronicler, Bernardino Zambotti of Ferrara (c. 1460–after 1504), studied at the university from about 1476 until taking his degree in civil law in 1485. He then held minor judicial and administrative posts in the communal government of Ferrara. His chronicle offers a vivid picture of Ferrara in the years 1476–1504, with much information on the university.

124. This is the estimate of Pinghini (1927, 134–35), derived from mathematical projections based on the number of degrees granted and the numerical relationship between matriculation records and degrees granted in future centuries.

125. Ginatempo and Sandri, 1990, 86, 88, 255. Not a major commercial center, Ferrara depended on a regional agricultural economy and the considerable military and political skills of its rulers for survival and prosperity.

the years 1475–79. Another student was the religious reformer of Florence Giro-lamo Savonarola (1452–98). He was the son of a Ferrarese doctor and grandson of the famous medical scholar Michele Savonarola (c. 1385–after February 1466), who taught at Ferrara earlier. Girolamo was an arts and medicine student in 1473 and perhaps earlier but left to become a monk in 1475.[126] Ludovico Ariosto (1474–1533) studied law in the 1490s but took no degree. Theophrast Bombast von Hohenheim, called Paracelsus (1493/94–1541), the great innova-tor in medicine and chemistry, probably studied medicine at Ferrara, but the dates are unknown.

The University of Ferrara conferred at least 1,436 doctorates (25 per year) between 1442 and 1499.[127] Unlike other Italian universities, Ferrara awarded slightly more arts and medicine degrees than law degrees from1442 through 1459. Guarino Guarini probably attracted many Italians and ultramontanes who wished to learn about humanism at the feet of the most prestigious (and oldest) pedagogue of the movement. Then, beginning in the 1460s, Ferrara began to award a few more law degrees than arts and medicine degrees. This tendency accelerated. By the period 1500 through 1555, Ferrara awarded approximately 3.2 times as many law as arts and medicine degrees.[128] Many students from Germany, the Netherlands, Austria, France, Spain, England, Poland, and else-where obtained degrees. By the 1540s one-third or more of the degree recipients came from beyond Italy, a high percentage for an Italian university.

But not all the students who obtained degrees spent much time in Ferrara. Perhaps two-thirds of the students who won doctorates from Ferrara had pre-viously studied at other universities including all the other Italian universities, especially Bologna and Padua, plus Avignon, Dôle, Louvain, Paris, Toulouse,

---

126. Verde, 1995, 96–97.

127. Pardi (1970) provides names, homelands, disciplines, other universities attended, promoters, and key witnesses for degree recipients for the years 1402–1555. He supplements and sometimes corrects Venturini, 1892, and Secco Suardo, 1894, 202–6.

128. The precise figures are as follows, organized by decade:

	Law	Arts / Medicine	Theology
1442–48	42	53	1
1451–59	102	101	24
1460–69	129	114	36
1470–79	155	105	22
1480–89	129	78	5
1490–99	154	124	62
1500–1503	74	40	13
1512–16	51	39	3
1520–29	18	12	0
1530–39	186	60	1
1540–48	299	57	3
1550–55	237	64	16

From Pardi, 1970. It should be remembered that there are some gaps in the records and that the university suffered several closures between 1505 and 1529.

Valence, Cologne, Fribourg, Heidelberg, Ingolstadt, Leipzig, Mainz, Tübingen, Erfurt, Luther's Wittenberg, Oxford, Vienna, Cracow, and others.[129] Ferrara was a place where men, especially ultramontanes who had probably done the bulk of their studying elsewhere, came to obtain degrees quickly. Nicolaus Copernicus (1473–1543) is an example. He began his university studies at Cracow and then studied canon law and astronomy at the University of Bologna from 1496 to about 1501. He studied medicine at Padua for all or most of two academic years 1501–3 but took a doctorate in canon law at Ferrara on May 31, 1503. Copernicus probably spent a few months, possibly only weeks, in Ferrara.[130]

Students came to Ferrara for degrees after studying elsewhere for reasons of convenience, cost, and tradition. Ferrara is only 45 kilometers north of Bologna and 85 kilometers south of Padua on the flat plain of the Po River. Bolognese and Paduan students could easily journey to Ferrara for degrees. Although all degrees were expensive, a Ferrara degree probably cost less than those taken elsewhere. And once students began going to Ferrara for degrees, sons, kinsmen, friends, and fellow countrymen would follow. Ferrara seems to have been something of a diploma mill.[131]

Very limited matriculation records suggest that the students who spent more time at Ferrara were mostly Italians. In 1534 and 1535, for example, 116 of 119 known matriculants in the faculty of arts and medicine were Italians. But about a third of the 55 degree recipients in those two years were non-Italians.[132] It may be that foreigners came for degrees, while Italians came to learn.

The Studio Ferrarese attracted a few academic stars, beginning with Guarino Guarini, who taught from 1442 to 1460. Men of lesser distinction from Ferrara families increasingly filled professorial ranks in the second half of the sixteenth century. The majority of professors taught for many years, giving the university pedagogical continuity.

The University of Ferrara was a princely creation. The Este rulers obtained a charter and created a university in 1442. It taught alongside one of the most brilliant courts of the Italian Renaissance, the place where Matteo Maria Boiardo, Ludovico Ariosto, and Torquato Tasso (1544–95, who taught mathematics at Ferrara in the years 1575–77) wrote literary masterpieces. Just as they sur-

129. Ibid.

130. The record of his degree states that he studied at Bologna and Padua, but it does not mention any Ferrara study. Ibid., 110–11.

131. Collett (1994) analyzes the careers of a number of Englishmen who obtained degrees at Ferrara, about 1460–1502. He argues that they imbibed the ideology of Guarino Guarini, who viewed humanistic studies as contributing to the common good and believed that humanists should serve the commonweal. Upon returning to England, these men took positions with the government and helped create the links between Crown and learning which characterized the Tudor dynasty. Although the article is persuasive, it is not always clear how much time these Englishmen spent at Ferrara. Romano (1995) lists Sicilian law students and professors who came to Ferrara.

132. Franceschini, 1975, 155; Pardi, 1970, 122–25. To be precise, non-Italians took at least seventeen of fifty-five doctorates. One must caution that matriculation records, in the few cases in which they survive, tend to be incomplete and that many students were not required to matriculate.

rounded themselves with talented writers, musicians, and artists, so also the Este created a good medium-rank university. Ferrara's intellectual strengths were humanistic studies and a supportive climate for innovation.

Este rule over the university ended in 1597. When Duke Alfonso II (ruled 1559–97) died without male heirs, Ferrara passed into papal hands, because the Este had ruled as papal vicars. A papal governor arrived, and the Este family moved to Modena. The University of Ferrara remained, no longer the pride of the Este but the fifth university in the papal state.[133]

CATANIA, 1445

Catania, on the eastern shore of Sicily, had been the capital of the Kingdom of Sicily. But when Alfonso I (the Magnanimous) became king of Aragon, Castile, Sardinia, and Sicily in 1416, he made Palermo the capital of Sicily. The idea of compensating Catania for its loss of status with a university emerged in 1434.[134] In addition, Catania and other Sicilian communes had been giving their young men subsidies to study at mainland universities; a local university would make this unnecessary. Commune and king approached the pope for a charter, but nothing happened because Alfonso had further territorial ambitions. When dynastic anarchy weakened the nearby Kingdom of Naples, he conquered it in 1442, entering the city of Naples in triumph in 1443. Alfonso then moved to mend fences with the pope, who had supported the deposed Neapolitan ruler. A mollified Pope Eugenius IV issued a bull authorizing a university at Catania, a small town of 6,000 to 7,000 inhabitants, on April 18, 1444.[135] The University of Catania began in late October 1445 with six professors. It issued its first doctorate (in civil law) to a Sicilian from Siracusa in November 1449.

The initial 6 professors included a theologian, 2 professors for civil law, 1 for canon law, a professor of medicine, and a grammarian.[136] They earned a total of 66 oncie (ounces), a money of account worth 4.5 ducats at that time, hence, 297 ducats.[137] The proceeds from an export tax levied on goods shipped from the port of Catania up to the amount of 1,500 ducats (equal to 333 oncie) were designated for the university. But it never saw more than half that amount in the fifteenth century.[138]

The university remained very small. It had 10 professors in 1485 (1 theologian,

133. It appears that the years 1597–1602 were very lean for the university, but recovery followed. Visconti, 1950, 73–80; *I maestri di Ferrara,* 1991, 49–65.

134. This account is based on Sabbadini, 1975; Catalano-Tirrito, 1975; and Catalano, 1934. Giuffrida (1981, 250–81) adds some interesting financial details. Rashdall (1936, 2:57–58) offers a very brief sketch.

135. For the population, see Ginatempo and Sandri, 1990, 192.

136. This list comes from a financial roll of 1455 which probably duplicated that of 1445. See Catalano, 1934, 24–26, for the surviving rolls.

137. Doc. 60 of July 31, 1445, in Sabbadini, 1975, 60. An ounce equaled 2.5 scudi in the late sixteenth century; Catalano, 1934, 24. Although comparing salaries between universities is difficult, it is clear that Catania's salaries were low.

138. Giuffrida, 1981, 260–64.

3 professors of civil law, 2 for canon law, 1 for medicine, 1 for philosophy, 1 logician, and a humanist), who earned 83 oncie (374 ducats). The faculty expanded to 12 in 1498 with the addition of a second professor of medicine and 1 for surgery, earning 167 oncie (752 ducats). The number and distribution of professors across the disciplines remained about the same through the sixteenth century. Salaries increased after 1540, when a viceroy contributed additional funds on condition that he might have ultimate approval over appointments. In the late sixteenth century, 12 professors earned 1,900 scudi (760 oncie), still low for university salaries across Italy.

The commune of Catania ruled the university, subject to the supreme authority of viceroys who governed Sicily on behalf of the Aragonese kings in the fifteenth century and for Spain after 1504. Viceroys seldom asserted their power but did occasionally confer lifetime appointments on professors. The commune, preferring annual contracts, probably limited such actions through vigorous protests. At first the communal council named the professors; later three Riformatori dello Studio, prominent and sometimes learned local men, in conjunction with the treasurer of the university, made these decisions. At times this small group was expanded to include others, including student representatives. But student participation in electing professors ended by 1522.

The majority of professors were Sicilians, often with degrees from Catania, with non-Sicilians added as needed. Turnover in the ordinary professorships of law and medicine was low. Although professors frequently enjoyed local or Sicilian fame, they did not attract wider attention through their scholarship. The commune required professors of medicine to perform additional duties that nearly transformed them into communal physicians. The morning ordinary professor of medicine had to visit the communally run hospital twice daily, and the professor of surgery was obliged to care for the poor without pay and to examine those desiring licenses in practical surgery.

Enrollment was low. A document of 1460 lamented that the enrollment was only thirty students; hence, the commune asked the monarch for help in appointing additional professors whose presence would attract more students.[139] Because communes issued such appeals at moments of crisis, the figure should not be taken as average. Nevertheless, the total of forty-five known doctoral degrees awarded between 1449 and 1500 also suggests very low enrollments.[140] Hence, it is not likely that enrollment rose above eighty before the end of the century. Although Sicilians were obligated to attend Catania, many continued to go to universities on the mainland.

The University of Catania grew in the following century. A single surviving matriculation document (probably incomplete) of 1579 listed 186 students, of whom 153 studied law. On the basis of these and similar isolated records, the average annual enrollment may have been about 100 in 1500 but rising to more than 300 in the last decades of the sixteenth century. The students were over-

139. Sabbadini, 1975, 85, doc. 119.
140. Catalano-Tirrito, 1975, 40–41. The following enrollment estimate of eighty is mine.

whelmingly Sicilian. The number of graduates rose from about 10 a year early in the sixteenth century to an average of 25 to 50 annually by the end of the century.[141] The town of Catania also grew, to 8,000 to 11,000 in the later fifteenth century, 14,000 in 1500, and 20,000 to 24,000 by the middle of the sixteenth century.[142]

The tiny university did not innovate. Moreover, Catania dropped its humanities professorship. Throughout the fifteenth century and the first half of the sixteenth, the roll included a professor of grammar, sometimes grammar and poetry, as well as a professor of Greek and Latin for the single year 1463–64. Then in 1556 the Jesuits established in Catania a secondary school for the humanities which accepted external (non-Jesuit) students. The viceroy ordered the commune to grant the Jesuit college a subsidy in return for educating some of the boys of the town. The commune opposed the college and only grudgingly paid the subsidy. Then in 1575 the Catania Jesuits offered to introduce the university subjects of theology, philosophy, and logic into the college, asking in turn that the commune increase its subsidy. Deeply divided over the issue, the commune eventually agreed, but the new viceroy, Marc'Antonio Colonna, said no. The Jesuits then asked that they be given some positions in the university. The commune refused, and the viceroy supported the commune. But in 1579 Viceroy Colonna decreed that the university would eliminate its single professorship in the humanities and would appoint no professors of rhetoric, grammar, or humanities in the future, because the Jesuit college would teach these subjects. Thus, the humanistic post disappeared from the university after 1580.[143]

University classes met in a house on the Piazza del Duomo until it was torn down in 1559 in order to create a larger piazza intended to include a university building. Since this project failed to materialize, the university continued to meet in rented quarters and a monastery until it received in 1684 its own building near the church of San Marco. After the earthquake of 1693 destroyed much of Catania, the commune erected a new building in the present Piazza dell'Università, approximately a block from the cathedral. It still serves the university today.

The University of Catania was the most modest of Italian universities. It never expanded beyond a skeleton faculty, nor did it recruit famous scholars. Nevertheless, by the late sixteenth century, it granted a surprisingly large number of degrees to its Sicilian student body.

141. The enrollment estimates for the sixteenth century come from Catalano, 1934, 44, who also extrapolated from the number of degrees granted. For the number of degrees awarded, see also Novarese, 1995, 338.

142. Ginatempo and Sandri, 1990, 179, 183, 192.

143. Catalano, 1934, 26, 88–91; Scaduto, 1974, 354–56; Scaduto, 1992, 238.

CHAPTER 4

The Third Wave

Macerata, Salerno, Messina, and Parma

fter a pause of nearly one hundred years, communes and princes again created universities. Three new universities appeared in the second half of the sixteenth century and another in 1601. Other communes tried and failed to establish universities. Sometimes they got no further than an incomplete or paper university.

MACERATA, 1540–1541

Macerata is a hilltop town above the Potenza River valley on the Adriatic slope of the Apennine Mountains some 65 kilometers south of coastal Ancona. Despite its isolation, Macerata was a regional agricultural center and an administrative hub because the papal legate ruled the Marches from there. Estimates put the population at 4,000 in 1550 and 13,000 to 14,000 in 1600. A census of 1656 counted 8,839, after the plague period of 1630 to 1633.[1] The communal government created a university in a twelve-month period in 1540 and 1541.

Limited earlier pedagogical activity prepared the way. Pope Nicholas IV conferred on Macerata a bull authorizing the establishment of a university in 1290, but nothing happened at that time. In 1518 Pope Leo X authorized the college of legists of Macerata to grant degrees under certain conditions. It had a communal Latin school and may have had the occasional law lecturer. But no university existed in the fourteenth, fifteenth, and early sixteenth centuries.[2]

The commune of Macerata decided to erect one. In 1536 it appointed an

---

1. The 1550 estimate, which may be low, comes from Ginatempo and Sandri, 1990, 148; the estimate for 1600, from Barbieri, 1977, 32; and the figure for 1656, from Cecchi, 1979, 154.

2. Marongiu, 1948, 3–11, and Adversi, 1988, 3–10. These two works are the fundamental studies for the university. *Studium Maceratense 1541 al 1551* (1998) and *Studium Maceratense 1551 al 1579* (1999) publish some of the archival documents, especially conferrals of degrees. Colini-Baldeschi (1900) and Donati (1924, 195 n. 2) also deny the existence of a university before 1540.

Institutes lecturer. From 1534 through 1539 the commune repeatedly petitioned its overlord, the pope, for the right to establish a university. Paul III granted its wish in a bull of July 1, 1540.[3] Unlike most other Italian governments, the papacy did not block the creation of new universities within its state in order to protect an existing *studium*. Hence, Macerata would become the fourth university, after Bologna, Rome, and Perugia, in the papal state. In September 1540 the commune decreed that the grinding tax (the tax imposed on the service of grinding grain into flour) should be quadrupled and that the taxes on wine and meat would be raised. The additional income would fund the university.[4] Throughout the process, the commune of Macerata looked to the University of Bologna as an example to follow. It asked Bologna for a copy of its statutes and apparently obtained a copy of the Bolognese faculty roll of 1536. In September 1541 the commune deputized a commission of four to compile a roster of houses to be made available to students at reasonable rents, another Bolognese practice.

The commune began to hire professors in the fall of 1540 and continued to do so throughout the academic year of 1540–41. Two of the first legists came from the University of Siena. The civilian Alessandro Sozzini (1508–41), the modestly accomplished son of Mariano Sozzini the Younger, the most famous jurist of the day, arrived in Macerata in early 1541 but died on April 28. The other Sienese legist taught for the academic year 1540–41 and then returned to Siena.[5] A few other professors may have joined them in the first year. Not until the academic year 1541–42 did Macerata have a complement of nine teachers covering the core university subjects.

Thus, the original faculty consisted of seven legists and two arts professors. It appears that Fra Bartolomeo taught natural philosophy and logic separately in two daily lectures. Five professors came from Macerata, and a sixth carried the name of a prominent Macerata family. The outsiders were two Sienese legists and an arts professor from Imola, also part of the papal state.

Macerata looked to Siena for faculty, because the republic's troubles made its professors, especially the legists, receptive to overtures. As Florence, France, and Emperor Charles V threatened the independence of a state already weakened by civic strife and economic decline, Macerata moved to lure away some of its professors. The papal legate governing the Marches and residing in Macerata at this moment was a Sienese noble who probably helped persuade some of his countrymen to come. Although the Sienese professors were not so renowned as their counterparts at Padua and Bologna, they did teach at an old university that emphasized law. The Sienese natural philosopher Francesco Piccolomini (1523–

---

3. Foglietti, 1878, 38–51; Marongiu, 1948, 11–12. The bull, *In eminenti dignitatis apostolicae specula,* can be found in ASM.

4. Fresco, 1901, 30–32.

5. Marongiu, 1948, 14, and Minnucci and Košuta, 1989, 505, for Sozzini's death date. For more on the Sozzini dynasty of legists, see Chapter 13. The other Sienese legist was Francesco Cosci, or Coscia (d. 1576). He went to Pisa in 1543. Nardi, 1975, 201–2, 205, 213–15; Minnucci and Košuta, 1989, 500 and index; *Studium Maceratense 1541 al 1551* (1998, 11–12 n. 19) lists the earliest known appointments.

TABLE 4.1
University of Macerata Roll, 1541–1542

Civil law, ordinary A.M.	Girolamo Malavolti of Siena[a]
Civil law, ordinary P.M.	Marcantonio Bellarmati of Siena[b]
Civil law, extraordinary	Giovanni Battista Bracconi of Macerata[c]
Civil law, extraordinary	Francesco Costa of Assisi[d]
Civil law, *Institutes*	Giovanni Pellicani of Macerata
Canon law, ordinary	Camillo Costa of Macerata
Law unspecified	Ottavio Ferri of Macerata
Medicine, logic, or theology[e]	Filippo Teodosi of Imola
Natural philosophy and logic	Fra Bartolomeo of Macerata

Source: Marongiu, 1948, 16–17.

[a]Malavolti (1507–60) studied and taught at Siena before going to Macerata. In 1544 he moved to the University of Pisa, where he taught civil law for the rest of his life. Marongiu, 1948, 70, 71; *Studium Maceratense 1541 al 1551,* 1998, 8 and see index; Minnucci and Košuta, 1989, 394, 406 n, 414, 428, 502; Cascio Pratilli, 1975, 120 n. 5; Barsanti, 1993, 523.

[b]Bellarmati (1500–1544) obtained his degree in civil law at Siena in 1524, was heavily involved in Sienese politics, and taught at Siena possibly before 1535, and certainly from 1535 through 1541, then at Macerata (1541–44). He was called to the University of Pisa but died on February 7, 1544. Bellarmati wrote several legal works, all but one published posthumously. Marongiu, 1948, 69, 71; *Studium Maceratense 1541 al 1551,* 1998, 7–8; Craveri, 1965; Nardi, 1975, 201–3, 205, 209–10; Minnucci and Košuta, 1989, 394, 400, 403, 406, 410, 490, 497, 499, 546.

[c]*Studium Maceratense 1541 al 1551* (1998, 11–12 n. 19) states that Bracconi was appointed to the first ordinary afternoon civil law position in 1540. He also held high civic office.

[d]The students elected Francesco Costa, a fellow student, to lecture; he took his degree in canon and civil law in October 1542. Marongiu, 1948, 21; *Studium Maceratense 1541 al 1551,* 1998, 5, 6, 15–16. Obviously, Macerata was copying the practice of other universities, such as Bologna, by awarding lectureships to students in their last year of study. Although Francesco was listed as "of Assisi," the Costa (including Camillo below) were a prominent Macerata family. Stumpo, 1984, 167; Foglietti, 1878, 99–100.

[e]It is not clear if Teodosi taught medicine, logic, or theology, because the documents suggest all three at various times. Marongiu, 1948, 17, 70; *Studium Maceratense 1541 al 1551,* 1998, 34 nn. 71, 72.

1607) also accepted a Macerata appointment. From the leading Sienese family, Piccolomini took his degree at Siena in 1546 and began teaching there. He taught at Macerata for one year, 1549–50, at Perugia 1550–60, and from 1560 onward at Padua, where he became famous.[6] The Sienese professors helped Macerata in its early years but did not stay long. Macerata relied less on the Sienese pipeline as it became established.

The University of Macerata took root as a small institution. It had 9 to 10 professors (the maximum was 12 and the low 7) in the forty years after 1541.[7] Law dominated: a typical roll of 10 professors had 5 or 6 civilians and 1 canonist. The remaining 3 or 4 arts professors taught logic, natural philosophy, humanistic studies, medicine, and theology. They often taught two subjects, such as natural

6. Baldini, 1980, 390–93. Marongiu (1948, 37, 52) incorrectly states that Piccolomini taught at Macerata for five years. See *CHRP,* 831, for further bibliography.

7. This is based on seventeen complete and partial rolls from 1544–45 through 1580–81 published in Marongiu, 1948, 50–67.

philosophy and logic, or theology and logic. They either lectured twice daily or, more likely, taught one subject the first half of the year and the other in the second half. Medicine, the dominant arts subject in other universities, never had more than one professor and was not taught in some years. The roll of 1544–45 is typical (see table 4.2). As the roll shows, the university now drew its faculty overwhelmingly from Macerata and elsewhere in the Marches (Fermo and Osimo). None of the 1544–45 professors was a prominent scholar.

Over time the distribution of professorships among the disciplines evolved slightly. A single professor of medicine became a regular part of the roll in the mid-1550s. But the rhetoric or humanities position disappeared; the commune may have felt that those desiring humanities instruction could attend the thriving local Jesuit school founded in 1561.[8] By 1580 theology had become a separate professorship, always filled by an Augustinian friar from the local monastery.[9] The creation of the theology position coincided with the growing number of degrees awarded in that subject.

From the early 1580s through the 1620s, the University of Macerata had 7 or 8 legists and 4 artists.[10] The legists consisted of an ordinary morning professor of civil law, an ordinary afternoon professor of civil law (who normally received the highest salary), a canonist, and 3 or 4 professors who taught *Institutes*. Occasionally someone teaching Bartolo's works or legal practice replaced one of the *Institutes* professors.[11] The artists consisted of a theologian, a logician, a natural philosopher, and a professor of medicine.

8. The Society of Jesus had arrived in 1556. A local youth, Matteo Ricci (1552–1610), joined the order. His missionary work in China made him one of the most renowned Jesuits in the history of the order. For the strong Jesuit presence in Macerata, see Scaduto, 1964, 412–13, 426–29; Scaduto, 1974, 392–96; and Scaduto, 1992, 208–12. By 1591–92 the Jesuits received a modest annual subsidy of 400 florins from the commune. ASM, Archivio Priorale, F. 194, f. 101ᵛ (1591–92); F. 195, f. 26ʳ; F. 197, f. 124ʳ, and passim. The commune may have paid the Jesuits for teaching local boys (Jesuit schools were free to the pupils) and for their charitable activities. This was a common arrangement; see Grendler, 1989, 368.

9. It appears that theology and logic began to separate in the 1570s. Then in October or November 1579, Father Domenico Berardelli, O.S.A., "lettore di theologia et logica," died. He was replaced by Father Nicola Massio, O.S.A., who received a four-year contract to teach theology only. ASM, Archivio Priorale, F. 664, Salariati, ff. 23ᵛ–24ʳ, 78ᵛ. Massio taught theology at least through 1589.

10. The following is based on communal financial records, because no rolls for the period after 1581 have been found. The teaching faculty can be reconstructed from the payment records in communal financial ledgers called "Camerlenghi, Introito ed esito." I have sampled these for the period 1579 through 1626: ASM, Archivio Priorale, FF. 191, 192, 194–201, 203, 206, 209, 212, 214, 216–18, and 664. Although the professors (*lettori*) are not always labeled in the records, one can usually identify them among the communal employees if a few names are known. The partial lists of professors in Foglietti, 1878, 116–19, and Adversi, 1988, 36–42, are helpful. One can also find individual appointment notices in the records of the communal council. For example, ASM, Archivio Priorale, F. 97, Riformanze, includes appointment notices, usually contract renewals, at ff. 4ʳ, 5ᵛ, 6ᵛ, 8ʳ, 15ᵛ, and so on for the period 1585–86. F. 99 covers 1589–95.

11. Claudio Giardini was described as "Lettore di Prattica" and "il Prattico" from 1605 through 1610. ASM, Archivio Priorale, Reformanze, F. 200, f. 41ʳ (1605–6); F. 201, f. 41ʳ (1606–7); F. 203, ff. 41ʳ, 130ʳ (1610–11). He became the "Straordinario di Bartolo" in 1613. Ibid., F. 206, f. 45ʳ; F. 209, f. 52ʳ (1615). See also Adversi, 1988, 41. In November 1579 Giovanni Battista Burgi was appointed

TABLE 4.2
University of Macerata Roll, 1544–1545

Civil law, A.M.	Girolamo Malavolti of Siena
	Camillo Costa of Macerata
Civil law, P.M.	Jubenzio Catilina of Velletri
	Francesco Giardini of Macerata
Institutes	Antonio Maria Paolini of Osimo
	Vincenzo Giotto of Fermo
Canon law, A.M.	Giovanni Battista Bracconi of Macerata
	Giovanni Pellicani of Macerata
Theology and logic	Fra Bartolomeo of Macerata
Philosophy and arts	Sebastiano of Montesanto
Latin and Greek Literature	Rodolfo Yracinto

Source: ASM, Archivio Priorale, F. 795, ff. 22ᵛ–23ʳ; also printed in Marongiu, 1948, 66, and *Studium Maceratense 1541 al 1551,* 1998, 47–49.

Note: I have given the names in Italian and have slightly rearranged the list in order to facilitate comparison with the roll of 1541–42.

Macerata was not an expensive university to maintain. The faculty of 11 or 12 professors, plus the beadle and bell ringer, received 10.6 percent of the communal budget (1,623 florins of a total budget of about 15,329 florins) in the calendar year 1606. The grinding tax yielded 3,450 florins that year, more than twice university expenses. Faculty salaries ranged from 494 florins paid to the afternoon ordinary professor of civil law, Ercole Bursatto, to only 30 florins received by a lowly *Institutes* professor. Bursatto was the highest-paid communal employee; he received nearly a hundred more florins than the second-best paid, the first communal physician (of three).[12] In the calendar year 1610 the faculty of twelve professors, plus the beadle and bell ringer, received about 1,725 florins from the communal budget of about 12,691 florins, about 13.6 percent of the total. Faculty salaries ranged from a high of 450 florins (the afternoon ordinary professor of civil law) to a low of about 30 florins (one of the *Institutes* professors).[13]

The best-known professors teaching at Macerata were legists. For example, Sforza degli Oddi (1540–1611) held the first afternoon ordinary professorship of civil law at Macerata (1583–88). A native of Perugia, he obtained his degree there and initially taught at Perugia. After Macerata, Oddi taught at the universities of

---

extraordinary lecturer on Bartolo. ASM, Archivio Priorale, F. 664, Salariati, ff. 13ᵛ–14ʳ. The new professorships on Bartolo and legal actions appeared in other universities as well; see Ch. 13, "Padua and Bologna."

12. ASM, Archivio Priorale, Camerlenghi, F. 200, ff. 35ʳ–44ᵛ, 47ʳ, 59ʳ, 71ʳ (for individual salaries), and 107ᵛ–108ʳ (summary figures). The *primo medico* received 400 florins. The terms *fiorini* and *scudi* are used interchangeably in the documents. But a florin seemed to be worth only 1 lira, rather than the Florentine or Paduan florin worth 3 or 4 lire. On Bursatto (d. 1613), from Mantua, see Foglietti, 1878, 115.

13. ASM, Archivio Priorale, Camerlenghi, F. 203, ff. 130ʳ–132ʳ for the summary figures, ff. 35ʳ–45ᵛ, 48ʳ, 59ʳ, for individual salaries. In the first ten months of 1607, university salaries claimed about 1,438 florins of communal expenses of 12,905 florins, about 11.1 percent. Ibid., F. 201, ff. 121ᵛ–123ᵛ.

Pisa (1588–92), Pavia (1592–97), Perugia (1597–99), Padua (1599–1600), and Parma (1601–11). He wrote several legal and other works.[14]

Despite their small number and general lack of eminence, the arts and medicine professors did boast the occasional scholar of wider reputation. Giovanni Battista Camozzi (1515–81) was born in Asolo in the Veneto, studied medicine and natural philosophy at the University of Bologna, and taught rhetoric there for one year, 1549–50. Expert in Greek, he edited a Greek edition in six volumes of Aristotle's *opera omnia* (which included some Greek commentaries by others) published by the Aldine Press in Venice between 1551 and 1553. Camozzi also edited Latin translations of Aristotle and some of the ancient Greek commentators on Aristotle. Finally, he wrote his own commentaries on Aristotle. Camozzi became professor of humanities and Greek at Macerata in 1554 and professor of natural philosophy later, remaining until 1564. Pope Pius IV then called him to Rome to undertake the translation of a corpus of Greek patristic writings, but only a partial translation of Theodoret ever appeared. Camozzi also taught rhetoric at the University of Rome between 1574 and 1580.[15]

Members of the Society of Jesus taught at the University of Macerata for two short periods. Between 1561 and 1563, Giovanni Domenico Fiorenzo (b. c. 1539; left the Jesuits in 1564) taught rhetoric, that is, the pseudo-Ciceronian *Rhetorica ad Herennium* the first year and Aristotle's *Rhetoric* the second year. Giovanni Catalano (birth name Blet; b. c. 1523; d. after 1564) taught Greek, that is, Demosthenes' *On the Crown,* in 1561–62 and an unknown text in 1562–63. Some members of the city council objected to the appointments, arguing that the Jesuits should stick to "divine duties" instead of teaching at the university. Indeed, the Jesuits did not appear in the next extant roll, that of 1564–65.[16] A Jesuit reappeared as a professor of logic in 1613. From that date through 1625, four different Jesuits held the logic professorship. The position's modest salary went to the Society's college in Macerata.[17]

The overwhelming majority of Macerata's students came from the Marches. The expected recruitment area for students was so limited that Macerata defined

14. See Foglietti, 1878, 111–12, and Cascio Pratilli, 1975, 168 n. 32, for a brief biography.

15. Marongiu, 1948, 37, 53, 54, 55, 56; Schreiner, 1974; Schmitt, 1983c, 37, 39, 138. The six-volume Greek Aristotle edition, sometimes called the *Aldina minor,* is described in Kallendorf and Wells, 1998, items 340–45. For Camozzi's Roman appointment, see *I maestri di Roma,* 1991, 89, 101, 111, 116.

16. Marongiu, 1948, 39, 58, 59. Jesuit sources offer more complete identifications, confirm that they taught at the university, and indicate the texts taught. See Scaduto, 1968, 16, 29, 57, and Scaduto, 1974, 394–95, 399 n. 17. This was only the second appearance of Jesuits in Italian university faculties. The first was in Rome, 1537–39; see Chapter 10, "Universities Teaching Theology Continuously."

17. The initial appointee was Father Livio Donati, S.J., in November 1613. He succeeded Fra Sebastiano d'Ancona, not further identified, who had filled the logic post for about fifteen years. ASM, Archivio Priorale, Camerlenghi, F. 206, f. 44ʳ. See also ibid., F. 209, 53ᵛ; F. 212, f. 46ʳ; F. 214, f. 44ʳ, F. 216, 44ᵛ. The last reference to a Jesuit logician is found in F. 217, f. 45ʳ: Father Antonio Ceccardi was paid for lecturing in logic for the first four months of 1625. He had no successor. Since the financial records for 1626 do not list a logician, the logic professorship may have been abolished at this time. Ibid., F. 218, f. 45ʳ.

nations, the traditional organizations of students from different regions of Europe and Italy found in larger universities, as students from different parts of the Marches. Macerata had 178 law students in 1574. Eighty-five were described as coming from the Marches without further qualification. Fifty-three came from "beyond the Chienti River," a river that paralleled the Potenza River some 10 to 12 miles south of Macerata. In other words, they came from the southern part of the Marches. Twenty students came from "outside the Potenza River," presumably north of the Potenza River, which flowed past Macerata in the valley below. Thus, they came from the northern part of the Marches. Twelve students came from "between the Chienti and Potenza rivers," that is, the villages and castles around Macerata. Finally, eight students came from outside the Marches. It appears that 170 of the 178 law students came from areas within a 50-mile (80-kilometer) radius of Macerata.[18]

These figures make possible an estimate of the size of the total student body in 1574. Students from the host town traditionally did not belong to a student nation. Hence, if one adds an estimated 15 law students from Macerata, and an estimated arts enrollment of 30 students from everywhere, to the 178 law students noted above, Macerata's total enrollment in 1574 might have been 223, an appropriate number for 10 or 11 professors.[19] (Macerata had not yet awarded any theology doctorates, suggesting that the university had no theology students at this time.) Since the number of degrees awarded climbed in the last twenty years of the century, the student body may have expanded as well.

The University of Macerata awarded its first doctorate (in civil law) in November 1541 and its second (*in utroque iure*) in April 1542. This small university awarded many more degrees in the next sixty years.

Like other universities, Macerata awarded an increasing number of doctorates in the late sixteenth century. By the 1580s, it conferred an annual average of 28 doctorates (18 in law, 3 in arts, and 7 in theology), a large number for a small regional university. The modest number of arts and medicine degrees reflected the limited number of professors in these subjects. About 13.6 percent of the law doctorates went to natives of Macerata.[20]

Although the university was founded for the purpose of educating men from the Marches, a handful of Germans, Spaniards, Frenchmen, and one Pole obtained degrees from Macerata in the sixteenth century.[21] Possibly the best-known law graduate was the Frenchman Marc'Antoine Muret (1526–85), who obtained a law degree *in utroque iure* on March 29, 1572. Muret, who had been teaching

18. Marongiu, 1948, 47–48. Any detailed map of the Marches makes the written descriptions clear.

19. My estimates for the number of law students from Macerata and the total number of arts students are roughly proportional to the law graduates from Macerata and the arts degrees noted in table 4.3. Puccini (1988, 87) estimates the size of the student body as 150 to 200 students in the late sixteenth and early seventeenth centuries.

20. Foglietti, 1878, 129–30; Marongiu, 1948, 46 n. 1. It is not known if this percentage of native-son graduates was typical for Italian universities.

21. Foglietti, 1878, 91.

TABLE 4.3
Doctoral Degrees Awarded at the University of Macerata, 1541–1600

Years	Law	Arts	Theology	Total
1541–50	28	3		31
1551–60	60	5		65
1561–70	86	8		94
1571–80	136	6	13[a]	155
1581–90	184	29	63	276
1591–1600	173	17	72	262
Total	667	68	148	887

Source: The 1541–50 figures come from Marongiu, 1948, 45; the rest come from Foglietti, 1878, 129–30, based on ASM, Archivio Priorale, Collegio di Dottori, FF. 795, 796, and 797, which list degrees. I have not redone Foglietti's work, because I have found him to be very reliable in areas that I have checked. Studium Maceratense 1541 al 1551, 1998, and Studium Maceratense 1551 al 1579, 1999, publish the contents of filze 795 and 796.
[a]The first theology doctorate was awarded in July 1577. Studium Maceratense 1551 al 1579, 1999, 299–300.

humanities and law at the University of Rome since 1563, had no previous degrees.[22]

The relatively large number of theology doctorates awarded is striking, because Macerata never had more than a single theologian. However, several mendicant orders, including all three Franciscan communities (the Conventual Franciscans, the Friars Minor, and the Capuchins), plus the Discalced Augustinians, had houses of study there. These monastic studia and the Jesuit college must have provided most of the theological instruction, while the university, with its papal charter, conferred the degrees in association with the local faculty of theology.[23]

Young men from the Marches seeking regional administrative posts and positions in the larger papal state attended the University of Macerata. Such a man was Cesare Costa (1530–1602). From a noble family of Macerata, Costa began to study law at the local university at nineteen. In 1549 he and nine other students offered to pay the rent and supply the furnishings for a house large enough for a Sienese professor, his family, and four boarding students, if the professor would come to Macerata. He did, but he returned to Siena after one academic year (1549–50).[24]

In July 1554, Costa received his law degree in utroque iure at Macerata and was immediately appointed to teach Institutes. By 1559 Costa was teaching civil law at the University of Rome, where he rose to first ordinary morning professor in

22. ASM, Archivio Priorale, F. 796, Collegio di dottori, f. 110ᵛ; now printed in Studium Maceratense 1551 al 1579, 1999, 224–25. The Macerata doctorate has escaped notice until now. For more on Muret and his degree, see Chapter 5, "The Cost of Degrees," and Chapter 13, "Pavia and Rome."
23. Masetti Zannini, 1977, 282; Paci, 1977, 295 and n. 43.
24. Marongiu, 1948, 15, 33. Stumpo (1984, 167) gives the date of the offer as 1550. The professor was Ludovico Borghesi (1494–1551); see Minnucci and Košuta, 1989, 498 and index; Nardi, 1975, 201, 205, 206–7; and Studium Maceratense 1541 al 1551, 1998, 194–95 n. 260..

1563. He then took a legal position in the papal curia. Most important, Pius IV entrusted Costa with overseeing the correction and editing of Gratian's *Decretum*, which task eventually became the publication of an improved edition of the entire *Corpus juris canonici* between 1582 and 1584. Costa also wrote a legal work, took orders, became bishop of Capua in 1572, and served the papacy in various capacities, including nuncio to Venice from 1585 to 1587.[25] Costa's legal training at a provincial university prepared him for a much larger career in the church, scholarship, and diplomacy.

The commune of Macerata created a new university in an isolated area of mountainous north central Italy. The leaders of the commune knew exactly what they wanted: a small law university that would train students from the Marches for governmental and legal careers. The city council made strenuous and largely successful efforts to recruit some of its first legists from a vulnerable university, Siena. Macerata's highest salaries did not equal the stipends that Bologna, Padua, and Pavia offered to legal stars, but they were enough to attract competent legists from lesser universities and scholars on their way to more prestigious posts.[26] Native sons from prominent local families and men from other towns in the Marches filled the rest of the professorships and earned less. Thus, Macerata followed the practice of Bologna and several other universities in faculty recruitment. Despite small size and skeletal arts faculty, Macerata produced a large quantity of graduates. The university fulfilled its founders' expectations and made Macerata into the intellectual center of the Marches.

The University of Macerata closed its doors only once in its long life, in the years 1805–16, during the Napoleonic era. It thrives today as a small university that still concentrates on law.[27]

SALERNO, C. 1592

Salerno had an early medieval medical school that failed to become a university in the thirteenth and fourteenth centuries. It did reach that goal at the end of the sixteenth century.

The School of Salerno, as it is commonly called, pioneered medieval medical pedagogy.[28] The physicians of Salerno had access to Greek and Arabic medical texts in Latin translation which they taught to others. The result was the devel-

25. *I maestri di Roma,* 1991, 28, 32, 34, rolls of 1559, 1561, and 1563. Other rolls are missing. The rest of this paragraph is based on Pastor, 1891–1953, 19:279–80; Marongiu, 1948, 15, 33; Stumpo, 1984; and *Studium Maceratense 1551 al 1579,* 1999, 49–50.

26. For example, Bartolomeo Carandini di Modena (c. 1566–1612) was appointed first ordinary afternoon professor of civil law in 1600 at 300 florins. In 1603 he agreed to a five-year contract at 400 florins, but he left for the University of Pavia in 1604. Donati, 1924, 193–99.

27. Macerata had many more professors of law than professors of letters and sciences when I visited in 1996.

28. The fundamental works are De Renzi, 1852–59, especially volume 1 with its history; and Kristeller, 1956b, who masterfully separates fact from myth. Additional bibliography on the medieval School of Salerno is not relevant here.

opment of a corpus of medical texts for pedagogical use and Europe's first medical school.

Salerno began to develop a university structure. It conferred degrees in the thirteenth century and had communally paid professors of medicine in the fourteenth century. But this happened just as the University of Naples expanded in the later thirteenth century. The Neapolitan rulers immediately barred all other higher instruction in the Kingdom of Naples with the exception of medicine at Salerno and reiterated the injunction many times through 1490.[29] Barred from expanding into a complete university, the School of Salerno declined to the extent that organized medical instruction may have disappeared completely in the fourteenth century and much of the fifteenth.[30]

An academic revival began in the last quarter of the fifteenth century. It coincided with the arrival of members of the Sanseverino family as rulers of Salerno. In 1463 King Ferrante I of Naples rewarded the mercenary captain Roberto Sanseverino (d. 1487) for his support by making him prince of Salerno. He and his successors were probably the wealthiest and most powerful nobles in the Kingdom of Naples after the king himself, and they supported learning to a limited extent.[31] Salerno also enjoyed a period of economic prosperity at this time. In these favorable circumstances a College of Physicians existed by 1473, the year that Salerno awarded its first extant doctoral diploma. In 1483–84, the commune appropriated 140 Aragonese ducats for the expenses of the *"studio,"* enough to support two to four professors at very low salaries, if they were appointed.[32]

Another prince of Salerno, Roberto II Sanseverino (d. 1508), brought the well-published and much-traveled Agostino Nifo (born in Sessa Aurunca just north of Naples in 1469/70; d. 1538) to teach natural philosophy and possibly medicine at Salerno in 1507. Nothing is known of his teaching, and he may have been more a learned courtier than a professor. He left in 1508.[33] When the next prince of Salerno, Ferrante (or Ferdinando; 1507–68), son of Roberto II, came of age, he also supported scholars.[34] He brought back Nifo to teach natural philosophy, and perhaps medicine, probably in 1522. Nifo was made prior and perpetual promoter of the Salerno College of Medicine. In January 1525 he conferred two doctorates: one in his capacity as prior of the College of Medicine and the other as count palatine, which honor Pope Leo X had bestowed on him in 1520. The

29. Monti, 1924, 23–24; Cortese, 1924, 164–65; Kristeller, 1956b, 541.

30. Kristeller (1956b, 548) refers to "the complete decay of the late fourteenth and of the fifteenth centuries." I have been unable to find any references, substantiated or otherwise, placing a professor at a University of Salerno in the fifteenth century beyond the very vague comments of De Renzi (1852–59, 1:371–73, 376–78).

31. There is no monograph on the princes of Salerno. Hence, their history has been pieced together from a variety of sources.

32. De Renzi, 1852–59, 1:402.

33. Cassese, 1958, 3. For brief summaries of Nifo's works and career, for which not all the dates are secure, see Lohr, 1979, 532–39; and *CHRP,* 828.

34. Antonaci, 1971–78, 2:12–16.

prince of Salerno, in turn, gave Nifo a lifetime pension in September 1525.[35]
Nifo probably remained in Salerno until 1531; after spending the academic year
1531–32 teaching at the University of Naples, he taught at Salerno again from
1532 to 1535.

Two other well-known scholars also came to Salerno, probably when Nifo was
not there. Marc'Antonio Zimara (c. 1475–1532) from Galatina (Lecce) taught
natural philosophy and theoretical medicine at Salerno from 1518 or 1519 to
1522.[36] The logician Girolamo Balduino (b. early sixteenth century; d. before
1553) from Puglia taught at Salerno for a brief period between 1529 and the early
1530s.[37]

These scholars followed similar career paths. All came from southern Italy, and
all studied and taught at Padua. They passed the bulk of their professional lives
elsewhere but came to Salerno when war closed the university at which they
were teaching. Finally, they were important scholars teaching university subjects.
As a result contemporaries used the term *studium* to describe the learned activity
at Salerno. For example, seven men who obtained doctorates from the University
of Ferrara between 1531 and 1551 stated that they had previously studied at the
Salerno *studium*.[38]

The patronage of the princes of Salerno came to an end. In 1547 Ferrante
Sanseverino allegedly participated in a rebellion against Spanish rule over the
Kingdom of Naples. The viceroy declared him a rebel, canceled the title "prince
of Salerno," and confiscated his properties. Ferrante became an exile who joined
the French forces against Charles V in 1552. He eventually moved to France,
where he became a Huguenot.

All the same, a limited amount of university-level teaching continued at
Salerno. Francesco Storella (1524/25–75) from Alessano (Lecce) taught logic and
natural philosophy at Salerno from 1555 or 1557 to 1558 and then moved to the
University of Naples.[39] Salerno also had some law instruction. The legist Giovanni Bolognetti of Bologna (1506–75) taught in the years 1540–43 and possibly
1562–64.[40] Alberto Bolognetti, also of Bologna (1538–85, no relation to Giovanni Bolognetti), received his doctorate at Bologna in 1562 and taught *Institutes*
there from 1562 to 1564. He then taught at Salerno from 1565 until 1574, during
which time he published two large legal works. He moved to Rome in 1574,
where he embarked on a papal diplomatic career and eventually received the cardinal's hat.[41] Angelo Spannochi (or Agnolo Spannocchi) of Siena (c. 1538–1614)
taught law at Siena (1568–70), then civil law at Salerno (1570–85), before mov-

35. Cassese, 1958, 16.

36. Lohr, 1982, 245–54; *CHRP,* 841.

37. Papuli, 1967, 60–67.

38. Three obtained doctorates in arts and medicine, four in both laws. So far as can be determined, they all came from southern Italy. Pardi, 1970, 121, 137, 139, 143, 155, 161.

39. Antonaci, 1966, 181–84; Lohr, 1982, 176–77.

40. Craveri, 1969.

41. Stella, 1964a, 17–18, 42–43, and passim; De Caro, 1969, 313. Alberto Bolognetti served as
papal nuncio to Tuscany, Venice, and Poland and became a cardinal in 1583.

TABLE 4.4
University of Salerno Roll, 1592

Civil law, A.M.	Giovan Jacobo Corbellese
Civil law, P.M.	Giovan Lorenzo De Ruggiero[a]
Civil law (Gloss)[b]	Giovanni Salato
Canon law	Vincenzo Quaranta
First lecturer in medicine	Metello Grillo[c]
Medicine	Francesco Alfano[d]
Logic (teaching the *Posterior Analytics* of Aristotle)	Orazio Gattola[e]
Logic	Giovan Battista Sarluca
Natural philosophy	Francesco Farao

Source: De Renzi, 1852–59, 1:403.

Note: I have slightly rearranged and expanded the descriptions of the professorships for the sake of clarity.

[a]Several members of the De Ruggiero family of Salerno were known as legists and physicians in the sixteenth century, but Giovan Lorenzo has not been identified. De Renzi, 1852–59, 1:406–7; Kristeller, 1956b, 549.

[b]De Renzi called Salato a *"glosista,"* a professor who taught "Text, Gloss, and Bartolo," sometimes shortened to "Gloss." The glossist was expected to teach the text of the *Corpus juris civilis,* the thirteenth-century gloss of Accursius, and Bartolo's commentary on the *Corpus.* He was to ignore the commentaries of fifteenth- and sixteenth-century legists. See Chapter 13, "Padua and Bologna."

[c]Metello Grillo was prior of the college of physicians in 1592. De Renzi, 1852–59, 1:403.

[d]Francesco Alfano was prior of the medical college in the 1580s and published a medical treatise in 1577. De Renzi, 1852–59, 1:389, 404–5; Kristeller, 1956b, 549; Nicolini, 1966, 597.

[e]A Salerno funeral monument of 1615 in honor of Orazio Gattola and another member of the Gattola family called him a physician. De Renzi, 1852–59, 1:409.

ing to Bologna, where he taught for the rest of his life.[42] The Sienese Girolamo Cerretani taught at Siena (1581–82) and then became ordinary professor of civil law at Salerno (1582–87), before returning to Siena to teach canon law from 1587 until 1602.[43] Pietro Soacio taught canon law at Pisa (1585–88) and then taught at Salerno for two years (1588–90) before moving to the University of Siena.[44] And at least one legist declined an offer from Salerno. Girolamo Benvoglienti of Siena (1520–1605), who taught at Rome and Siena through 1563, received an offer from Salerno in 1564 but remained at Siena when his salary was raised.[45] The communal government of Salerno probably paid these professorial salaries.

Thus, Salerno had a limited amount of university-level teaching in arts, medicine, and law a good part of the sixteenth century. But it is not known if other scholars flanked Nifo, Zimara, Bolognetti, and the others or how many other professors the prince of Salerno and, later, the commune of Salerno may have supported. Above all, it is not known if one or two distinguished outsiders were the nucleus of a small university primarily staffed by local scholars who have

42. Costa, 1903–4, 249–52. The Bolognese had some misgivings about Spannochi's modest achievements but appointed him because they were having difficulty filling the post. See also Dallari, 1888–1924, 2:220 and passim; Kristeller, 1956b, 548; and Cascio Pratilli, 1975, 28 and n. 23.

43. Cascio Pratilli, 1975, 75.

44. Ibid., 150 n. 51; Barsanti, 1993, 534.

45. Morandi, 1966, 703.

escaped notice. Until evidence for six to eight scholars simultaneously teaching the core university subjects is located, the answer has to be that Salerno had an incomplete university of one, two, or three teaching professors.

If the commune of Salerno was working toward a complete university, it achieved its goal by the end of the century. The first and only known roll for the University of Salerno is that of 1592, presumably for the academic year 1592–93. At that time Salerno had four legists and five professors of arts and medicine.

In contrast to the University of Macerata, which concentrated on law, Salerno achieved a balance that favored arts and medicine. The University of Salerno continued into the seventeenth century. In 1603 the communal government appropriated 729 Aragonese ducats (466 for the legists and 263 for professors of arts and medicine) for university salaries, probably enough to maintain a university of nine or ten professors on modest salaries.[46] The University of Salerno continued until the Napoleonic governor of southern Italy suppressed it in 1812.

Salerno began to move toward a complete university in the early sixteenth century with the appointment of a distinguished professor of natural philosophy or medicine or both), usually a southerner who had studied and taught in northern Italy. It added a legist or two in the third quarter of the century. Salerno achieved a teaching and degree-granting university with a core faculty of nine in 1592. The town of 6,000 to 7,000 souls (in 1532) could easily find housing for the 100 to 200 students who would attend a small university.[47]

MESSINA, 1596

The commune of Messina had begun its efforts to establish a university 160 years earlier. In 1434 Pope Eugenius IV granted to King Alfonso I (the Magnanimous) of Aragon, king of Naples and Sicily, a charter authorizing a Sicilian university.[48] Both Catania and Messina immediately applied to the king for permission to establish a university. But Catania won the king's favor and formed a university in 1445. Undaunted, Messina obtained a second university charter from King John I of Aragon (Spain) in 1459. Nothing came of this or later fifteenth-century attempts to establish a university at Messina.[49] Catania remained the only institution in Sicily authorized to award degrees.

When the Society of Jesus established its first European school in Messina in 1548, the communal government saw this as an opportunity to create a university.[50] The Jesuits also wanted a university. Hence, the Society obtained a papal

---

46. De Renzi, 1852–59, 1:403. Nevertheless, this was not a great deal of money for a university.

47. Ginatempo and Sandri, 1990, 190, for the population.

48. Even though the king of Naples ruled both the Neapolitan kingdom and Sicily at this time, the two were different political units and separated by water. This may explain why Neapolitan kings blocked a university at Salerno on the mainland, 80 kilometers south of Naples, but permitted a university in Sicily. Neapolitan views did not matter after Spain took control of Sicily in 1479.

49. Cesca, 1900, 6. The two privileges plus the bull of Pope Paul III of 1548 (mentioned in the next paragraph) are printed in Tropea, 1900, 85–92.

50. For the story of the University of Messina, start with Cesca, 1900. Tropeo (1900) and

bull (November 16, 1548, executed on February 12, 1549) authorizing a *studium generale* with the right to grant degrees in all fields. Moreover, the bull explicitly rejected Catania's claim to be the only institution in Sicily empowered to grant doctorates. The Jesuits and the commune of Messina agreed in 1549 that the university would have two parts. The commune would appoint and pay the salaries of professors of law and medicine. The Jesuits would provide the professors (the number varied in the negotiations) to teach philosophy, theology, humanities, and possibly mathematics, with salaries to be paid by the commune. All that remained was to settle details over the structure and finances.

But agreement did not come. The commune of Messina quickly issued statutes (June 1550) giving it authority over all appointments, including the Jesuit arts professors, and complete governance of the university. The Jesuits insisted on control over their half of the university. The statutes of 1550 and subsequent negotiations demonstrated that commune and Society had fundamentally different conceptions of a university.[51] The commune wanted an Italian-style university, modeled on Bologna, which would focus on law and medicine, to be ruled by the city. The Jesuits seemed to have in mind a collegiate university, such as Paris or Salamanca, which had as its center a residence college. There a group of clergymen would teach and guide spiritually students of arts, philosophy, and theology.

Another issue was money: How much would the commune pay the Society for its teaching in the university? The commune offered various sums over the years, but never enough, in the view of the Jesuits.[52] Nor could the Jesuits compromise much on the money. Although the commune provided a subsidy to the Jesuit preuniversity school in Messina, which offered free education to boys, the Messina Jesuits had other needs. Money from university teaching would help support the whole Jesuit establishment and apostolate in Messina, which included church, school, living quarters, preaching, catechetical instruction, and ministries to various groups in society.[53]

Romano (1900) print valuable documents. Scaduto (1948) added new material from the Archivum Romanum Societatis Iesu, and Romano (1992) reviewed the Jesuit part of the story. Moschea (1991b) and especially Novarese (1994) now provide the most comprehensive analyses and much new documentation. My account is based on all, but especially Moschea and Novarese.

51. Moschea (1991b, 92) and Novarese (1994, 78–79) make this point.

52. For the financial negotiations between commune and Jesuits, see Scaduto, 1948. Different ways of judging the value of professors kept them apart. When the sums offered by the commune to the Society were divided by the number of Jesuit professors who would teach, the average salary was quite modest and not commensurate with the services to be provided and the abilities of the Jesuit teachers, in the view of the Jesuits. Indeed, several of the Jesuits who taught at the Jesuit school at Messina were learned scholars. However, the commune probably intended to pay large salaries to one to three star professors (probably outsiders) in law and medicine and modest to very low salaries to the rest, who would be local men happy with the honor of teaching at the university. The commune probably saw Jesuits who would teach the less important arts subjects in the same way.

53. For a brief summary of Jesuit activity in Messina, see Scaduto, 1964, 68, 71, 248 n. 9, 375, 391, and Scaduto, 1974, 356–61, 441, 542, 608, 638, 732.

Most important, Catania opposed the proposed university at Messina with every weapon at its disposal, including threatened retaliation against the Jesuits, who had a preuniversity school in Catania.[54] The viceroy, ruler of Sicily for the Spanish crown, issued an ambiguous ruling. In April 1550 he accepted the papal bull and ruled that Messina might appoint professors, so long as the rights of both parties (Messina and Catania) were respected.[55] The practical effect was that Catania had to be mollified. But Catania refused to share with Messina the right to grant degrees of higher education in Sicily, and the Spanish crown did not force Catania to give way. The practical result was that Messina might appoint professors to teach, but it could not award degrees.

With this setback, negotiations between Messina and the Society of Jesus petered out.[56] The Jesuits went their own way, adding to their preuniversity school a little higher instruction in philosophy, theology, and mathematics. But the commune kept working toward a university. It promulgated new university statutes in 1565 and funded a limited amount of higher education in the 1560s, 1570s, and 1580s. The names of 17 teaching scholars (8 in law, 5 in medicine, 1 for natural philosophy and metaphysics, and 1 each in mathematics, metaphysics, and theology) have been located for those years.[57]

The legist Giovanni Bolognetti, previously mentioned, may have been the best known. Born in Bologna, he took his law degree *in utroque iure* there in 1533 and taught at Bologna from 1533 to 1540, Salerno from 1540 to 1543, Naples from 1543 to possibly 1562, Salerno probably from 1562 to 1564, then Messina from 1564 until 1571 or 1572. According to a contemporary account, he began with very few students but had two hundred by October 1570. He moved to the University of Pavia in 1572. Bolognetti produced six folio volumes of commentaries and another of *consilia* (advisory opinions on cases undertaken by others).[58]

The commune also paid the Jesuits to teach a limited amount of philosophy, theology, and cases of conscience in the 1570s but then abruptly gave that charge to the local monastery of Dominicans from 1578 to 1592.[59] Overall, it does not seem likely that Messina ever had enough professors (six to eight teaching simul-

---

54. On the Jesuit school in Catania, see Scaduto, 1974, 354–56.

55. In his letters on the matter, the viceroy approved the papal bull but with a qualifying legal clause: "salvis juribus utriusque partis coram delegatis" (with the rights of both parties remaining intact in the presence of the delegates). I am grateful to Erika Rummel for the translation. I do not know the source of the clause; perhaps it comes from the *Corpus juris civilis*. See Moschea, 1991b, 107, 201–2 (doc.); Novarese, 1994, 70–71, 367–68 (doc.).

56. Although they would have liked to have a university in Messina, the Jesuits did not see it as essential. The Society had other avenues for awarding and obtaining degrees. In 1552 Pope Julius III granted to the Society the right to award doctoral degrees in philosophy and theology to graduates of their own schools who passed rigorous examinations. Other popes confirmed this in 1556, 1562, 1567, and 1571. Cesca, 1900, 15.

57. Novarese, 1994, 127–35.

58. Craveri, 1969; Novarese, 1994, 92 n. 35, 130–31.

59. Novarese, 1994, 121–24.

taneously) to constitute a university. Nor could Messina award degrees. Some students initially studied at Messina but then went elsewhere for degrees.

The commune of Messina finally won the right to award degrees through bribery and legal action. In 1590 it made a "free donation" to the Spanish monarchy of 500,000 scudi (200,000 oncie, or ounces). In return, the crown in 1591 authorized Messina to establish a university and to confer doctorates.[60] The commune was permitted to levy a tax on wheat and flour entering the city in order to pay the costs. In 1593 Messina obtained a papal ruling authorizing the erection of a university without the Jesuits, thus altering the papal bull of 1548. And in April 1596 Messina defeated a legal challenge from Catania brought before the Spanish crown. The way was clear for a university.

Messina announced the opening of its university on December 15, 1596. The ceremony was held on December 22, with the inaugural lecture delivered on December 23 in the church of San Domenico. Classes met in the Dominican convent through June 1598.[61] The commune proclaimed statutes for the new university in March 1597. They listed thirteen or fourteen professorships, with assigned salaries for the majority. For law, the statutes created five positions: first and second positions in civil law, one position in *Libri feudorum* (feudal law), one for *Institutes*, and one for canon law. The faculty of arts and medicine included a professor of theology, a professor of medical theory, another for practical medicine, one for medical botany, one or two natural philosophers, one logician, one metaphysician, and either a professor of anatomy and surgery or one for the humanities (*humanità*).[62]

Rolls do not survive, but some of the professors who taught in the first three decades have been identified.[63] Giacomo Gallo (1544–1618) was the most reputed and best-paid legist. A native of Naples, Gallo received his doctorate of law from Naples in 1563 and immediately began to teach civil law there, becoming in time the highest-paid member of the law school. He resigned his Neapolitan professorship in 1591 in order to practice law in Rome. Gallo successfully argued before a papal tribunal Messina's case that the papal bull of 1548 could support a university without the Jesuits. The grateful commune appointed him first professor of civil law at the very high salary of 1,150 scudi in 1596. Gallo taught at Messina until 1602, when he was again sent to Rome to argue a case for the city. Gallo won the case, but while in Rome he accepted an appointment to the University of Padua. The angry commune moved to confiscate his property but

60. Ibid., 105–06.

61. Ibid., 125.

62. The statutes are printed in Romano, 1900, 158–76; see 169–70 for two lists of professorships that differ slightly. The first lists thirteen professors including the humanist, the second fourteen with many salary figures. The latter list omits the humanist but adds a second natural philosopher and an anatomist/surgeon. The statutes are unusual in that they listed the positions in detail and because they were written in Italian rather than in Latin. They are the earliest Italian university statutes written in the vernacular known to me.

63. Earthquakes, fires, and the bombardment of the municipal archive in 1848 have destroyed university records. Cesca, 1900, 31 n. 1. But see Romano, 1900, 170, and Novarese, 1994, 213–23, 230–35, 499–564, who have identified many professors from other documents.

then let him go without retribution. Like other minor universities, Messina could not hold an ambitious legal star. Gallo died in Padua in 1618.[64]

The initial professor of canon law was Ottavio Gloriozo (1536–1623), a Calabrian who obtained his degree, practiced law, and taught privately, always in Naples, until called to Messina. Like Gallo, Gloriozo defended Messina in various legal cases; unlike Gallo, he taught there for the rest of his life.[65] The first natural philosopher was Antonino Mazzapinta. Bartolomeo Castelli of Messina, a professor of medicine, delivered the inaugural lecture in 1596.[66] The best-known medical scholar to teach at Messina in these years was Giovanni Battista Cortesi of Bologna (1553/54–1633/34). A poor man who worked initially as a barber-surgeon, Cortesi acquired a medical degree from the University of Bologna in 1583, taught there until 1599, and then moved to Messina, where he taught anatomy, practical medicine, and medical botany. He was known for his expertise in plastic surgery and for his numerous publications. He complained about a lack of cadavers to dissect, perhaps a sign of the university's limitations.[67] And Messina had a professor of Greek from 1599 onward.[68]

No matriculation records or estimates of the number of students are available for the first years. However, as a result of another dispute with the University of Catania, the Spanish crown ordered the University of Messina to force all students to matriculate annually. Thus, Messina had reliable matriculation records for a few later years.

Thus, Messina had a university of 13 or 14 professors who taught 400 to 450 students. With about 60,000 inhabitants in 1600, the city could easily support this number of students.[69] Sixty-eight percent of the students came from Messina and its province, 29 percent came from the rest of Sicily, and 3 percent came from elsewhere, notably Malta, in the years 1634 to 1638.

The University of Messina continued in the seventeenth century as a small university with a group of professors who produced considerable traditional scholarship.[70] There were two exceptions. Giovanni Alfonso Borelli (1608–79), known for his research in mathematics, astronomy, and iatromechanics (the use of anatomy and mechanics in order to describe physical motions of the body), taught mathematics at the University of Messina from about 1635 to 1656. He returned for the years 1667–72 but may not have taught at that time.[71] Another major exception was Marcello Malpighi (1628–94), pioneering microscopic and comparative anatomist. Italy's most distinguished medical scholar of the century

64. Buscemi, 1900, 59–62. For his Neapolitan career, see Cannavale, 1980, 71–76, 82, and Cortese, 1924, 318. For his Paduan career, see Facciolati, 1978, pt. 3, 136.

65. Buscemi, 1900, 62–64.

66. De Ferrari, 1978b. Castelli published in 1597 an elementary medical textbook that went into several editions, plus two other works. His birth and death dates are unknown.

67. De Ferrari, 1983b; Novarese, 1994, index.

68. Moschea, 1991b, 122 n. 67; Novarese, 1994, 233, 503–7, 520–23.

69. Ginatempo and Sandri, 1990, 181.

70. For the list of the professors at Messina in the years 1636–74, see Arenaprimo di Montechiaro, 1900. For a discussion of their writings in all fields, see Dollo, 1984, esp. chs. 4–6.

71. Baldini, 1970, and Settle, 1981.

TABLE 4.5
Matriculation at the University of Messina, 1634–1638

Year	Law	Medicine and Surgery	Philosophy	Theology	Total
1634–35	338	14	75	8	435
1635–36	342	23	62	21	448
1636–37	297	32	75	20	424
1637–38	291	30	42	17	380
Percentage of total:	75	6	15	4	

Source: Moschea, 1991b, 155–66, esp. 160–61.
Note: Students had to renew their matriculation annually. If they matriculated only once in their university careers, Messina would have had annual enrollments of 1,500 to 2,000 students, because students needed about five years of study before taking degrees. But such high enrollments were not possible at a provincial university. Although additional matriculation data are available for the academic years 1638–39 through 1643–44, the number dropped to 159 in 1638–39, then 158, 125, 152, 94, and only 58 in 1643–44. Obviously, matriculation was no longer rigorously enforced. Indeed, the decline in matriculations began in 1637–38.

and Europe's premier anatomist, Malpighi wrote some of his most important works in his four years at Messina (1662–66).[72]

Thus, after much effort and against the bitter opposition of Catania, Messina established an effective regional university. It was a larger university with more accomplished scholars than Catania, possibly because the commune of Messina appropriated almost three times as much money for its university. Indeed, some students who studied at Catania came to Messina to take law degrees.[73] Although Messina emphasized law, its most famous scholars were professors of mathematics and medicine. When a large number of Messina's professors and students participated in an uprising against Spain between 1674 and 1678, the Spanish authorities closed the university in 1682. It revived in 1838 and continues to this day.

PARMA, 1601

Parma tried and failed to restore its medieval university in the fifteenth century. After becoming an independent state, the city tried again in the middle of the sixteenth century and finally succeeded in 1601. The political fortunes of the city always determined the history of the university.

In the thirteenth and fourteenth centuries Parma supported a handful of scholars and a structure that local historians believe constituted a university.[74] Whatever its size and scope, the medieval *studium* continued after the Visconti family of Milan took control of the city in 1346. When Giangaleazzo Visconti

---

72. There is a large bibliography; start with Belloni, 1981.

73. The budget figures from about 1600 were Messina, 2,000 ounces; Catania, 770 ounces. Moschea, 1991b, 125 n. 73. For Catania students who obtained degrees at Messina in the years 1636–50, see Novarese, 1995, 341–42.

74. Gualazzini (1978, chs. 1–3) argues for the existence of a medieval University of Parma. Rashdall (1936, 2:333–34) denies that it existed.

became ruler of Lombardy in 1385, he designated Pavia the sole university of the state. In 1387 he ordered all his subjects to study at Pavia. Higher education at Parma, which may have been very modest by this time, came to a halt.

When in 1402 Giangaleazzo Visconti suddenly died, his centralized northern Italian state disintegrated. Subject towns hastened to escape the inept rule of his underage son. One of the fugitives was Parma, which in 1409 came under the more benign authority of Marquis Niccolò III d'Este of Ferrara. Parma petitioned its new ruler for permission to open a university and received it in September 1412.[75] The schismatic Pope John XXIII (elected 1410; abdicated 1415) bestowed various privileges on the university, but not the power to award degrees.

The commune of Parma immediately issued a call for scholars and students from other universities; it offered excellent salaries to the former and generous privileges to the latter. Some distinguished scholars heeded the call. The legist Cristoforo Castiglioni (1345–1425) came to Parma in 1414 and stayed at least a year, but no more than two and one-half years.[76] The famous medical scholar Ugo Benzi (1376–1439) taught from 1412 to 1416.[77] The natural philosopher Biagio Pelacani da Parma (c. 1350–1416) was prior of the College of Doctors of Arts from 1412 until his death on April 23, 1416, and may have taught.[78] The renowned logician Paul of Venice (Paolo Nicoletti, 1369/72–1429) apparently taught for an indeterminate period between 1412 and 1416.[79]

A few other names appeared as members of the degree-granting colleges of arts and law. Although John XXIII had not given Parma the power to award degrees, the local colleges of doctors did so anyway, claiming much earlier authorization by emperor and pope. However, no bull or charter has come to light. Parma awarded its first doctorate in December 1412 and twenty known law doctorates and twelve in arts and medicine through 1416.[80] In addition, Parma drafted statutes for its colleges of doctors of arts and medicine (1415) and law (1416) and for an organization (*universitas*) of law students (1414). A matriculation record, which is probably incomplete, listed seventy-one law students in 1414.[81]

75. Piana (1986) gives an excellent account of the revived University of Parma. This summarizes the less-focused information found in Piana, 1963, 307–24, and Gualazzini, 1978, chs. 4–5. See also Petti Balbi, 1995, and Greci, 1998.

76. Castiglioni, a native of Milan, had taught for many years at Pavia and held high legal offices in Milan. He left the University of Pavia in 1412 after two brothers of his wife assassinated Giovanni Maria Visconti, duke of Milan. He must have felt compromised by their actions. Castiglioni taught at Parma during the academic year 1414–15 and possibly the following year. He was at the University of Siena in April 1417 and returned to Pavia in 1419. Mari, 1979.

77. Benzi, 1966, 721.

78. Federici Vescovini, 1979, 39.

79. Lohr, 1972, 314.

80. For the degrees, see Piana, 1963, 333–63; see also Gualazzini, 1978, xx–xxiv, xliii–liii. In 1512 Pope Julius II conferred on Parma the right to grant degrees in all fields. Piana, 1963, 514. By that time Parma had already conferred more than three hundred doctorates.

81. See Gualazzini, 1978, 3–190 for the statutes, and 191–93 for the list of students. See Piana, 1963, 333–36, for the text of the doctoral degree in arts of 1412 with the names of promoters.

Exactly how many teaching professors Parma had at this time is unknown because of the lack of documentation. Indeed, the evidence for the presence of Benzi, Castiglioni, Pelacani, and two or three other scholars comes from their names on a handful of documents in which colleges conferred degrees between 1412 and 1416. This suggests, but does not prove, that they taught, because degree-granting colleges had many nonteaching members. Still, Parma may have had enough professors (six to eight) in canon and civil law, medicine, natural philosophy, logic, and rhetoric to constitute a teaching university for a handful of years after 1412.

The university did not survive. When the Visconti regime in Milan recovered its strength, it moved against the Parmese institution. Duke Filippo Maria Visconti (ruled 1412–47) ordered his subjects (naming several) teaching or studying at Parma to transfer to Pavia within fifteen days under threat of heavy penalties. Governments routinely ordered their subjects to study at the university within the state, but this decree was stronger than usual. Worse, Filippo Maria Visconti regained political control of Parma in September 1420. The University of Parma immediately ceased to exist. It came back to life for a year or so when the Ambrosian Republic of Milan replaced Visconti rule in 1447. But Francesco Sforza, who took control of Parma in February 1449 and all of Lombardy in 1450, again made Pavia the sole university of the state, and Parma closed again. In the late 1470s Parma had a professor of civil law and one for philosophy and a professor of medicine in 1492. But that was all.[82]

After ceasing to be a teaching institution in 1420, Parma became a paper university, one that conferred degrees without teaching. Parma awarded 287 doctoral degrees (145 in law, 42 in arts and medicine, 96 in theology, and 4 unknown), an average of 3.15 per year, from 1432 through 1522. In the initial decades after 1432 the typical recipients were northern Italians who had studied at Bologna, Pavia, or Padua, and sometimes all three, before obtaining law degrees at Parma.[83] Parma's degree may have been cheaper than those at active universities, or its examinations may have been easier to pass.

In the late fifteenth century an increasing number of non-Italians (Germans, Spaniards, Frenchmen, and men from the Low Countries) came to Parma for degrees. After 1500, the majority were French. For example, fourteen Frenchmen obtained law doctorates at Parma in 1505 and 1506.[84] They followed on the heels of the French monarchs and armies who marched through Piedmont-Savoy and ruled Lombardy from September 1499 through the early 1520s. These Frenchmen typically began their studies at French universities and then went to Turin and Pavia, and occasionally a third northern Italian university, before going to Parma for degrees. When war closed the University of Pavia, more came to

---

82. Greci, 1998, 89–93.

83. The degrees are found in Piana, 1963, 363–502, and Piana, 1966, 515–61. Piana cautions that these degrees should not be taken as a complete tally. See Piana, 1963, 376–78, for two typical degree recipients of 1445 and 1447 who had studied elsewhere.

84. Piana, 1966, 524–37.

nearby Parma. Thus, although the foreign invaders defeated Italy's armies, they respected its universities and Parma's doctoral colleges.

Parma also had a college of theologians with the power to confer degrees from at least 1448. It awarded its first known theological doctorate in 1460 and many more from the 1470s onward, reaching a high of fifteen in the year 1498. The mendicant order friars who obtained theology doctorates at Parma were overwhelmingly Italians from the northern third of the peninsula. But how much theological instruction, if any, the monasteries of Parma offered is unknown.

The leaders of Parma never gave up the hope of creating a functioning university. As the wars continued, Parma again escaped Milanese rule and came under papal control in 1521.[85] Under the benign eye of Pope Clement VII (ruled 1523–34), it tried, unsuccessfully, to revive its university. Then in September 1545, Parma and nearby Piacenza became an independent dukedom under Pier Luigi Farnese, son of Pope Paul III (ruled 1534–49). The citizens of Parma immediately petitioned their new ruler for a university; Pier Luigi agreed, and Pope Paul III issued a papal bull for it. By early 1547 the commune had hired three professors to teach *Institutes*, logic, and Greek and Latin humanities.[86] Although members of the Piacenzan nobility assassinated Pier Luigi Farnese in September 1547, these professors continued to teach. But the commune diverted university funds to the military in 1551, and the tiny partial university closed. Nevertheless, Parma continued to award degrees in law, arts, and medicine in the late sixteenth century.[87]

Despite the assassination of its first ruler, Parma and Piacenza remained in Farnese hands as an independent dukedom under Spanish protection. Then in 1599, Duke Ranuccio I Farnese (b. 1569; ruled 1592–1622) approached the Society of Jesus with a proposal.[88] In 1564 the Jesuits had founded in Parma a school to teach at the preuniversity level.[89] The arrangement was typical: the city provided a subsidy to support the school, which offered free Latin education to boys from about the ages of ten to sixteen. Duke Ranuccio I now proposed the creation of a university that would include the Jesuits.

After some bargaining, agreement was reached: the Society would provide professors for logic, natural philosophy, mathematics, and theology, in return for

85. For the following, see D'Alessandro, 1980, 20–25. Parma was ruled by the French in the years 1499–1512, by the papacy 1512–15, by the French 1515–21, and by the papacy from 1521 until the creation of the Farnese dukedom in 1545.

86. Exactly how much teaching took place is impossible to say. Brizzi (1980, 136) dismisses the attempt to revive the university between 1547 and 1551 as "ephemeral."

87. D'Alessandro, 1980, 39, 44–52.

88. For the following, see Berti, 1967, 23–39; D'Alessandro, 1980; and Brizzi, 1980, the latter two with valuable documents. D'Alessandro and Brizzi offer much richer accounts than Berti but are distinctly hostile to the Jesuits and to Duke Ranuccio I to a lesser degree. Berti is neutral. In addition, D'Alessandro and Brizzi posit a contrast between the free, autonomous Renaissance university of an earlier era and what they see as a restricted and Jesuit-dominated University of Parma. In reality, Renaissance universities enjoyed only as much, or as little, autonomy as commune and prince allowed long before 1601.

89. D'Alessandro, 1980, 27–30, and Scaduto, 1992, 316–21.

TABLE 4.6
University of Parma Roll, 1601–1602

Theology (*de Deo*)	François Remond of France, S.J.[a]
Theology (*de iure et iustitia*)[b]	unfilled
Canon law	Teodoro Testa of Parma
Civil law, ordinary P.M.	Sforza degli Oddi of Perugia[c]
	Vincenzo Francolino of Fermo
Civil law, ordinary A.M.	Annibale Marescotti of Bologna
	Innocenzo Canoso of Parma
Institutes (civil law)	Gaspar Trincadino of Parma
	Marco Antonio Bottoni of Parma
Metaphysics	Ottaviano Trecca of Parma, S.J.
Natural philosophy	Vittorio Premoli, S.J.[d]
Medical practice	Alberto Sanseverino of Parma
	Alessandro Recordati of Bologna
Medical theory	Giovanni Talentono of Fivizzano[e]
Mathematics	Jean Verbieri of Belgium, S.J.
Anatomy	Pompilio Tagliaferri of Parma[f]
Logic	Marco Garzoni of Venice, S.J.[g]
Rhetoric	Paolo Bombino of Cosenza, S.J.[h]
Simples (medical botany)	Pompilio Tagliaferri of Parma

Source: ASPr, Istruzione pubblica farnesiana, Bu. 1, no pag.; it is accurately printed in D'Alessandro, 1980, 60–61, which is followed here.

Note: The professorships are listed in the order given in the document. I have changed the Latin descriptions and names into Italian, French, and English and have added "S.J." in order to identify the Jesuit professors.

[a]Remond (1560/62–1631) was born in Dijon, received a doctorate from Padua, and then entered the Jesuit order. He taught rhetoric, philosophy, and theology at Rome, Padua, Parma, Bordeaux, and Mantua, where he died of the plague while attending stricken soldiers. He wrote numerous orations, elegies, epigrams, panegyrics, and theological works. Sommervogel et al., 1960, vol. 6, cols. 1652–56.

[b]This may have been intended to be a professorship in casuistry.

[c]See the first section of this chapter for a brief biography of Oddi.

[d]Premoli (1566–1630) published a confessor's manual, and taught philosophy and theology at Jesuit schools in Padua, Rome, and Bologna. Sommervogel et al., 1960, vol. 6, cols. 1203–4.

[e]Fivizzano is a small hill town near the Ligurian coast in northeastern Tuscany.

[f]From a Parmese noble family, Tagliaferri (c. 1560–1639) studied medicine at Padua and Bologna and took his degree at Rome. He also taught medical theory and anatomy during his long teaching career at Parma and was the first to detect the plague in Parma in 1630. He received several honors from the commune. Rizzi, 1948, 27; Affò, 1969, 19–20.

[g]Garzoni (1571–1630) apparently published little or nothing. Sommervogel et al., 1960, vol. 3, col. 1250.

[h]Bombino (1575–1648) published an expurgated edition of Catullus, various orations, and lives of Ignatius Loyola and Edmund Campion. Sommervogel et al., 1960, vol. 1, cols. 1682–84.

TABLE 4.7
University of Parma, Law and Medicine Professors, 1609–1610

Canon law, ordinary A.M.	Francesco Maria Vaghi of Parma, 100 ducatoni[a]
Civil law, ordinary A.M.	Paolo Tusignani of Bologna, 685 ducatoni
	Marco Antonio Bottoni of Parma, 160 ducatoni
Institutes, ordinary A.M.	Giovanni Battista Aiata of Brescia 70 ducatoni
	Antonio Longo(ghi) of Parma,[b] 27.4 ducatoni
"Repetitione di Bartolo," A.M.	Febo Bellacappa,[c] 40 ducatoni
Civil law, student extraordinary A.M.	Orazio di Nottaro of Crema, 6.8 ducatoni
Canon law, ordinary P.M.	Rev. Vincenzo Mazzoli of Pisa, 500 ducatoni
Civil law, ordinary P.M.	Sforza degli Oddi of Perugia, 1,200 ducatoni
	Gaspare Rodici of Piacenza, 300 ducatoni
	Fabio Ranucci of Macerata,[d] 300 ducatoni
Institutes, ordinary P.M.	Alessandro Carissimi, 27.4 ducatoni
	Giulio Biardi, 27.4 ducatoni
Civil law, student extraordinary P.M.	Stefano Stortiliono of Milan, 6.8 ducatoni
Medical theory, ordinary A.M.	Alberto Sanseverino of Parma, 400 ducatoni
Medical practice, ordinary A.M.	Accurso Accursi of Parma, 80 ducatoni
Medical practice, extraordinary A.M.	Francesco Martini,[e] 27.4 ducatoni
Surgery, extraordinary A.M.	Pietro Magnani,[f] 27.4 ducatoni
Medical theory, extraordinary P.M.	Paolo Simonetti of Parma,[g] 27.4 ducatoni
Medical practice, ordinary P.M.	Alessandro Recordati, 330 ducatoni
Anatomy, ordinary, and simples P.M.	Pompilio Tagliaferro of Parma, 400 ducatoni
Natural philosophy, student extraordinary	Matteo Greco of the Grisons, 6.8 ducatoni
Medicine, student extraordinary P.M.	Cristoforo Sardi 6.8 ducatoni

Source: ASPr, Archivio del Comune di Parma, Studio, Bu. 1913, a ledger entitled "Delli lettori e altri provisionati nel Studio rifformato," ff. 1ʳ–22ʳ, which lists payment records for the period October 1609–October 1610.

Note: Payments were made quarterly and recorded in ducatoni or in lire for those receiving the lowest salaries. All have been converted into ducatoni. I have listed the professors in the order found in a university roll. I have also added the place of birth when missing, if possible, so that it easily can be seen which were local men.

[a]Vaghi taught at Parma from 1606 to 1618 and died in 1619. Rizzi, 1948, 30.

[b]Longhi taught *Institutes* (1609–15) and then canon law (1615–27). Rizzi, 1948, 30.

[c]Bellacappa taught at Parma from 1609 to 1622. Rizzi, 1948, 41.

[d]Ranucci taught *Institutes* at Macerata from about 1578 through 1606 and then apparently moved to Parma. Bartolomeo Vecchi of Siena replaced Ranucci in mid–academic year, also at 300 ducatoni per annum.

[e]Martini taught at Parma from 1609 to 1620. Rizzi, 1948, 26.

[f]Magnani taught at Parma from 1609 to 1620. Rizzi, 1948, 25.

[g]Simonetti taught at Parma from 1609 to 1625. Rizzi, 1948, 25.

payment of 1,000 ducatoni (large ducats of account, worth 7 lire 6 soldi instead of the normal 6 lire 4 soldi). Duke and commune would choose the professors of law and medicine. The city government of Parma created a magistracy, the familiar Riformatori dello Studio found elsewhere, to oversee the university, and the duke promulgated university statutes in 1601. He also petitioned the pope for the right to award degrees and the usual privileges, even though Parma had been awarding degrees for centuries. A prince or commune reviving a university often wanted a fresh papal or imperial document in order to legitimate and advertise the renewed institution. At least one Jesuit began to lecture in the fall of 1599, and some law and medical lectures may have started in 1600–1601. The full university began in the fall of 1601. The University of Parma began with seventeen professors offering eighteen daily lectures in 1601–2.

Thus, 6 civilians and 1 canonist taught law, 4 professors taught medicine (with the anatomist also teaching medical botany), 5 Jesuits taught arts subjects, and 1 Jesuit taught theology in 1601–2. At least 7 of the professors were local men, and the rest of the lay professors came from northern Italy. Unlike almost all other Italian universities at this time, Parma had 2 non-Italians in its faculty, both of them Jesuits. Within a few years the University of Parma expanded.

In 1609–10 the University of Parma had 12 law professors and 7 medical professors, plus 4 student lecturers, 2 in law, 1 in medicine, and 1 in philosophy. Seven to 9 Jesuits, with some of them lecturing twice a day (see table 4.8) completed the faculty. The 23 legists and medical professors earned a total of 4,756.6 ducatoni; the 2,000-ducatoni payment to the Jesuits brought the total to 6,756.6 ducatoni, making Parma a reasonably expensive university.[90] At least seven of the law and medicine professors were natives of Parma, and an eighth came from nearby Piacenza. The University of Parma reached 26 professors delivering 31 daily lectures in 1617–18. This roll includes the Jesuits.

The University of Parma had 11 legists, 7 medical professors, and 9 artists, with the latter offering 13 daily lectures in arts, in 1617–18. (This roll had no student lecturers.) Local men continued to fill the majority of the positions: at least 10 of the 18 law and medicine professors came from Parma, and another came from Piacenza. Two of the 8 Jesuits came from Parma. Parma also had considerable faculty stability, as professors remained 15 to 20 years. The law faculty boasted one star, Francesco Accarigi, and at least 3 of the Jesuits were well published. With 26 professors and 31 daily lectures Parma was a medium-sized university with several established scholars.[91]

---

90. This seems to have been an average figure. In another academic year between 1602 and 1609 the salary expenses of the law and medical professors were 4,910 ducatoni (for 7 legists, 5 medical professors, and 4 student lecturers) plus 136 ducatoni for the salaries of 2 beadles and incidental expenses, especially the cost of erecting the temporary anatomical theater. With the 2,000 ducatoni paid to the Jesuits, the total academic salary expenses were 6,910 ducatoni. ASPr, Istruzione pubblica farnesiana, Bu. 2, unpaginated document entitled "Nota delle provisioni che ogni anno si devono alli ss.ri lettori nel studio di questa città di Parma." The names of the professors indicate that the year is neither 1601–2 nor 1609–10, but a year in between.

91. Bologna, Ferrara, Padua, Pavia, Pisa, and Siena were larger; Naples, Rome, and Turin were

At 2,000 ducatoni for 9 professors delivering 13 daily lectures, the Jesuits were a great educational bargain. Indeed, the Jesuits felt that their services were undervalued and sought more. Duke Ranuccio I did not increase the annual payment but promised future compensation by means of a substantial legacy in his will. But when he died in 1622, the dukedom was so heavily in debt that there was no legacy. The Jesuits never received the promised bequest.[92]

Duke Ranuccio's university was part of an ambitious educational, cultural, and social program rivaling those of larger city-states. He founded a university featuring the Society of Jesus, some of whose members were established philosophers, mathematicians, and theologians. While other universities had turned a stony countenance to the Jesuits, Ranuccio had welcomed them. He promised a physically safe university, and the presence of the Jesuits implied a morally upright environment. Ranuccio also built an awesomely large palace housing an elegant theater. Students who enrolled at Parma might become acquainted with the duke, who took a personal interest in the university. As he was a feudatory of the king of Spain, other benefits might flow from the contact. Princely absolutism was the order of the day across Italy and Europe, but few princes made it so attractive as the duke of Parma.

All of this must have impressed young men and parents searching for a university where they or their sons would learn and make useful contacts. Some northern Italians saw Parma as a welcome alternative to older universities plagued by student violence and weakened by pedagogical abuses (see Ch. 14). Parma, with a full complement of law and medical courses and professors comparable to most other universities, offered effective competition, especially to Padua. Although Venetian subjects were required by law to attend the University of Padua, many defected to Parma. The Venetian governor of Vicenza wrote in 1603 that "an infinite number of gentlemen [were] sending their sons to the University of Parma," using the excuse that Venetian nobles were also abandoning Padua.[93]

---

about the same size as Parma; and Catania, Macerata, Messina, Perugia, and Salerno were smaller at this time. It should be kept in mind that university faculties were shrinking in the seventeenth century.

92. See, for example, a document of Sept. 5, 1612, arguing that 2,000 ducatoni were not enough for the Jesuits. ASPr, Istruzione pubblica farnesiana, Bu. 1, no pag. On the failed legacy, see Brizzi, 1980, 206–7 n. 84.

93. "Non voglio restar per fine di queste parte di dire che infiniti gentilhuomeni mandano li loro figlioli nel Studio di Parma con tutto che fossero pubblicate le leggi in questo proposito, et si escusano che vedendo la nobiltà venetiana abbandonar il Studio di Padoa." *Relazione* (concluding summary report) of Nicolò Pizzamano, governor of Vicenza, Oct. 8, 1603, as quoted in Brizzi, 1980, 202 n. 47. How many young Venetian nobles attended the University of Parma is unknown, because of the lack of matriculation records.

In 1611 the Venetian governor of Padua also complained that many Venetian subjects were attending other universities, especially Parma, at the expense of Padua. "Non però posso tacere che in quel Studio [Padua] si ritrovi molto minor numero di sudditi di quello che raggionevolmente doveria esservi . . . se ne passano in altri Studij d'Italia et a quello di Parma in particolare." He went on to point out that some Venetian subjects, particularly those from Lombard cities in the western part of the Venetian mainland state, felt more comfortable at Parma. *Relazione* of Angelo Correr, Mar. 8, 1611, in *Relazioni,* 1975, 132.

TABLE 4.8
University of Parma Roll, 1617–1618

Law
  Morning

Canon law, ordinary A.M   Rev. Francesco Maria Vaghi of Parma
                                                 Rev. Antonio Longhi of Parma
Civil law, ordinary A.M.   Francesco Accarigi of Siena[a]
                                                 Marco Agostino Bottoni of Parma[i]
Civil law, extraordinary A.M.   Febo Bellacappa
Institutes, A.M.   Camillo Accarigi of Siena[b]

  Afternoon

Institutes, P.M.   Ottavio Rossi of Parma[c]
                                                 Giovanni Francesco Lucchetti of
                                                     Parma[d]
Civil law, ordinary P.M.   Bartolomeo Vecchi(o) of Siena[e]
Canon law, ordinary P.M. ("De usurius")   Gaspar Rodesio
Canon law, ordinary P.M. (*Decretals*)   Rev. Giovanni Battista Strata

Medicine
  Morning

Medicine, extraordinary A.M. ("De febribus")   Francesco Martini
Medical theory, ordinary A.M.   Accurso Accursi of Parma[f]
                                                 Alberto Sanseverino of Parma[g]
Medicine, extraordinary ("De ulceribus et de   Pietro Magnani of Parma
    morbo gallico")

  Afternoon

Medical theory, extraordinary P.M.   Paolo Simonetti of Parma
Medical theory, ordinary P.M.   Domino Albasini of Piacenza
                                                 Pompilio Tagliaferri of Parma

Arts and Theology
  Morning

Theology   Girolamo Serravale of Bologna, S.J.[h]
Natural philosophy / Metaphysics   Jacopo Filippo Tresio, S.J.[i]
Natural philosophy   Francesco Rossano of Forlì, S.J.[j]
Logic (Aristotle's *Organon*)   Niccolò Zucchi of Parma, S.J.[k]
Rhetoric (Cicero's *Partitiones oratoriae*)   Francesco Milanino of Parma, S.J.
Theology ("leget de sacramentis minoribus")   Bernardo Cessi of Modena, S.J.

  Afternoon

Moral philosophy ("leget de preceptis   Domenico Zanetti of Ferrara, S.J.
    decalogi")
Mathematics   Giuseppe Biancani of Bologna, S.J.[l]
Theology   Vittorio Premoli of Cremona, S.J.[m]

Natural philosophy / Metaphysics	Jacopo Filippo Tresio, S.J.[n]
Natural philosophy	Francesco Rossano of Forlì, S.J.
Logic	Niccolò Zucchi of Parma, S.J.
Humanities	Francesco Milanino of Parma, S.J.[o]

Source: ASPr, Archivio del Comune di Parma, Studio, Bu. 1909, no pag.

Note: Although the roll often does not give titles of the professorships, these can be deduced from the texts taught.

[a]Although born in Macerata, Accarigi (d. 1622) spent much of his life in Siena and was viewed as Sienese. He received his doctorate at Siena in 1580 and then taught there from 1581 to 1613. He was the first holder (1589–93) of the new *Pandects* professorship intended to teach humanistic jurisprudence, but he combined *mos italicus* and *mos gallicus* in his teaching. He moved to Parma in 1613 at the very high salary of 1,300 ducatoni plus the influential post of ducal councillor. He finished his career at Pisa (1618–22). The author of several works, Accarigi was the star legist in this roll. Rossi, 1906, 45, 49–60; Cascio Pratilli, 1975, 73 n. 199, and see index.

[b]The son of Francesco, Camillo Accarigi later taught at Pisa and died in 1633. He wrote two works. Rizzi, 1948, 35; Ascheri, 1991, 140.

[c]Rossi taught at Parma from 1613 to 1618; Rizzi, 1948, 39.

[d]Lucchetti/o taught at Parma from 1613 to 1622 and wrote one book. Rizzi, 1948, 39.

[e]Vecchi taught at Parma from 1609 to 1626. Rizzi, 1948, 34.

[f]Accursi died in 1622. Rizzi, 1948, 25.

[g]Sanseverino (1553–1623) taught the *Aphorisms* of Hippocrates, a statutory medical text. Rizzi, 1948, 25.

[h]Serravale's teaching was described as lecturing on "S. Thomae de sacramentis in genere et de Eucharistia." Serravale (c. 1572–1645) was later rector of the Jesuit college of Parma. Sommervogel et al., 1960, vol. 12, col. 811.

[i]Tresio (not further identified) taught Aristotle's *De generatione, De anima,* and *Metaphysics,* a combination of the standard texts for natural philosophy and metaphysics.

[j]Rossano taught Aristotle's *Physics,* book 8, *De caelo,* and *De generatione,* book 1, standard fare for natural philosophy.

[k]Zucchi (1586–1670) published works on mechanics and optics, as well as numerous vernacular devotional works. He had his own idea for making a telescope in 1616 and discovered the first of the craters on Jupiter. He later taught mathematics at the Collegio Romano, knew Kepler, and preached at the papal court. Sommervogel et al., 1960, vol. 8, cols. 1525–30.

[l]Biancani (1566–1624) taught Euclid's *Elementa* and "sphero," presumably astronomy. He published several works on mathematics and astronomy. Sommervogel et al., 1960, vol. 1, cols. 1436–37.

[m]Premoli taught "de vitiis et peccatis," either moral theology or casuistry.

[n]Tresio, Rossano, and Zucchi taught the same texts in the afternoon as they taught in the morning. Whether they repeated their morning lectures or continued their expositions, giving a course of lectures double the length of the norm (and requiring students to come twice a day), is unknown. In any case, these three Jesuits plus Milanino lectured twice a day.

[o]Milanino (not further identified) taught Cicero's *Verrines* and Virgil's *Aeneid,* book 2.

Other Terraferma subjects followed: more than 30 young Brescians studied at the University of Parma in 1610 or 1611.[94] Overall, Parma probably had 300 to 400 students in the early seventeenth century. The town, with a population of at least 20,000, perhaps reaching 30,000, could easily host this number of students.[95]

Students might attend Parma for sound intellectual reasons. But religious politics probably also persuaded some Venetians and Terraferma subjects to study there. In the late sixteenth century, the Jesuits had established schools in several towns of the Venetian state, including Padua. But vehement opposition from some professors and students at the University of Padua persuaded the Venetian Senate to suppress the Paduan school in December 1591, on the grounds that it was competing with the university (see Ch. 14, "Competition from Religious Order Schools"). The Venetian government then banished the Jesuits from the entire Venetian state in 1606 for taking the side of the papacy during the Interdict conflict of 1606–7 and kept them out until 1657. The remaining Jesuit schools in the Venetian state had to close. The republic also forbade its subjects on April 18, 1606, from attending Jesuit schools outside the Venetian state.

However, Ranuccio I had founded in 1601 a boarding school for boys of certified noble lineage, which the Jesuits directed and staffed from 1604 on. The Parma boarding school attracted noble boys aged eleven to twenty, the majority from Italy, the rest from elsewhere in Europe. As a sign of his favor, Ranuccio opened his private hunting preserve to the boys and gave them seats of honor at public ceremonies. Despite the Venetian prohibition, the Parma boarding school for nobles attracted several hundred students from Venice and the Venetian state in the course of the seventeenth century.[96] Sending their sons to the Jesuit-run school for nobles may have expressed the opposition of some nobles to the anti-Jesuit policies of the government. (And enrolling sons of Venetian nobles must have been satisfying for the Jesuits.) Many nobles of Brescia, Verona, and other mainland cities also sent their progeny to the boarding school in violation of the republic's prohibition. Inevitably, some boys at the boarding school would elect to continue their studies at the University of Parma.

94. "Più di trenta gioveni Bresciani siano andati à studiare in Parma." Copy of a letter to the Venetian governors (*rettori*) of Brescia from the Venetian governors of Padua, no date but 1610 or 1611, in ASVe, Riformatori dello Studio di Padova, Bu. 420, no pag. The letter went on to reiterate the law that Venetian subjects had to study at Padua and to request that the governors of Brescia tell fathers that their sons must transfer to the University of Padua within fifteen days. See also another letter with the same message to the Brescian *rettori* of Sept. 3, 1611, and notation of a similar letter addressed to the *rettori* of Verona. Ibid., no pag.

95. The enrollment estimate is mine. For population figures, see Ginatempo and Sandri, 1990, 87, 88, 255.

96. "In questo Collegio si trovano al presente 34 figlioli di Nobili Venetiani." From an anonymous and undated (but c. 1606) Venetian denunciation of the Parma school printed in Brizzi, 1980, 190. See also Brizzi, 1976, 38, 68 n. 115, and Brizzi, 1994, 496–97, 502–3, 511, who counts 171 students from Venice, Brescia, and Verona between 1600 and 1649. After 1657, the enrollment from the Venetian state greatly increased. Overall, the Parma boarding school for nobles attracted nearly twice as many students from the Republic of Venice as from any other Italian state.

Thus, after several attempts over more than two centuries, Parma had a university. Even more than Ferrara in 1442 and Pisa in 1473, the University of Parma owed its existence to a determined prince, who made a pact with the Society of Jesus. The resultant University of Parma was a traditional university with the Jesuits teaching theology and all the arts subjects, except medicine.[97] This new university offered strong competition to the established universities of Pavia, Ferrara, Padua, and Bologna.

INCOMPLETE UNIVERSITIES

Italy had sixteen universities between 1400 and 1601. Other towns offered a limited amount of advanced instruction, but not enough professors to constitute a university. Sometimes these incomplete universities awarded doctoral degrees.

Modena had an incomplete school of higher learning. The city offered advanced study, and possibly enough of it, to claim to be a university in the thirteenth century.[98] But this structure disappeared by 1338. In its place, the city established three public lectureships over the course of the next 150 years: grammar (later called humanities) beginning in 1364, law and notarial art from 1424, and medicine (begun in 1488, on a continuing basis from 1524). The three lecturers followed the forms of a university. They adhered to an academic calendar, they taught at set hours with bells announcing the beginning and end of classes, and they were paid by the commune. Carlo Sigonio (1522/23–85), a native of Modena, held the humanities lectureship from 1546 through 1552. He initially taught beginning and advanced Greek and added a humanities course in 1547, apparently teaching three classes daily. He also published the first of his many books on ancient Roman history while at Modena. Sigonio left for a post at the Scuola di San Marco in Venice in 1552 (see below) and then became a distinguished professor at the universities of Padua and Bologna. Even though the instruction of these three lectureships was probably university level, Modena did not award degrees. The commune of Modena suspended the three lectureships in 1590 for lack of money. The city finally established a university in the early 1680s with an imperial charter of 1685.

Piacenza, like Parma a part of Lombardy and ruled by Milan, briefly hosted the University of Pavia between the autumn of 1398 and May 1402. The commune longed to establish a university after the Pavian *studio* left, but its Milanese rulers did not permit this. Pavia, which feared that its own university might once again be transferred to Piacenza, also sought to prevent the Piacenzan College of Legists from awarding degrees. Piacenza did have a single law lecturer for *Institutes* in 1435 and again in 1485. Then, as with Parma, the tides of war freed

---

97. D'Alessandro (1980) and Brizzi (1980) argue that the Jesuits increasingly viewed their part of the university as distinct and separate from the teaching of law and medicine. More research on all aspects of the University of Parma is needed to prove or disprove this statement.

98. Mor, 1952, 13–62. For Sigonio, see McCuaig, 1989, 3–13.

Piacenza from its Milanese anchor. The French occupied Piacenza from November 1499 through June 1512, and the papacy ruled the city until September 1545. During this period, Piacenza established several lectureships in an obvious attempt to create a university. It had an *Institutes* lecturer in 1509 and added a Scripture lecturer in 1513, a second law lecturer by 1537, a humanities lecturer in 1527, and a logician in the early 1540s.[99] Although not all posts were continuously filled, Piacenza may have had 5 or 6 professors teaching simultaneously in the early 1540s: single professors for the humanities, logic, and Scripture, plus 2 or 3 legists with an emphasis on the *Institutes*, but no medicine. One of the law professors was Niccolò Bellone of Casale Monferrato (c. 1500–1552), a man of several publications and some distinction. He had taught at Pavia from 1535 until 1540, when war caused the university to close; he moved to Piacenza in 1540 or 1541 but left in 1542.[100]

The 1540s marked the apex of Piacenza's quest to establish a university. In 1545 it became part of the dukedom of Parma and Piacenza. After several Piacenzan nobles assassinated Pier Luigi Farnese in 1547, the Spanish viceroy in Milan took control. He ruled Piacenza until 1556, when the city was restored to the reconstituted Farnese dukedom of Parma and Piacenza. Piacenza's effort to create a university gradually lost momentum after midcentury. By the late 1550s it had only a single *Institutes* lectureship, which lasted through the eighteenth century. The Scripture professorship ceased to exist in 1567, and humanities and logic disappeared in 1584. The colleges of doctors of law, arts and medicine, and theology may have awarded degrees throughout the sixteenth century, but the records have not survived. Piacenza could not get beyond an incomplete university.

Two famous but tiny schools in Venice offered instruction at an advanced level but did not confer university degrees. The Scuola di Rialto (sometimes called the School of Philosophy) began in 1408 and consisted of a single professor.[101] Like the University of Padua, the Scuola di Rialto taught Aristotelian natural philosophy and English terminist logic in the fifteenth century. A Venetian noble always held this lectureship in the sixteenth century, and the instruction, while remaining Aristotelian, became more diverse. The Scuola di San Marco began in 1446 as a single professor to teach Latin grammar and rhetoric to boys training to become governmental secretaries and notaries.[102] A second professor was added in 1460 to teach poetry, oratory, and history; this post became a professorship of advanced humanities and Greek and was held by some distinguished humanists. Thus, Venice had three professors, at least two of them lecturing at an advanced level, teaching a combination of logic, natural philosophy, the humanities, and Greek.

99. This and the following paragraph are based on Nasalli Rocca, 1948, esp. 220, 227–29, and Del Fante, 1980a.

100. Criniti, 1965.

101. See B. Nardi, 1971, 3–98, and Lepori, 1980.

102. Ross, 1976, is the indispensable guide with much additional bibliography. See Palmer, 1983, 48–49, and Grendler, 1989, 62–63, 269, for brief summaries.

The Venetians went further by establishing professorships of mathematics in 1530 and Scripture in 1532, both of which lasted a few years. In 1575 the Venetian government hired a professor to teach *Institutes*, notarial art, and criminal law. This combination post, intended to provide introductory legal training especially for the notaries who served the ducal chancery, lasted through 1603.[103] Had the Scuola di Rialto, the Scuola di San Marco, and the professorships of mathematics, Scripture, and introductory legal studies existed simultaneously, and had they been combined with the limited medical instruction and power to grant degrees of the Venetian College of Physicians (see below), Venice would have had a small university. But the Venetian government did not permit this to happen. When Paolo dalla Pergola, who lectured at the Scuola di Rialto from 1421 until his death in 1455, tried in 1445 to transform the Scuola di Rialto into a university, the Venetian government sharply rebuked him.[104] The Venetian government had designated Padua the only university of the Venetian state and suppressed potential rivals.

Arezzo had a university in the thirteenth century; it disappeared in the middle of the fourteenth. The city tried again in the fifteenth century. In 1452 the Aretines obtained a new university charter from Emperor Frederick III. In 1464, and again in 1466, Arezzo proclaimed a roll of 4 to 6 professors, but they did not teach. The city then appointed 5 professors, 2 for civil law, 1 for canon law, 1 for arts, and 1 for logic, who taught during the academic year 1468–69. The roll had a sixth (apparently unfilled) position for *Institutes*. The commune also repeatedly urged Florence to move its university to Arezzo; one way or another, the Aretines would have a *studio*. But the teaching of 1468–69 was the closest they came to success. In 1473 the Florentines moved most of their university to Pisa, not Arezzo. The latter made one more attempt in 1512 by appointing a professor of law and one in medicine and by promulgating university statutes. But no further progress occurred. Arezzo did award at least 32 doctorates in law, arts, and medicine between 1452 and 1493. But the small subject city lacked the resources and political strength needed to re-create past university glory.[105]

The Jesuit Collegio Romano, founded in 1551, was an extraordinarily important institution of higher learning in the Catholic world. It offered advanced instruction in the humanities, ancient languages, Aristotelian logic and natural philosophy, metaphysics, theology, and mathematics, plus preuniversity school-

---

103. "Per instruction principalmente delli nodari della cancellaria nostra ducale." Copy of the Senate appointment notice of June 7, 1578, in AAUP, F. 737, f. 281ʳ–ᵛ. This second appointee at a salary of 220 ducats was "Francesco Detiano [*sic*]." He may have been Gian Francesco Deciani (1537–90), a legist son of Tiberio Deciani (1509–82), the first holder of the new criminal law professorship at Padua. Spagnesi, 1987, 539, 540. The first holder of the Venetian *Institutes* professorship was Emilio Maria Manolessi, 1575–78. Fabrizio Cecconi, who held the position from 1581 to 1592, went on to teach *Institutes* at Padua from 1592 until his death in 1599. See also Paternoster, 1883, 16–17; Lepori, 1980, 605 n. 387; and Palmer, 1983, 49.

104. B. Nardi, 1971, 24–26; Ross, 1976, 530; Lepori, 1980, 550–52.

105. Black, 1985b and 1988, and the documents in *Studio e scuola in Arezzo*, 1996, 179–302.

ing. It boasted internationally known scholars and had the right to award the doctorate of theology and the license degree in philosophy from 1556 onward. But because it did not teach law and medicine, it was not a university in the Italian meaning of the term.[106]

PAPER UNIVERSITIES

A commune holding a papal or imperial charter and having colleges of doctors of law, arts and medicine, or theology could award university degrees even if little or no advanced instruction occurred. This was a paper university.[107]

Probably every major city in Italy and some minor ones had colleges of law and medicine composed of prominent local legists and physicians with doctorates. Their chief duties were to regulate the practices of law and medicine in the town.[108] But when pope or emperor conferred a university charter on a commune, the local colleges of doctors of law, medicine, and theology might also examine candidates and confer degrees. Of course, the candidates studied elsewhere.

The most important paper university was the College of Physicians (Collegio dei Medici) of Venice. It had received the power to grant doctorates, but only to Venetian citizens, from Pope Nicholas V in 1447.[109] Emperor Frederick III (ruled 1440–93), who seems to have handed out university charters wherever he went, awarded the Venetian College of Physicians the title of *studium generale* and the right to award degrees universally on February 14, 1469, during a visit to Venice.[110] Pope Paul II, a Venetian noble, added a papal university privilege on January 18, 1470. With the authority of these multiple charters, the Venetian College of Physicians examined and awarded 603 doctorates of medicine between 1501 and 1602. But the Venetian College of Physicians had no professors, no students, and no teaching, with the minor exception noted below. Hence, medical students studied elsewhere, the majority of them at the University of Padua, and then came to the Venetian College of Physicians for their degrees. They did this because the Venetian doctorate cost 10 ducats, and the Paduan doctorate 18, through most of the sixteenth century.[111] In addition, Venetian doctorates of medicine, or arts and medicine, seem to have been just as esteemed

106. See Villoslada, 1954, 33–42, 89–105. For mathematics at the Collegio Romano, see Lattis, 1994, ch. 2, with much additional bibliography.

107. "Paper university" comes from Rashdall, 1936, 2:325, who defines them as "universities for which Bulls were granted, but which never came into actual existence." I define a paper university as one that had a charter and awarded degrees but did not teach.

108. Park (1985, 37–42) gives a good brief description of the College of Physicians in Florence.

109. B. Nardi, 1971, 25.

110. The following is based on Palmer, 1983.

111. These are average figures for most of the century. The Paduan college tried to charge 20 to 30 ducats early in the century, but Venetian competition forced it to lower the price. And in 1578 the Venetian college raised its fee to 12 ducats. There were other price variations and some reductions for poor students. Surgery degrees cost less: 12 to 14 ducats at Padua and 7 to 9 in Venice. Ibid., 31–34.

as Paduan doctorates. They were probably more useful if the recipient intended to practice in Venice.

Even though Venice did not offer medical instruction, the College of Physicians did contribute a little to the training of physicians. The University of Padua required its medical students to spend at least one year practicing medicine with a physician. Some medical students fulfilled this requirement by accompanying prominent Venetian physicians on their rounds. The experience probably induced some students to obtain their medical doctorates at Venice. The College of Physicians also sponsored an annual anatomical dissection. Although it was intended for local physicians and surgeons, some students may have attended, if they could get places. The Venetian government converted the annual anatomical dissection into a lectureship in anatomy in 1628. The government also established a lectureship of medical theory in 1585, but it does not seem to have lasted very long.[112] These contributions to medical training fell far short of university training.

Other paper universities preceded and followed the Venetian College of Physicians. As described earlier, Parma had a paper university from 1420 to 1547 and in the last thirty to forty years of the sixteenth century. The politically independent commune of Lucca started to create a university but then abandoned the attempt. Lucca obtained an imperial charter from Emperor Charles IV in 1369 and a papal bull from Urban VI in 1387 authorizing a *studium generale* with the right to confer doctoral degrees in all fields except theology. Lucca appointed a single professor to teach natural and moral philosophy, logic, and rhetoric in 1376 and planned to appoint a professor of medicine in 1388 but did not do so. The Luccans tried again in 1455, as the city council appropriated 4,000 florins for a university, more than enough for a small institution. But nothing came of the attempt. In 1476 Lucca appointed a Dominican friar to teach logic and philosophy; how long he taught is unknown. Lucca did award doctoral degrees, as 138 men sought degrees between 1403 and 1487. Because of the incompleteness of the records, it is not clear how many succeeded. The city government also supported financially at least 82 Luccans who studied at various Italian universities in the fourteenth and fifteenth centuries.[113]

Genoa and Urbino also awarded degrees without teaching. Pope Sixtus IV, a native of Genoa, in 1471, and Emperor Maximilian I, in 1513, formally recognized Genoa as a *studium generale* with the right to award degrees. The colleges of law and medicine conferred a large number in the sixteenth and seventeenth centuries. But Genoa had no university-level teaching before the mid-seventeenth century.[114] Urbino received the power to confer degrees in law from Pope Pius

112. Ibid., 44–51.

113. Barsanti, 1980, 68–99, 198–99, 201–9, and Davies, 1997–99. I am grateful to Dr. Davies for a prepublication copy of his article.

114. Isnardi, 1975, vol. 1, esp. chs. 17 and 18, pp. 200–235. See Savelli, 1990, for a study of the law doctorates awarded by the college of legists in Genoa.

IV in 1564 and had a communally funded *Institutes* lecturer in 1576. But a full teaching university appeared only in 1671.[115]

CONCLUSION

Although each commune followed its own path, the reasons for and against establishing a university were much the same everywhere. Renaissance Italians believed strongly in the value of higher education; they wanted to learn. In addition, they believed that a university conferred fame and honor on the host city. A university also trained the civil servants, legists, judges, physicians, surgeons, teachers, and scholars needed by government, the local community, and society at large. A university aided the local economy, because wealthy foreign students—anyone who was neither a native son nor a subject was a foreigner—spent a great deal of money on fees, food, lodging, servants, tutoring, and books.

The thirst for higher learning led many Italian communes to attempt to create universities. But after obtaining a charter, a town often failed to establish a university, most often because of external political opposition. Other reasons included high costs, the lack of suitable housing for out-of-town students, or unwillingness to make available housing at reasonable cost. Sometimes townspeople and city council refused to pay the anticipated price in injured citizens and molested daughters for the honor of hosting a university.[116] Then a commune had the solace of an incomplete or paper university, which were typical Renaissance combinations of exaggerated claims and disappointing reality. Nevertheless, even incomplete and paper universities yielded some benefits.

Despite the difficulties, Italy established sixteen teaching universities in Italy in three waves. After legal instruction at Bologna evolved into a university in the late twelfth century, Padua, Naples, and Siena quickly followed, then Rome and Perugia after a hiatus of about sixty years. This initial wave of foundations ended in 1308 with six lasting universities. A second wave of university creations coincided with the first century of the Renaissance, from the maturity of Petrarch to the death of Leonardo Bruni (1444). Six more Italian universities, beginning with Florence in 1348 and ending with Catania in 1445, appeared. Then came a century-long pause, until the late Renaissance saw the creation of four more universities between 1540 and 1601. After another hiatus, Italians added additional universities in the second half of the seventeenth century.

The successive waves of Italian university foundings roughly paralleled the rest of Europe. While the university was the quintessential institution of the Middle Ages, the Renaissance more than doubled the number.[117]

115. Marra, 1975, vol. 1.

116. When in the middle of the sixteenth century the prince-archbishop of Trent proposed the establishment of a university, city council and citizenry strongly opposed him on these grounds. He abandoned the idea. Barsanti, 1980, 94.

117. See the list of university foundation dates through 1500 in Verger, 1992, 62–65; see Grendler, 1999b, for new universities of the sixteenth century.

CHAPTER 5

The University in Action

he Italian Renaissance university in action was a complex organization that behaved a little differently than its medieval predecessor or
northern European counterpart.

THE ORGANIZATION OF INSTRUCTION

The ceremonial opening of the academic year usually occurred on October
18, the Feast of Saint Luke the Evangelist.[1] It began with orations; the humanities
professor often represented the entire university with an oration praising all
disciplines but especially *studia humanitatis.* But lectures usually began only after
the consecutive religious holidays of All Saints' Day and All Souls' Day, November 1 and 2. And individual professors might further delay lectures for more or
less legitimate reasons. For example, in the faculty of arts at the University of
Padua in 1592, one professor began lecturing on November 2, fourteen on
November 3, and one each on November 7, 8, 9, 12, 18, and December 13 (the
newly appointed Galileo Galilei).[2]

Once the academic year began, three to five liturgical feasts interrupted the
teaching calendar every month. Universities marked with holidays the feast days
of the four early doctors of the church, most of the Twelve Apostles, and local
and regional patron saints and events in the lives of Jesus and Mary. In addition, the Christmas vacation usually started on December 21, the feast of Saint
Thomas the Apostle, and lasted the rest of the month, to be followed by the
holidays of January 1 and 6. A three-day Carnival vacation anticipated the beginning of Lent but could stretch to a week or longer.[3] The Easter vacation began on

1. Dallari, 1888–1924, 1:viii. The following is based on the 1387 statutes of Florence in Gherardi,
1973, 55–58, and the 1432 statutes of the legists at Bologna in Malagola, 1966, 102–3. For the Ferrara
calendar, see Secco Suardo, 1983, 158–59, and Thorndike, 1944, 335–37. This is just a sampling of
the available information.

2. Favaro, 1966, 2:116–17.

3. For a fifteen-day Carnival holiday at Siena, see Minnucci and Košuta, 1989, 571.

Palm Sunday and lasted until the Sunday after Easter, a total of fourteen days. The academic year was supposed to last until July 15, sometimes until mid-August. But few professors taught beyond the end of June, and some stopped earlier.

Renaissance universities had ordinary and extraordinary days of instruction. The ordinary teaching days were Monday, Tuesday, Wednesday, Friday, and Saturday; the extraordinary teaching days were Thursdays and holidays. However, Thursday might become an ordinary teaching day if a holiday occurred during the week.[4] No regular teaching took place during the extended holidays of Christmas, Carnival, and Easter. But the annual public anatomical dissection might be held during the Christmas or Carnival holidays. Because cold weather preserved the corpse longer, and because the dissection went on continuously for days and nights, attracting numerous students and professors from across the university, an extended winter vacation period was the best time. If the public anatomy took place in a nonvacation time, such as late January, other arts and medicine lectures were suspended.[5]

University calendars listed about 135 ordinary teaching days and about 45 extraordinary teaching days. However, students often transformed the vigils of feast days into holidays and extended the longer holidays, thus shortening the academic year. And citing tradition, a celebration, or a grievance, they sometimes refused to attend lectures on ordinary days. By the early seventeenth century so many unauthorized vacation days had crept into the calendar that the teaching year was reduced to half the mandated ordinary days and about 30 extraordinary days (see Ch. 14, "Private Teaching and Other Pedagogical Abuses").

Italian university rolls listed four kinds of professorships: ordinary (*ordinarius*), extraordinary (*extraordinarius*), holiday (*dies festivi*), and university (i.e., student) lectureships (*lecturae universitatis*).[6] Ordinary professors taught on the ordinary teaching days, and holiday professors taught on the holidays. But extraordinary professors and student lecturers might teach on either ordinary or extraordinary days, depending on local practice. One to several of each of the four kinds of professors taught major subjects in large universities. Ordinary professors of civil law, medical theory, medical practice, and natural philosophy were the university's most important men.

---

4. "Dal principio del Studio dunque fino alla vigilia de San Thomaso si devria per quel comandono li Statuti legger ogni giorno eccetto le domeniche et li giovedì, quando non occorre fra la settimana altre feste, le qual però se publicano per le Schole dalli Bidelli." Description of the University of Padua by Giovanni Francesco Trincavello, no date but second half of 1552, printed in Gallo, 1963, 76. Also: "Gli ordinarii leggono tutti i giorni di lavoro nei tempi soliti a leggersi, dal giovedì in poi (= in fuori) destinato a vacanza; e gli straordinarii leggono il giovedì, et tutti gli altri giorni delle feste." From an anonymous description of the University of Padua written about 1580, found in the archive of the University of Bologna and printed in Favaro, 1915, 249.

5. See Trincavello's comment of late 1552 approving the practice of Bologna: "Nel Studio di Bologna, nel qual non è lecito far l'Anatomia se non nelle vacationi o di Natale, overo di carnesciale, et non nelli tempi che si legge per non interromper le lettioni ordinarie." Gallo, 1963, 78–79 (quote 79). I have not attempted to discover how many universities did the same as Bologna.

6. The rolls of Bologna found in Dallari, 1888–1924, make these distinctions clear. However, the rolls of other universities seldom do so.

Ordinary professorships in major subjects usually had multiple occupants, so that students had several opportunities to hear lectures on statutory texts. For example, in a typical year Bologna had two ordinary professors of medical theory teaching in the morning and three more in the afternoon.[7] Several universities had five or six ordinary professors of civil law, half teaching at the same hour in the morning, and the other half teaching simultaneously in the afternoon. Other things being equal, teaching in the morning or afternoon did not manifest a difference in prestige. Possibly the star ordinary professor in a subject such as civil law taught either in the morning or the afternoon according to his preference.

Two or more ordinary professors teaching the same text at the same hour were concurrents competing for students. But they were seldom equal in prestige and salary. A medium-sized university might have two or three ordinary professors of medical theory, designated in the roll as first, second, and third. The first normally received a higher salary than the second, and the second more than the third.[8]

Medium to large universities also had one, two, or more holiday professorships in major subjects. A subject considered minor might be taught only as a holiday professorship; for example, moral philosophy was only a holiday professorship at Bologna for most of the fifteenth and early sixteenth centuries. Holiday professors enjoyed considerably less prestige and salary than ordinary professors.

Extraordinary professors mattered less than ordinary professors. That is the only generalization that can be made, because different universities imposed different obligations on extraordinary professors. Despite the title, perhaps a majority of extraordinary professors taught on ordinary days.[9] Some taught the same subjects and texts as ordinary professors on the ordinary days, but at different hours. For example, ordinary professors of law taught in the morning, and extraordinary professors of law taught in the afternoon at Padua in the fifteenth century.[10] On the other hand, extraordinary professors were required to lecture on different texts than the ordinary professors at the University of Pisa.[11] Some-

7. Dallari, 1888–1924, 1:124 (1484–85).

8. Padua was a partial exception. By the mid-sixteenth century, the Venetian government paid first- and second-place ordinary professors in a subject nearly the same salaries and occasionally paid the second a little more than the first. This may have been a means of encouraging competition and rewarding a second-place professor with superior abilities. (Some professors seem to have won higher salaries through their scholarship, others by securing the support of prominent Venetian senators.) But first and second ordinary professors never exchanged positions at Padua; the second-place professor had to wait until the first professor died or left before succeeding him.

9. For example, Padua in the mid-sixteenth century had extraordinary professors who taught on ordinary days and extraordinary professors who taught on extraordinary days. See Gallo, 1963, 66, 68–72. A further complication for the researcher is that the majority of surviving lists of professors are only unofficial rolls or salary lists. Neither distinguish between ordinary and extraordinary professors and provide only brief and inconsistent descriptions of positions. By contrast, the Bolognese rolls published by Dallari, 1888–1924, are official rolls.

10. Belloni, 1986, 77–79.

11. Marrara, 1993, 132–33.

times extraordinary professorships taught less prestigious subjects, such as a new field within civil law, on the ordinary teaching days. When a subject rose in status, the extraordinary professorship became an ordinary professorship. Finally, some extraordinary professors did teach only on the extraordinary days, becoming de facto holiday professors.

Almost all professors held only one position, even if it was only a low-paying holiday lectureship. Thus, a professor lectured once a day. Ordinary and some extraordinary professors lectured five days a week, fewer if a holiday occurred. Holiday lecturers delivered one or two lectures per week. But they did not teach on the most solemn holidays, such as Easter. Occasionally an ordinary professor added a holiday lectureship to his duties. Pietro Pomponazzi simultaneously held the first ordinary professorship of natural philosophy and the holiday lectureship in moral philosophy at Bologna from 1514 through 1521 (see Ch. 11, "Moral Philosophy in Other Universities"). He must have added the moral philosophy lectureship because he wanted to teach the subject; he certainly did not need the small additional income.

Universities had one-year student lectureships of two kinds. The student rectors of the arts and law student organizations almost always taught during the year of their rectorships. These student rector lectureships were listed at the head of the law and arts rolls, a reminder of their former importance. In addition, Bologna, Macerata, Parma, Pisa, and Siena appointed one or more students in the last year of study to teach. Bologna had the most elaborate program of student lectureships; it appointed up to eleven, typically five in law and six in arts, distributed over various subjects. Students had to have successfully completed a formal disputation and be within a year of taking the doctoral examination. The chosen students taught for one year at modest salaries but received cost-free degrees, a prize of considerable value. Pisa had four student lecturers, one each in canon law, civil law, arts, and medicine, again chosen after they had disputed. They taught on holidays.[12]

Lectures were distributed throughout the day according to a twenty-four-hour clock. The teaching schedule of Rome, a medium-sized university, in 1567–68 was typical, except for the six theologians lecturing at different hours. Most universities had only two theologians, perhaps one lecturing at the first morning hour and the other at the first afternoon hour. Or they lectured as concurrents. Professors lectured for one hour, although a university occasionally ordered two-hour lectures. However, students sometimes complained that professors did not lecture even one hour.

Rome's lecture schedule was designed to meet student needs. Lectures were distributed throughout the day so that a student could attend them in several subjects if he wished. Introductory subjects and less important professorships in major subjects (e.g., the extraordinary lecturers in natural philosophy and medi-

_____

12. See below for a detailed explanation of the disputations involved in the Bolognese student lectureships. For Pisa, see Verde, 1973–94, 2:613–27; Mango Tomei, 1976, 61–63; and Marrara, 1993, 126–27.

TABLE 5.1
Lectures at the University of Rome, 1567–1568

Morning	Afternoon
Hour 13 (7 A.M.)[a]	**Hour 20 (2 P.M.)**
Theology	Theology
Metaphysics	Hebrew
Institutes (three professors)	Natural philosophy, extraordinary
Greek (two)	Medical theory, extraordinary (two)
Surgery	Humanities
	Institutes (two)
Hour 15 (9 A.M.)[b]	**Hour 21 (3 P.M.)**
Theology	Theology
Canon law	Canon law (two)
Medical theory (two)	*Pandects* (humanistic law)
Logic (two)	Medical practice (two)
Hour 16 (10 A.M.)	**Hour 22 (4 P.M.)**
Theology	Theology
Civil law (two)	Civil law (two)
Natural philosophy (two)	Natural philosophy (two)
Mathematics	

There was also a holiday lectureship in medicinal simples.

Source: I maestri di Roma, 1991, 51–55.

Note: The lecture schedule changed very little over the next twenty-five years.

[a]Renaissance Italians divided the day into twenty-four one-hour segments beginning at sunset. Sunset was hour zero; hour one was one hour after sunset, hour two was two hours after sunset, and so on. The time of day according to the modern North American clock has been added. For the modern hours it is assumed that sunset occurred at 6 P.M. in early November, the beginning of the academic year. The lecture hours expressed according to the modern clock changed as the hour of sunset advanced in December and receded after December 21.

[b]It does not appear that those who taught at the thirteenth hour lectured for two hours, but that there was a gap in the teaching day.

cal theory) appeared in the first morning and first afternoon hours. Five different professors lecturing at two different hours taught *Institutes,* considered a foundation course needed by all law students. Logic, judged useful to both arts and law students, occupied the second morning hour. No scheduling conflict existed between the ordinary lectures in natural philosophy, medical theory, and medical practice, all essential for medical students. The surgery lecture, which sometimes included anatomy (this roll is silent on the matter), met at a different hour than other medical lectures. Civil law lectures were held at preferred hours in the late morning and in the middle of the afternoon. The schedule distributed throughout the day subjects, such as mathematics and humanities, considered useful and desirable but not essential. Finally, Rome, like most middle-sized universities, had two or three concurrents in all the major subjects but none in the less essential subjects. Small universities had very few concurrents, whereas Bologna,

with the largest faculty in Italy, had concurrents (up to six teaching simultaneously) almost everywhere in the timetable.

The student career of Francesco Guicciardini (1483–1540) illustrates some of
the pedagogical choices in courses, professors, and universities which a student
might make.[13] He began his studies at the University of Pisa (then located in
Florence) at the end of November 1498 by attending lectures on the *Institutes*. He
was only fifteen, two or three years younger than the average beginner. In the
academic year 1499–1500 he continued to attend the lectures on *Institutes* from
the same professor in the afternoon plus lectures on civil law in the morning. In
1500–1501 he heard the civil law lectures of Filippo Decio, the star civilian, in the
morning and another series of lectures in civil law from a different professor in
the afternoon.

But in March 1501 he moved to the University of Ferrara. Although his father
believed that young Francesco would study harder at a university outside Florence and had always intended to send him away, politics made it imperative. As
enemies threatened Florence, Guicciardini Senior wanted a member of the family outside Florence in case he had to move his fortune in a hurry. Francesco
remained at Ferrara for about a year and a half, always attending both a morning
and an afternoon series of lectures in civil law.

Dissatisfied with Ferrara, he moved to the University of Padua in the fall of
1502. He attended the afternoon civil law lectures of Carlo Ruini, the most
famous legist at Padua, all three of his years there. During the first two, he
attended the morning civil law lectures of Cristofano Alberizio da Pavia, a minor
figure who did not please Guicciardini, from November to Easter and the canon
law lectures of Filippo Decio, his former teacher at Pisa / Florence, from Easter to
the end of the year. Guicciardini also lodged in Decio's house for two years,
1502–4. In 1504–5, his last year of study, Guicciardini attended the civil law
lectures of a little-known professor in the morning and the famous Ruini in the
afternoon. He returned to Florence to take his doctorate in civil law on November 15, 1505, at the age of twenty-two and one-half, some two or three years
younger than the average. The degree cost him 26 ducats. He decided not to take
a degree *in utroque iure,* because "the degree in canon law was of little value" and
would have cost another 12.5 ducats.[14] Despite this economy, Guicciardini Senior spent more than 500 gold ducats on his son's seven years of study.

Guicciardini attended three universities, moving from the local institution to a
second-rank university and then to the prestigious Padua. Because the curricular
texts on which professors lectured were the same everywhere, such moves produced little academic dislocation. The diligent Guicciardini always attended two
series of ordinary lectures, morning and afternoon; many students attended only
one lecture a day.[15] On the other hand, Guicciardini did not mention attending

13. The following comes from Guicciardini's *Recordanze,* his diary. Guicciardini, 1936, 54–57;
English translation, Guicciardini, 1965, 129–33.

14. Guicciardini, 1965, 133.

15. Francesco Gandolfo, professor of canon law at Bologna, lamented that very few students

any holiday lectures. He began with two years of lectures on the *Institutes* and then spent the rest of his student career listening to lectures on civil law, plus a year of lectures in canon law. Guicciardini heard the lectures of both academic stars and obscure professors. On four occasions he attended the lectures of a professor for more than one year. Because the law curriculum at Padua required four years of morning and afternoon lectures to cover all of the *Corpus juris civilis* (see Ch. 13, "Padua and Bologna"), Guicciardini probably heard lectures on different books from year to year. And if he heard lectures on the same books, going over the same material more than once may have deepened his understanding. Preference for one professor over others obviously helped determine his classroom choices, but possibly so did self-interest: Decio and Ruini were influential legists whose support might be useful to a young man. And if Guicciardini had taken his degree at Padua, they would have been notable promoters.

The single-minded Guicciardini did not mention attending lectures on any subject except law. Other students had broader tastes. For example, in 1597 students at Padua complained that students who heard the humanist professor could not attend the *Institutes* lecture, and vice-versa, because they met at the same hour.[16] Arts and medicine students expected to hear lectures in logic, natural philosophy, medical theory, and medical practice and to attend the annual anatomical dissection.

Guicciardini's comments on his brief teaching career underscored the competitive nature of concurrency. On October 31, 1505, Guicciardini was appointed to teach *Institutes* at the University of Pisa, temporarily located in Florence. He received the low salary of 25 florins and began teaching on November 9. He competed effectively for students with three concurrents.

> My concurrents were messer Giovan Battista Gamberelli, or Lastraiuolo, who was one of the most senior doctors in Florence, but not very learned, and messer Iacopo Modesti da Carmignano, whose *Institutes* lectures I had attended, and messer Francesco di Bartolommeo Pandolfini who had started to lecture the year I began attending the university. We began on November 9th and in spite of their greater experience messer Giovan Battista and messer Francesco had fewer listeners than I had, while messer Iacopo and I were more or less equal. Actually if there was a difference he had the advantage of me, more because of the nobility of some of his pupils rather than greater numbers.[17]

---

attended both morning and afternoon classes. ASB, Assunteria dello Studio, Bu. 79, unpaginated letter, no date but 1592 or 1593.

16. "Lamentandosi molti scholari, che ascoltano l'Humanista, che non possono ascoltare l'Instituta, et molti, che ascoltano l'Instituta, che non possono ascoltar la Rhetorica, proprio instrumento della scienza civile." Letter of an officer of the student arts organization to the Riformatori, Nov. 8, 1597, in ASVe, Riformatori dello Studio di Padova, F. 419, no pag. Note the use of "Humanista" and "Instituta" to describe the professors in these subjects.

17. Guicciardini, 1936, 56; English translation, with slight modifications, from Guicciardini, 1965, 132–33. These professors are found in Verde, 1973–94, 2:234–35, 306–7, 388–89.

If Guicciardini had intended to pursue an academic career, he would have begun writing legal treatises and angling for a higher professorship at Florence or elsewhere. Instead, the university closed in 1506, and Guicciardini began to practice law. He retained a connection by examining degree candidates as a member of the Florentine college of doctors of law for several years (see below).

Attendance at a professor's lectures ranged from ten to more than a hundred. In early December 1489 the beadle listed the attendance at the lectures of five legists and six professors of arts and medicine at the University of Pisa, then located in Pisa. Bartolomeo Sozzini, a famous professor of civil law, had 115 to 120 students, the canonist 40 students, the civilian Filippo Decio 36, and the other two legists 20 to 22 and 10 to 12 students, respectively. Two concurrent professors of medical theory had 14 to 15 and 8 to 10, respectively. Two concurrent professors of practical medicine had 12 to 14 and 9 to 10 students. The two concurrent professors of logic had 20 to 22 and 16 to 18 students. The total enrollment was between 220 and 275 students.[18] Larger universities probably did not have individual classes any larger than Sozzini's 120 but had many more classes in the range of 40 to 70 students. For example, Baldassare Rasini, ordinary professor of rhetoric at Pavia, stated that he had 63 students attending his lectures in 1448.[19]

Professors who taught many students asked for higher salaries. In 1602 or 1603 an anonymous petitioner pleaded for a higher salary for Paolo Beni, the ordinary professor of humanities at Padua. He merited a salary increment because he taught a large number of students and had brought the humanities professorship back to life, according to the petitioner. Antonio Riccobono, Beni's predecessor, had had an average of no more than a dozen students, despite teaching for more than thirty years, he wrote. But Beni had taught "hundreds" of students in his first two years (he began teaching at Padua in March 1600); he taught more students than the first ordinary professor of *Institutes* and many other lecturers. And 60 or 70 students were attending his lectures in the current year (1602–3). Beni's full classes were even more remarkable because he taught at the same hour as ten other principal lecturers in an era of declining enrollments at Padua. And Beni had to compete with a horde of private teachers who drew students away from the university lectures, the petitioner concluded.[20]

18. Verde, 1973–94, 4:865, letter of Dec. 2, 1489, Pisa. Fuller identifications of the professors are found in ibid., 1:337–39, with additional information in ibid., vol. 2, see the index. For a short biography of Bartolomeo Sozzini (1436–1506), see Chapter 13. These were the most important ordinary professors; the official did not give the attendance at the lectures of the other twenty-five professors. See Verde, 1973–94, 4:143–44 (Nov. 22, 1474), 800 (Mar. 28, 1489), for similar class attendance figures.

19. Sottili, 1982, 527.

20. "Primo. che il suo antecessare havea letto più di 30 anni senza passar ordinariamente una dozzena di scolari, non ostante che lo studio in quei tempi fosse fioritissimo dove che il Beni lesse i due primi anni come centinaia di scolari, remettendo quella catedra in piedi . . . nonostante che lo studio sminuito assai di scolari, e che all'hora ch'egli legge, leggano X altri lettori principali, e che di più i lettori di logica, per gara ch'hanno insieme, in quell'hora nimenino dalle scole a casa i loro

There is no reason to doubt the general accuracy of the attendance claims, because the beadle could verify or deny the figures. And Padua's university building had some large rooms capable of holding a hundred or more students. Even if the account exaggerated Beni's popularity, the fame and competence of a professor and the importance of the subject certainly caused attendance to rise or fall. A first ordinary professor probably attracted more students than his concurrents or extraordinary professors teaching on ordinary days. The number of students hearing holiday lecturers is difficult to estimate, while student lecturers probably attracted few listeners.

In addition to classroom instruction, university towns hosted numerous informal study circles. Professors, students, and amateurs met to read, discuss, enjoy one another's company, and win friends and make contacts. A wealthy nobleman might serve as host; out-of-town visitors added fresh perspectives. Indeed, the presence of a university almost ensured international participation. For example, Italian, English, and northern European professors, students, and nonstudents gathered in the luxurious household of Reginald Pole (1500–1558) in Padua between 1521 and 1526 to air humanistic, philosophical, and religious issues. Niccolò Leonico Tomeo (1456–1531), Greek scholar and former professor, was their intellectual leader.[21] One doubts that such a group could have come together beyond a university town.

LATIN

Latin was the language of lecture hall, disputation, and text. Hence, professor and student needed to speak Latin fluently and well. As one professor warned, if you possess more knowledge than Avicenna and more experience than Galen but must search for words when disputing or conversing, you will be a laughing stock. You must become fluent in Latin. Speak it in the university, at table, while studying, at rest, and when walking alone. Only then will you be able to dispute and to discuss scholarly matters with other students.[22]

---

scolari, senza lasciarli ascoltar' Humanita come si costumava: e che all'istess'hora molt'altri dottori etiandio che non siano lettori di studio, leggano a casa, e ne' monasteri, con spogliar lo studio della solita frequenza e far pratiche straordinarie per divertir i giovani dallo studio publico. La onde sicome quest'anno ordinariamente ha letto con 60, e 70 scolari come ogniun' ha veduto. . . . : tanto che i due anni adietro ha finito di leggere con più numero di scolari che il primo Institutario e molti altri lettori principali." Unsigned and undated (but 1602–3) petition to the Riformatori in ASVe, Riformatori dello Studio di Padova, Bu. 420, no pag.

The petition can be dated from the statement that the current academic year was Beni's third at Padua. Although the petition lacks an author, one can be certain that Beni knew of it. The petitioner also added two more reasons for a raise: Beni had written many books, and he had a good Latin style. It is not known if Beni's salary was raised at this time. Incidentally, the petitioner very slightly exaggerated Riccobono's tenure: he taught at Padua twenty-eight years, 1571–99, not more than thirty years.

21. Fenlon, 1972, 24–27, and Woolfson, 1998, 110–17. See Chapter 8, "Greek Texts and Commentaries," for more on Tomeo.

22. Lombardelli, 1594, 39ᵛ–40ʳ.

In practice, the quality of spoken Latin varied. Much was probably serviceable rather than eloquent. In an Italian-dominated student body and professoriat, it is likely that professors and students sometimes, perhaps often, abandoned classical usage in favor of Italianate word forms and analytic word order.[23] And it could be worse. In the 1560s and 1570s the beadle strongly criticized the professor of surgery at the University of Rome for speaking poor Latin and for slipping into Italian. Because students did not want to listen to his poor Latin, he had few students.[24] In 1589 the University of Siena permitted the anatomist, the lecturer on medical botany (*semplicista*), the mathematician, and the Italian lecturer to lecture in Italian.[25] No other university authorized such a radical change.

A handful of attempts were made to introduce professorships of Italian, in order to teach foreign students the Italian language, not the glories of Italian literature. On the request of its German nation, Siena in 1589 established a professorship "di lingua Toscana," with enrollment restricted to German students.[26] Citing the Sienese precedent, the German nation at Padua requested such a post in the early seventeenth century. Ingolfo de' Conti, the Paduan professor charged with finding ways to check the decline of the university, endorsed the proposal on the grounds that it would attract more students. But nothing happened.[27] Foreign students had to learn the language of the street and the majority of students on their own. Wealthy students hired tutors.

DISPUTATIONS

Learning in the Renaissance university took place in a verbal arena. The ability to argue strongly and well, always in Latin, was a highly prized skill. Although lecture and degree examination were also oral performances, the disputation best expressed the verbal character of the Renaissance university.

The disputation was a formal debate in the presence of an audience. It may have developed out of *quaestiones,* that is, explorations of contested points, pursued by medieval professors in their lectures. Disputations became regular occur-

---

23. See the interesting comments of William McCuaig on a surviving fragment of a series of lectures on poetics by Carlo Sigonio, who taught at Padua and Bologna. McCuaig, 1983, 49–50.

24. "D. Benalbus Brancalupus . . . hic non satis colet linguam latinam, et legit sermone vulgari." And "Hic paucos habet scholares. De hoc conqueruntur scholares ob imperitiam linguae latinae veteranique non satis dignantur suas adire lectiones." Comments of the beadle, Alessio Lorenzani, in *I maestri di Roma,* 1991, 39 (1566), 60 (1568–69). For other comments and references to Benalba (or Menalba) Brancalupo, who taught surgery at Rome from at least 1563 through 1582, see ibid., 35, 51–52, 65–66, 76, 86, 99, 110, 115, 122.

25. Marrara, 1970, 161; Cascio Pratilli, 1975, 91.

26. Rossi, 1910; Beccaria, 1970; Marrara, 1970, 20, 44–45, 161, 163, 228, 231, 232, 233, 235, 236, 238, 240, 241, 243, 245, 247, 248; Cascio Pratilli, 1975, 79–81, 83–84 n. 22, 188; and Maraschio and Poggi Salani, 1991.

27. See an undated (but 1613 or 1614) three-page memorandum on the subject by Angelo Ingegneri in ASVe, Riformatori di Studio di Padova, Bu. 429, no pag., plus other references scattered throughout the busta. See also AAUP, F. 630, "Discorso di Ingolfo de' Conti di Padova circa il regolare i scolari dello Studio di Padova," f. 266ʳ, no date but 1615.

rences in northern European universities by the mid-thirteenth century. Disputants might focus on a particular question (*quaestio disputata*) or on any subject (*disputatio de quolibet*).[28] Two or more disputants argued according to Aristotelian principles of argumentation for and against various propositions in order to arrive at the truth and convince the audience. Victory, rather than consensus, was the goal. The skills needed to win a disputation—drawing distinctions according to logical principles, stating one's views forcefully, pointing out errors in the statements of opponents, and quoting authoritative texts from memory—were considered useful in all areas of professional life.[29]

Even some humanists praised this quintessential Scholastic activity. Leonardo Bruni put warm praise for disputations into the mouth of Coluccio Salutati in book 1 of his *Dialogi ad Petrum Histrum* (1401): "What sharpens the intellect, rendering it more clever and versatile, better than disputation, since in a brief space of time one must apply one's self to the topic and thence reflect, discourse, make inferences, and conclusions?" Bruni had Salutati say, "When I was a young student of grammar in Bologna I spent every hour of every day in disputation. I challenged my comrades and questioned my teachers."[30] On the other hand, some early Italian humanists were unenthusiastic about the disputation, because they identified it with late medieval terminist (i.e., British) logic.[31]

Numerous university professors and students swept aside doubts. They praised disputations and emphasized their importance in university education. Communicating and disputing imprint on the mind what one has heard or read better than any other exercise, wrote one commentator in 1588. For understanding and penetrating deeply into subtleties, there is nothing more valuable than the disputation. Continual questioning develops the ability to recognize the truth. Many shy and faint-hearted students become eager and bold through argument.[32] Flee those young men who have doctorates but have done little disputing, wrote a Sienese professor in 1578.[33]

Disputations helped professors build reputations for learning. The medical professor Girolamo Cardano (1501–76) boasted that no one in Milan, Pavia, Bologna, France, or Germany had ever bested him in a disputation. He was particularly proud of his ability to discomfit his opponent by quoting passages

28. See Kenny and Pinborg, 1982, 21–29; Maierù, 1989; and Cobban, 1990, 167–71, 200.

29. Cobban (1990, 14, 161–62) makes this point well. See also Brugi, 1922, 58–61.

30. The English translation in Bruni, 1987, 64, 65, is quoted.

31. See Chapter 7, "Teaching and Research," and Gilbert, 1971.

32. Bartolomeo Meduna, *Lo scolare* (Venice: Pietro Fachinetti, 1588), as quoted extensively in Volpicelli, 1960, 385. From Friuli, Meduna (fl. mid-to late sixteenth century) was a Franciscan Conventual with a theological degree. See Volpicelli, 1960, 599–600.

33. Lombardelli, 1594, 40ᵛ. This appears in a long letter of advice of 1578 to his brother who was studying at the University of Pisa. Lombardelli (1540/45–1608) taught humanities at the University of Siena, then at the seminary there. The encyclopaedist Tommaso Garzoni (1549–89) added more praise for disputing: "Sopra tutto bisognarebbe, che spessissime fiate disputassero con gli altri perche la disputa . . . è quella ch'aguzza l'intelletto, & lo fa penetrare dove la lettura & lo studio non perviene." Garzoni, 1601, discorso 101, p. 727. First published in 1585, this book was reprinted eleven times through 1665.

from memory. A successful disputation attracted students to a professor's lectures, while a poor performance diminished him in the eyes of colleagues and students.[34]

Success in disputing earned rewards. For example, the University of Bologna offered up to eleven one-year lectureships (five in law, the rest in six different arts subjects) to students. The holders had to be foreign (i.e., non-Bolognese), poor (undefined, but possibly only relatively poor), and near the conclusion of their studies. Most important, a student qualified for a lectureship by successfully disputing in the subject in which he wished to lecture. The student's disputation performance probably determined whether he received a lectureship in the following academic year.

A placard announced these formal student disputations.[35] A notice (see fig. 5) proclaimed that Iacobus Ebelinus Germanus would dispute on astrology (meaning astronomy in this case) on March 29, 1509. He would dispute under the authority of the student rector of arts and the supervision of Professor Galeotto Beccadelli, an ordinary professor of medical theory. The principal question (*dubium*) was, Do celestial bodies shine by their own light or do they reflect light from another body? Six consequent theses (*conclusiones*), two with corollaries, were also to be disputed. Theses and corollaries were usually drawn from, or based on, curricular texts, especially those of Aristotle. Ebelin would hold the position that celestial bodies produce their own light.[36] This disputation seemed fairly simple; some involved many more theses, corollaries, and additional problems (*impertinentia*) spread over several subjects.

At the appointed place and time, and in the presence of as many students and professors who came, Jacob Ebelin took on all comers. It is likely that the disputation lasted two or three hours or longer, that a good number of students and professors participated, and that it was noisy. Jacob Ebelin must have disputed well, because he held the student lectureship in astronomy for the academic year 1509–10.[37]

Professors also engaged in formal disputations. Giovanni Domenico Albertazzi, a priest who taught logic at the University of Bologna from 1592 to 1594, announced that he would hold a public disputation on November 28, 1592, at the fifteenth hour (about 9 A.M.). Calling himself a philosopher, he offered to dispute one hundred theses in humanistic studies, logic, natural phi-

34. Cardano, 1982, ch. 12, pp. 60–62. He particularly mentioned a three-day disputation against a rival professor at Pavia. See also the comments of Francesco de' Vieri (Francesco Verino il Secondo), a professor of natural philosophy at Pisa, writing in 1587. Del Fante, 1980b, 402.

35. The following is based on ASB, Riformatori dello Studio, "Dispute e ripetizioni di scolari per ottenere letture d'università, 1487–1515," which includes numerous disputation notices through 1520. Matsen (1977, 1985, and 1994) analyzes these documents well. Piana (1984, 92*–102*) and Verde (1973–94, vol. 4, pt. 3, pp. 1378–83) print some material from these documents.

36. ASB, Riformatori dello Studio, "Dispute e ripetizioni di scolari per ottenere letture d'università, 1487–1515," f. 278. Matsen (1994) provides descriptions of several Bolognese disputation notices, including this one on p. 547. For Beccadelli's appointment, see Dallari, 1888–1924, 1:201. He taught at Bologna from 1497 through 1511.

37. Dallari, 1888–1924, 1:206; Matsen, 1994, 547–48 n. 82.

¶IMPETRATA Prius licentia a Magnifico ac generoſo
uiro Domino Hieronymo Tigrino de Bagnacauallo Arti
ſtarum et Medicorum Alme uniuerſitatis Bononie Recto
re digniſſimo. Iacobus Ebelinus Germanus artium Magi/
ſter minimus inter medicine Scolares infra dubium cum ſu
is Concluſionibus: et Correlariis. Sub excellentiſſimo arti/
um et medicine Doctore Magiſtro Galeoto de Bicadellis
ſuſtinere conabitur. Die Veneris penultima Martii.

Dubium Aſtrologicum

Vtrum corpora celeſtia ſint de ſe lucida uel ab alio lumen re
cipiant.

P. cocluſio. Sol exiſtens in medio planetarum non omnimodam eis luci/
ditatem preſtat.

.ii. cocluſio/ Oppoſitio corporis celeſtis ad aliud corpus celeſte non impe
dit eius lumen.

.iii. cocluſio Luciditatem maiorem eſſe in ſole q̃ in aliis aſtris firmiter te/
nemus.

iiii. cocluſi. Non quelibet pars celi eſt eiuſdem denſitatis et raritatis cum
reliqua.

Correlariũ. Non quelibet pars celi eſt eiuſdem diaphaneitatis et lumino/
ſitatis cum reliqua.

.V. coclu. Omnem partem celi de ſe eſſe luminoſam ſuſtinere conabi/
mur.

.VI. cuclu. Omnia corpora celeſtia per ſuum lumen cauſare caliditatem
in iſtis inferioribus concedimus.

Correlariũ. Aliquod corpus per ſuum lumen in iſtis inferioribus non tan
tum cauſare caliditatem ſed etiam combuſtionem non ne/
gamus.

Cõ. Reſpõ. Pars affirmatiua dubii eſt uera.

Fig. 5. Printed notice for the disputation of student Iacobus Ebelinus Germanus,
University of Bologna, on March 29, 1509. *ASB, Riformatori dello Studio,* "Dispute e
ripetizioni di scolari per ottenere letture d'università 1487–1515."

losophy, metaphysics, mathematics, moral philosophy, and especially theology (theses 39–100).[38]

The most famous disputation of the Renaissance never happened. In early December 1486, Giovanni Pico della Mirandola published his *Conclusiones nongentae,* offering to defend them in a disputation to be held in Rome sometime after January 6, 1487. The nine hundred theses drew upon a vast array of reading covering practically every university subject, plus material that was not part of the curriculum. Pico sent copies to Italian universities, inviting philosophers and theologians to come and dispute with him. One wonders what professors and students made of Pico's grand proposal. But the papacy condemned thirteen of the theses, and the disputation never took place.[39]

But many other formal and informal disputations went forward. University statutes required professors and students to dispute formally. For example, all professors at Padua were required to engage in formal disputations twice a year, before and after the Easter holidays.[40] Sometimes these led to memorable (and lengthy) confrontations. Many universities also required frequent "circular disputations" (*disputationes circulares*). At the end of each lecture, or once a week, professor and students were required to gather in a circle outside the classroom, often in the piazza, in order to dispute with one another and the professor over the conclusions reached in the lecture.[41] At Padua circular disputations occurred daily in the late afternoon (hour twenty-three) with professors and students required to attend. The statutes threatened professors who absented themselves with small fines (20 soldi) and admonished students to be polite and quiet.[42] Some professors did not like circular disputations and tried to avoid them.

Students practiced disputing. Residence colleges usually required their students to participate in disputations on a regular basis. For example, the Collegio della Sapienza at Pisa held student disputations every Saturday afternoon. One

38. ASB, Assunteria dello Studio, Requisiti dei Lettori, Bu. 30, item 10a, a fourteen-page printed pamphlet listing the theses. The date and time of the disputation have been filled in by hand. See Dallari, 1888–1924, 2:245, 249, for his teaching appointments.

39. For a modern edition, Italian translation, and account of the circumstances, see Pico della Mirandola, 1995.

40. *Statuta artistarum Achademiae Patavinae,* 1496, bk. 2, ch. 19, Sig. G^r–^{v}. The requirement dates from at least 1465, as this work prints the 1465 statutes with additions. The disputation requirement appears in subsequent editions of the statutes, for example, in *Statuta artistarum et medicorum Patavini Gymnasii,* 1589. For the same requirement for the law professors, see *Statuta iuristarum Patavini Gymnasii,* 1550, bk. 2, ch. 11, ff. 77^v–79^r. For the disputation requirement at Siena, see Minnucci and Košuta, 1989, 116–18.

41. Maierù, 1994, 64 n. 111, with quotes from the statutes of the universities of Bologna, Padua, and Pisa. For Macerata, see Foglietti, 1878, 72. For Perugia, see Ermini, 1971, 454–56. For Pisa, see Mango Tomei, 1976, 61; Spagnesi, 1993, 222–23; and Verde, 1998, 117. For Siena, see Minnucci and Košuta, 1989, 38–39. For Rome, see Conte, 1998, 174–75, 178.

42. *Statuta artistarum Achademiae Patavinae,* 1496, bk. 2, ch. 23, Sig. G^r–^{v}; repeated in *Statuta artistarum et medicorum Patavini Gymnasii,* 1589. Legists were also required to participate in circular disputations: *Statuta iuristarum Patavini Gymnasii,* 1550, f. 79^r–^{v}, referring to a 1474 ducal decree.

student, chosen by lot fifteen days earlier, defended one or two theses against three or more other students who took the opposite side, all done in the presence of professors.[43]

Although invariably exhorted or required to conduct disputes in courteous tones and with respect for opponents, students and professors did not always do so.[44] A student at Pavia offered this advice to deflect sharp attacks: if you must cede a point, make it appear as if you are doing so through politeness. This is a secret style that serves shrewd professors well in circular disputations.[45] But the format of the disputation encouraged attacks. And strong statements combined with the Renaissance habit of invective produced some nasty verbal and written confrontations.[46]

CIVIL AUTHORITY AND STUDENT POWER

Civil governments made all significant university decisions because they paid professorial salaries and other expenses. Students had little formal power but still sought to influence university policy through persuasion.

Commune or prince usually ruled the university through an intermediate body. The highest authority elected or appointed a magistracy of three to nine men to oversee the university. Called Riformatori dello Studio (Bologna, Ferrara, Padua, Parma, Pavia, and Turin), Assunteria di Studio (Bologna in the sixteenth century),[47] Savi dello Studio (Siena), or Ufficiali dello Studio (Florence), the magistracies consisted of leading citizens and officeholders who often possessed doctoral degrees from the local university. The Riformatori represented the university to the highest councils of government and vice versa. They listened to students or professors. They decided when to suppress or create professorships and whom to appoint, and they suggested salary figures. Prince or governing council then issued decrees or passed legislation. The Riformatori promulgated disciplinary regulations for professors and students—and often saw them ignored.

However, Riformatori did not administer the university in a modern sense. Indeed, universities had no administrative staff beyond one or two beadles and a bell ringer. The former visited classrooms daily to make sure that professors showed up for classes and that the required minimum number of students were in attendance. Universities mostly ran themselves on a daily basis.

---

43. Toniolo Fascione, 1980, 84–85. The Collegio Ferdinando at Pisa and the Ghislieri and Borromeo colleges at Pavia also required students to dispute on a regular basis.

44. For examples of advice to students to dispute politely, see Lombardelli, 1594, 44ʳ; Roero, 1604, 70–72; and Volpicelli, 1960, 385–86, passages from Meduna, *Lo scolare* of 1588.

45. "Se cederai, parrà che tu ceda per cortesia, e questo è uno stile secreto che servano gli aveduti lettori ne' circoli." Roero, 1604, 72.

46. McCuaig (1989, 43–49, 64–65, 203) gives examples from the career of Carlo Sigonio.

47. As explained in Chapter 1, Bologna added a second magistracy (the Assunteria) to oversee the university in the 1520s. It gradually assumed control over more important university matters at the expense of the Riformatori.

The University of Pisa after 1543 was the major exception; there no magistracy intervened between university and ultimate civil authority. The Medici grand duke of Florence and his chief minister exercised direct control over the University of Pisa by means of an appointed civil servant called a *provveditore.* The latter gradually assumed control over all aspects of the university and reported all to the grand dukes, who made decisions (see Ch. 3).

The student *universitas,* that is, the students organized in order to hire professors and to lead the community of students and masters, were only shadows of their medieval selves in the Renaissance. In the early fifteenth century students still voted for the occupants of some professorships. But over the course of two centuries, governments citing the argument that such elections produced fighting and public disorder removed the right to choose professors for all except a handful of junior positions. For example, the Venetian Senate eliminated the remaining student-elective positions at Padua in 1560.[48] If displeased, student leaders still threatened to move the entire student body to another city. When the communal authorities decided to execute a student for a crime of violence, students charged that this violated their traditional immunity from local prosecution and threatened to leave. But no significant student migrations occurred in the fifteenth and sixteenth centuries. The most important, at least to the students, remaining privilege was the right to bear arms. Civil authorities had little success eliminating or restricting this right.

As in centuries past, the students annually elected their leaders, a rector and councillors for both the arts and law *universitates.* Although still boasting ceremonial and symbolic prestige, rectors had little real power, and some gradually disappeared. At Bologna rectors sometimes served more than one year for lack of a successor in the early sixteenth century. Only a single rector was elected for both arts and law in the mid-1550s. The office often stood vacant in the 1560s and 1570s, and it disappeared completely after 1579–80. The same happened at Perugia.[49]

Although their power had eroded, student organizations still sought to influence governments. When they wanted something, they sent their leaders to speak, and governments usually listened. For example, the Venetian authorities always paid attention to the German law nation, because it was a large, well-organized group of wealthy students who brought considerable prestige to the university and income to the local economy. Students sometimes campaigned for the appointment of an individual scholar. The arts organization and some law students of Padua asked the Riformatori to establish a lectureship in botany in 1532 (see Ch. 9, "Medical Botany"), and the student arts organization and the German arts nation urged the Venetian Senate to suppress the Jesuit school at Padua in 1591 (Ch. 14, "Competition from Religious Order Schools"). The government did as the students wished in these cases. But because nonstudents,

48. Dupuigrenet Desroussilles, 1980, 646; De Bernardin, 1983, 77.
49. Sorbelli, 1940, 12–17; Ermini, 1971, 203, 208.

especially professors, also sought these goals, it is impossible to determine if student pressure was the deciding factor.

PROFESSORS

Professors were the most important part of the university. Prominent scholars attracted students, while high enrollments, especially of students of noble status, built the reputation of the university. The qualities, careers, salaries, and movements of professors mattered both to themselves and to universities.

Academics, communal officials, and students agreed that the ideal professor should possess three qualities: an acute intellect, a good memory, and a fluent and forceful delivery.[50] First and foremost, the able professor could explicate a passage or text subtly and convincingly. He worked his way through the maze of commentaries, resolved contradictions, refuted opposing views, and arrived at a satisfactory solution. This ability was prized because professors lectured on texts on which many previous scholars had written. And a professor needed to surpass his concurrent lecturing on the same text. Moreover, the ideal professor explicated a text in such a way that even students of modest abilities could grasp the meaning.

Second, the good professor possessed a trained and well-stocked memory. He was expected to be able to recite passages from memory in order to prove his points. A good memory also helped him to lecture in an orderly manner. And, paradoxically, a capacious memory helped create spontaneous teaching, which university culture prized. Students did not want a professor to read his lectures; someone who did was a *doctor chartaceus* (paper doctor). In 1592 and 1596 the Venetian government forbade professors at Padua from reading their lectures under pain of a salary reduction of 20 ducats.[51] A prodigious memory helped the professor to lecture without notes. One senior scholar advised future academics to develop the capacity of their memories at a young age, and he urged colleagues to exercise theirs daily. Memory was an essential tool in the pedagogical arsenal.

Third, the good professor expressed himself fluently and forcefully in good Latin. He needed a strong presentation in order to imprint the principles of his discipline on the minds of listeners, especially the slower students. The professor should not have to search for the appropriate Latin word. Good students would be offended if the professor hesitated or made mistakes, wrote one professor. He had to deliver his lectures with enough eloquence and energy that his listeners

50. The description is an amalgam of three discussions on the qualities of an ideal professor. The first is a letter of 1583 of a Bolognese official reporting on a professor from Salerno being considered for the afternoon first ordinary professor of civil law at Bologna. He measured the candidate against the ideal. Costa, 1903–4, 250–51. The second is that of Paolo Beni, professor of humanities at Padua, written 1600–1610. ASVa, Archivio Beni, Ms. 123, pp. [36, 39–49]. The third is by Annibale Roero, who studied law at Pavia between 1596 and 1602. Roero, 1604, 28–29.

51. Facciolati, 1978, pt. 3:29–30; Brugi, 1922, 89–90. However, Paolo Beni did not object to a professor using notes in order to summarize the principal points. And he endorsed bringing a book to class, if the professor had to quote a text at length. ASVa, Archivio Beni, Ms. 123, pp. [43–44].

would remember the points. If a professor speaks only languidly, one student groused, he might as well send a servant in his place to read his lecture.

In addition to these primary qualities, communal officials searching for a star professor wanted someone of high reputation who would attract students. This meant a scholar boasting numerous publications, such as the ubiquitous law and medicine *consilia*. By contrast, students seem to have paid little attention to publications. They wanted professors who would explain the texts well enough so that they would pass the doctoral examination.

The majority of professors obtained university appointments immediately after receiving doctorates; a minority, especially medical men, practiced their profession for a few years before assuming academic posts. A handful accepted professorships after practicing their professions for many years. Professors normally received contracts (*condotte*) of one to four years without guarantee of renewal. Lifetime appointments were extremely rare and given only to professors of mature years whom the government particularly favored.[52] Nevertheless, contracts were almost always renewed indefinitely at the same or a higher salary. Even though the modern concept of academic tenure did not exist, professors were seldom dismissed or failed to receive contract renewals.[53] At the same time, a few poorly paid introductory positions were reserved for recent graduates and limited, at least by custom, to one or two years. Examples include the medical lectureship on the third book of Avicenna, an introductory logic position, and the moral philosophy professorship until 1560, all at Padua, and some *Institutes* professorships at Siena.[54] When the year or two ended, the young scholar either moved to another position or left the university to pursue a professional career. And in the late sixteenth century Pisa used the logic appointments of one to three years as testing grounds for young scholars. Those who taught satisfactorily advanced to professorships of natural philosophy. Those who did not left (Ch. 7, "Logic at Other Universities").

Local communes normally paid professorial salaries, even if a prince or a more distant government determined the amounts. Like other communal employees,

---

52. For example, Girolamo Fabrici d'Acquapendente, professor of anatomy and surgery at Padua, received a lifetime appointment in 1610 at about seventy-seven years of age. It turned out to be a mistake; see Chapter 14, "Private Anatomy Teaching at Padua."

53. Only two exceptions have been noted. The natural philosopher Girolamo Borri (1512–92) lost his position at Pisa in 1586 because of his quarrelsome nature. He immediately obtained a professorship at the University of Perugia. See Grendler, 1996a, 39–42. And when Turin turned humanities instruction over to the Jesuits in 1568, it did not renew the contract of the Latin humanist. See Chapter 6, "The Sixteenth Century." Of course, it is possible that professors who knew that their contracts would not be renewed left of their own accord.

54. See the list of holders of these positions in Riccobono, 1980, sigs. F4^r–^{v}, G^v, G3^v–G4^r, and Tomasini, 1986, 322–23, 326–27, 336–38. The moral philosophy professorship became a more important position filled by a midcareer or senior scholar in 1561; see Chapter 11, "Moral Philosophy in Other Universities." At Siena, newly graduated legists who were Sienese citizens had to teach *Institutes* for one year. Prunai, 1959, 84, 98; Minnucci and Košuta, 1989, 334, 397, 406; Cascio Pratilli, 1975, 87. Student lectureships, whether held by the rector or won through a disputation, were always one-year, predoctoral positions.

professors received periodic payments. Many communes paid professors in three equal installments (*terzerie*), typically November 1, March 1, and August 1. But Parma paid its professors quarterly, and Macerata paid every two months and monthly for a brief time.[55] Professors occasionally received part of their salary in kind, for example, bolts of cloth at Naples in the late fifteenth century.[56]

Some communes reduced a professor's salary if he missed lectures without permission, if he did not teach the full period (either one hour or two hours), and for each lecture that failed to attract a minimum number of students. The commune of Bologna deducted 30 soldi (= 1 lira 10 soldi) from a professor's salary for each lecture attracting fewer than five listeners, or for a missed lecture, in the late fifteenth and early sixteenth centuries. A professor who delivered a lecture lasting only half the period lost 10 soldi. An official called a *punctator* checked each class daily.[57] It was theoretically possible for poorly paid professors attracting few students or missing many lectures to receive no salary. Professors at the University of Pavia were expected to attract at least four students to each lecture in 1448, and six students in 1449, under pain of an unspecified salary deduction.[58] Communes might also impose other salary reductions: for example, in the 1560s Bologna forced professors to bear part of the cost of the construction of the university building through salary deductions.

Salaries were not always paid on time. Then professors threatened to stop teaching and occasionally went on strike. At Pavia some professors, possibly a majority, stopped teaching in April 1453 because they had not been paid. The alleged leader of the strike, a modestly paid ordinary professor of medical theory named Francesco Sachetti, was discharged. But he was restored to his professorship upon begging forgiveness of the duke of Milan.[59] At Turin in January 1470 the commune agreed to increase the salaries of professors who refused to continue teaching.[60] And professors at Siena went on strike at the beginning of the academic year in November 1532 and achieved their demands (see Ch. 2).

A large number, perhaps a majority, of professors enjoyed professional income beyond their salaries. In the early fifteenth century, Bolognese arts professors received small supplementary fees, sometimes called "bench money," from the students who attended their lectures.[61] Numerous professors earned fees for par-

---

55. For Florence, see the detailed records in Verde, 1973–94, vol. 5; for Parma, see ASPr, Archivio del Comune di Parma, Bu. 1913, which contains various ledgers including salary records for 1610–16; for Macerata, see ASM, Archivio Priorale, FF. 191–218 passim.

56. De Frede, 1960, 47.

57. See ASB, Riformatori dello Studio, Appuntazioni dei lettori, 1465–1526, 1531–37, no pag. This busta contains a loose collection of reports by *punctatori* on various professors.

58. Maiocchi, 1971, vol. 2, pt. 2, pp. 540, 546.

59. *Documenti di Pavia*, 1994, docs. 28–32 for complaints about the lack of pay; docs. 71, 119, and 121, for the strike and its aftermath; and doc. 195, the roll of 1455–56, which shows that Sachetti was again teaching (p. 192).

60. Bellone, 1986, 82.

61. The statutes of 1405 permitted the arts professors to collect annual fees ranging from 5 to 40 soldi from each student in class. Malagola, 1966, 248, 251–53; English translation in Thorndike, 1944, 274–78. I do not know if the practice continued.

ticipating in degree examinations (see below). Many engaged in private teaching; some lodged and boarded private pupils. Medical professors and legists had the greatest opportunity to earn additional income. Both could practice privately and write *consilia,* that is, advisory opinions on cases undertaken by other physicians and lawyers. *Consilia* were an especially important source of income for law professors, some of whom wrote hundreds.[62] By contrast, professors did not earn significant income from their publications, because the Renaissance publishing industry lacked effective systems of author royalties and copyright protection. Private practice also enabled professors to maintain close ties with princes and members of the communal government. Legists gave legal advice to the commune, medical professors served as court physicians, and some humanists tutored the prince's children.

A few medical scholars and legists moved into and out of the academy. Shortly after publication of his famous *De humani corporis fabrica* in 1543, Andreas Vesalius left the University of Padua in order to become physician to Emperor Charles V.[63] A small number of established law professors left in order to become judges or advisors to princes. A larger number of new law graduates held minor legal lectureships for one or two years before entering private practice, never to return to the university. Like Francesco Guicciardini, they saw a junior professorship as a bridge between study and practice. But the vast majority devoted their entire professional lives to university teaching. Once settled on a university career, few left.

Professors had neither mandatory retirement nor pension plan. When he became old or was unable to teach, an academic could only petition the government for assistance. For example, in 1593 Benalbo Brancalupo, the Roman professor of surgery who spoke Latin poorly, petitioned the pope for a pension. He wrote that he had taught surgery at the university for twenty-four years but was now eighty-one years of age and could not continue. He was promised help during the pontificate of Sixtus V (1585–90) and was now asking for a pension in order to sustain life. Whether or not Brancalupo received a pension is unknown; certainly some professors did.[64] But the majority of professors taught until death, partly because life was often short.

Communes expected professors, and sometimes students, to wear a long academic gown, a form of dress which set them apart from the rest of society. Civic authorities were not pleased when professors failed to wear it; an official in Siena complained in 1581 that professors went about dressed like rascals and failed

---

62. For surviving *consilia* written by fifteenth-century Paduan medical professors, see Pesenti, 1984. See the numerous *consilia* listed in the works of fifteenth-century Paduan law professors in Belloni, 1986. Cavallar (1991) documents that Francesco Guicciardini, a young attorney at law, wrote dozens of *consilia,* earning 1 or 1.5 florins for each.

63. His official title was *medicus familiaris ordinarius,* "regular physician to the household" of the emperor. O'Malley, 1964, 26, 27, 189 (quote), 190. Other considerations also moved Vesalius. Born in Louvain, Vesalius was a subject of the emperor, and his father had served as imperial pharmacist. Vesalius later planned to return to a teaching post at Padua but died prematurely.

64. Brancalupo's petition is in ASR, Archivio dell'Università di Roma, R. 86, f. 3ᵛ, Nov. 15, 1593. For another petition for a pension, see ibid., f. 24ʳ. For one that was granted at Bologna, see ASB, Assunteria dello Studio, Requisiti dei lettori, Bu. 30, fasc. 41 (1610).

artisans. They were supposed to wear the long gown because they were like fathers to students; they were not their comrades in love affairs.[65] In 1591 the commune of Macerata complained that some *dottori* with little regard for their rank had introduced the practice of dressing in short clothes like everyone else. Since doctors wished to enjoy the prestige of their teaching office, they were to wear the long robe (*vestire di longo*) and a long soutane for the dignity of the doctorate and of the city, the commune huffed.[66] Similar complaints surfaced at Pavia and Perugia.

Students showed their respect for a professor by accompanying him to the lecture hall. When the hour for the lecture approached, students went to his home to escort him to class. The longer the column of students following the professor to class, the greater his honor. Inevitably, the practice got out of hand. In 1586 the Bolognese government decreed that only two students might accompany a professor to class. If the number was greater, the professor would lose his post for three years.[67] On the other hand, respect for professors did not always extend to courteous classroom behavior, as students talked, made noise, and interrupted lectures.

Governments promoted academic localism. Almost all demanded that their subjects attend the university within the state and then chose professors from its graduates. Encouraged and protected by such policies, some families in university towns begot dynasties of professors for the local institution. Some prominent Bolognese family names appeared repeatedly on the university's rolls between 1400 and 1600.[68] Since a university professorship secured an honored place in society, this was a happy outcome for the fortunate individuals and families. In addition, prince or commune sometimes forbade subjects from accepting professorships elsewhere.

Faculties were stable because the majority of professors, including gifted scholars, taught at a single university.[69] Very rarely did a government try to improve the

65. Catoni, 1991, 51.

66. "Sendosi visto che molti dottori, con poca reputatione del grado loro, hanno introdotto stile di vestire di corto come ciascun'altro privato, che per decoro della dignità del dottorato, et della città insieme, volendo detti ss.ri dottori godere le preheminenze del magistraro debbano vestire di longo, et con la sottana del continuo, et quelli che recuseranno non godano tali preheminenze, ma entrino negli altri luoghi come gli altri cittadini non dottori, et il presente decreto si debba intimare a tutti acciò non possano pretenderni ignoranza." ASM, Archivio Priorale, F. 99, Reformanze, ff. 122ᵛ–123ʳ, Sept. 19, 1591. The same was true at Siena (Marrara, 1970, 163, and Cascio Pratilli, 1975, 91) and at Perugia (Ermini, 1971, 444). The Senate of Milan ordered both professors and students at Pavia to wear long gowns. *Memorie di Pavia,* 1970, pt. 2, doc. 18, p. 18, Aug. 27, 1541. Students did not always obey; see Negruzzo, 1995, 48–49.

67. For the prohibition, see ASB, Assunteria di Studio, Bu. 1, a printed pamphlet of 1586 with rules for the university, sig. A2ᵛ. I have no evidence that the penalty was ever imposed. For the practice at Pavia, see Roero, 1604, 38, and Vismara, 1963, 446; for Perugia, see Ermini, 1971, 444.

68. One finds many professors at Bologna bearing the names Albergati, Aldrovandi, Bolognetti, Fantuzzi, Gozzadini, and Paleotti over the two centuries.

69. Charles Schmitt makes the point several times that Italian professors moved about a great deal. Perhaps his strongest statement is "During the fifteenth and sixteenth century academic careers were built on a sort of free-enterprise system in which services were sold to the highest bidder. Only rarely

university by massive recruitment from elsewhere. An exception proves the rule. In response to the perceived decline of Padua, the Venetian government made offers to scholars at Ferrara, Florence, Pavia, Rome, and Siena in the last fifteen years of the fifteenth century, persuading several to come (see Ch. 1, "Padua, 1222"). More commonly, governments pursued only a single star professor, and then only when a vacancy occurred.

Cataclysmic events, especially the wars of the first half of the sixteenth century, stimulated more mobility than "raiding." Pavia and Turin had many interruptions between 1500 and 1560, Pisa suffered several closures between 1504 and 1543, and Rome was closed from 1527 to 1539. When war closed a university, its professors were moveable. To cite one example, when the War of the League of Cambrai closed the University of Padua in 1509, the natural philosopher Pietro Pomponazzi and the civilian Carlo Ruini moved to Bologna, never to return. By contrast, the relatively quiet first half of the fifteenth century and the peaceful second half of the sixteenth century saw little academic movement.

A small number of professors could change positions at will. The civilian Mariano Sozzini the Younger (1482–1556) of Siena took his degree at Siena and then taught at Siena in the years 1504–17, Pisa 1517–21, Siena again 1521–25, Padua 1525–42, and at Bologna from 1542 until death (see Ch. 13). Star civilians had the most opportunities to move, because governments believed that they had a magnetic effect on enrollment. On the whole, winning favorable attention outside one's own university, and beyond the academy itself, enabled a professor to transfer from one university to another. Sometimes a professor's scholarly excellence shone so brightly that it is easy to understand why he was in demand. At other times it is difficult to comprehend the reasons for a professor's high reputation.

Communes carefully planned and executed campaigns to lure a well-known professor. Ambassadors and fellow countrymen made discreet inquiries through third parties. They tried to determine the professor's current salary, how much it would take to move him, and how receptive he would be to an offer. Governments expected a native son to be willing to return to his *patria* for less money than his current salary.[70]

But famous professors did not always move from a lesser to a greater university, or shuttle between Bologna and Padua, solely for money or prestige. Personal

---

do we find a professor who stayed at a university for his entire career." His examples are Biagio Pelacani da Parma, most of whose career was in the fourteenth century, Giorgio Valla, and Agostino Nifo, all three atypical. Schmitt, 1983e, 117. Certainly a handful of the most famous professors, especially legists, moved from university to university. But probably 80 percent taught at one university their entire careers, and most of the rest moved only once. The evidence comes from rolls.

70. For two such campaigns, see ASB, Assunteria di Studio, Bu. 34, Requisiti dei Lettori C, fascs. 5 and 6. In the former, a letter states that Giovanni Campeggi (1448–1511), a Bolognese citizen currently ordinary professor of civil law at Padua at a salary of 1,000 gold ducats, would return to Bologna for 600 florins. In 1503 Campeggi did move to Bologna for the lower salary. Mazzacane, 1974.

reasons might weigh heavily. Girolamo Cardano (1501–76) left Pavia for Bologna in 1562 because his son, who lived in Cardano's house, had murdered his unfaithful wife and had been decapitated.[71] The desire to leave behind grief and public scandal must have been a powerful inducement to move. Carlo Sigonio began teaching at Padua in 1560, but a nasty quarrel with a colleague caused him to move to Bologna in 1563.[72]

Bologna and Padua clearly had greater reputations than the other universities.[73] Pavia ranked third and was joined by Pisa after 1543. The group of Ferrara, Perugia, Florence, Siena, and Rome filled the middle range. Naples came at the head of the next group, which also included Turin. Catania, Macerata, Salerno, and Messina were too small or too new to have high status, and Parma was founded only in 1601.

Observers' subjective perceptions and concrete facts created the reputations that set Bologna and Padua apart. Professorial mobility, described above, offers convincing evidence of their high standing plus impressionistic evidence for the lower status of other universities. A number of well-known scholars taught at both Bologna and Padua but seldom left either for lesser universities. The presence or lack of famous professors also offers evidence of a university's rank. False advertising confirms this. Siena in the sixteenth century consistently listed on its faculty rolls Paduan professors who were offered posts at Siena but declined to come.[74] Siena, the lesser university, hoped to attract students with the (false) promise of the presence of professors from Padua, the greater university.

Size mattered: large universities had better reputations than small universities. Bologna and Padua had the largest faculty complements and student enrollments, while Catania, Macerata, and others were small in size and reputation. The presence of a large number of non-Italian students, especially Germans of noble blood and deep pockets, was a mark of distinction. Again Bologna and Padua probably led, and Pavia also had many foreign students.[75] Finally, the number of leading members of society—nobles and future princes and prelates—who attended a university helped raise or lower its reputation. Florentine nobles went to Pisa rather than Siena, and future leaders of Venice studied at Padua. The Univer-

71. M. Gliozzi, 1976, 760.

72. McCuaig, 1989, 43–47, 54–55.

73. What follows are my assessments based on a variety of direct and indirect evidence. Obviously, it is subjective and disputable, but perhaps no more so than the current published rankings of American and Canadian universities. These are averages for the whole period, 1400–1600, even though some universities improved or declined at one point or another. For example, Pisa was moribund in the first half of the fifteenth century but challenged Pavia for third position in the period 1550–1600. Pavia had a high reputation in the fifteenth century but was often closed on account of war in the first half of the sixteenth century. Turin rose in importance and reputation after 1566.

74. For example, Siena advertised that Mariano Sozzini the Younger was teaching there when he was at Padua. Minnucci and Košuta, 1989, 396, 400 (roll of 1533–34), 403 (1535–36), 410 (1539–40), 414 (1541–42). The rolls listed additional professors teaching elsewhere.

75. This is an estimate. I know of no study comparing the number of non-Italian students at various universities.

sity of Bologna produced far more popes, bishops, and cardinals than did Rome, Perugia, and Macerata, also located in the papal state.[76]

STUDENT LIVING

Students came to the university from different backgrounds and for a variety of motives. The sons of princes, nobles, and prominent urban families came for the intellectual polish of university training and to meet others of equal rank. The sons of administrators, lawyers, and physicians came for the degrees that would enable them to follow in their fathers' footsteps. Ambitious young men from provincial villages and rural castles came to acquire the degree that would enable them to climb the social ladder. Wealthy foreign students from lands lacking prestigious universities came for the degree that would guarantee a prominent position back home. But men who loved learning, the future scholars and professors, also came. Students coming from elsewhere relied on letters of credit to pay daily expenses.[77] They made living arrangements according to their circumstances and preferences.

The student Ercole Gonzaga (1505–63) lived like the prince that he was. The second son of the ruling family of Mantua, already a bishop and intended for the cardinal's hat, Gonzaga arrived at the University of Bologna in December 1522 at the age of seventeen and a half.[78] He established a household filled with servants and advisors and began to study. Well prepared in Latin and Greek, Gonzaga pursued an education that combined university lectures, private instruction, and fine living.

In the morning Gonzaga attended a logic lecture at the university. Then in the early afternoon, Lazzaro Bonamico (1477/78–1552) came to his residence to lecture to him on the classics, especially Cicero. A well-known humanist and fervent proponent of Ciceronian Latin, Bonamico taught at the universities of Bologna, Rome, and Padua during his long career. At this moment he was a well-paid (170 ducats per annum) tutor. Gonzaga also attended at least one anatomical dissection and many banquets in the company of his patrician friends.

The famous natural philosopher Pietro Pomponazzi, a fellow Mantuan, directed Gonzaga's philosophical studies. On the days that he lectured at the university, the philosopher came to Gonzaga's residence in midafternoon. While students often came to a professor's residence to escort him to the lecture hall, Pomponazzi came to the student, and they walked together to the university.

Pomponazzi was a friend and mentor as well as teacher to the young aristocrat. His death in May 1525 grieved Gonzaga deeply and made him end his university studies. Although he never took a degree, Gonzaga studied ancient languages, humanistic texts, philosophy, and theology for the rest of his life with a series of

---

76. Of course, papal service was a tradition among the Bolognese nobility.

77. "Anzi tutti gli scholari forestieri, vivono per lettere di chambio dì per dì." Letter of the beadle of the University of Pisa, Oct. 18, 1479, Pisa, in Verde, 1973–94, vol. 4, pt. 1:345.

78. The following is based on Murphy, 1995, ch. 1, 24–41. See also Luzio, 1886.

tutors in the midst of a very active ecclesiastical and political career. And he became a passionate bibliophile.

Other nobles imitated Gonzaga so far as their finances allowed. Carlo Borromeo (1538–84), the second son of a Lombard count and also intended for an ecclesiastical career, went to the University of Pavia in 1552 to study law.[79] His father's agent found a house consisting of six rooms, plus stalls for two horses. It rented for 14 scudi, whether for the year or a shorter period is not clear. The house sheltered four persons: Carlo, another youth to serve as companion, a priest hired to tutor Carlo, and a woman who served as cook and housekeeper. In his first year Carlo attended university lectures and received private lessons on the *Institutes.*

The priest tutored, supervised the household, and reported regularly to Carlo's father on the boy's conduct and studies. Unfortunately, the priest turned out to be a quarrelsome man who had to be replaced. Nor did the companion, the son of an administrator serving Carlo's father, prove satisfactory. He spent little time in the house, refused to be seen with Carlo outside it, and got into scrapes that dishonored the Borromeo name. And the household was not lavish. Carlo's father, who had his own financial problems, kept his son on such a tight financial leash that Carlo more than once lacked money to buy the legal texts needed for his studies. Carlo's only extravagance was a music teacher who taught him to play the lute in 1554. Although Carlo was a keen scholar who spent five or six hours a day at his books, he did not lead a carefree student life. He attended the University of Pavia from November 1552 through early 1558, with a few interruptions, a total of about five and one-half academic years. He left the university in July 1558 when his father died, but he returned to take his doctorate in civil and canon law in December 1559.

Many students formed groups of four or five and rented an entire house.[80] At Padua in the 1540s, 1550s, and 1560s, the annual rent for a house ranged from 9 to 31 ducats and averaged 20. They often hired a cook or a servant (or both) to run the house, not always with happy results. Several German students at Padua rented a house and hired an old female servant to cook in 1575. She pilfered a gold chain worth 200 crowns.[81]

A document from Pavia estimated the expenses for room and board for five students in 1547. It assumed that the students rented a house and hired two servants, a man and a woman, to clean and cook.[82] The expenses were rent, salary

79. This and the following paragraph are based on Maiocchi and Moiraghi, 1984, a fascinating account of Borromeo's student days with many quotations from his letters and those of his tutors.

80. Roero (1604, 12–13) listed the choices open to students and recommended renting a house ("tener a casa"). See also Mango Tomei, 1976, 55–56.

81. Ronchi, 1967, 296–301, 314. These house rents do not include Alessandro d'Este, cousin of Duke Alfonso II of Ferrara, who rented an entire palace in 1589 for 40 ducats annually. It must have been a modest palace.

82. ASPv, Università 33, Acta Studii Ticinensis 1500–1550, fasc. 121, an undated document (but c. May 1547, like the preceding document) entitled "Scruttino per le dozzene de scolari. A boche cinque per giorno." Since the document accompanied an anonymous letter protesting that foreign

and board for the servants, and the food consumed by the students: pasta, wine, meat, fruit, cheese, animal fat, olive oil, vinegar, salad greens, rice, and the ingredients for the evening *minestra* (soup). Food costs doubled on the weekends, as the students laid in oranges, lemons, candied fruits, and artichokes to entertain fellow students. The five also had to purchase firewood, candles, linens, and utensils. The total estimated cost was 0.8 lira (= 16 soldi) per student per day, or 4 lire per day for the group of five students. The living expenses for an academic year of eight months (November through June) were about 192 lire (0.8 lira/day × 30 days × 8 months) per student. This was the equivalent of about 28 Venetian ducats, a widely used money of account, for the academic year. The per student room and board cost for the academic year was about two-thirds the annual wage of a worker in the Venetian building trades at this time.[83] Of course, students had the additional expenses of books, clothes, and transportation.

Renting a house was common enough that city and university authorities issued many regulations in order to ensure that the town had enough rental housing at reasonable cost to accommodate students. In 1582 the Bolognese government appealed to townspeople to rent houses to students at fair prices and offered to compile a listing of the available houses. Nevertheless, students often complained about rapacious landlords.[84]

Students also roomed and boarded with a family. Some lived, boarded, and studied privately with university professors. The humanist Gasparino Barzizza, teaching at the University of Padua (1407–21), and the mathematician Galileo Galilei, also at Padua (1592–1610), were among the professors who earned additional income in this way. Sometimes called an academy or *paedagogicum,* the establishment might consist of the professor, his wife or domestic help (or both), an assistant teacher (*ripetitore*) who drilled the students, and from three to twenty student boarders, some of whom might be of preuniversity age. Students boarded with professors to receive additional instruction and to reap the benefits of closer association with the learned man. Convinced that the private instruction of *paedagogica* undermined university lectures, communal authorities tried to restrict them, especially in the later sixteenth century.[85] But they never abolished the private academies.

All the above students came from reasonably affluent sectors of society. A poor

---

professors and students should not have to pay a higher tax, it probably came from students or communal authorities fearful that the tax increase would drive away students.

83. For the computation, 20 soldi = 1 lira; 124 soldi or 6 lire 4 soldi = 1 Venetian ducat of account in the sixteenth century. A scudo was worth 5 or 6 lire, roughly equivalent to a ducat. Workers, not masters, in the Venetian building trade earned about 20 soldi per day in the 1550s and early 1560s. If they worked 275 days per year, they earned 5,500 soldi (20 x 275) or 44 ducats (5,500 divided by 124) per annum. Of course, any estimates can only be very approximate. For daily wages in the Venetian building industry, see Pullan, 1968, 158.

84. ASB, Assunteria di Studio, Bu. 94, fasc. 6, memorandum of July 18, 1582. See also Brizzi, 1984, 26. For living arrangements, regulations for renting, and governmental efforts to relieve a shortage of student housing at Pisa in the sixteenth century, see Mango Tomei, 1976, 53–56.

85. Mercer, 1979, 106–9, 121–24, 168; Brizzi, 1984, 19–21. See Chapter 14 for complaints against private teaching.

student at the University of Rome described a very different life in 1576. He came from a large family in a rural area of the papal state. Since his father could not afford to send him to a Latin school, he had learned that difficult language at home and then supported himself by teaching others in his hometown plus Ancona and Naples. Eventually an employer had given him enough money to study. He then walked from Naples to Rome in order to begin university studies. He lived in one room, dressed in secondhand clothes, and sold his books in order to eat, as he studied for a law degree, which he was about to receive.[86] One wonders how many others, faced with such obstacles, dropped out.

RESIDENCE COLLEGES

A small percentage of students lived in residence colleges. These were the modest Italian counterparts of the famous residence and teaching colleges that played such an important role at Paris, Oxford, and Cambridge. But Italian residence colleges never developed a significant teaching role. They only provided accommodation to a very small number of students who met strict entry requirements. In a few cases governments created them in order to attract students.

The Italian collegiate movement began in the thirteenth century with a single college; many more were added in the next two centuries, although not all lasted.[87] A wealthy clerical or lay donor, the latter often a professor, left a bequest to establish a college, usually named for himself, in a university town. The bequest typically provided a house and income intended to board free of charge four to thirty poor students. But because the endowment frequently did not meet expenses, the colleges often demanded fees. The donor commonly restricted admission to students who came from a particular geographical area, such as the region of his birth. He might limit enrollment to students studying a designated discipline or two. Very occasionally, students had to be ecclesiastics. They were normally permitted to stay for six or seven years, although the period might be as short as four and as long as ten. Students were obliged to conform to rules reminiscent of a monastery. A constitution and an elected student rector provided governance.

A commune or another civic organization might create a residence college for local youths studying at a university. In 1531 a confraternity in Bergamo founded

86. ASR, Archivio dell'Università di Roma, R. 100, fasc. 9, no pag., Mar. 9, 1576. Similar accounts are found in ibid., fasc. 5, May 9, 1573, and fasc. 100, Apr. 26, 1577. Every year the College of Legists of the University of Rome paid the doctoral degree expenses (25 scudi) of a limited number of poor students. In order to obtain the graduation subsidy, students told their stories of poverty, which the college verified by questioning acquaintances.

87. One college was founded in the thirteenth century: the Avignonese college in Bologna in 1257. Brizzi, 1984, 11, 51. Denley (1991a, 75) gives the date as 1256. Next came the Bresciano in Bologna in 1326, followed by seventeen more across Italy in the rest of the fourteenth century. The following is based on Brizzi, 1984, and Piana, 1984, 76*–90* for Bolognese colleges; and especially on Denley, 1991a, who summarizes well the existing scholarship on Italian residence colleges to 1500. See also Marti, 1966; *I collegi universitari*, 1991, with articles on Perugian, Pisan, and Sienese colleges; and the articles in *Vocabulaire des collèges*, 1993.

a residence college in Padua to house five local youths. The confraternity chose young men aged seventeen or older on the basis of their probity, poverty, good morals, and ability and sent them to the college, a rented house in Padua. After a maximum of seven years' residence, they were expected to return with doctorates in civil law, canon law, or medicine. The confraternity sent thirteen young men from Bergamo to the Paduan college between 1531 and 1546, and seven obtained degrees. But another five were expelled from the college for misbehavior, and the fate of the last is unknown. The miscreants skipped lectures, took unauthorized vacations, partied, got into fights, and spent money frivolously. The Bergamo confraternity abandoned the residence college as a failure.[88] It returned to a policy of providing financial subsidies to individual youths, a policy that several towns pursued. Communes supported the university studies of local men in order to acquire the civil servants, lawyers, judges, physicians, surgeons, and teachers needed by the town, and because they believed that learned citizens contributed to the common good.[89]

Bologna, Padua, and Pavia had six to twelve residence colleges each in the fourteenth and fifteenth centuries. All were small, and some disappeared by 1500.[90] The total number of students living in colleges in each of these large universities in the late fifteenth century may have been 100 or fewer, a small fraction of enrollments ranging from 700 to 1,500. By contrast, a state-supported residence college could play a key role in the life of a smaller university. The residence college for foreign students founded by the commune of Siena became an integral part of the university, even though no teaching occurred within its walls.

The success of the Sienese Casa della Sapienza persuaded the grand-ducal government of Tuscany to establish two state-supported residence colleges at the University of Pisa. The Collegio della Sapienza of Pisa opened its doors to 40 students in 1545, and the Collegio Ferdinando of Pisa accepted 35 in 1595. While their organization and rules were similar to those of the Casa della Sapienza of Siena, the students were needy subjects of the grand dukes of Tuscany rather than foreigners. Upon presentation of evidence of poverty and passing a Latin examination, the residents might live, board, and study for free for up to six years. In turn, the college residents were required to swear perpetual fealty to the grand duke of Tuscany. The opportunity for free room and board was so highly prized and so rare that potential students tried year after year to win places. The Pisan colleges clearly helped some young men to rise in the world. But the government also benefited, through the acquisition of trained and loyal civil servants.[91] Nev-

---

88. Carlsmith, 1998.

89. See the example of Lucca; Barsanti, 1980, 68–83; and Davies, 1997–99.

90. Denley, 1991a, 75–77, plus the bibliography listed in note 87. The number of students living in colleges is only a rough estimate, because in many cases it is difficult to determine if, and how long, a college survived.

91. On the Collegio della Sapienza of Pisa, see Toniolo Fascione, 1980 and 1991; on the Collegio Ferdinando of Pisa, see Biagi, 1980. See also Cascio Pratilli, 1975, 122–23, 163–65.

ertheless, the two state colleges lodged only 75 students in a total enrollment of about 600 around 1600, while Pisa had only two tiny private colleges.[92]

New residence colleges appeared in the last third of the sixteenth century. Although named for famous clergymen of the Catholic Reformation, they resembled earlier colleges.[93] Pope Pius V (Michele Ghislieri) created the Collegio Ghislieri at Pavia in 1567. It housed 24 students, almost all from the region of Alessandria, the pope's *patria*. The students, who had to be at least eighteen years of age, received free lodging, could study any of the major subjects, and might stay for seven years. In a break from tradition, the Collegio Ghislieri began to play a small pedagogical role by the middle of the seventeenth century. It organized an academy, which included external scholars, for formal discussions. It paid university professors to give lectures in the college on university nonteaching days. Examinations were conducted and degrees awarded in the college. And in the late eighteenth century, the library of the Collegio Ghislieri became the university library of Pavia.

The Collegio Borromeo in Pavia followed a similar path. The brainchild of Cardinal Carlo Borromeo, it welcomed its first boarders in 1581. It had thirty-five students, both laymen and future clerics, in 1582–83. This was not a free college; students paid 5.5 scudi per month plus the cost of boarding a servant, if accompanied by one. Since students had to prove that they possessed considerable family assets in order to be considered for admission, most came from the upper ranks of Milanese society. The future Cardinal Federico Borromeo (1564–1631), a younger cousin of Cardinal Carlo, joined the first class and graduated with a theology degree in 1585.[94] The Ghislieri and Borromeo colleges still serve as student residences at Pavia.

In the seventeenth century the collegiate movement prospered in some universities but declined in others. At Padua fourteen residence colleges lodged 129 students in 1614, while thirteen colleges housed only 40 students in 1640. Financial mismanagement of endowment income and the acceptance of dissolute students lacking academic commitment caused the Paduan colleges to decline.[95]

---

92. Two small private residence colleges were established at Pisa in 1568 and 1605. Cascio Pratilli, 1975, 165.

93. Although some scholars tend to see the quasi-monastic rules of the new colleges of the late sixteenth century as a manifestation of the religiosity of the Catholic Reformation, their rules were only slightly more rigorous than those of colleges founded in the late Middle Ages or the Casa della Sapienza in Siena. And students did not necessarily obey the rules. For example, the future comic dramatist Carlo Goldoni, then sixteen years of age, was expelled from the Collegio Ghislieri in 1723 for writing a satirical and salacious poem. Casalino Astori, 1970, 134. On the Collegio Ghislieri, see Bendiscioli, 1961, 362–67; Marcocchi, 1966; and *Il Collegio Universitario Ghislieri,* 1966–70.

94. Bascapè, 1955, esp. 47–56; Bendiscioli, 1961, 368–70; and *La riforma cattolica,* 1967–70, 2:159–61.

95. The figure of 129 students in fourteen residence colleges in 1614 comes from the papers of Ingolfo de' Conti in ASVe, Riformatori dello Studio di Padova, Bu. 429, no pag. The figure of 40 students comes from De Bernardin, 1975, 480. The Venetian governors of Padua periodically reported the problems of the colleges; see *Relazioni,* 1975, 150 (Sept. 16, 1614), 172 (Nov. 28, 1617),

Italian residence colleges did not become northern-style teaching colleges for institutional and political reasons.[96] Paris and Oxford developed combination residence and teaching colleges, because they had numerous young students thirteen to eighteen years of age, and regent masters, that is, new masters of arts required to teach younger arts students for about two years.[97] Parents and authorities believed that students in their early and middle teens needed a place to live under adult supervision. The regent masters, who were often clergymen, lived in the college. They taught and guided the students, thus creating the teaching college.

By contrast Italian universities lacked very young students; they enrolled students eighteen to twenty-five years of age studying for doctorates in law and medicine. Professors hired by the commune taught them; no regency system existed. Since Italian universities lacked young students needing instruction and supervision, and regent masters, the teaching college could not develop. To ensure this, Italian communes never permitted formal teaching to occur outside what they called the "public university." The statutes of Italian residence colleges always insisted that students attend university lectures.

THE DOCTORATE

The culmination of university study was the doctoral degree with the right to teach anywhere in Christendom. But the doctorate was almost detached from the university. The groups and individuals who examined candidates and awarded degrees did not necessarily teach at the university.

Italian Renaissance universities awarded only doctorates. Barely a handful of bachelor's degrees in law, medicine, and arts have come to light in the late fourteenth century and the first half of the fifteenth, and none thereafter.[98] The term *bachelor* appeared very rarely in Italian university documents. When it did, *bachalarius* meant only an advanced student, not the holder of a bachelor's degree

---

379 (June 1660). But the story of the Paduan colleges has yet to be written. See AAUP, FF. 600–607, for much material from the seventeenth and eighteenth centuries and copies of earlier documents.

96. There were three very limited exceptions. The Spanish College in Bologna taught a small amount of theology to the thirty resident students. Marti, 1966, 22–23, 30, 32. For more on the Spanish College, see the studies in *Albornoz y el Colegio de España*, 1972. In Rome the Collegio Capranica (in operation by 1476) and the Collegio Nardini (begun c. 1484), each hired a theologian to deliver lectures on theology in exchange for room and board. The justification offered in the statutes was that the University of Rome did not offer much theological instruction, which was true at the time. The Capranica also had a canonist, while the Nardini had a moral philosopher who came to the college to deliver lectures on the ethical texts of Aristotle. See Esposito, 1992 and 1993. All three of these colleges were quasi-ecclesiastical institutions, halfway between mendicant order *studia* and university, and the residents were mostly clergymen. See Esposito, 1992, 50.

97. Fletcher, 1986, 185–87; he also points out that Oxford modified the regency system in the sixteenth century.

98. Sottili notes that the Pavian law statutes of 1395 mention an examination for a bachelor of both laws, and he has found four bachelor's degrees in canon law (1385, 1399, 1404, and 1446) and one in medicine (1441). *Lauree Pavesi*, 1995, 17–18. That is all.

won by means of an examination and conferred in a formal ceremony. Some-times the advanced student had disputed and was lecturing.[99] For example, very occasionally a university appointed a student not yet a doctor to an ordinary teaching position rather than to a student lectureship. The appointee might be called *bachalarius,* possibly in order to distinguish him from professors with doc-torates.[100] The bachelor's degree survived only in theology, conferred by faculties of theology, but was not universally awarded in that subject.[101]

Why the bachelor's degree disappeared and how Italian universities became exclusively doctoral institutions are not known. The only near contemporary explanation comes from Jacopo Philippo Tomasini in 1654, who believed that the bachelor's degree fell into disuse because students did not want to bear the expense of acquiring both bachelor's and doctoral degrees.[102]

The history of Italian universities, which developed differently than northern universities, supports Tomasini's view. Bachelor's degrees were strongly identi-

99. Martinotti, 1911, 24–25; Sorbelli, 1940, 176–78; Bellomo, 1979, 248–51; Trombetti Bu-driesi, 1988, 155–56; and Maierù, 1994, 55–56, all of whom rely on early Bolognese statutes. See the quotation from the Paduan law statutes of 1445 concerning "bachelors" disputing in Belloni, 1986, 60. See also Ermini, 1971, 567; Denley, 1981, 197; and *Lauree Pavesi,* 1995, 17–18, 274.

100. See the Bolognese roll of 1426–27: "D. Iacobus de Verbon bachalarius in decretis deputatus ad lecturam Sexti et Clementinarum ordinariam." Dallari, 1888–1924, 4:*Aggiunte,* p. 51. Iacobus de Verbon taught only one year.

101. "Baccalaureatus verò vestigium in Italia apud religiosos viros adhuc remanet." Tomasini, 1986 (but first published in 1654), 200. For theology degrees, see Chapter 10, "Faculties of Theology" and "Doctorates of Theology."

102. "Baccalaurei olim Battelaurei & Lytae vocabantur, Iuris nodos solvere incipientes. Sed ex usu Academiae Parisiensis Bacciliarii appellantur, à bacillo ipsis exhibito, in signum auctoritatis docendi quam consequuntur. Initio multi quidem paupertate, aliave causa quum se nolint subiicere rigoroso examini Cl. Collegii in artibus Medicinae, vel in Iure, baccalaureatus, vel Doctoratus gradum à Comitibus Palatinis, aut Lateranensibus sumbant. Postea verò sublata hac consuetudine Gymnasii Rector, sive substitutus convocatis duobus Professoribus bina puncta dabantur, iisque recitatis & diligentis excussis, illis gradus Baccalaureatus conferebatur, privilegiumque ab Univer-sitatis Notario sigillo firmatum concedebatur. Haec olim ratio compendiosior fuit quam Doc-toratus, qui paulo sumptuosior erat. Baccalaureatus verò vestigium in Italian apud religiosos viros adhuc remanet. . . . Licentiandi, praesertim in Iure communi, erat Patavii usus frequentior, antequam constitueretur Collegium Venetum, de quo supra diximus." Tomasini, 1986, 200.

The part of Tomasini's explanation which seems most convincing is that the bachelor's degree disappeared because it seemed an unnecessary extra expense. But his introduction of the counts palatine confuses the issue. Bachelor's degrees had disappeared long before the sixteenth century, when count palatine degrees became common. Moreover, the dual mention of counts palatine degrees and the establishment of the Venetian College of Doctors (arts in 1616, extended to law in 1636) to grant doctorates echoes the official Venetian justification for founding the Venetian College. The Venetian government founded a new degree-granting college in order to eliminate count palatine degrees taken by students in order to avoid the normal, but more expensive, route through the colleges of doctors of law and arts, which granted degrees on the basis of papal authorization. The Venetian College of Doctors also offered in a new way the service that counts palatine provided to non-Catholics: they conferred the doctorate without insisting on an oath of allegiance to Catholi-cism. Naturally, the Venetian authorities did not mention publicly the latter reason. See below, "Doctorates from Counts Palatine," and Chapter 14, "Positive Developments," for more explanation.

Facciolati (1978 [but first edition 1757], pt. 2:10, and pt. 3:206) also reports that the bachelor's degree in law and arts became obsolete at Padua but offered no explanation.

fied with arts and theology in northern universities. Paris and Oxford awarded numerous bachelor's and master's degrees in arts and theology because they taught these subjects almost exclusively. But Italian universities concentrated on law and medicine from the beginning. They viewed the arts subjects as preparation for medicine, not as ends in themselves to be recognized with a degree. They taught no theology until the second half of the fourteenth century, and only a limited amount thereafter. Hence, medicine and law students, who wanted doctorates in order to practice their professions, saw no need to acquire bachelor's diplomas, and the degree fell into disuse.

After attending lectures for four to seven or more years and disputing, the student decided that he was ready to present himself to be examined for the doctorate (*laurea*). Colleges of doctors, rather than groups of professors, examined candidates. Colleges of doctors were independent bodies composed of small groups of local men possessing doctorates in a particular field. For example, at Bologna the College of Doctors of Civil Law had twenty members, the College of Doctors of Canon Law had twelve, the College of Doctors of Arts and Medicine had twelve, and the College of Doctors of Theology had twenty-four. Each also had three supernumeraries, who served as alternates.[103] The size varied from university to university, and sometimes a single college of legists examined candidates for both civil and canon law. At Bologna all members of colleges, plus their ancestors, had to be Bolognese citizens, had to have obtained a doctoral degree at Bologna, and had to have taught there for three years. These requirements were typical, if a little more restrictive than elsewhere.

Local notables with doctoral degrees numerically dominated colleges of doctors. Francesco Guicciardini was an example. He taught for only one year as a very junior law professor but later served for several years as member, later prior, of the College of Legists of Florence.[104] His position as the scion of a leading local family and his growing law practice probably gained him entry.

Prominent professors easily gained admittance to colleges of doctors if they were native sons. But colleges of doctors did not welcome all the professors at the university into their ranks. They usually accepted ordinary professors who were citizens and academic stars, even if they were foreigners. But they accepted others only grudgingly and under pressure from the civil government. They excluded junior professors as well as many middle-rank and foreign professors.[105]

103. This is based on Simeoni, 1940, 13, and Piana, 1984, 31*–42*; for Ferrara, see Secco Suardo, 1983, 159–65; Visconti, 1950, 30–31; and Del Nero, 1996, 97; for Florence, see Verde, 1973–94, 2:644–46; and Davies, 1998, 36–43; for the Roman college of physicians, see Carlino, 1999, 70–77; for Turin, see Catarinella and Salsotto, 1998, 557–67. Colleges of doctors of theology, that is, faculties of theology, are discussed in Chapter 10.

104. Cavallar, 1991, 41, 87–90, 322–24, 337, 341, 342, 351, 356, 357, 364. Guicciardini even served as a promoter on two occasions.

105. For example, the Venetian government ordered the College of Physicians of Padua to enroll the first-place ordinary professors of natural philosophy and medical theory and to enroll professors who were foreigners. AAUP, F. 653, ff. 157ʳ (Feb. 15, 1569), 160ʳ (July 8, 1592). But other documents in this filza show that the Venetian government engaged in an ongoing struggle to get the College of Physicians to include more professors. Paolo Beni in the early seventeenth century urged that all the

Of course, a college of doctors could grant exemptions from its own rules. If it wished to add a distinguished professor who was not a citizen, the commune granted him citizenship and enrolled him. If it wished to add someone who had not taught at the university, had not taught the minimum number of years, or had obtained his doctorate elsewhere, it did so.

Examination of the candidate and conferral of the degree required several steps.[106] First, the candidate held a preliminary meeting with the college of doctors. The candidate informed the appropriate college in which subject(s) he wished to be examined. Law students took degrees in civil law, in canon law, or both simultaneously (*in utroque iure*). Nonlegists might obtain doctorates in arts, medicine, arts and medicine, and very occasionally surgery.

At this meeting promoters, that is, professors, some chosen by the candidate, others named by the college, were assigned to represent and help the candidate throughout the process. At this point they testified that the candidate was ready to be examined. The candidate usually had to affirm or offer evidence, such as a statement from a professor, that he had studied for the required number of years (four to seven, depending on the degree sought and university regulations) at the current university or others (or both) and had disputed the required minimum of times (at least once, more commonly twice). However, evidence of university study was not closely scrutinized, and exceptions occurred. A candidate for the doctorate of medicine might also have to present evidence that he had worked with a physician. The college fixed the date for the beginning of the examination and informed the candidate of the cost.

The candidate had to surmount two examinations, the first of which determined whether he would win the doctorate, and a second pro forma examination for the degree. Historians usually call them private and public examinations, despite varying terminology in the documents. The college fixed a date for the first (private) examination, the one that mattered. When the day arrived, the candidate attended mass in the morning and then went to the appointed place, usually an ecclesiastical venue, such as a church or the bishop's palace.

The candidate now received from the prior of the college the *puncta* (points) on which he would be examined. These were two, three, or four brief passages selected at random from the statutory texts in the subject matter of the desired degree. If he wanted a degree in canon law, the *puncta* came from the *Corpus juris canonici;* for civil law, from the *Corpus juris civilis;* for both laws, one or more from

---

first- and second-place foreign professors be enrolled in the appropriate colleges of doctors, which suggests that this was not the norm. See ASVa, Archivio Beni, Ms. 123, p. [38].

106. This summary of the procedure for arts and law doctorates is based on the following descriptions of the procedure at different universities but passes over some details and local variations. Secco Suardo, 1983, 165–70; Visconti, 1950, 31–34; Simeoni, 1940, 36–37; Marongiu, 1948, 42–45; *Acta Graduum 1501 ad 1525,* 1969, ix–xi; Verde, 1973–94, 2:635–46; Palmer, 1983, 34–39, a good detailed account; *Acta Graduum 1601 ad 1605,* 1987, xii–xv; Trombetti Budriesi, 1988, 153–65; Davies, 1995–96, 69–72; Del Nero, 1996, 97–98; and Davies, 1998, 43–48. This is not an exhaustive bibliography. The procedure for theology degrees was a little different; see Chapter 10, "Doctorates of Theology."

Fig. 6. Diploma of Theseus de Coloredo of Forlì, doctorate in civil law from the University of Padua, June 12, 1504. *AAUP.*

each. For arts, the *puncta* came from Aristotle, perhaps the *Physics* and a logical work. If he sought a degree in medicine, the *puncta* were drawn from the *Canon* of Avicenna, Galen, or the *Aphorisms* of Hippocrates. A candidate wanting a degree in arts and medicine received *puncta* from both Aristotle and medical texts. For theology the *puncta* came from Peter Lombard's *Sentences*.[107]

The candidate had a limited time, normally twenty-four hours, to prepare. His promoters, three to ten strong, were permitted to help him. The next day the candidate and his promoters came to the appointed place where the prior and members of the college were assembled. The candidate began by expounding and explaining the *puncta*. Then members of the college proposed counter-arguments to which the candidate responded. Even though the *puncta* were brief passages, the examination could be very wide ranging if the examiners wished it so. A candidate for a medical doctorate might also be required to give his opinion on a medical case proposed to him. Throughout the private examination the promoters sat with the candidate and prompted him when necessary. After the candidate finished, he and his promoters withdrew while the members of the college voted; a two-thirds' favorable vote was required.[108] It does not appear that candidates ever failed. However, if the candidate received a majority, but not two-thirds, of favorable votes, he might attempt the examination again after an interval of a few months. Girolamo Cardano received enough favorable votes for his doctorate of medicine degree at Padua only on the third attempt.[109]

If the candidate received the necessary votes, he proceeded to the second (public) examination and the conferral of the degree after a short period. The same procedure was followed at the public examination. But since the examiners had already satisfied themselves as to the candidate's competence, the public examination was invariably successful. The graduation ceremony followed, sometimes on the same day. An ecclesiastical personage, such as the bishop or his vicar, presided. Members of the college, the promoters, and the candidate's friends, often students from his student nation, attended and were recorded as witnesses. The chief promoter praised the candidate, who then received symbols of his new dignity from the bishop in his capacity as chancellor of the university or his vicar. He received books in his subject, first closed to symbolize the knowledge within the book, then opened to signify that the doctor would teach these books. Next came a gold ring which represented the marriage between the doctor and his subject. Finally came the doctor's biretta (the three-cornered hat of the scholar), which he

107. The degree documents in *Studium maceratense 1541 al 1551*, 1998, and *Studium maceratense 1551 al 1579*, 1999, give the *puncta*, and the editor has located the exact law references.

108. Some historians (e.g., Del Nero, 1996, 97) state that the candidate received the license degree (permission to teach) after the initial examination. While theological candidates often received the license of theology degree separately from the doctorate of theology, this does not appear to have been the case in law, medicine, and arts. Further research on the point is needed.

109. Cardano, 1982, ch. 4, p. 42. Although this was in 1526 or 1527, I have been unable to locate his degree in *Acta Graduum 1526 ad 1537*, 1970.

was entitled to wear.[110] He was now a doctor, recognized as a master of his subject, possessed of the right to teach it to others, and an honored member of society. A festive dinner and celebration followed. The elaborate procedure and ceremony certified to the graduate and the world his new dignity.

A few scholars obtained doctorates in arts initially, then in medicine a few years later. A famous example was Pietro Pomponazzi, who took a doctorate in arts in 1487, immediately began teaching, and, without halting his lecturing, took a doctorate in medicine in 1495, all at Padua.[111] The practice of obtaining two doctorates largely disappeared in the sixteenth century.

Students were required to study and to take degrees from the university, or universities, within the state. Every government, except the papacy, ordered its subjects to do so. They repeatedly passed laws imposing large fines on violators. They especially insisted that students take degrees at the university within the state by threatening to bar from civic office subjects lacking them. But numerous students, including sons of the most prominent families in a city or state, ignored the decrees and were never punished, so far as is known. Of course, princes and communes could grant dispensations from their own rules, and colleges of doctors might wink at regulations. But there were other considerations as well. Prohibitions against studying and taking degrees outside the state collided with the reality that every government wanted foreign students. The presence of students from beyond the state conferred prestige on the university and economic benefits on the town. If a government enforced regulations against external study on its own subjects, it would probably suffer reprisal, which would hurt enrollment in the local institution. So governments contented themselves with noisy threats, hoping that this would discourage some of their subjects from going elsewhere.

THE COST OF DEGREES

The doctorate cost a great deal. For example, in August 1602, one Alfonso Belgio received his law degree from the University of Parma. The new doctor had to pay fees to thirty-seven different individuals. Belgio paid 7 lire 6 soldi (= 1 ordinary Parmese ducatone) to the bishop's vicar. He then paid 9 lire 15 soldi (a ducatone of higher value) to the prior of the college of law, and the same amount to the priorate, that is, the office. Then 9 lire 15 soldi went to each of ten other individuals, probably members of the college, only one of whom may have been a professor. Belgio paid Sforza degli Oddi, the leading ordinary professor of civil law at Parma, 19 lire 10 soldi because he was a promoter and a member of the college. Belgio paid 12 lire 3 soldi to a second promoter, an ordinary professor of civil law, and the same amount to a third, who taught *Institutes* but was not

110. Davies (1998, 47 n. 242) provides an excellent summary of the ceremony of books, ring, and hat.

111. For Pomponazzi, see Pine, 1986, 44. See Piana, 1966, 147, 150, 153, 165, for a scholar who took an arts degree in 1425 and a medical degree in 1428, and another man who did the same in 1427 and 1433.

described as a promoter. Next, the new doctor paid eighteen other unnamed men, possibly additional members of the college of legists, a total of 43 lire 17 soldi, an average of 2 lire 9 soldi each. Next in line with hands outstretched were four nonacademic officials: the vicar's notary, the university beadle, and the law college beadle. Each received 7 lire 6 soldi, while the bell ringer received 1 lire 16 soldi. Finally, Doctor Belgio paid 7 lire 6 soldi for the use of the room in the episcopal palace for the examination. The grand total was 264 lire 8 soldi, a little more than 36 Parmese ducatoni (valued at 7 lire 6 soldi).[112] This did not include the cost of the expected celebratory banquet hosted by the new graduate or gifts to the witnesses.

The cost of a degree in Parma may have been a little higher than elsewhere or earlier, but not remarkably so. Paduan medical degrees cost a minimum of 15 Venetian ducats (a ducat was worth 6 lire 4 soldi) for poor students to a maximum of 30 ducats in the sixteenth century. A price war with the nonteaching Venetian college of medicine held down the Paduan cost. On average, doctorates cost 22 to 40 ducats or scudi in the fifteenth and sixteenth centuries.[113] Doctorates in law, especially civil law, generally cost more than doctorates in arts and medicine, probably because the candidates more often came from higher ranks of society and expected to enjoy greater professional earnings than arts and medicine graduates. The high cost of degrees made the handful of free degrees (perhaps two in law and two in arts and medicine annually) which every university awarded on evidence of poverty very desirable.

Members of colleges of doctors and professors who served as promoters earned supplementary income for little effort. For a highly paid star such as Sforza degli Oddi at Parma, who received a salary of 1,200 ducatoni (worth 7 lire 6 soldi each) at Parma in 1609–10, another 2 or 3 ducatoni for serving as a promoter could not

112. This summarizes a document entitled "Lista della spesa del Dottorato del S.r Alfonso Belgio nella sala del Palazzo episcopale di Parma," dated October 1602, in ASPr, Istruzione pubblica farnesiana, Bu. 1, no pag. Although the document does not indicate the identity of the college or the subject matter of the degree, it had to be civil law. The document does not identify which were professors, but comparison with the Parma roll of 1601–2 identifies three of them (Oddi, Innocenzio Canoso, and Marco Antonio Bottoni) as civilians. A fourth ("Rev. S. Dottor Marescotto") may have been Annibale Marescotti, another ordinary morning professor of civil law. The document gives the total amount as 264 lire 8 soldi, although the sum of the individual disbursements comes to 252 lire 14 soldi, if I have interpreted the multiple disbursements correctly.

113. Palmer, 1983, 31–34. The number of people involved and the costs of the Parma doctorate of 1602 can be compared with similar information for a doctorate in arts and medicine at Padua on May 19, 1521, which included fees of 143 lire (about 23 Venetian gold ducats) for more than fifty-five people. *Acta Graduum 1501 ad 1525*, 1969, doc. 860, pp. 338–39. At Ferrara in the fifteenth century, the candidate for an arts doctorate had to deposit almost 22 ducats before he began the process, and it may not have covered the full cost. Secco Suardo, 1983, 165, 168, 170. For a list of the payments (a minimum of 105 lire) and who got them for a doctorate of law at Bologna in 1432, see Malagola, 1966, 150–52. For other degree prices in 1577–78 (Padua, 50 scudi; Bologna a little less; Siena, 34 scudi; Ferrara, 28 scudi), see Brugi, 1907. Because the candidate could negotiate the cost of the degree with the college, and because it is difficult to compare the monetary systems of different towns or to estimate the extent to which inflation reduced the value of money over time, it is not possible to make more precise comparisons between universities and the two centuries.

have meant very much. But to an *Institutes* professor earning 27 or 28 ducatoni per annum, an additional 1 to 2 ducatoni for assisting in a degree examination must have been very welcome.[114] But well-paid famous professors were more likely to be members of colleges of doctors and to serve as promoters than lowly *Institutes* professors. One student advised degree candidates to invite all the ordinary professors with whom he had studied in order to show his gratitude.[115] Eventually some universities attempted to limit the number of promoters.

ALTERNATE PATHS TO THE DOCTORATE

Some men, however, acquired doctorates by examination after little or no attendance at lectures. Occasionally a ruler exploited the freedom of colleges of doctors to award degrees as they wished in order to obtain a doctorate for a visiting dignitary. On November 14, 1475, Duke Galeazzo Maria Sforza, the ruler of Lombardy, wrote to the college of doctors of law of the University of Pavia informing them that the ambassador of the duke of Burgundy would visit the city. The duke noted that the ambassador was a learned man and should be awarded the doctorate of canon law. Moreover, the duke felt that the ambassador should not have to pay for the degree. Not surprisingly, the college of legists agreed on both counts. The ambassador arrived in Pavia on November 16, was examined and awarded the doctorate of canon law on the 17th, and left on the 18th.[116]

The doctorates of two well-known Renaissance humanists also illustrate how the regulations could be ignored. The Faculty of Theology (i.e., the college of doctors of theology) of the University of Turin awarded Erasmus of Rotterdam a doctorate of theology on the basis of an examination. Erasmus had studied theology at Paris in a desultory fashion and with numerous absences between 1495 and 1499. But he did not acquire a degree and probably satisfied few, if any, of the numerous and lengthy requirements for the doctorate of theology. Nor did he study at Turin, as no lectures were held in the late summer. Nevertheless, Erasmus arrived in Turin about the middle of August 1506 and passed the doctoral examination and received his degree on September 4, 1506.[117]

Marc'Antoine Muret (1526–85) received his doctorate of law *in utroque iure* from the University of Macerata after an even shorter visit. So far as is known, Muret never studied at a university or took an earlier degree. Born in Limousin, France, Muret taught humanities in various preuniversity schools in provincial France, before accusations of sodomy drove him out of the country at the end of 1553. He then taught privately in Venice and Padua and at the University

114. These salaries come from the 1609–10 Parma roll; see Chapter 4, "Parma, 1601."

115. Roero, 1604, 85.

116. Sottili, 1982, 519–21, 563–64. The diploma is printed in *Lauree Pavesi,* 1995, 354–56, but with the date Nov. 13, 1475. It also states that the ambassador already possessed a licentiate in canon law from the University of Heidelberg.

117. For the story, see Grendler, 1998.

of Rome from 1563 until his death. In 1572 Muret took advantage of the Easter vacation in order to travel the approximately 150 miles over the Apennine Mountains to the University of Macerata. He was examined and received the degree on the Saturday before Palm Sunday, March 29; he probably returned to Rome in time to resume teaching after the Easter vacation, now as Doctor Muret. He did not attend lectures at Macerata during the Easter vacation, nor did he have any other known connection with the university.[118]

Obviously the college of theologians at Turin and the college of legists at Macerata decided on the basis of the doctoral examination, and probably the scholarly reputation of the candidates, that Erasmus and Muret merited degrees. It is likely that many other less learned candidates also obtained doctorates by examination after limited university study. For example, ten English clergymen obtained doctorates of theology and five English laymen obtained doctorates in law from the University of Turin between 1496 and 1511. Indeed, one received his doctorate of theology on the same day as Erasmus. From what little is known of their careers, it does not appear that these fifteen Englishmen spent years studying at Turin or at any other Italian university.[119] As noted earlier, more than 600 men obtained doctorates in medicine from the Venetian College of Physicians between 1501 and 1602, and 283 obtained doctorates in law, medicine, arts, and theology at Parma between 1432 and 1522, when neither Venice nor Parma had a teaching university. Moreover, most newly chartered universities of the late fourteenth, fifteenth, and sixteenth centuries began to award doctorates in the first and second years of existence, before candidates could have fulfilled local residence requirements.

The diplomas of men obtaining doctorates without studying at the conferring university sometimes mentioned study at other institutions, but not always. It appears that many students, especially non-Italians, obtained doctorates by examination without spending much time attending lectures in Italy. Northern Europeans sometimes sneered at such degrees as doctorates *per saltum* ("by leap"), that is, by leaping over the requirements in order to win the degree through examination.[120] But Italians did not seem to hold such degrees in lesser esteem than those won by following the statutory path. Indeed, the Italian practice made possible the first university degree awarded to a woman. Elena Lucrezia Cornaro Piscopia (1646–84) studied privately in Venice. She went to Padua only a few

118. For Muret's degree, see ASM, Archivio Priorale, F. 796, f. 119ᵛ, now printed in *Studium Maceratense 1551 al 1579,* 1999, 224–25. So far as can be determined, Muret scholars are unaware of the degree. For his early life and biography, see Chamard, 1951; Trinquet, 1965; and Renzi, 1986. For Muret's teaching at Rome, see *I maestri di Roma,* 1991, 35–123 passim; for the calendar of the year 1572, see Cappelli, 1983, 66.

119. Bellone, 1994, and Grendler, 1998, 58.

120. See Bubenheimer, 1977, 40–53, and Elsener, 1972. The 1485 and 1501 statutes of the Faculty of Theology of Louvain denied membership in the faculty to anyone graduating from another university *per saltum* or *per bullam* (see below). Jongh, 1980, 141–42, 3*. For corruption of the degree process at the University of Florence involving Florentines, see Davies, 1995–96, 72–80.

days before her doctoral examination in philosophy, conducted by the College of Doctors of Arts and Medicine of the University of Padua on June 25, 1678. It was successful, and she obtained the degree.[121]

Individuals could also award doctorates. Just as emperor and pope delegated to colleges of doctors their authority to award doctorates, they also delegated this power to individuals. Then the person acting for pope or emperor conferred the doctorate. Those who received doctorates in this way were sometimes called doctors "*bullati*" or "*per bullam,*" because the doctorate came from an individual possessing a papal bull or an imperial document.[122]

A pope might grant to a high churchman or curial official the power to award degrees. For example, the master general of the Dominican order received from the pope the authority to confer the doctorate of theology on members of his order during general chapter meetings. In a noted case, the master general of the Dominican order conferred the doctorate of theology on Tommaso da Vio Gaetano (Cajetan) (1469–1534) in a May 1494 meeting of the chapter, after Cajetan had brilliantly defended theses against all comers, including Giovanni Pico della Mirandola. Cajetan had been a formal theology student for only one year.[123] An emperor might confer the power to grant doctorates on a feudatory, who then awarded degrees as he saw fit.[124] Those who obtained degrees *per bullam* often did so because they could not afford the high costs of a degree obtained in the normal fashion. Or, as Jews, they were not part of the mainstream of Christian society. It is very difficult to determine whether the recipients of degrees *per bullam* attended lectures for several years and were examined by professors.

Even though statutes insisted on many years of study, colleges of doctors could ignore regulations and award degrees as they saw fit. Their independence and distance from the teaching university offered students a great deal of flexibility. These factors encouraged the mobility so characteristic of Italian universities, as students often studied at two, three, or four universities before taking a degree. But the same freedom also opened the door to abuses. Because the degree candidate had to pay fees to those who examined him and to the promoters, greed may have encouraged colleges of doctors and professors to award degrees through examination without concern for residence. Foreign students came to Italian universities to study at the leading research centers in Europe for the

121. Maschietto, 1984, 85–90, 119–27.

122. See Franceschini, 1975; Bubenheimer, 1977, 46–48; Piana, 1984, 63*; and Davies, 1995–96, 73.

123. Hinnebusch, 1973, 64–65, and Gargan, 1971, 156–57.

124. In 1559 Galeazzo Gonzaga awarded doctorates in arts and medicine to several Jews in Ferrara. His privilege came from Emperor Charles V and was conditional upon the candidates being examined by at least three doctors from the Ferrara College of Doctors. Franceschini, 1975, 170–73. A clergyman and poet, Galeazzo was a member of the Gonzaga ruling family of Mantua. But the nature of his privilege is unclear; it does not appear that he was a count palatine. Since the Gonzaga were feudatories of Charles V and enjoyed various favors from the emperor, it is possible that the emperor conferred this power on Galeazzo, perhaps when he visited Mantua in 1532. I am grateful to Paul V. Murphy for information on Galeazzo Gonzaga.

humanities, law, medicine, science, and mathematics, although not in theology. Some came in order to obtain easy degrees from colleges of doctors.

DOCTORATES FROM COUNTS PALATINE

Counts palatine also granted doctorates outside the normal procedures. The office and title of count palatine originated in the Lombard kingdom of northern Italy (c. 575–774), when kings granted to individuals the authority to act in their absence in various legal and judicial matters.[125] Charlemagne and his successors continued to name counts palatine in Italy; the Holy Roman Emperor Otto III (983–1002) seems to have named a large number. The early title for such an official was "count of the palace" (*comes palatii*) or "count of the sacred palace" (*comes sacri palatii*), which signified that the official functioned as a member of the administration of the king or emperor. In time, "count of the sacred Lateran palace" (*comes sacri Lateranensis palatii*) or "count palatine of the sacred Lateran palace" (*comes palatinus sacri Lateranensis palatii*) became the common description of the office, even though the connection with the ancient Roman Lateran palace was tenuous.[126] Whatever the exact title, "count palatine" became the generic name for these officials, possibly because *palatinus* meant "belonging to the imperial palace."

Counts palatine initially had the authority to create notaries and judges, legitimize bastards, name guardians for minors, and exercise other legal powers on occasion.[127] Most important, the title and authority of a count palatine were inherited in perpetuity by males in the direct legitimate line. This suggests that kings and emperors originally saw the office of count palatine as a means of creating an Italian aristocracy loyal to monarchy or empire. On rare occasions counts palatine sought political power. In Pavia a group of counts palatine over-

125. The following is based on Ficker, 1961, vol. 1, paragraphs 170–77, pp. 312–23; vol. 2, paragraphs 244–66, pp. 66–118; Mayer, 1968, 2:42–43, 86, 154, 187–89, 191–93, 319, 363–66; and Bascapè, 1935, esp. 281–90.

126. For example, when in 1519 Benedetto Porcellini conferred a doctorate at Padua, the notarial document described him as follows: "nos Benedictus de Porcellinis, milles [*sic*] et comes palatinus et sacri Lateranensis palatii apostolicis et imperialis ac utriusque iuris doctor ex privilegio imperatoris domini Fedrici tercii Romanorum et omnium christianorum regis Austrie, Siritie, Chirintie, Cornioli ducem et comitem Chiriolis ex privilegiis datis Venetiis prime die mensis iunii anno 1452." *Acta Graduum 1501 ad 1525*, 1969, doc. 770. Thus, Emperor Frederick III Habsburg conferred the title of soldier/knight and count palatine of the sacred Lateran apostolic and imperial palace on an unnamed ancestor (it was Vittorio Porcellini; Martellozzo Forin, 1999, 88) of Benedetto at Venice on June 1, 1452.

The ancient Lateran palace belonged to the Roman imperial government. When the empire became Christian in the fourth century, the Lateran palace was given to the pope as his residence at a time when the pope was probably under imperial tutelage. It remained the pope's residence until the papacy moved to Avignon. Including the Lateran palace in the title of count palatine may have been an effort to claim that the count enjoyed universal authority sanctioned by both emperor and pope.

127. For example, counts palatine created numerous notaries in the Veneto in the fifteenth century. See Grubb, 1996, 125, 170–71. And the Giovio family used its count palatine authority to legitimize Paolo Giovio's illegitimate son. Zimmermann, 1995, 150, 334 n. 69.

turned the communal government and ruled the city for a few years in the late thirteenth century and early fourteenth.[128] But this seems to have been an isolated event. Emperors continued to create counts palatine throughout the Middle Ages and Renaissance. Popes also exercised the powers of counts palatine at the expense of the Roman aristocracy in the twelfth and thirteenth centuries and may have begun creating counts palatine beyond the papal state in the fourteenth century.[129]

Emperor Charles IV of Luxemburg (ruled 1347–78) may have been the first to add the right of conferring university degrees to the powers of counts palatine. In 1357 he named one Fenzio di Albertino da Prato count palatine of the sacred Lateran palace with the power of conferring the license and doctorate of civil law.[130] In 1363 he did the same for Giacomo Santacroce, doctor of civil law and a native of Padua, and his son Francesco.[131] The legal justification for the right to confer degrees is unknown; perhaps the emperor saw it as a corollary of the power to create notaries.

Once conferring degrees became one of the office's powers, emperors and popes began to name professors counts palatine. Emperor Sigismund of Luxemburg (ruled 1410–37) made Giovanni Francesco Capodilista (c. 1375–1452), a Paduan native and longtime professor of canon and civil law at Padua, count palatine in 1434. Other Paduans and Venetians, not all of them professors, received the same privilege.[132] Pope Paul II named Ludovico Carbone, professor of rhetoric and *humanae litterae* at the University of Ferrara, in 1459.[133] Emperor Frederick III Habsburg named Baldo Bartolini, professor of civil law at the University of Perugia, in 1469.[134] And so on. Emperors conferred the privilege as a reward for services rendered or a financial donation.

Counts palatine apparently conferred few doctorates before the last decade of the fifteenth century. For example, counts palatine conferred about 157 known degrees at Padua from 1443 through 1500 (an average of 2.7 annually), but more than half of them between 1490 and 1500.[135]

The number of counts palatine and the number of degrees they conferred

---

128. Bascapè, 1935, 291–377.

129. Mayer, 1968, 2:43 n. 104; Ficker, 1961, vol. 2, paragraphs 257 and 265, pp. 95–96, 113–14.

130. "Doctoresque in iure civili constituere in omnibus civitatibus imperii nostri, terris et locis, diligenti prius examinatione adhibita a doctoribus collegii civitatum habentium privilegia studii, ipsisque sic examinatis et approbatis licentiam tribuere sacratissimas leges legendi et docendi locorum ubique nostre dictionis vel imperii." Charter of Charles IV conferring the title and powers of count palatine of the Lateran palace on Fenzio di Albertino da Prato, Aug. 15, 1357, Prague, printed in Ficker, 1961, vol. 4, doc. 524, pp. 539–41 (quotation p. 540). See also Ficker, 1961, vol. 2, paragraph 253, pp. 107–8.

131. Martellozzo Forin, 1999, 82, 112–14 (text).

132. Ibid., 115–18, for the text of the decree; and ibid., passim, for other creations. See Tocci, 1975, 638, and Belloni, 1986, 254–58, for more on Capodilista and his descendents.

133. Paoletti, 1976, 700.

134. Abbondanza, 1964a, 594. Bartolini also received the Knighthood of the Golden Spur, a title that sometimes accompanied the count palatine office in the Renaissance.

135. Martellozzo Forin, 1999, 92–95.

increased in the sixteenth century. Since legitimate male descendents inherited the title, every new count palatine had the potential of begetting a line of counts palatine. For example, eight descendents of Giovanni Francesco Capodilista, including two sons who taught law at Padua, conferred degrees as counts palatine from 1452 through 1508.[136] Another four Capodilista awarded degrees between 1548 and 1605. Every degree flowed from the original count palatine authority granted Giovanni Francesco in 1434.[137] So far as can be determined, none of the sixteenth-century Capodilista counts palatine taught at the University of Padua or anywhere else.[138]

The Capodilista were not unique. Eight other counts palatine, including five members of the Porcellini family, conferred degrees from 1501 through 1525 at Padua.[139] In addition, emperor and pope awarded new titles to famous professors (Andrea Alciato, Agostino Nifo, and Andreas Vesalius), little-known professors, and nonscholars in the sixteenth century. Counts palatine awarded degrees in all disciplines. But the number of count palatine doctorates still constituted only a small fraction of the total known doctorates. For example, 89 of the approximately 1,100 known doctorates awarded at the University of Padua from 1501 through 1525 were counts palatine degrees; this amounted to about 3.5 per year and 8 percent of the total.[140]

The procedure for a count palatine doctorate was similar to that for a college-awarded degree but less elaborate. Notarial documents recording the particulars of count palatine degrees at Padua mentioned *puncta,* an examination, and a vote.[141] In some cases professors are recorded as examining the candidate. In addition, after 1568 the appropriate student rector or his representative had to be

---

136. Ibid., 82–88, 92–95. The two sons who taught at Padua were Francesco (c. 1405–62/63) and Federico (c. 1410–c. 1466). See Belloni, 1986, 188–89, 194–99, and Trenti, 1975.

137. Transalgardo Capodilista, another Francesco Capodilista, and Girolamo Capodilista conferred doctorates between 1548 and 1568. Sigismondo Capodilista conferred doctorates in 1588, 1595, 1596, 1597, 1599, 1600, and thirty doctorates from 1601 through 1605. Veronese Ceseracciu, 1980, 158–68; *Acta Graduum 1601 ad 1605,* 1987, docs. 37, 226, 239, and the index. On Apr. 25, 1602, Sigismondo Capodilista conferred a doctorate of philosophy and medicine on William Harvey of England. *Acta Graduum 1601 ad 1605,* 1987, doc. 394. Sometimes the documents indicated that the degree was conferred on the basis of the title originally granted to Giovanni Francesco Capodilista in 1434. See *Acta Graduum 1501 ad 1525,* 1969, doc. 498.

138. Facciolati (1978, pt. 3:54) lists a Sigismondo Capodilista holding the (ordinary?) third position in civil law in 1509. But he did not award degrees.

139. *Acta Graduum 1501 ad 1525,* 1969, see index.

140. Ibid. Although the volume includes 1,149 documents, occasionally two documents dealt with one graduate. As always, the numbers can not be absolute, because one can count only known degrees.

141. For example, the record for a count palatine doctorate of May 23, 1503, included the statement "prius recitato puncto." *Ibid.,* doc. 218, p. 74. And the record for a count palatine doctorate in philosophy and medicine awarded to a Paduan Jew on Mar. 19, 1602, included the following statement: "examinandum curavimus, qui-in omni-periclitatione adeo egregie-se gessit-ut-nemine penitis atque discrepente-idoneus-philosophus et medicus fuerit iudicatus;-nos itaque praefactum d. Samuellem philosophiae et medicinae doctor-facimus." *Acta Graduum 1601 ad 1605,* 1987, doc. 338, pp. 123–24.

present at count palatine degree ceremonies in Padua.[142] The records also listed promoters, witnesses, and sometimes the place.

Students sought count palatine degrees because they cost less than degrees conferred by colleges of doctors. The latter had statutory procedures involving many individuals, all of whom had to be paid. A count palatine examination and degree involved fewer promoters and examiners; indeed, the count might act alone. It took place in a private venue, often the home of the count palatine, and with little solemnity. All the above meant less expense. Sometimes students obtained one degree (e.g., civil law) from the college of doctors and a second (e.g., canon law) from a count palatine. Hence, they paid full price for the first degree and a lower amount for the second. Students also sought out counts palatine in order to shorten the years of study required by colleges of doctors, for example, five for civil law and another two for canon law at Padua. Counts palatine did not necessarily demand so many years of study. Finally, ties of friendship and patronage led students to take degrees from a count palatine rather than from a large impersonal college of doctors. A number of non-Italian students lived in Capodilista and Porcellini households in Padua and then took degrees from count palatine members of these families.[143] Whether Italians viewed count palatine doctorates as less prestigious than those conferred by colleges of doctors is unknown.

Counts palatine also provided a route to the degree for individuals completely outside the university. In 1469 Emperor Frederick III awarded the title of count palatine with the power to confer doctorates in medicine to an eminent Jewish physician, Judah Messer Leon da Montecchio. The latter then awarded doctorates in medicine to at least four other Jews in the following three years. The notarial record of one such degree stated that the recipient had studied for "many years," but it did not mention a university. The record also indicated that Judah Messer Leon did everything himself: he gave the candidate the *puncta,* examined him, and then conferred the books, gold ring, and biretta.[144] The proliferation of counts palatine awarding doctorates undermined the link between teaching and degree, but the full effects would not become apparent until the late sixteenth and early seventeenth centuries.

THE COUNTER REFORMATION

The intellectual atmosphere in Italian universities was less free in the last third of the sixteenth century than earlier. But professors and students, Italians and non-Italians, enjoyed different levels of intellectual and religious freedom.

142. On Mar. 24, 1601, leaders of the student arts organization wrote to the Riformatori dello Studio di Padova. They referred to a Venetian Senate law of 1568 which stated that the student rector or his representative must be present for any degree awarded by imperial or papal authority, including count palatine degrees. However, the college of theologians was ignoring the law, according to the students. ASVe, Riformatori dello Studio di Padova, F. 419, no pag.

143. Martellozzo Forin, 1999, 97–108.

144. Luzzati, 1994, esp. the notarial document on 51–53.

A handful of professors were imprisoned, lost their positions because of religious beliefs, or had to change passages in their books.[145] In 1547 Bernardino Tomitano (1517–76), first ordinary professor of logic at Padua, published under his own name a vernacular translation of Erasmus's *Paraphrasis in evangelium Matthaei*. The 1554 Venetian Index of Prohibited Books listed it as Tomitano's work and banned it. In 1555 he spontaneously appeared before the Venetian Inquisition to declare that it was Erasmus's work and that he had never assented to Erasmus's views. The Inquisition ordered him to prepare an expiatory oration criticizing Erasmus and praising religious orthodoxy. Tomitano suffered no other penalty.[146]

Matteo Gribaldi Mofa (c. 1500–1564) gave up his professorship of civil law at Padua because of his religious beliefs.[147] He came from a patrician family of Chieri (near Turin) but moved to a castle in the Swiss Alps about 20 miles from Geneva sometime before 1535. The Protestant Republic of Berne took this territory from Piedmont in 1536. At some point Gribaldi became a Protestant with leanings toward Anabaptistism and anti-Trinitarianism. He was also a well-known legist who taught at the universities of Toulouse (1535–36), Cahors, Perugia (1540?), Valence (1540–41), and Grenoble (1543–45). The University of Padua hired him as a second-place afternoon ordinary professor of civil law in 1548. Gribaldi applied to the Bernese government, to which he swore that he was an Evangelical Protestant even though he was strongly anti-Trinitarian by this date, for permission to accept the position and received it. As there was no first-place ordinary professor of civil law at that time, Gribaldi was a key figure. By 1551–52 he earned 1,100 florins, the highest salary in the university.[148]

While at Padua, Gribaldi made little secret of his religious views. He did not attend mass, probably expressed himself freely, and opened his home to ultramontane Protestant students. He also spent his vacations at his castle in Protestant Switzerland. The Paduan bishop became suspicious, and Gribaldi's concurrent denounced him. The Venetian governors of Padua protected Gribaldi but asked that he rebut the accusations. Instead, Gribaldi left Padua on April 22, 1555. The University of Tübingen in Lutheran Württemberg immediately hired him; indeed, Gribaldi had probably made this arrangement before leaving Padua. A few of his students followed him to Tübingen.

145. The following discussion omits individuals who were arrested for Protestant beliefs long after studying or briefly teaching at a university. For example, Girolamo Donzellini of Brescia (1513–87) earned a medical degree at Padua in 1541, taught in 1541–42 as second-place extraordinary professor of medical theory at Padua, and then left the university. He was a steadfast Protestant who smuggled heretical books into Italy, was tried four times by inquisitions and abjured twice, and was finally drowned as a relapsed and obstinate heretic in 1587. Grendler, 1977, 108–10; Facciolati, 1978, pt. 3:367; and especially Schutte, 1992.

146. See Grendler, 1977, 101–2, and especially Davi, 1995, 24–35, for more detail and bibliography.

147. For what follows see Ruffini, 1955, 45–140, the most important study; Stella, 1969, 136–42, 146–51; and Hudon, 1996, all with additional bibliography. Several studies of Italian religious exiles discuss his religious views, but little has been written on his academic career.

148. Facciolati, 1978, pt. 3:140–41; Tomasini, 1986, 257. See the legists' roll of 1551–52 in Gallo, 1963, 67, 96. For his Perugia appointment, see Ermini, 1971, 531.

Gribaldi further developed his anti-Trinitarian views and arguments for religious toleration. He became an intellectual founder of future Unitarianism and condemned Calvin for approving the burning of Michael Servetus. But attacks from academic rivals continued to disrupt his university career. A fellow Italian religious exile denounced him to the Lutheran prince of Württemberg for his anti-Trinitarianism, and he lost that position in 1557. The Catholic University of Grenoble hired him for the second time in 1559. As at Padua, a fellow professor denounced Gribaldi for his religious views, but academic differences may also have separated them. The accuser championed *mos gallicus,* the humanistic approach to legal studies, whereas Gribaldi taught *mos italicus,* the traditional method. Practitioners of the two rival methods often fought. Gribaldi again lost his professorship and retired to his Swiss mountain home, where he died in 1564. So far as is known, Gribaldi was the only scholar to lose professorships in both Catholic and Lutheran universities because of his religious views.

Carlo Sigonio (1522/23–84), the distinguished first ordinary humanities professor at Bologna, published a series of works from 1571 on recounting the history of late Roman and early medieval Italy. After publication of the initial titles, the censors of the Roman Congregation of the Index found much to criticize. Sigonio rejected the Donation of Constantine and viewed the growth of papal temporal power in the Middle Ages as a complicated historical process marked by advances and retreats. By contrast, papal censors wished to see papal temporal power as a seamless unity from the fourth century onward. Sigonio and the censors argued their positions back and forth. In the end Sigonio had to accept some changes, including endorsement of the Donation of Constantine, in revised editions of his books and in future works.[149] His books were never banned, nor did Sigonio suffer any institutional consequences. Indeed, his salary rose to great heights. But he was not permitted to describe historical truth as he saw it.

On October 6, 1570, the Bolognese Inquisition arrested Girolamo Cardano, first ordinary professor of medical theory at Bologna. He spent seventy-seven days in prison and another eighty-six days under house arrest. On February 18, 1571, the Roman Congregation of the Holy Office insisted that Cardano make a solemn abjuration. Instead, Cardano abjured in a less formal way on March 10. He also promised not to publish any additional works and relinquished the last two years of his teaching contract in return for a pension. Upon the advice of Cardinal Giovanni Morone, papal legate of Bologna and a firm supporter, Cardano went to Rome in order to place himself under the protection of the pope. Pius V received him warmly but did not give him a pension; Gregory XIII did in 1573. In return, Cardano destroyed some 120 of his tracts that were judged "confused," and he offered to correct his errors. In 1575 Cardano was permitted to practice medicine in Rome. But the aging scholar spent his last months

149. For the complex history of the censures, see McCuaig, 1984 and 1989, 251–90, and William McCuaig, "The Ecclesiastical Censures of 1581–1583 against Carlo Sigonio and his replies. A critical edition with introduction and notes." An online publication of the Centre for Reformation and Renaissance Studies, Victoria College, University of Toronto. URL: http://crrs.utoronto.ca.

writing his autobiography, *De propria vita liber,* which has had an immense *fortuna*. He died in September 1576.[150]

Cardano wrote about two hundred works in which he discussed algebra, arithmetic, astrology, astronomy, divination, gambling, the occult power of gems, geometry, magic, mathematics, mechanics, medicine, natural history, natural philosophy, prognostication, Roman history, and other subjects. He was immensely curious, iconoclastic, and original but also credulous (e.g., he accepted the existence of mermaids) and very disorganized. Cardano is chiefly remembered for his original contributions in algebra, the first attempt at formulating a theory of probability, his tentative efforts to formulate a non-Aristotelian philosophy of nature, and his innovative approaches to medicine.

Without the trial records of the Bolognese Inquisition (of which little survives), it is not possible to determine which ideas were found objectionable and which errors he abjured. Certainly Cardano expressed views that ecclesiastical authorities might have found offensive.[151] He strongly endorsed astrology and prepared a horoscope for Christ. He held Christianity to be the true religion but criticized religious writers, especially in the early church, for foolish statements. He wrote a defense of Nero in which he noted that the criteria for judging historical figures were historically conditioned and often wrong. He marveled at men who willingly endured martyrdom for various religious systems, not just Christianity. At times Cardano seemed to adopt a relativistic view toward the world's religions, and he seemed indifferent to the institutional church. He strongly defended the immortality of the soul but implied that many contemporaries doubted an afterlife. A number of thinkers of the later sixteenth and seventeenth centuries judged Cardano to have been an atheist. Possibly his combination of philosophical, religious, and historical iconoclasm led to strong suspicion of heresy, which could not be proven. Eventually, the *Index librorum prohibitorum* of 1596 insisted that all Cardano's nonmedical works had to be corrected.[152]

Fabio Nifo (d. after 1599) from Sessa, Campania, had moved in Huguenot circles in France before studying medicine. He received his doctorate of medicine from the Venetian College of Physicians in February 1575. In October he was appointed second-place extraordinary professor of practical medicine at Padua.

150. The best brief biography is M. Gliozzi, 1976. See also Antonio Ingegno's introduction in Cardano, 1982, 9–29. For some of the correspondence concerning his hiring, see ASB, Assunteria di Studio, Bu. 34, Requisiti dei Lettori C, fasc. Girolamo Cardano, no pag. For Cardano's career at Bologna, see Dallari, 1888–1924, 2:155, 159, 161, 164, 167, 170, 173, 176, 179, 182 (replacement); Costa, 1905; and Simili, 1956, 391–93.

151. There is an immense literature on Cardano, including the following recent studies, all of which list additional bibliograpy. See Thorndike, 1923–58, 5:563–79, for a brief overview; see Ingegno, 1980; Fierz, 1983; Siraisi, 1997; and Grafton, 1999; for comprehensive studies. *Girolamo Cardano,* 1994, contains articles on many aspects of Cardano's thought. Zanier, 1975, and di Rienzo, 1994, deal with Cardano's religious thought. See Shumaker, 1982, 53–90, for the horoscope of Christ. M. Gliozzi, 1981, summarizes his mathematical contributions. See Spini, 1983, 29–33 and passim, for Cardano's posthumous reputation as an atheist and libertine. There are many editions and translations of Cardano's *De propria vita liber;* Cardano, 1982, is a good Italian translation.

152. *Index de Rome, 1590, 1593, 1596,* 1994, 487–89 and index.

The Venetian Holy Office arrested him in January 1576, but Nifo escaped. (Since the Venetian government emptied the jails during the plague of 1575–77, it may not have been a real escape.) He then lived and practiced medicine in Poland, Transylvania, Oxford, and Leiden.[153]

Three other professors had difficulties with the Index or Inquisition because of their philosophical views. Girolamo Borri at Siena was imprisoned, probably for denying the soul's immortality; he later resumed his academic career. Cesare Cremonini at Padua was questioned for the same reason and saw one work placed on the Index, but he did not suffer imprisonment or any other penalty. And Francesco Patrizi at Rome had to make changes in his Neoplatonic *magnam opus* (see Ch. 8 for all three).

As these examples show, professors sometimes had to make corrections in their published works. On the other hand, they were permitted to hold prohibited books. Ulisse Aldrovandi (1522–1605), professor of natural philosophy at Bologna from 1561 to 1600, left his large collection of about thirty-four hundred books, some of them prohibited, to the city. In his papers was a document from the Congregation of the Holy Office of 1566 permitting Aldrovandi to hold some prohibited titles. Of course, Aldrovandi added many other books, not all of them allowed, after that date. Upon his death the city asked the Congregation if the "suspect and perhaps prohibited" books in his collection could be retained and used by the professor who succeeded him. The Congregation replied yes, so long as the books were expurgated according to the *Index expurgatorius* of Rome (1607, which contained guidelines for expurgating the works of a handful of authors, chiefly Erasmus), and so long as the names of heretics, and passages against the faith, or offensive to pious ears, or contrary to free will, were deleted. In similar fashion, professors at the University of Pisa in the late sixteenth and seventeenth centuries routinely received permission from the local Inquisition to hold prohibited books.[154] Professors in other universities probably also held prohibited titles, with or without permission.

Thus, neither professors nor Italian students could espouse non-Catholic views, even if they held prohibited books.[155] But Italian civil governments granted much more religious freedom to foreign students.

Italian authorities ignored the numerous ultramontane Protestants studying at Italian universities for nearly half a century. For example, between 1544 and 1553 the University of Ferrara awarded eleven doctorates to Germans who had previously studied at the University of Wittenberg. It is very unlikely that these

153. Palmer, 1983, 169; Facciolati, 1978, pt. 3:358; Tomasini, 1986, 316.

154. ASB, Assunteria di Studio, Bu. 100, pt. 2, no pag. The inventory of his printed books is ninety-four pages long. Although I did not examine the list in detail, I spotted a number of prohibited titles, mostly works on nonreligious topics by northern European Protestant scholars. For Pisa, see Prosperi, 1999, 271–72, 276.

155. If discovered, Italian students holding Protestant views were arrested and prosecuted. There is the tragic case of Pomponio de Algerio of Nola (c. 1531–56), a student at Padua, who was arrested for Lutheran views. Refusing to recant, he was executed by burning in Rome. Rosa, 1960.

students were Catholics.[156] Only in the 1560s did the papacy attempt to enforce religious orthodoxy. The papal bull *In sacrosancta beati Petri* of November 13, 1564, insisted that all students make a profession of the Catholic faith before receiving degrees from universities in Catholic lands. After the preliminary meeting with the college of doctors but before the first examination, the candidate had to swear that he was a Catholic in the presence of the bishop or his representative. University professors and other teachers also had to swear the oath in order to teach.

The bull did not have the intended result because counts palatine awarded degrees to Protestant, Jewish, and Orthodox students who refused to swear the oath.[157] (Counts palatine also conferred degrees on Catholics who willingly swore the oath.) Count palatine degrees enabled Italian universities to continue to be international institutions in an age of religious division. More important, governments developed policies of tacit toleration of Protestant students from Germany, the land that traditionally sent the largest number of foreign students to Italian universities. It was a major breech in the wall of the Counter Reformation.

The story of the German Protestants at Padua is best documented. Germans had always been the most numerous, most influential, and, reputedly, the wealthiest foreign students at Padua. When *In sacrosancta beati Petri* was promulgated in Padua in March 1565, the German students refused to swear the oath and demanded that the Venetian government reject it. The government did not do as they wished but turned a blind eye as they obtained doctorates from counts palatine.[158]

A long memorandum by the papal nuncio in 1566 summarized his discussions with the Venetian government over its policy of toleration.[159] Venice permitted Protestant students to live within their lodgings as Protestants (eating meat on Friday, reading heretical books, and so on) for three reasons. The Venetian government did not want to offend German rulers with whom they traded. In addition, the approximately two hundred German students at Padua spent 25,000 to 30,000 ducats annually. Finally, the Germans swelled enrollment, thus enhancing the reputation of the university.

The nuncio advanced counterarguments. Protestant princes should not be offended if Venice obliged German Protestant students to live as Catholics, because German princes, England, and Geneva did the same. Indeed, Protestant governments forced all strangers living in their midst to conform to the local religion within three days. Moreover, not all the Protestant students would leave Padua if forced to live as Catholics. Some would stay willingly, others because

156. Pardi, 1970, 137, 141, 147, 149, 159, 161, 163, 167.

157. For Jews who obtained doctorates at Padua, see Veronese Ceseracciu, 1980; Carpi, 1986; and Ruderman 1987 and 1995, ch. 3.

158. See ASVa, Ms. Barbarino Latino 5195, ff. 58ᵛ–59ʳ, for a summary of papal complaints that students obtained doctorates from counts palatine without swearing the oath.

159. Letter and memorandum of Nuncio Giovanni Antonio Facchinetti of Sept. 14, 1566, in *Nunziature di Venezia*, 8, 1963, pp. 105–9. See also Stella, 1964b.

Germany lacked famous universities and professors. Even better, an influx of Italian Catholic students would more than replace any departing Protestants. Many pious parents did not allow their sons to study at Padua because of the Protestant presence there; if the Protestants left, they would send their sons. Obliging Protestant students to live as Catholics would also protect from heresy the one hundred and more sons of Venice who studied at Padua. The Venetian government responded to this argument by saying that Italian Catholic students had no contacts with the Germans. The nuncio, who had taken a degree in law at Bologna, answered that this was not so. Students converse with all, he wrote. Indeed, because the Germans were rich and entertained lavishly, they were very popular. The Venetians replied that they had tolerated the Protestants for many years without ill effects on their own sons or on the Paduans who served the German Protestants in their lodgings and taught them Italian and music. The nuncio and the government reached an impasse.

Why did German Protestant students continue to attend Italian Catholic universities after the establishment of Protestant universities? The nuncio correctly pointed to the major reason, the weakness of German universities, especially in the subjects in which Italian universities excelled, *mos italicus* law and medicine. Even though both Protestant and Catholic regions of Germany increasingly adopted Roman law, German universities were not leaders in the field. And the average German university had only two or three professors of medicine, none of them famous, compared with fifteen to twenty at Bologna, including leading scholars.[160] In addition, foreign students came to Italian universities in order to meet students from many lands, not just Italians.[161] Italy probably still attracted more students from abroad than the universities of any other part of Europe. Indeed, an astonishingly large number of European intellectuals studied in Italian universities both before and after the beginning of the Protestant Reformation in 1517.

The Venetian government never barred Protestant students. It tacitly permitted them to live as they wished in their lodgings. But they were forbidden to practice their religion openly, to proselytize, and to show their contempt for Catholicism. Naturally, the students did not always behave circumspectly. They turned their backs when the host was elevated at mass. They posted anonymous notices attacking Catholicism. They urinated in holy water fonts.[162] Nevertheless, the Venetian government would not permit the Paduan Inquisition to make any arrests on the grounds that the identity of the suspected culprits was uncertain or that the charges were hearsay.

---

160. Strauss, 1986, on Roman law in Germany. Freedman (1985, 132–34, 136) points out that the universities of Vienna, Heidelberg, Giessen, and Helmstedt had only two or three professors of medicine at any one time in the sixteenth and early seventeenth centuries.

161. Martellozzo Forin (1971, 76–79) makes this point.

162. "Ma palesemente mostravano disprezzo della religione con voltar le spalle nelle chiese mentre s'alsava il S.mo Sacramento, con spander urina ne' vasi dell'acqua santa, con attaccar cartelli in publico contro la religione cattolica." Report of the former nuncio Alberto Bolognetti, no date but 1581, in Stella, 1964a, 277–79 (quote 278).

The German arts and law nations at Padua wanted more. They spurned the demands of the bishop of Padua that they live and act as Catholics,[163] and they frequently asked the Venetian government for a written guarantee of protection. Finally in 1587, the Venetian government apparently gave the German nations of arts and law a document guaranteeing them immunity from the Paduan Inquisition. Again, nothing was said publicly, and no document has been located. Overall, Padua had two hundred or more Germans annually in attendance, the vast majority Protestants, in the last third of the century.[164]

Padua was not unique in its toleration of Protestant students. In 1581 a young English Protestant in Padua praised Italians for not inquiring into the religious views of foreign visitors. He wrote that he felt more secure in the Republic of Venice than in France and had heard the same about Tuscany.[165] He was correct. The grand dukes of Tuscany protected German and other Protestant students who studied at the University of Siena. The ducal official charged with overseeing the university summarized the policy in 1602. Probably a quarter of the German students were heretics, he wrote, but they were left alone so long as they did not engage in contemptuous acts against Catholicism in public, acts that Rome would notice. This was enough for the government, because the Germans spent "doubloons by the bale" (*spendono doble a balle*), and their presence honored the city. The father inquisitor, an obedient subject of the grand duke, would not act without the permission of the civil government, he concluded.[166]

How many Germans studied at Siena is unknown, but there were enough that the government contemplated constructing a residence for them in 1596. Siena also had Bohemian, Flemish, and Polish students, some of whom may have been Protestants, in the late sixteenth century. Siena's tolerance for German Protestant students could produce surprising student itineraries. One Jeremias Wild of Augsburg studied at the universities of Heidelberg and Basel, then the Geneva Academy, all Calvinist institutions, and finally at the University of Siena, between

163. In 1579 the bishop of Padua and Girolamo Mercuriale, professor of medicine and protector of the German nation of artists, presented a list of rules by which the Germans were to live while in Padua. They were to burn their heretical books and observe Lenten fasting regulations but were not asked to attend mass. The German students rejected the demands out of hand and denounced Mercuriale, who humbly begged their pardon. *Atti degli artisti,* 1911, 149–50; Brugi, 1905, 92–93.

164. Former nuncio Bolognetti gave the number as "quasi sempre il n.° di 200" in 1581. Stella, 1964a, 277. This number is consistent with other information. More than 6,000 (i.e., 60 per year) different Germans matriculated into the two German nations, artists and legists, between 1550 and 1599. Approximately 1,000 men matriculated in the German nation of artists between 1553 and 1600, and the numbers rose in the last quarter of the century. *Matricula Germanicae Artistarum,* 1986. Since students normally studied for several years, this suggests 200 to 300 Germans were annually in attendance. Another piece of evidence is that 100 to 300 German law students annually voted for the leaders of the German nation of legists between 1564 and 1597. Contemporaries and Brugi concur that the majority of the German students were Protestants. Brugi, 1905, 41, 73, 85.

165. The English traveler was Nicholas Faunt (1554–1608), who later held political office in England. Woolfson, 1998, 128, 233–34.

166. Letter of Scipione Naldi of July 30, 1602, quoted in Marrara, 1970, 140. For the story of the toleration of ultramontane heretical students at Siena from 1570 onward, see Marrara, 1970, 139–43; Prunai, 1959, 122–29; and Cascio Pratilli, 1975, 26, 41–45, 49, 58–60.

1598 and 1616. He eventually became a professor at the Calvinist Academy of Lausanne.[167]

Bologna followed the same path. In 1553–54 the Bolognese Inquisition tried nine Spanish students, including five theology students, at the Spanish College, on charges that were largely theological overstatements. The trial yielded one abjuration and light penances for the rest.[168] As this was the only known trial of students at Bologna, it appears that the local Inquisition did not pursue Protestant students. Indeed, the Bolognese commune and Pope Gregory XIII assured the German nation that its privileges would be honored. The commune sent out letters encouraging German students to come.[169] A limited number of German Protestants also studied in other Italian universities. Perugia, for example, enrolled more than four hundred German students between 1579 and 1600, a minority from Protestant territories. It is likely that some of these students were Protestants.[170]

While the story of the German students is best known, Protestant students from other lands also continued to attend Italian universities. For example, in 1555 the papacy protested to the Venetian government that four hundred Germans and Englishmen lived at Padua as heretics, scandalizing the townspeople and corrupting Catholic students.[171] The Venetian government did nothing. While the figure may have been exaggerated, Protestants who fled England during the reign of Mary Tudor (1553–58) swelled the number. These wealthy Englishmen attended lectures and dined well but did not always matriculate or graduate. When Elizabeth I came to the throne, many returned to England to assume prominent places at court and in English society. But English Protestants continued to come to Padua to study for the rest of the century and beyond.[172] A small number of Protestant students from France and elsewhere also studied at Padua without difficulty.[173]

Italian universities were as tolerant, or more tolerant, of religious dissent than Protestant universities. After becoming Protestant, the University of Heidelberg imposed Calvinist or Lutheran oaths, depending on the religion of the ruler, on its professors and students. A new religious oath sometimes led to the dismissal of Protestant professors adhering to different creeds.[174] The governments of Edward

167. Maag, 1995, 167. Even stranger, the Geneva Academy apparently had a German Catholic student in 1615. Ibid., 101. From 1584 students at Geneva had to swear only that they would live according to the Word of God and that they rejected papal superstitions and manifest heresies. It was a much milder oath than in Calvin's lifetime. Ibid., 52.

168. Battistella, 1901.

169. Simeoni, 1940, 9–11, 69; ASB, Assunteria di Studio, Bu. 94, fasc. 5, a series of letters of the 1560s and 1570s encouraging German students to come.

170. Weigle, 1942, esp. 136, 144, 162, 164.

171. Stella, 1969, 142.

172. Woolfson (1998) provides a comprehensive study and list of English students at Padua in the years 1485–1603.

173. For French Huguenot students at Padua, see Rodinis, 1970; for Polish students, who were not necessarily Protestants, see Sambin, 1964.

174. Maag, 1995, 156, 160–61, 168.

VI (1547–53) and Elizabeth I (1558–1603) expelled, or compelled to resign, numerous officers and students for holding, or suspicion of holding, Catholic views in a series of purges at Oxford.[175] In 1559 the Crown imposed an oath accepting royal supremacy in the church and renouncing papal authority as a condition for receiving degrees. Enforcement became stronger in the 1570s, as a few students were annually denied their degrees. The Crown increased the pressure with new statutes of 1581 insisting that all students sixteen or older had to subscribe to the royal supremacy over the church and the English articles of religion as a condition of matriculation into any college or residence hall. Undergraduates learned Calvin's catechism. Tudor and Stuart governments eventually executed nearly seventy English Catholics with University of Oxford connections.[176] Overall, the English Crown insisted on greater public and private religious conformity at Oxford than Italian civil rulers did in their universities.[177]

Certainly the intellectual atmosphere in the last third of the sixteenth century was less free than it had been earlier. Italian professors, like their colleagues all across Europe, had to swear oaths and conform outwardly to the prevailing religion. They had to write more cautiously than in the past. But there was still considerable room for philosophical speculation, so long as scholars couched their views within prescribed boundaries or acceptable formulations. Even though it is impossible to know the extent of self-censorship resulting from Index and Inquisition, the restrictions were not drastic for the times. Indeed, professors at Italian universities may have had as much, or more, freedom to express their views as colleagues elsewhere.[178] Italian professors continued to correspond with their northern European Protestant counterparts and to publish works with Protestant publishers. Banned books continued to enter Italy in violation of the Index of Prohibited Books.[179] The Counter Reformation did not greatly change Italian universities. Professors and students had as much freedom of inquiry and religion as the times allowed, and possibly a little more than some of their counterparts elsewhere in Europe.

175. Mary Tudor (reigned 1553–58) deposed some Oxford college officials and had three bishops burned at Oxford for their activities elsewhere. But her reign had less impact on the university than those of Edward and Elizabeth. McConica, 1996, 47–49.

176. See Loach, 1986, esp. 381, 384–86, 388, 390; Williams, 1986, esp. 407–13, 433; and the comprehensive study of McConica, 1996. Outside of England, there is very little scholarship on the treatment of Catholics in Protestant universities. Several articles in *Universities in Early Modern Europe,* 1996, raise the issue, but there is no extended discussion.

177. Two circumstances help explain the severity: the English Crown was dealing with its own subjects, because Oxford had very few foreign students, and the papal bull *Regnans in excelsis* of Feb. 25, 1570, had called on English Catholics to depose Elizabeth I.

178. For example, professors at the Faculty of Theology of Paris had to stop teaching about tyrannicide when Henry IV entered Paris in 1594. And the librarian of the Collége de Clermont, who owned pamphlets favoring tyrannicide, was hanged. Brockliss, 1987, 298–99.

179. See the comments in Tedeschi, 1991, 339–45, and Grendler, 1977, 286–93.

PART II

TEACHING AND RESEARCH

he Renaissance university inherited a teaching curriculum and some research topics from the Middle Ages. The curriculum in 1400 embraced grammar and rhetoric; logic; natural philosophy; medicine and surgery; theology; mathematics, astronomy, and astrology; canon law; civil law; and a very limited amount of metaphysics and moral philosophy, always linked to natural philosophy. Much of the arts curriculum drew on Aristotle, and medical teaching depended on Galen, Aristotle, and Arabic scholarship.

The medieval names of the professorships continued for the most part, as did the broad outlines of some research questions. But the Renaissance university introduced much innovation in the next two hundred years. It created new professorships, such as anatomy and medical botany. Theology, once barely taught, had more friars teaching the subject within the university. Metaphysics and Scripture professorships closely tied to theology joined the curriculum. Moral philosophy became an independent discipline. Mathematics dominated the tripartite mathematics, astronomy, and astrology position, and professors of mathematics focused more on practical applications. Canon law declined in the number of professors and significance, while civil law created new specializations, each with its own professorship.

Humanism drove much of the curricular and research innovation. After joining university faculties, humanists transformed the study of grammar and rhetoric into the *studia humanitatis*. Once humanistic studies and humanists became established in the university, scholars in other disciplines acquired their philological and linguistic expertise, along with the humanistic ideology that viewed ancient texts as the true source of learning, and medieval scholarship as a barrier to them. Humanistically inclined scholars changed the content of instruction and research in all disciplines except theology. Although the Renaissance university never severed its medieval roots, its teaching and research differed substantially by 1600.

CHAPTER 6

The *Studia Humanitatis*

You should not be so parsimonious with the professors of Latin and Greek
whose letters are called humane. Indeed, they are the foundation of all learning.
—Pietro Bembo, letter of November 2, 1527

he introduction of humanistic studies may have been the most
important innovation in the Renaissance university. The humanists
joined the university and introduced new texts and a new approach
to ancient texts. Eventually their methodology transformed other
disciplines as well.

GRAMMAR AND RHETORIC IN
THE FOURTEENTH-CENTURY UNIVERSITY

In 1387 the University of Pavia appointed Giovanni Travesi da Cremona (c.
1350–c. 1418) to a professorship in "grammar, rhetoric and authors" (*grammatice,
rhetorice et auctorum*), which he held, with minor absences, until death.[1] This
program, with *ars dictaminis* as part of rhetoric, constituted humanities instruction
in the fourteenth-century university. Based on ancient texts and medieval manuals, it prepared students to learn the necessary skills to become notaries, secretaries, and chancery officials.

A fragment of the statutes of the University of Bologna at the beginning of the
fifteenth century summarized the degree requirements for grammar and rhetoric

Epigraph: See n. 138 below for the full quote in Italian and the reference.

1. The appointment notice for 1391–92 changed the terms slightly: Travesi was to teach "greater
authors, rhetoric, and speculative grammar" (*Ad legendum auctores magnos, rethoricam et grammaticam
speculativam*). Speculative grammar was a medieval logical approach to grammar. Rossi, 1901, 24, 25.
See also Maiocchi, 1971, vol. 2, pt. 1:167.

of the preceding century. The candidate for a doctoral degree in grammar had to offer two discussions (*lectiones*) at his doctoral examination. The first was to be based on a "point" (passage) taken from books 17 and 18 of the *Priscianus minor*, that is, books 17 and 18 of the *Institutiones grammaticae* of Priscian, the early-sixth-century grammarian who taught in Constantinople. *Priscianus minor* dealt with syntax. The second discussion had to be based on a passage taken from *Priscianus maior*, that is, the first sixteen books of the *Institutiones grammaticae*.[2] This explained morphology (the internal structure and forms of words) and phonology (phonetics).

For rhetoric, the degree candidate had to offer two *lectiones*, the first based on a passage from the pseudo-Ciceronian *Rhetorica ad Herennium* (often called *Rhetorica nova*), written c. 86 to 82 B.C. by an unknown author. Jerome believed Cicero to have been the author, and Renaissance printings of the text perpetuated this belief, even though some doubted Cicero's authorship and Rafaello Regio rejected it in 1491. The second *lectione* had to be based on a passage from Cicero's *De inventione* (often called *Rhetorica vetus*), written when he was nineteen.[3] Both were dry, technical manuals of rules, principles, and definitions of numerous rhetorical figures. Much fourteenth-century *ars dictaminis* instruction was based on these two works. The Priscian, *Rhetorica ad Herennium,* and *De inventione* requirements remained in place in some universities through the fifteenth century.[4]

The studies of Giovanni Conversini (1343–1408) illustrate the curriculum. In 1359 he attended the course on *ars dictaminis* based on the *Brevis introductio ad dictamen* of Giovanni di Bonandrea (1240/41–1321, a professor at Bologna for more than thirty years) offered by Pietro da Forlì, professor of rhetoric at the University of Bologna. At Easter 1360 Conversini shifted to a course on the *Rhetorica ad Herennium*. He was such a youthful prodigy that he was elected to one of the student lectureships (presumably for the following year) in which he taught the *Rhetorica ad Herennium* and the *Brevis introductio ad dictamen* to a large audience, according to his account.[5] After studying *ars dictaminis* at the university for a year or more, the fourteenth-century student might obtain, with additional study of about two years, a notarial diploma, rather than proceeding to an arts degree, which took longer. Giovanni Conversini took a notarial diploma in 1362 at the age of nineteen instead of going on for an arts degree. The combination of grammar, rhetoric, *ars dictaminis,* and *ars notaria* prepared him for the chancellor positions he held in later life.[6]

---

2. "Promovendus vero in gramatica, servato ordine supradicto, recipiat ponta pro prima lectione in prisiano minor, pro 2.ª lectione in prisiano maiori, et in examine ordo servetur, ut supra." Malagola, 1966, 488.

3. "Promovendus vero in retorica, primo, servato ordine dato, recipiat poncta pro prima lectione in retorica nova, et pro secunda lectione in retorica veterj tulij, et in examine servetur modus predictus." Malagola, 1966, 488. For the *fortuna* of the *Rhetorica ad Herennium* and *De inventione* in the Middle Ages and Renaissance, see Ward, 1978, 1983, and 1995.

4. See the 1448 statutes of the University of Turin. Vallauri, 1970, 1:101–2.

5. Sabbadini, 1924, 23–24.

6. Ibid., 25 and passim; Kohl, 1983b.

Ars dictaminis meant the art of composing formal Latin letters according to complex forms and rules. Rather than trying to imitate ancient classical prose, the student learned the rules of classical rhetoric and then followed model letters, or parts of letters, found in manuals prepared by *dictatores,* usually thirteenth-or fourteenth-century university professors of rhetoric. For example, Francesco da Buti (1324–1405) wrote an *ars dictaminis* treatise while he taught at the University of Bologna between 1366 and 1376.[7] The manuals taught a structure and style very different from the letters of Cicero, which were very little known.

The close bonds between grammar, rhetoric, and *ars notaria* meant that universities had professors to teach notarial art. From 1370–71 through 1405–6, the University of Bologna arts and medicine rolls always included at least one, normally two, and sometimes three professors teaching notarial skills.[8] The roll of 1386–87 directed the two professors of notarial art to teach the "Summam notarie," that is, the *Summa artis notariae* (mid-thirteenth century) of Rolandino Passaggeri, twice in the course of the year.[9] In 1395–96, the university charged one of the three notarial professors to do three things: teach the *Summa artis notariae* twice in the year, lecture on the *Institutes* (see below) once during the year, and lecture on the "Flores notarie" (not identified) on holidays.[10] It seems that the professor was to deliver two series of lectures on the *Summa artis notariae* and one series of lectures on the *Institutes* in the ordinary teaching days of the academic year and to lecture on the "Flores notarie" on holidays throughout the year.

Toward the end of the fourteenth century notarial skills began to be linked to law, rather than to grammar and rhetoric. At the University of Bologna the professorship was sometimes listed as "teaching notarial skills and the *Institutes.*"[11] Part of the *Corpus juris civilis,* the *Institutes* was an introductory manual containing the principles of civil law. In similar fashion, the one or two professors of notarial art at the University of Pavia from 1387 through the mid-fifteenth century were listed with the law professors.[12]

Closely linked to *ars dictaminis* in the fourteenth century, notarial studies lost their place in the faculty of arts in the fifteenth century when humanistic studies replaced *ars dictaminis.* Despite academic inertia, the University of Bologna au-

7. Banker, 1971, 273, and ch. 6 for the role of *ars dictaminis* in society.

8. The following discussion is based on the rolls for the appropriate years in Dallari, 1888–1924, vols. 1, 2, and 4: *Aggiunte.* The arts faculty at Padua taught notarial students until well in the fourteenth century. Siraisi, 1973, 41.

9. "Dominus Stephanus Dominici Tolomey qui legit in Studio Bononie Sumam notarie et dictam Sumam bis in anno legere debet." Dallari, 1888–1924, 4: *Aggiunte, 12.*

10. "D. Hostexanus de Hostexanis ellectus ad lecturam Notarie. . . . Et teneatur legere, prosequi et finire totam Summam notarie bis in anno et totam lecturam Institutionum semel in anno et Florem notarie diebus festivis." The ellipsis is in Dallari's text. Dallari, 1888–1924, 4: *Aggiunte,* 18.

11. "Lecturam Notarie et Institutionum." Dallari, 1888–1924, 4: *Aggiunte,* 5 (quote, 1376–77), 13, 15, 19; vol. 1:7.

12. Maiocchi, 1971, 1:118, 153, 185, 228, 312, 422. For the fifteenth century, see Maiocchi, 1971, vol. 2, pts. 1 and 2. One or two men held the post for many years at stipends that placed them in the lowest quartile, sometimes the second lowest quartile, of faculty salaries.

thorities in 1457–58 finally confirmed the severance of the link between *ars notaria* and literary studies which had occurred in scholarly practice some time earlier by moving the notarial professorship to law.[13] Notarial art continued to be taught in the Bolognese faculty of law by a single professor to 1600 and beyond.[14]

The fourth element of fourteenth-century humanities instruction, and the most important for the future, was *auctores*. The term in medieval usage meant curriculum authors, that is, those authors and texts to be taught in schools at various levels.[15] At the university level, the *auctores* of the medieval teachers often meant the four ancient Roman poets—Vergil, Statius, Lucan, and Ovid—whom the Middle Ages loved, plus Boethius's *De consolatione philosophiae*.[16] For example, the commune of Bologna in 1321 hired Giovanni del Virgilio to teach Vergil, Statius, Lucan, and Ovid at the University of Bologna.[17]

Pietro da Moglio typified the professor of grammar and rhetoric who also taught some classical authors. A Bolognese born early in the fourteenth century, Pietro da Moglio was probably a pupil of Giovanni del Virgilio. He then taught grammar and rhetoric at the preuniversity level in Bologna as an independent master with a boarding school for many years. He next appeared on Bolognese communal payment records as a university professor of "the science and art of rhetoric" (*scientie et artis retorice*) in 1352 at a salary of 50 Bolognese lire. He held this position until 1362 without relinquishing his boarding school. He then taught at the University of Padua from 1362 until 1368, before returning to Bologna as professor of grammar and rhetoric from 1368 until death in 1383.[18]

Pietro da Moglio offered much standard fourteenth-century university fare in his teaching.[19] He lectured on the *Rhetorica ad Herennium* and Cicero's *De inventione* at the university. He taught *ars dictaminis* to Coluccio Salutati (1331–1406) when the latter attended (1345 or 1346 to 1348) his boarding school in Bologna. (Salutati then pursued the two-year course in *ars notaria* at the University of Bologna.)[20] He interpreted the *De consolatione philosophiae* of Boethius as well as the *De quattuor virtutibus* of pseudo-Seneca.[21]

13. This is a point made by Calcaterra, 1948, 167.

14. Dallari, 1888–1924, 1:48 (roll of 1457–58), and vols. 1 and 2.

15. For a tentative list of medieval *auctores*, see Grendler, 1989, 111–17.

16. Giuseppe Billanovich (1965, 147, 152) emphasizes the inclusion of Vergil, Ovid, Lucan, and Statius in the medieval *auctores*.

17. The document of Nov. 16, 1321, reads in part: "Cum . . . in civitate Bononie presentialiter non sint alliqui doctores versifficaturam poesim et magnos auctores, videlicet Virgilium Stacium Luchanum et Ovidium maiorem." As quoted in Kristeller, 1961, 182 n. 5.

18. Sorbelli, 1912, 317; Calcaterra, 1948, 137–39; Frati, 1935; and Dallari, 1888–1924, 4: *Aggiunte*, 4, 5, 6, 7. The post was listed as "scientia Retorice" in 1370–71 and "grammar and rhetoric" subsequently.

19. Giovanni Billanovich (1963–64) has assembled information about Pietro da Moglio's teaching primarily from student comments found in various manuscripts. Because he taught both at the university and in his boarding school, which had some preuniversity students, it is sometimes difficult to determine the audience for lectures on a particular text.

20. Witt, 1983b, 14–23.

21. Although attributed to Seneca in the Middle Ages, it is the *Formula avitae honestae,* a treatise on the four cardinal virtues intended for laymen, by Saint Martin of Braga (c. 520–80).

At the same time, his friendly contacts with Petrarch and Boccaccio demonstrated an interest in early humanistic scholarship. Perhaps as a consequence Pietro da Moglio taught a broad range of classical texts. He taught and wrote a commentary on the *Facta et dicta memorabilia* of Valerius Maximus.[22] He composed a Latin poem of 249 hexameters modeled on Ovid which discussed Anna's lament for her dead sister Dido (*Aeneid,* bk. 4, lines 670 ff.). In addition, Pietro da Moglio commented on the comedies of Terence and the tragedies of Seneca. Because the commentaries do not survive, it is not clear how extensive was his knowledge and understanding of these works or if his approach differed in any way from standard medieval fare. And between 1369 and 1371 he apparently introduced into his university lectures discussion of the Latin bucolic poetry of Dante (*Eclogae*) and Petrarch (*Bucolicum carmen*).[23]

His popular name, "Pietro della Retorica," testified to his fame in his own lifetime and after. Salutati and other students remembered him with great affection. But it is doubtful that Pietro da Moglio can be seen as a transitional figure who anticipated the teaching of humanistic studies in Italian universities in the fifteenth century. The works of Boethius, pseudo-Seneca, Valerius Maximus, Ovid, and Vergil which he taught and on which he commented were typical of the classics that medieval scholars knew; they did not point to the future *studia humanitatis*. And Guarino Guarini severely criticized his Latin prose style as obscure and unclassical, or un-Ciceronian, in 1415.[24]

Like Pietro da Moglio, other professors of grammar and rhetoric taught both *ars dictaminis* and a limited number of ancient classical texts. For example, Bartolomeo del Regno from Puglia (d. before 1415) succeeded Pietro da Moglio as professor of "grammar, rhetoric, and authors" at Bologna in 1383, remaining at least through the academic year 1406–7. He lectured on Terence, Plautus, Livy, and the *De officiis* of Cicero.[25] Francesco da Buti (1324–1405), who taught at the University of Pisa from about 1355 until his death, commented on Persius and Horace as well on as the *Doctrinale* (c. 1199) of Alexander de Villedieu. He also wrote an *ars dictaminis* treatise and a grammatical text.[26]

Lectureships on Dante as an "author" were an anomalous feature of instruction in late-fourteenth-century universities. About 1385 Francesco da Buti began to lecture publicly on Dante's *Commedia* in Siena, presumably at the university.[27] One "Blasio of Perugia" lectured on "the book of Dante" on holidays as a student lecturer on rhetoric at Bologna in 1395–96.[28] Other universities also had short-

22. Schullian, 1984, 338–40. Unfortunately, his commentary is lost.

23. Giovanni Billanovich, 1963–1964, pt. 1:203–23,

24. Guarini, 1967, 1:85–86; Sabbadini, 1964b, 176–77.

25. Dallari, 1888–1924, 1:5, 7, 10; 4: *Aggiunte,* 9, 10, 12, 14, 16, 18, 23, 26, 27, 30. The position was called "grammar" in 1383–84, was renamed "grammar and rhetoric," then became "grammar, rhetoric, and authors" in 1388–89. See also Martellotti, 1964.

26. Mazzoni, 1970; Fioravanti, 1993, 266.

27. This culminated with the completion in 1395 of his vernacular commentary on the *Commedia,* for which he is remembered. Mazzoni, 1970.

28. "Magister Blaxius de Perusio ellectus ad lecturam Recthorice per Universitatem. . . . non

lived Dante lectureships. In 1396 the University of Siena appointed Giovanni di Ser Buccio da Spoleto (c. 1370–after 1445) to lecture on Dante's *Commedia* on holidays in addition to his regular appointment to teach grammar and rhetoric. Giovanni di Ser Buccio continued to teach at the Sienese *studio* probably without interruption until 1445, but it is not known how many years he lectured on Dante.[29] In 1399–1400 Filippo da Reggio taught "Dante et Auctores" at the University of Pavia, then temporarily located in Piacenza.[30] The lectureship was gone by 1403–4, the next extant roll.

Only Florence continued to have a Dante lectureship in the fifteenth century, but as a "city" lectureship intended for all, not just students. It began in 1373–74, when the university was closed, as the government appointed Giovanni Boccaccio to teach Dante *in civitate*.[31] After a hiatus of thirty-eight years, Giovanni Malpaghini da Ravenna (1346–1422?) was appointed in 1412 to teach "the book of Dante" on holidays, again *in civitate,* for five years. The appointment was renewed for another five years in 1417. In 1415 the commune also appointed Giovanni Gherardi da Prato (1367–c. 1444), another prominent Florentine intellectual, to lecture on Dante *in civitate.* Thus, Florence had two Dante lecturers, as Gherardi held the lectureship through 1426. After a three-year hiatus, it was renewed in 1429 as a holiday lectureship that lasted, with brief interruptions, through 1446. Francesco Filelfo held the position, now called "Dante and moral philosophy," from 1431 to 1433; he delivered vernacular lectures at the cathedral. The position became "Dante and theology" when a Dominican friar held the post in the early 1440s, but it then disappeared for good.[32] In the end, Dante did not become a part of the curriculum of the Renaissance university.[33]

In the fourteenth century, the university professor of grammar and rhetoric explicated the technique for writing letters and speeches according to the principles found in the *Rhetorica ad Herennium,* Cicero's *De inventione,* and the rules of *ars dictaminis.* He also taught a few, mostly poetic, authors from the ancient Latin world. Together with logic, these lectures gave the student the skills to proceed with the rest of the university curriculum. Or else the student took the shorter course in *ars notaria* and left the university for a career in civil administration. By the end of the fourteenth century *ars dictaminis* was declining in importance. Thanks to Petrarch and his followers, humanistic rhetoric was gaining favor.[34]

---

obstante quod non sit doctoratus. Et teneatur legere librum Dantis in diebus festivis." Dallari, 1888–1924, 4: *Aggiunte,* 18. I have not identified Blasio of Perugia.

29. Goffis, 1971. Zdekauer (1977, 27) quotes from a Sienese archival document of October 1397, which suggests that this was a city lectureship intended for the educated public: "refirmaverunt magistrum Ioannem Ser Buccii de Spuleto in magistrum gramatice, rectorice et lecture Dantis civitatis Senarum, pro duobus annis."

30. Maiocchi, 1971, 1:421; vol. 2, pt. 1: 38–40, and Nasalli Rocca, 1970.

31. Gherardi, 1973, 344–45; Park, 1980, 265; Garfagnini, 1988, 194.

32. See the appointment notices in Gherardi, 1973, 388, 393, 395–96, 401, 404. See the payment notices in Park, 1980, 274–83, 286, 288, 290, 292–95, 297, 300, 301, 303. For Filelfo's lectures on Dante, see Garin, 1969, 194.

33. For the ways in which Florentine intellectuals interpreted Dante, see Garin, 1969, 179–213.

34. See Witt, 1982, 1983a, 1986, and 1988.

The *Rhetorica ad Herennium* practically disappeared from the university curriculum in the fifteenth and sixteenth centuries but continued to be taught at the preuniversity level. The *De inventione* disappeared from both.[35]

HUMANISTS AVOID THE UNIVERSITY, 1370–1425

Universities had only one or two modestly paid professorships of grammar, rhetoric, and authors. If a humanist took such a position and imbued his students with the values of humanism, the *studia humanitatis* would enter the university curriculum. But from the emergence of Petrarch in the 1340s until about 1425, only one leading figure of the humanist movement spent significant time teaching in universities.

The famous men of letters who composed the first, second, and third generations of humanists did not want to teach in universities. Petrarch and Boccaccio fled from university teaching as if it were the plague. Coluccio Salutati was a chancellor, not a university professor. The famous humanists born about 1370 were no different. Leonardo Bruni (1370–1444) served as chancellor of Florence. Pier Paolo Vergerio (c. 1368–1444) taught logic at Bologna in 1388–89 as a student lecturer, and possibly at the University of Padua, 1391–97, while he continued his studies in rhetoric and law. He spent the rest of his life as a princely tutor and serving various rulers.[36] The famous humanist pedagogue Guarino Guarini of Verona (1374–1460) only became a university professor very late in life, in 1442.

There were exceptions. Giovanni Malpaghini had served as Petrarch's amanuensis and secretary from 1364 to 1368. He then lived in Rome and Avignon until about 1375. He reappeared in Florence about 1390, making friends with Salutati and probably teaching privately.[37] The University of Florence appointed him to teach rhetoric in the autumn of 1394. The commune renewed the appointment for another three years in September 1397 at a salary of 100 florins. He was expected to teach a historian, a moralist, and a poet, apparently one per year, a prescription that suggested a commitment to humanistic studies. Malpaghini continued to teach at the university at least into the autumn of 1402 at a salary of 70 florins. The appointment was now more conventionally described as "rhetoric and authors." The Florentine *studio* then closed in 1406 and did not reopen until the autumn of 1413. But in June 1412 the commune appointed Malpaghini to teach "rhetoric" and "greater authors" *in civitate Florentie* and, as noted earlier, to lecture on "Dante's book" on holidays, at a salary of 8 gold florins per month.[38]

35. Grendler, 1989, 212–14 and passim, for preuniversity teaching.

36. See Vergerio, 1969, xiv–xv, 23, 26, 107, 471; McManamon, 1996, 17, 33–34, 52.

37. For short biographies of Malpaghini, see Sabbadini, 1924, 241–46, who disentangles him from Giovanni Conversini; Sabbadini, 1933; Martines, 1963, 270, 308–9, 315, 316, 319, 323, 324; Resta, 1971; and especially Witt, 1995, who corrects Sabbadini on some points. Appointment notices for Malpaghini are found in Gherardi, 1973, 369–70, 374, 377, 388, 393.

38. "Cum vir doctissimus dominus Iohannes de Malpaghinis de Ravenna, hactenus in civitate Florentie pluribus annis legerit et diligentissime docuerit Rethoricham et Autores maiores, et ali-

However, the rhetoric and authors appointment of 1412 may not have been a university appointment. The notice was unusual in several ways. It never mentioned the university (*studium*) but did mention Malpaghini's poverty, his young sons, and the lack of a teaching salary for some time. The fact that Malpaghini did not appear in university payment records after the *studio* reopened in 1413 supports the surmise that the appointment was at the preuniversity level.[39] This may have been an attempt to relieve his poverty by paying him to teach at the preuniversity level. Malpaghini certainly had friends in high places, starting with Leonardo Bruni, willing to help.

Malpaghini is important because he is believed to have taught Bruni, Pier Paolo Vergerio, and other famous humanists, who remembered him fondly. He may have impressed on his students the conviction that Cicero should be the model for Latin prose style, a key element in fifteenth-century humanism.[40] But much of his teaching probably took place outside the university. And because Malpaghini wrote almost nothing, it is impossible to determine the character of his teaching. In any case, his appointment did not leave a strong humanistic mark on the University of Florence.

The same can be said about the famous appointment of Manuel Chrysoloras. Coluccio Salutati persuaded Manuel Chrysoloras of Constantinople (1350–1415), an eminent Byzantine scholar, to come to Florence to teach Greek. Chrysoloras arrived in February 1397 to teach Greek literature and grammar for five years at the excellent salary of 150 gold florins, later raised to 250.[41] But the details of his contract suggest that it was not a university appointment. Chrysoloras was not subject to the Ufficiali dello Studio, the civic officials who oversaw

---

quando librum Dantis, et multos instruxerit in predictis in non modichum decus civitatis; et quod iam certo tempore elapso non fuit dicto domino Iohanni de salario provisum a Republica . . . et ipse dominius Iohannes pauper, cum parvulis filiis, sine salario lecture vacare non posset; . . . Quod dictus dominus Iohannes . . . sit conductus et solepniter deputatus, pro tempore quinque annorum . . . ad legendum publice et omnibus audire volentibus in civitate Florentie Rectoricham ac etiam de Auctoribus maioribus. . . . Et insuper etiam librum Dantis, quem legat diebus festivis . . . pro quolibet et quolibet mense dicti temporis florenos otto auri." Gherardi, 1973, 388, June 9, 1412. See also Davies, 1998, 15–16.

39. At this time the Florentine commune began to pay two or three grammar masters to teach at the preuniversity level. See Park, 1980, 274, for a rhetorician and two grammarians at the low salaries of 35 and 25 florins in 1415–16. These and subsequent similar appointments for preuniversity instruction continued through midcentury and beyond. For further explanation and documentation, see Grendler, 1989, 24–26. (However, the date "1413" on p. 24, line 5 up, should be "1415.") One caution: the suggestion that Malpaghini's appointment in 1412 was at the preuniversity level is tentative. Many documents are missing, the Florentine *studio* did not have a serene existence, and appointment notices were not always clear. Witt (2000, 350) argues that Malpaghini taught at the University of Florence from 1413 until death in 1422.

40. Witt (2000, 340–51, 374, 384, 390–91, 393–94, 428, 443, and 445) argues that Malpaghini had considerable influence on humanists in Florence and elsewhere. See also Davies, 1998, 108–9.

41. For his appointment, see the documents in Gherardi, 1973, 365, 367, 370, 372–73, and Davies, 1998, 15. For his teaching and influence, see Cammelli, 1941, 34–106; Thomson, 1966; Weiss, 1977, 233–38; Witt, 1983b, 303–9; Hankins, 1990, 39, 44–45, 105–9; and Wilson, 1992, 9–12.

the university. And he taught in his home, not in university quarters. Salutati brought him to Florence to teach Greek to himself and his circle, most of whom were beyond university age.

Chrysoloras taught in Florence until the end of October 1399, when, because of the plague, he received permission to move to a country villa. When his emperor, Manuel Palaeologus, came to Italy, Chrysoloras left Florence in March 1400, never to return. He was not replaced. Chrysoloras taught in Florence for only thirty-three months, or a shorter period, if he suspended teaching during the summers. Nevertheless, he securely established Greek studies among the Florentine humanists. His teaching and personality left a permanent mark on the group of young and mature Florentines who sat at his feet.[42] But his impact on the university and its students was slight.

The first humanist to spend significant time in university teaching was the transitional figure Gasparino Barzizza (1360–1430). Born near Bergamo, Barzizza studied grammar and rhetoric with Giovanni Travesi da Cremona at the University of Pavia, where he took his doctorate in grammar and rhetoric in 1392. In the next few years he taught privately at Bergamo and may have had a position at the Visconti court in Milan. In 1403 Barzizza appeared as a professor of grammar and authors and, later, grammar, rhetoric, and authors at the University of Pavia. But this appointment came to an end in early 1407, when the university dismissed him in order to bring back Travesi.[43] Barzizza went to Venice, where he taught several sons of Venetian nobles as an independent master for several months. In October 1407 the Venetian Senate appointed him to teach rhetoric and moral authors ("in Rhetoricis et Moralibus [Auctoribus])" at the University of Padua at a salary of 120 florins. It is possible that the patrician fathers of Barzizza's pupils secured the appointment for him.[44]

Little is known of Barzizza's ordinary lectures, which probably followed traditional paths. However, he also operated a boarding school, where he taught boys of both preuniversity and university age. And he delivered "voluntary" lectures, that is, special lectures outside the regular curriculum for which the listeners paid the lecturer a fee announced in advance.[45] It is likely that he did his most humanistic teaching for the benefit of the boys and young men from northern Italian noble families, the most famous of whom was Leon Battista Alberti, in his boarding school and in the special lectures.

Barzizza's teaching and scholarship blended new and old. He pioneered in the development of grammar and rhetoric based on ancient Latin classics, the foundations of the *studia humanitatis*. Although trained in speculative grammar, Barzizza rejected it in favor of grammar based on the usage of ancient authors. He

---

42. The only non-Florentine known to have been a pupil was Pier Paolo Vergerio, a member of Salutati's circle. McManamon, 1996, 86–87.

43. Maiocchi, 1971, 1:208 for his degree; vol. 2, pt. 1:40, 68, 84, 85–88, for his appointments and dismissal.

44. Mercer, 1979, is the fundamental study on Barzizza; see 27–28, 38–39, for the above. Martellotti, 1965a, provides a succinct biography.

45. Mercer, 1979, 42.

composed works on Latin orthography and punctuation which followed classical norms. Barzizza particularly loved the works of Cicero and searched for manuscripts, then emended the corrupt texts of *De oratore, Orator,* the *Letters to Atticus,* and the *Tusculan Disputations,* as well as Quintilian's *Institutio oratoria.* This was before the discoveries of complete texts of *De oratore* and *Orator* in 1421 and of Quintilian in 1416.[46] Although Barzizza lacked the techniques of textual criticism, his activity and values were clearly those of the early humanistic movement. At the same time, much of his teaching, even in his boarding school, remained traditional. He relied on such medieval pedagogues as the grammarian Alexander de Villedieu and Giovanni Balbi, author of a medieval glossary. He wished to reform rather than discard *ars dictaminis.*

In late 1421 Barzizza returned to Lombardy to copy and edit Cicero's rhetorical manuscripts found in the cathedral library of Lodi in early 1421. He was listed as a professor at Milan at the high salary of 350 ducats for the academic year 1421–22.[47] He may have continued copying and editing while teaching at Milan in the next few years, but documentation is lacking. Barzizza then appeared as a professor of "rhetoric and poetry" at the University of Bologna for two academic years, 1426–28.[48] The lectureships had assumed the typical humanistic title of later years, "rhetoric and poetry." He then taught rhetoric at the University of Pavia for the academic year 1429–30, before dying at the end of June 1430.[49] Barzizza was the first humanist to hold a university appointment for an extended period of time.

It appeared that Barzizza might inaugurate a humanist succession in the rhetoric position at Padua. After he left Padua, the university appointed Vittorino da Feltre to the professorship of grammar and rhetoric for the academic year 1422–23. But Vittorino resigned after only six months to become a schoolmaster. He preferred to mold youngsters rather than teach dissipated university students, as he saw them. After Vittorino, the position reverted to minor figures through the middle of the century, men who participated minimally in the humanist movement.[50] Malpaghini, Chrysoloras, and Barzizza were precursors, not the builders of significant humanistic studies in Italian universities.

The reasons why humanists did not become university professors are easy to

46. Ibid., 72–76.

47. Maiocchi, 1971, vol. 2, pt. 1:198. Barzizza's name appeared with the notation "In Mediolano" at the end of the list of professors of the University of Pavia. For more on humanist professors at the Milanese court, see below.

48. Dallari, 1888–1924, 4: *Aggiunte,* 53, 54, and Mercer, 1979, 135.

49. Maiocchi, 1971, vol. 2, pt. 1:267, and Mercer, 1979, 136, for his death.

50. For the roll of 1422–23 with Vittorino's appointment and the notice of his successor, see Ch. 1, table 1.2. In 1430–31, Cristoforo Barzizza, a nephew of Gasparino, taught rhetoric but soon became a professor of practical medicine. Sambin, 1965, and Pesenti, 1984, 42–48. On Oct. 29, 1433, Antonio Pezini was hired to replace Cristoforo Barzizza; he is called "Antonio Picino (or Piceno) da Bergamo" in the rolls of 1434–37. See AAUP, F. 648, ff. 54ʳ, 73ʳ, 79ᵛ, 80ᵛ, 81ᵛ. See also the printed rolls in Cessi, 1909, 143, and Tomasini, 1986, 155–58, 279. Egidio Carpo taught in 1436 and was succeeded by Matteo da Rido Patavino at an unknown date, according to Facciolati, 1978, pt. 1:liii. And so on.

find. Teaching grammar, rhetoric, and authors in the university was poorly paid and lacked prestige. A humanist could earn a higher salary as chancellor to a republic or secretary to a prince. Most important, the chancellor or secretary was highly visible and could possibly shape events through his presence at the prince's elbow.

For those humanists drawn to teaching, tutoring boys appealed more. The early humanists believed strongly in the power of the *studia humanitatis* to inculcate good morals as well as elegant expression; they expected their young charges to become responsible and upright leaders of society. Since they believed that the boy was father to the man, what better place to shape the mind and character of future rulers than in elementary and secondary schools? The best possible venue was in the familial atmosphere of the small boarding school of twenty aristocratic boys presided over by the humanist as surrogate father. Teaching grammar and rhetoric to university students aged eighteen to twenty-five could not compete with this vision. Finally, the humanist movement had not built up enough public support to make government leaders feel that they should appoint committed humanists to university faculties.

HUMANISTS JOIN THE UNIVERSITY, 1425–1450

Universities only began to appoint humanists to professorships about 1425.[51] The humanists born about 1400 constituted the first generation to take university positions in significant, but not large, numbers. They began to win university professorships in the same quarter century that humanistic studies triumphed at the preuniversity level in northern and north central Italy.[52]

The University of Bologna introduced humanistic studies and humanists into the faculty in 1424–25 with the appointment of Giovanni Aurispa to teach Greek. This was the first Greek professorship in an Italian university since Leonzio Pilato taught at the University of Florence (1360–62).[53] Aurispa (1376–1459) was less a scholar than a dealer in Greek manuscripts. In the course of two extended trips to Constantinople he learned Greek and brought back and sold numerous important Greek manuscripts. After a year at Bologna, he taught Greek at the University of Florence for one year, 1425–26. But he was dismissed for one or more of several possible reasons: enemies among the patriciate, poor teaching skills, and reduced university funding as war loomed. Aurispa never returned to university teaching.[54] At Bologna Theodorus de Candia replaced Aurispa for the

51. For some general comments about humanism and humanists in fifteenth-century Italian universities, see Kristeller, 1985, 5–6, 8–10; for the University of Bologna, see Sorbelli, 1940, 254–65, and Kristeller, 1956c, 316–20.

52. Grendler, 1989, 125–41.

53. Although Manuel Chrysoloras was in Lombardy, including Pavia and Milan, between 1400 and 1403 and did some teaching, it is doubtful that it was under university auspices. Indeed, most of the University of Pavia was in Piacenza between 1398 and May 1402. Cammelli, 1941, 107–30.

54. Dallari, 1888–1924, 4: *Aggiunte,* 49, as "Iohannes Hisparus"; Bigi, 1962b; Robin, 1991, 31–32; Wilson, 1992, 25–27. However, Aurispa is not listed in the payment records of the University of Florence for 1425–26. Park, 1980, 283.

next two academic years, 1425–27. Theodorus's low salary of 35 Bolognese lire in his second year of teaching suggests that he was not viewed as a major appointee.[55] In 1426, as noted above, the university hired the aging Gasparino Barzizza to teach rhetoric and poetry for two academic years.

Then the University of Bologna hired Francesco Filelfo (1398–1481) for 1427–28. Filelfo had attended the University of Padua, where he studied rhetoric with Gasparino Barzizza, but he did not take a degree, so far as is known. Now this young humanist of large reputation was hired to teach "Greek and Rhetoric" at 100 Bolognese lire.[56] Thus in 1427–28, Barzizza and three lesser figures taught Latin rhetoric and poetry, while Filelfo taught Latin rhetoric and Greek. The simultaneous appointments of four lecturers for rhetoric and poetry, and one for rhetoric and Greek, was a vote of confidence for the new *studia humanitatis*.[57] But it did not endure. Barzizza left at the end of the academic year in 1428, and Filelfo did not tarry in Bologna. The three minor figures who also taught may not have approached their subject humanistically.

The University of Pavia also began to appoint humanists. On March 15, 1430, it appointed Antonio Beccadelli, called il Panormita (1394–1471), to the single rhetoric position, renewed the following year. But Beccadelli left to become official poet to the Milanese court.[58] In autumn 1431 the University of Pavia filled the vacant rhetoric professorship with the twenty-four-year-old Lorenzo Valla at a salary of 50 florins. Although he was listed in the faculty of medicine and arts, the nomination came from the student rector of the faculty of law.[59] As described in Chapter 3, the student organizations at Pavia annually presented a proposed list of professors to the ducal government, which made the appointments, with changes as it saw fit. Since the rector of law nominated Valla, at least some of the law students wanted him. It is also possible that Beccadelli suggested Valla to the students. Whatever the circumstances, the appointment argues that university opinion favoring the *studia humanitatis* had grown to the point that the students wanted and got a precocious young humanist. His appointment was renewed for 1432–33 at the same salary.

But Valla did not reside peaceably in a university dominated by law.[60] On Sunday, January 22, 1433, a public degree examination of a candidate in law was

55. Dallari, 1888–1924, 4: *Aggiunte*, 49, 51, 53; Zaoli, 1920, 229. Theodore de Candia was not the better-known Theodore Gaza but has not been further identified.

56. Dallari, 1888–1924, 4: *Aggiunte*, 56; Zaoli, 1920, 232. There is an immense bibliography on Filelfo; see especially *Francesco Filelfo*, 1986, and Robin, 1991.

57. The three other teachers of rhetoric and poetry were Franciscus de Campania, Matheus de Foro Iullij, and Robertus de Arimino. They have not been further identified.

58. Maiocchi, 1971, vol. 2, pt. 1:267, 269, 272, 278–79; Resta, 1965, 401.

59. "Ad lecturam Rethorice. M. Laurentius de Scrivanis positus in Rotulo porrecto per Rectorem Iuristarum flo. l." Unfortunately, the name of the student rector of law is not known. In the following year the roll read: "M. Laurentius de Placentia, qui leget anno presenti flor. quinquaginta." The Pavian florin was worth 32 soldi at this time. Maiocchi, 1971, vol. 2, pt. 1, 293, 305. See also Sottili, 1990, 443–44.

60. The following is based on Speroni, 1979, who adds new information, summarizes the bibliography, and corrects previous accounts, and Sottili, 1990, 443, who clarifies some points.

in progress in the cathedral. At the point in the proceedings where anyone in the audience might oppose granting the degree, Valla rose and apparently did exactly that, no doubt with sharp comments about the ignorance and barbarous language of the legist. The student rector of law, whose presence was required by the statutes, defended the candidate and legal instruction generally, while the student rector of arts, also a required participant, took Valla's side. The presiding bishop ordered Valla's arrest for precipitating the breach of decorum. Valla fled the church with law students in hot pursuit.

Valla reported that a legist boasted that no work of Cicero could compare with the briefest text of Bartolo da Sassoferrato, his *De insigniis et armis*. In one night in February 1433 Valla wrote a slashing attack denouncing the practice and teaching of civil law and its major figures, the revered Accursio, Bartolo, and Baldo degli Ubaldi. He attacked their barbarous language, ridiculed their syllogisms, and lashed them for their ignorance of history. Valla praised the language of ancient Rome as found in the *Digest* but alleged that Bartolo did not understand it. He concluded by charging Bartolo with ignorance of the Latin language and distortion of the meaning of legal passages. His was the first of several humanist attacks on traditional legal studies.

The Pavian legists were enraged. Whether or not Valla had to flee for his life, as some accounts have it, he did leave Pavia and his teaching post. Pavia was not ready for Valla's revolutionary humanism. On March 19, 1433, the Milanese government appointed Beccadelli and Antonio d'Asti to complete the academic year. Antonio d'Asti, who has not been further identified, continued in the rhetoric professorship the following year.[61]

Despite the unhappy experience with Valla, the University of Pavia did not give up on humanistic studies. In March 1435 the commune of Pavia addressed a petition to the duke of Milan asking him to appoint to the professorship of rhetoric one Baldassare Rasini. The petition is notable for its praise of humanistic studies. The commune began by averring that profit and honor would come to the commune if the university had a learned man to lecture on rhetoric and the outstanding works of the poets. There were many youths in the city who were very eager to cultivate those studies called "most humane" (*istis studiis, que humanissima vocant*) if they had a wise teacher to instruct them in the art of oratory and the sweetness of sacred poetry. Fortunately, such a man was available: Baldassare Rasini, most excellent in the art of speaking, had devoted himself for many years to "humanistic studies" (*studiis humanitatis*). The commune asked that Rasini be given a lectureship in "most sweet poetry and rhetoric" at an adequate salary.[62]

---

61. Maiocchi, 1971, vol. 2, pt. 1:308, 309, 310. Beccadelli left for the Neapolitan court and did no further university teaching.

62. "Maximum equidem fructam et decus, illustrissime Princeps, hec vestra inclita Comunitas consequeretur si eruditum virum haberet qui Rethoricam et egregia poetarum opera ornate apud eam perlegeret. Sunt enim hac in urbe multi adulescentes qui summopere cupiunt istis studiis, que humanissima vocant, solertem operam adhibere, si sapietem in illis preceptorem possent imitari, qui artis oratorie singularia precepta et sacre poësis eos suavitatem edoceret. Nam si illud commode

The petition is as important as the appointment. The rhetoric of praise indicated the relatively high esteem that humanism enjoyed with some segments of influential opinion. While the position was the traditional professorship of grammar and rhetoric, the language of the petition (drafted by Rasini himself?) demonstrated that those imbued with the ideology of humanism wished to claim the post as their own.

The object of this praise was probably born between 1400 and 1405, the son of a Milanese nobleman. Rasini took a doctorate *in utroque iure* at Pavia in 1427. He taught civil law at Pavia from 1427 to 1429; the following six years are blank. Thanks to the commune's petition and a favorable ducal response, he began to teach rhetoric alongside Antonio d'Asti in the autumn of 1435 at a salary of 60 florins. Rasini continued to teach rhetoric with many increases in salary at the University of Pavia for the rest of his life, which ended in 1468. Rasini was a minor humanist who wrote a number of short orations and letters, interpreted Plautus and Livy, praised the Milanese dukes, and won the approval of the German students.[63] He fit the university community of Pavia much better than did Valla.

The University of Florence also moved to appoint a humanist just before 1430. For the academic year 1428–29 it appointed Francesco Filelfo to teach rhetoric and poetry, and he apparently began teaching in spring 1429. He had enormous initial success, with four hundred and more attending his lectures, according to Filelfo's own account. In the autumn of 1431 the commune gave him a new three-year contract that added the holiday lectureship on Dante and moral philosophy to his ordinary professorship of rhetoric and poetry. His salary was 350 florins, second only to the ordinary morning professor of civil law, who received 500 florins.[64]

In 1431 the university added another humanist, Carlo Marsuppini (1399–1453), to teach "poetry, rhetoric, philosophy, Greek, and ethics" at a salary of

---

assequi possent fieret profecto hec vestra Respublica doctior ac locupletior, ita ut pro status vestri salute apta magis redderetur. Quas ob res, humanissime Princeps, cum hic in presentiarum sit egregius dominus Baldassar Rasinus, in arte dicendi clarissimus, qui usque ab ineunte etate studiis humanitatis summa cum gloria studuit, quem vestra prefata Comunitas affectat magnopere, suis pro virtutibus innumeris, publice legentem intueri, dignetur piisima Dominatio Vestra, premissis attentis, prenominatum dominum Baldessarem ad ipsam lecturam dulcissime poësis et rethorice nunc cum salario competenti deputare, quod non ambigimus, vestra pro singulari in nos omnes clementia, consecuturos esse, cum sempre Dominatio Vestra studuerit ea omnia libenter experiri, que ad commoda vestre huiusce Reipublice redundarent. Deus optimus maximusque statum vestrum diu ad vota felicitare dignetur. Ex Papia, xviiij martii, mccccxxxv." The names of six communal councillors follow. Maiocchi, 1971, vol. 2, pt. 1, 347. Thorndike (1944, 312–13) provides an English translation. However, he incorrectly states that the petition came from the students and gives a wrong date of March 18.

63. Maiocchi, 1971, vol. 2, pt.1:353, 357. For his appearance on university rolls, see ibid., pts. 1 and 2:226 (as a student), 239, 246, 394, 423–25, 432, 470, 481, 485, 495, 518, 528, 538. See also Hammer, 1940 and 1948; Sottili, 1982, 525–27, 568–72; and McManamon, 1989, 20, 31, 108, 286–87.

64. Park, 1980, 287–90, and Gherardi, 1973, 245, 415–19, 424, 426–27.

140 florins, soon raised to 150.[65] The son of a wealthy Aretine who moved to Florence, Marsuppini studied under Malpaghini and apparently studied Greek with Guarino Guarini in Florence. Although he published very little, he had a vast reputation, at least locally, for his prodigious memory and for his poetry. Hence, for a brief period, the University of Florence had two well-paid humanist professors.

But politics snarled humanistic studies at the Florentine *studio*.[66] Filelfo and Marsuppini would have been rivals in any case, but civic politics was the core issue. The political struggle between the Medici and the oligarchic republicans led by the Albizzi faction was nearing its climax. Filelfo, the outsider, had begun teaching with the support of Cosimo de' Medici, but he saw the appointment of Marsuppini, a Medici paladin, as undermining his position. Filelfo now aligned himself with the opposition to the Medici. He denounced local humanists tied to the Medici; they responded in kind. His lectures on Dante, delivered in the Florentine cathedral, seemed to lend ideological support to the Albizzi faction. Then in May 1433, a person hired by an associate of Cosimo's attacked Filelfo with a knife in an attempt to drive him from the city. Filelfo blamed the Medici for the attack, which left a scar on his face.

In the larger world, the Medici were exiled in October 1433 and recalled in triumph in October 1434, at which time Cosimo banished Filelfo from Florence. The government of Siena, no friend of Florence, immediately hired him to teach at the University of Siena from 1434 to 1438 (see below). While at Siena, Filelfo participated in a failed assassination attempt against Cosimo de' Medici in 1436. It is clear that civic politics and competition for patronage complicated the teaching of humanistic studies at the Florentine *studio*. The humanist professor was a public intellectual. His learned lectures on the classics—Filelfo taught several texts of Cicero, Aristotle's *Nicomachean Ethics,* and Dante—were, or were heard as, partisan political statements.

Despite Filelfo's banishment, the University of Florence remained committed to hiring humanists. Marsuppini, supported by the Medici, taught at Florence in the years 1434–37, 1440–42, and 1451–52 and probably during some of the interim years for which information is lacking. But Florence continued to seek a distinguished outsider as well. It appointed George of Trebizond (1395–1472/73), a Greek born in Crete and possibly the ablest of the émigré scholars, to teach poetry and rhetoric. He first taught in 1438–39, a year in which Marsuppini did not appear in university payment records, at a salary of 120 florins. Another man

65. "Carolus de Aretio, ad legendum Poesiam, Rethoricam, Physolofiam, Grecum et Eticam, pro dicto anno, cum salario florenorum centum quadraginta, ad dictam rationem." Gherardi, 1973, 414. See ibid., 441, and Park, 1980, 288, 291, 293, 294, 298, 299, for additional appointment notices for 1434–37 and 1440–42. The discussion of Marsuppini is based on Vespasiano, 1951, 315–17; Martines, 1963, 127–31, 332–33; Zippel, 1979, 198–214; Brown, 1979, see index; Black, 1985a, index; and Field, 1988, 78–81 and index.

66. On Filelfo's Florentine career, see Vespasiano, 1951, 349–51; Voigt, 1968, 1:346–65; Zippel, 1979, 214–53; Field, 1988, 62–63, 83–84; Robin, 1991, 17–21, 40–41; Viti, 1997, 614–16; and Davies, 1998, 83–85, 110–12.

held the rhetoric and poetry position the following year. Then both George of Trebizond and Marsuppini taught for two years, 1440–42.[67] Florence had two highly visible humanist lecturers.[68]

Thus, humanists and humanistic studies began to enter the university in the years following 1425. But the path was neither smooth nor direct. Those who avoided controversial topics and enjoyed strong extrauniversity political support found the way easier. Humanists had a foothold in the university, but they did not occupy much space.

HUMANISTIC STUDIES FLOURISH, 1450–1520

The position of humanistic studies improved decisively at midcentury, especially at the universities of Florence, Bologna, Rome, and Ferrara. Between 1450 and about 1520, major humanists sought and obtained university professorships.

In August 1451 the Florentine government made another of its periodic attempts to improve the university. Lamenting the fact that many Florentine citizens and subjects studied at the universities of Padua, Bologna, and Siena "at great peril and expense," the government proposed to improve the local *studio* by allocating 1,700 florins, still a modest amount in comparison with other universities, for faculty appointments. But the proposed distribution of funds demonstrated that the commune intended to give humanistic studies greater prominence and support. The order of disciplines is that of the plan:[69]

Rhetoric and poetry instructors	350 florins
Civil law	440
Canon law	300
Medicine	300
Ethics, philosophy, and theology on festival days	70
Astrology (one instructor)	40
Surgery (one instructor)	40
Civil law (*Institutes*)	20
Logic (one instructor)	20[70]

This plan would appropriate more money (350 florins) for humanistic studies than for medicine and surgery (340 florins), a highly unusual allocation of re-

---

67. Park, 1980, 296–99. For his teaching and writing in Florence, see Vespasiano, 1951, 297–98, and Monfasani, 1976, 41–53. For the chronology of George of Trebizond's movements, see Monfasani, 1976, 36–39; and modified in George of Trebizond, 1984, 856.

68. Marsuppini soon reached a higher civic position. Thanks in part to his friendship with the Medici, he became chancellor of Florence in 1444 and served until death in 1453. He was honored with a funeral monument in the church of Santa Croce. See Black, 1985a, 72–74, 104–5, 110–111, and chs. 5 and 6.

69. Gherardi, 1973, 260–62.

70. The total for university professors is 1,580 florins. Another 120 florins went to grammarians who taught at the preuniversity level, even though the plan did not state this explicitly.

sources. The commune wanted to emphasize humanities teaching, which had fallen to a low ebb.[71] By contrast, natural philosophy, so important in every other university, was to be combined with ethics and theology and relegated to a holiday lectureship. The proposal went on to affirm that one professor of medicine and one for "oratory and rhetoric" would be exempt from a communal law limiting professorial salaries to 150 florins.

Naturally, the commune had someone in mind for the high-salaried humanistic position: it appointed Carlo Marsuppini, now chancellor of the Florentine republic, to a humanities professorship at a salary of about 300 florins for the academic year 1451–52.[72] Unfortunately, Marsuppini died in April 1453, leaving the Florentine *studio* again bereft. The quest to appoint someone who would also serve as the leader of upper-class Florentines with humanistic interests began anew. Several local scholars plus Francesco Filelfo from Milan offered their services, each with some support from the Florentine political and intellectual elite.

The professorship of rhetoric and poetry eventually went to Cristoforo Landino (1425–98). From an old Pratovecchio family (about 50 kilometers outside Florence) but born in Florence, Landino may have studied at the University of Pavia and definitely studied with Marsuppini. He worked his way up the Florentine academic ladder, helped by his friendly relations with the Medici party. Landino taught privately, may have served as a notary in the Florentine chancery, and probably was a communally supported grammar teacher at the preuniversity level in 1452 and 1454 at a salary of 35 florins. He probably also held the Dante lectureship, paying 45 florins, in 1456–57. In January 1458, the university appointed him to teach rhetoric and poetry at a salary of 100 florins. He held the post with distinction for thirty-nine years, published numerous works, and saw his salary rise to 300 florins. Although a distinguished Latin scholar, Landino had little expertise in Greek. So the commune appointed Francesco da Castiglione to this position, which, despite many absences, he held between 1446 and 1462.[73]

71. Comparison with the nearest extant roll confirms this. In 1447–48 the university had eighteen professors in various subjects earning a total of 1,845 florins but no one teaching rhetoric and poetry. Park, 1980, 308–9. It is possible that the roll is incomplete.

72. See Brown, 1979, 11 n. 35, for an archival notice that Marsuppini received on Feb. 29, 1452, payment of 466 lire, 13 soldi, and 4 pence for teaching rhetoric and poetry; also noted in Davies, 1998, 178. Since university salaries were paid in thirds and the florin was then worth 96 soldi (Goldthwaite, 1980, 430), Marsuppini had an annual salary of at least 292 florins. Probably the other two payments were slightly higher in order to reach 300 florins. Marsuppini would have needed an exemption from Florentine law in order to hold simultaneously the chancellorship and a teaching post at the *studio*. His high standing with Cosimo de' Medici and Florentine intellectuals would have made this possible. See also Field, 1988, 79–80.

73. On the competition to replace Marsuppini, see Field, 1983 and 1988, 77–106. On Landino and his appointment, see Gherardi, 467; Park, 1980, 309–10; Field, 1988, 231–36, esp. 234 n. 10; Verde, 1973–94, 2:174–77; and Davies, 1998, 113, 181–84. For Francesco da Castiglione, see Field, 1988, 88 n. 36, 98, and Davies, 1998, 112–13, 161, 185. He taught irregularly at the Florentine *studio* from 1446 to 1462. John Argyropoulos taught Aristotelian philosophy, not humanities, at the University of Florence from 1456 until about 1471, at the high salary of 400 florins. Field, 1988, 55–57, 107–26, and Davies, 1998, 121, 186–88.

Thus, at mid-century the University of Florence elevated humanistic studies by giving the subject a significant fraction of the budget and appointing a major figure.

Although the university moved to Pisa in 1473, the humanists stayed in Florence. In 1480, the commune added Angelo Poliziano (1454–94), who taught at Florence until his death. Thus for fourteen years Florence had two of the most important humanistic scholars of Italy teaching at different hours.[74] In addition, Demetrius Chalcondylas came from Padua in 1475 to teach at the Florentine *studio* until 1491. Several lesser or younger scholars also taught poetry and rhetoric, or Greek, in the late fifteenth century.[75]

The major humanists who taught at Florence commanded high salaries. For example, in 1489–90 Landino and Poliziano each earned 300 florins and Chalcondylas 250, the same as the upper one-third to one-fourth highest-paid professors at Pisa. But they worked hard for their money, delivering two lectures daily rather than the customary one.[76] And in the academic year 1491–92, Poliziano was required to teach four lectures daily, two in the morning and two in the afternoon, probably to fill the gap caused by the departure of Chalcondylas. But he received 450 florins, a figure surpassed only by one legist and two professors of medicine at Pisa. Even after John Lascaris was hired to teach Greek, Poliziano continued to receive 450 florins.[77] Of course, the Florentine humanists were not just teaching young students. They were available to teach all Florentines who wanted to learn and to grace the Medici court with their learning. By contrast, Pisa paid little attention to the humanities at this time.[78]

The studia humanitatis also became a more important part of the University of Bologna in the second half of the fifteenth century. The expansion had three stages. First, the number of humanistic appointments gradually increased. Second, a Greek lectureship became part of the teaching program. Third, major humanists of considerable accomplishment held long-term appointments.

At midcentury, the University of Bologna had two or three professors of rhetoric and poetry but no Greek lecturer, in a total professoriat of about 100 and an arts contingent of 42 to 45. Then the humanities grew. The number of humanists expanded to 4 or 5 in the 1460s, to half a dozen from about 1471 to 1477, and receded to 4 or 5 for the rest of the century. The figure often included a

74. "Alia hora quam dominus Christophus Landinus." Clause in Poliziano's three-year contract for 1482–85 quoted in Verde, 1973–94, 2:27.

75. For the contracts of the humanists who taught at Florence from 1473 to 1503, see Verde, 1973–94, 2:22–23, 24–25, 26–29 (Poliziano), 84–91 (Bartolomeo Della Fonte or Fonzio, 1446–1513), 174–77 (Landino), 178–79 (Chalcondylas), 194–95, 260–61, 362–63 (Ioannes Lascaris), 476–77, 502–3. There is information on the teaching of Poliziano, Landino, and Della Fonte in Verde, 1973–94, vol. 4. On Della Fonte, an important figure in his own right, see Zaccaria, 1988. On Chalcondylas, see Petrucci, 1973.

76. Verde, 1973–94, 2:85, 175.

77. See the rolls in Verde, 1973–94, 1:343–45, 348, 351.

78. Pisa had two (later one) professors of poetry and rhetoric, always minor figures, from 1473 to 1503. See Verde, 1973–94, 1:293; 2:94–101, 424–25.

professor of Greek. The humanities expanded while the total faculty size contracted to 80 to 90 and the arts component shrank to about 35.[79]

At first the university appointed young men, local men, and the sons of famous humanists to the professorships in rhetoric and poetry. Niccolò Perotti (1429–80) taught rhetoric and poetry at Bologna for two years, 1451–53, before embarking on an ecclesiastical career. A native son, Lianoro de' Lianori (1425–78), studied with Guarino Guarini at Ferrara and then taught Greek for four years, 1455–59, at the University of Bologna before embarking on a successful ecclesiastical career that included an apostolic secretaryship in Rome.[80] Battista Guarini (1435–1505), son of the famous Guarino Guarini, taught at Bologna for two years, 1456–58, before returning to Ferrara. Giovanni Mario Filelfo (1426–80), son of Francesco, taught rhetoric and poetry, plus Greek, then just rhetoric and poetry, for two years, 1461–63. It appears as if the university hoped that it might acquire reflected glory by hiring at low cost the sons of the century's most famous humanists.[81] But none of these men could have accomplished much at Bologna in their short tenures. Indeed, their scholarly achievements were in the future (Perotti) or modest at any time. While the outsiders came and went, several obscure local men faithfully taught rhetoric and poetry for many years while publishing little or nothing.[82]

The situation changed with the appointment of Francesco Dal Pozzo, called Puteolano (d. 1490), in 1467.[83] Born in the territory of Parma sometime in the first half of the century, he became a Sforza courtier in Milan. In 1467 he obtained a professorship of rhetoric and poetry at the University of Bologna, possibly through the influence of Ginevra Sforza, wife of Giovanni II Bentivoglio, ruler of Bologna. Dal Pozzo tutored the very young Bentivoglio children (the eldest son, Annibale, was born in 1469)[84] and performed other courtly duties in addition to university teaching. While at Bologna, he edited and saw through the press the *editio princeps* of Ovid (1471) and an edition of Catullus's *Epigrammata* and Statius's *Sylvae* (1473). In addition, he began work on a new edition of the works of Tacitus, including the previously unprinted *De vita Iulii Agricolae,* published after he left Bologna. Later editors praised his textual emendations on Tacitus. Dal Pozzo had a significant pedagogical impact on future Bolognese humanists, especially on Filippo Beroaldo the Elder. After ten years at

79. Dallari, 1888–1924, 1:29–176 passim.

80. Frati, 1930.

81. Dallari, 1888–1924, 1:31, 34, 43, 46, 49, 51, 59, 62, for the above appointments. For Giovanni Mario Filelfo, see Pignatti, 1997, 628. Although Dallari (1:87) lists Francesco Filelfo teaching rhetoric and poetry at the University of Bologna in the academic year 1471–72, I have been unable to confirm this.

82. The unknowns included Nicolò Volpe and Matteo de Gypso.

83. Dallari, 1888–1924, 2:76–105 passim, under the name "Franciscus de Parma"; Raimondi, 1956, 334–35; Raimondi, 1987, 54–58, 76, 83; Contarino, 1986; Ianziti, 1988, 212–13, 216, 226–33.

84. Ady, 1935, 157. Giovanni II Bentivoglio and Ginevra Sforza were married May 2, 1464, and had sixteen children, with the birth dates of some of the daughters uncertain. In any case, Dal Pozzo's charges were extremely young. See the genealogical table of the Bentivoglio in Ady, 1969, xvii, and p. 139 for the marriage.

the Bolognese *studio,* Dal Pozzo returned to the Sforza court at Milan, where he resumed a courtier's life, which included rewriting Milanese history in order to improve the Sforza image.

Humanistic studies at the University of Bologna reached a high plateau in the last quarter of the century, as major humanists taught there for long periods. The leading humanist was Filippo Beroaldo the Elder (1453–1505), from a local noble family. He studied with Dal Pozzo and was appointed to a professorship in rethoric and poetry at Bologna at the precocious age of nineteen in 1472, teaching until 1475. After spending time in Parma and Paris, he returned to Bologna, where he taught rhetoric and poetry from 1479 until his death in 1505, twenty-nine years overall. He was an enormously popular teacher. In 1493 a visitor to his lectures reported that three hundred students were in attendance. Another contemporary reported that two hundred ultramontane students abandoned the Bolognese *studio* when he died. Even if the figures were exaggerated, Beroaldo was a major figure at the university. The commune recognized this by raising his salary from 150 Bolognese lire to 600 in the course of his career.[85]

Next came Antonio Cortesi Urceo, called il Codro (1446–1500). After suffering the loss of his books in a fire while teaching in Forlì, he took the name "Codro" from an ancient poet who suffered similar disaster, as described in Juvenal, *Satires,* I, 2; III, 203–11. Born near Reggio Emilia, the son of a notary, Codro studied at Ferrara with Battista Guarini and then went to Forlì, where he taught the ruler's son. After dynastic upheaval at Forlì, Codro became professor of grammar, rhetoric, and poetry at the University of Bologna in 1482. In the academic year 1485–86 he added the second post of holiday professor of Greek and held both positions for the rest of his life.[86] Beroaldo the Elder and Codro had a number of pupils, including Filippo Beroaldo the Younger (1472–1518), a cousin of Beroaldo the Elder, and Giovanni Battista Pio (1475/76–1542?), who also taught at the university and were productive scholars.[87]

85. For the teaching positions held by Dal Pozzo, Beroaldo the Elder, Codro, Beroaldo the Younger, Giovanni Battista Pio, and lesser humanists through 1510, see Dallari, 1888–1924, 1:90–205 passim. For overall studies of Bolognese humanism, see Raimondi, 1956; Raimondi, 1987 (emphasizes Codro); and D'Amico, 1984, 361–69. For the size of Beroaldo's student audience and his salary, see Fantuzzi, 1965, 2:114; Frati, 1908, 212; and especially Beroaldo the Elder, 1995, introduction by Lucia Ciapponi, p. 3, for the figure of three hundred students. For Beroaldo the Elder's life and scholarship, see Fantuzzi, 1965, 2:111–35, and 9:53–55; Rizzi, 1953; Raimondi, 1956, 341–46; Garin, 1961, 359–87; Gilmore, 1967; Krautter, 1971; Garin, 1974; Garin, 1975, 197–218; Casella, 1975; D'Amico, 1984, 361–62; Raimondi, 1987, 76–93 and index; D'Amico, 1988, index; Fera, 1988; and Beroaldo the Elder, 1995. Despite these studies, there is much to be done on Beroaldo the Elder.

86. Codro was listed as "Antonius de Forlivio" in the university rolls. On Codro, see Raimondi, 1987, and Gualdo Rosa, 1983.

87. Beroaldo the Younger taught rhetoric, poetry, and grammar, or rhetoric and poetry, at Bologna from 1498 or 1499 until sometime during the 1502–3 academic year, when he left for Rome. Pio taught rhetoric and poetry in the years 1494–95, 1500–1506, 1507–12, 1514–27, and 1532–33, a total of twenty-six years. Dallari, 1888–1924, 1:157, 176–212 passim, 2:9–49 passim, 69. For Beroaldo the Younger, see Fantuzzi, 1965, 2:136–45; Frati, 1908, 217–23; and Paratore, 1967.

Thus, the University of Bologna had a significant group of humanists linked to one another through teaching and scholarly interests in the last quarter of the fifteenth century.[88] They produced a very large body of commentaries, critical studies, and editions of ancient texts, and they wrote prodigious numbers of orations and poems. Beroaldo the Elder produced editions and annotations on portions of the texts of Propertius, Frontinus, Cicero's *Philippics* and *Tusculan Disputations,* Suetonius, Juvenal, Apuleius's *Golden Ass,* Aulus Gellius's *Attic Nights,* Lucan's *Pharsalia,* Pliny the Elder's *Natural History,* and other texts. His *Annotationes centum,* resolutions through emendation and explanation of 104 philological problems found in a variety of ancient texts, displayed Beroaldo's erudition and served as a model of humanistic historical and philological scholarship. He also wrote numerous orations, letters, occasional works, and some poetry. After the death of Poliziano in 1494, Beroaldo the Elder's productivity, intelligence, and teaching at a premier Italian university made him Italy's leading humanist.[89]

Codro is best known for his commentary on Plautus's *Aulularia,* but he also wrote other works including much Latin poetry. Beroaldo the Younger is remembered for his *editio princeps* (1515) of the first six surviving books of the *Annals* of Tacitus. And Giovanni Battista Pio produced the first Renaissance commentary on Lucretius and studied other late Roman archaizing writers. Some, possibly most, of this scholarship came from the classroom. Bologna competed with Rome for the title of leading university center for humanistic scholarship between about 1480 and 1505.[90]

The University of Rome also became a major center for humanistic studies in the mid-fifteenth century. Because of the lack of university records, probably destroyed in the sack of 1527, the story cannot be followed from the beginning or in detail. Nevertheless, it is clear that Nicholas V (1447–1555) securely planted humanistic studies in Rome. Humanists came initially in order to participate in Nicholas's project to translate Greek classics into Latin or to obtain lucrative curial posts. Cardinal Bessarion (1403–72) also supported humanists, especially Greeks and those interested in translating ancient sources. Other cardinals offered household positions to humanists.[91] Humanists who came to Rome for other reasons often stayed to teach at the university, partly because under the benevo-

For Pio, see Dionisotti, 1968, 81–128; Raimondi, 1987, 108–13; Raimondi, 1974; and D'Amico, 1984, 362–63.

88. In addition, Vincenzo da Bologna (not further identified) taught Hebrew from 1464–65 through 1489–90. But the study of Hebrew does not seem to have been part of humanistic studies at Bologna. Indeed, only a tiny number of fifteenth-century Italian humanists learned Hebrew.

89. This is the judgment of Dionisotti (1968, 80). For a good analysis of Beroaldo's method in the *Annotationes centum,* see Beroaldo the Elder, 1995, 6–15.

90. Of course, nonuniversity venues, such as the Aldine circle in Venice for Greek studies and the Neapolitan court, were also important centers for humanistic studies.

91. The best account of Roman support for humanists and humanistic studies through the curia, papal court, and the households of prelates is D'Amico, 1983, chs. 1–3. The entire work explores the themes of Roman humanism in exemplary fashion.

lent papal gaze teaching could be combined with another post, giving the humanist a double income.

Humanists began to fill Roman professorships just before midcentury. George of Trebizond bought a curial scriptorship in 1440 and then taught privately in Rome. By 1449 he began to teach rhetoric at the Studium Urbis to such acclaim that he was considered the leading rhetorician at the university.[92] However, other humanists joined the university and challenged his claim. In early 1450, Theodore Gaza (1408/10–76), another volatile Greek who, with the support of Nicholas V, had come to Rome in order to translate Greek works, apparently stood up during George's lecture to charge him with error and stupidity in his use of an example taken from natural philosophy. To make matters worse, Lorenzo Valla (1407–57), who had come to Rome from Naples in 1448, began to teach rhetoric at the university in March or April 1450, possibly at the same hour as George. The extremely combative Valla took issue with George on the question, Who were the greatest military commanders of the ancient world, the Greek generals led by Alexander the Great (George) or Roman generals (Valla)? The public debate ended when George stopped lecturing at the university in 1451 and left Rome in 1452. Valla continued to teach there until his death in March 1457. George then returned to Rome to teach for an indeterminate period during the pontificate of Calixtus V (1455–58). Thus, two major humanists, perhaps flanked by one or two minor figures, taught at the University of Rome at about the same time in the middle of the century. Both published voluminously, including some of the most important works of the humanist movement.[93]

In the 1470s, 1480s, and 1490s, the University of Rome had a large contingent of teaching humanists: 3 to 8 professors of rhetoric and 1 to 3 professors of Greek simultaneously in a teaching faculty of 45 to 75 professors.[94] The university also had in 1482 a professor of "tre lingue," possibly Latin, Greek, and Hebrew. Some of the humanistic professors were major figures. Possibly the most important, and with the longest tenure, was Pomponio Leto (1427–98), who taught rhetoric at the Studium Urbis from 1468 until 1496, except for absences for travel in 1472–73 and 1479–83. Domizio Calderini (1446–78) had a very productive eight years (1470–78) teaching Latin rhetoric and Greek at the University of Rome. He lectured on the Silver Age authors Martial, Juvenal, Statius, Suetonius, Silius Italicus, and Pliny the Elder. Calderini also held an apostolic secretaryship from

92. For the beginning of Trebizond's Roman career, see Monfasani, 1976, 44–45, 53.

93. On George of Trebizond and Valla, see Monfasani, 1976, 79–83, 112, 140, 165; Renazzi, 1971, 1:131–32, 149–52; and the brief comments in Grafton and Jardine, 1986, 66–67. For Gaza, see Geanakoplos, 1989, 68–90. Renazzi (1971, 1:160–63) and Lee (1978, 173–74) believe that Gaza taught at the University of Rome; Bianca (1999) does not.

94. Because rolls are lacking, information comes from payment records for the years 1473, 1474, 1481, 1482, 1483, 1494, 1495, and 1496, supplemented by other data; see Lee, 1978, 151–92; Dorati da Empoli, 1980; and Lee, 1984; especially the tables in Dorati da Empoli, 1980, 107; and Lee, 1984, 145. These studies supersede and sometimes correct Chambers, 1976. Renazzi, 1971, 1:228–42, is still useful. For the professor of "tre lingue" Gugliemo de Ramondo (not further identified), see Dorati da Empoli, 1980, 125.

1471 until his death.[95] Even the peripatetic Francesco Filelfo lectured at the university for five months in the first half of 1475 and another few months in early 1476. There were many others.[96]

Humanistic studies continued to flourish in the Studium Urbis during the pontificate of Leo X (1513–21). The roll of 1514 listed 18 professors of rhetoric and 3 professors of Greek, in a roll of 87. Six rhetoricians, including the best-known Tommaso Fedra Inghirami (1470–1516), Filippo Beroaldo the Younger, Giovanni Battista Pio, and Raffaele Brandolini (d. 1517), taught in the morning and another 5 in the afternoon. Three more taught on holiday mornings and 4 on holiday afternoons. The 3 professors of Greek taught in the morning, in the afternoon, and on holidays.[97] They constituted the largest group of humanistic professors in any university during the Renaissance.

The University of Rome rivaled Bologna and Florence as the leader for humanistic studies between 1450 and 1500 and surpassed them in the early sixteenth century. Moreover, the combination of the university, the curia, the papal court, the academies, and prelatial households made Rome the largest and most important gathering of humanists in Europe. Humanistic studies may have declined a little at the Studium Urbis in the years after 1514 because of financial stringency and the deaths or departures of humanist professors. The sack of Rome in 1527 struck down the university and Roman humanistic studies.

The smaller University of Ferrara also embraced humanistic studies in the second half of the fifteenth century, although not as enthusiastically as Florence, Bologna, and Rome. Humanistic studies at Ferrara made their mark through their influence on pupils and scholars in other subjects. When Ferrara began in 1442, Guarino Guarini delivered the prolusion, the formal celebratory lecture. He stressed the civic role of the university and humanistic studies. Good letters aided the commonwealth by making good men. Rhetoric taught leaders to make good laws and institutions. Medicine conserved and restored health, civil law punished vice and rewarded virtue, and so on.[98]

With this beginning and the presence of Guarini, the revived university made room for humanists. Guarini himself taught until his death in 1460. He was succeeded by his youngest son, Battista Guarini, who taught at Ferrara for the rest

95. The standard monograph on Pomponio Leto is Zabughin, 1909–12. D'Amico, 1983, 91–102, gives a good summary of Leto and his circle with additional bibliography. For Calderini, see Perosa, 1973. For more on the teaching of the Roman humanists, see Grafton and Jardine, 1986, ch. 4.

96. For Filelfo, see Viti, 1997, 620. Giovanni Sulpizio da Veroli taught rhetoric at the university in the years 1481–84 and 1494–96 and presumably in the intervening years for which no records are available. Martino Filetico taught both Latin and Greek in 1473–74 and 1481–83, and probably in between. Antonio Vosco (or Volsco) taught rhetoric in the years 1481–83, in 1494, and probably during the years without records. Antonio Mancinelli (1452–1505) taught at the University of Rome in the years 1486–91 and 1500–1505. Lesser scholars taught for shorter periods.

97. *I maestri di Roma*, 1991, 1–5. Renazzi (1971, 2:66–78) identifies most of the humanistic professors. D'Amico (1983, index) provides much information and further bibliography. The future historian Paolo Giovio taught moral philosophy in 1514, but whether he approached the subject humanistically or in an Aristotelian manner is not known.

98. Del Nero, 1996, 38–39, 48–49.

of his life. Although he was an able humanist with a command of Greek, Battista seems to have published only one significant work, *De ordine docendi et discendi* (1459), a loving syllabus of humanistic studies based on his father's teaching. Ludovico Carbone (1436–82), one of Guarino Guarini's favorite pupils, was appointed to teach rhetoric and "humanae litterae" in 1456 and also continued until death. A prolific author of Latin dialogues, orations, and poetry, Carbone edited the *editio princeps* (1471) of the letters of Pliny the Younger and other works. The Greek émigré Theodore Gaza taught various Greek authors (among them Homer, Demosthenes, Xenophon, Aristophanes, and Plato) at Ferrara (1446–49) while he was studying medicine. He did much to promote Greek studies at Ferrara, according to his pupil, Carbone. The most important humanist appointee was Nicolò Leoniceno (1428–1524), who began to teach in 1464. Even though he spent most of his long career teaching medicine rather than rhetoric and poetry, his application of humanistic historical and philological criticism to ancient medical texts, and his humanistically based hostility to the medieval approach to medical texts, inaugurated medical humanism and was immensely influential (see Ch. 9).[99]

The two Guarini, Carbone, and Leoniceno attracted a number of foreign and Italian pupils to Ferrara, some of whom spread humanistic studies widely. The Hungarian Janos Pannonius (Joannes de Csezmicze, 1434–72) studied with Guarini Senior at unknown dates and with Gaza in the 1440s and brought humanistic studies to Hungary. The German Rudolf Agricola (1444–85), who studied at Ferrara between 1475 and 1479, played a major role in bringing humanistic rhetoric to northern Europe through his *De inventione dialectica*.[100] Aldo Manuzio (c. 1450–1515) studied at Ferrara in the late 1470s and did not leave permanently until 1482. The cultural environment of Ferrara played a major role in shaping Manuzio's commitment to make ancient Greek texts available; he fondly recalled his Greek studies with Battista Guarini at Ferrara.[101]

COURT AND CLASSROOM: CHANGING EMPLOYMENT FOR HUMANISTS

In the second half of the fifteenth century, humanists added university teaching to their list of preferred careers. Numerous major and minor humanists began

---

99. For the major humanist professors at Ferrara, see Chiellini, 1991. *I maestri di Ferrara,* 1991, lists tentative rolls and information on individuals which, for the lack of documentation, is not always complete or accurate. For Battista Guarini's scholarship, see Piacente, 1995. For Carbone, see Paoletti, 1976, who gives his dates as 1430–85. For Carbone's funeral orations, see McManamon, 1989, 30–31, 32, 58, 80–81, 137, 147, 160–61, 261–62. Gundersheimer (1973, 164–67) sees Carbone and Battista Guarini as courtier-humanists. True, but they were also important university professors. For Gaza, see Monfasani, 1994b, and Bianca, 1999, 739. For Leoniceno, see the bibliography in Chapter 9, "Medical Humanism."

100. Vasoli, 1968a, 153–62, for Ferrarese influence on Agricola.

101. Lowry, 1979, 51–53, 114.

to spend most or all of their professional lives as university professors. But they did not abandon the court or communal government, because humanism remained an educational program with broad appeal. A leading humanist attracted attention from within and outside the university.

The world viewed the humanist professor as more than someone lecturing to university students seeking degrees. Except for the public anatomy (see Ch. 9, "University Anatomy after Vesalius"), the humanities lecture was the teaching event most likely to attract listeners from beyond the university community. The nature of humanism practically guaranteed the humanist a broader audience than just university students, most of whom studied law and medicine. The reasons were obvious. Humanism instructed men to speak and write eloquently, taught them to interpret classical works, and exhorted them to live honorably. As the purveyor of such learning, the humanist might become an intellectual leader of adults, especially well-born young men. Filelfo seems initially to have filled this role for the losing faction in a political struggle; Marsuppini influenced two generations of Florentine intellectuals. Humanists entered the homes and villas of the city.

The humanist professor might have closer personal contact with the leaders of the city or court than other university professors. A professor of civil law put his legal skills at the service of the prince when needed and was richly rewarded. Professors of medicine treated the prince and members of the court and were also handsomely remunerated. But they offered only technical expertise; they did not teach the classics as a guide to life.

In light of the perceived significance of humanistic studies, it is hardly surprising that the leaders of Florence, Bologna, and other towns took a greater interest in university humanities posts than their predecessors had shown toward professorships of grammar and rhetoric. Court or commune might seek out a major humanist from elsewhere or nominate someone from its circle. Civic factions tried to impose their choice on the magistracy determining university appointments. When Carlo Marsuppini, humanist professor and chancellor of Florence, suddenly died in 1453, several candidates offered their services. Groups of Florentine intellectuals tried to persuade the commune to appoint a leading humanities professor who would also serve as mentor for their extrauniversity studies. An anti-Medici circle wanted to bring back Francesco Filelfo or to appoint the Greek John Argyropoulos, while the Medici supported the local man Cristoforo Landino. Eventually a compromise was reached: the university hired Argyropoulos to teach natural philosophy in 1456 and Landino to teach Latin rhetoric in January 1458 but would not have Filelfo.[102] The contest underscored the point that the humanities appointment mattered a great deal to civic factions.

Consequently, the humanist who wanted a professorship worked as hard to ingratiate himself with local ruling families as he did on his scholarship. Indeed, friendship with civic leaders often led to a professorship. Marsuppini, Landino,

102. Field, 1983 and 1988, 77–106.

and Poliziano all had close ties with the Medici family. Poliziano first served as
Lorenzo de' Medici's secretary. Then in the summer of 1475 he became tutor to
Lorenzo's son, Piero (b. 1472), then Giovanni (b. 1475), the future Leo X. The
famous humanist professor began his pedagogical career by teaching the ABCs to
a three-year-old. Even though their mother dismissed him in May 1479, Poliziano maintained his friendship with Lorenzo (and hung on to the benefice and
villa given him) and basked in Piero's affection. Poliziano got his professorship in
the autumn of 1480.[103] *La culla* (the cradle) led to *la cattedra* (the university chair.)

Bolognese university humanists also maintained excellent relations with the
court. Dal Pozzo, Beroaldo the Elder, and Codro had close and affectionate links
to the ruling family. Dal Pozzo had a room in the Bentivoglio palace and tutored
the children of Giovanni II Bentivoglio. The latter, in turn, attempted to obtain
ecclesiastical benefices for Dal Pozzo. Beroaldo the Elder and Codro tutored
some of the sixteen Bentivoglio children, and all wrote eulogistic pieces for
weddings and other family occasions. Beroaldo the Elder, a Bolognese citizen,
also held minor offices and performed diplomatic tasks for the ruler.[104] These
major humanist scholars practiced secondary professions as tutors and affable
house guests.

Because humanist training was so desirable, the rulers of Renaissance city-
states wanted it immediately available to themselves and their circle. So they
sometimes made the capital a center of humanistic scholarship at the expense of
the humanities at the university located elsewhere in the state. In Lombardy
the university was in Pavia, but the court was in Milan. Hence, Visconti and
Sforza dukes appointed humanist professors to teach at the Milanese court. These
court humanists taught anyone who came to listen and performed other useful functions.

When the University of Florence moved to Pisa in 1473, Lorenzo de' Medici
kept the humanistic section of the departed university in Florence for the benefit
of local men with a taste for learning. The university-level humanists formed the
apex of a small publicly supported grammar and humanities establishment for
Florentines. The commune paid the salaries of a handful of grammarians who
taught Latin at the preuniversity level.[105] More advanced students then attended
the lectures of Landino, Poliziano, and others. By contrast, minor scholars taught
humanities to the university students at Pisa.

Venice, another capital city lacking a local university, adopted a different path
to the same goal. In 1446 the Venetian government founded the Scuola di San
Marco, a non-degree-granting university-level humanistic school with two professors, who were sometimes major figures. They taught humanistic studies to

---

103. Bigi, 1960, 692, 695; Bigi, 1986, 478–79; Verde, 1973–94, 4:199, 347–49.

104. Frati, 1908, 212; Ady, 1935; Ady, 1969, 144–45; Raimondi, 1987, 32, 58–59, 131–32, 198–
99, 203–6, 213, 225, 259, 261, 293.

105. The number of schoolmaster grammarians ranged from two to six but averaged three or four
between 1473 and 1503. Verde, 1973–94, 1:296–383 passim.

noble youths and future chancery secretaries.[106] Supporting humanistic studies at the court or capital city prevented universities from becoming important humanistic centers until later (Padua) or never (Pavia and Pisa).

A high post in the chancery of a republic or princedom or a curial position in Rome remained highly desirable, if hard to get. Landino was an unsuccessful candidate for chancellor of the Florentine republic in 1458. But he later held a secretaryship in the Florentine chancery and served as "chancellor" (i.e., secretary) to the Guelf party simultaneously with his university lecturing.[107] Other humanists sought ecclesiastical preferment, which offered income and leisure to study. Some humanists, such as Giovanni Gioviano Pontano at Naples, became courtier-administrators.

Thus, a large number of major and minor humanists became university professors in the second half of the fifteenth century. They earned considerably higher salaries and enjoyed greater esteem than professors of grammar and rhetoric of the late fourteenth and early fifteenth centuries. But they did not completely abandon commune or court.

HUMANISTIC STUDIES AT OTHER UNIVERSITIES

Humanistic studies and humanists entered the faculty of almost every university in the second half of the fifteenth century. But development was often slow or partial for a variety of reasons.

The University of Padua did not emphasize the *studia humanitatis* or appoint very many humanists of the first rank in the fifteenth century. After Gasparino Barzizza left in 1421, the University of Padua had one, occasionally two professors of rhetoric. The important figures were Raffaelo Regio (d. 1520), who probably taught in the years 1482–86 and 1503–9, and Giovanni Calfurnio (1443–1503), who taught from 1486 to 1502.[108] Both were able scholars, but not on the level of Filippo Berolado the Elder or Poliziano

Padua did establish a professorship of Greek in 1463, filling it with the Greek Demetrius Chalcondylas at a high salary of 300 florins. He left in 1475 and later taught at the University of Florence (1475–91) and in Milan (1491–1511). Not an original scholar, Chalcondylas wrote a Greek grammar and edited uncritically the printed *editiones principes* of several Greek texts: an anthology, twenty-one orations of Isocrates, and a Byzantine lexicon. Lesser figures followed, except for Marco Musuro of Crete (1470–1517), who taught in the years 1503–4 and 1505–

---

106. See Ross, 1976, and Grendler, 1989, 62–63, 65, 138, with additional bibliography.

107. Brown, 1979, 45, 186, 202–3; Black, 1985a, 105–7, 170–72, 182, 212–13.

108. For the professors of rhetoric from 1423 to 1450, see above, n. 50. The lack of records leaves the period 1450–70 blank. Bullengero da Sicilia taught in 1470 and perhaps earlier, Domenico da Rubea of Brescia was teaching in 1472 and 1474, Angelo da Rimini in 1476, and Cataldo Pariso from Sicily in 1486. See Facciolati, 1978, pt. 1:lii–lvi, who is sometimes vague, and Favaro, 1918, 75–77, for the faculty of arts role of 1500–1501. See Ward, 1995, 234–44, on the scholarship of Calfurnio and Regio.

9 before moving to Venice, where he collaborated with Aldo Manuzio in the publication of Greek texts.[109]

The University of Pavia had 2 or 3 professors teaching rhetoric, with the number occasionally dropping to 1 or rising to 4, in an average faculty of 60, between 1450 and 1500.[110] But the Sforza court in Milan, with 1 to 4 humanists, was the center for humanistic scholarship in Lombardy. The better-known humanists taught at high salaries in Milan, while minor or young humanists taught for low salaries at Pavia. In 1485–86, for example, three humanists (the well-known Giorgio Merula [1431–94] and Francesco Dal Pozzo, along with the obscure Pavero Fontana) taught at Milan, earning 920 florins collectively. Three unknowns (Matteo Trovamala, Pietro Lazzaroni, and Francesco Marianna) taught at Pavia, earning a total of 520 florins.[111]

The University of Siena did little to support humanistic studies in the fifteenth century. Various minor figures taught grammar and rhetoric in the late fourteenth century and early fifteenth. For example, Giovanni di Ser Buccio da Spoleto (c. 1370–after 1445) taught grammar, rhetoric, and poetry probably continuously from 1396 until 1445 and had San Bernardino of Siena, Maffeo Vegio, and Aeneas Sylvius Piccolomini among his pupils. But his scholarship, if any, has not survived.[112] Then Siena offered Francesco Filelfo the opportunity to escape his troubles at Florence. In autumn 1434 Filelfo was hired to teach oratory plus Greek and Latin literature for two years at the Sienese *studio* at the handsome salary of 350 florins per year.[113] As at Florence, Filelfo immediately animated Sienese humanistic studies both in and outside the university. He attracted a large circle of young admirers from the leading families; some remembered him fondly in later years. But Filelfo taught at Siena only through 1438 and then left for the Milanese court.

109. Cammelli, 1954, and Petrucci, 1973. After Chalcondylas came Alessandro Zeno, 1475–79, then Lorenzo Camers, called "il Cretico," because he studied in Crete for seven years, from 1479 to his death in 1505. Facciolati, 1978, pt. 1:lv–lvi. John Monfasani believes that Padua ranks higher as a humanistic center than I have suggested.

110. There are numerous rolls of the 1470s, 1480s, and 1490s, in ASPv, Università, Bu. 22, 23, and 32. Verde (1973–94, 1:384–92) prints Pavian rolls for 1480–81 and 1482–83. See Porro, 1878, for the roll of 1498–99. See also Sottili, 1982, 539–44, 548.

111. Sottili, 1982, 540–41, for the salaries, and Sottili, 1997, who also judges humanistic instruction at Pavia to be of secondary rank. *Memorie di Pavia* (1970, 1:159–68 passim) and Bianchi (1913, 160–65) add further information on the humanist professors at Pavia and Milan. For a brief summary of the career of Merula, known especially for his editing of the classics for the Venetian presses in the 1470s and 1480s and his teaching at the Scuola di San Marco in Venice before moving to Milan in 1484, see Gardenal, 1986, and King, 1986, 400–402.

112. Goffis, 1971; Fioravanti, 1981, 50 n. 3. More generally, see Fioravanti, 1991a, 261–63.

113. "Deliberaverunt conducere et conduxerunt Dominum Francischum Filelfum de Tolentino ad lecturam artis oratorie et licterarum gregarum [*sic*] et latinarum pro duobus annis proxime futuris . . . com salario declarando per Sapientes Studii, non ascendendo summam trecentorum quinquaginta florenorum pro anno qualibet." As quoted in Zdekauer, 1977, 6 n. 2, document of September or October 1434. See also Viti, 1997, 616. For Filelfo's impact, see Fioravanti, 1981, 12, 28–29, 32–34, 51–53, and passim, and P. Nardi, 1974, 36–37.

After Filelfo, no major humanist would set foot in Siena, lamented Agostino Dati (1420–78), the leading local humanist.[114] But local humanists did not teach at the university. For example, Dati, author of many orations and historical works, held political offices and the post of chancellor of Siena for the last twenty-six years of his life. The first surviving university roll, that of 1492–93, listed 2 professors of poetry and 2 for grammar in 45 professors, but none of the 4 was a known humanistic scholar. The roll of 1500–1501 included 4 professors "In Humanità," again unknowns, in a faculty of 52.[115] A professorship of Greek was noticeably absent from the rolls. Although humanistic studies mattered to some of the local elite, the government, which decided university policy, did not share their view.

At Perugia the one or two professorships of grammar and authors became professorships of rhetoric and poetry in the first half of the fifteenth century.[116] But as a small university with a strong tradition in legal studies, Perugia had difficulty attracting and holding humanists. Francesco Filelfo declined to come in 1438, as did several other major figures. Perugia also lacked a Greek professorship.[117]

Then the commune hit upon a way to make the position more attractive. Aware that humanists preferred the post of chancellor to that of professor, Perugia decided to combine the two: the humanist chancellor would also teach oratory at the university. After suffering one rebuff, Perugia succeeded in appointing Tommaso Pontano da Camerino (d. 1450), known for his expertise in Latin and Greek and as a poet, to the two posts in 1440. He held them with increasing stipends until his death. A second, minor humanist taught beside the chancellor-professor.

Perugia continued to try to combine the posts for the rest of the century. Some humanists still declined offers, while others accepted but stayed only briefly. The most famous humanist by far to come was Giovanni Gioviano Pontano (1426–1503), nephew of Tommaso Pontano. Born into an Umbrian family from near Spoleto which lost its wealth in an uprising, Pontano studied at Perugia before winning a post with the king of Naples in 1448. He returned to Perugia in 1465 with the promise of a triennial appointment to the double post, but the pope, the Perugian overlord, refused to ratify his chancellorship. Probably his service with two Neapolitan kings, sworn enemies of the papacy, rendered him unacceptable. Hence, after three years of teaching at Perugia, Pontano returned to the Neapolitan court in 1468, where his humanistic and administrative career soared.

Finally, the native son Francesco Maturanzio or Matarazzo (1443–1518), a

---

114. Fioravanti, 1981, 51; for Dati, see also Viti, 1987.

115. Zdekauer, 1977, 191–93, for the roll of 1492–93; Mondolfo, 1897, for the roll of 1500–1501.

116. Ermini, 1971, 590–609, and Bini, 1977, 599–602, for the discussion in this and the next three paragraphs. Zappacosta, 1977, surveys the scholarship of the Perugian humanists. On Giovanni Gioviano Pontano, see also Bentley, 1987, 127–28.

117. Perugia may have had a professor of Greek in 1467; if so, it was the only year. Ermini, 1971, 604–5.

scholar of middling stature, provided continuity for humanistic studies. He began as secretary to the papal governor of Perugia in 1475 and may have begun teaching at the *studio* by 1477; he certainly taught there from 1486 to 1492. After teaching elsewhere, he returned as professor of oratory and poetry in 1498. The chancellorship was added in 1503, and he held the two posts until his death in 1518. A keen Ciceronian, Maturanzio wrote a number of orations, commentaries on Cicero's *Philippics* and Statius, and a chronicle of Perugia.

The University of Naples embraced humanism late but initially with enthusiasm. Humanists appeared on the roll in 1465–66, when the university reopened after being closed for nine years.[118] The roll of twenty-two professors included four humanists, including Constantine Lascaris, who taught Greek. Lascaris left in disgust after ten months, because he believed that the Neapolitans lacked enthusiasm for Greek studies. Nevertheless, the humanistic component remained at the high level of three to five competent, if not outstanding, scholars through the academic year 1470–71. Lorenzo Valla and Florentine scholarship much influenced humanistic studies at the University of Naples.

The leading figure was the Neapolitan Giuniano Maio (c. 1430–93), who taught rhetoric between 1465 and 1488, except for the various closures. He published a classical Latin dictionary (1475) that had six incunabular printings, an edition of the letters of Pliny the Younger, a selection of Cicero's orations, and other works, but he never received more than a modest salary for his labors. Maio and other fifteenth-century university humanists at Naples also tutored princelings of the Neapolitan royal family; this cemented relations with the court and provided income when the university was closed. But humanistic studies dwindled to one professor of rhetoric by the end of the fifteenth century. The frequent closings of the university clearly hampered their development. The Neapolitan court, with a gathering of major humanistic scholars led by Giovanni Gioviano Pontano, was the true center of Neapolitan humanism.

The tiny University of Catania had a professor of grammar when it opened its doors to students in 1445. This post seems to have become grammar and poetry in 1455 and humanity, grammar, and rhetoric in 1467, suggesting that humanistic studies had reached Sicily. In 1463–64 the university introduced a professorship of Greek filled by a Greek, but it lasted only one year.[119] The small University of Turin appears to have had little instruction in grammar and rhetoric of any kind, and no humanists, in the fifteenth century.[120]

With the exception of Turin, all the above universities welcomed the *studia humanitatis* in the second half of the fifteenth century. But none of them emphasized the humanities as strongly as Florence, Bologna, Rome, and Ferrara. Governmen-

118. De Frede, 1960, 191–96 for a complete list of the humanists at the university, 46–57 for Maio, and 80–95 for Lascaris. See Santoro, 1980, 145–58, 269–72, for the intellectual interests of the Neapolitan university humanists.

119. Sabbadini, 1975, 21, 36; Catalano, 1934, 24–25, 84–87.

120. The lack of rolls makes discussion difficult, but Bellone (1986) has found no teaching humanists in the fifteenth century.

tal decisions to make the capital or court the center for humanistic studies, lack of size, or a preference for legal studies rendered humanistic studies less important.

THE SIXTEENTH CENTURY

The humanities were a recognized discipline by 1500, strong in some universities, weak in others. In general, those universities that had emphasized humanistic studies before 1500 continued to do so. Other universities paid them little heed or dropped them from the curriculum.

The Bolognese government maintained the humanities at a high level. In 1513 the Bolognese Senate decreed that the university might appoint four non-Bolognese professors, one each in law, philosophy, medicine, and humanistic studies.[121] The positions were to be filled by the most eminent scholars to be found. That the ordinary afternoon professor of humanistic studies (*Ad humanitatis studia horis pomeridianis*) was to be one of the star professors, along with the first ordinary professor of civil law, the first ordinary professor of medical theory, and the first ordinary professor of natural philosophy, signaled the high status of humanistic studies. These four professors were expected to attract students and to lead the university. They were always men of great reputation and usually of high scholarly achievement.

The decree was not fully implemented until the wars had subsided. Then the Bolognese devoted a great deal of time and effort to filling the humanist post with major scholars. Bologna initially appointed Romolo Amaseo of Udine (1489–1552) in 1538.[122] He had previously taught rhetoric and poetry at Bologna (1513–20 and 1524–38) and now held the humanities professorship until he left for the University of Rome in 1544. The Bolognese then hired Sebastiano Corradi (or Corrado) da Arceto, c. 1510–56, then teaching in Reggio Emilia; he held the post from 1545 until his death in 1556. Next came Francesco Robortello of Udine (1516–67), who was persuaded to leave the University of Padua for 1,200 Bolognese lire. He taught in Bologna from 1557 to 1561 before returning to Padua. His return to Padua caused his academic enemy, Carlo Sigonio of Mantua, then teaching at the University of Padua, to accept the Bologna humanities professorship in 1563. Although all the previous occupants of the position had been men of scholarly achievement and famous in their day, they paled in com-

121. Costa, 1902–3b, 330 n. 24, Senate decree of 1513 repeated in 1540 and 1578; Zaccagnini, 1930, 146–47. The key significance of the decree was to designate these four positions as preeminent. While the wording seemed to limit the number of non-Bolognese professors to four, this was not necessarily the case. Although Bolognese citizenship was a prerequisite for university employment, the government either did not always observe the requirement, or it granted citizenship to a limited number of non-Bolognese academics.

122. Costa, 1907a, provides an excellent overview of the humanities post and its occupants. For Amaseo, see Avesani, 1960; for Corradi, see De' Angelis, 1983a. See Simeoni, 1940, 32, for some salary figures. For Robortello's salary, see ASB, Assunteria di Studio, Bu. 53, Requisiti dei Lettori. Lettera R. Vol. 24, fasc. 30b.

parison with Sigonio. A very popular lecturer and author of numerous monographs, Sigonio was the most important historian of ancient Rome and early medieval Italy before the nineteenth century. After starting at 1,210 Bolognese lire, his salary steadily rose to 2,400 Bolognese lire in 1579, the third highest in the *studio*.[123]

After Sigonio's death in 1584, the Bolognese persuaded Aldo Manuzio the Younger to come for one year, 1585–86, at 1,400 Bolognese lire. A scholarly mediocrity bearing a famous name, Manuzio demanded three times as much in salary and perquisites, plus a post for his nephew, to continue at Bologna. The Bolognese wisely refused to renew his contract. Tommaso Correa (1536–95), a Portuguese scholar, held the post from 1586 until his death in 1595. Then in an effort to restore former glory, the Bolognese turned their eye to the Flemish Justus Lipsius (1547–1606), then teaching at Louvain. A founder of neo-Stoicism and editor of Seneca and Tacitus, Lipsius was the most famous humanist in Europe. The pope, various cardinals, and other high officials joined in the effort to woo him. The commune offered a great deal of money, while Bolognese representatives, and even cardinals, explained away Lipsius's tendency to switch religions when he changed universities. But after a long courtship, he declined to come.[124]

Bologna certainly viewed humanistic studies as an important and distinct discipline. The appointment of a distinguished scholar documented this. So did the shift in terminology from professors of "rhetoric and poetry" to professors of "*humanitatis studia.*" And the humanities were not limited to one famous professor. Rather, he was the leader of a group of five, which included a morning professor of the humanities, an extraordinary holiday professor in the humanities, a professor of Greek, and a student lecturer in rhetoric.[125]

Modest bureaucratic evidence further supports the judgment that the university viewed humanistic studies as a distinct discipline. As elsewhere, the beadle at

123. McCuaig, 1989, ch. 1, esp. 61–62.

124. For Correa, see De' Angelis, 1983b. For the extensive correspondence on the humanist and other appointments in the last twenty years of the sixteenth century, see ASB, Assunteria di Studio, Bu. 75, Lettere dall'ambasciatori agli Assunti, 1571–1694 (especially for Lipsius), and Assunteria di Studio, Bu. 79, Lettere di diversi all'Assunteria, 1575–1691.

125. See Dallari, 1888–1924, vol. 2. Although the extraordinary professor of the humanities disappeared after a few years, the humanistic complement usually remained at five because the morning ordinary professorship expanded to two. Late in the century the humanist contingent dropped to four but still included the professor of Greek.

The rolls also continued to list teachers of rhetoric and poetry, but these were preuniversity teachers, as accompanying minutes made clear. For example, in the roll of 1538–39 under the heading "Ad Rhetoricam et Poeticam" and before the names of six teachers appeared the following minute: "Legant quilibet duas lectiones, unam in oratoria, alteram in poetica arte. Ad primam horam legere possint in scholis suis privatis, in quibus et pueros grammaticam doceant cum conditione grammaticis apposita ut infra." Dallari, 1888–1924, 2:88. The direction that they might teach "in their private schools" rather than "in studio" and that they "teach grammar to boys" under the same condition (that they teach four paupers without charge) required of the grammarians indicated preuniversity instruction. For more on the primary- and secondary-school teachers on the rolls of the University of Bologna, see Grendler, 1989, 26–29.

Bologna visited daily to see if the professor lectured, if he taught the full hour, and that he had the minimum required number of students (three or five) in attendance. Those who fell short in any way were assessed per diem financial penalties to be deducted from their salaries. The beadle noted the transgressions and then added them up every three months to find the sum, if any, to be deducted, from professors' salaries.

The beadle's summary records survive for intermittent months between May 1531 and July 1537. Some of these little packages of chits are labeled in contemporary hands as "canonisti legisti e umanisti ordinarii," that is, professors of canon law and ordinary humanist professors. Other packets were labeled "artisti e filosofi ordinarii," again in a contemporary hand.[126] Probably the groupings arose because of the location of their teaching. Perhaps canonists and ordinary humanists lectured at one location (the Archiginnasio, which would later house all the lectures, was not yet built), and professors of other arts subjects and ordinary professors of natural philosophy taught elsewhere. In any case, the labels on the documents suggest that the humanists were viewed as a distinct part of the faculty.

Rome continued to emphasize the humanities in the smaller university that followed the sack of 1527. It reopened in 1535 with 2 professors of rhetoric and a professor of Greek in a faculty of 18.[127] This increased to 3 rhetoricians and a professor of Greek in a faculty of 24 in 1539. Rome maintained an average of 4 humanists (1 or 2 rhetoricians, 1 or 2 professors of Greek, and a professor of Hebrew) until 1587 in an average faculty of 37. The beadle regularly commented that even though the professor of Hebrew attracted few students, it was a necessary lectureship.[128] The papacy may have encouraged Greek and Hebrew studies at the university in order to help train scholars for the large editorial projects (the Bible and patristic authors) under way. Rome also had a professor of Arabic in 1575–76. The faculty then decreased to an average of 29 in the remaining thirteen years of the century, at which time the professorship of Greek disappeared, leaving 2 professors of rhetoric and a professor of Hebrew. Contemporaries then complained that rhetoric was in decline in the university.[129]

126. ASB, Riformatori dello Studio, Appuntazioni dei lettori, 1465–1526, 1531–37, a box of material organized chronologically. The box contains lists of professors with the dates of their missed lectures, plus notes and working papers used to calculate the amounts to be deducted.

127. For what follows, see *I maestri di Roma*, 1991, 7–151 passim.

128. "Hic, etsi paucos habeat scholares, lectio tamen eius necessaria est." Comment of beadle Alessio Lorenzani on the Hebrew lectureship in *I maestri di Roma*, 1991, 89. There are similar comments elsewhere in the rolls. For the Arabic lecturer, see ibid., 103.

129. McGinness, 1995a, 604–5. In an effort to improve rhetoric, the University of Rome invited Justus Lipsius to come and teach, but he declined, according to Vincente Blas Garsia, a local humanist. Garsia addressed a *Libellus supplex ad Summum Pontificem, scriptus nomine quorundam studiosorum iuvenum* to Pope Clement VIII on behalf of the students of the university sometime in the late 1590s. It is published in Garsia's *Orationes Romanae aliaque nonnulla*. Valencia, R. Patricius, 1603. See p. 463 for the reference to Lipsius. I am grateful to Frederick McGinness for providing me a copy of the *Libellus*. Garsia lamented the decline of the university, especially in rhetoric, and reviewed the professors who taught there and those who did not come. Although the University of Bologna, with the pope's approval, made an offer to Lipsius, I am unable to confirm that La Sapienza did.

The best-known and ablest humanistic scholar at Rome was Marc'Antoine Muret, who taught moral philosophy (Aristotle's *Ethics*) in the years 1563–67, humanistic jurisprudence (the *Pandects*) 1567–72, and then rhetoric from 1572 until his death in 1585. He was a figure of European distinction. Romolo Amaseo, who came from Bologna, taught at Rome from 1544 to 1550 and was a humanist of high reputation, if not great scholarly achievement. Pompeo Ugonio, who taught rhetoric from 1586 through 1612, published works on Christian antiquities in Rome. Others were middling scholars or little known. Although the humanities at the University of Rome after 1535 did not reach the numbers and distinction achieved in the late fifteenth century, they continued to be important.

The University of Ferrara also maintained a strong tradition in humanistic studies in the sixteenth century. The university normally had 3 and sometimes 4 humanists in a faculty of 45 to 50 professors between 1540 and 1600.[130] They included an ordinary morning professor to teach "Latin rhetoricians, orators, and poets," an ordinary afternoon professor for the same subject, and a Greek professorship called "Greek humanities" (*Ad lecturam humanitatis Graecae*) or simply "Greek language" (*Ad lecturam linguae Graecae*). There was also an extraordinary professor of Greek or Latin authors *in vacationibus generalibus.* He probably lectured during the lengthy vacation breaks such as Carnival and Easter. Sometimes the faculty rolls gave these four posts the collective heading "Humanistae" or "Humanisti." As at Bologna, the term suggests that the humanities were seen as a separate discipline within the university.

Two men dominated humanities instruction at Ferrara. Giovanni Battista Giraldi Cinzio (1504–73) taught in 1532–33, perhaps in the next few years when rolls are missing, and definitely from 1541 through 1563, when he left for the University of Turin. Giovanni Battista Nicolucci, called il Pigna (1529–75), taught from 1550–51 until his death. He held the ordinary morning professorship of Latin rhetoric, oratory, and poetry and for many years (1553–75) also held the extraordinary professorship. Both Giraldi and Pigna were closely tied to the Este court, often simultaneously teaching and serving as secretaries to the prince or the government.

The University of Pisa grew in importance in several scholarly fields after 1543, but not in the humanities. It had only a Latin humanities professor and a professor of Greek between 1543 and 1566, and just the Latinist from 1566 to the end of the century. Only Francesco Robortello, who taught in the years 1543–49, his first university post, was an established scholar.[131]

By contrast, the Florentine rump of the university continued to offer humanities scholarship of a high order. Two humanists taught at Florence through the sixteenth century.[132] Pier Vettori (1499–1585) of Florence held one post from

---

130. This and the following paragraph are based on Solerti, 1892, 24–51; Pardi, 1972, 225–50; Franceschini, 1970, 266–70; *I maestri di Ferrara*, 1991, 20–49 and passim; and Chiellini, 1991.

131. See the lists in Barsanti, 1993, 565–66.

132. See FN, Ms. Corte d'appello, 3, ff. 32ʳ, 34ʳ, 36ʳ, 38ʳ, 39ᵛ, 42ʳ, 44ᵛ, 47ʳ, 49ʳ, 50ᵛ–51ʳ, 52ᵛ, 54ᵛ–55ʳ, for the professors at Florence from 1557–58 through 1568–69. Vettori received 300 florins and Adriani 200 throughout these years. Cascio Pratilli, 1975, 196–97, lists the Florentine professors for

1538 until 1583. The ablest textual critic in the Italy of his generation and the true successor to Poliziano, Vettori edited and commented on numerous ancient Latin and Greek texts.[133] Giovanni Battista Adriani (1511–79), also a Florentine, held the other post from 1549 until his death. Adriani is best known for writing a vernacular history of Italy for the years 1536 to 1574 and for numerous Latin orations. Vettori and Adriani were fervent republicans who made their peace with the Medici. Adriani then wrote works justifying the regime of Cosimo I de' Medici; Vettori did not.

The University of Padua had 1 or 2 professors in the humanities in a faculty of 50 to 60 from 1517 until the end of the century: a professorship of Latin rhetoric, considered the higher post, and a professorship of Greek at a lower salary. However, about half the time the two posts were combined into one position, called "Greek and Latin Humanities" (*Ad humanitatem Graecam et Latinam*).

Despite the limited number of positions, the humanities at Padua were more important than in the fifteenth century, because most of the humanists were able scholars.[134] The Venetian Senate appointed Marino Becichemo from Dalmatia (probl. 1468–1526) to the professorship of Latin rhetoric in 1517, and he held it to his death. Like Poliziano and Beroaldo the Elder, he published critical notes and comments on passages in many ancient texts, especially the *Rhetorica ad Herennium,* Quintilian, and book 1 of Pliny the Elder's *Natural History.* The Senate then appointed Romolo Amaseo to the professorship of Greek in 1521, a post he held until departing for Bologna in 1524. Giovanni Antonio de Marostica taught Greek in the years 1524–26, followed by Bernardino Donato of Verona (1480/90–1543), who taught Greek from January 1526 through the middle of 1527.[135] Then in 1530 the Senate appointed Lazzaro Bonamico (1477/78–1552) to the combined professorship of Latin and Greek humanities. Bonamico, a strict Ciceronian, wrote very little but had a large reputation that has not endured. He

---

1567–68. In addition, Andrea Dazzi (1473–1548) was appointed in January 1548 to teach "lettere grece et Latine d'humanità" in Florence. FN, Ms. Corte d'appello, 3, f. 14ᵛ. Dazzi had previously taught Greek at Florence in 1502 and may have continued to 1515. See Verde, 1973–94, 2:22–23. He then taught at Pisa in the years 1515–17 (Fabroni, 1971, 1:400) before returning to teach at Florence by 1519. Diminished sight forced him to give up that post about 1520 in favor of private teaching. Then in January 1548 he was restored to his post in Florence but died in July. He wrote numerous Latin poems and orations and taught Vettori. See Vivoli, 1987.

133. See Pecoraro, 1986, for a brief summary of Vettori's career and more bibliography. Grafton (1983, 52–70, 85–95, 167–72, 184–85, 248–57) discusses Vettori's textual criticism and its influence. See Aguzzi-Barbagli, 1988, 111, 113–14, for Vettori's commentary on Aristotle's *Poetics.* For Adriani, see Miccoli, 1960a.

134. See AAUP, FF. 651 and 242, and Inventario 1320 for sixteenth-century rolls of the faculty of arts and a few appointment notices with salaries. Many rolls are missing, and there are some discrepancies. Riccobono, 1980, 28ᵛ–30ʳ; Tomasini, 1986, 340–42; and Facciolati, 1978, pt. 1:lvi–lix, provide additional information that is not always complete or correct. Marangoni, 1901, pt. 1:118–51, provides a listing of the humanists, 1500–1530. For Becichemo, see Clough, 1965, and Nauert, 1980, 352–56; for Amaseo, see Avesani, 1960; for Bonamico, see Marangoni, 1901, and Avesani, 1969. Despite his minimal accomplishments, Bonamico earned high salaries (300 florins in 1530–31), which enabled him to become a substantial landholder. See Piovan, 1988.

135. See Biadego, 1895, esp. 12–13.

taught alone until 1545, when Giovanni Faseolo (or Fasolo) of Padua was appointed to teach Greek. He translated into Latin some of the commentaries on works of Aristotle by Simplicius (c. 500–after 533), a Greek Neoplatonic author. Faseolo, who did not otherwise distinguish himself, taught at Padua until his death in January 1572.

Francesco Robortello of Udine succeeded Bonamico in the professorship of Latin rhetoric.[136] He taught at Padua in the years 1552–57, went to Bologna, and then returned to teach at Padua from 1561 to 1567. Although he wrote on several subjects, Robortello is best known for his detailed Latin commentary on Aristotle's *Poetics* (1548), which greatly influenced literary criticism. His bitter enemy, Carlo Sigonio, taught at Padua from 1560 to 1563. Upon Robortello's death, Faseolo was promoted to the Latin rhetoric post. Antonio Riccobono (1541–99) was added to teach Greek in the autumn of 1571. When Faseolo died, Riccobono became professor of Latin and Greek humanities, a post he held until death. Riccobono published a new Latin translation of Aristotle's *Poetics* (1579), a Latin commentary on the *Poetics* (1585), and a treatise on the art of history (1568). Paolo Beni of Gubbio (1553–1625) then held the combined post from March 1600 until his death and wrote numerous interesting works. Overall, the humanities were better served at Padua in the sixteenth century than earlier.

However, the university did not make the humanities a priority. An incident illustrates the point. As noted above, Bernardino Donato taught Greek at Padua for a year and a half, at a salary of 100 florins, before leaving for a nonuniversity post in provincial Capodistria, probably because it paid more. Donato was an accomplished scholar who edited works of Saint John Chrysostom and Saint John Damascene in Greek and works of Priscian and Macrobius in Latin. He wrote a treatise comparing Aristotle and Plato and perhaps a Latin grammar.[137] In the search for Donato's replacement, one of the Riformatori dello Studio di Padova asked the eminent humanist and Venetian noble Pietro Bembo (1480–1547) for advice. Bembo replied with an angry letter, here paraphrased.

I have made it clear to you, Bembo wrote, that the honored and well-attended University of Padua greatly needs a professor of Greek, which subject is just as necessary as any other and greatly in demand. You asked me in Venice about someone who wanted that post. I did not answer because I did not want to speak ill or to lie. I regret that you dismissed Bernardino Donato who was a learned and active scholar. I know his situation now. If you would reappoint him with a small increment in salary, he would come back from Capodistria. Since you give a thousand florins to a legist, you should not be so parsimonious with the professors of Latin and Greek whose letters are called humane. Indeed, they are the foundation of all learning.[138]

136. There is no modern biography of Robortello. For bibliography see *CHRP,* 835. For the *Poetics,* see Aguzzi-Barbagli, 1988, 105, 106, 111, 112–13, 156–57. For Sigonio, see McCuaig, 1989. For Riccobono, see Mazzacurati, 1961. For Beni see Mazzacurati, 1966, and especially Diffley, 1988.

137. See Biadego, 1895, and *STC Italian,* 1958, 224.

138. "Fo intender a V. S. che in questo onorato e frequentissimo Studio ha gran bisogno d'un lettor Greco, la qual lettura per l'universal disiderio di quelle lettere, non è men necessaria che verun

Nothing needs to be added to the letter. The University of Padua paid very high salaries to legists, but humanistic studies were not important enough for the authorities to award a small increment to a modestly paid professor of Greek. While significant in themselves, humanistic studies played their most important role in Padua through their influence on other disciplines, above all medicine.

Humanistic instruction at the University of Pavia shriveled to a husk in the sixteenth century. The university normally had only a single professor from 1536 onward, often described as teaching *arte oratoria greca e latina,* in a faculty of 50 to 60.[139] With the exception of Giraldi, who held the post between 1568 and 1572, the Pavian humanists were obscure figures. One is remembered for his later religious career. Celio Secondo Curione (1503–69), who taught humanities for three academic years (1536–39), was a Protestant who fled Italy in the summer of 1542. He eventually became a humanities professor at the University of Basel (1546–69). There he published several Protestant religious works and many commentaries, editions, and translations of the classics.

The universities of Siena and Perugia, which emphasized law, paid more attention to humanistic studies in the sixteenth century than they had in the fifteenth but did not make them a priority. Perugia had two ordinary professors and a vacation lecturer in the Latin humanities but apparently no professor of Greek on a regular basis. The occupants of these positions were very minor figures.[140] The Sienese *studio* had 1, 2, even 3 humanists, including a professor of Greek, in a faculty of 40 between 1531 and 1541. But humanistic studies shrank to a single position, normally Latin humanities, in the second half of the century. The Sienese humanists were minor figures whose names did not resonate beyond

---

altra. E perchè voi mi domandaste in Vinegia della qualità d'uno, che disiderava questo luogo che io non vi volli rispondere, non per cagion che io non avessi che dirvi, che avea pur troppo, ma perchè nè volea dir male, nè sapea mentire, increscendomi che aveste data licenzia a M. Bernardin Donato, che era a dotto ed atto a queste fatiche, ho voluto bene intendere dello stato suo; e informato a bastanza, dico che se voi il ricondurrete con alcun poco accrescimento di salario, egli verrà, solo che vostre Sig. scrivano a nome della città in Capo d'Istria, che vi rendano il vostro lettore. Vi ricordo bene, che se date mille fiorini ad un leggista, non siate così parco ne' Lettori o Greci o Latini di quelle Lettere che umane si chiamano, che sono pure il fondamento a tutte le scienze, che perfettamente apprender di debbono. L'amore ch'io porto a questo così eccellente studio, ed all'onor di voi mi fa così parlare. State sano. Al secondo di novembre 1527. Di Villa." The letter was addressed to Marin Zorzi. Pietro Bembo, *Lettere* (Verona, 1743), 2:163, as quoted in Biadego, 1895, 13.

139. See the many rolls, almost year by year, in ASPv, Università, Cartone 20, no pag. Rizzo, 1987, prints the roll of 1584–85 on 75–76 n. 35. For the names of the humanities professors at Pavia from 1500 to 1600, see *Memorie di Pavia,* 1970, 1:169–76 passim, and Bianchi, 1913, 165–72. There are probably some inaccuracies in these old lists. For a list from 1536 onward, see Zorzoli, 1986, 280–81 n. 177. For Curione, see Biondi, 1985. There is one fascinating exception to the generally bleak picture. Giovanni Federici of Pavia and Paolo Ricci of Pavia taught Hebrew in 1520 and 1521. See ASPv, Università, Cartone 22, f. 3ᵛ. Because no rolls are available for those war-torn years, an archivist of an earlier century searched through city notarial records for names of professors, turning up these two. They are also mentioned in *Memorie di Pavia,* 1970, 1:169. Ricci (d. 1541) was a converted Jew who published a series of religious and philosophical works, some based on the Talmud and the Cabbala. He spent most of his career in Germany. Bietenholz, 1987. Federici is unidentified.

140. Ermini, 1971, 234–36, 608–15.

their classrooms. But some traditions continued. One humanist who taught in the late 1520s and early 1530s became chancellor of the republic in 1533.[141]

The University of Turin had two rhetoricians in 1532–33 and 1534–35, but the number dropped to one by 1565. Then in 1568 the duke of Piedmont-Savoy dismissed the Latin humanist and decreed that the Jesuit college of Turin would teach humanities to university students. The university did add a professor of Greek, in effect, a replacement for the Latin humanist, but at less than half the salary. The professorship of Greek was gone by 1600.[142]

The University of Naples had only a single humanistic professor, who taught rhetoric and sometimes Greek, through the sixteenth century. Catania had one professor of grammar, who probably taught the rest of the *studia humanitatis* as well, through the first eighty years of the sixteenth century. The university eliminated the position in 1580 on the grounds that the Jesuit college in Catania would provide instruction in "humanità."[143] The statutes of Macerata, another university which emphasized law, required the humanities professor to deliver the prolusion opening the academic year.[144] It had a professor (Giovanni Battista Camozzi) of humanities and Greek in the 1550s, who later taught natural philosophy as well. But this limited humanities instruction soon disappeared. Messina and Salerno had no discernible teaching in the humanities. Parma had a single professor of rhetoric, a Jesuit, in the early seventeenth century. In general, university humanistic studies were less important at the end of the century than they had been in 1500.

CURRICULAR TEXTS

In 1552 a student describing the University of Padua noted that the humanist was free to lecture on the text that pleased him most.[145] He meant that, in contrast with other subjects, the statutes imposed no required curricular texts for the humanities. Moreover, the humanists' outlook disposed them to independence in teaching and research, possibly because they spent little time as university students. Filelfo, Poliziano, and Sigonio lacked degrees, and Muret acquired his by examination at the age of forty-six. Of this illustrious group only Poliziano and Sigonio even studied at universities.[146] By contrast, the overwhelming ma-

141. For six rolls for the years 1531–41, see Minnucci and Košuta, 1989, 395–416, and 517–19 for biographical information on the humanists. For the period 1563–90, see the rolls in Cascio Pratilli, 1975, 175–89; for rolls 1589 to 1602, see Marrara, 1970, 159–61, 227–49. The humanist professor turned chancellor was Marcantonio Zondadori; see Minnucci and Košuta, 1989, 518–19.

142. See Vallauri, 1970, 1:135–39, 205–7, for the rolls of 1532–33, 1534–35, and 1565, and Chaiudano, 1972a and 1972b, esp. 77–78, 93–94, and 1972c, for developments from 1566 onward.

143. Catalano, 1934, 25–26, 86–91. For Naples, Macerata, Messina, Salerno, and Parma, see Chapters 2 and 4.

144. Marongiu, 1948, 30.

145. "Et così dell'Humanista, alli quali è lecito trattar, o legger quel che più gli piace." Letter of Giovanni Francesco Trincavello, no date but second half of 1552, printed in Gallo, 1963, 90. Trincavello took a law degree in 1555.

146. Poliziano apparently attended lectures of Landino and other Florentine professors in the

jority of professors of law, medicine, natural philosophy, and other subjects held doctorates and often went directly from the degree to university teaching. Free of statutory restraints, with limited experience of university study, and sometimes disdainful of university habits, the humanists taught a wide variety of ancient Latin and Greek texts.

Barzizza's teaching at Padua, Milan, Bologna, and Pavia in the early fifteenth century combined traditional medieval methods and the foundations of humanistic studies. He continued to use some medieval texts, while introducing his students to new classical works. He taught ancient Latin orthography and punctuation as an aid to understanding ancient works. He also emphasized the importance of Cicero as a prose model.[147] Barzizza was a beginning point, nothing more.

After Barzizza, the humanist professors began to teach a greater variety of texts. Francesco Filelfo seemed in a hurry to lecture on everything available in ancient Latin literature. For example, he taught Cicero's *Tusculan Disputations* and "Rhetorica," possibly the *Rhetorica ad Herennium,* at Florence between 1429 and 1434. He also taught Aristotle's *Ethics,* Sallust's *Bellum Iugurthinum,* and Augustine's *De civitate Dei* there. He lectured on Cicero's *De natura deorum* and *De oratore* and the *Aeneid* at Siena from 1434 to 1438. He taught Aristotle's *Politics* in Milan in 1471–72. And he returned to Cicero's *Tusculan Disputations* at Rome in 1475.[148]

In the second half of the fifteenth century, humanist professors concentrated on the major Latin poetic and rhetorical works. Cristoforo Landino at Florence taught mostly major poetic texts over an eleven-year period.[149]

1458–59	probably Cicero, *Tusculan Disputations*
1459–60 or 1460–61	Horace, *Odes*
1461–62	Juvenal, *Satires,* and Persius
1462–63	Vergil, *Aeneid,* books 1–7
1463–64	*Aeneid,* books 7–12, plus probably other texts of Vergil
1464–65	"precepts of the arts of poetry and rhetoric," plus Horace, *Ars poetica*
1464–65 or later	Petrarch, *Canzoniere*
1465–66	the art of writing letters with commentary on Cicero's *Ad familiares*
1467–69	*Aeneid, Eclogues,* and possibly other works of Vergil

1470s. Sigonio studied for three years at Bologna and one year at Pavia, about 1538–42, but disliked what he called university pedantry. McCuaig, 1989, 6.

147. Mercer, 1979.

148. Resta, 1986, 16–17 n. 28. The Greek authors taught are not known.

149. The chronology is that of Cardini, 1973, 16–17, 334–41, as slightly modified by Field, 1986, 21–22, and Field, 1988, 236–38.

Because Landino saw poetry as embodying philosophy, he believed that the teacher should interpret the mind of the poet in order to uncover his manifold wisdom.[150]

Angelo Poliziano ranged even more widely.[151] He was required to deliver daily two lectures on Latin or Greek texts of his choosing, and four daily lectures from 1491 onward, an unusually heavy teaching schedule. Thanks to the printing press, scholars now had access to a broader range of ancient Latin texts. Poliziano took full advantage.

1480–81	Quintilian, *Institutio oratoria;* Statius, *Silvae;* Ovid, *Heriodum epistolae*
1481–82	*Rhetorica ad Herennium;* Ovid, *Fasti;* perhaps Hesiod, *Works and Days*
1482–83	Vergil, *Bucolica;* Theocritus, *Idylls*
1483–84	Vergil, *Georgica;* Hesiod; Aesop, *Fables*
1484–85	Terence, comedies; perhaps Suetonius; Horace, *Satires;* perhaps Persius, *Satires*
1485–86	Juvenal, *Satires;* Homer, *Iliad*
1486–87	Homer, *Iliad* and *Odyssey;* Vergil, *Aeneid;* lectures on poetry in general
1487–88	*Iliad* and *Odyssey;* perhaps *Aeneid* and lectures on poetry
1488–89	*Iliad* and *Odyssey;* perhaps poetry in general
1489–90	*Iliad* and *Odyssey;* perhaps poetry in general
1490–91	Aristotle, *Ethics* and *Physics;* Suetonius, *De vita Caesarum;* Quintilian, *Institutio oratoria,* book 5
1491–92	Aristotle, *Categories, On Interpretation,* and *On Sophistical Refutations;* Porphyry (c. 234–301), *Isagoge;* and *Liber sex principiorum* of Gilbert of Poitiers (c. 1075–1154)
1492–93	Aristotle, *Prior Analytics;* Cicero, *Tusculan Disputations*
1493–94	Aristotle, *Posterior Analytics* and *Topica;* Ovid, *Tristia*

Poliziano first followed the common pattern of lecturing on a Latin rhetorical text and a Latin poetic work, including the ubiquitous Vergil. But soon he branched out to the Roman satiric poets, followed by the Greek poetry of Homer. In the 1490s he began to lecture on Aristotle's *Ethics* and *Physics.* He also taught Aristotle's logical works along with a medieval commentary. Such works were normally the focus of professors of moral philosophy, natural philosophy, and logic, respectively. For Poliziano a humanities professorship meant the op-

150. On Landino's teaching and writing, see Cardini, 1973; Kallendorf, 1983 and 1989, 129–65; and Field, 1988, 240–68.

151. The list, which summarizes the research of Branca and previous scholars, is found in Branca, 1983, 86 n. 22. His private teaching has been omitted. A number of Poliziano's manuscripts including teaching notes and lecture material have been edited in recent years. For the Suetonius course of 1490–91, see Gardenal, 1975; for the comment on Terence's *Andria,* see Poliziano, 1973.

portunity to roam widely through ancient Latin and Greek poetry, rhetoric, history, philosophy, and logic. Scholars lacking his ability and imagination had to be less venturesome.

The humanist professors of the University of Rome offered instruction on various texts in the 1470s, 1480s, and 1490s, but especially Cicero, who was so important to Roman humanism. Martino Filetico taught the philosophical works (*Paradoxa Stoicorum, Cato maior de senectute, Laelius de amicitia, Tusculan Disputations, De officiis*) as well as some of the rhetorical works, such as *De oratore*. He also taught poetry, such as Horace and the more complex *Satires* of Juvenal and Persius, over a number of years. Giovanni Sulpizio of Veroli taught Vergil and the historians Lucan and Silius Italicus in the 1480s and 1490s.[152] Like Beroaldo the Elder and Codro at Bologna, the Roman humanists reached out to study more challenging Latin authors, whose works exhibited complex syntax and allusions to little-known aspects of the ancient world.

The curriculum expanded again after 1530 or 1540. Fresh Greek texts entered the lecture hall after recovery, translation into Latin, and printing. Aristotle's *Rhetoric* could provide the theoretical framework that the *Rhetorica ad Herennium* and Quintilian had earlier furnished, and Aristotle's *Poetics* could do the same for poetry. More Roman historians appeared. Humanist professors still taught a good amount of Cicero, but they ranged more widely through his speeches.

The humanists at Padua offer an example of the greater variety of humanist teaching in the sixteenth century. Lazzaro Bonamico taught the oration *Pro lege Manilia* of Cicero in 1530–31. Then in 1539–40 he innovated by teaching Livy and Thucydides.[153] Later in the century the Paduan humanists emphasized Latin and Greek orators, plus Aristotle's *Poetics* and *Rhetoric*. Sigonio lectured on *Pro Milone* and possibly other speeches of Cicero in the academic years 1560–61 and 1561–62 and on Aristotle's *Poetics* probably in 1561–62.[154] In the academic year 1568–69 Giovanni Faseolo taught Cicero's speech *Pro Rabirio perduellionis reo.*[155] In 1569–70 Faseolo lectured on Cicero's *Pro Cluentio* and an oration of Isocrates. In 1571–72 Antonio Riccobono taught Aristotle's *Rhetoric,* and Faseolo did Cicero's speech *Pro lege Manilio* and Isocrates' oration *Panathenaicus* (a comparison of Athens and Sparta). In 1574–75 Riccobono, now alone, discussed another oration of Cicero plus book 3 of Aristotle's *Rhetoric.* In 1575–76 Riccobono lectured on Cicero's *Tusculan Disputations* and again Aristotle's *Rhetoric.* In 1594–95 Riccobono taught Cicero's *Topica* and Sophocles' *Oedipus tyrannus.*

Students at universities with several humanists in nonconcurrent positions had considerable choice. For example, the University of Rome offered four humanities lectures at three different hours in 1579–80. One rhetorician taught Aristotle's *Rhetoric* at the 17th hour (mid- to late morning, depending on the

152. Lee, 1978, 176, 184–85, and Grafton and Jardine, 1986, 83–94. D'Amico (1983, ch. 5) explains the importance of Cicero in Roman humanism.

153. Avesani, 1969, 535, 537.

154. McCuaig, 1983 and 1989, 43, 46, 53.

155. The rest of the information on the texts taught comes from rolls of the faculty of arts in AAUP, Inventario 1320. Only a few named the texts taught.

season). Marc'Antoine Muret lectured on the *Aeneid* at the 21st hour (early to midafternoon), and a third rhetorician taught Vergil's *Georgics* at the 23rd and last lecture hour in the late afternoon. The professor of Greek taught the first *Olynthiac* of Demosthenes and the grammar manual of Theodore Gaza at the 21st hour.[156]

Even the single humanist, occasionally joined by a second, at the University of Pisa taught both a Latin and a Greek author and ranged widely, especially in Greek.[157]

1565–66	Homer, *Odyssey;* Cicero, unspecific speeches
1567–68	Homer; Sallust
1568–69	Sophocles, *Oedipus tyrannus;* Aristotle, *Ethics*
1569–70	Aristotle, *Politics;* Cicero, *De provinciis consularibus*
1571–72	Pindar; Cicero, *Pro Balbo*
1572–73	Pindar; Caesar, *Bellum civile*
1573–74	Homer; Cicero
1574–75	Homer; Cicero
1576–77	Homer; Cicero
1581–82	Cicero, *De provinciis consularibus*
1583–84	Pindar; Aristotle, *Nicomachean Ethics*
1584–85	Sophocles, *Antigone;* Aristotle, *Rhetoric*
1585–86	Sophocles, tragedies; Aristotle, *Poetics*
1587–88	Homer, *Iliad,* book 1; Cicero, *Pro Milone*
1588–89	Sophocles, *Oedipus tyrannus;* Cicero, *Partitiones oratoriae*
1589–90	Sophocles, *Ajax;* Horace, *Ars poetica*
1590–91	Aristotle, *Poetics;* Tacitus
1591–92	Horace
1596–97	Isocrates, *Oratio ad Demosthenem;* Vergil, *Aeneid,* book 1
1597–98	Hesiod, *Works and Days;* Horace, *Carmina.* book 1
1598–99	Isocrates; Cicero, *Pro Archia*
1599–1600	Homer, *Iliad;* Vergil, *Georgics*

The Pisan humanists emphasized Greek poetry, with some discussion of oratorical prose, plus Latin oratorical works.

Humanists at small universities, however, usually stayed with Vergil and Cicero, the most popular poetic and rhetorical authors. Humanist professors at the University of Siena during the 1530s and early 1540s lectured on two texts annually, each for half the year. In 1532–33 one taught Cicero's *De officiis* and Vergil's *Georgics,* canto 2; the same humanist then covered *De officiis,* book 2, and the *Georgics,* canto 3, in 1539–40. Another humanist taught Cicero's *Philippics* and the *Aeneid,* book 6, in 1539–40. In 1542–43 he discussed Cicero's *De oratore.* A

---

156. *I maestri di Roma,* 1991, 116, 118. A similar choice was available in 1575–76; see ibid., 101–3.

157. The list has been compiled from Pisan archival documents by Schmitt, 1983f, 23 n. 13. It is briefly summarized in Schmitt, 1972, 254.

third humanist taught unnamed orations of Cicero and Demosthenes in 1534.[158] Teaching mostly the prose of Cicero and the poetry of Vergil was an unadventuresome pedagogical path followed by secondary school teachers across Italy.[159]

The profile of the university texts demonstrates that the humanist professors steadily expanded their command over the literature of the ancient world. After Barzizza's foundational teaching, which gave students the basic tools with which to read ancient Latin texts, the humanist professors extended their range. By the end of the fifteenth century they were teaching some of the most difficult literary and historical works of ancient Rome but few Greek texts. Not surprisingly, the ablest humanistic scholars exhibited the greatest imagination and variety in their teaching texts. In the sixteenth century, the humanists increasingly taught Greek texts as well. Indeed, universities with a single humanist professor expected him to teach annually both a Latin and a Greek work. Professors often added Aristotle's *Poetics* and *Rhetoric* to aid in the theoretical analysis of literature. Despite the greater variety of texts, the poetry of Vergil and the speeches of Cicero still commanded most attention.

TEACHING AND RESEARCH

Although few humanist university lectures have survived, their content sometimes did in other forms. A course of lectures typically began with the introductory lecture, or prolusion (*praelectio*), which offered a general description of the course with the theoretical and methodological principles to be followed. Professors sometimes published these in collections of short works or as introductions to editions of the text. Moreover, the detailed analyses delivered orally in the lecture hall might appear in a diffused and discursive way as the scholia to a published text.[160] For example, the humanist professor Sebastiano Corradi published in 1552 a book on the *Brutus* of Cicero which included "almost all the words" (*totidem paene verbis*) of a course that he had taught over a three-year period at Bologna.[161]

What does survive confirms that university humanists employed the paraphrase-commentary format as the basic teaching approach. The professor might begin by reading through the section of the text to be discussed that day, followed by a brief general explanation of the meaning. He would then launch into a word-by-word analysis of the text, explaining grammatical, rhetorical, historical, and interpretive points. The paraphrase-commentary was thorough and comprehensive. Its disadvantages were that the professor had to deal with questions as they arose in the text and that it could not be adapted easily to address general issues.[162] The professor could vary the scholarly depth and emphases within the

---

158. Minnucci and Košuta, 1989, 517–19.

159. See Grendler, 1989, 203–50.

160. Renzi (1985, 39–40 and passim) makes this point well. See also Renzi, 1986.

161. The phrase was Corradi's from the introduction to the published work, as quoted in Costa, 1907a, 31.

162. This was the method recommended by Guarino Guarini and followed by Landino, among

paraphrase-commentary according to his wishes and student expectations. Flexibility was necessary, because the humanist probably attracted a greater range of students with more varied expectations than did professors in other disciplines.

Ulisse Aldrovandi, a professor of natural philosophy, made this point in 1573 in a memorandum proposing a rearrangement of the teaching schedule at the University of Bologna. He noted that some humanists and the extraordinary professors of theoretical medicine taught at the same time, the fourth hour of the morning. This presented no conflict because they lectured to different groups: the younger students attended the humanities lectures while more advanced students attended the lectures of the extraordinary professors of theoretical medicine.[163]

However, *the* humanist, meaning the star ordinary afternoon professor of the humanities, and the ordinary professors of natural philosophy (which included Aldrovandi) taught at the third hour of the afternoon. These two sets of lectures fitted well together, because when the legists finish lecturing, the "majority of the learned [*studiosi*] who delight[ed] in good letters [would] hear the excellent humanist," who was Carlo Sigonio. Others would attend the lectures of the ordinary natural philosophers.[164] This suggests that advanced students, and perhaps anyone who took "delight in good letters," attended the humanities lectures of the brilliant Sigonio.

Aldrovandi wanted to attract to his lectures some of the *studiosi* who attended Sigonio's lectures. So he proposed that he move to the second hour of the morning. If that happened, some "gentlemen who delight[ed] in good letters" and some legists would come to hear him.[165] In other words, Aldrovandi schemed to get himself a more advantageous lecture hour in order to attract to his lectures the same broad audience of students and "gentlemen" who attended

---

others. Field, 1988, 255. For a brief account of the paraphrase-commentary at the preuniversity level, see Grendler, 1989, 244–50.

163. "4th hora & ultima il Theorio sopraordinario nella qual hora leggeva il Curtio, il Vittorio, il Francanzano et ultimamente il Cardano, quali huomini celeberrimi: et in questa hora leggavano gli Humanisti. Di modo che queste due classi si compatiscono per essere la letture dell Humanità ascoltata da giovinetti e quella del Theorica [*sic*] sopraordinario da provetti e versati già più anni nei studij." BA, Ms. B 3803, Ulisse Aldrovandi, "Informatione del Rotulo del Studio di Bologna de' philosophi et medici all'illustrissmo Card. Paleotti" (Explicit: Di casa li 26 di Settembre 1573), f. 4^r. This is a copy of the autograph original, which is in the Archivio Arcivescovile in Bologna. All those named had been professors of medical theory at Bologna in earlier years: Matteo Corti (also called Curzio or Curtio; 1538–41); Benedetto Vittori (1512–31, 1539–61), Antonio Francanzano (1562–64), and Girolamo Cardano (1563–70). On Corti, see De Ferrari, 1983c, and Siraisi, 1987, 188–92.

164. "All'hora 3.a sucedono li Philosophi ordinarij et Humanista che è l'Eccellente Sigonio, e queste due letioni stanno bene insieme: et una non impedisce l'altro: perche cessando all'hora di leggere li leggisti, possono la maggior parte dei studiosi che si dilettano di belle lettere udira l'Eccellente Humanista e gl'altri professori dell'arte odono i philosophi ordinarij." BA, Ms. B. 3803, f. 4^{r-v}. The term *i studiosi* may mean all who were interested, including professors, students, and outsiders.

165. "Appresso questo sappia che alcuni gentilhuomini che si dilettano di belle lettere, mi vengono ascoltare, et ancora alcuni leggisti, à quali questa hora è commoda." "Non tacerò che ancora alcuni che si dilettano di lettere humane che per leggere gli humanisti dopo me questa hora li trova commoda." BA, Ms. B 3803, ff. 8^v, 9^r.

Sigonio's lectures. (It does not appear that the university changed the schedule to accommodate him.)

The memorandum also suggests that Bologna with its four or five humanists offered different levels of humanistic instruction. The morning humanists probably taught a general, more introductory approach to the literature of the ancient world, while Sigonio presented the results of his original research on the social structure of ancient Roman society. But a single humanist at a small university probably had to content himself with teaching standard texts and emphasizing elegant expression, civil wisdom, and some knowledge of the ancient world. This would be particularly true for a humanist professor who had to teach both a Latin and a Greek author every year.

The different levels of student expectations help explain the varying approaches to lecturing and research of humanist professors. Three kinds of humanities teaching and research can be discerned.[166] The first might be called teaching the classics for elegance, wisdom, and knowledge. The professor explained the grammatical, rhetorical, historical, civic, and moral meaning of a text. He identified unfamiliar persons, places, and customs. He gave the derivations of words. And he interpreted the passage, perhaps placing it in a broad philosophical or civic context by means of allegoresis. In the broadest terms he taught the classics as preparation for the active life.

The student learned to understand and appreciate the beauty of ancient words and sentiments. He learned more about the wondrous world of Greece and Rome. He learned how to express himself elegantly. He might hear an uplifting moral or civic lesson inspiring him to emulate the good example found in the text. Many students probably wanted just such learning from the humanities lectures. It is quite likely that this kind of instruction accounted for much of the popularity of "humane letters" among the members of leading families who took a great interest in the humanities lectures at the local university.

A second form of instruction might be called researching the classics. The professor approached the ancient text as an object of detailed research; it was an artifact of the past to be studied carefully for its own sake. The professor asked and resolved such questions as, What exactly did the ancient poet mean in a particular passage? What were the Greek sources behind the words of a Latin satirical poet? What is the meaning of an obscure name or word? Was the received text accurate, or should it be corrected? How does one determine this?

Beginning in the last quarter of the fifteenth century, some humanist professors, especially the ablest, embraced this problem-oriented research, at least in their published work.[167] Rather than presenting a paraphrase-commentary of an entire work—which would mostly repeat the content of previous commentaries—they discussed the text selectively. They solved precise, limited problems

166. Some of what follows was suggested by Grafton, 1985, and Grafton and Jardine, 1986, chs. 3 and 4.

167. See Grafton, 1988b, esp. 26–32, an essay first published in 1977. Branca, 1983, makes some of the same points for Poliziano only. Beroaldo the Elder, 1995, is an excellent example of problem-oriented research. See also Perosa, 1973, 601, discussing Calderini.

within the work. They might improve a corrupt passage or explicate the meaning of an obscure word. The student learned by following the professor through the resolution of a problem. After solving a number of limited problems in one text or a series of issues in several texts, the humanist published a volume of these problems and solutions. Possibly Domizio Calderini in the 1470s inaugurated this form of scholarly monographic publication; Poliziano, Beroaldo the Elder, and others followed. Poliziano used this method of monographic publication for his studies in order to develop an understanding of how manuscripts might be used to establish the text.[168] The ultimate end of research-oriented teaching was a monographic study to be read by other scholars. It enabled the author to display his learning and to point out the shortcomings of other scholars. Humanist professors did a great deal of both.

Sometimes a change of professors produced an immediate shift of approach. Upon Poliziano's death in 1494, Marcello Virgilio (Berti) Adriani (1464–1521) succeeded him as professor of poetry and oratory in Florence. Adriani taught through at least 1502. In addition, he was elected first secretary in the Florentine chancery in 1498 and held the post through various changes of government. In contrast to Poliziano's intricate philological analysis, Adriani sought elegant expression, good citizenship, and republican values in the classics. His approach recalled the civic humanism of Leonardo Bruni of the early fifteenth century, an emphasis that he thought his Florentine listeners would value in the present. Not surprisingly, Adriani focused on the best-known Latin classics, such as Vergil.[169]

At the other extreme, some sixteenth-century humanities professors became historians of the ancient world. In his maturity, Sigonio devoted himself to detailed historical research on the offices, institutions, and social stratification in ancient republican Rome. He aimed at a historical reconstruction of ancient government and society and published his findings in numerous historical monographs, some quite technical in nature.[170] Marc'Antoine Muret's research and teaching on such authors as Tacitus was also critico-historical.

However, sometimes higher authorities felt that professors got carried away by their research. So they reminded them that students did not always want lectures full of detailed research. In 1578 Cardinal Guglielmo Sirleto, scholar, Vatican librarian, and member of the commission of cardinals overseeing the University of Rome, suggested to Marc'Antoine Muret that, for the sake of the

---

168. See Grafton, 1988b, 32–52; Branca, 1983, esp. ch. 10; and D'Amico, 1988, 21–27. Each work lists much more bibliography.

169. The contrast between Poliziano and Adriani is the major theme of Godman, 1998. Although he calls Adriani's approach to the classics "public humanism," it really was "civic humanism." On Adriani, see also Miccoli, 1960b, and Verde, 1973–94, 2:476–77, under the name Marcellus Berti.

170. Costa, 1907a, traces a historically oriented *studia humanitatis* through Romolo Amaseo, Sebastiano Corradi da Arceto, Francesco Robortello, and Carlo Sigonio, at Bologna. Costa calls this humanistic research antiquarianism, that is, scholarship detached from concern with contemporary issues. Avesani (1960, 662) agrees. However, McCuaig (1989, esp. chs. 2 and 3) demonstrates that a fervent belief in the republican liberties of northern Italian city-states accompanied Sigonio's historically oriented research on ancient Rome and early medieval Italy. Sigonio believed that the roots of city-state liberties were to be found in the earlier societies that he studied.

students, he should teach an easier text than the one that he had taught the previous year. According to Muret, Sirleto said the following to him:

> Since in the past year you devoted your lectures to the *Politics* of Aristotle, it would be appropriate if this year you would choose a little easier theme. Indeed, not all those for whom you should labor are capable of understanding such complex matters; neither can one expect that the great majority will love Greek. It is a question of those who at the beginning of the new year unwillingly approach the content of books already more than half explicated; (it would be) almost like a banquet tasted and consumed by others. Therefore, I invite you to choose some historian; and, if you will listen to me, no one is more preferable than Sallust. He expresses himself in excellent Latin; he is serious and rich in content, full of civil wisdom and stylistically similar to Thucydides, something that I know matters much to you. Besides, since the book is not too long, you could easily explicate it completely in a few months.[171]

Sirleto's admonition suggests several points. Muret had ventured beyond the usual texts used in humanities courses in order to present a very detailed and lengthy analysis of Aristotle's *Politics*. But the students found Aristotle difficult. They lacked the command of Greek needed to grasp some of the points made by Muret, who must have used the Greek text to some extent. Because he presented such a detailed analysis, Muret had gone through only half the *Politics* the previous year and intended to continue in the present academic year. But students who had not attended the previous year's lectures would be confused and resentful if forced to begin at the halfway point. So Sirleto recommended that Muret lecture this year on a shorter, easier, well-written Latin historical text. Moreover, Sallust was "full of civil wisdom" from which a broad range of students might profit. In other words, for the sake of the students, Sirleto urged Muret to deliver a series of lectures on Sallust which would teach good style and civic wisdom.

It appears that Muret took Sirleto's advice and taught Sallust during the academic year 1578–79.[172] Sallust's *Bellum Catilinae,* an account of the Catiline conspiracy, is so full of self-righteous and obvious moral *sententiae* that Muret probably did not find it much of a challenge, even though students could derive pithy commonplaces and civil and moral lessons from it. Muret soon returned to his first love. During the academic years 1580–81 and 1581–82, he taught what

---

171. Quando, inquit, superioris anni curriculum in Aristotelis Politicis consumpsisti, non alienum fuerit hoc anno aliquid paullo levioris operae adsumere. Nam neque omnes ii, quorum te commodis servire oportet, capaces sunt tam arduarum disputationum; & a plerisque impetrari non potest, ut Graecas litteras ament; & sunt, qui anni principio, ad dimidiatos libros, tamquam ad delibatas ab aliis ac prope semesas epulas non libenter accedant. Quare auctor tibi sum, ut aliquem historicum sumas; ac, si me audis, non alium potius, quam Sallustium. Nam & egregie latine loquitur, & gravis ac densus est, & civilis sapientiae plenus, &, quod tu quanti facias scio, Thucydideus; & ut exiguis liber est, paucis illum mensibus totum explicare facili poteris. From Muret's "Interpretaturus C. Sallustium de Catilinae coniuratione" of Nov. 3, 1578, in Muret, 1737, 1:250. It is also quoted by Renzi, 1985, 45–46 n. 26.

172. Muret, 1737, 1:250.

appears to have been an intense, detailed course on the first three books of Tacitus's *Annales,* a difficult historical text.[173]

Teaching the classics for elegance, wisdom, and knowledge and researching the classics were not mutually exclusive. The humanist professor might employ a combination of both in the classroom. He might favor one approach at one time and another for a different text.

The third and most memorable form of teaching and research might be called conquering new fields. The humanist used his unique skills, critical awareness, and iconoclastic outlook to venture into new areas of learning, to look at the world in new ways, or to reexamine the bases of knowledge. Here the humanist's freedom from statutory curricular demands and his wide-ranging critical faculties became most apparent. The humanist's presumption that most medieval learning was wrong-headed also spurred him to innovate.

Lorenzo Valla, although a university professor for only about eight and one-half years, applied his critical skills and iconoclastic spirit to many intellectual assumptions and found them lacking. He was not alone. Scholars used their knowledge of Greek and philological skills to reexamine the ancient texts on which much of university learning was based and sometimes produced revolutionary results. Medical humanism (see Ch. 9) was the prime example.

The humanist professors created the new field of literary criticism. Robortello, Giraldi Cinzio, and Riccobono explained its principles as found in Aristotle and Horace, and Sigonio published a treatise on the poetics of dialogue (*De dialogo liber,* 1561).[174] Elaborating on the insights of Aristotle and Horace became a major preoccupation of humanistic teaching and research in the second half of the sixteenth century.

The freedom from statutory constraints permitted humanist professors to apply Aristotelian and Horation definitions of poetry to contemporary vernacular poetry. For example, Giraldi and Pigna argued that Ludovico Ariosto's *Orlando furioso* (1516) was a poetic masterpiece, despite the fact that it was a romance that violated Aristotelian rules of poetry. Giraldi and Pigna also argued that the romance was a genre comparable to, or superior in worth to, the classical epic. Unfortunately, the simultaneous publication of their findings in 1554 led to an acrimonious quarrel. Pigna denounced Giraldi for plagiarizing his work, and Giraldi accused Pigna of making unwarranted use of what he had learned as a pupil in Giraldi's classroom.[175] The publication of Torquato Tasso's *Jerusalem Liberated* (1581) produced a new wave of discussions and arguments about the nature of epic poetry.

---

173. Renzi, 1985, 33. The article discusses the teaching and publication of Muret's commentary on Tacitus.

174. See Snyder, 1989, 39–86. The poet Torquato Tasso was Sigonio's pupil at Padua, 1560–62.

175. There is a large literature on the debate over *Orlando furioso.* Weinberg (1961, chs. 19 and 20, 954–1073 and passim) provides a summary and further bibliography. For the pioneering efforts of Giraldi and Pigna to canonize the poem as a classic, see Javitch, 1991, 21–29, 39–41, 71–72, 90–93, 126, 132–33, 160, 163, 168, 172. For the split between Giraldi and Pigna, see Bongi, 1890–97, 1:427–29.

The humanists' critical interest in the forms of vernacular literature led them to write in the vernacular. Although Giraldi and Pigna lectured in Latin, they published vernacular literary works rather than editions and studies of the Latin and Greek classics. Giraldi wrote vernacular tragedies in an effort to create Italian tragedy, *novelle,* a vernacular commentary on Ferrarese history, and an important work in literary criticism. Pigna published a book on the duel, another on the prince, a history of the Este family, and his own work of literary criticism, all in the vernacular. By contrast, Giraldi wrote only a few works in Latin, notably orations, and Pigna a Latin commentary on Horace's *Ars poetica.*[176]

HUMANISTS IN THE UNIVERSITY: A SUMMATION

The humanists' journey from private scholar to professor was neither quick nor easy, largely because of their own hesitations. Nevertheless, they found a congenial home in the university. Humanistic studies had a far more important place in the Renaissance university than did grammar, rhetoric, and *ars dictaminis* in the fourteenth-century university.

Humanists entered Italian universities without opposition from professors of other disciplines. Part of the reason was that a revolution in preuniversity education accompanied the entry of humanists into university faculties. Certainly by 1500, and probably earlier, the vast majority of university professors in all disciplines had received a humanistic preuniversity education. Hence, they were well acquainted with the *studia humanitatis* and saw no reason to oppose adding humanists to the faculty. Moreover, rulers wanted humanists in the university.

In northern Europe, where the development of humanistic studies came later in both university and preuniversity education, theologians often strongly opposed the appointment of humanists to university faculties. Northern humanists, in turn, denounced theologians in the most insulting terms, arguing that humanistic grammatical-philological criticism better explicated the word of God in Scripture than did Scholastic dialectics. The conflict was bitter and prolonged, because the stakes were university turf in this life and salvation in the next.[177]

No such conflict occurred in Italy, because humanists and theologians did not compete for students or tell each other how to get to heaven. Theology had a very small presence and little prestige in Italian universities. Most theological instruction took place in the mendicant order *studia,* not in the classrooms of the civic university (see Ch. 10). Theologians had limited contact with other professors. By contrast, theology was central to northern universities. Nor did Italian humanists invade the territory of the theologians. With the notable exception of Lorenzo Valla, Italian university humanists wrote relatively little on theological issues and seldom applied philological skills to Scripture. When fifteenth-century

176. The most convenient and nearly complete listing of the works of Giraldi and Pigna is found in *STC Italian,* 1958, 305, 334, 519.
177. See Nauert, 1973 and 1998, and Rummel, 1995.

Italian humanists did write about religious issues, they formulated a *theologica rhetorica,* which did not attack but bypassed Scholastic theology.[178]

From about 1450 onward, humanistic studies played a major role in university education, not only in the study of the classics but also through their influence on other disciplines. The century and a quarter from about 1450 to about 1575 was a golden age for university humanists. Then signs of decline began to surface.

Jesuit schools challenged the university's role as the primary provider of humanities education. The Jesuit colleges across Italy strongly emphasized the humanities and taught them well. Consequently, penny-pinching rulers eliminated humanistic studies from the universities of Turin and Catania on the grounds that students could learn at the free local Jesuit school. One also wonders if the presence of a Jesuit school at Macerta from 1561 explains the absence of humanistic studies at the University of Macerata. Observers judged that the teaching of rhetoric prospered at the Jesuit Collegio Romano but was declining at the University of Rome at the end of the century.[179] The number of humanities professors in Italian universities was considerably lower in 1600 than in 1500, and fewer memorable scholars could be found among them. A lustrous era of university humanistic instruction and research had ended.

178. Trinkaus, 1970.
179. McGinness, 1995a.

CHAPTER 7

Logic

lisse Aldrovandi, a professor at Bologna, saw logic as a preparatory subject.[1] In his 1573 analysis of the University of Bologna time-table, he noted that logic and medical theory were taught at the same hour. Teaching these two subjects at the same hour produced no conflict, because those who attend the logic lectures were "youths and beginners not yet able" to benefit from medical lectures. By contrast, students attending the medical theory lectures had already been introduced to dialectic.[2]

On the other hand, in 1587 a Pisan professor of natural philosophy defined logic in lofty fashion as "an instrumental faculty, [the] regulator of the operations of the rational soul of man, to the end that he can distinguish true from false in the speculative sciences, and good from evil in the active and effective [ones]." If students receive good training in logic, they will produce great fruit in the sciences, in medicine, and everything else, he concluded.[3]

They were both right. By the late sixteenth century logic was both an introductory subject and an opportunity for advanced speculation. It showed students how to formulate tight arguments, a useful skill for all subjects. But professors of logic also dealt with scientific method. They pondered the proper approach to finding truth through scientific inquiry in natural philosophy and mathematics.

1. Because contemporary sources, especially university rolls, overwhelmingly preferred the term *logic* to *dialectic,* it is used here. The instances in which Renaissance scholars drew a distinction between logic and dialectic are neither numerous nor relevant.

2. "I logici e theorici di Medicina: le quali due letioni stanno bene insieme nè l'una è impedimenti [*sic*] all'altra, perche ordinariamente quelli che odono logica sono giovinetti, e principianti che anco non sono atti ad udire Medicina: ne meno quelli che odono la Theoria hanno bisogno di dialettica, per esser già introdotti in quella." BA, Ms. B 3803, "Informatione del Rotulo. . . . 1573."

3. "Una facoltà stormentale [= strumentale] regolatrice dell'operazioni dell'anima razionale dell'uomo, a fine che egli distingua nelle scienze speculative il vero dal falso, et nell'attive et fattive il bene dal male." From the "Parere o vero Giudizio di m. Francesco de' Vieri, detto il Verino secondo intorno al famoso et nobile studio di Pisa" of 1587, as quoted in Del Fante, 1980b, 413. Verino's description of logic as an instrumental faculty suggests an acquaintance with the work of Francesco Zabarella. See below.

They debated the classification of disciplines and their priority. Although the majority of professors of logic were poorly paid young scholars, a few senior professors of stature commanded higher salaries and respect.

Logic began in 1400 as a thoroughly medieval subject, but by 1600 it had come under humanist influence and had been adapted to the needs of scientists. One thing remained constant: from Paul of Venice in 1400 through Jacopo Zabarella at the end of the sixteenth century, Padua was the leading university for logic.

LOGIC AT PADUA

Very little is known about the teaching of logic at Padua before 1400. Peter of Abano (c. 1257–1315), who taught astrology and mathematics there from about 1306 until his death, argued that logic was a necessary preparation for both medicine and law. But only five logicians have been identified as teaching at Padua in the late thirteenth and early fourteenth centuries.[4]

The most important logician of the late fourteenth and fifteenth centuries was Paul of Venice (Paolo Nicoletti da Udine, 1369/72–1429). An Augustinian Hermit at the order's Paduan convent, Paul studied at Oxford between 1390 and 1393, where he assimilated terminist logic. Upon returning to Italy, he probably began to teach at the University of Padua in 1395. He wrote his best-known work, the *Logica parva* (also called *Summulae*) in 1395–96, followed by many others. He held professorships of logic and natural philosophy at Padua until 1420. However, involvement in ecclesiastical and political affairs kept him out of Padua for months and years. The Venetian government exiled him for alleged heresy in 1420. Paul then taught at the University of Siena in 1420, may have taught at Bologna or Perugia (or both) in 1424, and again taught at Siena in 1427 and early 1428. Allowed to return to the Venetian state, he resumed lecturing in natural philosophy at Padua in 1429 but died almost immediately thereafter. His several works summarizing late medieval Oxford terminist logic became widely used textbooks.[5] Paul of Venice solidified the hold of English logic on the curriculum of Italian universities.

---

4. Siraisi, 1973, 58–65, 175.

5. This short biographical sketch comes from Lohr, 1972, 314–20; Perreiah, 1967; and Bottin, 1983, 85–97. See also *CHLMP,* 875; and *CHRP,* 830. There is a very large bibliography on Paul of Venice, including several articles in *Aristotelismo veneto,* 1983, and Perreiah, 1984. Paulus Venetus, 1984, is an English translation of the *Logica parva.*

Older sources state that Pier Paolo Vergerio (c. 1368–1444), the famous early humanist, taught logic at Padua for up to seven years. See Facciolati, 1978, pt. 1:1. This cannot be confirmed. After acquiring a doctorate of arts at Bologna, Vergerio arrived in Padua by January 1391. He lived and studied at Padua in the years 1391–97 and 1400–1405, with some absences. Vergerio may have supported himself by teaching logic in the university, but the evidence is not clear. In the spring of 1405 Vergerio took a doctorate in arts and medicine, followed by a doctorate in canon and civil law, and then left Padua. Leonardo Smith, Vergerio's biographer and editor, printed the relevant sources and indicated the uncertainty about his teaching. See Smith, 1926–28, pt. 1:151, 152, 155, and pt.

After Paul of Venice's departure and death, Padua had a single logician through much of the fifteenth century, usually a young scholar who had probably just earned his doctorate. In most cases he taught logic for a few years before moving up to a more prestigious lectureship or leaving the university. All were disciples of Paul of Venice to greater or lesser degree; they pursued fourteenth-century English and Parisian formal logic with its emphasis on terms and suppositions. Ironically, whereas Oxford logic stagnated intellectually in fifteenth-century England, it flourished in Italy.[6]

Gaetano da Thiene from Vicenza (Caietanus de Thienis, 1387–1465), who taught logic at Padua from 1422 to 1430, was the best known of the logicians. He was an influential and well-published scholar of Averroist tendencies who wrote four works on logic.[7] A more typical Paduan logician was Domenico de' Domenichi (or Domenico Dominici, 1416–78), who took his doctorate in arts in January 1436 and then taught logic in the years 1435–37 and perhaps until 1441. He then became a bishop, theologian, papal diplomat, and orator, always with humanistic inclinations.[8]

In 1487 the Venetian Senate added a new logic post usually called *De Sophistica,* because the duties included teaching the *Regulae solvendi sophismata* of William of Heytesbury (see below, "Teaching and Research").[9] Padua now had first, second, and third ordinary professors of logic, plus a lecturer on sophisms, which position was sometimes doubled, making a total of four or five logicians. The arts students, who elected the second ordinary logician and the one or two sophisms professors, normally chose young scholars who had just completed their degrees. In addition, the third ordinary professorship was one of the poorly paid third positions ("terzi luoghi") reserved to Paduans by a Senate decree of 1467.[10] Turnover was high, because most logicians were young scholars who either ascended to better positions in natural philosophy or left the university. Only the first ordinary professor of logic might be a scholar of consequence.

Most logicians earned salaries in the bottom quartile of the professoriat. For example, in 1509–10 the three ordinary logicians received 35, 35, and 20 florins, and the sophisms professor received 30. In 1535–36, the figures were 124 (an

---

2:92–96 and passim, and especially Vergerio, 1969, xv, 275–76 n. 1; 483–86, and the letters for the years 1390–1405. McManamon (1996, 17–18, 33–34) believes that Vergerio did teach logic at Padua. However, Vergerio did not mention teaching at Padua in his surviving letters for those years.

6. Vasoli, 1981, 47; Maierù, 1982; Ashworth and Spade, 1992, 60.

7. He was appointed to teach logic on Oct. 18, 1422, at a salary of 40 florins. AAUP, F. 648, f. 35ᵛ. See also Facciolati, 1978, pt. 2:114. For his thought, see Di Napoli, 1963, 97–105; Silvestro da Valsanzibio, 1967; Lohr, 1967, 390–92; Vasoli, 1981, 45–46; *CHLMP,* 860; *CHRP,* 818–19; and Lawn, 1993, 62–63. See Facciolati, 1978, pt. 2:113–16, for a list of the logicians who taught at Padua in the fifteenth century.

8. Tomasini, 1986, 157, 158, 279; Facciolati, 1978, pt. 2:114; King, 1986, 363–65; D'Amico, 1983, 218, 315; Smolinsky, 1991.

9. Facciolati, 1978, pt. 2:114, 118–19.

10. Bertolaso, 1959–60, explains the *terzi luoghi.*

unusually high salary), 35, and 20 florins for the three ordinary logicians and 20 florins each for two sophisms professors.[11]

The importance of logic changed at Padua in the mid-sixteenth century. It continued to be an introductory subject but also provided the basis for research into scientific method. Now the first ordinary professor of logic who pursued such research became a significant scholar of long tenure and a much higher salary. For example, in 1551–52 the first ordinary professor of logic (Bernardino Tomitano) received a good salary of 200 florins.[12] But the rest of the logicians remained at a low level, 20 to 36 florins, and the sophisms professorship disappeared in 1560. From that date to the end of the century, only two (very occasionally three) logicians taught at Padua.[13]

Bernadino Tomitano typified the new Paduan logician. He obtained his doctorate in arts in 1535 and later a doctorate in medicine. He began as third ordinary professor of logic in 1539, moved to second position in 1540, and ascended to first ordinary professor of logic in 1543, which post he held until 1563, earning a highest salary of 300 florins. He then abandoned university teaching in order to practice medicine. He reportedly taught more than two hundred Venetian patricians over his long career, which probably helped his salary to rise. Tomitano lectured on most of the logical texts of Aristotle, publishing some of his lectures but leaving the majority in manuscript. Tomitano also added commentary and notes to several of the logical works of Aristotle and Averroës (Ibn Rushd, 1126–98) for the revised second edition of the Aristotle and Averroës edition published by the Giunti press in 1562 (see below, "Teaching and Research"). And he explored demonstrative regress (see below).[14]

The most important logician at Padua, and in Italy, was Jacopo Zabarella (1533–89), a Paduan known for his analysis of demonstrative regress. He obtained his doctorate from the University of Padua in 1553 after studying with Tomitano in logic and Marc'Antonio de' Passeri in natural philosophy. Zabarella was appointed first ordinary professor of logic at 60 florins in 1564, succeeding Tomitano. He then became second extraordinary professor of natural philosophy in 1568, first extraordinary professor of natural philosophy in 1577 at 260 florins rising to 350, and second ordinary professor of natural philosophy in 1583 at 410

---

11. AAUP, F. 651, ff. 1^v–2^r for the roll of 1509–10, and f. 129^{r-v} for the roll of 1535–36. Other rolls in F. 651 and Inventario 1320 list similar salaries for logicians.

12. Gallo, 1963, 72, for salaries from the roll of 1551–52.

13. See Facciolati, 1978, pt. 3:295–97, 301–3, 306–7, 309–12; Riccobono, 1980, sigs. G2^v–G4^r. See also the various rolls in AAUP, Inventario 1320; the rolls of 1553–54 and 1584–85 in AAUP, F. 651, ff. 207^v, 302^r; the roll of 1571–72 in Riccobono, 1980, sigs. I1^r–I2^r; and the roll of 1577–78 in ASB, Assunteria di Studio, Bu. 100, fasc. 5, also printed in Favaro, 1915, 256. After 1560, the two sophisms positions disappeared, even though the posts were sometimes listed as "vacant" in drafts of rolls; see the rolls of 1568–69 and 1569–70 in AAUP, Inventario 1320. It appears that the government abolished the position by not filling it.

14. See Facciolati, 1978, pt. 3:296, 302, 306; Riccobono, 1980, sig. G3^r; Lohr, 1982, 201–4 with bibliography. Camerini, 1962–63, vol. 1, pt. 1:426–27.

florins.[15] Through his brilliance Zabarella partially overcame Venetian resistance to appointing Paduans to major professorships. Even though he spent only four years teaching logic, Zabarella studied the subject throughout his career. He published many treatises, some written in disputes with another Paduan logician, Bernardino Petrella (1529–95), who taught logic at Padua from 1562 to 1567 and from 1569 until his death.[16]

Padua emphasized logic more than any other university by creating a relatively large number of positions and through the scholarship of its logicians. Paul of Venice wrote a widely used textbook, while Jacopo Zabarella led the discussion of scientific method in the sixteenth century.

LOGIC AT OTHER UNIVERSITIES

No other university had such important logicians as did Padua. But they all taught the subject and sometimes had several logicians.

The University of Bologna had a large number of logicians, but they were minor scholars. Bologna taught logic from the last quarter of the thirteenth century.[17] The earliest surviving roll, that of 1351–52, listed a professor of dialectic earning 50 Bolognese lire, a salary in the middle of the modest pay scale.[18] Through the 1370s, 1380s, and 1390s, Bologna had two or three logicians, sometimes combined with natural philosophy.[19] The roll of 1388–89 had three logicians, including the youthful humanist Pier Paolo Vergerio as a student lecturer.[20] Bologna continued to have two or three logicians, divided into morning and afternoon ordinary professorships, in the early fifteenth century.[21]

As the size of the faculty expanded, so did the number of logicians. For example, Bologna had 5 logicians in 1458–59, 2 teaching in the morning, another 2 in the afternoon, plus a student lecturer. This pattern continued. The number of logicians numbered 5 or 6 (occasionally 4 or 7) in a faculty of 80 to 100 for the greater part of the fifteenth century.[22] Bologna deemphasized logic some-

---

15. For his appointments and salaries, see Facciolati, 1978, pt. 3:280, 284, 289, 296. For biographical and bibliographical information, see Edwards, 1976; Schmitt, 1981d; Lohr, 1982, 233–44; and *CHRP*, 841.

16. For Petrella, see Lohr, 1979, 577–79.

17. Siraisi, 1981, 6, 34, 44, 115, 127, 140, 241.

18. Sorbelli, 1912, 316. The dialectician was Pietro da Crema, who has not been identified further.

19. Dallari, 1888–1924, 1:1–7 passim; 4: *Aggiunte*, 1–23 passim.

20. "Ad lecturam Loyce. Magister Petruspaulus electus pro Universitate cum salario librarum L. bon." Dallari, 1888–1924, 1:7. Confirmation comes from an undated letter of Vergerio in which he announced this fact: "de petitis lecturis, ut credo, nosi quod magister Aldrovrandinus suam obtinuit, ego logicam." Vergerio, 1969, letter 11, p. 23; see also pp. xiv–xv. "Electus pro Universitate" meant that he was chosen for one of the lectureships reserved for advanced students in the last year of study. See Matsen, 1994, 532–33. The statutes limited student lectureships to one year.

21. Dallari, 1888–1924, 4: *Aggiunte*, 50–51.

22. Ibid., vol. 1, and p. 51 for the roll of 1458–59.

what in the sixteenth century. Beginning about 1515, the university eliminated the afternoon ordinary logic lectureship, thus reducing the number to 2, occasionally 3 or 4, logicians. The number of logicians again rose to 4 in the last quarter of the sixteenth century.[23]

Very few established scholars taught logic at Bologna. Occasionally a young man taught the subject for one to three years before advancing to a professorship in a more prestigious discipline and becoming well known in the latter field. For example, Ludovico Boccadiferro (or Buccaferrea, 1482–1545) earned his doctorate in arts and medicine from Bologna in 1516; he taught logic there for three years (1515–18) and then natural philosophy for the rest of his life. Boccadiferro became a well-known philosopher of Averroist orientation who frequently differed with Pomponazzi.[24] Ulisse Aldrovandi taught logic in 1554–55, the year following his doctorate, and then moved to natural philosophy.[25] But most of the logicians at Bologna were unknown figures who held the position for many years.

The University of Pavia had a single logician (in scientia loice, later simply "logic"), in a faculty of 30 to 40, from the late 1380s until the 1430s, then 2 or 3 logicians in a faculty of 50 to 70, from the 1430s through the end of the century. The title of the lectureship was often "logic and sophistries" (Ad lecturam logicae et sophistariae). From about 1540 through 1600, Pavia had an average of 3 logicians, in a faculty of about 50. The university viewed logic professorships as long-term posts, rather than as temporary positions for young scholars. Some Pavian logicians rose to teach natural philosophy, but less often than those at Padua and Bologna. Logicians' salaries remained in the bottom quartile throughout the two centuries.[26]

The University of Ferrara averaged 2 or 3 logicians in an arts faculty of 20 to 25 in the second half of the fifteenth century. Then from 1540 through the late 1560s, 4 or 5 logicians taught in an arts faculty of about 35. The number of logicians dipped to 2 or 3 through the 1570s and early 1580s, before rising again to an average of 4 or 5 from the mid-1580s to the mid-1590s, when the arts faculty numbered 30 to 35. The title of the post was most often "logic" and sometimes "dialectic."[27]

23. Ibid., vol. 2. All the student lectureships in arts, including logic, had disappeared by this time.

24. Ibid., 2:12, 15, 18, for the logic appointments. See Rotondò, 1969, and Lohr, 1974b, 282–86, for Boccadiferro.

25. Dallari, 1888–1924, 2:133, 136.

26. Maiocchi, 1971; Memorie di Pavia, 1970, pt. 1:153–76, passim; Sottili, 1982, 548–49; Verde, 1973–94, 1:387, 391; ASPv, Università, Cartone 20, various rolls, no pag., and Cartone 22; and Rizzo, 1987, 76 n. 35, for roll of 1584–85.

27. I maestri di Ferrara, 1991, 3–49, 154–55, 162–63, and passim for individual professors. However, the listings for logic in I maestri di Ferrara seem to be more incomplete and inconsistent with other sources than in other disciplines. For example, I maestri di Ferrara (15) lists only eleven arts professors (including two logicians), while Secco Suardo (1983, 287) lists twenty-eight arts professors (including six logicians). Hence, in order to estimate the number of logicians, I have relied more heavily on other sources: Solerti, 1892; Secco Suardo, 1983; Pardi, 1972; and Franceschini, 1970, 258–61.

The Ferrara logicians were an undistinguished lot with one exception. Antonio Musa Brasavola (1500–1555) taught logic in 1519, later publishing his lectures on Porphyry. After obtaining his doctorate in arts and medicine in 1520, Brasavola continued to teach logic through the academic year 1527–28, apparently writing several commentaries on Aristotle's logical works, which may have been his lectures. He then taught natural philosophy and medicine, publishing numerous works in the last field.[28]

The University of Florence had a single logician in the 1360s, 2 in the 1390s, but only a single logician in an arts faculty of 10 to 12 in the fifteenth century. The logicians received salaries that placed them in the bottom rank.[29] Although logic was considered indispensable preparation for natural philosophy and medicine, Florence, which did not emphasize these disciplines, may have felt that a single logician was enough. Indeed, some Florentine humanists strongly criticized medieval logic.

When the university moved to Pisa in 1473, it became a more conventional institution focusing on medicine. Consequently, the number of logicians at Pisa rose to 3 or 4 in an arts faculty of almost 20, and 4 or 5 in the period 1515–25. As elsewhere, many logicians taught that subject only briefly before rising to professorships of natural philosophy or medicine, if they acquired a doctorate in the latter. Pisa had 2 or 3 logicians on the faculty from 1543 to the end of the century.[30]

In the late sixteenth century Pisa used the logic professorships as proving grounds for young arts scholars wishing to pursue academic careers. The new graduate taught logic for one, two, or three years. If he proved satisfactory, the university advanced him to a natural philosophy post; if found wanting, his contract was not renewed.[31] This practice may have existed elsewhere but was not acknowledged explicitly.

One Pisan natural philosopher criticized the practice. Francesco Verino il Secondo (or Francesco de' Vieri, 1524–90) had taught logic at Pisa in 1553–54, then moved up to become extraordinary, later ordinary, professor, of natural philosophy, but again taught logic from 1570 to 1575. Verino argued that logicians should be kept in place and made happy with excellent salaries. He offered the Paduan practice as a model: Paduan logicians were not promoted to other positions but focused on logic. He noted that Bernardino Tomitano had "taught logic 22 or 24 years" (the correct number was 24) at Padua, while Bernardino Petrella had taught "an infinite number of years" (25 in 1587) "with a great

---

28. See G. Gliozzi, 1972; Lohr, 1974b, 275–76; and Chiellini, 1991, 221. Brasavola's logic and natural philosophy teaching is not listed in *I maestri di Ferrara,* 1991, 201–2.

29. Spagnesi, 1979, 271; Park, 1980.

30. Verde, 1973–94, 1:293–383 passim, plus profiles of individual logicians in vol. 2. See Del Gratta, 1993a, 501–2, and Fabroni, 1971, 1:393–96, 2:470–71, for lists of logicians. See Cascio Pratilli, 1975, 193, 195, for rolls of 1543–44 and 1567–68, and Galilei, 1966, 34, 39, 41, for rolls of 1585–86, 1589–90, and 1590–91.

31. Cascio Pratilli, 1975, 153–54 n. 63. There are many examples. See the lists of professors in Barsanti, 1993, 562–65 and passim.

reputation." Employing senior professors to teach logic had borne "great fruit with students" at Padua, in his opinion.[32] But Pisa did not change its policy.

The University of Rome had 1 or 2 logicians in the 1470s, 1480s, and 1490s. This grew to a temporary high of 4, 2 ordinary and 2 for holidays, in the bloated roll of 1514. From 1535 through the end of the century, Rome returned to 2 ordinary logicians, initially teaching at the same hour, later teaching morning and afternoon. They received modest stipends in the lower one-third of the salary range but were not at the bottom. Roman logicians did not attract attention for their scholarly achievements.[33]

As noted above, Paul of Venice taught at the University of Siena in 1420 and again in 1427–28. But from then on Siena treated logic as an introductory position to be held by a young academic. Siena had 3 very poorly paid logicians in an arts faculty of 21 in 1493, and 4 in an arts faculty of 18 in 1500.[34] University statutes of 1544–45 permitted new doctoral graduates to teach logic in the year following graduation, but how many took advantage of the opportunity is unclear.[35] Siena had 2, occasionally 3, logicians in the sixteenth century until the reforms of 1589 set the number at 2. The reforms of 1589 also decreed that a scholar needed only a doctorate to hold the ordinary professorship of logic but needed 4 to 8 years of university teaching experience in order to hold ordinary professorships of law, medicine, and natural philosophy.[36] This, and the lowest salaries in the university, confirmed the inferior status of Sienese logicians. None were known scholars.

The University of Naples had 1 or 2 logicians in the fifteenth and sixteenth centuries.[37] Perugia had a single logician in the fifteenth and sixteenth centuries.[38] Turin had 1 or 2 in the 1530s and 2 ordinary professors of logic after its restoration in 1566. The logicians with long tenure eventually received salaries in

---

32. "Fermi in esse, contentandogli et ristorandogli con buoni et honoratissimi salarij, come e' fecero già al'Eccellentissimo logico messer Bernardino Tomitano, che lesse la logica 22 o 24 anni continui, né mai potette salire più sù, così il Petrella l'ha letta una infinità d'anni con gran sua reputazione et utilità et con gran frutto degli scolari." Verino's "Parere o vero Giudizio . . . intorno al famoso et nobile studio di Pisa," as quoted in Del Fante, 1980b, 402–3. Verino's accurate information on the teaching careers of Tomitano and Petrella is one piece of evidence among many that professors kept a close eye on other institutions.

33. Dorati da Empoli, 1980, 107, 118–20, 123, 127, for the 1470s through 1490s; I maestri di Roma, 1991, 4–156 passim, 1040–42, 1046, for the rolls and professors, 1535 through 1601. Rome had four logicians once, in 1549–50.

34. See Zdekauer, 1977, 192, for the roll of 1492–93; Mondolfo, 1897, for the roll of 1500–1501; Minnucci and Košuta, 1989, 407, 412, 415, for various rolls 1537–38 through 1541–42, and 508–10 for the careers of some logic professors; Cascio Pratilli, 1975, 175–88 passim, for various rolls 1563–64 through 1589–90; Marrara, 1970, 229–49 passim, for rolls 1589–90 through 1600–1601; and Prunai, 1959, 155–56, for some additional names of logicians of the 1560s and 1570s.

35. Marrara, 1970, 125, and Cascio Pratilli, 1975, 87.

36. Marrara, 1970, 49 plus 237, 240, 244, 247, 248, for examples of use of the rule, and Cascio Pratilli, 1975, 88 n. 43.

37. See Cannavale, 1980, 43–81 passim and 86–87; Filangieri di Candida, 1924, 185–86; and Cortese, 1924, 334–35.

38. See Nicolini, 1961, 149, for the roll of 1443–44, and Ermini, 1971, 234–35.

the low average range.[39] At Catania, natural philosophy and logic were a combined position until 1485, when logic became a separate professorship.[40] A professor taught both logic and another subject, often theology, in the early years of the University of Macerata. A separate professorship of logic existed by the 1580s. Salerno had a professor of logic (teaching Aristotle's *Posterior Analytics*) in 1592. Messina had a single professor of logic in the late sixteenth century, as did Parma in the early seventeenth century. None of the logicians at these universities were known scholars.

Because logic was a preparatory subject imparting the methodological training needed for the study of natural philosophy, medicine, and law, universities had a significant number of logicians. But logic did not enjoy high status or earn handsome salaries for its professors. Some universities (Bologna, Ferrara, Pisa, and Siena) awarded the post to recent graduates who were expected to teach logic briefly before moving up to natural philosophy and medicine or departing the university. A few universities (Pavia, Rome, and Turin) relied on long-term appointees. The number of logicians in the arts faculties declined slightly by 1600 in several universities.

TEACHING AND RESEARCH

Medieval logic consisted initially of Aristotle's *Categories* and *De interpretatione* along with Porphyry's *Isagoge;* the three were collectively called the "Old Logic" (Logica vetus). Aristotle's *Prior Analytics, Posterior Analytics, Topics,* and *Sophistici elenchi,* collectively known as the "New Logic" (Logica nova), became available in the twelfth century. Medieval scholars worked over this material and prepared textbooks, the most famous of which was Peter of Spain's *Tractatus* (also called *Summule logicales*), probably written in the 1230s. But there were numerous other developments in an era enamored of logic.[41]

Italian universities inherited this logical program at the dawn of the Renaissance. The 1405 statutes of the University of Bologna decreed that the logicians were expected to lecture on all the above texts of the Old and New Logic, plus the *Liber sex principiorum* of Gilbert of Poitiers, over a three-year period. In addition, they were to teach the *Tractatus* of Peter of Spain, with the exception of the section on fallacies, for which Thomas Aquinas's *De fallaciis* should be substituted.[42]

But just as these statutes appeared, Italian logic changed as a result of the

---

39. See Vallauri, 1970, 1:135–39; Chiaudano, 1972b, 87–117 passim; Chiaudano, 1972a, 161–73 passim. No logicians have turned up in the few records of the fifteenth century. Bellone, 1986.

40. Catalano, 1934, 24–26, 83.

41. There is an enormous bibliography on medieval logic. Start with the articles in *CHLMP.*

42. Malagola, 1966, 251; with corrections by Dallari, 1888–1924, 2:xiv–xv. The *Book of Six Principles* was a widely used textbook in logic. Thomas's work was *De fallaciis ad quosdam nobiles artistas* (1244–45), written when the author was about twenty years old and a student. Based on Peter of Spain's *Fallaciae maiores,* it examines fourteen kinds of syllogistic errors to be found in sophistical argumentation. Weisheipl, 1974, 34–35, 386.

invasion of the "Britanni," that is, logicians and natural philosophers, especially at Merton College, Oxford, who flourished in the second quarter of the fourteenth century and later. They included Thomas Bradwardine (c. 1295–1349), Walter Burley (or Burleigh, c. 1275–1344/45), Richard Feribrigge (or Ferrybridge, fl. 1360s), William Heytesbury (before 1313–72/73), Ralph Strode (fl. 1360s), Richard Swineshead (or Swyneshed, fl. 1340–55), and Roger Swineshead (d. c. 1365). They were also called the "Oxford Calculators" for their work in kinematics. They set the dominant program of Scholastic logic until 1500, and beyond that date in some parts of Europe.[43]

Italian mendicant friars who studied at Oxford from 1340 to 1380 brought the works of the Oxford logicians to Italy. Manuscript evidence documents the presence of their works in Padua, Bologna, Florence, and Pisa, especially in monastic houses of study.[44] English logic entered Italian universities by the end of the fourteenth century. One Angelo da Fossombrone taught Heytesbury's two most influential works, the *Regulae solvendi sophismata* and *Sophismata,* at the University of Bologna in 1395–96. Clearly a follower of the "Britanni," he wrote several logical works, including a commentary on part of Heytesbury's *Regulae.*[45] Paul of Venice then codified and spread English logic through his teaching and textbooks.

Fifteenth-century professors of logic in Italian universities taught the works of Paul of Venice, the English logicians, and the Aristotelian texts, as seen through the eyes of the Britanni. At Padua, Gaetano da Thiene, a disciple of Paul of Venice, wrote commentaries on the works of Feribrigge, Heytesbury, and Strode.[46] At Perugia in 1443–44, the logician taught Aristotle's *Posterior Analytics* in the morning and the "Old Logic" and Paul of Venice (presumably the *Logica parva*) in the afternoon.[47] Fra Giovanni Dolce da Venezia (d. 1499), a Carmelite, did the same at the University of Pisa from 1473 until his death. According to the funeral eulogy, Fra Giovanni composed treatises on, and undoubtedly taught, the *Logica parva* of Paul of Venice, Walter Burley, the *Regulae solvendi sophismata* of Heytesbury, and the *Posterior Analytics* of Aristotle.[48]

The 1496 statutes of the faculty of arts of the University of Padua codified this

---

43. While there is much bibliography, Ashworth and Spade, 1992, is an excellent short survey. Lawn, 1993, offers a good survey of the rise and decline of Oxonion logic across Europe.

44. See Siraisi, 1973, 62–64; Courtenay, 1982; and the other studies in Maierù, 1982, and Lawn, 1993, 54–63.

45. "M. Angellus de Foresinfraneo [*sic*] ellectus ad dictam lecturam Loyce. Et teneatur legere sophystarias et regullas Hesberi et Sophysmata Hesberi." Dallari, 1888–1924, 4: *Aggiunte,* 19 (quote), 22, 23. *Hesberus* was a common Latin version of Heytesbury in Italy. Angelo da Fossombrone taught natural philosophy (1397–99) and then the same subject at Padua (1400–1402). Nothing else is known about his life. See Leonardi, 1961; Federici Vescovini, 1982; and Lawn, 1993, 59–60.

46. Vasoli, 1981, 45–47.

47. Nicolini, 1961, 149.

48. "Compose in dicta facultà Sopra la loichetta di Paulo Veneto; Sopra Burleo; Sopra la Posteriora; Sopra le Regole d'Entisbero et circa quatordici questione molte risolute et artificate." Eulogy from a convent archival record as quoted by Verde, 1973–94, 2:380–85 (quotation on 384). The book of "Fourteen Questions" has not been identified. See also Fioravanti, 1993, 279–82.

curriculum by naming the texts that the holders of the new post in sophisms had to teach.[49] They were the "Logic" (probably the *Logica parva*) of Paul of Venice, the *Consequentiae* of Ralph Strode along with the *Dubia* on that text of Paul of Pergola, and the *Regulae solvendi sophismata* of William of Heytesbury, which had just been printed in Pavia (1481), as well as in Venice (1491 and 1494).[50] English logic dominated Italian universities.

But early humanists rejected English logic and ridiculed the Oxford logicians. "I britanni" became "i barbari britanni" (barbarous Brits) for the humanists. The humanists saw late medieval logic in general, and British logic in particular, as a useless exercise contributing nothing to learning. Petrarch set the tone between 1364 and 1366: "Dialecticians arise these days who are not only ignorant but insane, and like an army of black ants from the recesses of some rotten oak they burst forth to plunder all the fields of true learning. They condemn Plato and Aristotle, they ridicule Socrates and Phythagoras. And this they do, good God, with what foolish authorities!"[51] He also objected to the fact that medieval logicians treated their subject as an end in itself, rather than as a means toward further knowledge. Coluccio Salutati and Leonardo Bruni added numerous equally colorful denunciations. The humanists particularly enjoyed ridiculing the names of the British logicians, which sounded strange to Italian ears: "Tisbero" for Heytesbury, "Ferabrich" for Feribrigge, and so on.[52] Later humanists joined the chorus of condemnation.

The humanists' objections were broad and fundamental. They believed that late medieval logicians treated the technical problems and elaborate terminology of the discipline as ends in themselves. Logic, in their view, contributed nothing to a humanistic education of eloquence, good morality, and civic responsibility. Pier Paolo Vergerio criticized universities for paying too much attention to logic, and not enough to moral training, at about the same time (c. 1388) that he taught logic at Bologna.[53] The humanists objected to the logicians' "barbarous" Latin, to their metalanguage full of technical terms. And they objected to the logicians' focus on medieval works at the expense of ancient texts.

Lorenzo Valla offered an alternative in his *Dialectica*. He drastically reduced the scope of medieval logic, made it a minor part of rhetoric, and called for a return to the rhetorical approach of Cicero and Quintilian, which sought to persuade and convince by a variety of "inventions" or devices. For Valla, the highly

49. Facciolati, 1978, pt. 2:114, 118–19.

50. Paul of Pergola (c. 1380–1455) taught at the Scuola di Rialto in Venice (a state-sponsored lectureship of Aristotelian philosophy) from 1421 to 1454. He had studied with Paul of Venice and was a strong adherent of the English logicians. Strode's *Consequentiae* and Paul's *Dubia* were printed together at Venice in 1477, 1481, 1484, 1488, and 1493. On the Scuola di Rialto and Paul of Pergola, see B. Nardi, 1971, esp. 18–29, and *CHRP*, 830.

51. *Rerum Senilium,* bk. 5, letter 2, as translated in Petrarch, 1992, 2:163–64.

52. The fundamental study is Garin, 1969, 43–79, and esp. 139–66. See also Vasoli, 1968a, 9–27; Gilbert, 1971; Perreiah, 1982; and L. Jardine, 1988, 176–78, which includes an often quoted passage from Bruni attacking English logicians by name. See these same authorities for the following paragraph.

53. McManamon, 1996, 27–28.

technical classification and investigation of different kinds of proof of late medieval logic were simply irrelevant.[54] But humanistic attacks did not persuade
fifteenth-century Italian university logicians to change their ways. So far as is
known, they never taught Valla's *Dialectica* or any other humanistic or rhetorical
logic text in the fifteenth and sixteenth centuries.[55]

But change did come, initially through the typically humanist desire to study
Aristotle's logical works in new Latin translations meeting humanistic standards.
Throughout the Middle Ages scholars used Latin translations of Aristotle's logical
works prepared by Boethius between 510 and 522.[56] This finally changed when
the Byzantine émigré John Argyropoulos (c. 1415–87) made new translations.
Argyropoulos taught logic (1456–57), then natural philosophy (1458–71), at the
University of Florence. He translated Aristotle's *De interpretatione, Prior Analytics,
Posterior Analytics,* and *Categories,* plus the *Isagoge* of Porphyry, between about
1456 and the early 1460s.[57] Aristotle's logical works appeared in Greek in the
Aristotle edition published by Aldo Manuzio in 1495–98. This edition also
bestowed the collective title of *Organon* to the six logical texts of Aristotle and
imposed on them a chronological ordering that may not be correct.

The humanistic impulse to produce better Latin translations based on the
original Greek gathered strength in the sixteenth century. A junior logician at
Padua played a key role, and other Paduan logicians contributed to a large collective effort. Giovanni Francesco Burana of Verona (c. 1475/80–after 1503), about
whom little is known, obtained his arts doctorate at Padua in 1500 and began to
teach logic in the same year.[58] He continued to teach logic at Padua through
1503, then abandoned an academic career in order to become a physician in

54. Valla began working on a book about dialectic possibly while teaching at the University of
Pavia in 1432–33 and completed the third version in the last year of his life, 1457. He gave the three
versions of the work different names. *Dialecticae disputationes,* a title given by a sixteenth-century
editor, is most commonly used today. The critical edition goes under the name *Repastinatio dialectice et
philosophie;* see Valla, 1982. Monfasani and Trinkaus (see below) prefer the simpler *Dialectica.* There is
a large literature on it, of which only a few items are mentioned here: Vasoli, 1968a, 28–77; Monfasani, 1984 and 1988, 191; L. Jardine, 1988, 178–81; Monfasani, 1990b; and Mack, 1993, 22–116.
The *Dialectica* also included a general attack on Aristotelian natural philosophy; see Trinkaus, 1993.

55. George of Trebizond's *Isagoge dialectica* (published c. 1440) and Rudolf Agricola's *De inventione
dialectica* (begun when Agricola was in Italy, completed in 1479, and printed in 1515) were much
more influential in northern Europe than in Italy. On the contrasting northern European diffusion,
but lack of influence in Italy, of the logical works of Valla, George of Trebizond, and Agricola, see
Monfasani, 1976, 328–37; Monfasani, 1984, 193–94; Monfasani, 1988, 191, 197; Monfasani, 1990b,
191–92; Lawn, 1993; and Mack, 1993, 15, 114–16, 256–302.

56. Dod, 1982, 53–54, 74–75.

57. Garin, 1947–50, 82–87, 99, for the translations. For further information and bibliography on
Argyropoulos, see Bigi, 1962a; Field, 1988, 55 and passim; *CHRP,* 808; and Monfasani, 1990a, 60–
63. Argyropoulos earlier taught at the University of Padua (1441–44) and later taught at Rome
(1471–77), Florence again (1477–81), and Rome again (1481–87).

58. This and the following paragraph are based on Facciolati, 1978, pt. 2:115, pt. 3:291, 302, 330,
353, 357; Riccobono, 1980, sig. G3ʳ; Vasoli, 1963; Risse, 1964, 225, 229–34; Stabile, 1972; Lohr,
1974b, 255–56, 284; Cranz, 1976a, 124, 126–27; Schmitt, 1979b, 129, 132, 136, 138–39, 141–42.

Verona, and apparently died soon after. Remarkably skilled in languages, Burana possessed competence in Greek, Hebrew, Arabic, and Syriac. He prepared, but did not publish, new Greek-to-Latin translations of Aristotle's *Prior Analytics* and *Posterior Analytics* with his own commentaries, plus translations from Arabic of four of Averroës's commentaries on the *Prior Analytics* and *Posterior Analytics*. At his death, Burana left his works in the care of a pupil, with instructions that they be published.

The pupil was Gerolamo Bagolino of Verona (b. 1470/80; d. after 1535), who taught natural philosophy at Padua (1517–24), then practical medicine (1524–35). Bagolino published Burana's works with additions and emendations in 1524. Burana's translation of the *Prior Analytics* and *Posterior Analytics* and of Averroës's commentaries eventually became part of the great eleven-volume Aristotle and Averroës Latin edition published by the Giunti press of Venice between 1550 and 1552.[59] Gerolamo Bagolino largely organized the edition; his son, Giovanni Francesco Bagolino (who taught logic at Padua in 1533–34) and Marco Oddi (d. 1589, who taught logic at Padua in the late 1540s and theoretical medicine later), edited and completed the edition after Gerolamo died.[60] Burana's new translations, with corrections by father and son Bagolino, of the Aristotelian and Averroistic logical works were often reprinted. As mentioned above, Bernardino Tomitano added notes and additional commentary to the 1562 edition. Thus, a group of University of Padua logicians of humanist outlook produced new translations from the Greek of Aristotelian logical works, new translations of Averroës's commentaries on these works, plus their own commentaries.

This scholarly activity began to produce change in the teaching of logic. Angelo Poliziano, professor of rhetoric and poetry at the Florentine branch of the University of Pisa, anticipated the change. Poliziano taught all six parts of Aristotle's *Organon,* plus Porphyry's *Isagoge* and the *Liber sex principiorum* of Gilbert of Poitiers in the last three years of his life, 1491–94. His prolusions to the lectures show that he approached logic rhetorically and from a humanist perspective.[61]

Poliziano's approach to logic departed significantly from the norm. Poliziano lectured on Aristotle, rather than on late medieval logical texts. He did not like the "acrobatics" of the "sophists," and he criticized such "barbarous moderns" as Burley, Heytesbury, William of Ockham, and Strode. Poliziano preferred Aristotle himself, preferably in Greek, with the Greek commentators of late antiquity such as Theophrastus, Alexander of Aphrodisias, Themistius, Simplicius, and John Philoponus as his guides. He placed logic in a broader framework than discussion of the significance of terms. Logical arguments and proofs, including probable arguments, were only useful parts of a broader art of discourse, in his

59. The 1550–52 Aristotle-Averroës edition (with the logical works in volume 1) is described in Camerini, 1962–63, pt. 1:382–86.

60. The sources differ on when Marco Oddi taught logic. Facciolati, 1978, pt. 3:291, gives 1549–52; Riccobono, 1980, sig. G3ʳ, gives 1546–48.

61. For the texts on which he lectured, see Branca, 1983, 86 n. 22. For an analysis of his prolusions, see Vasoli, 1968a, 116–31, and L. Jardine, 1988, 194–95.

view. Finally, Poliziano allied logic with rhetoric, although it is not clear if he was influenced by Lorenzo Valla.

Logic continued to evolve. Early-sixteenth-century Italian university logic, as seen in the logical works of Agostino Nifo, presented a mixed face to the world. Nifo never taught logic, so far as is known, but he did write commentaries on five of the six works of Aristotle's *Organon* and a textbook, the *Dialectica ludicra,* published in 1520. Strongly influenced by Lorenzo Valla's *Dialectica,* Nifo's work manifested a humanistic approach toward logic. Nifo focused on Aristotle, rec- ognized the usefulness of the Greek commentators, and had sharp things to say about medieval logicians. In humanist fashion, he broadened the perspective of logic to embrace arguments more appropriate to public oratory. He discussed the syllogism and discarded much of the more technical aspect of medieval logic (suppositions, *insolubilia, consequentiae,* etc.). But his work also relied on medieval authors and repeated much medieval material.[62]

University logicians in the middle and the second half of the sixteenth century continued to move away from the formal, technical logic of the late Middle Ages. For example, Bernardino Tomitano concentrated on Aristotle's logical works and less on late medieval logical authors.[63] These scholars had the linguistic skills to consult the Greek texts of Aristotle and the ancient Greek commentaries; they read Averroës's commentaries. They increasingly concentrated on method as found in Aristotle. The rolls show the change: professors of logic at Bologna, Padua, and Rome taught the *Posterior Analytics,* which contained Aristotle's major discussion of method, in the last third of the sixteenth century. For example, the Bolognese logicians taught books 1 and 2 in alternate years during the late 1580s and the 1590s. Even though logicians doubtlessly went beyond this text in their teaching, the emphasis was significant.[64]

Most important, Italian university logicians, especially those at Padua, directed their attention to broader issues, such as the nature of logic itself and the principles of demonstration. They explored scientific method, what might be called the epistemology of the sciences. They queried how researchers might progress from sense evidence to demonstrative proof. They investigated the claims of mathe- matical certainty and explored the logical validity of astronomical hypotheses.[65]

62. For Nifo's career, works, and additional bibliography, see Mahoney, 1981; Lohr, 1979, 532– 39; and *CHRP,* 828. The differing analyses of Ashworth, 1976, and L. Jardine, 1981 and 1988, 195– 97, should be read together.

63. On Tomitano's logic, see Riondato, 1960; Simionato, 1973; and Davi Daniele, 1983; plus the brief discussions in Crescini, 1965, 150–53; Vasoli, 1968b, 293–97 and passim; and Vasoli, 1981, 63–64.

64. For the teaching of the *Posterior Analytics* in Bolognese rolls, see Dallari, 1888–1924, 2:234, 237, 241, 245, 249, and so on; for Padua, see AAUP, Inventario 1320, rolls of 1568–69, 1569–70, and 1594–95; and F. 651, f. 302ʳ, roll of 1584–85; for Rome, see *I maestri di Roma,* 1991, 52, 61, 66, 76, 87, 99, 115 (various rolls 1567–68 through 1579–80).

65. N. Jardine, 1988, is a good summary of these developments. There is not space to discuss other important writers on logic, such as Marco Antonio Zimara (1460–1532; see Antonaci, 1971–78) and Girolamo Balduino (d. c. 1550; see Papuli, 1967). Risse (1964, 216–307) and Crescini (1965, chs. 5 and 6) offer good surveys of Italian developments, while Vasoli, (1981, 47–73) provides an overview of the Paduan logicians.

DEMONSTRATIVE REGRESS

Beginning with Agostino Nifo in the early sixteenth century, professors of logic and some in natural philosophy began to discuss demonstrative regress, a logical technique permitting the scholar to reason from an observed effect (fact) to its proximate cause and then to reason back (regress) from the cause to the effect where the reasoning began.[66] It was a procedure of rational demonstration which offered a means of drawing truthful and convincing conclusions from physical evidence, always within an Aristotelian context. Demonstrative regress was basically a method of reasoning enabling the scholar to move from phenomena grasped by the senses to universal principles and back again.

Demonstrative regress began with some statements in Aristotle's logical works, notably the *Posterior Analytics* I, 13, but also the *Prior Analytics* II, 5, 8, 20, and *Topics* II, 2. Further statements are found in the *Physics* I, 1; *Nicomachean Ethics* I, 2, 3; and *Metaphysics* V, 11.[67] Aristotle in the *Posterior Analytics* made a distinction between demonstration "of the fact" (*quia*) and demonstration "of the reasoned fact" (*propter quid*). The fact is known by sense experience: one can see that the moon is round. The "reasoned fact" is an explanation of the cause: the fact that the moon is round explains that it has phases. But one can also return from the cause to the fact: the moon has phases because it is round. Aristotle also commented on the appropriateness of demonstrative regress for different sciences.

However, Aristotle's brief remarks raised questions. How does the scholar progress and regress? By what logical method can he move between the fact and the reasoned fact? To which forms of scientific knowledge could demonstrative regress best be applied? Averroës, Peter of Abano, and Paul of Venice, among others, discussed the issue. The natural philosophers Pietro Pomponazzi and Agostino Nifo weighed in. Demonstrative regress and related matters became a focus of intense discussion in the late sixteenth century, especially after the Greek text of Aristotle became available and scholars possessed the necessary Greek skills to use it. Professors of logic at Padua, notably Girolamo Balduino and Bernardino Tomitano, took the lead. The effort to understand Aristotle became an inquiry into scientific method.

Jacopo Zabarella was the ablest and the most influential of the new logicians who concentrated on method. He wrote several treatises on Aristotle's *Posterior Analytics*. Most important, he wrote nine short works on logic, including *De regressu*, which he published together in 1578 as *Opera logica*. Zabarella also wrote commentaries on Aristotle's *Physics*, the *Meteorology*, and *De anima*, plus several works in natural philosophy.[68]

66. This definition is closely modeled on those of N. Jardine (1988, 686) and Wallace (1995, 78).

67. For what follows, see Wallace, 1995, and Wallace, 1996, 300–308.

68. There is a large bibliography on Zabarella, of which only part can be listed here. For this and the following two paragraphs, see Risse, 1964, 278–93; Crescini, 1965, 168–88; Vasoli, 1968b, 308–42; Poppi, 1972, notably 131–68 on the nature of logic; especially Mikkeli, 1992; and Ventrice, 1992–93. Gilbert (1960, 167–73), N. Jardine (1988, 689–93), and Copenhaver and Schmitt (1992, 117–21) offer good succinct summaries of key points. Several studies in *Method and Order* (1997)

Zabarella continued and expanded the approach of Tomitano. Logic was not an end in itself or a skill to resolve linguistic puzzles with metaphysical overtones, in his view. Rather, Zabarella saw logic as an instrumental or functional discipline enabling the user to acquire knowledge in the sciences. He believed that this was Aristotle's essential goal for logic. Logic provided a method of permitting the acquisition of new knowledge from principles or evidence already known. Logic enabled the natural philosopher, medical scholar, or mathematician to move from either sense evidence or first principles to new knowledge and to be certain that he had demonstrated the truth of his conclusions.

In his commentary on the *Posterior Analytics* and in *De regressu,* Zabarella amplified Aristotle's demonstrative regress. He called reasoning from cause to effect the demonstrative method. Demonstrative method, in which causes were better known than effects, was basically one of composition, which might also be called synthesis. Demonstrative method could be found in a perfect science, such as mathematics. For example, a mathematical principle or formula, of which one is certain, can produce numerous effects, that is, individual results.

The other, less sure method was resolutive, which was reasoning from effect to cause and might also be called analysis. The scholar starts from effects, because causes were generally not known. He seeks causes from their effects in order, later, to know the effects from their causes.[69] It was a method for getting behind effects in order to learn causes. It could move from sense experience to the level of scientific knowledge.

Zabarella elaborated on the resolutive, or analytic, method of discovery. There were two forms of resolutive method. The first was demonstration from effects, which could enable the scholar to discover objects that are obscure and hidden. The other resolutive method was demonstrative induction, that is, reasoning from particular facts to a general principle. The scholar should examine carefully selected examples until the mind noticed essential connections, despite different particulars. Even with confusion between which is cause and which is effect, mental examination led to consideration of the cause. Eventually the mind removes the confusion. Now the regression can move from a conjectural argument to a true demonstration. Finally, the whole process of scientific knowing can include both demonstration of the fact (*quia*) and of the reasoned fact (*propter quid*). Resolution was a weaker form of method than demonstration. But it could be used to uncover principles that were otherwise not demonstrative. Resolution was a typical and useful method to be used in the natural sciences, because the scholar had to start from effects in order to discover causes.

The new developments in Aristotelian logic and especially the discussion of demonstrative regress resonated widely, because they dealt with scientific method. Scholars could use the new logic as a tool in their investigations and as a

---

discuss Zabarella at length or in passing. For his biography, works, and natural philosophy, see Di Napoli, 1963, 376–79; Lohr, 1982, 233–42; Schmitt, 1969, 1981d, and 1983c, 10–11, 17–18, 31, 47, 56, 102, 148; Kessler, 1988, 530–34; Michael, 1993; and *CHRP,* 841, for more bibliography.

   69. Again I am following closely Wallace, 1995, 90–93, and Wallace, 1996, 301–3.

way of persuading others of the truth of their assertions. It had the greatest impact in the investigation of the natural world but also touched mathematics and medicine. Aristotelian logic as explained and interpreted by sixteenth-century Italian logicians had considerable influence on the young Galileo Galilei. He learned of demonstrative regress through his study of the manuscript summaries of courses in natural philosophy taught by several Jesuits at the Collegio Romano in the 1580s and from his professors of natural philosophy, especially Francesco Buonamici and Jacopo Mazzoni, at the University of Pisa, during his student days (1581–85) and as a junior professor of mathematics (1589–92). He used demonstrative regress in an innovative way.[70]

For Galilei the key was the regress, the examination of the proposed cause. This was the process of testing, investigating, and eliminating possibilities in order to determine which cause was necessary wherever the effect was present. Galilei used *experimentum* (test or experiment) to determine regress. This was a physical test, such as dropping objects of different weight to see if they arrived at the ground at the same time in his examination of the motion of falling bodies in *De motu* (c. 1590). The action tested the proposed cause, that is, his theory that two dropped objects of different weights will hit the ground at the same time. The test demonstrated the reasoned fact. This was demonstrative regress, reasoning from the effect back to the cause or basic principle. Of course, other elements, above all his reliance on mathematics, contributed to Galilei's scientific investigations, and he later rejected Aristotle in his new science of mechanics. Nevertheless, Aristotelian logic as developed by Zabarella and others played a role in Galilei's early scientific work in the period before 1610.

The logic of Zabarella and others in Italian universities of the late sixteenth century was a logic of scientific method. It was not the logic of Paul of Venice or the humanistic rhetorical logic of Rudolph Agricola, which was so influential in northern Europe. Rather, it was a renewed Aristotelian logic of scientific epistemology appropriate to the needs of students and professors in universities dominated by Aristotelian natural philosophy and medicine. Zabarella was not a precursor to modern experimental science of the seventeenth century. He was a thorough Aristotelian who filled in the gaps of Aristotelian science.[71]

The logic of which Zabarella was the leading proponent usefully explored the methods of reasoning to be employed in natural philosophy, metaphysics, medicine, and mathematics. It helped to defend the autonomy of natural philosophy, which focused on a variety of scientific issues, from metaphysics, increasingly linked to theology in the sixteenth century. Zabarella's scientific method differentiated between natural philosophy and medicine by viewing the latter as an empirical and productive art lacking demonstration of causes. Professors of natural philosophy, who felt threatened by the claims of medicine based on anatomical research to be a true science, found this support useful.[72] Scholars in Italy and

70. The following is based on Wallace, 1992 and 1998, which summarize more detailed studies.
71. This is a point established by Schmitt, 1969, esp. 123–38, and often echoed in the literature.
72. Mikkeli makes a good point: "Moreover, the interminable discussion of the methodology of

Europe read, praised, and discussed the work of Zabarella and others until the gradual demise of Aristotelian science in the second half of the seventeenth century.

CONCLUSION

Renaissance universities mostly viewed logic as a propaedeutic discipline. Students needed to acquire dialectical skills as tools for study and research in other areas. Positive and negative institutional consequences flowed from this view. On the one hand, logic was essential to the curriculum. Hence, every university had logicians, occasionally up to a half dozen. But the position was often relegated to poorly paid, short-term junior scholars. Padua, whose faculty boasted the most important logicians throughout the Renaissance, was a major exception.

Logic, the quintessential medieval Scholastic discipline, underwent great change between 1400 and 1600. Late medieval terminist logic, as summarized by Paul of Venice, flourished in fifteenth-century Italian universities despite humanist attacks. But if humanist criticism failed to change the logic curriculum, the application of humanistic skills to the basic texts of logic eventually brought about change in the content. Sixteenth-century Italian university logicians increasingly turned away from late medieval logic.[73] They paid attention to the original Greek of Aristotle's texts and prepared better Latin translations. They chose to follow ancient Greek commentaries rather than Heytesbury and Paul of Venice. But unlike some of their counterparts in northern Europe, they did not turn to rhetorical logic, as found in Rudolph Agricola's *De inventione dialectica*. Rather, the ablest sixteenth-century logicians used their new skills and broader perspective to transform logic into an investigation of the nature of scientific method, always within an Aristotelian universe.

---

arts and sciences in the sixteenth century may be seen as an attempt to defend the scientific status of either the recently founded autonomous sciences or, on the other hand, the empirically based productive arts. The discussions of orders and methods, resolutions, compositions and *regressus* are, therefore, not merely further elaborations of an old Aristotelian tradition, but also expressions of opinions in a lively debate concerning the changing relationships between various arts and sciences in sixteenth-century Italian universities." Mikkeli, 1997, 228.

73. It is telling that the only Italian logician discussed in Ashworth's survey of traditional (i.e., medieval) logic in the Renaissance was Crisostomo Javelli (1470–1538), a Dominican friar who never taught in a university. Ashworth, 1988, 162, 167–68, 170; Lohr, 1977, 730–33; *CHRP,* 822.

CHAPTER 8

Natural Philosophy

atural philosophy meant science in Italian Renaissance universities. The approach differed from the modern conception. Now science is commonly divided into life sciences and physical sciences. Further subdivisions include psychology, biology, botany, and zoology in the life sciences, and physics, chemistry, and geology in the physical sciences. Each modern scientific discipline examines a part of reality or the same reality according to its disciplinary approach.[1] By contrast, the Italian Renaissance university taught aspects of both the life sciences and physical sciences as Aristotelian natural philosophy without subdivisions. They had professors of natural philosophy, rather than professors of life sciences, physical sciences, or individual subjects such as psychology and physics. Renaissance natural philosophy excluded metaphysics and moral philosophy, which had their own professors and were considered less important.[2]

Italian universities strongly emphasized natural philosophy. It claimed the second highest number of professors in the faculty of arts, trailing only medical theory by 1 or 2, in large and medium-sized universities. Bologna had an average of 5 professors of natural philosophy from 1400 until the 1560s, when the number

1. In practice there may be considerable overlap between some subdivisions.

2. At the beginning of the fifteenth century a university might appoint little-known figures to teach two philosophical subjects. For example, Baldassare da Cesena taught both natural philosophy and metaphysics at the University of Bologna in 1406–7, and Agostino de Codio and Niccolò da Faba taught natural philosophy and moral philosophy there in 1406–7, again in 1410–11, and possibly in the intervening years. Dallari, 1888–1924, 4:*Aggiunte,* 25, 28, 30, 31, 32. However, it appears from the wording of some of these rolls that the university appointed the professors to teach two distinct subjects, rather than a mixture of two kinds of philosophy. It is likely that they taught one or more texts for natural philosophy in one half of the year and a different text or texts for moral philosophy in the other half. Professorships teaching two philosophical subjects soon disappeared, except in the tiniest universities. Universities considered natural philosophy, moral philosophy, and metaphysics to be separate subjects to be taught by different professors throughout the fifteenth and sixteenth centuries.

rose to 8 and occasionally 10.[3] The majority of universities (Ferrara, Padua, Pavia, Perugia, Pisa after 1543, Rome, Siena, and Turin) boasted 3 to 5 natural philosophers. Florence and Naples had 2; Messina, Parma, and Salerno 1 or 2. Even the tiny universities of Catania and Macerata had a single professor of natural philosophy, who occasionally also taught logic.[4] The number of natural philosophers was about half of all medical professors combined (medical theory, medical practice, surgery, anatomy, and medical botany). Natural philosophy did not decline in importance in the Renaissance but held a larger fraction of the faculty in the last quarter of the sixteenth century.

High salaries manifested its prestige. The first ordinary professor of natural philosophy normally received the highest nonmedical salary in the faculty of arts. The exceptional natural philosopher enjoyed a salary equal to, and occasionally higher than, the best-paid professor of medicine. Pietro Pomponazzi, for example, received the highest salary in the faculty of arts, and the second highest overall, in the University of Bologna in 1523–24.[5]

Italian universities emphasized natural philosophy more strongly than did universities elsewhere in Europe, because they viewed it as a preparation for, and a complement to, medical studies. The link between philosophy and medicine began in the ancient world. Despite some differences, Aristotle, the Hippocratic corpus, and Galen shared a common scientific-medical outlook. Hippocrates and Galen accepted much of Aristotle's analysis of the world, of animals, and of humans, and believed that natural philosophy played an important role in the education of a physician. Aristotle, in turn, had an intense interest in medical matters and wrote medical works that survive only in fragments. The symbiosis continued in the training of physicians in ancient Alexandria, in the medieval Arab world, and at the school of Salerno from the late eleventh century through the early thirteenth. When medicine became the most influential part of the arts curriculum in medieval Italian universities, key early figures in the development of the curriculum insisted on the link between Aristotelian natural philosophy and medicine. Medical men in particular reiterated the importance of natural philosophy for the good training of physicians. Philosophers accepted the link, but also saw their discipline as autonomous, with its own issues and quests.[6]

Students studied natural philosophy to acquire an understanding of the physical world as the foundation for the study of medicine, especially medical theory.

---

3. For example, Bologna had 10 natural philosophers in a faculty of 48 artists in 1600–1601. Dallari, 1888–1924, vols. 1 and 2 passim, and 2:269–72 for the 1600–1601 roll. Whenever rolls at Bologna or elsewhere listed only "philosophy," instead of "natural philosophy," this meant natural philosophy. Moral philosophy and metaphysics were separate professorships, almost always with their own names.

4. See Chapters 1–4.

5. Pomponazzi received a salary of 2,100 Bolognese lire, trailing only Carlo Ruini, who taught civil law for 4,320 lire. Another civil legist ranked third, earning 1,000 lire, followed by a canonist and two professors of theoretical medicine at 600 lire. ASB, Assunteria di Studio, Bu. 92, fiscal roll of 1523–24, no pag.

6. Schmitt, 1985, explains the philosophers' point of view very well. For the medical perspective, see Lockwood, 1951, 4–9; Bylebyl, 1985b; and Siraisi, 1990, 2–3, 12, 67, 79–85, 100, 146, and 191.

The practical art (*ars*) of medicine depended on the scientific knowledge (*scientia*) of physical phenomena. Renaissance natural philosophers sometimes animadverted on the statement "Where the natural philosopher finishes, there begins the physician."[7] University statutes codified this principle.

At the same time, natural philosophy was an autonomous discipline. University statutes stipulating the texts to be taught and to be used for degree examinations made this clear. Many, perhaps most, professors of natural philosophy pursued research topics lacking relevance to medicine; they demonstrated the independence of their discipline through their scholarship. Probably most professors of natural philosophy did not see their teaching as limited to the preparation of future physicians.

ARISTOTELIAN CURRICULAR TEXTS

Natural philosophers taught and commented on a range of Aristotle's scientific and philosophical texts. The vast scope of Aristotle's knowledge, along with the new availability of Latin translations of his works at the birth of universities, had made him the foundation of scientific learning. Oxford and Paris planted Aristotle into the curriculum in the thirteenth century, and the rest of Europe followed. The Aristotelian curricular texts defined the content of natural philosophy at the beginning of the fifteenth century.

The Bolognese statutes of 1405 prescribed the texts to be taught for natural philosophy.[8] The ordinary professors were obliged to teach a three-year cycle of Aristotle's works. In the first year they taught the entire text of Aristotle's *Physics,* plus book 1 of Aristotle's *De generatione et corruptione,* which dealt with elements and compounds. In the second year they taught Aristotle's *De caelo et mundo,* which examined the causes and properties of the heavens, plus the *Meterology,* which dealt with atmospheric science. They also taught Aristotle's *De sensu et sensibilis.* In the third year the ordinary professors of natural philosophy were to teach book 1 of Aristotle's *De anima* "except the errors found therein."[9] *De anima*

7. This version (in Latin, *Ubi desinit physicus, ibi medicus incipit*) comes from Simone Simoni (1532–1602) and is quoted by Schmitt, 1985, 12. However, the subordinate role of natural philosophy should not be exaggerated. Schmitt (1985, 4) states that "the normal career structure [for professors] was to progress from logic, through natural philosophy, to medicine." Some professors followed this career pattern, but it was not normal. The vast majority of professors of natural philosophy never held professorships of medicine, and the majority of professors of medicine never held professorships of natural philosophy. Ulisse Aldrovandi, the example cited by Schmitt (1985, 274 n. 27), does not prove his point. Aldrovandi taught logic, then the medicinal properties of plants for one year, then natural philosophy, which focused on plants, animals, and fossils, for forty years. He really taught natural history; indeed, Aldrovandi was one of the century's greatest natural scientists.

8. The following is based on the 1405 statutes in Malagola, 1966, 274. Thorndike (1944, 279) provides an English outline summary with one minor error. Cranz (1971) and Cranz and Schmitt (1984) offer a good listing of sixteenth-century printings of Aristotle's works.

9. "Exceptis erroribus primij," Malagola, 1966, 274. One wonders if the alleged errors were the views attributed to Aristotle by Averroës that the world was eternal and that the human soul was mortal. See below, "The Debate on the Immortality of the Intellective Soul."

dealt with the general features of living beings. They were also to teach parts of the *Metaphysics:* the prelude only of book 1, followed by books 2, 5–10, and 12.

The extraordinary professors of natural philosophy also followed a three-year cycle without duplicating the teaching of the ordinary professors. In the first year, the extraordinary professors were obliged to teach book 2 of *De generatione et corruptione,* followed by *De somno et vigilia* (On sleep and wakefulness; part of the *Parva naturalia*), and then the *Physiognomia,* a pseudo-Aristotelian work.[10] In the second year they were to teach the "de substantia orbis" (unidentified, but perhaps part of the pseudo-Aristotelian *De mundo*), plus Aristotle's *De memoria* (Memory and recollection), and *De respiratione* (On breath), both parts of his *Parva naturalia.* In the third year of the cycle, the extraordinary professors were to teach part of book 4 of Aristotle's *Metaphysics,* plus *De longitudine,* and *De motu animalium* (On the motion of animals). The *Parva naturalia* dealt with different organisms, including humans. Hence, the extraordinary professors of natural philosophy provided a program of study which focused on the activities of living beings.

The professors of natural philosophy at Bologna also lectured on additional Aristotelian texts for which they might charge small fees. Many of these dealt with zoology: *De generatione animalium, Historia animalium, De partibus animalium, De motu animalium,* and *De progressu animalium,* the first three of which were sometimes known collectively as *De animalibus.* They also might lecture on the "Ethics" (presumably the *Nicomachean Ethics*), the *Politics,* the pseudo-Aristotelian *Economics* (*Oeconomica*), and the *Rhetoric,* probably because it contains a section (bk. 2, ch. 2) analyzing the emotions, a part of psychology. Natural philosophers were also supposed to teach Aristotle's *Posterior Analytics,* which discussed the methodology of scientific knowledge or demonstration. And they taught logical texts, namely, Aristotle's *Prior Analytics, De sophisticis elenchis,* and the *Liber sex principiorum* of Gilbert of Poitiers.[11]

Despite this smorgasbord of Aristotelian texts, the rolls suggest that professors of natural philosophy increasingly concentrated on the *Physics* and *De anima,* and paid less attention to other works, in the next two hundred years. At the University of Perugia in 1443–44 the ordinary professor of natural philosophy taught *De anima,* and the holiday professor of philosophy taught *De generatione et corruptione.*[12] The 1448 statutes of the University of Turin indicated that degree candidates in philosophy were to be examined on points taken from the *Physics, De anima,* and "de ortu et interitu," another name for *De generatione et corruptione.*[13]

The emphasis on the *Physics* and *De anima* increased in the sixteenth century. By the late sixteenth century Padua had arranged its schedule so that students could hear lectures on all the texts offered by the ordinary and extraordinary professors in three years. In the first year the ordinary professors lectured on *De*

10. Schmitt and Knox (1985, 45–50) list eleven different works with this title.

11. Malagola, 1966, 252; English translation in Thorndike, 1944, 277–78. It is not likely that the *Rhetoric* to which the statutes referred was the pseudo-Aristotelian *Rhetorica ad Alexandrum.*

12. Nicolini, 1961, 149–50.

13. Vallauri, 1970, 1:101.

anima, book 3, and the extraordinary professors on *De anima,* books 1 and 2. In the second year the ordinary professors lectured on the *Physics,* book 8, and the extraordinary professors on the *Physics,* books 1 and 2. In the third year, the ordinary professors lectured on *De generatione et corruptione* and the extraordinary professors on *De caelo et mundo.* The ordinary and extraordinary professors exchanged texts for the next three-year cycle. With this schedule students could also hear a single professor lecture on all the statutory texts in six years. For example, from 1590 through 1629 Cesare Cremonini taught the following texts in a six-year rotation: year one: *De anima,* 3; year two: *Physics,* 8; year three: *De generatione et corruptione;* year four: *De anima,* 1 and 2; year five: *Physics,* 1 and 2; year six: *De caelo.* In the seventh year he began to repeat the cycle.[14]

Bologna in the sixteenth century also concentrated on the *Physics, De caelo et mundo,* and *De anima* in a three-year cycle organized in such a way that ordinary and extraordinary professors did not teach the same texts in the same year. Because Bologna had many more professors than did Padua, some natural philosophers added other texts, especially after the middle of the century. Then the *Meteorology, De generatione et corruptione,* and the *Parva naturalia* appeared regularly along with the *Physics, De caelo et mundo,* and *De anima.*[15]

At the University of Rome the ordinary professors of natural philosophy normally taught Aristotle's *Physics, De anima,* and *De caelo* in the second half of the sixteenth century. Lesser professors of natural philosophy occasionally taught different Aristotelian texts. In 1567–68, the extraordinary professor of natural philosophy, a young scholar teaching without a stipend, taught Aristotle's *De sensu et sensibilis.* In 1579–80 the second ordinary professor of natural philosophy taught book 2 of *De generatione et corruptione,* and the extraordinary professor taught "De motu," which could be either *De motu animalium* or "De motu cordis," the last chapter of *De vita et morte,* both part of the "animal books" of Aristotle.[16] Concentration on the *Physics* and *De anima* meant that issues concerning the physical world and the nature of humans dominated research and lecturing.

GREEK TEXTS AND COMMENTARIES

The traditional Aristotelian texts in new linguistic clothes, accompanied by fresh texts, began to enter the teaching and research of natural philosophy in the 1490s. Some philosophy professors acquired the ability to read Aristotle in Greek. Like the humanists, they criticized medieval Latin translations and commentaries and preferred ancient works in the original language.

14. The clearest explanation is found in Kuhn, 1996, 88–90 n. 5. See also AAUP, Inventario 1320, various faculty of arts roles. The statutes of 1589 made one change: the extraordinary professors were to teach the last four books (5–8) of the *Physics,* instead of just book 8. *Statuta artistarum et medicorum Patavini Gymnasii,* 1589, 68ᵛ. The extent to which this was carried out is not known.

15. Dallari, 1888–1924, vol. 2.

16. See the rolls of 1567–68, 1568–69, 1569–70, 1570–71, 1574–75, 1575–76, and 1579–80 in *I maestri di Roma,* 1991, 53, 55, 61, 63, 67, 69, 77, 79, 88, 91, 100, 104, 116, 117, 118.

The first professor known to teach a natural philosophy text of Aristotle in Greek was the Byzantine émigré Andronicus Callistus of Constantinople (d. c. 1475), one of several who came to Italy at midcentury. In 1458–59 he held an ordinary professorship of Greek at the University of Bologna. Then from 1462 through 1466, Callistus was both ordinary professor of Greek and holiday (*diebus festivis*) lecturer of moral philosophy. He taught a variety of Greek texts, including Aristotle's *Physics*.[17] However, because he was not a professor of natural philosophy, he would not give detailed attention to the *Physics*. His impact on natural philosophy had to be slight. And his students probably lacked the necessary Greek to take full advantage of his lectures. Nevertheless, it was a beginning. John Argyropolous, another Byzantine émigré, taught the *Physics* and *De anima* from the Latin text at the University of Florence from 1456 to 1471. But he did refer to the Greek text now and then.[18] Other Byzantine émigrés teaching Greek or rhetoric in Italian universities began to create new Greek-to-Latin translations of Aristotle's works.[19]

Teaching the natural philosophy texts of Aristotle from the Greek and applying humanistic textual criticism to medieval Latin versions began in earnest at the University of Padua in the 1490s with Francesco Cavalli (after 1450–1540). Nothing is known of his early life and career except that he came from Brescia. In 1492 he became a professor of practical medicine at Padua with a salary of 150 florins. According to a sixteenth-century source, Cavalli began to teach Aristotle in Greek at Padua sometime between 1492 and 1497.[20]

Cavalli made other contributions to Greek Aristotle studies. He published *De numero et ordine partium ac librorum physicae doctrinae Aristotelis* (*GW* 5832, Venice, no date, between 1492 and 1495), the first work of textual criticism on Aristotle. It proposed a "correct" order and structure of the Aristotelian corpus and paid particular attention to the works on animals, plants, and medicine. Cavalli discussed the authenticity of some works, speculated on possible lost works, and referred to ancient Greek commentators. Since no Greek edition of Aristotle had yet appeared in print, Cavalli based his scholarship on manuscript sources. He next collaborated in the monumental *editio princeps* of the Greek Aristotle published by Aldo Manuzio in Venice between 1495 and 1498. The edition's ordering of the works of natural philosophy followed that proposed by Cavalli in *De numero,* while some works he judged spurious were omitted.

Cavalli was a popular teacher with seventy-five students in 1508. One likes to think that they came for his Greek learning. In any case, the pleased Venetian

17. Dallari, 1888–1924, 1:51, 62, 64, 65, 67, 70; Bigi, 1961; Monfasani, 1990a, 52–53, 63; Wilson, 1992, 95, 111–12, 114, 116–18. Callistus was also an important copyist of Greek manuscripts.

18. Bigi, 1962a; Field, 1988, 55, 107–26 and passim; Monfasani, 1990a, 61–63.

19. Monfasani, 1990a.

20. The source is Francesco Patrizi da Cherso, in a work published in 1581, quoted by Schmitt, 1983a, 288–89 n. 4. This and the following two paragraphs are based primarily on Schmitt, 1983a. See also Pesenti, 1984, 70–72, and Palma, 1979.

government raised his already handsome salary of 400 florins to 460. Cavalli continued to teach practical medicine at Padua to 1509, when the university closed.

In April 1497 the Venetian Senate took another step to promote the teaching of the Greek Aristotle at Padua. The rector of the arts and medicine student organization came to the Venetian Senate with a petition: the students requested the creation of a Greek lectureship for the purpose of explaining the texts of Aristotle "in [natural] philosophy and medicine," and they asked that Niccolò Leonico Tomeo be given the position. In other words, they wanted a new professorship to expand what Cavalli had begun. The Senate quickly agreed; it appointed Tomeo to do exactly what was requested at a salary of 100 florins.[21] Tomeo's post was not a traditional appointment in natural philosophy, medicine, or humanities but embodied aspects of all three; his scholarship did the same. The relatively low salary also confirms that the post was a special one.

Of course, the new professorship was created too quickly and easily to have been only a spontaneous student initiative. The more likely scenario is that key professors and Venetian senators had already made up their minds to create the new position. Cavalli's example, or the arguments of humanistically minded students and professors, may have persuaded them that teaching Aristotle in Greek would advance medical and scientific learning. Moreover, the Senate was clearly primed to appoint Tomeo. The new position was one of several Venetian initiatives to improve the university at this time.

Tomeo justified the support of Senate and students. Born in Venice the son of a Greek immigrant, Tomeo (1456–1531) studied at Padua, then at Florence and Milan under Demetrius Chalcondylas, before taking his doctorate in arts at Padua in 1485.[22] Upon inheriting considerable family property, he settled in Padua in 1497. Thus, he was already on the scene when appointed. Tomeo taught at the university for about ten years, 1497 to 1506; after leaving his post he remained in Padua, possibly teaching privately. Tomeo influenced a wide circle of humanists and students, especially from England. He produced many new Latin translations of ancient Greek works, notably Aristotle's works on medicine, animals, natural history, and the pseudo-Aristotelian *Quaestiones mechanicae,* plus commentaries. Tomeo also published original works and searched for manuscripts. His scholarship demonstrated extensive use of ancient Greek commentators on Aristotle, including Alexander of Aphrodisias, Priscianus Lydus, and

21. The key part of the petition reads: "Venit in hanc urbem nostram rector artistarum Gymnasii nostri Patavini . . . petiit et supplicavit . . . nomine omnium illorum scolarium cupientium habere lectorem in lingua greca et explanatorem textuum aristotelicorum maxime in philosophia et medicina, pro coadiuvandis eorum studiis, ut ad talem lecturam constitueretur vir eruditissimus et doctor utriusque lingue peritissimus magister Nicolaus de Thomeis dictis omnibus scolaribus supra quam dici possit gratissimus et acceptissimus." Quoted in De Bellis, 1980, 41, with the date Apr. 21, 1497. Dupuigrenet Desroussilles (1980, 623) gives a shorter version with the same key words from a Senate document of Apr. 7, 1497.

22. The discussion of Tomeo is based especially on De Bellis, 1975 and 1980. See also Facciolati, 1978, pt. 1:lv–lvi; King, 1986, 432–34; Geanakoplos, 1989, 114–29; and Woolfson, 1998, 103–18 and passim, for his influence on English students.

Michael Ephesius. Finally, Tomeo translated a section of Plato's *Timaeus* along with Proclus's commentary, an early example of a strong interest in Platonic and Neoplatonic philosophy by a university professor.

Cavalli and Tomeo pioneered a new approach to the Aristotelian texts in the natural philosophy curriculum by turning to the Greek text of Aristotle as the basis for teaching and research. They then produced new Latin translations that employed the humanistic "meaning of the text" method of translation, rather than the medieval "word for word" approach. The new wave of scholars believed that their work was superior to the medieval Latin translations, some of which had been based on intermediate Arabic versions. The new Latin translations became the foundation for teaching and research for numerous university professors, who added classroom discussion of Greek words when necessary.

Greek authors and commentators on Aristotle of late antiquity became part of university natural philosophy. Between 200 to 600, five to nine centuries after Aristotle's death in 322 B.C., several Greek scholars wrote perceptive and often critical commentaries on his works. They also composed original studies within the Aristotelian tradition but from the perspective of the more eclectic philosophical culture of late antiquity. Their works also included material derived from earlier Greek philosophy but not found in Aristotle or Plato. Medieval scholars knew little of the commentators of late antiquity and then only in Latin translations. And they approached them from their own viewpoints. Then, between 1495 and 1540, practically all the surviving works of the Greek commentators on Aristotle, plus additional ancient works, were printed in Greek and translated into Latin, often for the first time. Other works were translated anew by scholars with a better command of Greek and a broader knowledge of Greek philosophy than their medieval predecessors.

It is sometimes forgotten that all the early printings of the collected works of Aristotle included commentaries and occasionally independent works written by other authors. The first comprehensive printed edition of Aristotle, a Latin edition in seven volumes published in Venice in the years 1472–74, included most of Aristotle's works plus commentaries by Averroës.[23] The edition added Averroës because medieval university learning viewed Aristotle and Averroës as a package.

Aldo Manuzio and his collaborators probably produced the monumental five-volume edition of the Greek text of Aristotle primarily for the use of university scholars in natural philosophy.[24] Like the earlier Latin printings, Aldo's edition included numerous commentaries. But he included Greek commentaries of late antiquity, plus other Greek scholars, always in Greek, while excluding medieval commentaries. Indeed, the Aldine Aristotle was a humanist effort to replace the medieval university trio of Latin Aristotle, Averroës's Latin commentaries, and Avicenna's Latin commentaries with a Renaissance trio of Greek Aristotle,

---

23. For this and the following paragraphs, see Minio-Paluello, 1972, 483–500.

24. On the Aldine Aristotle, see Minio-Paluello, 1972, 489–94; Lowry, 1979, see index; and Schmitt, 1981a.

Greek commentaries on Aristotle, and other ancient Greek scientific works. Indeed, the three middle volumes of the edition offered an encyclopedia of ancient Greek natural history.

After the publication of the Greek Aristotle, the Aldine Press and other Venetian presses printed many other Greek works in the first thirty years of the sixteenth century which greatly influenced the development of natural philosophy. For example, Alexander of Aphrodisias (fl. c. A.D. 200), an Aristotelian through and through, wrote a series of independent works plus commentaries, of which those on the *Prior Analytics, Topica, Meterologica, De sensu,* and *Metaphysics* survived. His name also became attached to a number of spurious works. Although some of Alexander's writings circulated in the Middle Ages, his works played a much more important role in Renaissance debates on the intellective soul, fate, and free will after the printing of the Greek edition between 1513 and 1516 and the appearance of Latin translations of some of his previously unavailable works.[25]

Other ancient Greek commentators on Aristotle became available. Simplicius (c. 500–after 533) wrote long commentaries on Aristotle's *Physics, Categories, De anima,* and *De caelo* from a Neoplatonic perspective. He also sought to harmonize Plato and Aristotle. Medieval scholars knew the commentaries on the *Categories* and *De caelo* in Latin, thanks to the indefatigable translator William of Moerbeke (1220/35–after October 1286). But his other works and the Greek originals did not reach Western scholars until the end of the fifteenth century and especially the sixteenth century, with Greek printings appearing in 1499 and 1527. They became a key part of Renaissance debates on Averroës's interpretation of Aristotle's views on the intellect and on astronomy.[26] Another influential figure was Themistius (317?–c. 388), who paraphrased and summarized Aristotle's works while teaching at Constantinople. His works were known in Latin translation in the Middle Ages but attracted new attention in the Renaissance.[27]

Later in the sixteenth century scholars began to pay attention to John Philoponus, also called "the Grammarian," a Greek Christian and Platonist who lived in Alexandria probably between 490 and the 570s. He wrote extensive and very critical commentaries on the key scientific and logical works of Aristotle; his commentaries on the *Physics, Posterior Analytics, Meterology, De generatione et corruptione, De anima,* and the *Metaphysics* survive, although not all in complete form.[28] But the Christian West knew only the commentary on *De anima.* The other works became available only in the last years of the fifteenth century and in the sixteenth. Renaissance scholars began to cite the Greek manuscript of Philoponus's commentary on the *Physics,* of which the first four books survive in

25. Cranz, 1960–1971, is the indispensable guide.

26. B. Nardi, 1958 (365–455), is the key study on Simplicius; see also Verbeke, 1981a. Grafton (1988a, 776–91) offers a brief guide to the rediscovery of ancient authors important for Renaissance natural philosophy. See also Park and Kessler, 1988, 459–61.

27. Verbeke, 1981b.

28. The discussion of Philoponus is based on Schmitt, 1987, and Sambursky, 1981. For more, see the studies in *Philoponus,* 1987.

entirety and books 5 through 8 in fragments, in the early sixteenth century. The Greek text of the *Physics* was first printed in 1535; a Latin translation appeared in 1539 and another in 1558. These two Latin translations were printed at least nine times in the sixteenth century, always in Venice.

In his commentary on the *Physics,* Philoponus strongly criticized parts of Aristotle's scientific system. He pinpointed some of its most evident weaknesses, such as Aristotle's confusing views on the vacuum. Aristotle had rejected the possibility of a vacuum except under limited "unnatural" circumstances. The normal absence of a vacuum determined Aristotle's discussion of the motion of bodies: a body's motion must be motion through a medium and, consequently, relatively slow. Philoponus, by contrast, saw the space around a body as basically empty, that is, a vacuum. Since there was nothing around a body, a body's motion came from the motive power of the moving body or the force that propelled it. Thus, the propellant force determined the velocity of a moving body; since the body met little or no resistance in a void, its velocity could be very quick. This was the theory of impetus, which led to the modern explanation of "momentum" or "kinetic energy," beginning in the seventeenth century.

Of course, medieval scholars discussed the problem of the vacuum and had some notion of impetus without acquaintance with Philoponus or, at best, with a vague awareness of his ideas through Avicenna. By contrast, sixteenth-century scholars, including Galilei, now read and used Philoponus in their own ways. Anti-Aristotelians gleefully seized on Philoponus as an authoritative ancient club with which to beat Aristotle. Fervent Aristotelians sought to refute Philoponus. And a middle group of scholars carefully studied Philoponus as they developed their own scientific views.

In addition, ancient Greek writers who did not comment on Aristotle were rediscovered. Theophrastus (372/370–288/286 B.C.) was Aristotle's successor as leader of the Peripatetic school in ancient Greece and a voluminous writer. But most of his surviving writings only became available in manuscript in the late fifteenth century and in print in 1497, when they were included in the Aldine Greek Aristotle. The sixteenth and early seventeenth centuries saw additional Greek editions and Latin translations. Theophrastus was especially important to sixteenth-century botanical studies.[29]

By the middle of the sixteenth century, practically all the ancient Greek scientific writers had been recovered, translated or retranslated into Latin, edited, and printed. Together they brought a richer understanding of Aristotle and ancient Greek science generally to university scholarship and teaching. Because Plato influenced many of the ancient Greek authors, some Platonic seasoning garnished the Aristotelian meal. The ancient writers also lent support to attempts to harmonize Plato and Aristotle.

A historical Aristotle, that is, Aristotle in his own language, in the scientific context of his own era, and subject to criticism from scholars of late antiquity, emerged. Since Aristotle's system was so complex and his language often elusive,

29. Schmitt, 1971; McDiarmid, 1981.

commentaries explicating his meaning had always accompanied him, like an entourage surrounding a modern celebrity. And just as today's entourage controls access and interprets the famous person to the public, so also did Aristotle's commentators provide entry and explanation to the scholars who studied him. The Middle Ages had an Averroistic Aristotle, a Thomistic Aristotle, an Albertine Aristotle, and so on. Now the Renaissance began to have an ancient Greek Aristotle, or better, several ancient Greek Aristotles.

By no means did the printing of the Greek Aristotle and ancient Greek commentaries drive out medieval translations and commentaries. These also were edited and printed, sometimes in excellent new editions. It was difficult to discard the medieval Latin translations, because much of the technical vocabulary came from these works. Ciceronian Latin, so beloved of humanists, did not offer good substitutes for *anima, intellectus, sensitivum,* and so on.[30] A monumental example of the continued importance of the medieval Latin Aristotle was the eleven-volume folio-sized Aristotle-Averroës Latin edition issued by the Giunti Press of Venice between 1550 and 1552. This edition included all the known extant works of Aristotle, including some now considered spurious, in Latin translation. Some of the translations were new humanistic versions, others improved medieval translations. Some Aristotelian works were offered in more than one translation. And practically every title was accompanied by Averroës's commentary in a medieval or new translation. Overall, the sixteenth-century printings of Averroës presented to the reading public thirty-four of the thirty-eight known extant works of Averroës dealing with Aristotle. The Middle Ages, by contrast, had had only fifteen such works in Latin.[31]

By the end of the sixteenth century, a basic library for the study of natural philosophy was both similar to and different from that of a hundred years earlier. For example, in 1594 the directions for a state-sponsored residence for students about to open at the University of Pisa listed the texts that the library had to have. For natural philosophy they were the *opera omnia* of Aristotle and Averroës and (unspecified) commentaries of John Philoponus and Simplicius on Aristotle. The library should also include the *opera omnia* of Thomas Aquinas and Plato, which might also be useful for natural philosophy.[32]

Aristotle remained the foundation of natural philosophy in all its parts as he had been in the Middle Ages. Natural philosophers pursued most of the same issues and questions as before. But the discovery, printing, translation, and study of the Greek works of antiquity in the years just before and after 1500, plus better access to the medieval Aristotle, produced "Eclectic Aristotelianism" or "Eclectic Aristotelianisms."[33] Philosophers offered arguments that incorporated a wide range of sources in order to interpret correctly "the master of those who know."

30. Cranz (1976b, 361–65) makes this point well.
31. The edition is described in Camerini, 1962–63, pt. 1:382–86. See the discussion by Schmitt, 1979b.
32. Biagi, 1980, 113. The residence was the Collegio Ferdinando, which opened in 1595.
33. The terms come from Schmitt, 1983c, 99–103.

Primum Volumen.

ARISTOTELIS
STAGIRITAE
Organum.

AVERROIS CORDVBENSIS
IN EO COMMENTARIA,

Epitome, Quæsita nonnulla, ac Epistola vna.

*Leui Gersonidis in nonnullos Aristotelis & Auerrois
libros annotationes.*

Arabum quorundam Quæsita, & Epistolæ.

Quæ omnia vti olim latinitate donata fuerant, ita nunc summo studio,
singulariq; diligentia castigata leguntur.

BERNARDINI TOMITANI PATAVINI
in Aristotelis & Auerrois dicta, Animaduersiones quædam,
& Contradictionum Solutiones.

Quæ vero in hoc continentur, pagina versa monstrabit.

VENETIIS APVD IVNCTAS.
M. D. LXII.

FIG. 7. Title page of volume 1 (of 11 volumes in 15 parts) of Latin Aristotle and
Averroës edition, Venice: Giunti, 1562. This is the second edition of the famous work
first published in Venice: Giunti, 1550–52. *Annenberg Rare Book and Manuscript Library,
University of Pennsylvania.*

This was particularly true at Padua from the 1490s to 1509. Alessandro Achillini, Agostino Nifo, Pietro Pomponazzi, Nicoletto Vernia, and Marc'Antonio Zimara all taught natural philosophy at Padua, sometimes as concurrents, always as rivals, in these years.[34] While of this group only Nifo mastered Greek, all were open to the new material to some degree. Eclectic Aristotelianism then spread to other universities.

INANIMATE WORLD, SCIENTIFIC METHOD, AND THE SOUL

Renaissance natural philosophers inherited many issues from the Middle Ages. But thanks to a better understanding of ancient Greek science, much enthusiasm, and the conviction that they could do better than their medieval predecessors, they approached them in new ways. And they raised new questions. Teaching and research in natural philosophy embraced three broad areas, each guided by its appropriate Aristotelian curricular texts.

The study of the inanimate world, what might be called the physical sciences in modern terminology, came first. Aristotle's *Physics* explicated the basic principles, and *De caelo et mundo* and *De generatione et corruptione* discussed the heavens, elements, compounds, and the atmosphere. Seeing a stone, a star, or a flame, Aristotle asked, what is it made of? (its matter); what is its essential character? (form); what external or internal agency produced it? (cause); what is its purpose? (end).[35] The natural philosopher paid particular attention to the attributes of the physical world, which were earth, air, fire, and water. Following Aristotle's texts, the scholar focused on physical change, which Aristotle called motion: its variety, its regularity, and especially its causes.

In his analysis, the natural philosopher relied greatly on Aristotelian physical principles and only to a limited extent on observation of the physical world. In order to prove his conclusions, the natural philosopher enunciated a principle and then demonstrated by philosophical reasoning (premises followed by logically necessary conclusions) that his analysis of the physical phenomena was true. He did not test his conclusions by much further observation, and he practically ignored mathematics.

The second part of natural philosophy might be called scientific method. Relying on Aristotle's *Posterior Analytics* as well as the *Physics* and the *Topics,* the scholar posited a methodology to solve scientific problems. The methodology was dialectical: conclusions must come from necessary premises. The natural philosopher shared this research with professors of logic, and by the mid-sixteenth century, the latter concentrated most on scientific method (see Ch. 7, "Demonstrative Regress").

The third part of natural philosophy was what might be called "the study of

34. Antonaci (1971–78, 1:106–26) captures the atmosphere well. See especially Mahoney, 1968, 1970a, 1970b, 1976a, 1976b, 1982, 1983, and 1986, on Vernia and Nifo.

35. This succinct description is based on Owen, 1981, 250–51, and Wallace, 1988, 202–3. For a broader treatment, see Wallace, 1996, chs. 1 and 2.

nature." According to Aristotle, every living thing had an organic soul, which is the form or life principle appropriate to it. The organic soul was the source that directed those life functions tied to the bodies of living beings and dependent on them: sensation, memory, reproduction, digestion, and much else. Obviously, plants had organic souls considerably different from those of animals; humans and animals had organic souls both similar to and different from each other's. The Aristotelian approach to understanding different kinds of organic souls was to study their faculties, that is, their various powers. Each faculty was responsible for a distinct operation, such as digestion or sensation. The organic soul of the plant caused its growth and reproduction. The organic soul of an animal caused its growth, reproduction, and sensation. At the same time, a common approach toward all living things enabled the scholar to develop a model. From that model he might postulate various operations of living things and form a basis from which to explain differences.

Natural philosophers might study the life activities of any organism in the world, but the majority concentrated on the life activities of humans. Much of this study might be called *psychology*, a term first coined in 1575.[36] Psychology meant studying the natures and activities (forms and faculties in Aristotelian terminology) of living things. *De anima*, especially books 2 and 3, provided the approach and direction of these studies; the *Parva naturalia* and the animal books of Aristotle furnished much additional data through comparison with animals. The texts discussed human activities, such as sleep and waking, youth, and old age.

Renaissance natural philosophers pursued topics that might be called scientific studies of the organic soul. They attempted to locate the center of certain life activities in different organs of the body, or the origin of the organic soul in a particular organ. Here natural philosophers shared some areas of research with the medical studies of physiology and anatomy.[37] But natural philosophers also studied memory, dreams, and mental illness. Most important, psychology had its own unique areas of investigation.

Unlike an animal, a human had an intellective soul, which performed all the functions of an organic soul and at the same time was the seat of rational knowledge, will, and responsible action. According to Aristotle and his followers, the intellective soul was not identical with the body, despite the fact that it controlled the body's many activities. Hence, close investigation of the relationship between

36. The German humanist Joannes Thomas Freigius first used the term. Park and Kessler, 1988, 455. Psychology is the heading of section 9 in *CHRP*, comprising chapters entitled "The Concept of Psychology," "The Organic Soul," and "The Intellective Soul." The following is based on the first two of those chapters; Park and Kessler, 1988; and Park, 1988. Although there is no comprehensive account of psychology in the Renaissance, these studies make an excellent beginning. See also Michael, 1993, 65–69. For a broader perspective, see Wallace, 1996, 107–13 and passim.

37. One of the consequences was that a limited number of natural philosophers took doctorates in medicine after a doctorate in natural philosophy. A few taught both natural philosophy and medical theory, but only Alessandro Achillini taught both simultaneously (at Bologna in the first decade of the sixteenth century). See Chapter 1, "Bologna in the Sixteenth Century." However, taking degrees in and teaching both subjects became increasingly rare in the sixteenth century, probably because both became more specialized.

sense perception and cognition was an important topic in Renaissance psychology. The human intellective soul (*mind* is a close synonym) might be defined as the source of a person's thoughts and actions; it was not a material part of a person but something higher, a realm of immaterial matter, that is, thought in the broadest sense. The most important scholarly pursuit carried on in this part of natural philosophy was the attempt to analyze human cognition, how a person knows.

As they studied and taught *De anima* and other texts, natural philosophers wrote a great deal about the faculties of the organic soul. But this scholarship attracted little attention from contemporaries outside a specialized readership and little curiosity from later historians.[38] By contrast, both contemporaries and historians have been preoccupied with what natural philosophers had to say about the human intellective soul. What was its nature? How did it function? The most controversial issue in natural philosophy was the attempt to define the human intellective soul. It attracted much attention in the classroom and beyond.

THE DEBATE ON THE IMMORTALITY OF THE INTELLECTIVE SOUL

Aristotle in *De anima* III, 4–5, discussed the questions, how does the human intellect know, and what is the relationship between sense knowledge and abstract thought?[39] They led almost immediately to consideration of the nature of the intellective soul, the human mind. Does it exist independently from the body and immaterially, because it can "know" independently of sense experience? Or does the intellective soul depend entirely on sense experience and is it, therefore, dependent on the body and material in substance? If the latter is the case, the intellective soul dies with the body. Or is the intellective soul somehow both material and immaterial, dependent and independent of sense experience and the body? Christian patristic theology, which approached the question from a different perspective, had its own authoritative texts, and often relied on Plato and Neoplatonists, concluded that the intellective soul existed independently of the body and was immortal. But medieval scholars had to take into account Aristotelian science before reaching a conclusion. Since Aristotle was ambiguous and confusing on the question, a philosopher's answer, indeed, his overall approach to human psychology and cognition, had to rely as much on Aristotelian commentators and his own analysis as on the Philosopher himself.

Medieval philosophers discussed these issues at length. The great Islamic scholar Averroës denied the immortality of the human intellective soul. Led by Thomas Aquinas and John Duns Scotus (c. 1265–1308), medieval Scholastic philosophers in northern universities developed a Christian Aristotelianism.

38. Park (1988, 476) points out that the literature on the organic soul is voluminous but largely unexplored by historians.

39. Cranz (1976b) offers a fascinating account of the basic problem in *De anima,* the relationship between sensation and intellection, and outlines some of the ways that medieval and Renaissance authors faced it.

They articulated a broad metaphysics that comprehended all reality including God defined as First Cause.[40] Their views won acceptance; philosophers in northern universities are not known to have adopted Averroist positions after about 1350.[41]

However, Italian natural philosophers approached the intellective soul from a different direction than their colleagues in northern universities for two reasons. First, because of the prominence of medical studies in Italian universities, natural philosophers paid close attention to the body and sensation (sense experience) in the process of cognition. Second, Italian natural philosophers saw their discipline as separate and detached from theology and its concerns. The absence, or minimal presence, of theology in the curriculum of Italian universities in the fourteenth and early fifteenth centuries encouraged separation: theological issues could be ignored because theologians were seldom there in the next classroom to present them. By contrast, Christian theological concerns could not be ignored in northern universities, because university theologians were present and numerous. Hence, an Italian habit of discussing certain issues independently of theological considerations arose. Philosophers might base their arguments about the human intellective soul on Aristotle and Averroës, rather than Christian revelation.

Hence, natural philosophers in Italian universities from the late fourteenth century onward leaned toward a naturalistic approach to the intellective soul. They centered their discussion on humans' functions, the operations of the body as well as the mind, in cognition. This was fertile ground for intensive and favorable discussion of Averroist views. Biagio Pelacani (Blasius of Parma, c. 1350–1416), who taught at Bologna and Padua, argued that because intellectual operations depended on natural processes, the soul was mortal. On the other hand, Gaetano da Thiene, who taught natural philosophy at Padua from 1430 to 1462, sought to harmonize an Averroist position with Christian doctrine; he asserted that the intellective soul was individual and immortal. His position also anticipated some principles of humanism, notably that a person was a being intermediate between the natural and spiritual extremes.

Slowly a broad question emerged that touched Christian belief: Can Aristotelian natural philosophy confirm personal immortality? Two incidents at the University of Pisa in the academic year 1473–74 illustrated the climate of philosophical discussion. Some students contacted one of the civic officials (Ufficiali dello Studio) who oversaw the university to protest against the teaching of the ordinary professor of natural philosophy, Dominic of Flanders (Balduin Lottin, c. 1425–79). A Dominican and major Thomist theologian, Fra Dominic knew the full range of philosophers from Plato, Alexander of Aphrodisias, and Themistius to Averroës and Renaissance thinkers. However, the students complained that

40. Lohr, 1988b. However, the precise question that so exercised Renaissance natural philosophers, whether the immortality of the individual human soul can be demonstrated philosophically, was not a major issue in the Christian Middle Ages. See Kristeller, 1979b, 181–87.
41. Monfasani, 1993, 248.

Fra Dominic, who may have been lecturing on *De anima,* based his opinions on Thomas Aquinas, rather than "according to common philosophical opinion" (*iuxta communem philosophantium opinionem*). As a Thomist, he would have defended the demonstrability of the immortality of the soul, if this was one of the issues on which the students were exercised.[42]

Also at Pisa in 1473–74, a long disputation on logical questions involving students, assisted by their professors, raised the issue of the immortality of the soul. The disputants made a sharp distinction between theological and philosophical conceptions (the latter based on Aristotle and Averroës) of the immortality of the soul and argued that Thomas had not interpreted Aristotle correctly.[43]

It seemed to many Renaissance professors of natural philosophy that they had three alternatives.[44] The first was that there was one immortal universal intellect. An individual human intellect simply participated in the universal intellect for the brief period in which he or she lived. This was the position of Averroës. Second, individual human intellects existed but died with the body, the position of Alexander of Aphrodisias. Third, the individual immortal intellective soul existed and could be demonstrated philosophically, the position of Albertus Magnus and Thomas Aquinas.

By the late fifteenth century some philosophers, especially at Padua, found the third position philosophically untenable and adopted the first or second position. For example, both Nicoletto Vernia, who taught natural philosophy at Padua from 1465 to1499, and Agostino Nifo, who taught at Padua from 1492 to 1499, favored Averroës and denied the demonstrability of the immortality of the individual soul.[45]

Given the importance of the issue to Christianity, it is hardly surprising that an ecclesiastical authority became concerned. On May 4, 1489, the bishop of Padua, in conjunction with the Paduan father inquisitor, issued a decree entitled "Edictum contra disputantes de unitate intellectus" (Edict against disputants on the unity of the intellect) addressed to all the professors of philosophy of Padua and their students.[46] The decree addressed a key part of the larger issue. Aristotle taught that the process of abstraction involved two functions. The individual must receive sense images and must abstract universal content from them. He used the terms *possible* or *receptive intellect* and *agent* or *active intellect*. But he did little to explain the duality of the two intellects or how they worked together, so

42. Verde, 1973–94, vol. 4, pt. 1:41 (quote), 88–90; vol. 2:190–91. See also Fioravanti, 1993, 271, and Vasoli, 1998b, 96–99, 132–33, with additional bibliography. Fra Dominic also relied on Plato in his defense of the immortality of the soul.

43. Verde, 1973–94, vol. 4, pt. 1:105–19, esp. 105–6, 116–18. See also Fioravanti, 1993, 270–71.

44. Kessler (1988, 519) makes this point.

45. Ibid., 492–94, 496–500, and *CHRP,* 828, 839, for additional bibliography. For Nifo, see especially Mahoney, 1970a.

46. The decree from the Archivio Curia Vescovile in Padua is printed in Ragnisco, 1891, 8–9, who is followed here. B. Nardi (1958, 100, 155) and Di Napoli (1963, 185–86) print the key section of the edict. Di Napoli (1977, 1980) provides an Italian translation.

it was left to commentators to interpret his meaning. Scholars in the Averrroist tradition saw intellect as single (unity of the intellect), not dual, and the same for all people. Consequently, the individual human intellect was not immortal.

The edict began with an analogy. Anyone who leaves a poison (*venenum* = potion or poison, but also medicine in some contexts) openly on the table is guilty of a crime even if no one dies of the poison. Because poison is so dangerous but at the same time can be used to cure diseases, governments strictly regulate pharmacists who handle it. Since this is done for a poison that kills only the body, one must be even more warned against the poison that kills souls.

The edict then warned about the deceptions of philosophy. Those who study philosophy should do so in such a way that they will not unlearn Christian philosophy, and those who teach should remember that they are also Christians. These dangerous philosophers are those who dispute about the unity of the intellect ("eos qui de unitate intellectus disputant"). This doctrine removes the (supernatural) rewards of virtue and the pains of vice, leaving persons thinking that they may freely commit the gravest crimes. Therefore, the bishop and inquisitor forbid public disputations on "the unity of the intellect." Nor may anyone dispute that position publicly by calling it "the doctrine of Aristotle according to the interpretation of Averroës, a learned but wicked man" (et si hoc ex Aristotelis sententia fuisse secundum Averroin hominem doctum quidem sed scelestum). The edict threatened automatic excommunication for violators. The bishop ordered a copy of the edict to be posted on the doors of the cathedral and the basilica of Sant'Antonio.[47]

Bishop Pietro Barozzi (1443–1507) promulgated the edict. A Venetian noble from a family whose members specialized in acquiring ecclesiastical offices, Barozzi studied law and other subjects at Padua from 1461 to 1471, although no evidence of a degree has come to light.[48] With the support of the Venetian government Barozzi became bishop of Belluno in 1471 and bishop of Padua in 1487, which post he held until death. He was keenly interested in humanistic studies, theology, Platonic studies, and mathematics. Barozzi collected an excellent library of 355 volumes and penned numerous orations, works of consolation, poetry in a humanistic vein, political theory based on Aristotle, and saints' lives. At Padua he was an energetic bishop who worked hard to improve the standards of the clergy and to help the poor through the establishment of a *monte di pietà* offering small loans. Sixteenth-century Catholic reformers rightly hailed him as a model reforming bishop.[49] A concern for the care of souls clearly motivated Barozzi to issue the edict. He did not want professors teaching and students learning philosophical positions that contradicted Catholic doctrine.

Barozzi's edict forbade public disputations on the unity of the intellect. Dis-

47. Gios, 1977, 294.

48. *Acta Graduum 1461 ad 1470*, 1992 (see the index), offers ample evidence of his presence as witness to others' degrees but does not include a degree for Barozzi. The volume for the 1470s has not yet appeared.

49. The standard work is Gios, 1977; see also the brief accounts of Gaeta, 1964, and King, 1986, 333–35. Barozzi merits further study.

putations were public events announced in advance and usually held in a church or another common meeting place. They attracted students, professors, and anyone else who wished to listen, as students and professors showed off their dialectical and oratorical skills in noisy debate. The disputation format encouraged participants to defend their positions strongly. Hence, a student or professor who denied the immortality of the soul in a disputation would do so in strong, contentious terms and might attract much attention. These circumstances probably were a major reason for the ban.

However, Bishop Barozzi did not ban lectures defending Averroist positions.[50] As his analogy of the poison that can both kill and cure indicated, Barozzi wanted Averroist teaching to be used with care and regulated. Banning all discussion of Averrorist views would have disrupted philosophy teaching to an unprecedented degree. Moreover, the professor in the lecture hall could be seen as explaining Averroës in the midst of a series of lectures on Aristotle's *De anima,* rather than as defending Averroës.[51] In addition, lectures were routine daily occurrences before a limited audience of the professor's own students. They did not normally attract a broader audience, as disputations probably did.

Still, the positions condemned by the bishop had circulated since the thirteenth century and had been taught in greater or lesser degree at Padua and elsewhere in the fourteenth and fifteenth centuries. Other philosophical and institutional changes under way probably moved the bishop to act.

A strong countermovement to Averroës, asserting that philosophy could demonstrate the immortality of the soul, had arisen. Renaissance Platonism greatly strengthened the anti-Averroist position among Italian philosophers and prelates. Marsilio Ficino wrote his major work, *Theologia Platonica de immortalitate animorum* (Platonic theology on the immortality of souls) between 1469 and 1474 (printed in 1482) and published his Latin translation of Plato in 1484. Ficino and his followers strongly held that philosophy could prove the immortality of the soul, and they condemned philosophers who held Averroist views.[52] Ficinian Platonism held as a fundamental tenet that Christian theology and philosophy, whether Aristotelian or Platonic, agreed, because both led to God. Indeed, Renaissance Platonism lent support to all those seeking concord between Christianity and Aristotelian-based natural philosophy. Although Platonism was not part of the university curriculum until later (see below), it certainly influenced professors of natural philosophy, some of whom saw philosophy and Christian theology as in accord.[53] As Renaissance Platonism spread through philosophical

50. B. Nardi (1958, 156) noted this; reiterated by Mahoney (1968, 271 n. 11).

51. Monfasani (1993, 250 n. 18) makes this last point. In my view, a series of classroom lectures by an informed scholar is likely to be more persuasive than one public event in a heightened atmosphere. Nevertheless, civic and university authorities, then and now, seem to worry more about the impact of a single public lecture on a controversial topic than a year's worth of teaching.

52. Kristeller (1979b, 188–91) makes this point. The best overall interpretation of Ficino's thought remains Kristeller, 1964b.

53. For example, Andreas Camuzio (c. 1512–c. 1587), who taught logic, natural philosophy, and theoretical medicine at the universities of Pavia and Pisa, wrote as follows in 1541: "The professors of

and theological circles, its supporters increasingly saw the Averroist position as both antireligious and philosophically wrong-headed. Barozzi himself owned several of Ficino's books and may have been sympathetic to such views.[54]

Additional support for the view that philosophy could demonstrate the immortality of the soul came from Italian philosophers and theologians who were members of mendicant religious orders. Following Saint Thomas Aquinas (c. 1225–74), almost all Dominican philosophers and theologians of the Renaissance strongly affirmed that reason could demonstrate the truths of Christianity, including the soul's immortality. Some lay philosophers also accepted Thomist views.[55] The Franciscan John Duns Scotus argued that it could not be determined if reason could demonstrate certain key points that Christian revelation revealed to man. However, some Franciscan Scotist theologians and philosophers of the fifteenth and sixteenth centuries (including Antonio Trombetta; see below) abandoned Duns Scotus and argued that reason could demonstrate such points as the immortality of the soul.[56]

Another group supported the Italian anti-Averroists through their absence. William of Ockham (c. 1285–1347/49) and his nominalist followers denied that philosophy could prove the immortality of the soul, thus undercutting the Christian position as effectively as Averroës. (However, unlike Averroës, Ockhamists argued that a person knew by faith [fideism] that he or she had an immortal soul.) Although nominalists and realists battled for supremacy in northern European universities, Italy had no Ockhamists, and few Italian theologians were fideists.[57] Had there been an Italian Ockhamist presence, it would have diluted the anti-Averroist campaign of the mendicants.

The views of the mendicant order philosophers and theologians would not have mattered much if they were still restricted to their own *studia*. However, members of mendicant orders now had a presence within the University of Padua. In 1442 the Venetian Senate had established a professorship of Thomist metaphysics, appointing a Dominican friar to the post. In 1474 the Senate created a concurrent Scotist metaphysics post, which was filled by a Franciscan. Since metaphysics was seen as preparation for the study of theology, the Venetian Senate created a professorship of theology in 1476–77, appointing a Franciscan Scotist to fill it. Finally, in or about 1490 the Senate created a professorship of

---

sacred Scripture and of philosophy may argue against it, but I am of the opinion that the doctrines of sacred theology are in no way contrary to the teachings of Aristotle and Plato: rather they agree in all ways." Translation by Schmitt, 1982a, 183.

54. Di Napoli, 1963, 222–23, and especially Monfasani, 1993, 267–70, who explains the web of influence which Ficino and his followers exercised on Barozzi and the framers of *Apostolici regiminis*.

55. On the importance of Thomism in Renaissance philosophy, see Kristeller, 1974, 27–91, with much additional bibliography; and Mahoney, 1976a. Tommaso de Vio Cajetan (see below) was the Dominican exception who denied that philosophy could demonstrate the soul's immortality.

56. Offelli, 1954, 18–33; Poppi, 1979; and Monfasani, 1993, 264. Trombetta differed strongly from Scotus on whether philosophy could demonstrate anti-Averroist positions.

57. Monfasani, 1993, 256–58. The Franciscan professors at the important convent *studium* of Sant' Antonio (il Santo) in Padua blocked any attempt to introduce Ockhamist nominalism. Poppi, 1989, 6.

Thomist theology filled by a Dominican.[58] Thus, four mendicant order clergy-men taught theology and religiously oriented metaphysics at Padua in the 1490s. They were there to point out the contradictions between Averroist views and Christian theology found in the teaching and writing of their colleagues in natural philosophy.

One of the mendicant order professors led the anti-Averroist group. Antonio Trombetta (1431–1517), a Franciscan and native of Padua, taught Scotist meta-physics at the university from 1476 or 1477 until 1511. Influential and respected, he wrote several works strongly criticizing his Averroist-inclining colleagues. And he worked closely with Bishop Barozzi to prepare the edict.[59]

The battle between Averroists and anti-Averroists was fundamentally a strug-gle between two schools of philosophy, albeit with much variation from scholar to scholar within each school. If church authorities could be persuaded to sup-port one side or the other, so much the better for that side. The institutional presence of the mendicant order clergymen, led by Trombetta, probably tipped the balance. The local bishop then lent his support to the anti-Averroists for religious reasons.

Barozzi's edict of 1489 did not name names, but its chief target was Nicoletta Vernia (1420–99). Vernia received his doctorate from Padua in 1458 and became extraordinary professor of natural philosophy in 1465 and ordinary professor in 1468. He was the most influential natural philosopher at Padua and highly es-teemed by the Venetian authorities.[60] Vernia had already written a treatise es-pousing an Averroist position and saw himself as a target.[61]

If Vernia was the chief target, Bishop Barozzi's edict accomplished its purpose. By 1492 Vernia had written another treatise (published posthumously in 1504) in which he reversed his position. He now argued against Averroës, affirming the immortality of the individual intellective soul and denying the unity of the intellect. An exchange of letters with Barozzi included in the book indicated that Vernia was aware of Barozzi's criticism and had altered his position.

It is not certain, however, that Vernia changed his position because of the bishop's edict. In the second treatise Vernia cast his net widely in order to embrace many questions in addition to immortality of the intellective soul. One of the first to use extensively the Greek commentators freshly available in hu-manistic Latin translations, Vernia now criticized all medieval commentators, including Averroës. Much like Giovanni Pico della Mirandola (1463–94), Vernia

---

58. Brotto and Zonta, 1922, 93–99; Poppi, 1981, 12–13. See Chapter 10 for details.

59. Poppi, 1962 and 1964; these articles are reprinted with additional bibliography in Poppi, 1989. See also Mahoney, 1976b; Gios, 1977, 295 n. 11, 300–302, 383; and Vasoli, 1998b, 110–12, 138.

60. The Venetian government raised his salary from 200 to 250 florins in November 1481 and to 300 florins in October 1488. AAUP, F. 648, ff. 238ʳ (Nov. 8, 1481); 268ʳ (Oct. 20, 1488). Facciolati (1978, pt. 2:106) adds that in 1482 the government permitted him to teach without a concurrent professor and that his salary rose to 365 florins in 1491. Student protest persuaded the Venetian government to restore a concurrent for Vernia in 1487. B. Nardi, 1958, 121–22.

61. Mahoney, 1976b, 144–49, for his treatise. For this and the following paragraph, see Gios, 1977, 301–3. See Di Napoli, 1977, p. 1981, for Italian translations of portions of letters between Barozzi and Vernia.

employed Neoplatonic sources and even some nonphilosophical texts in his search for a common truth underlying the various schools. Vernia even tried to reconcile Aristotle and Plato on the nature of the soul and of knowledge, an early such effort.[62] Vernia attributed his changed views to his reading of Plato and an array of Greek commentators on Aristotle. It is also possible that his desire for a benefice enabling him to retire from teaching caused him to change his views in an effort to curry favor with Bishop Barozzi. Whatever the reasons, the more important point is that the discussion had broadened considerably to go beyond Averroës.[63] Agostino Nifo also changed his position, which he attributed to reading Aristotle in Greek.[64]

However, Paduan philosophers continued to teach views contrary to Christian doctrine, according to Bishop Barozzi. In 1504 he wrote to the Venetian government arguing for a higher salary for the professor of Scotist theology. On the Scotist's teaching Barozzi commented, "[It] is like a medicine for the errors on the eternity of the world, on the unity of the intellect, on nothing coming from nothing, and so forth, which abound among the philosophers; and without it [the professorship of Scotist theology], one could say that in this university nothing is taught which is not also taught in a university of pagans."[65]

Debate on the intellective soul continued in the universities. Alessandro Achillini, who taught at Bologna in the years 1484–1506, Padua 1506–8, and Bologna again 1508–12, wrote important works on the subject. So did the restless Agostino Nifo, who taught at Naples (twice), Salerno (on three occasions), Rome, and Pisa after leaving Padua. Like Vernia, Achillini and Nifo increasingly relied on the ancient Greek sources, especially Alexander of Aphrodisias, Themistius, and Simplicius, and on Platonic texts in order to see matters in more complex ways. They concluded that the individual intellective soul was immortal, not just because Christian revelation asserted it but because philosophy demonstrated it. Achillini and especially Nifo sought agreement between philosophy and revealed Christianity and among various ancient philosophers. And they developed many other topics in human psychology.[66]

62. Di Napoli, 1963, 181–93; B. Nardi, 1958, chs. 4, 5; Mahoney, 1976b, 149–63; Kessler, 1988, 492–94.

63. Scholars differ on the sincerity of Vernia's reversal. B. Nardi (1958, 109), Gios (1977, 303 n. 32), and Monfasani (1993, 250–51 n. 21) doubt the sincerity of his altered position. Di Napoli (1963, 193) and Mahoney (1976b, 162) accept it as sincere.

64. Mahoney, 1970a, 459. Nifo was also familiar with Plato and the Greek commentators on Aristotle. Mahoney, 1968.

65. "La lectura di theologia secondo la via de Schoto, la quale è come una medicina de li errori *de eternitate mundi, de unitate intellectus, et de hoc quod de nihilo nihil fiat* et altri simili, i quali pullulano da li philosophi: senza la quale el se poteria dire che in quel Studio non se lezesse cossa la quale non se lega anche in Studio de' pagani." Letter of Barozzi of Feb. 23, 1504, in Sanudo, *I Diarii*, 1969, col. 884; reprinted in Gios, 1977, 383, and Monfasani, 1993, 265. The translation is Monfasani's with my slight modifications. The appeal was for the Irish Franciscan Maurice O'Fihely.

66. Start with B. Nardi, 1958, chs. 4, 5, 8, 9, 13, and 14. On Achillini, see B. Nardi, 1960; Matsen, 1974 and 1976; and Kessler, 1988, 495–96. For Nifo, and comparisons between Vernia and Nifo, see

The philosophers' argument over the soul's immortality reached the ears of Rome. Various preachers and scholars raised the issue in their sermons before the papal court in the late fifteenth and early sixteenth centuries. Six of the seven preachers who discussed the issue at length concluded that philosophy could demonstrate the soul's immortality.[67]

Given the importance of the issue and the attention it was receiving, it was only a matter of time before the church would officially consider the demonstrability of the soul's immortality. This happened at the Fifth Lateran Council meeting in Rome (1512–17). One of the commissions appointed to prepare the work of the general sessions drafted a statement. Because belief in life after death was an essential part of Christianity and Trombetta was a member of the commission, its conclusion was not surprising. The council produced a bull entitled *Apostolici regiminis sollicitudo,* which followed in the footsteps of Barozzi's edict of 1489. The eighth session approved it with two dissenters, who argued that philosophy should not be bound by theological positions, on December 19, 1513.[68]

The bull began by denouncing "some extremely pernicious errors": "especially on the nature of the rational soul, with the claim that it is mortal, or only one among all human beings, and since some, playing the philosopher without due care, assert that this proposition is true at least according to philosophy . . . we condemn and reject all those who insist that the intellectual soul is mortal, or that it is only one among all human beings, and those who suggest doubts on this topic."[69]

The bull then ordered a remedy.

We strictly forbid teaching otherwise to be permitted. . . . Moreover, we strictly enjoin on each and every philosopher who teaches publicly in the universities or elsewhere, that when they explain or address to their audience the principles or conclusions of philosophers, where these are known to deviate from the true faith—as in the assertion of the soul's mortality or of there being only one soul or of the eternity of the world

---

Mahoney, 1968, 1970a, 1970b, 1976b, 1981, 1983, and esp. 1986, and Kessler, 1988, 496–500. For further bibliography on all three figures, see *CHRP,* 806, 828, 839, and Copenhaver and Schmitt, 1992, see index and bibliography.

67. O'Malley, 1979, 152–55. Many other preachers referred in passing to the soul's immortality.

68. The commission dealt with other matters as well. For its membership, see Price, 1985. The most important dissenter was the eminent Dominican Tommaso de Vio Cajetan (1468; cardinal 1517; d. 1534). In 1504 he argued that philosophy could demonstrate the soul's immortality; O'Malley, 1979, 154. But in 1509 he changed his view, writing that philosophy could not prove the soul's immortality, a position that he held for the rest of his life. Cajetan taught Thomistic metaphysics at the University of Padua (1495–97), Thomistic theology at the University of Pavia (1498–99), and philosophy and Scripture at the University of Rome (1501–8), at which time he was elected general of the Dominican order. He published many works. See Di Napoli, 1963, 214–26; Kessler, 1988, 504; Iorio, 1991, 159–83, esp. 173; *Memorie di Pavia,* 1970, pt. 1:190–91; Wicks, 1983, 10–36; and Negruzzo, 1995, 187–97. See *CHRP,* 812, for further bibliography. The other dissenter was Niccolò Lippomano, bishop of Bergamo, about whom little is known. See also Monfasani, 1993, 269 n. 128.

69. For the Latin text and English translation, see *Decrees,* 1990, 1:605–6.

and other topics of this kind—they are obliged to devote their every effort to clarify for their listeners the truth of the Christian religion, to teach it by convincing arguments, so far as this is possible, and to apply themselves to the full extent of their energies to refuting and disposing of the philosophers' opposing arguments, since all the solutions are available.

The key point was obvious: leaders of the Catholic Church worried that much contemporary philosophical discussion contradicted Christian doctrine and endangered the salvation of the souls under its care, and they wanted to stop it. Hence, the bull condemned the Averroist view of the unity of the intellect, the position of Averroës and Alexander of Aphrodisias that the individual human soul was mortal, as well as the position attributed to Aristotle that the world was eternal (and not God's creation at some point in time).

However, the bull did not prohibit discussion of "the conclusions of philosophers . . . [that] deviate from the true faith." Rather, it insisted that philosophers "clarify . . . the truth of the Christian religion . . . so far as this [was] possible" and that they refute the philosophers' opposing arguments. This was a significant concession compared with later condemnations. For example, Indexes of Prohibited Books later in the century banned outright not only heretical views but also the reading, possession, publication, and sale of books presenting them. *Apostolici regiminis* only demanded that philosophers present the Christian position and that they refute objectionable views. The bull further demanded that philosophers demonstrate philosophically the truths of Christianity "so far as this [was] possible." This clause seemingly acknowledged that not everyone agreed that all truths of Christianity could be demonstrated philosophically. It was an escape clause. Overall, the bull was something of a compromise: it affirmed a central element of Christian belief while allowing limited philosophical discussion about its demonstrability. The bull did two things: it promulgated doctrine and set guidelines for the teaching of philosophy.[70]

Still, *Apostolici regiminis* insisted on a major change in university teaching. It ordered philosophers reaching scientific conclusions opposed to Christian theology to correct themselves and to defend the Christian position. The bull might become a means of restricting philosophical freedom.

This did not happen. Instead, the ensuing philosophical debate after *Apostolici regiminis* freed natural philosophy from all but nominal theological constraints. Pietro Pomponazzi, then teaching at the University of Bologna within the papal state, published his famous *Tractatus de immortalitate animae* (Treatise on the immortality of the soul) in 1516. Pomponazzi, who had been working on the book for years, began by announcing that he would deal with the immortality of the

70. Minnich (1986, 326–27) makes this point and also suggests that it was a compromise document. Indeed, the three cardinals who probably drafted the final form of the decree came from different philosophical backgrounds and were protectors of rival religious orders whose traditional philosophies took differing positions on the demonstrability of the soul's immortality. They were Niccolò Fieschi (protector of the Dominicans), Domenico Grimani (protector of the Franciscans), and Bernardino Lopez de Carvajal (protector of the Minims). Minnich, 1986, 326–27 n. 21.

soul strictly on philosophical terms. And he would try to determine Aristotle's views on the question.[71] He strongly criticized the positions of both Averroës and Thomas Aquinas before developing his own position, which was based on the operations of the human intellect.

Pomponazzi argued that the human intellectual soul could not function, that is, it could not know, without images (*phantasmata* = phantasms or images). Images, in turn, were dependent on sense experience, an operation of the body. Finally, soul and body were tightly unified. Therefore, the individual intellective soul, while immaterial and immortal in some ways, was essentially material and mortal. This was the only possible truth that philosophy based on Aristotle and supported by an accurate understanding of human psychology (that is, man's operations that enabled him to know) could reach, in his view.

Pomponazzi then rigorously drew the religious and moral consequences of the soul's mortality. The major religions of the world were not divinely inspired but fictions by which lawgivers used the threat and promise of eternal life in order to persuade the majority of humans, who would not otherwise do good, to behave well. But the wise man did not need religion in order to live the ethically good life. Borrowing from Stoic ethics, Pomponazzi argued that the wise man would do good and avoid evil without the promise of eternal reward, because good was its own reward.

Having argued on the basis of human philosophical reasoning for the soul's mortality, Pomponazzi finished the treatise by stating that faith, whose evidence was revelation and canonical Scripture, proved that the soul was immortal. Philosophy could not do so. Pomponazzi firmly supported the position that faith proved Christian truths. But he also defended the difference between philosophical and religious proof and affirmed the usefulness of philosophical speculation.[72]

Pomponazzi in this and other works asserted in the strongest possible terms the different conclusions that philosophy and theology might reach. He declared the independence of philosophy from belief. And he exploited the escape clause in *Apostolici regiminis* which permitted professors to "explain . . . the . . . conclusions of philosophers, where these [were] known to deviate from the true faith." On the other hand, he certainly did not "devote every effort to clarify . . . the truth of the Christian religion."

Pomponazzi's book provoked denunciations from clergymen and one public burning of the work but no negative personal consequences, even though he

71. "Leaving aside revelation and miracles, and remaining entirely within natural limits, what do you yourself think in this matter? And, second, what do you judge was Aristotle's opinion on the same question?" These are the questions posed by Pomponazzi in the introduction to his work. I use the English translation of *Tractatus de immortalitate animae* by William Henry Hay II found in Cassirer, Kristeller, and Randall, 1948 (257–381 for Randall's introduction and the treatise, 281 for the quotation). Of the very large literature on Pomponazzi, only a few mostly recent works can be listed: Oliva, 1926; Di Napoli, 1963, 227–64; Kristeller, 1964a, 72–90, 174; B. Nardi, 1965; Poppi, 1970; Trinkaus, 1970, 2:530–51, 803–9; Pine, 1986; Kessler, 1988, 500–504; Lohr, 1988a, 602–5; Iorio, 1991, 114–35; Copenhaver and Schmitt, 1992, 104–9.

72. Ch. 15 of *De immortalitate animae* in Cassirer, Kristeller, and Randall, 1948, 377–81.

PETRI POMPONATII MANTVANI TRACTATVS DE IMMORTALITATE
ANIMAE.
PROEMIVM continens intentionem/seu Libri materiam & causam intentionis.&c.

RATER HIERONYMVS Natalis Ragufeus Ordinis Predicatogȝ/Cū aduerfa
laboraré ualitudine/Sicuti eft Vir humaniffimus/noftriȝ amantiffimus/ad nos fe
frequentius recipiebat:Cumqȝ quodam die minus me uexari a morbo confpiceret/
Vultu adeo demiffo fic orfus eft:Cariffime Preceptor/fuperioribus diebus cū pri/
mū de cælo nobis exponeres/pueniffefqȝ ad locū illū in quo Ariftoteles ingenitum
& icorruptibile coüerti pluribus argumétationibus cötendit oftédere/Dixifti diui Thomæ aqui
natis pofitioné de aiogȝ imortalitate qq̄ uerā/& i fe firmiffimā nullo pacto ambigeres/Ariftotelis
tamé dictis minime cöfonare cenfebas:ea pp nifi tibi moleftū effet/abfre duo itelligere maxime
defiderare:Primū/f.quid reuelationibus/& miraculis femoris/pfiftendoqȝ pure infra limites na
turales hac in re fentis:Altegȝ uero/quā nā fententia Ariftotelis in eadé materia fuiffe cenfes: At
ego qum omniū ibi aftantiū/idé maximū defideriū cöfpiceré (Et.n.multi aderāt) Sic tūc ipfi.Di
lectiffime fili uofqȝ cæteri/Et fi nõ pagȝ petis/altiffimū.n.huiufmodi negotiū eft/cū oés fere illu/
ftres Phylofophi i hoc laborauerint: Quoniā tamé nõ nifi ré quā poffum/quid.f.exiftimé poftu
las/facile &.n.eft hoc tibi aperire:ideo libenti aio tibi moré gerā:Cætegȝ uero/an ita fe habeat res
ut exiftimo/peritiores cöfules: Rem ig itur deo duce aggrediar.

Caput primū i quo oftéditur hominen effe ancipitis naturæ mediūqȝ iter mortalia/& imortalia

NITIVM autem cöfiderationis noftræ/hinc fumendū duxi/hominé.f.nõ fim
plicis/fed multiplicis/nõ certæ fed ancipitis naturæ effe/mediūqȝ inter morta/
lia & imortalia collocari:hoc aüt uidere apertū eft fi eius effentiales operatio/
nes ex quibus eéntiæ notificátur infpexerimus: Eo &.n.quod uegetatiuæ/&
fenfitiuæ opera exercet/quæ ut.z.de aia &.z.de generatione aialiū capire.3.tra
ditur/fine inftruméto corporali caducoqȝ exerceri non poffunt/mortalitatem
induit: Eo aüt quod intelligit & uult/quæ operationes/ut p totū librū de aia/
& primo de partibus aialium cap.primo: Et.z.de generatione aialium cap.3.habetur/fine iftru
méto corporali exercentur:qd̄ feparabilitaté & i materialitaté arguit/hæc uero imortalitatem
iter imortalia cönumerádus eft. Ex quibus tota colligi pót cöclufio/non fimplicis.f.naturæ effe
cū tres aias ut fere ita dixerim includat:uegetatiuā uidelicet/fenfitiuā/& intellectiuā:ancipitéqȝ
naturā fibi uendicare/cū neqȝ fimpliciter mortalis/neqȝ fimpliciter imortalis exiftat/uegȝ utráqȝ
naturā amplectitur:Quapp bene enunciauerút antiqui cū ipfum inter æterna/& téporalia ftatue
runt/ob eam caufam:qȝ neqȝ pure æternus/neqȝ pure téporalis fit:cū de utraqȝ natura participet:
ipfiqȝ fic in medio exifteti data eft poteftas utrā uelit naturā induat:quo factū eft:ut tres modi
hominū inueniantur:Quidá náqȝ inter deos cönumerati funt/licet p pauci. Et hi funt qui fubis
gatis uegetatiuæ/& fenfitiuæ/quafi toti röales effecti funt:Quidá uero ex toto neglecto itellectu/
foliíqȝ uegetatiuæ/& fenfitiuæ incūbétes/quafi in beftias trāfmigrauerunt: Et hoc fortaffis uo/
luit Apologus pythagoreus cū dixit aias humanas in diuerfas beftias tranfire: Quidá uero puri
homines nuncupati funt:Et hi funt qui mediocriter fecundū uirtutes morales uixerūt:nõ tamé
ex toto intellectui incubuere neqȝ prorfus uirtutibus corporeis uacauere:hogȝ tamé modorum
unufquifqȝ magnā hét latitudine/ficuti uidere apertū eft:Huic ét cöfonat quod i pfalmo dicitur
Minuifti eum paulominus ab angelis:&c.

Caput.z.in quo ponuntur modi quibus dicta multiplicitas humanæ naturæ intelligi poteft.

Ifa itaqȝ multiplici/ancipitiqȝ hominis natura/nõ ea quidé quæ ex cöpofitione materiæ
& formæ refultat/fed ea que ex parte ipfius formæ feu animæ.Videndū reftat cum im
mortale/& mortale oppofita fint/quæ de eodé affirmari nequeūt/merito quis ambiget
quo fieri modo poffit:ut hæc fimul de humana aia dicátur:Etenim hoc uidere non leue:Quare
uel una & eadé natura ftatuef/quæ fimul mortalis & imortalis fit/aut altera & altera: quod fi fe
cūdū def.hoc tribus modis intelligi poterit:Aut igȝ fecūdū numegȝ hominū erit numerus mor/
taliū/& imortaliū/utpote in Socrate erit una imortalis/& una aut duæ mortales/ & fic de cæte/
ris/fic qȝ unufquifqȝ homo/ppriā mortalem/& imortalem habeat:Aut porius in oibus homini
bus una tantū ftatuetur imortalis/fecundū unumquéqȝ aüt hominé mortales funt diftributæ &
multiplicatæ/an magis ecöuerfo:imortalem multiplicatā/mortalé uero oibus comunem pone

A ij

FIG. 8. Title page of first edition of Pietro Pomponazzi's *Tractatus de immortalitate animae*. Bologna: Giustiniano da Ruberio, November 6, 1516. *Annenberg Rare Book and Manuscript Library, University of Pennsylvania.*

taught at the major university within the papal state.[73] Indeed, in response to an offer from another university, the Bolognese government in 1518 raised his salary to a very high level (see Ch. 1, "Bologna in the Sixteenth Century"). The only sign of caution is that Pomponazzi did not publish two other controversial works, perhaps for fear of the consequences.[74]

Thus, the 1513 bull failed to bring natural philosophy and theology into harmony. Instead, the bull and Pomponazzi's treatise inadvertently established the grounds for their divorce.

THE IMMORTALITY OF THE SOUL AFTER POMPONAZZI

The debate continued. Philosophers wrote many more treatises on the immortality of the soul and on what might be labeled "human psychology," that is, sense perception and the operation of the human intellect. Probably the majority of Italian professors of natural philosophy defended the proposition that reason could demonstrate the immortality of the soul. As the war of books went on, the end result became clear: natural philosophers on both sides of the question accepted the separation between what natural philosophy taught and what theology taught.[75]

Teaching that the human soul was mortal according to philosophy sounded a discordant note in the harmony of the Catholic Reformation. Preachers sometimes denounced philosophers who held that the soul was mortal. Fra Cornelio Musso (1511–74), a Franciscan and possibly the most famous preacher in Italy, studied at the University at Padua and later taught theology at the universities of Pavia and Bologna. In several sermons he denounced the Averroist views that the soul was mortal, the world eternal, the intellect unitary, and that devils did not exist.[76]

Since practically all students in the faculty of arts and medicine attended lectures in natural philosophy, the question of the demonstrability of the immortality of the human soul may have resonated in the university and beyond more than anything else taught there. And it could surface outside the university in unusual circumstances. For example, in January 1572 the Venetian Inquisition investigated the religious views of one Teofilo Panarelli. The Holy Office questioned his sister, who stated that the accused denied purgatory "as a philosopher."

73. Pine, 1986, 124–31.

74. They were *De naturalium effectuum admirandorum causis seu de incantationibus* and *De fato*, published in Protestant Basel in 1556 and 1567, respectively. The former work was placed on the Index of Prohibited Books in 1596.

75. Di Napoli, 1963, 254–421; Pine, 1986, 124–233; Kessler, 1988, 504–7, 518–34; Iorio, 1991, 141–289; and Michael, 1993.

76. See Musso, 1558, 296; Musso, 1580, 29–30; Musso, 1610, 345, 406, 412, 496; and Poppi, 1989, 127–41, for more. Fra Francesco Panigarola (1548–94), another famous preacher, denounced the concept of the eternity of the world and the universal intellect of the Averroists. But he also seemed to make a distinction between what the philosopher can know about the soul through reason and how much more the theologian aided by Scripture can know. This included certainty that the soul is immortal. Panigarola, 1617, 145, 332.

She probably meant that Panarelli had learned and accepted the philosophical position that the soul was mortal. Denial of purgatory followed logically.[77]

Panarelli had studied medicine at the University of Padua between 1554 and 1559.[78] Although his sister never stated with whom Panarelli studied, the likeliest candidate to teach that the soul was mortal was Marcantonio Genua de' Passeri (1490/91–1563), first ordinary professor of natural philosophy from 1531 to 1563 and a popular figure with students and the Venetian authorities. Differing somewhat from Pomponazzi, Genua held with Averroës to a universal eternal intellect in which humans participated. But man's participation through his individual intellect perished with his body. Hence, in a more complicated way Passeri also denied philosophically the immortal human soul.[79]

But Panarelli's alleged philosophical denial of the soul's immortality was not the whole story. Further investigation revealed that Panarelli was a fervent Calvinist who instructed others in Calvinist beliefs. Why, then, had his sister testified that Panarelli denied the immortality of the soul "as a philosopher?" The probable answer is that she was trying to distract the tribunal from uncovering the true reason for her brother's denial of purgatory, a Protestant position, by claiming that he held an acceptable philosophical position. The Inquisition would not prosecute Panarelli for denying the philosophical demonstrability of the soul's immortality. But it did prosecute him for believing in John Calvin. The Venetian Inquisition extradited Panarelli to Rome, where he was hanged as an obstinate and unrepentant heretic in 1572.[80]

As the century wore on and the next began, some professors continued to teach that the individual human intellective soul was mortal according to philosophy.[81] They exploited the escape clause in *Apostolici regiminis* to claim the right to teach that Aristotelian philosophy, properly understood, denied the soul's immortality. And they did not necessarily teach the Christian position. Cesare Cremonini (1550–1631) was an example.

Cremonini, who taught at the universities of Ferrara (1578–1590) and Padua

---

77. "Hà negato il purgatorio come Filosofo." Testimony of Virginia Panarelli, sister of Teofilo, of Jan. 19, 1572, in ASVe, Santo Uffizio, Bu. 32, Processo Teofilo Panarelli, Virginia Panarelli, Catherina Panarelli, Francesco Rocca libraro, Giulio Gemma, et Hieronimo de Padua, f. 7ʳ.

78. Testimony of Teofilo Panarelli of Jan. 18, 1572, in ibid., Processo Teofilo Panarelli e Ludovico Abioso, no pag. This is a separate fascicle from the one cited in the preceding note.

79. Di Napoli, 1963, 348–50; Kessler, 1988, 523–27, esp. 525. For praise of Passeri, see the 1549 report of Bernardo Navagero, Venetian governor of Padua, in *Relazioni*, 1975, 25.

80. Panarelli was a key figure in a network of religious dissenters under investigation. See Grendler, 1977, 104–5, for a summary of the story.

81. For example, Marcantonio Genua de' Passeri and Jacopo Zabarella at Padua and Francesco Buonamici (1533–1603; see Helbing, 1989, 341 n. 36) at Pisa, among others, held that the immortality of the soul could not be demonstrated philosophically, and they had no difficulty. Girolamo Borri, or Borro (1512–92), a conservative Aristotelian who taught natural philosophy at the universities of Perugia and Pisa, renounced the view that the soul was mortal in Rome in 1583, served a year in prison, and then returned to teaching. He is the only person known to have been imprisoned for holding that the soul was mortal. But he was also imprisoned on two other occasions on suspicion of Protestantism and for holding prohibited books. It is likely that neither his complete views nor the full story is known. See Grendler, 1996a, 39–42.

(1591–1629) was probably the most prominent and best-paid professor of natural philosophy in Italy in his time. He was denounced to the Paduan Inquisition and had to respond several times between 1604 and 1626.[82] One of the charges was that Cremonini was not simply explaining Aristotle's position but personally held that the soul was mortal and taught this view to students.

The major confrontation came in 1619. Cremonini published a cosmological work entitled *Disputatio de coelo* in 1613. The Roman Congregation of the Holy Office forwarded to the Paduan Inquisition a long list of its objections to Cremonini's book in July 1614 and again in September. Cremonini eventually replied with a *Responsio* at the end of 1614, to which the papacy had further objections. In general, the Congregation objected that Cremonini's interpretation of Aristotle did not conform to Christian truth. Cremonini, on the other hand, insisted on a separation between the thought of Aristotle and Christian revelation and refused to correct his own book. If it had to be corrected in order to make it conform to Christian truth, this was a task for a theologian, he stated. In 1616 he published an *Apologia* repeating and elaborating his position.[83]

The Congregation in Rome returned to the issue in the summer of 1619 with a renewed demand that Cremonini make changes in his work. The inquisitor of Padua relayed the demands to Cremonini, informing him that he must follow the decree of the Fifth Lateran Council. Cremonini had to refute Aristotle's position and defend the Catholic faith. And he had to correct the book himself; this was his duty as "a Christian and Catholic philosopher."[84]

Cremonini rejected the idea that he had to be a Christian philosopher. Against the decree of the Fifth Lateran Council that philosophers must teach Christian truth, Cremonini argued that philosophers should not have to do the work of theologians. As an Aristotelian philosopher, Cremonini would not make the changes demanded. If it wished, the Inquisition could get a professional theologian to correct the work by refuting the erroneous opinions of Aristotle. But as a philosopher, Cremonini could not and would not do this. He was a philosopher who taught what could be demonstrated philosophically and nothing more. He

---

82. The following is based on Poppi, 1993, which reviews Cremonini's encounters with the Inquisition on the basis of new documents that he has discovered. He also includes important documents previously available. For other aspects of Cremonini's life and thought, see Della Torre, 1968; Lohr, 1975, 728–39; Schmitt 1980, 1983c, 10–12, 27, 31, 33, 102, 138–39, and 1984b; Spini, 1983, 155–59 and passim; and Kuhn, 1996. See *CHRP,* 814–15, for bibliography. For a summary of his Ferrara career, see Chiellini, 1991, 226–27, and *I maestri di Ferrara,* 1991, 217.

83. This was his *Apologia dictorum Aristotelis de quinta coeli substantia adversus Xenarchum, Ioannem Grammaticum et alios* (Venice, 1616).

84. "La Santità di Nostro Signore m'ha ordinato ch'io faccia sapere a Vostra Signoria che nella sua *Apologia* non solo non ha sodisfatto alla corettione del primo libro inscripto *Disputatio de Coelo* secondo la dispositione del Concilio Lateranense sciogliendo le ragioni d'Aristotele confutandolo, e manifestamente difendendo la fede Catholica. . . . Per tanto Vostra Signoria corega per se stessa il primo libro secondo il prescritto del Concilio Lateranense, et essendo questo debito suo, e non de' Theologi e d'altri, Vostra Signoria lo deve fare così per obligo di Coscienza, essendo quel Philosopho Christiano e Catholico che dice di essere." Letter of Father Paolo Sansoni, inquisitor of Padua, to Cremonini, July 3, 1619, as printed in Poppi, 1993, 102–3, quote on 102.

was paid to teach Aristotle as he understood him and would do so. If he did anything else, he would have to return his salary, because he would not be doing the job for which he had been hired.[85] There the matter rested. The Congregation of the Index placed *Disputatio de coelo* on the Index of Prohibited Books in 1623, but did nothing to Cremonini.[86]

Cremonini offered a ringing declaration of the independence of philosophy from theology. And he delivered as strong an affirmation of the freedom of the lecture hall to be found anywhere in Europe at this time. The unwavering support of the Venetian government enabled him to defy ecclesiastical authorities. But the Italian university tradition of teaching Aristotle independently of theological considerations, a tradition that began in the Middle Ages, as acknowledged by *Apostolici regiminis,* affirmed by Pomponazzi, and invoked by Cremonini, played the key role. Despite concern for souls who might be led astray by a professor teaching that philosophy could not demonstrate the soul's immortality, Rome did not overturn the methods of teaching Aristotelian philosophy. Aristotle was more powerful than a papal bull.

The only way that religious authorities might have ensured that all university philosophers taught that the soul was immortal would have been to control appointments, which was impossible. Only at Parma were they able to secure this result. During negotiations in 1599 to found the University of Parma, Father Antonio Possevino of the Society of Jesus insisted in his discussions with Duke Ranuccio I Farnese, duke of Parma and Piacenza, that the professors of philosophy should be Jesuits rather than laymen. If a philosopher was not first a good theologian, then he would inevitably introduce "pestilential errors on the mortality of the soul or the like."[87] Possevino got his way. When the new University of Parma opened in 1601, Jesuits held the professorships of natural philosophy.

Except for Parma, Aristotelian natural philosophy remained secular. Its professors discussed a range of philosophical and scientific issues alongside professors of medicine who studied the organic parts of humans and other animals. They confirmed and strengthened the separation of natural philosophy from theology. Metaphysics and moral philosophy, by contrast, became more bonded to theology (see Chs. 10 and 11). After Pomponazzi, "philosophy would no longer be identical with Aristotle, nor Aristotle with St. Thomas and the teaching of the

85. "Vedremo anco insieme il Concilio Lateranense, et così farò quella ocorrerà, ma quanto al mutar il mio modo di dire, non so come poter io promettere di trasformar me stesso. Chi ha un modo, chi un altro. Non posso ne anco retrattare espositioni d'Aristotele, poiché l'intendo così, e son pagato per dichiararlo come l'intendo, e nol facendo sarei obligato alla restitutione della mercede; così anco non posso retrattare considerationi haute circa li Interpreti, e refutationi ch'habia[te] fatte delle loro esplicationi: ci va l'honor mio, l'interesse della Cathedra, e per tanto del Prencipe." Reply of Cremonini to the Paduan inquisitor, no date but 1619, as printed in Poppi, 1993, 104–5, quote on 105. See also Poppi's comments on 30–31. The statement is also found in Della Torre, 1968, 59–60.

86. Poppi, 1993, 36.

87. "Altri potrebbono pretendere letture di filosofia benché fossero secolari, la quale quando è letta da chi non è prima buon Teologo, serve spessissimo per introdurre pestilenti errori della mortalità dell'anima, o di altro." Possevino's account of discussions between the duke and himself in an undated (but late 1599) document printed in Brizzi, 1980, 183–89, quote at 188.

church; a philosopher could be a Thomist, an Aristotelian, a Platonist or anything else, provided that his philosophy was conclusive and coherent."[88] Natural
philosophy became increasingly eclectic.

PLATONIC PHILOSOPHY IN THE UNIVERSITIES

The most significant new philosophical influence was Platonism accompanied by Neoplatonism from the ancient world and the Renaissance. Plato became much better known through Marsilio Ficino's translation and the Platonism
and Neoplatonism found in ancient Greek writers. Although the natural philosophy curriculum inherited from the Middle Ages had no room for Plato, three
universities introduced Platonic natural philosophy in the sixteenth century.
Francesco Patrizi attempted to substitute a comprehensive Platonic natural philosophy for that of Aristotle.

A Latin Plato began to appear in the first half of the fifteenth century, as Italian
humanists prepared Latin translations of works not previously available.[89] After
Marsilio Ficino's Latin translation was printed in 1484, scholars could more easily
study, comment on, and teach Plato's works, if they wished. Ficino himself may
have introduced Plato into the university classroom. He taught natural philosophy at the University of Florence in 1466, probably as an extraordinary lecturer
and at a low salary. A contemporary stated that Ficino lectured publicly on Plato's
Philebus to a large audience in the late 1460s, but whether as a university professor
or privately is unknown.[90]

The first secure notice of university teaching of a Platonic text occurred when
Theodore Gaza taught Greek and eloquence at the University of Ferrara between
1446 and 1449. Gaza began by teaching Demosthenes' *On the Crown,* which was
soon followed by Plato's *Gorgias,* a work critical of rhetoric which also, in Gaza's
opinion, demonstrated the power of rhetoric. Thus, Gaza used one dialogue of
Plato as part of his rhetorical instruction.[91] The Greek émigré scholars did not
promote Platonic philosophy but concentrated on translating and teaching Aristotle, because this helped them to get university professorships.

The second known example of formal university lectures on a Platonic text
came from Henry Cornelius Agrippa von Nettesheim (1486–1535), the German
scholar of the occult, who taught at the University of Pavia from 1512 to 1515
and at the University of Turin between 1515 and 1517. He lectured on Plato's
Symposium at one of the two universities and also taught the Hermetic and
Neoplatonic *Pimander* at Pavia in 1515.[92] The much more influential Niccolò
Leonico Tomeo, who taught Aristotle from the Greek text at Padua between

88. Kessler, 1988, 507. See Lohr, 1988a, 604–5, for a similar conclusion.

89. The fundamental study of the fifteenth-century translations and commentaries is Hankins,
1990. To be sure, a certain amount of Platonism and Neoplatonism was present in the Middle Ages
and influenced such figures as Thomas Aquinas.

90. See Davies, 1992, which is summarized in Davies, 1998, 122–23.

91. Monfasani, 1983, 180, and 1990a, 59–60; and Bianca, 1999, 739.

92. *Memorie di Pavia,* 1970, pt. 1:169; Nauert, 1965, 39, 40, 41, 45, 46, 51, 52; Schmitt, 1976b, 99.

1497 and 1506, also taught Plato. But how he did it, and the role that Plato played in his teaching, are unclear.[93]

As Platonic and Neoplatonic views became available, Aristotelian professors of natural philosophy took note. They did not lecture on Platonic texts but made use of Platonic and Neoplatonic views in other ways. Finding a particular Aristotelian opinion questionable, the professor might substitute one taken from Plato or a Neoplatonist in an overall Aristotelian or eclectic argument. A philosopher might use material from a pseudo-Aristotelian work accepted as genuine, even though many of these works reflected a good deal of ancient Neoplatonism. Some natural philosophers with syncretic tendencies noted similarities between Aristotle and Plato. Finally, some Aristotelians relied on and borrowed from the works of modern Neoplatonists such as Marsilio Ficino.[94]

Committed Platonists spread their views outside the university through their writing, private teaching, and the numerous informal literary and philosophical academies found in Italy in the first three quarters of the sixteenth century. Much vernacular literature was drenched in Platonism and Neoplatonism. On the very rare occasions in which a Plato enthusiast obtained a university post, he might introduce Platonic material into the required lectures on Aristotelian texts and express his allegiance to Plato in other ways. Francesco Cattani da Diacceto (1466–1522) was an example.

A Florentine from a noble family with close connections to the Medici, Cattani was a pupil of Ficino's whom contemporaries saw as Ficino's successor as the leader of Florentine Platonists. Cattani wrote various works on Plato, probably taught Plato privately, and participated in informal discussion groups, including the well-known gatherings at the Orti Oricellari (the gardens of the Rucellai family palace). Then in 1502 he was appointed to teach both natural philosophy and moral philosophy as part of the small group of professors who remained in Florence after the university moved to Pisa. Although Cattani had studied at the University of Pisa from 1490 to 1493, the appointment notice mentioned that he had no doctorate and had not disputed publicly. He received a salary of 100 florins, quickly raised to 200. Cattani held the post through 1521, teaching only natural philosophy from 1516 onward, at which time he was paid 525 florins.[95]

93. See the evidence for his Platonic teaching collected by Schmitt, 1976b, 99 and nn. 25 and 26 on p. 103.

94. See Schmitt, 1982a, 180; Mahoney, 1970a, 456–57; and Mahoney, 1986. On the pseudo-Aristotelian works, on which much needs to be done, see Schmitt and Knox, 1985, and Schmitt, Kraye, and Ryan, 1986, 3–14. Federico Pendasio (1522/25–1603), who taught logic at Pavia for an unknown period of time then was ordinary professor of natural philosophy at Padua (1564–70) and Bologna (1571–1603), offers an example of the interest in Plato. He composed a series of lectures on the differences between Aristotle and Plato. Purnell, 1974, 20 n. 10. See also Di Napoli, 1963, 369–74; Iorio, 1991, 264–71.

95. Fabroni, 1971, 1:392, for the 1502 appointment. Further information is found in Verde, 1973–94, 2:218–23; vol. 3, pt. 1:284–85 (Cattani as student); and vol. 4, pt. 3:1460–63. Payment notices for 1516 to 1521 at an annual rate of 525 florins are found in ASF, Studio fiorentino e pisano, 8, "Stipendia per la [sic] studio di 1514 al 1521," ff. 131ᵛ, 134ʳ, 135ʳ, 136ᵛ, 139ʳ, 143ʳ, 161ᵛ, 163ᵛ, 168ʳ, 171ʳ. For Cattani's lecturing and writing, see Kristeller, 1956a, and Kristeller, 1979a.

He lectured on Aristotle's *De caelo et mundo, De anima*, the *Physics,* book 8, and possibly the *Meterology,* all standard texts for natural philosophy, and the *Nicomachean Ethics,* a standard text for moral philosophy.

Although Cattani lectured on the required Aristotelian texts, he devoted most of his writing to Plato and Platonic themes. In his works he attempted to show that Aristotle agreed with Plato on such issues as the soul and space. But Cattani followed Plato when they differed. For example, in his discussion of Aristotle's *De caelo et mundo,* he often departed from Aristotle in order to endorse Plato's views. Cattani greatly respected Aristotle and ancient Peripatetics but had only contempt for modern Aristotelians. On the reasonable assumption that his works indicated the direction of his teaching, it is likely that Cattani inserted a good deal of favorable comment on Plato into his university teaching. Writing on Plato, while teaching Aristotle and inserting into his lectures as much Plato as his audience would allow, was the path that a committed Platonist with a university position had to follow.

Platonism attracted some scholars because it offered a concordist alternative to the conflict between faith and reason argued by many Aristotelians. For example, in a public disputation at Pavia in 1536, Andreas Camuzio (1512–87), a professor of logic and natural philosophy at Pavia, argued that Plato, Aristotle, and Christian Scripture were in agreement. He repeated this assertion at another public disputation at Milan in 1541.[96] This was in the tradition of the concordist Platonism of Ficino and Giovanni Pico della Mirandola. Some outside the university agreed: the preacher Cornelio Musso, who denounced secular Aristotelianism, praised Plato for intuiting divine truth.[97]

Cattani and Camuzio were fifth columnists infiltrating some Platonism into an Aristotelian land. Although support for Platonism was growing, it had no formal position in the curriculum until Pisa and Ferrara appointed professors of Platonic philosophy within a year of each other. Rome and Pavia followed later.

The University of Pisa appointed the Florentine Francesco Verino il Secondo (also called Francesco de' Vieri; 1524–91) to lecture on Plato on holidays, that is, days on which ordinary lectures were not held, beginning in the academic year 1576–77.[98] The new post was an unpaid extraordinary lectureship that Verino held in addition to his ordinary lectureship in (Aristotelian) natural philosophy. The appointment came about on Verino's request, with the indispensable support of Grand Duke Francesco de' Medici and his consort, Grand Duchess Joanna of Austria. They continued a tradition of Medici support for Platonic studies which had begun when Cosimo de' Medici financed Ficino's Platonic

96. Schmitt, 1982a, 181–84, and *Memorie di Pavia,* 1970, pt. 1:169.

97. Musso, 1610, 412, and especially Poppi, 1989, 134, 137.

98. "Ad lecturam Platonis diebus festivi D. Franciscus Verinus Florentinus," as quoted from the archival source by Schmitt, 1972, 263 n. 103. See ibid., 263–64, for further information. See also Schmitt, 1976b, 99–100, and Barsanti, 1993, 538, 562. Verino enrolled at the University of Pisa in 1544 and obtained his doctorate there in 1552. For what follows, see Fabroni, 1971, 2:340–51; Del Fante, 1980b; and Gibba, 1995–96.

studies a century earlier. Verino taught the *Timaeus* the first year and the *Hipparchus* the following two years.[99]

Verino had definite philosophical and pedagogical goals in mind. In the first year he intended to demonstrate that Plato and Christianity were compatible, that Plato's notion of a creator and the Christian God of love were the same. In the second year he would explain the agreement between Plato and Aristotle, that both asserted the immortality of the human soul. In the third year he would elucidate aspects of Plato's philosophy. Verino also responded to the objections that Plato was unsystematic and that his teaching could not provide demonstrative proof necessary for scientific investigation. Plato provided probable reasons that could be grasped by a broad audience, not just those with university training, argued Verino. Moreover, Plato could be taught in simple language understood by all.

Verino's colleagues did not welcome the innovation. Verino complained of persecution and that others tried to dissuade his students from studying Plato.[100] When Verino published a book arguing for concord between Plato, Aristotle, and Christianity, Andrea Cesalpino (1524/25–1603), professor of medical botany and practical medicine at Pisa, harshly criticized him. Cesalpino was very scandalized that Verino should take up the arguments of heretical teachers of philosophy and medicine, from whom one learned wicked principles and deduced wicked conclusions, complained Verino. The conservative Aristotelian Girolamo Borri (1512–92), Verino's concurrent in the ordinary professorship of natural philosophy, also strongly objected to the attempt to reconcile Plato and Aristotle.[101] The critics apparently won. After a three-year period, for which Verino pleaded in vain for a salary for his Plato lectureship, he abandoned it in 1579.

The University of Ferrara went much further. It established an ordinary professorship of Platonic philosophy in 1577, the first such in Europe, and appointed Francesco Patrizi (Franjo Petrić in Croatian) to the post.

Patrizi came to the professorship via a circuitous route. Born in Cherso, a large island in the Adriatic Sea just south of the Istrian peninsula, he was the son of a minor noble. After a little schooling, his father sent Francesco on a seagoing galley captained by his uncle, apparently in the service of Venice during a three-cornered struggle between Venice, the Turks, and Dalmatian pirates.[102] During

99. See Verino's undated letter (possibly early 1580s) printed in Verde, 1983, 92.

100. "Harei seguitato, ma hebbi gran persecutori che mi levavano gli scolari con dissuadergli dallo studio di esso Platone." Verino's undated letter (early 1580s) printed in Verde, 1983, 92.

101. "El dottore [Andrea] Cesalpino, al quale io per commissione di Vostra Signoria Clarissima detti uno di quei libretti delle *conclusioni platoniche, theologicha et peripatetici* da me dedicatole, mi ha trovato et si è meco fortemente scandalezzato che io riprenda coloro i quali hanno uditi maestri heretici in filosofia et in medicina, da' quali si imparano cattivi principii, onde poi ne deducono cattive conclusioni." Letter of Verino to Baccio Valori, ducal secretary in Florence, of Feb. 7, 1590, Pisa. Printed in Verde, 1983, 84–86, quotation on 84. On Cesalpino, see De Ferrari, 1980. For additional evidence of hostility toward Verino's Platonic teaching and writing, see Schmitt, 1976a, 469–71; Del Fante, 1980b, 408; and Gibba, 1995–96, 146–47.

102. The following account of Patrizi's university studies and subsequent career is based on his

his years on the galley, he forgot how to read. But finding a copy of the *Fior di virtù,* a book of popular culture often used as a primary reader, he taught himself to read again and quickly passed to chivalric romances, always in Italian. When the galley returned to Venice in 1542, his uncle sent him to school in Venice to learn vernacular abbaco (commercial arithmetic) and bookkeeping, so that he might become a merchant. But his father, seeing the thirteen-year-old's eagerness to read, provided a tutor to teach him Latin. He next sent him to study in Ingolstadt, Bavaria, for fifteen months before the outbreak of war brought him back to Cherso for more schooling. He then went to the University of Padua in May 1547 to begin medical studies.

That summer, before he began attending formal lectures, Patrizi picked up a copy of Xenophon in Greek and Latin. Having earlier learned the rudiments of Greek, Patrizi now improved it "without any guide or help" (*senza niuna guida o aiuto*). He learned it so well that at the beginning of the academic year in November he began to read the Greek text of Aristotle's "logic" (some part of the *Organon*) plus its Greek commentaries. In the next three years at Padua, he pursued the studies of a medical student: he progressed from logic, to natural philosophy, and on to medicine at the feet of some of the most famous professors of the day. But Patrizi was dissatisfied with the Aristotelian logic and natural philosophy that he heard.

Then, sometime between 1548 and 1550, Patrizi heard a Franciscan friar sustain Platonic conclusions and "fell in love with Plato." He asked the friar if he would set him on "the Platonic way." The friar told him to read Ficino's *Theologica Platonica,* which Patrizi did with great enthusiasm.[103] This was the beginning of his lifelong devotion to Platonism. When his father died in 1551, Patrizi sold his Galen and other medical works and left the university. He did many different things in Rome, Venice, Padua, Ferrara, Cyprus, Spain, and elsewhere in the next decade and a half. Despite sometimes living far from the academic world, Patrizi published books on utopianism, honor, poetry, history, and rhetoric in Italian. In 1571 he published the *Discussiones peripateticae,* a sustained attack on Aristotle and Aristotelianism.

Returning from Spain in 1576 or 1577, Patrizi found himself in Modena, where he met Alfonso II Este, duke of Ferrara. There he also renewed his acquaintance, begun years earlier, with Antonio Montecatini (1537–99), professor of natural philosophy in the years 1567–1594, at the University of Ferrara. Although most of his publications dealt with Aristotle, Montecatini appreciated Plato as well. He published an epitome of Plato's *Laws* in 1561 and a commentary on the *Republic* in 1591.[104] Montecatini was also secretary to Duke Alfonso II and

---

own letter of Jan. 12, 1587. in Patrizi da Cherso, 1975, 46–51. For the *Fior di virtù* and the preuniversity curriculum generally, see Grendler, 1989, 275–80 and passim.

103. The friar's identity is a mystery. He could have taught at a convent *studium* in Padua or could have been a fellow student or someone passing through.

104. For Montecatini's teaching positions and lists of his printed and manuscript works, see especially Lohr, 1978, 595; Vasoli, 1989, 210–11; *I Maestri di Ferrara,* 1991, 252–53; and Chiellini, 1991, 235–36.

a powerful voice in Ferrara's intellectual life. Through Montecatini's influence, Patrizi, age forty-eight and lacking a university degree, was appointed ordinary professor of Platonic philosophy at the University of Ferrara in 1577, the first such position in a European university. Patrizi began teaching at the end of 1577 or the beginning of 1578. His appointment was listed as *Ad lecturam Reipublicae Platonis* in 1578–79 and *Ad lecturam philosophiae Platonicae* thereafter.[105]

In a broad sense, the professorship was the culmination of the growing interest in Platonic philosophy among Italian scholars. Locally, it reflected Montecatini's enthusiasm for Plato and probably Ferrara's strong interest in Greek studies, which had begun in the late fifteenth century and embraced both literature and medicine. Ferrara had a professorship of Greek orators and poets (*Ad lecturam oratorum et poetarum Graecorum*) from 1540 through 1575. It had two, and sometimes three, professors teaching the Greek works of Hippocrates (*Ad lecturam Graecam operum Hippocratis*) through the 1570s and much of the 1580s. And it had a professorship in the Greek language (*Ad lecturam linguae Graecae*).[106] Now Ferrara added a professor of Platonic philosophy.

Patrizi received an initial salary of 390 lire di marchesini, which rose to 400 lire in 1587–88 and 500 lire in 1591–92.[107] He earned less than did the leading professors of natural philosophy (500 to 800 lire), while Montecatini received a salary of 1,200 lire (the highest in the university), raised to 1,400 lire in 1583–84. But Montecatini's salary reflected additional responsibilities as ducal secretary and one of the Riformatori of the university. Patrizi earned a middling stipend, below the leading professors of medicine, law, and natural philosophy but comfortably above a cluster of minor legists, logicians, theologians, lesser humanists, mathematicians, and surgeons, who earned only 100 to 200 lire.[108] Ferrara saw the position as significant but not a star appointment.

Patrizi was a strong and original philosopher. Whereas previous Renaissance Platonists tried to find points of agreement between Aristotle and Plato, Patrizi rejected Aristotle completely. In his *Discussiones peripateticae* (1571; expanded edition 1581) Patrizi used humanistic philological techniques and his extensive knowledge of ancient Greek sources in order to subject the received picture of Aristotle to sharp historical criticism.[109] Patrizi concluded that ancient biographical sources proved that Aristotle had lived a dissolute life. He argued that Aristotle wrote only 4 of the 747 titles attributed to him at one time or another. Rather than being an original researcher in such fields as natural history, Aristotle was a mere compiler of the work of earlier Greek scientists. (Modern scholars believe that Aristotle did not write all of the *Historia animalium* and are uncertain

105. Franceschini, 1970, 265–66; Muccillo, 1992, 201–2 n. 6.

106. Franceschini, 1970, 250–51, 269–70.

107. See Muccillo, 1992, 201–2 n. 6; and Chiellini, 1991, 239.

108. Salary figures come from Solerti, 1892, 27–51 passim; Pardi, 1972, 248–50; Franchesini, 1970, 219–70 passim; and Chiellini, 1991, 235–36, for Montecatini and passim. All figures are lire di marchesini.

109. This summary is based on the excellent articles of Muccillo, 1981 and 1996, 73–193.

about the extent of his zoological research.)[110] Patrizi then reconstructed the history of the Aristotelian tradition in order to determine at what point the Stagirite had become an unquestioned authority. According to Patrizi, the earliest followers of Aristotle had freely criticized their master, but philosophical freedom vanished with Alexander of Aphrodisias in the second to third centuries A.D. In an impressive display of erudition and humanist historical criticism, Patrizi sought to demythologize, then to bury, Aristotle.

In his larger subsequent work *Nova de universis philosophia* (A new philosophy of universes; 1591), Patrizi offered his alternative to the Aristotelian system. The four-part work is a vast encyclopedia of natural philosophy based on Plato. Part 1, entitled *Panaugia,* deals with both the metaphysical and physical properties of light. From the first light (*prima lux,* or God) proceeds the illumination (*lumen*) of the world, which is both corporeal and incorporeal. In the physical world light is the source of movement and life. Part 2 is *Panarchia,* defined as "a series of all principles";[111] it deals with hierarchy in a Platonic sense. The third part is *Pampsychia,* "the theory of the all-soul." Soul appears in an intermediary position between the spiritual and corporeal world. This section discusses at some length the world-soul, which is the animating principle of the corporeal universe.

Part 4, entitled *Pancosmia* (the theory of the all-cosmos), discusses the physical world and is the most original part of the work. Here Patrizi offered an alternative to Aristotelian physical science. Rejecting Aristotle's four elements of earth, air, fire, and water, Patrizi proposed space, light, heat, and fluid or humidity. These substances combine with one another in different proportions to form mixed bodies, such as heaven, ether, air, stars, water, and earth. Patrizi began with space, seeing it as prior to all bodies and even to light. Patrizi's concept of space comprehended vacua and physical infinity, which Aristotelian science could not readily encompass. Patrizi also made a distinction between mathematical and physical space, something that Aristotelian natural philosophy could not do. Indeed, Patrizi raised mathematics to a higher level of importance than did Aristotelianism. Mathematics, especially geometry, was prior to physics; mathematics was needed to comprehend space. Patrizi also left room for empirical observation. The fourth part of the work has novel views (e.g., the stars move freely in ether rather than remain in solid spheres) that would influence or stimulate future scholars of the physical world and the heavens. Thus, as an alternative to Aristotle, Patrizi offered a powerful natural philosophy based on Plato and a panoply of ancient Greek sources, such as Lucretius and the Neoplatonic commentaries of Simplicius and John Philoponus. His system somewhat resembled the innovative natural philosophy of Bernardino Telesio but was still highly original.

110. Balme, 1981, 258–59; *Greek Literature,* 1985, 807.
111. The quotations come from Kristeller, 1964a, 121–22. There are good brief summaries of his thought with comprehensive bibliographies in Kristeller, 1964a, 110–26, 175–77, 186–87; Garin, 1966, 2:661–65, 712–13; Vasoli, 1983, 527–83; Muccillo, 1981, 1986b, 1992, and 1996; Vasoli, 1989; Leinkauf, 1990; and Copenhaver and Schmitt, 1992, 187–95.

Patrizi had a religious agenda as well. Throughout he argued for the compatibility of Platonism and Christian theology on God, including the Trinity. He wanted to substitute Plato and a coalition of ancient philosophers and texts, including Neoplatonists, some pre-Socratics, especially the *Corpus Hermeticorum*,[112] and Church Fathers, notably Saint Augustine, for the atheistic Aristotle, who denied creation in time, affirmed the eternity of the world, and saw only a First Mover rather than a personal God. It would be a "perennial philosophy" compatible with Christian revelation.[113] Aristotelianism was both a bad philosophical system and incompatible with Christianity. Platonism in the eclectic form developed by Patrizi was the superior philosophical system and compatible with Christianity.

In addition to explaining his philosophy, *Nova de universis philosophia* was probably part of Patrizi's campaign for a position at the University of Rome so that he might bring his philosophy to the center of Catholicism. He dedicated the book as a whole to Pope Gregory XIV, who reigned just long enough (December 5, 1590–October 15, 1591) to be the chief dedicatee, and the eleven parts of the book to a phalanx of cardinals who directed Rome's cultural agenda. Patrizi had become acquainted with several of them when he and they studied at the University of Padua.[114]

Then Cardinal Ippolito Aldobrandini, one of the dedicatees, became Pope Clement VIII on January 30, 1592. He immediately invited Patrizi to teach Platonic philosophy at the University of Rome. The pope's circle of supporters warmly welcomed Patrizi upon his arrival on April 18. He moved into the palace of Cardinal Cinzio Aldobrandini, the pope's favorite nephew and a major patron of learning, and joined the discussions of an informal academy organized by the cardinal.[115] Patrizi became ordinary professor of Platonic philosophy (*In philosophia platonica*). He received a four-year contract, which was unusually long, and 600 scudi per annum, a figure that tied him for the highest salary at the university with professor of practical medicine Andrea Cesalpino, newly arrived from Pisa.[116] Obviously, the papacy viewed Patrizi with esteem and the introduction of Platonic philosophy as an important initiative.

Patrizi began teaching at the University of Rome sometime between May 15 and June 6, 1592. He lectured on Plato's *Timaeus* to a large audience that included

---

112. See Copenhaver, 1992, an English translation with a historical account and extensive notes.

113. Muccillo, 1992, 205–7. On *philosophia perennis* in the Renaissance, see Schmitt, 1966; Schmitt, 1970; and Copenhaver and Schmitt, 1992, 184–85, 335–37.

114. Muccillo, 1992, 208–9. Many future prelates studied in universities in order to obtain doctorates in law. More of Italy's future leaders, clerical and lay, seem to have studied at Padua than at any other university.

115. On Cinzio Aldobrandini (1555–1610), see Guarini, 1960, and Grendler, 1977, 241, 267, 269, 272–73, 278. Cinzio Aldobrandini is best remembered as the friend and patron of Torquato Tasso, who also lived in the palace. Muccillo, 1992, 210–15.

116. See *I maestri di Roma*, 1991, 1:130 (Cesalpino), and 132, 136, 141, 146 (Patrizi) for their places on the rolls.

many cardinals, according to his own account. In the following academic year he lectured on book 2 of Plato's *Laws*.[117]

Despite papal favor, Patrizi's daring philosophical program immediately ran into trouble. A Spanish Dominican, Fra Pedro de Saragoza, charged that some theses in the *Nova de universis philosophia* were heretical; he also objected to Patrizi's attacks on the great figures of the Dominican order, Albertus Magnus and Thomas Aquinas. The accuser was a close associate of Bartolomeo de Miranda, another Dominican friar who was Master of the Sacred Palace. In that capacity he oversaw press censorship in Rome and was an ex officio member of the Congregation of the Index, which ruled on censorship matters for the Catholic world.[118] On November 7, 1592, the Congregation of the Index summoned Patrizi to answer the charges. Thus began a two-year struggle between Patrizi and the Congregation.

Patrizi defended himself in various ways.[119] He argued that some statements by pre-Christian authors should not be understood literally and that some philosophical issues were unresolvable. He stated that various of his statements, and some taken from ancient authors, found theologically objectionable by his accuser, referred to the physical world and not to theological matters. Patrizi also argued that his accuser had misquoted him and had taken statements out of context. Throughout Patrizi affirmed the importance of his philosophical synthesis of Plato, the early Neoplatonists, pre-Socratics, Hermetic authors, and Church Fathers and that it was compatible with Catholic Christianity. At the same time, Patrizi reiterated that Aristotle was the suborner of Christianity, because he denied divine creation, held the world to be eternal, and denied the immortality of the human soul. Patrizi also constantly professed his willingness to accept the tribunal's judgment and to emend his text, if required. He sought favorable opinions from learned clerics. And he pleaded for permission to publish an emended version, which appeared in Venice with the date 1593, although it may have been printed in 1594.

---

117. Muccillo, 1992, 219.

118. Unfortunately, the text of the denunciation has not been found. Little is known of Fra Pedro (d. 1623) except that he was associated with Bartolomeo de Miranda (d. 1597) during the latter's six years as Master of the Sacred Palace. See *Scriptores Ordinis Praedicatorum*, n.d., vol. 2, pt. 1:321, 432, for brief biographies of the two Dominicans. The Master of the Sacred Palace was also the pope's personal theologian and his closest theological advisor, if the pope so wished. Clement VIII did not. For the office of Master of the Sacred Palace, see McCuaig, 1989, 261–62, and Grendler, 1994, 273.

Whether Fra Bartolomeo or the Congregation of the Index directed Fra Pedro to examine the book or whether he did it on his own initiative is unknown. More generally, one wonders if an Aristotelian at the university, or one of the many Scholastic theologians in Rome, first brought Patrizi to the attention of the friar or the Master of the Sacred Palace. It will be recalled that Andrea Cesalpino opposed the milder Platonism of Francesco Verino when he taught at Pisa.

119. For Patrizi's battle with the Congregation of the Index, see the following works replete with documents: Firpo, 1950–51, 159–73; Firpo, 1970 (an English version of the former lacking full notes); Gregory, 1953; Gregory, 1955; Patrizi da Cherso, 1970 and 1993; and Muccillo, 1992, 229–32. There is more bibliography, but these are the essential works.

Above all, Patrizi fought to persuade the Congregation not to place his mag-
num opus on the revised Index of Prohibited Books nearing completion.[120] The
Congregation, in turn, delayed a decision while it sought advice from scholars.
No doubt the breadth, complexity, originality, and polemical tone of the work
made a decision difficult. Finally, the Congregation asked the Jesuit Cardinal
Francisco de Toledo, a convinced Aristotelian and a leading figure in neo-
Scholasticism (also called Second Scholasticism) of the late sixteenth century, to
evaluate the work.[121] His judgment was very negative. On July 2, 1594, the
Congregation accepted Toledo's view; it banned *Nova de universis philosophia* and
ordered copies to be destroyed. However, the new Index of Prohibited Books,
finally promulgated in 1596, eased the condemnation: the book was prohibited
unless corrected by the author subject to the approval of the Master of the Sacred
Palace.[122] But it was never published again.

Patrizi continued to teach at the University of Rome throughout the controversy. But whether he taught beyond 1596 (his four-year contract probably ended
in June 1596) is unknown, because the rolls for 1595–96 and 1596–97 are missing. Patrizi died on February 7, 1597, in the palace of Cardinal Cinzio Aldobrandini. Upon his death and despite the controversy, the papacy sought to continue
the Platonic initiative by appointing another Platonist, Jacopo Mazzoni (1548–
98).[123] Earlier he had been a concordist, but in 1597 he published a book emphasizing the differences between Aristotle and Plato (see below). Unfortunately, he
died in 1598, before he could have made much of an impact.

At about this time, Clement VIII, who still inclined toward continuing the
Platonic post, asked Cardinal Robert Bellarmine for advice. The erudite neo-
Scholastic Jesuit responded that because Platonism had such a close affinity with
Christianity, it more easily led minds into error than did other pagan philosophies. Hence, it was more dangerous than Aristotelianism. Taking Bellarmine's
advice, the pope terminated the professorship of Platonic philosophy upon the
death of Mazzoni.[124] Thus ended the most important attempt to make Platonic

120. Throughout the controversy over Patrizi's book, the Congregation of the Index was preoccupied with the completion and promulgation of a new index, the first revision since 1564.
Versions of 1590 and 1593 were completed and then withdrawn; the Clementine Index finally
appeared in 1596. For the lengthy negotiations and battles involving the Congregations of the Index
and the Inquisition, several popes, other Vatican figures, and the Venetian government, see Grendler,
1994; *Index de Rome, 1590, 1593, 1596,* 1994; and Fragnito, 1997, 143–98.

121. Although his condemnation of Patrizi's work has not survived, the minute of the Congregation of the Holy Office indicates that it was very negative. Toledo (1532; cardinal 1593; d. 1596)
taught philosophy and theology at the Jesuit Collegio Romano and wrote commentaries on Aristotle's logic, *Physics, De generatione et corruptione,* and *De anima,* and Thomas Aquinas's *Summa Theologiae.* He also wrote various exegetical works on the New Testament and advised the papacy on
several diplomatic issues. For a short sketch, see Pérez Goyena, 1913. For his extensive involvement in
papal affairs, see Pastor, 1891–1953, vols. 19–24, index.

122. "Francisci Patritii Nova de universis philosophia, nisi fuerit ab auctore correcta et Romae
cum approbatione R. Magistri Sacri Palatii impressa." *Index de Rome 1590, 1593, 1596,* 1994, 549–50.

123. Muccillo, 1992, 234–36, esp. nn. 89 and 90.

124. The story comes from a 1631 biography of Bellarmine and is repeated in Firpo, 1950–51,

philosophy a part of the ordinary curriculum of Italian Renaissance universities. The controversy with the Congregation of the Index buried Patrizi's grand plan under the suspicion of heresy. Given the opposition, it is remarkable that Clement VIII supported the Platonic professorship as long as he did.

Patrizi's ordinary professorships at Ferrara and especially Rome marked the high point of university Platonism. After the elimination of the Platonic position at Rome, Platonism gradually subsided everywhere. In 1591, after Verino's death in the same year, Jacopo Mazzoni, already an ordinary professor of natural philosophy, renewed the Platonic holiday lectureship at Pisa, which had been dormant since 1579. This time the lectureship lasted longer, from 1591 through 1604, then 1609–21 and 1633–35, when it disappeared.[125] The statutes of the state-supported student residence Collegio Ferdinando (which opened in 1595) offered support of the lectureship by insisting that its library should include the *opera omnia* (whether in Latin or Greek is not indicated) of Plato.[126]

The University of Pavia followed the Pisan example for a few years in the early seventeenth century. It added an extraordinary holiday lectureship on Plato between 1606 and 1614, taught by Leonardo Maurizi (or Leo Mauritius) of Arezzo, an ordinary professor of natural philosophy who added the Platonic post to his duties. Nothing more is known about the position.[127] The University of Bologna considered creating a Plato lectureship, to be filled by either Mazzoni or Flaminino Pappazoni, then teaching logic at the University of Pavia, in 1588. But Bologna did not create a Plato lectureship and, perhaps, never took the idea seriously. Pappazoni (c. 1550–1613), a native of Bologna, came to Bologna in 1589, but as an ordinary professor of natural philosophy teaching the standard Aristotelian texts.[128]

166; Firpo, 1970, 278; and Muccillo, 1992, 235–36. Firpo believes that the encounter occurred in 1597 after Patrizi's death, but Muccillo places it in 1598 after Mazzoni's death.

125. Carlo Tomasi filled the position from 1598 to 1604, Cosimo Boscagli from 1609 to 1621, and Girolamo Bardi from 1633 to 1635. All were minor figures. Barsanti, 1993, 508, 510, 536, 562. The texts taught in the years 1617–19 were the *Timaeus, Phaedrus,* and *Republic.* Schmitt, 1976b, 100.

126. Biagi, 1980, 113, statute of 1594. Whether Plato's works were actually acquired for the library is not known.

127. *Memorie di Pavia,* 1970, pt. 1:176, under the name of "Maurizio Aretino Leone." As "Leo Mauritius Aretinus" he is listed as the first ordinary professor of natural philosophy in the roll of 1601–2. ASPv, Università, Cartone 20, Rotoli originali 1506–1601, no pag. Maurizi earlier taught logic at the University of Pisa (1588–95). See the rolls of 1589–90 and 1590–91 in Galilei, 1966, 39, 41, and Barsanti, 1993, 525.

128. Letter of ambassador Camillo Paleotti to Bologna of June 11, 1588, Rome, in ASB, Assunteria di Studio, Bu. 79, Lettere di diversi all'assunteria, 1575–1691, no pag. Paleotti had spoken to Cardinals Agostino Valier and Federico Borromeo about the matter, which he said had been often discussed by the Bolognese government. Costa (1907b, 90 n. 55) adds details. The cardinals had initially proposed the Plato appointment, but the Bolognese authorities saw such an appointment more as a frill than a necessity: "E ben vero che altre volte s'è ragionato d'introdurre in questo Studio la lettura di Platone più per ornamento che per necessità, ma però fin qui non si è concluso di farlo." Letter of the government to the ambassador of Aug. 6, 1588, quoted in Costa, 1907b, 90 n. 55. Tutor and friend of Federico Borromeo, Pappazoni was ordinary professor of natural philosophy (1580–83) and of logic (1583–88) at Pavia. *Memorie di Pavia,* 1970, pt. 1:175. He appears in the roll of 1584–85

The effort to make Platonism a significant part of the teaching and research of the university failed. Beyond Patrizi's problems in Rome, there were broader scientific, pedagogical, and religious reasons for its failure to win a place in the university curriculum. Even though institutional inertia embodied in university statutes opposed change, when a coalition of professors and civic authorities became convinced that change would be useful, it happened. The introduction of professorships of humanistic studies, Greek, Vesalian anatomy, medical botany, and new positions in law demonstrated that Italian universities could change. But the majority of professors and civil authorities were not convinced of the utility of Platonic philosophy.

Plato did not offer nearly as much material of a scientific nature as did Aristotle and other authors in the Peripatetic tradition.[129] Because the faculty of arts emphasized scientific and medical studies, professors naturally turned to the authors who offered more appropriate material, and a greater quantity of it, for research and teaching. The alliance of Aristotle and Galen, even modified by Vesalian anatomy, offered much more scientific and medical matter to study than did Plato and the Neoplatonists of the ancient world and the Renaissance.

Plato's works were ill suited pedagogically for philosophy instruction. His unsystematic dialogues could not easily be adapted to the *quaestio,* commentary, and disputational techniques of university instruction. Francesco Verino reported the views of his colleagues and students on this point in 1590. They said that Plato did not deserve to be taught in universities, because Plato did not proceed with "method" or true order, which aids the memory, Verino wrote. They complained that his reasons were "topical" and probable, and not as demonstrative and productive of *scienza* (knowledge or science) as were those of Aristotle.[130]

Finally, church authorities rejected the religious agenda of Renaissance Platonism. Platonists from Ficino through Patrizi argued that Platonism and Catholicism were in accord: both led people to God. The visionary Patrizi wanted an eclectic Platonism enriched with other ancient traditions to become the philosophy of the Catholic Church. But the unresolved philosophical problems in harmonizing Platonism, Neoplatonism, Hermeticism, and so on with Catholicism left churchmen uneasy at best, hostile at worst.

Hence, the papacy and its leading theologians reaffirmed Catholicism's com-

printed in Rizzo, 1987, 76 n. 35. For Pappazoni's teaching at Bologna (1589–1605), see Dallari, 1888–1924, 2:234, 238, 241, 245, 249, 253, 256, 259, 261, 264, 271, 286. For his life and thought, see Camerota, 1997.

129. Some of the following comes from Schmitt, 1982b, esp. n. 55 on 328–29, and Copenhaver and Schmitt, 1992, 186.

130. "Altri dicono che Platone non merita di esser pubblicamente esposto per gli Studii si perché non procede con Methodo o vero ordine, che conferisce alla Memoria, sì ancora perché le sue ragioni son topiche et probabili et non come quelle di Aristotile demonstrative ed producitrici negli animi nostri di scienza." Francesco Verino il Secondo, *Vere conclusioni di Platone conformi alla Dottrina Christiana et a quella d'Aristotile* (1590), as quoted in Muccillo, 1992, 212 n. 26; also quoted in Del Fante, 1980b, 409 n. 99. Earlier in his book Verino commented on the hostility and "insolence" that his efforts to teach Plato encountered.

mitment to Aristotelian-based neo-Scholasticism. Thomist Scholasticism was
the philosophy of the Dominican order, whereas Franciscans followed Scotist
Scholasticism. Now the Society of Jesus, the greatest intellectual force in late
Renaissance European Catholicism, embraced a neo-Scholasticism that relied on
an Aristotelian logical and metaphysical framework and Thomism. The learned
and politically powerful Jesuit philosopher-theologians, Cardinals Toledo and
Bellarmine, expressed the neo-Scholastic opposition to Platonism. At the same
time that the academic world preferred a secular scientific Aristotelianism to
Platonism, the leaders of Catholicism preferred a neo-Scholastic metaphysical
Aristotelianism, despite the fact that a prominent strand of Aristotelianism denied
the demonstrability of fundamental truths of Christianity.

Even though Platonism did not win a place in the curriculum, it did influence
developments in natural philosophy by helping to point the way toward the
mathematical approach of Galilei. The work of Jacopo Mazzoni demonstrates the
point. Appointed to the University of Pisa in 1588 to teach natural philosophy,
Mazzoni lectured on the *Physics* of Aristotle. As noted above, he took on the
added charge of the extraordinary holiday lectureship on Plato in 1591. Earlier
Mazzoni had attempted to find agreement between the two great Greeks. Now
he changed his mind.

In his major work, *In universam Platonis et Aristotelis philosophiam praeludia, sive
de comparatione Platonis et Aristotelis* (published in 1597), Mazzoni attempted to
locate exactly where Plato and Aristotle differed and to weigh the merits of each
on specific points of natural philosophy.[131] Mazzoni's most important conclusion
was that they differed significantly in the degree to which they relied on mathematics to study physical phenomena. Mazzoni pointed out that Aristotle did not
use mathematical demonstration but a physics of causation. Plato, by contrast,
ranked mathematics higher than a physics of causation as a means of explanation.
Mazzoni preferred Plato's use of mathematics to understand the physical world.
With mathematics one could develop abstract analysis without considering vari-
eties of matter and motion, which were key parts of Aristotelian analysis. Mathematics enabled the natural philosopher to deal abstractly with such areas as the
vacuum and dynamics, in which the rejection of mathematical reasoning left
Aristotelianism in a quandary. Although Mazzoni found much that was useful in
Aristotelian physics, he also demonstrated the inadequacies of traditional Aristotelian physics in some areas. He found in Plato a champion of a better, mathematical approach.

Mazzoni was a popular professor and the mentor of a group of junior colleagues who came together for wide-ranging discussions. Galileo Galilei was
a member of Mazzoni's circle during his Pisan tenure (1589–92). How much
Mazzoni influenced Galilei, or Galilei influenced Mazzoni, is difficult to determine. But it is significant that Plato was the authority for a mathematical
approach to physics which Mazzoni endorsed and which Galilei brought to
perfection.

131. The following is based on Purnell, 1972.

CONTINUITY AND DECLINE OF ARISTOTELIAN
NATURAL PHILOSOPHY

Besides Platonism, the only alternatives to Aristotelian natural philosophy
were the so-called new philosophies of nature elaborated by Bernardino Telesio
(1509–88), Giordano Bruno (1548–1600), Tommaso Campanella (1568–1639),
and Girolamo Cardano, to a lesser extent. They shared a visceral dislike of Aristotelianism and delighted in pointing out its difficulties. They all emphasized that
the philosopher must study "nature" and underscored sense perception as a
means of learning. Beyond that, agreement evaporated. Each proposed innovative philosophies of spirit and matter and discussed cosmology, physics, and
metaphysics in ways that defy summary.[132] But of the new philosophers of nature,
only Cardano held a university post, and he taught medicine at Pavia and Bologna. The new philosophies of nature lacked a presence in the university.

Hence, Italian professors continued to teach Aristotelian natural philosophy
into the seventeenth century. Indeed, more Latin commentaries on Aristotle
were written between 1500 and 1650 than in the thousand years between Boethius (d. 524) and 1500.[133] Of course, the Aristotelian natural philosophy encountered after 1550 was often very different from that found before 1490. It was
a transformed Aristotelianism, or Aristotelianisms, with the best or most functional aspects of the medieval Aristotle preserved and fused with the fruits of
humanism.[134]

However, the quality of university Aristotelian natural philosophy in the late
sixteenth and early seventeenth centuries varied from university to university and
scholar to scholar.[135] On the one hand, there was Jacopo Zabarella at Padua. He
approached Aristotle with an open mind and dealt with the Greek text of Aristotle with philological precision. Most important, Zabarella affirmed that he
would accept Aristotle's authority only when it derived from reason. To some
extent he approached the physical and biological world empirically by paying
attention to observation and experience. Zabarella was the best kind of talented
Renaissance professor of Aristotelian natural philosophy.

Ulisse Aldrovandi, professor of natural philosophy at the University of Bologna, demonstrated the broad range and eclectic nature of Renaissance Aristotelianism by becoming an encyclopedist natural historian. After having taught logic
and medical botany earlier, he received in 1560 a appointment not found anywhere else: an ordinary professorship in the "natural philosophy of fossils, plants,
and animals" (*Legat philosophiam naturalem ordinariam, de fossilibus, plantis et ani-*

132. The following offer summaries with considerable additional bibliography: Kristeller, 1964a,
91–109, 127–44, 174–75, 177–78; Ingegno, 1980 and 1988; and Copenhaver and Schmitt, 1992,
284–328.

133. Lohr, 1974b, 228. In addition, see the excellent discussion of Aristotelian textbooks published from about 1470 to about 1620, most of them intended for university use, in Schmitt, 1983c,
34–63.

134. Schmitt, 1983b, 112–13.

135. Schmitt makes this point several times, most strongly in Schmitt, 1983c, ch. 1. For Zabarella,
see Chapter 7 in the present volume.

malibus). He held it until 1600.[136] In discharge of his duties, Aldrovandi lectured on the standard Aristotelian texts but emphasized plants, animals, fossils, and minerals. He published books on birds, insects, fish, plants, metals, and so on and supplemented and corrected Aristotle's texts on the basis of his own vast natural history collections. Aldrovandi was an Aristotelian professor of natural history who concentrated on plants and animals.

Although much influenced by Aristotle, Aldrovandi often criticized the master for not having personally verified the information in his biological works and for other inadequacies. In the attempt to develop his own classification system of plants and animals, Aldrovandi relied greatly on observation.[137]

At the other end of the Aristotelian universe were very conservative Aristotelians such as Girolamo Borri. From Arezzo, Borri was a student at the University of Siena in 1533, and in 1535 he obtained his doctorate in philosophy, medicine, and theology, probably at Padua. He taught briefly at the University of Perugia, then natural philosophy at the University of Pisa from 1553 to 1559 and 1575 to 1586. He may have taught elsewhere as well. Borri paid no attention to the Greek commentaries and ignored humanist textual criticism. He accepted only Aristotle, garnished with very limited observation of the physical world. Borri practiced a kind of conservative Aristotelianism which Charles Schmitt aptly called "scruffy medievalism."[138]

Hostile to medieval Aristotelianism but very conservative in other ways was the highly esteemed Cesare Cremonini, who denied the demonstrability of the immortality of the soul. Cremonini was extremely popular with students and the Venetian nobility. As many as four hundred students attended his lectures, according to his own account, and generations of young Venetian aristocrats praised his teaching. Cremonini took a leading role in university affairs and was richly rewarded with very high salaries, which reached the extraordinary figure of 2,000 florins by 1629.[139]

Cremonini saw his task as teaching the Aristotle of the printed page without deviation. He would not rely on empirical evidence or observe nature, as his colleague and friend Galilei urged him to do. Cremonini refused to look through Galilei's telescope, according to a seventeenth-century account. Whatever the truth of the story, it accurately described Cremonini's attitude. Galilei, in turn, probably had Cremonini in mind when he satirized philosophers who would not raise their eyes from the printed page in order to look at nature.

Whether old fashioned or up to date, rigidly conservative or open to new evidence, Aristotelian natural philosophy dominated Italian university instruction through the mid-seventeenth century. For example, in 1651 the ordinary

136. Dallari, 1888–1924, 2:150 (quote), 153, 156, and passim for his position. See also Tugnoli Pattaro, 1981, 151.

137. Tugnoli Pattaro, 1981, 75–94, 141–43, and passim; Montalenti, 1960, 121–23; and Findlen, 1994.

138. Schmitt, 1983c, 18. See also Stabile, 1971; Schmitt, 1976a; Schmitt, 1978; Minnucci and Košuta, 1989, 466, 531; and Grendler, 1996a, 39–42.

139. Schmitt, 1980 and 1984b.

professors of natural philosophy at the University of Bologna were required to lecture on the *Physics, De caelo et mundo, De generatione et corruptione, Meterology, De anima,* and *Parva naturalia.*[140] The same was true elsewhere. Claudio Guillermet di Beauregard (Berigardo in Italian; c. 1590–1663) taught at Pisa from 1627 to 1639, becoming ordinary professor of natural philosophy in 1634. He moved to Padua in 1639 as second ordinary professor of natural philosophy, becoming first professor at the very high salary of 1,400 florins in 1661. At Padua Beauregard lectured on Aristotle's *Physics, De anima, De caelo,* and *De generatione et corruptione* in the 1650s and 1660s. In his early books he strongly condemned Galilei's views. He later shifted to an ambiguous position but clung tenaciously to Aristotle throughout.[141] Others, such as Scipione Chiaramonti (1565–1652; ordinary professor at Pisa [1627–36] and possibly elsewhere), wrote numerous books defending traditional Aristotelian natural philosophy and attacking Galilei.[142]

All Aristotelians saw the world as a living, biological entity and analyzed reality as ordered structure. They all believed that defining the essential nature of things and demonstrating the attributes of a piece of reality produced scientific knowledge.[143] All understood motion as a process of change from one state of being to another. All relied on a methodology of syllogistic reasoning.

From these principles flowed difficulties. Mathematical explanations, which ignored the quality or essence of reality but simply measured it, did not fit into Aristotelian science. Because Aristotelianism could not integrate mathematical evidence into its developmental approach, most Aristotelians rejected or paid little attention to mathematical proof. In similar fashion, Aristotelians willingly observed nature and sought a limited amount of empirical evidence but looked with Aristotelian eyes. They did not make full use of empirical data because they did not satisfy their demands for philosophically demonstrable proof, that is, conclusions based on a series of logically unassailable affirmative and negative statements. In their quest for demonstrable proof, Aristotelians did not recognize or admit how much their own analysis of the physical world and human psychology was based on dialectical argumentation.

Eventually an accumulation of contrary principles and evidence undermined Aristotelian natural philosophy. The scholarship of Galilei, Descartes, and others could neither be rebutted nor incorporated into Aristotelianism. Copernicanism was too convincing to be ignored. The many experiments that disproved Aristotle's views on the vacuum, space, and other issues could not be dismissed. Schol-

---

140. ASB, Assunteria di Studio, Bu. 91, a handwritten booklet dated 1651 listing required texts for all subjects. However, the professor of natural philosophy for fossils, plants, and animals (Aldrovandi's old position) was free to lecture on any texts he chose.

141. Soppelsa, 1974, 92–112, esp. 92 n. 2 for his teaching, and Beauregard, 1965.

142. See Soppelsa, 1974, index; Benzoni, 1980; and Barsanti, 1993, 513. Schmitt describes Chiaramonti's *Philosophia naturalis methodo resolutiva tradita* (1652): "In short, it is a textbook for teaching natural philosophy which takes . . . nothing of the last half century into account, although there are various cosmetic attempts to bring conventional scholastic teaching up to date." Schmitt, 1983d, 221–22 (quotation on 222).

143. See the summary comments of Schmitt, 1969, 124, and Lohr, 1988a, 537.

ars more and more realized that they could understand nature better through mathematics than Aristotle's doctrines.[144] So Aristotelian natural philosophy collapsed in Italian universities between 1650 and 1700.

In the second half of the seventeenth century, Italian professors of natural philosophy and mathematics embraced the views that their predecessors had rejected. Moving quickly to make up for lost time, they proposed hypotheses, advanced proofs, and engaged in experiments according to the new science. University reorganization recognizing the new science followed. For example, in 1739 the Venetian Senate established at the University of Padua a professorship in experimental philosophy. Aristotelian *philosophia naturalis* became *philosophia experimentalis*.[145] When this happened, the incredibly durable and adaptive natural philosophy based on Aristotle, the heart of the medieval and Renaissance faculty of arts, came to an end.

144. Schmitt, 1983c, 5–7, 103–8; Wallace, 1988, 233–35; and Schmitt, 1983d, 220, for an eloquent summary. The sea change was the scientific revolution of the seventeenth century, about which much has been written.

145. Soppelsa, 1974, 115–208, esp. 117, 141–54, for the first professor of experimental philosophy.

CHAPTER 9

The Medical Curriculum

Men learned in languages as well as in medicine.
—Agostino Gadaldino, preface to 1541 Galen edition

he Italian university of 1400 inherited the medical curriculum established in the preceding 100–150 years. The statutory curriculum and the core system of medical professorships remained much the same between 1400 and 1600. But the content of medicine—what was researched, written, and taught—changed greatly, because of the increased emphasis on anatomical study through dissection. The rise of medical humanism added professorships of anatomy and medical botany and helped create clinical medicine. The innovations were both significant and characteristically Renaissance in nature.

MEDIEVAL MEDICAL KNOWLEDGE

Renaissance universities inherited a set of ancient and medieval texts with which to teach the traditional medical subjects. Medieval medicine was based on ancient Greek medicine, namely, Hippocrates, Aristotle, and Galen. The name of the ancient Greek physician Hippocrates of Cos (c. 460–c. 370 B.C.), about whom nothing is known, became attached to a corpus of about sixty brief

Epigraph: "Deinde adhibitis nonnullis doctis & tam linguarum peritia quàm medicina eruditissimis viris, libros omnes Galeni & qui nondum fuerant latinate donati, in latinum vertendos." Agostino Gadaldino's undated preface to Galen, 1541, sig. ij ʳ. O'Malley (1964, 103) first noted this passage. Gadaldino (1515–75) was the chief editor of the monumental seven-volume Latin edition of Galen. By stressing that the translators had consulted "ancient manuscripts," he proclaimed the importance of the humanist historico-critical method.

medical treatises written between 430 and 380 B.C.[1] A half dozen tracts of the Hippocratic corpus became medieval and Renaissance curricular texts. Aristotle (384–322 B.C.) wrote several treatises on biology, zoology, and other subjects pertinent to medicine. Above all, he provided a philosophical framework that organized biological learning and made it possible to fit in new material.

The most important of the Greek trio was Galen (probably 130–200), a physician who spent much time in Rome. Galen summarized previous Greek medicine and added a great deal more through his own observations heavily based on animal dissection. He then wrote up the total in an encyclopedic corpus of works of which about ten thousand pages survive and probably another three thousand have disappeared. Galen's works covered the entire spectrum of medical knowledge as he saw it: method, medical theory, practical medicine, anatomy, surgery, and pharmacology.

Many of the Greek works first became available in Latin, often via Arab intermediate translations, in the twelfth century. These epochal translations were done at about the same time that students began to gather at the feet of distinguished teachers at Salerno. The physicians at Salerno between the late eleventh and the early thirteenth centuries introduced Greek and Arab medicine into Christian Europe.[2] They formulated the initial group of texts with which to teach Hippocratic and Galenic medicine. These brief treatises, called collectively the *articella,* consisted of the Hippocratic *Aphorisms* and *Prognostics,* Galen's introductory treatise that bore several names (*Ars medica, Ars parva, Tegni,* or *Microtechne*), and the *Isagoge* of Joannitius, a collection of brief medical opinions attributed to "Joannitius," who is thought to have been the Arab Hunain ibn Ishaq of the ninth century.[3] Some tracts on pulse and urine, essential diagnostic tools for the medieval physician, completed the list.

The medieval medical synthesis was firmly rooted on a Greek understanding of human physiology as explicated by Galen. This physiology was a complex analysis of the body which began with things natural: complexion, humors, and systems.[4] Complexion (or temperament) was the balance of the qualities of hot, wet, cold, and dry in the human body. When all was in balance, the body was healthy. But there was no absolute measure of the right complexion, such as 98.6 degrees Fahrenheit for the temperature of the human body in modern medicine. Individuals had varying complexions: some were hotter than others. The physician determined the proper complexion of the individual when healthy by observation and judgment. Ill health occurred when the body was out of balance, meaning that the individual's complexion was too hot or too cold. The physician judged what the individual's proper, healthy complexion should be. He then attempted to attain it by prescribing medicine or foods that would correct the

1. There is a large body of literature on Hippocrates and the corpus. I have used Hippocrates, 1886, which contains English translations of seventeen of the treatises; Levine, 1971; and Joly, 1981.

2. See the important studies of Kristeller, 1956b and 1986.

3. See Siraisi, 1987, 39 n. 65, for the identification.

4. The following paragraphs are based on Siraisi, 1990, 97–128. See also Siegel, 1968 and 1970, and Temkin, 1973.

imbalance by adding or subtracting heat to the complexion. He might also prescribe therapy, such as bloodletting, in order to relieve the body of an excess of the humor responsible for the complexional imbalance. When the complexion was back in balance, or restored to what was normal, the patient was cured.

The four humors were body fluids essential to the functioning of the body. They were blood, phlegm, bile (also called choler, red bile, or yellow bile), and black bile (melancholy). Phlegm was a general term for secretions that were colorless or whitish, such as the fluid in the brain. Red or yellow bile was the fluid found in the gallbladder; black bile, that found in the spleen. Blood was particularly important and subject to intricate analysis. Together the four humors largely determined the complexional balance.

The body also had principal organs and the systems associated with them, which had virtues (general powers of action) and faculties (specific abilities). The two principal ancient physiological authorities did not agree on the importance and rolls of the major organs. Aristotle taught that the heart ruled the whole body. Galen argued that the heart, brain, and liver each governed a separate group of organs and functions. Physiological systems based on principal organs enabled the medical scholar to classify physiological activity and to understand the structure.

The activity and structure of blood vessels received special mention. According to the Galenic explanation, the venous and arterial blood vessel systems were entirely separate. The veins were part of the system connected to the liver; they carried blood that nourished the body. The arteries were connected to the heart and carried a mixture of *spiritus* and blood. *Spiritus* was a substance manufactured in the heart from air and carried throughout the body by the arteries. It really was the vital principle of the body. Since the veins and arteries carried different liquids with different purposes according to Galenic physiology, it made sense to see them as separate. The only link between the two according to Galen was that a small amount of blood allegedly crossed from one side of the heart to the other through supposed pores in the central septum (the heart wall) in order to mix with the *spiritus*. This is a very simplified account of Galenic physiology as understood by medieval medical men.

Some Aristotelian and Platonic philosophical principles undergirded Galenic physiology. Although the description of the body and its functions relied partly on anatomical knowledge, physiological theory dominated. Dissection of human bodies mostly confirmed theory, and the theory was laced with Greek philosophy. The writing and teaching of medicine were closely allied to natural philosophy because Galen and Aristotle were philosophers as well as medical scholars. They saw medical knowledge within a broader philosophical, that is, scientific, context. Consequently, medieval and Renaissance medical writers also stressed the links between medicine and natural philosophy. In addition, medieval scholars in all fields liked to see individual bits of knowledge as parts of a larger whole. So it was with medicine: medical scholars saw a diseased organ as part of a whole body in ill health and prescribed accordingly. Treating one part of the body with little attention to the rest, which seems to be a characteristic of modern medical specialization, did not exist.

Reading some of the ancient and medieval medical texts suggests additional features. Ancient and medieval medical men were keen observers of the sick; they justly prided themselves on the accuracy of their observations and ability to predict the course of a disease. For example, Hippocrates' *Prognostics,* a standard curricular text for centuries, repeatedly stated that if the patient exhibited certain symptoms, he or she was likely to die. And if the patient exhibited other symptoms, he or she would recover. "When the bladder is hard and painful, it is an extremely bad and mortal symptom, more especially in cases attended with continued fever."[5] Indeed, such symptoms suggest blockage of the urinary tract and internal infection that, if unrelieved, will prove fatal. Ancient, medieval, and Renaissance medical men were skilled in diagnosis (although they did not have the wide range of medical names for diseases available in later centuries) and in prognosis. What was missing was an arsenal of therapies with which to fight the disease.

On the other hand, when ancient, medieval, and Renaissance medical men faced an external manipulative problem, such as setting a broken limb, they could be very skillful. For this they could follow the detailed instructions in Hippocrates' *Fractures* and set the limb properly.[6] Overall, medieval and Renaissance medical men could justly claim that their medicine was a *scientia,* a body of demonstrable knowledge, because it enabled them to diagnose a problem, predict what would happen, and sometimes cure the patient.

In addition to the corpus of Greek medicine, medieval university teaching relied heavily on Arab medical works that summarized, reorganized, and added to Greek medicine. Because the Arab world had assimilated Greek medical works before Christian Europe, scholars such as Avicenna and Averroës did a better job of summarizing, reorganizing, and adding to the Greek corpus. The same men who translated Galen and Hippocrates also translated major Arab medical texts into Latin in the twelfth century.[7] Because of their highly organized encyclopedic nature, some of the Arab medical treatises seemed the best available teaching tools. Like teachers everywhere, medieval medical professors often relied on good summary texts to convey the essence of the subject to their students.

By the fourteenth century medical knowledge had so advanced that there were numerous medical works: the ancient sources, Arab authorities, and numerous commentaries on both by medieval writers. Naturally, the texts did not always agree. The university medical scholar used Scholastic analysis to deal with conflicting authorities and to arrive at conclusions.

In Scholastic analysis, the professor first isolated the key sentences in conflicting authoritative texts. He then listed their points of agreement and disagreement. Next he resolved the differences, most often by reconciling the two, perhaps by finding a higher principle that overrode the differences. Finally he

5. Hippocrates, 1886, 1:208.
6. See the comments of the surgeon and translator Francis Adams in the preface to *Fractures* in ibid., 2:25–26.
7. Lemay, 1981.

disposed of objections to the solution. If he succeeded in his endeavor, the medical scholar could claim that medicine was *scientia,* rather than simply *ars,* a manipulative skill. Almost all medical works, from commentaries on Galen to *consilia* dealing with individual cases, written between 1300 and 1500 employed Scholastic method.

As a result the professor of medicine was a man skilled in dialectical disputation as well as in medicine. He studied logic early in his university career in order to acquire the dialectical method he would use to understand and to manipulate the content of medicine. As a professor he used Scholastic dialectic and demonstrative reasoning to explain his points in his lectures, commentaries, and medical *consilia.* A fixed body of knowledge based on authoritative texts, a good memory, and skill in oral disputation produced a successful professor of medicine. Ugo Benzi (1376–1439), the most famous professor of theoretical medicine of his era, who taught at Bologna, Florence, Padua, Parma, Pavia, and Siena, exemplified this kind of professor. His fame came from his brilliant oral disputations in which he vanquished his foes with subtle reasoning. All other professors of medicine also possessed and used dialectical skills with greater or lesser skill.[8]

Scholastic method was very useful, because it sought to reconcile differences in order to arrive at a systematic and coherent statement of truth. But it had disadvantages for the study of medicine. Because it relied heavily on authoritative texts and their interpretation, its practitioners paid less attention to observation of phenomena. And when they did locate observable evidence, they often employed ingenious dialectical reasoning to fit the new phenomena into the received theory. In other words, Scholastic method gave priority to established and systematic knowledge at the expense of new knowledge and evidence that did not fit the pattern. Nevertheless, it was the method that medical scholars used to organize and teach the corpus of medical knowledge found in authoritative texts.

THE MEDICAL CURRICULUM IN 1400

The earliest surviving, and the most important, statutes with information on the medical curriculum were those of the University of Bologna of 1405. These required texts codified medieval practice and remained largely in effect in Bologna and elsewhere through 1600.

Avicenna's *Canon* and Galen dominated. The Arab Avicenna (Ibn Sina, 980–1037) wrote a very large encyclopedia of medicine in five books covering, respectively, general principles of medicine, simple drugs, diseases of individual

---

8. For Benzi and the structure of medical writing, see Lockwood, 1951, and Benzi, 1966. Lockwood's description of university medical knowledge and teaching at the time is worth quoting: Medicine was "a complicated inert mass of data on which the university professors exercised their wits. Their wits, however, were keen. . . . They commanded a vast store of factual knowledge—nine-tenths of which was worthless or false, of course, but accepted as 'scientific truth' in their day. Their command of this traditional lore was immediate and personal. In bitter rivalry, in subtle and merciless debate, they made public demonstration of their powers and their erudition. It was a vigorous, arrogant, ostentatious pedantry." Lockwood, 1951, 8.

organs, general diseases of the whole body or occurring in various parts of the body (fevers, boils, wounds, poisoning, and the like), and the preparation of complex prescriptions and poison antidotes.[9] The title, which should be *Canon of Medicine*, comes from the Arabic *Qanun*, meaning code of laws or series of principles. The *Canon* presented a compendium of ancient Hippocratic and Galenic medicine with Arab additions. Translated into Latin by Gerard of Cremona (1114–87), it quickly became a major medical text for Christian Europe. The work's thorough organization probably facilitated its acceptance: each book was subdivided several times into smaller sections to the point that some sections consisted of only a sentence or two. Its comprehensiveness also made it attractive as a pedagogical text. But the book was not structured from beginning to end in such a way as to fit the progression of medical teaching in Italian universities. Hence, the Bolognese statutes excerpted parts of the *Canon* according to their approach to the divisions of medicine.

Individual treatises of Galen made up most of the rest of the curriculum. Although Galen and Avicenna taught the same medicine, they presented it differently.[10] Galen made his points through lengthy descriptions of physical manifestations in numerous short treatises. Moreover, he made comparisons, for example, pointing out that the flesh of the heart was drier and harder than that of the spleen, kidneys, or liver. He took time to criticize other medical men. By contrast, Avicenna listed the organs in descending order of dryness without comment. Galen was leisurely, discursive, and full of examples. Avicenna was schematic, brief, and comprehensive. Each had pedagogical virtues.

The medical faculty of Bologna, and all other universities, had professors of three subjects: medical theory, medical practice, and surgery. The Bolognese statutes of 1405 directed the professors of each to teach an intricate four-year sequence of texts. Medical theory was the most important. As many professors taught theoretical medicine as practical medicine and surgery combined, and the leading ordinary professor of medical theory usually received the highest salary in the arts and medicine faculty. Hence, the Bolognese statutes devoted most attention to the texts to be taught for medical theory.

The statutes began with the texts to be taught by the men who filled the morning ordinary professorship of medical theory (four in the early years of the fifteenth century). The statutes further divided the texts into those to be taught in a "first lecture" (*primo lectione*) and a "second lecture" (*pro secunda lectione*). This meant that some texts were to be taught in the first half of the academic year ending at the pre-Easter vacation, and other texts were to be taught after Easter.[11]

---

9. Shah (1966, 427–29) provides a brief summary of the contents of books 2–5, which have never been translated into English so far as I know and are available in Latin only in fifteenth- and sixteenth-century editions.

10. See Siraisi, 1987, 33–40, for a comparison of the approaches of Galen and Avicenna.

11. This conclusion about the meaning of first and second lecture comes through a process of elimination. First, the statutes also divided the curriculum for surgery into first and second lectures, even though surgery sometimes had only one professor. Second, if the statutes meant that the professor was required to switch from one group of texts to others at the midpoint of a two-hour

For the first half of the first year, the morning ordinary professors of medical theory taught book 1, fen 1, doctrines 1–4 and 6 (excluding the sections on anatomy), of the *Canon* of Avicenna.[12] ("Fen," meaning "part," came from the translator's adaptaion of an Arabic term.) In these approximately sixty pages (in a modern English translation), Avicenna outlined physiology, that is, the principles of the composition of a living body. Avicenna began with a definition of medicine and then presented an Aristotelian discussion of the elements (earth, air, fire, and water). Thus, Avicenna positioned medicine within the context of Aristotelian natural philosophy and made it scientific in the contemporary understanding of the term. The work went on to a Galenic discussion of the humors of the body, followed by a discussion of the balance of hot, wet, cold, and dry in living bodies. The sixth doctrine of fen 1 dealt briefly with the principles of growth, nourishment, and reproduction.[13] Next came five doctrines in fen 3 on the causes of health and disease, the inevitability of death, the diseases of children, and the regimens of food, liquid intake, and "sleep and wakefulness." These doctrines also dealt mostly with general principles of medicine, as a part of what might be called bodily regimen and general hygiene.[14]

In the second half of the first year, the ordinary morning professors of medical theory taught five treatises of Galen: *De differentiis febrium* (On the differences of fevers); *De simplicibus medicinis* (Of medicinal simples), omitting book 6; *De diebus criticis* (On critical days), book 1; *De complexionibus* (On complexions); and *De mala complexione* (On bad complexion or health).

In the first year the ordinary afternoon professors of medical theory (five of them in 1407–8) teaching at the canonical hour of nones (about 3 P.M. through much of the year) covered Avicenna's *Canon,* books 4, fen 2 (dealing with medical prognostication), and 2 (on medicines), and much of three treatises of Galen: "De interioribus," that is, his *De locis affectis* (On the state of ill health), omitting

---

lecture, the statutes might have referred to "first hour" and "second hour." Moreover, such a division would make little pedagogical sense. Third, if the statutes meant to divide the ordinary morning professors into two groups, with some teaching the "first lecture," and the others the "second lecture," they would have used different terminology. Moreover, this would have violated concurrency, which was such a firm principle in universities that the statutes would have explained and defended the violation. Finally, dividing the year at the midpoint reflected student preferences. They sometimes shifted their attendance from one lecturer to another in the same subject at Easter. See the example of Francesco Guicciardini in law mentioned in Chapter 5, "Organization of Instruction."

12. The discussion of the Bolognese medical curriculum in 1405 is based on Malagola, 1966, 274–76. Thorndike (1944, 280–81) provides a useful diagrammatic summary. But he fails to distinguish between the two sections of the morning ordinary professorships of theoretical medicine and calls the ordinary afternoon professors "extraordinary professors." The rolls demonstrate that Bologna did not have extraordinary professors of medicine at this time; they appeared later in the century. Park (1985, 245–48) has done an excellent job of summarizing the statutes and identifying the texts. Although my analysis was done independently, I have followed her lead in a handful of cases. Siraisi (1981, 107) lists many of the Galenic texts mentioned. See also Siraisi, 1987, 55–58.

13. See Shah, 1966, 1–46, 125–37, for an English translation from the Arabic and Siraisi, 1987, 23–29, for a summary.

14. Shah, 1966, fen 3, introduction plus doctrine 1, ch. 3; doctrine 2, chs. 7–9 (pp. 279–83, 291–98, 309–27).

book 2; *De regimine sanitatis,* book 6; and *De diebus criticis,* book 2; plus the *Aphorisms* of Hippocrates, omitting part 7.

In the second year of the four-year cycle, the morning ordinary professors began with Galen's *Tegni,* followed by the *Prognostica* (Prognostics, one of the *articella*) without commentary and *De morbis acutis* (On acute diseases) of Hippocrates again without commentary and omitting book 4, and part of Avicenna's *De viribus cordis* (On the strength of the heart, a minor work) in the first half of the year. They taught a group of Galen's works in the second half: *De accidenti et morbo* (On accident and disease); *De crisi* (On the crisis); *De diebus criticis,* tract 1 on fevers from *Ad Glauconem de medendi methodo* (On the method of healing to Glaucon); *De tabe* (On plague); and *De utilitate respirationis* (On the usefulness of breathing).

In the second year the afternoon ordinary professors of medical theory also divided the academic year into two. In the first half they taught Avicenna's *Canon,* as was done by the first ordinary morning professors in the first year. In the second half they taught Avicenna's *Canon,* book 4, fen 2, plus most of four works of Galen: *De differentiis febrium, De mala complexione, De simplicibus medicinis,* omitting book 6, and *De diebus criticis,* book 1.

In the third year of the four-year cycle, the morning ordinary professors of medical theory taught Hippocrates' *Aphorisms,* except for the seventh and last section, in the first half of the year. In the second half they taught several parts of the *Colliget* (also called *Universalis de medicina*), a medical encyclopedia of Averroës, excluding the material on medical botany. They also taught more Galen: books 7–13 of his *Liber terapeutice* (Book of therapeutics), also called *De methodo medendi* (The method of healing), a major work; part of *De virtutibus naturalibus* (On natural virtues); and book 2 of *De diebus criticis.* The afternoon ordinary professors repeated in the first half of the second year what the morning ordinary professors had taught in the first half of the first year. They taught five works of Galen (*De accidenti et morbo; De crisi; De diebus criticis,* bk. 3; *De complexionibus;* and *De febribus ad Glauconem,* bk. 1) in the second half.

Almost all the teaching in the fourth year repeated what had been done earlier. The morning ordinary professors of medical theory taught Avicenna's *Canon* in the first half of the year, as they had done in the first year, and book 4, fen 1 (on fevers), and book 2 (medicinal simples) of the *Canon,* plus two works of Galen, *De locis affectis,* omitting book 2, and *Regimen sanitatis*), and Hippocrates' "De natura" (probably *De natura fetus* [On the nature of the fetus]) in the second half. The afternoon ordinary professors taught Hippocrates' *Aphorisms,* omitting part 7, in the first half of the year, followed by the same texts as the morning ordinary professors had taught in the second half of the third year, omitting only Galen's *De diebus criticis.*

Thanks to this complex and irregular alternation of texts for medical theory, almost all were taught twice, and some three times, in a four-year cycle. Thus, in any given year a student had a 50 to 75 percent chance of hearing lectures on any required text of medical theory. The rotation of texts enabled a student to begin his studies at any point in the four-year cycle. Bolognese statutes were able to prescribe a full and complex rotation of lectures on required texts because Bologna had more professors than any other university, from fifteen to twenty-five professors of medicine in the fifteenth century. Such ample coverage probably attracted students and made it easier for them to move from one university to another. By contrast, most northern European universities had only two to eight medical professors even in the sixteenth century.[15] Smaller Italian universities followed the same curriculum as Bologna for theoretical medicine but could not provide multiple opportunities to attend lectures on prescribed texts.

On the other hand, the sequence demonstrated limited logicality. The student began with an introduction and overview of physiology by means of lectures on Avicenna's *Canon*, book 1, an appropriate starting point. Indeed, professors used this part of the *Canon* as an introduction to medicine through the sixteenth century. But it is difficult to discern a logical pattern in the cornucopia of texts and portions of texts that followed.

A canon of texts develops through choice, chance, availability, and habit. For example, possibly an influential professor, perhaps the pioneering Taddeo Alderotti, who taught at Bologna from the mid-1260s until the early 1290s, decided to teach complexion with the text he considered the best. Others would follow. Or a particular text might be the only one available when professors were developing the curriculum. Once texts entered the curriculum, habit kept them there. Whatever the reasons for individual texts, the statutes codified pedagogical practice.

The Bolognese statutes of 1405 prescribed a similar four-year cycle for practical medicine, taught by five or more ordinary professors lecturing concurrently in the early years of the fifteenth century. Practical medicine differed from theoretical because it focused on the anatomical, pathological, and therapeutic knowledge needed to cure the sick. Teachers systematically dealt with parts of the body from top to bottom. Using Avicenna's *Canon*, book 3, throughout, the professors of practical medicine discussed the head and brain in the first year. They passed on to the lungs, heart, and chest in the second year; moved to the liver, stomach, spleen, and intestines in the third; and finished with the urinary and reproductive systems in the last year.[16]

Surgery dealt with the manual operations needed to restore health. Surgical instruction meant teaching students how to make incisions, prepare and administer medicine, and set broken bones. It was the least important part of university medicine. Italian universities awarded few degrees in the subject, because most surgeons did not attend university: they learned through apprenticeship with an established surgeon.[17] The 1405 statutes of the University of Bologna decreed four texts for the teaching of surgery, taught by two concurrent professors of surgery, who lectured at the nineteenth hour (beginning anywhere between 1 P.M. and 3 P.M. depending on the season of the year). They were to begin every academic year with the *Chirurgia* of Bruno da Longoburgo of Calabria, com-

15. Bylebyl, 1982, 201.
16. Malagola, 1966, 276–77; Park, 1985, 247–48; Siraisi, 1987, 55–56.
17. Siraisi, 1981, 108–10; Park, 1985, 62–66.

pleted at Padua in 1252.[18] This was followed by "The Surgery of Galen," which was a section of his *De methodo medendi* dealing with wounds.[19] The professors then went on to portions of Avicenna's *Canon* dealing with fractures, wounds, ulcers, and the like and the seventh book of the *Liber Almansoris* of Rhazes (al-Razi, d. 925). The latter was another Arab medical encyclopedia, more clinical and empirical in approach than that of Avicenna.

The remarkably detailed Bolognese statutes of 1405 were in force through the fifteenth and the sixteenth centuries, even though university rolls did not list the full range of texts to be taught.[20] Nor did the structure of professorships change much. In the last twenty years of the fifteenth century Bologna created a medical lectureship to teach book 3 of Avicenna's *Canon,* which dealt with diseases of particular parts of the body beginning with the head and working down.[21] It was another position in practical medicine. Padua added the same lectureship in the first half of the sixteenth century, dropped it in 1579, and then reintroduced it in 1591.[22]

Other universities taught the same texts as did Bologna. Two examples, one from the fifteenth century and the other from the sixteenth, serve for many. The University of Perugia in the academic year 1443–44 had four medical lectureships. Two ordinary morning professors of theoretical medicine taught Avicenna's *Canon,* book 1, fen 1. Another morning professor of theoretical medicine taught Hippocrates' *Aphorisms.* The afternoon ordinary professor of practical medicine taught the *Canon,* book 4, fen 1, which dealt with fevers. And a professor who combined the posts of surgery and practical medicine taught the *Canon,* book 4, fen 2, described as "De apostematibus, erniis et pustulis" (On abscesses, hernias, and pustules).[23] These were the texts named by the university rolls, in other words, the leading text to be taught, probably accompanied by others. The similarity to Bologna is not surprising, because Perugian statutes of 1457 decreed that the university's medical students had to attend lectures on all the texts required for graduation at Bologna or Paris.[24] Fifteenth-century professors of medicine also wrote numerous commentaries on Avicenna, Galen, and Hippocrates.[25]

Paduan professors of medicine taught a similar group of texts in the sixteenth

18. Bruno composed two works, a *Chirurgia magna* of about twenty folios in the 1498 printing, and a *Chirurgia parva* of three folios. The statutes do not specify which work. For surgery, see Malagola, 1966, 247; Siraisi, 1981, 108–10; and Park, 1985, 248.

19. Siraisi, 1990, 162, 214 n. 17.

20. Surviving rolls give an incomplete, generic indication of the texts to be taught in a lectureship, and most fail to list any. Nevertheless, they are essential for understanding the curriculum.

21. The lectureship is described as follows: "Ad lecturam tertij Avicenne de egritudinibus a capite usque ad pedes (diebus festis vel ordinarijs pro voluntate autorum)." Dallari, 1888–1924, 1:107, roll of 1478–79. Hieronymus de Ranutijs, not further identified, held the position from its inception through 1496–97. It was suppressed after the 1499–1500 academic year.

22. See, for example, the roll of 1543–44 in AAUP, Inventario 1320, no foliation. See Siraisi, 1987, 111–12.

23. Ermini, 1971, 446–47 n. 99. Ermini mistakenly refers to fen 3, which deals with poisons.

24. Ibid., 468.

25. See the list of publications of medical professors in fifteenth-century Padua in Pesenti, 1984.

century. In the academic year 1568–69, the ordinary professors of theoretical medicine taught Avicenna's *Canon,* book 1, fen 1, while the extraordinary professors of theoretical medicine taught Galen's *Ars medica.* The ordinary professors of practical medicine taught book 9 of *Liber Almansoris* of Rhazes, while the extraordinary professors of practical medicine taught book 10 of the same work. In the following academic year, the ordinary professors of theoretical medicine taught Hippocrates' *Aphorisms,* while the extraordinary professors taught Avicenna's *Canon,* book 1, fen 1. In practical medicine, the ordinary professors taught Avicenna's *Canon,* book 4, fen 1 (on fevers), while the extraordinary professors taught book 9 of the *Liber Almansoris.* The professor of surgery taught "De tumoribus" (On tumors; probably Galen's *De tumoribus praeter naturam*) and "De vulneribus" (On wounds; probably a section from Galen's *De methodo medendi*) both academic years. Of course, professors taught other texts as well.[26]

This was the medical curriculum developed in the Middle Ages and taught in the fifteenth century. Although the traditional texts continued to be taught, medical education changed considerably in "the medical Renaissance of the sixteenth century."[27]

MEDICAL HUMANISM

Change in medical research and training began at the end of the fifteenth century and in the early years of the sixteenth, as a group of scholars usually called "medical humanists" applied humanistic philology and ideological criticism to ancient medical texts. Nicolò Leoniceno (1428–1524) of Vicenza originated medical humanism and taught others.[28]

Leoniceno drank at the purest humanistic spring. At Vicenza, he received an excellent humanist education and learned Greek at an early age in the school of Ognibene Bonisoli, a pupil of Vittorino da Feltre's and a significant pedagogical

26. See the rolls of 1568–69 and 1569–70 of the faculty of arts in AAUP, Inventario 1320, no foliation. It was the same at Bologna in the late sixteenth century. Every year the ordinary and extraordinary professors of theoretical medicine taught two of the following: the *Tegni* of Galen, the *Aphorisms* of Hippocrates, and Avicenna's *Canon,* bk. 1, fen 1. The professors of practical medicine taught Avicenna's *Canon,* bk. 1, fen 4 (on humors); the *Canon,* bk. 4, fen 1 (on fevers); and "De morbis particularibus," which may have been book 9 of Rhazes' *Liber Almansoris,* which briefly described more than a hundred different complaints or diseases. See the rolls from 1586–87 through 1599–1600 in Dallari, 1888–1924, vol. 2. The same texts continued to be taught at Bologna through much of the seventeenth century. The professors of theoretical and practical medicine taught the same above texts at Rome. In addition, the professor of surgery at Rome taught *De fracturis* (On fractures) of Hippocrates, a work called "De vulneribus" (On wounds; probably a text of Galen), and Galen's *De tumoribus praeter naturam.* See the rolls of 1567–68, 1568–69, 1569, 1570–71, 1574–75, and 1575–76 in *I maestri di Roma,* 1991, 52–54, 61, 65–68, 75–76, 78–79, 86–87, 89–91, 99, 101–3. See also Siraisi, 1987, 84–93.

27. The term appears frequently, even as a book title; see *Medical Renaissance,* 1985.

28. See Bylebyl, 1979, 340–41; Bylebyl, 1981b and 1985b; Mugnai Carrara, 1979 and 1991; and Nutton, 1997, 3–8. Although born in Vicenza, Leoniceno was often called Niccolò da Lonigo, possibly because his grandfather was Alberto da Lonigo. Leoniceno is sometimes confused with the previously mentioned Niccolò Leonico Tomeo.

humanist in his own right.[29] Leoniceno had a superb command of Greek by eighteen. In 1446 he went to the University of Padua, where he acquired a degree in arts and medicine in 1453; his lifelong epilepsy probably led him to a medical career. He may have taught natural philosophy at the University of Padua from 1462 to 1464; in the latter year he moved to the University of Ferrara, teaching practical medicine in the years 1464–73, moral philosophy 1474–75, then theoretical medicine 1485–87. Although his teaching cannot be documented after 1487 because of the lack of records, the inscription on his tomb stated that he taught at Ferrara for sixty years, that is, from 1464 until his death, except for brief absences.[30] He was also a physician to the Este court. He may have taught at Bologna in 1483 and was first ordinary afternoon professor of medical theory as well as extraordinary (holiday) lecturer in Greek philosophy at the University of Bologna in 1508–9.[31] Leoniceno was a passionate collector of Greek texts. His library, numbering at least seventy-five Greek manuscripts at his death, was the largest private collection of Greek medical, scientific, and philosophical works of his time. Leoniceno knew and corresponded with his major humanist contemporaries, notably Giovanni Pico della Mirandola, Angelo Poliziano, and Erasmus. He helped Aldo Manuzio assemble and edit Greek texts.

As a medical humanist, Leoniceno made contributions of lasting importance. He began the process of locating, editing, and translating into Latin the Greek Galen, arguing that the Greek texts should be the basis of medical study. Leoniceno edited the first Greek printing of Galen, his *Methodus medendi* and the *De arte curativa ad Glauconem,* printed in Venice in 1500. Aldo Manuzio promised a complete Greek edition of Galen as early as 1495, and the Aldine Press fulfilled the promise after his death with the five-volume Greek *editio princeps* of 1525, prepared by various scholars. Leoniceno ultimately produced new Latin translations of eleven of Galen's works.

The editing and translating of Galen according to humanistic principles culminated in 1541, when the Giunti Press of Venice, the most active publisher of medical texts in Italy, brought out a folio-sized, ten-part Latin edition of most of Galen's works. Various northern Italian humanistic medical academicians, notably Agostino Gadaldino, Giovanni Battista Da Monte, and Andreas Vesalius, edited or translated many titles in the Giunti edition. The new Latin translations steadily replaced medieval translations. More than six hundred printings of one or more works of Galen in Latin appeared across Europe in the sixteenth century, about two-thirds between 1525 and 1560.[32]

---

29. See Grendler, 1989, 133–35, on Bonisoli.

30. *I maestri di Ferrara,* 1991, 238. Even if advancing age limited his university teaching, his presence and influence in Ferrara are undeniable.

31. Dallari, 1888–1924, 1:201, 202.

32. Galen, 1541, for the first volume. The Giunti edition has ten sections divided into seven volumes (sometimes bound into six). Camerini (1962–63, pt. 1, item 457) describes the edition, which was reprinted eight times between 1550 and 1625. See Durling, 1961, for a global census of Renaissance Galen editions and commentaries. See Bylebyl, 1979, 339–41, on humanistic medicine and Galen.

FIG. 9. Title page of volume 1 (of 7) of Latin Galen edition, Venice: Giunti, 1541. Agostino Gadaldini, Giovanni Battista Da Monte, Andreas Vesalius, and other medical humanists edited and translated Galen's works for the edition. *Annenberg Rare Book and Manuscript Library, University of Pennsylvania.*

Leoniceno attacked the medieval Arab medical scholars, especially Avicenna and Averroës, for their bad translations, mistaken interpretations, and errors in transmitting and systematizing Greek medicine. He also pointed out the mistakes of Christian commentators. Invoking the familiar humanist distinction between "words" (*verba*) and "things" (*res*), Leoniceno insisted on concentrating on things, which meant freeing the ancient texts from the mistakes and confusion of the Arab commentators and giving greater emphasis to such practical aspects of medicine as anatomical structure, treatment of specific diseases, and medicinal herbs. Leoniceno wanted to make it possible to practice medicine as the ancients had. If they did so, he believed that modern physicians would more often cure disease and relieve suffering.

Leoniceno argued for methodological change. In a treatise of 1508 he analyzed the comments on method found in the prologue to Galen's *Ars medica*.[33] Galen had stated that one might teach a subject in three ways: analysis according to the end or purpose of the topic, synthesis, or by creating a series of definitions. This last teaching method might be useful for organizing the whole of a discipline, he noted. But the looseness of Galen's terminology, his philosophical eclecticism, and his lack of clarity left his readers puzzled. Medieval scholars resolved the difficulty by viewing this prologue through Aristotelian eyes; they reduced Galen's method to Aristotelian demonstration and dialectic. By contrast, Leoniceno freed Galenic method from enveloping Aristotelian dialectic. He pointed out that Galen wrote about techniques of teaching, not methods of philosophic inquiry. Leoniceno then argued that Galen offered support for the idea that there were two different general methods to be employed in medicine or any other science: (1) a method relying on logical demonstration to be used for discussing particular aspects or questions in the science of medicine and (2) a broader method, not necessarily logical demonstration, which might order the entire contents of a science.

The details of Leoniceno's discussion about scientific method were intricate. The effect of his treatise was to proclaim methodological freedom: there were ways to organize medical and other scientific knowledge other than Aristotelian logic. The second approach of Leoniceno (and Galen), that of ordering the entire contents of a science along fresh lines, attracted immediate and widespread support. Medical scholars increasingly wrote independent treatises on a topic, rather than commenting on a curricular text, the traditional approach. Vesalius's *De humani corporis fabrica*, structured as a new anatomical treatise rather than a commentary on Galen, was a spectacular example. Leoniceno also inaugurated a debate about the accuracy of Pliny the Elder which had significant impact on the humanist approach to medical botany (see below).

Leoniceno taught others, especially at the University of Ferrara.[34] His initial

33. See Gilbert, 1960, 12–23, 98–107; Wightman, 1964; Bylebyl, 1981b, 249; and Edwards, 1976, for what follows.

34. For what follows, see especially Nutton, 1997, 8–19; Wightman, 1964, 369–72; and Mugnai Carrara, 1994. The lack of records makes it difficult to document the complete teaching careers of

and most important disciple was Giovanni Manardo (1462–1536), who studied with Leoniceno and then taught medicine at Ferrara from 1482 to 1492. He returned to teach there for brief periods early in the sixteenth century and from 1518 until his death. Manardo embraced Leoniceno's approach; indeed, he dismissed Avicenna's *Canon* in its medieval Latin version as "a dense cloud and infinite chaos of obscurities" in 1521.[35] Manardo substituted a broad knowledge of the ancient sources, plus an emphasis on clinical medicine, botany, and medical botany. He believed that medicine should be separated from Aristotelian philosophy. Antonio Musa Brasavola (1500–1555), pupil of Leoniceno and Manardo, took a doctorate in medicine and philosophy at Ferrara in 1520 and taught logic and natural philosophy there. He taught theoretical and especially practical medicine from 1540 until his death, always at Ferrara. He shared Leoniceno's views and published many works, especially in medical botany. Manardo and Brasavola were strong Galenists, who nevertheless criticized him when necessary.

The small University of Ferrara made a major contribution to Renaissance medicine through its emphasis on medical humanism from the 1490s through the first half of the sixteenth century, not least because several important anatomists studied there. Leadership then passed to the larger University of Padua in the 1540s. And medical humanism spread to other scholars and places.

The medical humanists with their superior Greek and comprehensive knowledge of the classical corpus uncovered the variety and nuances of ancient medicine underneath the medieval syntheses. Awareness of the differences in the ancients helped to free medicine from the Galenic-Aristotelian unity of the medieval commentators and to stimulate scholars to look at things with fresh eyes. Medical humanism prepared the way and provided the foundation for new developments in anatomy, clinical medicine, and medical botany.

THE ANATOMICAL RENAISSANCE

Medical humanism and the Renaissance interest in the human body generated the most important innovation in medicine, a new approach to the study of human anatomy.[36] The central figure was Andreas Vesalius. Although Vesalius merits every bit of acclaim he has received, the accompanying story of the impact of anatomy on university medical education is just as important.

Italian universities began anatomical dissection of the human body in the later Middle Ages. Emperor Frederick II decreed in 1240 that medical education had

---

Manardo and Brasavola at Ferrara. See *I maestri di Ferrara,* 1991, 202–3, 244–45, for what is known and for lists of their works. For biographical information and further bibliography on Manardo, start with Cotton, 1981; for Brasavola, see G. Gliozzi, 1972.

35. As quoted and translated in Siraisi, 1990, 190.

36. Historians of medicine often use the term "Anatomical Renaissance" to describe the accomplishments of Vesalius and other anatomical scholars, most of them Italians, of the sixteenth century. For example, *The Anatomical Renaissance* is the title of Cunningham, 1997. Of the vast scholarly literature on the subject, only a fraction can be cited. The following account focuses on the university context and the impact of the new anatomy on medical faculties.

to include study of the anatomy of the human body ("anatomiam humanorum corporum in scholis didicerit"). Whether this meant that anatomical dissection was practiced at this time is unclear but seems unlikely.[37] Italian dissections for teaching purposes and autopsies are fully documented at the end of the thirteenth century and the beginning of the fourteenth.

Italian universities performed anatomical dissections and autopsies, and many more of them, long before northern universities, because northern Europeans often objected to dismembering a corpse. Italians seldom objected; indeed, a grieving family member might ask for an autopsy, in the hope of discovering the cause of death of a loved one, so that family members might take action to avoid a similar fate. In this climate of opinion, university anatomical dissection became an integral, if small, part of Italian medical education. Dissection probably was begun in relative privacy, as a professor cut open a corpse before a small group of favored students. But it developed into a special event, with attendance required for advanced medical students, by 1400. By contrast, the first known dissection of a human body at the University of Paris occurred in the late 1470s and the first known public anatomy at Heidelberg, done by an Italian, only in 1574.[38]

University statutes of Florence, Bologna, Padua, and elsewhere of the late fourteenth and early fifteenth centuries decreed that dissections (usually called "an anatomy" or "public anatomy") should be performed in the presence of students.[39] Both a male and a female body were to be dissected annually, with advanced medical students required to attend. A professor of medicine read and commented on the required text, the *Anatomia Mundini* (written in 1316), by Mondino de' Liuzzi (c. 1270–1326). Another man did the dissecting, while a third person might point out the relevant parts of the body. The public anatomy was almost always done in January or February because of the lack of refrigeration, and it normally lasted five to fifteen days but could last three weeks or more if flesh was boiled from the bones. A public anatomy illustrated what was written in textbooks and aided student memories. Dissection was not yet a research technique intended to reveal new information about the human body. As the number of students invited to attend might be limited to twenty or thirty, it was still a small part of medical education.

The state provided bodies of condemned criminals, especially "foreigners," meaning those who were not natives of the town and its immediate surrounding territory. The need for bodies for dissection might mean a less painful death for a

37. Alston (1944–45, 225–26; quote on 226 n. 20), believes that Frederick II's decree meant that dissection of the human body was already being practiced. Park (1995) and Carlino (1999, 153–54, 170) doubt it. Premuda and Ongaro, 1965–66; Siraisi, 1990, 78–97; and Carlino, 1999, 170–80, are useful surveys of late medieval anatomical developments.

38. For Paris, Alston, 1944–45, 230–31, and Park, 1995, esp. 114–15 n. 16; for Heidelberg, Nutton, 1985, 96.

39. For Florence, see the statutes of 1387 in Gherardi, 1973, 74–75, and Park, 1985, 60–61. For Bologna, see Malagola, 1966, 289–90; English translation in Thorndike, 1944, 283–84; for Padua, see Premuda and Ongaro, 1965–66, 129, 135. For a description based on the statutes, see Bylebyl, 1979, 353–57.

convicted criminal. The Florentine statutes of 1387 stated that a woman condemned to death by burning for witchcraft should be hanged instead and her body given to the university for dissection. A man condemned to beheading and mutilation should be hanged if his body was intended for an anatomy.[40] If no body was available locally, the government sent one from elsewhere. For example, in late November 1458 the duke of Milan ordered a woman, condemned to death for witchcraft in a distant part of Lombardy, to be sent to Pavia for the use of the university. Presumably, she was sent to Pavia, hanged, and her body dissected.[41]

Scholarly interest in the study of human anatomy through dissection greatly increased at the end of the fifteenth century. Gabriele Zerbi (c. 1435–1505), who taught theoretical medicine at Bologna, Rome, and Padua but also published an anatomical work; Alessandro Benedetti (c. 1450–1513), who taught practical medicine at Padua; and Iacopo Berengario (Barigazzi) da Carpi (c. 1460–c. 1530), professor of surgery at Bologna from 1502 to 1527, were leaders.[42]

Interest in the human body was not confined to medical scholars and students.[43] Treatises on man's dignity and greatness expressed the Renaissance fascination with human beings and kindled a desire to penetrate the inner mysteries of the body. Artists were particularly eager to learn about the human form. The public anatomy was the natural place to satisfy this interest. As the dissector displayed parts of the body, viewers might marvel at God's handiwork.

Berengario reported a growing interest in his public anatomies in Bologna, as students from all over the university clamored to attend. For example, Ercole Gonzaga, a student of the humanities, philosophy, and theology, attended at least one, perhaps more, public anatomies when he was at Bologna (1522–25; see Ch. 5, "Student Living"). Civic officials attended at least the opening sessions. No doubt the time of the year, often Carnival season, and the nearly continuous action, as the dissection went on through the night with torches illuminating the corpse, heightened the atmosphere.

The medical humanists now turned their critical gaze on anatomy. They demanded that Galen's works on anatomy be read in the original Greek and disseminated in new, accurate Latin translations. Giorgio Valla (1447–1500), Benedetti, and especially Leoniceno led the way.[44] In 1529 Demetrius Chalcondylas published his Latin translation of Galen's *De anatomicis administrationibus* (On anatomical procedures), never previously translated into Latin. A native Greek

40. Gherardi, 1973, 74–75.

41. Panebianco, 1969. This is the first documentary evidence for anatomical dissection at Pavia, although it probably began earlier.

42. For more information, see Cunningham, 1997, 58–87. Ongaro (1981, 75–99) and Schmitt (1977, 58–67) present good surveys of Paduan medicine, especially anatomical study, before Vesalius. For the career and publications of Zerbi, see Pesenti, 1984, 213–16. For Benedetti, see Crespi, 1966, 244–47; Schullian, 1981; and Pesenti, 1984, 48–53. For Berengario, see Berengario da Carpi, 1959, 3–29; Ascari and Crespi, 1964; O'Malley, 1981a; and French, 1985.

43. Some of what follows has been suggested by Ferrari, 1987.

44. Recent scholarship strongly emphasizes the contribution of medical humanism to the Anatomical Renaissance. See Nutton, 1988, and Cunningham, 1997.

but not a medical scholar, Chalcondylas made some mistakes. In 1531, Johann Guinther of Andernach, one of Vesalius's teachers at Paris, brought out a better Latin translation that was often reprinted.[45]

Galen had done a great deal of animal dissection and some vivisection. He also summarized the results of a considerable amount of anatomical research by earlier medical scholars whose works have not survived. Overall, Galen provided much more anatomical detail and information on dissection technique than medieval writers on the subject. And he insisted on the importance of anatomy. But medical men knew little of this until all of Galen's anatomical works appeared in Latin translation in the 1520s and 1530s. Now they could follow Galen better than before, as they dissected bodies. Believing that Galen was far superior to all the anatomists who followed, they tried to duplicate what he had done. The key figure was Vesalius.

Andreas Vesalius of Brussels (1514–64) studied in Louvain, where he dissected small animals, and at Paris, a center of Galenic revival in the 1520s and 1530s, where he did human dissections and became convinced of the importance of anatomical study.[46] Vesalius took a bachelor's degree from Louvain in 1537; in the autumn of that year he came to Padua, where he immediately won a medical doctorate through examination. In December 1537 the Venetian Senate appointed Vesalius the combined first and second ordinary professor of surgery (although Padua normally had only one) with the requirement that he teach anatomy. The appointment renewal for 1540–41 emphasized "with the obligation to dissect human bodies."[47] Vesalius initially received 40 florins, subsequently raised to 70, then to 200. During his tenure at Padua, he visited the universities of Bologna and Pisa, where he performed public anatomies to much attention and acclaim. His strong personality and showmanship on such occasions helped convince onlookers of his novel views. He left the University of Padua to become one of Charles V's physicians in 1543 and never returned to academic life.

Vesalius was very much a medical humanist with a good knowledge of Greek. He translated one anatomical work of Galen and emended the translation of *De anatomicis administrationibus* for the Giunti Latin edition. Like other medical humanists, Vesalius criticized the medieval Arabic medical writers and wished to restore medicine to the tradition of the ancients.

At Padua Vesalius embarked on an intensive program of dissecting as many human cadavers as possible, with an ambitious publication program his goal. He became convinced that Galen's description of the human body had numerous errors because it was based on the dissection of animals. Vesalius's intense activity

45. Durling, 1961, 237–39, 283, on Guinther's translation.

46. The account of Vesalius's career and the *Fabrica* is mostly based on O'Malley, 1964, which includes extensive translated material from the *Fabrica*. Vesalius, 1950, reproduces the illustrations, accompanied by some translated text, from Vesalius's works. See also Cunningham, 1997, 88–142, and Carlino, 1999, index. There is much more scholarship on Vesalius than can be listed here.

47. For Vesalius's salary, see AAUP, F. 651, ff. 138ᵛ, 140ᵛ, 144ᵛ ("Andrea Vasalio Germano con obligo di tegliare li corpi humani"), 151ᵛ, 158ᵛ, 162ᵛ, 164ᵛ.

at Padua culminated in the publication of *De humani corporis fabrica* (On the fabric [or structure] of the human body) in Basel in 1543. This most famous and most beautiful of all medical books of the Renaissance, and perhaps of all time, raised the study of anatomy to a new level.

The *Fabrica* innovated in content and presentation. First, Vesalius provided much more information and considerably more detail on the human anatomy than any previous text. Although he did not announce any spectacular individual discovery, the amount of new material and the detail was overwhelming. Second, Vesalius attempted to base everything in his book solely on examination of the human body, although he did not completely succeed. Nevertheless, he constantly affirmed the principle. Third, his anatomical illustrations were far superior to any earlier book or manuscript. Vesalius deliberately emphasized illustrations far more than his predecessors, and he integrated text and illustration more closely. Fourth, he insisted that students should dissect and study cadavers at first hand rather than rely on lectures and books. In order to encourage human anatomical study, Vesalius explained how to dissect as he went through the body. Vesalius emphasized that he did his own dissection. Fifth, Vesalius criticized Galen whenever he believed that Galen was incorrect, which was often. Finally, Vesalius tried to develop a standard terminology for the parts of the body based on the Greek names or Latinized versions of Greek names. He also included anatomical names in Arabic and Hebrew for reference and rejected many medieval Latin terms. The revised edition of 1555 corrected mistakes and added new material.

Like humanistically inclined scholars in other fields, Vesalius had a deep reverence for the ancient authorities. But he tempered that respect with his own experience. For example, Vesalius lectured three times on Galen's *De ossibus ad tyrones* (On the bones for beginners), a Latin translation of which just became available in 1535, before he began to criticize the text.[48] Vesalius combined ancient wisdom and his own research in order to create a new Renaissance study of anatomy.

BODIES FOR DISSECTION

Although Vesalius's achievement was personal, neither he nor the anatomists who followed could have done much anatomical research outside the university environment or without the strong support of the Venetian civil authorities. The latter brought Vesalius to Padua, rushed him through a doctorate, and gave him a lectureship at the age of twenty-three. Most important, they provided him with numerous cadavers.

Beyond the public anatomies, Vesalius had additional bodies at his disposal to

---

48. O'Malley, 1964, 111. As Bylebyl, 1979, 360–61, put it, "it was only because he [Vesalius] had so thoroughly mastered the content of Galenic anatomy for teaching purposes that he could go on to become the effective founder of modern anatomy."

dissect privately or in the company of a few students. Indeed, he kept some bodies, or parts of them, in his living quarters for several weeks! Although Vesalius never indicated exactly how many human bodies he dissected for the *Fabrica,* he specifically mentioned two female cadavers before Padua and seven more during the five years of preparation at Padua.[49] Since male bodies were far easier to obtain, it is possible that he had two to three times as many male corpses to dissect, making a total of twenty to thirty, while at Padua.

As in other universities, the Venetian governors of Padua made available the bodies of executed foreign (i.e., not Venetian, Paduan, or possibly other residents of the Venetian state) criminals for university public anatomies. Moreover, they scheduled executions to suit Vesalius's needs. In the *Fabrica,* he publicly thanked a Venetian governor of Padua for providing him with bodies "scarcely dead." When Vesalius wanted a female cadaver for a public anatomy at the University of Pisa, Duke Cosimo I de' Medici removed the body of a nun from its burial vault in Florence and sent it to Pisa by barge.[50]

Nevertheless, the demand for bodies by Vesalius and other anatomists quickly exceeded the supply of criminals to be executed, because Italian Renaissance governments employed capital punishment sparingly.[51] Additional bodies came from charitable hospitals, where foreigners and others lacking relatives and friends died.[52] Again, this required the cooperation of hospital authorities and government.

If anatomists did not have enough bodies, they procured them illegally. Vesalius encouraged his students to rob graves and snatch bodies. Indeed, wherever Vesalius went, a rash of body snatchings occurred! Since he took little trouble to hide his incitement of students to grab bodies, the authorities clearly winked at this for the sake of science. On the other hand, accusations of human vivisection which dogged Vesalius and other anatomists are unfounded.[53] The anatomists did employ animal vivisection.

The authorities continued to condone body snatching for the sake of Padua's anatomical dissections after Vesalius left. In December 1556, Gabriele Falloppia (1523–62), then professor of surgery and anatomy, wrote to the Riformatori dello Studio asking for cadavers. He invoked a threat guaranteed to stir them into action: German and Polish students were beginning to leave for Bologna and Ferrara for lack of an anatomical dissection. Three days later the Riformatori wrote to the Venetian governor of Padua asking him to provide Falloppia with the body of an executed criminal. If no execution was imminent, he should

49. O'Malley, 1964, 113, 436–37 n. 7.

50. Ibid., 201, 370 (quote), 436 n. 5.

51. Park (1994, 13–14) makes this point, which can be supported from other evidence. For example, the authorities of the large city of Venice executed only 168 persons (about 1.7 per year) in the sixteenth century, the majority in the last third of the century. Grendler, 1977, 58. The bodies of executed heretics—of whom there were very few in Italy—were not dissected, so far as is known.

52. Ferrari, 1987, 60–61; Park, 1994, esp. 13–21.

53. Park, 1994, 19–20.

permit those hired to assist the anatomy to procure "covertly" the body of someone "lowborn and unknown." This would be a great benefit to the university, the Riformatori concluded.[54]

In other words, the Riformatori told local authorities to look the other way while Falloppia's assistants stole the body of someone lacking mourners or for whom the protests of relatives might be ignored. The episode also makes the point that anatomical dissection had become so important to medical education that students threatened to leave for its lack or delay. Only a university strongly supported by civil authorities could provide the needed bodies for extended anatomical research.

UNIVERSITY ANATOMY AFTER VESALIUS

As anatomical study grew in importance, the appointment entitled "Surgery," and later "Surgery and Anatomy," changed its nature. The statutes charged the professor holding this appointment to teach the statutory texts for surgery, which meant teaching students how to heal wounds, set broken bones, and so on. In addition, the professor was required to preside over the annual public anatomy. The appointee apparently was not required to deliver a series of lectures on human anatomy.

Despite the statutes, teaching anatomy, rather than surgery, through one or two public anatomies, by means of private dissections before a small group of students, and through lectures, with a part of a human or animal body (or both) at hand, became increasingly important. Vesalius fulfilled his obligation to lecture on surgery in a relatively short time but spent much more time lecturing on anatomy.[55] His successors probably did the same. Positions in surgery, or surgery and anatomy, became de facto lectureships in which anatomy dominated, not least because anatomical research enabled professors to make new discoveries. Indeed, from the 1540s onward, all the major Italian universities had accomplished anatomists who made discoveries about the human body. Traditional surgery did not provide this opportunity.[56]

Padua illustrates the point. After Vesalius, Realdo Colombo (see below) taught briefly at Padua, to be followed by a minor figure. Then Gabriele Falloppia of Modena was appointed in 1551. Falloppia had begun to dissect bodies before he

54. "Et non havendo suggieto da far morire vogli permetter che li masari possino covratamente procaciarsi di qualche corpo quando li venga occasione di persona ignobile et non cognosciuta, per che questo serà di gran giovamento a tutto questo studio." Letter of the Riformatori di Studio di Padova to the *podestà* of Padua, Dec. 15, 1556, printed in Favaro, 1928, 227. Falloppia's letter of December 12 is on 226–27. The *massari* (literally "managers" or "stewards") were two men chosen and paid by the student organization to prepare the anatomy. Before the erection of permanent anatomical theaters, they selected the site, purchased the lumber, and oversaw the construction of a temporary theater. They also collected fees from the students and viewed the dissection. As the letter indicates, at times they were expected to find a cadaver.

55. O'Malley, 1964, 79–80.

56. However, Nutton (1985) makes the valid point that there was "humanist surgery," that is, surgery based on classical texts, in the sixteenth century.

began his medical studies at the University of Ferrara, where he took his degree, probably in 1547, and then taught surgery and anatomy at the University of Pisa (1548–51).[57] Padua appointed Falloppia to teach surgery and medical botany with partial responsibility for the public anatomy at a salary of 200 florins, later raised to 270. Falloppia was initially relegated to the secondary role of dissecting, while a senior professor explained the body.[58] But at the anatomy of January 1555, the students loudly demanded that Falloppia be given sole responsibility. The university agreed.

Falloppia lectured on, and published commentaries on, surgical and anatomical texts, including Hippocrates' *De vulneribus capitis* (On wounds of the head) and Galen's *De ossibus ad tyrones* and *De tumoribus praeter naturam* (On tumors contrary to nature). Most important, his dissections of the bodies of adults, fetuses, newborn infants, and small children led to important discoveries about the kidneys, teeth, ear muscles, nerves, and especially female reproductive organs. The fallopian or uterine tubes are named for him. Falloppia was considering an offer to move to the University of Bologna as professor of practical medicine at a salary of 400 scudi when he died of tuberculosis in 1562.[59]

After Falloppia's premature death the Paduan post went in 1565 to his pupil Girolamo Fabrici da Acquapendente (c. 1533–1619), who held it until retirement in 1613. Fabrici lectured on Galen's texts, conducted the public anatomies (which he neglected in later years), and dissected throughout the year.[60] He also did pioneering work in comparative embryology and was the teacher of William Harvey during the latter's studies (1598 or 1599 through 1602) at Padua. Popular with Venetian senators, Fabrici was extremely well paid, his salary eventually reaching 1,400 florins. Even though the major focus of his appointment was anatomy, it continued to be called "Surgery and Anatomy" until 1609, when for a few years anatomy and surgery were divided between two professors, before being combined again in 1619.[61]

Anatomy also became important in middle-rank universities, such as Rome. Dissections probably began in Rome as early as the fourteenth century, and a

57. Favaro, 1928. The professors of surgery and anatomy at Padua are listed in Tomasini, 1986, 302–3; Facciolati, 1978, pt. 3:385–90; Bertolaso, 1959–60, 29–31; and in the various rolls found in AAUP.

58. His appointment was described in 1553–54 as "Chirurgia semplici et obligo di tagliar l'anatomia." AAUP, F. 651, f. 206ᵛ.

59. Favaro, 1928, 133–41.

60. "Leget de partibus similaribus, & dissimilaribus, & earundem actionibus [on similar and dissimilar parts and their actions], de ossibus [on bones], de anatome [on anatomy]. Item de luxationibus, & fracturis [of laxations and fractions] hora 3. mane." These are probably all texts of Galen. The lecture began at the third hour of the morning, that is, three hours after sunrise. Description of Fabrici's duties in the roll of 1594 found in AAUP, Inventario 1320, no pag., and fig. 3 of this book. On Fabrici, see Adelmann, 1942; Zanobio, 1981; and Muccillo, 1993b, each with additional bibliography. For similarities and dissimilarities between Fabrici and Harvey and an informative account of anatomy instruction at Padua at this time, see Whitteridge, 1971, 9–40. On Fabrici's failure to perform the public anatomy in later years and his hostility to a rival, see Chapter 14, "Private Anatomy Teaching at Padua."

61. See the Faculty of Arts roll of 1610–11 in AAUP, Inventario 1320, no pag.

university dissection is documented in 1512.[62] The university appointed Realdo Colombo (c. 1510–59), who began teaching at Padua and then taught at Pisa (1546–48), professor of anatomy, which position he held from 1549 until his death in late 1559. In 1556 he performed a postmortem dissection of Saint Ignatius Loyola. The roll of 1559–60 listed Colombo's appointment as *In Anathomia* and his salary as 220 scudi, which tied him with three others for the second highest salary in the university.[63] The stipend signified the esteem in which Colombo was held and the growing importance of anatomy.

Colombo originally planned to produce a book on anatomy jointly with Michelangelo Buonarotti, who was keenly interested in the subject. Although the artist's advancing age prevented this project from coming to fruition, Colombo did produce an important book, *De re anatomica libri XV* (1559), published just as he died. He tried to replicate the practice of the anatomists in ancient Alexandria, and he sometimes corrected Vesalius. He is best remembered for the discovery of the pulmonary circulation of the blood, that is, that all the blood goes from the right ventricle of the heart through the lungs before returning to the left ventricle. His discovery denied Galen's view that blood passed from right to left ventricle through minute pores in the septum, the dividing wall in the heart. Colombo's understanding of the activities of the heart and lungs partially anticipated William Harvey's famous book of 1628.

After Colombo's death, the University of Rome lacked a professor of anatomy and had no public anatomy for some years in the 1560s. The authorities tried to assign the public anatomy to the surgery professor, whose Latin was so poor that he sometimes lectured in Italian. But he did not wish to do the anatomy, and the students complained.[64] In 1570–71 a professor of medical theory lectured on anatomy but did not perform the public anatomy. Finally, a youthful professor of surgery, Costanzo Varoli (1543–75), arrived in 1572, lectured on anatomy to considerable praise, and presided over the public anatomy while another scholar did the cutting. Varolio was another talented medical scholar who made important discoveries about the optic nerve and the brain.[65] After Varoli's sudden death, the public anatomy, which was "very important," according to the beadle, was not held in 1575–76.[66] It resumed in 1579–80. The beadle praised the new professor and the cutter, who continued to dissect until the body stank! From that date through the rest of the century and beyond, Rome had a professor, whose appointment was usually described as surgery and anatomy, to do public ana-

62. Carlino, 1999, 87–92, who surveys public anatomies in sixteenth-century Rome.

63. *I maestri di Roma*, 1991, 30, and Renazzi, 1971, 2:193–94, for his appointment. On Colombo see Whitteridge, 1971, 41–77; Bylebyl, 1981a; Colombero, 1982; and Cunningham, 1997, 143–66.

64. "Chyrurgus scuta 100: Benalbus Brancalupus. Hic noluit facere Anathomiam sibi assignatam; hic non satis colet linguam latinam, et legit sermone vulgari." Comments of the beadle, Alessio Lorenzani, in *I maestri di Roma*, 1991, 39 (1566). The beadle reported that there was no anatomy in 1568–69 or in the following year. Ibid., 63, 70.

65. *I maestri di Roma*, 1991, 89; Renazzi, 1971, 2:194–95; O'Malley, 1981d; and Carlino, 1999, 90.

66. "Anatomia, quae maximi momenti est, hoc anno non habita est." *I maestri di Roma*, 1991, 106.

tomies and to lecture on anatomy. In most cases the professor lectured and a surgeon, not necessarily from the university, dissected.[67]

Other medical scholars at Rome besides professors of anatomy or surgery dissected as well. Bartolomeo Eustachi (1500/1510–74), another medical humanist who read Greek and Arabic, came from the court of Urbino to Rome in 1549 and became a professor of medicine at the university sometime in the mid-1550s, although the title of the initial appointment is unknown. By 1559 he was professor of practical medicine, which he held at least through 1563, when severe gout forced him to resign. Eustachi did many dissections on bodies delivered to him from the hospitals of Rome. He began as a supporter of Galen in opposition to Vesalius and then made improvements on Vesalius and major new discoveries. Eustachi published a series of treatises on the kidneys, teeth, and other parts of the body. The eustachian tube between the nose and the ear is named for him.[68]

The individuals and pattern of events at Rome illustrated the changes that the growing interest in anatomy brought to the hierarchy of university medical instruction. A large gap in education, activity, prestige, and money traditionally separated professors of theoretical and practical medicine and the surgeons. Many surgeons were not university trained; those who were and taught in universities were not major scholars. They were modestly paid, were seldom published, played little role in medical research, and did not ascend to professorships of practical medicine. The Latin-challenged professor of surgery at Rome who declined to do the public anatomy, possibly because he did not understand well the texts of Galen, typified the traditional professor of surgery.

The new anatomists were different. Even though their appointments might be surgery, or surgery and anatomy, they were very well educated, fired by the skills and approach of medical humanism, dedicated to reviving ancient anatomy, and capable of original research. Although professors of anatomy did not always do the cutting in the public anatomy, they dissected on other occasions. They published monographs with major discoveries about the human body, received higher salaries than professors of surgery in the past, and sometimes ascended to ordinary professorships of practical medicine. At the same time, theoretical and especially practical medicine based on traditional texts moved closer to anatomy, as some professors of these subjects embraced anatomical dissection.

Unlike Padua and Rome, the University of Bologna did establish an ordinary professorship of anatomy. It had a history of distinguished anatomists. Mondino de' Liuzzi, who wrote the standard medieval textbook on anatomy, probably taught at Bologna at the end of the thirteenth century and in the first

---

67. *I maestri di Roma*, 1991, 119 (beadle's comment), 122, 126, 131, 135, 140, 145, 149, 153, 157, 983, 986. Some rolls are missing. Carlino, 1999, 91–92.

68. For his appearances on the rolls, see *I maestri di Roma*, 1991, 30 (1559), 33 (1561), 35 (1563). Most of the rolls of the 1550s are missing. See also Renazzi, 1971, 2:189–91; O'Malley, 1981b; and Muccillo, 1993a.

quarter of the fourteenth.[69] Jacopo Berengario (Barigazzi) da Carpi, whose 1521 commentary on Mondino's *Anatomia* succeeded the latter as the standard pre-Vesalian text, taught surgery and did the public anatomy at Bologna between 1502 and 1527.[70]

In 1560 Giulio Cesare Aranzio (c. 1530–89), professor of surgery at the university since 1556, began petitioning the Bolognese government for appointment as professor of anatomy.[71] He noted that he had performed both public and private dissections without payment. His numerous petitions finally bore fruit in 1570, when the apostolic legate in Bologna decreed the establishment of an ordinary professorship of anatomy (*Ad anathomiam ordinariam*) and awarded the post to Aranzio, to be added to his surgery professorship, at the low salary of 100 lire. But Aranzio had to bear all the costs of the annual anatomy, which probably consumed much of the salary. And the legate undercut Aranzio's position by authorizing other professors to dissect publicly and privately, so long as they did not do so at the time of Aranzio's annual public anatomy.

The last provision inevitably led to conflict. In 1579 the Bolognese authorities decreed that another professor of surgery, Gaspare Tagliacozzi (1545–99), would receive annually the second available cadaver for dissection. When both the first and second bodies were mistakenly given to Aranzio in 1584, students supporting Tagliacozzi threatened a mass migration. Upon Aranzio's death in 1589 the university named all four professors of surgery ordinary professors of anatomy as well, with Tagliacozzi first in precedence. They were simultaneously professors of surgery and of anatomy. However, the four anatomists did not do four public dissections annually but rotated the task, obviously now an honor, each performing every fourth year. The three idle anatomists did not receive the extra salary of 100 or 200 lire in the years in which they did not dissect publicly. Of course, each may have conducted dissections in the presence of students when they could find bodies.

Despite its awkward compromise on the appointment, the university had confirmed the importance of anatomy by establishing an ordinary professorship in the subject. This was how universities recognized a significant new area of scholarship. The concession that other professors might do anatomical dissections acknowledged the fact that various professors besides the professor of anatomy did such research and that they should not be stopped. The student threat offered evidence that anatomy was important to them. And both Aranzio and Tagliacozzi did important anatomical research. Aranzio published a major work on

69. Bullough, 1981; Siraisi, 1981, 66–69 and see index.

70. On Berengario, see Ascari and Crespi, 1964; French, 1985; and Dallari, 1888–1924, 1:181–214 passim, 2:5–49 passim. Berengario da Carpi, 1959, is an English translation of his *Isagogae breves* (A short introduction to anatomy) of 1522.

71. Discussion of the institution of anatomy professorships at Bologna is based on Martinotti, 1911, esp. 80–83; Forni, 1948, 75–77, 80–97; and Gnudi and Webster, 1950, 58–63, 97–101, 146–48. For Aranzio, see Mondella, 1961, and Dall'Osso, 1981. See Dallari, 1888–1924, 2:179–270 passim, for the relevant rolls.

pregnancy and the fetus based on his anatomical observations.[72] Tagliacozzi published the first major work on plastic surgery in 1597.

Other universities joined the anatomical Renaissance quickly or slowly. At Pavia, anatomy appeared in the rolls for the first time in 1536 in the form of a professor charged with teaching both surgery and anatomy. A professorship devoted solely to anatomy appeared in 1554. The holder initially received a salary of 100 scudi, half for lecturing on anatomy ("pro lectura anatomiae") and half for performing the anatomical dissection ("pro incisione cadaveris humani").[73]

Fired by medical humanism, some of the medical professors at Ferrara were keenly interested in the new anatomy and did excellent work in the subject. Both Antonio Maria Canani (1490/1500–1578) and especially his cousin Giovanni Battista Canani (1515–79) performed anatomical dissections at Ferrara in the 1530s and 1540s. The latter, who did the public anatomies at Ferrara in the years 1544–52, was a friend of Vesalius's and published a study of muscles in 1541. It was the first anatomical work to use copper engravings, which could present finer detail than the woodcuts that illustrated the books of Vesalius and others. The Canani were professors of surgery, practical medicine, and theoretical medicine, rather than professors of anatomy, at the time. Anatomy became an ongoing holiday (*diebus festivis*) professorship in 1570.[74]

After reopening in 1543 the University of Pisa appointed Realdo Colombo to teach anatomy and surgery (1546–48), followed by Gabriele Falloppio (1548–51). Falloppio may have dissected seven or eight bodies annually at Pisa. After these two departed, Pisa in 1552 established a holiday professorship of anatomy, filled by a lesser figure. Beginning in 1557 Pisa had an ongoing ordinary professorship of anatomy. But none of the men who followed compared to Colombo and Falloppio.[75]

The University of Turin (then temporarily at Mondovì) had an ongoing professorship of anatomy beginning in 1564–65.[76] Anatomy entered the University of Perugia in 1580 with a professor of anatomy and surgery, which became two by 1600.[77] Siena only hired a professor of anatomy, rather than surgery and

72. Mondella, 1961; Dall'Osso, 1981.

73. *Memorie di Pavia*, 1970, 125, 127; Palumbi, 1961, 101. See ASPv, Università, Cartone 20, no pag., rolls of 1556–57, 1559–60, 1561–62, 1562–63, and so on for descriptions of the appointment.

74. *I maestri di Ferrara*, 1991, 151, which summarizes the rolls found on pp. 10–49. More cautious and reliable is Franceschini, 1970, 247. *I maestri di Ferrara*, 10, lists one Girolamo Molino teaching anatomy in the years 1460–63. Closer inspection reveals that Molino was the student rector of arts from 1461 to 1463, that he served as a witness for degrees, and that he obtained his own doctorate of medicine on Feb. 14, 1463. Pardi, 1970, 39, 41–43. He may have held a student lectureship in medicine, but it is very unlikely that he held an anatomy position. For the two Canani, see G. Gliozzi, 1974a and 1974b, and Muratori, 1981. Broader studies of anatomy and medicine at Ferrara are Muratori and Bighi, 1963–1964, and Raspadori, 1991.

75. Barsanti, 1993, 558–59, for the list, and passim for individual professors. Fabroni, 1971, 2:71–85; Cascio Pratilli, 1975, 148–49, 151 n. 54.

76. Vallauri, 1970, 1:205, 207.

77. Ermini, 1971, 236, 571.

anatomy, in 1587; he was permitted to lecture in Italian after 1588.[78] Naples did not establish a professorship of anatomy, or surgery and anatomy, in the sixteenth century, although Giovan Filippo Ingrassia (c. 1510–80), professor of practical medicine from 1547 to 1553, was known for his anatomical studies and probably taught anatomy.[79] Catania did not have a professorship of anatomy but did have an annual anatomical dissection beginning in 1595.[80] Messina probably had a professor of anatomy and surgery in the late 1590s. Neither Macerata nor Salerno had professors of anatomy in the sixteenth century. Parma had a professor of anatomy, who also taught medical botany, from the foundation of the university in 1601 to at least 1610 and probably beyond.

As anatomy grew in importance and popularity, permanent anatomical theaters replaced the temporary rough wooden platforms. The theaters were probably small, circular wooden amphitheaters constructed within the larger university building and suitable for fifty or more tightly crammed spectators. Pavia erected an anatomical theater in 1552. Pisa apparently had one by 1569.[81] Ferrara had an anatomical theater, whose construction was financed by the students, in 1551, and another within the new university building in 1588.[82] Bologna built a permanent wooden anatomical theater within the Archiginnasio shortly after 1595. The authorities replaced it with a splendid amphitheater holding several hundred spectators in 1637. The latter was designed more for public spectacles than to enable students to look closely at a body.[83] Padua's anatomical theater, built in 1594 within the Palazzo del Bo, is the best known surviving Renaissance anatomical theater.

As indicated above, the mobility of the anatomists and rising salaries indicated the subject's growing importance. The hierarchy of university medicine remained the same, but professors of anatomy, or surgery and anatomy, sometimes ascended to the more important professorships of practical and theoretical medicine in the second half of the sixteenth century. At Bologna Tagliacozzi began his university teaching as a professor of surgery and anatomy at 100 lire in 1570 but was earning 1,140 lire as an ordinary professor of theoretical medicine at his death in 1599.[84] Such ascents did not occur in the fifteenth century.

Of course, anatomy's importance transcended salaries and positions. Those who taught anatomy and dissected bodies made numerous significant discoveries. Given the complexity of the human body and previous ignorance, this is not surprising. But it does not diminish the achievement. Most important, anatomical study became part of the research and teaching of numerous medical scholars. Professors of theoretical and practical medicine increasingly emphasized anatom-

78. Cascio Pratilli, 1975, 75–76, 186, 188; Piccinni, 1991, 149.

79. Cortese, 1924, 330–31; O'Malley, 1981c.

80. Catalano, 1934, 91.

81. Ferrari, 1987, 72 n. 76.

82. Quinterio, 1991, 90.

83. Ferrari, 1987, 72–82.

84. Gnudi and Webster, 1950, 227. A second doctorate in philosophy in 1576 and his success in rebuilding the noses of injured princes and nobles through plastic surgery probably also helped.

ical knowledge. They referred to anatomical detail in order to establish the structural bases for physiology. They used autopsies to illustrate the effects of disease. To be sure, a wide gap still separated physiology studied by means of traditional texts and Scholastic dialectic from anatomy based on observation.[85]

By the last quarter of the sixteenth century, both students and university authorities greatly appreciated anatomical studies. In or about the academic year 1579–80, the vice rector of the University of Pisa wrote a letter to Grand Duke Francesco I de' Medici, ruler of Tuscany, concerning the needs of the University of Pisa and included a judgment on anatomy. The public anatomy was "one of the most honored, useful, indeed, necessary things that [could] possibly be done."[86] No other event in the academic year attracted so much attention.

In the seventeenth century anatomical study continued to be essential to medical research and education. But the public anatomy, which Vesalius used so effectively to promote the new anatomy, diminished in importance and value. Advances in anatomical knowledge now came by means of detailed analyses of particular systems of the body, such as the circulation of the blood. The newly invented microscope, the magnifying glass, and minute study of parts of the body became important. This anatomical research was best done in an intimate and private setting, far from the open and sometimes carnivalesque atmosphere of the public anatomy.[87] But it followed the path blazed by Vesalius, Falloppia, Colombo, and others. The anatomical Renaissance was the single most important contribution of Italian universities to medicine.

CLINICAL MEDICINE

Giovanni Battista Da Monte (or Montanus) introduced clinical medicine, the next innovation in medical education, in the early 1540s.[88] Born of a noble family in Verona in 1489, Da Monte received a broad education with a humanistic emphasis at Padua. He learned Greek well enough to translate a Greek literary work. He then studied medicine with Leoniceno at Ferrara and counted himself a disciple. A medical degree from the College of Physicians at Venice followed in 1520. He traveled extensively through Italy, including visits with the humanist Giovanni Pontano at Naples, before practicing medicine at Brescia for several years. Da Monte's growing medical reputation culminated in appointment as first ordinary professor of practical medicine at Padua in the autumn of 1539 at a salary

85. Bylebyl, 1979, 363; Bylebyl, 1985a, 223–25; and Siraisi, 1987, 304–10, 324–44.

86. "L'Anatomia si faccia ogni anno, al freddo, d'huomo e di donna o almeno d'huomo solo; ella è una delle più honorate et utili, anzi necessarie cose che si possino fare, et è stato danno già grandissimo 'l dismetterla." Letter of Lodovico Villani da Prato, vice rector of the University of Pisa, no date but 1579–80, printed in Del Fante, 1980b, 420. In Rome the beadle put it this way in 1570–71: "Anatomia, quae maximi momenti est in arte medica." *I maestri di Roma,* 1991, 80; see also p. 106 (1575–76).

87. Ferrari, 1987, 90.

88. The following is based on Bylebyl, 1979, 345–52; Ongaro, 1981, 119–26; Bylebyl, 1982; and Muccillo, 1986a. See Palmer, 1983, 78, for Da Monte's medical degree.

of 500 florins. While at Padua he helped prepare the Giunti Latin Galen edition of 1541, and he supported the founding of the university botanical garden. In 1543 Da Monte became first ordinary professor of theoretical medicine at Padua at a salary of 700 florins, a position he held until death in 1551.

Some universities insisted that the future physician serve an apprenticeship with an established doctor. For example, fifteenth-century university statutes required an aspiring doctor to practice with a certified physician (for six months at Pavia and twelve months at Padua) before taking the degree.[89] But Da Monte was the first to make clinical medicine a regular and integrated part of medical teaching. Contemporaries fixed the date as 1543, although he had started earlier.

At that time Da Monte led his students from the Palazzo del Bo, where professors lectured, to the Hospital of St. Francis next door, where he was a physician. At the hospital he lectured to his students on the symptoms, diagnosis, pathology, and cure of diseases in the presence of a patient who could be examined. (Unless the patient understood Latin, he did not know what Da Monte was saying about his disease and condition; this may have spared him bad news.) Da Monte also took students to the bedsides of his private patients. Further, he turned the circular disputations, the required discussions between professor and students after a lecture, into free-ranging clinical discussions of cases. These regular, systematic clinical discussions at the hospital and in the circular disputations came to be called the "collegium Montani" (Montanus's College). Students took notes that became highly prized. Clinical medicine was Da Monte's attempt to bridge what he saw as an artificial division between medical theory and practice. He tried to create a universal medicine uniting the two.

After his death, former pupils won attention for his method by publishing accounts of his hospital lectures, his numerous medical *consilia,* and his university lectures, along with paeans of praise. Paduan professors of medicine continued to analyze diseases at hospitals. The Venetian Senate formally endorsed clinical medicine in 1578: two professors were to visit a hospital at an appointed hour to discuss individual cases and diseases with students invited to come. This approach was like that of botany instruction, in which a teacher made himself available at a specified time in the university botanical garden (see below). Other Italian universities followed Padua's example. Clinical medicine, nonexistent in northern Europe, greatly attracted ultramontane students, who spread news of the practice. The initial northern clinical school was established at Leiden in 1636.

MEDICAL BOTANY

Spurred by the humanists, medical scholars paid increasing attention to the ancient sources for medical botany and then began to observe plants directly.[90]

89. Park, 1985, 61; Palmer, 1983, 45.

90. Although the sources often referred to the lectureship as the teaching of simples, and the professor sometimes as the *simplicista,* medical botany seems the best term, as will become clear. Alternatives, such as botanical medicine and pharmacology, are less satisfactory.

The expanding interest in plants led universities to introduce the new professor-ship of medical botany and to found botanical gardens. Even though the major reason for studying plants remained medical, scholars moved close to studying plants for themselves by the end of the sixteenth century.

Medieval scholars studied plants as sources of medicine and coined the term *simple*. From the classical Latin adjective *simplex, simplicis* (undivided), *simple* acquired the meaning of medicinal plant in the Middle Ages, possibly as a conse-quence of Gerard of Cremona's Latin translation of the Arabic version of a text of Galen. Gerard's translation of Galen's work was usually entitled *De simplicium medicamentorum facultatibus* (On the powers of medical simples), or *De simplici-bus medicinis,* or just *De simplicibus* (On simples). *Simple* came to mean a single plant that produced a single medicinal substance, or simple drug, rather than a compound drug made from several plants. Several vernacular languages em-braced the term.

Medieval medical education placed little emphasis on teaching the medicinal properties of plants. As noted earlier, the 1405 statutes of Bologna ordered the ordinary professors of theoretical medicine to teach Galen's *De simplicibus,* except for book 6, in the first year of the four-year cycle and to do the same in the third year. The statutes specifically mentioned the section in the fifth book, which discussed "the necessity of mixing compound medicines."[91] But these were the only references to teaching medical botany in the four-year Bolognese medical curriculum filled with other texts. Professors might also teach simples from a medical encyclopedia, such as book 2 of Avicenna's *Canon,* although Bologna did not prescribe it.

The two major ancient sources for simples and plantlore, Dioscorides and Pliny the Elder, available in Latin translation, were little used in the Middle Ages. Peter of Abano lectured on Dioscorides' *De materia medica* at Padua around 1300, but this seems to have been an isolated case. Epitomes and encyclopedias dissemi-nated a limited amount of the information found in Dioscorides and Pliny the Elder. But medieval university professors teaching simples spent little time exam-ining plants directly, if at all.

The humanists' growing expertise in, and enthusiasm for, ancient Greek learning in the second half of the fifteenth century led them to Dioscorides' *De materia medica.*[92] Probably a physician born in what is now Turkey, the Greek Dioscorides (fl. A.D. 50–70) compiled by far the largest and most important pharmaceutical guide in antiquity and for the next fifteen hundred years. *De materia medica* was a catalogue of more than six hundred plants, thirty-five ani-mal products, and ninety minerals. For each plant Dioscorides presented mul-tiple names, origin and physical characteristics, medicinal uses, and instruc-tions on preparing a medicine from the plant, although the descriptions were

91. "Legatur liber de simplici medicina, excepto sexto libro eiusdem." "Quo lecto, legatur de quinto usque ad illud capitulum in quo incipit determinare de simplicibus medicinis, quo lecto, legantur capitula ultima quinti libri, ubi determinat de necessitate compositionis medicinarum com-positarum usque ad finem quinti libri." Malagola, 1966, 275.

92. The following is based on Riddle, 1980 and 1981.

often so brief and sketchy that they led to confusion and controversy. Although Dioscorides sometimes relied on older authorities, he emphasized that he examined plants himself whenever possible. He told his readers that knowledge of plants had to be gained through experience.

The humanists recognized the importance of Dioscorides and turned their attention to the text, which had become much altered through rearrangement, interpolations, and copying errors. They also heeded Dioscorides' advice to examine plants personally. The Venetian humanist Ermolao Barbaro (1453/54–92) made a new Latin translation about 1481, intended to replace a fourteenth-century translation, and added a commentary partially based on examination of plants, some found in his own garden of simples in Padua. His translation with commentary was not printed until 1516. Leoniceno and Giorgio Valla gathered manuscripts for the first Greek edition of Dioscorides, published by Aldo Manuzio in 1499, with a revised edition of 1518. Numerous other editions, translations, and commentaries followed. The publications signaled a growing interest in medical botany based on the ancients.

The humanists soon turned to the *Historia naturalis* of Pliny the Elder (A.D. 23/24–79). Pliny's work is a sprawling, poorly organized encyclopedia of natural history in the broadest sense of the term in thirty-seven books, of which 20 through 27 dealt with botany.[93] Medieval scholars knew Pliny's work fairly well but never used it as a university text, so far as is known. Instead, they pillaged it for their own works. By contrast, the humanists recognized its importance as a source of ancient natural history so early that the first printed edition appeared in 1469. Unfortunately, the received text had become very corrupt. The numerous unusual names of plants and Pliny's Greek quotations had led to many scribal errors. Some of the ablest and most important Italian humanists set to work to correct the text, a process that continued in northern Europe through the mid-sixteenth century. The discussions and disagreements about the text in the late fifteenth and early sixteenth centuries are usually called the "Pliny controversy."

Most of the controversy dealt with the textual errors in the manuscripts of Pliny. Ermolao Barbaro and most other humanists blamed them on medieval copyists and editors, the typical humanist attitude. But Leoniceno introduced a new perspective in a little work entitled *De Plinii et plurium aliorum medicorum in medicina erroribus* (On the medical errors of Pliny and many other physicians) of 1492. He argued that Pliny had made many of the errors himself. Pliny was particularly responsible for the incorrect terminology (plants and drugs incorrectly labeled, the use of different names for the same herb) found in the work. Leoniceno asserted that Pliny had often garbled the information found in his Greek sources. He emphasized the possible medical consequences of such mistakes: physicians could kill their patients if, following Pliny, they prescribed the wrong drug.

Although the majority of humanists who worked on the difficult text rejected

---

93. The following is based on Thorndike, 1923–1958, 4:593–610; Reeds, 1975, 32–33; Mugnai Carrara, 1979, 195–96; Nauert, 1979 and 1980; D'Amico, 1988, 72–98.

Leoniceno's argument, later medical botanists accepted Leoniceno's point that even a treasured ancient source had to meet standards of factual accuracy and utility. Leoniceno did not propose personal observation and experimentation on plants as a means of checking the accuracy of the ancient source, but later medical botanists did.

Monasteries, wealthy individuals, and scholars began to maintain gardens of simples for pleasure, study, or profit, another sign of the growing interest in botany. Ermolao Barbaro's garden in Padua has been mentioned; others could be found in Venice and nearby. Producing costly drugs from plants was commercially important. Venetian access to the Near East made it easier for northern Italian scholars to obtain rare plants, which could be compared with the descriptions in Pliny.[94]

The expanding enthusiasm for medical botany led to separate lectureships on the subject, the first at the University of Rome in 1514. The roll listed a certain Giuliano da Foligno to teach medicinal simples (*Ad declarationem Simplicium Medicinae*) at a salary of 80 florins. The use of the phrase *ad declarationem* (to explain, or to demonstrate through reasoning) instead of the more common *ad lecturam* (to read or lecture) may signify that Giuliano was expected to explain or demonstrate from the plants themselves, in addition to lecturing about them from books. But this remains only speculation for the lack of additional information. Nothing is known of Giuliano, and the lectureship may not have continued. The next surviving roll (1535) of the University of Rome lacked it. But from 1539 through the end of the century and beyond, Rome had a medical botanist, either as an ordinary or a holiday professor. The men who held the position were not distinguished and did not receive high salaries.[95]

Padua established the first continuing lectureship on medical botany. In June 1532, officers of both the arts and law student organizations approached the Venetian governors of Padua. They requested that the University of Padua establish a new lectureship on simples, arguing that it would be very useful and necessary to medicine. They praised the accomplishments of Giovanni Manardo, then teaching at Ferrara, in this field. The students clearly wanted the appointment to go to Manardo, a medical humanist and follower of Leoniceno, known for his scholarship in medical botany. The governors relayed the request to the Venetian Senate. The latter established an ordinary professorship (*Ad lecturam simplicium*) in the autumn of 1533.[96] The Senate did not appoint Manardo, choosing instead a scholar of modest accomplishment, Francesco Bonafede (1474–1558), then second ordinary professor of practical medicine at Padua. Bonafede held the position until 1549, when the Riformatori retired him. Gabriele Falloppia next taught the

94. Palmer, 1985b.

95. *I maestri di Roma*, 1991, 5, 10, 14, 18, 22, 30, 33, 35, 47, 55, 63, 69, 92, 105, 110, 119 (with few students in 1579–80), 122, 126, 131, 135, 140, 145, 149, 153, 1098–99; Renazzi, 1971, 2:65–66, 239, 245–46.

96. The account from Sanudo's diaries is reprinted in Favaro, 1918, 126. See AAUP, F. 651, f. 113ʳ, for Bonafede's appearance in the roll of 1533–34. Also see Giacomini, 1969; Cotton, 1981; Ongaro, 1981, 126–27; Facciolati, 1978, pt. 3, 405–6; Tomasini, 1986, 95–98.

trio of medical botany (lecturing on book 5 of Dioscorides), anatomy, and surgery at Padua until his death in 1562.

Other universities followed the lead of Rome and Padua. Luca Ghini (1490–1556) became the first professor of medical botany at Bologna. After taking his degree at Bologna in 1527, he was appointed one of several ordinary professors of practical medicine. But his passion was medical botany; it is likely that he had attended the lectures of Nicolò Leoniceno at Bologna (1508–9) or at Ferrara, and he spent much time gathering plants. In the academic year 1534–35, no doubt after much urging, the Riformatori of the university appointed him to an ordinary professorship of medicine in which he could also teach simples by lecturing on Galen's *De simplicibus* (*Ad lecturam Medicinae statim post lectionem in tertiis.* [*Legant de simplicibus*]). He received 100 Bolognese lire, the same salary he had previously earned. But the university was not yet convinced of the importance of medical botany, so he left in 1536. He was reappointed in the autumn of 1539 to teach only medical botany: *Ad lecturam de simplicibus medicinalibus.* Ghini was to demonstrate simples plus comment on Galen, other ancient texts, and "recent books" at an increased salary of 300 Bolognese lire.[97] The description was significant: Ghini was to show and describe plants themselves, whether from his teaching lectern or elsewhere is unclear. He was to lecture on both ancient and modern botanical texts, a clear recognition of the growing importance of contemporary botanical scholarship. In general, Ghini emphasized personal examination of plants, and he sometimes treated ancient texts with skepticism.

Ghini was also the first professor of medical botany at the University of Pisa. He moved there in 1544, partly because Bolognese stipends were not paid on time, and stayed until 1555. This was the beginning of the botanical professorship at Pisa.[98] His student, Andrea Cesalpino (1524/25–1603), succeeded Ghini, teaching medical botany at Pisa from 1555 to 1571. Cesalpino developed a physiological taxonomy for plants based on Aristotelian categories. Because he paid little attention to the medicinal uses of plants but focused on the plants themselves (stems, leaves, seeds, and fruit), he helped to make botany an independent branch of knowledge. Although he later taught practical medicine at Pisa and Rome and worked out much of the circulation of the blood, he is best remembered for his attempt to establish the principles of botany.[99] Other medical botanists followed Cesalpino at Pisa.

Ghini returned to Bologna in 1555, this time at 600 Bolognese lire, but died soon after. Although he published nothing during his lifetime, Ghini was a driving force in Italian botanical scholarship and the teacher of Cesalpino, Ulisse

---

97. "Simplicis medicinae tradendae et monstrandae munus, eamque ex Galeni et aliorum medicorum veterum, et recentiorum libris in publicis scholis interpretandum." From a Bolognese archival document of Aug. 30, 1539, quoted by Sabbatani, 1926, 32. This paragraph is based on Sabbatani, 1926; Keller, 1981; and Meschini, 1999. For his appointments, see Dallari, 1888–1924, 2:52–102 passim, esp. 75 (1534–35 appointment and quote) and 91 (1539–40 appointment and quote).

98. For what follows, see Cascio Pratilli, 1975, 148; Garbari, Tongiorgi Tomasi, and Tosi, 1991, 15–51; Garbari and Tongiorgi Tomasi, 1993, 363–70; and Barsanti, 1993, 559.

99. De Ferrari, 1980, and Mägdefrau, 1981.

Aldrovandi, and William Turner (see below). Ghini obtained plants from the length of the Mediterranean basin and compared them with descriptions in Dioscorides and Pliny. He pioneered the technique of *hortus siccus* ("dry garden" but really the modern herbarium), that is, pressing and drying a plant, which was then attached to a card. It could be kept as a reference or sent to others.

Ferrara came next. Leoniceno had apparently lectured on simples as part of his other teaching at Ferrara. The medical humanist Antonio Musa Brasavola carried on botanical research at Ferrara in the 1530s, supported by a botanical garden in the palace of Duke Alfonso I d'Este and possibly his own garden. The University of Ferrara then added a medical botany lectureship in November 1543, filled by Gaspare Gabrieli (1494–1553).[100] A Paduan noble, Gabrieli took a medical degree at Padua in or before 1525. He taught at the University of Ferrara in 1537–38 and as professor of natural philosophy in the years 1541–43. His new post was described as "Lectura simplicium medicamentum," paying 150 lire, later reduced to 100 lire. Surviving lecture notes show that he commented on Dioscorides. Gabrieli continued to teach in Ferrara through the 1546–47 academic year and then returned to Padua, where he devoted himself to letters and to cultivating his own garden of simples. The position continued through the rest of the century and beyond.

University botanical gardens followed on the heels of the professorships. Padua and Pisa almost simultaneously founded the first university botanical gardens of Europe. Padua's story is better known because the documentation is ample and precise.

Bonafede, seconded by the first and second professors of theoretical and practical medicine, and the ordinary professors of natural philosophy repeatedly asked the Venetian government to establish a garden of simples in Padua. The leaders of the student arts organization also endorsed the project with a petition of November 1543. They evoked all the famous ancients who had written on natural history: Dioscorides, Theophrastus, Galen, and other Greeks; Pliny the Elder and various Romans. The petition then noted the contributions of the moderns, especially Ermolao Barbaro, Leoniceno, Manardo, and the northern European scholars, Leonhart Fuchs (1501–66) and Otto Brunfels (c. 1489–1534). Praise by students at a leading Italian university for the contributions of two German Protestants showed the existence of an international community of botanists. The students then pledged that a botanical garden would enable them to learn more in two years than they could have learned in all of the past. They argued that the Venetian Senate should not permit the University of Padua to fall behind its rivals. A botanical garden would expand the reputation of the *studio* and bring in more students. Every sector of the university—medicine, law, and "humane letters"—wanted the garden, concluded the petition.[101]

---

100. For Musa Brasavola, see Nutton, 1997, 14–16; for Gabrieli, see Gioelli, 1970. See also *I maestri di Ferrara,* 1991, 173, 226, and Bruni, 1991.

101. The petition of Nov. 8, 1543, to the Riformatori dello Studio di Padova, is printed in Azzi Visentini, 1984, 25, 245 (document).

The campaign succeeded. In late June 1545 the Venetian Senate authorized construction of a botanical garden.[102] Construction followed quickly enough that the garden had a curator and earned the praise of learned visitors by the summer of 1546. Expenses for the garden and the salary of its curator came from the tax that funded the university. In 1552 the Riformatori dello Studio di Padova ordered the manure collected from the streets of Padua to be delivered to the garden. Obtaining an adequate supply of water was a constant problem, which was partially solved by digging a canal and adding a waterwheel. It diverted water into the garden from one of the canals running through Padua. A printed catalogue of 1591 listed twelve hundred species of plants. The botanical garden of the University of Padua remains where it was built, attracting visitors to this day.

The professor of medical botany lectured in the university building, while the curator cared for the garden. However, when the medical botany professorship became vacant after 1567, Melchior Giulandino (c. 1520–89), the curator of the botanical garden since 1561, assumed the additional responsibility of teaching about plants. He taught at the garden instead of lecturing in the university building.[103] In addition, from the feast of Saint Mark the Evangelist (April 25) through the month of July, Giulandino made himself available in the garden in the last three hours of daylight to anyone who wished to learn about plants. He showed any plant, teaching its Greek, Latin, and German names and its species, to all who came to see. For these combined duties he received a salary of 600 florins, the fourth highest stipend in the faculty of arts.[104] The combination of positions in the person of Giulandino probably shifted the emphasis of the teaching from their medical use to the study of the plants themselves.

After Giulandino's death, Padua returned to two positions, a professor of medical botany and a curator-demonstrator in the botanical garden. The Paduan roll of 1594–95 listed two names under *Ad lecturam simplicium*. The first, Prospero Alpino (1553–1616), taught Galen's *De simplicium medicamentorum facultatibus*, which suggests an emphasis on the medical uses of plants, at the third hour of the afternoon. The second, Giacomo Antonio Cortusi (1513–1603), the curator of

102. For the story, see Azzi Visentini, 1984, especially the documents on 245–61.

103. "Leggere, dichiare, e mostrare nel medesimo horto li semplici." Ongaro, 1981, 129, quoting from AAUP, F. 666, f. 29ʳ. "Ad lectura simplicium. Locus vacat in gymnasio sed Exc. d. Melchior Giulandinus (ut sui moris est) docebit in horto medicinali suo tempore et more solito." From the roll of 1584–85, in AAUP, F. 651, f. 302ʳ. Other rolls of the period also describe the medical botanical professorship as vacant.

104. "Il Giulandino deputato alla cognitione de simplici non legge altramente nelle scole; ma finito il giorno di S. Marco, seguendo per tutto il mese di Luglio stà continovamente dopo le vintiun' hora fino à notte nel giardino de simplici, et ad ogn'uno che li mostra qualsivoglia herba, insegne subito il nome greco, latino, tedesco; et delle speciare [*sic*]; et ha di stipendio fiorini 600." ASB, Assunteria di Studio, Bu. 100, fascicle 5, "Stato dello Studio di Padova," fols. 2ᵛ–3ʳ. No date but about 1580. This roll of Padua's professors, with detailed information on teaching and salaries, by an anonymous Bolognese observer, demonstrates how closely the two leading universities kept track of each other.

the botanical garden, demonstrated plants in the botanical garden in the late afternoon (twenty-second hour) beginning May 2, 1595.[105]

Pisa's botanical garden began about the same time as Padua's. Land clearance for a university botanical garden in Pisa may have begun in late 1544. Luca Ghini was gathering plants in the nearby mountains for the garden in July 1545. Thus, it may have had plants to study by late summer of 1545 and certainly did in 1546. Pisa's botanical garden also had a curator and a distinguished history and survives today.[106] Ferrara established the third university botanical garden in 1550, and Bologna followed in 1568.

Several other universities established professorships of medical botany. The University of Pavia created a lectureship of medical botany in 1546, held by Giorgio Dordoni until 1570, with an assistant added by 1551. Beginning in 1558, Pavia had two professors of medical botany, both charged with "explanation of simples and the garden" (cum declaratione et viridario Simplicium). These two positions continued through most of the rest of the century and beyond. Possibly the first, higher-paid professor concentrated on teaching the medicinal qualities of plants, while the second taught the properties of plants (i.e., botany) and oversaw the garden plot. Pavia probably had a small garden by the 1550s located in a courtyard within the sprawling university building. The Milanese government ordered the creation of an official university botanical garden in 1559, but nothing happened until 1773![107]

Perugia apparently established a professorship of medical botany at the early date of 1537, but nothing is known about it. By 1600–1601 it had a professor of pharmacological theory and another for pharmacological practice.[108] The University of Turin, temporarily located in Mondovì, had a medical botanist in 1566.[109] The University of Siena established a professorship of medical botany only in 1589; its occupant might lecture in Italian. Siena lacked a formal university botanical garden until the eighteenth century, although provision was made for demonstrating plants.[110] Messina had a professor of medical botany in the late 1590s. Parma had a professorship of medical botany, taught by the same person who held the anatomy professorship, from 1601 at least through 1610.[111] Catania,

---

105. The duties of Alpino were "Leget libros de simplicum medicamentorum facultatibus hora 3. post. merid." The duties of Cortusi were "Incipiet docere, in horto die secunda Maii 1595 hora 22." Roll of 1594–95 in AAUP, Inventario 1320, no pag.; see fig. 3 of this book. It should be noted that little or no lecturing occurred after the end of May. The roll of 1597–98 presents the same division of duties, except that Alpino was to teach one of the books of Dioscorides' De materia medica. AAUP, Inventario 1320, roll of 1597–98, no pag. But when Cortusi died, Alpino assumed both charges. For comments on Alpino's teaching and research, see Premuda, 1984, 131–34.

106. Cascio Pratilli, 1975, 148 n. 43, 153 n. 61; Keller, 1981, 383; and esp. Garbari, Tongiorgi Tomasi, and Tosi, 1991. Ghini also helped establish a botanical garden in Florence in 1550.

107. Giacomini, 1959, and Ciferri, 1961, 153–55.

108. Ermini, 1971, 236, 570.

109. Vallauri, 1970, 1:207.

110. Nannizzi, 1909; Cascio Pratilli, 1975, 81, 83, 186, 188; Piccinni, 1991, 149.

111. For Messina and Parma, see Chapter 4, "Messina, 1596" and "Parma, 1601."

Macerata, Naples, and Salerno did not establish professorships of medical botany in the sixteenth century, nor did they have botanical gardens.

Galen's *De simplicibus* and Dioscorides' *De materia medica* were the normal teaching texts for medical botany.[112] But instruction and research increasingly centered on the direct observation of plants. This led to study of the classification of plants and something closer to modern botany with the second generation of botanists, such as Andrea Cesalpino, previously mentioned, and especially Ulisse Aldrovandi at Bologna.

Aldrovandi studied several disciplines and traveled a great deal before taking a degree in philosophy and medicine at Bologna in 1553. After teaching logic for a year, he moved to natural philosophy and then became one of two lecturers on medical botany in 1556–57. For a few years he taught both medical botany and traditional natural philosophy based on Aristotelian texts. The roll of 1560–61 indicated something new: Aldrovandi taught "fossils, plants, and animals" in his ordinary professorship of natural philosophy ("Legat philosophiam naturalem ordinariam, de fossilibus, plantis et animalibus").[113] He did this for the rest of his teaching career, which ended in 1600. Thanks to his influence within and outside the university, Aldrovandi played a major role in persuading the Bolognese authorities to establish a botanical garden in 1568.

Aldrovandi passionately collected every sort of plant, animal, or stone. He then made valiant, if not always successful, efforts to classify the products of the natural world according to scientific criteria. The results of his labors began to appear in print toward the end of his life, and his manuscripts continued to be published through the mid-seventeenth century. Aldrovandi willed his immense collection to the University of Bologna, which became a museum of natural history attracting wide attention. With Cesalpino and Aldrovandi, medical botany had expanded to become natural history.

Medical botany developed in a series of steps.[114] Inspired by medical humanism, scholars gathered all the information available in ancient sources. They next attempted to confirm that information through observation. Inevitably, they found that ancient (and medieval) works contained sketchy descriptions, confused multiple names for plants, and outright mistakes. The inadequacies of the ancient texts probably stimulated the development of Renaissance medical botany more than accurate descriptions of plants would have. The medical botanists published new herbal books with superior observations and illustrations. They began to classify plants descriptively. Finally, they interpreted the characteristics of the plants. The original study of medicinal simples became botany and the beginning of natural history. Botany gradually became a separate science rooted

112. In addition to what has already been mentioned, see Sabbatani, 1926, 37, and Riddle, 1980, 10. The Roman medical botanist was teaching Dioscorides in 1574–75. *I maestri di Roma*, 1991, 92.

113. Dallari, 1888–1924, 2:150 and passim for his annual teaching appointments. There is a large bibliography on Aldrovandi; start with Montalenti, 1960; Castellani, 1981; Tugnoli Pattaro, 1981; and especially Findlen, 1994.

114. In addition to the material above, some of what follows has been suggested by Schmitt, 1975b, 39–44; Palmer, 1985a; and Bruni, 1991.

in the study of empirical data gathered throughout Europe, the Near East, and eventually America and Asia. Like their counterparts in anatomy, professors of medical botany began to write specialized monographs on their subject.

More than any other Renaissance scholars, botanists were a closely knit scholarly community who shared dried plants, bulbs, seeds, and knowledge despite the religious divisions of Europe. One of these was William Turner (1508–68), the first English botanist and natural historian. He studied briefly at Padua, then at Ferrara and at Bologna under Ghini, between 1540 and 1546, taking a medical doctorate at either Ferrara or Bologna. He also lived in Protestant regions of Switzerland, Germany, and the Netherlands during Mary Tudor's reign (1553–58). Despite his fervent Protestantism—he wrote religious tracts that referred to the "Romish pox" and Catholicism as spiritual fornication—he maintained contacts with Italian Catholic botanists.[115]

As with anatomy, universities played a crucial role in the development of medical botany by creating professorships and botanical gardens. The latter provided a range of plants and herbs to study, including some that were rare and costly. Although medical botany did not attract such wide attention or spontaneous praise for its importance within the university as did anatomy, it was the third part of the medical Renaissance trio.

CONCLUSION

Medical humanism was the driving force for change in Italian university medical education. It applied humanist scholarly principles and ideology to the study of medical texts and to medicine generally. By the early sixteenth century, a student who entered a university had received a thorough preparation in humanistic studies and, to an increasing extent, classical Greek.[116] Equally important, those who took medical degrees had imbibed the humanist ideology that strongly believed that the texts of ancient Greece and Rome in their original languages were the highest repositories of learning and that the knowledge and wisdom learned from ancient texts was immediately applicable to the present.

Medical humanism began in Ferrara but soon became a pan-university commonwealth of medical scholars who read one another's works, followed similar research paths, and imbued students with their values. The wartime disruptions of the first quarter of the sixteenth century may have delayed the arrival of medical humanism into university faculties. When it did come, the resulting innovations were swift and decisive. The University of Padua introduced Vesalian anatomy, clinical medicine, and medical botany between 1533 and 1543. Other universities followed. Adding new professorships, botanical gardens, and permanent anatomical theaters, or the failure to do so, divided universities into stronger and weaker centers for medical instruction.

115. Webster, 1981, and Woolfson, 1998, 87, 101–2, 278.
116. This meant that the professor could insert brief phrases or quotations in Greek into his lectures and books and expect to be understood. Siraisi, 1987, 97.

A resultant development was the growing importance of practical medicine. In the fifteenth century the first ordinary professor of theoretical medicine was the most prestigious and best-paid member of the medical faculty. By the end of the sixteenth century the first ordinary professor of practical medicine drew equal to, then surpassed, his counterpart in prestige and salary.[117]

Although much changed, the outward structure of the medical curriculum remained the same. New lectureships were added, but they did not displace older ones. Professors continued to lecture on many of the same ancient and medieval texts as before, because the statutes required this, and because they still found them useful. Hippocrates, Galen, and Avicenna remained at the core of the medical curriculum.

However, professors treated the traditional texts more freely. Lecturers took a more critical stance. They judged a medical text according to its fidelity to its Greek origins and how well it conveyed accurate and useful information.[118] They criticized Galen when necessary. The lecturer also added material acquired from anatomical dissection, bedside observation, and medical botany. Medicine was becoming more "hands-on," thanks to anatomical observation, the study of plants, and clinical medicine. Medical knowledge began to resemble an eclectic collection of information rather than a system.

The style of medical lecturing also changed somewhat. Professors loosened the Scholastic commentary and dialectical format. Now the professor presented a lecture more akin to an essay.[119] Research changed, as medical professors more often wrote treatises on precise topics (i.e., monographs), rather than commentaries on traditional texts. The medical scholar himself changed. The philosopher-physician of the fifteenth century, that is, the scholar shaped by Aristotle who taught both natural philosophy and medicine, gave way to the humanist-physician in the later sixteenth century, that is, the scholar shaped by humanism, as well as Aristotle and Galen, who taught only medicine.

Despite the continuity imposed by statutes, enough changed that the physician of the fourteenth and fifteenth centuries might have had trouble finding his way through the teaching and research of Italian universities after 1550. In the following centuries, the Aristotelian-Galenic structure disintegrated.

---

117. For example, at Padua about 1580 the first ordinary professor of medical theory (Bernardino Paterno) and the first ordinary professor of medical practice (Girolamo Mercuriale) were both paid 900 florins. The second ordinary professor of medical theory was paid 300 florins and the second ordinary professor of medical practice 520 florins. ASB, Assunteria di Studio, Bu. 100, fascicle 5, f. 2ʳ–ᵛ. In 1598–99 at Padua, the first ordinary professor of practical medicine earned 1,000 florins and the first ordinary professor of medical theory 900. Riccobono, 1980, 147ʳ. In 1616–17, again at Padua, the first ordinary professor of medical practice earned 1,000 florins, and the first ordinary professor of medical theory earned 800 florins. AAUP, F. 651, f. 425ʳ. Rome produced the most startling change. Three professors of practical medicine were paid 500 to 700 scudi each, two professors of medical theory were paid 150 to 280 scudi, and the professor of surgery and anatomy 225 to 280 scudi, in the 1590s. *I maestri di Roma*, 1991, 130, 131, 135, 140, 145, 149. See also Siraisi, 1987, 99–100, 110–11.

118. This is a point made by Siraisi (1987, 201 and passim).

119. Siraisi, 1987, 195–96, describing mid-sixteenth-century Paduan lecturers on Avicenna's *Canon*.

CHAPTER 10

Theology, Metaphysics, and Sacred Scripture

heology never had the prominence in Italian universities which it enjoyed in some northern universities. Theology arrived late, had few instructors, and remained peripheral to the main purposes of the university. Indeed, some Italian universities went many decades without any theological instruction at all. Instead, mendicant order general schools (*studia generalia*), located in university towns but separate from the university, taught theology. Only gradually did the university move to include theology by appointing one or two friars from the mendicant order *studia* to theological professorships. In like fashion, the universities created a limited number of professorships of metaphysics, viewed as complementary to theology, and Holy Scripture, to be filled by friars. Only after the Council of Trent concluded in 1563 did the number of theology, metaphysics, and Scripture professorships increase a little. Universities then awarded more theology doctorates than in the past. Nevertheless, theology, metaphysics, and Scripture remained minor subjects in universities dominated by arts, medicine, and law.

FROM MENDICANT ORDER *STUDIA* TO FACULTIES
OF THEOLOGY

As universities were being established, Paris and Oxford enjoyed a quasi monopoly of the right to award degrees in theology. The papacy refused to grant the authority to confer theological degrees with the corresponding right to teach theology anywhere in Christendom (*ius ubique docendi*) to other towns across Europe.[1] Faced with this situation and the need to educate their members, the mendicant monastic orders established their own schools beginning in the second quarter of the thirteenth century.

The Dominicans, Franciscans, Augustinian Hermits, Carmelites (Order of Our Lady of Mount Carmel), Cistercians, Servites (Servants of Mary), and other

---

1. For a good brief summary of the development of theology at Paris and Oxford, see Asztalos, 1992, 409–33.

orders erected elaborate educational pyramids.² General chapter meetings, the supreme authority in orders, directed each local monastery to establish a school, which might be a single teacher instructing the younger members. In addition to preparatory studies, the monastery typically offered daily lectures on the Bible and the *Sentences* of Peter Lombard, along with daily repetition exercises and a weekly disputation covering the week's material.

After two years of study, those with greater aptitude for learning were sent to a provincial school (*studium*). These were schools in designated monasteries within the province, administered by the provincial leadership, and open to all members in the province. Large orders, such as the Dominicans, had three levels of provincial *studia*. The lowest were "arts" schools, teaching logic, not arts, based on Aristotle's logical works and standard medieval manuals. After two or three years in a logic school, gifted students went on for another two years at a provincial school for philosophy, where they studied Aristotle's *Physics* and *De anima*. After two further years, a few favored students advanced to a provincial theological school, where they again studied the Bible and Peter Lombard's *Sentences* for another two years or so.

Friars commonly moved from *studium* to *studium* within their order, just as lay students moved from university to university, except that the friars traveled more. Educational travel enabled the order to exchange ideas and persons; it contributed to the unity and universality of the order and its scholarship. Although the number of schools was large, enrollments were probably small: six, eight, perhaps ten students, taught by one lecturer. Moreover, the number of years a friar spent in a particular school varied. And his education was interrupted if his convent called him back to teach or take on other duties.

An order's *studia generalia* (general schools) stood at the apex of its educational pyramid. These were schools under the direction of general chapter meetings and open in limited numbers to all members of the order who had passed through the lower schools. For example, the Dominicans decreed in 1316 that every province, which might comprise thousands of members, might send two students to each general school of the order. Either the home convent or the province paid the expenses of members sent to general schools. General schools offered the familiar combination of lectures on the Bible and on Peter Lombard's *Sentences* at the most advanced level. They attracted the best scholars of the order. From the *studia generalia* came the order's most important preachers, its generals and provincial superiors, bishops, and major theologians.

By the early fourteenth century, the two groups of Franciscans (Friars Minor of St. Francis and Franciscan Conventuals) had about thirty general schools across Europe, the Dominicans about twenty, the Augustinian Hermits about twenty, the Carmelites about sixteen, and the smaller orders fewer. In Italy each of the

2. A number of excellent studies document the growth of monastic order education in the Middle Ages. For the Dominicans, see Hinnebusch, 1973, chs. 2 and 3, and Mulcahey, 1998; for the Franciscans, see Moorman, 1968, ch. 13, and pp. 365–68, and Iriarte, 1982, 149–54; for the Augustinian Hermits, see Gutierrez, 1983, 121–28, and Gutierrez, 1984, ch. 6; for the Carmelites, see Lickteig, 1981; for an overview, see *Le scuole degli ordini mendicanti*, 1978.

mendicant orders had established *studia generalia* in convents in five or more urban centers. The Dominicans had theological *studia generalia* in convents in Milan, Genoa, Venice, Bologna, Florence, Orvieto, and Naples by the 1330s. The two groups of Franciscans had *studia generalia* in convents in Asti, Milan, Genoa, Padua, Venice, Bologna, Rimini, Florence, Pisa, Assisi, Perugia, Siena, Todi, Rome, Naples, and Barletta (near Bari on the Adriatic coast in southern Italy). The Augustinian Hermits had *studia generalia* of theology in Milan, Bologna, Florence, Siena, Rome, and Naples. The Carmelites had *studia generalia* in theology in Milan, Bologna, Florence, Naples, and Catania in 1345.[3]

The mendicant orders located their *studia generalia* of theology in convents in university towns, while their curricula imitated the preparation for, and teaching of, theology at the University of Paris. But unlike the situation in northern Europe, where monastic schools were often integrated into the university and members of monastic orders often became university professors, the monastic orders forged no links with Italian universities at this time. The four or more mendicant order *studia generalia* located in convents in a university town lacked ties with the civic university of law, medicine, and arts and had no links to schools of other orders. Their ties were to other convent schools of the order. Nor could a monastic order *studium generale* award degrees in theology.

Then, in the mid-fourteenth century, the papacy decided that it would no longer support the near monopoly of Paris. It authorized other universities to award degrees in theology with the right to teach the subject anywhere in Christendom. Papal irritation at the strong support for nominalism and conciliarism of the Paris theologians played a role in the decision. In addition, the monastic orders sought the right to award theological degrees. Such authority would raise the prestige of their *studia generalia* in university towns. Further, the monastic orders desired the opportunity of obtaining theology doctorates for their members without the difficulty and expense of sending them to Paris, even though the latter remained the most prestigious place for theology. For their part, communes wanted the authority to award theological degrees for the prestige that this right would add to the local university and the town. For example, in 1363 the commune of Padua prayed, and students pleaded with the pope, to authorize a faculty of theology in Padua.[4]

The Avignonese popes cheerfully acquiesced, and the papacy continued this policy after its return to Rome in 1378. True to their contrary nature, the majority of the Paris theologians supported the Avignonese antipopes during the Great Schism, 1378 to 1418. Provoked, the Roman pontiffs completed the destruction of the Paris-Oxford theological near monopoly by issuing additional theological charters.[5]

The result for Italy was the establishment of faculties of theology in university towns so that theological degrees carrying the name of the university could be

---

3. D'Alatri, 1978, esp. 57–58, 66–67, 69, 70.
4. Brotto and Zonta, 1922, 26, 253 (text of the 1363 bull).
5. Verger, 1978, 194–95; Kristeller, 1985, 5; Lytle, 1981, 76, 80–82.

awarded. Papal decrees authorized the establishment of faculties of theology at Pisa in 1343[6] and Florence in 1349.[7] The Florentine commune was so grateful that when the first doctorate of theology was about to be conferred, it rang the bells of the city. Officialdom and many citizens came to the ceremony on December 9, 1359.[8] Papal decrees also authorized faculties of theology at Bologna (bull of 1360, faculty of theology established in 1364),[9] Padua (1363),[10] Perugia (1371),[11] Pavia (1389, statutes in 1393),[12] Ferrara (faculty of theology possibly founded as early as 1391, certainly functioning in 1403),[13] Siena (1408),[14] Naples (sometime between 1332 and 1428),[15] Turin (possibly 1418, certainly by 1428),[16] and Catania (1444).[17] The foundation charters of the later universities of Macerata, Messina, and Salerno authorized them to award degrees of theology. Parma had a faculty of theology with the power to confer degrees from at least 1448, although a full university did not exist until 1601. The University of Rome awarded theological degrees from its beginning in the thirteenth century through the authority of the papacy.

Thus, the older Italian universities founded without the power to award degrees in theology during the Parisian near monopoly added the right to have a faculty of theology with the authority to grant theological degrees. The foundational charters of the new universities of the fourteenth, fifteenth, and sixteenth

6. Clement VI's foundation bull of Sept. 4, 1343, for the University of Pisa included the right to establish a faculty and to award degrees in theology. Picotti, 1968, 19. For limited information on the teaching of theology in the mid-fourteenth century, see Picotti, 1968, 23, and Fabroni, 1971, 1:55–56. For the statutes of 1475, see *Statuta collegii theologorum Pisanae,* 1910.

7. Shortly after the Florentine government established the university, it petitioned Pope Clement VI in Avignon for a charter authorizing it to have all the faculties including theology and to award degrees in all fields including theology. Clement VI obliged with a bull dated May 31, 1349. See Villani, 1980, vol. 1, bk. 1, ch. 8, p. 16, for a contemporary account; Gherardi, 1973, 116–18, for the bull; and Spagnesi, 1986, 129–32, for details.

8. This is the description of the joyful occasion by the chronicler Matteo Villani (d. 1363) in Villani, 1980, vol. 4, bk. 9, ch. 58, pp. 245–46.

9. See Ehrle, 1932, 7–78, for the statutes and much additional material. See also Piana, 1977, 20, 21.

10. Brotto and Zonta, 1922, 23–31, and 253–54; Poppi, 1981, 6.

11. Ermini, 1971, 33–34. Pope Gregory XI granted a faculty of theology upon request of the commune of Perugia.

12. Andreoli Panzarasa, 1989, 36–37; Bernuzzi, 1989.

13. Piana, 1968, 116; Dal Nero, 1991, 246, 248; Samaritani, 1995, 44–48; Del Nero, 1996, 111–23.

14. Bertoni, 1968, 3–5.

15. Monti (1924, 29–30, 64–66) argues that no faculty of theology existed at Naples in 1332, but there was one in 1428, although the foundation date is unknown. See also Filangieri di Candida, 1924, 174–75.

16. The foundation bull of 1411 included theology, but it is not clear that a faculty of theology began immediately. The bull is printed in Vallauri, 1970, 1:239–41. Bellone (1986, 38) suggests that a faculty of theology existed in 1418; Vallaro (1936, 41–42) says definitely by 1428.

17. Catalano, 1934, 13–16. The date comes from the foundation bull; the university did not begin teaching until the fall of 1445.

centuries included the right to grant theological degrees. Because the papacy also granted the same power to old and new northern European universities, it won the gratitude of theologians across Europe, if not in Paris and Oxford.

The establishment of faculties of theology made mendicant order *studia generalia* in university towns more important. The others did not necessarily disappear, especially if located in a major political center. For example, the Dominican *studium generale* at the convent of Sant'Eustorgio in Milan continued, even though it could not award doctoral degrees.[18] A handful of faculties of theology with the power to award doctorates of theology were established in nonuniversity towns, but they came to little.[19]

FACULTIES OF THEOLOGY

The term *faculty of theology* did not mean the structure of a teaching faculty of professors, students, and lectures *within* the civic university of arts, medicine, and law. Although the statutes employed such wording as "faculty of sacred theology of the gracious university in the famous city of the Sienese," the civic university did not necessarily teach theology.[20] At best it taught a limited amount of the sacred science. Some communes appointed one or two professors of theology and allied subjects for the university, while others did not. Instead, most theological instruction took place in, and members of the faculty of theology came from, the mendicant order *studia generalia* located in university towns.

The faculty of theology was a kind of confederation of the *studia monastica* under the name of the civic university but with limited participation by the latter.[21] Nevertheless, the establishment of faculties of theology meant that suc-

---

18. Airaghi, 1984.

19. Orvieto and Fermo were examples. Cremascoli, 1989, 188.

20. As an example, see the opening words of the 1434 statutes of the faculty of theology of Siena: "In isto libro sacrae Theologicae facultatis almae Universitatis inclitae civitatis Senarum subscribentur omnes incorporationes tam revendorum magistrorum." Quoted in Bertoni, 1968, 4.

21. Scholars have gradually learned more about Italian faculties of theology and their links to the civic university of arts, medicine, and law. Kristeller (1956c, 316) wrote: "No separate faculty of theology was ever formed after the model of Paris and of the other northern schools, but merely an examining body (*collegium*) which comprised the more learned members of the various religious houses." For similar views, see Kristeller, 1974, 45–46, and 1985, 7. In similar fashion, Gieysztor (1992, 110) wrote: "The faculty of theology was in the hands of the mendicant orders and existed on the fringe of the *studium generale*," (i.e., the university of arts, medicine, and law). Kristeller's view has been modified. Poppi (1981, 11 n. 35, and 15 n. 46) has corrected Kristeller and sees theology as a real presence within the Italian universities after the establishment of faculties of theology. Further clarification has come from Monfasani (1993, 252–56), who emphasizes that Italian universities did not offer "a coherent body of university courses that would enable a candidate to take a degree on the basis of university courses" (254). Finally, the best account to date of an Italian faculty of theology is Negruzzo, 1995, on Pavia.

My view, elaborated in this chapter, can be summarized: (1) Poppi is correct that the establishment of faculties of theology made a difference. Theology had a limited but real presence in the majority of Italian universities most of the time between 1400 and 1600. (2) The size and significance

cessful theological students might receive license and doctorate degrees from the university authorizing them to teach anywhere in Christendom, just like doctors of law, medicine, and arts.

In the broadest sense the term *faculty of theology* embraced everyone teaching, studying, or obtaining degrees in theology in a town. In this large meaning, faculties of theology in Italian university towns had three structural components. First was the organization, headed by a deacon, that is, the administrative leader, of the faculty of theology and its theologians. It and they oversaw instruction and awarded degrees through the authority of the papal charter granting this right under the name of the university. Second came the mendicant order *studia* to whom teachers and students belonged and where most of the teaching occurred. The third and smallest element consisted of the one or two theologians (sometimes joined by one or two metaphysicians and a biblicist) holding university professorships. But university professors of theology, metaphysics, and biblical studies were always members of the regular clergy and affiliated with local mendicant order *studia*.

The fundamental unit of a faculty of theology was the individual convent *studium generale* and its members. The most important person in the *studium* was the regent (*reggente*) or director of studies, who was usually the chief lecturer as well. Then came one or two, occasionally three or four, lecturers on the Bible or the *Sentences*. These were probably advanced students fulfilling lecture requirements on the path toward the doctorate of theology. Next came one or two *magistri studentium* (masters of students), assistant teachers who oversaw the repetitions, lectures, and disputations. Then came two to ten students, who simply attended lectures and studied. This was the structure and membership of the Dominican convent of San Tommaso in Pavia between 1478 and 1530, a typical *studium*.[22] Smaller convent *studia* might have only a single teaching doctor of theology and one or two students.

The well-known and important Franciscan convent of Sant'Antonio (called il Santo) in Padua in 1475 was larger. It had a regent who may also have taught, the well-known Antonio Trombetta mentioned in chapter 8; a lecturer in theology, presumably with a doctorate; three bachelors of theology, one of whom lectured plus two *magistri studentium;* a lecturer of philosophy, presumably metaphysics; a bachelor of philosophy; a lecturer in biblical studies, probably a student on the road to a doctorate; and a master of the *studium* who guided the students and oversaw disciplinary matters but did not teach. And it probably had more than ten students. But only Trombetta, and possibly the theology lecturer and the

---

of that presence and the amount of theological instruction offered varied from university to university. (3) While formal links between faculty of theology and university of law and medicine were lacking, governments took account of theology when planning for the civic university. (4) The quantity of theology, metaphysics, and Scripture instruction offered within Italian universities expanded between 1400 and 1600.

22. Negruzzo, 1995, 75–85.

metaphysics lecturer, if they possessed doctorates in theology, would be involved in examining candidates for degrees.[23]

A university town always had at least four or five convent *studia generalia* from the major religious orders, while major university cities could have ten or more.[24] The size and importance of a faculty of theology closely paralleled the size and prominence of the local university.

Bologna's faculty of theology embraced twenty institutions, many of them small and practically inactive. In order of importance, they were the four major mendicant order *studia* (Dominican, Franciscan, Augustinian, and Carmelite), followed by that of the Servites, the Collegio di Spagna, the cathedral chair of theology, and others.[25] Padua's theological establishment consisted of convent *studia* of the Dominicans, Franciscan Conventuals, Augustinian Hermits, Carmelites, Servites, Humiliati, Celestines, and Benedictines, plus a cathedral chair of theology for some decades, and a few other teachers in the city, in the fifteenth century.[26] The faculty of theology at Florence comprised five significant theological *studia generalia:* the Dominican *studium* at the convent of Santa Maria Novella, the *studium* of the Friars Minor of St. Francis at Santa Croce, the Augustinian Hermit *studium* at Santo Spirito, the Carmelite *studium* at Santa Maria del Carmine, and the Servite *studium* at Santissima Annunziata. There were also shadowy *studia* at San Marco, San Lorenzo, the episcopal palace, and the Humiliati convent at Ognissanti, making a total of nine.[27]

Since each convent *studium generale* in the university town had at least a regent master who probably taught, the number of lecturers in theology (excluding students teaching as part of the requirements for the doctorate) was at least as many as the number of convent *studia* in the town. If the larger convent *studia,* such as those of the Dominicans, Franciscans, and Augustinian Hermits, had an additional lecturer or two, the number would be higher.

The term *faculty of theology* also referred to the local theologians with doctorates who examined candidates and conferred degrees. In this sense faculty of theology meant a college of doctors of theology like the colleges of doctors of law and medicine and arts.[28] This group was drawn from the mendicant order friars

---

23. Cortese, 1975, 286–87.

24. Pavia had twenty-five male monasteries in 1590, although it is unlikely that all had *studia generalia*. Negruzzo, 1995, 53.

25. Piana, 1960 and 1976, 1:100 n. 4, and Ehrle, 1932, 9 n. 9. For the Franciscans at Bologna, see Pergamo, 1934. On the limited theological instruction at the Collegio di Spagna, see Marti, 1966, 22–23, 89–90.

26. Brotto and Zonta, 1922, 81–85, 88–90; Poppi, 1981, 8. The Humiliati were a small penitential order founded in the early twelfth century and suppressed in 1571.

27. Piana, 1977, 62–131. Florence had 19 male convents within the city walls and another 11 within a 5-mile radius of the center of the city in the late fifteenth century. Florence had about 750 monks and friars in 1427 and probably more than 800 in the late fifteenth century. Brucker, 1990, 42–46.

28. Scholars sometimes use the terms *faculty of theology* and *college of theology* interchangeably. See Bertoni, 1968, 4: "Per tracciare un periodo della storia della facoltà [of Siena], più propriamente del

with doctorates teaching in their own convent *studia,* those teaching theology in
the civic university, and possibly other local doctors of theology. But the examining committee or college did not necessarily embrace all teachers with doctorates
or all local doctors of theology. In Padua in 1497, sixteen *magistri* (doctors of
theology) appeared for the examination and conferral of a doctoral degree. They
included the two metaphysicians (with doctorates in theology) then teaching in
the civic university but not the two theologians teaching there.[29]

Nevertheless, the number of examiners at Padua in 1497 gives a rough idea of
the minimum number of the teaching theologians with doctorates in the city. If
all sixteen examiners were teaching and the university theologians are added,
Padua had at least eighteen senior theology instructors with doctorates in 1497. It
is likely that Padua had additional theologians with doctorates in its various
convent *studia,* perhaps teaching metaphysics.[30]

Although the faculty of theology did not teach as an unified body, it exercised
limited supervision over the teaching carried on in the convent *studia* by setting
degree requirements. As a collective body it enjoyed a place in religious and civic
ceremonies. The faculty of theology exercised at least nominal doctrinal authority in the city. When requested by city governments, it offered theological opinions on disputed matters.[31] Such requests were infrequent, because Italian communes tended to be fiercely independent on religious matters. Colleges of legists
and colleges of physicians played greater roles in civic affairs.

DOCTORATES OF THEOLOGY

Faculties of theology established the requirements for degrees in theology.
Their degree requirements replicated those of the Faculty of Theology of Bologna of 1364, which closely followed those of the University of Paris. Statutes and
practice also reflected the educational structures of the mendicant orders.

Collegio teologico." See also Vallaro, 1936, 42; Gargan, 1971, 13, 14, 15, and passim; Piana, 1976,
1:203 and passim; and Piana, 1977, 60, 197, 273, and passim. For the sake of clarity, *college* here means
the group of doctors of theology who examined candidates for doctorates, and *faculty* refers to all
members of the faculty involved in teaching or studying theology in the mendicant order *studia* and
the university.

29. Sbriziolo, 1973, 171–72. The group included five Franciscans, four Augustinians, three
Dominicans, two Carmelites, one Servite, and a secular priest.

30. Il Santo also taught logic and metaphysics to the younger members of the order. Gargan, 1971,
11; d'Alatri, 1978, 53, 59, and passim.

31. For example, in the mid-fourteenth century the Florentine faculty of theology gave its views
on whether the Florentine government might convert forced loans (*prestanze*) to the state into
perpetual government bonds. Piana, 1977, 231–45, including other issues on which the faculty of
theology or individual members gave their views. In 1530 four theological faculties in Italy gave
opinions on whether King Henry VIII might divorce Catherine of Aragon. Bologna, Padua, and
Pavia said yes. Piana, 1977, 232; Monfasani, 1993, 252–53. Ferrara said no; Dal Nero, 1991, 256. But
requests from civic and ecclesiastical authorities seem to have been infrequent. Italian faculties of
theology did not play nearly so large a role as arbiters of theological orthodoxy as did the faculty of
theology in Paris. See Farge, 1985, chs. 3–5. On the role of university faculties of theology in general,
see Lytle, 1981.

Having acquired competence in arts, the theological student was then required to attend lectures in theology in his order's *studia* for six years.[32] Peter Lombard's *Sentences* and the Bible were the basic texts. After completing these studies and having reached the age of thirty, the candidate next spent three or more years lecturing on the Bible; he annually lectured on one book from the Old Testament and one from the New Testament. Since these initial lecture series were considered to be rapid or cursory (*cursorie*), in which the lecturer did not venture his personal opinions on more complex issues, the lecturer was commonly called a *cursor*. At some point the *cursor* became a *baccalarius biblicus* (bachelor of the bible), or simply *biblicus*, who was expected to deliver more detailed lectures with more extended exegetical and theological commentary. However, no baccalaureate degree was conferred. "Bachelor" meant only that a student had attained a certain level of achievement. He was acknowledged to be en route to the license and doctorate, still several years distant.

Upon finishing his biblical lectures of perhaps one year, the candidate became a *baccalarius Sententiarii* (bachelor of the *Sentences*) and lectured on Lombard's *Sentences* for two or more years. He also engaged in a series of increasingly elaborate disputations. Having completed this requirement, he became a *baccalarius formatus* (formed bachelor). At this point he was permitted to preach to the academic community, as sermons were considered part of his training. Finally the candidate was ready to be examined for the license and doctorate of theology. He had to prepare a discussion on some *puncta* drawn from Peter Lombard's *Sentences,* pass the private and public examinations conducted by members of the faculty of theology, and deliver a lecture. Italian statutes required a minimum of twelve or thirteen, and sometimes fifteen to sixteen, years of study beyond the arts training for the doctorate in theology. Late-fourteenth-century statutes also required candidates to be over thirty-five years of age.

However, the long road to the doctorate became shorter in the fifteenth century. At Padua, for example, the candidate was admitted into the faculty of theology after successfully proving his competence through an examination.[33] How long it took to reach that level obviously varied from student to student. Upon admittance into the faculty of theology, the student at Padua lectured for only one year on a book of the Bible as a *baccalarius biblicus* and for two years as a *baccalarius Sententiarii* in his order's *studium*. He also successfully completed several disputations. After three years of lecturing and disputations, he presented himself

32. See Ehrle, 1932, for the 1364 Bolognese statutes and some subsequent revisions. This and the following paragraph are based on Bertoni, 1968, 10–12, who uses the statutes of the faculty of theology at Siena; Bernuzzi, 1989, who prints the Pavian theological statutes of 1393; Dal Nero, 1991, esp. 251–53; and Del Nero, 1996, 123–30, on the statutes of Ferrara; Negruzzo, 1995, 59–63, for Pavia; Verde, 1973–94, 2:643–44, for Florence; Smalley, 1969, 200–202; and Asztalos, 1992, 417–20, which is based on statutes from several northern European and Italian faculties. The summary omits minor steps and does not take into account small variations from place to place. See Farge, 1985, 11–28, for the Paris requirements.

33. This is based on the practice at the Dominican *studium generale* at Sant'Agostino in Padua. Gargan (1971) summarizes the statutes of 1406 and 1424 on pp. 13–18 and presents careers of students on pp. 40–172.

for the examinations for the license, then doctorate of theology, which often followed within a few days. But not always; sometimes several years separated the two degrees. Fifteenth-century statutes also often lowered the age threshold for the doctorate to thirty years of age and then failed to hold students to the lower standard. Pope Eugenius IV (1431–47) criticized the Florentine faculty of theology for not insisting on the age requirement of thirty and for shortening the length of study.[34]

In practice, the order may have had more authority over a student than the faculty of theology. It probably decided how fast the candidate moved through the requirements before the doctoral examination. The monastic orders never did follow strictly statutes modeled on Paris, especially after the Black Death created a shortage of teachers. And some candidates received doctorates outside the authority of the faculty of theology. For example, various popes granted the Dominican order the right to confer degrees on members of the order during general chapter meetings.[35] Or the commune or another powerful voice would request that a friar be given the doctorate, and the pope or a willing count palatine (who might lack theological expertise) conferred it. Bypassed faculties of theology objected, to no avail.[36]

Eased requirements and special powers enabled brilliant students to obtain doctorates quickly. Tommaso de Vio Gaetano (Cajetan) was born in 1469, entered the Dominican order, began his studies at Naples in 1484, and continued them at Bologna in 1488. He came to Padua in 1491 and was formally accepted as a student in the faculty of theology there on March 19, 1493. At a meeting of the general chapter of the order at Ferrara in May 1494, he disputed brilliantly against Giovanni Pico della Mirandola in the presence of the duke and members of his order. Cajetan responded to a hundred objections from Pico and was carried off in triumph. The master-general of the order immediately conferred the doctorate of theology on Cajetan on May 18, 1494. Thus, after only one year of study as a formal candidate for the degree, Cajetan was a doctor of theology at the age of twenty-four or twenty-five. He went on to a brilliant scholarly career and a cardinal's hat.[37]

---

34. An undated bull discussed by Piana, 1977, 268–69.

35. Gutierrez, 1983, 123–25, for the Augustinian Hermits; Hinnebusch, 1973, 64–65, for the Dominicans.

36. Piana, 1977, 272–76, for examples from Florence.

37. Gargan, 1971, 156–57; Del Nero, 1996, 135. Another student who moved quickly through his theological studies was Martin Luther. After four years of university philosophy study, Luther entered an Augustinian Hermit convent in late July 1505 at the age of twenty-one. He professed vows in 1506 and began his theological studies in the summer of 1507. At the urging of his superiors, Luther moved rapidly through his theological studies. The statutes of the theological faculties of Erfurt and Wittenberg permitted members of religious orders to do this. He received his doctorate of theology in October 1512, one month short of his thirtieth birthday and five years and a few months after he began his studies. During his theological studies, Luther lectured on the Bible and *Sentences*. He also lectured on Aristotle's *Nicomachean Ethics*, not as a requirement but to fill a gap in the teaching schedule created by the absence of a philosopher. Luther's studies were also interrupted by his five-

Certainly some brilliant, and not so brilliant, candidates became doctors of theology before the age of thirty and without studying for ten or more years. But a pattern is hard to find. While some students moved quickly, other friars took many years, possibly because other activities or lack of funding and support from the order interrupted their studies. Many men were probably well over thirty upon obtaining the doctoral degree.[38] Despite the easing of the age, study, and teaching requirements in the fifteenth century, the doctorate (*laurea*) of theology still demanded the longest period of training and had the highest age threshold of any degree awarded in Italy. By contrast, men in their mid-twenties normally became doctors of law, medicine, or arts after only five to seven years of university study.

The number of theological doctorates awarded varied greatly from faculty to faculty. In general, faculties of theology located in major university centers awarded many more doctorates than those located in less important centers.

Padua awarded some 408 doctorates in theology between 1424 and 1532, a little more than 4 per year.[39] Bologna awarded an average of 4 annually in the sixteenth century, with the majority coming in the second half of the century.[40] Pavia awarded 1 to 3 theology doctorates annually in the fifteenth century. Little information is available for the period 1500 to 1550, because the university was often closed. Then the number gradually increased to 3 to 4 annually in the 1560s, to an average of 8 annually in the 1570s, and 10 to 15 annually in the last two decades of the sixteenth century.[41]

Next came smaller centers. The Florentine faculty of theology awarded 301 known doctorates in theology between 1413 and 1567, an average of nearly 2 per year.[42] The faculty of theology at Ferrara awarded 179 doctorates in theology

month journey to Rome in 1510–11 and his transfer from Erfurt to Wittenberg. Thus, Luther received his doctorate after no more than five years of study and after having been a monk for only six and one-half years. Brecht, 1985, 91–104, 125–27.

38. For example, there was the Dominican Paolo da Padova, who became a student at Sant'Agostino in Padua in 1422, cursor in 1425, bachelor in 1431; received his license in 1436, his doctorate in 1440; and died in 1441. Gargan, 1971, 75. There were many similar cases.

39. Poppi, 1981, 10. They included 143 Franciscans, 101 Dominicans, 76 Augustinians, 54 Carmelites, 43 Servites, 24 diocesan clergymen, 2 Humiliati, 1 Celestine, and 1 Benedictine. See Gargan, 1971, 166–72, for the list of Dominicans.

40. Simeoni (1940, 122) gives the figure of 108 for 1500–1550, and 329 for 1551–1600. The figure seems low, especially for the late sixteenth century. It should be remembered that all counts are based on the number of degrees for which documentation has been located. How many degrees have escaped notice is impossible to determine. Nevertheless, since most of the figures given in these paragraphs come from surviving faculty of theology records, rather than from searches in notarial archives, the theological degree totals may be pretty complete.

41. This is based on BUPv, Ms. Ticinese vol. 5, fascicle 2, "Matricula Collegii Theologorum Papiae (1397–1632)," and ASPv, Università, Doctoratus, Busta 1 (1525–65), 2 (1566–72), 3 (1573–77), 6 (1587–90), and 8 (1596–99). Negruzzo (1995, 266–86, esp. 273, 282, and 284) located 345 theological doctorates, 1460 through 1599.

42. Piana, 1977, 447–74, for the list. The breakdown of theological doctorates (*lauree*) by religious order is 76 Dominicans, 62 Augustinians, 62 Servites, 61 Franciscans, 32 Carmelites, 5 secular priests,

1460 through 1579, an average of 1.5 annually. However, the number of doctorates rose to as many as 12 or 14 annually at Ferrara in last twenty years of the
sixteenth century.[43] The University of Siena awarded 61 doctorates of theology
1484 through 1486 and 1496 through 1579, about 1 annually. Theology accounted for only 5.6 percent of the total of 1,675 known Sienese doctorates
conferred in these years.[44] Other faculties of theology awarded few theology
doctorates. Naples and Perugia may have awarded about the same number as
Siena annually. The University of Turin awarded the fewest known doctorates,
only 34 in the fifteenth century.[45] The figure for Catania may have been no
greater than at Turin.

The number of doctorates of theology awarded rose dramatically in the last
twenty to thirty years of the sixteenth century. The University of Pisa offered the
most startling evidence. The increase in Pisan doctorates of theology was much
greater than in law or arts and medicine; indeed, the percentage of theological
doctorates rose from almost nothing in the 1540s to 19 percent of the annual total
in the 1590s. The number of theology doctorates approximately equaled the
number of medicine and arts doctorates in the last twenty years of the century.

The University of Macerata, founded in 1540–41, offers additional evidence.
It awarded its first doctorate of theology only in 1577 but added another 147
through 1600. Thus, Macerata conferred an average of 10.6 doctorates of theology annually, 1577 through 1600 (see table 4.3 in Ch. 4).

The increase in the number of theological doctorates came mostly from the
secular clergy. Very few secular priests obtained doctorates in theology in the fifteenth century and the first half of the sixteenth. Then the atmosphere changed.
The Council of Trent decreed that cathedral canons must have doctorates in
theology or canon law or comparable training (Session 22, canon 2, September
17, 1562). Bishops sometimes insisted that secular clergymen obtain degrees as
prerequisites for holding benefices.[46] The new religious orders of the Catholic
Reformation dedicated themselves to training clergymen, some of whom would
pursue doctorates in university faculties of theology. The combination of exhor-
tation, degree requisites for benefices, and enhanced educational opportunity
had the desired result, especially with the secular clergy. For example, more
secular priests than members of the regular clergy obtained doctorates of theol-

---

2 Humiliati, and 1 unidentified. The Dominicans made up one-fourth (25.2%) of the total. Verde
(1973–94, 2:648–729) found evidence of 34 theology doctorates at the University of Pisa/Florence
in the years 1474–1505, about one per year. This was 10 percent of the total number of doctorates of
344 awarded in all subjects during those years.

43. The distribution by order of the doctorates (1460–1579) was 70 Franciscans, 58 Dominicans,
28 Servites, 8 Carmelites, 6 Augustinians, and 9 secular clergymen. Thirty-four of the 179 (19%)
were Ferrarese. Dal Nero, 1991, 253, 257.

44. Minnucci and Morelli, 1998, xxiii. However, their research has not reached the last twenty
years of the century, when most universities awarded more doctorates of theology.

45. Bellone, 1986, 136. Because of the lack of records, this figure is probably incomplete.

46. Negruzzo, 1995, 134, 274.

TABLE 10.1
Doctorates at the University of Pisa, 1543–1599

Years	Theology	Medicine and Philosophy	Law	All Fields Combined
1543–49	1	36	92	136
1550–59	12	158	352	524
1560–69	10	131	505	647
1570–79	96	121	634	852
1580–89	121	138	613	872
1590–99	176	156	592	923

Source: Adapted from Del Gratta, 1980, table 3a, no pag.
Note: The total number of doctorates in all fields combined is slightly higher than the sum of the doctorates in various fields because in a few cases the subject area of a doctorate could not be determined. See Del Gratta, 1980, 1.

TABLE 10.2
Growth in Theology Doctorates at the University of Pisa, 1543–1599

Years	Annual Average of Theology Doctorates	Theology as % of all Doctorates
1543–49	0.1	—
1550–59	1.2	2.3
1560–69	1.0	1.5
1570–79	9.6	11.3
1580–89	12.1	13.9
1590–99	17.6	19.1

ogy from Pavia in the last quarter of the sixteenth century.[47] This new group of students, when added to the regular clergy, whose demand for degrees did not slacken, meant an unprecedented number of theology students.

It is not clear how members of the secular clergy managed simultaneously to support themselves and to satisfy the degree requirements. Mendicant order convents provided room and board for their student members. A secular clergyman needed support from benefice, patron, or his own funds in order to study. Members of the regular clergy were able to satisfy the teaching requirements by teaching in convent *studia,* an opportunity not available to secular clergymen. It is likely that faculties of theology made adjustments and compromises to enable secular clergymen to obtain degrees. They may have accepted teaching in seminaries or other educational venues or waived the teaching in favor of examinations. Much remains to be learned.

It is difficult to estimate the number of regular and secular clergymen studying for theological degrees in Italian universities and the local convent *studia* at any

47. See ibid., 272–74.

one time. As with other subjects, probably fewer than half of the students who studied theology obtained doctorates. Perhaps 20 to 30 doctoral students were in residence in the major centers in the fifteenth century and 50 to 60 by the end of the sixteenth century. Smaller centers had fewer students.

THEOLOGY, METAPHYSICS, AND SACRED SCRIPTURE AT THE UNIVERSITY OF PADUA

The civic universities of law and medicine and their ruling governments responded in different ways to the establishment of faculties of theology. A majority welcomed a small theological presence. They created one or two professorships to teach theology, and sometimes metaphysics, almost continuously from the late fourteenth century or from the foundation of the university in the fifteenth or sixteenth centuries. Some added a biblicist in the second half of the sixteenth century. Pavia, Florence, Pisa, Rome, Turin, Siena, Catania, Macerata, Messina, and Parma followed this path.

Other universities did little. They did not teach theology and metaphysics continuously in the fifteenth century and only created permanent professorships of theology, metaphysics, and Scripture during the Catholic Reformation in the last third of the sixteenth century. Bologna, Ferrara, Perugia, and Naples took this route, while Salerno lacked a theologian in its only sixteenth-century roll, that of 1592.

Padua followed neither path but approached theology in an innovative and pragmatic fashion. Despite the early establishment of a faculty of theology, Padua taught no theology or metaphysics until the mid-fifteenth century. Then the Venetian Senate added these posts in order to strengthen the university and to attract students. In the sixteenth century the Senate created a permanent post in Scripture, making Padua the first Italian university to have one.

Convent *studia* in Padua were active as early as the late 1220s. Albertus Magnus taught at the Dominican convent of Sant'Agostino, while Saint Anthony of Padua also taught between 1227 and 1231 at the Franciscan Conventual convent of Santa Maria Mater Domini, which was later called "il Santo" in his honor. A papal bull of 1363 established the faculty of theology of Padua, and statutes from 1406 survive.[48] But the university taught no theology at this time.

Then in 1433 the arts and medicine students asked the Venetian Senate to establish a theology professorship at a salary of 40 florins. As was often the case with such requests, they had someone in mind, a Franciscan friar with a theological doctorate from Paris. He had been a member of the Paduan faculty of theology since 1415 and was probably a teacher in a local convent *studium*. The Senate refused, because it had decided in 1428 not to spend more than the 4,000 florins already allocated to the university. New posts would have to come from other

---

48. The fundamental work on the Paduan faculty of theology is Brotto and Zonta, 1922; see chs. 1–5 for the early history. Poppi (1981, 3–7) summarizes it. Also see Gargan, 1971. See Boaga, 1984, for the Carmelite *studium generale* in Padua.

income. So in 1439 the communal government of Padua asked the local bishop to obtain from the pope the diversion of some benefice income to the funding of six professorships, including theology. The effort failed. Nevertheless, the bishop did pay the stipend of a theologian who taught under the auspices of the cathedral.[49]

Although the Senate refused to create a theological lectureship, it did establish a professorship of metaphysics in 1442, appointing a Dominican friar, Graziadio d'Ascoli, from the local faculty of theology and Dominican convent of Sant'Agostino.[50] The initial professorship of metaphysics became a permanent part of the university's arts roll as Thomistic metaphysics (*Ad metaphysicam in via s. Thomae*) and was always filled by a Dominican. In 1474 the Senate authorized a second metaphysics position *in via Scoti,* that is, according to the teaching of John Duns Scotus (1266–1308). The Senate appointed the distinguished English Augustinian Hermit Thomas Penketh (d. 1487).[51] The Scotist professor of metaphysics represented the other great current in medieval metaphysics. Both Thomist and Scotist metaphysicians taught Aristotle's *Metaphysics* at the same time (hour 13, the second lecture hour of the morning) as concurrents through the sixteenth century.[52]

Metaphysics *in via s. Thomae* or *in via Scoti* meant Aristotelian metaphysics interpreted from the perspective of one or the other of the two most influential Scholastics. Aristotelian metaphysics became the preferred method for explaining being, seen as essential preparation for the study of theology. As Étienne Gilson put it, this was "an Aristotle that was neither Averroës, nor Thomas Aquinas, nor even Aristotle himself, but . . . an 'Aristotle not contrary to faith.' "[53] Already at home in convent *studia* curricula, Aristotle, the Christian metaphysician, now moved into the University of Padua.

The Venetian Senate next created a professorship of theology as part of an effort to arrest an enrollment decline in the local convent *studia* and the faculty of theology. The number of students had dropped, perhaps because the fees were

49. Brotto and Zonta, 1922, 86–89. Although the 1439 request did not name the subject matter for the proposed six professorships, it was obvious from other comments that theology would have been one of them. In this discussion, salary figures are always given in florins, because professors were paid in florins, even when the Senate spoke in terms of the more valuable ducats.

50. Contarini, 1769, 131–33; Brotto and Zonta, 1922, 190; Poppi, 1981, 12–13. Brotto and Zonta (1922, 130) believe that the introduction of metaphysics taught by a friar was meant to counter the Averroist denial of the immortality of the individual human soul. Perhaps, but Gaetano da Thiene, Padua's leading natural philosopher in these years, already taught that the intellective soul was individual and immortal.

51. Brotto and Zonta, 1922, 93–97. Antonio Trombetta succeeded Penketh in the university professorship of Scotist metaphysics. Poppi, 1962, 353.

52. Although the surviving arts rolls of the sixteenth century found in AAUP, Inventario 1320 and F. 651, do not list teaching hours, they always list the two metaphysicians together. Another source confirms that they lectured at the same hour. In 1577–78, the Dominican Tommaso Pellegrini taught Thomistic metaphysics, and the Franciscan Conventual Salvatore Bartoluzzi taught Scotist metaphysics at the same time. ASB, Assunteria di Studio, Bu. 100, fascicle 5, "Stato dello Studio di Padova," no foliation, f. [2ʳ]. On Pellegrini, see Contarini, 1769, 164–66; on Bartoluzzi, see Simioni, 1934, 69.

53. Gilson, 1955, 471.

high, perhaps as part of the precipitous decline in the number of students in all disciplines which struck the University of Padua in the mid-fifteenth century.[54] The disappearance of the cathedral lectureship and of posts in smaller convent *studia* by the 1470s left fewer teaching theologians to attract students. Even though the convent *studia* and faculty of theology were not its responsibility, the Venetian Senate helped them by creating a publicly funded professorship in theology beginning in 1476–77. Penketh, who had been teaching Scotist metaphysics, became professor of Scotist theology, the first theologian in the university.[55] Another friar replaced him as Scotist metaphysician.

In 1490 the Venetian Senate added a professorship of Thomist theology. According to its own words, the Senate created this position because theology was fundamental to the Catholic faith and because the rector of arts and many students had requested it. The Senate appointed the Dominican Fra Lodovico dei Valenza da Ferrara (1453–96), who had taught theology at the University of Ferrara (1486–87) and was currently teaching natural philosophy there. Thus, rather than appointing someone from a local convent, the Senate treated the theology professorship like any other university position. It raided another university for a theologian, typical Venetian policy at this time. Obviously, the Dominican order agreed to the move, a sign of the growing influence and importance of the university in the teaching of theology. Fra Lodovico was appointed "to teach theology according to the doctrine of St. Thomas" (*Ad legendum theologiam iuxta doctrinam s. Thomae*) at 60 florins, the same salary that the Scotist theologian received.[56] The Thomist theologian became the concurrent of the Scotist theologian, as theology (teaching at hour 14, the third lecture hour of the morning) immediately followed metaphysics in the schedule.[57]

The four posts were truly university professorships. The Venetian government funded them and chose the occupants. The professors taught in the rooms rented for the university, rather than in their own convents.[58] Thus, the Venetian Senate added metaphysics and theology to arts and law and in so doing strengthened both the faculty of theology and the university.

Pressures from several directions helped to introduce metaphysics and theology into the University of Padua. The theologians and students of the faculty of theology wanted to arrest the decline in their numbers. The bishops of Padua, who served the university as chancellors, probably worked behind the scenes to

54. See Chapter 1, "Padua, 1222."

55. Brotto and Zonta, 1922, 90–92, 95–101, 178–81, 203.

56. Ibid., 99–100, 185–86, 266–67 (quotation from Senate decree of Oct. 21, 1490). See also Contarini, 1769, 11–21, who includes a list of Fra Lodovico's many publications. For his Ferrara appointments, see *I maestri di Ferrara*, 1991, 17, 18, 281.

57. See the rolls in AAUP, Inventario, 1320, and in F. 651; and ASB, Assunteria di Studio, Bu. 100, fascicle "Stato dello Studio di Padova," f. [2r–v].

58. In 1484 the Venetian Senate granted a salary increase to Francesco Securo di Nardò, the Dominican metaphysics lecturer, so that he could live outside his convent near the university lecture room. The aging friar could no longer make the long walk from his convent to the lecture hall. Although his age is unknown, he had held the Thomist metaphysics post since 1464 and died in 1489. Brotto and Zonta, 1922, 100, 195–97; Contarini, 1769, 133–36.

create the positions. Since the bishops were always Venetian nobles with family connections to members of the government in Venice, they would be heard. The arts students added their voices. And the Venetian governors of Padua, concerned for the prosperity of the city, probably joined the chorus.[59] Friars coming from afar to live and study in convents had to be fed, and their orders paid high fees when they earned degrees, all of which contributed to the local economy. The Venetian Senate acceded to the requests, because it saw the addition of metaphysics and theology as measures that would make Padua a more prestigious scholarly center. The second metaphysics post and the two theological posts established between 1474 and 1490 were part of a broad effort by the Venetian government to improve the university in those years.

Although both Thomism and Scotism were Scholastic metaphysical and theological systems, significant differences separated them.[60] In the Thomistic tradition, salvation is the happy consequence of cooperation between God's grace and human nature. Man's nature includes his intellect, which can reflect in some partial way about God and yearn for union. Human beings are drawn toward God to fulfill their nature; the human intellect helps bring men and women toward God. God offers them his saving grace; when they freely accept God's grace, they can reject sin and be saved. Thus, moral perfection and salvation come through man's knowing cooperation with God.

Scotist theology, by contrast, sees God and humans as more distant from each other and places greater emphasis on man's will. God's design for men and women is less clearly imprinted in their nature and less well understood by their intellects. But God infuses humans with grace, which disposes them to contrition, love, and obedience. Through an act of will, man loves God, obeys his laws, and is saved. Compared with Thomism, Scotism emphasized God's power and human weakness more, had a less optimistic view of human capabilities, and subtly reduced the importance of works. Of course, both Thomist and Scotist theologians developed many nuances on the major themes of their traditions. And they sometimes borrowed from each other and from external sources.

Unlike arts and law, theology had no separate roll of professors, because it lacked a traditional student organization (*universitas*) with a rector, the origin of the rolls.[61] So civic authorities inserted the theologians into either the law or arts roll. Most often, they listed the theologians and metaphysicians at the beginning

59. The claim of the student rector of arts of 1495 supports this hypothesis. Writing in 1496, he credited himself, Bishop Pietro Barozzi, and Alvise Bragadino, one of the two Venetian governors of Padua in 1492, for the revival of theology at Padua. Brotto and Zonta, 1922, 101–2. He apparently referred to the 1490 creation of the Thomist theological professorship. A similar combination of students, bishop, and governor may have helped win approval for the earlier posts.

60. The following comparison is based on Giacon, 1944–1950, 1:17–22; Gilson, 1955, 361–83, 454–71; Copleston, 1962, chs. 31–41 (Thomas), chs. 45–50 (Scotus); Panteghini, 1976, 415–17; and Collett, 1985, 18–22. Two cautions: the discussion here considerably simplifies the two traditions and touches on only one theological point. There is much bibliography on medieval Thomism and Scotism but little on the two philosophies during the Italian Renaissance. Two exceptions are the discussion of Thomism in Kristeller, 1974, 29–91, and Vasoli, 1998b.

61. Negruzzo, 1995, 33.

of the arts and medicine roll. Padua did so, always grouping the four friars in this order: the Thomist theologian, the Scotist theologian, the Thomist metaphysician, and the Scotist metaphysician. The professor of Sacred Scripture, when added in 1551, was listed between the Scotist theologian and the Thomist metaphysician.[62]

Dominican friars always held the Thomistic professorships of metaphysics and theology from their inauguration in the fifteenth century through 1600 and beyond. Franciscans and one Augustinian held the Scotist professorships of metaphysics and theology. Although these friars came from every part of Italy and beyond (including Maurice O'Fihely from Ireland and Tommaso Penketh from England), they normally had taken theological degrees at Padua and resided in local convent *studia*.[63] While the Venetian Senate jealously guarded the power to choose all professors, it appears that the bishop of Padua was consulted on these appointments.[64]

Metaphysicians and theologians received salaries in the middle range of arts and medicine professors, with the metaphysicians often paid more than the theologians. For example, in 1509–10, the Scotist metaphysician, Antonio Trombetta, earned 150 florins; the Thomist metaphysician, Girolamo da Monopoli, earned 100; the Scotist theologian, Maurice O'Fihely, earned 100, and the Thomist theologian, Gaspare Mansueti da Perugia, earned 60. Their salaries were far below the first ordinary professor of theoretical medicine (496 florins) and the first ordinary professor of natural philosophy, Pietro Pomponazzi at 370 florins, but far above the three logicians, paid 35, 35, and 20 florins; the moral philosopher, paid 15 florins; and the extraordinary professors of natural philosophy, paid 47, 20, and 20 florins. The metaphysicians and theologians were paid in the same range as the Greek lecturer Marco Musuro at 140 florins, the rhetorician Raffaele Reggio at 100 florins, and the professor of astronomy and mathematics Bernardino Trinca at 70 florins.[65] As with professors in other fields, accomplishments, perceived prestige, and length of service raised or lowered the salaries of the metaphysicians and theologians within a limited range. Trombetta had taught the

---

62. See the arts rolls from the sixteenth century in AAUP, Inventario 1320, and F. 651.

63. Also called Maurice du Port, O'Fihely (d. 1513) taught Scotist theology at Padua from 1497 to 1512, wrote several books, edited works of Scotus, participated in the Fifth Lateran Council, and became a bishop. See Scapin, 1976.

Contarini (1769, 16–72, 109–21, 130–70) lists the Dominican professors of metaphysics, theology, and Scripture through the early seventeenth century. Brotto and Zonta (1922, 179–207) list the Thomist and Scotist professors of metaphysics and theology through the early sixteenth century. They are in agreement except for the first Thomist metaphysician. Also see Rossetti, 1976, for Franciscans who taught at the university through the eighteenth century.

64. Brotto and Zonta (1922, 94) believe that the bishop had to approve the metaphysics appointees. And Bishop Pietro Barozzi (bishop 1487–1507), in concert with the governors of Padua, made representations to the Senate in order to get the metaphysics and theology appointees that he wanted and to secure adequate salaries for them. Gios, 1977, 299–301.

65. See the 1509–10 roll with salaries in AAUP, F. 651, ff. 1ʳ–2ʳ. This pattern continued. In 1536–37, the two metaphysicians were paid 100 florins each, the theologians 130 and 60. Again they were in the middle range of arts salaries. AAUP, F. 651, f. 129ʳ–ᵛ.

longest (since 1476–77), and he, Girolamo da Monopoli, and O'Fihely had published more than the younger Gaspare Mansueti.[66]

In 1551 the Venetian government created the new lectureship of Sacred Scripture at the University of Padua. The Senate decree noted that the professor of Thomistic metaphysics had already been lecturing on Scripture for the past year to an audience as large as any in the university. Well satisfied with his efforts, and adding that such a professorship was appropriate for the times, the Senate appointed the Thomistic metaphysician, the Dominican priest Adriano Valentico, to the new professorship at a salary of 100 ducats. The Senate then chose another Venetian Dominican to assume the vacated Thomistic metaphysics post at a salary of 70 florins.[67] Dominicans held the Scripture professorship about two-thirds of the time from 1551 through 1600.[68]

Padua established the first permanent Scripture professorship in an Italian university, fifteen years before any other university acted and thirty-six years before the University of Rome. Indeed, several Italian universities never created Scripture professorships in the sixteenth century. Although the Council of Trent in 1546 had instructed princes and city governments to introduce lectureships of Sacred Scripture into universities lacking it (i.e., all Italian universities), the Tridentine decree does not appear to have influenced the Venetian Senate very much, if at all.[69] Since the papal nuncio to Venice never mentioned the matter, papal pressure apparently played no role.[70]

---

66. For Trombetta, see Poppi, 1962, 1964, and 1983. These three studies are reprinted in Poppi, 1989. For Girolamo da Monopoli, see Contarini, 1769, 21–27; Brotto and Zonta, 1922, 187–89; and Simioni, 1934, 59. For O'Fihely, see Brotto and Zonta, 1922, 183–85, and Scapin, 1976. For Mansueti, see Contarini, 1769, 27–30; Brotto and Zonta, 1922, 189–90; and Simioni, 1934, 59–60.

67. "Quanto convenga alli presenti tempi, che nel studio nostro di Padoa si lega la lettione della scrittura sacra a cadauno puo esser manifesto: il che etiam Dio, è, stato l'anno passato con l'effetto cognosciuto però che havendo letto quella lettione il R.do padre maestro Adriano dell'ordine di predicatori, è, stato cosi volentieri udito, et con tanto frequentia di scolari quanta altra lettione di quel studio, et però devendosi continoare la preditta lettione ad honor de'l signor Dio, et di quel studio nostro essendo massimamente certi della dottrina, et religione del p.to R.do maestro: L'Andera parte, che esso maestro Adriano sia condutto à legere nel p.to studio la lettione della scrittura sacra à beneplacito della sig.a nostra et gli sia constituito salario de ducati cento all'anno." ASV, Senato, Terra, Registro 38, f. 26ʳ, Sept. 10, 1551. I am grateful to Guido Ruggiero for providing me with a transcript of this document. A Riformatore dello Studio di Padova proposed the measure, which passed by the overwhelming vote of 183 yes, 3 abstentions, and 1 opposed. Valentico (born in Venice in 1506; d. 1572) taught Thomistic metaphysics (1543–51) and Scripture (1551–64) at the University of Padua. He then served as inquisitor of Venice (1564–66) and bishop of Capodistria (1566–1572). For his career, see Contarini, 1769, 109–12, 160–62, 204; Simioni, 1934, 67, 70; and Grendler, 1977, 49 n. 71.

68. Contarini, 1769, 109–30, 160–62, 204; Simioni, 1934, 67, 70.

69. See paragraph 7 of the second decree on instruction and preaching of the fifth session (June 17, 1546) in Decrees, 1990, 2:668–69, Latin with English translation.

70. See Nunziature di Venezia, 5, 1967. Two eighteenth-century sources offer another explanation. The rivalry between the Thomist and Scotist theologians had become so sharp that the study of Scripture, the source of theology, had become threadbare and degraded. Dissatisfied, the Riformatori dello Studio di Padova decided to create a professorship exclusively for Scripture. Facciolati, 1978, pt. 3:267. This was first printed in 1757. Contarini (1769, 109–10) repeats it. The explanation, with its whiff of Enlightenment disdain for Scholastic theology, is too distant from the event to be convincing.

Venice's traditional policy of maintaining and improving the university in order to attract more students probably led to the professorship. Riformatori and Senate created the position during a period of intense activity designed to invigorate the intellectual and spiritual life of the Venetian state and the university during the tenure of Doge Francesco Donà (1545–1553). The government authorized the construction of a botanical garden in Padua in 1545 and it expanded preuniversity schooling in Venice in 1551. It reorganized the teaching of law.[71] The Paduan medical revolution of anatomy, clinical medicine, and medical botany came to fruition at this time. And Venice created a joint church-state Inquisition to deal with heresy in 1547.

With two theologians, two metaphysicians, and a biblicist, Padua had the largest religious studies offering of any Italian university outside of Rome at midcentury. Much of the convent *studium* curriculum for the theological doctorate had entered the university. Padua had 5 professors of religious studies in an average faculty of 30 in arts and 26 in law in the second half of the sixteenth century. With the new Scripture professorship and all the other changes, Padua was a far broader and more diverse university than before.

The university theologians and metaphysicians avoided taking public positions in the sharpest Italian ecclesiastical and jurisdictional dispute of the day, the Venetian interdict of 1606–7. In April 1606, Pope Paul V placed Venice under interdict for the republic's refusal to hand over two clergymen accused of crimes and its failure to revoke laws asserting civil jurisdiction over church lands. Led by Paolo Sarpi, a Servite friar employed as theologian to the Venetian government but with no teaching position, several clergymen from Venetian convents strenuously argued the Venetian position against Cardinals Robert Bellarmine and Cesare Baronio and other theologians on the papal side.[72] But only one professor of theology or metaphysics at the University of Padua took a public stance. Father Angelo Andronico (1543–1629), a Venetian Dominican from the convent of SS. Giovanni e Paolo in Venice who taught Thomistic metaphysics from 1583 to 1593 and Thomistic theology from 1593 to 1628, signed a Venetian protest against the interdict on May 6, 1606.[73]

UNIVERSITIES TEACHING THEOLOGY CONTINUOUSLY

Some universities taught theology practically continuously from the late fourteenth century or from their creation in the fifteenth and sixteenth centuries. The larger universities of this group expanded their offerings in religious studies

---

71. Grendler, 1989, 63–67, for preuniversity education; and Chapter 13, "Padua and Bologna," for law.

72. For a list, see Pirri, 1959, 313. See Grendler, 1977, 280–82, for a brief summary of the interdict crisis.

73. For his involvement in the dispute, see Benzoni, 1970, 48, 51. For his career, see Facciolati, 1978, pt. 3:254, 260; Contarini, 1769, 68–72, 166–67; and Simioni, 1934, 63, 68. His close connections with some Venetian patricians, and the fact that he spent a good deal of time in Venice, may have led him to sign the protest document.

in the second half of the sixteenth century. The smaller universities maintained the status quo.

Pavia

The University of Pavia paid an Augustinian Hermit, Bonifacio Bottigella of Pavia, to teach theology in 1374. Thus, Pavia had a professor of theology before the creation of its faculty of theology in 1389. Fra Bottigella continued to teach both theology and moral philosophy through 1391 at least and was replaced by a Franciscan in 1393. Pavia continued with a single theologian through 1400.[74] In the early fifteenth century the number expanded to two and sometimes three friars from the major mendicant orders. They now taught theology only. However, in 1430 Duke Filippo Maria Visconti of Milan reduced theology to a single professor at the low salary of 30 florins. A Dominican, an Augustinian, and a Franciscan alternated annually in the post. The single theologian was initially listed at the beginning of the law roll but moved to the head of the arts roll in 1443–44.[75]

In 1444–45 a second theologian was added.[76] From the 1460s to the end of the century, two, sometimes three, and once four (1488–89) theologians taught. At least one, and occasionally two, were Dominican friars; a Carmelite or a Franciscan (or both) completed the group.[77] One of the theologians sometimes also taught metaphysics on holidays.[78] With a few exceptions, their salaries were at the bottom of the scale.

Although the rolls did not indicate what approach the professors took to the sacred science, Dominicans and Carmelites undoubtedly followed Aquinas to greater or lesser extent, while Franciscans and Augustinians were Scotists. Thomism received a boost in 1480, when the university appointed a Dominican to teach the works of Thomas Aquinas. This meant that he might expound Thomas's works directly, rather than lecturing on the *Sentences* and using Aquinas

74. Maiocchi, 1971, vol. 1, doc. 33, p. 28 (1374); doc. 252, p. 117 (1387); doc. 305, p. 151 (1389); doc. 366, p. 184 (1391); doc. 430, p. 220 (1393); doc. 432, p. 227 (1394); doc. 472, p. 311 (1395); doc. 751, p. 420 (1399–1400 at Piacenza). These are all payment records rather than rolls. See also Volta, 1898; Andreolli Panzarasa, 1989, 37; *Memorie di Pavia*, 1970, 185–86; and the review of the early years in Negruzzo, 1995, 10–15. Negruzzo is the fundamental study of theology at Pavia.

75. Maiocchi, 1971, vol. 2, pt. 1, doc. 415, p. 279, and doc. 417, p. 283. Andreolli Panzarasa, 1989, 41. For the rolls from 1430 through the 1440s, see Maiocchi, 1971, vol. 2, pts. 1 and 2. See Maiocchi, 1971, vol. 2, pt. 2, doc. 611, p. 469, for the move to the arts roll.

76. Maiocchi, 1971, vol. 2, pt. 2, doc. 623, p. 481 (1444–45) and passim, and *Documenti di Pavia*, 1994, 199, for the roll of 1455–56.

77. See ASPv, Università, Cartone 22, ff. 153^r–154^v (roll of 1469–70), 155^r–157^r (1472–73), 158^r–159^v (1475–76), 165^r–167^v (1480–81), and passim to ff. 221^r–225^r (1499–1500). The roll for 1483–84 is also found in ASPv, Università, Cartone 20, no pag. Negruzzo (1995, 346–48) lists the theologians found in these documents. Verde (1973–94, 1:384–92) prints the rolls of 1480–81 and 1482–83 from a Florentine source. See also Sottili, 1982, 529–30.

78. See, for example, the roll of 1482–83, in which "d. M. Gometius [Gomez] hispanus, ordinis minorum" taught both theology on regular teaching days and metaphysics on holidays. Verde, 1973–1994, 1:388, 391.

to explicate Peter Lombard. This first known lectureship dedicated to Thomas's works both reflected and added to the importance of Italian Thomism. The Dominicans now had the numerical advantage of holding two of the three or four theological posts in the 1480s and 1490s, with one of them concentrating on the order's leading theologian. Lecturing on Thomas's works continued through 1499–1500, with the major Renaissance Thomist Tommaso de Vio (Cajetan) filling the position in 1497–98.[79]

Pavia had a combination metaphysics and natural philosophy professorship (in addition to several natural philosophers) part of the time in the first forty years of the fifteenth century.[80] When in 1441–42 metaphysics became a separate holiday lectureship, taught by the ordinary theologian, it joined the religious studies group.[81] Metaphysics remained a holiday lectureship, often taught by one of the ordinary theologians, until it became a daily lectureship in 1496–97.[82] But pay was low and turnover frequent.

This pattern continued through the first half of the sixteenth century, although the university was more often closed than open. One well-known figure, the Franciscan Conventual and famous preacher Cornelio Musso (1511–74), taught metaphysics at the University of Pavia between 1536 and 1538, before going on to Bologna.[83] Some archival documents called the theology position Scholastic theology (*Ad lectura theologiae scholasticae*) as early as 1519. This was the first known appearance of this title in an Italian university roll; it became the norm at Pavia from 1566 onward. Also in 1566–67, the new professorship of Scripture (*Ad lecturam Sacrae Scripturae*) appeared, initially filled by a Carmelite. It continued through the rest of the century and beyond.[84]

From the 1580s onward, the University of Pavia had 4 or 5 professors of religious studies (2 Scholastic theologians, a Scripture professor, and 1 or 2 metaphysicians) in a total complement of 47 to 50 professors.[85] The Dominicans no

---

79. Andreolli Panzarasa, 1989, 43. "Paulus de Monilia, Ordinis Praedicatorum qui legat opera Beati Thomae de Aquino." ASPv, Università, Cartone 22, f. 165ᵛ, roll of 1480–81. See other rolls in the latter source, passim through f. 225ʳ. The same is found in the rolls of 1480–81 and 1482–83 printed in Verde, 1973–1994, 1:384, 388. See also Sottili, 1982, 529–30; *Memorie di Pavia*, 1970, 190–91; and Negruzzo, 1995, 346–47, and 190–92, 348, for Cajetan.

80. The post was usually described as *Ad lecturam Methaphisice et lecturam que de Parvis Naturalibus Aristotelis appellatur* at the very low salary of 30 florins. Maiocchi, 1971, vol. 2, pt. 1, doc. 272, p. 185 (1419–20); doc. 338, p. 222 (1425–26); doc. 367, p. 240 (1427–28); doc. 378, p. 247 (1428–29); doc. 431, p. 292 (1431–32); doc. 451, p. 304 (1432–33); doc. 497, p. 356 (1435–36).

81. Maiocchi, 1971, vol. 2, pt. 2, p. 430.

82. See the rolls in Maiocchi, 1971, vol. 2, pt. 2, pp. 470 (1443–44), 485 (1445–46), 496 (1446–47), 520 (1447–48), 539 (1448–49), and the rolls for the rest of the century in ASPv, Università, Cartone 22, as cited in n. 77. See also *Memorie di Pavia*, 1970, 157–69 passim, and Sottili, 1982, 530–31.

83. Negruzzo, 1995, 209–17; plus Cantini, 1941, 151; Bartman, 1945, 251; and Odoardi, 1948, 227. *Memorie di Pavia* (1970) lists Musso as teaching metaphysics at Pavia in 1537 (p. 170) and a "Cornelio" teaching theology in 1537 (p. 191).

84. ASPv, Università, Cartone 20, roll of 1566–67, no pag.

85. A fairly complete set of fiscal rolls, 1538–39, then from 1550–51 through 1601, can be found in ASPv, Università, Cartone 20, no pag. Zorzoli (1982, 567 n. 48) gives the roll of 1548–49 based on a manuscript source. Rizzo (1987, 75–76 n. 35) prints the roll of 1584–85. Negruzzo (1995, 346–65,

longer enjoyed the dominant position; the posts were evenly spread among the Dominicans, Franciscans, Augustinian Hermits, and Carmelites. Contrary to the provincialization of Pavia's faculty in other subjects in the sixteenth century, the majority of the teaching friars did not come from Pavia and Lombardy.[86] And their salaries had improved. The religious studies professors now earned the same as the majority of lesser professors of medicine and a little more than the least important legist and the ill-paid mathematician.[87] Overall, religious studies expanded in numbers and importance at the University of Pavia over the course of two centuries.

Florence and Pisa

The University of Florence also taught theology continuously from its early decades. Between 1358 and 1363, 1 to 3 mendicant order friars simultaneously taught theology in the university. Between 1363 and 1369, 4 theologians (a Dominican, a Carmelite, an Augustinian, and a Franciscan) taught. Thus, theologians accounted for 4 of the total faculty of 16 to 22. Then theology declined to a single friar, in a larger university of 20 to 30 professors, over the next century to 1473.[88] The position was sometimes called "Sacred Scripture" rather than theology, and the appointees came from various backgrounds. For example, the Dominican Bartolomeo Lapacci de' Rimbertini (1402–66), who knew Greek and had a distinguished career as bishop before becoming a theology lecturer, was appointed to teach the Epistles of Saints Paul and Jerome in 1461.[89] By contrast, the University of Florence never had a professorship of metaphysics. In the second half of the sixteenth century, long after the university had moved to Pisa, one theologian continued to teach in Florence as part of the Florentine contingent of 3 or 4 professors.[90]

A theologian taught at the University of Pisa in the 1360s, and another theologian may have been teaching in the first decade of the fifteenth century. Although

summary on 366–71) lists the theologians, metaphysicians, and professors of Scripture found in archival sources. There are some differences in the sources and a couple of typographical errors in her list. Names of theologians and metaphysicians are also found in *Memorie di Pavia*, 1970, 171, 174–76, 192, 193.

86. Negruzzo, 1995, 39 and passim.

87. ASPv, Università, Cartone 20.

88. Spagnesi, 1979, 270, with the roll of 1391–92 listing a theologian and a biblical lecturer; Park, 1980; Piana, 1977, 24–37, who reprints appointment notices for theologians, 1359–1428, from Gherardi, 1973, and adds other material; and Davies, 1998, 176, 191, for two theologians, 1461–63 and 1464. Some rolls of the 1420s, 1430s, and 1440s did not list a theologian. It should be remembered that almost all knowledge of Florentine professors comes from fiscal records, which have many gaps.

89. In 1462 he was called "Lettore in sagra teologia" and in 1463 was paid to teach "in sagra scrittura," according to payment records. Davies, 1998, 53, 94, 176.

90. "Francesco da Studiglio Hispanus" (Francesco De Astudillo) taught theology in Florence at a salary of 200 florins from 1557 through 1563 and then from 1566 to 1569. He taught theology at Pisa as a holiday lecturer (*diebus festivis*) from 1563 to 1566. FN, Ms. Corte d'appello, 3, ff. 32^r, 34^r, 36^r, 38^r, 39^v, 42^r, 50^v, 52^v, 55^r. See also Cascio Pratilli, 1975, 196; Fabroni, 1971, 2:463; and Barsanti, 1993, 516, 540.

there was no instruction, Pisa awarded twelve doctorates of theology in the years 1469 through 1472.[91] After the university came back to life in 1473, Pisa had a single theologian, who also sometimes taught metaphysics, among its 25 to 40 faculty members through 1526. All were Franciscans, except for one Augustinian.[92] When the University of Pisa reopened in 1543, it had 2 theologians and 2 metaphysicians. The university added a holiday professorship of Scripture in 1589–90, which became permanent. Hence, at the end of the century Pisa had 5 professors of religious studies in a professoriat of about 45.[93] Friars sometimes moved from one position to another in the religious studies group. Servants of Mary, perhaps because of their Tuscan origins, and Franciscans dominated the positions, followed by three Augustinians and a lone Dominican in the half century, but none achieved scholarly distinction.

Rome

The papal curia offered limited and irregular theological instruction in Rome, possibly from the origins of the university in the 1240s. For example, a theologian received payment from the papal treasury for lecturing to the clerical members of the curia and papal court between 1299 and 1302.[94] Theological instruction at the papal curia sought to inform members of the curia about disputed points under current discussion. Although important to the intellectual life of the curia, the instruction was irregular and unsystematic. These lectures may have continued through the fourteenth and early fifteenth centuries as the papacy and curia moved from place to place, but documentation is lacking. The Master of the Sacred Palace, the pope's personal theologian, delivered some theological lectures at the curia and examined candidates for theological degrees. By the mid-fifteenth century, various clergymen, especially members of the mendicant orders and visitors with lofty reputations, discussed theological *quaestiones* at the papal court. So far as is known, the informal instruction at the papal court did not include regular cycles of lectures on the texts required for theological degrees.[95]

The various mendicant order convent *studia* in Rome also offered theological

91. Picotti, 1968, 23–24, and Davies, 2000, 216–18.

92. Verde, 1973–94, 1:293–303, for the rolls 1473–1503, and 2:122–25, 270–83, 360–63, 464–57, 482–83, and 544–45, for more information about the theologians. For the period 1503–25, see Fabroni, 1971, 1:379, 392–93, and Del Gratta, 1993a, 492, 501.

93. Fabroni, 1971, 2:463–64; Barsanti, 1993, 540–42 and passim; and the Pisan rolls of 1543–44 and 1567–68 in Cascio Pratilli, 1975, 192, 194.

94. See Paravini Bagliani, 1989, 67–69, and Frova and Miglio, 1992. These works refine and correct Renazzi, 1971, 1:21–56.

95. For the role of the Master of the Sacred Palace, see Creytens, 1942, esp. 74–79. See the account of the life and works of the Augustinian canon Niccolò Palmieri (1401–67), who discussed poverty and riches in the church, the conception of Christ, and other disputed issues at the papal court on a number of occasions. Monfasani (1991–92, 33) writes: "But the most important aspect of these texts [of Palmieri] is their very existence. They prove that the public argument of [theological] *quaestiones* constituted a normal part of the intellectual life of the Roman Curia in the fifteenth century." See also Monfasani, 1992. For sermons at the papal court, see O'Malley, 1979.

instruction. For example, Thomas Aquinas lectured on theology at the Dominican *studium* in the convent of Santa Sabina between 1265 and 1268.[96] Although the religious orders often furnished lecturers for the curia and for the university later, the history of the Roman convent *studia* and the Roman faculty of theology remains to be written. It is known that a professor of theology taught at the University of Rome in the academic year 1460–61.[97] And one to four friars annually taught theology, and sometimes metaphysics and Scripture, at the university in the 1470s, 1480s, and 1490s.[98] The first surviving roll of 1514 listed 2 theologians among the 87 professors.[99]

Theology became important in the University of Rome only in the 1530s and later. Upon reopening after the sack of 1527, the university had 2 or 3 theologians in a faculty complement of 20 to 25 in the mid-1530s and in the 1540s.[100] By midcentury it had reached the level of 40 professors, including 5 theologians, where it would remain until the mid-1580s.[101] A single metaphysician, occasionally joined by a second and a third, also taught.[102] Thus, the religious studies component of the University of Rome numbered 6, and occasionally up to 10, professors in a total of about 40, a larger theological and metaphysical component than found in any other Italian university. A single professor of Sacred Scripture joined them in 1587–88.[103] When the size of the faculty declined to 25 to 30 in the last fifteen years of the century, it included 2 theologians, a metaphysician, and the Scripture professor. As elsewhere, the religious studies professors had no separate place in the rolls. The theologians, and often the professor of Scripture, were listed at the head of the legists, while the metaphysicians were inserted into the middle of the artists.

Friars from the mendicant orders filled these posts with two surprising exceptions. In November 1537 Pope Paul III appointed two Jesuits, Pierre Favre (1506–46) and Diego Laínez (1512–65), to teach theology at the University of

96. Mulcahey, 1998, 278–306.

97. Fernando of Cordova (1422/26–86) was described as "in studio Urbis facultatem theologiae publice legis" in 1460. For his career, see Monfasani, 1992, esp. 23–24, 61 (quote). Renazzi (1971, 1:21–56 passim, 165–66) offers several names of professors of theology. But the evidence presented is not clear enough to determine if they taught in convent *studia* or university. See also the cautions of Frova and Miglio, 1992, 30–31, 36–39.

98. Dorati da Empoli, 1980, 107, 133–35. The fiscal data may be incomplete, and the names are sometimes difficult to identify.

99. *I maestri di Roma*, 1991, 2, 1102.

100. Rolls of 1535–36, 1539–40, and 1542–43, in *I maestri di Roma*, 1991, 7–16, 1102.

101. This is based on the rolls of 1548 through 1582, with many gaps, in *I maestri di Roma*, 1991, 17–124, 1102–4. In several years, the theological component was higher, for example, 9 of 40 in 1549 and 7 of 37 in 1568–69. See Renazzi, 1971, 2:168–73, 3:28–30, for brief information about some of the theologians. However, I have been unable to verify his statement (2:171–72) that Fra Felice Peretti, the future Pope Sixtus V (1585–90), taught theology at the University of Rome in the late 1560s. Nor does Pastor (1891–1953, vol. 21) mention it.

102. *I maestri di Roma*, 1991, 4–149 passim, and the summary list on 1073, which omits a few names.

103. See the rolls of 1587 through 1599, with several gaps, in *I maestri di Roma*, 1991, 125–51, 1094, 1104.

Rome. Both came from the original band of ten Jesuits who gathered together at the University of Paris between 1528 and 1536, but neither had advanced degrees in theology, so far as is known. Laínez taught Scholastic theology, lecturing on the *Sacri canonis missae . . . expositio* (Explanation of the sacred canon of the mass; first ed. 1488), by the German nominalist theologian Gabriel Biel (c. 1410–95). This was an often printed manual of practical pastoral theology, rather than a nominalist treatise. Favre taught "positive theology," that is, the history of doctrines, paying particular attention to Scripture. Favre and Laínez taught at the University of Rome for two academic years before stopping in the summer of 1539.[104] Laínez later became an immensely influential theologian at the Council of Trent and general of the order.

These were the only Jesuit professors of theology to be found in Italian universities in the sixteenth century. Even though they taught theology in universities in Spain, Portugal, and German-speaking Europe, the Jesuits did not crack the mendicant order monopoly on theology, metaphysics, and Scripture studies in Italy. They had to be content with their own Collegio Romano (founded 1551), a scholarly center for theology, philosophy, ancient languages, rhetoric, and grammar. The other new religious orders of the Catholic Reformation had no more success in winning Italian university theology posts than the Jesuits during the sixteenth century. So they taught in their own preuniversity schools and novitiates for junior members.

The University of Rome spread the positions among the major mendicant orders, giving each the opportunity to display its theological wares in the center of Catholicism. For example, the five teaching theologians of 1576–77 and 1579–80 included a Carmelite, a Franciscan, an Augustinian, a Dominican, and a Servite.[105]

The friars who taught at the University of Rome might be major figures with wide responsibilities beyond the university. Often the procurator general of an order taught theology at the university. Third in the order's hierarchy after the general and vicar-general, the procurator general represented his order and protected its privileges at the papal court. He preached at the papal court and might be tapped for other duties. Fra Giovanni Battista Bernori di Piombino, professor of Sacred Scripture at the University of Rome and procurator general of the Augustinian Hermits (1592–1607) illustrates the point.[106] In 1594 he petitioned the congregation of cardinals that oversaw the university for an increase in salary. Fra Bernori listed his teaching career and his service to the papacy. He had taught for eighteen years at Salamanca, then in various *studia* in Italy, and at the University of Rome since 1586. While in Rome he had helped to expurgate the Tal-

104. To be sure, Favre and Laínez were not officially Jesuits before formal approval of the order in 1540. Tacchi Venturi, 1950, 93, 102; Salmerón, 1907, 734–35; *Fontes narrativi*, 1943, 122–23; and Schurhammer, 1973, 411. I am grateful to John W. O'Malley for providing me with photocopies of the last three references. University of Rome rolls do not survive for 1537–38 and 1538–39, and the pair are not listed in the roll of 1539–40. *I maestri di Roma*, 1991, 9–10.

105. *I maestri di Roma*, 1991, 109, 110, 114–17.

106. McGinness, 1995b, 64, 70, 246, 247, 249.

mud, had preached in Hebrew to the Jews, and had served five Vatican congregations. He had examined candidates in benefice "competitions."[107] The cardinals eventually responded. His salary remained at 100 scudi through 1595 but rose to 120 scudi in 1599, 130 scudi in 1603, and 150 scudi in 1609.[108]

As his petition indicated, Bernori contributed to many of the papacy's initiatives for scholarly renewal and the suppression of dissent. Expurgating the Talmud referred to papal decrees of 1592 and 1593 banning much Hebrew literature, and demanding expurgation of other works, for alleged anti-Christian sentiments.[109] Preaching to the Jews in Hebrew meant the obligatory (for Roman Jews) sermons begun in 1584 with the goal of converting Jews to Catholicism.[110] Fra Bernori assisted the Congregation of the Index in revising the Tridentine (1564) Index of Prohibited Books, which culminated in the promulgation of the Clementine Index of 1596.[111] Fra Bernori also helped to prepare a new Latin Vulgate Bible meeting the standards of humanistic biblical scholarship, which the papacy issued in 1590 and 1592.[112] He served the congregation (founded 1588) that oversaw the Vatican Press (founded in 1587). The Typographia Apostolica Vaticana issued numerous works of religious scholarship prepared by Roman scholars, including the Vulgate, liturgies, and editions of patristic and medieval Scholastic authors.[113]

The Congregation of Rites and Ceremonies (established 1588), which Bernori assisted, corrected the manuals of church ceremony and ritual, examined the prayers associated with various saints, and checked canonization cases for historical accuracy and precedent.[114] Examining benefice "competitions" meant that Fra Bernori assisted the Congregation of the Segnatura di Grazia (founded 1588) in judging competing claims for favors and benefices.[115] Then in 1597, three years after his petition for a higher university salary, the pope appointed Bernori to the commission charged with resolving the bitter controversy over Molinism, that is, the role of grace, free will, and predestination in Catholic theology.[116]

107. "In Salamanca, in diversi studi d'Italia, et in Roma anni otto, oltra l'haver servito in questa cortesamente [word missing?] per ispurgar il Talmud, predicare in lingua hebrea all'hebrei, nelle Congregationi dell'Indice, cerimonie, Bibbia, Tipographia, et nelli concorsi de benefitij esaminatore." ASR, Archivio dell'Università di Roma, R. 86, f. 10ʳ, letter of Bernori, called Giovanbattista Piombino here and in the rolls. Thus, Bernori began teaching at the University of Rome in 1586. That roll is missing, but he appeared as professor of Scripture in 1587. *I maestri di Roma*, 1991, 125.

108. See *I maestri di Roma*, 1991, 125, 129, 134, 139, 143, 149 (increase to 120 scudi), 152, 156 (130 scudi), 160, 164, 168 (150 scudi), and p. 1094 (summary).

109. Pastor, 1891–1953, 24:218–21.

110. Stow, 1977, 19–21.

111. Grendler, 1994, and Fragnito, 1997, 143–93.

112. For part of this story and additional bibliography, see Pastor, 1891–1953, 21:208–22, and Grendler, 1977, 241–43.

113. On the Typographia Apostolica Vaticana, see Pastor, 1891–1953, 21:209, 258; 22:199–201, and Grendler, 1977, 230, 241, 244, 248, 251. For a list of some of its publications, see Ascarelli, 1972, summary list on 353–54 and passim.

114. Pastor, 1891–1953, 21:54–57.

115. Ibid., 254.

116. For mention of Bernori, see ibid., 24:322, 334, 336.

In brief, Fra Bernori, a biblicist with a command of Hebrew, was a versatile soldier in the army of clerical scholars who created Catholic renewal. The theologians, metaphysicians, and professors of Scripture of the university provided the papacy with scholarly expertise in many areas. They may have played a larger role in the life of the church beyond the classroom than by teaching theology.

Despite the large number of theologians, the University of Rome did not award a commensurate number of doctorates in theology. The beadle reported that the university awarded "few" (*pauci*) or "some" (*nonnulli* or *aliqui*) theology doctorates annually between 1567 and 1580. By contrast, the university awarded forty to ninety-three law doctorates annually in those years.[117]

Turin, Siena, Catania, Macerata, Messina, and Parma

Turin had professors of theology, always mendicant order friars, in the fifteenth and early sixteenth centuries. But which ones taught in the university and which in convent *studia* is impossible to determine because of the absence of records.[118] After closures, the university resumed a full existence in Turin in 1566. From that date through the end of the century, Turin had a theologian (usually a Dominican) and a metaphysician (usually a Franciscan). The university added a professorship of Scripture in 1580–81, raising the religious studies total to three of a total faculty of about thirty-three.[119]

Just as legists might become political and legal advisors to the prince, professors of medicine court physicians, and humanists tutors to the sons of the prince, so a theologian might become the duke's confessor and exert influence. The Dominican Giovanni Ambrogio Barbavaro (d. c. 1594) came from a Milanese noble family, entered the convent of Sant'Eustorgio in Milan, studied at Paris and Padua, held offices in his order, wrote about twenty titles, and taught theology at the University of Padua from 1562 to 1573. He then taught theology at the University of Turin from 1573 until 1580, when Duke Emanuele Filiberto appointed him confessor to his son. The latter almost immediately became Duke Carlo Emanuele I (1562; ruled 1580–1630), who ruled with Barbavaro at his side.[120]

The University of Siena, which emphasized law, seemed to treat theology and metaphysics as interchangeable. The handful of surviving fifteenth-century rolls sometimes listed either a metaphysician or a theologian but not both.[121] From

---

117. See the reports for 1567–71, 1574–76, and 1579–80 in *I maestri di Roma*, 1991, 51, 59, 64, 74, 85, 96, 113.

118. Bellone, 1986, 131–41; Vallauri, 1936, 74. See Vallaro, 1936 and 1937, for the Dominicans at Turin.

119. See the summaries of the rolls in Chiaudano, 1972b, 87–117 passim, and Chiaudano, 1972c, 161–80 passim. Three rolls are found in Vallauri, 1970, 2:28–29, 48–49, 76–78. The Scripture professor was a priest, but his order, if any, is not given.

120. Chiaudano, 1972b, 108–16; see especially Contarini, 1769, 56–60, and Vallaro, 1936, 87–88, for short biographies.

121. Someone taught both "philosophy" and theology in 1339, and a Dominican taught theology

1531–32 through 1541–42, Siena lacked a theologian but normally had two metaphysicians. The metaphysicians were always mendicant order friars, normally held doctorates in theology, and were members of the Sienese faculty of theology.[122] One wonders if they combined metaphysics and theology in their teaching. From the 1560s on, Siena separated the two: one theologian and one metaphysician, both always members of mendicant orders. In the last decade of the sixteenth century, a Franciscan taught theology and a Dominican taught metaphysics.[123] The university did not have a professor of Scripture at any time.

At the tiny University of Catania, a lone clergyman taught both "philosophy" (presumably natural philosophy) and theology in the first decades after its founding in 1445. Then theology acquired its own professorship, shared between the Augustinian, Benedictine, Carmelite, Dominican, and Franciscan orders between 1476 and 1600. Catania never had a professor of metaphysics or Scripture.[124]

At the small university of Macerata a friar taught both theology and another subject, usually logic, from its beginning in 1540–1541 until the 1570s. At some point in the late 1570s, theology became a separate professorship, initially filled by an Augustinian. Messina had a theologian and a metaphysician at the end of the sixteenth century. Parma had a theologian and a metaphysician, both Jesuits, when it began in 1601, and three theologians and a metaphysician, always Jesuits, in 1617–18. (See Ch. 4 for all three universities.)

UNIVERSITIES RELUCTANT TO TEACH THEOLOGY

Some universities did not welcome theology and metaphysics. They taught them only intermittently in the fifteenth and early sixteenth centuries. Not until after the conclusion of the Council of Trent in 1563 did they teach theology, metaphysics, and sometimes Scripture on a continuous basis.

Bologna received papal authorization to award doctorates in theology in 1360 and had a faculty of theology in 1364. But Bologna rarely taught theology. The subject appeared only four times (two theologians in 1387–88, a single theologian in 1395–96, 1404–5, and 1412–13) in the late fourteenth and early fifteenth centuries.[125] Metaphysics was even more absent from the university. The roll of

---

in 1404. Prunai, 1950, 30, 50. An undated roll that might be 1474 listed neither theologians nor metaphysicians; Minnuci and Košuta, 1989, 119–21. The roll of 1492–93 had no theologians but did have four "philosophers" and one metaphysician, the positions filled by two Franciscans, an Augustinian, a Carmelite, and a Dominican. Zdekauer, 1977, 192. By contrast, the roll of 1500 had three theologians but no metaphysicians. Mondolfo, 1897, 415.

122. Minnucci and Košuta, 1989, 397–416 for the rolls, and 515–16 for information on the metaphysicians.

123. Cascio Pratilli, 1975, 21, 38, 52, 74, 83, 86–87, 90, 175–88 passim, for comments and rolls from the 1560s through 1589–90; Marrara, 1970, 228–45, for rolls 1589–90 to 1600; and Prunai, 1959, 98, 137, 148–49, although some of his statements have not been verified.

124. Catalano, 1934, 56, 70–73, 80–83. The incomplete records do not always indicate the religious order affiliation.

125. Dallari, 1888–1924, vol. 4: *Aggiunte*, 16, 19, 26, 35.

1415–16 listed a lecturer for the two subjects of astrology and metaphysics, followed by three lecturers for astrology and metaphysics in 1416–17. Metaphysics and theology then disappeared for the rest of the century.[126]

Theology and metaphysics briefly reappeared in 1507. Perhaps as papal influence over the city increased in the early sixteenth century, papal governors persuaded the Bolognese Senate to create theology and metaphysics posts.[127] In any case, a Dominican and a Franciscan, each lecturing in his own convent but as university professors, taught theology 1507 through 1512. After a one-year hiatus, a different Franciscan theologian, again lecturing in his own convent, appeared in 1513–14. A Franciscan and a Servite began to teach metaphysics in 1507–8.[128] But theology vanished, and only a single metaphysics position survived after 1514.[129] The civic authorities clearly did not want the friars to enter the university. Theology briefly returned for two years in the form of a lone Franciscan (1528–30) and again in 1537–38 with the appointment of Fra Cornelio Musso. His lectureship had the unusual title of "sacred evangelical theology" (*Ad lecturam sacrosantae Theologiae evangelicae*). After teaching at Bologna for two years, Musso left for Rome, and the position disappeared.[130]

Theology did not secure a permanent place in the faculty of arts and medicine at Bologna until 1566–67. The new bishop, Cardinal Gabriele Paleotti, who had assumed his duties in early 1566, and the papal governor of Bologna persuaded the Bolognese Senate to create it, and a Servite friar was appointed. The Senate cited the urging of the Council of Trent as explanation for the new professorship.[131] This time it became permanent, as one and often two friars taught theology in the next twenty-two years. The title changed from "sacred theology" to "scholastic theology" (*Ad lecturam Theologiae scholasticae*) in 1588–89.[132]

In 1579–80, the University of Bologna inaugurated a professorship in Scripture. Again Cardinal Paleotti brought it about, and his personal theologian, an Augustinian Hermit, became the first holder. From 1579–80 through the end of the century, one or two professors of biblical studies taught in the University of Bologna. Paleotti also wanted the university to create posts in Hebrew and

---

126. Ibid., 36, 38, 40. The terms *astrology* and *astronomy* were often used interchangeably at this time.

127. This is a tentative hypothesis. Examination of the relationship between the Bolognese government and the papacy concerning the university is badly needed.

128. The listing of 1508–9 is typical: "Ad Theologiam. (Quam legere possint in scholis monasteriorum suorum.) D. M. frater Eustachius de Bononia, ordinis Praedicatorum. D. M. frater Hieronymus de Bononia ordinis Minorum." Dallari, 1888–1924, 1:198, 202 (quote), 205, 209, 212, 2:5.

129. Ibid., 2:8, 11, 15, 18, 21, 25, and so on.

130. For the 1528–30 position, see ibid., 56–59. For Musso, see ibid., 84, 87. Cantini (1941, 151), Bartman (1945, 251), and Odoardi (1948, 227), all based on a sixteenth-century life of Musso, mistakenly state that the post was in metaphysics. Also see Poppi, 1989, 127–41.

131. The Senate decree of Oct. 29, 1566, is printed in Piana, 1976, 1:108. Prodi (1959–67, 2:225) provides additional evidence of the efforts of Paleotti and the governor. See also Dallari, 1888–1924, 2:167. Simeoni (1940, 121) has the wrong dates for the beginning of the permanent theological and Scripture professorships and is unaware of the previous short-term professorships of theology.

132. Dallari, 1888–1924, 2:231.

biblical Greek in order to teach the ancient languages needed for critical biblical studies. But the Senate did not create these positions.[133]

In 1589–90, the University of Bologna had five professors of religious studies: three theologians, a metaphysician, and a professor of Scripture. The number remained at five, with the mixture varying a little, through the end of the century.[134] The positions were not grouped together but scattered throughout the arts roll. Franciscans dominated; Servites, Augustinians, and Carmelites held a few positions. The Dominicans were conspicuous by their absence.

Thus, religious studies did not find a permanent place in the University of Bologna until two hundred years after the establishment of a faculty of theology in 1364. A lay tradition in the university and satisfaction with the status quo probably explained their long absence. Despite its location in the papal state and the presence of a papal governor, the Senate of Bologna created permanent theology positions only in the last third of the sixteenth century through the efforts of one of the ablest bishops of the Catholic Reformation and the urging of the Council of Trent.

Ferrara followed the Bolognese example and taught theology only sporadically before the conclusion of the Council of Trent. A single professor taught Sacred Scripture between 1448 and 1466, plus theology in 1456. After a hiatus of a decade, an ordinary professorship of theology appeared in 1475–76 and lasted through 1508–9. One, two, and occasionally three theologians simultaneously taught. Theology then disappeared for more than sixty years until revived in the form of a single professor in 1569–70, rising to two in 1575–76, three in 1591–93, but dropping to two in 1593–94. Franciscans, Carmelites, and Servites filled the posts, but no Dominicans.[135] Ferrara had a metaphysician in 1473–74 and another in 1532–33. Metaphysics finally became an ongoing position in 1540, with a single metaphysician teaching through 1544, rising to two in 1544–45, and remaining at that figure for the rest of the century. Except for a Dominican in the years 1540–45, all sixteenth-century metaphysicians were Franciscans, Servites, and Carmelites.[136]

133. Ibid, 204; Prodi, 1959–67, 2:226–27.

134. For the theological, metaphysics, and Scripture professorships from 1566–67 to the end of the century, see Dallari, 1888–1924, 2:167–268 passim.

135. The mid-fifteenth-century professor of Sacred Scripture was "Giovanni da Ferrara," of whom nothing is known. Another "Giovanni da Ferrara" taught theology at Ferrara in 1514–15, the lone appearance of a theologian between 1509 and 1569. Their religious orders are unknown. *I maestri di Ferrara,* 1991, 4, 7–11 passim, 15–23 passim, 39–49 passim, 174, 222. As noted earlier, the lists for the fifteenth century are based on a variety of older sources whose information cannot be verified and is sometimes not accurate. For more information on theology in the fifteenth century, see Piana, 1968; Dal Nero, 1991; Samaritani, 1995; Lombardi, 1995; and Del Nero, 1996, 111–45. Franceschini (1970, xvi–xvii, 264) lists the sixteenth-century theologians and metaphysicians with their religious orders. He also opines (xvii) that theology was added as a consequence of the Council of Trent.

136. The metaphysician teaching in 1473–74 was a layman, Ludovico Carri detto Tosetto (c. 1450–1539), who also taught natural philosophy and theoretical medicine at various times. *I maestri di Ferrara,* 1991, 210; Chiellini, 1991, 223. The metaphysician teaching in 1532–33 was Roberto Sacrati, possibly also a layman, who later taught natural philosophy (1540–56). All the other meta-

The University of Perugia may have had the occasional friar teaching theology in the fourteenth and fifteenth centuries.[137] In the sixteenth century a single theologian, either a Dominican or a Franciscan, was added to the roll on a regular basis. In 1566, a continuing professorship of Scripture, filled by a Dominican, appeared. Perugia also had an extraordinary vacation lecturer in metaphysics in the sixteenth century.[138] The University of Naples had an occasional professor of theology in the fifteenth century but no regular position and no metaphysician. In the sixteenth century the university had a single ordinary professor of theology, an ordinary professor of metaphysics, and an extraordinary professor of metaphysics between 1575 and 1581. Dominicans almost always filled both the theological and the metaphysical posts. Naples had no professorship of Scripture.[139] Salerno had no religious studies professorships in the late sixteenth century.

ERASMUS'S DOCTORATE OF THEOLOGY

On September 4, 1506, the University of Turin awarded a doctorate of theology to Desiderius Erasmus of Rotterdam (c. 1466–1536). It is the most famous and surprising doctorate of the Italian Renaissance. Erasmus did not spend years studying, teaching, and disputing in Turin. Instead, he arrived in Turin in mid- or late August, obtained the degree on September 4, and left shortly thereafter.[140]

Some foreigners viewed Italian faculties of theology as places where clergymen could get theological doctorates with little difficulty. Erasmus was among them. He broached the idea of obtaining an Italian doctorate in theology as early as the spring of 1498. He opined that he intended to go to Italy that year "to study theology for *a few months* [emphasis added] at Bologna, taking my doctorate there."[141] In other words, Erasmus judged that even the famous university and faculty of theology of Bologna would waive most of the requirements in order to award him the degree after a brief period of residence.

Instead, Erasmus went to the University of Turin, a small, isolated institution of little renown where foreigners could get doctorates in even briefer periods of time. Indeed, ten English clergymen obtained doctorates of theology from the University of Turin between 1496 and 1511, and none are known to have spent much time there. Turin conferred a doctorate on Erasmus, an Augustinian canon and priest with permission to live outside his convent but with a growing reputation in letters and the ability to pay the fees.

---

physicians were members of religious orders. See Franceschini, 1970, 256–58, and *I maestri di Ferrara,* 1991, 14, 25–49 passim, 168–69.

137. Bini (1977, 242–63, 594) lists several friars who may have taught theology in the university in the mid-fifteenth century. But the information is vague.

138. Ermini, 1971, 226 n. 8, 235–36, 239, 619–21; Nicolini, 1961, 142, 149. Unfortunately, little is known about these lectureships.

139. Filangieri di Candida, 1924, 157, 168, 186; Cortese, 1924, 328–30.

140. What follows is a brief summary. For the full story including the Latin text and English translation of Erasmus's diploma, see Grendler, 1998.

141. *Erasmus,* 1974, letter 75 [Paris, c. April 1498], lines 15–16, p. 151.

Erasmus's diploma stated that a local Franciscan friar promoted his candidacy. It then stated that the Dominican deacon of the faculty of theology and other doctors of theology examined him, finding him sufficiently learned to merit the license and doctorate of theology. The vicar-general of the archbishop of Turin, in his role as vice-chancellor of the university, then conferred on Erasmus the license and doctorate of theology.

Obviously, Erasmus did not fulfill the requirements of years of study, teaching, and disputing in his fortnight in Turin. Nor had he satisfied them during his desultory and minimal theological studies at Paris between the autumn of 1495 and the summer of 1499. He was out of Paris as often as he was there and while in the city spent most of his time cultivating humanists and writing.[142] Beyond the examination, Erasmus met only the age requirement for the license and doctorate of theology: he was about forty years old in September 1506. In short, Erasmus exploited a minor university's willingness to give him a quick and easy doctorate. He obtained the degree in the hope that it would lend authority to his attacks on what he saw as wrong-headed Scholastic theologians and erring clergymen. Unfortunately, or perhaps with justice, the Paris theologians never recognized Erasmus's doctorate and heaped scorn on the university (never named by Erasmus) that conferred it.

TEACHING TEXTS

As in most other disciplines, professors of theology, metaphysics, and Scripture lectured on standard texts, the same texts taught in convent *studia*.

Aristotle's *Metaphysics* was always the basic text for metaphysics lectures. Indeed, the 1589 statutes of the school of arts and medicine of Padua required the metaphysicians to begin with the first book and to teach the whole over three years.[143] In practice, the Paduan metaphysicians concentrated on books 1, 7, and 12. For example, in 1568–69, both the Thomist and Scotist metaphysician taught book 12; in 1594–95 both taught book 7.[144] At Rome the metaphysicians also taught books 1, 7, and 12, in the last third of the sixteenth century.[145]

The reasons for concentrating on these three chapters (of fourteen) in the *Metaphysics* are easy to understand. Book 1 outlines the characteristics of metaphysics, which Aristotle also called "first philosophy," "wisdom," and even "theology" at times. It then offers a good survey of earlier Greek philosophy on

142. For Erasmus's Paris years and hostility toward the Scholastic theology taught there, see Farge, 1999.

143. *Statuta artistarum et medicorum Patavini Gymnasii,* 1589, p. 68ᵛ.

144. AAUP, Inventario 1320, no pag., rolls of 1568–69 and 1594–95; F. 651, f. 301ʳ, roll of 1584–85. Facciolati (1978, pt. 2:98) also points out that the metaphysicians concentrated on books 1, 7, and 12. Also see Poppi, 1981, 14.

145. *I maestri di Roma,* 1991, 51 (bk. 12), 60 (bk. 1), 65 (bk. 7), 75 (bk. 12), 86 (bk. 1), 88 (bk. 6), 98 (bk. 7), 100 (bk. 12), 114 (bk. 12), in rolls 1567–68 through 1579–80. As is the case everywhere, only a minority of the surviving rolls listed the books to be taught. Professors undoubtedly also referred to other books of the *Metaphysics,* and other works, in their lectures.

metaphysics, finding it inadequate. Book 7 discusses in detail his conception of substance, with forays into essence, form, and matter. Building on substance, book 12 develops Aristotle's famous argument for the Unmoved Mover or God.[146] The three books are the heart of Aristotle's work and were an appropriate metaphysical foundation for Scholastic theology.

The basic text for theology was the *Four Books of Sentences* of Peter Lombard (c. 1095–1160), a northern Italian who spent most of his career in Paris. More a compilation than an original work, the *Sentences* (written c. 1150) so effectively combined extensive quotations from biblical, patristic, and medieval authorities with clear dialectical organization that it became the basic theological textbook of the Middle Ages and the Renaissance.[147] Book 1 treated God, the Trinity, God's attributes, predestination, and evil. Book 2 discussed creation, angels, demons, the fall of man, grace, and sin. Book 3 dealt with the incarnation of God in Jesus, the redemption of man, the virtues, and the Ten Commandments. Book 4 analyzed the sacraments, death, judgment, hell, and heaven. The book covered the whole of Christian theology in a series of questions, which were further divided into subsections, or "distinctions," and smaller questions. Each book had forty to fifty distinctions that led the reader through all the major theological issues and controversies. Thanks to its dialectical presentation, a lecturer following the *Sentences* could present the past history of a question and then offer his own views within the scholarly tradition.

A professor of theology usually focused on one of the four books for his year's lectures. For example, in 1568–69 both the Scotist and Thomist theologians at the University of Padua taught book 1 of the Sentences. In the following year they both taught book 2.[148] Each lecturer probably used the commentaries on the *Sentences* written by the respective champions of their orders, Thomas Aquinas and Duns Scotus, plus other works in the Thomist and Scotist traditions.

The University of Rome with its four to six theologians offered a greater variety of theological lecturing but still used the *Sentences* as the basic text. Rather than teaching at the same hour as concurrents, the Roman theologians taught at different hours. For example, in 1579–80, the five teaching theologians offered the following instruction. The Dominican taught "de tractatu angelorum" from the first part of Thomas's *Summa theologiae* (probably part 1, questions 50–64) at the fourteenth hour (c. 9 A.M. in the autumn). The Augustinian Hermit taught book 1 of the *Sentences* at the fifteenth hour (10 A.M.). The Franciscan taught book 2 of the *Sentences* at the sixteenth hour (11 A.M.). The Servite taught book 4 of the *Sentences* at the twentieth hour (3 P.M.). And the Carmelite taught book 3 of the *Sentences* at the twenty-first hour (4 P.M.). The same pattern occurred in

---

146. See the English translation in Aristotle, 1941, 680–926.

147. Only three works from an immense bibliography on the *Sentences* and its influence will be mentioned here: de Ghellinck, 1948; *Miscellanea Lombardiana,* 1957; and Delhaye, 1961.

148. See these two rolls in AAUP, Inventario 1320, no pag. They did not lecture on all four books in a four-year cycle but concentrated on books 1 and 2, so far as can be determined. However, the 1589 statutes dropped the *Sentences* requirement and permitted the theologians to teach what they wished. *Statuta artistarum et medicorum Patavini Gymnasii,* 1589, 68ᵛ.

other years. Indeed, in 1570–71 an indefatigable student could attend daily lectures of all six theologians at six different hours.[149]

The Scripture lecturers had no statutory text but preferred Paul's Epistles. For example, at Padua the Scripture lecturer taught Paul's Epistle to the Hebrews in 1568–69 and the Book of Genesis in 1569–70. Other Paduan biblical lecturers taught the Epistle of Paul to the Romans in 1583–84, Galatians in 1584–85, and Hebrews from the fifth chapter onward in 1594–95. These books plus Paul's letters to the Corinthians were particularly favored.[150]

THE REPUTATION OF THEOLOGY

Even though theology, metaphysics, and biblical studies found secure homes in Italian universities, other members of the university community did not respect them.

Professors in other disciplines commonly dismissed metaphysics as of little importance. In 1573 Ulisse Aldrovandi, professor of natural philosophy and natural history at the University of Bologna, addressed a long memorandum to the chancellor of the university arguing for a reorganization of the teaching schedule. Metaphysics did not merit a prime time, because it was not a difficult subject. Aldrovandi was almost scornful. The majority of those who attended metaphysics lectures were friars; only a few "scholars" (*studiosi*) and beginners came. Students could learn metaphysics by themselves without lectures. Metaphysics "was not very necessary."[151]

Francesco Verino il Secondo, who taught natural philosophy and Platonic philosophy at the University of Pisa, also noted this attitude in 1587. Many considered metaphysics to be of secondary importance, and, for that reason, the metaphysicians were poorly paid, he wrote. Verino regretted this state of affairs and urged the authorities to pay the metaphysicians better. But he criticized the theological teaching at his university. Theologians should expound the sacred texts directly without mixing in human philosophy, he wrote. He wanted theology instruction to be based on the original texts without the Scholastic overlay, a typical humanistic approach.[152]

Paolo Beni (1553–c. 1625), professor of humanities at the University of Padua from 1600 to 1623, had little use for metaphysics and Scholastic theology as

---

149. *I maestri di Roma*, 1991, 75–79, 115–17. See also the rolls of 1567–68, 1568–69, 1569–70, and 1575–76, in ibid.

150. See AAUP, Inventario 1320, for the 1569–70 and 1594–95 rolls, and AAUP, F. 654, f. 290ᵛ, letter of Dec. 2, 1583, for what the Scripture professor was teaching in 1583–84; and F. 651, f. 301ʳ, for the 1584–85 roll. In 1577–78, the Scripture professor taught unspecified Epistles of Saint Paul. ASB, Assunteria di Studio, Bu. 100, fascicle 5, "Stato dello Studio di Padova," f. 2ᵛ. See also Poppi, 1981, 14.

151. "Perche alla metaphysica la maggior parte sono frati che l'ascoltano: e pochi altri studiosi e principianti, perche redendo philosophia continuamente li studiosi, da se possono intendere metaphysica sanza altre lettioni." And elsewhere, metaphysics "per non esser lettura tanto necessaria." BA, Ms. B 3803, Ulisse Aldrovandi, "Informatione del Rotulo del Studio di Bologna de' philosophi et medici all'Ill.mo Card. Paleotti," ff. 8ᵛ, 9ʳ.

152. Verino's memorandum of 1587 as quoted in Del Fante, 1980b, 403, 411.

taught by the friars.[153] Noting that some said that metaphysics lectures were useless and damaging to those who heard them, Beni posed the question, Should metaphysics be retained or changed in the university? In his complicated response, Beni did not reject Aristotelian metaphysics completely. Instead, he argued that a Platonic metaphysics better handled nonmaterial substances, while the disciplines of logic, natural philosophy, and mathematics, along with Aristotelian metaphysics, could teach other parts of the subject. But he had little use for Aristotelian metaphysics as preparation for Scholastic theology or the close links between the two.

Beni saw discussion of abstract and intricate metaphysical subtleties as harmful: "There is no doubt that scholastic theology is in good part reduced to metaphysical digressions and questions."[154] He wished that metaphysics would be taught without following either Duns Scotus or Thomas. And he criticized the mendicant order lecturers who taught the subject. They had no respect for the foundations and style of the Latin language; they lacked knowledge of languages, especially Greek, which were needed to study Aristotle. Every day they invented such abstruse, abstract, inaudible, horrible, and portentious terms that they ended up obscuring Aristotle rather than explaining him. It was no wonder that only members of a friar's own religious order came to hear his metaphysics lectures, Beni expostulated.[155]

However, Beni recognized that metaphysics taught by friars would not be eliminated. So he proposed moving them to a lesser position in the timetable. At Padua the two concurrent ordinary metaphysics professors lectured at the second morning hour (hour 13), followed by the two concurrent theology lecturers in the next hour. Beni did not think that such a useless subject should have one of the best hours of the morning. Metaphysics should be relegated to a holiday lectureship and its prime morning hour given to the professor of Scripture. The university had made the Scripture lectureship a holiday lectureship (teaching on Thursdays and holidays) about 1580; Beni wanted to restore it to ordinary status at a good hour.[156] Although differing in several ways, Aldrovandi, Verino, and

153. The following is based on ASVa, Archivio Beni, Ms. 123, autograph manuscript entitled "Discorso intorno alla riforma dello Studio di Padova." He intended it for the Venetian authorities overseeing the university, but whether he submitted it is not known. The material cited here is Beni's chapter 19, ff. [77–82].

154. "Perche non si vede a che uso poi serva l'haver' atteso a disputar così astratte et intricate sottigliezze se non fosse alla teologia scholastica . . . (poiche non è dubbio che la teologia scholastica par buona parte ridotta a digressioni o questioni metafisiche)." ASVa, Archivio Beni, Ms. 123, f. [80].

155. "Finalmente è cosa certa che gli ordini claustrali a quali vuol nelle publica università incaricarsi la lettura metafisica . . . de' loro (the friars') studij poco stimano o fondamenti di lingua latina o coltura di stile o cognitione di lingue massime Greca la qual'è tanto necessaria in Aristotele o eruditione. . . . Anziche inventano ogni giorno più termini così abstrusi, astratti, inauditi; per non dir' horribili e portentosi . . . tanto per dichiarar' Aristotele quanto per finir d'oscurarlo." "Laonde non mi maraviglio io poi, che non esse gli uditori di tal lectione altri quasi che religiosi dell'istess'ordine." ASVa, Archivio Beni, Ms. 123, ff. [81–82].

156. ASVa, Archivio Beni, Ms. 123, f. [82]. For Scripture as a holiday lectureship, see ASB, Assunteria dello Studio, Bu. 100, fascicle "Stato dello Studio di Padova," f. [2^{r}–^{v}]. See also the rolls of

Beni agreed that metaphysics and Scholastic theology did not measure up to other university disciplines.

ITALIAN CONVENT AND UNIVERSITY THEOLOGY, 1400–1600

Italian theology based on medieval Scholasticism resisted major change through the fifteenth and sixteenth centuries. Lorenzo Valla, who taught at the University of Rome in the years 1450–57, attacked Scholastic theology and offered the new approach of a biblical theology based on applying humanistic critical principles to the study of sacred texts. Some humanists followed his lead.[157] But despite the general humanist disdain for Scholastic theology, humanists and theologians in Italian universities did not battle each other as they did in northern European universities.

In northern Europe humanists struggled to gain admission into university faculties or to win more and better positions within them.[158] Feeling threatened, the established Scholastic theologians tried to bar them entry. The two forces launched missiles of bitter and often colorful invective against each other from the 1490s onward, as the humanist tide surged or receded. But in fifteenth-century Italy the humanists easily won a secure place in faculties of arts, where the theologians barely had a foothold. They were in no position to keep anyone out. And why should they care? Their primary home was the convent *studium,* from which the humanists, mostly laymen, were excluded and which did not interest them in any case. There was little common turf over which to fight.

A second reason for the struggle in northern universities was that the northern humanists "put their sickles into other men's crops," a complaint frequently voiced by northern theologians.[159] They felt that the humanists had invaded theology's sanctuary by using historical and philological criticism to interpret sacred texts. And adding insult to injury, the interlopers scornfully dismissed Scholasticism. The theologians fought back against the unqualified "grammarians" and "poets" who told them in haughty terms how better to serve the queen of sciences. Again, little of this occurred in Italy. After Valla, Italian university humanists did little biblical textual criticism but concentrated on classical texts. They did not "put their sickles into other men's crops." Italian university theologians and humanists mostly ignored each other.

Italian alternatives to traditional Scholastic theology came almost exclusively from humanistically inclined churchmen outside the universities and convent *studia.* A group of Roman humanists holding curial or other ecclesiastical positions articulated a classicizing theology between 1480 and 1520.[160] It did not

---

1594–95, 1597–98, and 1610 in AAUP, Inventario 1320, no pag. Facciolati (1978, pt. 3:267) sees it as a holiday lectureship from the beginning. But this does not appear to have been the case.

157. See Trinkaus, 1970, especially pt. 4; Trinkaus, 1988; and Vasoli, 1998d, all with much bibliography.

158. Rummel, 1995, esp. ch. 4.

159. Ibid., 84–85.

160. D'Amico, 1983, ch. 6. More generally on "humanist theology," see Vasoli, 1998a and 1998c.

enter the convents or universities. From the early 1520s into the 1540s, a number of Italians known collectively as *spirituali* developed an unsystematic theology that emphasized Pauline doctrines of sin and grace. Influenced by Luther's justification by faith but outside university circles, the movement lacked doctrinal cohesion. When some *spirituali* became Protestants, it withered.[161]

Within the religious orders, a group of Benedictine monasteries led by Santa Giustina of Padua developed a patristic theology that offered a convent alternative to traditional Scholasticism.[162] Based on Greek patristic writers, especially John Chrysostom, the Benedictines focused on the argument that man could be saved through restoration of his shattered human nature by faith. But so far as is known, none of these Benedictines taught theology, metaphysics, or Scripture in universities. Nor do they seem to have had much influence within the faculty of theology at Padua. Their theology went into decline after 1546, when the Council of Trent rendered doctrinal decisions that cast the shadow of heresy on their views.

A few prelates and theologians at the Council of Trent strongly challenged traditional theology in April and May 1546.[163] Following humanist principles, they wanted to discard Scholastic method in favor of placing primary emphasis on the Bible. To accomplish this, they wanted the council to order each religious order *studium* to establish a biblical lectureship, which would be the most important lectureship in the convent and would lead theological instruction. The goal was nothing less than the replacement of Scholastic theology with biblical theology. A secondary goal was to break the mendicant order monopoly of theological instruction through the establishment of biblical lectureships outside the convents.

Domiñgo Soto (1494–1560), the Dominican professor of theology at the University of Salamanca and Emperor Charles V's theological representative at the council, fought back. He argued that Scholasticism was essential to the teaching of theology and that religious orders should make their own decisions about the place of Scholastic theology. In effect, he argued for the continuing Scholasticism domination. Unable to agree, the council opted for a compromise. It ordered convents and monasteries to teach Scripture, but without specifying the position or role of such teaching. It also ordered universities to establish professorships of Scripture, and some did. But the council did not decide Scholasticism's fate at this time. In effect, the council endorsed the status quo, because convent *studia* already had Scripture instruction, but in a secondary position to the teaching of Peter Lombard's *Sentences* and Thomist or Scotist Scholasticism.

The 1546 debate at Trent was the closest the Catholic Church came to significant change in the teaching of theology or to breaking the monopoly of the mendicant orders in Italy. When the council returned to the subject of clerical

---

161. There is a large literature on this subject, especially on those figures who became Protestants. Prominent members were Cardinals Gasparo Contarini and Reginald Pole.

162. This is the subject of Collett, 1985.

163. See Jedin, 1961, 99–124, for the debate, and *Decrees*, 1990, 2:668–69, paragraphs 4, 5, and 6, for the decrees of June 17, 1546. The representative from the Benedictine Congregation of Santa Giustina was a leading critic of Scholasticism in the debates. See Collett, 1985, ch. 9, esp. 194–95.

training in 1563, it took the route of establishing diocesan seminaries, rather than discussing methodological innovation. But seminaries did not displace convent *studia* and university faculties of theology, both of which continued to play the major role in advanced training in theology.

Theological change came in the form of a revitalized Scholastic theology, usually called "New Scholasticism" or "Second Scholasticism," in the last third of the sixteenth century.[164] Thomism, endorsed by Dominicans and Jesuits, dominated Second Scholasticism.

Several factors made Thomism triumphant in New Scholasticism. First, Thomism may already have been stronger than its rivals by the late fifteenth century, as the teaching of Thomas's works at Pavia indicated. It may have had more distinguished, or more influential, representatives than did Scotism. And Thomas was the preferred Scholastic at the papal court in the late fifteenth century.[165] Second, the Thomist explanation of the economy of salvation was closest to the Tridentine formulation that both grace and works were needed for salvation. Thomism was a world-affirming theology suited to an Italy and Catholic Europe much influenced by the humanist emphasis on man's dignity and potential. Third, Pius V, a Dominican, gave the papal stamp of approval to Thomism in 1567 by conferring the title "Doctor of the Church" on Thomas Aquinas. He was the first new Doctor of the Church proclaimed after the eight patristic doctors (Gregory the Great, Ambrose, Augustine, and Jerome of the Latins, and John Chrysostom, Basil, Gregory Nazianzen, and Athanasius of the Greeks) so honored in the Middle Ages. By contrast, John Duns Scotus was never canonized or designated a Doctor of the Church.[166] Finally, Jesuit theologians, while somewhat eclectic, had an optimistic view of man's nature which was closer to Thomism than Scotism. In 1586 and 1599, the Society of Jesus adopted Thomism as the theology and metaphysics to be taught in all the schools of the order.[167]

However, Italian mendicant order theologians teaching in convent *studia* and universities did not lead Second Scholasticism.[168] Dominican theologians teaching in Spain, such as Francisco de Vitoria (1483/92–1546), Domiñgo Soto, Bartolomé Carranza (1503–76), and Bartolomé de Medina (1527–81), did. Dominicans and Carmelites in Italian convents and universities taught Thomism as followers. The most intellectually forceful New Scholastics teaching and writing in Italy at the end of the sixteenth century were Jesuits, such as Robert Bellarmine (1542–1621) and Francisco de Toledo (1532–96). But they taught in their

164. See Giacon, 1944–50, esp. vol. 1. Much additional bibliography can be found in specialized studies.

165. O'Malley, 1979, 148–49.

166. The Franciscan Scholastic Saint Bonaventure of Bagnorea (1221–74) was named Doctor of the Church in 1587, but his theology, with its mystical bent, did not become a major stream in Scholastic theology.

167. There is an enormous amount of material on the adoption of Thomism in *Monumenta Paedagogica Societatis Iesu*, 1986, 1992a, and 1992b.

168. This is not to diminish the contributions of the Dominican Thomists, Cajetan and Francesco dei Silvestri da Ferrara (1474–1528).

own institutions, like the Collegio Romano, rather than in Italian universities or convent *studia*. Meanwhile, Franciscans and Augustinians continued to teach Scotism into the seventeenth century.

Scholars do not hold fifteenth- and sixteenth-century Italian mendicant order theology in high regard. The distinguished historian of theology and philosophy Antonino Poppi has characterized European theology in general, and Italian theology in particular, after 1378 as an epoch of "speculative weariness" and one of the bleakest periods in the history of Western theology. In his view, theology lacked creativity because it was overly reverential to the great thirteenth-century syntheses. Hence, fifteenth-century theologians concentrated on nominal and gnoseological (cognitive) subtleties, plus ecclesiastical issues.[169]

Since research on the rank and file of Italian theologians is sparse, judgments must be tentative.[170] Nevertheless, the fact that universities and convents taught Thomism and Scotism supports Poppi's fundamental criticism; they certainly honored these medieval syntheses. And the numerous treatises for and against conciliarism, on the role of riches and poverty in the church, and for and against the doctrine of the Immaculate Conception document his contention that theologians spent much intellectual energy on ecclesiastical issues. Most important, all the signs suggest that the vast majority of the Dominicans, Franciscans, Augustinians, Carmelites, and Servites in Italian universities continued to teach medieval Scholasticism of their predecessors with little originality. Very few theologians who taught in Italian universities and convent *studia* are remembered today.[171]

By the end of the sixteenth century, Italian universities had more religious studies positions and had conferred many more doctorates of theology than in the fifteenth century. But faculties of theology did not become full teaching schools, like schools of law and arts and medicine, within the university. If the instruction of the mendicant orders had been fully incorporated into the civic university, lay authorities would have insisted on appointing all the theologians and would have intervened in other ways. Such intervention might have—or might not have—changed theological instruction. Free of civic control, faculties of theology and individual mendicant order *studia* preserved their autonomy and went their own ways.[172] The price was that theology seems to have been the least innovative of university disciplines during the Renaissance.

169. Poppi, 1981, 16–17. While noting the deference to the great medieval Scholastics, Brotto and Zonta (1922, 131–32) and Vasoli (1998b) are less critical. One hastens to add that the criticism is leveled against theology only. Members of the mendicant orders made valuable contributions to Renaissance humanism and learning generally. See Kristeller, 1974, 95–158.

170. Italian theology of the fifteenth and sixteenth centuries is the least studied of all scholarly disciplines in the Italian Renaissance.

171. It is striking how few Italian names appear in the survey of Catholic theology in the fourteenth, fifteenth, and sixteenth centuries of Grabmann (1961, 92–122, 148–85).

172. Cremascoli (1989, 189) makes this point.

Moral Philosophy

f the few universities that taught moral philosophy, Padua was the most important, especially in the second half of the sixteenth century. Aristotle's moral books provided the texts, but humanism had a major impact on the teaching.

MORAL PHILOSOPHY IN THE LATE MIDDLE AGES

University teaching of moral philosophy did not begin until medieval scholars translated Aristotle's *Nicomachean Ethics, Politics,* and the pseudo-Aristotelian *Economics* into Latin. Robert Grosseteste made the first complete Latin translation of the *Nicomachean Ethics* in 1246 and 1247, and William of Moerbeke finished his Latin translation of the *Politics* about 1260. An anonymous Latin translation of the *Economics* appeared in the early thirteenth century, followed by a translation of books 1 and 3 by Durandus of Auvergne about 1295. The Middle Ages and Renaissance held the *Economics* to be Aristotle's work—despite its mixture of Aristotelian concepts and material from Xenophon and the Stoics.[1]

Some notable northern European Scholastics taught and published commentaries on these texts in the late thirteenth century and in the first third of the fourteenth. Northern European universities, especially those in central Europe, sometimes required students to attend lectures on the *Nicomachean Ethics* and (less often) the *Politics* and *Economics* in the late fourteenth and the fifteenth centuries.

---

1. Although written about the same time, the three books of the *Economics* may have been the product of several hands. A pupil of Aristotle may have been written book 1, which sometimes follows closely the *Politics,* between 325 and 275 B.C. Book 2, with its non-Aristotelian anecdotes and discussion about raising money, differs considerably from book 1. The Greek text of book 3 is lost. The Latin text of book 3 seems to add Stoic material from the second and third centuries A.D. See Soudek, 1968, 54 n. 2, and Bruni, 1987, 301, 388–89 n. 6. The *Eudemian Ethics* (which considerably overlaps the content of the *Nichomachean Ethics*), the pseudo-Aristotelian *De virtutibus et vitiis,* and the *Magna moralia,* about whose authenticity scholars differ, played very minor roles in Aristotelian moral philosophy of the Renaissance and are not discussed in this chapter.

Moral philosophy was a lesser subject on the road to the master of arts, not the doctorate.[2]

Medieval Italian universities gave moral philosophy a minor place as supplementary instruction in other subjects, medicine in particular. Bolognese medical professors included material on the *Ethics, Politics,* and *Economics* in their lectures, and one of them delivered a series of lectures on the *Economics,* between 1265 and 1325. The material fitted into a broad conception of medical instruction. For example, the professor might supplement his lectures on human conception and birth with comments on marriage, family, parents, and children from the *Economics.*[3] The 1405 statutes for arts and medicine at Bologna recognized the irregular presence of the *libri morales,* which were not required for any subject. If a professor wished to offer extraordinary lectures on them, he might charge 20 soldi for lectures on the *Ethics,* 20 soldi for the *Politics,* and 5 soldi for the *Economics.*[4] Italian convent *studia* sometimes also taught the *libri morales* as preparation for theology. For example, in 1315 a Dominican friar taught moral philosophy at the convent *studium* of Sant'Eustorgio in Milan by lecturing on the *Ethics, Politics, Economics,* and *Rhetoric.*[5]

Moral philosophy occasionally appeared as a subject in university rolls in the late fourteenth and early fifteenth centuries. The University of Bologna had one or two professors in the 1380s and 1390s; they received very low salaries and sometimes taught another subject as well.[6] In the first quarter of the fifteenth century, one to three professors taught natural philosophy and moral philosophy together at Bologna.[7] The holders of these ill-paid combined positions were unknown figures.

Moral philosophy also appeared irregularly and infrequently at the University of Pavia. From the late 1380s through 1408, a single professor taught moral philosophy plus another subject. In 1387–88, a friar taught moral philosophy and theology. In 1389–90 a layman taught the unusual combination of moral philosophy and astrology. From 1391–92 through 1394–95, a friar again taught moral philosophy and theology. These combination positions were poorly paid, usually 20 to 60 florins. Then from 1403–4 through 1408, the well-known Biagio Pelacani of Parma (c. 1365–1416) taught moral philosophy, astrology, and mathematics.[8]

2. Wieland, 1982; Dunbabin, 1982; Overfield, 1984, 41–42, 212; and Siraisi, 1981, 73.

3. Siraisi, 1981, 72–95. On the other hand, it does not appear that the *Ethics, Politics,* and *Economics* were taught at the University of Padua before 1350. Siraisi, 1973.

4. Malagola, 1966, 252; also noted by Siraisi, 1981, 87.

5. The Dominican lecturer was Galvano Fiamma; Airaghi, 1984, 357–58.

6. Dallari, 1888–1924, 1:4 (1384–85), 5, 7 (1388–89). The salaries were 25 Bolognese lire or nothing.

7. Ibid., 4:*Aggiunte,* 28, 30, 32, 34, 36, 38, 40, 41, 43, 45, and 1:9. See also Lines, 1996, 172–74.

8. Maiocchi, 1971, 1:117, 129, 153, 184, 220, 227; vol. 2, pt. 1:40 (quotation below), 68, 84, 98. Pelacani's appointment was listed as follows: "M. Blaxius de Parma simul cum lectura Philosophie moralis, Astrologie et cum mathematicis." Not all annual rolls are available. A list of moral philosophers from the late fourteenth century through 1600 is found in *Memorie di Pavia,* 1970, 153–76, 185–

Francesco da Conegliano taught both natural philosophy as an ordinary professor and ethics on holidays at the University of Florence from 1365 through 1370. Then between 1391 and 1397, Florence had one or two moral philosophers who sometimes also taught natural philosophy. Next, from 1414–15 through 1421–22, a single professor, often a friar, taught moral philosophy, sometimes with natural philosophy, either as ordinary professor or as a *diebus festivis* lecturer.[9]

Moral philosophy based on the three Aristotelian moral texts had little weight in Italian universities in the late fourteenth and early fifteenth centuries. Indeed, northern European scholars produced many more commentaries on the three Aristotelian moral texts than Italians did.[10]

HUMANISTIC MORAL PHILOSOPHY AT THE UNIVERSITY OF FLORENCE

In September 1362 the Venetian government hailed Petrarch as the greatest moral philosopher and poet of Christendom.[11] The description was appropriate, if exaggerated, because Petrarch and his followers saw moral philosophy as central to the *studia humanitatis* and their vision of man. Although they seldom taught in universities, numerous humanists wrote treatises on moral philosophy. They created a humanistic moral philosophy that entered the University of Florence.

The generation of humanists reaching maturity around 1400 concluded that universities failed to teach men how to live and wrote treatises to remedy the deficiency.[12] Early-fifteenth-century Florentine humanists in particular saw the *Ethics, Politics,* and *Economics* as texts teaching appropriate conduct for the active life. Leonardo Bruni led the way by publishing a translation of the *Nicomachean Ethics* in 1416–17, an annotated translation of the *Economics* in 1420, and a translation of the *Politics* in 1437.[13] Since the *Politics* dealt with the conduct of government, the *Nicomachean Ethics* with the individual's ethics in society, and the *Economics* with the management of the family and its wealth, all three were essential elements of civic humanism. In the words of Eugenio Garin, "It is not

---

89, passim, but the listings are incomplete and sometimes at variance with the rolls. Lines, 1996, 183–88, is much better.

9. Park, 1980, 260–64, 273–81, passim; Spagnesi, 1979, 271–72; Lines, 1996, 167–69.

10. See Lohr, 1967, 1968, 1970, 1971, 1972, 1973, and 1974a.

11. This happened as Petrarch came to take up residence in Venice, at the government's expense. Wilkins, 1961, 186.

12. See *Cambridge Translations,* 1997, for English translations of treatises of moral philosophy, or parts of them, of Petrarch, Coluccio Salutati, Francesco Filelfo, and Poggio Bracciolini. See Trinkaus, 1970.

13. The following is based on Garin, 1947–50; Garin, 1961, 60–72; Soudek, 1968; and Field, 1988. See Bruni, 1969, 20–49, 70–96, 120–21, for the relevant texts and prefaces to his translations of the *libri morales* of Aristotle. For English translations of Bruni's *Isagogue,* the *Life of Aristotle,* and other relevant texts, plus an excellent commentary, see Bruni, 1987, 254–317, 377–90. For the story within the broader European context, see Schmitt, 1979a, and 1983c, 64–88.

an exaggeration to affirm that all of Florentine civic humanism of the early fifteenth century moved under the sign of a rediscovered moral Aristotle."[14]

Bruni abandoned the medieval word-for-word translation method and attempted to turn the Aristotelian Greek into coherent and elegant, but less technical, Latin. At the same time, the originality and humanistic quality of his translations varied, because Bruni sometimes simply adapted medieval translations to humanistic tastes. Nevertheless, his efforts won the approval of humanists south and north of the Alps, and his translations of the three texts had an enormous *fortuna*. Bruni also wrote an *Isagogue of Moral Philosophy* between 1424 and 1426 and a *Life of Aristotle* in 1429, both of which argued for an Aristotle congruent with Florentine civic humanism. A few years later the Florentine humanist Donato Acciaiuoli (1429–78), who, like Bruni, was not a university teacher, published influential commentaries on the *Ethics* (1464) and *Politics* (1472).[15]

Perhaps as a result of the activities of the civic humanists outside the university, moral philosophy entered the University of Florence in humanistic dress with the Augustinian Hermit and humanist Andrea di Piero da Milano, or Andrea Biglia (c. 1395–1435). Born in Milan, Biglia learned Greek in his youth, joined the Augustinian order, studied at Padua, and enjoyed close rapport with several major humanists. When he moved to the convent of Santo Spirito in Florence in 1418, Biglia joined the humanist circle of Leonardo Bruni and Niccolò Niccoli. In 1419–20 Biglia began teaching moral philosophy at the Florentine *studium,* which became moral philosophy and natural philosophy in the following two years, 1420–22.[16]

Then the title of Biglia's Florentine professorship changed to "moral philosophy, poetry, and rethoric" (*Filosofiam moralem, Poesiam et Rhettoricam*) at a salary of 35 florins in 1422–23.[17] Whether or not Biglia taught differently than before, the new title indicated the union of moral philosophy and humanism in the university. Indeed, Biglia was an active humanist who wrote a history of Milan, an account of the decline of Eastern Christianity, and a number of funeral orations, all in humanistic oratorical style. Biglia also wrote commentaries on Aristotle's *Metaphysics* and book 4 of *De caelo et mundo,* which gave proof of his competence in natural philosophy. But he did not write commentaries on the *libri morales* of Aristotle, so far as is known.

Biglia left Florence in 1423. After a hiatus of eight years, the University of

14. Non è esagerato affermare che tutto l'umanesimo civile fiorentino del primo '400 si muove sotto il segno del ritrovato Aristotele morale, 'aureo fiume' d'eloquenza. Garin, 1961, 66. See also Soudek, 1968, 95. Baron, 1966, is the key work for civic humanism.

15. See *Cambridge Translations,* 1997, 47–58, for a translation of book 2, chapter 7, of the commentary on the *Ethics.* It is surprisingly Scholastic in form and content. See also Field, 1988, 202–30 and passim.

16. For the teaching appointments, see Park, 1980, 278–81, and Lines, 1996, 169. For additional information on Biglia in this and the following paragraph, see Biglia, 1968; Baron, 1966, 393; Lohr, 1967, 358; Webb, 1976a and 1976b; Piana, 1977, 35; Black, 1985a, 206, 217, 227–28; Ianziti, 1988, 17–18; and McManamon, 1989, index.

17. For the appointment notice, see Gherardi, 1973, 402.

Florence in 1431 added two humanists whose responsibilities included teaching moral philosophy. The Florentines gave the famous Francesco Filelfo, who had been teaching at Florence since 1429, a three-year contract to teach rhetoric and poetry as ordinary professor, plus Dante and moral philosophy on holidays. He began a course of lectures on the *Nicomachean Ethics* on December 30, 1431, presumably to fulfill his moral philosophy obligation.[18] Also in 1431 the university appointed Carlo Marsuppini, a local favorite who published little, to teach "poetry, rhetoric, philosophy, Greek, and ethics" at a lower salary.[19] The two descriptions demonstrated that moral philosophy had been subsumed into humanistic studies.

Filelfo left Florence after two years, and Marsuppini's appointment notice dropped ethics after 1434. After a lapse of several years, a Dominican friar taught philosophy (presumably natural philosophy) and ethics in 1438–39, and another priest taught logic, ethics, and "moral politics" (*politica moralis*) in 1439–40.[20] Moral philosophy then disappeared from the rolls of the University of Florence.

Nevertheless, some professors of Florence continued to study Aristotle's *libri morales* in a humanistic context. Nicolò Tignosi da Foligno (1402–74) taught logic briefly at the University of Bologna and medical theory at Perugia in the 1420s. He then joined the humanists enjoying Medici patronage in Florence. Tignosi taught medical theory at the University of Florence in 1439–40 and again in 1450–51. In 1459 or 1460, Tignosi completed an extensive commentary on the *Nicomachean Ethics*. Using Bruni's translation, he affirmed a civic humanist interpretation of the work, praising Cosimo de' Medici as a great civic example, while also providing a philosophical examination of the different activities of humans. Tignosi later taught philosophy and medicine at the University of Pisa 1473–74.[21] A medical professor with broad knowledge (he also wrote a commentary on Aristotle's *De anima*), Tignosi became caught up in the humanist enthusiasm for the moral works of Aristotle.

John Argyropoulos prepared a new Latin translation of the *Nicomachean Ethics* in the late 1450s when lecturing on the text at the University of Florence.[22] He criticized Bruni's translation of the *Nicomachean Ethics* and did not offer a civic interpretation of the *Ethics*. Although Argyropoulos's translation was superior,

18. For Filelfo's appointments, see Park, 1980, 288, 290; Gherardi, 1973, 245, 415–19, 424, 426–27; and Lines, 1996, 169. See Zippel, 1979, 232, for his course on the *Ethics*. Years later, in 1473, Filelfo began to write *De morali disciplina*, a large work of moral philosophy on a broad metaphysical canvas which included reconciling Plato and Aristotle. Although left unfinished, it testified to Filelfo's strong interest in moral philosophy. See Robin, 1991, 149–66, 226–46, for a discussion of book 1 and additional bibliography.

19. For Marsuppini's appointments, see Gherardi, 1973, 414, 441; Park, 1980, 288, 291; and Lines, 1996, 169. For further bibliography on Marsuppini, see Chapter 6, note 65.

20. Park 1980, 296–97; Lines, 1996, 169.

21. Rotondò (1958) stresses the civic aspect of Tignosi's commentary, while Field (1988, 38–58) notes its broader philosophical dimension. See also Lohr, 1972, 306–7, and Verde, 1973–94, 2:504–5.

22. Field, 1988, 114, 115 n. 28, 123–24, 126; Lines, 1996, 169–70.

Bruni's translations of the *Economics* and *Politics* continued to be widely used through the end of the sixteenth century. Indeed, the civic humanists' embrace of the *libri morales* of Aristotle probably led to the introduction of moral philosophy into the University of Florence and bringing the discipline into the humanistic orbit.

MORAL PHILOSOPHY IN OTHER UNIVERSITIES

Elsewhere, moral philosophy oscillated between humanistic studies, natural philosophy, and the Christian Aristotle of the friars. The discipline began as a shared appointment with another discipline or two and then gradually became an independent professorship in its own right. But many universities ignored moral philosophy.

Andrea Biglia, who had previously taught moral philosophy, poetry, and rhetoric at Florence, illustrated the mixed nature of moral philosophy elsewhere. He taught the combination of natural and moral philosophy at the University of Bologna for three academic years, 1424–25 through 1427–28.[23] After a brief stay in Pavia, Biglia also taught moral and natural philosophy at the University of Siena in 1429–30. He added theology on festival days, thanks to a doctorate of theology acquired at some point. But he also remained a humanist, because he praised oratory in his oration of October 1430 inaugurating the Sienese academic year. He may have continued to teach at Siena until his premature death in 1435.[24]

Moral philosophy emerged as an independent subject taught by an extraordinary professor on holidays (*diebus festivis*) at the University of Bologna in the 1430s.[25] It remained an extraordinary holiday lectureship taught by two, three, or four professors through the rest of the fifteenth century and into the sixteenth. It then briefly gravitated into the theological orbit. From 1507–8 through 1513–14, one or both of the mendicant order friars who taught metaphysics added the holiday teaching of moral philosophy to their duties. Then in a radical change of direction, Pietro Pomponazzi added the extraordinary holiday moral philosophy post to his ordinary professorship in natural philosophy (1514–21). A second, minor figure occasionally also taught moral philosophy alongside him. Unfortunately, the contents of Pomponazzi's moral philosophy lectures are unknown, and he left no commentaries on Aristotle's *libri morales*.[26] Given his embrace of a non-Christian Stoic ethics in the *De immortalitate animae*, it is likely that his moral philosophy lectures were very different from those of the friars.

After Pomponazzi relinquished the holiday moral philosophy professorship, a

---

23. Dallari, 1888–1924, 4:*Aggiunte*, 48, 50, 55. Webb (1976a) does not note Biglia's teaching appointment at the University of Bologna. Lines (1996, 174) does.

24. Biglia, 1968, 414; Fioravanti, 1981, 17.

25. Dallari, 1888–1924, 1:12, 13, and passim; Lines, 1996, 154–55, 174–78.

26. Dallari, 1888–1924, 1:198, 202, 205, 209, 215; 2:5, 8, 11, 15, 18, 21, 25, 27. Lohr, 1980, 645–70, for the lack of commentaries on the *Ethics, Politics,* and *Economics.*

single professor held the position from 1521–22 through 1528–29. It then disappeared until 1563. It reappeared as a single ordinary professorship of moral philosophy, which continued through the end of the century.[27] No well-known scholar held the position after Pomponazzi.

The University of Padua lacked a moral philosophy professorship in the first three decades of the fifteenth century.[28] In 1430, Padua hired an Augustinian Hermit to teach moral philosophy and logic at the very low salary of 15 florins. Another lecturer teaching only moral philosophy followed in the mid-1430s.[29] The university then had only the occasional moral philosopher over the next sixty years. The Venetian noble and humanist Ermolao Barbaro the Younger (1453/54–93) taught Aristotle's *Nicomachean Ethics* in 1475–76 and the *Politics* in 1476–77 at Padua, plus Aristotle's *Rhetoric* in 1479–80. Barbaro then abandoned university teaching for a political career and private studies.[30]

Moral philosophy became a minor ordinary professorship at Padua in the sixteenth century. The Venetian Senate suspended the post in 1506 but revived it in 1509 at the very low salary of 15 florins.[31] After the years of closure and near

27. Dallari, 1888–1924, vol. 2. The post was doubled for five years, 1587–88 through 1591–92. See also Lines, 1996, 178–79.

28. Facciolati (1978, pt. 2:119) stated that Gasparino Barzizza taught moral philosophy on holidays in addition to his ordinary professorship of rhetoric from 1407 through 1421; and Poppi (1976, 106, 138 n. 12) agrees. However, Mercer (1979, 38–40) doubts this. He points out that Barzizza's appointment was "in Rhetoricis et Moralibus (Auctoribus)." Mercer further demonstrates that Barzizza taught Seneca, Cicero, Valerius Maximus, Vergil, and Terence, which were standard humanities fare, rather than the Aristotelian *libri morales*. In his lectures on the above authors, Barzizza referred to Aristotle's *Nicomachean Ethics* but never lectured directly on it. Archival evidence supports Mercer's contention. A partial list of professors of Sept. 12, 1407, includes "Mag. Gasparo [Barzizza] de Pergamo [= Bergamo] in Retoricis" but makes no reference to moral philosophy. AAUP, F. 648, f. 10ᵛ. See also the roll of 1422–23 in table 1.2.

29. See the arts roll of 1430–31 in AAUP, F. 648, f. 54ʳ; it is printed accurately in Cessi, 1909, 143. See also Facciolati, 1978, pt. 2:119–21. The arts rolls of 1434 through 1437 list Venanzio da Camerino teaching moral philosophy *in diebus festivis*. See AAUP, F. 648, ff. 79ʳ–ᵛ, 80ʳ–ᵛ, 81ʳ–ᵛ. Tomasini (1986, 155–57) accurately prints these rolls. Poppi (1976, 138–39 n. 12) gives a complete list of the moral philosophers at Padua through 1560 based on AAUP, F. 668. His study is fundamental. Lines (1996, 179–83) also provides a full list of the Paduan moral philosophers through 1624.

30. Facciolati, 1978, pt. 2:120. There is some disagreement concerning the dates of Barbaro's teaching. Barbaro's lectures on the *Ethics* were published posthumously as *Compendium Ethicorum librorum* in 1544, with a date of "Patavii pridie kal. decembris 1474" (Padua, Nov. 25, 1474), according to Lohr (1968, 237). Paschini (1957, 13) notes that Barbaro completed his lectures on the *Politics* on Feb. 20, 1476, and believes that this date was Venetian style, that is, 1477. If Paschini is correct, Barbaro lectured on the two texts in the years 1475–77 instead of 1474–76, as Bigi (1964, 96) stated. Paschini adds that Barbaro also taught Aristotle's *Rhetoric* in 1479 at Padua. Poppi (1976, 138 n. 12) lists Barbaro as appointed to teach moral philosophy on Jan. 27, 1477 (if Venetian style, this would be 1478). Whichever dates are correct, Barbaro taught moral philosophy at Padua for a limited time in the late 1470s, before the Venetian government in 1477 and 1479 forbade its nobles from teaching there. By 1484 Barbaro had returned to Venice and begun a diplomatic career. See King, 1986, 322–23, for the rest of his career and more bibliography.

31. Facciolati, 1978, pt. 2:120–21. For confirmation, see the roll of 1500–1501 printed in Favaro, 1922, 75–77, and that of 1509–10 with salaries, in AAUP, F. 651, ff. 1ʳ–2ʳ.

closure (1509–17), Padua had an ordinary moral philosophy professorship from 1518 until 1561, with the occupant changing practically every year.[32] Moral philosophy was a temporary position for new graduates. Almost all laymen in their early twenties, they had just received their degrees, sometimes on the same day they were appointed to teach moral philosophy. They taught for one year and then disappeared. The stipend remained at 15 florins, at the lowest level of professorial salaries.[33]

Then in 1561, the Venetian Senate called from Bologna the humanist Francesco Robortello to come and hold the positions of ordinary rhetoric and poetry and ordinary moral philosophy at the very high salary of 400 florins.[34] Robortello may have wanted to add the minor professorship of moral philosophy in order to strengthen his position against Carlo Sigonio, who had been appointed to teach rhetoric and poetry in 1560. Each saw himself as Padua's leading humanist. Both laid claim to the lecture hall normally used by the humanist professor, forcing students and Venetian senators to choose sides. Differing in their interpretations of ancient Roman history and much else, they hurled invectives until Sigonio moved to the University of Bologna in 1563. Robortello remained at Padua, teaching both rhetoric and moral philosophy, until his death on March 18, 1567.[35] Beyond the personal quarrel, the decision to combine rhetoric and moral philosophy had other consequences. The university authorities had raised the status of moral philosophy and saw it as closely allied to the humanities.

Upon Robortello's death, the Venetian Senate left the moral philosophy position vacant for ten years. It reappeared in 1577 with the appointment of Giason

32. See the lists in Riccobono, 1980, 26[r]–[v]; Tomasini, 1986, 322–23; Facciolati, 1978, pt. 3:313–15; and especially Poppi, 1976, 107, 138–39 n. 12. There are a few differences from list to list; nevertheless, the rolls found in AAUP confirm their overall accuracy. See AAUP, Inventario 1320, numerous rolls, and F. 651, ff. 120 [r]–[v] (roll of 1534–35), 129[r]–[v] (1535–36), 206[r]–[v] (1553–54), all of which list a single ordinary moral philosopher paid 15 florins.

33. See, for example, the roll with salaries of 1535–36 in AAUP, F. 651, f. 129[r]–[v]. Nine arts professors (of the total of 29) were paid 10, 15, or 20 florins. They included the lowest-paid extraordinary professors of practical and theoretical medicine, three ordinary logicians, two third-position teachers of Avicenna, the professor of surgery, and the moral philosopher. The rest of the arts and medicine salaries ranged from 50 to 400 florins, and 400 to 800 ducats, worth more than the florin.

34. Poppi, 1976, 107–8, 139 n. 15, citing an AAUP document describing the appointment as "Ad philosophiam moralem ordinariam et politicam, et ordinariam rhetoricam et poeticam." However, the rolls simply refer to moral philosophy.

35. For the dispute between Sigonio and Robortello, see the excellent discussion in McCuaig, 1989, 43–49. See in particular the descriptions of Robortello's combined professorship from archival records in McCuaig, 1989, 44 n. 126. There is one minor error in McCuaig's account. On p. 44, he states "there had never been an ordinary chair in moral philosophy" at the University of Padua. The evidence cited above demonstrates that it did exist as a minor and poorly paid ordinary professorship. It must be said that the archival sources often fail to distinguish between ordinary and extraordinary professorships and that it is sometimes difficult to determine which was which. With the appointment of Giason De Nores in 1577 (see below), moral philosophy became a well-paid extraordinary professorship. On Robortello's position, see also Tomasini, 1986, 323; Facciolati, 1978, pt. 3:315; and Riccobono, 1980, 26[v]. See AAUP, F. 651, f. 154[v], for Robortello's death.

De Nores (c. 1530–90) as extraordinary professor of moral philosophy. De Nores taught on holidays at the considerable salary of 200 florins, subsequently raised to 250, then 300 florins.[36] A Cypriot noble who came to Venice after the fall of Cyprus to the Turks in 1570, De Nores was an active scholar who published on Aristotle's *libri morales,* plus a variety of ancient authors who were the normal objects of research of humanist professors of rhetoric and poetry. With this continuing appointment at a good salary, moral philosophy became a significant, humanistically oriented professorship at the University of Padua.

After De Nores's death, the post remained vacant for two years. Then in 1592 Niccolò Colonio of Bergamo, another scholar with humanistic interests, took the position at 200 florins. He quickly became involved in a controversy with the humanist professor Antonio Riccobono over Horace's *Epistola ad Pisones.* Possibly the moral philosopher had ventured into territory that the humanist felt was his.[37] Colonio left the university in 1594 and was replaced by a Paduan clergyman, the canon Giovanni Belloni. The latter received a salary of 150 florins, which eventually rose to 650, as he continued in the post until his death in 1624.[38] Belloni seems to have been humanistically inclined, and he had an interest in Plato, but he published very little.[39] From Belloni in 1594 through the end of the eighteenth century, all the professors of moral philosophy were clergymen, either Paduan canons, mendicant order friars, or members of the new religious orders of the Catholic Reformation. They brought both humanistic and theological interests to the post.[40]

While Padua elevated the status of moral philosophy, other universities did not. The University of Pavia had a single ordinary moral philosopher between 1418–19 and 1428–29 and again in the 1440s.[41] In the second half of the fifteenth century moral philosophy became a holiday lectureship taught by one or two unknown figures, sometimes friars, at salaries as low as 12 florins. The moral philosopher sometimes taught theology or natural philosophy as well.[42] After

---

36. He taught at the first afternoon hour at a salary of 200 florins, according to the description of the University of Padua found in ASB, Assunteria di Studio, Bu. 100, fascicle 5, "Stato dello Studio di Padova," f. 2ᵛ, no date but c. 1580. See also AAUP, F. 651, f. 302ʳ; Riccobono, 1980, 79ʳ; Tomasini, 1986, 323; Facciolati, 1978, pt. 3:315–16; Lohr, 1979, 541–42; G. Patrizi, 1990; and Lines, 1996, 183.

37. For the dispute, see Facciolati, 1978, pt. 3:316; see also Poppi, 1976, 108, 139–40 n. 17. Riccobono had a strong interest in the Aristotelian moral works. He translated books 3, 4, and 8 of the *Nicomachean Ethics,* commented on the whole work, and wrote some "Notae" on the *Politics.* Lohr, 1980, 689–91.

38. Riccobono, 1980, 79ʳ; Tomasini, 1986, 323; Facciolati, 1978, pt. 3:316; Poppi, 1976, 108, 140 n. 18; Lines, 1996, 183. See also the roll of 1594–95, which lists Belloni teaching "Ad Philosophiam Moralem Aristotelis" on "diebus festivis." AAUP, Inventario 1320, no pag. See AAUP, F. 651, f. 425ᵛ, for the roll of 1616–17.

39. Belloni published in 1601 a work in Italian on naiads in Homer. See Pontani, 1981, 156–57.

40. Poppi, 1976, 106, 137–38 n. 7.

41. Maiocchi, 1971, vol. 2, pt. 1:167, 185, 222, 232, 240, 247, 395; vol. 2, pt. 2:433, 485, 496.

42. For example, see the rolls from 1469–70 through 1499–1500, with gaps, in ASPv, Università, Cartone 22, ff. 153ʳ–225ʳ, passim, and the roll of 1483–84 in ASPv, Università, Cartone 20, no pag. See also Verde, 1973–94, 1:387, 392, rolls of 1480–81, 1482–83, and Sottili, 1982, 548, 549.

years of war in the early sixteenth century, the roll of 1538–39 listed a single holiday moral philosopher. The post then disappeared.[43] Moral philosophy seems to have been a casualty when the university reduced the nonmedical part of its arts faculty in the second half of the sixteenth century.

The University of Rome had a little moral philosophy, with the subject initially seen as close to, or part of, the humanities. In 1514–15 the young humanist Paolo Giovio and an unidentified "Damianus" taught it. In 1563–64 Marc'Antoine Muret, an eminent humanist, taught moral philosophy; his post became "moral philosophy and good letters" (*In philosophia morali et candidioribus litteris*) in 1566–67.[44] Since Muret published commentaries on the *Nicomachean Ethics*, the *Economics*, and the *Rhetoric*, and numerous other classical literary and historical texts, he clearly viewed moral philosophy as part of humanistic studies.[45] In 1567–68 Muret abandoned the position to teach humanistic jurisprudence and later rhetoric. After a hiatus of twenty years, the university reestablished in 1586 or 1587 a moral philosophy professorship, which continued to the end of the century and beyond.[46] The subject matter was now Aristotle. Thus, moral philosophy at Rome changed from a rarely taught humanities subject into a lectureship on Aristotle's *libri morales*.

Two other universities taught moral philosophy on a limited basis. The University of Ferrara had a regular professorship in the subject, taught by an unknown figure at a low salary, only for the twenty-year period 1547–67.[47] After the reforms of 1523–28, Perugia added a vacation-time lectureship in moral philosophy.[48] The universities of Catania, Macerata, Messina, Naples, Pisa, Salerno, and Turin never had professorships in moral philosophy. In 1617–18 Parma had a Jesuit teaching moral philosophy described as "teaching the Ten Commandments" (see Ch. 4, table 4.6).

Moral philosophy reached its highest point at the University of Florence in the fifteenth century and Padua in the late sixteenth century. In both cases the bonds with humanism helped elevate the discipline. Other universities linked moral philosophy to natural philosophy or theology or ignored it.

43. ASPv, Università, Cartone 20, no pag., numerous rolls from 1538–39 through 1600–1601. Rizzo (1987, 75–76 n. 35) prints the roll of 1584–85.

44. *I maestri di Roma*, 1991, 4, 35, 41 (quote). Since the partial summary on p. 1081 is not completely accurate, one must reconstruct the post from the rolls.

45. Lohr, 1978, 601–2. On Muret, see Renzi, 1985 and 1986

46. *I maestri di Roma*, 1991, 127, 131, 136, 141, 147, 150, 154. The moral philosopher who taught from 1586 or 1587 through 1601 was Lelio Pellegrini from Sonnino, known as an orator. See Muccillo, 1992, 222 n. 56, and especially McGinness, 1995b, 64, 101, 126, 167–68, 170–72.

47. *I maestri di Ferrara*, 1991, 29–38 passim, 157, 238, and Franceschini, 1970, 265, 266. The professor was Giovanni Leoni da Vercelli, about whom nothing is known. In addition, Giovanni Battista Coatti taught "operam Aristotelis" between 1561 and 1567, which Franceschini believes was also moral philosophy. The medical humanist Nicolò Leoniceno may have taught moral philosophy at Ferrara for one year, 1473–74, while two moral philosophers appeared on the roll of in the year 1505–6. *I maestri di Ferrara*, 1991, 21, 157, 238. Moral philosophy became a continuing professorship only in 1602.

48. Ermini, 1971, 234–35.

TEACHING MORAL PHILOSOPHY

The teaching of moral philosophy meant lecturing on Aristotle's *libri morales,* especially the *Nicomachean Ethics.* At Bologna, the professor of moral philosophy lectured on different parts of the *Ethics* through a five-year cycle in the 1590s. In 1591–92 he lectured on the *quintum librum de iustitia et iure* (fifth book on justice and law). Indeed, the fifth book of the *Nicomachean Ethics* discusses the nature of justice and its different forms, including legal justice. In 1592–93 the moral philosopher lectured *de virtutibus contemplativis* (on contemplative virtues), the topic of book 6 of the *Nicomachean Ethics.* In 1593–94 he discussed *amicitia* (friendship), that is, books 8 and 9 of Aristotle's work. In 1594–95 he lectured *de foelicitate in universali* (on happiness in general), the second half of book 10 of the *Nicomachean Ethics.* In 1595–96 he lectured *de attinentibus ad virtutes morales,* that is, books 2 and 3, chapters 1–5, which discussed the nature and different kinds of virtue. In 1596–97, he lectured *de virtutibus moralibus,* which could have been part or all of books 2 through 5. And so on.[49]

Paduan professors did the same. As noted earlier, Ermolao Barbaro taught the *Nicomachean Ethics* and the *Politics* at Padua in the years 1475–77. Sixteenth-century rolls often described the post as *Ad philosophiam moralem Aristotelis.* In 1543–44 the moral philosopher was described as "teaching the book of the Ethics." In 1594–95 the moral philosopher taught "the first book of the Ethics." In 1610 he taught the sixth book of the *Ethics.*[50]

Overall, the content of Aristotle's works, especially the *Nicomachean Ethics,* provided the structure and themes for the teaching of moral philosophy. Discussions of the supreme good (*summum bonum*), different kinds of virtues, moral virtue as a mean, and similar themes dominated. These issues led easily into questions that went beyond Aristotle, such as whether pagan ethics were compatible with Christian teaching.[51]

Moral philosophy's links with other disciplines also influenced teaching and scholarship. It is likely that a scholar teaching both natural and moral philosophy viewed the latter through the lens of Aristotle's *De anima, Physics,* and similar works. At other times, moral philosophy accompanied theology and was taught by a friar. In this circumstance, a Scholastic approach, especially that of Thomas Aquinas, exerted considerable influence.[52] The third approach was humanistic.

49. Dallari, 1888–1924, 2:242, 245, 249, 253, 256, 259, 262, 264, 271. For an English translation of the *Nicomachean Ethics,* see Aristotle, 1941, 927–1112.

50. Rolls of 1543–44, 1594–95, and 1610–11 in AAUP, Inventario 1320, no pag.

51. Kraye (1988) offers an excellent, European-wide survey of Renaissance philosophy based on an abundance of works written by academics and nonacademics alike. See also *Cambridge Translations,* 1997, with excerpts from numerous moral philosophy treatises. Most interesting is that of Verino or Francesco de' Vieri (pp. 166–76), who argued for a Platonic ethics. See also Poppi, 1976, 108–37, who summarizes the contents of a limited number of treatises on moral philosophy written at Padua and Venice by scholars both within and outside the university. I have been unable to consult David A. Lines, "Teaching Virtue in Renaissance Italy: Latin Commentaries on Aristotle's *Nicomachean Ethics*" (Ph.D. diss., Harvard University, 1997). What follows are a few supplementary remarks.

52. Kraye (1988, 316–17, 326–27) makes this point. It should also be noted that a significant

For some professors of moral philosophy with humanistic tendencies, teaching meant presenting to future leaders of society a philosophy for the active and civic life. University lectures would prepare young nobles to govern themselves, their families, and their states. The Venetian government's appointment notice for Giason De Nores made this clear. It began: "Since moral philosophy is so useful to the civic life, our ancestors acted prudently in establishing in our University of Padua a professor who could teach this very fruitful part of philosophy to our young men."[53]

Giason De Nores tried to fulfill this charge in such works as *De constitutione partium universae humanae et civilis philosophiae, quam Aristoteles sapienter conscripsit* (On the arrangement of all human and civil philosophy that Aristotle so wisely composed) of 1584. In his preface, De Nores stated that this year, as in the past, he was offering a comprehensive outline of "all human and civil philosophy" as an introduction to his university lectures on the first book of the *Nicomachean Ethics*.[54] An outline of "human, active, and civic philosophy" based on the three *libri morales* of Aristotle followed. To emphasize his theme and to aid his students' memories, De Nores included thirty pages of tables outlining the many parts of a human, active, and civil philosophy. This visual summary in tabular form included references to the various books of the three Aristotelian treatises.[55]

De Nores offered the same moral philosophy for the active life in a longer treatise written in the vernacular, obviously intended for a broader audience: *Breve institutione dell'ottima republica di Iason De Nores, raccolta in gran parte da tutta la philosophia humana di Aristotile, quasi come una certa introduttione dell'Ethica, Politica, & Economica* (Brief instruction on the best republic by Jason De Nores, collected in great part from all the human philosophy of Aristotle, almost like a reliable introduction to the *Ethics, Politics,* and *Economics*) of 1578. In this expanded format, De Nores argued that the ultimate good of all the different actions of the diverse individuals who constituted society was the well-ordered republic. De Nores paid particular attention to "the way of living of the famous and illustrious men who attend to the government of states and republics . . . this being almost the goal of

---

number of Italian clergymen wrote commentaries on the *libri morales* of Aristotle in the fifteenth and sixteenth centuries. See the surveys of Lohr, 1967–82. Of course, laymen teaching moral philosophy might also be influenced by Thomas and Scholasticism generally.

53. Essendo la philosophia moral tanto utile alla vita civile prudentemente fecero li maggiori nostri nel instituire nel studio nostro di Padova un lettore che havesse ad insegnare così fruttuosa parte della Philosophia alli nostri giovani. AAUP, F. 668, f. 322ʳ, dated June 22, 1577, as quoted in Poppi, 1976, 139 n. 16.

54. De Nores, 1584, sig. 2ᵛ. The tables mentioned next are found on pp. 21ʳ–35ᵛ. Please see figure 10. The roll of 1584–85 stated that De Nores would teach the *Ethics* that year. AAUP, F. 651, f. 302ʳ.

55. See Schmitt, 1983c, 56–59, for the growing use of tables to summarize information visually in late-sixteenth-century textbooks. His comment that northern Europeans used tables more often than did Italians is undoubtedly true. Nevertheless, De Nores used them very extensively, and one wonders if he was influenced by Peter Ramus.

DE
PRINCIPVM PARTIVM
VNIVERSAE HVMANAE,
ET CIVILIS PHILOSOPHIAE
CONSTITVTIONE,

QVAM ARISTOTELES DECEM LIBRIS
Ethicorum, Octo Politicorum, & Duobus Oecono
micorum sapienter conscripsit,

Tabulæ per diffinitionem, & diuisionem.

Philosophia Humana, Actiua, & Ciuilis est disciplina dirigens
societatem ciuilem ad propriam felicitatem per optimã
rempublicam, eiusque leges, tam publicas, quam
familiares.

Huius Philosophiæ Humanæ, Actiuæ, & Ciuilis,

Prima pars	secūda pars	Tertia pars	Quarta pars sūt Le-
est, Summū	est	Ciuitas	est Optima	ges, tāquā instrumē
bonum hu-	ipsa, quæ fe	Respublica,	ta inanimata ītrodu
manum ci-	licitatem ci	hoc est op	cendæ felicitatis.
uile, hoc est	uilem intro	timus ordo	Harum legum,
felicitas ip-	ducendam	magistra--	
sa ciuilis in	in se recipi	tuum, qui	Aliæ sūt / Aliæ sūt
troducenda	at, quæ inde	tāquam in-	publicæ, / familia-
in ciuitatē,	sit propriū	strumentū	quæ in- / res, quæ
quę inde sit	subiectum	animatum	troducāt / introdu
propriū su-	pertractan-	introducat	felicita- / cant fe-
biectūm p̄	dum in pri	felicitatem	tem ci- / licitatē
tractādum	mo libro	ciuilem in-	uilem in / ciuilem
ī prioribus	politicorū,	ciuitatem,	ciuitatē, / infami-
decē libris	ut patet ex	quę inde sit	quæ in- / lias, quę
1	2	3	4 5 F

FIG. 10. Beginning of an extensive tabular outline of "human, active, and civic philosophy" based on Aristotle's *Ethics, Politics,* and the pseudo-Aristotelian *Economics* in Giason De Nores, *De constitutione partium universae humanae et civilis philosophiae, quam Aristoteles sapienter conscripsit.* Padua: Paolo Meietti, 1584, f. 21ʳ. Thomas Fisher Rare Book Library, University of Toronto.

civic life."[56] De Nores's example of the best republic was, naturally, Venice, and he included brief comments on Venetian governmental institutions. As in his other work, De Nores summarized in a series of tables the active, human, and civic philosophy based on the *Ethics, Politics,* and *Economics* that he taught. At the same time, De Nores also praised those who devoted themselves to contemplation.

To this point De Nores's moral philosophy teaching was conventionally Aristotelian. But in another book he struck out in a new direction by marrying the moral philosophical principles of Aristotle to the eloquence of Cicero: *In M. T. Ciceronis universam philosophiam de vita et moribus* (Towards a general philosophy for life and morals according to Marcus Tullius Cicero) of 1581.[57] This was a natural development for De Nores, who also published extensively on humanistic and literary topics: studies on Aristotle's *Rhetoric* and *Poetics,* on oratory, on Horace, on comedy and tragedy, plus a literary polemic on the pastoral. The premise of *In M. T. Ciceronis universam philosophiam* was that the well-structured *Nicomachean Ethics* could not inspire men to act virtuously, while the eloquent Plato lacked order. Only Cicero offered the best of both worlds: his combination of eloquence, example, and method produced effective moral philosophy.

De Nores posed the objection that one could not teach Aristotelian moral philosophy without Aristotle. He responded that individual works of Cicero corresponded to specific texts and chapters of the *libri morales* of Aristotle. Cicero's *De finibus* corresponded to the *Nicomachean Ethics,* book 1; *De officiis* to the *Ethics,* books 2 through 6; the *Tusculan Disputations* to the *Ethics,* book 7; *De amicitia* to the *Ethics,* books 8 and 9; *De republica* to Aristotle's *Politics,* books 1–7; and *De legibus* to the *Politics,* book 8. Finally, Cicero's *Familiar Letters* (with its many letters to or about Cicero's wife and daughter) corresponded to the *Economics,* the treatise on domestic life and family. Thus, Aristotle's principles of moral philosophy could be found in Cicero's words. As in his other works, De Nores summarized his message in a series of tables. It is not likely that De Nores delivered this material to his students directly in the form of a series of lectures on Cicero, because the professor of moral philosophy was required to lecture on the Aristotelian works. Instead, he probably interpolated the Ciceronian material.[58]

---

56. La terza maniera di vivere è de gli huomini chiari & illustri, che attendono al governo de' Stati, & delle Republiche, i quali reputano la felicità esser l'Honore, essendo egli quasi il fine della vita civile. De Nores, 1578, p. 5ʳ. The tables outlining his thought are found on pp. 51ʳ–56ᵛ.

57. De Nores, 1581. See pp. 20ᵛ–21ʳ for the comparisons between Cicero and Aristotle in the next paragraph, and pp. 65ʳ–75ᵛ for the tables. Kraye (1988, 326) pointed out De Nores's comparison between Cicero and Aristotle. For a list of De Nores's publications, see Patrizi, 1990.

58. Although De Nores did not state that this was classroom material, it is likely that it was. In addition to the structure of the work and the tables, a further sign of the book's university origins was its dedication to the three Venetian patricians then filling the office of Riformatori dello Studio di Padova, the magistracy that oversaw the university and determined professorial salaries. See the title page of De Nores, 1981. The three dedicatees were Giovanni Donà, Giovanni Soranzo, and Paolo Tiepolo. Soranzo and Donà served as Riformatori from May 4, 1580, until Mar. 3, 1581; Tiepolo from Apr. 14, 1581, until Apr. 13, 1583. See AAUP, F. 508, list of Riformatori, no pag. The trio were among the most important Venetian politicians of their generation. For their political careers, see Grendler, 1979, 316–17, 319–23.

De Nores's moral philosophy, intended to prepare students for participation in civic affairs, continued fifteenth-century civic humanism, but with significant limitations. The original civic humanism developed outside the university, as chancellors of communes, freelance humanists, Florentine merchant-statesmen, and Venetian patricians wrote treatises. De Nores had the same goal as his predecessors, but he transformed fifteenth-century civic humanism into abstract academic moral philosophy. Missing was the analysis of wise and foolish civic actions of the ancients. De Nores's work lacks an immediate and pressing historical context. And he never mentioned any of the moral dilemmas of political action which Machiavelli raised in his (now banned) works. The framework of a philosophy for the civic life remained, but De Nores seemed more concerned to organize moral philosophy into neat tables than to raise and answer difficult questions.

Despite its limitations, university moral philosophy offered principles for the civic life deemed appropriate for future leaders of Renaissance states. De Nores provided a philosophical foundation for the civic and political thought of Venetian patricians of the late Renaissance. That group included Paolo Paruta (1540–98), the most important Italian political and historical author of his generation. Indeed, Aristotelian moral philosophical principles undergirded much of Paruta's writing.[59] By demonstrating that one could learn an appropriate ethics through Cicero, De Nores also made explicit the strong links between Aristotelian moral philosophy and the *studia humanitatis*.

Whether the approach was humanistic, through natural philosophy, or theological, moral philosophy attempted to teach students how to live, rather than to impart a body of scientific knowledge. With the partial exception of humanistic studies, moral philosophy was the only university subject to attempt this. But because the Italian Renaissance university was overwhelmingly a professional and scientific institution, moral philosophy was not taught in all universities, nor was it of first-rank importance in those that did teach the subject. Northern universities and Iberian universities influenced by the Jesuits gave moral philosophy greater prominence.[60] Instead, Italian universities emphasized the humanistic dimension of Aristotelian moral philosophy.

59. See Paruta's *Della perfezione della vita politica* (1579), *Discorsi politici* (published 1599), his histories of Venice, and his extensive diplomatic correspondence. The scholarship on Paruta is too vast to list here. Because Paruta's works were grounded in historical and contemporary political reality, they are far more interesting and perceptive than those of De Nores. Nevertheless, the professor De Nores and the statesman Paruta viewed the world in the same way, through an Aristotelian lens with a humanistic tint. *Della perfezione della vita politica* relied heavily on Aristotle's *Nicomachean Ethics*. Incidentally, Paruta studied at Padua between 1558 and 1561, before De Nores arrived. Bouwsma, 1968, 199.

60. Schmitt, 1979a, 94–95. Evidence comes from a variety of sources. Northern Europeans and scholars from the Iberian Peninsula published more commentaries on the *libri morales* in the fifteenth and sixteenth centuries than did Italians. Moreover, many sixteenth-century commentaries written by Italians were the efforts of clergymen teaching in convent *studia*, rather than professors in universities. Lohr, 1967–82. The survey of Kraye, 1988, also reveals a greater interest in moral philosophy in northern Europe.

CHAPTER 12

Mathematics

he Renaissance university inherited from the medieval university a professorship combining mathematics, astronomy, and astrology. Over the course of the fifteenth and sixteenth centuries, the professorship and the disciplines within it changed greatly. The recovery of ancient Greek mathematical texts produced innovation and led Renaissance mathematicians to rethink their discipline. Algebra and geometry grew in importance and sophistication. Mathematics added fresh practical applications. Astronomy advanced revolutionary theories about the planetary system and the universe, while astrology declined in importance. In the seventeenth century mathematicians challenged Aristotelian conceptions of the physical universe.

The changes in content and emphasis produced a change in name. In 1400 most universities called this professorship astronomy, astrology, and mathematics. By the end of the sixteenth century mathematics was the preferred single name for it. Astronomy sometimes became a separate professorship, while astrology disappeared from the title.

STATUTORY TEXTS

The twelfth and thirteenth centuries saw a flowering of mathematics which produced the teaching program of the early Renaissance university. Medieval scholars translated into Latin (sometimes through intermediary Arabic translations) significant Arabic and Greek texts. Western authors adapted these texts and the material in them for scholars and students. The 1405 statutes of the University of Bologna codified the curriculum. They prescribed an elaborate four-year cycle of ancient and medieval texts for the teaching of a combination of mathematics, astronomy, and astrology, to which they gave the single name "astrology." To a great extent this curriculum remained in the statutes and teaching for the next two centuries.

The mathematics was Euclidian, the astronomy and astrology Ptolomaic, with the astrology supplemented by Arabic texts. The professor taught introductory mathematics (basic arithmetic and geometry) and astronomy in the first year. He continued the study of mathematics and astronomy and added astrology in the second year. The lecturer provided instruction in all three in the third year. Using the arithmetical and geometric skills acquired earlier, the lecturer concentrated on astrology and astronomy in the fourth year. Overall, mathematics was treated as a lesser skill in the service of astronomy and astrology.

The reasons for teaching Euclid's geometry are easily understood, as are the links between mathematics and astronomy. University mathematical studies included astrology because of its links with medicine.[1] Medical men assumed that heavenly bodies could influence the progress of a disease and, properly used, might aid in its cure. Hence, physicians needed to be able to calculate the movements of the heavens so that they might apply a medical procedure at the most advantageous moment. Astronomical calculations from tables and observations located the positions of the stars, making possible the plotting of astrological conjunctions. Expertise in arithmetic and geometry was needed to make astronomical measurements. Overall, the statutes viewed the three disciplines as complementary.

It appears that the Bolognese curriculum became simpler in the course of the next two centuries. The two mathematicians, teaching at different hours at the University of Bologna in the late sixteenth century, taught three different series of lectures described as "Euclid," "the theory of planets," and "the astronomy of Ptolemy."

4th hour morning	4th hour afternoon
1591–92: Euclid	theory of the planets (or *De sphaera* of Sacrobosco)
1592–93: theory of the planets	astronomy of Ptolemy
1593–94: astronomy of Ptolemy	Euclid

The cycle then repeated.[2]

The Bolognese statutes imposed three additional duties. The professor was required to produce an annual almanac, which would include the calendar, seasons, the relative positions of the planets, stars, and moon, and other data. The appearance of the Gregorian calendar in 1582 made this much easier than before.[3] He also had to produce a set of predictions ("iudicia," or judgments) for the year, to be held by the beadle so that they might be consulted. The predictions embraced both judicial astrology, that is, foretelling future events in the lives of persons and nations, and natural astrology, that is, predicting natural occurrences, such as floods, storms, and eclipses. Numerous sets of predictions noting the rise

1. Nancy Siraisi has made this point repeatedly: Siraisi, 1973, 83–84, 93; Siraisi, 1981, 139–45; Siraisi, 1990, 68–69, 128–29, 134–36.

2. Dallari, 1888–1924, 2:242 (quote below), 245, 246, 249, 250, 253, 256, 259, 260, and so on. In 1591–92, the teaching of the afternoon professor was described in more detail as "Legant spheram Sacro Busto [*sic*] vel theoricam planetarum."

3. There is an almanac for 1586 in ASB, Assunteria di Studio, Bu. 88.

TABLE 12.1
Statutory Texts for "Astrology" at Bologna, 1405

Year One

Algorismus on fractions and integers[a]
Euclid, *Elements,* book 1 with the commentary of Campanus of Novara[b]
Alfonsine Tables with *Canons* (probably by John of Saxony)[c]
Theory of the Planets[d]

Year Two

Sacrobosco, *De sphaera*[e]
Euclid, *Elements,* book 2
Jean de Linières, *Canons* on the *Alfonsine Tables*[f]
Messahala (Māshā'allāh), *A Treatise on the Astrolabe*[g]

Year Three

Alcabitius (Al-Qabīṣī), *Introduction to the Art of Astrology*[h]
Pseudo-Ptolemy, *Centiloquium* with commentary of Haly Rodohan[i]
Euclid, *Elements,* book 3
"Treatise on the Quadrant"[j]

Year Four

Ptolemy, *Quadripartitus* (or *Tetrabiblos*), entire[k]
"Book on unseen urine"[l]
Ptolemy, *Almagest,* "third part"[m]

Note: The following is a summary from Malagola, 1966, rubric 78, 276, who identifies some of the texts. Thorndike, (1944, 281–82) provides an English translation and also identifies some texts.
[a]Several treatises circulated under the name *Algorismus.* A likely candidate is the *Algorismus* of Johannes de Sacrobosco (John of Holywood, d. 1244 or 1256), a widely used textbook. Another possibility is *Algorismus de minutiis,* an arithmetic on fractions attributed to Sacrobosco by late medieval authors, but not the same as the *Algorismus.* In any case, the text taught was an introduction to arithmetic and algebra. For an English translation of selections of Sacrobosco's *Algorismus,* see Grant, 1974, 94–101. On Sacrobosco, see Daly, 1981.
[b]"Legatur primus geumetrie [*sic*] Euclidis cum commento Campani." Malagola, 1966, 276. That is, the lectures should deal with book 1 of Euclid's *Elements* using Campanus's work, which is a combination of reworked translation, commentary, and expansion of the great work of geometry of Euclid (fl. c. 295 B.C.). Book 1 of the *Elements* focuses on plane geometry, specifically "the geometry of points, lines, triangles, squares and parallelograms." It also offers definitions and basic postulates and axioms. Bulmer-Thomas, 1981a, 417 (quote). Campanus of Novara (d. 1296) wrote this textbook version of Euclid about 1259, and it was widely used through the sixteenth century. Toomer, 1981b, and Murdoch, 1981, 446–47. Possibly the professor was supposed to lead his students through the relevant sections of Campanus's work.
[c]The *Alfonsine Tables* are the mathematical calculations from Ptolemy's *Almagest* with limited modifications. Since the *Tables* enable the user to determine and predict the positions of heavenly bodies, they were a basic tool for Ptolemaic astronomy. Tradition has it that scholars supported by King Alfonso X of Castile prepared them about 1250 to about 1275—hence, the name. However, Poulle,

1988, argues that they were prepared in Paris about 1321, possibly by John of Murs and associates. In any case, John of Saxony (fl. 1327–55) recast them into a different form and added Latin precepts in 1327. John of Saxony's immensely influential version was probably used at Bologna. For selections in translation of John of Saxony's version of the *Alfonsine Tables,* see Grant, 1974, 465–87.

[d]The anonymous *Theorica Planetarum* was an elementary textbook that explained Ptolemaic astronomy in terms that students could understand. Possibly written in the second half of the thirteenth century, it was still used in the sixteenth century. For excerpts in translation, see Grant, 1974, 451–65. See also Pedersen, 1981, and North, 1992, 349–50. Surviving medieval manuscripts of the *Theorica planetarum* usually included a package of the *Theorica planetarum,* a set of astronomical tables, and a treatise or two on instruments such as the quadrant or astrolabe. This may have been the intent at Bologna. See Grant, 1974, 451.

[e]"Tractatus de spera," which has to be *De sphaera* (c. 1220) of Sacrobosco. This work summarizing Ptolemaic astronomy was the most used and commented on astronomical work of the Middle Ages and Renaissance. See Thorndike, 1949, and Daly, 1981.

[f]Jean de Linières (c. 1300–c. 1350), who taught John of Saxony, wrote this astronomical work about 1320.

[g]Māshā'allāh (fl. 762–c. 815) was an Egyptian Jew at the Baghdad court who wrote numerous astrological works, of which *A Treatise on the Astrolabe* (in Latin translation) was the best known. Pingree, 1981b.

[h]Al-Qabīṣī (fl. c. 950 in Aleppo, Syria) wrote this introductory textbook in astrology. Pingree, 1981a.

[i]The *Centiloquium* is an often mentioned astrological treatise attributed to Ptolemy in the Middle Ages. Haly Rodohan (Ali ibn Ridwan, c. 998–1061) from Cairo was a medical author who also wrote astrological works.

[j]A number of treatises on the quadrant circulated, such as the *De quadrante* of Campanus of Novara; it briefly explained how to use the quadrant to solve some astronomical and measuring problems. Toomer, 1981b, 27. But there were other treatises as well.

[k]A famous astrological work.

[l]"Legatur liber de urina non visa." Malagola, 1966, 276. Thorndike (1944, 282) suggests a work by "William of England," who has not been further identified. Because examining urine was an important part of medical diagnosis, various treatises on urine circulated in the Middle Ages. The inclusion of such a treatise in the statutory texts for mathematics suggests that this was a work of medical astrology, that is, the use of astrology to assist the doctor in determining when to prescribe a medicine or medical procedure.

[m]"Legatur dictio tertia almagestj." Malagola, 1966, 276. The *Almagest* of Ptolemy of Egypt (c. A.D. 100–170) was the foundation of astronomy until well into the seventeenth century. A complete textbook for studying all the known heavenly bodies, it summarized ancient astrononical knowledge and added Ptolomey's own observations. "Dictio tertia" may mean book 3 discussing solar theory (equinoxes, solstices, motion of the sun, and calendar problems). Although the 1405 statutes postponed lecturing on the *Almagest* until the fourth year, Ptolemaic theory undergirded all the astronomy and astrology taught. See Toomer, 1981c, for an overall view and bibliography.

and fall of princes and states, whether the Turk would menace Italy, the fate of crops, coming lunar and solar eclipses, and so on survive.[4] Finally, the Bolognese professor of astrology was required to give free predictions to students within a month of the request.[5] Other universities also imposed the requirement of preparing an almanac.[6]

Although the Bolognese statutes were unusually elaborate, other universities followed the same general pattern. For example, the 1448 statutes of the University of Turin decreed that the mathematician should teach the elementary *De arithmetica* of Boethius (c. 480–524/25), Sacrobosco's *Algorismus,* Euclid's *Elements,* and part of Ptolomy's *Almagest.*[7]

The 1543 statutes of the University of Pisa required mathematicians to teach Euclid, Sacrobosco's *De sphaera,* and unspecified texts of Ptolemy in a three-year cycle. Hence, in the 1570s the professor of mathematics taught Sacrobosco's *De sphaera* in the first year, book 7 of Euclid's *Elements* in the second, and Ptolemy's *Almagest* plus book 10 of Euclid in the third. For the Ptolemaic requirement the professors taught his astrological *Tetrabiblos* and his *Geography,* a work in cosmography. However, the Pisan professors also went beyond the statutory authors in order to teach the *Theoricae novae planetarum* of George Puerbach (1423–61) and the *Sphaera* of Orance Finé (1494–1555).[8]

In 1575–76, the mathematician at Rome taught three books of Euclid, Sacrobosco's *De sphaera,* and the *Theorica planetarum,* either the thirteenth-century work or the *Theoricae novae planetarum* of Puerbach. In 1579–80 he taught books 1 and 6 of Euclid, Sacrobosco's *De sphaera,* the *Theorica planetarum,* and "judicial astrology as permitted by the holy Council of Trent."[9] These examples and the teaching of Galileo Galilei (see below) indicate that professors of mathematics generally taught the texts inherited from the medieval university, but not so faithfully as their counterparts in other disciplines. They also taught some Renaissance texts, notably Puerbach.

4. See Thorndike, 1923–58, vols. 4, 5, and 6, for several chapters surveying manuscript and printed annual predictions. See especially vol. 5, chap. 12, 234–51, which studies predictions issued by sixteenth-century Bolognese astrologers, many of whom taught at the university.

5. Malagola, 1966, 264, rubric 60; English translation in Thorndike, 1944, 282. See also Bortolotti, 1947, 11. The requirement to produce an almanac and predictions is not found in the 1405 statutes but was often indicated in the rolls. For example, see the roll of 1493–94: "Ad Astronomiam de mane diebus continius et ordinarijs. (Et fiat iudicium et tacuinum.)." Dallari, 1888–1924, 1:153.

6. For example, Florence, Sept. 26, 1402: "Ad legendum Astrologiam et faciendum Taccuinum." Gherardi, 1973, 377.

7. Vallauri, 1970, 1:102.

8. Schmitt, 1978, 54, 57. Puerbach's *Theoricae novae planetarum* (finished 1454) was a popular textbook of Ptolomaic planetary theory which criticized and improved on the medieval *Theorica planetarum.* Pedersen, 1978. and Hellman and Swerdlow, 1981. Finé was a French mathematician who taught at Paris. See Poulle, 1981.

9. "Mathematicus: librum primum et 6. Euclidis et Spheram sacribusti et Theoricas planetarum ac iudiciariam ut permissum est a sacrosanto Concilio Tridentino." In other years, the rolls simply stated that the mathematician taught Euclid. Rolls of 1567–68, 1568–69, 1569, 1570–71, 1574–75, 1575–76, and 1579–80 in *I maestri di Roma,* 1991, 53, 61, 67, 77, 89, 101, 116 (quote).

THE RENAISSANCE OF MATHEMATICS

The medieval flowering of mathematics codified in the statutes came to a halt about 1300, because it had satisfied the needs of universities dominated by Aristotelian logic and natural philosophy. For example, Campanus of Novara's version of Euclid brought out the philosophical aspects of the *Elements* at the expense of geometric proofs.[10] Scholastic Aristotelianism needed only relatively simple mathematics.

The great recovery of ancient Greek mathematical texts occurred in the middle and late fifteenth century and produced the Renaissance of mathematics of the next century.[11] Humanists with a strong interest in mathematics sought out Greek mathematical manuscripts as enthusiastically as they pursued those in other subjects. By the end of the fifteenth century almost all ancient Greek mathematical writings had been recovered, although contemporary mathematicians made little use of them. Mathematicians of humanistic outlook and the required linguistic capabilities translated, or retranslated, the Greek texts into Latin, wrote commentaries, and assimilated them into their own work in the second half of the sixteenth century.

Archimedes (c. 287–212 B.C.), the greatest mathematician of the ancient world, was the most important figure in the mathematical Renaissance.[12] Although most of his works were available in Latin by 1300, medieval scholars made little use of them. Archimedes first came to the attention of humanists for his reputation as an inventor and builder of practical machines. Then his skill in dealing mathematically with the physical sciences of mechanics and hydrostatics entranced sixteenth-century scholars. A new Latin translation of his works (excluding *On Floating Bodies*) was done about 1450 but not printed at this time. A Greek edition of most of Archimedes' works accompanied by the fifteenth-century Latin translation was printed in 1544. Federico Commandino (1509–95) published another Latin translation in 1558, plus a Latin translation with mathematical emendations of the important *On Floating Bodies* and *Equilibrium of Planes* in 1565. Archimedes' studies on dynamics and statics found in the latter two works particularly influenced Galilei.

The discovery of Diophantus's (fl. A.D. 250) *Arithmetica* in the 1460s, its use in 1572, and its Latin translation in 1575 greatly stimulated the development of algebra.[13] Pappus of Alexandria's (fl. A.D. 300–350) *Mathematical Collection,* a

---

10. Rose, 1976, 76–89. A similar thing happened to Archimedes' *On the Measurement of the Circle* in the fourteenth century; see Clagett, 1981, 226.

11. The story is the theme of Rose, 1976, which provides the title of this section. See also Rose, 1973.

12. See Rose, 1973 and 1976, and Clagett, 1981. See Clagett, 1964, for the detailed history up to 1300, summary on 1–14; for the period about 1450 to 1565, see Clagett 1978, esp. 1, 225–46 for a summary, and Laird, 1991.

13. For Diophantus, see Vogel, 1981a. For Pappus of Alexandria, see Boyer, 1971–76, and Bulmer-Thomas, 1981b. For Apollonius, see Toomer, 1981a. For Hero of Alexandria, see Drachmann and Mahoney, 1981.

work that covers almost all of Greek geometry and is important for mathematical analysis and synthesis, was first used in a printed mathematical text in 1566 and was published in Latin translation in 1588. The latter included an account of the *Mechanics* of Hero of Alexandria (fl. A.D. 60). The *Conica* of Apollonius (c. 250–175 B.C.), with its complex mathematics to measure cones, was published in Latin in 1566.

Finally, the pseudo-Aristotelian *Mechanica* or *Questions of Mechanics* played an important role in the development of mathematical techniques to solve physical problems. Written in the third century B.C., it was ignored in the Middle Ages. Aldo Manuzio first printed it, in Greek, in 1497. A Latin translation followed in 1517, while Niccolò Leonico Tomeo published a second, better Latin translation in 1525, which became the standard. Italian translations and commentaries followed. The *Mechanica* stimulated mathematicians, because it combined mathematics and physics in order to solve problems in dynamics, statics, weights, and velocity as Aristotle had not done.[14]

In addition to rediscovering ancient Greek works, Renaissance mathematicians also paid more attention to the greatest medieval mathematician, Leonardo Fibonacci (or Leonardo of Pisa, c. 1170–after 1240). Expert in many techniques and blessed with inventive genius, Fibonacci had a profound knowledge of both ancient Greek and medieval Arab mathematics. However, medieval university mathematicians ignored the bulk of his corpus, rich in algebra and geometry and very original in indeterminate analysis and number theory.[15] Luca Pacioli (c. 1445–1517) brought him to the attention of the Renaissance by including a good deal of Fibonacci's material in his encyclopedia of mathematics, the *Summa de arithmetica, geometria, proportioni et proportionalità* (1494; reprinted 1523). Sixteenth-century algebraists cited and used Fibonacci through Pacioli; indeed, Fibonacci's works were not printed until the nineteenth century.[16]

With new texts, skills, and confidence in the power of mathematics, university scholars addressed topics that might be described as the practical application of mathematics. They had always done this to a limited degree, but it became the norm in the second half of the sixteenth century. And as the mathematicians expanded their horizons, they began to interest themselves in matters traditionally the province of Aristotelian natural philosophy. For example, when studying statics and tides from a mathematical perspective, they investigated motion, a topic in natural philosophy.[17] A clear sign of change was that mathe-

14. For the *Mechanica*, see *Mechanics*, 1969, 11 and passim; Rose and Drake, 1971; and Laird, 1986. Dynamics is the study of the action of force on bodies in motion or at rest; it embraces kinetics, kinematics, and statics. The last is the study of bodies, masses, or forces in equilibrium.

15. North (1992, 342) summed it up well: Fibonacci was "a lonely figure, too great for his contemporaries to appreciate properly." The exception was his *Liber abaci* (1202; revised 1228), a treatise on commercial mathematics which exerted a continuous influence through the preuniversity vernacular abbaco schools. But universities did not teach abbaco.

16. Vogel, 1981b; Bortolotti, 1947, 27–33; and Rose, 1976, 2, 20 n. 26, 27, 29, 34, 55, 76, 79, 82–83, 89, 143–47, 190–91, 205, 208, 214, 264.

17. Schmitt, 1975a, 504–7; Schmitt, 1975b, 44–49; and Schmitt, 1982b, 308–13.

maticians wrote treatises contrasting the certainty of mathematical truth with what they saw as the uncertainty and error found in philosophy and astrology. And they wondered how the syllogisms of logic could be reconciled with the axiomatic proofs of mathematics.[18]

The confidence and expansion of mathematics led inevitably to the questioning of traditional Ptolemaic astronomy and Aristotelian physics. The potential for doubt had always been there, because a basic incompatibility divided Ptolemaic astronomy and Aristotelian natural philosophy. According to Aristotle, the motion of celestial substances should be circular and regular around a fixed point. But Ptolemy's heavenly bodies with their eccentrics and epicycles did not behave that way. Most medieval astronomers ignored the conflict and adopted a compromise: Aristotelian natural philosophy supplied the reasons for celestial motion, but mathematics calculated the paths of heavenly bodies.[19] This worked because scholars viewed mathematical techniques as fictions: they provided useful information for computing heavenly positions but did not describe reality.

When the conflict was finally addressed, the results contradicted traditional views. Scholars applying mathematics to the physical world in such areas as mechanics, motion, tides, calendar reform, and fortifications eventually found it difficult to maintain the view that mathematics was only a useful fiction measuring, but not describing, physical reality. The separation between the Aristotelian view of physical reality and mathematics as hypothesis made no sense to Galilei, who concluded that what could be measured mathematically should be described mathematically.

Such was the eventual result of the renewal of mathematics of the sixteenth century. The road to the seventeenth-century Galilean revolution led largely, but not exclusively, through the teaching and research of sixteenth-century professors of mathematics who transformed the field.[20]

PROFESSORS OF ASTROLOGY, ASTRONOMY, AND MATHEMATICS

The number of professors of astrology, astronomy, and mathematics at a university was normally one or two and did not change between 1400 and 1600. But the professorship gradually became independent of the concerns of natural philosophy and medicine, and its name evolved from astrology, to astronomy, and finally to mathematics. The name change reflected the revolution in the discipline, while the accomplishments of those who held the post determined the

18. Rose, 1976, 6, 97, 101, 110, 161, 169–70, 172, 176–78, 185, 188, 195, 206, 266, 268, 281, 286, 290; Gilbert, 1960, 81–92. See also Crapuli, 1969.

19. Kren (1983, 238–40) makes this point neatly. See also N. Jardine, 1988, 697–700.

20. Nonuniversity mathematicians also played key roles in the mathematical Renaissance of the sixteenth century. For example, Niccolò Tartaglia (1499/1500–57) was an abbaco teacher, Federico Commandino (1509–75) a court mathematician and physician, and Rafael Bombelli (1526–72) an engineer-architect. Giovanni Battista Benedetti (1530–90) was a court mathematician, while Guidobaldo dal Monte (1545–1607) was a nobleman of independent means. See Rose, 1976, for some of their contributions. However, this account focuses on university teachers.

degree to which a university participated in the revolution. Padua and Bologna were the most significant universities for mathematics. Several other universities had a single mathematician, occasionally of some distinction, and a few practically ignored the discipline.

Padua

Several men taught astrology at the University of Padua in the fourteenth century, apparently always in conjunction with other subjects. The lack of rolls makes the statement tentative, but it appears that a professor of medicine with an interest in astrology, astronomy, or mathematics added this subject to his teaching and research.[21] The peripatetic Biagio Pelacani taught natural philosophy and astrology at Padua in 1384 and perhaps for the next three to four years; he returned to teach the same subjects from 1407 to 1411.[22]

Padua began to have an independent professorship of mathematics, which it called astrology, in the first quarter of the fifteenth century.[23] The first documented occupant was Prosdocimo de Beldemandis or Beldomandi (1370/80–1428), who taught astrology from 1422 to 1428 at a salary of 40 florins and published works on astronomy, astrology, and algorism. One famous figure taught briefly. Johannes Müller of Königsberg, called Regiomontanus (1436–76), possibly the most important astronomical author of the century and a contributor in other mathematical fields, taught at Padua in 1463–64. Regiomontanus had come to Venice in the entourage of Cardinal Bessarion when the latter was named papal legate to Venice and left with him in 1464.[24] In 1482 the name of the position became astronomy and sometimes mathematics in the 1490s.

In 1506 the Venetian government stated that since the lectureships of mathematics and astronomy had been left vacant, it would appoint one man to fill both.[25] The decision simply put a good face on the status quo, because it does not

21. Jacopo Dondi dall'Orologio (c. 1293–1359) taught medicine, or medicine and astrology, from about 1343 until his death. He introduced the *Alfonsine Tables* to Padua and published a work on tides still taught at Padua in the sixteenth century. His son Giovanni Dondi dall'Orologio (c. 1330–88) taught medicine at Padua (1343–61, 1366–67, and 1368–79) plus astrology (1359–60, and possibly in other years). Maddison, 1981; Siraisi, 1973, 90–93, 123–27; and Pesenti, 1992a and 1992b.

22. Favaro, 1922, 24–29; reprinted, but without most of the notes, in Favaro, 1966, 1:78–105. See also Federici Vescovini, 1979.

23. For the fifteenth-century mathematicians at Padua, see Favaro, 1922, 30–54, who summarizes, corrects, and adds greatly to the material found in older sources, of which the key ones are Facciolati, 1978, pt. 2:116–18, and Tomasini, 1986, 155–58. Sambin (1974) adds a little additional information on the mathematicians of the 1490s. The majority of the teaching mathematicians of the fifteenth century were little-known figures. For a brief biography of Beldemandis, see Vasoli, 1965; for Cando Candi (taught 1434–35), see Troncarelli, 1974; for Francesco Capuano (taught c. 1475–95), see G. Gliozzi, 1976.

24. Favaro, 1922, 38–49; Rosen, 1981c.

25. For the sixteenth-century mathematicians up to Galilei, see Favaro, 1922, 50–70 (55–56, 60 for the document of 1506). Favaro subsumes and corrects Facciolati, 1978, pt. 3:320–22, and Riccobono, 1980, 28r–v. Biagioli (1989, 92–93) provides a brief summary list of the mathematicians at

appear that Padua ever had two professors. Throughout the sixteenth century it had a single professor, who was expected to divide his time between astronomy, astrology, and mathematics. In 1521 Federico Delfino (c. 1477–1547) was paid 40 florins to teach astrology and 20 florins to teach mathematics.[26] However, the surviving rolls do not list separate lectures, that is, astronomy part of the year and mathematics for the remainder. The likely meaning in both 1506 and 1521 was that the mathematician would lecture on an astronomical text one year and a mathematical text the following year, which was the practice later in the century. Delfino, who taught at Padua from 1520 to 1547, wrote an often cited treatise on tides and several works on other mathematical topics, all published posthumously.

By midcentury, Paduan mathematical research and teaching manifested the impact of the mathematical Renaissance. The mathematicians increasingly used ancient Greek texts and lectured on a growing number of practical topics. The professorship was now called mathematics. The university appointed Pietro Catena (1501–76) as Delfino's successor in 1547. In alternating years Catena lectured on mathematical texts, such as the *Elements* of Euclid, and astronomical texts, such as the *De sphaera* of Sacrobosco and *Geography* of Ptolemy. He also lectured on the *Mechanica* in 1564 and 1573, but poorly, in the judgment of some contemporaries.[27]

The expansion of mathematics and the emphasis on ancient Greek texts became stronger at Padua as the century progressed. A second lecturer in mathematics appeared in 1559–60. Francesco Barozzi (1537–1604) lectured without salary on Proclus's *Commentary on Euclid,* an ancient mathematical text emphasizing a Platonic approach. A manuscript collector with a good knowledge of Greek, Barozzi was a key figure in the revival of Greek mathematics. He published a Latin translation of Proclus's commentary in 1560 as well as a number of other mathematical works. Whether Barozzi lectured at Padua more than one year is not known; in any case, he had left the city by 1565.[28]

Giuseppe Moletti (1531–88) succeeded Catena, holding the mathematical

---

Padua and bibliography. Rose (1975 and 1976, 283–87 and see index) and Carugo (1984) provide additional information and bibliography.

26. Favaro (1922, 61) quotes the document; see also AAUP, F. 654, f. 35ᵛ. Delfino's salary rose to 120 florins by his death. See Bianca, 1988.

27. For Catena, see Favaro, 1922, 63–64, and Giacobbe, 1979. See Rose and Drake, 1971, 93, and Laird, 1986, 58–59, for the negative judgments on his lectures on the *Mechanica*. Paduan statutes of the sixteenth century do not make it clear if the mathematician was required to lecture on certain texts. *Statuta artistarum et medicorum Patavini Gymnasii,* 1589, 68ᵛ. In practice, they lectured on both traditional texts and new ones.

28. See Favaro, 1922, 65–66. A document with the terms of the Paduan appointment is printed in Rose, 1977, 171. Catena lectured in the afternoon and Barozzi in the morning. As both Favaro and Rose point out, Barozzi's appointment violated the Venetian Senate decree of June 25, 1477, prohibiting Venetian patricians from teaching, even as unpaid lecturers, at Padua. For more information on Barozzi, see Barozzi, 1964; Crapuli, 1969, 55–62; Rose, 1976, index; Rose, 1977; and Carugo, 1984, 153–64.

position from 1577 until his death. Moletti began at 200 florins in 1577; after publication of his book on calendar reform, the Senate raised it to 300 florins and eventually to 500 florins, high figures for a mathematician. Moletti interested himself in a variety of physical mathematical issues. He lectured on the *Mechanica* in 1581–82 and 1585–86, treating it within an Aristotelian framework. He also lectured on Euclid's *Optics* (a treatise on perspective), cosmography (a combination of astronomy and geography), anemography (measuring the velocity and direction of winds), hydrography (the study and mapping of bodies of water), and geography. This was in addition to Euclid's *Elements* and Sacrobosco's *Sphaera*.[29]

After the position lay vacant for four years, Galileo Galilei came from the University of Pisa to take the professorship of mathematics in 1592.[30] Galilei, who had earlier failed to obtain a post at Bologna, taught at the third hour of the afternoon (hour 23, or late afternoon according to the modern clock), the traditional lecture hour for mathematics at Padua. Galilei taught Euclid frequently, plus *De sphaera* (presumably of Sacrobosco), and the *Theorica planetarum*.[31] He also lectured on the *Mechanica* in 1593–94 and again in 1598–99.[32] And about 1600 he wrote a treatise on mechanics which completed the integration of Archimedean statics into the study of moving weights and started a new path. Galilei also continued to write on practical mathematical issues, such as military fortifications and engineering. In 1609 he built his own telescope, which enabled him to see the four moons of Jupiter.

The Paduan years were immensely important for the maturation of Galilei's ideas. But he did not develop mathematical instruction much, nor did he create a "Galilean school" at Padua. As he admitted, he devoted little time or effort to his university lecturing, and, so far as can be determined, his instruction was conventional. Galilei complained that the majority of the attendees at his lectures were medical students, who were not very interested in mathematics or capable of understanding advanced concepts. By contrast, he did a great deal of private teaching, which produced considerable income.[33]

Nevertheless, the Venetian government treated Galilei very well. He initially received a four-year appointment at 180 florins, raised to 320 in 1598 and to 520 in 1606. In recognition of his telescope, whose use he demonstrated to various Venetian patricians, the Senate in August 1609 authorized a lifetime appoint-

29. Favaro, 1922, 67–70; Laird, 1986, 60–62; and Laird, 1987. For the salary of 300 florins and that he taught at the third hour of the afternoon, see ASB, Assunteria di Studio, Bu. 100, fascicle 5, "Stato delle Studio di Padova," f. 2ᵛ. It was later raised to 500 florins, according to Rose, 1976, 286. For the roll of 1584–85, in which he taught Euclid and Sacrobosco, see AAUP, F. 654, f. 302ʳ.

30. The Venetian Senate appointment notice of Sept. 26, 1592, is printed in Favaro, 1966, 2:107. See also ibid., 106–302, for numerous documents on Galilei's Paduan career.

31. See the documents in Galilei, 1966, 119–20, or Favaro, 1966, 2:114–15.

32. Galilei, 1966, 120, and Laird, 1986, 62–64. Although none of his Paduan lectures have survived, Favaro (1968, 185–209) prints a student version of the 1593–94 lectures on the *Mechanica*.

33. For assessments of Galilei's career at Padua and his teaching, see Carugo, 1984, 186–92 (see 191 for his confession that he did not spend much time on his university teaching), and Pastore Stocchi, 1984, 37–66 (complaints about his students on 49 n. 43 and p. 63). For his private teaching, see Galilei, 1966, 149–58, and Chapter 14, "Private Teaching and Other Pedagogical Abuses."

ment for Galilei at a salary of 1,000 florins, an unprecedented figure for a professor of mathematics. The lifetime appointment, a rare concession for any professor, would take effect in the fall of 1610, at the expiration of his existing four-year contract. But in 1610 Galilei left to become "Primary Philosopher and Mathematician" to the Medici grand duke in Florence at a salary of 1,000 scudi, thus angering the Venetian Senate and the patricians whom he had lobbied for the lifetime appointment and high salary.[34] Nevertheless, in 1631 a Venetian official asked him through an intermediary if he would consider returning to the University of Padua.[35] Either the ill will generated by his abrupt departure had dissipated, or Galilei was so famous that it could be overlooked. But he never returned to university teaching.

Mathematics at Padua began as an adjunct to medicine and then became an independent professorship early in the fifteenth century. The name changed from astrology to astronomy, then to mathematics in the mid-sixteenth century. The astrological part of the teaching declined in importance but did not disappear. The Paduan mathematicians significantly broadened their mathematical interests, as Delfino, Catena, Moletti, and Galilei studied practical and physical applications.[36] The Venetian authorities raised the salary of the university mathematician considerably over the course of the sixteenth century, thus tacitly approving the new directions of the subject.

Bologna

A handful of scholars taught astrology in combination with another subject in the thirteenth and fourteenth centuries at the University of Bologna.[37] The earliest surviving rolls listed a professor of astrology (1351–53), as did the next surviving roll, that of 1370–71.[38] Between 1379 and 1383, Bologna had an astrologer plus Biagio Pelacani da Parma, who taught natural philosophy and astrology. Pelacani returned to teach the same subjects in 1387–88. The astrology post flourished, with two to four professors through the 1380s and 1390s.[39]

The fifteenth-century university had two professors for the position.[40] By the

34. See Galilei, 1966, 111–19, for the Venetian government documents on his appointments, and Biagioli, 1993, 36–45. Biagioli (44) makes the common mistake of believing that Paduan professors were paid in ducats rather than florins. The florin was worth 5 lire (= 100 soldi), as opposed to the Venetian ducat of account worth 6 lire 4 soldi (= 124 soldi).

35. A former student at Padua wrote to Galilei on behalf of one of the Riformatori dello Studio di Padova. He offered an inducement. At the time Galilei was having difficulty getting his *Dialogue Concerning the Two Chief World Systems* published. The letter writer suggested that it could easily be published in Venice. Galilei's response, if any, has not come to light. Favaro, 1917, 111; Favaro, 1966, 2:16–17.

36. Some of this has been suggested by Schmitt (1975b, 44–49, and 1982b, 308–13).

37. Bortolotti, 1947, 13–16; Siraisi, 1981, 6–7.

38. Sorbelli, 1912, 316–17; Dallari, 1888–1924, 4:*Aggiunte,* 4.

39. Dallari, 1888–1924, 1:5, 7, and 4:*Aggiunte,* 6–25 passim. On Pelacani, see Federici Vescovini, 1979.

40. The rolls also listed another mathematical position that was not a university professorship. The

1450s, the rolls used the names "astrology" and "astronomy" interchangeably to describe the position; in the second half of the century, the post became astronomy and, occasionally, astronomy and mathematics.[41] Domenico Maria Novara (1454–1504), who held an astronomy post from 1483 until his death, was an active astronomer who made observations.[42]

Nicolaus Copernicus (1473–1543) was the most famous student to take advantage of mathematics and astronomy instruction at the University of Bologna. He arrived in 1496 to study canon and civil law but pursued astronomical studies as well with Novara. Copernicus made his earliest recorded astronomical observation at Bologna in March 1497 and lectured on mathematics in Rome on November 6, 1500. After five years' study at Bologna, Copernicus returned to Poland in the summer of 1501 in order to obtain permission for medical studies. He then studied medicine at the University of Padua for two academic years, 1501–3. He took a doctorate in canon law from the University of Ferrara on May 31, 1503, and returned to Poland, never again to visit Italy. Although his interest

---

1384–85 roll listed a new position called arithmetic ("In Asmetricha [*sic*]"). In addition to his teaching duties, the arithmetician was obliged to serve the commune by measuring fields and walls, by supervising construction work on the walls, and by auditing communal accounts. This post was immediately renamed abbaco ("Ad lecturam Abbachi") and commonly went by this name for the rest of the fourteenth, fifteenth, and sixteenth centuries. Dallari, 1888–1924, 1:5 (full description of his duties, repeated briefly in other rolls), 7, and 4:*Aggiunte,* 14, 16, 18, for the fourteenth century. Dallari, 1888–1924, vols. 1 and 2, for the fifteenth and sixteenth centuries. Two to four or five men taught abbaco at any one time.

The abbaco position was a communally funded preuniversity teaching post for the purpose of instructing boys in commercial mathematics and elementary accounting. Abbachists taught (always in the vernacular) boys intended for merchant careers how to solve business-related problems, such as calculating interest, discounting loans, money exchange, partnership divisions, measurement and distance problems, and alligation exercises, that is, determining how much gold or silver to add or subtract to an existing metallic mixture in order to obtain coins of a certain purity. The mathematics employed combined arithmetic, algorism, algebra, geometry, and what might be called ingenious reasoning. See Grendler, 1989, 306–29, for examples and more bibliography. University professors, by contrast, taught (in Latin) mathematics, astronomy, and astrology based on Euclid, Sacrobosco, and Ptolemy to men who would become physicians, philosophers, legists, and humanists.

The abbachists, the four to six grammarians paid by the Bolognese commune to teach Latin grammar and literature to boys in various quarters of the city, and the one to three writing masters for various parts of the city constituted an embryonic public school system. See Grendler, 1989, 22–29, with examples from other towns as well. They were listed on the university rolls only for the administrative reason that the commune of Bologna appointed and paid them.

Contemporaries knew that they were not university teachers. For example, in his 1573 proposal to rearrange the teaching hours of the university, Ulisse Aldrovandi never mentioned the abbaco/arithmetic, Latin, or writing teachers. BA, Ms. B3803, "Informatione del Rotulo del Studio di Bologna . . . 1573." Finally, the salaries demonstrated that the abbachists, grammarians, and reading and writing masters taught at the preuniversity level. The preuniversity teachers normally received 25 to 50 Bolognese lire, and a maximum of 100 lire. Professors received 100 lire and higher. ASB, Assunteria di Studio, Bu. 92, fascicle 4, salaries for 1523–24 and 1526–27.

41. Dallari, 1888–1924, 2:31–175 passim. For the title "Ad lecturam Astronomie et Mathematice," see ibid., 2:37, 40 (1453–55).

42. Ibid., 1:121–85 passim. Novara appears as "Dominicus Maria" and "Dominicus Maria de Ferraria." See also Bortolotti, 1947, 20–21, and Rosen, 1981b.

in mathematics and astronomy predated Italy, these interests flourished during his years in Italy. But the impact of his university studies on the evolution of his thought is difficult to evaluate.[43]

Having changed its name from astrology, the astronomy (or astronomy and mathematics) post continued in the sixteenth century. In 1508–9 the ordinary professorship of astronomy became a holiday professorship (*diebus festivis*); two, three, or four astronomers taught under this title into the 1560s.[44] The year 1555–56 saw another name change: in that year the university had a professor of mathematics (*Ad praxim mathematicae*), who taught alongside the two astronomers. For the next fifteen years, Bologna had a mathematician, an astronomer or two, and a student astronomy lecturer.[45] The talented algebraist Ludovico Ferrari (1522–65) held the mathematical post for the last year of his life, 1564–65.[46] From 1572 the position, now restored to an ordinary professorship, was called mathematics. From that date through 1587–88, Bologna had an ordinary professorship of mathematics plus a student lectureship in astronomy. From 1588–89 through the end of the century, the university had two ordinary professors of mathematics, one teaching at the fourth hour of the morning and the other teaching at the fourth hour of the afternoon. The student astronomy lectureship disappeared in the 1590s.[47]

In 1573 Ulisse Aldrovandi noted that only a few students attended the lectures of the mathematician. One wonders if the reason was his lack of distinction.[48] Then in 1576 the university appointed the accomplished and versatile Egnazio Danti (1536–86), who remained through 1583. A Dominican friar, Danti had previously taught mathematics, and had performed a variety of tasks involving the practical use of mathematics, at the Medici court in Florence. Danti studied or published works on geography, cosmography, mapmaking, the astrolabe, military architecture, perspective, mechanics, gnomonics (constructing sundials), and calendar reform, as well as traditional mathematical and astronomical topics.[49]

Pietro Antonio Cataldi (1552–1626) replaced Danti as ordinary morning professor of mathematics sometime in the academic year 1583–84 and held the position until his death. Cataldi wrote numerous works, always in the vernacular, in theoretical and practical arithmetic, algebra, geometry, and astronomy. He was

---

43. The outline of Copernicus's Italian university years is found in Rosen, 1981a, 401–2. For a study of what is known about his Bolognese years, see Sighinolfi, 1920. For a review of the scholarship on Copernicus's Paduan career, see Bilinski, 1983.

44. See Dallari, 1888–1924, 1:201, for 1508–9.

45. Ibid., 2:136, 139, 142, 144, 146, and so on.

46. Ibid., 162, and Jayawardene, 1981b.

47. Dallari, 1888–1924, 2:121–272 passim.

48. BA, Ms. B. 3803, "Informatione del Rotulo del Studio di Bologna," f. 9ᵛ. The undistinguished mathematician was Francesco Burdino, who taught from 1570 to 1579. Nothing is known about him.

49. Dallari, 1888–1924, 2:195, 198, 201, 204, 206, 209, 212, 215, 218. Bologna had two mathematicians in the years 1576–79. Danti was a member of the commission to reform the Julian calendar from 1580 and became bishop of Alatri in the fall of 1583. See Righini-Bonelli, 1981; Fiore, 1986; and Settle, 1990.

an innovative algebraist who is remembered for his explication of infinite number series and unlimited continuous fractions.[50] Overall, the Bolognese mathematicians of the sixteenth and early seventeenth centuries made significant contributions in algebra.[51]

Thus, Bologna had at least two, and sometimes three or four, mathematicians, more than any other university, throughout the Renaissance. The Bolognese rolls also document the evolution of the name of the position. It was called astrology in the fourteenth and early fifteenth centuries. The name "astronomy" dominated from about 1450 to about 1550, while the name "astrology" disappeared from the rolls, although not in instruction. The name "mathematics" first appeared in the rolls of the 1450s and remained a minority name for a century or so. Mathematics pulled even with astronomy in the 1560s, and replaced astronomy in the 1570s, for the rest of the century. Astronomy remained only as the title of the student lectureship, which was left unfilled in the 1590s. In contrast to the practical bent of Paduan mathematicians, Bolognese mathematicians of the sixteenth century achieved major advances in technical mathematics, especially algebra.

Other Universities

None of the other universities was as important as Padua and Bologna in mathematics. But they manifested the same pattern of change. The University of Florence usually had a professor of astrology in the fourteenth and fifteenth centuries. Often the post was a holiday lectureship (*diebus festivis*), and sometimes the subject was taught in conjunction with one of the medical lectureships. From 1435–36 through 1441–42, one Bernardo di Andrea Bonaventura taught the unusual combination of surgery as an ordinary professor and astrology as holiday lecturer. He then taught only astrology from 1442 through 1448. The astrologer received a low salary, usually 25 to 72 florins, throughout.[52]

When the university moved to Pisa in 1473, it lacked a mathematician until the appointment of Luca Pacioli to teach Euclid in the years 1500–1503 and 1504–6. An astrologer also taught from 1501 to 1503 and another mathematician

---

50. Dallari, 1888–1924, 2:215 and subsequent years. See also Bortolotti, 1947, 81–93; Carruccio, 1981a; and De Ferrari, 1979a, all with additional bibliography.

51. On the other hand, two distinguished local mathematicians did not teach the subject at the university. Rafael Bombelli (1526–72), the greatest Bolognese algebraist of the century, was an engineer who neither studied nor taught at the University of Bologna. Jayawardene, 1981a; Rose, 1976, 146. Girolamo Cardano, known for his work in algebra, probability theory, game theory, and mechanics, published much of his mathematical work before going in 1562 to the University of Bologna, where he taught medicine. M. Gliozzi, 1976 and 1981, and Rose, 1976, see index, each with additional bibliography.

52. For the professors of astrology, see Park, 1980, 262–63, 280, 282–83, 285, 287–88, 290–92, 294, 296–303, 308 (292, 294, 296–303, 308, for Bonaventura), and Gherardi, 1973, 261, 402 414, 444. For 1391–97, see Spagnesi, 1979, 272. The one exception to low salaries was Fra Batista da Fabriano, who was paid 140 florins to teach natural philosophy and astrology in 1447–48. Park, 1980, 308. No doubt most of his salary was for teaching natural philosophy.

from 1516 to 1522.[53] Upon reopening in 1543, Pisa often had two professors of mathematics, the new name for the position, from 1543 until 1588, then one from 1588 to the end of the century and beyond.[54] Two of them rose above the ordinary. Filippo Fantoni (d. 1591), who taught in the years 1560–67 and 1581–89, wrote a work on calendar reform, a compendium of cosmography and astronomy which incorporated material on the New World, a treatise on mathematical certitude, and a work on motion.[55] He was succeeded by the youthful Galilei (age twenty-five), who taught at Pisa from 1589 to 1592, at a salary of 60 scudi. It was a suitable, even generous, stipend for an unproven young man in a lectureship whose stipend was usually found in the lowest quartile of university salaries.[56] Galileo Galilei taught books 1 and 5 of Euclid in his first two years (1589–91), and book 1 plus "hypotheses on celestial motion" (*celestium motuum hipotheses*) in 1591–92. His concentration on mathematics, and omission of Ptolemy, medieval texts, and astrological works, indicated the direction of his mind.[57] While teaching at Pisa, Galilei wrote *De motu,* in which, under the influence of Archimedes, he departed from Aristotle in order to treat motion mathematically.[58]

The University of Perugia had an astrology position in the fifteenth century. In the late sixteenth century, Perugia had two mathematicians, both vacation lecturers, in mathematics and "spheres and mathematics," which suggests astronomy. Two well-known mathematicians taught at Perugia: Luca Pacioli in the periods 1477–80, 1486–88, and 1510–11, and Pietro Antonio Cataldi, who taught at Perugia from 1569 to 1583 before moving to Bologna.[59]

The University of Rome did not emphasize mathematics. A professor of medicine, who also lectured on astrology, taught from 1481 to 1483.[60] The initial surviving roll, that of 1514, listed a mathematician, Luca Pacioli, and an astrol-

---

53. See Verde, 1973–94, 1:375, 378, 382. On Pacioli and Marsilio Rosati, the astrologer of 1501–3, see ibid., 2:462–65, 482–83; Fabroni, 1971, 1:392–93; and Del Gratta, 1993a, 492, 502.

54. See the list in Barsanti, 1993, 566. Schmitt, 1972, 255–63, is the fundamental source. Some rolls have been printed: those of 1543–44 and 1567–68 in Cascio Pratilli, 1975, 192–95, and rolls of 1585–86 and 1589–91 in Galilei, 1966, 32–35, 37–42.

55. Schmitt, 1972, 256–57; Barsanti, 1993, 518, 566; and the roll of 1585–86, which lists Fantoni, in Galilei, 1966, 34. On Fantoni, see Schmitt, 1978, with the list of his teaching on 57.

56. See the listing of Galilei in the rolls of 1589–91 in Galilei, 1966, 39, 41, and another document on 43. It is sometimes claimed that Galilei was very ill paid at Pisa, for example, Cascio Pratilli, 1975, 166. This was not the case; Galilei received an appropriate salary given his inexperience and the salary structure in Renaissance universities. Indeed, he did a little better than expected, because ten professors (of the total of forty-five), including some civil law professors, were paid only 45 florins in 1589–90.

57. Schmitt, 1972, 255–63, with the quote describing Galilei's teaching from an archival document on 262.

58. See Schmitt, 1969, especially 106–38.

59. Ermini, 1971, 234–35, 584–87; De Ferrari, 1979a, 288, for Cataldi. Another mathematician was Girolamo Bigazzini (1480–1564), who probably taught in the 1540s and 1550s. See Comparato, 1968. The list in Biagioli, 1989, 93–94, fails to note that the two abbachists taught at the preuniversity level.

60. This was Giovanni Doddo (or Doddi) da Padova. See Dorati da Empoli, 1980, 107, 130; and Lee, 1984, 145.

oger.[61] After the sack of 1527, the renewed university practically ignored mathematics until 1566.[62] From that date through the end of the century and beyond, a single mathematician regularly appeared on the rolls.[63] One Roman mathematician participated in the revival of Greek mathematics. Anton Maria Pazzi, who taught mathematics in the years 1559–60 and 1566–71, had an excellent command of Greek and may have translated works of Hero and Pappus. He also found a manuscript of Diophantus's *Arithmetica* in the Vatican Library. He worked with Rafael Bombelli to prepare a translation but never completed it, probably because of his bad health. The beadle several times commented that Pazzi's sickly condition caused him to miss lectures, with the result that he had few students.[64] By the end of the century, mathematics had declined; beginning in 1601, a single professor taught the unlikely combination of mathematics and moral philosophy. The Jesuits at the Collegio Romano exercised mathematical leadership in Rome in the late sixteenth and early seventeenth centuries.[65]

Mathematics at Pavia gradually became an independent subject and underwent the usual name change from astrology to mathematics. In the late fourteenth and early fifteenth centuries, astrology was an addendum to natural philosophy. Biagio Pelacani taught natural philosophy, moral philosophy, and astrology, or the combination of moral philosophy, astrology, and mathematics, in 1377–78, 1387–88, and from 1389 to 1407 or 1408. Pelacani's mathematical interests included astrology, astronomy, optics, weights, and the velocity of motion.[66] A lowly paid professor of astrology or another professor teaching natural philosophy and astrology, or both, occasionally joined Pelacani.

After a hiatus of more than a decade, an ordinary professorship of astrology appeared in 1418–19. The position had two professors in the 1430s but declined to one astrologer in the second half of the fifteenth century. In addition, Giovanni Marliani often added astrology to his medical lecturing in the 1450s, 1460s, and 1470s. The post had changed its name to mathematics in the mid-sixteenth century. A single ordinary professor of mathematics taught at Pavia for the rest of

---

61. *I maestri di Roma*, 1991, 4; Renazzi, 1971, 2:50–51.

62. Of the nine surviving rolls 1535 through 1563, only two (1535 and 1559) listed a mathematician. *I maestri di Roma*, 1991, 8, 30, 1047.

63. Ibid., 40, 48, 53, 61, 67, 77, 89, 101, 111, 116, 123, 132, 136, 141, 146, 154, 157, 162, 165, 170 (1566 through 1609, with gaps), 1047. The post was doubled three times and is missing from two rolls. See also Renazzi, 1971, 2:176–77 and 3:36.

64. Rose, 1976, 146–47, 149, 207–8; Jayawardene, 1981a, 280. For his teaching, see *I maestri di Roma*, 1991, 30, 40, 48, 53, 61, 77 (comment of beadle).

65. See Wallace, 1984. Christoph Clavius (1537–1612), who taught at the Collegio Romano from 1565 until his death, was the best-known mathematician there.

66. For the rolls through 1407–8, see Maiocchi, 1971, 1:119, 153, 154, 186, 225, 228, 312; vol. 2, pt. 1:40, 68, 84, 98. Pelacani continued to teach when the university was in Piacenza (1399–1402). On Pelacani, see Thorndike, 1923–58, 4:65–79, 652–62; Vescovini, 1979; and *CHRP*, 809, with additional bibliography. *Memorie di Pavia* (1970, pt. 1:147–50) lists those who taught mathematics at Pavia. The list in Biagioli, 1989, 93, is very incomplete. For a brief survey of mathematics at Pavia which concentrates on the post-Renaissance period, see Galafassi, 1961.

the century and beyond. The only important mathematician at Pavia was the medical professor Girolamo Cardano, who never taught mathematics in the university, so far as is known.[67]

Ferrara, with its strong emphasis on humanism, paid little attention to mathematics. The university usually had a single professor of mathematics, with the position occasionally rising to two, or left unfilled, in the second half of the fifteenth century.[68] But the common pattern was for a scholar with primary expertise in another discipline to teach mathematics briefly before moving on to another lectureship.

In the sixteenth century mathematics became an independent professorship with a variety of names: astrology, astronomy, and most often "Spheres and Euclid" (*Ad lecturam Spherae et Euclidis*), which indicated that the texts taught were Sacrobosco's *De sphaera* and Euclid. However, those who held the position still tended to be scholars whose major expertise was elsewhere. For example, the poet Torquato Tasso (1544–95) taught "spheres and Euclid" at Ferrara for two academic years, 1575–77.[69] Only at the beginning of the seventeenth century did the position finally become "mathematics."

The University of Siena had a professor of astrology in 1492–93 and 1500–1501.[70] The next available rolls, those from 1531–32 through 1539–40, listed a single professor of astronomy, whose title became mathematics in 1539–40.[71] The mathematical position disappeared in the 1560s, 1570s, and 1580s but reappeared after the reorganization of the university in the 1590s.[72] None of the holders of the position was a mathematician of distinction.

There is no evidence of a mathematician at the University of Turin in its first

67. For the period 1418–19 through midcentury, see Maiocchi, 1971, vol. 2, pt. 1:167, 185, 222, 232, 240, 247, 265, 269, 282, 293, 304, 318, 356, 395; vol. 2, pt. 2:432, 433, 469, 470, 484, 485, 495, 496, 520, 528. For the second half of the fifteenth century, see Sottili, 1982, 548; *Documenti di Pavia*, 1994, 193 (roll of 1455–56); Verde, 1973–94, 1:387, 391; and ASPv, Università, Cartone 20, various rolls, no pag., and Cartone 22. For rolls of 1538–39, and many rolls in the second half of the sixteenth century, see ASPv, Università, Cartoni 20 and 22. The roll of 1538–39 called the post astronomy, but the next surviving roll, 1553–54, and all subsequent rolls called it mathematics. See Rizzo, 1987, 76 n. 35, for the roll of 1584–85. On Cardano as a mathematician, see M. Gliozzi, 1981, and Rose, 1976, index.

68. *I maestri di Ferrara*, 1991, 6–20, plus the brief summaries of the teaching and publications of individual professors. The information for the fifteenth century is not always reliable. See also Secco Suardo, 1983, 266.

69. In addition, the natural philosopher Cesare Cremonini taught "Spheres and Euclid" in 1588–89. *I maestri di Ferrara*, 1991, 20–50 passim, 41–42 for Tasso, 46 for Cremonini; Franceschini, 1970, 263.

70. Zdekauer, 1977, 193; Mondolfo, 1897, 417. On the other hand, Siena had no astrologer in 1474–75. Minnucci and Košuta, 1989, 119–21.

71. Minnucci and Košuta, 1989, 398, 401, 404, 408, 412. The list of mathematicians at Siena in Biagioli, 1989, 95, is incomplete.

72. For eight rolls, 1563–64 through 1589–90, see Cascio Pratilli, 1975, 175–88. A mathematician appears in eleven of the twelve rolls from 1590–91 through 1601–02. Marrara, 1970, 230–47, passim.

century and a half. But from 1566 on it had a single mathematician.[73] The University of Naples never had an ongoing professorship of mathematics in the fifteenth and sixteenth centuries and began teaching the subject regularly only in 1653.[74] The universities of Catania, Macerata, Salerno, and Messina lacked mathematicians. Parma had a professorship of mathematics, always held by a Jesuit, from its beginning in 1601 (see Ch. 4, tables 4.6 and 4.8).

LUCA PACIOLI

Luca Pacioli attracted more attention than any Renaissance mathematician before Galilei, even though he contributed no original concept or technique. Rather, he was a successful traveling salesman for the discipline.

Born in Sansepolcro about 1445, Pacioli may have studied mathematics with the most famous son of the town, the painter and excellent mathematician Piero della Francesca (1410/15–92). Pacioli learned abbaco and became an abbaco teacher at the preuniversity level, especially in Venice. He was the guest of Leon Battista Alberti (1404–72) in Rome for several months and then joined the Franciscan order sometime between 1470 and 1477. After his religious studies, Fra Pacioli returned to the lay world as an itinerant professor of mathematics. He probably taught initially at the University of Perugia for three years, 1477 through 1480.[75] The next few years of his life are blank until he appeared again as a professor at the University of Perugia (1486–88). He may have taught at the universities of Naples and Rome in 1489 and 1490, but documentation has not been located.[76]

In 1493 or 1494 Pacioli came to Venice to see his magnum opus, the *Summa de arithmetica, geometria, proportioni et proportionalità* (1494; second edition 1523) through the press. Dedicated to the duke of Urbino, Guidobaldo da Montefeltro, who may have been a pupil, this encyclopedia summarized much of the available mathematical learning and implied a program for the future. During the academic year 1493–94 Pacioli visited Padua and may have taught at the university, either for a few lectures or as professor for the whole year.[77] He next appeared as a professor at the ducal court in Milan in 1497–98 and 1498–99, teaching geome-

73. No mathematicians are listed in Bellone, 1986, or in the rolls of 1532–33 and 1534–35 in Vallauri, 1970, 1:135–39. Nevertheless, as noted earlier, the 1448 statutes of Turin listed texts to be taught in mathematics. For the rolls from 1566 through 1630, see Chiaudano, 1972b and 1972a.

74. Naples had two professors of astrology in 1469–70, a professor of logic and geometry from 1512 to 1515, and a professor of mathematics in 1533–34. Cannavale, 1980, 47, 55–57, 64; Filangieri di Candida, 1924, 185; Cortese, 1924, 303, 336; and the list in Biagioli, 1989, 92.

75. Ermini, 1971, 585–86, who gives archival references for all the years of Pacioli's teaching at the University of Perugia. For Pacioli, the best short sketch is Jayawardene, 1981c; see also Rose, 1976, index. Taylor, 1942, is well written and gives much information but is not the greatly needed scholarly biography of Pacioli. The articles in *Luca Pacioli*, 1998, discuss aspects of his work.

76. Renazzi (1971, 1:227) states that Pacioli taught at the University of Rome between 1480 and 1490 and then moved to the University of Naples.

77. Favaro, 1922, 46.

try and arithmetic at a salary of 200 florins.[78] While at Milan he became the friend of and mathematical advisor to Leonardo da Vinci. When the city fell to the French in September 1499, Pacioli and Leonardo moved to Florence.

Pacioli shared quarters with Leonardo da Vinci in Florence for a time. He also taught mathematics at the University of Pisa, temporarily located in Florence, for five of the next six academic years, 1500–1503 and 1504–6. He received a salary of 60 florins, with the obligation to give private lessons to those who wanted them, the first year. His fame as a mathematician and his association with Leonardo da Vinci probably attracted Florentine patricians. Pacioli received 80 florins the second year and 100 florins (on condition that he teach all the books of Euclid) the third year.[79] After the University of Pisa (still in Florence) closed in 1506, Pacioli was in Venice by August 1508. There he lectured to Venetian patricians and supervised publication of two more works, *De divina proportione* and a Latin translation of Euclid, both of 1509. In 1510–11 Pacioli again taught at the University of Perugia. His final appointment was as professor of mathematics at the University of Rome in 1514–15, at a salary of 120 florins.[80] He died in Sansepolcro in 1517.

Although not an original thinker, Pacioli summarized a great deal of information, especially in algebra. As noted earlier, he made available the advanced algebra and number theory of Leonardo Fibonacci. Renaissance algebraists followed the framework established by Pacioli in the *Summa* and cited him often. Pacioli's greatest accomplishment was to stimulate enthusiasm for mathematics through his university teaching, his private tutoring, and possibly through the fame of his association with Leonardo da Vinci. He crisscrossed Italy telling anyone who would listen the glories of mathematics; the major achievements of the mathematical Renaissance came shortly thereafter.

THE PROGRESS OF MATHEMATICS

In 1400 university mathematics seemed to be a skill to be learned in order to comprehend astronomy and astrology, including astrological medicine. Over the next two centuries, mathematics became much more an independent discipline to be studied for its own sake and its practical applications in the physical world. Calendar reform, mechanics, motion, perspective, the study of tides, and the mathematics of military fortifications all received increased attention. The Greek mathematical revival of such authors as Archimedes focused attention on mathematics lacking astrological relevance. Indeed, mathematicians engrossed in the

---

78. "Mag.r Lucas de S.to Sepulcro Ordinis Minorum, qui legat Geometriam et Aritmeticam. Flor. CC." ASPv, Università, Cartone 22, ff. 217ᵛ, 222ᵛ (quote). This appointment has not been previously noticed.

79. Verde, 1973–94, 1:55, 375, 378, 382; 2:462–65; Fabroni, 1971, 1:392; and Del Gratta, 1993a, 489. Pacioli apparently did not teach at the University of Bologna in 1501–2, despite his appearance on its roll. Dallari, 1888–1924, 1:178.

80. *I maestri di Roma*, 1991, 4.

revival of Greek mathematics began to attack astrology as uncertain. For these and other reasons astrology declined in importance.[81] Thus, it was no accident that the professorship was renamed "mathematics" in all universities except Ferrara by the mid-sixteenth century. The new name indicated the new orientation and greater importance of mathematics at the expense of astrology and, to some extent, astronomy.

With new techniques and confidence, mathematicians broadened their inquiry into areas traditionally claimed by natural philosophy. They wrote treatises on mathematical certainty, a sign of their growing confidence.[82] They offered mathematical demonstration as an alternative to traditional syllogistic reasoning. Galilei's research, although not necessarily his university teaching, was the culmination of this process.

Some universities participated in the mathematical revival much more than others. Even though the number of professors of mathematics was always low, most often one, the accomplishments of those who held the posts at Padua and Bologna made them the leading mathematical universities. Padua emphasized what might be called mathematical engineering, that is, the use of mathematics to solve practical problems in the physical world. Bologna had two to four mathematicians and led in the development of increasingly sophisticated algebra and geometry.

The expansion of mathematics into new areas continued in the following century. Galilei's *Dialogue Concerning the Two Chief World Systems* of 1632 and *Two New Sciences* of 1638 announced a sweeping reorientation in mathematics and physical sciences. In the latter he treated statics, kinematics, and motion physically and mathematically in ways that provided foundations for modern science. His method and studies of the physical world raised fundamental questions that occupied mathematicians and natural philosophers. Some rejected Aristotle in favor of a science based on mathematics, experiment, and empiricism. Others tried to reconcile Galileo and Aristotle by inserting Galilean mechanics into an eclectic, if ramshackle, Aristotelianism. On the whole, seventeenth-century Italian university mathematicians and natural philosophers assimilated Galilei within a short time. The acceptance of a new mathematically oriented experimental science, along with the abandonment of Aristotelian physics, was indisputable by the late seventeenth century.[83]

Galilei aided the process in ways other than through his books. He had great influence on Italian university mathematicians through his correspondence and his patronage, which helped followers to obtain university positions at Bologna and Pisa and, to a lesser extent, at Padua. Most of them continued and developed

81. This statement seems valid for universities as a whole, despite the evidence that Schmitt (1972, 259) offers for the continuing importance of astrology at Pisa between 1543 and 1589. For an attack on astrology, see Rose, 1976, 172.

82. N. Jardine, 1988, 693–702.

83. This is the theme of Soppelsa, 1974; see especially the conclusions on 201–8. See also Torrini, 1979; Soppelsa, 1986; and Schmitt, 1983d, esp. 220.

his ideas.[84] They coped with the difficulties created by the papal condemnations of Copernicanism as reality (it could be held as a hypothesis) in 1616 and of Galilei in 1633.

Bonaventura Cavalieri (1598?–1647), professor of mathematics at the University of Bologna from 1629 until his death, is a case in point. Cavalieri, who considered himself a follower of Galilei, is best known for his original work on infinitesimals in geometry, but he taught Copernican and Galilean astronomy as well. His lectures for two academic years, 1642–44, seemed to give equal time to Ptolemy, Copernicus, and Tycho Brahe. For example, Cavalieri lectured on "the construction of the universe" according to the theories of Ptolemy, Copernicus, and Brahe, respectively, on successive days in November 1642. The assigned texts to explicate Ptolemy were the *Almagest,* Regiomontanus's *Epitome* of the *Almagest,* and the *Theories* of Puerbach. For Copernicus, "which [was] set forth merely as a hypothesis," students were to read the "corrected" form of his masterwork, *On the Revolution of the Orbs,* and Johann Kepler's *Epitome* of Copernican astronomy.[85] The schedule of lectures balanced tradition and novelty. But it is very likely that Cavalieri taught Copernican and Galilean views quite sympathetically.

Universities eventually created new positions that gave institutional recognition to the larger scope of mathematics. In 1650 Bologna established a professorship of mechanics.[86] In 1678 the Venetian Senate divided the single mathematics post at Padua into two. From that date, one professor taught mathematics, and the other held a new position called astronomy and meteorology.[87] Given curricular conservatism, these were significant changes.

The first holder of the Paduan astronomy and meteorology position was Geminiano Montanari (1633–87), who had previously taught mathematics at Bologna (1664–78). His broad research interests included acoustics, atmospheric phenomena, hydrology, hydrostatics, meteorology, optics, and photometrics. In 1664 he charted the exact position of a comet with the aid of instruments he invented or improved; he later discovered variable stars. A follower of Galilei who was familiar with the works of Descartes, Montanari pursued an empirical methodology and published a book ridiculing astrology.[88] Such examples could be multiplied. The Italian Renaissance of mathematics of the sixteenth century came to fruition in the new science of the seventeenth century.

84. For an overview, see Segre, 1991, ch. 3 and passim. For Pisa, see Iofrida, 1993, 305–16, and Maccagni, 1993, 353–56. For Bologna, see Cavalieri below. For Padua, see Favaro, 1917, 96–121; Favaro, 1966, 2:7–17; and Carugo, 1984, 192–99.

85. Thorndike, 1944, 393–405, quotations on 394, 396 (booklist). On Cavalieri, see Bortolotti, 1947, 11–12, 81–82, 94–95, 101–8; Carruccio, 1991b; and De Ferrari, 1979b.

86. Bortolotti, 1947, 82. Pietro Mengoli (1625–86) held the position from 1650 to 1678.

87. Soppelsa, 1974, 117. See also the roll of 1737 in AAUP, Inventario 1320, no pag., which listed the two posts. At that time the mathematician taught the elements of geometry and military architecture.

88. Soppelsa, 1974, 119–32, and Rosino, 1988. For further discussion of the development of mathematics at the University of Padua in the seventeenth and eighteenth centuries, see Soppelsa, 1986.

CHAPTER 13

Law

When the opinions of the doctors are in disagreement, that of Bartolo should
prevail as greater than all the others.
—Annibale Roero, *Lo scolare*, 1604

aw mattered in the Renaissance. The civil state used law in order to
expand its jurisdiction over society and individuals. To do this,
Renaissance governments needed a corpus of legal principles and a
growing army of administrators, advisors, judges, and officials with
some knowledge of law. Notarial training, once the prerequisite for important positions in civil society, was no longer considered adequate. Men increasingly needed law degrees in order to advance in civil administration and to
achieve noble status.[1] Those who opposed the expansion of government also
used the law. All this meant that an increasing number of men sought and
obtained law degrees.

The center of Italian legal instruction was ancient Roman law. Italian universities pioneered the study and teaching of Roman law and continued to offer the
most admired instruction in Europe. While continuing the traditions of medieval
Italian jurisprudence, Renaissance universities responded to new needs by introducing changes in the structure of professorships and teaching. They reduced the
number of canon law professorships and added professorships in civil law for

Epigraph: "Onde in alcuni paesi per statuto regio è stabilito, che ove sono discordanti le opinioni
de' Dottori, prevagli quella di Bartolo, come del maggiore di tutti gli altri." Roero, 1604, 14.

1. For example, a law degree replaced training in notarial art as the prerequisite for advancement,
especially for those who sought their fortune in the capital city of Florence, in the small Tuscan
commune of Poppi in the sixteenth and seventeenth centuries. Benadusi, 1996, 103–7. The preference for a law degree began early in the Renaissance.

specialized legal topics. They accepted humanistic jurisprudence to a limited degree. The changes were significant, if less dramatic than those in medicine.

MOS ITALICUS

The pedagogical tradition began when Emperor Justinian (ruled 527–65) ordered a compilation of the writings and opinions of classical Roman jurists going back to the early days of Rome. He also ordered the codification of existing Roman law.[2] This immense labor yielded several texts that became the *Corpus juris civilis,* a summary of Roman law and the last great achievement of the Roman Empire. In the following centuries, imperial authority disintegrated. A host of towns, lordly domains, kingdoms, and ecclesiastical jurisdictions, each issuing laws and decrees, took its place. The conflicts were infinite among the hundreds, probably thousands, of political units in Italy. Northern Europe, where customary law and feudal law dominated, had even more jurisdictions. Legists had to sort out the conflicting legal claims of these bodies and the rights of individuals in them. They eventually turned to the *Corpus juris civilis* to find a path out of the legal wilderness.

In the late eleventh century, scholars began to work through the *Corpus juris civilis* to develop a body of legal principles. While legal experts were to be found in several northern Italian towns, a group of them made Bologna the center of the Roman law revival. Their chosen method was the gloss, a word-by-word exegesis. The glossators, as they came to be called, began with the Bolognese Irnerius (1055–c. 1130) and concluded with the greatest and most prolific, Accursius (d. c. 1263). Other scholars and students came to Bologna to learn from Irnerio and his successors. The glossators wanted to understand the meaning of each word in the text, the legislator's intention behind the word, and, ultimately, the larger sense of the law. Legal scholars and practicing jurists began to regard Roman law as common law (*ius commune*) embodying principles of universal applicability. *Ius commune* could give some unity and coherence to the many different forms and examples of statutory, customary, and feudal law.

Gratian (fl. 1140s), a monk at a Bolognese monastery, did for church law what Justinian's legists had done for Roman law. About 1148 he published his *Concordia discordantium canonum,* usually called the *Decretum,* a collection of laws, including the decrees of the Second Lateran Council of 1139, and legal opinions.[3] It was the beginning of a legal code for the church. Scholars at Bologna and elsewhere adopted Gratian's *Decretum* as a textbook for the study of canon law.

Following the example of the glossators, canonists began to gloss Gratian's work. Called "Decretists," they continued their labors for a hundred years after

2. For the origins of medieval law in the universities, see the classic works of Savigny, 1834–51; Besta, 1925b, esp. 784–901; and Calasso, 1954; and the fresh appraisals of Radding, 1988; Bellomo, 1995; and Southern, 1995, 264–318. For briefer surveys, see Kuttner, 1982; Donahue, 1986; Ascheri, 1991, 131–32; and García y García, 1992.

3. In addition to the bibliography in note 2, see Chodorow, 1986.

Gratian; Hugutio (Uguccione) of Pisa (d. 1210) was the greatest of the tribe. Because the church was a living organism generating new laws and decrees, various popes issued, and Gratian's successors prepared, additional compilations. These texts and opinions eventually (by about 1500) became known collectively as the *Corpus juris canonici*. Thus, by the thirteenth century Italian legal scholarship had an agreed-upon core of legal texts and opinions to teach and a method (glossing) of instruction for both Roman and ecclesiastical law.

Medieval jurisprudence reached maturity in the school of the commentators of the fourteenth century. Having mastered the meanings of words and the sense of the texts, the postglossators investigated the law through the same Scholastic dialectical process used for natural philosophy and medicine. These legal scholars go by the name of postglossators, commentators, or "Bartolists," for its most famous figure, and the approach is called *mos italicus* (Italian method or style).

Instead of writing glosses investigating a word or a single point, the commentators applied Scholastic methodology to both civil and canon law in order to develop universal legal principles. The original texts from Justinian's Rome and Gratian's *Decretum* served as springboards for commentary applicable to medieval society. The commentators dismantled a text into its structural elements and logical moments and then reassembled the pieces into a coherent system. The commentator began with a statement and then began to develop the topic in all its ramifications, down to small details. He listed affirmative and negative views and then resolved the contradictions dialectically. In short, the commentators created a science of law. The process was rational and thorough, the Latin prose dull and turgid. But reasoning and comprehension mattered more than style.

The school of the commentators reached its highest point with Bartolo (Bartolus) of Sassoferrato (1313/14–57), the person whose name symbolized *mos italicus* throughout the Renaissance. Bartolo was born near Sassoferrato, a remote town in the Apennine Mountains about 70 kilometers northeast of Perugia in territory later ruled by Urbino. He was a precocious student who began his study of civil law at the age of fourteen under Cino (Sighibuldi) da Pistoia (c. 1270–1336), the pioneering postglossator, at the University of Perugia. Bartolo then took his doctorate at Bologna at the age of twenty or twenty-one.[4] He probably pursued a career as assessor (legal advisor) in various small towns in central Italy until he became a professor of civil law at the University of Pisa in 1339. In 1342 or 1343, he moved to the University of Perugia, where he taught for the rest of his short life, all the while writing voluminously.

The extraordinary number of manuscript and printed copies of his works testifies to Bartolo's influence long after his death. Hundreds, perhaps thousands, of manuscripts survive. The major Venetian printer Nicholas Jenson produced the first collected edition of Bartolo's works in eight volumes between 1477 and

4. For biographical information, see Sheedy, 1942, 11–27, and Calasso, 1964, 640–43. The bibliography on Bartolo is enormous; see Calasso, 1964, 667–69, for some of it. For a sampling of Bartolo's views in English translation, see Emerton, 1925, 119–54, and 255–84. See also Woolf, 1913, and Sheedy, 1942, for some of his opinions on the state, tyranny, family, city, and nobility.

1479; two additional eight-volume editions (Lyon and Venice) appeared before 1490, and there were nearly 140 incunabular editions in all. In the following century the Giunti of Venice, the leading legal publisher in Italy and perhaps in Europe, issued Bartolo's *opera omnia* in eleven double-columned folio volumes in 1567 and reissued that edition eight more times between 1570 and 1615.[5]

The other great fourteenth-century legal scholar, whose name marches in step with Bartolo, was Baldo degli Ubaldi (Baldus de Ubaldis).[6] Born in Perugia possibly in 1327, Baldo studied there, learning civil law from Bartolo. When and where he took his degree are unknown, but he was definitely teaching at the University of Perugia in 1351, remaining there until about 1357. Thus, the two most famous jurists of medieval Europe taught side by side for at least six years at the modest University of Perugia. Baldo's growing fame led to other positions. He taught at Pisa probably in 1357–58, at Florence 1358–64, in Perugia again 1365–76, at Padua 1376–79, at Perugia probably from 1379 to 1390, and finally at the University of Pavia from 1390 until his death in 1400. Baldo also wrote voluminously-more than seven million words, probably the most of any medieval legist—and had many followers.

Italian jurisprudence was modern in its goals. It created doctrines and a method that would enable the judge or lawyer to use Roman law principles to resolve contemporary legal issues. By focusing on ancient law, the Bartolists found the underlying meaning or reason of law. In their interpretations they paid particular attention to certain concepts that became part of the Western legal tradition. These included bestowing great authority on the ruler ("What pleases the prince has the force of law"); popular sovereignty (the prince is bound by the law); the status of persons; the distinction between public and private; the notion of property; and the principle of bringing legal action to redress injury.[7]

The ultimate reason for the dual (common and local) nature of law, and the dominant position of Roman law, is that Italians and Europeans were subject to both local and universal jurisdiction. Every individual was a subject of an Italian city-state or princedom with its own customs, which were being codified as statutes in the thirteenth and fourteenth centuries. Most Europeans and Italians were also subjects, at least theoretically, of a supranational civil authority, the Holy Roman Empire. And all except Jews and Muslims were members of a universal Catholic Church. Professors, lawyers, and judges needed common legal principles with which to thread their way through different systems. They found them in Roman law.

Because governments evolve and human beings have an infinite capacity to

5. Calasso (1964, 644–63) chronicles the manuscript history and, to a limited extent, the printing history of Bartolo's works. On Jenson's edition, see Lowry, 1991, 157–59 and ch. 6. For the Giunti *opera omnia* editions and additional information, see Camerini, 1962–63, pt. 2:24–27, 39–40, 66–67, 90–92, 118–19, 155–57, 180–81, 242–43, 290–91.

6. This biographical sketch comes from Canning, 1987, 2–6, 9. For some sixteenth- and seventeenth-century printings of Baldo's works, including five printings of his nine-volume *opera omnia*, see Camerini, 1962–63, pt. 2:45–46, 74–75, 89, 129–30, 175–76, 197–98, 290–92.

7. Kelley, 1991, esp. 68–70.

make things more complex, new legal issues arose which Roman law did not cover. The task of the professor was to reconcile Roman or canon law with the experience of the real world, to find the principle that would resolve the issue. *Mos italicus* worked because the commentators were eminently practical men who took great care when applying principles derived from ancient Roman law to contemporary life. Law professors kept in close touch with practicing lawyers and judges. They served as legal advisors to communes, cities, and guilds; they wrote innumerable *consilia* (advisory opinions) on current cases. Universities appointed law professors for their understanding of *ius commune* derived from the *Corpus juris civilis* and their skill in applying it in the resolution of particular cases of statutory law (*ius proprium*). They were not appointed for their expertise in local law. Students came to study with them because Europe's common legal tradition was strongest in Italy and the links to ancient Rome closest. This was the *mos italicus* that dominated Italian legal scholarship and education in the late Middle Ages, the Renaissance, and beyond.

Yet the commentators erected a curious jurisprudential edifice. The Bartolists believed that the compilations of Justinian provided a universal source for texts applicable to all cases in which a special or limited law was lacking. They did not seriously consider that a body of laws created for an ancient pagan society might not be appropriate for medieval Christian Europe. Moreover, although Italian communes and princes respected the legal system of the ancient Roman Empire, they mostly rejected the legal authority of the existing Holy Roman Empire. As one scholar put it, the commentators made the *Corpus juris civilis* into a kind of Roman imperial utopia.[8] Even worse, since the Bartolists were neither historians nor philologians, their interpretations might be mistaken and their theories at variance with the ancient sources. It did not matter so long as the interpretation dealt satisfactorily with the contemporary legal case and was accepted as such. This proved true for several hundred years.

TEACHING TEXTS

Legal instruction followed the organization of the texts in the *Corpus juris civilis* and *Corpus juris canonici*. For civil law, teaching the *Institutes* in four books, an abridgment of the *Digest* which Justinian ordered, was the introductory course in civil law. Every Italian university had a specific *Institutes* professorship, filled by one to three, occasionally more, men. Sometimes students read the *Institutes* with a tutor as preuniversity training. Next came lectures on the *Corpus juris civilis,* the heart of which was the *Digest* (also called *Pandects*) in fifty books comprising classical Roman writings on law over several centuries.[9] Medieval scholars divided the *Digest* into three parts: *Digestum vetus* (*Old Digest*), books 1 through 24.2; *Infortiatum,* books 25–38; and *Digestum novum* (*New Digest*), books 39–50.

8. See the comments of Del Giudice, 1923, 101–3, and Besta, 1925b, 873–80, with the metaphor of the "imperial utopia" at 874. See also Canning, 1987, 6–7.

9. *Digest of Justinian,* 1985, is a modern Latin and English edition.

Next came the *Codex* (*Code*) of Justinian in twelve books, a codification of imperial legislation. It was divided into the *Codex* itself (books 1–9) and the *Volumen parvum* (*Little Volume*), or simply *Volumen,* which comprised books 10–12. The *Volumen parvum* was also called *Tres libri* (*Three Books*), for obvious reasons.[10]

To these basic texts were added the *Novellae* (*Novels*), a collection of 134 imperial laws compiled in the sixth century. But medieval and Renaissance scholars usually called them *Authenticum* or, more often, *Libri authenticorum.* Sometimes a separate professorship was devoted to teaching them. Finally, in the 1150s a feudal judge in Milan wrote a treatise on the customs and practices of feudal law. Revised in the early thirteenth century, this became a collection called *Libri feudorum* (Books of feudal laws) and sometimes *Consuetudines feudorum* (Customs of feudal laws). Since feudal laws influenced medieval Italian communal statutes, some universities had professorships of *Libri feudorum.*[11]

After Gratian, canon law scholars collected a second group of church laws covering the period 1190 through 1226, with the decrees of the Third and Fourth Lateran Councils of 1179 and 1215 figuring prominently.[12] This collection was called the *Extravagantes,* that is, "outside" or "extraneous" to Gratian's *Decretum.* In 1234 Pope Gregory IX sent the faculties of law at Bologna and Paris a more uniform collection of texts to serve as a complete course of instruction. Called the *Decretals of Gregory IX,* it eventually supplanted Gratian's *Decretum.* Most Renaissance universities had professorships devoted to it.

The *Liber Sextus* (or simply *Sextus*), issued by Pope Boniface VIII in 1298, became the fourth part of the *Corpus juris canonici.* The fifth part was the *Clementinae,* issued by Pope John XXII in 1317 but named for his predecessor, Clement V (1305–14). This collection included new papal decrees plus the decisions of the Council of Vienne (1311–12). Finally, two later compilations, the *Extravagantes of John XXII* of 1325 and *Extravagantes communes* of 1501 and 1503, were considered to be part of the *Corpus juris canonici.* These collections seldom had professorships devoted exclusively to them. As time passed, university rolls, especially in the sixteenth century, sometimes simply listed canon law positions as ordinary professorships followed by a short phrase indicating the topic, such as usury, on which the professor would concentrate.[13] Other favorite topics included prebends, testaments, and the gifts and obligations of betrothal and marriage.[14] These replaced professorships devoted to specific sections of the *Corpus juris canonici.*

Thus, scholars and pontiffs created a body of legal materials to serve as the basis for university teaching. All sections of the *Corpus juris canonici* were teaching

---

10. Sometimes the term *Volumen parvum* embraced the *Volumen parvum, Institutes,* and *Novellae.*

11. Bellomo, 1995, 83–86, 167.

12. See Boudinhon, 1913, for a good explanation of the development of the *Corpus juris canonici.*

13. *I maestri di Roma,* 1991, 68 (1569), and Dallari, 1888–1924, 2:223, 226, 237, 263 (1586–87 through 1598–99) and passim.

14. *I maestri di Roma,* 1991, 54 ("de prebendis et dignitatibus," 1567–68), 62 ("de testamentis," 1568–69), 78 ("de donatione inter vir. et ux. et de sponsalibus et matrimonio," 1570–71).

collections of canons and canonists' views. They included numerous specific decisions but not every canon or papal decree. Inclusion seems to have depended on a judgment of the significance of a canon and its potential contribution to the development of legal principles. Although very different in origin, both the *Corpus juris civilis* and *Corpus juris canonici* provided collections of laws, canons, and opinions to serve as the foundation for teaching, research, and legal decisions. This teaching framework endured throughout the Renaissance.

Both civilians and canonists taught, wrote, and published several kinds of works.[15] The earliest was the gloss, a short comment explaining the meaning of a word with cross-references to other occurrences. The commentary on one of the major teaching texts, occasionally the whole *Digest,* more often one of its three major divisions, or a commentary on another significant work was the largest and most comprehensive form of legal writing.[16] Even though many legists taught both civil and canon law (but not simultaneously), few commented on both the *Corpus juris civilis* and *Corpus juris canonici.* Another form was the *repetitio* (literally "repetition," although the meaning was a treatise on a single topic). A *repetitio* might comment on a short passage, for example, "De verborum obligationibus" (On the words of obligation; *Digest,* bk. 45, ch. 1). This received much attention, because it dealt with the legal obligations coming from words, as in a contract. Another was "De verborum significatione" (On the meaning of words; *Digest,* bk. 50, ch. 16), crucial because it dealt with interpretation.

Legists also wrote for payment numerous *consilia,* advisory opinions on cases undertaken by others. Solicitors throughout the Italian legal world used *consilia* as a means of obtaining advice, assessing opinion, and garnering support. Francesco Guicciardini, a lawyer with a prosperous but not extraordinary practice in Florence and small Tuscan communes, wrote dozens of *consilia* or added his name to those written by others. He usually received a florin for each *consilium* or signature.[17] A well-known law professor wrote hundreds; Baldo degli Ubaldi wrote at least twenty-five hundred.[18]

HUMANISTIC JURISPRUDENCE

Italian Renaissance humanists launched a major assault on traditional law as taught by Italian jurists. Petrarch, who had "wasted" (his word) seven years studying law at Montpellier and Bologna, initiated the attack. He praised ancient legists and then turned to the "pettifogging lawyers in our own day." Petrarch leveled the charge against lawyers heard in all centuries—that they were tricksters more interested in money rather than justice—and added a new one: the lawyers

15. Although confusing in modern English, *civilian* seems a better term than *civilist* for a professor of civil law. *Canonist* is easily understandable.

16. The list of the works of fifteenth-century Paduan legists in Belloni, 1986, gives a good idea of the genres. For more detail, as well as other kinds of legal works not mentioned here, see García y García, 1992, 394–99, and Maclean, 1992, 30–34.

17. Cavallar, 1991, 306–73.

18. Canning, 1987, 14.

of his day cared nothing about the origins of Roman civil law. And they lacked eloquence based on the classics needed to be good lawyers.[19]

Lorenzo Valla added substance and insult to the humanistic criticism of law instruction. As noted in Chapter 6, "Humanists Join the University," Valla strongly attacked traditional jurisprudence when he was teaching at Pavia and had to flee the city. He expanded his rejection of medieval jurisprudence in his *Elegantiarum linguae latinae libri sex* (Six books of the elegances of the Latin language; written over many years and completed c. 1440). In the preface to book 3, Valla emphasized the importance of eloquence to the study of law. He noted that he had read the fifty books of the *Digest* with pleasure and admiration; he praised them for their gravity, balance, prudence, and elegance of expression. However, whereas ancient jurisprudents had been men of eloquence, "the Goths"—medieval glossators and commentators—were not. (He also dismissed without elaboration canon law, which also came from the "Goths.") Lacking a knowledge of the language and history of Rome, they were unable to understand the *Corpus juris civilis*. Hence, they elaborated foolish etymologies, made inappropriate definitions, and distorted the meanings of Latin words. No jurist could become an expert in his profession without humanistic philological and historical studies, Valla declared.[20]

For Valla, the *Digest* embodied ancient Roman civilization in its unity, which needed to be understood and restored insofar as possible. Advocating the same approach that he urged for theology, dialectic, and grammar, Valla wanted scholars to re-create the language of the ancient texts in its original purity in order to restore the discipline of law. The *Digest* had to be examined critically in the light of ancient Roman legal language and practice; then erroneous interpretations could be corrected. Other humanists echoed Valla's criticisms.[21]

The humanists, none of them practicing lawyers or professors of law, pointed out errors and called for an accurate historical study of the ancient texts. But their criticisms were largely irrelevant to the teaching and practice of law, because neither depended very much on a historical understanding of ancient Roman law. Ancient Roman law served as the foundation of contemporary law only because legists had adapted it to medieval and Renaissance Europe. In this monumental effort, barbarisms and other errors would have crept in, even if the glossators and commentators had been skilled humanists. Indeed, the legists had to invent new words, such as adjectives derived from nouns, in order to express concepts not found in classical Latin. Jurisprudence needed its own language.[22]

19. *Letters on Familiar Matters,* XX, 4, written between 1353 and 1361, in Petrarch, 1985, 132–38. See also Maffei, 1956, 35–36, and Gilmore, 1963, 29–30.

20. For the Latin text and an Italian translation of the preface to book 3 of the *Elegantiae,* see *Prosatori latini,* 1952, 606–13. See also Gaeta, 1955, 120–26; Maffei, 1956, 99–101; and especially Kelley, 1970, 39–43.

21. For example, Maffeo Vegio (1407–58), a friend of Valla's, also published a criticism of legists in 1433; see Speroni, 1976. For analysis of other attacks by Angelo Poliziano, Pietro Crinito, and Claudio Tolomei, see Maffei, 1956, 34–37, 41–49, 99, and Kelley, 1970, 46–50.

22. Brugi (1922, 87–88) makes this last point. See also Kelley, 1991, 74.

Bartolo and his followers also employed the dialectical tools of Scholasticism, which the humanists saw as impediments to true understanding, because law demanded a dialectic with which to express concurrence and disagreement.

Valla had an extremely limited, even naive, view of jurisprudence. Citing Quintilian, he argued that all of jurisprudence consisted either in interpreting the terms of the laws or in making distinctions between good and evil.[23] Valla's notion of interpreting the terms, that is, understanding the language in its original philological and historical meaning, was hopelessly incomplete for law. That the vast majority of fifteenth-century legists took no account of humanistic criticism is understandable.

Nevertheless, the humanists continued to criticize. They turned their attention to the text of the *Digest* itself. After the Justinian compilation in the sixth century, the *Digest* and other works had nearly disappeared until the Bolognese revival of the late eleventh century. That revival was based on a text of the *Digest*, called the *Vulgata* or common version, which had errors and interpolations.[24] Unknown to the glossators and commentators, a much earlier and better manuscript had survived the dissolution of Roman civilization. This was the famous Pisan-Florentine *Pandects* (also called the *Littera Pisana, Littera Florentina,* or *Littera Pisana-Florentina*), a complete and excellent text of all fifty books of the *Digest*.

The Pisan-Florentine *Pandects* came into Pisan hands by unknown means at an indefinite date. The story that the Pisans brought the manuscript back from Amalfi in 1137 seems to be a fourteenth-century invention. A tiny handful of scholars (e.g., Giovanni Boccaccio) had limited access to the manuscript in the late fourteenth century, but legists seem to have been unaware of its existence. In 1406 Florence conquered Pisa and brought the manuscript to Florence, placing it in a position of honor in the Palazzo Vecchio. Treated like a holy relic, it remained beyond the reach of scholars for many years.

In the 1480s the Medici permitted a few favored scholars to look at the manuscript. Angelo Poliziano, the humanist professor of rhetoric at Florence, opined that the Pisan-Florentine *Pandects* was an official copy prepared during the lifetime of Justinian (d. 565). In the summer of 1490, he made a collation of the manuscript and began the job of comparing it with the common version. But death in 1494 ended his labors.[25]

Possibly in response to the attacks of the humanists, two Bolognese professors became interested in the question of the accuracy of the texts of the *Corpus juris civilis*. In or about 1495, Pio Antonio Bartolini, who taught law at Bologna in

23. "Ut enim Quintilianus inquit, omne ius aut in verborum interpretatione positum est, aut in aequi pravique discrimine." *Elegantiae,* preface to book 3, in *Prosatori latini, 1952, 608*. The reference is to *Institutio oratoria,* XII. 3. 6.

24. This and the next paragraph are based on the excellent summary of the history of the text of the *Digest* in Astuti, 1984, 200–235; for the history of the other books of the *Corpus juris civilis,* see ibid., 173–200. See also Calasso, 1954, 85 n. 6, 267–341, 361–62; Maffei, 1956, 84–94; Kuttner, 1982, 300–301; Radding, 1988, 151–56; and Wilson, 1992, 2, 5–6.

25. Branca, 1983, 182–92, with much bibliography; Grafton, 1988b, 39–40; and Wilson, 1992, 109–11.

1495–96 but is otherwise unknown, published a short book entitled *Correctiones LXX locorum in iure civilis.* It corrected 49 corrupt passages in the *Digest,* 19 in the *Codex,* 1 in the *Institutes,* and 1 in the *Novels,* with philological acumen worthy of the humanists. Indeed, the later critical edition of the *Digest* accepted his emendations.[26]

Another Bolognese legist had the very ambitious idea of editing and printing the text of the Pisan-Florentine *Pandects.* Lodovico Bolognini (1446–1508) took his degree at Bologna and taught there (1468–73), at Ferrara (1473–79), and again at Bologna (1479–95) before becoming a judge and *podestà.* In 1490 he wrote to Lorenzo de' Medici for a transcription of a passage from the Pisan-Florentine *Pandects.* Poliziano sent it to him and answered other queries. In 1501–2 Bolognini moved to Florence, where he began to compile a list of the differences between the *Vulgata* and the Pisan-Florentine *Pandects.* At the end of 1507 he obtained from the pope a ten-year exclusive privilege for a printed edition of the Pisan-Florentine *Pandects,* but he died the following year. Despite his ambitions, Bolognini's surviving papers demonstrated that he lacked the knowledge of ancient Latin and the philological skills needed to realize his grand project. Nor did he realize that the *Vulgata* had to be corrected according to the older manuscript.[27]

Shortly after humanists and legists began to address the issue of the accuracy of the *Vulgata,* the first professor of law with true humanistic skills appeared in the person of Andrea Alciato (1492–1550).[28] Born into a prominent Milanese family, Alciato received excellent training in Latin and Greek under able humanists. He then studied law at Pavia and Bologna and took his doctorate *in utroque iure* at Ferrara in 1516. He had published several works applying humanistic techniques to legal issues even before obtaining his degree. At the same time, he wrote strictly philological studies on nonlegal texts, such as his *Annotationes in Tacitum* (1517). Alciato inaugurated a new era in which legists with humanistic training worked to achieve a historical reconstruction of ancient law and then based their legal commentary on a better understanding of the ancient texts than their predecessors had enjoyed. This was humanistic jurisprudence, which came to be called *mos gallicus iuris docendi,* or *mos gallicus* (French method), because its center was France.

With his reputation established before receiving his degree, Alciato embarked on a distinguished, and possibly the best-paid, academic legal career in the Renaissance. He taught first at Avignon (1518–22), then spent the years 1522–27 as a lawyer in Milan, returned to Avignon to teach (1527–29), and went on to the University of Bourges (1529–33). His French students and followers, especially at

26. Unfortunately, nothing else is known about Bartolini. One wonders if he was a member of the Bartolini family of jurists from Perugia. Abbondanza, 1964d; Maffei, 1956, 124–25.

27. Maffei, 1956, 90–91; especially Caprioli, 1969, with full bibliography; and Dionisotti, 1971.

28. The standard studies are Viard, 1926, and Abbondanza, 1960. For the following, see also Maffei, 1956, 52–54, 126–28, 132–36, and passim; Kelley, 1970, 87–88, 92–100; and Maclean, 1992, index. For his Bolognese career, see Costa, 1902–3a. For a recent discussion of Alciato as a humanist, see Avellini, 1990. For his teaching, see Belloni, 1995, who emphasizes his traditional side.

Bourges, created a historical school of law which was enormously influential in French jurisprudence, politics, and religion.[29]

Italians used the carrot and the stick to bring Alciato back to his native land. Enticing offers of high salaries for teaching in Italian universities attracted him, while political pressure from the duke of Milan, the Milanese Senate, and even Emperor Charles V made it very difficult to refuse. Alciato spurned Padua but taught at Pavia (1533–37), Bologna (1537–42), Ferrara (1542–46), and Pavia again (1546–50). Alciato continued to publish legal works during his Italian career, although at a slower pace than before.

Alciato lectured directly from the texts, correcting them when necessary. He substituted a humanistic *explication du texte* for a lengthy recitation of the opinions of earlier jurists and did it all in excellent classical Latin, which boosted his reputation. Although he wrote works of humanistic historico-philological criticism, Alciato probably did not introduce much of this material into his lectures, especially in Italy. A practical jurist through and through, Alciato did not sneer at Bartolo and other medieval commentators, as the humanists often did. He even criticized Valla. He accepted much traditional Italian jurisprudence. But he did renounce the vocabulary and style of Bartolo. Above all, he had the ability to cut through the verbiage of the commentators and see the heart of an issue. Hence, he could explicate a hundred laws in the course of a year's lectures while some of his colleagues did only a handful, because they masticated thoroughly all the comments. Less revolutionary than his French followers, Alciato added historical perspective and clarity to traditional jurisprudence.

Alciato's example and further humanistic concerns brought increased attention to the text of the *Corpus juris civilis*. Legists made several limited efforts to produce a critical edition of the *Digest* in the first part of the sixteenth century. But they paid little attention to the Pisan-Florentine *Pandects* manuscript. Other scholars with humanistic expertise sought to edit and print the precious manuscript. Lelio Torelli (1489–1576) and his associates succeeded.[30] Born in Fano, Torelli received a good humanistic education from his uncle in Ferrara and then took a law doctorate at Perugia in 1511. He served as *podestà* and legate in several places until appointed a judge in Florence in 1531, at which time he began to study the *Pandects* manuscript. Torelli published three short legal commentaries on passages of the *Corpus juris civilis* in the 1540s. In addition, two young legal scholars, the Spaniard Antonio Agustín (1517–86; doctorate from Bologna in 1541) and the Frenchman Jean Matal (c. 1520–86), both students of Alciato at Bologna,[31] collated the Pisan-Florentine *Pandects* in late 1541 and early 1542.

Torelli discovered that the last two leaves of the Florentine-Pisan *Pandects* were reversed. Since all other surviving manuscripts copied the mistake, this verified the remarkable fact that the Pisan-Florentine *Pandects* was the archetype, as To-

---

29. This is the theme of Kelley, 1970.

30. For what follows, see especially Gualandi, 1986, and the studies in *Le Pandette di Giustiano*, 1986. See also Grafton, 1983, 63–65, 252–54. Torelli lacks a monographic study; for brief biographies, see Cascio Pratilli, 1975, 45–46 n. 91, and Gualandi, 1986, 147–50.

31. Belloni, 1995, 148, 156.

relli announced in 1542. Agustín established in 1543 that the manuscript was a private copy made a few years after Justinian's death. Determined to publish the text, Torelli sought to bring to Florence a printer capable of printing the work. For this he needed permission and financial support from Duke Cosimo I de' Medici, which he failed to obtain. Then in October 1546 Torelli became the first secretary (effectively the chief advisor and executive officer) to Duke Cosimo I. Now the overseer of the regime's cultural patronage, Torelli brought to Florence in 1547 a printer from Brabant, Laurens Leenaertsz van der Beke, who became the ducal printer under the name of Lorenzo Torrentino. In 1553 Torrentino published the Pisan-Florentine *Pandects* in two (sometimes divided into three) folio-sized volumes.[32] Torelli and his son Francesco, who had a law degree from Pisa, prepared the work, with crucial help from Agustín and Matal. It was a landmark in legal scholarship and Renaissance textual criticism. In 1786 the manuscript itself was transferred to the Florentine Biblioteca Laurenziana, where it remains.

Torrentino never reprinted the famous work, and neither did any other Renaissance publisher, so far as is known. The lack of a reprint demonstrates that it did not replace the *Vulgata*. However, some later printings of the *Vulgata* added the variant readings from the 1553 *Pandects* in the margins.[33]

Despite the publication of the *Digest* and the efforts of Alciato, Italian law schools remained cool to humanistic jurisprudence. Indeed, several Italian jurists responded to humanistic attacks on *mos italicus* with vigorous defenses. Many saw humanistic jurisprudence as theoretical and historical scholarship, which was not helpful with contemporary legal issues.[34] They disliked what they saw as a division of law study into theory and practice. They knew that the comments indicating how the law was currently applied did matter. And because they relied on consensus and expressed their disagreements politely, they recoiled from the insults and harsh attacks that were the stock in trade of the humanists.

However, the universities created a small institutional place for the new method. Several created new positions called *Pandects* professorships (see below) for humanistic jurisprudence. The occupants were expected to explain the text of the *Digest* historically and philologically. At the same time, the *Pandects* professors inhabited the same legal world as their colleagues. They did not abandon the common opinions developed by Bartolo and held by most jurists. Occupants

32. The edition is briefly described in Moreni, 1989, 227–30. Theodor Mommsen published a modern edition of the text in 1870. For a recent Latin edition with English translation, see *Digest of Justinian*, 1985.

33. *Digestum vetus seu Pandectarum iuris civilis. Tomus Primus, Cum lectionum Florentinarum varietatibus, diligentius quàm antea in margine appositis. . . .* Venetiis, Apud Iuntas, 1598. Title page of volume I of an edition of 1598, from Camerini, 1962–63, pt. 2, item 1036. See also ibid., 262, item 1116, for the same notation on the title page of the Venice (Giunti, 1606) edition. Both these editions also contain commentaries by various legists. See also Brugi, 1921, 129–30. When Torrentino died in 1563, his heirs carried on the firm until its liquidation in 1570. The Florentine Giunti acquired the shop and its contents. *I Giunti di Firenze*, 1978, 46–47. Hence, it is logical that a Giunti publisher would bring out an edition that included the variants from the 1553 edition.

34. Some of the following comes from Brugi, 1921, 111–35, and Stein, 1988, 98–99.

of *Pandects* professorships provided teaching that was very humanistic, or less so, according to the individual's inclinations and abilities.

In the end, Italian jurisprudence remained traditional, but with some accommodation for humanistic jurisprudence. Alciato's followers found ordinary professorships in Italian law schools. In addition, professors following *mos italicus* incorporated some aspects of humanistic jurisprudence into their teaching. They could do this because the differences between *mos italicus* and *mos gallicus* were not great on the practical level of instruction and practice. Because both relied on their medieval predecessors and employed the same legal genres in their writing, they shared much common ground.[35]

The comprehensive nature of *mos italicus* also eased conflict. Many sixteenth-century Bartolists accepted the importance of teaching Justinian's texts corrected according to the principles of historical philology. While remaining faithful to "Bartolism," they modified the traditional dialectical exposition in favor of a freer exegesis that took into account humanistic insights into the meaning of words in their historical context.

By the late sixteenth century, Italian legal instruction had reached a modus vivendi with humanistic jurisprudence. In 1604, Annibale Roero, a young man who had studied law at the University of Pavia between about 1596 and about 1602, wrote a detailed description of his studies. He recommended a list of texts that students should purchase; it clearly indicated his preferences and must have reflected those of his professors as well.[36] The list included great names in both traditions. Roero praised Bartolo but also revered Alciato's *De verborum significatione* (Lyon, 1530), one of the touchstones of humanistic jurisprudence. Roero emphasized the importance of the ordinary gloss on the *Corpus juris civilis,* the *Summa* of Azzone (early thirteenth century), and the works of modern traditionalists Paolo di Castro (1360/62–1441), Giasone del Maino (1435–1519), and Filippo Decio (1454–1536). The student also recommended several works of sixteenth-century German, Dutch, and French humanistic jurisprudents. He did not mention Baldo degli Ubaldi, a conspicuous omission.

When the opinions of the doctors differed, the views of Bartolo should prevail, Roero wrote.[37] And he defended the legists' use of dialectic. But he also underlined the importance of reading "the pure texts," a fundamental principle of humanistic jurisprudence. Overall, legal training at Pavia seems to have been

35. One scholar summarizes the situation as follows: "Can one say that by the end of the sixteenth century, a new approach [to law] has been developed? What was the effect of the input of humanist material in the course of the fifteenth and sixteenth centuries? I would venture to reply: not very great. . . . Alciato's essay on meaning [*De verborum significatione* of 1530] . . . is very close to the approach of the postglossators." Maclean, 1992, 65–66, 85 (quote), 204.

36. Even though it is not known if Roero graduated, he provided concrete and detailed information on studies, professors, and student life which only a student would have. For this and the next paragraph, see Roero, 1604, 14–16. Vismara (1963, 451–69) identifies the authors and texts named.

37. "Le letture di Bartolo, il quale tutti gl'altri, meritamente precede. Onde in alcuni paesi per statuto regio è stabilito, che ove sono discordanti le opinioni de' Dottori, prevaglia quella di Bartolo, come del maggiore di tutti gli altri. " Roero, 1604, 14 (quote) and 105–7, for additional praise of Bartolo and defense of dialectic in law instruction.

traditional *mos italicus* but accepting of significant themes and works of humanistic jurisprudence.

Pavia was not unique. A number of Paduan professors employed humanistic jurisprudential concepts and techniques.[38] Even in Perugia, the birthplace of Bartolism, sixteenth-century professors taught a *mos italicus* tempered by humanistic insights.[39] Outside Italy, French law schools, the stronghold of humanistic jurisprudence, taught both traditional and humanistic legal approaches in the seventeenth century.[40] *Mos italicus* was a broad church that could embrace humanistic worshipers, so long as they bit their tongues and did not denounce their legal forefathers too strongly.

THE DECLINE OF CANON LAW

Other changes had greater impact on the structure and teaching of law in Italian universities. The number of canon law professorships relative to that of the civilians declined dramatically in the sixteenth century.[41] The number of canon law degrees awarded held steady, because students could add canon law to the civil law doctorate with little extra effort. But the degree had been devalued.

The first reason for the decline in the teaching of canon law was obvious, if difficult to measure: civil law and the state grew in influence at the expense of canon law and the church. Renaissance society became increasingly secular between 1400 and 1600, in the limited meaning that civil government with its courts, laws, and officials expanded its jurisdiction over the lives of its subjects at the expense of church courts, laws, and officials. Although both state and church claimed jurisdiction over marriage, family, some crimes, and usury, as well as the clergy, church institutions, and ecclesiastical lands under some circumstances, the state was winning.

A few church–state conflicts over jurisdictional issues attracted great attention. The papacy laid Venice under interdict in 1606 because the republic refused to revoke laws asserting civil jurisdiction over ecclesiastical lands and clergymen. The state won, because the papacy lifted the interdict in 1607 without forcing the republic to change its laws. Earlier and lesser administrative and legal moves also signaled that civil jurisdiction and law were claiming a larger share of the legal world. Students concluded that reading civil law would be more useful than studying canon law and voted with their feet. For example, Francesco Guicciardini in 1505 decided to take his doctorate in civil law only, because he wished to avoid additional expense and because "the degree of canon law was of little value."[42] University authorities took note and acted accordingly.

Universities were already eliminating canon law professorships before the Catholic Reformation. But then the papacy gave cause for further reductions.

---

38. Brugi, 1922, 86.
39. Ermini, 1971, 509–11, 514, 519–22, 533–37.
40. Brockliss, 1987, 289–90.
41. So far as can be determined, historians have not noticed the decline of canon law positions.
42. Guicciardini, 1965, 133.

The decrees of the Council of Trent set aside or changed many previous canons on benefices, eligibility for church offices, residence, marriage, and other topics, rendering a considerable amount of previous church law and decisions obsolete. Canon lawyers would have to build a new interpretive structure. But the papacy reserved to itself the interpretation of Trent's decrees.

Benedictus Deus of January 26, 1564 (promulgated on June 30), the papal bull accepting and proclaiming the Council of Trent, forbade publication without papal permission of all comments, glosses, observations, scholia, or any other interpretive material on the conciliar decrees. In case of dispute, application had to be made to the papacy, which alone would interpret the decrees of Trent.[43] The papacy then created the Congregation of the Council to interpret the disciplinary canons of Trent. The papacy wanted uniform application of the decrees and to assert its primacy as interpreter and executor of Trent's rules.[44]

The papal bull sharply limited the legal tradition to be erected on Trent. All previous compilations of canon law from Gratian's *Decretum* onward produced glosses, commentaries, and treatises for professors and lawyers to consult. But now canon lawyers and professors could not gloss, comment on, or write *consilia* interpreting Trent's canons. The prohibition may not have extended to interpreting the canons orally in teaching. But there was little to teach without published comments and glosses. Only papal agencies might interpret the Tridentine decrees through their decisions in particular cases. But these would normally be issued with little or no comment and would not be widely disseminated.

The combination of many new canons of Trent and prohibition against interpretation sharply reduced the corpus of canon law available for study. The papacy further trimmed the corpus when it decided in 1598 not to issue a new volume of papal constitutions to be added to the *Clementinae* of 1317.[45] In effect, the papacy closed the *Corpus juris canonici* by refusing to issue any new collections of canons, constitutions, and decisions to be studied and by prohibiting comments on the canons of Trent. It is ironic that both Protestants and Catholics simultaneously eliminated or reduced the teaching of canon law. Protestant universities abolished

43. "Ad vitandam praeterea perversionem, & confusionem, quae oriri posset, si unicuique liceret, prout ei liberet, in Decreta Concilii commentarios & interpretationes suas edere, Apostolica auctoritate, inhibemus omnibus, tam Ecclesiasticis personis, cuiuscumque sint ordinis, conditionis, & gradus, quam laicis, quocunque honore, ac potestate praeditis; Praelatis quidem sub interdicti ingressus Ecclesiae, aliis vero, quicumque fuerint, sub excommunicationis latae sententiae poenis, ne quis sine auctoritate nostra audeat ullos commentarios, glossas, annotationes, scholia, ullumve omnino interpretationis genus super ipsius Concilii Decretis quocumque modo edere, aut quiquam quocumque nomine, etiam sub praetextu maioris decretorum corroborationis, aut executionis, aliove quaesito colore, statuere. Si cui vero in eis aliquid obscurius dictum & statutum fuisse, eamque ob causam interpretatione aut decisione aliqua egere visum fuerit; ascendat ad locum, quem dominus elegit, ad Sedem videlicet Apostolicam, omnium fidelium Magistram, cuius auctoritatem etiam ipsa sancta Synodus tam reverenter agnovit." *Canones tridentini,* 1573, sigs. CC2 ʳ–CC5ᵛ (quotation at CC4ʳ–ᵛ). The bull is printed in all contemporary editions of the decrees of Trent examined. I am grateful to Nelson Minnich, who pointed to the importance of this bull.

44. See Pastor, 1891–1953, 16:5–11; Jedin, 1981, 332–34.

45. Pastor, 1891–1953, 24:230–31. The work was prepared in the 1580s and 1590s, but Clement VIII decided not to publish it.

the discipline, because it was part of the church which they rejected. The renewed papacy indirectly reduced the teaching of canon law, because it had less need for it.

The third and final reason for the decline in canon law was that many clerics opted for doctorates of theology rather than canon law after Trent. In the fifteenth century a canon law doctorate enabled churchmen, especially members of the secular clergy, to rise in the hierarchy. Now the Catholic Reformation put greater emphasis on theological training. Hence, Italian universities annually awarded six to ten times as many doctorates in theology in the last quarter of the sixteenth century than in the period 1400 to 1550 (see Ch. 10, "Doctorates of Theology").

Some professors agreed that canon law was no longer very important. Ulisse Aldrovandi, always ready to advise those who oversaw the university, was one of them. In his 1573 proposal to rearrange the lecture timetable, he stated that the "weakest" lectures were canon law (*Decretals*), taught at the first hour of the morning, and *Institutes,* meeting at the first hour of the afternoon, both ill attended. Linking *Decretals,* the most important part of canon law, with *Institutes,* the beginning course in civil law, already manifested his low opinion of canon law. But Aldrovandi went on: he wanted to give these two hours in the schedule to "more necessary and better attended lectures."[46]

Naturally, professors of canon law did not share this low opinion, nor did the timetable issue disappear. Writing in the early 1590s, Francesco Gandolfo, professor of *Decretals* at Bologna, protested a proposal to move canon law lectures, more precisely, to move *his Decretals* lectures, from the morning to the afternoon.

Gandolfo offered a spirited defense of canon law. It was as important or more so than civil law, because it dealt with "universal councils which refuted the malignant opinions of heretics." "[It is] the stable foundation of the Christian faith; it contains the ordinances and decrees of the holy fathers and popes." "It declares many articles of the faith." One could not be a good ecclesiastical administrator without canon law, he wrote. In addition, canonists had corrected many errors made by secular legislators on usury, slavery, and contracts. Still, he feared that if the canon law lectures were moved from morning to afternoon the canonists might be without students, because few law students attended lectures in both the morning and the afternoon.[47] Nevertheless, the university moved his teach-

---

46. "Li canonisti nella prima classe della mattina & gl'Instituti nel primo anche della sera . . . et invano queste sono manco frequentate classi che l'ordinari, però hanno havuto l'occhio di da più conveniente loco agli ordinarij, e più necessarie e frequentate letioni." BA, Ms. B 3803, "Informatione del Rotolo," f. 2^r–^{v}.

47. "Si tratta de concilij universali dove si reprobano li maligni opinioni delli heretici, fondamento stabil della Xpiana fede, in quella si contengono le ordinationi e decreti di santi padri e pontifici . . . si dechiarano molti articoli della fede." Undated letter of Francesco Gandolfo, in ASB, Assunteria dello Studio, Bu. 79, no pag. Gandolfo taught *Institutes* from 1579 to 1582 and then *Decretals* as ordinary morning professor at the first hour from 1582–83 until 1593–94, when he was moved to the third hour of the afternoon. Dallari, 1888–1924, 2:202–48 passim. The letter was obviously written shortly before the fall of 1593. Gandolfo, about whom nothing else is known, continued to teach until 1619. Simeoni, 1940, 243.

ing from the first hour of the morning to the third hour of the afternoon in 1593–
94. Whether or not the number of students in his lectures declined is unknown.
But Bologna did have a few more canonists than in the 1580s: three professors of
Decretals lecturing at the first hour of the morning and another three at the third
hour of the afternoon emphasizing a different topic.

Despite Gandolfo's defense, students seem to have spent little time studying
canon law compared with civil law. For those seeking degrees *in utroque iure,* the
statutes expected the degree candidate to devote an additional one or two years
beyond the civil law preparation, which was considered more demanding. For
example, the statutes at the University of Pisa in the 1480s required a student to
attend lectures for five years for either the civil or canon law degree and for seven
years if he wished a degree in both.[48] However, by the end of the sixteenth
century students seeking degrees in both laws no longer attended classes an extra
year or two but simply added a limited number of canon law lectures in the fourth
year of civil law study. Annibale Roero explained what they did.

Roero urged students to attend two lectures a day, the morning and afternoon
ordinary lectures in civil law, for three years. Then in the fourth year, the student
wanting a doctorate in both laws should also attend ordinary lectures in canon
law, if the university scheduled the ordinary lectures of canon and civil law at
different hours. With these lectures the student would learn canon law well
enough, he opined. But if the university scheduled ordinary civil and canon law
lectures at the same hour, the student should in the fourth year attend the
morning ordinary canon law lectures in place of the morning ordinary civil law
lectures. In other words, one series of canon law lectures heard for one academic
year was enough. He also noted that the majority of students began to attend
canon law lectures only two or three months before undergoing the doctoral
examinations. This was not enough; the student should begin hearing canon law
lectures from the beginning of the fourth year, he argued.[49]

Very few students took degrees in canon law only in the sixteenth century.
Even future prelates concentrated on civil law in their studies and teaching (see

48. Verde, 1973–94, 2:645. At Ferrara, students were expected to attend lectures for six years for
the canon law degree and eight for civil law. The number of years for degrees *in utroque iure* was not
indicated. Del Nero, 1996, 97. Such lengthy requirements were often shortened in practice.

49. "ANN. V. S. vuole ch'io vada così presto à sentir le lettioni de sacri canoni, se per lo più gli
scolari, come intendo, cominciano à sentirle due ò tre mesi prima, che ricever la laurea del dottorato,
& alle volte meno? SA. Non mi pare che tù far debba in modo tale: perche, come può alcuno
dottorarsi in legge canonica, & haverne studiato solamente tre mesi? come possono gli promotori
giurare che egli habbia il dovuto tempo studiato? forse che le materie canoniche non sono utili, e
necessarie? Io, insomma, voglio che tù al principio del quarto anno cominci à sentirle." Roero, 1604,
65–66 (quote on 66).

It is likely that students seeking only the canon law degree attended lectures for about four years,
because, like civil law students, they had to learn the principles, dialectic, and procedures of law
generally. But there were very few students of canon law only. And Roero makes it clear that the
majority of students (and their examiners) did not feel that much training in canon law was needed for
the double degree.

below). But the number of canon law degrees did not decline, because, unlike Guicciardini, most sixteenth-century students took degrees *in utroque iure*.[50] They could do this easily, because the additional canon law degree required no more time at university than the doctorate in civil law only. If students concentrating in civil law could add the canon law doctorate with a single series of lectures lasting two or three months to one year, universities did not need many professors of canon law.

PADUA AND BOLOGNA

Padua and Bologna, the most important universities for law, established a pattern that other universities followed to a greater or lesser degree. Both Padua and Bologna continued the tradition of *mos italicus* texts and professorships developed in the fourteenth century. But in the sixteenth century they reduced the teaching of canon law, added new professorships in criminal law, legal actions, and *Pandects,* and introduced a professorship devoted exclusively to Bartolo. Padua exhibited greater change, Bologna more continuity.

The morning and afternoon ordinary professorships in civil law, and the morning and afternoon ordinary professorships in canon law, led the law faculty at Padua. These men almost always received the highest salaries, with the leading civilian paid more than the leading canonist. At Padua each of these ordinary professorships had concurrent first- and second-place occupants. The Venetian government often appointed a more or less distinguished foreigner (someone not from the Venetian state) to the first place and a Paduan to the second.

Lecturing on the *Codex* and *Digest* constituted the largest part of civil law instruction. At Padua the morning and afternoon ordinary professors alternated their teaching annually, teaching half of a major part of the *Corpus juris civilis* each year. Hence, a student needed four years in order to hear lectures on all eight parts of the *Digest* and *Codex* if he attended both morning and afternoon ordinary lectures.[51]

By contrast, Bologna accelerated the alternation: a Bolognese ordinary professor covered the entire *Codex* or a major part of the *Digest* in one year. Hence, a student could hear the entire sequence in two years if he attended both morning and afternoon ordinary lectures (see below).

Padua followed a similar pattern for canon law. The morning ordinary professors of canon law taught book 1 of the *Decretals* the first year, book 2 the second year, and returned to book 1 in the third year. They also paid limited attention to

---

50. For example, the University of Pisa awarded 244 degrees *in utroque iure,* 11 in civil law only, and 7 in canon law only, between 1516 and 1528. Verde, 1998, 113. If anything, the tendency of students to take degrees in both laws became stronger later in the century at Pisa, Padua, and elsewhere. The fifteenth century was different. For example, Pisa awarded 87 degrees in civil law, 59 *in utroque iure,* and 56 in canon law between 1473 and 1505. Verde, 1973–94, 2:648–729.

51. Belloni, 1986, 66–68, and table 7 following p. 88. See also Gallo, 1963, 87–88. For more on teaching, see Brugi, 1915, 51–61, and Brugi, 1922, 12–19.

TABLE 13.1
Teaching of the Major Civil Law Professors at Padua

	Morning Ordinary Professors	Afternoon Ordinary Professors
Year 1	*Codex*, part 1	*Infortiatum*, part 1
Year 2	*Old Digest*, part 1	*New Digest*, part 1
Year 3	*Codex*, part 2	*Infortiatum*, part 2
Year 4	*Old Digest*, part 2	*New Digest*, part 2

the *Decretum*. The afternoon ordinary professors of canon law taught books 3, 4, and 5, of the *Decretals* over the course of two or three years.[52]

Although the statutes insisted that lecturers cover entire texts, or large parts of them, they probably did not do so in practice. Rather, they organized their teaching according to *puncta*, important passages to which they were expected to devote a specified number of days. At Padua on the last day allowed for a *punctum*, the beadle entered the classroom to announce that the professor would begin a new *punctum* in the next lecture. Professors who failed to follow this schedule ran the risk of angering their students, because doctoral examinations were based on *puncta*.[53]

In addition to the four major ordinary civil law professorships staffed by eight and later twelve professors,[54] Padua had extraordinary professorships of *Institutes* and notarial art. And there were others. A professorship of *Libri feudorum* appeared in the 1430s, again in 1462, and was taught continuously from 1476. It may have been intended especially for students from Germany, where feudal law mattered more. Professorships of *Libri authenticorum* and *Tres libri* (or *Volumen*) appeared on a very occasional basis but did not find permanent places in the curriculum in the fifteenth century. In canon law, extraordinary lectureships in the *Decretum,* and *Sextus* and *Clementinae,* existed for the whole fifteenth century. A single scholar normally staffed each of the extraordinary professorships.

Padua was a small law school in the first third of the fifteenth century with approximately a dozen legists, slightly more civilians than canonists.[55] The number grew, especially during the last third of the century, when the Venetian government made a determined effort to increase the size of the law faculty in

52. Belloni, 1986, 69–70, and table 6 following p. 88.

53. Brugi, 1922, 15–16.

54. In 1467, the Venetian government authorized the addition of four "third places," two in civil law and two in canon law. Reserved for recent graduates, they paid only 20 florins per annum. Finally, one or more "university lectureships," that is, a student in the last year of his studies lecturing at the salary of 10 florins, were added later in the century. The university lectureships were abolished in 1560. Dupuigrenet Desroussilles, 1980, 624; Belloni, 1986, 71–73.

55. The figures for the fifteenth century can only be estimates because only three legists' rolls have been discovered: 1422–23, 1424–25, and 1430–31. They are found in AAUP, F. 648, ff. 36ʳ–ᵛ, 37ʳ, 53ʳ, and are reprinted in Chapter 1, table 1.2, of this book (1422–23); Tommasini, 1986, 495 (1424–25); Cessi, 1909, 143 (1430–31); and Belloni, 1986, 45–48 (all three). However, the bio-bibliographical information on individual professors in Belloni, 1986, and Facciolati, 1978, pt. 2:23–76, offers enough additional information for some estimates to be made.

order to attract more students. Venice also persuaded well-known legal scholars from other universities to come to Padua in the last twenty years of the century.[56] By the first decade of the sixteenth century it had grown to about 25 professors of law, approximately 15 civilians and 10 canonists.[57]

When Padua rebuilt its faculty after the closing caused by the war of the League of Cambrai, it had about 25 legists from the 1520s until 1560.[58] The number of legists then briefly dipped to a low of 16, before recovering to about 20 in 1567–68 and for the rest of the century. The ordinary morning and afternoon professorships, two in civil law and two in canon law, anchored the law faculty throughout the century. The *Institutes* professorship and *Libri feudorum* posts continued.[59] So did the notarial art position, although it was only marginally a law position and of diminishing importance.

The Paduan law school began a period of experiment and innovation in the 1540s. First, Padua gave greater attention to specialized practical law, beginning with the creation of a professorship of criminal law. Although the expanding criminal justice systems in Italian republics and princedoms was heavily based on Roman law, universities had not devoted a professorship to the subject.[60] Then in 1532 Emperor Charles V promulgated a new criminal code, *Constitutio criminalis Carolina,* in a effort to standardize criminal law throughout the Holy Roman Empire. The *Carolina,* as it is usually called, urged judges lacking experience or practice in criminal law to seek advice from "the nearest university, city, or other source of legal knowledge."[61] The future judges and lawyers at Padua, especially the Germans, were quick to take the hint: the students began petitioning for a position in criminal law in the same year. The Venetian government obliged in December 1540 by creating a holiday professorship of criminal law at the good salary of 200 florins. It was the second in Italy; Padua trailed Bologna in this area (see below). The criminal law professor lectured on the books and passages in the *Corpus juris civilis,* especially in the *New Digest,* which the glossators had singled

56. For some examples of the recruitment of legists, see AAUP, F. 648, ff. 241^r, 242^r, 262^r, 277^r, 294^{r-v}, 295^{r-v}, 333^r, 339^r, 394^r.

57. The roll of 1500–1501 had 16 civilians and 12 canonists; the roll of 1506–7 had 14 civilians with 2 unfilled positions and 9 canonists with 1 unfilled position; the roll of 1507–8 had 14 civilians and 8 canonists. The roll of 1500–1501 comes from Sanudo's *Diarii* and is reprinted in Favaro, 1918, 76–77, and again in Belloni, 1986, 48–49. The second two come from AAUP and are reprinted in Belloni, 1986, 50–52.

58. This is based on numerous legists' rolls of the sixteenth century found in AAUP, F. 652 and Inventario 1320. Rolls of 1571–72 and 1598–99 are printed in Riccobono, 1980, 33^{r-v}, 146^v; a roll probably of 1580–81 is found in ASB, Assunteria di Studio, Bu. 100, fascicle 5, and printed in Favaro, 1915, 251–55; and the roll of 1551–52 with many names missing is found in Gallo, 1963, 67–69. One can also reconstruct much of the rolls from Facciolati, 1978, pt. 3:79–201.

59. There were minor variations in some posts. The notary position was doubled between 1518 and 1560, and the *Libri feudorum* position was suppressed between 1560 and 1577 and then restored. Facciolati, 1978, pt. 3:147–61, 165–69, 191–95; Brugi, 1922, 66, 68–69; Favaro, 1915, 251, 253, 255.

60. For the growth of the criminal law system in Florence and the role of Roman law in it, see Stern, 1994, xii, xiv, xx–xxi, 52, 239.

61. Translated quote from Strauss, 1986, 83.

out as dealing with criminal and penal law, with the ultimate selection left to the professor. The first appointment went to Pietro Filippo Mattioli of Perugia, where he had obtained his doctorate.[62]

In 1549 Padua appointed Tiberio Deciani (1509–82) to teach criminal law. After obtaining his law degree at Padua in 1529, he had pursued a political and judicial career, sometimes as a legal assessor alongside Venetian governors in the mainland state. It appears that the Venetian government wanted someone with practical experience in criminal justice. Deciani went on to a distinguished career at Padua, rising to first-position morning ordinary civil law in 1570. He wrote a comprehensive treatise on criminal law emphasizing the autonomy of the field and is considered one of the founders of modern criminal law. Indeed, the distinctions and interpretations that medieval and Renaissance jurists applied to Roman law softened the harsh criminal penalties found there and may have saved the lives of many criminals.[63] The introduction of criminal law as a separate teaching subject was one of the most important innovations of the sixteenth century.

Padua next drastically shaved the number of canon law positions. In 1544–45 the government abolished all six lesser canon law positions.[64] Canon law was left with the morning and afternoon ordinary professorships, which now focused on the *Decretals.* Each had 2 or 3 professors, making a total of 5 or 6 canonists. Civilians took their place, with dramatic results: in 1543–44 Padua had 11 canonists and 15 civilians; in 1545–46 Padua had 5 canonists and 21 civilians.[65]

In the place of the suppressed canon law slots, the government created several new civil law positions that affirmed the medieval foundational texts and interpreters. These new posts, all extraordinary professorships, began with one entitled "Text, Gloss, and Bartolo" (*Textus, Glossae, et Bartholi*), to be filled by two morning and three afternoon lecturers. The statutes enjoined the holders to read the same passage(s) from the *Corpus juris civilis* as did the ordinary professors, then the gloss (possibly the "great gloss" of Accursius), and then Bartolo's commentary, without omitting anything or losing time on disputes. The professorship and statutes reaffirmed the foundations of *mos italicus* and the importance of Bartolo. Students had demanded this professorship, probably because they felt that professors were spending too much time on later commentaries, including their own, and losing sight of the core of jurisprudence. The five places were reduced

---

62. AAUP, F. 652, ff. 198ᵛ, 200ᵛ, 208ᵛ, and passim. See also Tomasini, 1986, 260.

63. Facciolati, 1978, pt. 3:178–81; Favaro, 1915, 251; Brugi, 1922, 72; Dupuigrenet Desroussilles, 1980, 643; Gallo, 1963, 85, 88–89; and especially Spagnesi, 1987.

64. Facciolati, 1978, pt. 3:103–5, 108, 110, 115, 129, 132, 133; Dupuigrenet Desroussilles, 1980, 643–44. Both seem to have missed the drastic reduction of canon law professorships and the substitution of new civil law positions. Dupuigrenet Desroussilles sees the moves of 1544–45 as an effort to strip the student organizations of the power, never robust, to elect some professors, including several of the abolished positions. The government retreated from the move to check student electoral power in the face of stiff opposition at this time but eliminated the student right of election from almost all the legal posts in 1560. See Gallo, 1963, 94–95, for the Senate measure of Oct. 7, 1560. But the canon law positions were never restored.

65. Compare the two rolls in AAUP, F. 652, ff. 228ʳ⁻ᵛ, 252ʳ⁻ᵛ.

to four in 1560, and the professorship as a whole was abolished in 1579.[66] Also in 1544, the government created another new extraordinary post entitled *"Institutes with Text and Gloss"* (*Institutionum cum textu, et glossa*), with two places. The statutes obliged the professor to concentrate on the text and gloss of the *Institutes* without referring to the opinions of other scholars. This position lasted only until 1560.[67]

These two new professorships, filled by upwards of six men, expressed a movement *ad fontes* like that of humanistic jurisprudence, except that the "original sources" were the glosses and Bartolo's words written between the twelfth century and the mid-fourteenth. The professorships offered new respect for the foundations of medieval jurisprudence and reflected the conviction that current professors were not paying enough attention to them. The positions were intended to help students grasp the vision of *ius commune* as seen by its creators at a time when legists had lost their way in the thickets of commentary—or so students and the government believed.

Padua created another new extraordinary professorship with practical application called *De actionibus* (On legal actions) in 1544–45. It explained the kinds of legal actions which could be brought and the relations between them. But it only lasted until 1560.[68] In 1586, the government created a professorship entitled *De regulis juris* (On the rules of law). Exactly what this professorship taught that others did not is unclear; possibly it combined a study of the rules of legal procedure with an emphasis on juridical logic reminiscent of Baldo degli Ubaldi. If so, the post emphasized detailed practical concerns within traditional *mos italicus*. It continued into the eighteenth century.[69] A single professor held each of these new positions.

After affirming the roots of *mos italicus* and emphasizing the practical aspects of law, Padua moved in exactly the opposite direction by creating a professorship of humanistic jurisprudence. The German nation of law students wanted the position in 1578 and the humanist Marc'Antoine Muret, holder of the first Italian *Pandects* chair (at Rome, 1567–72), to fill it. But Muret was not interested. Nevertheless, the Venetian Senate established the post, decreeing that the lectures were to follow the pattern of humanistic jurisprudence as found in German universities and the example of Muret's lectures in Rome.[70] Perhaps the publica-

66. In addition to the numerous law rolls in AAUP, F. 652, see Facciolati, 1978, pt. 3:196–201; Brugi, 1922, 73–74; and Tomasini, 1986, 275. See Riccobono, 1980, 60ᵛ–61ʳ, for the text of the 1579 Senate decree abolishing the professorship.

67. Facciolati, 1978, pt. 3:162–64; Brugi, 1922, 72–73; Tomasini, 1986, 276.

68. AAUP, F. 652, f. 252ʳ; Facciolati, 1978, pt. 3:177; Brugi, 1922, 74; Tomasini, 1986, 276.

69. Facciolati, 1978, pt. 3:182–83; Riccobono, 1980, 59ʳ–ᵛ; Brugi, 1922, 74–75; Tomasini, 1986, 269.

70. The story is found in *Atti dei legisti*, 1912, 156, 209–11, 344, and Brugi, 1915. On Jan. 3, 1578, the law students of the German nation wrote Muret to ask him to come to Padua for the new post, but he declined in a letter of January 18. The exchange of letters exhibited a good amount of the rhetoric of humanistic jurisprudence, including condemnations of *mos italicus*. Muret, 1737, 2:298–301. Of course, the Venetian Senate, not the German nation, made appointments. If Muret had responded favorably, the German nation presumably would have then gone to the Venetian Senate,

TABLE 13.2

Professorships of Law at Padua, with Salaries, 1598–1599

Civil law, ordinary A.M.	1st (600 florins) and 2nd place (550)
Civil law, ordinary P.M.	1st (1,680), 2nd (500), and 3rd place (20)
Canon law, ordinary A.M.	1st (600 florins), 2nd (150), and 3rd place (20)
Canon law, ordinary P.M.	1st (450), 2nd (100), and 3rd place (20)
Criminal law	1 place (110)
Libri feudorum	1 place (50)
Pandects	1 place (200)
Institutes	1st (160), 2nd (50), and 3rd place (20)
"De regulis iuris"	1 place (60)
Notarial art	1 place (100)

Source: Riccobono, 1980, 146ᵛ.

Note: The salaries are given in Paduan florins.

tion of the famous Pisan-Florentine manuscript under that name led the Senate to call the position *Pandects* rather than the more common *Digest*. In any case, the name was used for all the humanistic jurisprudence professorships established in Italian universities. The lecturer was expected to explicate humanistically the ancient text by itself, ignoring contemporary practical applications. Angelo Matteazzi di Marostica, who held the position in the years 1578–1590 at a salary of 200 florins, later raised to 300, did exactly that. But his successors reverted to traditional legal instruction.[71]

The creation and abolition of professorships did not always mean the influx of fresh blood or efflux of old. Sometimes a person already on the faculty filled a new professorship, while a professor whose post had disappeared moved to a newly created one. Some legists moved from one minor professorship to another for twenty years and more.[72] More able or fortunate scholars rose from lesser positions to important ones, or from a second place to a first place, without changing specialities.

The new directions—specialized practical applications in civil law, reduction of canon law, renewed emphasis on the medieval foundations of *mos italicus,* and humanistic jurisprudence—did not constitute a coherent innovative program. Nevertheless, other Italian universities followed the same road in lesser degree. By the end of the sixteenth century the new positions in practical law and humanistic jurisprudence, and the reduction of canon law, remained at Padua. Table 13.2 summarizes the structure and salaries of law instruction.

---

which, if willing, would have entered into negotiations with Muret. But there was no guarantee that the Senate would have hired Muret, because accusations of pederasty and homosexuality dogged him. Moreover, the Venetian government often agreed to create professorships without appointing the person that students wanted. This reminded the students who ran the university. For the Senate decree citing Muret's lectures as the model, see Brugi, 1915, 108–9.

71. Facciolati, 1978, pt. 3:184–87; Riccobono, 1980, 58ʳ–59ʳ, who states that Matteazzi had many students; Brugi, 1922, 69–70; and Tomasini, 1986, 262–63.

72. See Martellozzo Forin, 1970, 145–47, for a scholar who obtained his degree at Padua in civil and canon law in 1536 and then occupied six different minor legal professorships there through 1556.

The total was 12 civilians, 6 canonists, and 1 notary. Padua had moved from slightly more civilians than canonists in the fifteenth century and 15 civilians and 10 canonists in the early sixteenth century.

Bologna

Bologna manifested the same tendencies as Padua, but with less innovation. Nevertheless, it introduced the first professorship in criminal law anywhere. And it had the largest number of law professors by a substantial margin throughout the Renaissance.

Bologna had more success than Padua in hiring the most famous, or at least the most expensive, legists.[73] It conferred an annual average of 11.6 civil law and *utroque iure* doctorates between 1374 and 1500, figures that do not include canon law degrees and are probably far from complete for civil law. Twenty-three percent were non-Italians. The number of law doctorates (civil, canon, and *utroque iure*) rose to at least 55 annually by the late sixteenth century.[74] Again the figures are probably far from complete. Because of its distinguished history, large faculty, famous professors, and high enrollment, contemporaries probably considered Bologna the premier law school in Italy and Europe.

For teaching civil law, Bologna used a system of alternation similar to that employed for the major texts in medicine and natural philosophy. In one year the morning ordinary professors of civil law taught the *Codex,* while the afternoon ordinary professors taught the *Infortiatum.* In the next year the morning ordinary professors taught the *Old Digest,* while the afternoon ordinary professors taught the *New Digest.* Even the well-known and highly paid professors participated in this system of rotation. Indeed, alternation virtually eliminated the distinction between ordinary and extraordinary professorships. For example, Andrea Alciato was afternoon extraordinary professor teaching the *New Digest* and the *Infortiatum* in alternate years during his four years at Bologna (1537–41).[75]

Alternation meant that in one year a large number of the civilians lectured on the *Codex* and *Infortiatum,* while the *Old Digest* and *New Digest* were practically ignored. In the following year, numerous professors taught the *Old Digest* and *New Digest,* while the *Codex* and *Infortiatum* were little taught.[76] Less important texts (*Volumen, Libri authenticorum, Libri feudorum,* and *Institutes*), were taught every year, albeit by fewer professors.

---

73. Costa (1903–4) describes the successful efforts to bring Alciato, Carlo Ruini, and other famous jurists to Bologna in the sixteenth century.

74. Trombetti Budriesi, 1988, tables 3 and 8 on 173 and 176, for 1374–1500. Simeoni, 1940, 65, for law degrees in the years 1583–99. Neither searched through notarial records, which may have additional doctorates.

75. Dallari, 1888–1924, 2:83, 87, 90, 92. His position was always "Ad lecturam Infortiati [or Digesti novi] vespertinam extraordinariam."

76. One can see this clearly by examining a three- or four-year period with little faculty turnover. A good example is 1450–54, in ibid., 1:27–37.

For example, the roll of 1450–51 had 28 professors and 4 student lecturers who taught civil law as follows:

Codex	8 professors and 1 student lecturer
Infortiatum	10 professors, the student rector, and 1 student lecturer
Volumen	1 professor and 1 student lecturer
Institutes	3 professors
Libri authenticorum	3 professors
Libri feudorum	3 professors

In the following year, 1451–52, 27 professors and 4 student lecturers in civil law taught as follows:

Old Digest	5 professors plus 1 unfilled position
New Digest	14 professors, 1 student rector, and 2 student lecturers
Volumen	1 professor and 1 student lecturer
Institutes	2 professors plus 2 unfilled positions
Libri authenticorum	3 professors
Libri feudorum	2 professors plus 1 unfilled position

Bologna made fewer structural changes than Padua. The most important innovation was the establishment of an ordinary professorship of criminal law in 1509–10, the first in Italy and Europe, so far as is known.[77] The criminal law professorship continued through 1512–13, disappeared, and then reappeared in 1536–37 under a different title: *Ad lecturam de maleficijs*.[78] Why it was dropped is unknown. However, it is likely that the proclamation of the *Constitutio criminalis Carolina* caused Bologna to revive the professorship and to gain a temporary edge on Padua in the competition for German students. The ordinary professorship of criminal law was filled by a single professor from 1536–37 through 1593–94. It expanded to two professors in 1594–95 and continued at this level into the following century.

A professorship in *Libri feudorum* began in 1440–41 and then left and reappeared in the curriculum several times in the next century and a half.[79] Like

77. "Ad lecturam Criminalium diebus continuis et ordinarijs. (Legat titulum Digesti ad legem Corneliam de siccarijs et veneficijs usque ad titulum de appellationibus etc.)." The appointee was "D. Hippolytus de Marsilijs." Ibid., 1:204 (quotation), 207, 211, 214. For another example: "Ad lecturam de Malefitijs. (Legant legem eorum Codicis de maleficis et mathematicis [*sic*])." Ibid., 2:262, roll of 1598–99.

78. Ibid., 2, 80–266 passim. It was occasionally a *diebus festivis* post, rather than an ordinary professorship.

79. *Libri feudorum* was taught in the years 1440–69 and 1536–70. In 1583 the Assunteria di Studio petitioned the Bolognese Senate to restore the lectureship, arguing that many other famous universities had it. Hence, it returned in the years 1586–93 and then disappeared for good. Ibid., 1:14–78

TABLE 13.3
Average Annual Number of Professors of Law at the University of Bologna, 1400–1600

Years	Civil Law	Canon Law	Notarial Art	Total
1400–1425	22	11	2	35
1426–50	30	21	2	53
1451–75	35	25	1	61
1476–99	28	25	1	54
1500–1525	24	20	1	45
1526–50	26	16	1	43
1551–75	26	9	1	36
1576–1600	20	11	1	32

Source: Dallari, 1888–1924, 1, 2, and 4: *Aggiunte*; Zaoli, 1920.
Note: Teaching student rectors and student lecturers are counted. However, these positions were not always filled after 1550, which explains part of the decline in numbers.

Padua, Bologna briefly had a professorship focusing on Bartolo: *Ad lecturam repeticionum Bartoli*. It was intended to be an intermediate course, coming after the introductory *Institutes* lectures and before the ordinary lectures on the *Codex* and *Digest*. Its purpose may have been to give students an understanding of the founder of *mos italicus* before they heard more detailed lectures concentrating on more recent commentators. It began in 1587–88 and ended in 1594–95.[80]

In 1457–58, the professorship of notarial art, earlier taught by two professors, now taught by a single professor, moved from the arts faculty to the law faculty, where it remained through 1600.[81] The move recognized a change in the perception of *ars notaria*. It had been closely linked to *ars dictaminis* in the thirteenth and fourteenth centuries. Now it was a handmaiden to law, especially commercial law, which grew in importance in the second half of the sixteenth century and the seventeenth.[82]

In contrast to Padua, Bologna did not make a serious effort to introduce humanistic jurisprudence until the seventeenth century. Bologna created a professorship of *Pandects* in 1588, giving it to a very young scholar. Because he had not yet reached the minimum of twenty-five years required to hold a professorship, he received no salary the first year and only a modest stipend thereafter. The position was suppressed in 1592. The Bolognese authorities revived it in 1606, appointing a fairly eminent scholar, who was paid a handsome salary and given a

---

passim; 2:80–175 passim, 223, 226, 229, 232, 236, 240, 243; and ASB, Assunteria di Studio, Bu. 94, fascicle 7 (1583). Colli (1990) discusses the minor legal professorships and their occupants in the fifteenth century, and Boris (1990) mentions a number of lesser legists in the sixteenth century.

80. Dallari, 1888–1924, 2:225, 229, 232, 236, 240, 243, 247; Costa, 1912, 77.

81. Dallari, 1888–1924, 1:46 (arts roll of 1456–57), 48 (law roll of 1457–58).

82. See the comments of Besta, 1925b, 881–84, and Del Giudice, 1923, 116–17. In 1596–97, the notary was to teach "de iudicijs," in 1597–98 "de contractibus," and in 1598–99, "de ultimis voluntatibus." Dallari, 1888–1924, 2:258, 260, 262.

concurrent. *Pandects* then had a continuous existence through the eighteenth century. However, by the 1640s the *Pandects* professors were teaching *mos italicus* like the ordinary professors of civil law.[83]

In canon law the *Decretum* received the most pedagogical attention in the 1350s, but by 1450 the *Decretals* had become more important and continued to be so through 1600.[84] Thus, in 1450–51, 24 professors and 4 student lecturers taught as follows:[85]

Decretum	7 professors, the student rector, and 1 student lecturer
Decretals	13 professors and 1 student lecturer
Sextus and *Clementinae*	4 professors and 1 student lecturer

The canonists taught the same texts every year. Some canon law instruction dealt with usury. For example, the ordinary morning lecturers on the *Decretals* taught the canons concerning usury (*Legant de usuris*) in the 1590s.[86] Indeed, the position was titled *Ad lecturam de usuris* in 1586–87.[87]

The canonists began in an inferior numerical position to the civilians in 1400, grew to near parity between 1476 and 1525, and then declined precipitously. The civilians outnumbered the canonists by nearly 2 to 1 in the 1530s, and 3 to 1 in the 1560s, 1570s, and 1580s, in the aftermath of the Council of Trent. The university reduced canon law by leaving several professorships, such as the *Sextus* and *Clementinae* positions and some of the *Decretal* places, vacant. However, in contrast to Padua and other universities, the Bologna canonists reclaimed part of the lost ground in the 1590s, as some of the vacant posts were again filled.

Numerous future prelates taught law, usually civil law, at Bologna. Ugo Boncompagni (1502–85), the future Gregory XIII, taught *Institutes* from 1530 to 1533 and then became a morning ordinary professor of civil law (1533–40).[88] Gabriele Paleotti (1522–97), future cardinal and archbishop of Bologna, taught *Institutes* from 1546 to 1550 and then was a morning ordinary professor of civil law (1550–56).[89] Although neither ever taught canon law, both moved from the university to the papal curia as judges.

Bologna introduced the first professorship of criminal law anywhere and broadened civil law instruction a little. Otherwise, Bologna changed less than Padua between 1400 and 1600.

---

83. Dallari, 1888–1924, 2:229, 233, 236, 240, and passim, and Costa, 1908.
84. See the rolls of 1351–53 in Sorbelli, 1912.
85. Dallari, 1888–1924, 1:27–28.
86. See, for example, the rolls of 1590–91 and 1598–99 in ibid., 2:237, 263.
87. Ibid., 223.
88. Ibid., 60–89 passim.
89. Ibid., 110–34 passim. For his teaching and legal views, see Prodi, 1959–67, 1:67–81.

PAVIA AND ROME

Next in importance came Pavia, a large and generally conservative law school favored by ultramontanes, especially Germans.[90] The Pavian press contributed to the city's reputation as a legal center by publishing many legal works, at least 171 editions in the sixteenth century.[91]

Legal instruction began in Pavia several centuries before the establishment of a university.[92] After the founding of the university in 1361, law instruction followed the same pattern as Bologna and Padua. It averaged about 28 legists (17 civilians, 10 canonists, and 1 notary professor) in the last fifteen years of the fourteenth century.[93] The star was Baldo degli Ubaldi, who taught most of the decade 1390–1400.[94]

The number of legists dropped to 10 to 15 in the first twenty years of the fifteenth century and then rose gradually to an average of 34 in the 1440s. In the second half of the fifteenth century the average number of legists eased to 28. Civilians constituted 55 to 65 percent of the total and canonists 35 to 45 percent. One or two notaries completed the legal professoriat in the second half of the fifteenth century.[95]

The University of Pavia emerged from the frequent closures of the first forty years of the sixteenth century as a smaller institution, with only 20 legists from the 1540s through the end of the century. As at Bologna and Padua, the number of canon law professorships declined drastically. A typical group of 20 legists included 16 civilians and 4 canonists in the last twenty years of the century. The notarial art professor disappeared.[96]

Pavia introduced a professorship *De actionibus* in 1520 and one for criminal law in 1578, both of which continued through the end of the century and beyond. In the 1590s the Milanese Senate ordered Pavian legists to focus on the "older

90. This is a major theme of Sottili, 1993, who offers much information about German law students at Pavia in the fifteenth century.

91. Cavagna, 1981, 20–21, 100–124, and passim. Although small compared with the presses of Venice, Rome, and Florence, the Pavian press was important in law. By contrast, the Bolognese press published very few legal texts.

92. Radding, 1988, 10–13, 74, 75, 78, 97, 171–74.

93. See the various rolls, 1387–88 through 1399–1400 with many gaps, in Maiocchi, 1971, 1:117–18, 151–53, 184–85, 220–22, 227–28, 311–12, 420–21. Besta (1925a) surveys the Pavian legists from 1361 to 1460.

94. Baldo is listed in payment records for 1393–94, 1394–95, 1395–96, and 1399–1400, when the university was in Piacenza. However, he does not appear in the records for 1391–92, and information for other years has not been located. Maiocchi, 1971, 1:223, 227, 311, 420.

95. For the rolls 1400–1450, see Maiocchi, 1971, vol. 2, pts. 1 and 2. For the second half of the fifteenth century, see ASP, Università, Cartone 20, no pag. (roll of 1483–84), and Cartone 22 (many rolls but also gaps). The rolls of 1480–81 and 1482–83 are published in Verde, 1973–94, 1:384–92. See also the summary in Sottili, 1982, 544.

96. This is based on the rolls in ASPv, Università, Cartoni 20 and 22. See also the summary statistics and the roll of 1584–85 printed in Rizzo, 1987, 73, 75–76 n. 35. Legists' rolls of 1541–42 and 1548–49 are found in Zorzoli, 1982, 567 nn. 47 and 48.

interpreters," that is, medieval jurists, and to avoid heaping up citations from more recent authors. This was Pavia's way of emphasizing "text, gloss, and Bartolo." Not until 1609 was a *Pandects* professorship added.[97]

Pavia competed with Bologna and Padua for the most eminent and expensive legists of the day in the fifteenth century and in the early sixteenth century, despite the wars and closures. It had some success. Giason del Maino, a famous and expensive jurist, taught at Pavia for more than thirty years, from 1467 to 1485, in 1490, and then from 1497 until the university closed its doors in 1512.[98] One of his students was Alciato, who taught at Pavia in the years 1533–37 and 1546–50. Another important figure was Gianfrancesco Sannazari della Ripa (c. 1480–1535), who was born in Pavia and took his law doctorate there between 1506 and 1508. He taught at Pavia from 1507 or 1508 until 1512 and then moved to the University of Avignon, where he became a famous and prolific jurist of *mos italicus*. Duke Francesco II Sforza brought him back to teach at Pavia in 1533 at the high salary of 1,000 florins and with an appointment as senator in Milan.[99]

After Sannazari della Ripa and Alciato, however, Pavia no longer tried to lure star legists from other universities. Instead, the commune of Pavia worked to advance the careers of native sons, and the Milanese Senate sought to reduce costs. Both efforts contributed to a less distinguished faculty of local men. Of 147 legists who taught in the sixteenth century, 98 were natives of Pavia, 19 were Milanese, and another 8 came from other parts of the Lombard state. Only 22 were foreigners. Moreover, a mere 18 of the 147 legists ever taught outside Pavia. The university promoted from within: professors typically advanced from the *Institutes* position, to criminal law, to ordinary morning professor of civil or canon law. As they advanced, their salaries did not increase as much as professors who moved from one university to another.[100]

Despite the difficulties, Pavia continued to attract law students from Italy and abroad in the second half of the sixteenth century. It awarded approximately 10 law doctorates annually in the period 1567 through 1572. That number grew to around 30 annually in the mid-1570s, to 61 in 1587, and 43 in 1596.[101]

---

97. Zorzoli, 1982, 570, 572–73. For the text of the Senate's statement of May 9, 1591, favoring medieval interpreters, see *Memorie di Pavia,* 1970, pt. 2:20.

98. Vaccari, 1957, 88–90; Belloni, 1986, 221–27.

99. Ascheri, 1970.

100. On the localization of university posts and the financial consequences, see Zorzoli, 1982, 568–69; Zorzoli, 1986, 186–88; Rizzo, 1987, 73, 77–79. At least one native son was an eminent scholar. Iacopo Menocchio (1532–1607) of Pavia began teaching *Institutes* there in 1555. He moved to the University of Turin (then at Mondovì) in 1566, on to Padua, and returned to Pavia in 1589, where he remained until his death. His salary reached the height of 6,000 lire in 1591–92, and possibly more later. ASPv, Università, Cartone 20, roll of 1591–92, no pag. He was also elected to the Milanese Senate and became president of a court in Milan. Devoted to *mos italicus* and a staunch defender of the rights of the state, Menocchio advised the Milanese Senate in the various church-state disputes that erupted around the turn of the century. Barbieri, 1912, 96–97; Del Giudice, 1923, 111.

101. The numbers were 12 in 1567, 10 in 1568, 5 in 1570, 7 in 1571, 13 in 1572, 27 in 1573, 32 in 1576, 61 in 1587, and 43 in 1596. This is based on a sampling of the doctorates awarded found in

The University of Rome had 17 to 30 legists in the 1470s and early 1480s, 60 percent of them civilians.[102] The number of legists remained high in the early sixteenth century, as the roll of 1514 had 30 legists (19 civilians and 11 canonists) in a faculty of 87 professors. Very few of the legists were recognizable names. The much smaller university that reopened in 1535 after the sack of 1527 had an average of 10 to 12 legists (7 to 9 civilians and 2 or 3 canonists) through the end of the sixteenth century.[103] A few legists teaching at Rome in the sixteenth century were well-known figures.

The most important innovation at Rome was the establishment of a *Pandects* professorship in 1567, the first in Italy. The learned French humanist Marc'-Antoine Muret, who had studied with humanistic jurisprudents in France, filled the position from 1567 to 1572 and then moved to rhetoric.[104] Muret's annual prelusions in these years asserted that eloquence and jurisprudence should be joined; one needed the *studia humanitatis* in order to study law properly. His letters praised French humanistic jurists and strongly criticized *mos italicus* as taught in Italy.[105] According to Muret, students flocked to his course, leaving the classrooms of other legists empty. Given the fact that Muret and the ordinary professors of civil law taught at different hours and that *mos italicus* dominated law at La Sapienza, his boast seems exaggerated. Muret also hinted that the other legists forced him to give up teaching the *Pandects* course, another claim that has not been verified.[106] After Muret, the *Pandects* position disappeared until revived

---

ASPv, Università, Doctoratus, Bu. 2 (1566–72), 3 (1573–77), 6 (1587–90), and 8 (1596–99). Each busta contains fascicles for discrete calendar years. Law doctorates made up 55 to 60 percent of the doctorates awarded. As usual, the records may not include all doctorates awarded.

102. The precise numbers are 27 legists in 1473, 20 in 1474, 17 in 1481, 30 in 1482, 27 in 1483, 22 in 1483, and 14 in 1484. The count for 1484 may be incomplete. See Dorati da Empoli, 1980, 107–17, and Lee, 1984, 145. Their counts, which differ slightly, are based on payment records. For 1514, see *I maestri di Roma*, 1991, 2–3. For information on some of the legists who taught in the late fifteenth and early sixteenth centuries, see Renazzi, 1971, 1:218–23.

103. *I maestri di Roma*, 1991, 7–171 passim, for the rolls 1535 through 1609, with many gaps. For comments on the legists, see Renazzi, 1971, 2:177–87; 3:37–39. However, Renazzi, a professor of law at the University of Rome when he published his history of the university (1803–6), was relentlessly hostile to *mos italicus* and warmly favorable to humanistic jurisprudence. His comments must be understood in this light.

104. *I maestri di Roma*, 1991, 47, 54, 62, 68, 78. Muret is listed in the next surviving roll, that of 1574–75, but without a subject. Renzi (1985, 28, and 1986, 263) states that Muret moved to a rhetoric professorship in 1572. Hence, the summary of the *Pandects* position in *I maestri di Roma*, 1991, 1024, needs to be corrected.

105. Four prelusions are found in Muret, 1737, 1:112–33. Those of 1567 and 1569 (112–16, 119–25) were particularly forceful. See also Muret's letters in ibid., 2:76–77 (Jan. 26, 1579), 120–22 (Sept. 13, 1580), and esp. 299–301 (Jan. 18, 1578). Renazzi (1971, 2:177–78) quotes from the last letter. See also Dejob, 1970, 177–87, who provides information on the *Pandects* professorship.

106. Muret, 1737, 3:300. The beadle Alessio Lorenzani made no reference to the size of Muret's audience, or to that of the other legists, or to their alleged hostility. *I maestri di Roma*, 1991, 47, 54, 62, 68, 78. Conte (1985b, 340, and 1998, 172–73) is also skeptical about Muret's attendance boast and provides useful information on some of the other legists at Rome.

in 1658. Thus, Rome had the first *Pandects* professorship in Italy because Muret wanted to teach the subject, rather than because the university believed in it. Rome emphasized *mos italicus*.[107]

Rome also established a professorship in criminal law in 1574–75, which continued into the seventeenth century.[108] The only other deviation from the norm was a holiday lectureship on Bartolo, which lasted only one year, 1570–71.[109] Although located at the center of Catholicism, the University of Rome did not emphasize canon law. But professors there helped produce a revised edition of Gratian's *Decretum*. Begun in 1560 under papal sponsorship and appearing in 1582, the revised text purged errors and incorrect references. It was a major work of legal scholarship.[110]

Despite its relatively small size, the law school at Rome awarded an extraordinary quantity of law degrees in the sixteenth century. The numbers steadily rose: 40 per year in the years 1548–60; 50 per year, 1561–70; 73 per year, 1571–80; 106 per year, 1581–90; 84 per year, 1591–1600; and 123 per year, 1601–10. About 92 percent of the degree recipients came from the papal state and southern Italy, about 7 percent from northern Italy, and 1 to 2 percent from outside Italy.[111] Although located at the center of an international church, La Sapienza's law school served a regional constituency. Rome was a significant second-line law school that produced a large number of graduates.

SIENA AND THE SOZZINI

Some law instruction existed in Siena in the twelfth century before the university was founded. The pioneering commentator Cina da Pistoia taught in Siena from 1321 to 1326 before moving to Perugia. Other known legists also taught in Siena, although the lack of rolls makes it impossible to reconstruct the law school in the fourteenth century.[112] In 1445 Siena had at least 7 civilians and 5 canonists.[113] By 1474 the law school had doubled to 13 civilians and 11 canonists, in a university of 45 professors.[114] The number remained at this level in the 1490s (e.g., 14 civilians and 8 canonists in a faculty of 43 in 1492–93) and grew to 13

---

107. Conte, 1985a, 72; Conte, 1985b, 339–40;

108. *I maestri di Roma,* 1991, 89–90, 101, and passim, 1019–20.

109. Ibid., 77.

110. Renazzi, 1971, 2:224–25; Pastor, 1891–1953, 19:279–80; Conte, 1985a, 17; Conte, 1998, 177–80.

111. Cagno, 1932, 168–72, 178–80. I have examined some of the archival evidence, for example, ASR, Archivio dell'Università di Roma, R. 227, "Registri dei Dottori e decreti togati, 3 marzo 1549–23 dicembre 1558." In addition, between 1567 and 1580 the beadle mentioned on six occasions the number of law degrees awarded annually. *I maestri di Roma,* 1991, 50, 59, 64, 74, 85, 97.

112. See Prunai, 1950, 30–41, and Minnucci, 1991, 111–14.

113. Nardi, 1974, 125–29. For a survey of law in the fifteenth century, see Zdekauer, 1977, and Minnucci, 1991, 114–16, 122–30.

114. See the undated roll, probably 1474, published in Minnucci and Košuta, 1989, 119–21.

civilians and 18 canonists in a faculty of 52 in 1500–1501.[115] Siena had become a large and significant law school.

Siena produced the most famous legal dynasty of the Renaissance, the Sozzini (or Socini) family of legists. Coming from a family in banking and commerce, Mariano the Elder (1397/1401–67) was the first to pursue a career teaching law. After winning his law degree, probably at Siena between 1425 and 1427, he began teaching canon law as a student lecturer in 1425 and as a professor in the autumn of 1427. He taught canon law at Siena for forty years, unusual stability for a prominent jurist. Mariano wrote numerous legal works that were widely used and printed in the fifteenth and sixteenth centuries. As a respected and prolific canon lawyer during the age of conciliarist agitation, he was much in demand for his opinions. He became quite influential at the Roman curia when his former pupil and close friend Enea Silvio Piccolomini (1401–64) became Pope Pius II in 1458. Although Mariano Senior enjoyed an Italian-wide reputation as a legist, he received relatively modest salaries until near the end of career.[116]

This was not true of his son, Bartolomeo Sozzini (1436–1506), who taught at the most famous law schools in Italy at much higher salaries than his father had enjoyed. Bartolomeo studied law at Siena under his father as well as at Bologna and Pisa. A civilian, he began teaching at Siena by 1461, remaining there until 1472. He taught at Ferrara (1472–73) and then at Pisa (1473–94), teaching both canon law and civil law, where his salary rose from 800 to 1,665 florins, by far the highest in the university. At Pisa he taught and examined for his canon law degree Giovanni de' Medici, the future Pope Leo X. The two most important law schools in Italy then pursued him, apparently judging that his star status outweighed his quarrelsome nature. He taught at Bologna (1496–98) and then at Padua (1498–1501) at the very high salary of 1,200 ducats. He returned to Siena in 1501. Now ill, he did not teach at the *studium* but served as promoter for some degree candidates, including his nephew (see below). Like his father, Bartolomeo was a prolific scholar whose works went into at least thirty incunabular editions and continued to be published later.[117]

Although Bartolomeo Sozzini taught outside Siena most of his professional

115. See Zdekauer, 1977, 191–93, for the 1492–93 roll; see Mondolfo, 1897, for the roll of 1500–1501. Why Siena had so many canonists in 1500–1501 is unknown. The increase was temporary.

116. Nardi, 1974, 6–113 passim, and Tedeschi, 1965, 282–87, for his life. His salary gradually rose from modest figures of 30, 60, 70, 80, 100, 110, 145, and 170 florins to a high of 500 florins in 1465. It then receded to 250 florins in his last contract awarded in the summer of 1467. The contracts specified that the Sienese gold florin was worth 4 lire. Nardi, 1974, 115, 116, 117, 119, 122, 124, 125, 129, 131, 133, 144, 147, for the salary documents. For a list of manuscript and printed editions of his works, see Nardi, 1974, 150–84.

117. Tedeschi, 1965, 287–91; Belloni, 1986, 168–71; Verde, 1973–94, 1:297–352 passim; 2:100–19; Dallari, 1888–1924, 1:162, 165; Costa, 1903–4, 216–17; Facciolati, 1978, pt. 2, 57–58; Secco Suardo, 1983, 262, 264; Bargagli, 1992; Del Gratta, 1993a, 490; and Minnucci and Košuta, 1989, 235–36, for comprehensive bibliography. Now see Bargagli, 2000, which arrived too late to use fully. Bartolomeo Sozzini's name appeared as examiner and promoter for Sienese law degrees in 1501 and 1502 but only once beyond 1502 (for his nephew in 1505). Minnucci, 1984.

FIG. 11. Bartolomeo Sozzini, *Consilia*. Part 4. No place or printer, 1537. *Special Collections Library, Biddle Law Library, University of Pennsylvania Law School.*

life, he maintained close ties with his native city and its leaders. This produced tense relations and angry encounters. The Sienese government exerted great pressure on Sozzini to teach in its university, and when he did not respond, it appointed him anyway. When Sozzini did not appear, the city denounced him as a traitor. On the other hand, Sozzini exploited the Sienese desire to bring him back: he accepted high civic offices (and salaries) even when teaching elsewhere. Sometimes he could combine his outside teaching appointments and Sienese public office. In the 1480s and 1490s when Bartolomeo taught at the University of Pisa, often located in Florence in these years, the Sienese sometimes elected him to serve as ambassador to Florence.[118]

The next Sozzini became even more famous. Mariano Sozzini the Younger (1482–1556) was the grandson of Mariano the Elder and nephew of Bartolomeo. He studied law at Siena and Bologna and took his degree in civil law at Siena in January 1505, with his uncle one of the promoters.[119] Mariano the Younger began teaching law at Siena in 1504 and stayed at least until 1517. He then taught at Pisa in the years 1517–23, was back in Siena in 1523, and then moved to Padua in 1525. He remained at Padua until 1542, rising to first afternoon ordinary professor of civil law at a salary above 1,000 ducats. He moved to Bologna for the academic year 1542–43 and remained there until his death in 1556.[120] In April 1552, Sozzini received 5,200 Bolognese lire (1,300 scudi), twice the sum of the second highest paid professor, plus various privileges and tax exemptions.[121] The university also appointed his son Celso ordinary professor of canon law.

Monarchs consulted Mariano the Younger on matters of European-wide importance, such as Henry VIII's divorce case. Although the cautious Venetian government forbade the Paduan professors to respond publicly to Henry's request for judicial opinions, Mariano did so anyway. He argued that the pope had lacked the authority to grant the dispensation permitting Henry to marry his brother's widow. Hence, Henry's first marriage to Catherine of Aragon was invalid, and he was free to marry Anne Boleyn. Mariano the Younger also wrote a well-known *consilium* on dueling, which was translated into Italian.[122]

Two sons of Mariano the Younger also held law professorships. Alessandro Sozzini (1508–41) took his degree at Siena, taught briefly there (1531–33), and then taught civil law at Padua (1533–35) before returning to Siena in 1537, although he was frequently absent from the city. He finished his career at Macerata in 1540–41.[123] Celso Sozzini (1517–70) initially taught at Siena and then received

118. Bargagli, 1992 and 2000, 92–131, 138–47.

119. His degree is noted in Minnucci, 1984, 72.

120. For this and the following paragraph, see Tedeschi, 1965, 292–98; Nardi, 1975, 199; Fabroni, 1971, 1:389; Facciolati, 1978, pt. 3:116, 134, 139; Costa, 1903–4, 226–28; Dallari, 1888–1924, 2:99, 101, 104, 107, 109, 112, 115, 118, 121, 123, 126, 129, 132, 134; Stella, 1988, 129–31, 150–53; and Del Gratta, 1993a, 490.

121. See the list of salaries printed in Cavina, 1988, 438.

122. Bryson, 1938, 236, plus 217–30 passim, which cites his *consilium*.

123. Tedeschi, 1965, 298–99; Facciolati, 1978, pt. 3:97, 126; Nardi, 1975, 199; Minnucci and Košuta, 1989, 505 and see index; Stella, 1988, 137–39, 153–55.

a canon law position at Bologna in 1551 as part of the arrangement that kept his father from leaving Bologna for another post. After his father's death in 1556, Celso moved into the ordinary civil law professorship vacated by his father. But he was not listed first and received a much lower salary than his father. Celso taught civil law at Bologna until 1563, when he returned to Siena.[124] The family name and their father's influence aided the careers of these two jurists of modest accomplishments.

The success of the Sozzini raised the prestige of the local university. All the Sozzini studied and taught at Siena, with Mariano the Elder spending his entire career there. As a result, the Sienese law school flourished at the end of the fifteenth century and in the early sixteenth and enjoyed a high reputation with ultramontane students, especially Germans.[125] Indeed, 77 percent of the degrees awarded between 1484 and 1579 were in law. And non-Italians received about 27 percent of them (see Ch. 2, "Siena, 1246").

The Sienese law school receded a little in size and greatly deemphasized canon law by the 1530s. At that time the law school consisted of 15 to 17 civilians and 3 to 5 canonists. The civilians usually included at least 3 newly graduated Sienese citizens, who were obliged to teach the *Institutes* for one year.[126] Combining deception and hope, the Sienese government listed Mariano Sozzini the Younger as professor of civil law in the rolls of the early 1530s, even though he taught at Padua. The Sienese used Sozzini's name to attract students and hoped that he would return to teach them. It did not happen, partly because the Sienese would not meet Sozzini's salary demands.[127]

As Charles V and Florence closed in on the city in the 1540s and 1550s, some Sienese legists left for other universities.[128] Following military defeat and the loss of independence in 1555, Siena was incorporated into the duchy of Tuscany in 1557. The Medici dukes promoted the Pisan *studio* at the expense of Siena. The Sienese law school dipped to its lowest point in two centuries, 6 civilians and 1 canonist, in 1563–64. But when the Medici crown prince, the future Francesco I, began to take an active role in the governance of the Tuscan state in 1567, the fortunes of the Sienese *studio* improved dramatically. In 1567–68 the law faculty had doubled to 13 civilians and 1 canonist. Under the benign eye of Francesco I, who became the ruler of Tuscany in 1574, the law school grew to 20 civilians and 5 canonists. Under the rule of Grand Duke Ferdinando I (1587–1609), who again favored Pisa, the Sienese law school settled at 17 legists (15 civilians and 2 canon-

124. Tedeschi, 1965, 299–300; Dallari, 1888–1924, 2:123, 126, 128, 131, 134, 137, 140, 143, 146, 149, 152, 155; Stella, 1988, 139, 141, 143.

125. See *I tedeschi dell'Università di Siena,* 1988, for the German students at Siena.

126. See Prunai, 1959, 84, 98; Minnucci and Košuta, 1989, 334, 397, 406; Cascio Pratilli, 1975, 87.

127. See the rolls of 1531–32, 1533–34, 1535–36, 1537–38, 1539–40, and 1541–42, in Minnucci and Košuta, 1989, 397–416, and Nardi, 1975, 201. Since the commune of Siena frequently awarded two-year contracts, each of these rolls probably covered the following year as well.

128. Nardi, 1975.

ists).[129] The civilian group included four or more newly graduated Sienese citizens obligated to teach the *Institutes*.

Always conservative, Siena became even less adventuresome. While other law schools added professorships in new fields, the only Sienese innovation in the second half of the century was a professorship of *Pandects* desired by the German students. It began in 1589–90 and continued into the next century. However, the holders of the position usually taught *mos italicus*.[130] The Sienese law school seldom appointed distinguished outsiders at any time in its history.[131] This did not matter so long as a number of native sons were learned jurists. By the end of the sixteenth century this was seldom the case.

Siena's importance came from its role as nurturer of legal talent and teacher of ultramontane students, especially Germans. It had the great good fortune that an eminent native son on the faculty became famous in the fifteenth century and that all the Sozzini taught locally, at least for a few years. Then political adversity forced Siena to settle for the position of second law school in Tuscany, although not far behind Pisa.

FLORENCE AND PISA

The commune of Pisa paid a legist to teach law to students as early as 1065. Other legists taught at Pisa between 1262 and 1283, long before the founding of the university in 1343.[132] Bartolo of Sassoferrato taught at Pisa from 1339 to 1342 and Baldo degli Ubaldi probably in the academic year 1357–58. Although few records survive, law continued to be taught in the late fourteenth century and the first years of the fifteenth.[133] Although instruction halted after Florence conquered the city in 1406, the college of doctors of canon and civil law awarded 42 law degrees (20 in canon law, 14 in civil law, and 8 *in utroque iure*) between 1406 and 1472. The majority of recipients were clergymen.[134]

129. See the rolls in Cascio Pratilli, 1975, 175–88, and Marrara, 1970, 228–48. For further discussion, see Prunai, 1959, 137–48; Cascio Pratilli, 1975, 11–115 passim, esp. 72–74; and Ascheri, 1991.

130. Rossi, 1906; Marrara, 1970, 228, 230, 231, 232, and passim; and Cascio Pratilli, 1975, 41, 73 n. 199, 87, 89 n. 45, 100.

131. Siena did appoint the Bolognese Gismondo Zannetti (or Zannettini), who taught at Siena from 1569 to 1576 at 700 to 787.5 florins, three and one-half to four times the salary of the next highest paid scholar. Prunai, 1959, 88–90, 143; Cascio Pratilli, 1975, 30–32, 35, 38, 56, 178, 181. However, Zannetti was teaching at the University of Rome in 1579–80. *I maestri di Roma*, 1991, 116. See also Ascheri, 1991, 135–36.

132. Fabroni, 1971, 1:16–45; Radding, 1988, 171, 173.

133. Spagnesi (1993) provides a good survey of law at Pisa from the beginning. See also Picotti, 1968, 24–25; Calasso, 1964, 641–42; Canning, 1987, 4. Benedetto Barzi of Piombino (c. 1350–1410), an influential jurist in his day, taught at Pisa in the years 1407–8 and then moved to Padua. Campitelli, 1965, 19. He should not be confused with Benedetto Barzi of Perugia (c. 1380–1459), also a legist. See Barzi, 1965.

134. Davies, 2000.

Law had an easier early life at the University of Florence . Four or 5 civilians, 3 canonists, and a notary normally taught in the fourteenth century. After leaving Pisa, Baldo degli Ubaldi taught civil law at Florence for six academic years (1358–64) and then moved to Perugia and Pavia.[135] The law faculty of the fifteenth-century University of Florence steadily expanded from 5 civilians, 3 canonists, and a notary at the beginning of the century to 6 or 7 civilians and the same number of canonists in the 1440s.[136] The notary position disappeared in the 1430s. The well-known Paolo di Castro taught civil law in the years 1401–3 and 1411–24 before moving to Bologna and Padua.[137]

From 1473 through 1503, the law faculty of the renewed University of Pisa, still often located in Florence, nearly doubled, from 12 to 14 legists to 23 to 25 legists (14 civilians and 11 canonists) in 1500–1501.[138] In the first quarter of the sixteenth century, the number of legists dropped slightly to an average of 18 to 19, with the balance between canonists and civilians remaining the same.[139] Filippo Decio of Milan, teaching both canon and civil law, was the other star law professor, alongside Bartolomeo Sozzini, for most of the period 1476 to 1526. Known for his skill and long-windedness—he once spoke for three hours without pause in a disputation—and for quarreling with his colleagues, Decio was a conservative follower of *mos italicus*.[140] He and his colleagues instructed many Florentines who took law degrees at Pisa, taught briefly in the lower ranks, and then opened private practices or entered governmental service.[141]

After closing in 1526, the University of Pisa reopened in 1543. At that time Duke Cosimo I de' Medici made a determined effort to hire Alciato, then at Ferrara, to add luster to the Pisan law faculty and to increase enrollment. Representatives of the duke wooed Alciato from early 1542 through early 1547, but without success, because the Milanese Senate wanted him for Pavia and held the ultimate trump card. The Senate called on Emperor Charles V, who made it clear that he did not want Alciato to move to Pisa. Alciato, a native of Milan and a

---

135. For rolls 1357–58 through 1369–70, see Park, 1980, 253–64; for law professors in 1388, see Abbondanza, 1959; for 1391–92 through 1396–97, see Spagnesi, 1979, 270. Baldo's salary began at 250 florins and rose to 300 florins. However, in 1362–63, Florence appointed Riccardo da Saliceto of Bologna at 800 florins. Park, 1980, 253–58; Canning, 1987, 4.

136. Gherardi, 1973, 376–77, for the roll of 1402–3, and passim for various appointment notices; Park, 1980, 268–310, passim.

137. D'Amelio, 1979, 229; Martines, 1968, 499–500; Park, 1980, 272–80 passim.

138. Verde, 1973–94, 1:293–383.

139. The rolls of 1504–6 and 1516–21 had 9 to 12 civilians and 8 or 9 canonists. ASF, Studio fiorentino e pisano, Bu. 8, ff. 131ʳ, 132ᵛ, 134ʳ, 135ᵛ, 138ʳ, and Fabroni, 1971, 1:379–90.

140. Decio taught at Pisa (1476–84), Siena (1484–87), Pisa (1487–1501), Padua (1502–5), Pavia (1505–12), Pisa (1516–28), and Siena (1528–36). He spent much of the time between 1512 and 1516 as a consultant on conciliar matters, as the Fifth Lateran Council met in those years. See Verde, 1973–94, 1:302–23, 331–373 passim; 2:570–79; Fabroni, 1971, 1:381–85 passim, 389; Mazzacane, 1987; and Spagnesi, 1993, 215–35, for the period 1473–1526. See Spagnesi, 1993, 222, for Decio's long disputation.

141. Martines (1968, 482–508 passim) lists many Florentines and a few outsiders who taught at the universities of Florence and Pisa from the 1360s to 1530.

subject of the emperor, was obliged to go to Pavia against his will, in the opinion of Cosimo's emissary.[142]

The University of Pisa had only 5 civilians and 2 canonists in 1543. The number then grew to 15 civilians and 7 canonists in 1567–68 and 13 to 18 civilians and 6 to 8 canonists in the late 1580s.[143] In the 1560s, the tiny Florentine branch of the University of Pisa included 1 poorly paid professor of *Institutes* among its 3 or 4 professors.[144] He was expected to teach this introductory text to Florentines before they went to Pisa for the bulk of their studies. The University of Pisa legists included some learned outsiders along with a large majority of undistinguished Tuscans from Florence, Pisa, and Arezzo.

Pisa created new positions in civil law but did not always make them permanent. A professorship of criminal law began in 1545 and lasted until 1588, when the government suppressed it. It was revived in 1604. The professorship of *Libri feudorum* began in 1559, was suppressed in 1588, and was revived in 1607. *Pandects* initially lasted only two years, 1591–93, because the person chosen for the chair lacked the necessary Greek and Latin skills to present a humanistic analysis of the text. *Pandects* reappeared in 1616.[145]

The University of Pisa awarded 202 law degrees between October 1, 1474, and the end of September 1505, an average of 6.7 annually, a small number by contemporary standards.[146] After 1543 the University of Pisa awarded many more law doctorates:[147]

Years	Annual average
1543–49	13
1550–59	35
1560–69	50.5
1570–79	63
1580–89	61
1590–99	59

142. See Abbondanza, 1958, for an account with many documents of the unsuccessful effort to bring Alciato to Pisa.

143. Fabroni, 1971, 2:464–68; Cascio Pratilli, 1975, 192–95; Galilei, 1966, 32–33, 37–38, 39–40; the lists in Barsanti, 1993, 544–51, 554; and Spagnesi, 1993, 236–48, for a survey of the period 1543–1650.

144. Antonio Malagonnelle was paid 50 florins annually to teach *Institutes* from 1563 through 1569. BNF, Ms. Corte d'appello 3, ff. 44ᵛ, 47ʳ, 49ʳ, 51ʳ, 52ᵛ, 55ʳ. The other professors in Florence in the 1550s and 1560s were normally two humanists and a theologian. It is not clear if the *Institutes* position existed in Florence before the 1560s, because earlier payment records in ASF, Studio, Bu. 8, fail to list the disciplines taught.

145. Fabroni, 1971, 2:466; Cascio Pratilli, 1975, 150–51 esp. nn. 52–53, pp. 168–69 esp. nn. 34–35; and Barsanti, 1993, 554.

146. Eighty-seven degrees in civil law, 56 in canon law, and 59 *in utroque iure* were awarded in the thirty years. The other degrees were 107 in arts and medicine, 34 in theology, and 1 in surgery. Hence, law doctorates accounted for 59 percent of the known doctorates awarded. Verde, 1973–94, 2:648–729 passim. These are the known degrees; there may have been others.

147. The figures come from Del Gratta, 1980, table 3a. Law degrees accounted for 70.49 percent of the doctorates awarded in the years 1543–99.

Fig. 12. Title page of Filippo Decio, *Consilia*. Volume 3. Lyon: Jean Marechal, January 8, 1533. An unknown hand has added the names of famous legists below the vignettes and Decio's name as the lecturer at the bottom of the page. *Special Collections Library, Biddle Law Library, University of Pennsylvania Law School.*

Overall, Florence had a relatively small law school of regional importance and with strong ties to the city. After the transfer of 1473, the revivified University of Pisa was more important, reaching a middle-rank position among law schools. But Pisa declined in quality in the late sixteenth century.[148]

THE OTHER UNIVERSITIES

Ferrara had a small law faculty of 12 legists in 1449–50, which increased to a medium- to large-sized school of 22 (13 civilians, 8 canonists, and 1 notary professor) in 1474–75.[149] The number remained at about 20 in the late fifteenth century. After the closures and other difficulties of the first thirty years of the sixteenth century, Ferrara emerged as a smaller law school in the 1540s. Ten to 13 civilians and 4 canonists made up the law professoriat until the 1580s, and 12 to 15 civilians and 3 canonists in the last two decades of the century. The professorship of notarial art disappeared in 1576.[150] Andrea Alciato, who had taken his degree at Ferrara in 1516 without attending classes there, taught at Ferrara for four academic years, 1542–46. He earned as much as the other 45 professors combined (see Ch. 3, "Ferrara 1442").

In addition to *Institutes* and the ordinary positions in canon and civil law, Ferrara had a single lecturer in *Libri feudorum* from 1540 onward. Feudal law became important at the end of the century, as the Este family sought to hold on to Ferrara against papal claims. If the task of the professor of feudal law was to disprove the ancient feudal fief that awarded the duchy to the papacy when Duke Alfonso II (1533; ruled 1559–97) failed to produce a legitimate male heir, he failed. The papacy, with the extralegal support of a large army, took over the duchy in 1598. Ferrara had a lecturer in criminal law from 1547–48, which became two in 1583–84. A professor *Ad lecturam Bartholi* or *Glossa et Bartholo* made an occasional appearance in 1555–56 and the 1560s, existed from 1569 to 1588, and then vanished. A professorship of *Pandects* appeared in the single year 1588–89.[151] Ferrara was more important as a university at which to obtain a degree than as a place to study law.

Perugia had the superb good fortune to be the place where the two greatest medieval legists studied and taught. Indeed, Bartolo da Sassoferrato and Baldo degli Ubaldi taught side by side at Perugia between 1351 and 1357. Although their tradition dominated legal instruction during the Renaissance, Perugia was less important as an institution.

148. Francesco Verino il Secondo (de' Vieri), a professor of natural philosophy at Pisa, had a more favorable opinion of the legists there in 1587. Del Fante, 1980b, 403–4.

149. Secco Suardo, 1983, 205–66 passim.

150. Franceschini, 1970, xiv–xv, 219–35; Pardi, 1972, 230–31, 238, 243, 248–49; Solerti, 1892, 24–51 passim.

151. Franceschini, 1970, xiv–xv, 231–34.

The fourteenth-century law faculty was quite small: 4 civilians and 3 canonists in 1339 and 3 civilians, 4 canonists, and a notary in 1396.[152] It expanded considerably in the fifteenth century, possibly because students wanted to study at the university that nourished Bartolo and Baldo. In 1429–30, Perugia had 19 legists (13 civilians and 6 canonists); in 1431–32 there were 21 legists but only 15 professors for arts and medicine. In 1443–44, Perugia had 13 civilians, 11 canonists, and a notary, while the rest of the university had only 11 professors.[153] In most universities, the faculty of arts had more professors than the faculty of law. But law dominated at Perugia. Perugia probably maintained a law faculty of about the same size in the later fifteenth and in the sixteenth centuries. For example, 15 civilians and 11 canonists taught in 1567–68. Only later did Perugia deemphasize canon law, with 21 civilians and 6 canonists in 1600–1601.[154]

Perugia did not add new professorships easily. In 1567–68 the university had professorships of criminal law and *Libri feudorum,* while two (of the four) *Institutes* professors also taught legal actions (*De actionibus*). But Perugia then dropped the criminal law and *Libri feudorum* posts for several years. They reappeared by 1600–1601 as holiday lectureships. Perugia had no *Pandects* professorship in the sixteenth century.[155]

Perugia had several eminent legists in the fifteenth century. They strongly maintained the tradition of Bartolo and Baldo to the point that some were renamed for their predecessors, for example, Baldo Bartolini (1409–90), called the "New Baldo" (Baldo Novello).[156] The law school remained large in the sixteenth century but declined in quality, as natives of Perugia, some of them descendents of Baldo degli Ubaldi, monopolized the teaching posts without attaining the eminence of their ancestors.

Naples had a significant law school during the thirteenth and fourteenth centuries. The law faculty reached the relatively high figure of 14 to 16 professors in the mid-fourteenth century but then receded in the fifteenth century, as the university was frequently closed. By the late fifteenth century, Naples had only 7 or 8 legists, equally divided between civilians and canonists. In the sixteenth century, the Neapolitan law school consisted of 7 civilians and 1 canonist, when all civilian posts were filled. Despite its small size, Naples attempted to add new professorships. At various times the civilian group included professorships in *De*

152. Ermini, 1971, 49–50, 85–86.

153. Nicolini, 1961, 141–50; Ermini, 1971, 226–27, 234.

154. Ermini, 1971, 229–30.

155. Ibid., 229–31. The lack of rolls makes more detailed analysis impossible.

156. See Abbondanza, 1964a. For other Perugian legists, see Ermini, 1971, 497–553; Bini, 1977, 594–96 and passim. For brief biographies of Onofrio Bartolini (c. 1350–c. 1415), see Abbondanza, 1964c; for Dionigi Barigiani (d. 1435), see Liotta, 1964; for Pier Filippo Della Cornia (1419/20–92), see Falaschi, 1988; and for Mariano Bartolini (1465/66–1509), see Abbondanza, 1964b.

actionibus, Libri feudorum, and "Text, Gloss, and Bartolo."[157] The Neapolitan law school had few well-known legists on its faculty.[158]

The Turinese law school had as many as 18 professors in 1452, 21 in 1472, and 16 in 1487, but the lack of rolls makes it impossible to determine if these were normal figures. In the early 1530s the law school had dropped to 7 civilians and 3 to 5 canonists. After the closures of the 1540s and 1550s, the restored university of the last third of the century normally had 1 or 2 canonists and 10 or 11 civilians, including a professor of feudal law, which continued with two professors in the early seventeenth century. Turin introduced criminal law in 1568. It lasted through 1586, disappeared at some point between 1586 and 1600, and then reappeared in 1604. The faculty usually included one well-known and highly paid civilian, such as Aimone Cravetta (1504–69), who taught from about 1562 to 1569, and Guido Panciroli (1523–99), who taught from 1569 to 1582. The star civilian sometimes earned as much as all the other legists combined.[159]

The University of Macerata had 5 or 6 civilians and 1 canonist between 1540 and 1580. The civilian posts included an extraordinary lectureship focusing on Bartolo in 1578–79, which was not continued. None of the legists achieved scholarly renown while teaching at Macerata. As noted in Chapter 4, Macerata awarded about 19 law degrees annually by the end of the sixteenth century.[160] The tiny University of Catania had only about 5 legists, usually 3 civilians and 2 canonists in the fifteenth century. This became 4 civilians and 1 canonist after 1541, when canon law was set at 1 position. Those who taught law at Catania tended to be local men from families filling communal administrative positions and civic offices. They did not attract scholarly attention beyond their own university.[161] Salerno had 3 civilians (one of them a "glossist") and 1 canonist in 1592.[162]

The 1596 statutes of the University of Messina created 4 professorships of civil law, including *Libri feudorum,* and 1 for canon law (see Ch. 4). Parma had 6

157. For the thirteenth and fourteenth centuries, see Monti, 1924, 74–84; for the fifteenth century, see Filangieri di Candida, 1924, 179–83, and Cannavale, 1980, 43–52, esp. the rolls 1478–80. For the sixteenth century, see Cannavale, 1980, 53–81 passim; Cortese, 1924, 302–3, 316–25. Cortese (1924, 322) also refers to an "extraordinary civil law or *Pandects*" professorship from 1565 through 1591 successively filled by Giulio Janua and Marcantonio Sorgente. Cannavale, by contrast, makes no mention of a *Pandects* post but does note that Janua and Sorgente held extraordinary civil law positions. Cannavale, 1980, 69–79 and see the index for the documents referring to Janua and Sorgente. In the absence of additional information, one cannot conclude that this was a position in humanistic jurisprudence. Indeed, Sorgente sometimes held the "Text, Gloss, and Bartolo" position, which approached law from the opposite perspective as humanistic jurisprudence.

158. The best-known jurist to teach at Naples may have been Alessandro Turamini (1556–1605), who taught there from 1592 to 1603.

159. Bellone, 1986, 91–113, esp. 97, 101, 103; for the 1530s, Vallauri, 1970, 1:135–38; for 1566–1630, see Chiaudano, 1972b, 98, for the introduction of criminal law; and Chiaudano, 1972a. Rolls for 1586–1600 have not survived. For Cravetta, see Olmo, 1984.

160. Marongiu, 1948, 50–73 passim; Bartolo lectureship on 63.

161. Catalano, 1934, 24–26, 58–70; Nicolosi Grassi, 1992.

162. De Renzi, 1852–59, 1:403.

civilians (including Sforza degli Oddi) and 1 canonist in 1601. The number rose to 10 professors (one of whom emphasized Bartolo) and 2 student lecturers in civil law and 2 canonists in 1609–10 and 7 civilians and 4 canonists in 1617–18. One canonist taught the legal aspects of usury in the latter year. Parma did not have any of the new professorships (such as *Pandects* or criminal law) in civil law, although the star civilian, Francesco Accarigi (d. 1622), blended *mos italicus* and *mos gallicus* in his teaching (see Ch. 4, "Parma, 1601").

CONCLUSION

The organization and structure of Italian law remained fundamentally the same from the age of Bartolo until that of Napoleon. Stability reigned, because the great glossators and commentators had successfully adapted ancient Roman law to the needs of European society.

Nevertheless, the Renaissance witnessed significant innovation. The most visible change was the steep decline in the teaching of canon law, a consequence of the growing power of the state and a papal decision to bar commentary on the canons of Trent. As with medicine, the Renaissance university created new professorships in order to teach specialized practical applications of the law. Eight universities established continuing professorships of criminal law: Bologna in the years 1509–13, then 1536–; Padua, 1540–; Pisa, 1544–88, 1604–; Ferrara, 1547–; Perugia, 1567, stopped at an unknown date, then 1600–; Turin, 1568–86, ceased between 1586 and 1600, restored 1604–; Rome, 1574–; and Pavia, 1578–. Several universities added *De actionibus* positions for part of the sixteenth century.

Italian universities made some room for humanistic jurisprudence. Alciato taught at Pavia, Bologna, and Ferrara between 1533 and 1550. Padua in 1578 and Siena in 1589 established ongoing *Pandects* chairs. Rome, Bologna, Ferrara, and Pisa had short-lived *Pandects* professorships in the second half of the sixteenth century, while Bologna, Pavia, and Perugia added continuing professorships of *Pandects* in the early seventeenth century.

Universities hesitated to introduce *Pandects* professorships, and professors wondered how they should teach the subject. If the professor of *Pandects* concentrated on philological and historical explanation of the text within the context of ancient Roman civilization, his lectures had little value for future lawyers, who had to deal with contemporary legal cases. If he tried to make his lectures more useful by introducing modern applications of the text, he risked duplicating the *Digest* lectures of the ordinary professors, who gave all their attention to this.[163] Professors not holding *Pandects* positions probably found the best solution for the Italian situation. They taught *mos italicus* lightly garnished with humanistic jurisprudence.[164]

Italian law schools also reaffirmed medieval jurisprudence. Padua, Ferrara,

---

163. Brugi (1916, 333) makes this point.

164. The statement is advanced cautiously, because much remains to be learned about the influence of humanistic jurisprudence in Italian classrooms and legal scholarship.

Bologna, Naples, Macerata, and Salerno created professorships of "Text, Gloss, and Bartolo" in the second half of the sixteenth century. The occupants of these chairs were expected to promote study of the great medieval jurisprudents at the expense of recent commentators. Finally, the composition of the professoriat changed. Except for Padua and Bologna, Italian universities filled faculty positions overwhelmingly with local men in the second half of the sixteenth century. Communes and princes seemed unwilling, or unable, to appoint distinguished and expensive outsiders.

Every university conferred more law degrees in the second half of the sixteenth century than earlier. Demand was high, because Italy and the rest of Europe had become societies in which the credential of a law degree mattered more than in the past. The increased demand probably originated with government. Italian and European states seem to have been expanding their jurisdiction and, therefore, needed more trained personnel with law degrees. The call for legal training may have started at the top. In Italy, for example, it is likely that the key advisors to princes and republics (counsellors and secretaries) and those who occupied high elective and appointive offices were more often men with legal training than the humanists and merchants of an earlier day. Perhaps men like the legist Lelio Torelli, chief advisor to Cosimo I de' Medici, filled more positions of trust and power than in the previous century. As Italy became blessedly free of war, but not of political differences, states fought more often with legal *consilia*, *consulti* (briefs combining historical, legal, and political matter in support of a course of action), and in the courts than with arms. Hence, governments needed more lawyers. The expansion of diplomacy, as large and small states maintained resident ambassadors and staffs at the capitals of many other states, required trained men, preferably with law degrees. A doctorate of civil law may have been added to humanistic studies as the ideal preparation for high servants of the state. All those going into state service at the higher levels had already acquired some knowledge of the classics, the ability to read and write Latin, and possibly moral wisdom and eloquence, because humanistic studies dominated preuniversity Latin schooling of the elite. A law education and degree completed the training.

In 1400 Italian law schools educated lawyers, judges, and administrators to govern Italian lay and ecclesiastical society. By 1600 Italian law schools graduated armies of Italian and ultramontane legists to govern and administer a Europe even more dependent on law.

PART III

RECESSIONAL

nternal decay and external threats appeared in the last years of the sixteenth century and intensified in the seventeenth. Professors did less lecturing in the university and more private teaching outside. Alternate paths to degrees undermined the university's importance to society. Fewer students came. Those who did spent little time in classrooms and more in rowdy behavior. Universities seemed unable to solve the problems. Most important, communal councils and princes, who had created the conditions for greatness of Renaissance universities and had met earlier threats with imagination and determination, now failed to respond and sometimes made matters worse. An era ended.

CHAPTER 14

The Decline of Italian Universities

 umerous contemporary observers believed that Italian universities were declining in the early seventeenth century. Even though they awarded record numbers of doctorates, civil authorities and professors saw external forces and internal abuses weakening Italian universities. They were correct. Religious order schools drew students away from universities. Students found easier paths to degrees than years of attending lectures. The growth of private teaching, the failure of matriculated students to attend classes, burgeoning student violence, and a shorter academic year undermined the university from within. Civil authorities could do little about the external threats and were unwilling to eliminate internal abuses. Finally, when the robust Italian economy of the sixteenth century gave way to recession by the 1630s or before, governments had little energy or money for universities. They made do with fewer professors, almost all of them local men.[1]

CONCERN FOR THE UNIVERSITIES

The Venetian governors of Padua often boasted about "their" university during the middle years of the sixteenth century. Expressions of concern crept into their reports late in the century. And cries of alarm and descriptions of abuses overwhelmed the pride in the seventeenth century. Observers elsewhere in Italy voiced similar concerns about universities.

The estimated enrollment at the University of Padua held up well through the early seventeenth century: 1,500 in 1609 and 1,200 in 1611, when 457 matriculated students were Venetian subjects.[2] But few of the enrollees resided in Padua

1. In addition to what follows, Roggero (1992, 49–89) offers a panoramic view of the problems of Italian universities between the sixteenth and the eighteenth centuries, and Rizzo (1987, 122–25) notes the strengths and weaknesses of Pavia between the late sixteenth and the early seventeenth centuries.

2. *Relazioni*, 1975, 114, 142; De Bernardin, 1983, 78 n. 81. When citing a *relazione*, I omit the name of the *capitano* or *podestà* who wrote it except for direct quotations. And only the year, not the

and heard lectures. A Paduan professor charged in 1614 that only one-third of the students actually attended lectures.[3] An outsider noticed the same thing. An official of the University of Pisa, a man who greatly admired the University of Padua, reported that Padua had 800 students in residence, including 30 Englishmen, in the second and third decades of the seventeenth century. But, he added, only 8 to 10 Englishmen attended classes; the rest spent their time in amorous adventures and military exercises.[4] It is not likely that students from other nations were more conscientious.

War and famine in the 1630s and 1640s then produced a dramatic drop in enrollment at Padua, whether or not the students attended classes. In 1640 the University of Padua had only 379 enrolled students, possibly the lowest figure of the century.[5] In 1644 a Venetian governor reported that the number of students did not exceed 700, a higher number than in the previous year.[6] Just as disturbing as the drop in enrollment was the disappearance of non-Italian students. Students from beyond the Alps accounted for 26 percent of the student body in 1611 but only 10 percent in 1677 and 5 percent in 1681.[7] By 1703 the total number of students in residence at the renowned University of Padua was only 400.[8]

Not only did total enrollment decline, but few Venetian nobles now studied at the University of Padua, despite the laws that barred them from going elsewhere. More than a hundred Venetian patricians may have been studying at the Univer-

---

month and day, is given in some cases. There is a gap in these useful records between Feb. 4, 1589, and Feb. 25, 1603, but they are very complete for the seventeenth century. De Bernardin (1975 and 1983) offers much additional information on Paduan problems.

3. De Bernardin, 1983, 79.

4. This is the undated statement of Girolamo da Sommaja, the government official charged with overseeing the University of Pisa between 1614 and 1636. Sommaja made it his business to correspond with officials from other universities, especially Padua. De Rosa, 1983b, 113.

5. De Bernardin, 1975, 481.

6. "Nella dispensa delle matricole risultano grave pregiudicij a publici datij, provandosi che annualmente ne vengono monificate mille trecento in circa, se bene li scuolari non eccedono mai il numero di settecento." *Relazione* of Podestà Alvise Foscarini in *Relazioni,* 1975, 342 (Feb. 20, 1646). There are other references in these years to the unreliability of matriculation figures as a consequence of unspecified financial abuses.

7. De Bernardin, 1975, 481.

8. This was despite a matriculation figure of 1,600: "poichè se si riflette che l'anno passato il numero di scolari effettivi, e legittimi fosse solo di quattrocento in circa, a quali giustamente si conviene una matricola per cadauno, e che siano state non ostante levate mille seicento matricole." He went on to say that the university had awarded about 120 doctorates. Statement of Podestà Ascanio Giustinian of May 11, 1703, who gave the figure of 400 "effective and legitimate" students three times, in *Relazioni,* 1975, 419 (quote), 420. Because matriculation figures do not give a true picture of the enrollment, I have not used the seventeenth-century numbers in Saibante, Vivarini, and Voghera, 1924, 177 and passim, and De Bernardin, 1975, 467, 470. Aware of the problem, De Bernardin uses them cautiously and for different purposes.

Brizzi (1988) provides a detailed study of Bolognese matriculation figures from the late sixteenth through the seventeenth centuries, along with many cautions about using them. Nevertheless, he concludes that the number of students at Bologna increased in the seventeenth century until the 1660s and then declined. In light of what is known about the nonresidence of matriculated students at Padua, this conclusion may be questionable.

sity of Padua in 1566.[9] A Venetian governor remembered, possibly from his own student days sometime between 1580 and 1600, when sixty and more Venetian nobles studied at Padua. But now in 1616 there were only seven or eight.[10] Matriculation figures supported his estimate: only a hundred Venetian patricians enrolled at Padua between 1592 and 1648.[11]

Padua's problems of slack attendance and enrollment decline were not unique. The University of Rome had only about 490 students—250 legists, 140 medical students, and 100 in other subjects—in 1628, a decline from the second half of the sixteenth century.[12] The number of matriculants at the University of Siena ranged from 50 to 150 annually between 1613 and 1624. While matriculation figures were notoriously incomplete, contemporary comments supported the view that Siena had fewer students.[13] Certainly the four new universities founded between 1540 and 1601 drew some students away from the older universities. But other changes had greater impact on all universities.

COMPETITION FROM RELIGIOUS ORDER SCHOOLS: THE JESUIT SCHOOL AT PADUA

The new religious orders of the Catholic Reformation offered free Latin humanistic schooling to boys. But instead of welcoming the schools for preparing more students for university educations, professors feared them as competitors. As the religious order schools grew in numbers, confidence, and scholarly achievement, they added courses in some university-level subjects. The Society of Jesus, with numerous schools, able scholars and teachers, and classes in logic, philosophy, and mathematics, offered the greatest threat. Professors and students at Padua responded with a fierce attack against the local Jesuit school.

The first Jesuit school in Italy which accepted external students (pupils who were not members of the Society) opened at Messina, Sicily, in 1548, and the number grew to forty-nine schools by 1600 and about eighty in Italy by 1630.[14] The foundation of Jesuit education was approximately six years' study of Latin grammar, rhetoric, and humanities instruction, including a limited amount of Greek, for boys aged ten to sixteen. The majority of Jesuit schools in Italy did not go beyond this preuniversity curriculum. But by the 1570s a few schools, espe-

9. The papal nuncio stated in 1566 that "a hundred and more" Venetian patricians were studying at the University of Padua. *Nunziature di Venezia,* 8, 1963, 108, memorandum added to letter of Nuncio Giovanni Antonio Facchinetti of Sept. 14, 1566. This figure cannot be confirmed and might be too high, but there is abundant evidence from the biographies of leading Venetian members of government of the sixteenth century that many of them studied at Padua. So did noble Venetian churchmen and an unknown number of other Venetians.

10. *Relazioni,* 1975, 167 (May 21, 1616). See also ibid., 184 (1619). There were also numerous laments that subjects in the Venetian state no longer studied in large numbers at Padua.

11. De Bernardin, 1983, 79–80.

12. ASR, Archivio della Università di Roma, R. 83, ff. 39^r–39bis^r.

13. Minnucci and Košuta, 1989, 319 n. 11; Catoni, 1991, 55–56.

14. The figures come from Brizzi, 1982, 919. For a brief overview of the development of Jesuit schools in Italy, see Grendler, 1989, 363–81.

cially in larger cities, added higher courses that duplicated university offerings. They taught logic, metaphysics, and natural philosophy, all based on Aristotle, as well as mathematics, theology, cases of conscience, and, at least in Milan, introductory canon law.[15]

The Jesuits established themselves in Padua in 1542, one of their earliest houses in Italy, and began to teach external students there in 1552.[16] In 1579 the Paduan Jesuit school added a philosophy class that immediately attracted 80 students. In 1582 the Paduan Jesuits opened a boarding school for students of noble birth; the entire school enrolled 450 students, including 70 nobles, in 1589. By this time the Jesuits offered a three-year philosophy curriculum based on Aristotle, consisting of logic the first year, natural philosophy with an emphasis on physical science the second year, and metaphysics and natural philosophy emphasizing psychology the third year.

Some university students were not pleased. Anonymous graffiti attacking the Jesuits appeared on walls. Then on two successive days in July 1591, students fired guns, broke windows in the Jesuit college, and scribbled anti-Jesuit graffiti in various places. On July 12, 1591, a group of university students, including some from prominent Venetian noble families, took off their clothes, wrapped themselves in sheets, and marched on the Jesuit house. Along the way they opened the sheets to display their genitals to women and children. Upon reaching the Jesuit college, they threw away their sheets and in full nakedness roundly abused the Jesuits and their students. Even though the Venetian government punished eight ringleaders with heavy fines, the episode opened the floodgates of a wave of hostility against the Jesuit school.

The student arts organization spoke to the Venetian Senate against the Jesuit school. So did a delegation of professors, consisting of two leading civilians, a canonist, and the first and second ordinary professors of natural philosophy, Francesco Piccolomini and Cesare Cremonini. Professors and students charged that the Jesuits had established an illicit rival university, an *anti-studio*.[17]

Cremonini summarized university grievances against the Jesuit school in a fiery oration to the Venetian Senate on December 20, 1591. He made several points. The Jesuits had stealthily and deliberately founded a rival university that drew students away from the University of Padua. This *anti-studio* was contrary to

15. See the description of the curriculum of the Jesuit Brera school in Milan in Rurale, 1992, 155–60. For the teaching of logic, natural philosophy, metaphysics, theology, and mathematics at Jesuit schools in Naples in the late sixteenth century, see Lewis, 1995, chs. 3 and 4. The move of the Jesuits into higher education in Italy has been little studied. But see Grendler, in press.

16. For what follows, Favaro, 1878, is the initial account and still valuable for the documents printed. Favaro, 1911, and Cessi, 1921–22, add additional information. Donnelly (1982) has located numerous additional Jesuit documents and gives the best account of the story. The latest review of the dispute is Sangalli, 1999, 187–275, who adds many interesting details. Zanardi (1994) offers an excellent survey of the Jesuits in the Venetian state from 1542 to1773; Cozzi (1994) studies Venetian attitudes toward the Jesuits in the years 1550–1657. The Jesuits called their houses in various towns *collegii* (colleges). But not all Jesuit colleges included a school for external students.

17. The term *anti-studio* occurs repeatedly in the documents, especially in Cremonini's oration against the Jesuit school.

Venetian law that had made Padua the sole university of the Venetian state and forbade the establishment of any other. In support of his claim that the Jesuits had illegally mounted an *anti-studio,* Cremonini noted that the Jesuits printed and posted a *rotulus,* a list of their teachers, classes, and the hours at which they met. He also blamed the July disturbances on the Jesuits: the very existence of the Jesuit school led "Gesuiti" and "Bovisti" (university students were called Bovisti because they attended lectures at the Palazzo del Bo) to fight like Guelfs and Ghibellines.[18] Cremonini added many other charges, most manifestly inaccurate. He concluded that the Venetian government had to suppress the illegal Jesuit "university," just as it had suppressed medieval rivals to Padua.

Professors and student leaders also attacked Jesuit teaching as superficial. They charged that Jesuit teachers did not teach directly from Aristotle but from modern manuals (*summisti*) not approved by university statutes. University professors, who lectured on Aristotle's texts and commentaries on them, considered the Jesuit program to be a superficial survey based on manuals that avoided thorny scientific problems. How could students become good philosophers without reading Aristotle, they asked?

The Jesuits responded that while they did print a list of professors and classes and rang a bell, they did not teach at the same hours as university professors of philosophy.[19] They could not be accused of conducting a rival university, because they did not teach medicine or law. Indeed, students who studied at the Jesuit school would go on to the university. To the charge of superficiality, the Jesuits responded that university professors failed to offer a coherent philosophical program, as the Jesuits did. Moreover, at the end of every month the Jesuit school held general disputations, in which natural philosophers disputed with logicians, and mathematicians with natural philosophers, exercises that were useful to all. If their teaching really was superficial, students would not attend Jesuit classes. Indeed, the Jesuit professors and their students produced scholarship comparable to that produced by university professors.[20] Student satisfaction with the Jesuits had not harmed the university but had compelled professors to teach more hours and to do a better job, the Jesuits responded.

The Jesuits pointed out that each Jesuit teacher of logic or philosophy delivered three hundred lectures annually, two to three times the number that professors delivered. One Jesuit respondent boasted that a Jesuit was more learned after ten years of study (the study and teaching before ordination) than anyone

18. Cremonini's oration is printed in Favaro, 1878, 93–100. Donnelly (1982, 62) notes three printings within three decades of delivery plus eleven manuscripts of Cremonini's oration. Thus, his words resonated widely.

19. Bencini (1970–71) provides the texts of five unpublished Jesuit responses to Cremonini and is followed here. Donnelly (1982, 61–71) summarizes well the arguments in the Jesuit responses.

20. An examination of thirteen Jesuit theses in natural philosophy written between 1612 and 1674 at Jesuit schools in Parma, Rome, Florence, and Milan showed that Jesuit Aristotelian natural philosophy was innovative and open to mathematics and experiment. Baroncini, 1981. This was not true of Cremonini and other conservative professors of natural philosophy. See also Baldini, 1994, who discusses Jesuit teachers and scholarship in the Venetian province of the Society.

else after twenty or thirty years of "negligent study," an obvious gibe at some of the Paduan professors. Finally, the Jesuits charged that Cremonini's real objection to the Jesuit school was that it taught a "Christian philosophy" diametrically opposed to his position that the human soul was mortal and the world eternal. But the Jesuit responses came too late and probably would not have made a difference in any case.

The Senate accepted the arguments of professors and student leaders. On December 23, 1591, three days after Cremonini's fiery oration, the Senate ordered the Jesuits to teach Jesuit students only. This had to be done in order to restore peace and order and to protect the university, the Senate stated. Indeed, the Senate decree repeated some of Cremonini's arguments. But the Senate action was hotly debated and far from unanimous. In the next few years some Venetian patricians and civic leaders of Padua made repeated efforts to get the ban lifted and to restore the Jesuit school for external students, at least for the lower classes, which did not compete with university lectures. But the Jesuits preferred to deploy their resources where they were more welcome.

The attack against the Jesuit school brought to the surface differences in pedagogy and learning as well as the hostility of the professoriat and some students. The Paduan professors pursued individual approaches to the Aristotelian texts in their lectures and writings. By contrast, the Jesuits offered an integrated survey of the Aristotelian texts. Like most university philosophers, Piccolomini and Cremonini separated natural philosophy and theology; the Jesuit curriculum closely linked the two subjects. However, some of the opposition also came from personal resentments and fears of lost income. Antonio Riccobono, who led the opposition against restoration of the Jesuit school after 1591, did not like the fact that the Jesuit school taught his subject, rhetoric, to a large number of students.[21] Professors probably blamed the Jesuits for lost income, because students who attended the free Jesuit school did not need to pay professors for private tutoring (see below). The German nation of arts students, which strongly opposed the Jesuit school, included an unknown number of Protestants, who were no friends of the Jesuits.

Political sentiments probably also played a part in the Senate's decision. The Jesuits were seen as philo-Spanish at a time when the Venetians feared Spanish power as a threat to their Mediterranean interests. Some saw the Society as the pope's ally at a time when a faction of Venetian patricians was strongly antipapal. Many other church-state and Venetian-papal disputes culminated in the crisis of 1606–7, when the papacy laid Venice under interdict. During the interdict the Venetian government banished the Society from the state. The Jesuits were not permitted to return until 1657, at which time they came back to Padua.[22]

21. See Riccobono, 1980, 103ʳ–106ᵛ; Favaro, 1878, 51, 55, 56, 88, 116–17; Mazzacurati, 1961, 129–30; and Donnelly, 1982, 72–74. It will be recalled that Riccobono had few students, according to an early-seventeenth-century commentator. See Chapter 5, "Organization of Instruction."

22. See Grendler, 1977, chs. 7–9, for other conflicts.

Despite the self-interest of professors and swirling political currents, the fundamental point was that a majority of the Venetian Senate accepted the argument that the Jesuits were drawing students away from the university. Since the government was worried about the prospects of the university, it eliminated what it saw as a competitor.

COMPETITION FROM RELIGIOUS ORDER SCHOOLS: SCHOOLS FOR NOBLES

The fierce attack against the Jesuits was symptomatic of university resentment against the schools of the Jesuits and other religious orders across Italy.[23] But only Padua succeeded in eliminating its rival. Professors won that battle but lost the war.

The Jesuits and other religious order schools drew highborn students away from universities through their schools for nobles. Beginning in the mid-1570s, the Jesuits began to operate schools limited to boys of noble blood. These were either independent boarding schools or special classes within larger Jesuit schools. Schools for nobles were not free but quite expensive. By the first quarter of the seventeenth century, the Jesuits operated schools for nobles in the university towns of Turin, Parma, Bologna, Ferrara, Siena, Rome, and Naples, as well as in the nonuniversity towns of Milan, Genoa, Brescia, Verona, Ravenna, Prato, Palermo, and Cagliari (Sardinia), plus those in the rest of Europe.[24] The Barnabites (the Clerks Regular of St. Paul) and the Somaschans (Clerks Regular of Somascha) also established boarding schools, some limited to nobles. When the Jesuits were expelled from the Venetian state in 1606, the Somaschans moved in to establish boarding schools for nobles in Bergamo, Brescia, and Verona.[25]

The religious order schools competed directly with the universities for the most highly prized students, those of noble blood. Throughout the Renaissance, the sons of the highborn had been attending universities, often without graduating. In the seventeenth century nobles increasingly attended Jesuit and other religious order boarding schools. Enrollment soared in northern Italian boarding schools for nobles. Indeed, enrollment at the Jesuit school for nobles at Parma rose from 550 in 1605, to 644 in 1646, and 905 in 1660. Approximately one-third of this enrollment was in the higher classes, which duplicated the first year or two of university studies. In 1606 an anonymous anti-Jesuit author claimed that 34 young Venetian nobles were attending the Parma school.[26] Whether or not this

---

23. For quarreling between the students of the Jesuit and non-Jesuit halves of the University of Parma, see D'Alessandro, 1980, 36, 82–85. For fighting at Pavia, see Zorzoli, 1986, 65–66.

24. Brizzi, 1976, 26.

25. See Grendler, 1989, 390–92, for a brief summary and additional bibliography.

26. See the highly vituperative anonymous denunciation of the Jesuits printed in Brizzi, 1980, 190; whole document pp. 190–92. Because some charges and information presented in this document are clearly inaccurate, the number of Venetian nobles attending the Parma school may be exaggerated.

the figure was accurate, numerous subjects of La Serenissima, many from Venice itself, attended such schools, despite the absolute prohibition against attending Jesuit schools imposed in 1612.[27]

The boarding schools offered a curriculum designed for the upper classes. In addition to humanities, philosophy, and theology, they taught horsemanship, French, and dancing, none of which universities offered. Noble boarding schools provided the opportunity to mingle with other young patricians from Italy and the rest of Europe. So did universities. But as more noble youths attended religious order boarding schools, they became the schools of choice for young nobles wishing to mingle with their peers. Religious order boarding schools offered a physically safe, religiously disciplined, and tightly structured education, in contrast to the violent life, licentious activities, and loosely organized curriculum of universities. Although the majority of the pupils at religious order boarding schools studied at the elementary and secondary levels, every young male student from about seventeen to twenty years of age there might have attended a university. Whether or not their schools were restricted to nobles, the religious order schools, and especially the boarding schools, offered an attractive alternative to the universities.

DEGREES FROM LOCAL COLLEGES OF LAW AND MEDICINE

However, religious order schools did not teach law and medicine, nor could they confer degrees in these disciplines. Local colleges of legists and physicians, or individual members, could do both.

Local professional colleges determined who might practice in the town, regulated the activities of their members, and worked with governments on legal and medical matters touching the entire community. Colleges in university towns also awarded degrees. Some colleges in nonuniversity towns also possessed the power to award doctorates, usually because they had at some time in the past acquired a university charter in the expectation of founding a university. Now many more local colleges of legists and physicians without university aspirations, or some of their members, acquired the power to award doctorates. Individuals became counts palatine, or else emperor or pope conferred count palatine powers on the college.

The lust for titles encouraged rulers to create many more counts palatine. Beginning in the last two decades of the fifteenth century, popes and emperors flooded Italy with new ones, awarding the title to professors and learned men, but more often to nonscholars bearing noble names.[28] Lawyers and physicians may have been particularly favored. It is possible that the majority of local professional

---

27. See Brizzi, 1980, 150–51, 167. Brizzi (1976 and 1980) documents that a large number of northern Italian nobles, including Venetians, attended Jesuit noble schools. For the Venetian prohibition against attending Jesuit schools, see Donnelly, 1982, 77.

28. Various popes awarded the title of count palatine to 408 individuals between 1484 and 1549. ASVa, Schedario Garampi 109 (index 552), ff. 98^v–116^r and 110 (index 553), ff. 186^v–195^r. A few well-known figures appear, for example, Jacopo Sadoleto (1513) and Pietro Bembo (1513), in Schedario Garampi 110, ff. 99^r and 100^r. Emperors also continued to create counts palatine.

colleges of legists and physicians across Italy had at least one member empowered to award degrees by the early seventeenth century.[29] Although Pope Pius V canceled the right of counts palatine to award degrees in 1568, it is not clear that this was retroactive.[30] And emperors continued to create counts palatine.

Popes and emperors also conferred the office of count palatine on entire colleges of legists and physicians lacking a university connection. Emperor Charles V granted the College of Legists of Milan the power to award the doctorate in civil law in 1529.[31] The commune of Pavia argued that only the university and its colleges of doctors should have this power in the Milanese state and that giving it to the Milanese college would damage the university. But the government in Milan rejected the appeal.[32] Charles V also conferred the title of count palatine on all the members of the degree-granting college of legists, and all the members of the college of physicians, of Bologna in 1530. And Pope Clement VIII conferred the title of count palatine on the College of Physicians of Milan in 1597.[33]

Colleges in small urban centers also acquired the right to award degrees. Emperors and popes conferred the power of awarding doctorates on colleges of legists in Cesena, Forlì, Imola, Ravenna, Reggio Emilia, and Rimini, all located within a small area of northern Italy, between 1504 and 1535.[34] And so it went across Italy. Local colleges conferred numerous doctorates over the next two hundred years.

Counts palatine, local professional colleges empowered to grant degrees, and the religious order schools joined forces to build a road to the doctorate which bypassed the university.[35] The aspiring future legist or physician might begin by studying logic and natural philosophy at a religious order school. For example, in 1584 the College of Physicians of Milan agreed that candidates for doctorates of medicine might count three years of philosophical studies at the Jesuit school in Milan toward the seven years of philosophy and medicine training required for the doctorate.[36] Aspiring legists could also study *Institutes* in courses sponsored by local professional colleges.[37]

29. Brambilla (1982, 101) opines that this was true in every professional college in Lombardy.

30. Penuti, 1998, 351.

31. Brambilla, 1982, 99–100, including n. 22.

32. See a letter of the commune of Pavia of Jan. 8, 1536, protesting the emperor's action in ASPv, Università, Cartone 30, f. 32ʳ. A letter from Milan of July 10, 1536, confirmed that the college of Milan would award doctorates. ASPv, Università, Cartone 33, fascicle 106.

33. Malagola, 1966, xiv–xvi (various popes confirmed these privileges), and Panebianco, 1966–67. See also Brambilla, 1982, 98, who notes that Pope Pius IV (1559–65) conferred the title of count palatine on corporate bodies, colleges, and academies throughout Italy.

34. Penuti, 1998.

35. Some of the following is based on Brambilla, 1982, 92–123, and Zorzoli, 1986, 228–55, 266–69, 272–77, 332–33, 338–45, 354–59, 364–65, who describe the process in Lombardy and the impact on the University of Pavia. The record of university problems and abuses elsewhere suggests that the same process occurred throughout Italy. See also Nasalli Rocca, 1948.

36. Rurale, 1992, 145–46.

37. Nasalli Rocca, 1948, 211–18; Zorzoli, 1986, 254–55, 266.

Having completed preliminary studies in logic and natural philosophy, the aspiring physician began to study medicine with a member of the local professional college. It was a far cry from hearing lectures in medical theory, practical medicine, anatomy, surgery, and medical botany at a university. In similar fashion, after attending the local *Institutes* course, the candidate for a law degree studied privately with a member of the local legal college. His legal education could not have been as comprehensive as that offered by the university; it might consist of little more than memorizing principles and titles and browsing through *opiniones communes.* Like an apprentice, the student also watched, assisted, and accompanied a physician or lawyer in his rounds, which may have been more valuable training. After an indefinite period of time, the student passed the examination given by his mentor's college. The college, or an individual member with count palatine authority, awarded the doctorate. And, of course, the new doctor's entry into the local professional college of legists or physicians was assured. Some students still wanted the more prestigious university doctorate. So, after religious order schooling and local study, they went to the university for a few months to obtain degrees. They evaded university residence requirements.

Studying and obtaining doctorates from local professional colleges instead of the university was part of a broader transformation of Italian society. Renaissance society, whose upper ranks were somewhat open to men of merit, was giving way to a closed Old Regime society of inherited local privilege. Princes, town councils, and professional bodies drafted rules that included or excluded men from participation in government and the professions on the basis of ancestors and occupations. A thicket of laws, regulations, and matriculation requirements created and surrounded a closed elite. Local colleges of legists dominated by members from powerful local families played a central role in the creation of a more closed society.[38] It is not surprising that they used their authority to choose and train whom they would admit into their ranks without reference to university study. For centuries universities had educated and created professional elites. Now local professional colleges were seizing that power.

PRIVATE TEACHING AND OTHER PEDAGOGICAL ABUSES

Competition from religious order schools and an easier road to the doctorate would not have affected universities so greatly if internal problems had not already weakened them. A series of pedagogical abuses undermined teaching and encouraged students to look elsewhere.

Private teaching, that is, instruction outside that offered by university lectures and medical demonstrations, was the most widespread and damaging abuse. Many students paid for private tutoring; sometimes they hired the same pro-

---

38. For this development in the Veneto, see Ventura, 1964, 285, 317–21, 324–25, 338–65; for Lombardy, see Zorzoli, 1986, 338–45, 354–65. For a detailed study of the aristocratization of one town, Brescia, and the position of lawyers, notaries, and physicians as part of the ruling elite, see Ferraro, 1993, esp. 51–71, 203–19.

fessors who lectured publicly to teach them privately or in small groups. Weaker or wealthier students had always sought out private teaching in order to supplement the lectures. Now many students abandoned the university lectures and relied on private teaching for their fundamental instruction. Worries about the corrosive impact of private teaching on the integrity of university instruction surfaced in the last years of the sixteenth century and became widespread in the seventeenth. Many denounced private teaching for undermining the "public" lectures, that is, the scheduled ordinary, extraordinary, and holiday lectures. But governments had little success in banning or restricting it.

A Paduan professor criticized private teaching as harmful to the professors involved and to the university as a whole. Paolo Beni studied at Padua in the mid-1570s and then taught at the University of Rome (1594–1600) and Padua (1600–1623). At some point in his Paduan career he drafted a treatise on the problems of Padua entitled "Discorso intorno alla riforma dello Studio di Padova," intended for Venetian authorities. It included strong criticism of private teaching.[39]

Beni counseled professors to avoid private teaching. University lecturing of a quality to win a reputation and to attract students was very fatiguing, especially for young professors, Beni wrote. If the professor also taught privately, he would not have the time to study and to prepare his public lectures. Beni expressed amazement that some academics were so occupied with private teaching that they entered the lecture hall ill prepared.

Private teaching also damaged the university, because it led students to "despise" (*vilipese*) the public lectures. What student would not prefer to have private instruction tailored to his convenience and need? Students became so enamored of private lessons that they scorned public lectures and misbehaved in class, Beni charged. Another problem was that students receiving private tutoring in the homes of professors some distance from the university were loath to ride or walk back to the university to hear public lectures. Beni rejected the argument that students needed private instruction in order to understand the public lectures or to deal with material omitted in the university lectures. A student did not need to employ a private teacher in order to learn the contents of book 2 of Aristotle's *Physics,* just because the university professor concentrated on books 1 and 8, Beni asserted. And if professors delivered the full complement of ordinary and extraordinary lectures, there would be ample time for the professor to teach, and the student to learn, all the necessary material. Then private teaching would not be needed, Beni concluded.

Private teaching flourished because students found it useful and professors found it profitable. Galileo Galilei's private teaching documents the latter point.

39. ASVa, Archivio Beni, Ms. 123, autograph manuscript, consisting of numerous unfoliated pages, some in fair copy, some in draft form. It is a comprehensive analysis of the problems of Padua and universities generally. Diffley (1988, 61, 257) describes the manuscript and promises an edition. The first quarto version, mostly in fair copy with marginal insertions, seems to be the final version and is used here. Chapter 14, pp. [49–60], the longest in the "Discorso," deals with private teaching. The material used here is found on pp. [49–55].

In his years at the University of Padua, Galilei taught numerous students privately: a few groups of indeterminate size, some in pairs, and many individuals.[40] Galilei earned an average of 2,306 lire annually from1601 through 1604 through private teaching. Until 1606, Galilei received a university salary of 1,600 lire (320 florins), which placed him in the middle of the Paduan scale. Thus, Galilei earned 44 percent more from private teaching than from university lecturing. (He also received an indeterminate amount from degree examination fees.) In 1606 the Venetian government raised his salary to 2,600 lire (520 florins). His private teaching income then dropped to an average of 607 lire annually from 1607 through 1609. It appears that Galilei reduced his private teaching as his university salary rose.

Professors taught the same material privately as in their lectures. In his private teaching, Galilei taught Euclid, Sacrobosco's *De sphaera,* the pseudo-Aristotelian *Mechanics,* arithmetic, perspective, the mathematics of fortifications, and "l'uso dello strumento," which was the use of geometrical and military compasses. Indeed, Galilei hired an artisan to construct compasses and then sold a pedagogical package of compass, training in its use, and instructional booklet to his private students.[41] With the possible exception of instruction on the use of the compass, this was the university mathematical curriculum. He taught privately Germans, Poles, Frenchmen, Englishmen, Bohemians, and Flemings, plus a limited number of Italians, including two Venetian nobles. Some of the students, especially the non-Italians, also boarded with Galilei.[42] Thus, he offered the entire university mathematical curriculum to private students willing and able to pay for individual or small group instruction. Galilei operated a profitable educational enterprise consisting of private teaching, compass package, and room and board.

Numerous critics called for a ban or severe restrictions on private teaching. In Bologna in 1583 a reform proposal demanded a ban on teaching at home, except for a handful of lessons in logic.[43] In 1586 the Bolognese government imposed such a ban. The decree lamented that the introduction of "academies," that is, a professor teaching students privately at home, had damaged the university lectures. Moreover, the decree continued, private teaching had caused traditional practices, such as class discussions that rendered students ready and subtle in

---

40. The payments for private instruction are found in Galilei, 1966, 149–58, and his university salary figures on pp. 112–15. The monetary value, as calculated by Galilei, of precious objects received in payment is included in the figures. Favaro (1966, 1:139–64) discusses his private teaching.

41. Galilei, 1966, 150; Biagioli, 1993, 8.

42. Galilei, 1966, 159–66. One wonders if the burden of running the household of boarders fell on Marina Gamba, the mother of Galilei's three illegitimate children, born 1600, 1601, and 1606. When Galilei left for the ducal court in Florence in 1610, he took the children with him but left Marina behind. When the two daughters reached the age of sixteen, Galilei placed them in convents but obtained the release of the elder to care for him in his old age. By contrast, he legitimized his son and made him his heir.

43. "Non si legga in casa escetto una o doe lettionij di logica, ne passino li logicij legger in casa altra lettione ch' di logica." ASB, Assunteria di Studio, Bu. 79, an anonymous "Avertimento per la Riforma dello Studio," Aug. 8, 1583, no foliation. This is the seventh of fourteen points in the "Avertimento."

argument, to fall into disuse. The government ordered professors not to teach privately during the academic year under pain of losing a year's salary for the first offense and revocation of the doctorate for the second offense. However, they might teach privately on holidays and during vacations.[44] The government repeated this ban in 1602 in modified form: it banned private instruction during regular teaching days and hours, while permitting it for the introductory subjects of logic and *Institutes* at any time.[45] The government repeated these and other regulations with similar threats in 1641 and 1713.[46] Illicit private teaching clearly continued.

Other universities also denounced private teaching and tried without success to regulate it. In Naples, students who had already studied the material privately made so much noise in the lecture hall that other students could not hear the lectures. Hence, the government forbade all private teaching with the exception of teaching *Institutes,* under penalty of three years' banishment to the island of Capri.[47] (Obviously, Capri was not the pleasure resort that it is today.) In 1623 the anonymous author of a reform memorandum for the University of Rome complained that private teaching was ruining the law school. Because the wealthy paid for private lessons, only the poor students came to hear the university lectures. The memorandum recommended that private teaching be delivered orally, not in writing. It should not cover the same material as university lectures, nor should it be scheduled during ordinary lecture hours.[48] On November 6, 1623, Pope Urban VIII issued an edict severely restricting private teaching.[49]

The restrictions on Roman private teaching produced immediate requests for higher salaries from the three professors who taught *Institutes*. Because they received university salaries of only 35 scudi annually and private teaching had been banned, they did not earn enough money to maintain home and family,

44. "Et perche le accademie, che si sono introdotto hanno partorito danno alle lettioni publiche, & annullati quei buoni & laudevoli riti antichi di argomentare alle scole alli Dottori, cosa che faceva li scolari pronti, sottili nell'argomentare, da che nasceva, che il Dottore per non perdere di riputatione bisognava che studiasse per forza. Ha statuto, che alcuno Dottore tanto leggista, come artista, ò altro non sia così ardito, che o si adunare scolari, ò altri in casa sua per fare accademie, ne lettioni private in quei tempi, che si leggono alle scole, ma solo le feste & nel tempo delle vacanze." Printed pamphlet entitled *Ordinationi fatte, et stabilite dall'illustri.mo et rever.mo Monsignor il Card. Caietano Legato & Molto Ill.mi Sig.ri Quaranta*. In Bologna Per Alessandro Benacci, 1586, sig. A2ʳ, in ASB, Assunteria di Studio, Bu. 1, no pag. This is an eight-page booklet of regulations for the university dated Sept. 25, 1586. The cardinal-legate and the Quaranta, the highest communal council, jointly ruled Bologna. "Argomentare alle scole alli Dottori" might also mean informal disputations held in the classroom or circular disputations.

45. Pamphlet entitled *Ordinationi fatte, et stabilite per conservare le dignità & reputatione del Studio di Bologna*. In Bologna per Vittorio Benacci. Stampator Camerale. 1602, sig. 3ʳ. The pamphlet is found in ASB, Assunteria di Studio, Bu. 89. Stampe e duplicati 1576–1660.

46. Costa, 1912, 76–82; Simeoni, 1940, 85.

47. Cannavale, 1980, ccxxviii–ccxxix, document 2270.

48. ASR, Archivio dell'Università di Roma, R. 83, ff. 27ʳ, 28ʳ⁻ᵛ, 30ʳ. This is a lengthy unsigned reform memorandum dated 1623.

49. Ibid., f. 32ʳ, printed edict.

they wrote.[50] Obviously these poorly paid professors teaching the introductory legal course relied on private teaching in order to make ends meet.

Private teaching went hand in hand with evasion of the residence requirements for degrees. All Italian universities required students to study at a university for five to seven years before receiving degrees. Universities further demanded that a student submit a statement testifying that he had studied for the statutory number of years before sitting for examinations. By the early seventeenth century, students routinely circumvented the residence requirement.

In 1614 a Venetian governor of Padua described what happened. The students came to Padua only in order to be drilled privately in the *puncta*, the brief passages from the statutory texts on which doctoral candidates were examined. Instead of attending university lectures in order to hear learned books methodically discussed by the principal professors of the university, the students learned "certain universal little rules" (*certe regolete universali*). Rather than studying for five or six years, they passed their examinations after one or two years, returning to their homes as superficially learned *dottoretti*. This is why there are so few students in Padua, he concluded.[51]

In 1638 the Venetian government sought to force students to fulfill residence requirements by ordering Venetian subjects desiring Paduan degrees to spent five years at Padua. But with the aid of false statements, Venetian subjects evaded the new rule.[52] Other students denied that they were Venetian subjects in order to obtain degrees in fewer than five years.[53]

Pavian professors winked at, and possibly knowingly signed, false residence documents. With the fraudulent testimonial in hand, the student presented himself for his degree examinations. Since professors collected fees for examining license and doctoral candidates, it was in their interest to examine as many students as possible, whether or not they had been attending lectures for five years.[54] In 1654 the Venetian governor complained that some students obtained

50. Ibid., R. 86, ff. 40^r, 43^v, letters of Fabricio Fabricii, Antonio Nanno, and Francesco Antonio Sgambati. Even though the archival register dates the letters as 1600, the only years in which all three taught together were 1622–23 and 1623–24. They earned salaries of 35 scudi at that time. Hence, the three *Institutes* professors probably wrote immediately after Urban VIII's edict. See *I maestri di Roma,* 1991, 193, 196, 995.

51. Podestà Giovanni Battista Foscarini in *Relazioni,* 1975, 146–47 (Sept. 16, 1614).

52. *Relazioni,* 1975, 304 (1638).

53. Ibid., and De Bernardin, 1983, 79. Paolo Beni also refers to matriculation fraud, which he would remedy by requiring students to give detailed information about themselves when matriculating: age, stature, skin, color, body size, and names of mother and father. He would also charge 10 soldi for each matriculation. ASVa, Archivio Beni, Ms. 123, pp. [33–34].

54. BUP, Ms. Ticinese, vol. 3, fascicle 25, f. 2^r–^{v}, a denunciation of abuses at the University of Pavia by an anonymous writer claiming thirty-three years' experience at the university (f. 4^r). The author's intimate knowledge of the University of Pavia suggests that he was a professor or beadle. The anonymous writer practically accused professors of complicity in the frauds by linking false residence *fedi* (certificates) with the information that professors earned 40 lire for each doctorate conferred. The document lacks a date but carries an internal date of 1684 corrected to 1679 (f. 1^r). Hence, the manuscript dates from about 1680.

their doctorates after only six months at the University of Padua.[55] And counts palatine on the faculty at Ferrara were willing to award degrees after very limited study.[56]

Another pedagogical abuse that subverted the statutes was "teaching the *puncta.*" In 1614 the Venetian Senate lamented that professors concentrated on the *puncta,* instead of the texts as a whole, with the result that students failed to grasp the "true discipline" of the subject. The Senate forbade this practice, even in private teaching, under pain of 100 ducats. But the Senate did permit professors to teach the *puncta* for fifteen days before students' doctoral examinations.[57] The Senate made a further compromise in 1665 when it ordered the Riformatori to designate two arts professors and two legists to teach the *puncta* for two months before students were examined for the license and doctoral degrees. The combination of private teaching, limited residence, and studying only the *puncta* undermined the university's instructional mission.

PRIVATE ANATOMY TEACHING AT PADUA

Students, however, sometimes had ample justification for seeking private instruction. The dispute over private anatomy teaching at the University of Padua demonstrated that on this occasion private teaching provided the training that the university failed to offer.

After Vesalius, anatomy became increasingly important in medical training at Padua. A single annual public anatomical dissection, held in the middle of winter and lasting fifteen to twenty days, was not enough. By the late sixteenth century, the anatomist carried out lengthy public anatomies during the Christmas and Carnival vacations, when the ordinary lectures did not meet, so that all interested students and faculty might attend. In addition, students apparently expected the professor of anatomy to do additional dissecting in the course of his lectures. He probably brought a body part to class.

In 1565 the Venetian government appointed Girolamo Fabrici d'Acquapendente (c. 1533–1619) the sole professor of anatomy and surgery.[58] Fabrici soon won deserved fame and a high salary from the Venetian government for his pioneering work in comparative embryology. In 1586 Fabrici persuaded the Venetian authorities to prohibit private dissections and lessons in anatomy. This was a departure from previous policy, as Paduan professors, like their colleagues in other universities, routinely carried out private anatomical dissections for their own

55. *Relazioni,* 1975, 364 (1654).

56. Visconti, 1950, 96–98.

57. "Che da lettori non si leggono à scolari li testi degli auttori di quelle professioni delle quali intendono far profitto, ma li punti soli che servono à conseguir il titolo del dottorato et non la vera disciplina della scienza che studiano, onde ne segue col danno de' studenti." AAUP, F. 491, ff. 6ʳ–7ʳ, copy of the Senate decree of Dec. 14, 1614. De Bernardin, 1983, 80–81, for the 1665 decree.

58. The following is based on Sterzi, 1909–10, especially the archival documents printed in pt. 2:71–104; De Ferrari, 1978a; and Muccillo, 1993b.

research and to instruct a few favored students.[59] Vesalius was known for this. And the Venetian government had authorized private anatomy teaching between 1562 and 1565, when the university lacked an anatomy professor. But something less noble than the integrity of university instruction motivated Fabrici: he wanted to eliminate a rival.

Giulio Cesare Casseri (c. 1552–1616), from a modest background in Piacenza, came to Padua, possibly as the servant of wealthy Piacenzan students. Casseri then became an assistant to Fabrici, living in his house and helping the latter in his anatomical dissections. The talented Casseri soon demonstrated skills equaling or surpassing those of Fabrici. After obtaining his medical degree in 1580, Casseri established a flourishing surgical practice in Padua while continuing his anatomical research. He taught and dissected privately for students who paid him until Fabrici stopped him in 1586. The ban initiated a struggle that lasted until the deaths of both. The dispute also revealed a pedagogical weakness in the university.

After the ban went into effect, the arts and medicine student organization and the German Nation of Artists bombarded the Venetian government with letters and representations asking that the ban on private anatomies be lifted. The heart of their complaint was that Fabrici did not do enough anatomical dissection. The students argued that the prohibition harmed students who had come to learn and that the ban infringed their rights. In 1591 they asked for the creation of an extraordinary professorship of surgery, obviously intended for Casseri.

The complaints about insufficient anatomy instruction were justified. Like most well-known medical professors, Fabrici also had a lucrative private practice, which led to absences from Padua. Moreover, age and illness, possibly arthritis, made it difficult for him to conduct the lengthy anatomical dissections, even if he did little or no cutting himself. In some years Fabrici held no public anatomies, on the grounds that no bodies were available. In other years he dissected for only a week or two, when the students expected three weeks and more. He often skipped the Christmas or Carnival anatomies, or both. When student protests to the government became louder, Fabrici increased his anatomical teaching; as the protests subsided, he reverted to his lackadaisical ways. But he fought Casseri throughout.

Meanwhile, Casseri built his own anatomical theater, continued his research, and taught anatomy and how to dissect privately. The German students particularly appreciated his work and paid him well. When the ban on private anatomy ban was strictly enforced, Casseri desisted. Student protests then escalated.

The Venetian government consistently supported Fabrici, no doubt because some leaders of the government held him in high regard.[60] For example, in

59. For private anatomy instruction at Bologna, see Martinotti, 1911, 29–35.

60. The three Riformatori dello Studio di Padova who supported Fabrici on Oct. 30, 1601, were Giacomo Foscarini, Girolamo Capello, and Giovanni Dolfin. Sterzi, 1909–10, pt. 2:84–85, doc. 12. It is hard to imagine more powerful supporters. For the political careers of Foscarini and Dolfin, see Grendler, 1979, 331–32, 337; for Capello, see Grendler, 1990a, 81. In addition, Fabrici dedicated his book on hearing and speech to Foscarini, Dolfin, and Leonardo Donà, another Riformatore, who went on to become doge. For Donà's political career, see Grendler, 1979, 338–39 and passim.

1601 the arts and medicine students made a particularly strong appeal to the Riformatori dello Studio di Padova to lift the ban on private anatomical teaching. The Riformatori asked the Venetian governors of Padua whether the ban should be lifted. The two governors praised the work of Fabrici, who in 1600 had been awarded his professorship for life, and called Casseri a troublemaker who incited students to steal bodies, an accusation (justly) leveled against most anatomists. The governors favored continuation of the ban on private anatomies, because the latter detracted from the university anatomy and created a shortage of bodies. But the governors also suggested that after the public anatomy was finished, they might be authorized to permit "particular anatomies" (*le anatomie particolari*), to be limited to those students who had not complained about or disturbed the public anatomy. The Riformatori issued orders echoing the advice of the governors.[61] In essence, Riformatori and governors supported Fabrici, threw the students a bone, and refused to acknowledge that a problem existed.

The situation worsened, because Fabrici's contract permitted him to omit the Christmas and Carnival anatomies when he reached forty years of teaching. This occurred in 1604 when he was about seventy-one years of age. The rivalry between Fabrici and Casseri continued. Almost simultaneously each published anatomical analyses of speech and hearing. A modern authority judges Casseri's work to have been greatly superior.[62]

The Riformatori eventually acted. When in 1608 Fabrici came to Venice to receive a Knighthood of St. Mark for having treated Paolo Sarpi for his stab wounds in an assassination attempt of October 1607, the Riformatori mildly criticized him for not doing enough anatomical teaching. Fabrici, in turn, asked the German Nation of Artists to write a testimonial praising his performance. The Germans refused. In 1609 the Venetian government finally acted: it divided the professorship of surgery and anatomy, leaving anatomy to Fabrici and giving surgery to Casseri, his first university appointment. But the salary difference was huge: 1,400 florins for Fabrici and 120 for Casseri. Moreover, on Fabrici's insistance, Fabrici taught at the prestigious and attractive third hour of the morning (10 or 11 A.M., according to the season of the year), whereas Casseri was relegated to the second or third hour of the afternoon (3, 4, or 5 P.M., according to the season). In 1613 Fabrici, now about eighty years of age, finally resigned his professorship, and Casseri became the professor of anatomy. Perhaps to make amends for their past treatment, the Venetian government also awarded Casseri a Knighthood of St. Mark. But he did not live long to enjoy professorship or knighthood, as he died in 1616.

The long dispute revealed more serious university weaknesses than the failure to force a senior professor to fulfill his obligations. The fundamental problem was that the university did not provide enough anatomical teaching to satisfy student

61. See in particular the letter of the Venetian governors of July 29, 1601, Padua, and the order of the Riformatori of Oct. 30, 1601, Venice, in Sterzi, 1909–10, pt. 2:82–85, docs. 11 and 12.

62. Sterzi, 1909–10, pt. 1:238–40.

demand. The medical revolution of the middle years of the sixteenth century had greatly increased the importance of anatomy. But the university had only a single professor of anatomy, who also taught surgery. Even if Fabrici had fully discharged his responsibilities, the anatomical instruction would have been insufficient. Dividing the professorship of anatomy and surgery in 1609 so that one professor could devote his time exclusively to anatomy was a step in the right direction. But it was not a permanent move. After Casseri died in 1616 and Fabrici in 1619, the position again became both anatomy and surgery taught by a single professor and remained so through the mid-seventeenth century. The Venetian government failed to create a needed separate professorship of anatomy. In its failure, Padua resembled most other universities.[63]

Second, the government's refusal to take effective action for more than twenty years (1586–1609) produced considerable student unrest. Its support of a malingering professor must have undermined student respect for university rules generally. Why should they honor residence requirements when the Venetian government permitted a senior professor to avoid dissecting?

Third, and most important, the officials who directly supervised the university, the Riformatori dello Studio di Padova, and the government failed to act. Their lethargy contrasted sharply with past decisive action. When the university seemed to be declining in the second half of the fifteenth century, the Venetian government imposed controls over absent and aging professors and raided other universities for new talent. In the mid-sixteenth century, the government helped create the medical revolution by appointing Andreas Vesalius, by adding a professorship of medical botany, and by founding a botanical garden. And when the Senate decided that the Jesuit school was a threat to the university, it moved very quickly. But the government failed to deal with the problem of insufficient anatomical teaching for more than twenty years and then did not create a permanent solution.

A contemporary report on the university underscored the fundamental problem: the Venetian government was out of touch with the university. In 1614 a new group of Riformatori commissioned Ingolfo Conti (c. 1572–1615), a Paduan nobleman newly appointed to a third ordinary position in logic, to investigate the problems of the university. His extensive report of 1615 began by noting that the government did not pay enough attention to the university. Conti pointed out that the Riformatori lacked firsthand knowledge of the university because they lived in Venice, far from professors and students.[64] Moreover, Conti continued, as major figures in the government, the Riformatori were so pre-

---

63. There were two exceptions. Bologna had separate professorships of anatomy and surgery, sometimes with two or more concurrents for each, in the late sixteenth and early seventeenth centuries. Dallari, 1888–1924, 2:189–271 passim. Ferrara had separate surgery and anatomy professorships through most of this period. Franceschini, 1970, 243–47; I maestri di Ferrara, 1991, 39–67 passim, 151, 153.

64. An anonymous denunciation of 1629 charged that the Riformatori never came to Padua. De Bernardin, 1983, 76–77. Because the Riformatori were elderly men in the highest ranks of the Venetian government, it is not surprising that they did not make the fatiguing trip to Padua.

occupied with affairs of state that they had little time for the university. The centralization of power, which left all significant university decisions, including appointments, in the hands of the Senate, was another problem.[65] The government did try to correct some university abuses, but it left the affairs of the university in the hands of distant and preoccupied Riformatori and the Senate. Neither responded in time to halt the decay.

THE SHRINKING ACADEMIC CALENDAR

The failure to teach the full complement of lectures was another major, peninsula-wide pedagogical abuse. Unwarranted vacation days and short lectures were not new abuses but became the norm in the seventeenth century.[66]

On April 30, 1477, the beadle at the University of Pisa happily reported that the professors had already delivered 104 lectures, 15 more than at this point in previous academic years. He predicted that professors would deliver a total of 145 lectures for the academic year 1476–77, instead of the customary 123.[67] In similar fashion, professors at the University of Pavia were obliged to deliver 128 lectures annually in 1548.[68] But in the second half of the sixteenth century, the number of mandated lectures at Pisa dropped from 150 to 120 and then to 110. Even this last number was ignored. By 1612 the academic year included 85 lectures, of which professors delivered only 60 to 70. Students would not permit the professors to teach on some teaching days, insisting that they were holidays or vigils of holidays.[69]

Paolo Beni vividly described the shrinkage of the Paduan teaching year in the early seventeenth century. The statutes decreed that teaching had to begin on October 19 and continue through August 15, with various holidays along the way, Beni began. However, in reality teaching began on November 5 and ended by June 10, he wrote. Moreover, in addition to the lengthy vacations at Christmas and Carnival and various statutory holidays on saints' feast days and the like, many unauthorized holidays had crept in, he continued. Although there should have been at least 135 days of ordinary lectures, unauthorized holidays had reduced the number to 85. Still worse, by custom professors did not lecture on about 12 of these days, leaving only a few more than 70. Student tumults prevented professors from lecturing on another 10 days. Hence, the statutory aca-

65. De Bernardin, 1983, 76 and passim. On Conti, see De Ferrari, 1983a, and Facciolati, 1978, pt. 3, 307. Certainly the government was preoccupied with the interdict crisis of 1606–7 and its aftermath.

66. Venetian authorities condemned and legislated against calendar abuses at Padua throughout the sixteenth century. See AAUP, F. 654, ff. 43^{r-v} (1503), 212^{r-v} (1544), 236^{r}–37^{r} (1555), 251^{r} (1569); and F. 491, ff. 3^{r}–4^{v} (1555). And the number of lectures delivered at the University of Bologna in the years 1556–58 and 1561–67 ranged from 70 to 103 through May, with little happening in the summer months. ASB, Riformatori di Studio. Minute de' rotoli, 1515–67, ff. 52^{r}, 56^{v}, 73^{r}, 75^{v}, 78^{v}, 82^{r}, 88^{v}.

67. Verde, 1973–94, vol. 4, pt. 1:263.

68. ASPv, Università, Cartone 33, fascicle 123, proclamation of Emperor Charles V of Jan. 30, 1548; also found in ASPv, Università, Cartone 36, pp. 20–21, Jan. 13, 1548.

69. De Rosa, 1983b, 103, and Marrara, 1993, 158–59.

demic teaching year of 135 days of ordinary lectures yielded only 60 days of actual teaching. In similar fashion, the calendar allowed for 45 days of extraordinary lectures, but abuses had reduced that number to 30. And even when they taught, professors sometimes lectured only half an hour, Beni concluded.[70]

The Venetian governors of Padua confirmed Beni's account. There were no more than 100 lectures—probably ordinary lectures—costing the government many thousands of ducats in professorial salaries, a governor lamented in 1614.[71] In 1638 the university had only 70 lectures in the law faculty and 100 to 110 in the arts faculty. The 1640–41 academic year had only 68 lectures.[72] And the governors reported another excuse for not teaching. On days on which a student received his doctorate, other students applauded him in class, and the lecture was canceled. The governor who reported this custom recommended that doctorates be awarded only on extraordinary lecture days.[73] The reduction in the number of public lectures increased the need and demand for private teaching, according to Beni.[74]

Some universities tried unsuccessfully to curb calendar abuses. The University of Bologna legislated that professors had to deliver at least 100 lectures in 1561, and it repeated the injunction periodically. In 1641 the government ordered professors to swear an oath that they would obey these and other regulations. But a group of professors argued that swearing the oath would endanger their immortal souls. They could not lecture when the students were in an uproar, nor could they do anything about unauthorized vacation days. If they swore to do something that they knew they could not do, they would be committing a sin, they concluded. The government eased the oath.[75]

The students' actions raise the question, Which abuse came first? Did an insufficient number of public lectures drive students to seek private instruction? Or did the growth of private teaching lead to a reduction of the number of public lectures, because students did not need them and professors did not want to deliver them? Whatever the answer, the University of Ferrara took the realistic route: it officially shortened its calendar in 1613.[76]

---

70. ASVa, Archivio Beni, Ms. 123, "Discorso," pp. [37, 56–60].

71. *Relazioni,* 1975, 149 (1614).

72. Ibid., 294 (1638), 314 (1641).

73. Ibid., 353–54 (1650).

74. ASVa, Archivio Beni, Ms. 123, "Discorso," p. [75], referring to the teaching of medicine.

75. Such regulations began to appear as early as 1545 and continued into the seventeenth century at Bologna. ASB, Assunteria di Studio, Bu. 91, no pag., a package of regulations on various university matters, including that each professor must deliver at least one hundred lectures between the beginning of the academic year and the end of August (Aug. 29, 1561), and the requirement that lectures must last one hour (Oct. 29, 1557). See also ASB, Assunteria di Studio, Bu. 89, four printed pages of rules of 1602, and Costa, 1912, 76–82, for the rules of 1641, with the protest against the oath on 78–79. It appears that the professors had learned a kind of specious casuistry.

76. According to the regulations of 1613, classes began after November 2 and lasted until December 12. They resumed after January 6 but stopped January 17. They resumed again at the beginning of Lent and stopped on the Sunday before Easter. They resumed again on the eighth day after Easter and

FINANCIAL PROBLEMS

Universities received the same or less money in the seventeenth century than earlier, despite the general rise in prices. Either the tax designated for the university failed to produce enough revenue, or governments diverted the money to other purposes.

At Padua the commercial tax whose proceeds supported the university failed to produce enough income to meet the payroll. The difference had to be made up from general revenues. As budgetary shortfalls increased in the mid- and later seventeenth century, salaries were not paid on time or only in part.[77] By 1660, Paduan professorial salaries were in arrears by 82,243 lire, which was equal to two-thirds to three-quarters of the annual academic salary budget.[78] Tardy payment of salaries had been a problem throughout the Renaissance, but the situation may have become much worse in the seventeenth century. No wonder professors taught privately.

Sometimes governments diverted the income designated for the university to other purposes. For example, the faculty of the University of Rome collectively received about 7,000 scudi in the 1580s and 1590s. The figure dropped to a little less than 6,000 scudi in the early seventeenth century and was fixed at 6,000 scudi in 1610.[79] The lower figure was not the result of inadequate proceeds from the tax on wine coming into the city, which financed the university and paid the salaries of fourteen preuniversity teachers. Indeed, this "Gabella dello Studio" took in 32,153 scudi in 1609. But the government spent only 5,765 scudi on faculty salaries, 1,135 scudi for other university expenses, and 430 scudi for the salaries of the fourteen preuniversity teachers. The rest of the money (24,823 scudi) went for noneducational purposes.[80] In these circumstances, university faculties inevitably shrank, as professorships went unfilled. Padua had seventeen vacancies,

---

continued until May 15, which was the end of the academic year. And, of course, there were many additional holidays along the way. Visconti, 1950, 78.

77. For example, in 1614 the tax produced 13,870 ducats in income while the University of Padua cost 15,542 ducats. In 1617, income was 13,706 ducats and expenses 17,452 ducats. *Relazioni,* 1975, 147 (1614), 171 (1617), and De Bernardin, 1975, 479.

78. *Relazioni,* 1975, 379 (June 1660). The amount of 82,243 lire was equal to 13,265 ducats of account valued at 6 lire 4 soldi, or 16,248 "academic florins," that is, florins worth 5 lire, the money in which Paduan professors' salaries were paid. The total expenses of the university were 22,410 ducats in 1655–56, including nonacademic salaries, the cost of the botanical garden, and some other expenses. Ibid., 368 (June 1656). If academic salaries constituted about 90 percent of the total, the salary arrears were about 66 percent of the annual faculty salaries (13,265 ducats divided by 90 percent of 22,410 ducats). If academic salaries constituted 80 percent of the total, the arrears were about 74 percent of annual faculty salary outlays. De Bernardin (1975, 479) adds additional information concerning salary arrears.

79. ASR, Archivio dell'Università di Roma, R. 86, ff. 260ʳ–261ʳ, a memorandum of 1656 summarizing the disbursements for faculty salaries from 1542 onward. See also Renazzi, 1971, 3:66–67.

80. ASCR, Decreti di Consiglio e Magistrati e Cittadini, Credenzone I, vol. 31 (1600–1611), pp. 282–84, financial summary of Jan. 16, 1610.

one-third or more of the total, in 1641.[81] The botanical garden also suffered and needed an infusion of fresh plants at midcentury.[82]

The deterioration of the Italian economy made it more difficult for students as well. An anonymous evaluation of the University of Rome of 1623 noted "the ruin of the money of the Kingdom [of Naples]." As a result, students from the Neapolitan state no longer came to Rome to study, because they could not afford to live away from home. The same was true for students from the papal state. They easily lived in Rome in the past, but this was no longer possible.[83]

FACULTY PROVINCIALISM

Subjects of the ruling government, especially local men, filled the vast majority of faculty positions in Italian universities, with the exception of Padua and Rome, throughout the Renaissance. At the same time, a little foreign yeast usually leavened the provincial dough, as universities appointed a limited number of professors from other parts of Italy and abroad. These "foreigners," (non-subjects) were often highly paid academic stars. But outsiders became increasing rare in the seventeenth century.

Bologna illustrates the point. The University of Bologna always had a limited number of distinguished foreigners in a faculty filled with local men and subjects. As described earlier, in 1513 the government codified this traditional practice by decreeing that the university had to have four non-Bolognese professors on its rolls. These positions became distinguished professorships in civil law, natural philosophy, theoretical medicine, and humanistic studies, filled by famous scholars paid the highest salaries in the university. The government spent considerable time and effort filling these professorships designated for outsiders with such outstanding scholars as Pietro Pomponazzi in natural philosophy, Carlo Ruini and Andrea Alciato in civil law, and Carlo Sigonio in humanistic studies.

The Bolognese government continued to make strenuous efforts to recruit distinguished foreigners through the sixteenth century. When Tommaso Correa of Portugal, the bottom filling the humanities chair, died in early 1595, the Bolognese surveyed the field and produced a list of ten humanists with their qualifications.[84] The list included Justus Lipsius of Belgium (1547–1606) along with his bibliography of twenty-seven titles published between 1577 and 1592.

81. *Relazioni*, 1975, 314 (1641). By contrast, the university had had 51 professors, 33 for arts and medicine and 18 for law, in 1617. Ibid., 171 (1617). Rome also had fewer professors; see Renazzi, 1971, 3:70–71.

82. *Relazioni*, 1975, 354 (1650), 379 (1660).

83. "La ruina delle monete di Regno [di Napoli] dove venivano molti scolari à Roma, li quali al presente mancano, non potevano mantenere; come ancora molti dello stato ecclesiastico, li quali prima potevano più facilmente mantenersi in Roma." ASR, Archivio della Università di Roma, R. 83, f. 28ᵛ.

84. For the wooing of Lipsius, see the letters of Camillo Gozzadini, the Bolognese ambassador to Rome, of Apr. 8 through June 3, 1595, and other documents, in ASB, Assunteria di Studio, Bu. 75, Lettere dell'ambasciadori agli Assunti, 1571–1694, no pag. See also Costa, 1907a, 52–58, with additional information and some excerpts from the letters.

The Bolognese quickly settled on Lipsius, then teaching at the University of Louvain. It was not a difficult decision, because Lipsius was the most distinguished humanist in Europe, the editor of Seneca and Tacitus, the founder of neo-Stoicism, and much else. He was also a man who changed his religious allegiance when he changed universities.

In order to pursue such a distinguished, controversial, and expensive scholar, the Bolognese needed the approval and support of the overlord of Bologna, the pope. It was common practice for princes to help in the wooing of distinguished scholars. Members of the Congregation of the Holy Office had doubts about the orthodoxy of Lipsius's famous book on politics and reason of state, his *Politicorum sive civilis doctrinae libri sex* (1589). But when contacted by the Bolognese ambassador, the cardinals of the Congregation of the Index dismissed the matter as of little consequence.[85] And nothing was said about his moves back and forth between Protestantism and Catholicism. The pope agreed that an offer should be made to Lipsius. When he rejected the initial offer as inadequate, Ulisse Aldrovandi, then teaching natural history at the university, and other Bolognese citizens pledged additional funds to help meet Lipsius's demands. In the end, Lipsius declined, citing health concerns as a reason not to journey so far from his native land and King Philip II's refusal to permit him to leave Louvain. The Bolognese then settled on a minor scholar, Roberto Tizzi da Sansepolcro, who began to teach in the 1596–97 academic year.[86]

The pursuit of Lipsius was the last real effort the Bolognese made to fill the four professorships with distinguished outsiders. After Tizzi left for the University of Pisa in 1606, the Bolognese left the post vacant until 1619, filled it for a few years, and then left it permanently vacant from 1634. They did the same with the other three professorships reserved for distinguished outsiders. In practical terms, the humanities professorship disappeared in 1634, the natural philosophy professorship in 1645, theoretical medicine in 1653, and civil law in 1655.[87]

Other universities made no effort at all to hire outside the ranks of local sons and subjects. Pavia's faculty became especially provincial. In the early seventeenth century, King Philip III, the ultimate ruler of the Lombard state, decreed that "dottori cittadini," (citizens of Pavia with doctorates) should be given preference over outsiders in appointments at Pavia.[88] The king's decree simply endorsed the status quo. Eighty-five percent (125 of 147) of the legists who taught at Pavia in the sixteenth century came from Lombardy, most from Pavia. Seventy-eight

85. See ASB, Assunteria di Studio, Bu. 75, letters of Camillo Gozzadini of Apr. 8 and May 10, 1595. A 1993 draft version of the revised *Index of Prohibited of Books* banned the book pending corrections. However, the promulgated 1596 *Index* did not ban or mention Lipsius's book. For Lipsius's appearance on the 1593 draft, see *Index de Rome, 1590, 1593, 1596,* 1994, 314, 318, 420–21, 827, 887.

86. Dallari, 1888–1924, 2:260, and Costa, 1907a, 58–62, who judges Tizzi to have been a scholar who contented himself with discussing the formal aspects of rhetoric, rather than investigating the life and thought of the ancient world.

87. Costa, 1912, 27–37.

88. ASPv, Università, Cartone 35, fascicle 171, edict of 1610 or 1611.

percent (61 of 78) of the legists who taught at Pavia in the seventeenth century came from Pavia and Lombardy.[89] In addition to satisfying local aspirants, the policy saved money, because local men, even if eminent, cost less than distinguished outsiders.[90]

Some scholars condemned university provincialism. Geminiano Montanari of Modena (1633–87), a distinguished and very productive astronomer and scientific generalist, was appointed to teach mathematics at the University of Bologna in 1664. At first pleased with the university, he became disillusioned with its provincialism. In 1677 he complained that those who ruled the university would not give any honors to an outsider (*forestiero*). They reserve them for local men, "who [are] for the most part little asses [*asinelli*], who enjoy their professorships through entitlement, because they are noted citizens."[91] He moved to the University of Padua in 1678.

STUDENT VIOLENCE

Pedagogical abuses, dwindling financial support, and fewer professors clearly harmed teaching and research. But probably the chronic student brawling had the most debilitating impact on the daily life of the university. The Venetian governor of Padua wrote in 1609 that the least little incident brought out the students, a hundred at a time, ready to fight; these daily brawls created so much trouble. He concluded that the greatest reason for the decline of the university was the restlessness of the students and their fighting.[92] Violence had been part of student life from the beginning but apparently became more pervasive and deadlier in the late sixteenth and the seventeenth centuries. Although students and townspeople had fought each other for centuries, fighting among students seems to have increased. Student violence disrupted classes, preoccupied the university community, and drove away students.

Perhaps the ultimate cause was to be found in the general social climate of increased lawlessness, as seventeenth-century Italy became a society of barons and *bravi* (hired bullies). The same governor of Padua who wrote that student violence was the greatest problem of the university went on to discuss the general violence that engulfed citizens and artisans as well. Nevertheless, he wrote, students were the worst transgressors, because they had little sense, had no property,

89. Zorzoli, 1986, 187. The total number of legists in the seventeenth century was smaller, because men stayed until they died. There was little faculty mobility.

90. Paolo Beni, himself an outsider, made this point while endorsing the continuing appointment of Paduans to the university there. ASVa, Archivio Beni, Ms. 123, "Discorso," p. [37].

91. "Che non fanno distinzione veruna da un forestiero, condotto per contratto, a questi suoi per la maggior parte asinelli, che godono le letture con titulo, perché sono noti cittadini." Quoted from a letter of Feb. 25, 1677, by Rosino, 1988, 175. See also Tabarroni, 1981.

92. "Che ben spesso si fanno vedere fino a cento in una volta per ogni picciola occasione, et portano non minor travaglio per le risse che ogni giorno succedono fra di loro." "È certo, che da niuna cosa è cagionata maggiormente la declinatione dello Studio fuorchè dall inquietudine delli scolari et dalle risse che seguono fra loro." *Relazione* of Tommaso Contarini, Sept. 24, 1609, in *Relazioni*, 1975, 114, 115.

and were outsiders, or sons of the family, meaning that, because they were still being supported by their families, they lacked a sense of responsibility.[93]

Other reasons for student violence can be found in the students' circumstances. Unsupervised young men who attended few lectures had much time on their hands; some filled it with fighting. The failure of governments to address teaching abuses or to enforce residence requirements may have bred contempt for law and order. The student organizations exerted little disciplinary authority; indeed, they engaged in practices that made matters worse. The quickness of students to resort to violence seems to have been greater than in the past and a product of the times.

Students carried weapons as a matter of honor; indeed, peers expected, even forced, them to do so. Leaders of the nations ordered incoming students to carry swords. If a student wanted to be honored and to remain in the university, he had to carry a sword, reported Annibale Roero shortly after he finished law studies at Pavia (1596–1602). If a student resisted carrying a sword, he was held to be a coward and subject to heavy penalties.[94] If he refused, he would have to flee the university as a coward. And he had to learn to use it: what a shame it would be to carry a sword and not know how to use it, Roero exclaimed. Roero urged all students to spend months practicing swordplay. And Roero advised his readers on their comportment when fighting. He mocked those who closed their eyes when hit in the face. The only reason for closing one's eyes was to avoid the blood spurting from an adversary's wound! Such braggadocio practically guaranteed a blood-spattered university career.

Swords were bad enough; firearms were worse. Student violence became more deadly when students began to use long and short arquebuses and pistols.

Firearms existed in Europe from the early fourteenth century but did not enter universities until they became easier to carry and use in the sixteenth century. Early firearms needed a reliable smoldering match or burning fuse, both of which required preparation, to explode the powder and propel the metal ball. The invention, possibly in Germany, of the wheel lock firearm around 1500 made possible self-igniting firearms. These were smaller firearms that could be concealed on one's person, carried, and fired more easily. The principle of the wheel lock was like that of a complicated cigarette lighter. The wheel lock had a rotating wheel, a mainspring, and various connected levers. Pulling the trigger released the spring, which turned the wheel, which created sparks at a point of contact between the metal and a hard stone, such as iron pyrites. The spark

93. "Li scholari sono i primi et più transgressori degli altri, perchè hanno poco cervello et manco robba, et sono forestieri or figliuoli di fameglia." Ibid., 115.

94. "Massime che chi non porta armi, non trova chi la voglia per se; ma tutti glie le danno, & è abborrito dalle compagnie. Di più li Consiglieri fanno agli studenti della sua nazione precetti sotto pene formidabili che debbono portare la spada, e molte volte altro che spada. E se il pupillo ricusa è tenuto per codardo. Oltre alle pene, che sono irremissibilmente esequite. e poi bisogna, se vuol stare in quello Studio, che porti la spada, se non che fuggavia." Roero, 1604, 133. The punctuation has been slightly modernized. The entire discussion about swords is on pp. 132–37. See also Vismara, 1963, 434–35, with quotations from the 1630 edition of the book.

exploded the powder, which moved the steel ball through the barrel. It was a self-igniting firearm, without match or fuse. The Italian term for wheel lock gun or arquebus was *archibugio da ruota* (or *rotta*), literally "wheel arquebus" or "wheel gun."[95]

The flintlock firearm appeared by 1547. Its chief feature was a hammer held in place by a spring. The hammer was drawn back to the catch. Pulling the trigger released the hammer, which hit a piece of flint, again producing sparks that fell into the pan holding the powder and firing the steel ball. The flintlock was a little simpler in construction than the wheel lock. The Italian term for a flintlock gun was *archibugio da focaia* (or *focea*), which was "flint arquebus" or "flint gun."

Both the wheel lock and flintlock arquebuses were immensely important inventions for warfare and for society. They were firearms that could be fired without a second piece of equipment, such as a lit fuse or smoldering match. The new arquebuses were smaller and more convenient; they could be carried safely, but were ready to fire. Moreover, wheel lock and flintlock made possible the shorter gun called the pistol. The new more portable firearms became fashionable among the upper classes of Europe, especially among wealthy young males quick to take offense and eager to prove their honor. This description exactly fit many university students.

The first reference to Italian university students carrying firearms came from the University of Siena in 1542. In that year new statutes of the Casa della Sapienza, the state-run residence for mostly non-Italian students, barred those living there from bringing into the Casa, or carrying outside, any kind of "offensive arms," especially "those of fire" and "wheels," a reference to wheel lock guns. Those possessing firearms had to dispose of them within two days under pain of banishment from the Casa for a month. However, students were permitted to wear a sword.[96] The decree suggests that some Sienese students had guns at this early date.

95. For descriptions of wheel lock and flintlock guns, see Blackmore, 1965, 19–35; Blair, 1968, 1–6, 162–65; and Morin, 1982, 21–41. I am grateful to Donald J. LaRocca for pointing out the differences between the two kinds of guns, the Italian terms for them, and the above bibliography. The documents that follow often refer to arquebuses, which were normally 3 to 5 feet long, which would seem to be too unwieldy to carry around town or into the lecture hall. However, swords and sixteenth-century pistols were also long, heavy, and awkward to carry. And some wealthy students had servants to carry the arms. The terms *pistola* (pistol) and *terzaruolo* (a short arquebus, about two-thirds the length of a normal one) appeared later and less often. It is possible that authorities used *archibugio* as a general term for all firearms, whatever their length.

96. "Non possino in alcuno modo o sotto alcuno colore li scolari di qual si vogli grado o conditione portare nela Casa dela Sapientia o fuore alcuna sorte d'armi offensibili, né manco possino tenere in alcuno modo nele loro camare o Casa dela Sapientia medesimamente alcuna sorte d'armi offensibili, escetto che una spada per ciascuno. E quelle che oltre a detta spada al presente si truovano in detta Casa o camare, tanto da fuoco, quanto d'altra sorte armi offensibili et rotelle, tutte fra due giorni prossimi dala pubblicatione de presenti capitoli debbino haverle portate e mandate fuore di detta Casa dela Sapienta." From chapter 10, "Sopra le armi," of the Statutes of Feb. 27, 1542, in Minnucci and Košuta, 1989, 358. Since the wheel lock gun may have been a German invention and the Casa della Sapienzia housed German students, one wonders if German students introduced firearms into the University of Siena.

Paduan students were carrying arquebuses as early as 1559 and 1560, at which time several suffered gunshot wounds during student elections.[97] An investigation into two homicides at Pavia in 1590 discovered that forty students "armed with diverse kinds of prohibited arms, especially wheel lock and flintlock arquebuses and pistols," were involved.[98] Some of the students who marched on the Jesuit school in Padua in 1591 carried long and short arquebuses.[99] Paduan students carried firearms into the lecture halls in 1611. Overall, students bearing and using arquebuses, *terzaruoli* (short arquebuses with barrels about 2 feet long, two-thirds the length of a standard arquebus barrel) and pistols were a constant problem through the seventeenth century.[100]

Attempts to ban arms failed. In 1579 the Spanish viceroy in Milan prohibited the students at Pavia from carrying swords, daggers, or any form of offensive and defensive arms, under pain of 100 gold scudi, a very large sum of money. If violators could not pay, they would be given three lashes in public. The stern decree apparently had little effect.[101] In 1593 the Bolognese government barred students from carrying swords to classes. The following year it allowed matriculated students to carry swords at night, but not during the day. However, the government did permit officials of the two student organizations to carry swords and unspecified "defensive arms" in daylight hours.[102]

Certain student practices caused students to reach for swords and guns. The most denounced was *spupillazione,* or *expupillatio.*[103] Because a *pupillo* was a minor under the guardianship of someone older, *spupillazione* came to mean that the new student had to pay in order to free himself from the "guardianship" of older students. At Siena students entering the Casa della Sapienza at the beginning of the academic year were obliged to host a dinner of pizza and wine for the older students. Jokes, hijinks, and the recitation of obscene poetry accompanied the dinner.[104] But elsewhere *spupillazione* was a hazing exercise in which older students extorted large sums of money from new students. Those who refused to pay were harassed physically and in other ways.

97. Dupuigrenet Desroussilles, 1980, 646.

98. "Armi di diverse sorte de arme prohibite, masime de archibugi da rotta et da foceo et pistole." ASPv, Università Cartone 33, Atti 1551–99, fascicle 158. The date "1590" has been added to the document in what may be a sixteenth-century hand.

99. Favaro, 1878, doc. 6, pp. 78, 80, July 16, 1591.

100. "Che publicamente nelle scole et nelle piazze erano da scolari portati li arcobusi, terzaroli et pistole." *Relazione* of Angelo Correr in *Relazioni,* 1975, 131 (Mar. 8, 1611). Additional references to students at Padua armed with these weapons are found in ibid., 115 (1609: "pistilla o di terzarolo" and "archibusi da ruota"); 220 (1627: "arcobuggi"); 294 (September 1638: "le pistolle"); 303 (November 1638: "le pistole"); 369 (1656: "armi da fuoco"); and 378 (1660: "armi longhe et curte da fuoco").

101. ASPv, Università, Cartone 33, Atti 1559–99, fascicle 152 for the decree of 1579. See also fascicle 156 for its repetition in 1588, and fascicles 154 (1585) and 158 (1590) for additional reports of armed students involved in violence.

102. ASB, Assunteria di Studio, Bu. 1, no pag., decrees of 1593 (no month or day) and Apr. 22, 1594.

103. Other terms found in the documents are *l'uso di dispupillare, il dispupillar i giovani,* and *spupille.*

104. Minnucci and Košuta, 1989, 569.

La spupillazione at Pavia went as follows. Upon arrival at the university, a new student was expected to recognize the older students of his nation by giving each a pair of gloves or a dozen pieces of silk lace, with additional gifts going to the counsellor, vice counsellor, and chancellor of his nation. He was to do this spontaneously in order to ensure the friendship of the older students. Students who were slow to pay suffered *la pupillagine* (guardianship) throughout the year. If the newcomer steadfastly refused to pay, the older students forcibly took his cloak (which identified him as a student) and continually invaded his room.[105]

A stubborn student who lived secure from invasion in quarters distant from the university was subject to action designed to collect payment or to inflict punishment. Annibale Roero described the elaborate practical joke played on a student who resisted *spupillazione* at Pavia. Although quite amusing, the story linked *la spupillazione* with threats to kill and firearms.

The counsellor of his nation came unarmed to the room of the new student, protesting his friendship. After he left, other students convinced the newcomer that the counsellor really intended to kill him; they persuaded the new student to carry an arquebus for protection. Next, an ambush was arranged: the counsellor stepped out of the shadows and threatened the new student. The latter's false comrades goaded the frightened student to fire his arquebus. But they had previously removed the bullet, leaving only a noisy powder discharge. Nevertheless, the counsellor fell down, apparently dead. Other students disguised as policemen rushed to the scene. They arrested the apparent killer, threatening trial and execution. But the false policemen agreed to let him go free in exchange for a bribe of 25 scudi. The terrified student then fled the city, abandoning his university career, while the "dead" counsellor and his confederates celebrated with the money extorted from the victim.

La spupillazione did not always produce amusement. At Padua the practice involved extortion and fighting. At the beginning of the academic year the new student at Padua was tricked into taking his comrades and roommates to an expensive dinner in luxurious surroundings. There older students from his own nation took over. They forced the neophyte to pay them 5 to 10 scudi and ripped the cloak off his back. If the victim fought back, the extortion attempt spawned large-scale student warfare, as other students came to the aid of the victim or joined his persecutors. The whole university was in an uproar just as classes were about to begin. Whatever the outcome of the initial skirmish, the desire for revenge may have produced more fighting during the academic year. Or else students fled to the religious order schools, where they might study in peace.[106]

105. This account including the practical joke that follows is based on Roero, 1604, 16–19. Vismara (1963, 435–36) summarizes Roero and includes quotations from the 1630 edition of Roero's book.

106. The fullest description of *spupillazione* at Padua is found in the *relazione* of Giovanni Battista Foscarini, a Venetian governor of Padua, of Sept. 16, 1614. "Vi è terzo lo abuso dello dispupillar i giovani, che novamente vengono allo Studio, il che si soleva già far con spesa di quattro o sei lire, che voluntariamente faceva mangiar in qualche gentilezza a compagni et concameranti il novello scolare; et hora è ridotto in una tirannide di scolari provetti delle nationi, li quali violentano il pupillo a pagarli

Numerous attempts to ban *spupillazione* failed.[107] It continued at Padua into the eighteenth century, at which time the sum extorted from new students was 20 ducats.[108]

City authorities did not use massive police action in order to quell student violence because they lacked the resources. In 1638 one of the Venetian governors of Padua complained that he had only six ill-paid policemen to deal with every sort of problem in the city. At the beginning of his tour of duty he had hired at his own expense additional officers to deal with the students. Later that same year the other governor added that there were only twenty officers to deal with the entire city and countryside of Padua.[109] When things got completely out of hand, the government in Venice sent troops to quell the students.[110]

Governments hesitated to confiscate swords and guns, or to crack down on student violence, for fear that students would leave. In an era of declining enrollment and brief residence, students, especially wealthy nobles, were essential to the economies of university towns, especially the small ones. Hence, governments tolerated a certain amount of student violence, which other students and townspeople had to endure.

POSITIVE DEVELOPMENTS

Not everything went badly for Italian universities in the seventeenth century; they also made significant innovations that nudged universities toward the modern world.

Renaissance universities lacked libraries, leaving students to plead for access to the collections of student nations, ecclesiastical institutions, professors, and bibliophiles.[111] Or they could buy their own copies. Stimulated by the founding of the Ambrosiana Library in Milan in 1609, Felice Osio, professor of humanities at Padua, petitioned the Venetian government to establish a library for the Univer-

---

cinque, sei, otto et dieci scudi, et gli levano d'attorno il ferarolo, et se fa resistenza, come pur alcuno se ne trova di animo nobile et risentito, che non vuol patir questa violenza et questo aggravio, vengono tra loro alle armi, et immediate si dividono le nationi in fattione, adherendosi non solamente li scolari, ma anco qualche lettore, in questo poco circospetto, chi all'uno chi all'altro; et si mette in confusione tutto lo Studio, all'hora apunto che principiano le lettioni; si feriscono et si ammazzano, et molti o richiamati da i padri, o per proprio desiderio di attender quietamente a i loro studij et viver fuori dei pericoli, si partano et vanno studiar altrove." *Relazioni,* 1975, 149.

107. Pavia banned it in 1595; see Vismara, 1963, 436 n. 35. It renewed the ban in 1618; see ASPv, Università, Cartone 35, fascicle 177, printed edict of the governor of Milan of Nov. 5, 1618. See also Marcocchi, 1966, 124–25. Padua banned it under pain of banishment and prison in 1615. AAUP, F. 491, no pag., proclamation of Nov. 3, 1615.

108. For references to the "dannate spupille," see *Relazioni,* 1975, 132 (1611), 270 (1634), 369 quote (1656), 378 (1660), 421 (1703). *Spupillazione* went on at the University of Pisa in the seventeenth century and probably elsewhere. De Rosa, 1983a, 24–25, 63.

109. *Relazioni,* 1975, 294–95 (Sept. 28, 1638), 304 (Nov. 9, 1638).

110. This happened twice in the 1640s. De Bernardin, 1983, 82.

111. At Padua, the German nation of artists had a library from 1586 onward, and the German nation of legists from 1596. Fedalto, 1984, 273. How many other student nations had libraries is unknown.

sity of Padua.[112] The Venetian Senate responded favorably in 1629 and appointed Osio the university librarian in 1631. The university library of Padua, the first in Italy, probably opened its doors in 1631. The regulations of March 1, 1631, mentioned a donation of fourteen hundred printed books and thirty-four manuscripts. The university library was first located in a building formerly occupied by the banished Jesuits. A series of decrees by the Riformatori dello Studio di Padova made it into a nonlending deposit library to be supported by the university community. All Venetian publishers had to give it a copy of each book printed or reprinted. Upon obtaining his degree, every new doctorate had to contribute 2 scudi to the library. Professors assuming Paduan posts for the first time, or moving to a different lectureship within the university, were assessed 10 percent of their first year's salary.[113] Donated books, especially from the libraries of deceased professors, also increased the size of the collection.

Although other universities did not immediately follow Padua's lead,[114] individuals and institutions slowly moved toward the establishment of libraries and museums open to students and, to some extent, to the general public. At Pisa, the students of the Collegio della Sapienza agreed in 1611 to donate the money collected from *spupillazioni* toward the purchase of books for the library of the Collegio.[115] This was an early example of how giving to a university was expected to purify ill-gotten gains. At Bologna, Ulisse Aldrovandi willed to the city of Bologna his library and his collection of plants, animals, and other objects from the natural world. After his death in 1605, these materials became a civic "museum of natural curiosities," which helped stimulate the development of museums of natural history.[116] Again Italy led the way.

The Venetian government also made it easier for Jews, Protestants, and members of the Greek Orthodox Church to obtain degrees without swearing that they were Catholics. The government came to this position in a roundabout way. The Venetian republic, like other states at this time, extended its control over the lives of its citizens. This meant eliminating the jurisdictional, ecclesiastical, and historical checks on state absolutism, especially those that came from external entities.[117] Counts palatine, whose authority originated with emperor or pope, were a classic example of a traditional exception to the power of the state. Hence, in 1612 the Venetian government abolished the rights of counts palatine in the

112. Osio had succeeded Paolo Beni in the humanities professorship in 1623. For the following, see Pesenti Marangon, 1979.

113. *Regole per la libraria instituta in Padova. Rescritte da gl'illustrissimi & eccelentiss. Signori Reformatori di quello Studio. A dì 1 Marzo 1631.* Stampate per Gio. Pietro Pinelli, Stampator Ducale. This is a four-page printed pamphlet found in AAUP, F. 737, ff. 78ʳ–79ᵛ.

114. New regulations of 1615 for the University of Naples stipulated that a library was to be created through donated books, but nothing happened. Cortese, 1924, 288.

115. De Rosa, 1983a, 24–25, 63.

116. The quote comes from Findlen, 1994, 24, which explores this phenomenon; see especially chs. 1, 3, and 6.

117. See Grendler, 1977, ch. 7, esp. 206–14. For what follows, see especially Rossetti, 1984; Sarpi, 1969, 562–85, which includes two of Sarpi's *consulti;* De Bernardin, 1975, 451–56; and De Bernardin, 1983, 71–72.

Venetian state. The republic objected primarily to the counts' authority to legitimize bastards, because it touched the all-important matters of inheritance and
patrimony. In similar fashion, Venice insisted that it alone should name notaries,
who were important civil officials. The power of counts palatine to confer doctorates was not the primary reason for the republic's move against them.

The non-Italian nations at the university responded with a storm of protests.
The government had forgotten, or had dismissed as a minor matter, the fact that
counts palatine conferred doctorates on non-Catholic students without demanding that they make a profession of allegiance to Catholicism, as required by the
papal bull of 1564. Venice had accepted the bull, agreeing that all those receiving
degrees through the authority of the colleges of law and arts and medicine would
swear the oath. But from 1565 onward, the republic had also permitted counts
palatine to award degrees to Jews, Protestants, and Orthodox Christians who did
not swear the oath.

The government quickly rescinded the decree abolishing counts palatine but
was left with a dilemma. How could it both eliminate the counts palatine and
allow non-Catholic students to receive degrees without swearing the oath? The
government created a new institution. On April 22, 1616, it founded a new
degree-granting college of artists and physicians, usually called the Collegio
Veneto, under the presidency of a well-known professor of medical theory,
Santorio Santorio.[118] After passing the usual examinations, a student received his
degree from this new college, whose authority came from the Venetian government. It stood alongside the traditional degree-granting colleges of law, and arts
and medicine, whose authority originated with a papal bull of 1264.

The papal nuncio and the bishop of Padua protested vigorously. The government then asked Paolo Sarpi, its major consultant on church-state jurisdictional
matters, for advice. As expected, Sarpi argued strongly in favor of the Venetian
position and for eliminating the oath: "Awarding the doctorate in philosophy and
medicine is a testimony that the student is a good philosopher and physician, and
that he can be admitted to the exercise of that skill. And saying that a heretic is a
good physician is not prejudicial to the Catholic faith."[119] Hence the Venetian
College went forward, awarding its first degree to a German. In 1636 the Venetian government added a Venetian College of Law, conferring its first law doctorate on an Englishman. One suspects that neither the German nor the Englishman
were Catholics. The Venetian colleges soon awarded many more degrees than
the traditional colleges; because they had fewer members, the examination was
easier to pass and the cost lower. Indeed, 597 German artists took degrees from

---

118. Other names included *Collegium Auctoritate Veneta,* the most accurate title; *Collegium al Bo;
Collegium Universitatis;* and *Collegium Publicum.* Santorio was the first ordinary professor of medical
theory (1611–24) and a major medical scholar. He also had ties to Sarpi and antipapal patricians. See
Sarpi, 1969, 36, 567, 569–73 passim, 600, and Siraisi, 1987, index.

119. Il dottorar in filosofia et medicina è un testificare che il scolare è un buon filosofo et medico,
et che si può admettere all'esercitio di quell'arte; et dicendo che un heretico sia un buon medico, non
si pregiudica alla fede catholica. From Sarpi's *consulto* of Feb. 8, 1617, as quoted in Rossetti, 1984, 373.
There is a similar statement in Sarpi, 1969, 583, his *consulto* of July 16, 1621.

the Venetian College, to only 76 from the traditional college, between 1616 and 1673.[120] Thus, Padua anticipated the modern arrangement in which a university confers degrees based on the authority of a civil government. But no other Italian university followed Padua's lead in the seventeenth century.

A WEAKENED INSTITUTION

Italian universities faced severe intellectual challenges as the seventeenth century opened. The humanistic impulse in university research and teaching had run its course, and Aristotelianism was disintegrating. The next step was to discard Aristotelianism in favor of mathematics and experimental science. This would have been a very difficult transition in the best of circumstances. But just when the university needed all its energy to make fundamental changes, external threats and internal abuses sapped its strength.

The seventeenth-century university did not offer a strong learning environment. The net result of the nonuniversity roads to degrees, competition from religious order schools, the failure of students to attend lectures, extensive private teaching, the shrinking academic year, and chronic student violence was that students learned less. Sooner or later, civic leaders, physicians, legists, and civil servants who learned little at universities, or avoided them altogether, would harm society through their ignorance. Perhaps the decline of the universities should be added to the reasons for Italian decadence in the seventeenth and eighteenth centuries.

Governments bore a significant part of the blame for the decline of the universities. In the fifteenth century, princes and city councils promoted humanistic studies in the universities. In the early sixteenth century, governments revivified universities closed by wars. In the middle of the century, civic authorities built botanical gardens, supported the medical Renaissance, and added new law professorships. But in the seventeenth century, governments failed to deal with abuses and sometimes made matters worse through neglect, provincialism, and financial stringency. Even though some individual professors had remarkable scholarly achievements, the seventeenth-century university was a weakened institution.

120. Fedalto, 1984, 273. This also suggests, but does not prove, that the majority of German students were not Catholics.

Conclusion

n 1412 the commune of Siena looked across the higher education landscape in Italy and found it barren: "All the universities of Italy and other lands are broken and almost non-existent."[1] This bleak assessment was accurate. The late fourteenth century had been a difficult time for Italian universities, and the new century promised worse. The University of Ferrara that tried to begin in 1391 had given up by 1404. The Pisan *studio* had died when Florence conquered the city in 1406. Naples hardly existed. Rome was open but did little, as the papacy struggled through the Great Schism. Pavia had declined to only nine professors in 1409–10. Florence had closed its doors in 1406 and would not reopen until 1413. Turin was struggling to begin. Siena, in great financial difficulty, had released all its Sienese-born professors in 1409. Only Bologna, Padua, and possibly Perugia were doing well.

Civic leaders and scholars did not know that Italian universities were about to take a decisive turn for the better. By midcentury every university except Pisa had revived, and the new universities of Ferrara and Catania had begun. The universities of Italy were far stronger in 1450 than before and poised to begin a revolutionary period in the history of learning.

The closures forced on universities by the wars of the first half of the sixteenth century only delayed the intellectual revolution gathering force. The universities of Padua, Pavia, Ferrara, Pisa, Rome, and Naples all closed for periods of years in the first half of the sixteenth century, and Turin closed a little later. When universities regained their strength—Padua, Ferrara, and Rome in the 1530s, Pavia and Pisa in the 1540s, and Turin in the 1560s—the delayed scholarly momentum coursed through the university like water through a breached dam. Scholarly innovation continued for the rest of the century. A strong desire for higher learning in parts of Italy without universities led to the founding of four new institutions between 1540 and 1601.

---

1. Quando tutti li Studii d'Italya e degli altri paesi son rotti et quasi mancati. From a deliberation of June 28, 1412, of the Sienese Consiglio Generale as quoted in Catoni, 1973, 164 n. 38.

Humanism was the major agent of change.[2] Leading humanists began to win
university professorships in the second quarter of the fifteenth century. By the last
quarter of the century, practically all universities had one or several humanists,
many of them major scholars. Although the humanities professorships, often
called "rhetoric and poetry," were never numerous and seldom well paid, humanism had a transforming effect on most other disciplines. Humanists, and humanistically trained and inspired scholars in other disciplines, began to criticize received scholarship and to innovate, which led to the scholarly breakthroughs of
the sixteenth century. The humanists first transformed rhetoric and poetry by
introducing new classical texts, a new methodology, and Greek. Before long,
medical scholars imbued with humanist values and armed with philological skills
created medical humanism, which generated vast changes in medicine. The
humanistic quest to find, read, and translate into better Latin the ancient and
early Christian era Greek commentators on Aristotle produced "Renaissance
Aristotelianisms"[3] and much change in natural philosophy. The humanistic
search for Greek mathematical texts led to more sophisticated mathematical
techniques. Although humanistic jurisprudence never toppled *mos italicus,* it
broadened the study of law.

Humanism was the primary, but not the only, agent of change. Because the
Catholic Reformation generated a demand for more degrees in theology, universities taught more theology, metaphysics, and Scripture. And when the Catholic revival bypassed traditional canon law, the number of canon law professorships declined.

Major structural changes in the distribution of professorships preceded, accompanied, and facilitated the intellectual innovations. Italian universities in
1400 had relatively small faculties focusing on law and medicine and only a
handful of professors in other subjects. Law, and arts and medicine, had about the
same number of professors, with law sometimes larger. By about 1450 the size of
the professoriat in most universities had expanded considerably, and the arts and
medicine professors usually outnumbered the legists. Italian universities concentrated on professional instruction in law and medicine before 1450 but began to
broaden their teaching and learning at midcentury. The diversification continued
through the rest of the fifteenth century and beyond. Humanistic studies, logic,
mathematics, medicine, and natural philosophy all saw remarkable innovation.
That most universities continued to award a larger number of doctorates in law
than in arts, medicine, and theology did not reflect the real change of emphasis in
scholarship and teaching. Law students more often pursued their studies to the
degree, because it was a required and useful credential. Knowledge mattered
more in arts and medicine; indeed, some distinguished professors outside law
lacked degrees.

The sixteenth-century university was more diverse structurally than that of
the fifteenth century. Specialization, the mark of modern scholarship and teach-

2. This is also the view of Rüegg, 1992.
3. This is the title of ch. 1 of Schmitt, 1983c.

ing, had begun. Universities created professorships of anatomy and medical botany. Medical theory and medical practice began to separate, and Vesalian anatomy influenced both. Civil law developed specialities, while canon law declined.
Moral philosophy grew in importance. Even theology became more important
within the university than it had been earlier. Mathematics, including its practical applications, became the dominant element in professorships previously
called mathematics, astronomy, and astrology. Astronomy declined, and astrology
nearly disappeared. Natural philosophy increasingly separated itself from medicine and never joined hands with theology. The unified Aristotelian and Galenic
edifice of learning began to crumble. From about 1475 through about 1600,
scholars at Italian universities produced innovations in every discipline except
theology.[4]

Governments established Italian Renaissance universities and helped them
achieve greatness. They wanted university-trained men to run the state and an
influx of wealthy students for the economic benefits that they rained on the
community. Princes and leaders of communes enjoyed having learned men in
their midst and basked in the prestige of hosting international centers of learning.
To make the university a success, towns spent considerable sums on higher
education and put up with student misbehavior. But governments did little to
arrest university decline in the seventeenth century.

Italian universities were the most important international centers of learning
in the Renaissance. The list of major intellectuals from across Europe who studied in Italian universities is very long. At the same time, universities were local
institutions. Men from the town and the state that hosted the university sought
and obtained most of the professorships. Colleges of doctors filled with local men
holding degrees from the university examined degree candidates. But universities
also appointed a limited number of distinguished outsiders, usually at higher
salaries than the locals received. Padua made a policy of searching out the best
available talent regardless of origin.

The development of alternate paths to degrees involving little or no university
study, internal problems, and diminished government support caused Italian
universities to decline in the seventeenth century. Nevertheless, from about 1475
to 1600 Italian Renaissance universities had one of the most productive and
extraordinary periods in the history of learning. Their influence continues to
this day.

---

4. The statement is tentative, because modern scholars have examined very little of Italian
university theological writing.

Faculty Size and Student Enrollments

This appendix summarizes information on the number of professors and student enrollments. The universities are listed in the order of their appearance in Chapters 1–4, where the documentation for the numbers, when available, is found. Table A.1 summarizes what is known about the size of the faculty of each university. Student rectors who taught (normally one for law and one for arts and medicine) and students who won lectureships in the last year of study are included. Where there are two or three numbers in a fifty-year period, it means that the faculty complement increased or decreased considerably, often as a result of near closure during a period of war. For more details, see the appropriate chapters. Sometimes table A.2 presents only estimates of student enrollments, that is, the number of students in residence.

Average Faculty Size, 1370–1599

University	1370–99	1400–1450	1450–99	1500–1550	1550–99
Bologna	52	73	93	87	82
Padua		29–50	50–60	60–19–58	58–49
Naples			20	15	15
Siena	12 est.	20–30	30–45	52–39	14–52–35
Rome			45–75	87–20–37	37–29
Perugia	16	36	36 est.	36	39
Pisa			30	30–42	45
Florence	11–30	8–27	2–5	4–8	3–4
Pavia	35–50	70–12–84	53–73	23–28	30–60
Ferrara			23–49	45*	45–50
Turin		6–20	20–30	24*	21–30
Catania		6	6–12	12	12
Macerata				9 (1541)	7–12
Salerno					9
Messina					13–14 (c. 1600)
Parma		6+ (1412-20)			17–27 (1601-17)

*When open, but frequently closed or nearly closed.

TABLE A.2
Estimated Student Enrollments, 1400–1600

University	1400–1450	1450–1500	1500–1550	1550–1600
Bologna	1,000	1,500	1,500–2,000	1,500
Padua	300–500	800–1,000	1,100–1,300	1,600–1,500
Naples		300	400	500
Siena	150–300	400–500	400–500	250–500
Rome			300–500	750–600
Perugia	300–400	300–400	200–300	200–300
Pisa		200–320	300	400–600
Florence	100–200	—	—	—
Pavia	600–700	600–700	0–350	500
Ferrara	430–500	0–400	500	
Turin	100	100–200	0–200*	500–400
Catania		30–80	100–200	200–300
Macerata				225
Salerno				50–100
Messina				400–450 (1630s)
Parma				300–400 (1601-50)

Bibliography

ARCHIVAL

Bologna, Archivio di Stato
  Assunteria di Studio
  Riformatori dello Studio
Florence, Archivio di Stato
  Studio fiorentino e pisano
Macerata, Archivio di Stato
  Archivio Priorale
Padua, Archivio Antico dell'Università di Padova
Parma, Archivio di Stato
  Archivio del Comune di Parma, Studio
  Istruzione pubblica farnesiana
Pavia, Archivio di Stato
  Università
  Università, Doctoratus
Rome, Archivio di Stato
  Archivio dell'Università di Roma
Rome, Archivio Storico Capitolino
  Registro di Decreti di Consiglio e Magistrati e Cittadini
Vatican City, Archivio Segreto Vaticano
  Archivio Beni, Ms. 123, Paolo Beni, "Discorso intorno alla riforma dello Studio di Padova." Autograph ms.
  Miscellanea Armadio
  Schedario Garampi
Venice, Archivio di Stato
  Riformatori dello Studio di Padova
  Santo Uffizio
  Senato, Terra

MANUSCRIPTS

Bologna, Biblioteca Archiginnasio

Ms. B 1283, "Miscellanea di memorie storiche bolognesi"

Ms. B 3803, Ulisse Aldrovandi, "Informatione del Rotulo del Studio di Bologna de' philosophici et medici all' illustrissimo Card. Paleotti." Explicit: Di Casa i 26 di Settembre 1573.

Florence, Biblioteca Nazionale Centrale

Ms. Corte d'appello, 3, "Deliberationes Supremi Magistratus et stantiamenta pro Studiis Florentino, et Pisano. Et Accademia Florentina"

Padua, Biblioteca Universitaria

Ms. 1673, "Manoscritti per servire alla storia dello Studio di Padova"

Ms. 1676, "Documenti per servire alla storia dello Studio di Padova"

Pavia, Biblioteca Universitaria

Ms. Ticinese, vol. 3, fascicle 25, Anonymous complaint concerning abuses at University of Pavia, c. 1680.

Ms. Ticinese, vol. 5, fascicle 2, "Matricula Collegii Theologorum Papiae (1397–1632)"

Vatican City, Biblioteca Apostolica Vaticana

Ms. Barberino Latino 5195, "Raccolta di alcuni negotij, e cause spettanti alla Santa Inquisitione nella Città e Dominio Veneto. Dal principio di Clemente VIII sino al presente mese di luglio MDCXXV"

PRINTED WORKS

Primary Sources, Collections of Documents, and Summaries of Documents

Acta Graduum 1406 ad 1450, 1970. *Acta Graduum Academicorum Gymnasii Patavini ab anno 1406 ad annum 1450*. Edited by Gaspare Zonta and Giovanni Brotto. 2nd ed. 3 vols. Padua.

Acta Graduum 1451 ad 1460, 1990. *Acta Graduum Academicorum Gymnasii Patavini ab anno 1451 ad annum 1460*. Edited by Michele Pietro Ghezzo. Padua.

Acta Graduum 1461 ad 1470, 1992. *Acta Graduum Academicorum Gymnasii Patavini ab anno 1461 ad annum 1470*. Edited by Giovanna Pengo. Padua.

Acta Graduum 1501 ad 1525, 1969. *Acta Graduum Academicorum ab anno 1501 ad annum 1525*. Edited by Elda Martellozzo Forin. Padua.

Acta Graduum 1526 ad 1537, 1970. *Acta Graduum Academicorum ab anno 1526 ad annum 1537*. Edited by Elda Martellozzo Forin. Padua.

Acta Graduum 1538 ad 1550, 1971. *Acta Graduum Academicorum ab anno 1538 ad annum 1550*. Edited by Elda Martellozzo Forin. Padua.

Acta Graduum 1601 ad 1605, 1987. *Acta Graduum Academicorum Gymnasii Patavini ab anno 1601 ad annum 1605*. Edited by Francesca Zen Benetti. Padua.

Adelmann, Howard B., 1942. *The Embryological Treatises of Hieronymus Fabricius of Aquapendente*. Edited, translated, and with commentary by Howard B. Adelmann. Ithaca, N.Y.

Alidosi Pasquali, Giovanni Niccolò, 1980. *I dottori bolognesi di teologia, filosofia, medicina, e d'arti liberali dall'anno 1000 per tutto marzo del 1623*. Bologna: Nicolo Tebaldini, 1623; rpt. Bologna.

Aristotle, 1941. *The Basic Works of Aristotle*. Edited by Richard McKeon. New York.

Atti degli artisti, 1911. *Atti della nazione germanica artista nello Studio di Padova.* Edited by Antonio Favaro. Vol. 1. Venice.

Atti dei legisti, 1912. *Atti della nazione germanica dei legisti nello Studio di Padova.* Edited by Biagio Brugi. Vol. 1: *1545–1609.* R. Deputazione Veneta di Storia Patria. Serie I, Documenti, vol. 16. Venice.

Berengario da Carpi, Jacopo, 1959. *A Short Introduction to Anatomy (Isagogae Breves).* Translation, introduction, and notes by L. R. Lind. Anatomical notes by Paul G. Roofe. Chicago.

Beroaldo the Elder, Filippo, 1995. *Annotationes centum.* Edited with introduction and commentary by Lucia A. Ciapponi. Binghamton, N.Y.

Bronzino, Giovanni, 1962. *Notitia doctorum sive catalogus doctorum qui in collegiis philosophiae et medicinae Bononiae laureati fuerunt ab anno 1480 usque ad annum 1800.* Milan.

Bruni, Leonardo, 1969. *Leonardo Bruni Aretino. Humanistisch-Philosophische Schriften mit einer Chronologie seiner Werke und Briefe.* Edited by Hans Baron. Leipzig and Berlin, 1928; rpt. Wiesbaden.

———, 1987. *The Humanism of Leonardo Bruni: Selected Texts.* Edited and translated by Gordon Griffiths, James Hankins, and David Thompson. Binghamton, N.Y.

Cambridge Translations, 1997. *Cambridge Translations of Renaissance Philosophical Texts.* Vol. 1: *Moral Philosophy.* Edited by Jill Kraye. Cambridge.

Canones tridentini, 1573. *Canones et decreta sacrosancti oecumenici, et generalis concilii tridentini.* Venetiis, Apud Hieronymum Polum.

Cardano, Girolamo, 1982. *Della mia vita.* Edited and translated by Alfonso Ingegno. Milan.

Cassirer, Ernst; Kristeller, Paul Oskar; and Randall, John Herman, Jr., eds., 1948. *The Renaissance Philosophy of Man.* Chicago and London.

Chartularium Studii Senensis, 1942. *Chartularium Studii Senensis.* Vol. 1: *1240–1357.* Edited by Giovanni Cecchini and Giulio Prunai. Siena.

Copenhaver, Brian, 1992. *Hermetica: The Greek "Corpus Hermeticum" and the Latin "Asclepius" in a New English translation, with Notes and Introduction.* Cambridge.

Dallari, Umberto, 1888–1924. *I rotuli dei lettori legisti e artisti dello Studio Bolognese dal 1384 al 1799.* 4 vols. Bologna.

Decrees, 1990. *Decrees of the Ecumenical Councils.* Edited by Norman P. Tanner, S. J. 2 vols. London and Washington, D.C.

De Nores, Giason, 1578. *Breve institutione dell'ottima republica di Iason De Nores raccolta in gran parte da tutta la philosophia humana di Aristotile, quasi come una certa introduttione dell'Ethica, Politica, & Economica.* Venetia, Appresso Paolo Megietti.

———, 1581. *In M. Tullii Ciceronis universam philosophiam de vita et moribus, ad illustrissimos & sapientissimos Patavina Academia Moderatores Ioannem Donatum, Ioannem Superantium Equitem, Paulum Theupolum, pariter equitem & dignissimum Divi Marci Procuratorem, Reip. Venetae, senatores amplissimos.* Patavij, Apud Paulum Meietum,.

———, 1584. *De constitutione partium universae humanae et civilis philosophiae, quam Aristoteles sapienter conscripsit.* Patavii Apud Paulum Meietum.

Digest of Justinian, 1985. *The Digest of Justinian.* Latin text edited by Theodor Mommsen, with the aid of Paul Krueger. English translation edited by Alan Watson. 4 vols. Philadelphia.

Documenti di Pavia, 1994. *Documenti per la storia dell'Università di Pavia nella seconda metà del '400.* Vol. 1: *1450–1455.* Edited by Agostino Sottili, Presentazione Ettore Cau. Bologna.

Ehrle, Francesco, 1932. *I più antichi statuti della facoltà teologica dell'Università di Bologna.* Bologna.

Emerton, Ephraim, 1925. *Humanism and Tyranny: Studies in the Italian Trecento.* Cambridge, Mass.

Erasmus, 1974. *The Correspondence of Erasmus: Letters 1 to 141, 1484 to 1500.* Translated by R. A. B. Mynors and D. F. S. Thomson, annotated by Wallace K. Ferguson. *Collected Works of Erasmus,* vol. 1. Toronto and Buffalo.

Fontes narrativi, 1943. *Fontes narrativi de S. Ignatio de Loyola et de Societatis Iesu initiis.* Vol. 1. Monumenta Historica Societatis Iesu, 66. Rome.

Galen, 1541. *Galeni omnia opera nunc primum in unum corpus redacta . . . Librorum indicem et diligentiam proximus quaternio demonstrabit.* Apud haeredes Lucaeantonij Iunte Florentini, Venetiis. The first volume of the monumental edition.

Galilei, Galileo, 1966. *Opere.* Nuova ristampa della edizione nazionale. Vol. 19: *Documenti.* Florence.

Gallo, Rodolfo, 1963. "Due informazioni sullo Studio di Padova della metà del Cinquecento," *Archivio veneto,* ser. 5, 73:17–100.

Garzoni, Tommaso, 1601. *La piazza universale di tutte le professioni del mondo, nuovamente ristampata & posta in luce, da Thomaso Garzoni da Bagnacavallo: Aggiontovi in questa nuova impressione alcune bellissime annotationi a discorso per discorso.* In Venetia, Appresso Roberto Meietti.

George of Trebizond, 1984. *Collectanea Trapezuntiana: Texts, Documents, and Bibliographies of George of Trebizond.* Edited by John Monfasani. Binghamton, N.Y.

Gherardi, Alessandro, ed., 1973. *Statuti dell'Università e Studio Fiorentino dell'anno MCCCLXXXVII.* Florence, 1881; rpt. Bologna.

Grant, Edward, ed., 1974. *A Source Book in Medieval Science.* Cambridge, Mass.

Gualazzini, Ugo, ed., 1978. *Corpus statutorum almi Studii Parmensis (saec. XV): Con introduzione su la storia della Università di Parma dalle origini al secolo XV.* 2nd enlarged ed. Milan.

Guarini, Guarino, 1967. *Epistolario di Guarino Veronese.* Edited by Remigio Sabbadini. 3 vols. Venice, 1915–19; rpt. Turin.

Guicciardini, Francesco, 1936. *Scritti autobiografici e rari.* Edited by Roberto Palmarocchi. Bari.

——, 1965. *Selected Writings.* Edited by Cecil Grayson; translated by Margaret Grayson. London, New York, and Toronto.

Hippocrates, 1886. *The Genuine Works of Hippocrates.* Translated by Francis Adams. 2 vols. in 1. New York.

Index de Rome, 1590, 1593, 1596, 1994. J. M. DeBujanda, Ugo Rozzo, Peter G. Bietenholz, Paul F. Grendler, *Index de Rome, 1590, 1593, 1596: Avec étude des index de Parme 1580 et Munich 1582.* Translated by Claude Sutto. Sherbrooke, Québec.

Lauree pavesi, 1995. *Lauree Pavesi nella seconda metà del '400.* Vol. 1: *1450–1475.* Edited by Agostino Sottili. Bologna and Milan.

Lombardelli, Orazio, 1594. *Il giovane studente. Nel quale con bellissimi Discorsi si ammaestra un Giovine, quasi dalle fasce, fin al tempo di darsi ad una professione.* In Venetia, Presso la Minima Compagnia.

I maestri di Ferrara, 1991. *I maestri di medicina ed arti dell'Università di Ferrara 1391–1950.* Edited by Francesco Raspadori. Florence.

I maestri di Roma, 1991. *I maestri della Sapienza di Roma dal 1514 al 1787: I rotuli e altre fonti.* Edited by Emanuele Conte. Fonti per la storia d'Italia, 116. 2 vols. Rome.

Maiocchi, Rodolfo, ed., 1971. *Codice diplomatico dell'Università di Pavia. Raccolta ed ordinato dal Rodolfo Maiocchi.* Vol. 1: *1361–1400.* Vol. 2, pt. 1: *1401–1440.* Vol. 2, pt. 2: *1441–1450.* Pavia, 1905–15; rpt. Bologna.

Malagola, Carlo, ed., 1966. *Statuti delle università e dei collegi dello Studio bolognese*. Bologna, 1888; rpt. Bologna.

Marti, Berthe M., 1966. *The Spanish College at Bologna in the Fourteenth Century: Edition and Translation of Its Statutes, with Introduction and Notes*. Philadelphia.

Matricula Germanicae Artistarum, 1986. *Matricula Nationis Germanicae Artistarum in Gymnasio Patavino (1553–1721)*. Edited by Lucia Rossetti. Padua.

Mechanics, 1969. *Mechanics in Sixteenth-Century Italy: Selections from Tartaglia, Benedetti, Guido Ubaldo, and Galileo*. Translated and annotated by Stillman Drake and I. E. Drabkin. Madison, Milwaukee, and London.

Memorie di Pavia, 1970. *Memorie e documenti per la storia dell'Università di Pavia e degli uomini più illustri che v'insegnarono*. 2 parts. Pavia, 1877–78; rpt. Bologna.

Minnucci, Giovanni, 1981a. *Le lauree dello Studio senese alla fine del secolo XV*. Milan.

———, 1984. *Le lauree dello Studio senese all'inizio del secolo XVI (1501–1506)*. Milan.

———, 1985. *Le lauree dello Studio senese all'inizio del secolo XVI*. Vol. 2: *1507–1514*. Milan.

Minnucci, Giovanni, and Košuta, Leo, 1989. *Lo studio di Siena nei secoli XIV–XVI: Documenti e notizie biografiche*. Milan.

Minnucci, Giovanni, and Morelli, Paola Giovanna, 1992. *Le lauree dello Studio senese nel XVI secolo. Regesti degli atti dal 1516 al 1573*. Florence.

———, 1998. *Le lauree dello Studio senese nel XVI secolo: Regesti degli atti dal 1573 al 1579*. Con la collaborazione di Silvio Pucci. Siena.

Monumenta Paedagogica Societatis Iesu, 1986. *Monumenta Paedagogica Societatis Iesu*. Edited by Ladislaus Lukács. Vol. 5: *Ratio atque Institutio Studiorum Societatis Iesu (1586, 1591, 1599)*. Rome.

Monumenta Paedagogica Societatis Iesu, 1992a. *Monumenta Paedagogica Societatis Iesu*. Edited by Ladislaus Lukács. Vol. 6: *Collectanea de ratione studiorum Societatis Iesu (1582–1587)*. Rome.

Monumenta Paedagogica Societatis Iesu, 1992b. *Monumenta Paedagogica Societatis Iesu*. Edited by Ladislaus Lukács. Vol. 7: *Collectanea de ratione studiorum Societatis Iesu (1588–1616)*. Rome.

Muret, Marc'Antoine, 1737. *Orationes, epistolae, et praefationes*. 2 vols. Roboreti, Ex Typographia Berniana.

Musso, Cornelio, 1558. *Prediche . . . fatte in diversi tempi, et in diversi luoghi*. In Vinegia, appresso Gabriel Giolito de Ferrari.

———, 1580. *Il Terzo libro delle prediche*. In Vinegia, appresso I Gioliti.

———, 1610. *Delle prediche quadragesimali . . . Parte prima*. In Venetia, appresso Andrea Muschio.

Nunziature di Venezia, 5, 1967. *Nunziature di Venezia*, vol. 5: *21 marzo 1550–26 dicembre 1551*. Edited by Franco Gaeta. Rome.

Nunziature di Venezia, 8, 1963. *Nunziature di Venezia*, vol. 8: *marzo 1566–marzo 1569*. Edited by Aldo Stella. Rome.

Panigarola, Francesco, 1617. *Prediche quadragesimali . . . predicate dal lui in San Pietro di Roma, l'anno 1577*. In Venetia, Appresso Pietro Miloco.

Pardi, Giuseppe, 1970. *Titoli dottorali conferiti dallo Studio di Ferrara nei sec. XV e XVI*. Lucca, 1900; rpt. Bologna.

Patrizi da Cherso, Francesco, 1970. "Francesco Patrizi da Cherso, Emendatio in libros suos novae philosophiae (a cura di Paul Oskar Kristeller)," *Rinascimento*, ser. 2, 10:215–18.

———, 1975. *Lettere ed opuscoli inediti*. Edited by Danilo Aguzzi Barbagli. Florence.

———, 1993. *Nova de universis philosophia: Materiali per un'edizione emendata*. Edited by Anna Laura Puliafito Bleuel. Florence.

Paulus Venetus, 1984. *Logica parva*. Translation of the 1472 Edition with Introduction and Notes by Alan R. Perreiah. Munich and Washington, D.C.

Petrarch, Francis, 1985. *Letters on Familiar Matters: Rerum familiarum libri XVII–XXIV.* Translated by Aldo S. Bernardo. Baltimore and London.

——, 1992. *Letters of Old Age: Rerum senilium libri I–XVIII.* Translated by Aldo S. Bernardo, Saul Levin, and Reta A. Bernardo. 2 vols. Baltimore and London.

Piana, Celestino, 1963. *Ricerche su le Università di Bologna e di Parma nel secolo XV.* Florence.

——, 1966. *Nuove ricerche su le Università di Bologna e di Parma.* Florence.

——, 1984. *Il "Liber secretus iuris caesarei" dell'Università di Bologna 1451–1500.* Milan.

Pico della Mirandola, Giovanni, 1995. *Conclusiones nongentae: Le novecento tesi dell'anno 1486.* Edited by Albano Biondi. Florence.

Platina, Bartolomeo, 1948. *Vita di Vittorino da Feltre.* Edited by Giuseppe Biasuz. Padua.

Poliziano, Angelo, 1973. *La commedia antica e l'Andria di Terenzio.* Edited by Rosetta Lattanzi Roselli. Florence.

Prosatori latini, 1952. *Prosatori latini del Quattrocento.* Edited by Eugenio Garin. Milan and Naples.

Relazioni, 1975. *Relazioni dei rettori veneti in Terraferma.* Vol. 4: *Podestaria e capitanato di Padova.* Milan.

La riforma cattolica, 1967–1970. *La riforma cattolica. Documenti e testimonianze.* Edited by Massimo Marcocchi. 2 vols. Brescia.

Roero, Annibale, 1604. *Lo scolare, dialoghi del Signor Annibale Roero, l'angusto intento. Ne' quali con piacevole stilo à pieno s'insegna il modo di fare eccellente riuscita ne' più gravi studij, & la maniera di procedere honoratamente.* In Pavia, ad instantia di Gio. Battista Vismara. No date, but dedicatory and publisher letters of 1604.

Salmerón, Alfonso, 1907. *Epistolae P. Alphonsi Salmeronis.* Vol. 2. Monumenta Historica Societatis Iesu, 32. Madrid.

Sanudo, *I Diarii,* 1969. *I Diarii di Marino Sanuto.* Edited by Federico Stefani. Vol. 5. Venice, 1881; rpt. Bologna.

Sarpi, Paolo, 1969. *Opere.* Edited by Gaetano and Luisa Cozzi. Milan and Naples.

Schmitt, Charles B.; Kraye, Jill; and Ryan, W. F., eds., 1986. *Pseudo-Aristotle in the Middle Ages: The "Theology" and Other Texts.* Warburg Institute Surveys and Texts, 11. London.

Shah, Mazhar H., 1966. *The General Principles of Avicenna's Canon of Medicine.* Karachi, Pakistan.

Statuta artistarum Achademiae Patavinae, 1496. *Statuta Dominorum Artistarum Achademiae Patavinae.* Colophon: Datae in nostro ducali palatio. Die X Iulii indictione xiiii Mccc-clxxxxvi. Expensis Magistri pasquini de roma et B. F. A. Copy: Venice, Marciana Library, 12.C.141

Statuta artistarum et medicorum Patavini Gymnasii, 1589. *Statuta almae Universitatis D. Artistarum, e Medicorum Patavini Gymnasii. Denuo correcta, & emendata.* Venetiis, Apud Iulium Painum stationarium almae universitatis artist., 1589. Colophon: Venetiis, Apud Nicolaum Morrettum. Copy: Venice, Marciana Library, Misc. 2395.1

Statuta collegii theologorum Pisanae, 1910. *Statuta collegii theologorum almae universitatis Pisanae anno domini MCCCCLXXV cum synopsi omnium theologiae lectorum ab initio collegii usque ad finem.* Edited by Carlo Fideli. Pisa.

Statuta iuristarum Patavini Gymnasii, 1550. *Statuta spectabilis et almae universitatis iuristarum Patavini Gymnasii.* Venduntur apud Hieronymum de Gibertis Civem Patavinum & bidellum almae universitatis dominorum iuristarum Paduae. 1550. Colophon: Venetiis, per Ioannem Patavinum, 1551. Copy: Venice, Marciana Library, 9.C.94.

Stella, Aldo, 1964a. *Chiesa e stato nelle relazioni dei nunzi pontifici a Venezia: Ricerche sul giurisdizionalismo veneziana dal XVI al XVIII secolo.* Vatican City.

Studio e scuola in Arezzo, 1996. *Studio e scuola in Arezzo durante il Medioevo e il Rinascimento. I documenti d'archivio fino al 1530.* Edited by Robert Black. Arezzo.

Studium Maceratense 1541 al 1551, 1998. *Atti dello Studium Generale Maceratense dal 1541 al 1551.* Edited by Sandro Serangeli. Turin.

Studium Maceratense 1551 al 1579, 1999. *Atti dello Studium Generale Maceratense dal 1551 al 1579.* Edited by Sandro Serangeli. Turin.

Thorndike, Lynn, 1944. *University Records and Life in the Middle Ages.* New York.

——, 1949. *The Sphere of Sacrobosco and Its Commentators.* Chicago.

Tropea, Giacomo, 1900. "Contributo alla storia della Università di Messina," in *CCCL anniversario della Università di Messina (contributo storico).* Messina, pt. 1, pp. 37–122.

Valla, Lorenzo, 1962. *Opera omnia.* Introduction by Eugenio Garin. Basel, 1540; rpt. Turin.

——, 1982; *Repastinatio dialectice et philosophie.* Edited by Gianni Zippel. 2 vols. Padua.

Verde, Armando F., 1973–94. *Lo Studio fiorentino 1473–1603: Ricerche e Documenti.* 5 vols. in 8 parts. Florence and Pistoia.

Vergerio, Pier Paolo, 1969. *Epistolario di Pier Paolo Vergerio.* Edited by Leonardo Smith. Rome, 1934; rpt. Turin.

Vesalius, Andreas, 1950. *The Illustrations from the Works of Andreas Vesalius of Brussels: With Annotations and Translations, a Discussion of the Plates and Their Background, Authorship and Influence, and a Biographical Sketch of Vesalius.* Edited by J. B. deC. M. Saunders and Charles D. O'Malley. Cleveland and New York.

Vespasiano da Bisticci, 1951. *Vite di uomini illustri del secolo XV.* Edited by Paolo d'Ancona and Erhard Aeschlimann. Milan.

Villani, Matteo, 1980. *Cronica di Matteo Villani a miglior lezione ridotta coll'aiuto de' testi a penna.* 6 vols. Florence, 1825–26; rpt. Rome.

Volpicelli, Luigi, ed., 1960. *Il pensiero pedagogico della Controriforma.* Florence.

Zambotti, Bernardino, 1937. *Diario ferrarese dall'anno 1476 sino al 1504.* Edited by Giuseppe Pardi. Rerum Italicarum Scriptores. New rev. ed. Vol. 24, pt. 7. Bologna.

SECONDARY SOURCES

Abbondanza, Roberto, 1958. "Tentativi medicei di chiamare l'Alciato allo Studio di Pisa (1542–1547)," *Annali di storia del diritto* 2:361–403.

——, 1959. "Gli atti degli Ufficiali dello Studio fiorentino dal maggio al settembre 1388," *Archivio storico italiano* 117:85–100.

——, 1960. "Alciato, Andrea." *DBI,* 2:69–77.

——, 1964a. "Bartolini, Baldo." *DBI,* 6:592–600.

——, 1964b. "Bartolini, Mariano." *DBI,* 6:613–16.

——, 1964c. "Bartolini, Onofrio." *DBI,* 6:617–22.

——, 1964d. "Bartolini, Pio Antonio." *DBI,* 6:624–25.

Accolti, 1960. No author. "Accolti, Francesco." *DBI,* 1:104–5.

Adorni, Giuliana, 1992. "L'Archivio dell'Università di Roma," in *Roma e lo Studium Urbis,* pp. 388–430.

——, 1995. "Statuti del Collegio degli Avvocati Concistoriali e Statuti dello Studio Romano," *Rivista internazionale di diritto comune* 6:293–355.

——, 1997. "L'Università di Roma e i suoi archivi," in *La storia delle università italiane: Archivi, fonti, indirizzi di ricerca.* Atti del Convegno, Padova, 27–29 ottobre 1994. Trieste, pp. 109–31.

Adversi, Aldo, 1988. "Le scuole," in *Storia di Macerata,* 2nd ed., edited by Aldo Adversi, Dante Cecchi, and Libero Paci. Vol. 3: *La cultura.* Macerata, pp. 3–76.

Ady, Cecilia M., 1935. "Francesco Puteolano: Maestro dei figlioli di Giovanni II Bentivoglio," *L'Archiginnasio* 30:156–59.

——, 1969. *The Bentivoglio of Bologna: A Study in Despotism.* Oxford, 1937; rpt.

Affò, Ireneo, 1969. *Memorie degli scrittori e letterati parmigiani.* Vol. 5. Parma, 1797; rpt. Bologna.

Aguzzi-Barbagli, Danilo, 1988. "Humanism and Poetics," in *Renaissance Humanism,* vol. 3, pp. 85–169.

Airaghi, Laura, 1984. "Studenti e professori di S. Eustorgio in Milano dalle origini del convento alla metà del XV secolo," *Archivum Fratrum Praedicatorum* 54:355–80.

Albornoz y el Colegio de España, 1972. *El Cardenal Albornoz y el Colegio de España.* Edited by Evelio Verdera y Tuells. Vol. 2. Zaragoza.

Alston, Mary N., 1944–45. "The Attitude of the Church towards Dissection before 1500," *Bulletin of the History of Medicine* 16:221–38.

Andreolli Panzarasa, Maria Pia, 1989. "Il convento di San Tommaso, la comunità domenicana e l'Università dal Tre al Cinquecento," *Annali di storia pavese* 18–19:29–47.

Antonaci, Antonio, 1966. *Francesco Storella, filosofo salentino del Cinquecento.* Galatina.

——, 1971–78. *Ricerche sull'aristotelismo del Rinascimento: Marcantonio Zimara.* Vol. 1: *Dal primo periodo padovano al periodo presalernitano.* Lecce and Galatina. Vol. 2: *Dal periodo salernitano al secondo periodo padovano.* Bari.

Arenaprimo di Montechiaro, Giuseppe, 1900. "I lettori dello Studio messinese dal 1636 al 1674. Notizie e documenti," in *CCCL anniversario della Università di Messina (contributo storico).* Messina, pp. 183–294.

Aristotelismo veneto, 1983. *Aristotelismo veneto e scienza moderna.* Edited by Luigi Olivieri. 2 vols. Padua.

Arnaldi, Girolamo, 1976. "Il primo secolo dello Studio di Padova," in *Cultura veneta,* vol. 2, pp. 1–18.

——, 1977. "Le origini dello Studio di Padova. Dalla migrazione universitaria del 1222 alla fine del periodo ezzeliniano," *La cultura,* 15:388–431.

Ascarelli, Fernanda, 1972. *Le cinquecentine romane. "Censimento delle edizioni romane del XVI secolo possedute dalle biblioteche di Roma."* Milan.

Ascari, Tiziano, and Crespi, Mario, 1964. "Barigazzi (Berengario), Iacopo." *DBI,* 6:360–64.

Ascheri, Mario, 1970. *Un maestro del "Mos Italicus": Gianfrancesco Sannazari della Ripa (1480 c.–1535).* Milan.

——, 1991. "La scuola giuridica senese in età moderna," in *L'Università di Siena,* pp. 131–44.

Ashworth, E. J., 1976. "Agostino Nifo's Reinterpretation of Medieval Logic," *Rivista critica di storia della filosofia* 36:355–74.

——, 1988. "Traditional Logic," in *CHRP,* pp. 143–72.

Ashworth, E. J., and Spade, P. V., 1992. "Logic in Late Medieval Oxford," in *The History of the University of Oxford.* Vol. 2: *Late Medieval Oxford,* edited by J. I. Catto and Ralph Evans. Oxford, pp. 35–64.

Asor-Rosa, Alberto, 1961. "Angeli, Pietro." *DBI,* 3:201–4.

Astuti, Guido, 1984. *Tradizione romanistica e civiltà giuridica europea: Raccolta di scritti.* Edited by Giovanni Diurni. Naples.

Asztalos, Monika, 1992. "The Faculty of Theology," in *Universities in the Middle Ages,* pp. 409–41.

Avellini, Luisa, 1990. "Per un profilo di Andrea Alciato teorico della lingua e della retorica," in *Sapere e/è potere*, vol. 1, pp. 281–92.

Avesani, Rino, 1960. "Amaseo, Romolo Quirino." *DBI*, 2:660–66.

———, 1969. "Bonamico, Lazzaro." *DBI*, 11:533–40.

Azzi Visentini, Margherita, 1984. *L'orto botanico di Padova e il giardino del Rinascimento*. Milan.

Bagarotti, 1963. No author. "Bagarotti, Bertuccio." *DBI*, 5:169–170.

Baldini, A. Enzo, 1980. "Per la biografia di Francesco Piccolomini," *Rinascimento* 20:389–420.

Baldini, Ugo, 1970. "Borelli, Giovanni Alfonso." *DBI*, 12:543–51.

———, 1994. "La tradizione scientifica dell'antica Provincia Veneta della Compagnia di Gesù: Caratteri distintivi e sviluppi (1546–1606)," in *I Gesuiti e Venezia: Momenti e problemi di storia veneziana della Compagnia di Gesù*. Atti del Convegno di Studi, Venezia, 2–5 ottobre 1990, edited by Mario Zanardi. Padua, pp. 531–82.

Balme, D. M., 1981. "Aristotle: Natural History and Zoology." *DSB*, 1:258–66.

Banfi, Luigi, 1983, "Scuola ed educazione nella Milano dell'ultimo Quattrocento," in *Milano nell'età di Ludovico il Moro*. Atti del convegno internazionale, 28 febbraio–4 marzo 1983. 2 vols. Milan, vol. 2, pp. 387–95.

Banker, James R., 1971. "Giovanni di Bonandrea's *Ars dictaminis* Treatise and the Doctrine of Invention in the Italian Rhetorical Tradition of the Thirteenth and Early Fourteenth Centuries." Ph. D. diss., University of Rochester.

Barbieri, Federico, 1912. "L'Università di Pavia durante il primo periodo della reazione cattolica," *Bollettino della società pavese di storia patria* 12:67–100.

Barbieri, Franco, 1977. "Macerata nel Seicento: Uno 'specimen' urbano," in *Studi maceratesi 11: Vita e cultura del Seicento nella Marca*. Macerata, pp. 32–40.

Bargagli, Roberta, 1992. "Documenti senesi per la biografia di Bartolomeo Sozzini (1436–1506)," *Bullettino senese di storia patria* 99:266–323.

———, 2000. *Bartolomeo Sozzini: Giurista e politico (1436–1506)*. Milan.

Baron, Hans, 1966. *The Crisis of the Early Italian Renaissance: Civic Humanism and Republican Liberty in an Age of Classicism and Tyranny*. Rev. one-vol. ed. Princeton, N.J.

Baroncini, Gabriele, 1981. "L'insegnamento della filosofia naturale nei collegi italiani dei Gesuiti (1610–1670): Un esempio di nuovo aristotelismo," in *La "Ratio studiorum": Modelli culturali e pratiche educative dei Gesuiti in Italia tra Cinque e Seicento*, edited by Gian Paolo Brizzi. Rome, pp. 163–215.

Barone, Giulia, 1978. "La legislazione sugli 'Studia' dei Predicatori e dei Minori," in *Le scuole degli ordini mendicanti (secoli XIII–XIV)*. Todi, pp. 205–47.

Barozzi, 1964. No author. "Barozzi, Francesco." *DBI*, 6:495–99.

Barsanti, Danilo, 1993. "I docenti e le cattedre dal 1543 al 1737," in *L'Università di Pisa*, pp. 505–66.

Barsanti, Paolo, 1980. *Il pubblico insegnamento in Lucca dal secolo XIV alla fine del secolo XVIII*. Lucca, 1905; rpt. Bologna.

Bartman, Roger J., 1945. "Cornelius Musso, Tridentine Theologian and Orator (1511–1574)," *Franciscan Studies* 5:247–76.

Barzi, 1965. No author. "Barzi, Benedetto." *DBI*, 7:20–25.

Bascapè, Giacomo C., 1935. "I conti palatini del regno italico e la città di Pavia dal Commune alla Signoria," *Archivio storico lombardo*, ser. 7, 62:281–377.

———, 1955. *Il Collegio Borromeo di Pavia: Contributo alla storia della vita universitaria*. Milan.

Battistella, Antonio, 1901. "Processi d'eresia nel Collegio di Spagna (1553–1554): Episodio della storia della Riforma in Bologna," *Atti e Memorie della R. Deputazione di Storia Patria per le Provincie di Romagna,* ser. 3, 19:138–87.

Battistini, Mario, 1919. *Il pubblico insegnamento in Volterra dal secolo XIV al secolo XVIII.* Volterra.

Beauregard, 1965. No author. "Beauregard, Claudio Guillermet." *DBI,* 7:386–89.

Beccaria, Gian Luigi, 1970. "Borghesi, Diomede." *DBI,* 12:643–46.

Bellomo, Manlio, 1979. *Saggio sull'università nell'età del diritto comune.* Catania.

——, 1995. *The Common Legal Past of Europe, 1000–1800.* Translated by Lydia G. Cochrane. Washington, D.C.

Bellone, Ernesto, 1986. *Il primo secolo di vita della Università di Torino (sec. XV–XVI). Ricerche ed ipotesi sulla cultura nel Piemonte quattrocentesco.* Turin.

——, 1994. "Laureati inglesi all'Università di Torino e Mondovì nel Cinquecento," *Studi Piemontesi* 23 (2): 439–46.

Belloni, Annalisa, 1986. *Professori giuristi a Padova nel secolo XV: Profili bio-bibliografici e cattedre.* Frankfurt am Main.

——, 1995. "L'insegnamento giuridico in Italia e in Francia nei primi decenni del Cinquecento e l'emigrazione di Andrea Alciato," in *Università in Europa: Le istituzioni universitarie dal Medio Evo ai nostri giorni. Strutture, organizzazione, funzionamento.* Atti del Convegno Internazionale di Studi, Milazzo 28 Settembre–2 Ottobre 1993, edited by Andrea Romano. Soveria Mannelli and Messina, pp. 137–58.

Belloni, Luigi, 1981. "Malpighi, Marcello." *DSB,* 9:62–66.

Benadusi, Giovanna, 1996. *A Provincial Elite in Early Modern Tuscany: Family and Power in the Creation of the State.* Baltimore and London.

Bencini, Serenella, 1970–71. "La lettura del Cremonini e le apologie inedite dei Gesuiti intorno alla controversia del 1591." Tesi di Laurea. Università degli Studi di Padova, Facoltà di Magistero.

Bendiscioli, Mario, 1961. "I collegi e l'università," in *Discipline e maestri dell'Ateneo Pavese.* Pavia, pp. 349–79.

Bentley, Jerry H., 1987. *Politics and Culture in Renaissance Naples.* Princeton, N.J.

Benzi, 1966. No author. "Benzi, Ugo." *DBI,* 8:720–23.

Benzoni, Gino, 1970. "I 'teologi' minori dell'interdetto," *Archivio veneto,* ser. 5, 91:31–108.

——, 1980. "Chiaramonti, Scipione." *DBI,* 24:541–49.

Bernuzzi, Marco, 1989. "Gli statuti della Facoltà teologica e il Collegio dei teologi a Pavia," *Annali di storia pavese* 18–19:121–35.

Berti, Giuseppe, 1967. *Lo studio universitario parmense alla fine del Seicento.* Parma.

Bertolaso, Bartolo, 1959–60. "I 'Terzi Luoghi' nello Studio padovano," *Acta Medicae Historiae Patavina* 6:1–15.

Bertoni, Luciano, 1968. "Il 'Collegio' dei teologi dell'Università di Siena e i suoi statuti del 1434," *Rivista di storia della Chiesa in Italia* 22:1–56.

Besta, Enrico, 1925a. "La scuola giuridica pavese nel primo secolo dopo la istituzione dello Studio Generale," in *Contributi alla Storia dell'Università di Pavia.* Pubblicati nell'XI centenario dell'Ateneo. Pavia, pp. 251–79.

——, 1925b. *Storia del diritto italiano.* Vol. 1, Parte seconda: *Fonti: legislazione e scienza giuridica dalla caduta dell'impero romano al secolo decimosesto.* Milan.

Biadego, Giuseppe, 1895. *Bernardino Donato grecista veronese del secolo XVI.* Nozze Fraccaroli-Rezzonica della Torre. Verona.

Biagi, Maria Grazia, 1980. "Gli statuti del Collegio Ferdinando di Pisa in età medicea," *Bollettino storico pisano* 49:87–118.

Biagioli, Mario, 1989. "The Social Status of Italian Mathematicians, 1450–1600," *History of Science* 27:41–95.

——, 1993. *Galileo Courtier: The Practice of Science in the Culture of Absolutism*. Chicago and London.

Bianca, Concetta, 1988. "Delfino, Federico." *DBI*, 36:552–54.

——, 1999. "Gaza, Teodoro." *DBI*, 52:737–46.

Bianchi, Dante, 1913. "La lettura d'arte oratoria nello Studio di Pavia nei sec. XV e XVI (1376–1550)," *Bollettino della società pavese di storia patria* 13:151–72.

Bietenholz, Peter G., 1987. "Ricius, Paulus," in *Contemporaries of Erasmus: A Biographical Register of the Renaissance and Reformation*, edited by Peter G. Bietenholz and Thomas B. Deutscher. Vol. 3: *N-Z*. Toronto, Buffalo, and London, pp. 158–60.

Bigi, Emilio, 1960. "Ambrogini, Angelo, detto il Poliziano." *DBI*, 2:691–702.

——, 1961. "Andronico, Callisto." *DBI*, 3:162–63.

——, 1962a. "Argiropulo, Giovanni." *DBI*, 4:129–31.

——, 1962b. "Aurispa, Giovanni." *DBI*, 4:593–95.

——, 1964. "Barbaro, Ermolao." *DBI*, 6:96–99.

——, 1986. "Poliziano, Angelo." *Dizionario critico della letteratura italiana*. 4 vols. Turin, vol. 3, pp. 478–89.

Biglia, Andrea, 1968. No author. "Biglia, Andrea." *DBI*, 10:413–15.

Bilinski, Bronislaw, 1983. "Il periodo padovano di Nicolò Copernico (1501–1503)," in *Scienza e filosofia*, pp. 222–85

Billanovich, Giovanni, 1963–1964. "Giovanni del Virgilio, Pietro da Moglio, Francesco da Fiano," *Italia medioevale e umanistica* 6:203–234; 7:279–324.

——, 1965. "Auctorista, humanista, orator," *Rivista di cultura classica e medioevale: Studi in onore di Alfredo Schiaffini* 7 (1–3): 143–63.

Bini, Vincenzo, 1977. *Memorie istoriche della perugina Università degli Studj e dei suoi professori*. Vol. 1: *Che abbraccia la Storia dei Secoli XIII, XIV e XV*. (Only volume published). Perugia, 1816; rpt. Sala Bolognese.

Biondi, Alberto, 1985. "Curione, Celio Secondo." *DBI*, 31:443–49.

Black, Robert, 1985a. *Benedetto Accolti and the Florentine Renaissance*. Cambridge.

——, 1985b. "The *Studio aretino* in the Fifteenth and Early Sixteenth Centuries," *History of Universities* 5:55–82.

——, 1988. "Higher Education in Florentine Tuscany: New Documents from the Second Half of the Fifteenth Century," in *Florence and Italy: Renaissance Studies in Honour of Nicolai Rubinstein*, edited by Peter Denley and Caroline Elam. London, pp. 209–22.

Blackmore, Howard L., 1965. *Guns and Rifles of the World*. London.

Blair, Claude, 1968. *Pistols of the World*. London.

Boaga, Emanuele, 1984. "Lo 'studium generale' dei carmelitani a Padova nel secolo XV," in *Riforma della Chiesa, cultura e spiritualità nel Quattrocento Veneto*. Atti del convegno per il VI centenario della nascita di Ludovico Barbo (1382–1443), Padova, Venezia, Treviso, 19–24 settembre 1982, edited by Giovanni B. Francesco Trolese. Cesena, pp. 345–57.

Bongi, Salvatore, 1890–97. *Annali di Gabriel Giolito de' Ferrari da Trino di Monferrato, stampatore in Venezia*. 2 vols. Rome; rpt. Rome n.d.

Boris, Francesca, 1990. "Lo Studio e la Mercanzia. I 'signori dottori cittadini' giudici nel Foro dei Mercanti nel Cinquecento," in *Sapere e/è potere*, vol. 3, pp. 179–201.

Borsetti, Ferrante, 1735. *Historia almi Ferrariae Gymnasii*. 3 vols. Ferrara.

——, 1970. *Adversus supplementum et animadversiones Iacobi Guarini*. Venice, 1742; rpt. Bologna.

Bortolotti, Ettore, 1947. *La storia della matematica nella Università di Bologna.* Bologna.

Bottin, Francesco, 1983. "Logica e filosofia naturale nelle opere di Paolo Veneto," in *Scienza e filosofia,* pp. 85–124.

Bottoni, Antonio, 1892. *Cinque secoli d'Università a Ferrara MCCCXCI–MDCCCXCI.* Bologna.

Boudinhon, Auguste-Marie, 1913. "Law, Canon," in *The Catholic Encyclopedia.* New York, vol. 9, pp. 56–66.

Bouwsma, William J., 1968. *Venice and the Defense of Republican Liberty: Renaissance Values in the Age of the Counter Reformation.* Berkeley and Los Angeles.

Bowsky, William M., 1970. *The Finance of the Commune of Siena, 1287–1355.* Oxford.

Boyer, Marjorie, 1971–76. "Pappus," in *Catalogus,* vol. 2, pp. 205–13; vol. 3, pp. 426–31.

Brambilla, Elena, 1982. "Il sistema letterario di Milano: professioni nobili e professioni borghesi dall'età spagnola alle riforme teresiane," in *Economia, istituzioni, cultura in Lombardia nell'età di Maria Teresa.* Vol. 3: *Istituzioni e società.* Bologna, pp. 79–160.

Branca, Vittore, 1983. *Poliziano e l'umanesimo della parola.* Turin.

Brecht, Martin, 1985. *Martin Luther: His Road to Reformation, 1483–1521.* Translated by James L. Schaaf. Philadelphia.

Brizzi, Gian Paolo, 1976. *La formazione della classe dirigente nel Sei-Settecento: I seminaria nobilium nell'Italia centrosettentrionale.* Bologna.

———, 1977. "Le istituzioni educative e culturali: Università e collegi," in *Storia della Emilia Romagna,* edited by Aldo Berselli. Vol. 2: *L'età moderna.* Bologna, pp. 443–461.

———, 1980. "Educare il Principe, formare le *élites*: I Gesuiti e Ranuccio I Farnese," in *Università, Principe Gesuiti: La politica farnesiana dell'istruzione a Parma e Piacenza (1545–1622).* Rome, pp. 133–211.

———, 1982. "Strategie educative e istituzioni scolastiche della Controriforma," in *Letteratura italiana.* Vol. 1: *Il letterato e le istituzioni.* Turin: Einaudi, pp. 899–920.

———, 1984. "I collegi per borsisti e lo Studio bolognese: Caratteri ed evoluzione di un'istituzione educativo-assistenziale fra XIII e XVIII secolo," in *SMUB,* n.s., vol. 4, pp. 9–48, apps. pp. 49–172.

———, 1988. "Matricole ed effettivi: Aspetti della presenza studentesca a Bologna fra Cinque e Seicento," in *Studenti e università degli studenti dal xii al xix secolo,* edited by Gian Paolo Brizzi and Antonio Ivan Pini. *SMUB,* n.s., vol. 7, pp. 225–59.

———, 1994. "Scuole e collegi nell'antica Provincia Veneta della Compagnia di Gesù (1542–1773)," in *I Gesuiti e Venezia. Momenti e problemi di storia veneziana della Compagnia di Gesù.* Atti del Convegno di Studi, Venezia, 2–5 ottobre 1990, edited by Mario Zanardi. Padua, pp. 467–511.

Brockliss, L. W. B., 1987. *French Higher Education in the Seventeenth and Eighteenth Centuries: A Cultural History.* Oxford.

Brotto, Giovanni, and Zonta, Gasparo, 1922. *La facoltà teologica dell'Università di Padova.* Pt. 1: *Secoli XIV e XV.* Padua.

Brown, Alison, 1979. *Bartolomeo Scala, 1430–1497, Chancellor of Florence: The Humanist as Bureaucrat.* Princeton, N.J.

Brucker, Gene A., 1969. "Florence and Its University, 1348–1434," in *Action and Conviction in Early Modern Europe: Essays in Memory of E. H. Harbison,* edited by T. K. Rabb and J. E. Seigel. Princeton, N.J., pp. 220–36.

———, 1982. "A Civic Debate on Florentine Higher Education (1460)," *RQ* 34:517–33.

———, 1988. "Renaissance Florence: Who Needs a University?" in *The University and the City,* edited by Thomas Bender. Oxford, pp. 47–58.

———, 1990. "Monasteries, Friaries, and Nunneries in Quattrocento Florence," in *Christianity and the Renaissance. Image and Religious Imagination in the Quattrocento,* edited by Timothy Verdon and John Henderson. Syracuse, pp. 41–62.

Brugi, Biagio, 1905. *Gli scolari dello Studio di Padova nel Cinquecento.* 2nd ed. rev. Padua and Verona.

———, 1907. "Giudizi di studenti tedeschi del secolo XVI sullo Studio di Padova," *Atti e memorie della R. Accademia di scienze, lettere ed arti in Padova,* n.s., 23:293–95.

———, 1915. *Per la storia della giurisprudenza e delle università italiane: Saggi.* Turin.

———, 1916. "Marco Antonio Mureto e la cattedra di Pandette nello Studio di Padova," *Atti e memorie della R. Accademia di scienze, lettere ed arti in Padova,* n.s., 32:325–34.

———, 1921. *Per la storia della giurisprudenza e delle università italiane: Nuovi saggi.* Turin.

———, 1922. "L'università dei giuristi in Padova nel Cinquecento: Saggio di storia della giurisprudenza e delle università italiane," *Archivio veneto tridentino* ser. 4, 1:1–92.

Bruni, Alessandro, 1991. "Le scienze botaniche, semplicistiche e terapeutiche nella Ferrara del Rinascimento: Un paradigma sull'evoluzione del concetto di farmaco," in *La rinascita del sapere,* pp. 274–92.

Bryson, Frederick R., 1938. *The Sixteenth-Century Italian Duel: A Study in Renaissance Social History.* Chicago.

Bubenheimer, Ulrich, 1977. *Consonantia Theologiae et Iurisprudentiae: Andreas Bodenstein von Karlstadt als Theologue und Jurist zwischen Scholastik und Reformation.* Tübingen.

Bueno De Mesquita, D. M., 1941. *Giangaleazzo Visconti, Duke of Milan (1351–1401): A Study in the Political Power of an Italian Despot.* Cambridge.

Bullough, Vern L., 1981. "Mondino de' Luzzi." *DSB,* 9:467–69.

Bulmer-Thomas, Ivor, 1981a. "Euclid: Life and Works." *DSB,* 4:414–37.

———, 1981b. "Pappus of Alexandria." *DSB,* 10, pp. 293–304.

Buscemi, Salvatore, 1900. "L'insegnamento del diritto civile nella antica Università di Messina," in *CCCL anniversario della Università di Messina (contributo storico).* Messina, pt. 2, pp. 57–78.

Bylebyl, Jerome J., 1979. "The School of Padua: Humanistic Medicine in the Sixteenth Century," in *Health, Medicine, and Mortality in the Sixteenth Century,* edited by Charles Webster. Cambridge, pp. 335–70.

———, 1981a. "Colombo, Realdo." *DSB,* 3:354–57.

———, 1981b. "Leoniceno, Nicolò." *DSB,* 8:248–50.

———, 1982. "Commentary," in *A Celebration of Medical History,* edited by Lloyd G. Stevenson. Baltimore, pp. 200–11.

———, 1985a. "Disputation and Description in the Renaissance Pulse Controversy," in *Medical Renaissance,* pp. 223–45, 331–38.

———, 1985b. "Medicine, Philosophy, and Humanism in Renaissance Italy," in *Science and the Arts in the Renaissance,* edited by John W. Shirley and F. David Hoeniger. Washington, London, and Toronto, pp. 27–49.

Cagno, Giorgio, 1932. "Gli studenti dell'Università di Roma attraverso il tempo dal XVI Secolo ai giorni nostri. Parte I," *Metron* 9:153–84.

Calasso, Francesco, 1954. *Medio evo del diritto.* Vol. 1: *Le fonti.* Milan.

———, 1964. "Bartolo da Sassoferrato." *DBI,* 6:640–669.

Calcaterra, Carlo, 1948. *Alma Mater Studiorum: L'Università di Bologna nella storia della cultura e della civiltà.* Bologna.

Camerini, Paolo, 1962–63. *Annali dei Giunti.* Vol. 1 in two parts: *Venezia.* Florence.

Camerota, Michele, 1997. "Flaminio Papazzoni: un aristotelico bolognese maestro di

Federico Borromeo e corrispondente di Galileo," in *Method and Order in Renaissance Philosophy of Nature: The Aristotle Commentary Tradition*, edited by Daniel A. Di Liscia, Eckhard Kessler, and Charlotte Methuen. Aldershot, England, pp. 271–300.

Cammelli, Giuseppe, 1941. *I dotti bizantini e le origini dell'umanesimo*. Vol. 1: *Manuele Crisolora*. Florence.

———, 1954. *I dotti bizantini e le origini dell'umanesimo*. Vol. 3: *Demetrio Calcondila*. Florence.

Campitelli, Adriana, 1965. "Barzi, Benedetto." *DBI*, 7:18–20.

Cannavale, Ercole, 1980. *Lo Studio di Napoli nel Rinascimento (2700 documenti inediti)*. Naples, 1895; rpt. Bologna.

Canning, Joseph, 1987. *The Political Thought of Baldus de Ubaldus*. Cambridge.

Cantini, Gustavo, 1941. "Cornelio Musso dei Frati Minori Conventuali (1511–1574): Predicatore, Scrittore e Teologo al Concilio di Trento," *Miscellanea Francescana* 41:145–74, 424–63.

Cappelli, Adriano, 1983. *Cronologia, Cronografia e Calendario Perpetuo: Dal principio dell'era cristiana ai nostri giorni*. Fifth ed. rev. Milan.

Caprioli, Severino, 1969. "Bolognini, Ludovico." *DBI*, 11:337–52.

Carafa, Giuseppe, 1971, *De Gymnasio Romano et de eius professoribus*. 2 vols. Rome, 1751; rpt. Bologna.

Cardini, Roberto, 1973. *La critica del Landino*. Florence.

Carlino, Andrea, 1999. *Books of the Body: Anatomical Ritual and Renaissance Learning*. Translated by John Tedeschi and Anne C. Tedeschi. Chicago and London.

Carlsmith, Christopher, 1998. "Il Collegio Patavino della Misericordia Maggiore di Bergamo 1531–c. 1550," *Bergomum* 93:75–98.

Carpi, Daniel, 1986. "Note su alcuni ebrei laureati a Padova nel Cinquecento e all'inizio del Seicento," *Quaderni* 19:145–56.

Carruccio, Ettore, 1981a. "Cataldi, Pietro Antonio." *DSB*, 3:125–29.

———, 1981b. "Cavalieri, Bonaventura." *DSB*, 4:149–53.

Carugo, Adriano, 1984. "L'insegnamento della matematica all'Università di Padova prima e dopo Galileo," in *Cultura veneta*, vol. 4, pt. 2, pp. 151–99.

Casalino Astori, Daniela, 1970. "Gli alunni non pervenuti alla laurea per espulsioni, decessi, ingressi in ordini religiosi (1567–1796)," in *Il Collegio Universitario Ghislieri di Pavia, istituzione della Riforma Cattolica (1567–1860)*. Milan, vol. 2, pp. 121–55.

Cascio Pratilli, Giovanni, 1975. *L'università e il principe: Gli Studi di Siena e di Pisa tra rinascimento e controriforma*. Florence.

Casella, Maria Teresa, 1975. "Il metodo dei commentatori umanistici esemplato sul Beroaldo," *Studi medievali*, ser. 3, anno 16, fascicle 2, pp. 627–701.

Cassese, Leopoldo, 1958. "Agostino Nifo a Salerno," in *Rassegna storica salernitana* 19, *Appendice*, pp. 3–17.

Castellani, Carlo, 1981. "Aldrovandi, Ulisse." *DSB*, 1:108–10.

Catalano, Michele, 1934. "L'Università di Catania nel Rinascimento," in *Storia della Università di Catania dalle origini ai giorni nostri*. Catania, pp. 3–98.

Catalano-Tirrito, Michele, 1975. *Storia documentata della R. Università di Catania nel secolo XV. Appendice*. Catania, 1913; rpt. Bologna.

Catarinella, Annamaria, and Salsotto, Irene, 1998. "L'università e i collegi," in *Storia di Torino*. Vol. 3: *Dalla dominazione francese alla ricomposizione dello Stato (1536–1630)*, edited by Giuseppe Ricuperati. Turin, pp. 523–67.

Catoni, Giuliano, 1973. "Genesi e ordinamento della Sapienza di Siena," *Studi senesi* 85:155–98.

——, 1991. "Le riforme del Granduca, le 'serre' degli scolari e i lettori di casa," in *L'Università di Siena,* pp. 45–66.

Caturegli, Natale, 1942–1944. "Le origini dello Studio di Pisa," *Bollettino storico pisano* 11–13:1–16.

Cavagna, Anna Giulia, 1981. *Libri e tipografi a Pavia nel Cinquecento: Note per la storia dell'Università e della cultura.* Milan.

Cavallar, Osvaldo, 1991. *Francesco Guicciardini Giurista: I ricordi degli onorari.* Milan.

Cavina, Marco, 1988. "Ricerche su Agostino Berò, canonista e consiliatore bolognese (1474 ca.–1554)," *Studi senesi* 100:385–440.

CCCL anniversario della Università di Messina (contributo storico). 1900. Messina.

Cecchi, Dante, 1979. *Macerata e il suo territorio: La storia.* Milan.

Cesca, Giovanni, 1900. "L'Università di Messina e la Compagnia di Gesù," in *CCCL anniversario della Università di Messina (contributo storico).* Messina, pt. 1, pp. 3–36.

Cessi, Roberto, 1909. "La biblioteca di Prosdocimo de' Conti," *Bollettino del Museo civico di Padova* 12:140–48.

——, 1921–1922. "L'Università giurista di Padova ed i Gesuiti alla fine del Cinquecento," *Atti del Reale Istituto veneto di scienze, lettere ed arti,* vol. 81, pt. 2, pp. 585–601.

Chamard, Henri, 1951. "Muret, Marc-Antonine," in *Dictionnaire des Lettres Françaises. Le seizième siècle,* edited by A. Pauphilet, L. Pichard, and R. Barroux. Paris, pp. 531–33.

Chambers, David S., 1976. "Studium Urbis and *gabella studii*: The University of Rome in the Fifteenth Century," in *Cultural Aspects of the Italian Renaissance. Essays in Honour of Paul Oskar Kristeller,* edited by Cecil H. Clough. Manchester, England, pp. 68–110.

Chiaudano, Mario, 1972a. "I lettori dell'Università di Torino ai tempi di Carlo Emanuele I (1580–1630)," in *L'Università di Torino nei sec. XVI e XVII.* Turin, pp. 139–217.

——, 1972b. "I lettori dell'Università di Torino ai tempi di Emanuele Filiberto (1566–1580)," in *L'Università di Torino nei sec. XVI e XVII.* Turin, pp. 69–137.

——, 1972c. "La restaurazione della Università di Torino per opera di Emanuele Filiberto," in *L'Università di Torino nei sec. XVI e XVII.* Turin, pp. 51–67.

Chiellini, Sabrina, 1991. "Contributo per la storia degli insegnamenti umanistici dello studio ferrarese (XIV–XVII secolo)," in *La rinascita del sapere,* pp. 210–45.

Chodorow, Stanley, 1986. "Law, Canon: After Gratian," in *Dictionary of the Middle Ages.* New York, vol. 7, pp. 413–17.

Ciferri, Raffaele, 1961. "Dal lettorato dei semplici all'istituto ed orto botanico ed istituti annessi," in *Discipline e maestri dell'ateneo pavese.* Pavia, pp. 153–64.

Clagett, Marshall, 1964. *Archimedes in the Middle Ages.* Vol. 1: *The Arabo-Latin Tradition.* Madison, Wisc.

——, 1978. *Archimedes in the Middle Ages.* Vol. 3 in four parts: *The Fate of the Medieval Archimedes, 1300–1565.* Philadelphia.

——, 1981. "Archimedes." *DSB,* 1:213–31.

Clough, Cecil H., 1965. "Becichemo, Marino." *DBI,* 7:511–15.

Cobban, Alan B., 1990. *The Medieval English Universities: Oxford and Cambridge to c. 1500.* Aldershot, England, 1988; rpt. Berkeley and Los Angeles.

Colini-Baldeschi, Luigi, 1900. "L'insegnamento pubblico a Macerata nel trecento e quattrocento," *Rivista delle biblioteche e degli archivi* 11:19–26.

Il Collegio Ghislieri, 1966–1970. *Il Collegio Universitario Ghislieri di Pavia, istituzione della Riforma Cattolica (1567–1860).* 2 vols. Milan.

I collegi universitari, 1991. *I collegi universitari in Europa tra il XIV e XVIII secolo.* Atti del Convegno di Studi della Commissione Internazionale per la Storia delle Università.

Siena-Bologna, 16–19 maggio 1988, edited by Domenico Maffei and Hilde De Ridder-Symoens. Milan.

Collett, Barry, 1985. *Italian Benedictine Scholars and the Reformation: The Congregation of Santa Giustina of Padua.* Oxford.

——, 1994. "Universities, Governments, and Reform: English Students at Ferrara during the Fifteenth and Sixteenth Centuries," in *Alla corte degli estensi: Filosofia e cultura a Ferrara nei secoli XV e XVI.* Atti del convegno internazionale di studi, Ferrara 5–7 marzo 1992, edited by Marco Bertuzzi. Ferrara, pp. 125–46.

Colli, Vincenzo, 1990. "Cattedre minori, letture universitarie e Collegio dei dottori di diritto civile a Bologna nel secolo XV," in *Sapere e/è potere,* vol. 3, pp. 135–78.

Colliva, Paolo, 1977. "Bologna dal XIV al XVIII secolo: 'Governo misto' o signoria senatoria?" in *Storia della Emilia Romagna,* edited by Aldo Berselli. Vol. 2: *L'età moderna.* Bologna, pp. 13–34.

Colombero, Carlo, 1982. "Colombo, Realdo." *DBI,* 27:241–43.

Comelli, Giambattista, 1912. "Laura Bassi e il suo primo trionfo," *SMUB,* vol. 3, pp. 197–256.

Comparato, Vittor I., 1968. "Bigazzini, Girolamo." *DBI,* 10:404–5.

Contarini, Giambattista, 1769. *Notizie storiche circa li pubblici professori nello Studio di Padova scelti dall'ordine di San Domenico.* Venice.

Contarino, Rosario, 1986. "Dal Pozzo, Francesco, detto il Puteolano." *DBI,* 32:213–16.

Conte, Emanuele, 1985a. *Accademie studentesche a Roma nel Cinquecento: De modis docendi et discendi in iure.* Rome.

——, 1985b. "Università e formazione giuridica a Roma nel Cinquecento," *La cultura* 2:328–46.

——, 1998. "Umanisti e Bartolisti tra i colleghi romani di Marc-Antoine Muret," in *L'università e la sua storia.* Origini, spazi istituzionali e pratiche didattiche dello *Studium* cittadino. Atti del Convegno di Studi (Arezzo, 15–16 novembre 1991), edited by Paolo Renzi. N.p., pp. 171–89.

Copenhaver, Brian P., and Schmitt, Charles B., 1992. *Renaissance Philosophy.* Oxford and New York.

Copleston, Frederick, 1962. *A History of Philosophy.* Vol. 2: *Mediaeval Philosophy.* Pt. 2: *Albert the Great to Duns Scotus.* Garden City, N.Y.

Cortese, Dino, 1975. "Rettifiche su alcuni maestri teologi al Santo tra Quattrocento e Cinquecento: Il maestro Sebastiano ed il maestro Nicolò Grassetto dell'Ordine dei Minori," *Il Santo: Rivista antoniana di storia dottrina arte* 15:275–95.

Cortese, Nino, 1924. "L'età spagnuola," in *Storia della Università di Napoli.* Naples, pp. 201–431.

——, 1965. *Cultura e politica a Napoli dal Cinque al Settecento.* Naples.

Cosenza, Mario E., 1962–67. *Biographical and Bibliographical Dictionary of Italian Humanists and of the World of Classical Scholarship in Italy.* 6 vols. Boston.

Costa, Emilio, 1902–3a. "Andrea Alciato nello Studio di Bologna," *Atti e memorie della R. Deputazione di storia patria per le provincie di Romagna,* ser. 3, 21:318–42.

——, 1902–3b. "Nuovi documenti intorno a Pietro Pomponazzi," *Atti e memorie della R. Deputazione di storia patria per le provincie di Romagna,* ser. 3, 21:277–317.

——, 1903–4. "La prima cattedra pomeridiana di diritto civile nello Studio bolognese durante il secolo XVI," *Atti e memorie della R. Deputazione di storia patria per le provincie di Romagna,* ser. 3, 22:213–52.

——, 1905. "Gerolamo Cardano allo Studio di Bologna," *Archivio storico italiano,* ser. 5, 35:425–36.

——, 1907a. "La prima cattedra d'umanità nello Studio bolognese durante il secolo XVI," *SMUB*, vol. 1, pp. 23–63.

——, 1907b. *Ulisse Aldrovandi e lo Studio bolognese nella seconda metà del secolo XVI.* Bologna.

——, 1908. "La cattedra di Pandette nello Studio di Bologna nei secoli XVII e XVIII," *SMUB*, vol. 1, pt. 2, pp. 181–95.

——, 1912. "Contributi alla storia dello Studio bolognese durante il secolo XVII," *SMUB*, vol. 3, pp. 1–88.

Cotton, Juliana Hill, 1973. "Caldiera, Giovanni." *DBI*, 16:626–28.

——, 1981. "Manardo, Giovanni." *DSB*, 9:74–75.

Courtenay, William J., 1982. "The Early Stages in the Introduction of Oxford Logic into Italy," in *English Logic in Italy in the 14th and 15th Centuries.* Acts of the 5th European Symposium on Medieval Logic and Semantics, Rome, November 10–14, 1980, edited by Alfonso Maierù. Naples, pp. 13–32.

Cozzi, Gaetano, 1994. "Fortuna, e sfortuna, della Compagnia di Gesù a Venezia," in *I Gesuiti e Venezia: Momenti e problemi di storia veneziana della Compagnia di Gesù.* Atti del Convegno di Studi, Venezia, 2–5 ottobre 1990, edited by Mario Zanardi, Padua, pp. 59–88.

Cranz, F. Edward, 1960–71. "Alexander Aphrodisiensis," in *Catalogus,* vol. 1, pp. 77–135; vol. 2, pp. 411–22.

——, 1971. *A Bibliography of Aristotle Editions 1501–1600 with Introduction and Indexes.* Baden-Baden.

——, 1976a. "Editions of the Latin Aristotle Accompanied by the Commentaries of Averroës," in *Philosophy and Humanism: Renaissance Essays in Honor of Paul Oskar Kristeller,* edited by Edward P. Mahoney. New York and Leiden, pp. 116–28.

——, 1976b. "The Renaissance Reading of the *De anima,*" in *Platon et Aristote à la Renaissance.* Paris, pp. 359–76.

Cranz, F. Edward, and Schmitt, Charles B., 1984. *A Bibliography of Aristotle Editions.* 2nd ed. with addenda and revisions. Baden-Baden.

Crapuli, Giovanni, 1969. *Mathesis universalis: Genesi di un'idea nel XVI secolo.* Rome.

Craveri, Piero, 1965. "Bellarmati, Marco Antonio." *DBI*, 7, pp. 607–09.

——, 1969. "Bolognetti, Giovanni." *DBI*, 11:326–27.

Cremascoli, Giuseppe, 1989. "La facoltà di teologia," in *Luoghi e metodi di insegnamento nell'Italia medioevale (secoli XII–XIV),* edited by Luciano Gargan and Oronzo Limone. Galatina, pp. 179–200.

Crescini, Angelo, 1965. *Le origini del metodo analitico: Il Cinquecento.* Udine.

Crespi, Mario, 1966. "Benedetti, Alessandro." *DBI*, 8:244–47.

Creytens, Raymond, O.P., 1942. "Le 'Studium Romanae Curiae' and le Maître du Sacré Palais," *Archivum Fratrum Praedicatorum* 12:5–83.

Criniti, N., 1965. "Bellone, Niccolò." *DBI*, 7:762–66.

Cunningham, Andrew, 1997. *The Anatomical Renaissance: The Resurrection of the Anatomical Projects of the Ancients.* Aldershot, England, and Brookfield, Vt., 1997.

d'Alatri, Mariano, 1978. "Panorama geografico, cronologico, e statistico sulla distribuzione degli *Studia* degli ordini mendicanti: Italia," in *Le scuole degli ordini mendicanti.* Todi, pp. 49–72.

D'Alessandro, Alessandro, 1980. "Materiali per la storia dello *Studium* di Parma (1545–1622)," in *Università, Principe, Gesuiti: La politica farnesiana dell'istruzione a Parma e Piacenza (1545–1622).* Rome, pp. 15–95.

Dall'Osso, Eugenio, 1981. "Aranzio, Giulio Cesare." *DSB*, 1:204.

Dal Nero, Domenico, 1991. "L'insegnamento della teologia in Europa e a Ferrara," in *La rinascita del sapere,* pp. 246–63.

Daly, John F., 1981. "Sacrobosco, Johannes de." *DSB,* 12:60–63.

D'Amelio, Giuliano, 1979. "Castro, Paolo di." *DBI,* 22:227–33.

D'Amico, John F., 1983. *Renaissance Humanism in Papal Rome: Humanists and Churchmen on the Eve of the Reformation.* Baltimore and London.

——, 1984. "The Progress of Renaissance Latin Prose: The Case of Apuleianism," *RQ* 37:351–92.

——, 1988. *Theory and Practice in Renaissance Textual Criticism: Beatus Rhenanus between Conjecture and History.* Berkeley, Los Angeles, and London.

——, 1993. *Roman and German Humanism, 1450–1550.* Edited by Paul F. Grendler. Aldershot, England.

Dao, Ettore, 1976. "Erasmus da Rotterdam (1469–1536) all'Università degli Studi di Torino per la laurea in Sacra Teologia: 4 settembre 1506," *Bollettino della Società per gli studi storici, archeologici ed artistici della provincia di Cuneo* 74:55–71.

Davi, Maria Rosa, 1995. *Bernardino Tomitano filosofo, medico e letterato (1517–1576): Profilo biografico e critico.* Trieste.

Davi Daniele, Maria R., 1983. "Bernardino Tomitano e la 'Quaestio de certitudine mathematicarum,' " in *Aristotelismo veneto e scienza moderna,* edited by Luigi Olivieri. 2 vols. Padua, vol. 2, pp. 607–21.

Davidsohn, Robert, 1977. *Storia di Firenze.* Vol. 4: *I primordi della civiltà fiorentina.* Pt. 3: *Il mondo della chiesa. Spiritualità ed arte. Vita pubblica e privata.* Translated by E. Dupré-Theseider. Florence, 1965; rpt. Florence.

Davies, Jonathan, 1992. "Marsilio Ficino: Lecturer at the Studio fiorentino," *RQ* 40:785–90.

——, 1995–1996. "Corruption of the Examination Process at the University of Florence," *History of Universities* 14:69–93.

——, 1997–99. " 'A Paper University'? The *Studio lucchese,* 1369–1487," *History of Universities* 15:262–306.

——, 1998. *Florence and Its University during the Early Renaissance.* Leiden, Boston, and Köln.

——, 2000. "The *Studio pisano* under Florentine Domination, 1406–1472," *History of Universities* 16:197–235.

Davies, Martin, 1988. "An Enigma and a Phantom: Giovanni Aretino and Giacomo Languschi," *Umanistica Lovaniensis: Journal of Neo-Latin Studies* 37:1–29.

De' Angelis, Francesca Romana, 1983a. "Corradi, Sebastiano." *DBI,* 29:322–23.

——, 1983b. "Correa, Tommaso." *DBI,* 29:419–21.

De Bellis, Daniela, 1975. "Niccolò Leonico Tomeo interprete di Aristotele naturalista," *Physis* 17:71–93.

——, 1980. "La vita e l'ambiente di Niccolò Leonico Tomeo," *Quaderni* 13:37–75.

De Bernardin, Sandro, 1975. "La politica culturale della Repubblica di Venezia e l'Università di Padova nel XVII secolo," *Studi veneziani* 16:443–502.

——, 1983. "I Riformatori dello Studio: Indirizzi di politica culturale nell'Università di Padova," in *Cultura veneta,* vol. 4, pt. 1, pp. 61–91.

De Caro, Gaspare, 1969. "Bolognetti, Alberto." *DBI,* 11:313–16.

De Ferrari, Augusto, 1978a. "Casseri, Giulio Cesare." *DBI,* 21:453–56.

——, 1978b. "Castelli, Bartolomeo." *DBI,* 21:685–86.

——, 1979a. "Cataldi, Pietro Antonio." *DBI,* 22:288–89.

——, 1979b. "Cavalieri, Bonaventura." *DBI,* 22:654–59.

——, 1980. "Cesalpino, Andrea." *DBI*, 24:122–25.

——, 1983a. "Conti, Ingolfo." *DBI*, 28:440–42.

——, 1983b. "Cortesi, Giovanni Battista." *DBI*, 29:763–65.

——, 1983c. "Corti, Matteo." *DBI*, 29:795–97.

De Frede, Carlo, 1960. *I lettori di umanità nello Studio di Napoli durante il Rinascimento.* Naples.

de Ghellinck, Joseph, 1948. *Le mouvement théologique du XIIe siècle.* 2nd enlarged ed. Bruges, Bruxelles, and Paris.

Dejob, Charles, 1970. *Marc'Antoine Muret: Un professeur français en Italie dans la second moitié du XVIe siècle.* Paris, 1881; rpt. Geneva.

Del Fante, Alessandra, 1980a. "Appunti sulla storia dello Studio di Piacenza durante l'età farnesiana," in *Università, Principe, Gesuiti: La politica farnesiana dell'istruzione a Parma e Piacenza.* Rome, pp. 97–131.

——, 1980b. "Lo Studio di Pisa in un manoscritto inedito di Francesco Verino Secondo," *Nuova rivista storica* 64:396–420.

Del Giudice, Pasquale, 1923. *Storia del diritto italiano.* Vol. 2: *Fonti: legislazione e scienza giuridica dal secolo decimosesto ai giorni nostri.* Milan.

Del Gratta, Rodolfo, 1980. *Acta Graduum Academiae Pisanae.* Vol. 1: *1543–1599.* Pisa.

——, 1983. *Libri Matricularum Studii Pisani, 1543–1609.* Pisa.

——, 1993a. "I docenti e le cattedre dal 1406 al 1543," in *L'Università di Pisa,* pp. 481–502.

——, 1993b. "L'età della dominazione fiorentina (1406–1543)," in *L'Università di Pisa,* pp. 33–78.

Delhaye, Philippe, 1961. *Pierre Lombard: Sa vie, ses oeuvres, sa morale.* Montréal and Paris.

Della Torre, Maria Assunta, 1968. *Studi su Cesare Cremonini: Cosmologia e logica nel tardo aristotelismo padovano.* Padua.

Del Nero, Domenico, 1996. *La corte e l'università: Umanisti e teologi nel Quattrocento Ferrarese.* Prefazione di Franco Cardini. N.p.

Denley, Peter, 1981. "Recent Studies on Italian Universities of the Middle Ages and Renaissance," *History of Universities* 1:193–205.

——, 1988. "Academic Rivalry and Interchange: The Universities of Siena and Florence," in *Florence and Italy: Renaissance Studies in Honour of Nicolai Rubinstein,* edited by Peter Denley and Caroline Elam. London, pp. 193–208.

——, 1991a. "The Collegiate Movement in Italian Universities in the Late Middle Ages," *History of Universities* 10:29–91.

——, 1991b. "Dal 1357 alla caduta della Repubblica," in *L'Università di Siena,* pp. 27–44.

——, 1993. "The Vocabulary of Italian Colleges to 1500," in *Vocabulaire des collèges universitaires (XIIIe–XVIe siècles),* edited by Olga Weijers. Turnhout, pp. 72–79.

De Renzi, Salvatore, 1852–59. *Collectio Salernitana: Documenti inediti e trattati di medicina appartenenti alla Scuola Medica Salernitana.* 5 vols. Naples.

De Rosa, Stefano, 1983a. *Una biblioteca universitaria del secondo '600: La Libraria di Sapienza dello studio pisano (1666–1700).* Florence.

——, 1983b. "Studi sull'Università di Pisa, II: La riforma e il paradosso: Girolamo da Sommaja Provveditore dello Studio Pisano (1614–1636)," *History of Universities* 3:101–25.

Diffley, P. B., 1988. *Paolo Beni: A Biographical and Critical Study.* Oxford.

Di Napoli, Giovanni, 1963. *L'immortalità dell'anima nel Rinascimento.* Turin.

——, 1977. "Religione e filosofia nel Rinascimento," in *Grande antologia filosofica,* edited by M. F. Sciacca, A. M. Moschetti, and M. Schiavone. Vol. 9: *Il pensiero della rinascenza e della riforma (Protestantesimo e Riforma Cattolica).* Milan, pp. 1855–2038.

Dionisotti, Carlo, 1968. *Gli umanisti e il volgare fra Quattro e Cinquecento.* Florence.

——, 1971. "Filologia umanistica e testi giuridici fra Quattro e Cinquecento," in *La critica del testo. II congresso internazionale della Società italiana di storia del diritto. Venezia 18–22 sett. 1967.* 2 vols. Florence, vol. 1, pp. 189–204.

Di Renzo Villata, Gigliola, 1992. "Dotti, Paolo." *DBI,* 41:543–48.

Di Rienzo, Eugenio, 1994. "La Religione di Cardano: Libertinismo e Eresia nell'Italia della Controriforma," in *Girolamo Cardano: Philosoph, Naturforscher, Arzt,* edited by Eckhard Kessler. Wiesbaden, pp. 49–76.

Discipline e maestri, 1961. *Discipline e maestri dell'Ateneo pavese.* Pavia.

Di Trocchio, Federico, 1979. "Cermisone, Antonio." *DBI,* 23:773–74.

Dod, Bernard G., 1982. "Aristoteles latinus," in *CHLMP,* pp. 45–79.

Dollo, Corrado, 1984. *Modelli scientifici e filosofici nella Sicilia spagnola (con inediti di G. Moleto, M. Malpighi, J. Caramuel).* Naples.

Donahue, Charles, Jr., 1986. "Law, Civil: *Corpus Iuris,* Revival and Spread." *Dictionary of the Middle Ages.* New York, vol. 7, pp. 418–25.

Donati, Benvenuto, 1924. "Lettore leggista e scolari modenesi all'Università di Macerata nei primi anni del Seicento," *Archivio giuridico* 92:189–209.

Donnelly, John Patrick, 1982. "The Jesuit College at Padua: Growth, Suppression, Attempts at Restoration: 1552–1606," *Archivum Historicum Societatis Iesu* 51:45–79.

Dorati da Empoli, Maria Cristina, 1980. "I lettori dello Studio e i maestri di grammatica a Roma da Sisto IV ad Alessandro VI," *Rassegna degli Archivi di Stato* 40:98–147.

Drachmann, A. G., and Mahoney, Michael S., 1981. "Hero of Alexandria." *DSB,* 6:310–15.

Dunbabin, Jean, 1982. "The Reception and Interpretation of Aristotle's *Politics,*" in *CHLMP,* pp. 723–37.

Dupuigrenet Desroussilles, François, 1980. "L'Università di Padova dal 1405 al Concilio di Trento," in *Cultura veneta,* vol. 3, pt. 2, pp. 607–47.

Durling, Richard J., 1961. "A Chronological Census of Renaissance Editions and Translations of Galen," *Journal of the Warburg and Courtauld Institutes* 24:230–305.

Edwards, William F., 1976. "Niccolò Leoniceno and the Origins of Humanist Discussion of Method," in *Philosophy and Humanism: Renaissance Essays in Honor of Paul Oskar Kristeller,* edited by Edward P. Mahoney. New York, pp. 283–305.

Elsener, Ferdinand, 1972. "Doctor in decretis 'per saltum et bullam'? Zur Frage der Anerkennung eines Doktorgrades im kanonischen Recht im Streit um eine Pfründenbesetzung beim Konstanzer Domkapitel," in *Festgabe für Paul Staerkle zu seinem achtzigsten Geburtstag am 26. März 1972.* St. Galler Kultur und Geschichte, 2. St. Gall, pp. 83–91.

Encyclopedia of the Renaissance, 1999. *Encyclopedia of the Renaissance.* Edited by Paul F. Grendler et al. 6 vols. New York.

Ermini, Giuseppe, 1971. *Storia della Università di Perugia.* Rev. and expanded ed. Vol. 1. Florence.

Esposito, Anna, 1992. "Le 'Sapientie' romane: I collegi Capranica e Nardini e lo 'Studium Urbis,'" in *Roma e lo Studium Urbis,* pp. 40–68.

——, 1993. "I collegi universitari di Roma: Progetti e realizzazioni tra XIV e XV secolo," in *Vocabulaire des collèges universitaires (XIIIe–XVIe siècles).* Turnhout, pp. 80–89.

Fabris, Giovanni, 1939–40. "Gli scolari illustri della Università di Padova," in *Atti e memorie della R. Accademia di scienze lettere ed arti in Padova,* Classe di scienze morali, vol. 56, pp. 287–342.

——, 1942. "Professori e scolari greci all'Università di Padova," *Archivio veneto,* ser. 5, vol. 30, anno 72, pp. 121–65.

Fabroni, Angelo, 1971. *Historiae Academiae Pisanae*. 3 vols. Pisa, 1791–95; rpt. Bologna.

Facciolati, Jacopo, 1978. *Fasti Gymnasii Patavini*. 3 vols. Padua, 1757; rpt. in one volume. Bologna.

Falaschi, Pier Luigi, 1988. "Della Cornia, Pier Filippo." *DBI*, 36:772–77.

Fanti, Mario, 1978. "Bologna nell'età moderna (1506–1796)," in *Storia di Bologna*. Bologna, pp. 197–282.

Fantuzzi, Giovanni, 1965. *Notizie degli scrittori bolognesi*. 9 vols. Bologna, 1781–94; rpt. Bologna.

Farge, James K., 1985. *Orthodoxy and Reform in Early Reformation France: The Faculty of Theology of Paris, 1500–1543*. Leiden.

——, 1999. "Erasmus, the University of Paris, and the Profession of Theology," in *Erasmus of Rotterdam Society Yearbook* 19:18–46.

Favaro, Antonio, 1878. *Lo Studio di Padova e la Compagnia di Gesù sul finire del secolo decimosesto*. Venice.

——, 1911. "Nuovi documenti sulla vertenza tra lo Studio di Padova e la Compagnia di Gesù sul finire del secolo decimosesto," *Nuovo archivio veneto*, ser. 3, 21:89–100.

——, 1915. "Informazione storica sullo Studio di Padova circa l'anno 1580." *Nuovo archivio veneto*, ser. 3, 30:247–61.

——, 1917. "I successori di Galileo nello Studio di Padova fino alla caduta della Repubblica," *Nuovo archivio veneto*, ser. 3, 33:96–182.

——, 1918. "Lo Studio di Padova nei Diarii di Marino Sanuto," *Nuovo archivio veneto*, ser. 3, 36:65–128.

——, 1922. "I lettori di matematiche nella Università di Padova dal principio del secolo XIV alla fine del XVI," in *Memorie e documenti per la storia della Università di Padova*. Padua, vol. 1, pp. 1–70. Only volume published.

——, 1966. *Galileo Galilei e lo Studio di Padova*. 2 vols. Florence, 1883; rpt. Padua.

——, 1968. *Galileo Galilei a Padova: Ricerche e scoperte, insegnamento, scolari*. Padua.

Favaro, Giuseppe, 1928. *Gabrielle Falloppia modenese (MDXXIII–MDLXII): Studio biografico*. Modena.

Fedalto, Giorgio, 1984. "Stranieri a Venezia e a Padova, 1550–1700," in *Cultura veneta*, vol. 4, pt. 2, pp. 251–79.

Federici Vescovini, Graziella, 1979. *Astrologia e scienza: La crisi dell'aristotelismo sul cadere del Trecento e Biagio Pelacani da Parma*. Florence.

——, 1982. "Il commento di Angelo di Fossombrone al *De tribus praedicamentis* di Guglielmo Heytesbury," in *English Logic in Italy in the Fourteenth and Fifteenth Centuries*, edited by Alfonso Maierù. Naples, pp. 359–74.

Fenlon, Dermot, 1972. *Heresy and Obedience in Tridentine Italy: Cardinal Pole and the Counter Reformation*. Cambridge.

Fera, Vincenzo, 1988. "Polemiche filologiche intorno allo Svetonio del Beroaldo," in *The Uses of Greek and Latin: Historical Essays*, edited by A. C. Dionisotti, Anthony Grafton, and Jill Kraye. London, pp. 71–87.

Ferrari, Giovanna, 1987. "Public Anatomy Lessons and the Carnival: The Anatomy Theatre of Bologna," *Past and Present* 117 (November 1987): 50–106.

Ferrari, Henri-Maxime, 1977. *Une chaire de medicine au xvᵉ siècle: Un professeur à l'Université de Pavie de 1432 à 1472*. Paris, 1899; rpt. Geneva.

Ferraro, Joanne M., 1993. *Family and Public Life in Brescia, 1580–1650: The Foundations of Power in the Venetian State*. Cambridge.

Ficker, Julius, 1961. *Forschungen zur Reichs- und Rechtsgeschichte Italiens*. 4 vols. N.p., 1868–74; rpt. Aalen.

Field, Arthur, 1983. "The *Studium Florentinum* Controversy, 1455," *History of Universities* 3:31–59.

———, 1986. "Cristoforo Landino's First Lectures on Dante," *RQ* 39:16–48.

———, 1988. *The Origins of the Platonic Academy in Florence.* Princeton, N.J.

Fierz, Markus, 1983. *Girolamo Cardano, 1501–1576: Physician, Natural Philosopher, Mathematician, Astrologer, and Interpreter of Dreams.* Translated by Helga Niman. Boston, Basel, and Stuttgart.

Filangieri di Candida, Riccardo, 1924. "L'età aragonese," in *Storia della Università di Napoli.* Naples, pp. 151–99.

Findlen, Paula, 1993. "Science as a Career in Enlightenment Italy: The Strategies of Laura Bassi," *Isis* 84:441–69.

———, 1994. *Possessing Nature: Museums, Collecting, and Scientific Culture in Early Modern Italy.* Berkeley, Los Angeles, and London.

Fioravanti, Gianfranco, 1981. *Università e città: Cultura umanistica e cultura scolastica a Siena nel '400.* Florence. This book reprints two articles that appeared in *Rinascimento,* ser. 2, 19 (1979): 117–67; and 20 (1980): 87–159.

———, 1991a. "Le *arti liberali* nei secoli XIII–XV," in *L'Università di Siena,* pp. 255–71.

———, 1991b. "La fondazione dello Studio fiorentino a Pisa ed un poemetto in lode di Lorenzo il Magnifico," in *Filosofia e cultura: Per Eugenio Garin,* edited by Michele Ciliberto and Cesare Vasoli. 2 vols. Rome, vol. 1, pp. 173–82.

———, 1993. "La filosofia e la medicina (1343–1543)," in *L'Università di Pisa,* pp. 259–88.

Fiore, Francesco Paolo, 1986. "Danti, Ignazio." *DBI,* 32:659–63.

Firpo, Luigi, 1950–51. "Filosofia italiana e Controriforma," *Rivista di filosofia* 41:150–73; 42:30–47.

———, 1970. "The Flowering and Withering of Speculative Philosophy———Italian Philosophy and the Counter Reformation: The Condemnation of Francesco Patrizi," in *The Late Italian Renaissance,* edited by Eric Cochrane. New York, pp. 266–84.

Fletcher, J. M., 1986. "The Faculty of Arts," in *The History of the University of Oxford,* vol. 3: *The Collegiate University,* edited by James McConica. Oxford, pp. 157–99.

Foglietti, Raffaelo, 1878. *Cenni storici sull'Università di Macerata.* Macerata.

Forni, G. G., 1948. *L'insegnamento della chirurgia nello Studio di Bologna dalle origini a tutto il secolo XIX.* Bologna.

Fragnito, Gigliola, 1997. *La Bibbia al rogo: La censura ecclesiastica e i volgarizzamenti della Scrittura (1471–1605).* Bologna.

Franceschini, Adriano, 1970. *Nuovi documenti relativi ai docenti dello Studio di Ferrara nel sec. XVI.* Ferrara.

———, 1975. *Spigolature archivistiche prime.* Ferrara.

Francesco Filelfo, 1986. *Francesco Filelfo nel quinto centenario della morte.* Atti del XVII convegno di studi maceratesi (Tolentino, 27–30 settembre 1981). Padua.

Frati, Lodovico, 1908. "I due Beroaldi," *SMUB,* ser. 1, vol. 2, pp. 207–28.

———, 1930. "Lianoro de' Lianori ellenista bolognese," *SMUB,* ser. 1, vol. 10, pp. 163–77.

———, 1935. "Nuovi documenti su Pietro da Muglio," *SMUB,* ser. 1, vol. 12, pp. 81–95.

Freedman, Joseph S., 1985. "Philosophy Instruction within the Institutional Framework of Central European Schools and Universities during the Reformation Era," in *History of Universities* 5:117–66.

French, R. K., 1985. "Berengario da Carpi and the Use of Commentary in Anatomical Teaching," in *Medical Renaissance,* pp. 42–74, 296–98.

Fresco, Ulisse, 1901. *Origine dello studio generale in Macerata.* Camerino.

Frova, Carla, and Miglio, Massimo, 1992. " 'Studium Urbis' e 'Studium Curiae' nel

Trecento e nel Quattrocento: linee di politica culturale," in *Roma e lo Studium Urbis,* pp. 26–39.

Gaeta, Franco, 1955. *Lorenzo Valla: Filologia e storia nell'umanesimo italiano.* Naples.

——, 1964. "Barozzi, Pietro." *DBI,* 6:510–12.

Galafassi, Vittorio Emanuele, 1961. "Le glorie dell'Università di Pavia nelle discipline matematiche e fisiche," in *Discipline e maestri dell'Ateneo pavese.* Pavia, pp. 63–92.

Gallo, Rodolfo, 1963. "Due informazioni sullo Studio di Padova della metà del Cinquecento," *Archivio veneto,* ser. 5, 73: 17–100.

Garbari, Fabio, and Tongiorgi Tomasi, Lucia, 1993. "Il giardino dei semplici," in *L'Università di Pisa,* pp. 363–76.

Garbari, Fabio; Tongiorgi Tomasi, Lucia; and Tosi, Alessandro, 1991. *Giardino dei Semplici: L'Orto botanico di Pisa dal XVI al XX secolo.* Pisa.

García y García, Antonio, 1992. "The Faculties of Law," in *Universities in the Middle Ages,* pp. 388–408.

Gardenal, Gianna, 1975. *Il Poliziano e Suetonio: Contributo alla storia della filologia umanistica.* Florence.

——, 1986. "Merula, Giorgio," *Dizionario critico della letteratura italiana.* 4 vols. Turin, vol. 3, pp. 160–62.

Garfagnini, Gian Carlo, 1988. "Città e Studio a Firenze nel XIV secolo: Una difficile convivenza," *Critica storica* 25 (2): 182–201.

Gargan, Luciano, 1971. *Lo studio teologico e la biblioteca dei domenicani a Padova nel Tre e Quattrocento.* Padua.

Garin, Eugenio, 1947–1950. "Le traduzioni umanistiche di Aristotele nel secolo XV," *Atti e memorie dell'Accademia fiorentina di scienze morali "La Colombaria"* n.s. 2, 16:55–104.

——, 1961. *La cultura filosofica del Rinascimento italiano.* Florence.

——, 1966. *Storia della filosofia italiana.* 2nd rev. ed. 3 vols. Turin.

——, 1969. *L'età nuova: Ricerche di storia della cultura dal XII al XVI secolo.* Naples.

——, 1974. "Note in margine all'opera di Filippo Beroaldo il Vecchio," in *Tra latino e volgare: Per Carlo Dionisotti,* edited by G. Bernardoni Trezzini et al. 2 vols. Padua, vol. 2, pp. 437–56.

——, 1975. *Rinascite e rivoluzioni: Movimenti culturali dal XIV al XVIII secolo.* Rome and Bari.

Garosi, Alcide, 1958. *Siena nella storia della medicina (1240–1555).* Florence.

Geanakoplos, Deno John, 1989. *Constantinople and the West: Essays on the Late Byzantine (Palaeologan) and Italian Renaissances and the Byzantine and Roman Churches.* Madison, Wisc., and Milwaukee.

Giacobbe, Giulio Cesare, 1979. "Catena, Pietro." *DBI,* 22:325.

Giacomini, Valerio, 1959. *Alle origini della lettura dei semplici (1546) dell'orto dei semplici (1558) e dell'orto botanico (1773) nell'Università di Pavia.* Pavia.

——, 1969. "Bonafede, Francesco." *DBI,* 11:491–92.

Giacon, Carlo, 1944–50. *La seconda scolastica.* 3 vols. Milan.

Gibba, Alessandra, 1995–96. "Francesco de' Vieri (1524–1591) and His Teaching at the University of Pisa," *History of Universities* 14:143–55.

Gieysztor, Aleksander, 1992. "Management and Resources," in *Universities in the Middle Ages,* pp. 108–43.

Gilbert, Neal W., 1960. *Renaissance Concepts of Method.* New York.

——, 1971. "The Early Italian Humanists and Disputation," in *Renaissance Studies in Honor of Hans Baron,* edited by Anthony Molho and John A. Tedeschi. Dekalb, Ill., and Florence, pp. 201–26.

Gilmore, Myron P., 1963. *Humanists and Jurists: Six Studies in the Renaissance.* Cambridge, Mass.

———, 1967. "Beroaldo, Filippo, Senior." *DBI,* 9:382–84.

Gilson, Etienne, 1955. *History of Christian Philosophy in the Middle Ages.* New York.

Ginatempo, Maria, and Sandri, Lucia, 1990. *L'Italia delle città: Il popolamento urbano tra Medioevo e Rinascimento (secoli XIII–XVI).* Florence.

Gioelli, Felice, 1970. "Gaspare Gabrieli. Primo lettore dei semplici nello Studio di Ferrara (1543)," *Atti e memorie della Deputazione Provinciale Ferrarese di Storia Patria,* ser. 3, 10: 1–74.

Gios, Pierantonio, 1977. *L'attività pastorale del vescovo Pietro Barozzi a Padova (1487–1507).* Padua.

Girolamo Cardano, 1994. *Girolamo Cardano: Philosoph, Naturforscher, Arzt.* Edited by Eckhard Kessler. Wolfenbütteler Abhandlungen zur Renaissanceforschung, 15. Wiesbaden, 1994.

Giuffrida, Tino, 1981. *Catania dalla dominazione sveva alla dominazione spagnola.* Vol. 2: *Storia, Personaggi, Cultura.* Catania.

I Giunti di Firenze, 1978. *I Giunti tipografi editori di Firenze, 1497–1570: Annali.* Edited by Decio Decia, Renato Delfiol, and Luigi Silvestro Camerini. Florence.

Gleason, Elisabeth G., 1993. *Gasparo Contarini: Venice, Rome, and Reform.* Berkeley, Los Angeles, and Oxford.

Gliozzi, Giuliano, 1972. "Brasavola, Antonio." *DBI,* 14:51–53.

———, 1974a. "Canani, Antonio Maria." *DBI,* 17:712–13.

———, 1974b. "Canani, Giovanni Battista." *DBI,* 17:714–16.

———, 1976. "Capuano, Francesco." *DBI,* 19:255–57.

Gliozzi, Mario, 1976. "Cardano, Gerolamo." *DBI,* 19:758–63.

———, 1981. "Cardano, Girolamo." *DSB,* 3:64–67.

Gnudi, Martha Teach, and Webster, Jerome Pierce, 1950. *The Life and Times of Gaspare Tagliacozzi Surgeon of Bologna, 1545–1599: With a Documented Study of the Scientific and Cultural Life of Bologna in the Sixteenth Century.* New York.

Godman, Peter, 1998. *From Poliziano to Machiavelli: Florentine Humanism in the High Renaissance.* Princeton, N.J.

Goffis, Cesare Federico, 1971. "Giovanni di ser Buccio da Spoleto," *Enciclopedia Dantesca.* 5 vols. and *Appendice.* Rome, 1970–78, vol. 3, p. 192.

Goldthwaite, Richard A., 1980. *The Building of Renaissance Florence: An Economic and Social History.* Baltimore and London.

Grabmann, Martin, 1961. *Die Geschichte der Katholischen Theologie seit dem Ausgang der Väterzeit: Mit Benützung von M. J. Scheebens Grundriss dargestellt.* Freiburg im Breisgau, 1933; rpt. Darmstadt.

Grafton, Anthony, 1983. *Joseph Scaliger: A Study in the History of Classical Scholarship.* Vol. 1: *Textual Criticism and Exegesis.* Oxford.

———, 1985. "Renaissance Readers and Ancient Texts," *RQ* 38:615–49.

———, 1988a. "The Availability of Ancient Works," in *CHRP,* pp. 767–91.

———, 1988b. "Quattrocento Humanism and Classical Scholarship," in *Renaissance Humanism,* vol. 3, pp. 23–66.

———, 1999. *Cardano's Cosmos. The Worlds and Works of a Renaissance Astrologer.* Cambridge, Mass., and London.

Grafton, Anthony, and Jardine, Lisa, 1986. *From Humanism to the Humanities: Education and the Liberal Arts in Fifteenth- and Sixteenth-Century Europe.* Cambridge, Mass.

Greci, Roberto, 1998. "Una duttile università 'di frontiera:' lo Studio parmense nel XV secolo," in *Le Università minori in Europe (secoli XV–XIX).* Convegno Internazionale di

Studi, Alghero, 30 Ottobre–2 Novembre 1996, edited by Gian Paolo Brizzi and Jacques Verger. Catanzaro, pp. 75–94.

Greek Literature, 1985. *The Cambridge History of Classical Literature.* Vol. 1: *Greek Literature.* Edited by P. E. Easterling and B. M. Knox. Cambridge.

Gregory, Tullio, 1953. "L'*Apologia ad censuram* di Francesco Patrizi," *Rinascimento* 4:89–104.

——, 1955. "L'*Apologia* e le *Declarationes* di F. Patrizi," in *Medioevo e rinascimento: Studi in onore di Bruno Nardi.* 2 vols. Florence, vol. 1, pp. 385–424.

Grendler, Paul F., 1977. *The Roman Inquisition and the Venetian Press, 1540–1605.* Princeton, N.J.

——, 1979. "The *Tre Savii sopra Eresia,* 1547–1605: A Prosopographical Study," *Studi veneziani,* n.s., 3:283–340.

——, 1989. *Schooling in Renaissance Italy: Literacy and Learning, 1300–1600.* Baltimore and London.

——, 1990a. "The Leaders of the Venetian State, 1540–1609: A Prosopographical Analysis," *Studi veneziani,* n.s., 19:35–85.

——, 1990b. "The University of Padua, 1405–1600: A Success Story," *History of Higher Education Annual* 10:7–17. Also in Grendler, 1995, study 11.

——, 1994. "Index de Rome, 1590, 1593, 1596: Introduction historique," in *Index de Rome 1590, 1593, 1596: Avec étude des index de Parme 1580 et Munich 1582.* Par J. M. De Bujanda, Ugo Rozzo, Peter G. Bietenholz, and Paul F. Grendler. Translated by Claude Sutto. *Index des livres interdits,* vol. 9. Sherbrooke and Geneva, pp. 271–309.

——, 1995. *Books and Schools in the Italian Renaissance.* Aldershot, England.

——, 1996a. "Intellectual Freedom in Italian Universities: The Controversy over the Immortality of the Soul," in *Le contrôle des idées a la Renaissance.* Actes de colloque de la FISIER tenu à Montréal en septembre 1995, edited by J. M. De Bujanda. Geneva, pp. 31–48.

——, 1996b. "Universities," in *The Oxford Encyclopedia of the Reformation,* edited by Hans Hillerbrand et al. 4 vols. New York, vol. 4, pp. 196–201.

——, 1998. "How to Get a Degree in Fifteen Days: Erasmus' Doctorate of Theology from the University of Turin," *Erasmus of Rotterdam Society Yearbook* 18, pp. 40–69.

——, 1999a. "Cornaro Piscopia, Elena Piscopia," in *Encyclopedia of the Renaissance,* edited by Paul F. Grendler et al. 6 vols. New York, vol. 3, pp. 86–87.

——, 1999b. "Universities," in *Encyclopedia of the Renaissance,* edited by Paul F. Grendler et al. 6 vols. New York, vol. 6, pp. 189–93.

——, in press. "Italian Schools and University Dreams during Mercurian's Generalate," in *The Society of Jesus during the Generalate of Evrard Mercurian, 1573–1580,* edited by Thomas M. McCoog. Rome.

Griffiths, Gordon, 1973. "Leonardo Bruni and the Restoration of the University of Rome (1406)," *RQ* 26:1–10.

Grubb, James S., 1996. *Provincial Families of the Renaissance: Private and Public Life in the Veneto.* Baltimore and London.

Gualandi, Giovanni, 1986. "Per la storia della *Editio princeps* delle Pandette fiorentine di Lelio Torelli," in *Le Pandette di Giustiniano: Storia e fortuna di un codice illustre.* Due giornate di studio, Firenze 23–24 giugno 1983. Florence, pp. 143–98.

Gualdo Rosa, Lucia, 1983. "Cortesi Urceo, Antonio, detto Codro." *DBI,* 29:773–78.

Guarini, Elena Fasano, 1960. "Aldobrandini, Cinzio." *DBI,* 2:102–3.

Guarini, Giacomo, 1970. *Ad ferrariensis Gymnasii historiam per Ferrantem Borsettum conscriptam supplementum et animadversiones.* 2 vols. in 1. Bologna, 1740–41; rpt. Bologna.

Gundersheimer, Werner L., 1973. *Ferrara: The Style of a Renaissance Despotism.* Princeton, N.J.

Gutierrez, David, 1983. *The Augustinians in the Middle Ages, 1357–1517.* Translated by Thomas Martin. Villanova, Pa.

——, 1984. *The Augustinians in the Middle Ages, 1256–1356.* Translated by Arthur J. Ennis. Villanova, Pa.

Hammer, William, 1940. "Balthazar Rasinus and His Praise of Studies at the University of Pavia," *Studies in Philology* 37:133–48.

——, 1948. "Balthazar Rasinus, Italian Humanist: A Critical and Bibliographical Appraisal," *Italica* 25:15–27.

Hankins, James, 1990. *Plato in the Italian Renaissance.* 2 vols. Leiden, New York, Kobenhavn, and Köln.

Hathaway, Baxter, 1962. *The Age of Criticism: The Late Renaissance in Italy.* Ithaca, N.Y.

Helbing, Mario Otto, 1989. *La filosofia di Francesco Buonamici, professore di Galileo a Pisa.* Pisa.

Hellman, C. Doris, and Swerdlow, Noel M., 1981. "Puerbach, Georg." *DSB,* 15:473–79.

Hinnebusch, William A., 1973. *The History of the Dominican Order.* Vol. 2: *Intellectual and Cultural Life to 1500.* New York.

Hudon, Wiliam V., 1996. "Gribaldi, Matteo," in *The Oxford Encyclopedia of the Reformation,* edited by Hans J. Hillerbrand et al. 4 vols. New York, vol. 4, pp. 194–95.

Hughes, Steven C., 1994. *Crime, Disorder and the Risorgimento: The Politics of Policing in Bologna.* Cambridge.

Hyde, J. K., 1972. "Commune, University, and Society in Early Medieval Bologna," in *Universities in Politics: Case Studies from the Late Middle Ages and Early Modern Period,* edited by J. W. Baldwin and R. A. Goldthwaite. Baltimore and London, pp. 17–45.

Ianziti, Gary, 1988. *Humanistic Historiography under the Sforzas: Politics and Propaganda in Fifteenth-Century Milan.* Oxford.

Ingegno, Alfonso, 1980. *Saggio sulla filosofia di Cardano.* Florence.

——, 1988. "The New Philosophy of Nature," in *CHRP,* pp. 236–63.

Iofrida, Manlio, 1993. "La filosofia e la medicina (1543–1737)," in *L'Università di Pisa,* pp. 289–338.

Iorio, Dominick A., 1991. *The Aristotelians of Renaissance Italy: A Philosophical Exposition.* Lewiston, N.Y, Queenston, Ontario., and Lampeter, Dyfed, Wales.

Iriarte, Lazaro, 1982. *Franciscan History: The Three Orders of St. Francis of Assisi.* Translated by Patricia Ross. Chicago.

Isnardi, Lorenzo, 1975. *Storia della Università di Genova.* 2 vols. Genoa, 1861–65; rpt. Bologna.

Jardine, Lisa, 1981. "Dialectic or Dialectical Rhetoric? Agostino Nifo's Criticism of Lorenzo Valla," *Rivista critica di storia della filosofia* 36:253–70.

——, 1988. "Humanistic Logic," in *CHRP,* pp. 173–98.

Jardine, Nicholas, 1988. "Epistemology of the Sciences," in *CHRP,* pp. 685–711.

Javitch, Daniel, 1991. *Proclaiming a Classic: The Canonization of Orlando Furioso.* Princeton, N.J.

Jayawardene, S. A., 1981a. "Bombelli, Rafael." *DSB,* 2:279–81.

——, 1981b. "Ferrari, Ludovico." *DSB,* 4:586–88.

——, 1981c. "Pacioli, Luca." *DSB,* 10:269–272.

Jedin, Hubert, 1961. *A History of the Council of Trent.* Vol. 2: *The First Sessions at Trent, 1545–1547.* Translated by Ernest Graf. London.

——, 1981. *Storia del Concilio di Trento*. Vol. 4, pt. 2: *Superamento della crisi per opera di Morone, chiusura e conferma*. Translated by Gino Cecchi and Giorgio Beari. Brescia.

Joly, Robert, 1981. "Hippocrates of Cos." *DSB*, 6:418–31.

Jongh, H. de, 1980. *L'anciènne faculté thèologie de Louvain au premier siècle de son existence (1432–1540): Ses débuts, son organisation, son enseignement, sa lutte contre Erasme et Luther: Avec des documents inédits*. Louvain, 1911; rpt. Utrecht.

Kallendorf, Craig, 1983. "Cristoforo Landino's *Aeneid* and the Humanist Critical Tradition," *RQ* 36:519–46.

——, 1989. *In Praise of Aeneas: Virgil and Epideictic Rhetoric in the Early Italian Renaissance*. Hanover and London.

Kallendorf, Craig, and Maria X. Wells, 1998. *Aldine Press Books at the Harry Ransom Humanities Research Center, The University of Texas at Austin: A Descriptive Catalogue*. Austin.

Keller, A. G., 1981. "Ghini, Luca." *DSB*, 5:383–84.

Kelley, Donald R., 1970. *Foundations of Modern Historical Scholarship: Language, Law, and History in the French Renaissance*. New York and London.

——, 1991. "Law," in *The Cambridge History of Political Thought, 1450–1700*, edited by J. H. Burns and Mark Goldie. Cambridge, pp. 66–94.

Kenny, Anthony, and Pinborg, Jan, 1982. "Medieval Philosophical Literature," in *CHLMP*, pp. 11–42.

Kessler, Eckhard, 1988. "The Intellective Soul," in *CHRP*, pp. 485–534.

King, Margaret L., 1986. *Venetian Humanism in an Age of Patrician Dominance*. Princeton, N.J.

Knod, Gustav C., 1970. *Deutsche Studenten in Bologna (1289–1562): Biographischer Index zu den Acta nationis Germanicae universitatis Bononiensis*. Berlin, 1899; rpt. Aalen.

Kohl, Benjamin G., 1983a. "Conti, Prosdocimo." *DBI*, 28:463–65.

——, 1983b. "Conversini, Giovanni." *DBI*, 28:574–78.

——, 1998. *Padua under the Carrara, 1318–1405*. Baltimore and London.

Krautter, Konrad, 1971. *Philologische Methode und Humanistische Existenz: Filippo Beroaldo und sein Kommentar zum Goldenen Esel des Apuleius*. Munich.

Kraye, Jill, 1988. "Moral Philosophy," in *CHRP*, pp. 303–86.

Kren, Claudia, 1983. "Astronomy," in *The Seven Liberal Arts in the Middle Ages*, edited by David L. Wagner. Bloomington, Ind., pp. 218–47.

Kristeller, Paul O., 1956a. "Francesco da Diacceto and Florentine Platonism in the Sixteenth Century," in Kristeller, *Studies in Renaissance Thought and Letters*. Rome, pp. 287–336.

——, 1956b. "The School of Salerno: Its Development and Its Contribution to the History of Learning," in Kristeller, *Studies in Renaissance Thought and Letters*. Rome, pp. 495–551. First published in 1945.

——, 1956c. "The University of Bologna in the Renaissance," *SMUB*, n.s., vol. 1, pp. 313–23.

——, 1961. "Un 'Ars dictaminis' di Giovanni del Virgilio," *Italia medioevale e umanistica* 4:181–200.

——, 1964a. *Eight Philosophers of the Italian Renaissance*. Stanford, Calif.

——, 1964b. *The Philosophy of Marsilio Ficino*. Translated by Virginia Conant. New York, 1943; rpt. Gloucester, Mass.

——, 1974. *Medieval Aspects of Renaissance Learning: Three Essays*. Edited and translated by Edward P. Mahoney. Durham, N.C.

——, 1979a. "Cattani da Diacceto, Francesco." *DBI*, 22:507–9.

——, 1979b. *Renaissance Thought and Its Sources.* Edited by Michael Mooney. New York.

——, 1985. "The Curriculum of the Italian Renaissance Universities from the Middle Ages to the Renaissance," *Proceedings of the PMR Conference,* Villanova, Pa., vol. 9, pp. 1–16.

——, 1986. *Studi sulla scuola medica salernitana.* Naples.

Kuhn, Heinrich C., 1996. *Venetischer Aristotelismus im Ende der aristotelischen Welt: Aspekte der Welt und des Denkens des Cesare Cremonini (1550–1631).* Frankfurt am Main.

Kuttner, Stephan, 1982. "The Revival of Jurisprudence," in *Renaissance and Renewal in the Twelfth Century,* edited by Robert L. Benson, Giles Constable, and Carol D. Lanham. Cambridge, Mass., pp. 299–323.

Laird, W. R., 1986. "The Scope of Renaissance Mechanics," *Osiris,* ser. 2, 2:43–68.

——, 1987. "Giuseppe Moletti's 'Dialogue on Mechanics' (1576)," *RQ* 40:209–23.

——, 1991. "Archimedes among the Humanists," *Isis* 82:629–38.

Lattis, James M., 1994. *Between Copernicus and Galileo: Christoph Clavius and the Collapse of Ptolemaic Cosmology.* Chicago and London.

Lawn, Brian, 1993. *The Rise and Decline of the Scholastic "Quaestio Disputata": With Special Emphasis on Its Use in the Teaching of Medicine and Science.* Leiden, New York, and Köln.

Lazzarini, Vittorio, 1950–51. "Crisi nello Studio di Padova a mezzo il Quattrocento," *Atti dell'Istituto veneto di scienze lettere ed arti,* Tomo 109, Classe di scienze morali e lettere, pp. 201–11.

Lee, Egmont, 1978. *Sixtus IV and Men of Letters.* Rome.

——, 1984. "Humanists and the 'Studium Urbis,' 1473–1484," in *Umanesimo a Roma nel Quattrocento,* edited by Paolo Brezzi and Maristella de Panizza Lorch. Rome and New York, pp. 127–146.

Leinkauf, Thomas, 1990. *Il neoplatonismo di Francesco Patrizi come presupposto della sua critica ad Aristotele.* Florence.

Lemay, Richard, 1981. "Gerard of Cremona." *DSB,* 15:173–92.

Leonardi, Claudio, 1961. "Angelo da Fossombrone." *DBI,* 3:227–28.

Lepori, Fernando, 1980. "La Scuola di Rialto dalla fondazione alla metà del Cinquecento," in *Cultura veneta,* vol. 3, pt. 2, pp. 539–605.

Levine, Edwin B., 1971. *Hippocrates.* New York.

Lewis, Mark W., 1995. "Preachers of Sound Doctrine, Followers of the True Religion, and Learned: The Social Impact of the Jesuit College of Naples, 1552–1600." Ph.D. diss., University of Toronto.

Lickteig, Franz-Bernard, 1981. *The German Carmelites at the Medieval Universities.* Rome.

Lines, David A., 1996. "The Importance of Being Good: Moral Philosophy in the Italian Universities, 1300–1600," *Rinascimento,* ser. 2, 36:139–93.

Liotta, Filippo, 1964. "Barigiani, Dionigi." *DBI,* 6:364–65.

Loach, Jennifer, 1986. "Reformation Controversies," in *The History of the University of Oxford,* vol. 3: *The Collegiate University,* edited by James McConica. Oxford, pp. 363–96.

Lockwood, Dean Putnam, 1951. *Ugo Benzi: Medieval Philosopher and Physician, 1376–1439.* Chicago.

Lohr, Charles H., 1967. "Medieval Latin Aristotle Commentaries: Authors A–F," *Traditio* 23:313–413.

——, 1968. "Medieval Latin Aristotle Commentaries: Authors G–I," *Traditio* 24:149–245.

——, 1970. "Medieval Latin Aristotle Commentaries: Authors Jacobus-Johannes Juff," *Traditio* 26:135–216.

——, 1971. "Medieval Latin Aristotle Commentaries: Authors Johannes de Kanthi-Myngodus," *Traditio* 27:251–351.

——, 1972. "Medieval Latin Aristotle Commentaries: Authors Narcissus-Richardus," *Traditio* 28:281–396.

——, 1973. "Medieval Latin Aristotle Commentaries: Authors Robertus-Wilgelmus," *Traditio* 29:93–197.

——, 1974a. "Medieval Latin Aristotle Commentaries: Supplementary Authors," *Traditio* 30:119–44.

——, 1974b. "Renaissance Latin Aristotle Commentaries: Authors A–B," *Studies in the Renaissance* 21:228–89.

——, 1975. "Renaissance Latin Aristotle Commentaries: Authors C," *RQ* 28:689–741.

——, 1976. "Renaissance Latin Aristotle Commentaries: Authors D–F," *RQ* 29:714–45.

——, 1977. "Renaissance Latin Aristotle Commentaries: Authors G–K," *RQ* 30:681–741.

——, 1978. "Renaissance Latin Aristotle Commentaries: Authors L–M," *RQ* 31:532–603.

——, 1979. "Renaissance Latin Aristotle Commentaries: Authors N–Ph," *RQ* 32:529–80.

——, 1980. "Renaissance Latin Aristotle Commentaries: Authors Pi–Sm," *RQ* 33:623–734.

——, 1982. "Renaissance Latin Aristotle Commentaries: Authors So–Z," *RQ* 35:164–256.

——, 1988a. "Metaphysics," in *CHRP,* pp. 537–638.

——, 1988b. "The Sixteenth-Century Transformation of the Aristotelian Natural Philosophy," in *Aristotelismus und Renaissance: In Memoriam Charles B. Schmitt,* edited by Eckhard Kessler, Charles H. Lohr, and Walter Sparn. Wiesbaden, 89–99.

Lombardi, Teodosio, 1995. "Presenza dei francescani nell'Università di Ferrara," in *"In supreme dignitatis . . .": Per la storia dell'Università di Ferrara, 1391–1991,* edited by Patrizia Castelli. Florence, pp. 53–59.

Lowry, Martin, 1979. *The World of Aldus Manutius: Business and Scholarship in Renaissance Venice.* Oxford.

——, 1991. *Nicholas Jenson and the Rise of Venetian Publishing in Renaissance Europe.* Oxford.

Luca Pacioli, 1998. *Luca Pacioli e la matematica del Rinascimento.* Atti del convegno internazionale di studi, Sansepolcro 13–16 aprile 1994. Edited by Enrico Giusti. Città di Castello.

Luzio, Alessandro, 1886. "Ercole Gonzaga allo Studio di Bologna," *Giornale storico della letteratura italiana* 8:374–86.

Luzzati, Michele, 1994. "Dottorati in medicine conferiti a Firenze nel 1472 da Judah Messer Leon da Montecchio a Bonaventura da Terracina e ad Abramo da Montalcino," in *Medicina e salute nelle Marche dal Rinascimento all'età napoleonica.* Atti del convegno Ancona-Recanati, 28–29–30 maggio 1992. 2 vols. Ancona, vol. 1, pp. 41–53.

Lytle, Guy Fitch, 1981. "Universities as Religious Authorities in the Later Middle Ages and Reformation," in *Reform and Authority in the Medieval and Reformation Church,* edited by Guy Fitch Lytle. Washington, D.C., pp. 69–97.

Maag, Karin, 1995. *Seminary or University? The Genevan Academy and Reformed Higher Education, 1560–1620.* Aldershot, England.

Maccagni, Carlo, 1993. "La matematica," in *L'Università di Pisa,* pp. 339–62.

Mack, Peter, 1993. *Renaissance Argument: Valla and Agricola in the Traditions of Rhetoric and Dialectic.* Leiden, New York, and Köln.

Maclean, Ian, 1992. *Interpretation and Meaning in the Renaissance: The Case of Law.* Cambridge.

Maddison, Francis, 1981. "Dondi, Giovanni." *DSB,* 4:164–65.

Maffei, Domenico, 1956. *Gli inizi dell'umanesimo giuridico.* Milan.

Mägdefrau, Karl, 1981. "Cesalpino, Andrea." *DSB,* 15:80–81.

Mahoney, Edward P., 1968. "Nicoletto Vernia and Agostino Nifo on Alexander of Aphrodisias: An Unnoticed Dispute," *Rivista critica di storia della filosofia* 23:268–96.

——, 1970a. "Agostino Nifo's Early Views on Immortality," *Journal of the History of Philosophy* 8:451–60.

——, 1970b. "Pier Nicola Castellani and Agostino Nifo on Averroës' Doctrine of the Agent Intellect," *Rivista critica di storia della filosofia* 25:387–409.

——, 1976a. "Agostino Nifo and Saint Thomas Aquinas," *Memorie Domenicane,* n.s., 7:195–226.

——, 1976b. "Nicoletto Vernia on the Soul and Immortality," in *Philosophy and Humanism: Renaissance Essays in Honor of Paul Oskar Kristeller,* edited by Edward P. Mahoney. Leiden and New York, pp. 144–63.

——, 1981. "Nifo, Agostino." *DSB,* 10:122–24.

——, 1982. "Neoplatonism, the Greek Commentators, and Renaissance Aristotelianism," in *Neoplatonism and Christian Thought,* edited by Dominic J. O'Meara. Studies in Neoplatonism: Ancient and Modern, vol. 3. Norfolk, Va., pp. 169–77, 264–82.

——, 1983. "Philosophy and Science in Nicoletto Vernia and Agostino Nifo," in *Scienza e filosofia,* pp. 135–202.

——, 1986. "Marsilio Ficino's Influence on Nicoletto Vernia, Agostino Nifo and Marcantonio Zimara," in *Marsilio Ficino e il ritorno di Platone: Studi e documenti,* edited by Gian Carlo Garfagnini. 2 vols. Florence, vol. 2, pp. 509–31.

Maierù, Alfonso, ed., 1982. *English Logic in Italy in the Fourteenth and Fifteenth Centuries.* Acts of the 5th European Symposium on Medieval Logic and Semantics, Rome, November 10–14, 1980. Naples.

——, 1989. "Gli atti scolastici nelle università italiane," in *Luoghi e metodi di insegnamento nell'Italia medioevale (secoli XII–XIV),* edited by Luciano Gargan and Oronzo Limone. Galatina, pp. 247–87.

——, 1994. *University Training in Medieval Europe.* Translated and edited by D. N. Pryds. Leiden, New York, and Köln.

Maiocchi, Rodolfo, and Moiraghi, Attilio, 1984. *San Carlo Borromeo studente a Pavia e gli inizi del collegio.* Pavia, 1912; rpt. Pavia.

Mango Tomei, Elsa, 1976. *Gli studenti dell'Università di Pisa sotto il regime granducale.* Pisa.

Marangoni, Giuseppe, 1901. "Lazzaro Bonamico e lo studio padovano nella prima metà del Cinquecento." *Nuovo archivio veneto,* ser. 3, 1: 118–51, 301–18; 2: 131–96.

Maraschio, Nicoletta, and Poggi Salani, Teresa, 1991. "L'insegnamento della lingua toscana," in *L'Università di Siena,* pp. 241–54.

Marcocchi, Massimo, 1966. "La personalità di Pio V e le direttive religiose, disciplinari e culturali delle costituzioni del collegio Ghislieri," in *Il collegio Ghislieri di Pavia: Istituzione della Riforma Cattolica (1567–1850).* Milan, vol. 1, pp. 91–129.

Mari, Paolo, 1979. "Castiglioni, Cristoforo." *DBI,* 22:140–46.

Marini, Gaetano, 1797. *Lettera . . . nella quale s'illustra il ruolo de' professori dell'Archiginnasio Romano.* Rome.

Marongiu, Antonio, 1948. "L'Università di Macerata nel periodo delle origini," *Annali della Università di Macerata* 17:3–73.

Marra, Filippo, 1975. *Chartularium per una storia dell'Università di Urbino. (1563–1799).* 2 vols. Urbino.

Marrara, Danilo, 1970. *Lo Studio di Siena nelle riforme del granduca Ferdinando I (1589 e 1591).* Milan.

——, 1993. "L'età medicea (1543–1737)," in *L'Università di Pisa,* pp. 79–190.

Marrou, Henri I., 1964. *A History of Education in Antiquity.* Translated by George Lamb. New York.

Martellotti, Guido, 1964. "Bartolomeo del Regno." *DBI,* 6:764–65.

——, 1965a. "Barzizza, Gasperino." *DBI,* 7:34–39.

——, 1965b. "Barzizza, Guiniforte." *DBI,* 7:39–41.

Martellozzo Forin, Elda, 1970. "Due professori di diritto alla ricerca di una condotta: Antonio da Burgos (1509) e Antonio Baculi da Cattaro (1549)," *Quaderni* 3:145–48.

——, 1971. "Studenti e dottori tedeschi a Padova nei secoli XV e XVI," *Quaderni* 4:49–102.

——, 1999. "Conti palatini e lauree conferite per privilegio: L'esempio padovano del sec. XV," *Annali di storia delle università italiane* 3:79–119.

Martines, Lauro, 1963. *The Social World of the Florentine Humanists, 1390–1460.* Princeton, N.J.

——, 1968. *Lawyers and Statecraft in Renaissance Florence.* Princeton, N.J.

Martinotti, G., 1911. "L'insegnamento dell'anatomia in Bologna prima del secolo xix," *SMUB,* vol. 2, pp. 1–146.

Maschietto, Francesco Ludovico, 1984. *Elena Lucrezia Cornaro Piscopia (1646–1684) prima donna laureata nel mondo.* Padua.

Masetti Zannini, Gian Ludovico, 1977. "Scuole maceratesi del Seicento nelle visite ad limina," in *Studi maceratesi 11: Vita e cultura del Seicento nella Marca.* Macerata, pp. 281–87.

Matsen, Herbert S., 1974. *Alessandro Achillini (1463–1512) and His Doctrine of "Universals" and "Transcendentals": A Study in Renaissance Ockhamism.* Lewisburg, Pa.

——, 1976. "Giovanni Garzoni (1419–1505) to Alessandro Achillini (1463–1512): An Unpublished Letter and Defense," in *Philosophy and Humanism: Renaissance Essays in Honor of Paul Oskar Kristeller,* edited by Edward P. Mahoney. New York, pp. 518–30.

——, 1977. "Students' 'Arts' Disputations at Bologna around 1500, Illustrated from the Career of Alessandro Achillini," *History of Education* 6:169–81.

——, 1985. "Selected Extant Latin Documents Pertaining to the 'Studio' of Bologna around 1500," in *Acta Conventus Neo-Latini Bononiensis.* Proceedings of the Fourth International Congress of Neo-Latin Studies, Bologna, August 26 to September 1, 1979, edited by R. J. Schoeck. Binghamton, N.Y., pp. 292–303.

——, 1994. "Students' 'Arts' Disputations at Bologna around 1500," in *RQ* 47:533–55.

Mayer, Ernst, 1968. *Italienische Verfassungsgeschichte von der Gothenzeit bis zur Zunftherrschaft.* 2 vols. Leipzig, 1909; rpt. Darmstadt.

Mazzacane, Aldo, 1974. "Campeggi, Giovanni Zaccaria." *DBI,* 17:449–53.

——, 1987. "Decio, Filippo." *DBI,* 33:554–60.

Mazzacurati, Giancarlo, 1961. *La crisi della retorica umanistica nel Cinquecento (Antonio Riccobono).* Naples.

——, 1966. "Beni, Paolo." *DBI,* 8:494–501.

Mazzoni, Francesco, 1970. "Francesco di Bartolo da Buti." *Enciclopedia Dantesca.* 5 vols. and *Appendice.* Rome, 1970–78, vol. 2, pp. 23–27.

McConica, James, 1996. "The Catholic Experience in Tudor Oxford," in *The Reckoned Expense: Edmund Campion and the Early English Jesuits.* Essays in Celebration of the First Centenary of Campion Hall, Oxford (1896–1996), edited by Thomas M. McCoog, S.J. Woodbridge, England, and Rochester, N.Y., pp. 39–63.

McCuaig, William, 1983. "Carlo Sigonio's Lectures on Aristotle's *Poetics*," *Quaderni* 16:43–69.

——, 1984. "Carlo Sigonio storico e la censura," *Atti e memorie della Deputazione di storia patria per le provincie di Romagna* 35:163–93.

——, 1989. *Carlo Sigonio: The Changing World of the Late Renaissance.* Princeton, N.J.

McDiarmid, John B., 1981. "Theophrastus." *DSB*, 13:328–34.

McGinness, Frederick J., 1995a. "The Collegio Romano, the University of Rome, and the Decline and Rise of Rhetoric in the Late Cinquecento," *Roma moderna e contemporanea* 3 (3): 601–22.

——, 1995b. *Right Thinking and Sacred Oratory in Counter-Reformation Rome.* Princeton, N.J.

McManamon, John M., 1989. *Funeral Oratory and the Cultural Ideals of Italian Humanism.* Chapel Hill, N.C., and London.

——, 1996. *Pierpaolo Vergerio the Elder: The Humanist as Orator.* Tempe, Ariz.

Mercer, R. G. G., 1979. *The Teaching of Gasparino Barzizza: With Special Reference to His Place in Paduan Humanism.* London.

Meschini, F. A., 1999. "Ghini, Luca." *DBI*, 53:767–71.

Method and Order, 1997. *Method and Order in Renaissance Philosophy of Nature: The Aristotle Commentary Tradition.* Edited by Daniel A. Di Liscia, Eckhard Kessler, and Charlotte Methuen. Aldershot, England, Brookfield, Vt., Singapore, and Sydney.

Miccoli, Giovanni, 1960a. "Adriani, Giovanni Battista." *DBI*, 1:308–9.

——, 1960b. "Adriani, Marcello Virgilio." *DBI*, 1:310–11.

Michael, Emily, 1993. "The Nature and Influence of Late Renaissance Paduan Psychology," *History of Universities* 12:65–94.

Mikkeli, Heikki, 1992. *An Aristotelian Response to Renaissance Humanism: Jacopo Zabarella on the Nature of Arts and Sciences.* Helsinki.

——, 1997. "The Foundation of an Autonomous Natural Philosophy: Zabarella on the Classification of Arts and Sciences," in *Method and Order in Renaissance Philosophy of Nature: The Aristotle Commentary Tradition,* edited by Daniel A. Di Liscia, Eckhard Kessler, and Charlotte Methuen. Aldershot, England, Brookfield, Vt., Singapore, and Sydney, pp. 211–28.

Minio-Paluello, Lorenzo, 1972. *Opuscula: The Latin Aristotle.* Amsterdam.

Minnich, Nelson H., 1986. "The Function of Sacred Scripture in the Decrees of the Fifth Lateran Council (1512–17)," *Annuarium Historiae Conciliorum* 18:319–29.

Minnucci, Giovanni, 1981b. "Rassegna bibliografica sulla storia dello Studio senese dalle origini fino alla prima metà del Cinquecento," *Studi senesi* 93:425–45.

——, 1991. "Professori e scolari giuristi nello Studio di Siena dalle origini alla fine del XV secolo," in *L'Università di Siena,* pp. 111–30.

——, 1995. "Il conferimento dei titoli accademici nello Studio di Siena fra XV e XVI secolo: Modalità dell'esame di laurea e provenienza studentesca," in *Università in Europa: Le istituzioni universitarie dal Medio Evo ai nostri giorni. Strutture, organizzazione, funzionamento.* Atti del Convegno Internazionale di Studi. Milazzo 28 Settembre–2 Ottobre 1993, edited by Andrea Romano. Messina, pp. 213–26.

Miscellanea Lombardiana, 1957. Novara.

Molho, Anthony, 1971. *Florentine Public Finances in the Early Renaissance, 1400–1433.* Cambridge, Mass.

Mondella, Felice, 1961. "Aranzio, Giulio Cesare." *DBI*, 3:720–21.

Mondolfo, Ugo Guido, 1897. "Il Ruolo dello Studio Senese del 16 ottobre 1500," in *Bullettino senese di storia patria* 9:412–17.

Monfasani, John, 1976. *George of Trebizond: A Biography and a Study of his Rhetoric and Logic.* Leiden.

——, 1983. "The Byzantine Rhetorical Tradition and the Renaissance," in *Renaissance Eloquence: Studies in the Theory and Practice of Renaissance Rhetoric,* edited by James J. Murphy. Berkeley, Los Angeles, and London, pp. 174–87.

——, 1984. Review of *Laurentii Valle Repastinatio dialectice et philosophie,* in *Rivista di letteratura italiana* 2:177–94. Also in Monfasani, 1994a, study 6, with the same pagination.

——, 1988. "Humanism and Rhetoric," in *Renaissance Humanism,* vol. 3, pp. 171–235. Also in Monfasani, 1994a, study 1.

——, 1990a. "L'insegnamento universitario e la cultura bizantina in Italia nel Quattrocento," in *Sapere e/è potere,* vol. 1, pp. 43–65.

——, 1990b. "Lorenzo Valla and Rudolph Agricola," *Journal of the History of Philosophy* 28:181–200. Also in Monfasani, 1994a, study 5.

——, 1991–92. *A Theologian at the Roman Curia in the Mid-Quattrocento: A Bio-biographical Study of Niccolò Palmieri, O.S.A.* Rome. This is a separate publication of the study appearing in *Analecta Augustiniana* 54 (1991): 321–81, and 55 (1992): 5–98.

——, 1992. *Fernando of Cordova: A Biographical and Intellectual Profile.* Transactions of the American Philosophical Society, vol. 82, pt. 6. Philadelphia.

——, 1993. "Aristotelians, Platonists, and the Missing Ockhamists: Philosophical Liberty in Pre-Reformation Italy," *RQ* 46:247–76.

——, 1994a. *Language and Learning in Renaissance Italy: Selected Articles.* Aldershot, England.

——, 1994b. "L'insegnamento di Teodoro Gaza a Ferrara," in *Alla corte degli Estensi: Filosofia, arte e cultura a Ferrara nei secoli XV e XVI.* Atti del convegno internazionale di studi, Ferrara, 5–7 marzo 1992, edited by Marco Bertozzi. Ferrara, pp. 5–17.

Montalenti, Giuseppe, 1960. "Aldrovandi, Ulisse." *DBI,* 2:118–24.

Monterosso Vacchelli, A. M., and Vasoli, Cesare, 1965. "Beldemandis, Prosdocimo de." *DBI,* 7:551–54,

Monti, Gennaro Maria, 1924. "L'età angioina," in *Storia della Università di Napoli.* Naples, pp. 17–150.

Moorman, John, 1968. *A History of the Franciscan Order from its Origins to the Year 1517.* Oxford.

Mor, Carlo Guido, 1952. *Storia della Università di Modena.* Modena.

Morandi, Ubaldo, 1966. "Benvoglienti, Girolamo." *DBI,* 8:702–3.

Moreni, Domenico, 1989. *Annali della tipografia fiorentina di Lorenzo Torrentino impressore ducale.* 2nd ed. Reprint edited by Mario Martelli. Florence, 1819; Florence.

Morin, Marco, 1982. *Armi antiche.* Milan.

Moschea, Rosario, 1991a. "Appendice. Eulogio di contropigilegio per lo studio (1630)," *Archivio storico messinese* 59:223–73.

——, 1991b. "Istruzione superiore e autonomie locali nella Sicilia moderna: Apertura e sviluppi dello *Studium Urbis Messanae* (1590–1641)," *Archivio storico messinese* 59:75–221.

Moyer, Ann E., 1992. *Musica Scientia: Musical Scholarship in the Italian Renaissance.* Ithaca, N.Y., and London.

Muccillo, Maria, 1981. "La vita e le opere di Aristotele nelle *Discussiones peripateticae* di Francesco Patrizi da Cherso," *Rinascimento,* ser. 2, 21:53–119.

——, 1986a. "Da Monte, Giovanni Battista." *DBI,* 32:365–67.

——, 1986b. "Marsilio Ficino e Francesco Patrizi da Cherso," in *Marsilio Ficino e il ritorno di Platone: Studi e documenti,* edited by Gian Carlo Garfagnini. 2 vols. Florence, vol. 2, pp. 615–79.

——, 1992. "Il platonismo all'Università di Roma: Francesco Patrizi," in *Roma e lo Studium Urbis,* pp. 200–47.

——, 1993a. "Eustachio, Bartolomeo." *DBI,* 43:531–36.

——, 1993b. "Fabrici d'Acquapendente, Girolamo." *DBI,* 43:768–74.

——, 1996. *Platonismo ermetismo e "prisca theologia": Ricerche di storiografia filosofica rinascimentale.* Florence.

Mugnai Carrara, Daniela, 1979. "Profilo di Nicolò Leoniceno," *Interpres* 2:169–212.

——, 1991. *La biblioteca di Nicolò Leoniceno. Tra Aristotele e Galeno: Cultura e libri di un medico umanista.* Florence.

——, 1994. "Nicolò Leoniceno e Giovanni Mainardi: aspetti epistemologici dell'umanesimo medico," in *Alla corte degli Estensi: Filosofia, arte e cultura a Ferrara nei secoli XV e XVI.* Atti del convegno internazionale di studi, Ferrara, 5–7 marzo 1992, edited by Marco Bertozzi. Ferrara, pp. 19–40.

Mulcahey, M. Michèle, 1998. *"First the Bow Is Bent in Study . . .": Dominican Education before 1350.* Toronto.

Muratori, Giulio, 1981. "Canano, Giovan Battista." *DSB,* 3:40–41.

Muratori, Giulio, and Bighi, Delfino, 1963–64. "Andrea Vesalio, G. B. Canano e la rivoluzione rinascimentale dell'anatomia e della medicina," *Acta medicae historiae Patavina* 10:59–95.

Murdoch, John, 1981. "Euclid: Transmission of the Elements." *DSB,* 4:437–59.

Murphy, Paul V., 1995. "Cardinal Ercole Gonzaga and Catholic Reform in Sixteenth-Century Italy (1505–1563)." Ph. D. diss., University of Toronto.

Nannizzi, Arturo, 1909. "I lettori dei Semplici nello Studio senese," *Bullettino senese di storia patria* 16:42–50.

Nardi, Bruno, 1958. *Saggi sull'aristotelismo padovano dal secolo XIV al XVI.* Florence.

——, 1960. "Achillini, Alessandro." *DBI,* 1:144–45.

——, 1965. *Studi su Pietro Pomponazzi.* Florence.

——, 1971. *Saggi sulla cultura veneta del Quattro e Cinquecento.* Edited by Paolo Mazzantini. Padua.

Nardi, Paolo, 1974. *Mariano Sozzini: Giureconsulto senese del Quattrocento.* Milan.

——, 1975. "Note sulla scuola giuridica senese negli anni della caduta della Repubblica," *Studi senesi* 87:195–220.

——, 1982. "Introduzione ad una ricerca sulle origini dello Studio di Siena," *Studi senesi* 94:348–61.

——, 1991. "Dalle origini al 1357." In *L'Università di Siena,* pp. 9–26.

——, 1996. *L'insegnamento superiore a Siena nei secoli XI–XIV: Tentative e realizzazioni dalle origini alla fondazione dello studio generale.* Milan.

Nasalli Rocca, Emilio, 1929. *Il trasferimento dello studio visconteo di Pavia a Piacenza dal 1398 al 1402.* Pubblicazioni della Università di Sacro Cuore. Serie V, Scienze storiche, vol. 8. Milan.

——, 1948. "Le cattedre di istituzioni legali nelle città italiane con particolare riguardo a Piacenza," *Rivista di storia del diritto italiano* 21:211–30.

——, 1970. "Filippo da Rocca," *Enciclopedia Dantesca.* 5 vols. and *Appendice.* Rome, 1970–78, vol. 2, p. 879.

Naso, Irma, 1997. "La scuola e l'università," in *Storia di Torino,* vol. 2: *Il basso Medioevo e la prima età moderna (1280–1536),* edited by Rinaldo Comba. Turin, pp. 597–615.

——, 1998. "Professori e studenti all'Università di Torino nel Quattrocento," in *Le università minori in Europa (secoli XV–XIX).* Convegno Internazionale di Studi, Alghero, 30

Ottobre–2 Novembre 1996, edited by Gian Paolo Brizzi and Jacques Verger. Catanzaro, pp. 103–17.

Nauert, Charles G., Jr., 1965. *Agrippa and the Crisis of Renaissance Thought.* Urbana, Ill.

——, 1973. "The Clash of Humanists and Scholastics: An Approach to Pre-Reformation Controversies," *Sixteenth Century Journal* 4:1–18.

——, 1979. "Humanists, Scientists, and Pliny: Changing Approaches to a Classical Author," *American Historical Review* 84:72–85.

——, 1980. "C. Plinius Secundus (*Naturalis Historia*)," in *Catalogus,* vol. 4, pp. 297–422.

——, 1998. "Humanism as Method: Roots of Conflict with the Scholastics," *Sixteenth Century Journal* 29:427–38.

Negruzzo, Simona, 1995. *Theologiam discere et docere: La facoltà teologica di Pavia nel XVI secolo.* Presentazione di Xenio Toscani. Bologna and Milan.

Nicolini, Fausto, 1966. *Saggio d'un repertorio biobibliografico di scrittori nati o vissuti nell'antico Regno di Napoli.* Naples.

Nicolini, Ugolino, 1961. "Dottori, scolari, programmi e salari alla Università di Perugia verso la metà del sec. XV," *Bollettino della deputazione di storia patria per l'Umbria* 58:139–59.

Nicolosi Grassi, Giuseppina, 1992. "L'insegnamento del diritto canonico nel primo secolo di vita dello 'Studium generale' di Catania (1444–1544)," in *Proceedings of the Eighth International Congress of Medieval Canon Law.* San Diego, University of California at La Jolla, August 21–27, 1988, edited by Stanley Chodorow. Vatican City, pp. 545–70.

North, John, 1992. "The *Quadrivium,*" in *Universities in the Middle Ages,* pp. 337–59.

Novarese, Daniela, 1994. *Istituzioni politiche e studi di diritto fra Cinque e Seicento: Il Messanense Studium Generale tra politica gesuitica e istanze egemoniche cittadine.* Milan.

——, 1995. "Strutture universitarie e mobilità studentesca nella Sicilia dell'età moderna," in *Università in Europa: Le istituzioni universitarie dal Medio Evo ai nostri giorni: Strutture, organizzazione, funzionamento.* Atti del Convegno Internazionale di Studi, Milazzo 28 Settembre–2 Ottobre 1993, edited by Andrea Romano. Soveria Mannelli and Messina, pp. 327–46.

Nutton, Vivian, 1985. "Humanist Surgery," in *Medical Renaissance,* pp. 76–99, 298–303.

——, 1988. "'Prisci dissectionum professores': Greek Texts and Renaissance Anatomists," in *The Uses of Greek and Latin. Historical Essays,* edited by A. C. Dionisotti, Anthony Grafton, and Jill Kraye. London, pp. 111–26.

——, 1997. "The Rise of Medical Humanism: Ferrara, 1464–1555," in *Renaissance Studies* 11:2–19.

Odoardi, Giovanni, 1948. "Fra Cornelio Musso, O. F. M. (1511–1574): Padre, oratore e teologo al Concilio di Trento," *Miscellanea Francescana* 48:223–42, 450–78.

Offelli, Siro, 1954. "Il pensiero del Concilio Lateranese V sulla dimostrabilità dell'immortalità dell'anima umana," *Studia patavina* 1:3–40.

Ohl, Ronald E., 1980. "The University of Padua, 1405–1509: An International Community of Students and Professors." Ph. D. diss., University of Pennsylvania.

Oliva, Cesare, 1926. "Note sull'insegnamento di Pietro Pomponazzi," *Giornale critico della filosofia italiana* 7:83–103, 179–90, 254–75.

Olmo, Antonino, 1984. "Cravetta, Aimone." *DBI,* 30:580–81.

O'Malley, C. D., 1964. *Andreas Vesalius of Brussels, 1514–1564.* Berkeley and Los Angeles.

——, 1981a. "Berengario da Carpi, Giacomo." *DSB,* 1:617–21.

——, 1981b. "Eustachi, Bartolomeo." *DSB,* 4:486–88.

——, 1981c. "Ingrassia, Giovanni Filippo." *DSB*, 7:16–17.

——, 1981d. "Varolio, Costanzo." *DSB*, 13:587–88.

O'Malley, John W., 1979. *Praise and Blame in Renaissance Rome: Rhetoric, Doctrine, and Reform in the Sacred Orators of the Papal Court, c. 1450–1521.* Durham, N.C.

Ongaro, Giuseppe, 1981. "La medicina nello Studio di Padova e nel Veneto," in *Cultura veneta,* vol. 3, pt. 3, pp. 75–134.

Origlia, Giangiuseppe, 1973. *Istoria dello Studio di Napoli.* 2 vols. Naples, 1753–54; rpt. Bologna.

Overfield, James H., 1984. *Humanism and Scholasticism in Late Medieval Germany.* Princeton, N.J.

Owen, G. E. L., 1981. "Aristotle: Method, Physics, and Cosmology." *DSB*, 1:250–58.

Paci, Libero, 1977. "Aspetti di vita ecclesiastica maceratese del Seicento," in *Studi maceratesi 11: Vita e cultura del Seicento nella Marca.* Macerata, pp. 288–358.

Palma, Marco, 1979. "Cavalli, Francesco." *DBI,* 22:724–25.

Palmer, Richard, 1983. *The "Studio" of Venice and Its Graduates in the Sixteenth Century.* Trieste and Padua.

——, 1985a. "Medical Botany in Northern Italy in the Renaissance," *Journal of the Royal Society of Medicine* 78:149–57.

——, 1985b. "Pharmacy in the Republic of Venice in the Sixteenth Century," in *Medical Renaissance,* pp. 100–17, 303–12.

Palumbi, Gennaro, 1961. "Profilo storico degli studi medico-biologici nell'ateneo ticinese," in *Discipline e maestri dell'ateneo pavese.* Pavia, 93–110.

Le Pandette di Giustiniano, 1986. *Le Pandette di Giustiniano: Storia e fortuna di un codice illustre.* Due giornate di studio, Firenze 23–24 giugno 1983. Florence.

Panebianco, Domenico, 1966–67. "I privilegi accordati dal Papa Clemente VIII ai medici del Collegio milanese nel 1597," *Archivio storico lombardo* 93–94:183–85.

——, 1969. "Un documento sull'anatomia a Pavia nel 1458," *Archivio storico lombardo* 96:313–15.

Panteghini, Gabriele, 1976. "La teologia speculativa al Santo dal Concilio di Trento al secolo XX," in *Storia e cultura al Santo,* edited by Antonino Poppi. Vicenza, pp. 415–83.

Paoletti, Lao, 1976. "Carbone, Ludovico." *DBI,* 19:699–703.

Papuli, Giovanni, 1967. *Girolamo Balduino: Ricerche sulla logica della Scuola di Padova nel Rinascimento.* Manduria.

Paratore, Ettore, 1967. "Beroaldo, Filippo, Iunior." *DBI,* 9:384–88.

Paravicini Bagliani, Agostino, 1989. "La fondazione dello 'Studium Curiae': Una rilettura critica," in *Luoghi e metodi di insegnamento nell'Italia medioevale (secoli XII–XIV),* edited by Luciano Gargan and Oranzo Limone. Galatina, pp. 57–81.

Pardi, Giuseppe, 1972. *Lo Studio di Ferrara nei secoli XV e XVI.* Ferrara, 1903; rpt. Bologna.

Park, Katherine, 1980. "The Readers at the Florentine Studio According to Communal Fiscal Records (1357–1380, 1413–1446)," *Rinascimento,* ser. 2, 20:249–310.

——, 1985. *Doctors and Medicine in Early Renaissance Florence.* Princeton, N.J.

——, 1988. "The Organic Soul," in *CHRP,* pp. 464–84.

——, 1994. "The Criminal and the Saintly Body: Autopsy and Dissection in Renaissance Italy," *Renaissance Quarterly* 47:1–33.

——, 1995. "The Life of the Corpse: Dissection and Division in Late Medieval Europe," *Journal of Medicine and Allied Sciences* 50:111–32.

Park, Katherine, and Kessler, Eckhard, 1988. "The Concept of Psychology," in *CHRP,* pp. 455–63.

Paschini, Pio, 1957. *Tre illustri prelati del Rinascimento: Ermolao Barbaro, Adriano Castellesi, Giovanni Grimani.* Rome.

Pastor, Ludwig von, 1891–1953. *The History of the Popes from the Close of the Middle Ages.* Translated by F. I. Antrobus et al. 40 vols. London and St. Louis.

Pastore Stocchi, Manlio, 1984. "Il periodo veneto di Galileo Galilei," in *Cultura veneta,* vol. 5, pt. 2, pp. 37–66.

Paternoster, Paolo, 1883. *Le scuole pubbliche a Venezia ai tempi della Repubblica. Nozze Levi-Rava.* Venice.

Patrizi, Giorgio, 1990. "Denores, Giason." *DBI,* 38:768–73.

Pecoraro, Marco, 1986. "Vettori, Piero." *Dizionario critico della letteratura italiana.* 4 vols. Turin, vol. 4, pp. 419–22.

Pedersen, Olaf, 1978. "The Decline and Fall of the *Theorica Planetarum:* An Essay in Renaissance Astronomy," in *Science and History: Studies in Honor of Edward Rosen.* Wroclaw, pp. 157–85.

———, 1981. "The Origins of the *Theorica Planetarum,*" *Journal for the History of Astronomy* 12:113–23.

Penuti, Carla, 1998. "Collegi professionali di giureconsulti con prerogativa di addottorare in area estense e romagnola," in *Le università minori in Europa (secoli XV–XIX).* Convegno Internazionale di Studi, Alghero, 30 Ottobre–2 Novembre 1996, edited by Gian Paolo Brizzi and Jacques Verger. Catanzaro, pp. 337–52.

Pérez Goyena, Antonio, 1913. "Toledo, Francisco." *The Catholic Encyclopedia.* New York, vol. 14, pp. 760–61.

Pergamo, Basilio, 1934. "I Francescani alla facoltà teologica di Bologna (1364–1500)," *Archivum Franciscanum Historicum* 27:3–61.

Perosa, Alessandro, 1973. "Calderini, Domizio." *DBI,* 16:597–605.

Perreiah, Alan R., 1967. "A Biographical Introduction to Paul of Venice," *Augustiniana* 17:450–61.

———, 1982. "Humanist Critiques of Scholastic Dialectic," *Sixteenth Century Journal* 13 (3): 3–22.

———, 1984. "Logic Examinations in Padua *circa* 1400," *History of Education* 13:85–103.

Pesenti, Tiziana, 1984. *Professori e promotori di medicina nello Studio di Padova dal 1405 al 1509: Repertorio bio-bibliografico.* Padua and Trieste.

———, 1992a. "Dondi dall'Orologio, Giovanni." *DBI,* 41:96–104.

———, 1992b. "Dondi dall'Orologio, Iacopo." *DBI,* 41:104–11.

———, 1992c. "Dottori, Stefano." *DBI,* 41:560–61.

Pesenti Marangon, Tiziana, 1977. "Michele Savonarola a Padova: L'ambiente, le opere, la cultura medica," *Quaderni* 9–10:45–102.

———, 1979. *La Biblioteca Universitaria di Padova, dalla sua istituzione alla fine della Repubblica Veneta (1629–1797).* Padua.

Petrucci, Armando, 1973. "Calcondila, Demetrio." *DBI,* 16:542–47.

Petti Balbi, Giovanna, 1995. "*Felix Studium viguit:* L'organizzazione degli studenti e dei dottori a Parma nel Quattrocento," in *Università in Europa: Le istituzioni universitarie dal Medio Evo ai nostri giorni: Strutture, organizzazione, funzionamento.* Atti del Convegno Internazionale di Studi, Milazzo 28 Settembre–2 Ottobre 1993, edited by Andrea Romano. Soveria Mannelli and Messina, pp. 37–50.

Philoponus, 1987. *Philoponus and the Rejection of Aristotelian Science.* Edited by Richard R. K. Sorabij. London.

Piacente, Luigi, 1995. "Battista Guarini: L'uomo e il letterato," in *"In supreme digni-*

tatis . . .": *Per la storia dell'Università di Ferrara, 1391–1991*, edited by Patrizia Castelli. Florence, 195–206.

Piana, Celestino, 1960. "La Facoltà teologica dell'Università di Bologna nel 1444–1458," *Archivum Franciscanum Historicum* 53:361–441.

———, 1968. "Lo Studio di S. Francesco a Ferrara nel Quattrocento: Documenti inediti," *Archivum Franciscanum Historicum* 61:99–175.

———, 1976. *Nuovi documenti sull'Università di Bologna e sul Collegio di Spagna.* 2 vols. Bologna.

———, 1977. *La facoltà teologica dell'Università di Firenze nel Quattro e Cinquecento.* Spicilegium Bonaventurianum, 15. Grottaferrata (Rome).

———, 1986. "L'Università di Parma nel Quattrocento," in *Parma e l'umanesimo italiano.* Atti del convegno internazionale di studi umanistici (Parma, 20 ottobre 1984), edited by Paola Medioli Masotti. Padua, pp. 97–120.

Piccinni, Gabriella, 1991. "Tra scienza ed arti: Lo Studio di Siena e l'insegnamento della medicina (secoli XIII–XVI)," in *L'Università di Siena,* pp. 145–58.

Picotti, Giovan Battista, 1968. "Lo Studio di Pisa dalle origini a Cosimo duca," in Picotti, *Scritti vari di storia pisana e toscana.* Pisa, pp. 11–48.

Pignatti, Franco, 1997. "Filelfo, Giovanni Mario." *DBI,* 47:626–31.

Pine, Martin L., 1986. *Pietro Pomponazzi: Radical Philosopher of the Renaissance.* Padua.

Pinghini, Carlo, 1927. "La popolazione studentesca dell'Università di Ferrara dalle origini ai nostri tempi," *Metron: Rivista internazionale di statistica* 7:120–168.

Pingree, David, 1981a. "Al-Qabīṣī." *DSB,* 11:226.

———, 1981b. "Māshā'allāh." *DSB,* 9:159–62.

Piovan, Francesco, 1988. *Per la biografia di Lazzaro Bonamico: Ricerche sul periodo dell'insegnamento padovano (1530–1552).* Trieste.

———, 1997. "Lauree edite e inedite in un diario padovano della prima metà del Cinquecento," *Quaderni* 30:95–109.

Pirri, Pietro, 1959. *L'interdetto di Venezia del 1606 e i Gesuiti: Silloge di documenti con introduzione.* Rome.

Plumidis, Giorgio, 1971. "Gli scolari greci nello Studio di Padova," *Quaderni* 4:127–41.

Pometti, Francesco, 1901. "Il ruolo dei lettori del MDLXVIII–MDLXX et altre notizie sull'Università di Roma," in *Scritti vari di filologia dedicata a E. Monaci.* Rome, pp. 67–93.

Pontani, Filippo Maria, 1981. "Il greco di Gianfrancesco Mussato, peritoso umanista," in *Rivista di studi bizantini e slavi: Miscellanea Agostino Pertusi.* 3 vols. Bologna, vol. 1, pp. 131–63.

Poppi, Antonino, 1962. "Lo scotista patavino Antonio Trombetta (1436–1517)," *Il Santo: Rivista Antoniana di storia dottrina arte* 2:349–67.

———, 1964. "L'antiaverroismo della scolastica padovana alla fine del secolo XV," *Studia patavina* 11:102–24.

———, 1970. *Saggi sul pensiero inedito di Pietro Pomponazzi.* Padua.

———, 1972. *La dottrina della scienza in Giacomo Zabarella.* Padua.

———, 1976. "Il problema della filosofia morale nella scuola padovana del Rinascimento: Platonismo e Aristotelismo nella definizione del metodo dell'etica," in *Platon et Aristote à la Renaissance.* Paris, pp. 105–46.

———, 1979. "L'averroismo nella filosofia francescana," in *L'averroismo in Italia.* Convegno internazionale (Roma, 18–20 aprile 1977). Rome, pp. 175–220.

———, 1981. "La teologia nell'università e nelle scuole," in *Cultura veneta,* vol. 3, pt. 3, pp. 1–33.

——, 1983. "Scienza e filosofia nelle scuole tomista e scotista all'Università di Padova nel Quattrocento," in *Scienza e filosofia*, pp. 329–43.

——, 1989. *La filosofia nello Studio francescano del Santo a Padova*. Padua.

——, 1993. "Cremonini, Galilei e gli inquisitori del Santo a Padova," *Il Santo: Rivista Antoniana di storia dottrina arte* ser. 2, 33, fascicles 1–2, pp. 5–112.

Porro, Giulio, 1878. "Pianta delle spese per l'Università di Pavia nel 1498," *Archivio storico lombardo* 5:507–16.

Poulle, Emmanuel, 1981. "Finé, Orance." *DSB*, 15:153–56.

——, 1988. "The Alfonsine Tables and Alfonso X of Castile," *Journal for the History of Astronomy* 19:97–113.

Premuda, Loris, 1984. "La medicina e l'organizzazione sanitaria," in *Cultura veneta*, vol. 4, pt. 2, pp. 115–50.

Premuda, Loris, and Ongaro, Giuseppe, 1965–66. "I primordi della dissezione anatomica in Padova (revisione critica)," *Acta medicae historia Patavina* 12:117–42.

Price, M. Daniel, 1985. "The Origins of Lateran V's *Apostolici Regiminis*," *Annuarium Historiae Conciliorum* 17:464–72.

Prodi, Paolo, 1959–67. *Il Cardinale Gabriele Paleotti (1522–1597)*. 2 vols. Rome.

Prosperi, Adriano, 1999. "Anime in trappola. Confessione e censura ecclesiastica all'Università di Pisa tra '500 and '600," *Belfagor* 54:257–87.

Prunai, Giulio, 1949. "Lo studio senese dalle origini alla 'Migratio' bolognese (sec. XII–1321)," *Bullettino senese di storia patria* 56:53–79.

——, 1950. "Lo studio senese dalla 'migratio' bolognese alla fondazione della 'Domus sapientiae' (1321–1408)," *Bullettino senese di storia patria* 57:3–54.

——, 1959. "Lo studio senese nel primo quarantennio del principato Mediceo," *Bullettino senese di storia patria* 66:79–160.

Puccini, Clemente, 1988. "La scuola medica e l'insegnamento della medicina legale," in *Storia di Macerata*, edited by Aldo Adversi, Dante Cecchi, and Libero Paci. 2nd ed. Vol. 3: *La cultura*. Macerata, pp. 82–113.

Pullan, Brian, 1968. "Wage Earners and the Venetian Economy, 1550–1630," in *Crisis and Change in the Venetian Economy in the Sixteenth and Seventeenth Centuries*, edited by Brian Pullan. London, pp. 146–74.

Purnell, Frederick, Jr., 1972. "Jacopo Mazzoni and Galileo," *Physis* 14:273–94.

——, 1974. "Jacopo Mazzoni as a Student of Philosophy at Padua," *Quaderni* 7:17–25.

Quinterio, Francesco, 1991. "Dal monastero al palazzo," in *La rinascita del sapere*, pp. 89–108.

Radding, Charles M., 1988. *The Origins of Medieval Jurisprudence: Pavia and Bologna, 850–1150*. New Haven and London.

Ragnisco, Pietro, 1891. *Documenti inediti e rari intorno alla vita ed agli scritti di Nicoletto Vernia e di Elia del Medigo*. Padua. Also in *Atti e memorie della R. Accademia di scienze, lettere ed arti in Padova*, n.s., 7 (1891): 275–302.

Raimondi, Ezio, 1956. "Umanesimo e università nel Quattrocento Bolognese," *SMUB*, n.s., vol. 1, pp. 325–56.

——, 1974. "Il primo commento umanistico a Lucrezio," in *Tra Latino e volgare: Per Carlo Dionisotti*, edited by G. Bernardoni Trezzini et al. 2 vols. Padua, vol. 2, pp. 641–74.

——, 1987. *Codro e l'Umanesimo a Bologna*. Bologna, 1950; rpt. Bologna.

Rashdall, Hastings, 1936. *The Universities of Europe in the Middle Ages*. Edited by F. M. Powicke and A. B. Emden. 3 vols. Oxford.

Raspadori, Francesco, 1991. "La facoltà medica di Ferrara," in *La rinascita del sapere,* pp. 264–73.

Reeds, Karen Meier, 1975. "Botany in Medieval and Renaissance Universities." Ph.D. diss., Harvard University.

——, 1976. "Renaissance Humanism and Botany," *Annals of Science* 33:519–42.

Renazzi, Filippo Maria, 1971. *Storia dell'Università degli Studj di Roma.* 4 vols. Rome, 1803–6; rpt. Bologna.

Renouard, Ant. Aug., 1953. *Annales de l'imprimerie des Alde, ou Histoire des trois Manuce et de leurs éditions.* 3rd ed. Paris, 1834; rpt. Bologna.

Renzi, Paolo, 1985. "*Taciti Annales, Mureti schola:* Note sulla didattica della storia allo Studium Romano nel secondo Cinquecento," *Annali del dipartimento di scienze storiche e sociali* 4:27–59.

——, 1986. "*Magna populi calamitas est uxorius princeps:* Educazione marziale e insegnamento della storia nel Cinquecento," in *Profili di donne: Mito immagine realtà fra Medioevo ed età contemporanea,* edited by B. Vetere and Paolo Renzi. Galatina, pp. 257–301.

Resta, Gianvito, 1965. "Beccadelli, Antonio, detto il Panormita." *DBI,* 7:400–407.

——, 1971, "Malpaghini, Giovanni." *Enciclopedia Dantesca.* Rome, vol. 3, pp. 795–96.

——, 1986. "Francesco Filelfo tra Bisanzio e Roma," in *Francesco Filelfo nel Quinto Centenario della Morte.* Atti del XVII Convegno di Studi Maceratesi. (Tolentino, 17–30 settembre 1981). Padua, pp. 1–60.

Riccobono, Antonio, 1980. *De Gymnasio Patavino commentariorum libri sex.* Padua: Francesco Balzeta, 1598; rpt. Bologna.

Riddle, John M., 1980. "Dioscorides,"in *Catalogus,* vol. 4, pp. 1–144.

——, 1981. "Dioscorides." *DSB,* 4:119–23.

Righini-Bonelli, Maria Luisa, 1981. "Danti, Egnatio (Pellegrino Rainaldi)." *DSB,* 3:558–59.

Riondato, Ezio, 1960. "Per uno studio di Bernardino Tomitano filosofo," in *Aristotelismo padovano e filosofia aristotelica.* Atti del XII Congresso Internazionale di Filosofia (Venezia, 12–18 settembre 1958), Vol. 9. Florence, pp. 221–29.

Risse, Wilhelm, 1964. *Die Logik der Neuzeit.* Vol. 1: *1500–1640.* Stuttgart-Bad Cannstatt.

Rizzi, Fortunato, 1948. *I professori dell'Università di Parma attraverso i secoli: Note indicative bio-bibliografiche.* Parma.

——, 1953. "Un maestro d'umanità: Filippo Beroaldo," *L'Archiginnasio* 48:77–111.

Rizzo, Mario, 1987. "L'Università di Pavia tra potere centrale e comunità locale nella seconda metà del Cinquecento," *Bollettino della società pavese di storia patria* 87 (n.s. 39):65–125.

——, 1989. "University, Administration, Taxation, and Society in Italy in the Sixteenth Century: The Case of Fiscal Exemptions for the University of Pavia," *History of Universities* 8:75–116.

Robin, Diana, 1991. *Filelfo in Milan: Writings, 1451–1477.* Princeton, N.J.

Rodinis, Giuliana Toso, 1970. *Scolari francesi a Padova agli albori della Controriforma.* Padua.

Roggero, Marina, 1992. *Insegnar lettere: Ricerche di storia dell'istruzione in età moderna.* Alessandria.

Romano, Andrea, 1992. "'Primum ac prototypum collegium Societatis Iesu' e 'Messanense Studium Generale': L'insegnamento universitario a Messina nel Cinquecento," in *La pedagogia della Compagnia di Gesù.* Atti del Convegno Internazionale, Messina 14–16 novembre 1991, edited by F. Guerello and P. Schiavone. Messina, pp. 33–72.

——, 1995. "Studenti e professori siciliani di diritto a Ferrara tra medioevo e età moderna," in *"In supreme dignitatis . . .": Per la storia dell'Università di Ferrara, 1391–1991,* edited by Patrizia Castelli. Ferrara, pp. 107–36.

Romano, Giacinto, 1900. "Gli statuti dello studio messinese," in *CCCL anniversario della Università di Messina (contributo storico).* Messina, pt. 1, pp. 123–208.

Ronchi, Oliviero, 1967. "Alloggi di scolari a Padova nei secoli XIII–XVIII," in Ronchi, *Vecchia Padova: Spigolature e contributi storici di arte urbanistica e cultura.* Padua, pp. 293–319. Also published as *Bollettino del Museo Civico di Padova* 56 (1967), pp. 293–319.

Rosa, Mario, 1960. "Algero, Pomponio de." *DBI,* 2:361.

Roscoe, William, 1805. *The Life and Pontificate of Leo the Tenth.* 4 vols. Liverpool.

Rose, Paul Lawrence, 1973. "Humanist Culture and Renaissance Mathematics: The Italian Libraries of the Quattrocento," *Studies in the Renaissance* 20:46–105.

———, 1975. "Professors of Mathematics at Padua University, 1521–1588," *Physis* 17:300–304.

———, 1976. *The Italian Renaissance of Mathematics: Studies on Humanists and Mathematicians from Petrarch to Galileo.* Geneva.

———, 1977. "A Venetian Patron and Mathematician of the Sixteenth Century: Francesco Barozzi (1537–1604)," *Studi veneziani,* n.s., 1:119–78.

Rose, Paul Lawrence, and Drake, Stillman, 1971. "The Pseudo-Aristotelian *Questions of Mechanics* in Renaissance Culture," *Studies in the Renaissance* 18:65–104.

Rosen, Edward, 1981a. "Copernicus, Nicholas." *DSB,* 3:401–11.

———, 1981b. "Novara, Domenico Maria." *DSB,* 10:153–54.

———, 1981c. "Regiomontanus, Johannes." *DSB,* 11:348–52.

Rosino, Leonida, 1988. "Geminiano Montanari astronomo della seconda metà del Seicento a Bologna e Padova," in *Rapporti tra le università di Padova e Bologna: Ricerche di filosofia medicina e scienza,* edited by Lucia Rossetti. Trieste, pp. 173–89.

Ross, James Bruce, 1976. "Venetian Schools and Teachers Fourteenth to Early Sixteenth Century: A Survey and a Study of Giovanni Battista Egnazio," *RQ* 39:521–66.

Rossetti, Lucia, 1974. "Edmund Davie, studente americano a Padova nel 1681," *Quaderni* 7:69–71.

———, 1976. "Francescani del Santo docenti all'Università di Padova," in *Storia e cultura al Santo,* edited by Antonino Poppi. Vicenza, pp. 169–207.

———, 1983. *L'Università di Padova. Profilo storico.* Milan, 1972; 2nd ed. Trieste.

———, 1984. "I collegi per i dottorati 'auctoritate Veneta,'" in *Viridarium floridum: Studi di storia veneta offerti dagli allievi a Paolo Sambin,* edited by Maria Chiara Billanovich, Giorgio Cracco, and Antonio Rigon. Padua, pp. 365–86.

Rossi, Pietro, 1906. "La prima cattedra di pandette nello studio senese," *Studi senesi* 23, pp. 39–62. This volume also appears under the title *Studi senesi. Scritti giuridici e di scienze economiche pubblicati in onore di Luigi Moriani nel XXX° anno del suo insegnamento.* Vol. 2. Turin.

———, 1910. *La prima cattedra di "lingua toscana" (Dai Ruoli dello Studio Senese 1588–1743).* Turin.

Rossi, Vittorio, 1901. "Un grammatico Cremonese a Pavia nella prima età del Rinascimento," *Bollettino della Società Pavese di Storia Patria* 1:16–46.

Rosso, Paolo, 1996. "I 'Rotuli' dell'Università di Pavia nella seconda metà del Quattrocento: Considerazioni sull'entità degli stipendi assegnati al corpo docenti," *Schede umanistiche,* n.s., 1:23–49.

Rotondò, Antonio, 1958. "Nicolò Tignosi da Foligno (Polemiche aristoteliche di un maestro del Ficino)," *Rinascimento* 9:217–55.

———, 1969. "Boccadiferro, Ludovico." *DBI*, 11:3–4.

Ruderman, David B., 1987. "The Impact of Science on Jewish Culture and Society in Venice (With Special Reference to Jewish Graduates of Padua's Medical School)," in *Gli Ebrei e Venezia secoli XIV–XVIII*, edited by Gaetano Cozzi. Milan, pp. 417–48.

———, 1995. *Jewish Thought and Scientific Discovery in Early Modern Europe.* New Haven and London.

Rüegg, Walter, 1992. "Themes," in *Universities in the Middle Ages*, pp. 3–34.

Ruffini, Francesco, 1955. *Studi sui riformatori italiani.* Edited by A. Bertola, L. Firpo, and E. Ruffini. Turin.

Rummel, Erika, 1995. *The Humanist-Scholastic Debate in the Renaissance and Reformation.* Cambridge, Mass., and London.

Rurale, Flavio, 1992. *I gesuiti a Milano: Religione e politica nel secondo Cinquecento.* Rome.

Sabbadini, Remigio, 1924. *Giovanni da Ravenna, insigne figura d'umanista (1343–1408).* Como.

———, 1933. "Giovanni da Ravenna," in *Enciclopedia italiana*, Rome, vol. 17, pp. 261–62.

———, 1964a and 1964b. *Guariniana.* 1. *Vita di Guarino Veronese* (first published in Genoa, 1891). 2. *La scuola e gli studi di Guarino Veronese* (first published in Catania, 1896). 2 volumes in one. Turin.

———, 1975. *Storia documentata della R. Università di Catania: Parte Prima: L'Università di Catania nel secolo XV.* Catania, 1898; rpt. Bologna.

Sabbatani, L., 1926. "La cattedra dei semplici fondata a Bologna da Luca Ghini," *SMUB*, vol. 9, pp. 13–53.

Saibante, M.; Vivarini, C.; and Voghera, G., 1924. "Gli studenti dell'Università di Padova dalla fine del 500 ai nostri giorni (Studio statistico)," *Metron* 4:163–223.

Salvioni, Giovanni Battista, 1890. "La popolazione di Bologna nel secolo XVII," *Atti e memorie della R. Deputazione di storia patria per le provincie di Romagna.* ser. 3, 8:19–120.

Samaritani, Antonio, 1995. "L'erezione dell'Università (1391) e la liberalizzazione delle terre (1392): Due collegate bolle di Bonifacio IX pretese dagli Estensi," in *"In supreme dignitatis . . .": Per la storia dell'Università di Ferrara, 1391–1991*, edited by Patrizia Castelli. Florence, pp. 27–50.

Sambin, Paolo, 1964. "Schede d'archivio per studenti e laureati polacchi a Padova nel primo Cinquecento," in *Relazioni tra Padova e la Polonia: Studi in onore dell'Università di Cracovia nel VI centenario della sua fondazione.* Padua, pp. 17–25.

———, 1965. "Barzizza, Cristoforo." *DBI*, 7:32–34.

———, 1974. "Professori di astronomia e matematica a Padova nell'ultimo decennio del Quattrocento," *Quaderni* 7:59–67.

Sambur.sky, S., 1981. "John Philoponus." *DSB*, 7:134–39.

Sangalli, Maurizio, 1999. *Cultura, politica e religione nella Repubblica di Venezia tra Cinque e Seicento. Gesuiti e Somaschi a Venezia.* Venice.

Santoro, Mario, 1980. "La cultura umanistica," in *Storia di Napoli.* Vol. 7: *Umanesimo e rinascimento.* Naples, pp. 115–292.

Savelli, Rodolfo, 1990. "Diritto e politica: 'Doctores' e patriziato a Genova," in *Sapere e/è potere*, pp. 285–319.

Savigny, Friedrich Carl von, 1834–51. *Geschichte des Römischen Rechts im Mittelalter.* 2nd ed. 7 vols. Heidelberg.

Sbriziolo, Lia, 1973. "'Magistri in sacra pagina' della seconda metà del Quattrocento," *Quaderni* 6:169–82.

Scaduto, Mario, 1948. "Le origini dell'Università di Messina," *Archivum Historicum Societatis Iesu* 17:102–59.

——, 1964. *L'epoca di Giacomo Lainez, 1556–1565: Il governo.* Rome.

——, 1968. *Catalogo dei gesuiti d'Italia, 1540–1565.* Rome.

——, 1974. *L'epoca di Giacomo Lainez, 1556–1565: L'azione.* Rome.

——, 1992. *L'opera di Francesco Borgia, 1565–1572.* Rome.

Scaglione, Aldo, 1986. *The Liberal Arts and the Jesuit College System.* Amsterdam and Philadelphia.

Scapin, Pietro, 1976. "Maurizio O'Fihely editore e commentatore di Duns Scoto," in *Storia e cultura al Santo,* edited by Antonino Poppi. Vicenza, pp. 303–8.

Schmitt, Charles B., 1966. "Perennial Philosophy: From Agostino Steuco to Leibniz," *Journal of the History of Ideas* 27:505–32. Also in Schmitt, 1981c, study 1, with the same pagination.

——, 1969. "Experience and Experiment: A Comparison of Zabarella's View with Galileo's in *De Motu,*" *Studies in the Renaissance* 16:80–138. Also in Schmitt, 1981c, study 8.

——, 1970. "*Prisca theologia e philosophia perennis:* Due temi del Rinascimento italiano e la loro fortuna," in *Atti del V. Convegno internazionale del Centro di Studi Umanistici: Il pensiero italiano del Rinascimento e il tempo nostro.* Florence, pp. 211–36. Also in Schmitt, 1981c, study 2.

——, 1971. "Theophrastus," in *Catalogus,* vol. 2, pp. 239–322.

——, 1972. "The Faculty of Arts at Pisa at the time of Galileo," *Physis* 14:243–72. Also in Schmitt, 1981c, study 9.

——, 1975a. "Philosophy and Science in Sixteenth-Century Universities: Some Preliminary Comments," in *The Cultural Context of Medieval Learning,* edited by J. E. Murdoch and E. D. Sylla. Dordrecht, pp. 485–530. Also in Schmitt, 1981c, study 5.

——, 1975b. "Science in the Italian Universities in the Sixteenth and Early Seventeenth Centuries," in *The Emergence of Science in Western Europe,* edited by M. P. Crosland. London, pp. 35–56. Also in Schmitt, 1984a, study 14.

——, 1976a. "Girolamo Borro's *Multae sunt nostrarum ignorationum causae* (Ms. Vat. Ross. 1009)," in *Philosophy and Humanism: Renaissance Essays in Honor of Paul Oskar Kristeller,* edited by Edward P. Mahoney. New York, pp. 462–76. Also in Schmitt, 1981c, study 11.

——, 1976b. "L'introduction de la philosophie platonicienne dans l'enseignement des universités a la Renaissance," in *Platon et Aristote à la Renaissance.* Paris, pp. 93–104. Also in Schmitt, 1981c, study 3.

——, 1977. "Thomas Linacre and Italy," in *Linacre Studies: Essays on the Life and Work of Thomas Linacre, c. 1460–1524,* edited by Francis Maddison, Margaret Pelling, and Charles Webster. Oxford, pp. 36–75. Also in Schmitt, 1984a, study 12.

——, 1978. "Filippo Fantoni, Galileo Galilei's Predecessor as Mathematics Lecturer at Pisa," in *Science and History: Studies in Honor of Edward Rosen.* Wroclaw, pp. 53–62. Also in Schmitt, 1981c, study 10.

——, 1979a. "Aristotle's Ethics in the Sixteenth Century: Some Preliminary Considerations," in *Ethik im Humanismus.* Beiträge zur Humanismusforschung, Band V, edited by W. Ruëgg and D. Wuttke. Bopard, pp. 87–112. Also in Schmitt, 1984a, study 7.

——, 1979b. "Renaissance Averroism Studied through the Venetian Editions of Aristotle-Averroës (with particular reference to the Giunta edition of 1550–2)," in *L'Averroismo in Italia.* Convegno internazionale, Roma, 18–20 aprile 1977. Rome, pp. 121–42. Also in Schmitt, 1984a, study 8.

——, 1980. *Cesare Cremonini: Un aristotelico al tempo di Galilei.* Centro Tedesco di Studi Veneziani. Quaderni, 16. Venice. Also in Schmitt, 1984a, study 11.

——, 1981a. "Alberto Pio and the Aristotelian Studies of His Time," in *Società, politica e cultura a Carpi ai tempi di Alberto Pio.* Atti del Convegno Internazionale (Carpi, 19–21 maggio 1978). 2 vols. Padua, vol. 1, pp. 43–64. Also in Schmitt, 1984a, study 6.

——, 1981b. "Borro, Girolamo." *DSB,* 15:44–46.

——, 1981c. *Studies in Renaissance Philosophy and Science.* London.

——, 1981d. "Zabarella, Jacopo." *DSB,* 14:580–82.

——, 1982a. "Andreas Camutius on the Concord of Plato and Aristotle with Scripture," in *Neoplatonism and Christian Thought,* edited by Dominic J. O'Meara. Studies in Neoplatonism: Ancient and Modern, vol. 3. Norfolk, Va., pp. 178–84, 282–86.

——, 1982b. "Philosophy and Science in Sixteenth-Century Italian Universities," in *The Renaissance: Essays in Interpretation.* London and New York, pp. 297–336. Also in Schmitt, 1984a, study 15.

——, 1983a. "Aristotelian Textual Studies at Padua: The Case of Francesco Cavalli," in *Scienza e filosofia,* pp. 287–314. Also in Schmitt, 1984a, study 13.

——, 1983b. "Aristotelianism in the Veneto and the Origins of Modern Science: Some Considerations on the Problem of Continuity," in *Aristotelismo veneto e scienza moderna.* Atti del 25° anno accademico del Centro per la storia della tradizione aristotelica nel Veneto, edited by Luigi Olivieri. 2 vols. Padua, vol. 1, pp. 104–23. Also in Schmitt, 1984a, study 1.

——, 1983c. *Aristotle and the Renaissance.* Cambridge, Mass., and London.

——, 1983d. "Galilei and the Seventeenth-Century Text-Book Tradition," in *Novità celesti e crisi del sapere,* edited by Paolo Galuzzi. Florence, pp. 217–28. Also in Schmitt, 1989, study 11.

——, 1983e. "Science, Philosophy, and Humanism in Fifteenth-Century Italy," in *Studia Mediewistyczne* 22:111–21.

——, 1983f. "The *Studio pisano* in the European Cultural Context of the Sixteenth Century," in *Firenze e la Toscana dei Medici nell'Europa del '500.* Vol. 1. Florence, pp. 19–36. Also in Schmitt, 1989, study 10.

——, 1984a. *The Aristotelian Tradition and Renaissance Universities.* London.

——, 1984b. "Cremonini, Cesare." *DBI,* 30:618–22.

——, 1985. "Aristotle among the Physicians," in *Medical Renaissance,* pp. 1–15, 271–79. Also in Schmitt, 1989, study 7.

——, 1987. "Philoponus' Commentary on Aristotle's *Physics* in the Sixteenth Century," in *Philoponus and the Rejection of Aristotelian Science,* edited by Richard R. K. Sorabij. London, pp. 210–30. Also in Schmitt, 1989, study 8.

——, 1989. *Reappraisals in Renaissance Thought.* Edited by Charles Webster. London.

Schmitt, Charles B., and Knox, Dilwyn, 1985. *Pseudo-Aristoteles Latinus: A Guide to Latin Works Falsely Attributed to Aristotle before 1500.* Warburg Institute Surveys and Texts. 12. London.

Schreiner, Peter, 1974. "Camozzi, Giovanni Battista." *DBI,* 17:297–98.

Schullian, Dorothy, M., 1981. "Benedetti, Alessandro." *DSB,* 1:603–4.

——, 1984. "Valerius Maximus," in *Catalogus,* vol. 5, pp. 287–403.

Schurhammer, Georg, 1973. *Francis Xavier: His Life, His Times.* Translated by M. Joseph Costelloe. Vol. 1. Rome.

Schutte, Anne Jacobson, 1992. "Donzellini, Girolamo." *DBI,* 41:238–43.

Scriptores Ordinis Praedicatorum, n.d. *Scriptores Ordinis Praedicatorum.* Edited by Jacobus Quétif and Jacobus Echard. 2 vols. in four parts. Paris, 1917–21; rpt. New York, n.d.

Le scuole degli ordini mendicanti, 1978. *Le scuole degli ordini mendicanti (secoli XIII–XIV).* Todi.

Secco Suardo, Girolamo, 1983. *Lo Studio di Ferrara a tutto il secolo XV.* Ferrara, 1894; rpt. Bologna.

Segre, Michael, 1991. *In the Wake of Galileo.* New Brunswick, N.J.

Seigel, Jerrold E., 1969. "The Teaching of Argyropulos and the Rhetoric of the First Humanists," in *Action and Conviction in Early Modern Europe: Essays in Memory of E. H. Harbison,* edited by Theodore K. Rabb and Jerrold E. Seigel. Princeton, N.J., pp. 237–60.

Settle, Thomas B., 1981. "Borelli, Giovanni Alfonso." *DSB,* 2:306–14.

——, 1990. "Egnazio Danti and Mathematical Education in Late Sixteenth-century Florence," in *New Perspectives on Renaissance Thought: Essays in the History of Science, Education, and Philosophy in Memory of Charles B. Schmitt,* edited by John Henry and Sarah Hutton. London, pp. 24–37.

Sheedy, Anna T., 1942. *Bartolus on Social Conditions in the Fourteenth Century.* New York.

STC Italian. 1958. *Short-Title Catalogue of Books Printed in Italy and of Italian Books Printed in Other Countries from 1465 to 1600 Now in the British Museum.* London.

Shumaker, Wayne, 1982. *Renaissance Curiosa.* Binghamton, N.Y.

Siegel, Rudolph, 1968. *Galen's System of Physiology and Medicine: An Analysis of His Doctrines and Observations on Bloodflow.* Basel and New York.

——, 1970. *Galen on Sense Perception: His Doctrines, Observations, and Experiments on Vision, Hearing, Smell, Taste, Touch, and Pain, and Their Historical Sources.* Basel and New York.

Sighinolfi, Lino, 1920. "Domenico Maria Novara e Nicolò Copernico allo Studio di Bologna," *SMUB,* vol. 5, pp. 205–36.

Silvestro da Valsanzibio, P., 1967. "Gaetano da Thiene," in *Enciclopedia filosofica.* 2nd ed. Florence, vol. 2, cols. 1557–59.

Simeoni, Luigi, 1940. *Storia della Università di Bologna.* Vol. 2: *L'età moderna (1500–1888).* Bologna.

Simili, Alessandro, 1956. "Gerolamo Cardano lettore e medico a Bologna," *L'Archiginnasio* 61:384–505.

Simionato, Giustina, 1973. "Significato e contenuto delle 'Lectiones' inedite di logica di Bernardino Tomitano," in *Quaderni* 6:111–24.

Simioni, Elisa, 1934. "I professori della facoltà teologica dell'Università di Padova nel Cinquecento," *Padova: Rivista mensile del Comune* 8:59–70.

Siraisi, Nancy G., 1973. *Arts and Sciences at Padua: The "Studium" of Padua before 1350.* Toronto.

——, 1981. *Taddeo Alderotti and His Pupils: Two Generations of Italian Medical Learning.* Princeton, N.J.

——, 1987. *Avicenna in Renaissance Italy: The "Canon" and Medical Teaching in Italian Universities after 1500.* Princeton, N.J.

——, 1990. *Medieval and Early Renaissance Medicine: An Introduction to Knowledge and Practice.* Chicago and London.

——, 1997. *The Clock and the Mirror: Girolamo Cardano and Renaissance Medicine.* Princeton, N.J.

Sitta, Pietro, 1892. "Saggio sulle istituzioni finanziarie del ducato estense nei secoli XV e XVI," *Atti della deputazione ferrarese di storia patria* 4:89–254.

Smalley, Beryl, 1969. "The Bible in the Medieval Schools," in *The Cambridge History of the Bible,* vol. 2: *The West from the Fathers to the Reformation,* edited by G. W. H. Lampe. Cambridge, pp. 197–220.

Smith, Leonardo, 1926–1928. "Note cronologiche vergeriane," *Archivio veneto tridentino* 10:149–57, and *Archivio veneto,* ser. 5, 4:92–141.

Smolinsky, Heribert, 1991. "Dominici, Domenico." *DBI*, 40:691–95.

Snyder, Jon R., 1989. *Writing the Scene of Speaking: Theories of Dialogue in the Late Italian Renaissance*. Stanford, Calif.

Solerti, Angelo, 1892. "Documenti riguardanti lo Studio di Ferrara dei secoli XV e XVI conservati nell'Archivio Estense," *Atti della deputazione ferrarese di storia patria* 4:5–51.

Sommervogel, Carlos, et al., 1960. *Bibliothèque de la Compagnie de Jésus*. 12 vols. Brussels and Paris, 1890–1930; augmented rpt. ed. by Marc Dykmans. Héverlé-Louvain.

Soppelsa, Maria Laura, 1974. *Genesi del metodo galileiano e tramonto dell'aristotelismo nella Scuola di Padova*. Padua.

——, 1986. "Le scienze teoriche e sperimentali tra Sei e Settecento," in *Cultura veneta,* vol. 5, pt. 2, pp. 271–345.

Sorbelli, Albano, 1912. "Gli stipendi dei professori dell'Università di Bologna nel secolo XIV," *L'Archiginnasio* 7:313–19.

——, 1940. *Storia della Università di Bologna*. Vol. 1: *Il medioevo (secc. XI–XV)*. Bologna.

Sottili, Agostino, 1982. "L'Università di Pavia nella politica culturale sforzesca," in *Gli Sforza a Milano e in Lombardia e i loro rapporti con gli Stati italiani ed europei (1450–1535)*. Milan, pp. 519–80. Also in Sottili, 1993.

——, 1984. "Tunc floruit Alamannorum natio: Doktorate deutscher Studenten in Pavia in der zweiten Hälfte des fünfzehnten Jahrhunderts," in *Humanismus im Bildungswesen des 15. und 16. Jahrhunderts,* edited by Wolfgang Reinhard. Weinheim, pp. 25–44. Also in Sottili, 1993.

——, 1990. "Università e cultura a Pavia in età visconteo-sforzesca," in *Storia di Pavia*. Vol. 3: *Dal libero comune alla fine del principato indipendente, 1024–1535*. Pt. 2: *La Battaglia di Pavia del 24 Febbraio 1525 nella storia, nella letteratura e nell'arte. Università e cultura*. Milan, pp. 359–451.

——, 1993. *Università e cultura: Studi sui rapporti italo-tedeschi nell'età dell'Umanesimo*. Goldbach, Germany.

——, 1997. "Der Rhetorikunterricht an der Universität Pavia in der zweiten Hälfte des 15. Jahrhunderts," in *Saeculum tamquam aureum*. Internationales Symposion zur italienischen Renaissance des 14.–16 Jahrhunderts am 17./18. September 1996 in Mainz, edited by Ute Ecker and Clemens Zintzen. Mainz, pp. 357–78

Soudek, Josef, 1968. "Leonardo Bruni and His Public: A Statistical and Interpretative Study of His Annotated Latin Version of the (Pseudo-) Aristotelian *Economics,*" *Studies in Medieval and Renaissance History* 5:49–136.

Southern, R. W., 1995. *Scholastic Humanism and the Unification of Europe*. Vol. 1: *Foundations*. Oxford.

Spagnesi, Enrico, 1979. *Utiliter Edoceri: Atti inediti degli Ufficiali dello Studio Fiorentino (1391–1396)*. Milan.

——, 1986. "I documenti costitutivi della provvisione del 1321 allo statuto del 1388," in *Storia dell'Ateneo fiorentino: Contributi di Studio*. 2 vols. Florence, vol. 1, pp. 107–45.

——, 1987. "Deciani, Tiberio." *DBI*, 33:538–42.

——, 1993. "Il diritto," in *L'Università di Pisa,* pp. 191–258.

Speroni, Mario, 1976. "Il primo vocabolario giuridico umanistico: Il "De verborum significatione" di Maffeo Vegio," *Studi senesi* 88:7–43.

——, 1979. "Lorenzo Valla a Pavia: Il libellus contro Bartolo," *Quellen und Forschungen aus italienischen archiven und bibliotheken* 59:453–67.

Spini, Giorgio, 1983. *Ricerca dei libertini: La teoria dell'impostura delle religioni nel Seicento italiano*. Rev. and enlarged ed. Florence.

Spufford, Peter, 1986. *Handbook of Medieval Exchange.* With the assistance of Wendy Wilkinson and Sarah Tolley. London.

Stabile, Giorgio, 1971. "Borri, Girolamo." *DBI,* 13:13–17.

——, 1972. "Burana, Giovanni Francesco." *DBI,* 15:386–89.

Stein, Peter, 1988. *The Character and Influence of the Roman Civil Law: Historical Essays.* London and Ronceverte.

Stella, Aldo, 1964b. "Tentativi controriformistici nell'Università di Padova e il rettorato di Andrea Gostynski," in *Relazioni tra Padova e la Polonia: Studi in onore dell'Università di Cracovia nel VI centenario della sua fondazione.* Padua, pp. 75–87.

——, 1969. *Anabattismo e antitrinitarismo in Italia nel xvi secolo: Nuove ricerche storiche.* Padua.

——, 1988. "Una famiglia di giuristi fra eterodossi padovani e bolognesi: Mariano e Lelio Sozzini (1525–1556)," in *Rapporti tra le università di Padova e Bologna: Ricerche di filosofia medicina e scienza,* edited by Lucia Rossetti. Trieste, pp. 127–60.

Stelling-Michaud, S., 1955. *L'Université de Bologne et la pénétration des droits romain et canonique en Suisse aux XIIIᵉ et XIVᵉ siècles.* Geneva.

Stern, Laura Ikins, 1994. *The Criminal Law System of Medieval and Renaissance Florence.* Baltimore and London.

Sterzi, Giuseppe, 1909–10. "Giulio Casseri, anatomico e chirurgo (c. 1552–1616)," *Nuovo archivio veneto,* ser. 3, 18:207–78; 19:25–111.

Stinger, Charles L., 1985. *The Renaissance in Rome.* Bloomington, Ind.

Storia dell'Ateneo fiorentino, 1986. *Storia dell'Ateneo fiorentino: Contributi di Studio.* 2 vols. Florence.

Stow, Kenneth R., 1977. *Catholic Thought and Papal Jewry Policy, 1555–1593.* New York.

Strauss, Gerald, 1986. *Law, Resistance, and the State: The Opposition to Roman Law in Reformation Germany.* Princeton, N.J.

Stumpo, Enrico, 1984. "Costa, Cesare." *DBI,* 30:167–69.

Tabarroni, Giorgio, 1981. "Montanari, Geminiano." *DSB,* 9:484–87.

Tacchi Venturi, Pietro, 1950. *Storia della Compagnia di Gesù in Italia.* Vol. 2, pt. 1: *Dalla nascita del fondatore alla solenne approvazione dell'Ordine (1491–1540).* 2nd ed. Rome.

Tangheroni, Marco, 1993. "L'età della Repubblica (dalle origini al 1406)," in *L'Università di Pisa,* pp. 5–32.

Tavilla, Carmelo E., 1991. "La controversia del 1630 sullo Studium: Politica e amministrazione della giustizia a Messina tra Cinque e Seicento," *Archivio storico messinese* 59:5–74.

Taylor, R. Emmet, 1942. *No Royal Road: Luca Pacioli and His Times.* Chapel Hill, N.C.

I tedeschi dell'Università di Siena, 1988. *I tedeschi nella storia dell'Università di Siena.* Edited by Giovanni Minnucci, translated by Raffaella Marcucci. Siena.

Tedeschi, John A., 1965. "Notes toward a Genealogy of the Sozzini Family," in *Italian Reformation Studies in Honor of Laelius Socinus,* edited by John A. Tedeschi. Florence, pp. 277–310.

——, 1991. *The Prosecution of Heresy: Collected Studies on the Inquisition in Early Modern Italy.* Binghamton, N.Y.

Temkin, Owsei, 1973. *Galenism: Rise and Decline of a Medical Philosophy.* Ithaca, N.Y, and London.

Thomson, Ian, 1966. "Manuel Chrysoloras and the Early Italian Renaissance," *Greek, Roman, and Byzantine Studies* 7:63–82.

Thorndike, Lynn, 1923–58. *A History of Magic and Experimental Science.* 8 vols. New York and London.

Tocci, Mirella, 1975. "Capodilista, Giovan Francesco." *DBI,* 18:638–40.

Tomasini, Iacopo Philippo, 1986. *Gymnasium Patavinum . . . libri V.* Udine, 1654; rpt. Sala Bolognese.

Toniolo Fascione, Maria Claudia, 1980. "Aspetti di politica culturale e scolastica nell'età di Cosimo I: L'istituzione del Collegio della Sapienza di Pisa," *Bollettino storico pisano* 49:68–86.

———, 1991. "Il Collegio della Sapienza di Pisa nella Toscana del Seicento: Provenienza culturale, sociale e geografica delle richieste di ammissione," in *I collegi universitari in Europea tra il XIV e XVIII secolo.* Atti del convegno di studi della commissione internazionale per la storia delle università, Siena-Bologna, 16–19 maggio 1988, edited by Domenico Maffei and Hilde De Ridder-Symoens. Milan, pp. 33–45.

Tonzig, Maria, 1973. "Elena Lucrezia Cornaro Piscopia (1646–1684), prima donna laureata," *Quaderni* 6:183–192

Toomer, G. J., 1981a. "Apollonius of Perga." *DSB*, 1:179–93.

———, 1981b. "Campanus of Novara." *DSB*, 3:23–29.

———, 1981c. "Ptolemy." *DSB*, 11:186–206.

Torraca, Francesco, 1924. "Le origini. L'età sveva," in *Storia della Università di Napoli.* Naples, pp. 1–16.

Torrini, Maurizio, 1979. *Dopo Galileo: Una polemica scientifica (1684–1711).* Florence.

Trenti, Luigi, 1975. "Capodilista, Francesco." *DBI*, 18:633–35.

Trinkaus, Charles, 1970. *In Our Image and Likeness: Humanity and Divinity in Italian Humanist Thought.* 2 vols. Chicago and London.

———, 1988. "Humanism and Scholastic Theology," in *Renaissance Humanism,* vol. 3, pp. 327–48.

———, 1993. "Lorenzo Valla's Anti-Aristotelian Natural Philosophy," *I Tatti Studies: Essays in the Renaissance* 5:279–325.

Trinquet, Roger, 1965. "Recherches chronologiques sur la jeunesse de Marc-Antoine Muret," *Bibliothèque d'Humanisme et Renaissance* 27:272–85.

Trombetti Budriesi, Anna Laura, 1988. "L'esame di laurea presso lo Studio bolognese: Laureati in diritto civile nel secolo XV," in *Studenti e università degli studenti dal XII al XIX secolo,* edited by Gian Paolo Brizzi and Antonio Ivan Pini. *SMUB,* n.s., vol. 7, Bologna, pp. 137–91.

Troncarelli, Fabio, 1974. "Candi, Cano." *DBI,* 17:752–53.

Tucci, Ugo, 1975. "Capodilista, Gabriele." *DBI,* 17:635–38.

Tugnoli Pattaro, Sandra, 1981. *Metodo e sistema delle scienze nel pensiero di Ulisse Aldrovandi.* Bologna.

L'Università di Torino nei sec. XVI e XVII. Turin, 1972.

Universities in Early Modern Europe (1500–1800), 1996. *A History of the University in Europe.* Vol. 2: *Universities in Early Modern Europe (1500–1800).* Edited by Hilde De Ridder-Symoens. Cambridge.

Vaccari, Pietro, 1957. *Storia della Università di Pavia.* 2nd rev. ed. Pavia.

Valentini, Roberto, 1936. "Gli istituti romani di alta cultura e la presunta crisi dello 'Studium Urbis' (1370–1420)," in *Archivio della Reale Società Romana di Storia Patria* 59:179–243.

———, 1944. "Lo 'Studium Urbis' durante il secolo XIV," *Archivio della Reale Società Romana di Storia Patria* 67:371–389.

Vallaro, Stefano, 1936. "I Domenicani in un documento antico dell'Università di Torino," *Archivum Fratrum Praedicatorum* 6:39–88.

———, 1937. "I professori Domenicani nell'Università di Torino," *Archivum Fratrum Praedicatorum* 7:134–90.

Vallauri, Tommaso, 1970. *Storia delle Università degli Studi del Piemonte.* 2 vols. Turin, 1845–46; rpt. Bologna.

Vasoli, Cesare, 1963. "Bagolino, Gerolamo." *DBI,* 5:267.

——, 1965. "Beldemandis, Prosdocimo de." *DBI,* 7:551–54.

——, 1968a. *La dialettica e la retorica dell'Umanesimo: "Invenzione" e "Metodo" nella cultura del XV e XVI secolo.* Milan.

——, 1968b. *Studi sulla cultura del Rinascimento.* Manduria, Italy.

——, 1981. "La logica," in *Cultura veneta,* vol. 3, pt. 3, pp. 35–73.

——, 1983. *Immagini umanistiche.* Naples.

——, 1989. *Francesco Patrizi da Cherso.* Rome.

——, 1998a. "The Crisis of Late Humanism and Expectations of Reform in Italy at the End of the Fifteenth and Beginning of the Sixteenth Centuries," in *History of Theology,* vol. 3: *The Renaissance,* edited by Giulio D'Onofrio, translated by Matthew J. O'Connell. Collegeville, Minn., pp. 371–457.

——, 1998b. "Italian Scholasticism and Ecclesiastical Culture in the Fifteenth Century: Continuity and Innovation," in *History of Theology,* vol. 3: *The Renaissance,* edited by Giulio D'Onofrio, translated by Matthew J. O'Connell. Collegeville, Minn., pp. 75–154.

——, 1998c. "The Mature State of Humanist Theology in Italy," in *History of Theology,* vol. 3: *The Renaissance,* edited by Giulio D'Onofrio, translated by Matthew J. O'Connell. Collegeville, Minn., pp. 188–247.

——, 1998d. "The Theology of Italian Humanism in the Early Fifteenth Century," *History of Theology,* vol. 3: *The Renaissance,* edited by Giulio D'Onofrio, translated by Matthew J. O'Connell. Collegeville, Minn., pp. 17–74.

Ventrice, Pasquale, 1992–93. "Giacomo Zabarella e Federico Pendasio: La nozione di matematica pura e mista," *Atti dell'Istituto Veneto di Scienze, Lettere ed Arti,* vol. 151, fascicle 2: Classe di scienze morali, lettere ed arti, pp. 505–66.

Ventura, Angelo, 1964. *Nobiltà e popolo nella società veneta del '400 e '500.* Bari.

——, 1983. "Contarini, Marcantonio." *DBI,* 28:237–41.

Venturini, Ottorino, 1892. "Dei gradi accademici conferiti dallo Studio ferrarese nel I° secolo di sua instituzione," *Atti della deputazione ferrarese di storia patria* 4:61–107.

Verbeke, G., 1981a. "Simplicius." *DSB,* 12:440–43.

——, 1981b. "Themistius." *DSB,* 13:307–9.

Verde, Armando F., 1983. "Il 'parere' del 1587 di Francesco Verino sullo Studio pisano," in *Firenze e la Toscana dei Medici nell'Europa del '500.* Vol. 1: *Strumenti e veicoli della cultura. Relazioni politiche ed economiche.* Florence, pp. 71–94.

——, 1995. "Studenti e professori fra l'Università di Ferrara e l'Università di Firenze: Fine del Quattrocento-inizio del Cinquecento," in *"In supreme dignitatis . . .": Per la storia dell'Università di Ferrara, 1391–1991,* edited by Patrizia Castelli. Florence, pp. 75–105.

——, 1998. "Il secondo periodo de [*sic*] Lo Studio Fiorentino (1504–1528)," in *L'università e la sua storia. Origini, spazi istituzionali e pratiche didattiche dello Studium cittadino.* Atti del Convegno di Studi (Arezzo, 15–16 novembre 1991), edited by Paolo Renzi. N.p., pp. 105–31.

Verger, Jacques, 1978. "*Studia* et universités," in *Le scuole degli ordini mendicanti (secoli XIII–XIV).* Todi, pp. 173–203.

——, 1992. "Patterns," in *Universities in the Middle Ages,* pp. 35–74.

Veronese Ceseracciu, Emilia, 1978. "Spagnoli e portoghesi all'Università di Padova nel ventennio 1490–1510," *Quaderni* 11:39–79.

——, 1980. "Ebrei laureati a Padova nel Cinquecento," *Quaderni* 13:151–68.

——, 1995. "Una sede dell'università artista (1474–1511)." *Quaderni* 28:183–88.

Viard, Paul Émile, 1926. *André Alciat, 1492–1550.* Paris.

Villoslada, Riccardo G., 1954. *Storia del Collegio Romano dal suo inizio (1551) alla soppressione della Compagnia di Gesù (1773).* Rome.

Visconti, Alessandro, 1950. *La storia dell'Università di Ferrara (1391–1950).* Bologna.

Vismara, Giulio, 1963. "Vita di studenti e studio del diritto nell'Università di Pavia alla fine del Cinquecento," *Archivio storico lombardo* 90 (n.s., vol. 3): 425–81.

Viti, Paolo, 1987. "Dati, Agostino." *DBI,* 33:15–21.

——, 1997. "Filelfo, Francesco." *DBI,* 47:613–26.

Vivoli, Carlo, 1987. "Dazzi, Andrea." *DBI,* 33:184–86.

Vocabulaire des collèges, 1993. *Vocabulaire des collèges universitaires (XIIIᵉ–XVIᵉ siècles).* Actes du colloque Leuven, 9–11 avril 1992. Edited by Olga Weijers. Turnhout.

Vogel, Kurt, 1981a. "Diophantus of Alexandria." *DSB,* 4:110–19.

——, 1981b. "Fibonacci, Leonardo." *DSB,* 4:604–13.

Voigt, Georg, 1968. *Il risorgimento dell'antichità classica ovvero il primo secolo dell'umanesimo.* 3rd German ed. rev. Translated by Diego Valbusa and Giuseppe Zippel. 3 vols. Florence, 1888–97; rpt. Florence.

Volpi Rosselli, Giuliana, 1993. "Il corpo studentesco, i collegi e le accademie," in *L'Università di Pisa,* pp. 377–468.

Volta, Zanino, 1898. "La facoltà teologica ne' primordi dello studio generale di Pavia," *Archivio storico lombardo* 25:282–316.

Wallace, William A., 1984. *Galileo and His Sources: The Heritage of the Collegio Romano in Galileo's Science.* Princeton, N.J.

——, 1988. "Traditional Natural Philosophy," in *CHRP,* pp. 201–35.

——, 1992. *Galileo's Logic of Discovery and Proof: The Background, Content, and Use of His Appropriated Treatises on Aristotle's Posterior Analytics.* Boston Studies in the Philosophy of Science, vol. 137. Dordrecht, Boston, and London.

——, 1995. "Circularity and the Paduan *Regressus:* From Pietro d'Abano to Galileo Galilei," *Vivarium* 33 (1): 76–97.

——, 1996. *The Modelling of Nature: Philosophy of Science and Philosophy of Nature in Synthesis.* Washington, D.C.

——, 1998. "Galileo's Pisan Studies in Science and Philosophy," in *The Cambridge Companion to Galileo,* edited by Peter Machamer. Cambridge, pp. 27–52.

Ward, John O., 1978. "From Antiquity to the Renaissance: Glosses and Commentaries on Cicero's *Rhetorica,*" in *Medieval Eloquence: Studies in the Theory and Practice of Medieval Rhetoric,* edited by James J. Murphy. Berkeley, Los Angeles, and London, pp. 25–67.

——, 1983. "Renaissance Commentators on Ciceronian Rhetoric," in *Renaissance Eloquence: Studies in the Theory and Practice of Renaissance Rhetoric,* edited by James J. Murphy. Berkeley, Los Angeles, and London, pp. 126–73.

——, 1995. "Quintilian and the Rhetorical Revolution of the Middle Ages," *Rhetorica* 13:231–84.

Webb, Diana M., 1976a. "Andrea Biglia at Bologna, 1424–7: A Humanist Friar and the Troubles of the Church," *Bulletin of the Institute of Historical Research* 49:41–59.

——, 1976b. "The Decline and Fall of Eastern Christianity: A Fifteenth-Century View," *Bulletin of the Institute of Historical Research* 49:198–216.

Webster, Charles, 1981. "Turner, William." *DSB,* vol. 13:501–3.

Weigle, Fritz, 1942. "Deutsche Studenten in Italien. Teil I: Die Deutsche Nation in Perugia," *Quellen und Forschungen aus Italienischen Archiven und Bibliotheken* 32:110–98.

——, 1954. "Die Bibliothek der Deutschen Nation in Perugia," *Quellen und Forschungen aus Italienischen Archiven und Bibliotheken* 34:173–202.

Weinberg, Bernard, 1961. *A History of Literary Criticism in the Italian Renaissance.* 2 vols. Chicago.

Weisheipl, James A., 1974. *Friar Thomas d'Aquino: His Life, Thought, and Work.* Garden City, N.Y.

Weiss, Roberto, 1977. *Medieval and Humanist Greek: Collected Essays.* Padua.

Whitteridge, Gweneth, 1971. *William Harvey and the Circulation of the Blood.* London and New York.

Wicks, Jared, 1983. *Cajetan und die Anfänge der Reformation.* Münster.

Wieland, Georg, 1982. "The Reception and Interpretation of Aristotle's *Ethics,*" in *CHLMP,* pp. 657–72.

Wightman, William P. D., 1964. "*Quid sit Methodus?* 'Method' in Sixteenth Century Medical Teaching and 'Discovery,' " in *Journal of the History of Medicine* 19:360–76.

Wilkins, Ernest Hatch, 1961. *Life of Petrarch.* Chicago and London.

Williams, Penry, 1986. "Elizabethan Oxford: State, Church, and University," in *The History of the University of Oxford,* vol. 3: *The Collegiate University,* edited by James Mc-Conica. Oxford, pp. 397–440.

Wilson, N. G., 1992. *From Byzantium to Italy: Greek Studies in the Italian Renaissance.* Baltimore.

Witt, Ronald G., 1982. "Medieval 'Ars Dictaminis' and the Beginnings of Humanism: A New Construction of the Problem," *RQ* 35:1–35.

——, 1983a. "Brunetto Latini and the Italian Tradition of *Ars dictaminis,*" *Stanford Italian Review* 3:5–24.

——, 1983b. *Hercules at the Crossroads: The Life, Works, and Thought of Coluccio Salutati.* Durham, N.C.

——, 1986. "Boncompagno and the Defense of Rhetoric," *Journal of Medieval and Renaissance Studies* 16 (1): 1–31.

——, 1988. "Medieval Italian Culture and the Origins of Humanism as a Stylistic Ideal," in *Renaissance Humanism,* vol. 1, pp. 29–70.

——, 1995. "Still the Matter of the Two Giovannis: A Note on Malpaghini and Conversino," *Rinascimento,* ser. 2, 35:179–99.

——, 2000. *"In the Footsteps of the Ancients": The Origins of Humanism from Lovato to Bruni.* Leiden, Boston, and Köln.

Woolf, Cecil N. Sidney, 1913. *Bartolus of Sassoferrato: His Position in the History of Medieval Political Thought.* Cambridge.

Woolfson, Jonathan. 1998. *Padua and the Tudors: English Students in Italy, 1485–1603.* Toronto and Buffalo.

Zabughin, Vladimiro, 1909–12. *Giulio Pomponio Leto: Saggio critico.* 3 vols. Rome.

Zaccagnini, Guido, 1930. *Storia dello Studio di Bologna durante il Rinascimento.* Geneva.

Zaccaria, Raffaella, 1988. "Della Fonte, Bartolomeo." *DBI,* 36:808–14.

Zanardi, Mario, 1994. "I 'domicilia' o centri operativi della Compagnia di Gesù nello Stato veneto (1542–1773)," in *I Gesuiti e Venezia: Momenti e problemi di storia veneziana della Compagnia di Gesù.* Atti del Convegno di Studi, Venezia, 2–5 ottobre 1990, edited by Mario Zanardi. Padua, pp. 89–179.

Zanetti, Dante, 1962. "A l'Université de Pavie au XVᵉ siècle: Les salaires des professeurs," *Annales: Économies Sociétés Civilisations* 17:421–33.

Zanier, Giancarlo, 1975. "Cardano e la critica delle religioni," *Giornale critico della filosofia italiana* 54:89–98.

Zanobio, Bruno, 1981, "Fabrici, Girolamo." *DSB*, 4:507–12.

Zaoli, Giuseppe, 1912. "Lo Studio bolognese e Papa Martino V (Anni 1416–20)," *SMUB*, vol. 3, pp. 105–88.

——, 1920. "Di alcuni 'rotuli' dello Studio della prima metà del secolo XV. (Contributo alla storia dello Studio dal 1420 al 1455)," *SMUB*, vol. 4, pp. 191–249.

Zappacosta, Guglielmo, 1977. "Il Gymnasium perugino e gli studi filologici nel Quattrocento," in *L'umanesimo umbro*. Atti del IX convegno di studi umbri. Gubbio, 22–23 settembre 1974. Gubbio, pp. 197–272.

Zdekauer, Lodovico, 1977. *Lo Studio di Siena nel Rinascimento*. Milan, 1894; rpt. Bologna.

Zimmermann, T. C. Price, 1995. *Paolo Giovio: The Historian and the Crisis of Sixteenth-Century Italy*. Princeton, N.J.

Zippel, Giuseppe, 1979. *Storia e cultura del rinascimento italiano*. Edited by Gianni Zippel. Padua.

Zorzoli, Maria Carla, 1982. "Interventi dei Duchi e del Senato di Milano per l'Università di Pavia (secoli XV–XVI)," in *Università e società nei secoli XII–XVI*. Pistoia, pp. 553–73.

——, 1986. *Università, dottori, giureconsulti: L'organizzazione della "facoltà legale" di Pavia nell'età spagnola*. Padua.

Index